"This will be one of the most widely read and cited anthologies ...
history. David Brotherton and Rafael Gude assembled a group of highly respected scholars, all
of whom have contributed rich reviews of the extant literature in their particular areas of critical
gang studies. There is, indeed, no other book like this one, and it is a useful, 'cutting-edge'
resource for researchers, teachers, students, practitioners, and policy makers."

Walter S. Dekeseredy, *Professor, West Virginia University, USA*

"Spanning the globe, this extraordinary book provides exciting and theoretically informed analyses
that challenge the status quo, provoke difficult conversations, and compel the reader to view social
justice and inequality as central to contemporary gang studies. A tour de force that will stimulate
and create pause for reflection, it is simultaneously a major chronicle of our times."

Rob White, *Distinguished Professor of Criminology,*
University of Tasmania, Australia

"Canvassing a broad swath of the sociological literature on street gangs, this anthology will
become a vital source of information for future gang researchers. No stone is left unturned.
The authors cover gangs from theoretical, practical, and historical perspectives to comparative
international viewpoints. It is an important contribution to critical gang studies."

Mark S. Hamm, *Professor of Criminology, Indiana State University, USA*

"This anthology of gang studies represents critical scholarship at its best. Written and edited
by leading scholars in the field, this work contributes to our understanding of the historical,
political, and cultural dynamics of the street gang on a global scale. It represents a refreshing
antidote to conventional views which tend to pathologize such groups. It is essential reading
for academics, practitioners, students, and anyone interested in a more humanist perspective."

Tara Young, *Lecturer in Criminal Justice and Criminology, University of Kent, UK*

"Gangs are much maligned, misunderstood and demonised while gang members are caricatured
as thugs, deviants, drug dealers and the criminals. Gangster is a term all too often mis-used to
stigmatise the marginal and criminalise racial groupings of young people. Yet, gangs can be
sites of resistance that offer marginalised young people a space for collective identify formation
to contest the militarised policing and suppression efforts of settler colonialism that lingers
in so many parts of the world. *The Routledge Handbook of Critical Gang Studies* unpacks these
caricatures. Drawing on original studies from Africa, Central and Latin America, Asia, Canada,
Europe and United States this compendium debunks the shortfalls of reactionary approaches,
such as gang suppression. Based on rich ethnographies, biographies and qualitative methods the
49 chapters apply theories from critical, cultural, de-colonial, Indigenous, Latina and southern
perspectives to unearth rich new understandings about gangs as spaces of identity, resistance
and belonging. It is essential reading for anyone remotely connected to the correctional and
criminal justice systems, such as social workers, police, lawyers, legislators and of course students
and academics from an array of disciplines in the social sciences, including criminology, law,
sociology, anthropology, social work, public policy, humanities, cultural studies and history."

Kerry Carrington, *Professor, QUT Centre for Justice, Queensland*
University of Technology, Brisbane Australia

Routledge International Handbook of Critical Gang Studies

Routledge International Handbook of Critical Gang Studies is rooted in the instability, inequality and liquidity of the post-industrial era. It understands the gang as a complex and contradictory phenomenon, a socio-historical agent that reflects, responds to and creates a certain structured environment in spaces which are always in flux. International in scope and drawing on a range of sociological, criminological and anthropological traditions, it looks beyond pathological, ahistorical and non-transformative approaches, and considers other important factors that produce the phenomenon, whether the historically entrenched racialized power structure and segregation in Chicago; the unconstrained state-abandoned development of favelas in Brazil; or the colonization, displacement and dependency of people in Central America. This handbook reflects and defines the new theoretical and empirical traditions of critical gang studies. It offers a variety of perspectives, including:

- A view of gangs that takes into consideration the global context and appearance of the "gang" in its various forms and stages of development;
- An appreciation of the gang as a socio-cultural formation;
- A race-ethnic and class analysis of the gang that problematizes domain assumptions such as the "underclass";
- Gender variations of the gang phenomenon, with a particular emphasis on their intersectional properties;
- Relations between gangs and the political economy that address the dominant mode of production and exchange;
- Treatments that demonstrate the historically contingent nature of gangs and their changes across time;
- The contradictory impact of gang repressive policies, institutions and practices as part of a broader discussion on the nature of the state in specific societies; and
- Critical methodologies on gangs that involve discussions of visual and textual representations and the problematics of data collection and analysis.

Authoritative, multi-disciplinary and international, this book will be of interest to criminologists, sociologists and anthropologists alike, particularly those engaged with critical criminology/

sociology, youth crime, delinquency and global social inequality. The *Handbook* will also be of interest to policy makers and those in the peacebuilding field.

David C. Brotherton is Professor of Sociology at the John Jay College of Criminal Justice and the Graduate Center at the City University of New York, where his research on youth resistance, marginalization and gangs led to the Street Organization Project in 1997. He has received numerous research grants from both private and public agencies and has published widely in journals, books, newspapers and magazines. Dr Brotherton currently co-directs the Social Change Project at the John Jay College of Criminal Justice and edits the Transgressive Studies book series at Temple University Press. In 2011, he was named Critical Criminologist of the Year and in 2015 was the recipient of the Praxis Award for contributions to social activism and justice.

Rafael Jose Gude is a Research Fellow with the Social Change and Transgressive Studies Project at John Jay College of Criminal Justice, CUNY. He has done extensive fieldwork with gangs in both El Salvador and Ecuador, where much of his research has focused on developing viable alternatives to the war on gangs. He has an MPhil in Latin American studies from the University of Oxford.

Routledge International Handbook of Critical Gang Studies

Edited by David C. Brotherton and
Rafael Jose Gude

Routledge
Taylor & Francis Group

LONDON AND NEW YORK

First published 2022
by Routledge
2 Park Square, Milton Park, Abingdon, Oxon OX14 4RN

and by Routledge
605 Third Avenue, New York, NY 10158

Routledge is an imprint of the Taylor & Francis Group, an informa business

British Library Cataloguing-in-Publication Data
A catalogue record for this book is available from the British Library

Library of Congress Cataloging-in-Publication Data
Names: Brotherton, David, editor. | Gude, Rafael Jose, editor.
Title: Routledge international handbook of critical gang studies / edited
by David C. Brotherton and Rafael Jose Gude.
Description: Abingdon, Oxon ; New York, NY : Routledge, 2021. | Series:
    Routledge international handbooks | Includes bibliographical references
    and index. | Identifiers: LCCN 2020054546 | ISBN 9781138616110 (hbk) | ISBN
    9780429462443 (ebk)
Subjects: LCSH: Gangs. | Criminology. | Equality.
Classification: LCC HV6437 .R68 2021 | DDC 364.106/6—dc23
LC record available at https://lccn.loc.gov/2020054546

ISBN: 978-1-138-61611-0 (hbk)
ISBN: 978-1-032-00885-1 (pbk)
ISBN: 978-0-429-46244-3 (ebk)

Typeset in Bembo
by Apex CoVantage, LLC

In memory of Roger Matthews (1948–2020) and Dwight Conquergood (1949–2004)

Contents

List of contributors   *xiv*
Acknowledgments   *xxvii*

PART I
Critical theories of the gang   **1**

1 Utilizing Southern criminology in the global North: applying
   Southern criminology to over-standings of English gang research   3
   Paul Andell

2 States of emergency: gangs, Benjamin, and the challenge to
   modern sovereignty   16
   Jon Horne Carter

3 The Birmingham School and critical gang studies   29
   Hugo Goeury

4 The gang as secret society   45
   Louis Kontos

5 On being affected: love, law and submission among gangsters   58
   Martin Lamotte

6 The Catholic Church and the gangs: toward a liberationist critique
   of gang violence   74
   Benjamin Jonathan Schwab

7 Gangs, space and the state: bringing Henri Lefebvre's spatial
   theory to critical gang studies   89
   Tilman Schwarze

Contents

PART II
Critical methodologies   109

8   Cultural criminology and gangs: street elitism and politics in
    late modernity   111
    Elke Van Hellemont and Michael Mills

9   Interviewing gang members: a note on research design   122
    Kevin Moran

10 New standards for social practice ethics? Researching processes
    of gang exit with former gang members   138
    Line Lerche Mørck

11 Filming (with) gangs: an essay on visual sociology in Barcelona   153
    Luca Queirolo Palmas

12 Why gang members are dehumanized in court   164
    John M. Hagedorn

13 Gang narratives and race-based policing and prosecution in
    New York City   177
    Babe Howell

PART III
Policies and repressive models   195

14 Securitization and the transnational governing of Central
    American gangs   197
    Markus-Michael Müller

15 Gangs and the garrison state: (in)security politics and democracy
    in Latin America   210
    Katherine Saunders-Hastings

16 Misguided strategy: New York City's decision to criminalize gangs   225
    Josmar Trujillo and Alex S. Vitale

17 Off the books and off the blocks: the dual economic marginalization
    of black gang members in Chicago   243
    Roberto R. Aspholm

18 Responding to exclusion in Hartford   257
    Albert DiChiara

PART IV
Global case studies 269

19 The war on gangs and gangsters: the Latino/a experience with settler
colonialism 271
Robert J. Durán and Jason A. Campos

20 Indigenous gangs in Western Canada 284
Sandra M. Bucerius, Daniel J. Jones and Kevin D. Haggerty

21 Transnationalism and postnational identities: the three lives of
a Latin King 298
Carles Feixa

22 Race and youth gangs in France: Denial, ambiguity, and recognition 316
Marwan Mohammed and Akim Oualhaci

23 Performing "gang-ness": the transformative "realness" of gang
violence in the Netherlands 328
Robert A. Roks

24 Stuck in between: a former *marero* in the "European capital" of
Salvadoran gangs 340
Paolo Grassi

25 A genealogy of gangs in Hong Kong 351
Alistair Fraser, Karen Laidler and Helen Leung

26 Reimagining the landscape of gangs: reflections from Bangladesh
and China 364
Sally Atkinson-Sheppard

27 Russian street gangs, their social construction and political use-value 376
Svetlana Stephenson

28 The fourth corner of the triangle: gang transnationalism,
fragmentation and evolution in Belize City 386
Adam Baird

29 Gang governance in the tropics: the political economy of violence
and social order in contemporary Nicaragua 399
Dennis Rodgers

Contents

30 Understanding the dynamics and functions of gang violence:
    the case of El Salvador   412
    Chris van der Borgh

31 The making of Central America's street gangs   426
    Sonja Wolf

32 A critical criminology of gangs and organized crime in Brazil   439
    Marcos Burgos

33 The legalization of the Latin Kings in Ecuador: the two hands of the
    state, from the production of marginalization to policies of inclusion   453
    Ana Rodríguez and Mauro Cerbino

34 Peace processes in Ecuador   469
    Fabricio José García Díaz

35 Gangs in the post-Chávez Bolivarian revolution: how *mano dura*
    policies and political pacts have organized crime in Venezuela   473
    Verónica Zubillaga, Rebecca Hanson and Andrés Antillano

36 Gangs in Kenya: work, manhood and security   489
    Naomi van Stapele

PART V
Culture and the gang   **503**

37 Identity and collective resistance among the Almighty Latin King and
    Queen Nation (New York)   505
    David C. Brotherton and Luis Barrios

38 "They treat us like criminals in front of our kids": gang-affiliated
    Chicanas and *trails of violence* in the barrio   518
    Katherine L. Maldonado-Fabela

39 "The city got my back so the city on my back": prisoner's negation
    of the states' claims of prisoner's humanity   537
    Amy Andrea Martinez

40 Performance narratives of gang identity and membership   556
    Vanessa R. Panfil

41 California placaso: the social construction of Chicanx gang graffiti   567
    Xuan Santos and Martin Leyva

42 "Gangbangers are gangbangers, hustlers are hustlers": the rap game,
   social media, and gang violence in Toronto   582
   Marta-Marika Urbanik

PART VI
Contexts and spaces   **601**

43 Prison gangs in the Northern Triangle: the critical contribution
   of prison studies to the theory of gangs   603
   Michele Miravalle

44 Doxa is dangerous: how academic doxa inhibits prison gang research   624
   Jennifer M. Ortiz

45 Prison gangs: rise, resistance, and reentry   633
   Calvin John Smiley

46 A legacy of mapping gang neighborhoods in LA   647
   Susan Phillips and Stefano Bloch

PART VII
Critical appraisals of major figures in gang research   **665**

47 Dwight Conquergood: an appreciation of his intellectual life and
   contribution to critical gang studies   667
   Kamran Afary and David C. Brotherton

48 The legacy of Joan Moore: a revolution in gang research   678
   Jorge David Mancillas and Robert Donald Weide

49 The legacy of James Diego Vigil: rebelde con causa   691
   Robert Donald Weide

Index   *706*

Contributors

Afary, Kamran

Kamran Afary, PhD, RDT, is Assistant Professor of Intersectional Identities, Relationships, and Social Justice in the Department of Communication Studies at Cal State LA. He completed his graduate studies at Northwestern University in the Department of Performance Studies with Dwight Conquergood as his adviser. Since 2017, he has taught health communication and interpersonal communication to incarcerated students pursuing a BA degree at Lancaster Prison. He is the author and editor of several books, including *Communication Research on Expressive Arts and Narrative as Forms of Healing* (2020), *Iranian Diaspora Identities: Stories and Songs* (2020) and *Performance and Activism: Grassroots Discourse After the Los Angeles Rebellion of 1992* (2009). He is also author of a forthcoming chapter in *The Routledge History of Police Brutality* and co-authored a chapter on Narradrama in *Current Approaches in Drama Therapy* (2020). Kamran is a registered drama therapist and a researcher, designing and delivering trauma-informed training for prison educators. He edits the *Prison BA Journal*, a student publication that provides incarcerated students in Lancaster Prison a platform to have their research and writing seen by others, and is a recipient of the 2020 Raymond Jacobs Memorial Diversity Award from the North American Drama Therapy Association.

Andell, Paul

Dr Paul Andell is a senior lecturer at the University of Suffolk, England. He has more than 25 years of experience of working in the criminal justice field undertaking work in practice, policy and research. Paul has worked in probation and youth justice in East London, became Head of the Criminal Defense Service for the Legal Services Commission and later Community Safety Manager for the Greater London Assembly. He was also Director of Communities for a Youth Leadership Charity, Brathay, and for 14 years was Vice Chair of the Lambeth Community Police Consultative Committee; this work involved improving community relations between residents and the police. Paul is a current member of EQUAL, an Independent Advisory Group tasked with reducing race discrimination in the criminal justice system in England and Wales.

Antillano, Andrés

Andrés Antillano is a professor and chair of criminology at the Escuela de Derecho de la Universidad Central de Venezuela and at post-graduate studies in Penal Ciencias at the Universidad Católica Andrés Bello. He has published several articles and book chapters about prisons, pólice, drugs, citizen security policies and urban violence. He is a collaborator of Red de Activismo e Investigación por la Convivencia REACIN.

Aspholm, Roberto R.

Roberto R. Aspholm has spent more than a decade working in community practice and research capacities on issues affecting young people in marginalized urban neighborhoods, particularly street gangs, community violence and violence prevention. His work in these capacities has taken place primarily on the South Side of Chicago and in East St. Louis, Illinois, an industrial suburb of St. Louis and the city with the highest homicide rate in the United States. He is a Minneapolis native and an avid fan of professional basketball and boxing. His book *Views from the Streets: The Transformation of Gangs and Violence on Chicago's South Side* came out in 2020.

Atkinson-Sheppard, Sally

Sally Atkinson-Sheppard is a criminologist and strategist from the United Kingdom. She was awarded her PhD from King's College London in 2015 following the completion of the ethnographic study discussed in this book. Sally began her career as a researcher for the Metropolitan Police Service (MPS) in London, where she represented the MPS in a collaborative study with the British Prison Service which explored the psychology of gang-related violence. She went on to advise for a variety of criminal justice reform projects in Bangladesh, including leading the Bangladesh Prison Directorate and the Bangladesh Anti-Corruption Commission through the development of their first strategic plans. Sally has recently returned to the United Kingdom after living and working in Beijing, where she led the first study into migrant children's involvement in gangs and organized crime in China.

Baird, Adam

Adam Baird holds a PhD from the Peace Studies Department at the University of Bradford. He is a trained ethnographer with a focus on crime, gang violence, citizen security and urban insecurity in Latin America and the Caribbean. He has used masculinities as a lens to understand gang membership in Medellín, Colombia, and has also worked across Central America and the Caribbean. His research has been funded by ESRC, OSF, IDRC and SSRC. Adam is an "Associated Expert" to the UNDP Crisis Response Unit for armed violence reduction and citizen security and has worked with the ICRC and Norwegian Red Cross, as well as NGOs and community-based organizations. His research has been used to design gang violence intervention projects in Belize.

Barrios, Luis

Dr Barrios is a board-certified forensic examiner and a professor of Latina/o psychology, Latin American studies, ethnic studies, qualitative research and methodology and cultural criminology at John Jay College of Criminal Justice's Department of Latin American & Latina/o Studies and a member of PhD faculties in social/personality psychology, Graduate Center, the City University of New York. Since 1988, Dr. Barrios has been a columnist of *El Diario La Prensa* in New York City, one of the oldest Spanish newspapers in the United States. He is the co-editor with Louis Kontos and David C. Brotherton of *Gangs and Society: Alternative Perspectives* (Columbia, 2003); co-author with David C. Brotherton of *Almighty Latin King & Queen Nation: Street Politics and the Transformation of a New York City Gang* (Columbia, 2004); and co-editor with Mauro Cerbino of *Otras naciones: Jóvenes, transnacionalismo y exclusión*, Quito: Ecuador: Facultad Latinoamericana de Ciencias Sociales. Dr. Barrios is also the author of *Josconiando: Dimensiones Sociales y políticas de la espiritualidad* (Editorial Aguiar, 2000), *Pitirreando: De la desesperanza a la esperanza* (Editorial Edil, 2004) and *Coquiando: Meditaciones subversivas para un mundo mejor* (Editorial Búho, 2008).

Bloch, Stefano

Stefano Bloch is a former graffiti writer and now cultural geographer and assistant professor in the School of Geography, Development & Environment at the University of Arizona. His recent work on crime, graffiti, gangs, policing, prison racialization, neighborhood change and gentrification has appeared in journals including *Progress in Human Geography*, *cultural geographies*, *Environment and Planning D: Society and Space*, *Critical Criminology*, *Geography Compass*, *Geographical Review*, *Geoforum* and the *Radical History Review*. His book, *Going All City: Struggle Survival in LA's Graffiti Subculture* (University of Chicago Press, 2019) provides an autoethnographic account of navigating poverty, gang and police violence and homelessness as a graffiti writer in 1990s Los Angeles.

Bucerius, Sandra M.

As an urban ethnographer and qualitative researcher, Dr Bucerius is interested in issues pertaining to prisons, victim/offender overlap, immigration and crime, radicalization and the opioid crisis. Dr Bucerius holds numerous research grants, including a SSHRC Partnership grant. Her contributions have been recognized through a number of major awards, including the 2016 University of Alberta's Martha Cook Piper Research Prize. Her ethnography on drug dealers won second place in the Deutscher Studienpreis Koerberstiftung competition in 2009 – the highest national award for social science dissertations in Germany. Her article "What Else Should I Do?", published in the *Journal of Drug Issues* in 2007, was awarded the Honorary Mention of the Migration Section of the *American Sociological Association*. She is the co-editor of the *Oxford University Press* Handbook series in criminology (alongside Michael Tonry) and Director of the University of Alberta prison project (UAPP). Dr. Bucerius published an acclaimed ethnography *Unwanted – Muslim Immigrants, Dignity and Drug Dealing* (Oxford, 2014) and is also co-editor of the *Oxford Handbook on Ethnicity, Crime and Immigration* and the forthcoming *Oxford Handbook on Ethnographies of Crime and Criminal Justice*.

Burgos, Marcos

Marcos Burgos was born in San Juan, Puerto Rico, and has lived and worked in the Caribbean, the United States and Brazil. Between 2010 and 2013, he was engaged in a grassroots movement of resistance against Rio's city government's plans to remove his neighborhood (the Laboriaux section of Rocinha) and dozens of other strategically located favela communities in Rio de Janeiro before the 2014 World Cup and 2016 Olympics. In 2016, Marcos completed his PhD in sociology from the Graduate Center, CUNY, and is currently a Research Fellow at the Center For Social Change and Transgressive Studies (CUNY) where he explores the sociospatial dynamics of violent crime in low-income communities of Latin America and the Caribbean, Brazilian street gangs and organized crime, drug trafficking, corruption, urban development schemes, public security policies and homicide reduction strategies. Marcos also works as a freelance social science researcher, urban ethnographer and journalist based in Rio de Janeiro's largest favela, Rocinha, where he has lived (intermittently) since 2001.

Campos, Jason A.

Jason A. Campos is a doctoral student in sociology at Texas A&M University. His primary area of interest is crime, law and deviance. Specifically, he seeks to analyze the interplay between immigration and crime in political narratives through the lenses of race and racial-ethnic identity. He also has a growing interest in Latino/a gangs, religious studies and hip-hop in the Afro-Latino/a diaspora. Prior to Texas A&M, Jason had the opportunity to research migrant farm workers, incarcerated immigrants and cycles of migration from different regions in Mexico.

He received his BA in ethnic studies and sociology from California Polytechnic State University, San Luis Obispo, and graduated with cum laude distinction.

Carter, Jon Horne

Jon Horne Carter is Assistant Professor and Co-Director of the AppState Ethnography Lab in the Department of Anthropology at Appalachian State University. He writes on baroque and gothic aesthetics, criminal underworlds, ethnographic methods, fictocritical anthropology, punk and black metal, criminality and policing, mass incarceration and undocumented migration out of Central America. He is currently finalizing a book manuscript for the University of Texas Press.

Cerbino, Mauro

Mauro Cerbino is a professor, researcher and former dean of the Facultad Latinoamericana de Ciencias Sociales in Quito, Ecuador, working primarily in the Department of International Studies and Communication. He is currently a counselor in the Consejo de Evaluación, Acreditación y Aseguramiento de la Calidad de la Educación Superior in Ecuador. He has taught several courses and seminars in a number of Ecuadorian, Latin American and European universities. He has been developing two lines of research for three decades. One on youth cultures and violence and the other around the articulation between the media, culture and politics. Based on the results of these investigations, he has published numerous books and articles in national and international newspapers and academic journals.

DiChiara, Albert

Albert DiChiara is Chair of the Department of Sociology and Criminal Justice at the University of Hartford. His interests revolve around neighborhood-level political radicalism and crime prevention. He is currently researching the legacy of Malcolm X's achievements in Hartford and the origins and continuing work of the Black Panther Party in Hartford.

Durán, Robert J.

Robert J. Durán is associate professor of sociology at Texas A&M University. He is the author of *Gang Life in Two Cities: An Insider's Journey* (2013) and *The Gang Paradox: Inequalities and Miracles on the U.S.–Mexico Border* (2018). He is currently working on a book with Oralia Loza focused on officer-involved shootings. All three books have been published by, or are under contract with, Columbia University Press.

Feixa, Carles

Carles Feixa (1962) is Professor of Social Anthropology at the Universitat Pompeu Fabra (Catalonia, Spain). He has investigated youth cultures and has conducted fieldwork in Spain and Latin America. He is the author or co-author of several books like *De jovenes, bandas y tribus* (1998), *Global Youth?* (2006), *Youth, Space and Time* (2016) and *El Rey. Diario de un Latin King* (2020). He has been Advisor for Youth Policies of the United Nations and Vice President of the International Sociological Association Research Committee "Sociology of Youth". In 2017, he obtained two of the highest recognitions for his research work: the ICREA Academia Award of the Generalitat de Catalunya and the Advanced Grant of the European Research Council (www.upf.edu/web/transgang).

Fraser, Alistair

Alistair Fraser is Senior Lecturer in Criminology and Director of the Scottish Centre for Crime and Justice Research at the University of Glasgow. Previously he spent four years as Assistant Professor in Criminology at the University of Hong Kong. He is the author of *Urban Legends: Gang Identity in the Post-Industrial City* (OUP, 2015) and *Gangs & Crime: Critical Alternative* (Sage, 2017).

García Díaz, Fabricio José

Fabricio Garcia has been a member of the organization Masters Of Street since 2003. Originally from the city of Montecristi, he has been a leader of the organization since 2006. In 2007, he was elected Secretary of the organization for the province of Manta and later named a delegate in the peace negotiations with other street organizations. He has been a militant of the Ecuadorian Communist Party since 2010 and in 2017 was chosen to participate in the national elections of 2017 as an alternate to the Andean Parliament. As a union organizer and a political campaigner for many years, Fabricio has been part of the struggle for workers' rights across Ecuador in many different contexts.

Goeury, Hugo

Hugo Goeury is pursuing a PhD in sociology at the Graduate Center, CUNY. His research focuses on the articulation between welfare and penal policies for the government of subaltern groups under neoliberalism.

Grassi, Paolo

Paolo Grassi is a social anthropologist (PhD, University of Verona, and master's, University of Milano Bicocca, 2007), with a specialization in development. He has also worked as a social worker, a teacher and a project manager assistant. Paolo is currently a post-doc fellow at the Polytechnic University of Milan (Department of Architecture and Urban Studies), lecturer in cultural anthropology at the University of Padua (Department of Linguistic and Literary Studies) and a local researcher for the "TRANSGANG project" (Universitat Pompeu Fabra Barcelona and University of Milan Bicocca). Over the past ten years, he developed interests in issues relating to gangs, urban segregation and violence and carried out ethnographic research in the Dominican Republic, Guatemala and Italy. He has published books and articles in English, French, Italian and Spanish. His last book, *Terreur à Guatemala-ville: Conflits territoriaux, violence et gangs* (L'Harmattan, 2018) describes the socio-spatial structure of the city, mapping out how the reality and imagination of the gangs connect disparate areas into a single, albeit partially segregated, entity.

Hagedorn, John M.

John Hagedorn is Professor Emeritus from the University of Illinois-Chicago. He has studied gangs in Chicago, Milwaukee and around the world for the past 40 years. He has written five books, edited two more and written dozens of popular and academic articles. Since the mid-1990s, he has turned his attention to the courtroom as an expert witness. His forthcoming book, *Gangs on Trial: Challenging Stereotypes and Demonization in Court*, tells stories from trials and sentencings of gang members. Rather than an examination of "them" – gangs – he turns his attention to "us" – how we all think in stereotypes and too easily demonize "the other". He lives in Milwaukee and is married to Mary Devitt, and together they have four children and ten grandchildren.

Haggerty, Kevin D.

Kevin D. Haggerty is Professor of Sociology and Criminology at the University of Alberta. He is a Killam Research Laureate and Tier I Canada Research Chair. He has been the executive editor of the *Canadian Journal of Sociology* since 2007. His research has been in the areas of surveillance, prisons, governance, policing and risk.

Hanson, Rebecca

Rebecca Hanson is Assistant Professor of Crime, Law and Governance at the University of Florida, with a joint appointment in the Department of Sociology and Criminology & Law and the Center for Latin American Studies. Her research analyzes policing, politics and violence in Venezuela and Colombia. She has published research in the *Journal of Latin American Studies; The Sociological Quarterly; Crime, Law, and Social Change*; and *REVISTA M. Estudos sobre a Morte, os Mortos e o Morrer*. She has also published extensively in outlets such as *The Christian Science Monitor, NACLA, The Conversation* and *Insight Crime*. In 2019, she published *Harassed: Gender, Bodies, and Ethnographic Research* (University of California Press) with Patricia Richards. Her current book manuscript asks how revolutionary politics in Venezuela transformed state security forces.

Howell, Babe

Babe Howell, Professor, teaches criminal law, criminal procedure, criminal trial advocacy, professional responsibility and lawyering. A graduate of Harvard College, Professor Howell received her JD from New York University School of Law, where she was a Root-Tilden Snow Public Interest Scholar. Howell's scholarship focuses on the intersection of the criminal justice system and race. In particular, she writes on the policing of minor offenses and gangs and the impact these prosecutions have on the legitimacy of the criminal justice system and communities of color. Before joining legal academia, Professor Howell was a practicing trial lawyer in the area of criminal defense in New York City for eight years. During this time, she worked at both the Legal Aid Society Criminal Defense Division in Manhattan and at the Neighborhood Defender Service of Harlem.

Jones, Daniel J.

Daniel J. Jones is an inspector with the Edmonton Police Service with 23 years experience. Daniel has worked in patrol, foot patrol, undercover operations and the gang unit as a constable; professional standards and homicide as a detective; patrol, equity diversion and inclusion as a staff sergeant; and investigative support and patrol operations as an inspector. Daniel's current role is the Inspector in charge of research for the Edmonton Police Service. He earned his master's degree in applied criminology and police management from the University of Cambridge and is currently a PhD candidate in criminology and criminal justice at the University of Huddersfield. Daniel's focus of research is the victim–offender overlap amongst incarcerated men and women, and he is a sessional lecturer at MacEwan University and the University of Alberta.

Kontos, Louis

Louis Kontos, PhD, is Assistant Professor of Sociology at John Jay College of Criminal Justice. Kontos has published articles on social theory, political movements, psychoanalysis, ethnography and street gangs, co-editing *Gangs and Society: Alternative Perspectives* (Columbia, 2003). He is currently completing a book on the politics of deviance and social control.

Laidler, Karen

Karen Joe Laidler is Professor of Sociology and Director of the Centre for Criminology at the University of Hong Kong. She has researched and published on youth gangs, violence, drug markets, women and imprisonment and several criminal justice issues in the United States and Hong Kong.

Lamotte, Martin

Martin Lamotte is a French anthropologist at the CNRS (Centre National de la Recherche Scientifique), affiliated to the Anthropology Department at Tours University and the EHESS. He is the Co-Editor of the journal *Monde Commun*, a French anthropological journal (https://monde commun.hypothe-ses.org/). His research focuses on gangs and their links to social movements, figures of social bandits and other forms of leadership and authority within criminal societies. For his PhD (anthropology at the EHESS-Paris and urban studies at the INRS-Montreal), he conducted a multi-sited ethnography between New York, Guayaquil City and Barcelona and followed the Ñetas international circulation. As a post-doctoral researcher, he conducted research in Puerto Rico and was invited to the College de France and Stanford University to carry out a project on social bandits. This research will be published in a book in the CRNS edition in September 2021. He is now working on a new project on predation within US inner cities.

Leung, Helen

Helen Wai-sze Leung is a researcher at Hong Kong Dignity Institute, focusing on mapping the modus operandi of human trafficking for sexual exploitation and forced criminal activities (drug trafficking) in Hong Kong. Previously, she led various research projects examining conflict and displacement in Syria under the Durable Solutions Platform and the Conflict, Stability and Security Fund. Helen was Column Editor at the *Oxford Monitor of Forced Migration*.

Leyva, Martin

Born on the West Side barrio in Santa Barbara, Martin Leyva grew up around gangs and barrio culture composed of art and graffiti. He is the Program Coordinator for Project Rebound at CSU-San Marcos. Leyva is a formerly incarcerated scholar and now a doctoral student at the University of California-San Diego in Education. Martin has a strong passion for social justice and human rights concerns. He institutionalized the Transitions Program, which offers therapeutic and educational opportunities for formerly incarcerated and system-impacted students. Leyva started chapters at different community colleges in California. He authored *From Corrections to College: The Value of a Convict's Voice*. Leyva is a motivational speaker who shares his academic journey with community organizations and universities throughout the United States. Leyva works with formerly incarcerated individuals by focusing on emotional intelligence and spiritual self-care and healing.

Maldonado-Fabela, Katherine L.

Katherine Maldonado is a mother of three, an underground scholar from South Central Los Angeles and a doctoral student in the Department of Sociology at UC Santa Barbara. She received her BA in Chicana/o studies from UCLA and MA in sociology at UC Riverside. Her research interests include gender, race and class inequality; socio-legal studies; family; and visual and feminist methodologies. Katherine is a Ford Foundation Pre-Doctoral Fellow, ASA Minority Fellow and AAHHE Fellow.

Mancillas, Jorge David

Jorge David Mancillas is a fourth-year PhD student in the Department of Sociology at the University of California, Los Angeles. His masters' thesis examined the relationship between the emotional distress that repeated traumatic loss causes and its role in the social reproduction of gang violence in Los Angeles. He is currently developing his dissertation research to include a focus on the association between gang members and the labor market, employment opportunities and income-generation strategies. Joan Moore's legacy is foundational to Mancillas' present work and inspires his future research endeavors.

Martinez, Amy Andrea

Amy Andrea Martinez is a first-generation system-impacted Xicana scholar-activist from a working-class neighborhood in Southern California. She is currently a doctoral candidate at John Jay College of Criminal Justice–City University of New York City. She holds a BA in sociology with an emphasis in crime, law, and deviance from UC Santa Barbara and MA in criminal justice from John Jay College of Criminal Justice. She is expected to graduate with her doctoral degree in criminal justice in spring 2022 and will be pursuing a career in academia. Her dissertation is a grassroots ethnographic exploration between the intersections of processes of racial dehumanization and the hyper-policing of Mexican/Chicano self-and/or state-identified gang-associated young people in Santa Barbara, California.

Mills, Michael

Michael Mills is a lecturer in criminology at the University of Kent (UK). His research interests centre on cultural criminology, narrative criminology, American subcultures of survivalism/prepping, political extremism, apocalypticism and ethnographic research methods.

Miravalle, Michele

Mr Michele Miravalle, PhD, is Research Fellow in Sociology of Law at the University of Turin, Department of Law, and Qualified Associate Professor in Philosophy of Law. He is the National Coordinator of the Italian Prisons Observatory, an independent body authorized by the Ministry of Justice to monitor the prison conditions and the fair application of the penitentiary law. His researches focus on critical prison studies, human rights and social control, law and psychiatry and cognitivism applied to criminal law. He also conducted empirical research into correctional facilities in Russia, Central America, Eastern Europe and the Middle East. He is involved in training activities for prison staff in many European countries as a team member of the European Prison Observatory.

Mohammed, Marwan

Marwan Mohammed is a sociologist at the Centre National de la Recherche Scientifique (France) based at the Maurice Halbwachs Centre in Paris. His main research interests are inequality, crime and racism. He is currently conducting comparative research on careers and markets in organized crime in France and the United States. He has published several books on youth gangs and desistance forme crime. His latest book is on the politicization of the word "communitarianism" (edited with Julien Talpin at the Presse Universitaire de France/La vie des Idées).

Moran, Kevin

Kevin Moran lectures on sociology at Seton Hall University. He has published articles on criminological theory in journals such as *Theoretical Criminology* and the *British Journal of Criminology*, as well as chapters on policing and decision-making in social movements. His scholarly interests include developing an ecological approach to researching desistance in prison and the use of interdisciplinary research to refine criminological theory and methods.

Mørck, Line Lerche

Line Lerche Mørck is Professor with special responsibilities in "Major identity formation, expansive learning and belonging – movement beyond gang involvement and radicalization" at The Danish School of Education, Aarhus University. In the book *Boundary Communities – Learning and Transcending Marginalization* from 2006, she develops a social practice theory focused on how local community projects across ethnic and social differences can create so-called border communities, which can support learning and partly transcend marginalization. In recent years, she has focused on community-building activities in socially deprived areas and social work projects in production schools, as well as interventions in gang conflicts and change of life conduct among ethnic minorities; (biker) gang communities; and persons diagnosed with autism spectrum diagnoses, ADHD and depression. In cooperation with Tina Wilchen Christensen, her research has focused on movements in and across the (biker) gang community and extreme groups. Line Lerche Mørck works in the cross-section between research and practice development in and across fields of education, social work and intervention with a focus on children, young people and adults in marginalized positions.

Müller, Markus-Michael

Markus-Michael Müller is a professor with special responsibilities in international development studies at Roskilde University, Denmark. His research focuses on transnational security governance, violence and (in)security and knowledge production, as well as new forms of South-South security cooperation, with a regional focus on Latin America. He is the author of *The Punitive City: Privatised Protection and Policing in Mexico City* (2016) and *Public Security in the Negotiated State. Policing in Latin America and Beyond* (2012). His work has been published in journals, including *Crime, Law & Social Change, Cooperation and Conflict, Geoforum, Geopolitics, Government & Opposition, Journal of Cold War Studies, Journal of Latin American Studies, Security Dialogue* and *Third World Quarterly*.

Ortiz, Jennifer M.

Jennifer Ortiz is an assistant professor of criminology at Indiana University Southeast. Dr Ortiz earned her PhD in criminal justice from John Jay College of Criminal Justice. Her research interests center on structural violence within the criminal justice system, with a focus on reentry post-incarceration and the treatment of gang-affiliated individuals. She is co-editor of the forthcoming volume *Critical and Intersectional Gang Studies*. Ortiz's most recent scholarship has been published in *The Prison Journal* and *Corrections: Policy, Practice, and Research*. In addition to her scholarship, Ortiz maintains a firm commitment to civil service and community activism. She serves as President of the New Albany, Indiana, Human Rights Commission and as an executive board member for Mission Behind Bars and Beyond, a Kentucky-based non-profit reentry organization. Ortiz also serves as Executive Counselor for the Division of Convict Criminology of the American Society of Criminology.

Oualhaci, Akim

Akim Oualhaci is a sociologist. His research primarily deals with the transformation of the cultural space of minority youths who live in segregated urban areas in France and the United States. He is the author of the book *Se faire respecter. Ethnographie de sports virils dans des quartiers populaires en France et aux Etats-Unis* (Presses Universitaires de Rennes, 2017).

Palmas, Luca Queirolo

Luca Queirolo Palmas is Professor in Sociology of Migration and Visual Sociology at Genoa University. Co-director of *Mondi Migranti, Journal of Studies and Research on International Migrations,* he also founded the Laboratory for Visual Sociology, devoted to spread visual forms of narrative and research in social sciences. He directed several European projects on gangs, youth cultures, borders and migrations. He has been visiting professor in Barcelona, Quito, San José de Costa Rica, Paris and Tunis.

Panfil, Vanessa R.

Vanessa R. Panfil is an ethnographer, criminologist, sociologist and advocate. She is the author of *The Gang's All Queer: The Lives of Gay Gang Members* (NYU Press, 2017), co-author of *Sex-Positive Criminology* (Routledge, 2021) and co-editor of the *Handbook of LGBT Communities, Crime, and Justice* (Springer, 2014; second edition forthcoming). Her research explores how intersections of gender and sexuality shape individuals' experiences with gangs, crime, victimization and the criminal and juvenile justice systems. She is currently an associate professor in the Department of Sociology and Criminal Justice at Old Dominion University in Norfolk, Virginia.

Phillips, Susan

Susan A. Phillips, PhD has studied gangs, graffiti and the US prison system since 1990. Phillips received her PhD in anthropology in 1998 from UCLA, where she taught for four years. Her books include *Wallbangin: Graffiti and Gangs in L.A.* (Chicago, 1999), *Operation Fly Trap: Gangs, Drugs, and the Law* (Chicago, 2012) and *The City Beneath: A Century of Los Angeles Graffiti* (Yale, 2019). Phillips has received numerous grants, including two Getty fellowships, a Soros Justice Media Fellowship and a Harry Frank Guggenheim research grant. Phillips is interested in theories of violence; relationships between small-scale social groups and the state; and intersections between urban history, material life and the built environment. She is currently a professor of environmental analysis and Interim Director of the Robert Redford Conservancy for Southern California Sustainability at Pitzer College.

Rodgers, Dennis

Dennis Rodgers is Research Professor of Anthropology and Sociology at the Graduate Institute of International and Development Studies, Geneva (Switzerland), and the PI of the ERC Advanced Grant-funded project "Gangs, Gangsters, and Ganglands: Towards a Global Comparative Ethnography" (GANGS). The latter is a five-year project that aims to systematically compare gang dynamics in Nicaragua, South Africa and France. More broadly, his research focuses on issues relating to the dynamics of conflict and violence in cities in Latin America (Nicaragua, Argentina) and South Asia (India). Much of his work involves the longitudinal study of youth gangs in Nicaragua, but he also works on the political economy of development, the politics of socio-spatial segregation, participatory governance processes, the historiography of urban theory and the epistemology of development knowledge. His recent publications include the edited volume *Ethnography as Risky Business: Field Research in Violent and Sensitive Contexts* (co-edited with Kees Koonings and Dirk Kruijt, Lanham: Lexington Books, 2019) and a special issue of the journal *Ethnography*, on "Ethnographies and/of Violence in Latin America and the Caribbean" (co-edited with Gareth A. Jones, volume 20, issue 3, 2019).

Rodríguez, Ana

Ana Rodríguez is a curator and researcher as well as a native of Quito, Ecuador. She is currently a member of URBAN FRONT, an international consultancy network that specializes in urban studies. She studied fine arts and philosophy at the Université Paris 1 Panthéon-Sorbonne in France and cultural studies at the Universidad Andina Simón Bolívar in Quito, Ecuador. Rodríguez served as Minister and Vice-Minister of Culture of Ecuador (2015–2016), directed the City Museums Foundation (2012–2014) and directed the Contemporary Art Center (2010–2012), all in Quito. Since 2000, she has served as Professor at the Universidad Central del Ecuador, Universidad Católica y Universidad San Francisco. At present, she works on public policies for cultural institutions as an associate researcher in FLACSO-Ecuador and continues to work with organizations in different fields, such as gang studies, food sovereignty and popular markets.

Roks, Robert A.

Robert A. Roks, PhD, is an assistant professor of criminology at Erasmus University of Rotterdam. His research interests include street culture, street gangs, outlaw motorcycle gangs and organized crime, with a preference for qualitative research methods and exploring alternative ways of collecting data (social media, digital communication and [rap] music).

Santos, Xuan

Xuan Santos is an award-winning associate professor in the Department of Sociology, Criminology & Justice Studies at California State University-San Marcos. He serves as the Faculty

Director for the CSUSM chapter of Project Rebound and the Criminology and Justice Studies Program in Temecula. His research interests are on gangs, barrio criminology, immigration, the informal economy and tattoos/graffiti. He co-authored "Apartheid Justice: Gang Injunctions and the New Black Codes", in *Race, Ethnicity and the Law*. Santos is a Chicano scholar-activist from Boyle Heights, a community east of the Los Angeles River, and participates in anti-gang injunction, anti-gentrification, and anti-police repression campaigns. He coined the term OG (an acronym that does not denote original gangster but opportunity giver). Opportunity givers understand the community struggles of marginalized persons and, at the same time, mobilize resources to empower people to become productive members of their communities.

Saunders-Hastings, Katherine

Dr Katherine Saunders-Hastings is Lecturer in Latin American Studies at UCL's Institute of the Americas, where she teaches and researches on urban and political anthropology. Prior to joining the Institute in 2016, Katherine was a postdoctoral fellow at Stanford University's Centre on Democracy, Development, and the Rule of Law. She earned her doctorate in socio-legal studies from the University of Oxford in 2015. She holds a BA in anthropology and history from McGill University and an MPhil in Latin American studies from the University of Cambridge and has worked with the International Centre for the Prevention of Crime (Montréal, Canada) and the Asociación para el Avance de las Ciencias Sociales (Guatemala City, Guatemala). Her research has been supported by fellowships from the Social Sciences and Humanities Research Council of Canada, the Clarendon Fund and the Harry Frank Guggenheim Foundation.

Schwab, Benjamin Jonathan

Benjamin Jonathan Schwab is a social scientist and Catholic theologian of German origin. He studied social work and theology in Munich, Germany. He holds master's degrees in anthropology and development studies from Radboud University, Nijmegen (The Netherlands) and in Latin American theology from Central American University (UCA), San Salvador (El Salvador). He has worked as a researcher and facilitator for a number of development and education projects in Europe, Asia, Africa and Latin America. As part of the theological research project "Violence and redemption" at UCA (El Salvador), he recently worked with victims of violence and vulnerable communities in El Salvador on hope and resistance in the midst of conflict and death. Currently he is a PhD candidate in theology/Christian social ethics at Julius-Maximilians-University, Würzburg (Germany), researching the contribution of liberation theology to contemporary social change and liberation processes.

Schwarze, Tilman

Tilman holds a PhD in international relations from the University of St Andrews. His research focuses on the production of urban spaces in marginalized urban communities in American cities, particularly Chicago. He uses Henri Lefebvre's theories of space as analytical frameworks in deciphering the complexity of everyday life and spatial production. His research foregrounds residents' lived experiences with territorial stigmatization and how this stigmatization contributes to gentrification-centered displacement processes. Tilman is also interested in the communicative and performative function of violence in inter- and intra-group contexts. His article *Social Rituals of Pain: The Socio-Symbolic Meaning of Violence in Gang Initiation* (with Jeffrey Murer) was recently published in the *International Journal of Culture, Politics, and Society* (2020).

Smiley, Calvin John

Calvin John Smiley is a critical sociologist and criminologist whose work focuses on issues related to social justice, inequality and race. He is an assistant professor in the sociology department of Hunter College-CUNY, where he teaches courses on the sociology of law, race and ethnic relations and criminal justice policy. Smiley has been published in several academic journals and is the co-editor of *Prisoner Reentry in the 21st Century: Critical Perspectives of Returning Home* (Routledge, 2020). For more information about Smiley's research, teaching and publications, please visit: www.cjsmiley.com.

Stephenson, Svetlana

Svetlana Stephenson is a Professor of Sociology at London Metropolitan University. She worked at the Russian Centre for Public Opinion Research (Levada centre) and was a Leverhulme Visiting Research Fellow at the University of Essex. Among her books are *Gangs of Russia. From the Streets to the Corridors of Power*, Cornell University Press, 2015 (awarded the 2015 Alec Nove Prize by the British Association for Slavonic and East European Studies); *Crossing the Line. Vagrancy, Homelessness and Social Displacement in Russia*, Ashgate, 2006; and *Youth and Social Change in Eastern Europe and the Former Soviet Union*, Routledge, 2012 (co-edited with Charles Walker).

Trujillo, Josmar

Josmar Trujillo is a writer and organizer based in New York City. He has organized around education, disaster recovery and policing. He currently organizes with the Coalition to End Broken Windows. He has written for the *Village Voice, NY Daily News, Newsday, Crain's, Truth Out* and *SchoolBook*.

Urbanik, Marta-Marika

Dr. Marta-Marika Urbanik is an assistant professor in the Department of Sociology at the University of Alberta. Her ethnographic and qualitative work examines marginalized neighborhoods, gang dynamics, the street code and inner-city policing.

van der Borgh, Chris

Chris van der Borgh (Centre for Conflict Studies, Utrecht University) is a lecturer, researcher and consultant specializing in issues of peace and security, political order and intervention. He has worked for the past 30 years on El Salvador. Recent publications focus on the politics of security provision in El Salvador.

Van Hellemont, Elke

Elke Van Hellemont is a lecturer at the University of Kent (UK), teaching cultural criminology and ethnography. Her research interests are multi-method research and ethnography, gangs, theoretical criminology, the seduction of deviance, cultural and critical criminology and anthropological perspectives on crime.

van Stapele, Naomi

Dr. Naomi van Stapele is an assistant professor in urban governance and development policy at the International Institute of Social Studies (ISS) in The Netherlands. One of her current research projects looks at the role of gangs in fighting violent extremism in Kenya. She has been involved in community-led action with gangs and sex workers in Nairobi since 1998, and from 2005 onwards, this has developed into community-led research and action (CLRA). In a recently concluded four-year-long research project, she studied security provision and community-led development by gangs in different cities in Kenya. Her PhD research explored the role of gender, economic uncertainty and political violence among gangs in Kenya. Cutting across all these projects is a focus on solidarity practices among and between multiple marginalized groups in highly volatile urban settings in East Africa and how these groups imagine and develop alternative economic, social and political action.

Vitale, Alex S.

Alex S. Vitale is Professor of Sociology and Coordinator of the Policing and Social Justice Project at Brooklyn College and a Visiting Professor at London Southbank University. He has spent the last 30 years writing about policing and consults with both police departments and human rights organizations internationally. Vitale is the author of *City of Disorder: How the Quality-of-Life Campaign Transformed New York Politics* and *The End of Policing*. His academic writings on policing have appeared in *Policing and Society, Police Practice* and *Research, Mobilization, and Contemporary Sociology*. He is also a frequent essayist, whose writings have been published in the *New York Times, Washington Post, The Guardian, The Nation, Vice News, Fortune* and *USA Today*. He has also appeared on CNN, MSNBC, CNBC, NPR, PBS, Democracy Now and The Daily Show with Trevor Noah.

Weide, Robert Donald

Robert Donald Weide is an assistant professor of sociology at California State University, Los Angeles. He holds an MA and PhD from New York University in Sociology and a dual major BA from UC Santa Barbara in political science and law and society, with an emphasis on criminal justice. His research agenda endeavors to dismantle narratives employed to demonize and criminalize marginalized populations and subcultures including graffiti writers, street and prison gangs. His book on racial division and interracial conflict between African American and Chicano gangs in Los Angeles, *Divide and Conquer: Race, Gangs, Identity and Conflict*, is forthcoming with Temple University Press.

Wolf, Sonja

Sonja Wolf holds a PhD in international politics (Aberystwyth) and is a *Cátedra CONACYT* assistant professor with the Drug Policy Program at the Centre for Economic Research and Teaching (CIDE), Mexico. Previously, she held research positions at the Autonomous Technological Institute of Mexico (ITAM), the National Autonomous University of Mexico (UNAM) and the Mexico City–based Institute for Security and Democracy (INSYDE). Dr Wolf's research interests focus on forced migration, violence, street gangs and security policies, especially in Central America. She is the author of *Mano Dura: The Politics of Gang Control in El Salvador* (University of Texas Press, 2017). Currently she is also a Visiting Fellow at the Latin America and Caribbean Centre (LACC) of the London School of Economics and Political Science (LSE).

Zubillaga, Verónica

Verónica Zubillaga (PhD, Catholic University of Louvain, Belgium) is an associate professor at the Universidad Simón Bolívar in Caracas and founder of Red de Activismo e Investigación por la Convivencia REACIN (www.reacin.org/). Her research focuses on youth gang and armed violence in Caracas, gender and public policy. Zubillaga has combined academia with public impact throughout her career, promoting an arms control and disarmament public policy in her home country of Venezuela and publishing in the local press. She was Craig Cogut Visiting Professor of Latin American Studies at Brown University (2014–15); Santander Visiting Scholar at the David Rockefeller Center for Latin American Studies, Harvard University (2016); and more recently Visiting Fellow at The Kellogg Institute for International Studies, Notre Dame University (2018–2019).

Acknowledgments

There are a lot of people to thank for their contributions to this volume and to the establishment of a field, a sensibility and a commitment to a social scientific praxis – a praxis that refuses to be complicit in the epistemic violence from which the gang as "folk devil" has usually been the end result. It has been a long road to get to this point when more than 50 authors from across the globe have been willing to share their renditions of the gang while maintaining a healthy skepticism of prevailing discourses so easily influenced by the "gang talk" (Hallsworth and Young 2008) of the day and the region. So where do we begin with our sincere mentions of appreciation?

First, of course, we want to thank all those who fill the following pages with their insightful analyses, revealing data, crafted theories and spirited conclusions. We aimed to bring as many critical voices to the page as possible to show how this other way of seeing and representing could take the research forward, and you all answered the call and much more. We cannot thank you enough. The idea for the book itself came from Tom Sutton, Routledge's senior editor and longstanding champion of criminological research, who thought it was time for a major compilation of new works on gangs in the critical tradition especially after an earlier intervention by one of the editors (see "Youth Street Gangs," Brotherton 2015). Jessica Phillips, also from Routledge, has guided us through the publication process with endless patience, resolve and seasoned judgment. We remain in your debt. A special mention must be made of the extraordinarily positive impact that Antonio Fernandez has had on the world of gangs, and without his vision and commitment to the cause of gangs as social movements, I doubt whether this work would ever have come into being. Similarly, the massive contributions of Luis Barrios to the communities whence gangs originate must be acknowledged. Meanwhile, we must express our appreciation to our comrades in Ecuador whose leadership and imagination made gang transformation possible: Manuel Zúñiga, Luis Varese, Gabriela Tavella, Alejandra Delgado and Fabricio Garcia, Ana Rodriguez and Mauro Cerbino. There is a lot to learn from Ecuador, and the research we conducted there was made possible through a PSC-CUNY grant, the Inter-American Development Bank and the Guggenheim.

Finally, my (Dave) institutions at John Jay College of Criminal Justice and the Graduate Center at the City University of New York have provided a home for this work for over two decades, and our recently formed Social Change Project will be the research hub to carry it forward. I single out my colleagues Jayne Mooney, Barry Spunt, Louis Kontos, Danny Kessler, Robert Garot, Antonio Fernandez, Clinton Lacey, Bahiyyah Muhammad and Rodrigo Martinez for their comradeship over many a year, as well as my many talented students who provided so much inspiration along the way, including Albert de la Tierra, Marcos Burgos, Robert Weide, Jennifer Ortiz, Peter Marina, Amy Martinez, Nick Rodrigo, Sarah Tosh, Edwin Grimsley, Jennifer Young, Matt Block and Marianne Madore. I would also like to thank Daniel

Stageman for all his support and last but not least Columbia University Press for permission to reprint chapter 37.

I'd (Rafa) also like to thank my colleagues in El Salvador who influenced me so much on how I came to view gangs through a critical lens – Adrian Bergmann, Jennifer Coreas, Jeanne Rikkers and Susan Cruz. Those are just a few names, but there are so many more. I also want to thank Mazi and Clayton for all their support. Their advice and our long conversations have helped to form my ideas the most over these past years. I'd also like to thank Ed Schortman and Dave Suggs for the continued friendship. These last few years have been very nomadic, and all of these people have helped me find a home wherever I was. And, lastly, I want to thank my family. I could never have asked for funnier and more creative people to surround myself with.

Part I
Critical theories of the gang

Utilizing Southern criminology in the global North

Applying Southern criminology to over-standings of English gang research

Paul Andell

Introduction

This chapter asserts that most criminological literature attending to English gangs has neglected a full consideration of the production of knowledge with respect to gangs and indicates the impact this has had on gang intervention policy. I address several core questions at the heart of what has become known as the UK Gang Thesis Debate (Pitts 2011; Hallsworth 2013; Andell 2019), such as: What is known of the problem and how do we know this? Who influences the problem definition and what impact does this have? And what are the problem representations and problem focus? It can be argued that the debate has mainly articulated assumptions and concerns about gangs either (i) from an over-idealized view, which sometimes fails to acknowledge the disproportionate negative impact on relatively deprived neighborhoods, or (ii) from a perspective focused on correcting gang problems, which tends to downplay the cultural and historical relevance of the participants caught up in gang street life.

The aim of the chapter is to problematize these dominant paradigms in contemporary English gang discourse by utilizing Southern criminology to illustrate how these paradigms manifest tensions created through knowledge production. The chapter offers a critical review of English gang studies utilizing the knowledge constructs underpinning "social homology" and "critical realism" in order to highlight some of the neglected issues and omissions. The chapter highlights the importance of specificity within the geographical, historical, social and cultural contextualization of the production of knowledge as well as the relevance and impact of failing to differentiate ontology and epistemology in gang studies.

Opposing reductionism

In an attempt to strengthen the credentials of Southern criminology, Travers (2017) calls for closer links with postcolonial thought and discusses potential conflicts in Southern criminology's philosophical and theoretical underpinnings. He calls for a deeper exploration of the conflicts within Southern criminology, between ideas of post-structuralism and critical realism, which this chapter begins to explore. Go (2016) summarizes the differences between social theory and postcolonial thought and their differing metaphysical propositions as follows,

> Postcolonial thought is primarily an anti-imperial discourse that critiques empire and its persistent legacies. If social theory was born from and for empire, postcolonial thought was born against it. Therefore, not only do social theory and postcolonial thought have different and divergent histories, they also embed opposed viewpoints and ways of thinking about the modern world in which we live.
>
> *(1)*

Travers (op cit.) provides an overview of some of the challenges facing a Southern criminology in shifting the focus from state criminal justice studies to global inequalities and transnational crime. In doing so, he invokes the philosophy of Guess to widen his critique and to support the radical potential of an epistemic and ontological rupture facilitated by a closer alignment to postcolonial studies which recognize the ubiquity of empire as a silent but pervasive force in shaping thoughts and actions. For Travers (op cit.), these discourses are inspired by the aims of a critical criminology of empowerment and emancipation rather than those of direction and discipline. Travers suggests that Southern criminology is but another name for post-colonial criminology, and in order to reach its full transformational potential, Southern criminology should fully adopt the philosophical and theoretical underpinnings of postcolonial studies. Early post-colonial scholars such as W. E. B. Du Bois, Aime Césaire, Frantz Fanon and Amilcar Cabral were part of a global landscape of anti-colonialism which highlighted colonial exploitation and the racist foundations of imperialism (Go 2016). Energizing all of them was a critique of empire and its multiple operations. The postcolonial thought they developed was a critical engagement with empire's ways of viewing, being and knowing – in short, its very culture. Later work such as that of Paul Gilroy (2004) built on these traditions to continue to deploy ontological and epistemic disruptions in defaming colonial knowledge claims and what he considered reified colonial knowledge production, which, in this view, precipitates a predatory universalism of western modernity. To date, it could be argued that postcolonial studies have successively maintained ontological and epistemological destabilization of grand theory in an attempt to highlight the proliferation of other discourses and a realization of other worlds. However, Vandenberghe suggests that there are some practical and intellectual disadvantages to over-destabilization or the complete dismantling of such knowledge bases. He argues:

> exploring and exposing the hidden connections between discourses power and practices . . . representations of reality within language do not so much repress as produce both the knowing subjects and the objects of knowledge as objects that are hailed by discourses that bring them into existence and subjected to the subtle workings of governmentality and power.
>
> *(Vandenberghe 2016: 16)*

Arguably, Gilroy (2002) embraces some of these techniques in his critique of policy-oriented criminology, suggesting that the primary object of state intervention is the moral regulation of citizens and property. In this view, laws are seen to identify with a national interest primed to exclude those who are not white British. Despite calls for closer ties with postcolonial studies, Travers (2017) also highlights the practical difficulties of this type of idealism in action. He suggests:

> there is a difference between overcoming them at a philosophical level and engaging with cultural and material realities in non-Western countries. The same mistakes have, arguably,

been made by critical criminologists in Western countries in having an idealized, positive view of the working class and its potential as a revolutionary force; and in not acknowledging the positive aspects of agencies such as the police, courts, and prisons in reducing the harms caused by crime.

Understanding the broader approach of Southern criminology

Despite calls for closer alignments of Southern criminology with postcolonial studies, Carrington et al. (2014) take a more inclusive approach in fleshing out the possible features of a Southern criminology. They acknowledge the impact that global divisions of power have had on knowledge production via the legacy of colonialism, which has often excluded the experiences of the global South but in doing so resists a relativism which undermines a criminological imagination that connects the individual experiences of crime to social structures and historical context (Carlen 1983).

Carrington and Hogg (2017) thus argue:

> Unlike post-colonial theory, southern epistemologies do imagine a prospect for intercultural translation between north and south, east and west which can produce ways of understanding that resist the universalizing tendencies of western thought (de Sousa Santos 2014: 212). Southern epistemologies have thus spawned a great deal of innovative new work in the social sciences which aims to bridge global divides and cross-fertilize intercultural thinking.
>
> *(Journal of Asian Criminology, p. 183)*

They make the case for developing a criminology which is more transnational and inclusive of the experiences and viewpoints of the global South, adopting methods and theories that transgress global divides, and include the political aim of the democratization of knowledge production. Carrington et al. cite Connell (2007) in broadening the definition of the global South, whereby,

> 'Southern' therefore references geographical divides in the world but is also used as a metaphor for the power relations embedded in 'periphery–center relations in the realm of knowledge'.
>
> *(viii)*

Carrington et al. (2014) take up this mantle when they argue for a non-homogenized critical criminology equipped to understand the nuanced experience of a range of local social and cultural factors which help to understand the experience of rural crime and victimization.

> Without a critical perspective of place, the realities of context can be lost. A new criminology of crime and place will help keep both critical criminology and rural criminology firmly anchored in the sociological – and by extension, criminological – imagination of C.W. Mills, William Chambliss, Stan Cohen, the Schwendingers, Ian Taylor, Jock Young, Pat Carlen, and Paul Walton, and all those other great critical minds on whose proverbial shoulders we stand upon today.
>
> *(Carrington et al. 2014: 474)*

Examples of the need for a critical perspective of place can be drawn from recent policy swings of denial and blame regarding gangs in England and Wales. Until recently, totalizing concepts were utilized by the National Crime Agency, which interchangeably described the personnel involved in County Line drug dealing networks as 'urban street gangs', 'organized crime groups' or 'dangerous dealer networks,' all of which presented challenges in assessing agency efforts organized through "taxonomic categories" of crime as opposed to understanding "relational and structured networks" which exist externally to the categories imposed (Andell 2019).

The advance of Southern criminology has the potential to weave across the boundaries of the global and the local, the specific and the general, particularly when Carrington et al. (2014) discuss Southern criminology not as a theory but as an approach or a tool to be used in analysis and understanding. They argue,

> The southern is also a metaphor for the other, the invisible, the subaltern, the marginal and the excluded. This is what we propose in speaking of something called 'southern' criminology. The division of the contemporary world into North and South loosely approximates older (but still common) ways of talking about global divides and global social relations.
>
> *(2014: 4)*

Carrington et al. are careful to highlight that it is not the intention of Southern criminology to further fragment the discipline of criminology but to nuance debates in order to contextualize historic, structural and cultural disadvantage. Moreover, they refute simple inversions of North and South approaches as being over-reductionist, which they deem to be caricaturing and essentializing Northern approaches while romanticizing Southern approaches.

Arguably, a useful direction for Southern criminology is in the attention it pays to critical specificity to avoid epistemic fallacies whereby analysis is replaced by description and every utterance is held as real. I argue that these ideas are also played out in the UK gangs thesis debate. In this debate, differences in understanding gangs are conceptualized by Hallsworth as arboreal versus rhizomic knowledge, whereby rhizomic knowledge allows for a non-essentialized view of street life, and an arboreal framework results in a Western over-corporatization of the gang (Hallsworth 2013). In order to analyze this proposition, we need to first deconstruct the UK gangs thesis debate before reconstructing a less polarized thesis of English gangs.

The UK gangs thesis debate

Recently, criminological debates regarding the existence and evolution of street gangs (and what is to be done about them) have re-invigorated theoretical criminological discussion in the United Kingdom, prompting a re-examination of realist–idealist discourses in critical criminology (Pitts 2009; Hallsworth 2013; Andell 2019).

Briefly, the realist critique suggests that idealists are removed from applied policies to reducing crime and victimization, while the Idealists assert that any improvements to the criminal justice system to combat gangs are meager liberal accommodations that tighten controls on the poor and disadvantaged (Tierney 2009). Arguably in this debate, it is suggested that idealism has a tendency to overstate the political significance of street culture, emphasizing state reactions and responses of the media. Conversely, realism tends to focus on the impact of crime on relatively poor neighborhoods, but in doing so, idealists argue they precipitate heightened levels of social control by fuelling what Stan Cohen (1972) calls "moral panics". Thus, if we moderately exaggerate the two positions, we can observe a discourse in which one perspective problematizes the social reaction to the offender and downplays the violence associated with gang involvement, which is contrasted with a perspective in which drives to address the gang phenomenon take priority over attempts to understand the socio-cultural nuances of the gang problem and of the social actors involved. If the gangs thesis debate is to further our understandings and interventions to reduce harms, then what is required is both theoretical rigor (Hallsworth 2013) and dynamic policy and practical application (Pitts 2008). The conceptualization of knowledge about urban street gangs is important, as different theories and methodologies can affect understandings of the ontology of gangs, leading to different approaches for intervention. Knowledge about gangs can be usefully demarcated in terms of idealism, naive realism and critical realism (Matthews 2014; Andell 2015; Pitts 2016).

Idealism and gangs

Preliminary reports about a recent possible phenomenon of English street gangs began to emerge in academic circles in the early 2000s (Bullock and Tilley 2008) following a series of violent incidents in a number of inner-city areas. Early criminological work investigating the possibility of a new gangs phenomenon in English cities by Hallsworth and Young (2008) questioned the existence of gangs in the United Kingdom. Arguably their analysis utilized constructivist epistemologies which did not separate the observed social realities of "violent street worlds" from the accounts given about them. This type of analysis led to well-meaning deviance denial in the form of idealistic noninterventionist approaches, which in the realms of political utility have done little to direct policy towards alleviating the strains experienced in relatively deprived neighborhoods, for example, early Youth Justice Board gang policy statements in England and Wales (Young et al. 2007).

However, other "idealist" literature, which also suffered from similar epistemic fallacies (Vandenberghe 2016) in its knowledge production, was discounted, perhaps because of a differing type of political inconvenience. This literature appeared in the form of 'true crime' books or biographies that provided personal descriptive accounts of gangs (for Birmingham, see Bassey 2005; for Manchester, see Walsh 2005; for London, see Pritchard 2008). These accounts have been viewed as problematic on the grounds that they:

> provide a distorted view of gangs, gang members, and their communities through their sensationalized, skewed, and superficial emphasis on crime and violence. Moreover, some of these publications overemphasize the relevance of ethnicity or immigration status as factors that 'explain' or define gangs.
>
> *(Aldridge et al. 2008: 34)*

However, by simply dismissing these accounts, potentially useful data may have been lost, as autobiographical descriptions may allude to the synchronic relationships by which social structures, social values and cultural symbols 'fit' together in a specific space and time, described by Willis (1978) as a social homology. It could be argued that such literature can provide data sources in the form of emergent or stratified social realities via accounts of largely hidden co-offending groups which are seldom utilized in criminological research (Windle 2018). Jack Katz (1988) argues,

> Academic social scientists will either learn how to think intelligently about using the genre of non fiction novels (and other new literary forms) about murders or they will leave this part of our social life and what ever these crimes might reveal about our lives more generally to journalists, politicians and literary critics.
>
> *(Seductions of Crime 1988)*

Katz (2002) further argues that "non-traditional" sources of information can package social life as data and assist in creating ideas that stratify social ontology. Despite Katz's commitment to foregrounding emotions of crime which facilitates an emergent theory, it is difficult to imagine that we interact without preconceived ideas of our own. In other words, we carry socially situated ideas into the field, and these ideas can constitute situated a priori concepts (Andell 2019). Thus, there is potential for Southern criminology to explore further the bridges between cultural criminology and critical realism through which ideas of a stratified ontology cross. This potential not only suggests a need to understand the presenting phenomenon and how this presenting phenomenon relates to background conditions but also how background conditions create underlying tendencies for actions or practices which precipitate as problems experienced (Matthews 2014).

Naive realism and gangs

In contrast to idealist approaches, empirically evidenced gang intervention work arrived in the United Kingdom through policy transfer from the United States (Andell 2015). These empirical approaches were mainly informed by statistical methods which could be termed "naive realist" (Matthews 2014), as the observed behaviors of these studies gave limited discernment to the causal tendencies which support observable experience or take account of cultural impacts. Policy transfer regarding gangs has sometimes initiated unpopular repressive interventions which threaten community relations. For example "gang call-ins" (Kennedy 2000) have resulted in accusations of racial profiling and coercion (Centre for Crime and Justice 2015). Problems associated with this type of approach appear to be rooted in over-generalizations of what constitutes a gang and who typically constitutes a gang member. These approaches of universalism may be deemed "Northern" definitions and may exhibit a reductionism which is often utilized for ease of measurement and comparison (Klein 2001). However, in doing so, this can lead to a narrow gauge being applied to a broad phenomenon. For example, gangs often have their roots in both local relative deprivation and international underdevelopment (Pitts 2008; Andell 2019); therefore, social history, geography and patterns of migration are also important to understand in the analysis (Gemert et al. 2008). Sayer (1992) suggests that interval scales can only be effectively developed for objects and processes that are qualitatively invariant. If these approaches are solely applied to gangs, there is a danger that scant attention will be paid to the causal mechanisms which help to explain the differing nature of gangs within specific neighborhoods at particular times (Andell 2019).

Young (2004) argues that the dry approach of statistics translates social relations into the arid language of mathematics. Thus, it is difficult to express the social processes that involve the grooming of some young people to feel safe or believe they have sound business opportunities as part of a street gang selling drugs. The use of theory therefore plays an important part in any contextual analysis in order to make sense of the many 'facts' that compose reality (Manicas 2006). Therefore, in this form of realism, not only is there an imperative, that the "flat ontology" of empiricism is required to be replaced with a stratified ontology, but also that the partiality of our epistemic approach should be acknowledged as relative.

In critiquing positivistic science, we should also be mindful of the limited and limiting repertoire of ideas and methods developed in the global North, which are sometimes believed to have universal relevance, albeit carrying a capacity to reproduce homogenized assumptions that can propagate stereotypes (Travers 2017) which at best ignore and at worse compound a full range of power inequalities in what can be termed "the real world" (Sweet 2018). To extend the reach of Southern criminology, it is necessary for the dualism of constructivism and realism to expand. Such a process requires support from mid-range theories, plural methods and inclusive participative practices for stakeholders, the choice of which will be dependent on the nature of the object under study. To expand our academic repertoire Southwards, it is useful to employ the reconstructive social theories of critical realism. This involves the interpretation of human meaning, intentions and actions but simultaneously the displacement of attention from aesthetics to ethics and politics in order to engage in radical reform to enable emancipatory practices.

Critical realism and gangs

Sweet (2018) argues that critical realism shares a post-positivist association with postcolonial studies and feminist standpoint theory. For example, Palmer and Pitts (2006) writing on gang and gun crime in West London, eschew positivism and utilize Ken Pryce's work (1979) to explain the "endless pressure" exerted on the African Caribbean communities residing in the housing estates of Harlesdon. These communities are not portrayed as passive victims but as active subjects engaging in networks of mutual support, resistance and solidarity. The study goes on to describe Wacquant's (1997) ideas regarding simultaneous upward and downward mobility for differing African American groups which result in the collapse of the African American ghetto. Palmer and Pitts (2006) utilize plural methodologies in their knowledge production. Similarly, Andell (2019) utilizes a range of methods in reconstructing a critical realist approach to gangs. He explains conflicts which arise in the UK gangs thesis debate between Pitts and Halsworth in terms of knowledge production debates, asserting that both Hallsworth (2013) and Pitts (2011) may not be as far apart in their analysis as they think they are. The reasons for this assertion are perhaps best explained utilizing Spivak's subaltern studies.

Spivak, Go and postcolonial realism. can the subaltern speak?

For Travers (2017), the main intellectual influence on a critical Southern criminology is knowledge that has been developed in the humanities and is rooted in postcolonial studies. He utilizes ideas of orientalism to critique western colonial thought as homogenizing. In contrast, Julian Go suggests that postcolonial thinkers have also relied on realist, sociological claims in order to propose their critiques. Go suggests that Frantz Fanon focuses upon new regularities of racial formation in France and makes causal assertions about how colonization produces new subjectivities in both the colonizer and the colonized. For Go, postcolonial theorists are mapping a social ontology, arguing that if claims are made regarding the assertion that knowledge has fuelled imperialism, then this involves a basic tenet of social science which insinuates that a world consists of observable regularities and patterns which can be known.

Go suggests we should advance realist, sociological ideas about colonization and empire if we are to comprehend a "postcolonial rationalism". Notwithstanding the significant diversity of subaltern groups, arguably, the one invariant characteristic is a notion of resistance to elite domination. In other words, resistance in its many forms is the similarity of their differences. Go utilizes the subaltern standpoint to address the links between observations and knowledge. He cites Spivak, who argues for a "strategic essentialism" in praxis for colonial categories when politically necessary. Ashcroft et al. (2007) also make this point in analyzing Spivak's work and point to her argument that no act of resistance takes place on behalf of an essential subaltern subject completely separate from the dominant discourse that furnishes the language and conceptual categories with which the subaltern voice speaks. Clearly, the existence of postcolonial discourse itself is an example of such speaking, and in most cases, the dominant language or mode of representation is appropriated so that marginal voices can be heard.

Strategic essentialism as formulations of street gangs

According to the previous line of argument, criminological phenomena such as street gangs can be investigated utilizing a strategic essentialism (or an a priori concept) which makes some knowledge claims before considering the layered and sometimes fragmented realities and understandings of them from the point of view of those involved. Here, the ontological premise is that social facts are constituted by the actions, thoughts and dispositions of socially situated actors (Vandenberghe 2016). The idea of socially situated actors not only has synergies with the UK gangs thesis debate but also with Carrington et al.'s broader ideas of who is included in the Global South. Thus, they argue,

> In this sense, theorizing from the subaltern allows for a "post-positivist realism," wherein we recognize that there is a world independent of what we say about it – power structures of colonialism and racism exist, really – but we cannot know about that world via the conventions of positivist science. Instead, we need methodologies and theories that are critical and situated.

Similarly, Go suggests that standpoints are not essences with clear pathways to better knowledge but structural entry points for developing "situated knowledge". This approach, it is argued, is always dependent on the observer and the lens of observation to generate "partial but objective truths" about the social world. Situated knowledge production lends itself to participative methodologies of action research in gang studies (Andell and Pitts 2017; Andell 2019), which prompts dynamic processes in reconstructing our theories and practices of street gangs. This approach to "theory building" takes account of a layered ontology and partial epistemology to avoid reifications which disqualify the potential for transitions of street gangs, either negatively towards local organized crime or positively towards formations and practices of self-help (Andell and Pitts 2018; Andell 2019; Brotherton 2015).

An example of situated knowledge production can be found in the work of both Bourdieu and Fanon, whose work is rarely brought together, as both forged different situated knowledges through their relationship with the war in Algeria in the 1950s, Bourdieu with a focus on class subjectivity and Fanon with a focus on colonized subjectivity. However, both share an understanding that colonization had a direct and violent effect on the colonized from their social organization to their subjectivity. Both thinkers shared an understanding of colonization as the imposition of foreign logic that ruptures the existence of the colonized and of social and cultural orders that give them meaning. The juxtaposition of Bourdieu with postcolonial studies allows for emergent insights into a "colonial habitus" (Ayling 2019).

Encouraging an emergentism through the relationalism of Bordieu

Go (2016) argues that Spivak's claim that the subaltern cannot speak should be read in terms of a "post-colonial" relationism. That is, as a voice subsequently constructed, a product of subject-object relations, the idea being that the centre and periphery are mutually constituted and consist of social relations as opposed to agents that exist outside of constitutive relations. Similarly, Left Realists argue that we cannot understand the actions of crime without simultaneously considering the reactions to them (Lea and Young 1984). These ideas can also be related to debates regarding subjectivity, for example, Spivak and the Subaltern Studies Group, whereby Spivak's critiques are implicit critiques of substantialist ontologies from the standpoint of relationalism.

Spivak elaborates on the problems of the category of the subaltern by examining the predicament of gendered subjects, specifically Indian women as both an object of colonialist historiography and as a subject of uprising.

Ideas regarding the subject and subjectivity directly affect "colonized" peoples' self-perceptions of identity and their capacities to resist conditions of domination or "subjection", and this indirectly has been a central feature of the UK gangs thesis debate, whereby over-essentializing the notion of a gang prevents room for "play" and the potential for the gang to transcend street life either negatively or positively.

The centrality of the autonomous human individual was a key feature of Enlightenment philosophy. Divine will or cosmic forces were no longer seen as a precept for human action; instead, the individual self was separate from the world and could employ understanding and imagination in thinking about and representing the world. However, this "Cartesian individualism" tended to downplay the significance of both social relations and language in formations of the self. Contemporary shifts in Enlightenment thinking are apparent in Freud and Marx. Freud's ideas of the unconscious suggests that there were parts of the mind that were not accessible by human thought, which blurred the distinction between subject and object. Marx also radically challenged ideas of autonomy in foregrounding economic structure and made the claim,

> It is not the consciousness of men that determines their being, but, on the contrary, their social being that determines their consciousness.
>
> *(Ashcroft et al. 2007: 202)*

Later elaborations of these ideas problematize the relationship between the individual and language, replacing human nature with ideas of the production of the human subject through ideology, discourse or language (op. cit.). In this reading, the dissemination of ideology is the dominant mechanism by which unequal social relations are reproduced. According to Althusser, power dynamics are propagated via interpolation; that is, the state apparatuses provide the conditions for subjectivities of a false consciousness to embed and occur (Ashcroft et al. 2007). Althusser was concerned with the nature of ideology and its materiality both within individuals and within the so-called "ideological state apparatuses". Althusser also postulates that ideology has a material existence, but he largely focused upon metaphysical and the imaginary dimensions of knowledge production. In contrast, Bourdieu (1991) draws attention to non-conscious and automatic bodily reaction to symbolic violence and domination, which for him are grounded in the dispositions that individuals acquire through interaction in the social field. Thus, for Bourdieu, the mechanisms of symbolic power are conceived as a social "field" in which competing social relations occur.

According to Go (2016), in Bourdieu's social field, actors compete for a variety of resources or varieties of "capital" that have the capacity to be changeable to each other. The concept of field, therefore, refers to the arrangement of actors (the multidimensional "field of forces") and the classificatory schemes and rules of the game, which actors utilize as they struggle for position (i.e., the "rules of the game") (Bourdieu and Wacquant 1992: 97). In this version of events, a field is a "network, or arrangement of objective relations between positions" (Bourdieu and Wacquant 1992: 97). Field theory thus offers a relational rather than substantialist view of the social. According to Bourdieu and Wacquant,

> To think in terms of fields . . . is to think relationally.
>
> *(1992: 96)*

Although fields have an intrinsic logic of conflict, they are not entities with stable and essential characteristics but are fluid and their borders shift. They are not "systems" or "structures" but are defined by relations of struggle and conflict. The identity and action of the agents or "players" in the field are confirmed by relations or positions within the field. Their relational position, not their innate qualities, defines their interests and actions. A field is a "space of position-takings, i.e. the discursive and non-discursive practices that actors carry out from the symbolic and material positions that they hold" (Go 2016). Thus, not all agencies and interventions located by social science and crime policy are inherently stigmatizing or disciplining, as postcolonial thought would have us believe, and much is dependent on the nature of the intervention at a particular time and place.

Conclusions: political praxis

Ideas have been explored regarding the utility of a Southern criminology, allowing for considerations of relational knowledge and emancipatory practices. I go on to analyze how this approach may provide the basis for progressive understandings in gang work rather than potential repressive over-standings of gang culture or liberal denials of gang harms. It is acknowledged that there are many groups of young people in the United Kingdom engaged in relatively harmless misbehavior, and the term 'gang' is sometimes over-used to describe them. I argue that conceptualizing the issues in a way which captures the influences of dynamic social trends is important, as it is acknowledged that it is difficult to apply static definitions to changing phenomenon.

The exploitation of vulnerable young people by street gangs involved in new drug distribution networks has recently been investigated and reported in the United Kingdom (Windle and Briggs 2015; Coomber 2015; Disley and Liddle 2016; Hallworth 2016; Andell and Pitts 2017, 2018; Jaensch and South 2018; Whittaker et al. 2018; Coomber R. and Moyle L. 2018). The irregular economy of drugs has international dimensions which are historically bound to western colonial expansion and structural violence (Jankowiak and Bradburd 2003). The arrival of new communities in the United States and Europe has often been met with threat and conflict, sometimes leading to gang formation or reliance on pre-existing gangs for protection and perceived progression. Following colonial expansion and the need for labor in "imperial homelands", patterns of migration have intertwined with structural and social factors, leading to threat, conflict and fear, which Decker et al. maintain is necessary for gang formation (Decker et al. 2009).

However, in order to analyze issues viewed or experienced as harmful, epistemologies should be utilized that separate justified belief from opinion. Conceptualization of the issues and collection and collation of data can assist initial directions of interventions but should also be viewed as starting points which may be subject to change depending on the inputs from a range of stakeholders by adopting an action research approach. Misjudgments currently occur which are said to be racially discriminatory and stigmatize young black men for the music they listen to or their behavior on social media. These misjudgments are said to be made through static conceptualizations of gang problems, as exemplified through the use of the gang matrix (Amnesty International 2018). These assessment tools are used to numerically order risk factors, and often this is done remotely from the neighborhoods in which the behaviors and attributes occur. Subsequently, the meanings which risk attributes carry are often misinterpreted or absented, and therefore explanatory power is lost (Matthews 2014; Andell and Pitts 2017). This can result in net widening and mis-targeted enforcement (CCJ 2015). It can be argued that this approach does little to build public confidence and can exacerbate problems in neighborhoods (Edmonds et al. 1995; Andell and Pitts 2017). Therefore, a more meaningful and dynamic approach needs to be developed in capturing data, assessing problems and devising interventions.

Our theories about gangs are historically, socially and culturally situated and always partial. Arguably at this moment in time, our best ideas about the underlying causal forces which precipitate gang problems involve social structures which have push and pull factors acting in conjunction with culturally enmeshed individuals with limited choices. The pushes of social exclusionary factors such as institutional racism and unemployment act in concert with pull factors of excessive consumerism and the search for respect through gangster culture. In light of these conflicts, the inclusion of cultural perspectives or the world view of those involved is crucial in formulating non-static and meaningful ideas about gang problems if we are to alleviate harms.

References

Aldridge, J., Medina, J. and Ralphs, R. (2008). Dangers and Problems of Doing 'Gang' Research in the UK. In F. van Gemert, D. Peterson, and I. Lein (Eds.), *Street Gangs, Migration and Ethnicity* (pp. 31–46). Cullompton, Devon: Willan.

Amnesty International (2018). *Trapped in the Matrix. Secrecy, Stigma, and Bias in the Met's Gangs Database.* Retrieved at www.amnesty.org.uk/files/2018-05/Trapped%20in%20the%20Matrix%20Amnesty%20 report.pdf?lJSxllcKfkZgr4gHZsz0vW8JZ0W3V_PD= (Accessed 8 December 2019).

Andell, P. (2015). *Thinking About Gangs.* University of Bedfordshire Doctoral Thesis, University of Bedfordshire Open Repository.

Andell, P. (2019). *Thinking Seriously About Gangs, Towards a Critical Realist Approach.* Basingstoke: Palgrave Macmillan.

Andell, P. and Pitts, J. (2017). *Preventing the Violent and Sexual Victimisation of Vulnerable Gang-Involved and Gang-Affected Children and Young People in Ipswich.* A Report for Suffolk County Council.

Andell, P. and Pitts, J. (2018). The End of the Line? The Impact of County Lines Drug Distribution on Youth Crime in a Target Destination. *Youth and Policy.* Retrieved at http:// www.youthandpolicy.org/ articles/the-end-of-the-line/ (Accessed 5 February 2018).

Archer, M. (1995). *Realist Social Theory. The Morphogenetic Approach.* Cambridge: Cambridge University Press.

Ashcroft, B. Griffiths, G. and Tiffin H. (2007). *Post Colonial Studies. Key Concepts.* 2nd edn. London: Routledge.

Ayling, P. (2019). *Distinction Exclusivity and Whiteness.* New York: Springer.

Bassey, A. (2005). *Homeboys: The Story of the Birmingham Gang.* Preston: Milo Books.

Bourdieu, P. (1991). *Language and Symbolic Power.* Cambridge: Polity Press.

Brotherton, D. (2015). *Youth Street Gangs: A Critical Appraisal* (New Directions in Critical Criminology). Oxfordshire: Routledge.

Bourdieu, P. and Wacquant, L. (1992). *An Invitation to Reflexive Sociology.* Cambridge: Polity Press.

Bullock, K. and Tilley, N. (2008). Understanding and Tackling Gang Violence. *Crime Prevention and Community Safety,* 10, 36–47.

Carlen, P. (1983). *Women's Imprisonment: A Study of Social Control.* New York: Routledge.

———. (1999). The Limits to, and Potential of, Feminist and Left Realist Perspectives. In R. Matthews and J. Young (Eds.), *Issues in Realist Criminology* (pp. 51–69). London: Sage.

Carrington, K., Donnermeyer, J. F. and Dekeseredy, W. S. (2014). Intersectionality, Rural Criminology, and Re-Imaging the Boundaries of Critical Criminology. *Critical Criminology,* 22(4), pp. 463–477.

Carrington, K. and Hogg, R. (2017). Deconstructing Criminology's Origin Stories. *Asian Journal of Criminology,* 12(3), pp. 181–197.

Centre for Crime and Justice (2015). *Met Criticised for Call-In Letter.* Retrieved at www.crimeandjustice. org.uk/news/met-police-criticised-gang-call-letter (Accessed 10 October 2017).

Cohen, S. (1972). *Folk Devils and Moral Panics the Creation of the Mods and Rockers*. London: MacGibbon and Kee Ltd.

Connell, R. (2007). *Southern Theory: The Global Dynamics of Knowledge in the Social Science*. Sydney: Allen & Unwin.

Coomber, R. (2015). A Tale of Two Cities: Understanding Differences in Levels of Heroin/Crack Market Related Violence – A Two City Comparison. *Criminal Justice Review*, 40(1), pp. 7–31.

Coomber, R. and Moyle, L. (2018). The Changing Shape of Street-Level Heroin and Crack Supply in England – Commuting, Holidaying and Cuckooing Drug Dealers Across 'County Lines'. *British Journal of Criminology*, 58(6), pp. 1323–1342.

de Sousa Santos, B. (2014). *Epistemologies of the South: Justice Against Epistemicide*. Boulder: Paradigm Publishers.

Decker, S. H., van Gemert, F. and Pyrooz, C. (2009). *D.C. International Migration & Integration*, 10, p. 393. Retrieved at https://doi.org/10.1007/s12134-009-0109-9 (Accessed 8 December 2019).

Disley, E. and Liddle, E. (2016). *Local Perspectives in Ending Gang and Youth Violence Areas: Perceptions of the Nature of Urban Street Gangs*, Research Report 88. London: Home Office.

Edmonds, M., et al. (1995). *Addressing Local Drug Markets*. London: Home Office.

Gilroy, P. (2002). *There Ain't No Black in the Union Jack: The Cultural Politics of Race and Nation*. New York: Routledge.

Gilroy, P. (2004). It's a Family Affair. In M. Forman and M. A. Neal (Eds.), *THaT'S the JOInt! The Hip-Hop Studies Reader*. New York: Routledge.

Go, J. (2016). *Postcolonial Thought and Social Theory*. Oxford: Oxford University Press.

Hallworth, J. (2016). *'County Lines': An Exploratory Analysis of Migrating Drug Gang Offenders in North Essex*. Dissertation Submitted in Part Fulfilment of the Requirements for the Masters Degree in Applied Criminology and Police Management, Cambridge.

Hallsworth, S. (2013). *The Gang and Beyond: Interpreting Violent Street Worlds*. Basingstoke, England: Palgrave Macmillan.

Hallsworth, S. and Young, T. (2008). Gang Talk and Gang Talkers: A Critique. *Crime, Media, Culture: An International Journal*. Sage. Retrieved at www.un~h.edu/ccrc/pdf/jvq/NatSCEV–Children's%20 ExposureFamily%20Violence%20final.pdf (Accessed 12 August 2019).

Jaensch, J. and South, N. (2018). Drug Gang Activity and Policing Responses in an English Seaside Town: 'County Lines, 'Cuckooing' and Community Impacts. *Journal of Criminal investigation and Criminology Revija za kriminalistiko in kriminologijo*, 69(4), pp. 269–278.

Jankowiak, W. and Bradburd, D. (Eds.). (2003). *Drugs, Labor and Colonial Expansion*. Tucson, AZ: University of Arizona Press.

Katz, J. (1988). *Seductions of Crime: Moral and Sensual Attractions in Doing Evil*. New York: Basic Books.

Katz, J. (2002). Start Here: Social Ontology and Research Strategy. *Theoretical Criminology*, 6(3), pp. 255–278. Sage.

Kennedy, D. (2000). Pulling Levers: Getting Deterrence Right. National Institute of Justice Journal (July 1998). Reprinted in *The Modern Gang Reader*. 2nd edn. Eds. Malcolm W. Klein, Cheryl L. Maxson, and Jody Miller. Los Angeles: Roxbury Press.

Klein, M. (2001). Resolving the Eurogang Paradox. In M. W. Klein, H. J. Kerner, C. L. Maxson and E. G. M Weitekamp (Eds.), *The Eurogang Paradox: Street Gangs and Youth Groups in the US and Europe*. London: Kluwer Academic Publishers.

Lea, J. and Young, J. (1984). *What Is to Be Done About Law and Order*. London: Pluto Press.

Matthews, R. (2014). *Realist Criminology*. London: Palgrave Macmillan.

Manicas, P. (2006). *A Realist Philosophy of Social Science, Explanation and Understanding*. Cambridge: Cambridge University Press.

Palmer, S. and Pitts, J. (2006). 'Othering' the Brothers: Black Youth, Racial Solidarity and Gun Crime. *Youth and Policy*, 91, pp. 5–22.

Pitts, J. (2009). *Reluctant Gangsters: The Changing Face of Youth Crime*. Cullompton: England: Willan.

Pitts, J. (2011). Mercenary Territory: Are Youth Gangs Really a Problem? In B. Goldson (Ed.), *Youth in Crisis? 'Gangs', Territoriality and Violence* (pp. 161–182). Abingdon, England: Routledge.

Pitts, J. (2016). Critical Realism and Gang Violence. In R. Matthews (Ed.), *What Is to Be Done About Crime and Punishment*. New York: Springer.

Pritchard, T. (2008). *Street Boys: 7 Kids. 1 Estate. No Way Out. The True Story of a Lost Childhood*. London: Harper Element.

Pryce, K. (1979). *Endless Pressure: A Study of West Indian Life-Styles in Bristol*. New York: Penguin Books.

Sayer, A. (1992). *Method in Social Science. A Realist Approach*. London: Routledge.

Sweet, P. (2018). *Julian Go's Post-Positivist, Postcolonial Realism Critical Realist Network*. Retrieved at http://criticalrealismnetwork.org/2018/04/25/julian-gos-post-positivist-postcolonial-realism/ (Accessed 28 October 2019).

Tierney, J. (2009). *Key Perspectives in Criminology*. Berkshire: McGraw-Hill Education, Open University Press.

Travers, M. (2017). The Idea of Southern Criminology? *Journal International Journal of Comparative and Applied Criminal Justice*, 43(1).

Vandenberghe, F. (2016). *What Is Critical About Critical Realism? Essays in Reconstructive Theory*. London: Routledge.

Van Gemert, F., Peterson, D. and Lien, L. I. (Eds.). (2008). *Street Gangs, Migration and Ethnicity*. London: Willan.

Walsh, P. (2005). *Gang War: The Inside Story of the Manchester Gangs*. Preston: Milo Books.

Wacquant, L. (1997). Three Pernicious Premises in the Study of the American Ghetto. In J. M. Hagedorn (Ed.), *Gangs in the Global City: Alternatives to Traditional Criminology* (pp. 34–54). Chicago, IL: University of Illinois Press.

Whittaker, A. J., Cheston, L., Tyrell, T., Higgins, M. M., Felix-Baptiste, C. and Harvard, T. (2018). From Postcodes to Profits: How Gangs Have Changed in Waltham Forest. Retrieved at https://www.lsbu.ac.uk/__data/assets/pdf_file/0018/128205/postcodes-to-profit-dr-andrew-whittaker.pdf (Accessed 29 March 2021).

Willis, P. (1978). *Profane Culture*. London: Routledge and Keegan Paul.

Windle, J. (2018). He Just Wasn't the Bloke I Used to Know': Social Capital and the Fragmentation of a British Organised Crime Network. In J. Windle, J. F. Morrison, A. Winter, and A. Silke (Eds.), *Historical Perspectives on Organised Crime and Terrorism* (pp. 75–90). Abingdon: Routledge. ISBN: 9781138652651

Windle, J. and Briggs, D. (2015). 'It's Like Working Away for Two Weeks', the Harms Associated with Young Drug Dealers Commuting from a Saturated London Drug Market. *Crime Prevention and Community Safety*, 17, pp. 105–119.

Young, J. (2004). Voodoo Criminology and the Numbers Game. In Ferrell, J., Hayward, K., Morrison, W. and Presdee, M. (Eds.), *Cultural Criminology Unleashed*. London: GlassHouse Press.

Young, J. (2011). *The Criminological Imagination*. Cambridge: Polity Press.

Young, T., Fitzgerald, M., Hallsworth, S. and Joseph, I. (2007). *Groups, Gangs and Weapons: A Report for the Youth Justice Board of England and Wales*. Youth Justice Board of England and Wales. ISBN 978-1-906139-06-3.

2

States of emergency

Gangs, Benjamin, and the challenge to modern sovereignty

Jon Horne Carter

In the great criminal this violence confronts the law with the threat of declaring a new law, a threat that even today, despite its impotence, in important instances horrifies the public as it did in primeval times.

– Walter Benjamin (CV, 283)

Introduction

What common ground could exist between street gangs in the urban landscapes of late capitalism in the West and a German literary and legal theorist of the high modern era? In my ethnographic fieldwork with gang communities in Central America, stretching from the mid-1990s to the present, I have always found a deep synergy between the historical materialism of Walter Benjamin, as he struggled to outmaneuver the Fascist law-makers of the Weimar Republic, and the challenge that street gangs have posed to the sovereign authority of the small republics of Honduras, El Salvador, and Guatemala over the last twenty years. In both contexts, that of Benjamin's time and the gang crisis in northern Central America today, one can ask how perpetrators of state violence attempt to legitimize their use of deadly force and how communities targeted by that violence in turn respond to that threat.

Though gang communities are not a universal type and evidence different characteristics wherever one might find them, always shaped within a particular lived context, it is vital to begin any analysis of modern gangs with the basic recognition that the one consistent commonality gangs share perhaps the world over is "threshold" relation to state power. Gangs exist at the threshold between law and community, where law is inconstant and selectively applied. Gangs are social worlds that take shape from within the margins of the state, shielding themselves and sometimes the broader community from economic and physical violence. Claiming power, where the narrative of state control and the ubiquity of its disciplinary mechanisms falters, is what makes gangs an alluring spectacle in state society going back to the nineteenth century. Charles Dickens, John Asbury, and other writers of the modern city described roving bands of children or neighborhood clans that considered themselves both fugitive and sovereign in a city increasingly controlled by the economically prosperous. We might also look farther back in time to the Middle Ages, when popular heroes that Hobsbawm called "social bandits" engaged in early modes of class struggle, sabotaging the practices of state formation built upon generations of primitive accumulation of capital (2000, 7–18). Similar to gangs in modern cities, bandits and brigands were not independent actors but the visible elements of broader social formations that challenged state authority in a given territory.

Whether in the early days of state formation or the contemporary era in which the nation-state is pulled apart by the varying forces of globalization, gangs are communities that emerge from the crisis of legitimacy of the state. While they may take on the role of political organizers, social workers, or organized crime rackets, at their most basic level, gangs are groups of individuals who take action to address the uneven authority of the state in their local worlds. The first signs of such activity often mean that police institutions are expanded and fortified in public campaigns that romanticize state intervention and in clandestine operations that infiltrate and dismantle local power structures.

In the following sections, I want to think about this tension between state and local power through the work of Walter Benjamin and the theorists who greatly inspired his writing on state power and political subjectivity, the French political philosopher Georges Sorel and the German legal theorist and jurist Carl Schmitt. Writing in the crucible of nationalism and high capitalism that shaped European modernity across the late nineteenth and early twentieth centuries, each asks how the powerful discourse of modernity, and its imbrication with consolidated power in the sovereignty of the modern state, might be disrupted – despite its iron grip on the history of the West. And while Benjamin was greatly influenced by Marxist and anarchist writers of the last century contemplating historical consciousness and history, it is his attention to aesthetics in politics and revolution that transcends the gap often inscribed between criminalized communities, such as street gangs, and political movements properly conceived.

Background

Walter Benjamin was born in Berlin in 1892 and came of age as the city was being transformed as the capital of the new German nation. The city population doubled between 1870 and the turn of the century, and the historical character of the Prussian city was overhauled as the modern seat of the German empire. Benjamin's childhood in Berlin, his education during the consolidation of German nationalism, and his witness to the transformation of the German state across two World Wars give his intellectual work a particular critical perspective on ideological underpinnings of modernity and statehood in the West (Benjamin 2002a). For urban ethnographers, Benjamin's attention to the social and material components of European modernity sets a high bar. His writings track the uneven and sedimented layers of modernization, which in turn, he points out, create the potential for powerful forms of disjuncture. The remains of a buried and effaced historical past were suppressed but all the more poised to erupt through the naturalized and totalizing ideological field of modern culture.

As the city around him was remade during his formative childhood years, with infrastructure and industry expanding faster than most other places in Western Europe, the young Benjamin was sheltered within the domestic interiors of bourgeois life. His father was a well-established businessman from a family of merchants in Cologne and his mother from wealthy and cultured family in eastern Prussia. The Benjamins were an assimilated Jewish family, who employed an extensive domestic staff to assist the household and the care of their three children, among whom Walter was the eldest (Eiland and Jennings 2014, 12–17). In Benjamin's essay "A Berlin Childhood Around 1900", he reconstructs moments from his outings with babysitters and family, as the heightened sensory awareness of childhood dovetailed with the varied temporalities to be found across the cityscape. As life in turn-of-the-century Berlin staged the discursive and ideological uniformity of European modernity, Benjamin sought out the repressed, excluded, and enchanted dimensions of urban life. Across his unfinished magnum opus *The Arcades Project* and classic essay *One-Way Street*, Benjamin excavates the interstices of alleyways and abandoned lots, the underworlds of street performers, ex-workers, and petty criminals, where the ideology of historical progress and rational organization of the material and social world were countered by other modes of worlding (2002b, 2016).

But like anyone in western Europe at the turn of the century, Benjamin's life and intellect were shaped by escalating conflicts that would explode into World War I. During his sheltered youth, Benjamin was educated by private tutors and then public secondary schools with rigid discipline. In middle school, he was sent to a boarding academy in central Germany where he encountered the experimental educator Gustav Wyneken, who awakened in Benjamin an awareness of what he would later call "the metaphysics of youth" – the struggle between academic knowledge and an awakening consciousness able to imagine alternative futures outside the continuum between past and present (Benjamin 1996, 6–17). This tension between inherited knowledge and other social possibilities put Benjamin and his university peers in the middle of debates about national culture and belonging that foreshadowed World War I.

The outbreak of armed conflict in 1914 did not directly impact Benjamin's life, though the wider context of inflation, insecurity, and the scramble for political power inside of Germany and the Weimar Republic shaped his interest in political economy, class struggle, and law. During the war years, Benjamin moved numerous times between Switzerland, Austria, and Germany, composing essays and reviews but also starting an extensive research project on the little-studied genre of baroque tragic theatre in Germany (2019). In this study, from the highly regarded Spanish traditions to the lesser-known German works, is an early incarnation of Benjamin's take on historical time, which would run through much of his later, and highly influential, essays. In the baroque, Benjamin saw the changing power structures of the medieval to the modern period, constituted aesthetically as theatre. In the baroque, human episodes stood across from the process and weight of natural history. The props were clumsy, the symbolism overwrought, and the arc of history bleak. But for Benjamin, baroque theatre staged a hopelessness that was desolate but also a clearing. The contrivances of power, juxtaposed with the inevitability of natural history, threw the mythological into a critical relief. Across Germany at the time of his writing, the Weimar government struggled to contain internal revolt by declaring a state of emergency. Both baroque theatre and the modern state of emergency, Benjamin noticed, had the power to stop historical time. In that clearing, he thought, is the chance to seize a vision of the future to come. It is in moments of disruption, rather than ideological coherence, that revolutionary chance appears.

States of emergency

Over the last twenty-two years, I have conducted numerous research trips to Honduras that total three years of residency in the country, living mostly in two residential zones on the periphery of the capital city of Tegucigalpa where gangs have held significant local authority since the mid-1990s. Since my first visit in 1997, Benjamin's thoughts on the state of emergency were never far from my mind. I think this is largely due to the fact that gangs, especially those of the post-conflict transition in Honduras, are native to emergency itself. When I first started ethnographic research in Honduras in the late 1990s, the country was emerging from one crisis and heading into another. It was caught between the impacts of Cold War counterinsurgent conflicts and the ascendant era of free-market liberalism that created new forms of economic and social dislocation for the poor (Grandin 2007, 193–197). During the Cold

War in Honduras, from 1980 to 1988, a counter-revolutionary army known as the Contras was funded by the United States and a network of international anti-communist militants, with the goal of overthrowing the newly victorious Sandinista government in Nicaragua. Most were former Nicaraguan National Guard ousted after the fall of Nicaraguan dictator Anastasio Somoza Debayle. While Honduras did not experience a civil war on the scale of Guatemala, El Salvador, and Nicaragua, the presence of the Contras and US military advisors had a deeply disruptive impact on the country. At its height, the Contra army numbered more than 20,000 mercenaries and internationals. The Honduran military being only 17,500 at the time, Honduran president Jorge Azcona supported US presence in Honduras if only so that the irregular counter-revolutionary army would not "become an uncontrollable group" of bandits in his country in the event that they lost US backing (Marshall et al. 1987, 146). US and Argentine covert action officials trained the death squadron known as Battalion 316, which targeted insurgents, labor leaders, students, and those suspected to be sympathetic to the political Left (Grandin 2007, 115–120). Refugees streamed out of the country, many to the United States (Blanchard et al. 2011). By the late 1990s, when I started visiting the country, the new free-trade policies put in place after the war hurt the working class, as currency was devalued, wages fell, and a deluge of imported commodities bankrupted domestic producers (Pine 2008, 19–22). In the middle of this political and economic transformation, thousands of young people whose families had fled during the military conflict were deported from the United States. Many belonged to gangs (Wolseth 2011). To witness their arrival, and social dislocation, was to see human lives as shaped by emergency: chased from one country, on to be persecuted and removed from another.

Starting in the late 1970s, the largest Central American refugee communities settled into the south-eastern side of Los Angeles, California, one of the most progressive sanctuary cities in the United States. In the district of Pico Union, Central American communities negotiated their presence between existing African American and Chicano gangs that for decades had been protecting their communities from the well-documented violence of the Los Angeles Police Department (Flores 2013). During the ensuing years, some Salvadoran refugees organized a community patrol group which, in time, would become the Mara Salvatrucha (MS13). Along with the Eighteenth Street gang (Barrio 18), both groups recruited from the youngest of Central American refugees (De Cesare 2013, 34–79). In 1996, two federal changes to immigration law (the Illegal Immigration Reform and Immigrant Responsibility Act and the Anti-Terrorism and Effective Death Penalty Act) expanded the criteria of deportability such that deportations quadrupled from 50,024 in 1995 to 188,467 in 2000 (Golash-Boza 2017, 42). In the small countries of northern Central America, the arrival of several thousand deportees each year was visible. Many had grown up in California where law enforcement of communities of color was historically aggressive. Many had experienced detention and incarceration in the criminal justice system of the United States. Honduran police targeted deportees as potential criminals based on their clothing, piercings, and tattoos. Some were members of MS13 or Barrio 18, though many were just typical adolescents, into hip-hop music and urban fashion. In the late 1990s, the idea of gangs in Tegucigalpa did not conjure images of the malevolent, predatory organizations that, in global media at least, are nearly synonymous with northern Central America today. At that time, these were young people, misfits and rebellious teenagers of different interests and styles, who came together as deportees or economically marginalized poor. Many deportees did not speak Spanish fluently, and if they arrived with tattoos, they were often marginalized as potential criminals, even within their own families. They arrived to Honduras as outsiders, and the majority remained so, with few social programs to support their integration into life in the city (Salomón et al. 1999).

By the early 2000s, the governments of Honduras, Guatemala, and El Salvador were all reporting rapid growth in street gangs in urban areas. As the domestic economy in Honduras continued to contract from impacts of NAFTA and neoliberal state policy, gangs offered a certain alternative at a time when economic and social resources for working people were shrinking. After the September 11, 2001, attacks in the United States, a wave of changes to national security practices swept over the hemisphere, including in Honduras (Wolf 2017). The war on gangs in Honduras began with a visit by President Ricardo Maduro to the United States, where advisors to the United States War on Terror shaped anti-gang policing in Honduras as an arm of hemispheric collaboration against terrorism (Zilberg 2011). In 2002, that plan was unveiled as Mano Dura (Iron Fist) policing, which integrated military and civil police forces for the first time since the 1980s (Carter 2014, 478–481). These special forces units had wide latitude for search, arrest, and detention of anyone suspected of gang membership and, on the first day of its roll-out, President Maduro walked the streets of Tegucigalpa surrounded by military tanks, urging citizens to overcome their fear of gangs and join in the liberation of their city. "Most of the joint military-police operations pit security forces against young alleged gang members, usually aged 15 to 19," writes Thelma Mejía, a political analyst in Tegucigalpa. "For the police, the youths' appearance – baggy pants and T-shirts, tattoos – is enough to signal that they are gang members and therefore subject to arrest, despite there being no law to justify this" (Mejía 2007).

Reflections on violence

In his meditations on law and modern sovereignty, Walter Benjamin's attention was focused on these moments of sudden escalation of state power, always with a preoccupation for how citizen resistance could respond. It was the retired French civil servant Georges Sorel who most influenced Benjamin's thinking at the early stages, with his landmark work *Reflections on Violence* (1908). The book examined the growing power of the syndicalist movement in France and the violent clashes between labor strikers and state forces, and it argued, controversially, that the working class's strongest position was to maintain itself apart from bourgeois society. That meant a confrontational stance that rejected the benevolence and compromises of capitalist and political classes, seeking to appease workers. Sorel's critique assailed the position of French Marxists who believed the contradictions in capital, left to their own devices, would create the conditions for proletarian revolution. He assailed "parliamentary socialism" and "civilized socialism" dependent upon a vanguard of the working class which negotiated terms with the state and capitalists, which, in Sorel's view, extended the existing scope of bourgeois morality into the working class itself. For Sorel, reform was the enemy. Only an uncompromising general strike had the power to destroy the state, which was the only option for creating a livable future. After spending years in Paris, Sorel was deeply influenced by anarchists of his time and suspicious of any utopian project. If the strike were led by syndicates, state power would not be handed over to the next ruling vanguard but rather would be diffused through the syndicates where new cultural and political practices could emerge.

Though it was published in French in 1903, Benjamin first read *Reflections on Violence* in 1920 while living in Switzerland, away from the economic volatility and bleak employment prospects in Germany. On his return to Berlin later that year, it served as the starting point for his own essay, "Critique of Violence", whose title acknowledged the influence of Sorel's ideas. What seems to have made Sorel's work especially exciting for Benjamin was his treatment of violence as a complex social phenomenon as opposed to middle-class understandings of violence as destruction that was either legitimate (state) or criminal (non-state). Sorel argues that across the nineteenth century, the idea of revolutionary violence was inextricably associated with the French Revolution, especially the Reign of Terror, in which anyone opposed to the Jacobin's utopian vision of the world was executed. If revolution only replaced one set of rulers with a new vanguard, always invoking the authority of "the people", then how could a new and fair society emerge? For Sorel, revolution had to destroy the state as the only possible form of governance. The question, then, was how? Sorel looked to warfare in ancient Greece, in which violence was not resentment but heroism without material reward. He does not give details of any general strike itself but focuses instead on the potential for the courageous actions of a few individuals to produce creative forms of identification and an instantaneous vision of the future socialist society. Contrary to the modeling and fulfillment of utopian ideas, Sorel offers the alternative of a "mythical" vision that inspires individuals to action. Socialist society would be knowable when the space was cleared for it to emerge, and not before. Proletarian violence, for Sorel, was the means to an end of institutionalized barbarism masquerading as the will of the people.

In 1997, when I started fieldwork on gangs in Tegucigalpa, the political Left, so crucial to Sorel's thinking, was in retreat. Labor organizing was still cautious after systematic persecution during the Contra war (Frank 2005). Targeting of suspected leftists had left 184 dead or disappeared, among whom were known leaders in the labor movement, agrarian reform movement, and anti-imperial Left (Comisionado Nacional de los Derechos Humanos 2002; Salomón 1994). The military, on the other hand, was dominated by politically conservative and pro-capitalist leadership that across the 1990s grew increasingly intertwined with private sector investors and lobbyists who would reshape the country along the Washington Consensus in preparation for regional economic integration (Ruckert 2010, 116–120; Salomón 2002). While the MS13 and Barrio 18 gangs grew exponentially in few years, it was easy to regard the numbers of under- or unemployed young people as continuous with working-class protest of the past. But that affinity was troubled by corporate media which quickly turned gang communities into spectacle, through cartoonish portrayals that demonized gang members as enemies of the public good, eroding national culture as much as public security (Pine 2008, 25–84).

Sovereignty

Benjamin's "Critique of Violence" begins by asking how existing forms of law, either natural or positive law, differed in their understanding of violence. Natural law regarded violence as a problem of human nature, constant over time. It was legitimate when it produced just ends, as anti-colonial violence disrupts oppression and institutes liberty. Positive law regarded violence as evolving historically and changing with human experience and time. Violence was legitimate in positive law insofar as its legitimacy could justify its ends, as state repression is permitted by but also demonstrative of the state itself. Both perspectives, Benjamin notes, approach violence as a means to an ends in a political system. Neither positive nor natural law can account for violence whose justification lies outside the existing legal order.

For the modern state, Benjamin argues there are two forms of violence. Law-making violence is that which establishes a legal order through foundational acts of violence. Law-preserving violence is that which sustains the authority of law-making violence in the form of institutions and ongoing practices. Together law-making and law-preserving acts are mutually constitutive and render the "mythical violence" of authority. Mythical violence, for Benjamin, is the self-referential space of legitimacy in which God is refashioned as secular, totalizing authority. The question that Benjamin took from Sorel's "proletarian strike" was how one might conceive of a form of violence that was neither law-making nor law-preserving but which would overturn the legal present. In opposition to mythical violence, Benjamin drew from Sorel to propose the concept of "divine violence", which, he suggested, did not serve idols but destroyed them, leaving nothing in their place.

> If mythical violence is law-making, divine violence is law-destroying; if the former sets boundaries, the latter boundlessly destroys them; if mythical violence brings at once guilt and retribution, divine power only expiates; if the former threatens, the latter strikes; if the form is bloody, the latter is lethal without spilling blood.
>
> *(Benjamin 1996 [1921], 23)*

Here Benjamin runs with Sorel and expands anti-state violence beyond the general strike, to revolutionary action that deposes an existing legal-mythical source of power.

What Benjamin called divine violence was of immediate concern to the ruling factions of Germany in the early 1920s. The Treaty of Versailles was signed in 1919 and imposed crippling reparations on the country. Economic and political instability led to armed uprisings in Munich, Dresden, Leipzig, and Braunschweig that were given support by the newly founded German Communist Party. The German right retaliated with violent suppression, as the right-wing mercenary groups calling themselves Freikorps unleashed paramilitary violence against uprisings and across the countryside (Theweleit 1987). As the new constitution of the Weimar Republic was underway, many Germans demanded that the leadership respond to insurgent violence by declaring a state of emergency. Within the emergency, uprisings from both the right and left could be quelled, after which the country could move forward. At the center of the ensuing debate between liberal and anti-liberal theories of sovereignty was the liberal legal theorist Hans Kelsen. Kelsen argued that the state of emergency was a logical impossibility within the legal system of the country, as the Weimar law and constitution formed a hermetic body in which everything was defined by law. Suspending the law undermined state sovereignty. Opposite Kelsen was the jurist and legal scholar Carl Schmitt, who was to become the core legal theorist of the Third Reich. Schmitt responded that political life was not limited and defined by its laws but responsible to the indisputable fact that the threat of violence was inescapable for human communities. Sovereignty, he argued, entailed defending the community from violence – naming the threat and acting against it ("friend-enemy distinction") (1996). Sovereignty, therefore, was prior to the legal order. When the legal order was threatened, the sovereign intervened to preserve it. Liberal governance, insofar as it was hamstrung by debate over individual and communal rights, could not act decisively during moments of danger and therefore put the nation at risk. Dictatorship was a governing arrangement that allowed for decisive action, declaring the emergency, after which liberal democratic governance could return. The critique of Kelsen was an attack on liberalism more broadly that Schmitt formalized in the book *Dictatorship* (2016).

But it was Schmitt's book *Political Theology* (1985) that, published a year later, is thought to be a direct reply to Benjamin ("Critique" was published in a journal where Schmitt's own work also appeared.) In *Political Theology*, Schmitt recuperates the emergency and "divine violence" within sovereignty itself. "Sovereign is he who decides on the exception," Schmitt writes in the book's opening salvo. The emergency was both an exception to law and also its locus of agency. Trained by Max Weber, Schmitt saw the rationalization of political life as a social fact, though hampered by a new dependence on technological and disembodied decision-making. He called his vision of sovereignty "political theology" insofar as with it, he attempted to restored a force of authority that could transcend an increasingly impersonal legal and governmental order. Sovereignty, like Weber's "iron cage", was a religious concept hollowed out by modern life while retaining its form. "The central concepts of modern state theory," Schmitt writes, "are all secularized political concepts" (36). Schmittian sovereignty was not beholden to the law but was itself the authority to suspend law. If divine violence struck with the power to depose a legal system, sovereignty struck to eliminate all existing alternatives. As the National Socialist Party shaped Germany over the next decade, those who decided what constituted an emergency held one of the primary tools by which Fascist violence was legitimized as a means to an end.

Political theology

In northern Central America, the primary mechanism of state repression of civil society during the 1980s was the emergency – the suspension of law in the name of preserving law from insurgents who (supposedly) would dismantle it. "Counter-insurgency" was both a euphemism which played down as a tactic the otherwise alarming idea of unchecked state power, as well as a shibboleth among the "power elite" for extending total domination of civil society in an ongoing manner, such that war and everyday life merge as to become indistinguishable.

In Honduras, the military death squad Battalion 316 was created, trained, and supported by US special forces and military veterans of the Dirty War in Argentina, creating a hemispheric network of theorists and tacticians acting within a constellation of state emergencies. But as demilitarization of northern Central American republics began in the early 1990s, the counter-insurgency brigades and military death squads proved somewhat resistant to dismantling. Many associated with human rights violations and death squads went into business in the private sector, establishing for-profit security firms that won state security contracts as policing and security work were privatized under neoliberal governance (Pine 2010, 249–261). As such, the Schmittian core of sovereign power was no longer located within military units but fragmented across networks of security contractors who purged the urban core of Tegucigalpa, making way for foreign investment capital expected to pull the country forward with the passage of a Central American free trade agreement to follow NAFTA. As security forces targeted homeless juveniles, those suffering addiction and substance abuse, and anyone whose physical appearance hinted toward involvement in gangs, the criminalization of poverty dramatized the public space as a theatre of law enforcement and criminalization. By the mid-1990s, the target of emergency powers had shifted from political dissent of the Cold War to security threats in the age of terrorism and narcotrafficking (Moodie 2012).

As Giorgio Agamben notes, the terror attacks on September 11, 2001, in the United States were fundamental to the vast expansion of Schmittian sovereignty by the turn of the 2000s (Agamben 2005). Anti-Islamic discourse across the West framed the threat of terrorism as an emergency that suffused daily life and required perpetual vigilance. While the United States expanded security, intelligence gathering, and military operations into a War on Terrorism, the countries of northern Central America enacted anti-gang security legislation that breached liberal norms (Paglen 2007). When anti-gang policing was introduced in El Salvador, Guatemala, and Honduras in 2002, it was cast as part of the necessary compromises to liberal norms that were required by a "global" war on terrorism (Zilberg 2011). The protocols for anti-gang called Mano Dura directed new US security aid to police and military units who could detain small groups on public corners, arrest anyone with tattoos, baggy clothing or particular hairstyles, conduct warrantless searches of private domiciles, and create general conditions of lawlessness as a basis for urban security (Gutiérrez Rivera et al. 2018; Rodgers 2009). In the first few years of Mano Dura, extra-judicial killing of young men and women increased dramatically. Investigations revealed the existence of off-duty police groups who assassinated suspected criminals, but were shielded by institutional corruption and exonerated of culpability (Stone 2012).

As anti-gang laws detained thousands of young men who languished in wards of the national prison system stretched far beyond its capacity, mysterious fires swept through dormitories where suspected gang members were isolated. In 2003, a fire in the Granja Penal in La Ceiba killed 69 people, and, a year later in 2004, a fire at the prison in San Pedro Sula killed 107 (Weiner 2004). On the day of the second fire, eye witnesses reported a masked firing squad on the prison lawn, executing any gang members who escaped (Hayden 2004). National uproar demanded investigations, and the aftermath of the fire initiated a shift in public opinion around Mano Dura. Photos of gang members in burn wards and of the charred remains of victims arranged in a grid inside the prison yard exposed the violence of sovereignty that is usually hidden under the rational veneer of modern bureaucratic and legal systems. Many of my neighbors in Tegucigalpa joined others in the streets, protesting for justice for gang members criminalized and brutalized without consequence, and commented to me later in the evening after we returned to the barrio, where gangs were still quite fearsome, that they were shocked to find themselves defending those whom they were accustomed to regarding as indefensible. Around Tegucigalpa, as I spoke to people in the aftermath of the fire in 2004, the protests for justice made fresh again memories of the 1980s and the deep resentment and sadness around the unresolved disappearances at the hand of Battalion 316. The theatricalized violence against gangs in the nation's prisons seemed to stage the violent core of sovereign power, where death squadrons are always ready, poised for the next emergency.

For Carl Schmitt, this force inside the concept of sovereignty was that of "political theology", a vengeful and lawless force that strikes against whatever dwells beyond its legal and political norms and whose existence is an existential threat to power. Toward the end of his life, Walter Benjamin pondered this continuity of the "emergency", cloaked within systems that conceal its absolute authority, and as Nazi forces occupied France in 1940 and threatened to take Paris, he recorded his thoughts as he prepared to flee. "The tradition of the oppressed teaches us that the 'state of emergency' in which we live is not the exception but the rule," Benjamin writes. "We must attain to a conception of history that is in keeping with this insight" (Benjamin 1969, 257). Benjamin asks us what a conception of history, as such, might look like. My question here is how gangs might help us imagine it.

Exception to the exception

As state violence against gangs in Honduras mounted across the early 2000s, gang tattooing began to change, particularly that of the MS13 and Barrio 18. Confined into overpacked prison barracks, gang members began covering their upper bodies and faces with interlocking images that formed a shroud over the body. This overflowing and excessing style was shocking even to a more liberal public, because the images were gothic figures of demons, skeletons, and naked bodies, with marijuana leaves, firearms, tombstones, and flames. It was both aesthetically and morally confrontational. Much of the writing on gangs focuses on testimonials of gang members as individuals, but the tattooing was also an overt statement, in a non-linear and unexpected style, asking for interpretation. Perhaps they ask us to consider how foisting oneself beyond the world of legality, making oneself a criminal in front of the state which criminalizes gang members, shifts the meaning of criminality?

One of Sorel's claims in *Reflections on Violence* that proved most controversial was that the working class was strongest, and most effectively confrontational, when it kept itself isolated from the temptations of compromise offered from capitalists and the political class. As mass incarceration of suspected gang members overwhelmed the prison system of a neoliberal state that allocated no funding for renovations, one of the unintended by-products of Mano Dura was a new and de facto social world of legal and political exteriority. In 2004, after the second prison fire, Honduran prison officials negotiated with human rights advocates to hand over authority inside of prison wards and empowered inmates to administrate prison interiors themselves in an arrangement that is often described as "co-governance" (Carter 2019). In Honduran prisons, this configuration opened a space where gangs were isolated from harm by controlling the flow of outsiders into their prison barracks and where their otherwise fugitive community was concentrated as never before. There, gang life transformed, as gang sociality expanded through processes of what anthropologist Kathleen Stewart, taking from Heidegger, calls "worlding" – the rhythms, relations, and movements by which spaces become inhabited and accrue into modes of existence (Stewart 2011, 445). Rather than thinking of "gangs" from a distant register that homogenizes their communities into copies beholden to an original or hegemonic chapter of MS13 or Barrio 18, I take from Stewart to urge that we think smaller and with the particular. For Stewart, an attention to "worlding" sticks close to the "proliferation of little worlds of all kinds that form up around conditions, practices, manias, pacings, scenes of absorption, styles of living, forms of attachment (or detachment), identities, and imaginaries, or some publicly circulating strategy for self-transformation" (2011, 446). By observing these shifts in the organization and aesthetic dimensions of gangs in Honduras in the early 2000s, one might be able to focus on the specific socially and historically situated conditions from which their communities have created themselves in dialogue with the political world whose powers of subjectification never cease.

In Walter Benjamin's "Theses on the Philosophy of History" (1996 [1940]), which was a companion piece to "Critique of Violence", he circled back after nearly twenty years to respond again to Carl Schmitt. In the essay, Benjamin meditates on the necessity of disrupting the mythical violence in sovereign power of modern states. And while the reader of Benjamin's work would have been familiar with the concept of "divine violence", which Benjamin opposes to mythical violence in his earlier essay, here he also introduces a temporality of disruption as a stoppage of time. The disruption of mythical violence arrests ideology and history into what he calls a "messianic cessation of happening", within which one has a chance to grasp the otherwise, which Benjamin calls "a revolutionary chance in the fight for the oppressed past" (1996, 263). We might think of the "oppressed past" as the history of those communities and individual lives buried beneath the wheel of mythical violence. It is this tension between past and present that animates human action in the moment that the political present is disrupted. Benjamin writes, "There is a secret agreement between past generations and the present one. Like every generation that preceded us, we have been endowed with a *weak* Messianic power, a power to which the past has a claim." That Messianic power is the present generation's unique place within history, which also meant its singular and unrepeatable relation to the past. Against mythical violence and the naturalized authority of sovereignty, "we shall realize that it is our task to bring about the real state of emergency," Benjamin goes on. That emergency is the legal system of sovereign power itself (1996, 257). The clarity of the Messianic moment was, for Benjamin, the scene of divine violence whose theatrical intervention into historical time drains state sovereignty of its greatest weapon – its sense of historical inevitability.

Conclusion

In this chapter, I have argued that the MS13 and Barrio 18 gangs of northern Central America might be regarded as more than sociological and criminological types but rather a critical study in the aesthetics of sovereignty and criminality. The history of gang communities in northern Central America is coeval with that of an excess of sovereign violence that does not begin in the Cold War period but attains there a legitimacy whose unfolding across subsequent decades has shaped gang life and in turn been shaped by it. Looking back at the formulation of Walter Benjamin's notion of divine violence, then, we can ask how this escalation of state violence against Leftists in the Cold War and then against gang members in the contemporary era made armed resistance difficult and even futile while it made room for other counter-performances. The tattooing of gang bodies with detailed portraits of infernal suffering and death mirrored the unadulterated violence of sovereignty and created a mimetic parabola that disrupted the familiarity of both visual and conceptual reality. It gives us pause. This disruption arrests the historical flow of an experience that is homogenized by ideological closure and produces what Benjamin called heterogeneous time – a rupture in the inevitability of the present, in which multiple historical futures become visible. That vision was a "dialectical image", the condensation of event and meaning across historical time. It is a site of investment, inspiration without a masterplan or an ideological name. Jacques Derrida, commenting on Benjamin's thought, called it a "messianicity without messianism" (Derrida 1992). The dialectical image, Benjamin tells us, flies up, and we are either to capture it or lose it forever. So how might we grasp it?

In answering this question, I think it is vital that we ask how these histories of gang life in Honduras have changed over the last decade and a half. Across the 2010s, they have changed dramatically, annexed by larger organized crime groups and transformed into an arm of narcotrafficking cartels. Today they are part of the systematized violence that drives Hondurans from the country in waves of refugees who make up the now familiar "migrant caravans". But as perpetrators of violence, it is crucial to realize that gangs are also now part of the criminal power of the state itself. In October 2019, as the president of Honduras, Juan Orlando Hernandez, was impugned in US courts for taking vast sums of money from cartels, Honduras is widely decried as a "narco-state", which folds gangs, cartels, and the sovereignty of the state into one another such that it is entirely possible to lose sight of what gangs often are – the target of state power rather than its perpetrators. If we think of gang politics in the late 1990s as a form of what Benjamin calls "divine violence" – shaking the myth of state lawfulness to its core and exposing the arbitrariness of state power with the laceration of their own bodies covered in occult imagery – then their history is impacted with potential for revolutionary interpretation of history, power, and possibility. If the breathless accounts of gang violence in northern Central America feel like so much ideological closure, perhaps it is a deep attention to the cultural and aesthetic registers of gang life, as resistance to state violence rather than an extension of it, that can open heterogeneous time and make social science writing into revolutionary critique.

References

Agamben, Giorgio. 2005. *State of Exception*. Translated by Kevin Attell. Chicago: University of Chicago Press.

Benjamin, Walter. 1969. "Theses on the Philosophy of History." In *Illuminations: Essays and Reflections*, edited by Hanna Arendt. Translated by Harry Zohn. New York: Schocken Books.

———. 1996. "Metaphysics of Youth." In *Walter Benjamin, Selected Writings Volume 1: 1913–1926*, edited by Marcus Bullock and Michael W. Jennings, 6–17. Translated by Rodney Livingstone. Cambridge: Harvard University Press.

———. 1996. "Critique of Violence." In *Walter Benjamin, Selected Writings Volume 1: 1913–1926*, edited by Marcus Bullock and Michael W. Jennings, 236–252. Translated by Edmund Jephcott. Cambridge: Harvard University Press.

———. 2002a. *The Arcades Project*. Translated by Howard Eiland and Kevin MacLaughlin. Cambridge: Harvard University Press.

————. 2002b. "Berlin Childhood Around 1900." In *Walter Benjamin, Selected Writings Volume 3: 1935–1938*, edited by Howard Eiland and Michael W. Jennings. Translated by Howard Eiland. Cambridge: Harvard University Press.

————. 2016. *One-Way Street*, edited by Michael Jennings. Translated by Edmund Jephcott. Cambridge: Harvard University Press.

————. 2019. *Origin of the German Trauerspiel*. Translated by Howard Eiland. Cambridge: Harvard University Press.

Blanchard, Sarah, Erin Hamilton, Nestor Rodríguez, and Hirotoshi Yoshioka. 2011. "Shifting Trends in Central American Migration: A Demographic Examination of Increasing Honduran and U.S. Immigration and Deportation." *The Latin Americanist* 55(4): 61–84.

Brotherton, David and Philip Kretsedemas. 2018. *Immigration Policy in the Age of Punishment: Detention, Deportation, and Border Control*. New York: Columbia University Press.

Carter, Jon Horne. 2014. "Gothic Sovereignty: Gangs and Criminal Community in a Honduran Prison." *South Atlantic Quarterly* 114(3): 475–502.

————. 2019. "Carceral Kinship: Future Families of the Late Leviathan." *Journal of Historical Sociology* 32: 26–37.

Comisionado Nacional de los Derechos Humanos. 2002. *Los Hechos Hablan Por Si Mismos:* Informe Preliminar Sobre los Desaparecidos en Honduras 1980–1993. Tegucigalpa: Editorial Guaymuras.

De Cesare, Donna. 2013. *Unsettled / Desasociego: Children in a World of Gangs / Los Niños en un Mundo de Pandillas*. Translated by Javier Auyero. Austin: University of Texas Press.

Derrida, Jacques. 1992. "Force of Law: The 'Mystical Foundation of Authority'." In *Deconstruction and the Possibility of Justice*, edited by Drucilla Cornell, Michel Rosenfeld, and David Gray Carlson, 3–67. New York: Routledge Press.

Eiland, Howard, and Michael W. Jennings. 2014. *Walter Benjamin: A Critical Life*. Cambridge: Harvard University Press.

Flores, Eduardo Orozco. 2013. *God's Gangs: Barrio Ministry, Masculinity, and Gang Recovery*. New York: New York University Press.

Frank, Dana. 2005. *Bananeras: Women Transforming the Banana Unions of Latin America*. Boston: South End Press.

Golash-Boza, Tanya. 2017. "President Obama's Legacy as 'Deporter in Chief.'" In *Immigration Policy in the Age of Punishment: Detention, Deportation, and Border Control*, edited by David Brotherton and Philip Kretsedemas. New York: Columbia University Press.

Grandin, Greg. 2007. *Empire's Workshop: Latin America, the United States, and the Rise of the New Imperialism*. New York: Holt Paperbacks.

Gutiérrez Rivera, Lirio, Iselin Åsedotter Strønen, and Margit Ystanes. 2018. "Coming of Age in the Penal System: Neoliberalism, 'Mano Dura' and the Reproduction of 'Racialised' Inequality in Honduras." In *The Social Life of Economic Inequalities in Contemporary Latin America. Approaches to Social Inequality and Difference*, edited by M. Ystanes and I Strønen, 205–228. London and Cham: Palgrave Macmillan.

Hayden, Tom. 2004. "Homies Were Burning Alive." *Alternet*, July 1, 2004. www.alternet.org/story/18843/ 'homies_were_burning_alive.'

Hobbsbawm, Eric. 2000. *Bandits*. London: Abacus Books.

Marshall, Jonathan, Peter Dale Scott, and Jane Hunter. 1987. *The Iran-Contra Connection: Secret Teams and Covert Operations in the Reagan Era*. Montreal, Canada: Black Rose Books.

Mejía, Thelma. 2007. "In Tegucigalpa, the Iron Fist Fails." *NACLA Report on the Americas*, July/August, 26–29.

Moodie, Ellen. 2012. *El Salvador in the Aftermath of Peace: Crime, Uncertainty, and the Transition to Democracy*. Philadelphia: University of Pennsylvania Press.

Paglen, Trevor. 2007. *Torture Taxi: On the Trail of the CIA's Rendition Flights*. New York: Icon Books.

Pine, Adrienne. 2008. *Working Hard, Drinking Hard: On Violence and Survival in Honduras*. Berkeley: University of California Press.

————. 2010. "Waging War on the Wageless: Extrajudicial Killings, Private Armies, and the Poor in Honduras." In *The War Machine and Global Health: A Critical Medical Anthropological Examination of the Human*

Costs of Armed Conflict and the International Violence Industry, edited by Merril Singer and G. Derrick Hodge, 241–276. Lanham, MD: Rowman and Littlefield.

Rodgers, Dennis. 2009. "Slum Wars of the 21st Century: Gangs, Mano Dura and the New Urban Geography of Conflict in Central America." *Development and Change* 40(5): 949–976.

Ruckert, Arne. 2010. "The Poverty Reduction Strategy Paper of Honduras and the Transformations of Neoliberalism." *Canadian Journal of Latin American and Caribbean Studies* 35(70): 113–139.

Salomón, Leticia. 1994. *La Violencia en Honduras, 1980–1993*. Tegucigalpa: CEDOH (Centro de Documentación de Honduras).

———. 2002. *Honduras: Reforma Policial y Seguridad Ciudadana*. Tegucigalpa: Foro Ciudadano.

Salomón, Leticia, Julieta Castellanos, and Mirna Flores. 1999. *La delincuencia juvenil: Los menores infractores en Honduras*. Tegucigalpa: CEDOH (Centro de Documentación de Honduras).

Schmitt, Carl. 1985. *Political Theology: Four Chapters on the Concept of Sovereignty*. Translated by George Schwab. Chicago: Chicago University Press.

———. 2016. *Dictatorship: From the Origin of the Modern Concept of Sovereignty to Proletarian Class Struggle*. Translated by Michael Hoelzl and Graham Ward. Cambridge, MA: Polity Press.

Sorel, Georges. 1950. *Reflections on Violence*. Translated by T. E. Hulme and J. Roth. Glencoe, IL: The Free Press.

Stewart, Kathleen. 2011. "Atmospheric Attunements." *Environment and Planning D: Society and Space* 29(3): 445–453.

Stone, Hannah. 2012. "Honduras' New Top Cop Comes With a Dark Past." *InSight Crime*, May 29.

Theweleit, Klaus. 1987. *Male Fantasies, Vol. 1: Women, Floods, Bodies, History*. Translated by Erica Carter, Stephen Conway, and Chris Turner. Minneapolis: University of Minnesota Press.

Weiner, Tim. 2004. "At Least 100 Are Killed in Prison Fire in Honduras." *New York Times*, May 18.

Wolf, Sonja. 2017. *Mano Dura: The Politics of Gang Control in El Salvador*. Austin: University of Texas Press.

Wolseth, Jon. 2011. *Jesus and the Gang: Youth Violence and Christianity in Urban Honduras*. Tucson: University of Arizona Press.

Zilberg, Elana. 2011. *Space of Detention: The Making of a Transnational Gang Crisis Between Los Angeles and San Salvador*. Durham: Duke University Press.

The Birmingham School and critical gang studies

Hugo Goeury

Introduction

In the 1960s and 1970s, groundbreaking research conducted by the Birmingham School changed the way we think about working-class youth by deconstructing the notion of subcultural deviance and bringing issues of resistance to the forefront of the analysis. If its early work emphasized the agency and potential for resistance of working-class youth, in a subsequent publication, Stuart Hall and his co-authors would shift their focus to the culture and institutions of social control of which those youths are the (un)privileged targets. While those theoretical and empirical interventions remain relevant for the field of gang studies, most mainstream, US-based criminologists have tended to neglect the Birmingham School's valuable insights.

This chapter reviews some of the main contributions of the Birmingham School, starting with the intellectual foundation on which it was built and then focusing on its work on subcultures and the subsequent publication *Policing the Crisis (PTC)*. The goal is to present some of the main ideas developed by the authors affiliated with the Birmingham School and to show how those can inform the work of scholars studying gangs from a critical perspective.

The origins of the "Birmingham School": working-class culture as opposition

In 1964, Richard Hoggart founded the Center for Contemporary Cultural Studies (CCCS) at the University of Birmingham. While the CCCS – which is usually considered the birthplace of cultural studies (Turner, 2003; Gelder, 2007) – remained active until 2002, it published its most influential work under the leadership of Stuart Hall, who directed it between 1968 and 1979.

As Hall himself (1980: 16) explained, the CCCS was greatly influenced by the seminal work of Hoggart (1992/1957), Williams (1983/1958) and Thompson (1966), who, together, represented the "original curriculum" that formed the Birmingham School's theoretical foundation. Hoggart and Williams both challenged the dominant, highly elitist paradigm of the time that tended to associate "Culture" with the middle and upper classes while discarding working-class culture as being insignificant and irrelevant. While both authors shared a certain nostalgia towards a "golden age" of working-class culture supposedly corrupted by the rise of the mass-consumption society, their work brought attention to the working-class culture's vitality rather than its presumed conformity and passivity. Without embracing the Marxist notion of class antagonism, Hoggart argued that a sense of "community" constitutes one of the most essential features of working-class culture which, following a "us" versus "them" division, sees bourgeois society, its institutions and representatives, as "strange and often unhelpful" (1992/1957: 53).

Thompson's *The Making of the English Working Class* built on the themes developed by Hoggart and Williams but approached them from an overtly Marxist perspective. Driven by his ambition to develop a "history from below," he shared their objective of putting the working class at the center of his analysis. His goal was not only to rescue the working class from the dustbin of history but to restore to its members a sense of agency of which most historical accounts had deprived them. By doing so, he challenged the dominant narrative that portrayed the working class as the victim of history to recast it in the role of the maker of history.

Even though he put greater emphasis on the relationship between modes of production and working-class cultural formations, he shared Williams and Hoggart's focus on working-class *culture*. As he famously put it, "class is a cultural as much as an economic formation" (Thompson, 1966: 12). However, he departed from their respective analyses by considering "culture" as a privileged space where class struggle takes place.

Thompson followed the Marxist tradition that insists on the relational nature of class structures and contends that one of the most essential features of the working class is that it exists in a position of subordination vis-à-vis the capitalist class which, in turn, relies on a wide array of mechanisms - both material and symbolic - to maintain its dominant position. The novelty of Thompson's analysis is that it defined working-class culture as being of an intrinsic oppositional nature. For him, working-class culture constitutes an alternative way of life through which the proletariat is able to subvert and oppose the norms and values of bourgeois society. This approach represented a challenge to the orthodox Marxist view that tends to discard culture as a secondary matter, a reflection of determining economic structures and a space whose revolutionary potential is seen as marginal at best. By centering his analysis on the subversive nature of working-class culture and by stressing its importance in fomenting working-class resistance, Thompson followed the path traced by Gramsci, overturning the traditional base-superstructure relationship.

Under Hall's leadership, the Birmingham School would expand the theories of Hoggart, Williams and Thompson to develop a new field of subculture studies which became the Center's hallmark. Similar to the three aforementioned authors, British working-class culture thus occupied a privileged topic of inquiry. Following Thompson's work, the Center emphasized the oppositional nature of working-class culture which, for the CCCS's members, constituted one of the most primordial areas where the working class could "*win space*" (Clarke *et al.*, 2006/1975: 35) against the prevalent hegemonic order. The Birmingham School also challenged Hoggart's negative vision on working-class culture in the post-war era. While Hoggart lamented the rise of the mass consumption society for having turned the vibrant "full rich life" of working-class culture into a superficial "candy-floss world" (1992/1957), Hall and his colleagues developed a different view of this phenomenon, seeing it as a site for new possibilities of symbolic resistance.

The Birmingham School and "subcultures"

The transformations of the post-war context

The CCCS's interest in working-class subcultures can be seen as a direct response and challenge to the dominant discourse of the post-war era in Britain. In 1957, in a context of economic growth and increasing purchasing power, Conservative Prime Minister Macmillan argued that the country was experiencing "a state of prosperity such as we have never had . . . in the history of this country," concluding: "most of our people have never had it so good" (Evans, 2010). It was also asserted that this new affluence was occurring at a time of broad political consensus between the two traditional political parties of the United Kingdom as the Tories and the Labour Party both agreed that a strong welfare state and a mixed economy constituted a vigorous model of socio-economic development. It was also professed that social conflict and class antagonism would wither away from British society. Commentators claimed that, as the working class was becoming increasingly similar to the middle class, the very notion of "social class" had lost all relevance. The Center's work responded with a virulent critique of what its members considered a complete "social myth" (Clarke *et al.*, 2006/1975: 17).

While the Birmingham School acknowledged that the post-war era was indeed a time of substantial change for the British working class, Phil Cohen (1980/1972) and others argued that the change was of a very different nature compared to the dominant discourse of affluence, consensus and bourgeoisification. For them, the post-war era was one of "social disorganization" (1980/1972: 66), and they argued that processes like the restructuring of the urban landscape, the disintegration of the "traditional working-class family" and changes in the country's economic structure had deprived the working-class youth of the work-centered, communal dimension that defined their parents' culture. The working-class youth of the 1960s was coming of age at a time when the "social cement of the community [was] in a state of crisis" (Cohen, 1980/1972: 70). In Clarke's words: "they were the 'dispossessed inheritors,' they received a tradition which had been deprived of its real social bases" (2006/1975: 81). Suffering, on the one hand, from the the destruction of manufacturing jobs and, on the other hand, from their inability to fully enter the new mass consumption society, the working-class youth of the 1960s "had the worst of all possible worlds" (Cohen, 1980/1972: 70).

It is in this context of change and instability that working-class subcultures emerged at the crossroads between "the familiar and the novel" (Hebdige, 1988/1979: 77); part of century old tradition of working-class resistance but taking new forms reflecting the specificties of the particular context in which they arose.

Resistance through rituals: subcultures and symbolic resistance

The connection between the cultural and the material or, in Marxist terms, between the superstructure and the base, is made explicitly clear by the members of the Birmingham School who insisted that, through culture, social groups "give *expressive form* to their social and material life-experience . . . culture is the way, the forms, in which groups 'handle' the raw material of their social and material existence" (Clarke *et al.*, 2006/1975: 4). Thompson's influence is unmistakable in this. Like the British historian, the CCCS focused on working-class subcultures as spaces of resistance, arguing that through the development and maintenance of their subcultures, members of the working-class youth are engaged in "the struggle to win symbolic and physical space from the [dominant] institution[s] [of bourgeois society] and [their] rules" (Willis, 2016/1978: 26). This vision builds on the notion of hegemony developed by Antonio Gramsci.

For Gramsci, hegemony relates to the capacity to create a new "common sense," to make appear as natural what are essentially particular class interests. Located in the realm of ideas and culture, it hides the exploitative reality of capitalism and the unequal power relations on which it rests, reframing them in a way that obscures and reifies their oppressive nature: "thus the unequal extraction of surplus value in production appears as 'a fair day's wage for a fair day's work'" (Hall *et al.*, 2013/1978: 195). By creating a sense of what is "natural" and by defining the field of possibilities – that is, what is feasible and desirable for society as a whole and the role that each social group is supposed to play in this grand narrative – hegemony creates the necessary conditions for the preservation of the status quo and the maintenance of existing structures of domination. Ultimately, stressing the importance of consent over coercion, it creates an environment which ensures that, from a working-class perspective, "unfree conditions [are] entered freely" (Willis, 2016/1978: 120).

However, this hegemonic order is, by definition, unstable. Due to the internal contradictions of capitalism, cracks frequently appear in this ideological construction, the oppressive nature of the system becoming increasingly apparent. As a result, the hegemonic order has to be constantly recreated and consolidated, opening up space for working-class resistance and contestation. It is through this lens of cultural resistance that subcultures have to be understood. They constitute what Hebdige (1988/1979: 19) defines as a "symbolic violation of the social order." While the subcultures studied by the CCCS were quite diverse, they all fulfilled the same functions for its working-class youth members.

At a time when the sense of "community" central to the crumbling parent culture was being lost, to belong to a subcultural group can be seen as an attempt to recreate this sense of "togetherness" and solidarity characteristic of working-class culture. This point is made particularly clear by Clarke (2006/1975: 80 emphasis in the original) in his study of the skinhead movement: "skinhead style represents an attempt to re-create through the 'mob' the traditional working-class community, as a substitution for the *real* decline of the latter." Until the mid-1960s, work was the pillar of working-class identity in industrialized countries. It was "the main orientation point, in reference to which all other life pursuits could be planned and ordered" (Bauman, 2005/1998: 17). However, with the rise of the mass consumption society and the decline of traditional blue-collar jobs, work and the workplace lost their centrality and their role of incubators of both individual and collective identity. As a result, consumerism gained in importance in defining one's identity (Miles, 1995, 1998; Winlow and Hall, 2006).

The more collective aspect of working-class community in the production-centered phase of capitalism tends to be contrasted with the rise of extreme individualism characteristic of consumer capitalism and its associated service economy. In that sense, the mods, the teds and the punks that captured the Birmingham School's attention were seen as a way to maintain this sense of community, in opposition to the extreme individualism of late capitalism.

The CCCS challenged the largely negative view that intellectuals like Hoggart and the Frankfurt School held regarding mass culture and mass consumption. Rather than seeing the working class as passively conforming to the messages of the "culture industry" and submitting to its ideology, the Birmingham School focused on the subcultures' potential for resistance. Subcultures are based on the subversion of the taken-for-granted symbolic signs associated with consumer goods. Ultimately, the punks, the teds, the rockers and the members of other subculutres are engaged in a dramatic and performative struggle over meaning. As Hebdige (1988/1979: 18) wrote, " 'humble objects' can be magically appropriated; 'stolen' by subordinate groups and made to carry 'secret' meanings: meanings which express, in code, a form of resistance to the order which guarantees their continued subordination." By insisting on the working-class youth's ability to subvert the social and symbolic meanings of consumer goods and to ascribe to them a new "cultural substance" that better reflects their own vision and semi-autonomous position in the world, the Birmingham School shed light on the power of agency of the actors they studied, moving away from the pessimistic vision of passivity that characterizes the Frankfurt School.

Hebdige (1988/1979) borrowed Lévi-Strauss's concept of *bricolage* to describe this process of symbolic appropriation, but he also drew attention to the fact that subcultures can also become co-opted and their subversive potential neutralized. This is particularly true, since, as styles, subcultures are essentially commodity centered. Indeed, Clarke *et al.* (2006/1975: 42) remind us that subcultures only emerged as a result of increased disposable income for working-class youth and the rise of a new consumer market targeting those same youths. Consequently, while subcultures are able to subvert the original meaning given to consumer goods, the result of such *bricolage* can eventually be reintegrated within the mass consumption society, diffusing its subversive potential. For example, the Sex Pistols, once a source of revulsion among the "decent" British middle class, have gone through the full circle, from being regarded as dangerous deviants by mainstream society to being fully integrated into the capitalist corporate entertainment culture. The ability of the capitalist system to successfully defuse and absorb what were originally acts of symbolic subversion helps us understand why the members of the Birmingham School were both optimistic and pessimistic about the transformative potential of the symbolic resistance offered by subcultural movements: "the cycle leading from opposition to diffusion, from resistance to incorporation encloses each successive subculture" (Hebdige, 1988/1979: 101).

The relative pessimism of the Birmingham School

Ultimately, it could be said that subcultures are a prime example of the kind of social bulimia described by Young (1999: 86), and which refers to the double process of "cultural inclusion and social exclusion." More fundamentally, it appears that the members of the Birmingham School were torn between recognizing, and celebrating, the symbolic resistance offered by subcultures while, at the same time, lamenting the very fact that this resistance remained confined to the symbolic realm. As Hebdige (1988/1979: 130) summarized it: "no amount of stylistic incantation can alter the oppressive mode in which the commodities used in subculture have been produced." While subcultures allow the working-class youths to "win space" and resist the dominant hegemonic order, they fall short of altering the capitalist relations of production that constitute the root cause of oppression.

Following Gramsci, Willis (2016/1978: 174) reminds us that "the cultural is part of the necessary dialectic of [capitalist] reproduction." Consequently, by rejecting the dominant, hegemonic cultural order, working-class youths engaged in subcultures *do* offer a form of resistance against capitalism. However, in the context of late capitalism, it seems like symbolic resistance represents a lesser threat to the dominant system. As noted previously, capitalism is a highly resilient system, able to accommodate subversive forms of symbolic resistance and to "commodify dissent" (Frank and Weiland, 1997; also see McGuigan, 2009).

Nonetheless, what subcultures and their "symbolic violation of social order" demonstrate is that the capitalist hegemonic order is never secured but is always contested, reminding us that "we have the logical possibility of radicalness" (Willis, 2016/1978: 175). However, the Birmingham School seems categorical that as long as this potential for radicalness is contained within the symbolic realm, the response offered by subcultures against capitalist exploitation "[is] fated to fail. . . . They 'solve', but in an imaginary way, problems which at the concrete material level remain unresolved" (Clarke *et al.*, 2006/1975: 35, 37). A similar mix of optimism and pessimism transpires in Willis's study *Learning to Labour. How Working Class Kids Get Working Class Jobs* (2016/1978). On the one hand, the author applauds the "working-class lads" he is studying for developing a counter-culture which opposes an educational system that does not address the needs and interests of working-class kids. On the other hand, he also points out that, by fully rejecting the opportunities for cultural capital formation offered by the educational system and by deriding all forms of intellectual labor, the "lads" also limit their options for upward social mobility, condemning themselves to a life of unskilled manual labor, a quintessential form of labor exploitation under capitalism. Consequently, "the counter-school culture becomes an always provisional, bare, skeptical yet finally accepting accommodation with the 'status quo'" (145). Subcultures could then be seen as an example of social reproduction (Bourdieu, 1973), creating the conditions that consolidate their members' subaltern class position and creating a self-perpetuating cycle in which working-class kids *keep* getting working-class jobs. While some CCCS members have pointed out that the prospects might be more promising for "the girls" (McRobbie and Garber, 2006/1975; Powell and Clarke, 2006/1975), it does seem that, overall, "there is no 'subcultural career' for the working-class lad, no 'solution' in the subcultural milieu, for problems posed by the key structuring experiences of the class" (Clarke *et al.*, 2006/1975: 35). Let us now turn our attention to the ways the Birmingham School's work on subcultures might inform the field of critical gang studies.

Subcultures and gang studies

As mentioned earlier, CCCS members were at pains to place the subcultures they were study-ing in the specific context in which they emerged. The same caution should also apply to gang scholars. Rather than studying gangs as if they existed in a vacuum, it is essential to take into consideration the specific context in which each gang appears and subsequently evolves.

As Brotherton (2015: 11) notes, gangs should be understood as "a social phenomenon that is said to emerge within the ebbs and flows of social, economic and political currents over time". Gang research in this vein can be seen in various contributions, from the work of Jensen (2014) and his emphasis on the legacy of territorial segregation in South Africa to Zilberg (2011) and her analysis of the impact that US immigration policies havee had in El Salvador. This kind of work allows us to better understand the various cultural and structural forces at play in each situation and of which the gangs are both a product of and a response to. Only by paying atten-tion to the social, political, economic and cultural environment which shapes each gang can we avoid the pitfall of pathologizing gang formation and activities. As the Birmingham School reminds us: "to blame the actions of individuals within a given historical structure, *without tak-ing that structure itself into account*, is an easy and familiar way to exercising the moral conscience without bearing any of its costs" (Hall *et al.*, 2013/1978: 181 emphasis in the original).

Furthermore, if we want to follow in the Birmingham School's footsteps and develop a true "history from below," it is essential to not only "plac[e] the gang *in history* . . . [but to also] contemplate the gang *with history*" ((Brotherton, 2015: 14 emphasis in the original). Gangs, just like subcultures, are not fixed; they have their own history. One has to know their past in order to understand their present. For example, when Hebdige (1974) analyzes the tribulations of the Rastafarian/Rude Boy subcultures, he traces them from colonial Jamaica to the streets of London. Brotherton and Barrios (2004) undertake a similar endeavor, studying the vari-ous traditions and influences that molded the transnational gang of the Almighty Latin King and Queen Nation, from Puerto Rico and Chicago to New York City. It is in this ground-breaking study that Brotherton and Barrios provide their own definition of what constitutes a "gang," a highly loaded term that they avoid, preferring the label "street organization" that is devoid of pejorative connotations:

> group formed largely by youth and adults of marginalized social class which aims to provide its members with a resistant identity, an opportunity to be individually and collectively empowered, a voice to speak back to and challenge the dominant culture, a refuge from the stresses and strains of barrio or ghetto life and a spiritual enclave within which its own sacred rituals can be generated and practiced. (p.23)

This definition could very well apply to the subcultures studied by the CCCS. By highlighting the gang's ability to offer its members a space of resistance against the dominant culture, Brotherton and Barrios follow the path set by the Birmingham School. They reject the emphasis put on illegal activities and stress the gangs' counter-hegemonic potential. What is more, since subaltern classes exist in a state of cultural domination, gang membership can be seen as fulfilling the same basic functions as belonging to a subculture. Borrowing from Bourgois (1995), it could be said that those who join the gang are "in search of respect." Ultimately, one of the most essential aspects of the gang, like any subculture, is that it recreates the sense of community and togetherness characteristic of working-class communities.

The communal dimension of the gang was highlighted early on (Thrasher, 1927) and has continued to be confirmed with such frequency that it could recently be affirmed: "although scholars, policy makers, police, and community organizations seldom agree on their approaches to gangs, there is one thing on which they do agree: When it comes to gangs, it is the group that matters" (Papachristos, 2013: 49–50). The importance of "territoriality" on which most gang scholars concur, some pointing out that "for [Chicano] gang members [of Los Angeles] the word for gang and neighborhood is identical" (Moore, 1978: 35), was also a defining feature of subcultural studies (Clarke et al., 2006/1975; Jefferson, 2006/1975; Clarke, 2006/1975). As Cohen (1980/1972: 74) put it, "territoriality is thus not only a way in which kids 'live' subculture as a collective behavior, but also the way in which the subcultural group becomes rooted in the situation of its community."

Just as the CCCS debunked the most alarmist accounts about subcultures, showing that "doing nothing" and "passing time together" constitute one of the most important aspects of belonging to a subculture (Corrigan, 2006/1975), critical gang scholars have shown that being in a gang is not so much about "terrorizing honest citizens" but about "hanging out in the 'hood" (Decker and Van Winkle, 1996; Conquergood, 2013/1994; Zilberg, 2011). It seems undeniable that for youths experiencing high levels of marginalization and discrimination from mainstream society, spending time among peers, donning the same clothes – in short, "reppin'" (Conquergood, 1992, 2013/1994 – represents a form of empowerment and a way to "*win space*" for the young gang members: "cultural space in the neighbourhood and institutions, real time for leisure and recreation, actual room on the street or street-corner" (Clarke et al., 2006/1975: 35). Conquergood has been at pains to underscore those various dimensions in his illuminating research on gangs (1992, 2013/1994, 1997).

While the dominant discourse about gangs insists on their supposedly intrinsic brutality and disrespect for human life, Conquergood shows that notions of love, respect and solidarity are at the center of gang culture. Drawing attention to the material and symbolic oppression from which the marginalized youths, predominantly ethnic minorities, who constitute the bulk of gang members suffer, he concludes: "against a dominant world that displaces, stifles, and erases identity, the homeboys create, through their communication practices, a hood: a subterranean space of life-sustaining warmth, intimacy, and protection" (Conquergood, 2013/1994: 248). Similarly, through the use of graffiti – which he defines as "counterliteracy" (1997: 354) – gang members are able to reclaim a sense of ownership over the "hoods" in which they have been segregated and subjugated to the degrading effects of over/under-policing which continuously reassert their status as second-class citizens (Rios, 2011). Overall, Conquergood insists on the counterhegemonic nature of gang culture, which rejects the prevalent individualism of bourgeois society. Along with Brotherton (2008, 2015, 2020; Brotherton and Barrios, 2004), he is one of the scholars who has gone to the greatest lengths to challenge the dominant accounts on gangs by developing a critical "history from below," thereby restoring a sense of agency to gang members. The influence of the Birmingham School in this critical research agenda is indisputable.

However, despite the similarities between gangs and the subcultures that fascinated the Birmingham School – to some extent, "gangsta culture" has also gone through the same cycle of incorporation into the mainstream (Kelley, 1994; Hagedorn, 2008) – an important difference relates to the material nature of those two phenomena. While subcultures constitute a form of escape and symbolic resistance for working-class youths, they do not offer any material solutions to their economic exploitation. The economic opportunities available to the segregated youths of the American inner-city neighborhoods are even more restricted than those of their British counterparts, mostly due to the extreme racial discrimination faced by African Americans and Latinos (Massey and Denton, 1993; Wacquant 2007). Already constrained in a position of extreme marginality, the residents of the American ghettos were hit particularly hard by deindustrialization and the rise of the service economy (Julius Wilson, 1997). In this context, gangs offer unique opportunities to address the material needs of a population ostracized in economically deprived neighborhoods (Sullivan, 1989; Jankowski, 1991). The gangs' economic appeal became all the more striking with the rise of international drug trade. Following Merton's classical typology (1938), gang members could be seen as innovators, seizing the opportunities provided by a lucrative business to increase their material well-being (Bourgois, 1995; Contreras, 2013). This situation led several authors to ponder the risks of social reproduction that weigh on gang members involved in such highly criminalized activities (Hagedorn, 1988; Bourgois, 1995; Macleod, 2009).

However, recognizing the material incentive associated with gang activities does not negate the notion of resistance. As the limited opportunities available to the working-class youths of the American ghettos are clustered in the most demeaning sectors of the labor market, refusing to submit to the dictates of the market, which reduces those youths to the most exploitable and disposable type of labor, can be seen as a form of resistance. This is the line of argument followed by Hall *et al.* (2013/1978: 380) in *Policing the Crisis* (*PTC*):

> the hustler was the product of the combination of racism and unemployment. But he also provided one of the few positive role models for young blacks on the block: one of the few not cowed by oppression, not tied to daily grind of low-wage poverty.

It is this other major publication of the Birmingham School which is the topic of the next section.

Crime, moral panics and social control

Policing the Crisis

Along with *Resistance through Rituals*, *PTC* is arguably the second most important contribution of the Birmingham School. As Hall and his co-authors wrote in the second edition of the book, the two publications "are two sides of the same coin" (2013/1978: xi). If *Resistance through Rituals* focused on the forms of symbolic resistance developed by working-class youths, *PTC* sheds lights on the culture and institutions of social control of which those youths are the (un) privileged targets. Using the so-called British "mugging crisis" of the early 1970s as their case study, the authors investigate both the processes through which a deviant act can turn into a "moral panic" and the function that moral panics can play in capitalist societies. In other words, the analysis shifts from the deviant act itself to the social construction of, and social reaction to, said act.

PTC starts by debunking the alarmist narrative around the "mugging crisis" in the United Kingdom, showing that this so-called "crisis" did not reflect an abrupt change in crime patterns as claimed by the various institutions – media, police, courts – fueling the moral panic over mugging. Having demonstrated that the so-called "mugging crisis" had no real material basis, they proceed to deconstruct the social meaning of the word "mugging".

The term emerged in the United States in the 1960s and came to embody a wide range of social anxieties revolving around the "Black ghettos." At a time of growing political consciousness and organization among African Americans, and in a period marked by rising civil unrest, "mugging" became associated with an alleged threat to the "American way of life." When the "mugging" label crossed the ocean and arrived in Britain in the early 1970s, it carried with it the images and social representations associated with the term in the United States. Transposed in the British context, "mugging" continued to be equated with rising poverty, growing racial tensions, unruly youths, loss of traditional values, banalization of crime and violence, and the undermining of law and order. In other words, "mugging" came to give substance to a latent feeling of social and moral crisis. Similar to what had occurred in the US, "mugging" was primarily associated with racial and ethnic minorities. At a time when Black youths were increasingly being defined as "problematic," they soon came to be portrayed as "potential muggers."

Focusing on its social construction, Hall *et al.* examine the ideological and social functions of crime. Following Durkheim's classical theory on the boundary-setting function of crime (1982/1894), the Birmingham School argues that crime plays a central role in our societies. Seen as a violation of the rules that organize life in community, crime is typically conceptualized as the quintessential offense against society. By breaking the law, the criminal excludes himself from society. Punishing him then serves as a sort of communal healing, a cathartic endeavor which reaffirms the social cohesion of society. Portrayed as a blind evil that affects society as a whole, rather than any social group in particular, "crime allows all 'good men and true' to stand up and be counted . . . in the defence of normality, stability and 'our way of life'" (Hall *et al.*, 2013/1978: 148).

Crime thus plays a vital ideological function in capitalist societies as it reinforces the myth of a cohesive society marked, not by unequal power relations, class antagonism, patriarchy, and racism, but by an essential division between "criminals" and "law-abiding citizens" of all backgrounds. This vision of a cohesive and consensual society is one of the most important features of the dominant hegemonic order: "it is what makes the rule of the few disappear in the consent of the many" (Hall *et al.*, 2013/1978: 213). The direct result of this ideological construct is to deny the necessity of bringing radical changes to the status quo. Tensions and conflicts might very well exist in society, but the punishment of criminals is presented as a proof that the existing institutional settings offer effective solutions to resolve social issues.

In *PTC*, the CCCS members demonstrate how the imposition of the "criminal label" on a specific social group partakes of a broad project of social control. By making certain behaviors illegal and labeling their perpetrators as criminals, the state is able to build a tight controlling net over potentially problematic social groups; those who would only "have their chains to lose and a world to win" (Marx and Engels, 2017/1848: 103) in a radical transformation of society. The association "mugger/Black youth" allowed for increased levels of surveillance and state control over second-generation immigrant youths at a time of rising political consciousness and challenges to the system of racial oppression that had maintained them in a subaltern position within British society. More than thirty years after the publication of *PTC*, Alexander (2010) would develop a similar argument about the "war on drugs" being disproportionately waged against African Americans, demonstrating that, under the guise of universalistic appeals to "law and order," the law can be mobilized effectively for targeted efforts of social control.

One of the most important contributions of *PTC* is that it analyzes the criminalization of certain social groups from the standpoint of a crisis of hegemony. A crisis of hegemony occurs when the gap between the ideological constructions deployed by the dominant classes to legitimize existing unequal power relations and the intrinsically exploitative nature of capitalism becomes so wide so as to pose a threat to the status quo. The internal contradictions of the capitalist system become so pronounced that the subaltern classes come to reject, and rebel against the hegemonic "common sense."

As noted previously, hegemony is most effective when consent outweighs coercion for the maintenance and consolidation of the status quo. Yet, when the very foundations of the system are considered to be in danger, when social instability is on the rise and class struggle threatens to take a more overt and confrontational turn, the state – which in Gramsci's theory of "integral state" is the central space where "historical blocs" of ruling classes are formed and the hegemonic order established (1971) – will deploy its coercive power to resolve the crisis. This shift from consent to coercion represents one of the most salient features of a hegemonic crisis: "the masks of liberal consent and popular consensus slip to reveal the reserves of coercion and force on which the cohesion of the state and its legal authority finally depends" (Hall *et al.* 2013/1978: 214). In the British case, as the post-war "we never had it so good" discourse was being increasingly discredited and challenged, it gave way to alarmist warnings that the "British way of life" was being threatened by gangs of muggers. Radical measures, it was argued, had to be implemented to avert this danger. A new "law and order" discourse emerged, legitimizing increasingly repressive measures as the only solution to save the "honest citizens" from the "hoodlums" wreaking havoc in the country. Hidden from view as long as consent prevails, the Leviathan state and its monopoly on legitimate violence rises again, curtailing civil liberties and deploying its repressive fist to supposedly protect society from those who terrorize it.

However, even when coercion becomes increasingly necessary to ensure the maintenance of the status quo, this shift must be perceived as legitimate by a substantial part of the subaltern classes. If this were not the case, an increase in repressive measures might potentially trigger a backlash of rising dissent rather than its diffusion (Francisco, 1996). It is in this context that moral panics become all the more important to gather popular support for repressive measures.

With the mass media playing a central role in this process, moral panics, and the mechanisms of exaggeration, distortion (Cohen, 2002/1972) and convergences (Hall *et al.*, 2013/1978) on which they rest, aim to construct the image of the "deviant other," which comes to be identified as the source of all evil in society. Moral panics fulfill the essential functions of maintaining boundaries between "us" and "them" and building consent for the criminalization of the "other" (Erikson, 1966; Cohen, 2002/1972; Young, 2011). The overall objective of a moral panic is then to: 1) build consensus for the state's shift towards coercion, 2) scapegoat and criminalize a specific social group which is seen as the source of the crisis and 3) divide the members of the subaltern classes and distract them from the real, structural causes of the crisis.

Building on those ideas, *PTC* makes the case that the "mugging crisis" represented, above all, such a moral panic organized to respond to the crisis of hegemony at play in the UK in the early 1970s. The authors also show that race played a central part in the manufacturing of the 'mugging crisis'. In that sense, *PTC* constitutes a great contribution to the century-long debate which, from Du Bois (2007/1935) to Roediger (2007) and Alexander (2010), has shown that race and its associated "wages of whiteness" have always played a crucial role in dividing the working class along racial lines, a fundamental feature which facilitates capitalist reproduction.

In the following section, we will see how the ideas developed in *PTC* remain relevant for the field of critical gang studies.

Gang bangers and muggers

From Phoenix (Zatz, 1987) to Sydney (Poyting *et al.*, 2001) and Vancouver (Katz, 2011), gangs have frequently constituted a prime target around which moral panics are organized. Presented as such a moral panic, *PTC* exposed the "mugging crisis" of the 1970s for what it truly was: a political project which, in a context of crisis of hegemony and corresponding shift from consent to coercion, scapegoated young Black men as the source of all evil in society. This strategy was used to divide the working class along an "us" versus "them" dichotomy and to redirect working-class anxieties, away from the internal contradictions of capitalism, and to a specific social group whose economic deprivation and ethnic composition made it a "perfect target." Forty years after its publication, the authors' invitation to shift our attention from "the *deviant act . . .* treated in isolation to *the relation between the deviant act and the reaction of the public and the control agencies to the act*" (Hall *et al.*, 2013/1978: 21) remains more pertinent than ever. Indeed, the same principles identified in the "mugging crisis" continue to be at play in the many consecutive moral panics organized around gangs since then:

> (1) the identification of a specific issue of concern; (2) the identification of a subversive minority; (3) 'convergence', or the linking, by labelling, of this specific issue to other problems; (4) the notion of 'thresholds' which, once crossed, can lead to an escalating threat; (5) the prophesy of more troubling times to come if no action is taken . . .; and (6) the call for 'firm steps.'
>
> *(Hall et al., 2013/1978: 223)*

Donald Trump's presidency in the United States is a case in point. Negative views about migrants have played a central role in Trump's political program and discourse, both on the campaign trail and once elected to the White House. Scholars who subjected his speeches to rigorous discourse analysis (Degani, 2016; Kreis, 2017; Liu and Lei, 2018; Sclafani, 2018) all reached a similar conclusion: "Trump uses an informal, direct, and provoking communication style to construct and reinforce the concept of a homogeneous people and a homeland threatened by the dangerous other" (Kreis, 2017: 607). As he infamously put it in his speech announcing his presidential bid:

> The US has become a dumping ground for everybody else's problems. . . . When Mexico sends its people, they're not sending their best. . . . They're sending people that have lots of problems, and they're bringing those problems with us. They're bringing drugs. They're bringing crime. They're rapists. And some, I assume, are good people.
>
> *(Washington Post Staff, 2015)*

Following his election, Trump frequently used gang violence as a strategy to build popular support in favor of his highly punitive migration and deportation policies. Between his inauguration in January 2017 and his 2019 State of the Union speech, he publicly referred to MS-13 more than 160 times (Miller, 2019). Time and again, Trump has maintained that the violent acts committed by MS-13 gang members, whom his administration officially defines as "violent animals" (White House, 2018), are a direct consequence of the supposedly permissive approach to border control of previous administrations. Contending that his government's migration policies aim at "protecting the freedoms of law-abiding Americans, . . . [by] going after the criminal gangs and cartels that prey on our innocent citizens" (White House, 2017), Trump (2018) has argued that "the scourge of MS-13 and other transnational criminal organizations will not abate until our Nation's borders are fully secure and those who seek to harm us are no longer able to exploit loopholes in our broken immigration laws."

The idea that illegal immigration, of which violent gang members supposedly represent the most glaring illustration, is the source of all the plights faced by the United States – "reduced jobs, lower wages, overburdened schools and hospitals, increased crime, and a depleted social safety net" (Trump, 2019) – has been one of the most important features of the Trump administration. There is, of course, a great irony to this discursive and political strategy, and not only because it fails to recognize that the United States had already entered an era of "mass deportation" during Barack Obama's presidency (Golash-Boza, 2015). More fundamentally, it is oblivious to the fact that, as Zilberg (2011) demonstrates, transnational gangs like the Mara Salvatrucha, Trump's favorite target, are a direct consequence of the same kind of punitive policies that the Trump administration advocates. Documenting the transnational implications of national security policies, Zilberg (2011: 130) concludes that "transnational formations like La Mara Salvatrucha and the 18th Street Gang are a somewhat ironic result of nativism and its work to criminalize immigrants." In other words, the very gangs that Trump presents as the most important reason for implementing harsher deportation policies might actually never have seen the light if it were not for . . . the implementation of harsher deportation policies in the United States. Of course, the Birmingham School teaches us that those factual elements have little significance when it comes to the social function that "muggers" or "gang members" fulfill for the maintenance of the status quo.

Muggers and gang bangers both represent the archetype of the "dangerous, racialized other," a subhuman figure marked by their pure evilness and against which the "rest of us," the "decent folks," should unite. And as Baker (2019) pointed out: "an us-against-them political strategy has been at the heart of Mr. Trump's presidency from the start." To be sure, this chapter is not trying to make the case that gangs do not exist or might not pose some serious issues for the communities in which they reside. Rather, following the line of inquiry developed by the Birmingham School, it contends, along with Zatz (1987: 30 emphasis in original), that if we shift the analysis away from the gangs to critically investigate the role that they fulfill from a social control perspective, the key issue becomes the "*social imagery* of . . . youth gangs, rather than their actual *behavior*." From this perspective, it appears that visions of unruly, violent youths of color threatening social order all coalesce in the figure of the Chicano gangs which have regained such high visibility in the discourse of the Trump administration. They represent the perfect boogeymen against which mainstream society can unite, diverting attention from other, more damaging, issues of capitalism. As noted previously, this is particularly true in times of crisis of hegemony. As Brotherton (2020) summarizes it:

> the gang as one of society's chief enemies, has a ubiquitous presence, becoming a key "floating" signifier in policing and regulating public and private spaces, all of which relate to protecting, reproducing, and reinforcing race/ethnic and class structures in the service of wealth and capital accumulation.

In conclusion, if the Birmingham School's work on subcultures can inform the field of gang studies by inviting scholars to move away from the more pathologizing approaches and to develop a more critical perspective emphasizing agency and resistance, *PTC* sheds light on another dimension of the "gang phenomenon," focusing on notions of social control and crisis of hegemony. While criminalizing gangs and designing moral panics around them play a crucial role in the consolidation of the status quo and the division of the working class, innovative measures like those implemented in Ecuador have fostered increased social inclusion for young gang members traditionally treated as social pariahs (Bortherton and Gude, 2018). In fact, moving away from punitive approaches might be a way to liberate the transformative potential of subcultures identified by the Birmingham School and to "transform [gang] *activity* into *activism*" (Zilberg, 2011: 156 emphasis in original).

References

Alexander, Michelle. 2010. *The New Jim Crow. Mass Incarceration in the Age of Colorblindness*. New York: The New Press.

Baker, Peter. 2019. "Trump Fans the Flames of a Racial Fire." *The New York Times*, July 14, 2019. www.nytimes.com/2019/07/14/us/politics/trump-twitter-race.html.

Bauman, Zigmunt. 2005/1998. *Work, Consumerism and the New Poor*. 2nd edition. New York: Open University Press.

Bourdieu, Pierre. 1973. "Cultural Reproduction and Social Reproduction." Pp. 71–112 in *Knowledge, Education and Cultural Change*, edited by Richard Brown. London: Tavistock.

Bourgois, Philippe. 1995. *In Search of Respect: Selling Crack in El Barrio*. Cambridge: Cambridge University Press.

Brotherton, David. 2008. "Beyond Social Reproduction: Bringing Resistance Back in Gang Theory." *Theoretical Criminology* 12(1): 55–77.

Brotherton, David. 2015. *Youth Street Gangs. A Critical Appraisal*. London: Routledge.

Brotherton, David. 2020. "Studying Gang Through Critical Ethnography" in *The Oxford Handbook on Ethnographies of Crime and Criminal Justice*, edited S. Bucerius, K. Haggerty and L. Berardi. New York: Oxford University Press.

Brotherton, David and Luis Barrios. 2004. *The Almighty Latin King and Queen Nation. Street Politics and the Transformation of a New York City Gang*. New York: Columbia University Press.

Brotherton, David and Rafael Gude. 2018. *Social Inclusion from Below. The Perspectives of Street Gangs and Their Possible Effects on Declining Homicide Rates in Ecuador*. Discussion Paper No IBD-DP-578. Washington, DC: Inter-American Development Bank.

Clarke, John. 2006. "The Skinheads and the Magical Recovery of Community." Pp. 80–83 in *Resistance Through Rituals*, edited by Stuart Hall and Tony Jefferson. 2nd edition. London: Routledge.

Clarke, John, Stuart Hall, Tony Jefferson and Brian Roberts. 2006. "Subcultures, Cultures and Class." Pp. 3–59 in *Resistance Through Rituals*, edited by Stuart Hall and Tony Jefferson. 2nd edition. London: Routledge.

Cohen, Phil. 1980/1972. "Subcultural Conflict and Working-Class Community." Pp. 66–76 in *Culture, Media, Language. Working Papers in Cultural Studies, 1972–79*, edited by Stuart Hall, Dorothy Hobson, Andrew Lowe and Paul Willis. London: Unwin Hyman.

Cohen, Stanley. 2002/1972. *Folk Devils and Moral Panics*. 3rd edition. New York: Routledge.

Conquergood, Dwight. 1992. *On Reppin' and Rhethoric: Gang Representations*. Evanston: Northwestern University, Center for Urban Affairs and Policy Research.

Conquergood, Dwight. 1997. "Street Literacy." Pp. 354–375 in *Research on Teaching Literacy Through the Communicative and Visual Arts*, edited by James Flood, Shirley Brice Heath and Diane Lapp. Mahwah: Lawrence Erlbaum Associates.

Conquergood, Dwight. 2013/1994. "Homeboys and Hood." Pp. 224–263 in *Cultural Struggles. Performance, Ethnography, Praxis*, edited by E. Patrick Johnson. Ann Arbor: The University of Michigan Press.

Contreras, Randol. 2013. *The Stickup Kids. Race, Drugs, Violence and the American Dream*. Berkeley: University of California Press.

Corrigan, Paul. 2006. "Doing Nothing." Pp. 84–87 in *Resistance Through Rituals,* edited by Stuart Hall and Tony Jefferson. 2nd edition. London: Routledge.

Decker, Scott and Barrik Van Winkle. 1996. *Life in the Gang: Family, Friends, and Violence.* Cambridge: Cambridge University Press.

Degani, Marta. 2016. "Endangered Intellectual: A Case Study of Clinton vs Trump Campaign Discourse." *Iperstoria* 8: 131–145.

Du Bois, W.E.B. 2007/1935. *Black Reconstruction in America: An Essay Toward a History of the Part Which Black Folk Played in the Attempt to Reconstruct Democracy in America, 1860–1880.* New York: Oxford University Press.

Durkheim, Emile. 1982/1894. *The Rules of Sociological Methods and Selected Texts on Sociology and its Method.* London: The Macmillan Press.

Erikson, Kay. 1966. *Wayward Puritans: A Study in the Sociology of Deviance.* New York: Wiley.

Evans, Martin. 2010. "Harold Macmillan's 'Never Had It So Good' Speech Followed the 1950s Boom." *The Telegraph,* November 10, 2010. www.telegraph.co.uk/news/politics/8145390/Harold-Macmillans-never-had-it-so-good-speech-followed-the-1950s-boom.html.

Francisco, Ronald. 1996. "Coercion and Protest: An Empirical Test in Two Democratic States." *American Journal of Political Science* 40(4): 1179–1204.

Frank, Thomas and Matt Weiland (eds.). 1997. *Commodify Your Consent: Salvos from the Baffler.* New York: Norton.

Gelder, Ken. 2007. *Subcultures. Cultural Histories and Social Practice.* London/New York: Routledge.

Golash-Boza, Tanya Maria. 2015. *Deported. Immigrant Policing, Disposable Labor, and Global Capitalism.* New York: New York University Press.

Gramsci, Antonio. 1971. *Selections from the Prison Notebooks.* New York: International Publishers.

Hagedorn, John. 1988. *People and Folks: Gangs, Crime, and the Underclass in a Rust-Belt City.* Chicago: Lake View Press.

Hagedorn, John. 2008. *A World of Gangs. Armed Young Men and Gangsta Culture.* Minneapolis: University of Minnesota Press.

Hall, Stuart. 1980. "Cultural Studies and the Centre: Some Problematics and Problems." Pp. 15–47 in *Culture, Media, Language. Working Papers in Cultural Studies, 1972–79,* edited by Stuart Hall, Dorothy Hobson, Andrew Lowe and Paul Willis. London: Unwin Hyman.

Hall, Stuart, Chas Critcher, Tony Jefferson, John Clarke and Brian Roberts. 2013/1978. *Policing the Crisis: Mugging, the State, and Law and Order.* 2nd edition. New York: Palgrave MacMillan.

Hebdige, Dick. 1974. *Reggae, Rastas & Rudies: Style and the Subversion of Form.* Birmingham: Centre for Contemporary Cultural Studies, University of Birmingham.

Hebdige, Dick. 1988/1979. *Subculture: The Meaning of Style.* London: Routledge.

Hoggart, Richard. 1992/1957. *The Uses of Literacy.* New Brunswick: Transaction Publishers.

Jankowski, Martín Sanchéz. 1991. *Islands in the Street. Gangs and American Urban Society.* Berkeley: University of California Press.

Jefferson, Tony. 2006. "Cultural Responses of the Teds." Pp. 67–70 in *Resistance Through Rituals,* edited by Stuart Hall and Tony Jefferson. 2nd Edition. London: Routledge.

Jensen, Steffen. 2014. "Intimate Connections: Gangs and the Political Economy of Urbanization in South Africa." Pp. 28–48 in *Global Gangs: Street Violence across the World,* edited by Jennifer Hazen and Dennis Rodgers. Minneapolis: University of Minnesota Press.

Julius Wilson, William. 1997. *When Work Disappears: The World of the New Urban Poor.* New York: Vintage Books.

Katz, Karen. 2011. "The Enemy Within: The Outlaw Motorcycle Gang Moral Panic." *American Journal of Criminal Justice* 36: 231–249.

Kelley, Robin. 1994. *Race Rebels: Culture, Politics, and the Black Working Class.* New York: Free Press.

Kreis, Romona. 2017. "The 'Tweet Politics' of President Trump." *Journal of Language and Politics* 16(4): 607–618.

Liu, Dilin and Lei Lei. 2018. "The Appeal to Political Sentiment: An Analysis of Donald Trump's and Hillary Clinton's Speech Themes and Discourse Strategies in the 2016 US Presidential Election." *Discourse, Context & Media* 25: 143–152.

Macleod, Jay. 2009. *Ain't No Makin' It: Aspirations and Attainment in a Low-Income Neighborhood*. 3rd edition. Boulder: Westview Press.

Marx, Karl and Friedrich Engels. 2017/1848. *The Communist Manifesto*. London: Pluto Press.

Massey, Douglas and Nancy Denton. 1993. *American Apartheid. Segregation and the Making of the Underclass*. Cambridge: Harvard University Press.

McGuigan, Jim. 2009. *Cool Capitalism*. London: Pluto Press.

McRobbie, Angela and Jenny Garber. 2006. "Girls and Subcultures." Pp. 177–188 in *Resistance Through Rituals*, edited by Stuart Hall and Tony Jefferson. 2nd edition. London: Routledge.

Merton, Robert. 1938. "Social Structure and Anomie." *American Sociological Review* 3(5): 672–682.

Miles, Steven. 1995. "Towards an Understanding of the Relationship Between Youth Identities and Consumer Culture." *Youth & Policy* 51: 35–45.

Miles, Steven. 1998. *Consumerism as a Way of Life*. London: Sage Publications.

Miller, Michael. 2019. "'Savage Gang': Despite Trump's Relentless Rhetoric, MS-13 Killings Are Down." *The Washington Post*, February 7, 2019. www.washingtonpost.com/local/savage-gang-despite-trumps-relentless-rhetoric-ms-13-murders-are-down/2019/02/06/9c6ace98–2662–11e9–81fd-b7b05d5bed90_story.html?noredirect=on&utm_term=.3a9eadbfc4a3.

Moore, Joan. 1978. *Homeboys: Gangs, Drugs and Prison in the Barrios of Los Angeles*. Philadelphia: Temple University Press.

Papachristos, Andrew. 2013. "The Importance of Cohesion for Gang Research, Policy, and Practice." *Criminology & Public Policy* 12(1): 49–58.

Powell, Rachel and John Clarke. 2006. "A Note on Marginality." Pp. 189–194 in *Resistance Through Rituals*, edited by Stuart Hall and Tony Jefferson. 2nd edition. London: Routledge.

Poyting, Scott, Greg Noble and Paul Tabar. 2001. "Middle Eastern Appearances: 'Ethnic Gangs', Moral Panic and Media Framing." *The Australian and New Zealand Journal of Criminology* 34(1): 67–90.

Rios, Victor. 2011. *Punished. Policing the Lives of Black and Latino Boys*. New York: New York University Press.

Roediger, David. 2007. *The Wages of Whiteness. Race and the Making of the American Working Class*. New York: Verso.

Sclafani, Jennifer. 2018. *Talking Donald Trump. A Sociolinguistic Study of Style, Metadiscourse, and Political Identity*. London: Routledge.

Sullivan, Mercer. 1989. *"Getting Paid": Youth Crime and Work in the Inner City*. Ithaca: Cornell University Press.

Thompson, E.P. 1966. *The Making of the English Working Class*. New York: Vintage Books.

Thrasher, Frederic. 1927. *The Gang. A Study of 1,313 Gangs in Chicago*. Chicago: The University of Chicago Press.

Trump, Donald. 2018. "Presidential Proclamation on National Gang Violence Prevention Week, 2018." www.whitehouse.gov/presidential-actions/presidential-proclamation-national-gang-violence-prevention-week-2018/.

Trump, Donald. 2019. "President Donald J. Trump's State of the Union Address." www.whitehouse.gov/briefings-statements/president-donald-j-trumps-state-union-address-2/.

Turner, Graeme. 2003. *British Cultural Studies. An Introduction*. 3rd edition. London and New York: Routledge.

Wacquant, Loïc. 2008. *Urban Outcasts: A Comparative Sociology of Advanced Marginality*. Cambridge: Polity Press.

Washington Post Staff. 2015. "Full Text: Donald Trump Announces a Presidential Bid." *The Washington Post*, June 16, 2015. www.washingtonpost.com/news/post-politics/wp/2015/06/16/full-text-donald-trump-announces-a-presidential-bid/?utm_term=.88b94827b57d.

White House. 2017. "President Donald J. Trump Taking Action Against Illegal Immigration." www.whitehouse.gov/briefings-statements/president-donald-j-trump-taking-action-illegal-immigration/.

White House. 2018. "What You Need To Know About the Violent Animals Of MS-13." www.whitehouse.gov/articles/need-know-violent-animals-ms-13/.

Williams, Raymond. 1983/1958. *Culture & Society: 1780–1950*. New York: Columbia University Press.

Willis, Paul. 2016/1978. *Learning to Labour. How Working Class Kids Get Working Class Jobs*. London: Routledge.

Winlow, Simon and Steve Hall. 2006. *Violent Night. Urban Leisure and Contemporary Culture*. Oxford: Berg.

Young, Jock. 1999. *The Exclusive Society. Social Exclusion, Crime and Difference in Late Modernity*. New York: Sage.

Young, Jock. 2011. "Moral Panics and the Transgressive Other." *Crime Media Culture* 7(3): 245–258.

Zatz, Marjorie. 1987. "Chicano Youth Gangs and Crime: The Creation of a Moral Panic." *Contemporary Crises* 11: 19–158.

Zilberg, Elana. 2011. *The Making of a Transnational Gang Crisis Between Los Angeles and San Salvador*. Durham: Duke University Press.

4

The gang as secret society

Louis Kontos

Introduction: the secretive organization and the secret society

Street gangs assume a variety of forms. Some are criminally oriented, while others are not. Some are assimilated within their communities, while others appear as intruders. As Thrasher (1936 [1927]) said, 'no two gangs are alike' (p. 5). But each of them is to some degree a secretive organization. The secrecy of the gang is a source of both its allure and its resilience. The more the gang resembles a secret society, the greater its immunity from intrusions of the outside world, including with regard to its generalized expectations and judgments, its demands for transparency, and its threats. For Simmel (1906), the allure of the secret society, whether religious, criminal, or political, becomes powerful when enough people reject the status quo but lack the means to change it; alternatively, when the change they seek to effect becomes realizable within the secret society. The allure is enhanced, in Simmel's view, with the appearance of 'despotism', which, in a modern legal-rational context, equates to arbitrary and secretive authority. The allure of street gangs is similar when vulnerable members of society lack protection, representation, and opportunity and, more generally, when undemocratic practices are pervasive. This chapter explores the resemblance between secretive street gangs and secret societies and further identifies reasons and causes of greater secrecy, self-alienation, and self-reference among both types of groups, which make of resemblance reality.

Thrasher's (1936 [1927]) early account of gangs highlighted the role of secrecy in hiding mischief and crime, as well as creating identity, solidarity, and mystique. The 'gang boys' were immersed in a 'universe of discourse' that was demoralizing to them, and yet they seemed to live by a code of their own. Thrasher described them as pioneers and, alternatively, as medieval and feudal.

> Gang leaders hold sway like barons of old, watchful of invaders and ready to swoop down upon the lands of rivals and carry off booty or prisoners or to inflict punishment upon their enemies. Sometimes their followers become roving, lawless bands, prowling over a large territory and victimizing the community.
>
> *(p. 6)*

Such gangs were integrated in neighborhoods, block by block. By contrast, Whyte's (1993 [1943]) 'corner boys' were better integrated in a homogeneous community – the Italian slum. Their activities were not limited to interstitial space, like the railroad or the docks, but extended through the center of city life, from the cafeteria to the barber shop to clubhouse. They claimed territory, like Thrasher's gangs but did not interfere with the routine activities of the membership of the community. In retrospect, the assimilated gang in the homogeneous community was a blip in time. Neighborhoods became more heterogeneous post-WWII, and the idea of public space became suddenly contested in the barrios and slums of American society. By the 1960s, the idea of territorial gangs evoked other kinds of images, including, for instance, of thuggish behavior in territorial disputes over public space that made such gangs troublesome to the community generally (see, for instance, Cloward and Ohlin's (1961) conflict-oriented gang subcultures).

But realizing space is different than claiming territory. As Simmel (2009 [1908]) puts it, 'social interaction among human beings is – apart from everything else it is – also experienced as a realization of space' (p. 545). Interaction evokes notions of membership, including in the distinction between insiders and outsiders and between partial insiders and strangers with reason for being in some place. The belonging of people to any space is only clear, Simmel (2007 [1908] states, when their roles are circumscribed; for example, 'the maid belongs to the house', but the cleaning lady does not (p. 55). But, unlike the cleaning lady in the space of the house, Simmel points out that there are members of society who are given official status (and documents) and thereby reason to think that they are full members, whereas they are not. They may be treated differently by authorities without explanation. They may be treated badly, depending on the authorities and upon the type of society. But rarely in any modern society are partial members labeled accordingly. It is merely an open secret and a fact validated by collective experience.

The secret society provides an integral response. Its membership is exclusive. Its typically long initiation process ensures not only that members become trustworthy but that they experience rebirth – that they break 'with what came before'. The secret society does not seek recognition or assimilation. Nor is the membership of the secret society forthcoming with reasons for self-alienation. As Simmel argues, silence is the more powerful choice. The individual who makes choices about what to disclose and to whom (including in the context of intimate relations) has thereby something in common with the type of person who takes an oath of secrecy and puts the brotherhood ahead of all else. But the individual who takes the latter decision has already veered away from, or turned his back on, the institutional matrix of the normative order. He is the type of deviant Erikson (2004 [1966]) described as an anomaly, because he can neither be threatened nor enticed toward conformity; that is, except that the member of a secret society is turning his back with others – as part of a brotherhood.

The sense of intense loyalty to a group is also to be found in the work of Shaw and McKay, Sutherland, Niederhofer, Miller, and other pioneer gang criminologists. But none of this work deals with the social-psychological dimension of belonging to a group that is already or might become a secret society, that is, where membership becomes the primary source of identity and cancels out 'what came before' that binds the member to outsiders historically and culturally. In the latter context, it doesn't (only) matter whether the secrets of the group are already known to the authorities or that they are made public in some way; what matters perhaps more is that the member does not disclose them. Such disclosure amounts not only to disloyalty and betrayal of the brotherhood but self-betrayal. The fact of membership includes that form of recognition and judgment.

The gang as a secret society

The transition of the secretive gang to a secret society comes with greater solidarity, not only greater secrecy. Whereas the street gang normally devotes effort to trying to protect itself from surveillance and infiltration, the gang as a secret society is doing much more than that. It is establishing a parallel universe of discourse which is uncontaminated by the expectations and judgments of outside others. The secret society, however, rarely approximates an ideological group, like what could be said about the cadres assembled by Lenin pre-1917, for instance. The secrecy of the secret society is more commonly about interpretation of established or emergent ideologies or religious doctrine. For instance, the Christians were a secret society under the Roman Empire before Christianity was adopted as its official religion. Secret societies also typically form for the purpose of protection, like the feudal Sicilian Mafia, which offered protection to newly freed serfs and peasants and which assimilated a great many of them. The street gang as a secret society is a relatively new phenomenon. This type of gang 'builds' its own culture and is simultaneously able to bind its membership to an oath to uphold the codes of that culture and to reject demands to reveal its secrets to outsiders.

The continuity of gangs in general is predicated on the replacement of people, not ideas, hence, much like the secret society, mitigating disruptions (Simmel, 1898). Disruptions include betrayals, internal rivalries, and external forms of reaction. In the current period, reaction includes the involvement of the FBI and ICE and the increased routine of gang 'sweeps', which, in each case, involve the arrest and prosecution of some members for the crimes of others, as well as people whose sole crime is associating with the gang. The result is broad, unaccountable police discretion. In the recent scandal in LA, hundreds of neighborhood youth were added to gang lists because the officers involved did not like the youth. The same officers were apparently surprised that oversight suddenly appeared over discretion. But the policy remains, as Banks (2020) describes it: 'police officers need to satisfy two criteria from a list that includes attire, tattoos, location, arrest record, associates, self-admission and the word of reliable, which could be another officer'. The phenomenon of unaccountable police discretion, along with an enhanced legal-juridical framework for actual gang crime, is part of what is called a war on gangs; which continues to intensify as gangs continue to exist and transform.

The logic of the secret society provides one direction. The secret society revolves around notions of brotherhood that are premodern in their intensity and exclusivity. In Simmel's (1906) view, this fact is reason enough for the secret society to prove seductive; since the modern concept of friendship is rather abstract, that is, it appears together with the desire for privacy, independence, and selective accountability (and transparency) and with the option to exit. Simmel adds,

> perhaps the modern man has too much to conceal to make a friendship in the ancient sense possible; perhaps personalities also, except in very early years, are too individualized for the complete reciprocality of understanding, to which always so much divination and productive phantasy are essential.
>
> *(p. 458)*

A sense of common struggle is solidified against alienated society, more directly when arbitrary authority is involved, for the difference is between the fair and unfair treatment of people as things. The more arbitrary the authority, the more justification appears for the self-alienating reflex of the secret society and of the street gang that, in degrees, becomes self-alienating and, in the process, approximates a secret society.

The secret society invariably embodies a counter-narrative against the logic and mandates of what Simmel labels 'the abstract world' (i.e., the society of things) and against ideational modes of exclusion and semi-inclusion that justify arbitrary authority. The common struggle of the membership of the secret society is always a story in the re-making, that is, in which the membership is the heroic protagonist, and, in the case of the street gang, the anti-hero. As such, folklore and history become indistinguishable. Vigil (2003) grasped this point when he described the established gang as a self-reproducing, self-referred entity in which continuity is secured through 'lore, legend, and even myth' (p. 101). Traditional Cholo gangs of the kind that Vigil studied have become secret societies in Simmel's sense by developing their own cultural system against conventional sources of historical interpretation and judgment and by excluding potential members who want to be part of a group but not a brotherhood, or not a subculture – or who do not wish to cut out the past. The Cholo subculture claims lineage from the Zoot Suit cliques and the anti-Mexican riots of the 1940s, which is to say, heroic and quasi-aristocratic lineage, and justifies its exclusivity accordingly.

At the same time, there are practical and instrumental reasons against secrecy in modern society; and therefore, for secretive street gangs and secret societies, there is always a necessary loosening of the code, that is, enough for the group member to function as a normal member of society. In a parallel process, members of gangs that are secret societies become 'associates' of other kinds of gangs when it seems possible and necessary, including, for instance, in places where there are multiple gangs but no single dominant gang and no gang wars. The FBI has labeled these formations 'hybrid gangs' (2013 National Gang Threat Assessment Report), thus obscuring the point that they are assemblages rather than types. Can a member of a Cholo gang become a member or associate of two or three 'crews' that were invented last week? The answer now is yes. The same member cannot, however, become a member of 18th Street. Hence, the hybrid gang is realized differently in the streets than in reports of law enforcement agencies, particularly the FBI, and via gang 'sweeps' where an assortment of people appear related to a singular hybrid entity due to their having been arrested together in the same space.

The greater the secrecy of any group, the more it is possible for observers to say practically anything they want about it. In that sense, there is a parallel between secret societies and gangs in general. The gang becomes visible through the discourses of law enforcement, politics, media, and academic research, in each case with 'unaccountable discretion' (Katz and Jackson-Jacobs, 2007). The fact that academic researchers were generally not preoccupied with gangs in the 1970s, that is, the period when the supergangs developed on the West Coast, followed by the Midwest, makes the problem of discretion vivid (cf. Bookin-Weiner and Horowitz, 2006). The resurgent interest over the past several decades in the street gang problem has served to pathologize it more thoroughly than what could be said about the same tendency in the 1950s, where it was tied to a theory of society – namely structural functionalism – that served to pathologize it.

In the most influential work at the time, Cohen (1955) related the idea of 'status frustration' to a broad consensus of norms and values that were deemed distinctly American and that were supposedly internalized as motives, aspirations, and sources of judgment and further embodied in symbolic systems through which the average conformist member of society gained recognition. None of that kind of heavy conceptual baggage appears in the work of contemporary mainstream criminologists, who relate the notion of frustration to status or more generally accumulated personal failures in life (e.g. Taylor, 2013; Agnew, 1992). In this case, it might be asked: what happened to the types of gangs that Thrasher (1936 [1927]) wrote about that were filled with life and the spirit of adventure. Are they merely part of a bygone past? What happened to the types of gangs with energy, vitality, and a sense of honor and dignity, which Cohen

(1955) both celebrated and pathologized? Are the new gangs radically different, or merely observed differently by criminologists and relevant others?

The claim about status frustration, when unrelated to a theory of society wherein frustrated people are plentiful, becomes merely a source of invidious distinction. People who are not in gangs, thereby, presumably, would seem happy with the workaday production of their status. But, as Matza and Sykes (1961) argue, leisure culture permeates every aspect American society, and deviant groups, like street gangs, thereby have much in common with the middle class and its children in their aversion to prolonged and degrading work, in which case, what matters about 'gangs' is their similarity to other kinds of groups (not only other types of gangs). And yet the claim about frustration refuses to die. And this mode of theorizing has been appropriated seamlessly within the discourse of law enforcement agencies, particularly the FBI. In this discourse, what matters about the assumed frustration of the gang member is that it harbors resentment, which is deemed (in the same discourse) not only potentially menacing, or potentially destructive, but also potentially traitorous. Frustration and resentment appear in the recent reports of the FBI (particularly the 2015 National Gang Report) as a sole reason for self-alienation and for the transformation of gangland into something akin to an alien invasion – replete with insiders who become outsiders or ally themselves with anti-American religious and ideological groups.

Gangs and terrorism?

There is no obvious reason gang criminologists should concern themselves with the topic of anti-American terrorism; nevertheless, the FBI and the US Department of Justice have already assumed and supported that concern. Therefore, as Decker and Pyrooz (2015) state, there is 'catching up' to do (p. 104). In 2015, they found that gangs, like terrorist groups, have norms, membership bonds, and some degree of hierarchy. Also, they found that gangs are not generally ideological but that political extremism does not require a political ideology (i.e. they found all of it in the same way that the FBI found it, without a single example of an American street gang becoming an anti-American extremist group that has used violence against civilians to further political ends, or that has otherwise been 'down with the Jihad'). They add that 'perhaps as much as $100 million has been spent on gang programming and yet we still do not know what works' (p. 107). Against what? Jihad?

This speculative criminology mirrors speculative law enforcement discourse. Not even the assimilationist logic of early gang criminology seems relevant to the current versions which seek to 'catch up' with terrorism. This is seen particularly in the work of Decker and Pyrooz, where no actual groups are compared, although there are plenty of suggestions for how that might happen. They advise us, for instance, to 'pay close attention to the role of prison', because 'in the U.S., prisons have been the site of producing radicalized beliefs including religious extremism, anti-government extremism and the tenets of hate groups' (p. 109). The authors apparently overlooked the research of Hamm (2008), which attends to the phenomenon of prison radicalization in great detail.

Hamm found that prison was the ideal site for radicalization because the inmates he observed were lost souls, trying to make sense of their lives and develop a sense of purpose. Some of them left their 'Judeo-Christian' origins because they found purpose within the Nation of Islam, which Hamm labels 'a traditional form of American Islam' (p. 15), against the Sunni version adopted by Kevin James, who took control of the Assembly of Authentic Islam (JIS) and wrote the JIS Protocol, which calls for the killing of infidels (p. 15). Though Hamm documents dozens of followers of this doctrine, it appears that none of them were good terrorists because none were good criminals. 'Although JIS's goal was "to die for Allah in a jihad," the members' criminal skills did not match their ideological fervor' (p. 16). Upon release, they were rearrested for a string of robberies ostensibly in the service of funding an attack on a US Army recruiting office four years to the day after 9–11. Hamm does not say what exactly needed funding. Did they have logistics? Or were they simply released convicts with some ideas from a jailhouse preacher with seemingly no other plan, purpose, or place of belonging? Hamm argues that 'terrorist recruitment' in prison is a serious problem and advises, among other things, the hiring of more chaplains.

As Hallsworth (2013) says, this piece of intrigue (political Islam) historically was missing in the war on gangs, but it now adds justification, that is, the idea that ordinary garden-variety American street gangs may be suddenly seduced by some group or set of ideas presented effectively to impressionable young people who might now channel their frustration into anti-American (or anti-British, etc.) attitudes. Such attitudes will presumably translate into a willingness and capacity for violence on a random and grand scale, all of which provide another justification for a war on gangs. The question, then, is why ideological street-gang terrorism has yet to happen. The isolated cases foiled by the police are too isolated and over-interpreted. In the most notable case, the El Rukns were foiled. But so was their founder, Jeff Fort, in 1972, for mismanaging government grants. The likely possibility is that the El Rukns were prepared to take money from Ghadaffy and do nothing. But the negotiations for money between an American street gang and the Libyan government, closely monitored by the FBI, appear enough not only to substantiate the intent of the group but also of other groups, at least potentially, or as a possibility. The El Rukns have not been forthcoming. Since their transformation (from Black P. Stone Nation), they have become more thoroughly a secret society. They neither affirm nor deny the radicalization imputed to them.

The illusion of transparency

'Radicalization' is a term with a long, ambiguous history in the social sciences, where reasons for the rejection of the status quo are routinely discovered. The current trend in academic discourse is to adopt definitions of the term 'radicalization' which bind it to political extremism and violence. Meanwhile, the FBI refers to the radicalization of street gangs as a given fact that warrants comparison with terrorist groups. Several researchers have forced the same comparison, despite the fact that the gangs they observe do not appear radical to them. But, then, what could radicalization possibly mean in the absence of an ideological worldview as the source? Long ago, Short and Moland (1976) tried to answer this question when they revisited two gangs from an earlier study. The gangs were the Nobles and the Vice Lords. The comparison was odd, because the Nobles were barely surviving by creating a hybrid version of their group, while the Vice Lords were an established group. Further, while over a thousand gang members were claimed as part of a 'roster' in the study, Short and Moland managed to get responses to their questions about politics and ideology from very few gang members and without accountable selection or anything resembling a representative sample. Nonetheless, it turns out that the Vice Lords were more 'radicalized' because they were more willing to answer 'yes' to the question of whether they support violence as a 'method' to achieve reform. What respondents understood by 'violence' and 'support'[1] is anybody's guess.

Counter-hegemonic ideas, interpretations, and logic routinely appear in the symbolic and discursive dimensions of gang culture, nonetheless (Brotherton, 2015; Conquergood, 1993). For instance, the oldest remaining street gang subculture, the Cholo, appropriated the derogatory label of the Spaniards for mixed-blood people of the Spanish Empire in Latin America;

likening them to mixed breed dogs, that is, 'mutts'. As Cummings (2003) put it, 'Despite, or because of, its long history of derogatory semantics, the term cholo was turned on its head and used as a symbol of pride in the context of the ethnic power movements of the 1960s' (p. 333). More typically, gang symbolism is arbitrarily related to the symbolism of other groups in order to establish distinction, for instance, when the color blue was adopted by the Crips after the Bloods adopted red. Other times, the symbolism is arbitrarily tied to a developing organizational logic. For instance, in the 1970s, the Almighty Latin King Nation named its belief system – Kingism – and moved toward a conservative stage, which is to say underground. The ALK(Q)N symbolizes its evolution through the colors black and gold – darkness and light – replete with an eschatology that includes engaging in 'organized' crime in order to build its resources to better support the community and battle its adversaries. The symbolic order of the gang (its universe of discourse) links generations of members. By contrast, MS-13 is unique among the established gangs in that it does not present its members with logic or symbolism that supports any claim to a sense of purpose. Self-mythologizing for MS-13 is about power. And yet, MS-13 maintains a concept of brotherhood. It has transformed itself from a small, defensively oriented group in the 1980s into a large secretive organization that increasingly resembles a secret society.

The FBI has been instrumental in the development of the public image of MS as a 'national' threat. The fact that the group is associated with spectacular forms of violence, including the use of machetes, provides reason enough for observers not to question the methods of information-gathering of the FBI with regard to this group. But then what to make of claims daily repeated by FBI officials that MS-13 mandates that each member commit murder? The recent police sweep of MS-13 included several years' worth of surveillance and resulted in roughly 200 arrests and 96 people charged with a range of crimes, including 28 murders since 2016 (Feuer, 2019). Other revelations from the same sweep include an internal MS-13 document stipulating that a member would have to commit four murders in order to gain advancement in the organization. Who knows what to make of such a document? Did ordinary members read it? How many of them committed four murders? The numbers certainly do not add up. The federal investigators involved in the sweep also reported the discovery of a 'New York Program' originating in El Salvador, where New York members are supposed to 'collect money and send it back to El Salvador'. What does any of this mean? All the relevant specifics are lacking. And the reader, including the researcher, has no real way of verifying or denying claim after claim about MS-13. But then there is reason to expect something more of a statement than 'collect money and send it back to El Salvador' (which is hardly unique in the Salvadorian community in NY) by authorities to justify their logic and methods. Inversely, the lack of information about MS-13 supports its mystique, as if it were a contemporary version of the Mafia – that is, something truly alien. Its connections to the old world are known among researchers as mostly the product of the flow of people in the mixture of migration and deportation. Yet imputations of conspiratorial 'connections' (that have not been verified by researchers) support the current nativist argument that undocumented immigration includes a portion of people with ties to an international criminal conspiracy and who use machetes to kill people.

It is worth recalling that part of the mystery of the Mafia was about its connections to the old world. How old was the brotherhood of the Mafia? What was the nature of the relation between old-world networks, traditions, codes of honor, and American criminal enterprise? For the nativist, Italian organized crime was merely part of a criminal alien invasion. The idea of spread from the 'old world' throughout American cities served the organized criminal syndicates well. Even before the appearance of Mafia, or La Cosa Nostra, there was the Black Hand, which claimed the same thing, which primarily extorted money through letters that contained specific threats of violence. And yet, while the letters were broadly circulated in newspapers, and while victims routinely sent money wherever they were told by the extortionists, it is not clear that any real organization by the name Black Hand ever existed (Lombardo, 2010). The Mafia, by contrast, certainly did exist. But mainstream criminologists reject the claim of old-world criminal networks, while the size and scope of Mafia dealings remain debatable. Conversely, the Kefauver Committee, 1950–1951, concluded that 'the Mafia is a direct descendent of a criminal organization of the same name originating in the island of Sicily' and recommended that 'immigration laws should be amended to facilitate deportation of criminal and other undesirable aliens' (quoted in Wade, 1996, p. 372). The McCarthy Committee hearings followed, 1951–1952, with a parallel emphasis, namely against the unrestricted speech and movement of insiders who become outsiders (i.e. communists).

Innocuous nativism

Nativist discourse, historically, obscures similarities between native and foreign groups, as well as the differences within native groups. In the United States, the concept of the native, as pertaining to progeny of European immigrants, is maintained around the singular claim that the country was built by a relatively homogeneous group of people from different shores.[2] Thus, nativism relies upon history less in the American context for support of a continuous, homogeneous community and more for the construction of unassimilated outsiders and public enemies. The gang becomes that entity repeatedly without much effort.

Mainstream criminology provides tacit support for reflexive nativism by comparing deviant groups to one another, for example, gangs to other gangs, rather than mainstream youth groups. And yet there are more similarities than differences among street gangs and mainstream groups. Long ago, Matza and Sykes (1961) made the cogent point that the primary 'subterranean value' American culture was not about devotion to the industrial labor process but aversion to it. The same groups that were making the argument that the newcomers did not want to work also understood that 'work is for suckers'. But such words are verboten in conventional society, even for the purpose of 'neutralizing' the meaning and consequence of any behavior in order to 'free the individual' (Sykes and Matza, 1957). The same individual who wants to steal from others is better off appealing to higher loyalties, or denying injury or responsibility for it, than claiming 'work is for suckers'. The techniques of neutralization work only where they are uncontroversial, that is, where conceptual vocabulary is drawn from the broader culture. The only controversial category in the list of 'techniques of neutralization' in Sykes and Matza's argument is 'condemning the condemners'. Why? Because the condemners are not merely part of anonymous bureaucracies but also part of a righteous community filled with cultural arbiters and warriors.

The righteous side of the culture wars

The rhetoric of the Trump administration has a gangster quality. Trump promises vengeance to the portion of the population that understands itself as both real America and as a submerged entity – not unlike Nixon's 'silent majority' – and also promises indifference to the idea of due process and the institutions through which it might be realized. Thus, while Trump routinely disparages federal judges, he also routinely heaps praise on racist cops – exemplified by a presidential pardon for Sheriff Arpaio after violating a federal court order to stop profiling Latinos. The anti-democratic impulse of the POTUS is nowhere more evident than when he embraces criminal cops as 'our' cops against the criminal alien, the thug, and the gangster, who are not 'ours'. Hostility toward professionalism and inclusivity alike was put on full display when Trump addressed the International Association of Chiefs of Police in Chicago in October 2109. Trump promised the audience the end of federal oversight, while repeating the story of an anonymous cop in Chicago who told him that he and his buddies could solve the crime problem in a week if given the chance (Couper, 2019). Earlier, Trump had threatened to 'send the Feds'. 'If Chicago doesn't fix the horrible "carnage" going on . . . I will send in the Feds! (Wagner and Berman, 2017). What this meant was anybody's guess, especially since 'the Feds' were already working with the CPD. The statement is the same in kind that formed the basis of Trump's Inaugural Address, where he referred to unemployment and crime together as 'carnage' inflicted on American society by invading foreigners, disloyal businesspeople, and overtly traitorous politicians. This type of talk resonated among the portion of the voting base that voted for Trump on the premise that he would restore a former glory to white-working class America, including in deindustrialized places like Chicago (Kontos, 2018).

In Chicago, Trump has incited hatred for public officials with inclusive policy initiatives – particularly Superintendent Johnson. About Johnson's 'sanctuary city' policies, Trump labeled him a disloyal American who puts 'criminals and illegal aliens before the citizens of Chicago' (Samuals and Carfant, 2019). In sanctuary cities across California, Trump has promised to do something more dramatic than sending the Feds, namely he promised that "illegal immigrants who can no longer be legally held (Congress must fix the laws and loopholes) will be, [sic] subject to Homeland Security, given to sanctuary cities and states!" (Bierman and King, 2019). This kind of talk is not only unprecedented in recent history in its lack of presidential decorum, but it is lacking in all specifics. It is merely nativism and authoritarian populism applied to any and every issue. It links the idea of sanctuary with the claim that liberal cities are soft on crime and gangs (notwithstanding the fact that these cities keep gang lists, surveil gang members, infiltrate gangs, engage in gang raids, etc.). Yet, for Trump, these cities await liberation, and thereby ICE is the only agency that deserves praise against not only invading hordes and proxy combat enemies but also against the bureaucracies that appear to him more concerned with due process than public safety. In his political sloganeering, ICE agents are combat heroes while they have 'liberated cities' (Fortin, 2018).

This logic, according to public opinion surveys (Kontos, 2011), appeals mostly to people who live outside these cities, just like the war on gangs appeals mostly to people who live in places without a gang problem. In a recent national survey, 85 percent of Trump voters told pollsters that they believed that MS-13 was a serious or very serious problem, and 50 percent added that they feared that they or their loved ones would be victimized by MS-13 (compared to 13 percent of people who voted for Clinton) (Birnbaum, 2018). The parallel is the gentrified urban environment which embodies new and different standards about where young people may congregate and more generally about what kind of people have the right to live in their neighborhood. The returning gentry do not want any of the problems from which they or their parents fled in earlier decades. Both the street-corner gang and the extra-territorial version appear troublesome in cities without undefined, interstitial space and little tolerance for people without objectively valid, transparent purpose (Ferrell, 2004).

Not only are gangs submerged in Chicago, Los Angeles, and New York City, but so are members of the immigrant and minority communities. Neighborhood youth are given reason to think that they'll be labeled gang members or criminals regardless of what choices they make and that at the end of the day, they have only each other to rely upon. In New York City, yet another innovation was added to the same scenario by relabeling profiling through stop-and-frisk (which was ruled unconstitutional) as gang policing. The latter was not presented as a 'switch' by the mayor or police commissioner but as a necessary, appropriate response to a new problem, namely the rise of gang crime. Yet Howell (2015) was able to rebut the NYPD's claim that half of violent crimes in the city are gang related through a Freedom of Information lawsuit in which the real (internal) numbers were revealed. (As it turned out, between 2005 and 2012, gangs ranked last and second to last as a cause of murder [p. 1], and less than 1 percent of felonies were gang related [p. 8].) Yet the propaganda machine still repeats the initial claims as if they have not been discredited. The repetition sends a message that a pretext for the differential treatment of neighborhood youth will not only be maintained but enhanced. Neighborhood youth will not only be stopped-frisked-surveilled but also possibly put on a gang list which may be used in criminal and deportation proceedings. Here it is possible to extrapolate from Simmel's (1906) notion of the secret society (which 'emerges everywhere as a correlate of despotism and of police control' [p. 472]). The fact is that the secretive street gang is more seductive where members are given reason to believe that they are born guilty, will be treated as criminals and gang members, even where they are innocent, and lack protection as well as recourse. Every established gang in American society involves some version of the claim that the authorities cannot be trusted and that members have to look after themselves.

Conclusion: nativism as method

I argue that the nativist turn in political culture reinforces gangster logic (by instantiating it) and further provides reason for the transition of secretive organizations into secret societies. History is thus repeated. The same kind of nativism was mobilized against previous newcomers, with ethnic organized crime as part of a system of reference against which the imagined community of natives could define itself. It refuses to die, shamelessly. Thus, former Attorney General Jeff Sessions was able to evoke Al Capone alongside MS-13, as if there were an obvious connection. Further, Sessions claimed to pledge the resources of the federal government in the war against specifically MS-13, in the same way that it did with Capone (Saul, 2017), seemingly forgetting that Capone was imprisoned for tax evasion, not racketeering, bribery, corruption, or any of the murders attached to his name. More importantly, there were no significant old-world connections within Capone's organization and no anti-American component – that is, the things that Trump and Sessions have said about MS-13. Capone was thoroughly Americanized; a quintessential American entrepreneur, as Merton (1938) labeled him.

Nativist claims and references do nothing to advance a discussion about the gang problem but instead provide fragmented, atomized, alienated society the feeling of unity in its moral outrage about problems that cannot be similarly isolated or named, including the growth and spread of ontological insecurity (Young, 1999). However, both populism and nativism are on shaky ground when the imagined community of 'real' Americans is held together only by selective feeling or experience and selective sources of recognition. The illusion of a homogeneous core of 'real' Americans against putative others is strengthened by a sense of collective victimization and by imputing to outsiders a willingness to deceive and take advantage of morally innocent and good-willed members of the imagined native community. The Trump administration has fortified the nativist fantasy through political sloganeering which redeems the assimilated immigrants and their progeny against the problems they experience and cause to others, such that others become the source of problems, or the source behind every apparent source. By contrast, the Clinton-Obama legacy of quasi-nativism confused audiences with statements that validated the moral worth of the alien worker against the alien criminal against a backdrop of policy initiatives (beginning with Clinton in 1994 and 1996), which made it possible for Obama to deport more people than any president since Truman and which provide tangible support for the nativist claim that immigrants are generally criminals.

With Trump, there is no confusion. In his political sloganeering on the campaign trail, Trump not only cast immigrants from Mexico, Central and South America, and Muslim countries as invading hordes with suspect motives for their arrival but also as possible subversives or proxy combatants from countries that 'sent' them here. As president, Trump added that the problem with immigration is that the wrong immigrants are coming to the United States. More from Norway would be good, in his estimation. The problem, in the view of the President of the United States, with immigration from Mexico, Central America, Africa, and the Caribbean, is that the countries are 'shitholes' (Kirby, 2018). Undocumented immigrants, including refugees and asylum seekers, are routinely labeled by the POTUS and a significant portion of the Republican Party as gang members or like them. Against this crude system of reference another materializes, whereby the people who are making these judgments demonstrate, in the process, their commitment to the imagined community of 'real' Americans. Being a real American in the nativist mode means ignoring a great deal of extra-legal violence on 'our' side, whereas outsiders are treated with scorn, ridicule, and held suspect for anti-American attitudes while self-proclaimed patriotic mobs continue to menace journalists, politicians, activists, and newcomers.

The nativist logic provides justification for cruel, disproportionate, arbitrary policies, including those which originate with Clinton, who bound immigration policy to crime and gangs, and Obama, who brought the legacy to fruition, alongside the augmentation of the surveillance power of the state. The secret society is already there or develops there to pick up the society's outcasts and throwaways, of which there are now many, with the added twist in contemporary American political culture that the distinction between the worker alien and the alien criminal has been made irrelevant. Moreover, there is no real protection for any of them. The secret society offers no specific protection outside the idea of brotherhood but makes the same idea all-encompassing. The secret society maintains a resilient, oppositional quality against demands for transparency and contrition from sources that have already demonstrated indifference to the notion of inclusivity and of democracy. The secret society realizes an integral place in modern society against the undemocratic state and the hypocrisy of normative groups, not otherwise.

Notes

1 Short and Moland would likely have obtained more 'yes' answers if they were interviewing random members of the public – particularly among the alt-right.
2 That is, bracketing the fact of European as a general category did not mean much until recently, that people from assorted European nations did not get along well throughout the late 19th and early 20th century, including decedents from the same nation (e.g. Northern and Southern Italians, Protestant and Catholic Irish, etc.).

References

Agnew, Robert. 1992. 'Foundation For a General Strain Theory of Crime and Delinquency'. *Criminology*. Vol. 20 (1): 47–88.

Banks, Sandy. 2020 (Jan. 21). 'In Scandal over LAPD Officers Falsely Tagging People as Gang Members, Video Confirms an Old Suspicion'. *Los Angeles Times. Latimes.com*.

Bierman, Noah, and Laura King. 2019 (Apr. 16). 'California Hits Back as Trump Threatens to "Dump" Immigrants in Sanctuary Cities'. *Los Angeles Times. Latimes.com*.

Birnbaum, Emily. 2018 (July 16). 'Overwhelming Majority of Trump Supporters Sees MS-13 as a Threat to U.S.: Poll'. *TheHill.com*.

Bookin-Weiner, Hedy, and Ruth Horowitz. 2006. 'The End of the Youth Gang'. *Criminology*. Vol. 21 (4): 585–602.

3

Louis Kontos

Brotherton, David, C. 2015. *Youth Street Gangs: A Critical Appraisal.* New York: Routledge.

Cloward, Richard, and Lloyd Ohlin. 1961. *Delinquency and Opportunity.* London: Routledge.

Cohen, Albert, K. 1955. *Delinquent Boys: The Culture of the Gang.* Glencoe, IL: Free Press.

Conquergood, Dwight. 1993. 'Homeboys and Hoods: Gang Communication and Cultural Space'. In *Group Communication in Context: Studies of Natural Groups.* Edited by L. Frey. Hillsdale NJ: Laurence Erlbaum.

Couper, David. 2019 (Nov. 1). 'Former Police Chief Says Trump Address to Cops Irresponsible, Dangerous: Reader View'. *USA Today.*

Cummings, Laura, L. 2003. 'Cloth-Wrapped People, Trouble and Power: Pachuco Culture in the Greater Southwest'. *Journal of the Southwest.* Vol 45 (3): 329, 348.

Decker, H. S., and David C. Pyrooz. 2015. '"I'm Down for a Jihad": How 100 Years of Gang Research Can Inform the Study of Terrorism, Radicalization and Extremism'. *Perspectives on Terrorism.* Vol. 9 (1): 104–112.

Erikson, Kai T. 2004 [1966]. *Wayward Puritans: A Study in the Sociology of Deviance,* Revised Edition. Boston: Allyn and Bacon.

Ferrell, Jeff. 2004. 'Boredom, Crime, and Criminology'. *Theoretical Criminology.* Vol. 8 (3): 287–302.

Feuer, Alan. 2019 (Dec. 20). 'MS-13 Gang: 96 Charged in Sweeping Crackdown on Long Island'. *New York Times. Nytimes.*

Fortin, Jacey. 2018 (July 1). 'Has Trump "Watched ICE Liberate Town From the Grasp of MS-13"? No'. *New York Times. NYTimes.com.*

Hallsworth, Simon. 2013. *The Gang and Beyond: Interpreting Violent Worlds.* London, UK: Palgrave-Macmillan.

Hamm, Mark, S. 2008 (Oct. 26). 'Prisoner Radicalization: Assessing the Threat in U.S. Correctional Institutions'. *nij.ojp.gov.* https://nij.ojp.gov/topics/articles/prisoner-radicalization-assessing-threat-us-correctional-institutions.

Howell, Babe K. 2015. 'Gang Policing: A Post Stop-and-Frisk Justification for Profile-Based Policing'. *Denver Criminology Law Review.* Vol. 5: 1–31.

Katz, Jack, and Curtis Jackson-Jackson-Jacobs. 2007. 'The Criminologist's Gang'. Chapter 5 In. *The Blackwell Companion to Criminology.* Edited by Colin Sumner. Hoboken, NJ: Wiley-Blackwell.

Kirby, Jen. 2018 (Jan. 11). 'Trump Wants Fewer Immigrants From "Shithole Countries" and More From Places Like Norway'. *Vox.com.*

Kontos, Louis. 2011. 'Media Distortion: A Phenomenological Inquiry into the Relation Between News and Public Opinion'. *Protosociology.* Vol. 27: 167–176.

Kontos, Louis. 2018. 'American Carnage: Political Culture in the Age of Trump'. *Socialism and Democracy.* Vol. 32 (2): 1–13.

Lombardo, Robert. 2010. 'The Hegemonic Narrative and the Social Construction of Deviance: The Case of the Black Hand'. *Trends in Organized Crime.* Vol. 13 (4): 263–282.

Matza, David, and Gresham M. Sykes. 1961. 'Juvenile Delinquency and Subterranean Values'. *American Sociological Review.* Vol. 26 (5): 712–719.

Merton, Robert, K. 1938. 'Social Structure and Anomie'. *American Sociological Review.* Vol. 3: 672–682.

National Gang Report, 2015. FBI.gov.

National Gang Threat Assessment Report, 2013. FBI.gov.

Samuals, Brett, and Morgan Carfant. 2019 (Oct. 28). 'Trump Blasts Chicago Police Chief in First Visit to City as President'. *TheHill.com.*

Saul, Josh. 2017 (Oct. 23). 'Sessions Says He's Going After MS-13 "Just Like We Took Al Capone off the Streets'. *Newsweek.com.*

Short, James, and John Moland, Jr. 1976. 'Politics and Youth Gangs: A Follow-Up Study'. *The Sociological Quarterly.* Vol. 17 (2): 162, 179.

Simmel, Georg. 2009 [1908]. 'Space and the Spatial Ordering of Society'. Pp. 543–620. In *Simmel, G. Sociology: Inquiries into the Construction of Social Forms, Volumes 1 and 2.* Translated and edited by A. J. Blasi, A. K. Jacobs, and M. Kanjirathinkal. Leiden and Boston. Brill Pub.

Simmel, Georg. 2007 [1908]. 'The Social Boundary'. *Theory, Culture and Society.* Vol. 24 (7–8): 53–56.

Simmel, Georg. 1906. 'The Sociology of Secrecy and of Secret Societies'. *American Journal of Sociology.* Vol. 11 (4): 441–498.

Simmel, Georg. 1898. 'The Persistence of Social Groups'. *American Journal of Sociology*. Vol. 3 (5): 662–698.

Sykes, Gresham M., and David Matza. 1957. 'Techniques of Neutralization: A Theory of Delinquency'. *American Sociological Review*. Vol. 22 (6): 664–670.

Taylor, Stanley, S. 2013. 'Why American Boys Join Street Gangs'. *International Journal of Sociology and Anthropology*. Vol. 5(9): 339–349.

Thrasher, Frederic, M. 1936 [1927]. *The Gang: A Study of 1313 Gangs in Chicago*. Chicago, IL: University of Chicago Press.

Vigil, Diego James. 2003. 'Urban Violence and Street Gangs'. *Annual Review of Anthopology*. Vol. 32: 225–242.

Wade, David, R. 1996. 'The Conclusion That a Sinister Conspiracy of Foreign Origin Controls Organized Crime: The Influence of Nativism in the Kefauver Committee Investigation'. *Northern Illinois University Law Review*. Vol. 16 (2): 371–410.

Wagner, John, and Mark Berman. 2017 (Jan. 25). 'Trump Threatens to "Send in the Feds" to Address Chicago "Carnage"'. *The Washington Post*.

Whyte, William Foote. 1993 [1943]. *Street Corner Society: The Social Structure of an Italian Slum*. Chicago and London: The University of Chicago Press.

Young, Jock. 1999. *The Exclusive Society: Social Exclusion, Crime and Difference in Late Modernity*. London, UK: Sage Publications.

5

On being affected

Love, law and submission among gangsters

Martin Lamotte

A true revolutionary is guided by great feelings of love.

Ernesto Che Guevara

As far as Dips remembers, it was a summer night in Puerto Rico. He had just returned from an evening out with two other members of the Ñetas, the gang in which he had been a lieutenant for several years. A feeling of fatigue and laxness drove them to a small bar near the edge of San Juan. Relaxing at a table with a beer, they forget their worries of the day as the night descends. In the months prior to their departure for Puerto Rico, rising tension was increasingly palpable among New York's Ñetas. Rudy Giuliani, the mayor of New York City, had launched his Zero Tolerance policy, starting a war on New York's gangs. In Brooklyn, Dips was responsible for managing conflicts with Papi Chulo gang members and a branch of the Latin Kings. That night, in the tropical air of his Caribbean homeland, Dips sought to distance himself from his problems and release some of the tension that had been building inside him. He had arrived in San Juan just a few days ago, maybe a week at most, looking to learn about the life of Carlos La Sombra, the founder of *La Asociación Pro-Derechos del Confinado*, also known as *Los Ñetas*.

Those evenings in Puerto Rico reminded Dips of his childhood and the family farm in the Sierra mountains. He grew up as a simple Jibaro, playing with goats and chickens. The transition to New York City was a shock. No open spaces, no trees, cold winters, and crowds of people filled the streets. Later that night, after finishing their beers, Dips and his fellow gang members went back to the hotel tired but relaxed, with Dips falling into a heavy sleep. It had been a pleasant evening during which he probably played pool, danced and chatted with the bar's regulars. Dips cannot remember too much about that night, but one thing was certain though: it was the 30th day of a month, the night that the group celebrates the *Grito*, in remembrance of its founder.[1] According to legend, Carlos was assassinated on this day in 1981, signalling the birth of *La Asociación* in Puerto Rican prisons before spreading to the New York prison system via Riker's Island. Indeed, constitutive of their development in prison, both in Puerto Rico and on the mainland, the Ñetas, like other similar marginalized groups, faced physical and structural violence typical of poor and criminalized young men and women (Curtis 1998; Brotherton & Barrios 2004; Godreau 2015).

The *Grito* is meant to be an evening of communion and abstinence. When Dips looks back on that night twenty years later, he does not remember it for the minutiae of the evening but rather the night that everything changed in his life. While he relaxed in his hotel room, Dips had no idea that on returning to New York City, he was about to face a *Mesa Disciplinaria* for having drunk alcohol and taken drugs on the night of the Grito. Denounced to the Junta Central by one of his two buddies, the leadership organization that leads the New York Chapter declared him to be "affected", in other words, guilty, and he would be sentenced to 100 strokes of the cane. Nonetheless, he still thinks it could have been worse. Indeed, they could have declared him persona non grata and executed him. These are, after all, the Ñetas' rules, and he knows them well, especially since he was tasked with implementing them in his own chapter. The humiliation he experienced, however, he never got over.

This kind of trial is rare for the Ñetas, despite being formally part of the group's codes of conduct. What he most remembers is the betrayal by his former companions, the decision by the internal court and the lingering hate that he maintains for Bebo, the person who launched and directed the Mesa Disciplinaria against him. To Dips, it was a story of pure vengeance for which he paid the price. Bebo was rising to power, and he took advantage of this situation to make an example of him and prevent him from being a future competitor. In essence, it was two birds with one stone and 100 lashes, which he accepted in addition to the sanctions against him. Despite this incident, and despite no longer being an active member of the Ñetas thanks to Bebo, Dips is still recognized as an important activist in his neighbourhood, and he neither rejects the Ñetas, nor does he regret bowing to the violent sanctions against him.

In many ways, this investment in the Ñeta law means submitting to a violent code of conduct. How then can we understand why Dips, and the Ñetas as a whole, voluntarily accept bowing to these rules and the accompanying violence? How can we explain the hold that these rules have on the lives of Ñetas?[2] How are we to understand the group's rule of law and its effect on the Ñetas? In this work, I will show how the Ñetas' code of rules encompasses a system of values and beliefs that structures and, most importantly, affects their lives.

"Power from below": domination, submission, affection

Upon hearing the sanctions handed down at the Mesa Disciplinaria, Dips tried to appeal. This was immediately disallowed, and he was forced to face the sentence. Did he have any another option? Nothing was stopping him from leaving the Ñetas, but he chose instead to accept the caning. Dips' involvement in *La Asociación* is not extraordinary regarding the complete commitment that is required of its members but does beg an important question about submission. Why comply with a code of law that makes use of this type of violence? How can we properly account for and describe the particularities of this willing submission?

As the philosopher Manon Garcia (2019) explains, there are a great number of articles about the intricacies of domination but little written about its other face – submission. In this chapter, I begin by asking questions that are ethical, epistemological and political in nature. The first involves finding a definition of submission. Following the feminist approach of Manon Garcia, analyzing submission is framed by two major pitfalls: sexist naturalization, which aims to explore how women are submissive by nature, and the moralizing explanation, which tends to argue that women are submissive as a result of moral or pathological failings. Within these frameworks, submission, rather than domination, tends to empower individuals by insisting on their dependence on rather than obedience to the power being exerted over them. In this interpretation, the act of submission is minimized, "the result of a desire to not actively resist domination" (32) and is viewed as a rational decision made in favour of passivity. This raises the following paradox and problem: how do we explain the fact that submission can be voluntary? Garcia responds that the submissive state is stable a priori, as it is based on voluntary non-violent dominance between two entities.[3]

I argue that Garcia's excellent analysis is also heuristically applicable to this chapter when seen as a daily experience that is both shared and commonplace. Her analysis is particularly useful when describing the act of submission as described previously when we locate the subject in his relationship to: (i) a colonized/settler regime, (ii) the colonial situation of Puerto Rico (Balandier 1951; Cooper & Stoler 1997; Ferguson 2013) and (iii) his racialized formation with a United States inner city (Bourgois 1995; Massey & Denton 1993; Wacquant 2008). There is, however, a "philosophical taboo" surrounding the discussion of this notion (i.e., submission). In traditional Western political philosophy, from La Boétie to Rousseau, submission is considered unnatural and something derived from a person's moral deficit. Indeed, Freud developed a psychoanalytical approach to submission, linking it to a form of masochism. However, while Freud attempted to provide psychoanalytical explanations of sadism, he had little to offer regarding the "enigma of masochism" (23) and taking pleasure in one's own suffering. Garcia notes that while most philosophy is silent on this act of voluntarily obeying and taking pleasure in one's own submission, the works of contemporary philosopher Simone de Beauvoir and her analysis of situation and the application of phenomenological methods are a counterpoint.

Garcia's work dovetails with the work of anthropologist Michel Naepels (2011, 2019) when it comes to the concept of vulnerability. Naepels argues that vulnerability only exists as a situation (Gluckman 1958; Agier 2009). In this perspective, we avoid labelling the subject an ontological victim or someone who is 'vulnerable'. Rather, submission is situational and differential and is visible only by examining individual and collective practises that activate it, that is, in situations of domination. By applying situational analysis, we can better understand the ways in which the mechanisms of submission are implemented, as well as the social, political and economic conditions of its existence. In short, it allows us to historicize submission. This means thinking of this relationship as the result of an unnatural process of oppression. Additionally, phenomenological analysis allows us to consider the experience of subjects in situations of submission while avoiding essentialization.

Garcia also states that studying the concept of submission is a shifting operation, moving from an examination of power and then analyzing it from below. In fact, we must consider the experience of submission itself and not think of power as moving in a single direction, from the top (the one with power) down (to those upon whom it is exerted). Studying submissive situations is part of a broader effort to understand dominant relationships, and it should not be done to the detriment of studying the way in which power is exercised (Foucault 1994). Analyzing submission, thus, allows us to broaden the analysis of power relations by thinking of power "as being indistinguishable in its effects and actions for those who submit to it" (100). This reversal is reminiscent of the pragmatic displacement proposed by Naepels from his study of typologies (or institutional processes) to his analysis of practised capacities (21). It is an effort to look at logics of action and the ways in which people act to put themselves in dominant situations. In the case of submission, we must carefully describe and understand how power is exerted, in which situation and upon whom it is exerted and take into account that submitted actors are stakeholders in the relationship. Garcia explains that this allows us to think of submission not as a blind obedience as described by La Boétie but rather as "the manner in which inter-individual domination is experienced by those upon whom it is exerted" (14). Nevertheless, the paradox of complicity in submission remains open and unexplained – as submission remains the action of allowing yourself to submit.

To better understand Dips' wholehearted commitment to the cause, as we will see later, and how he willingly submitted to *La Asociación's* violent application of the law, the idea of a traditional separation between affect and reason, as well as feeling and thinking, should not be replicated but just the opposite. To understand this power dynamic, we must consider how the Ñetas say they are "affected" (afectados) by their law. Here, I am basing myself on the works of anthropologist Ann Stoler (2004), for whom affective knowledge is the core of political rationality. It is through a type of emotional education called la *convivencia* where initiates become full members with rights that the love for *La Asociación* is instilled. This path of learning – that is, becoming a Ñeta and falling in love with the cause – is a process of affection in the Aristotelian sense,[4] that is, a form of learning that alters and transforms the interior. This path, as I seek to show, is intimately to tied to learning the Ñetas' rules of law. In short, this chapter is about submission and love in a context of structural and spatial violence and is the story of being affected. I argue that to understand how submission is exerted, including its terms and rationales, we must first analyze individual and collective practises. To do this, I followed Dips' involvement in the Ñetas up to the moment of his trial.

This chapter, therefore, is based on an ethnography that was done over more than four years with the Ñetas in New York, Guayaquil City, Barcelona and Madrid. I first met Dips in 2012 at a Puerto Rico Day parade in the Sunset Park neighbourhood and was introduced to him by other Ñetas that I had met that day. A few months earlier, I had been introduced to the president of the Ñetas through former members whom I had been following for two years on a daily basis. In New York, I joined in the activities of members, including spiritual ceremonies to honour the death of Carlos La Sombra, parties, chapter meetings and public group activities, including demonstrations against police violence and funeral gatherings on street corners where members had been killed. I also recorded several life histories and conducted formal and informal interviews. I then went to Spain where I was introduced to members via reference letters from a handful of leaders of the New York Ñetas, which opened doors to *La Asociación* in Europe. I spent two years there following the activities of several chapters. I briefly lived in the apartment of one of the local leaders, which allowed me to progressively integrate myself into the Barcelona Ñetas. From there, I went to Guayaquil, where I conducted brief fieldwork to contrast my data.

The first part of this chapter consists of a formal analysis of *La Asociación's* code of laws, as presented in the Ñetas' book, the Liderato. In the second portion, I will describe the *Convivencia* or the initiation process into the Ñetas, which requires learning the rules. In the third portion, I will look at the role of *el Corazón*, the heart, which is used as the symbol for the Ñetas commitment to *La Asociación*. This investment in love hides the asymmetrical and paternalistic power relations inside the group. I will then conclude with a discussion of what being affected means.

1 A look at the book: the problem with the nature of the Ñetas' rules

At 16 years old, Dips was a puny kid, smoking weed, taking acid and going out every night. To put his "name on the map", with his graffiti crew and on the street, he worked out with bricks in the basement of his building. He had a reputation to build, along with friends and girls to impress. He was also getting regularly beaten (jumped), so he started carrying a hammer when he went out.

This earned him the nickname "Hammer Guy", which suited him well, and people started to leave him alone. One night he was coming home after going out with friends when a fight started in the subway. Dips threw the first punch, which was soon followed by those of his friends. The man fell backwards, semi-conscious, and cracked his skull. The subway security cameras recorded the fight, and before the train could pull away, the police had circled the station. Dips ran, but he was quickly caught, along with most of his friends. Two of them received four and a half years in prison. Dips got six months in Rikers. It was the first time he went to prison, though he had been given house arrest several times as a minor. He still has vivid memories. He was in the adult world now, "with real criminals", he says. For the first few weeks, he tried to be the 'tough guy' to keep himself safe. He was afraid of being harmed or, worse, raped. But soon he encountered the Ñetas for the first time. He saw how they acted, the way they protected each other and stood up to the abuse from other prisoners and from the guards. He admired the way they followed a code and a lifestyle. It had a major impact on his behaviour, and everything he learned on the street started to crumble away. You don't need to be a tough guy, to act or pretend, he thought. He didn't join the Ñetas right away, but he was heavily influenced by their conduct and how they obeyed a code of law. All of this was still a secret, though, as the Ñetas didn't accept just anybody into their ranks. They were shrouded with a certain mystery and romanticized, which appealed to Dips. It wasn't until Dips became a Ñeta that he learned and understood the Ñetas' twenty-five rules of law.

The book

As Pirie (2013) noted, anthropologists working on the law generally avoid classifying their object of study too closely. They often avoid using the term 'law' at all, preferring instead to talk about processes, social standards and legal pluralism. The focus is often on what the law does, the role it plays in the process of control and how it is used as a tool to exercise hegemony or even to resist power. Pirie asks, how do we categorize the law? What is specific to the law and our notion of law? How do people apply it; why do they do so and to what effect? Pirie states that to analyze the nature of law, we must start by looking at its form before its function. One way of doing this is to look at the laws in the books and the way the laws are codified and written before delving into the ways in which they are used, manipulated and applied.

The Ñetas' laws are given in Chapter 7 of the *Liderato*, written in the mid-90s in New York. This book was then circulated across *La Asociación*'s chapters, including those in Latin America and Europe. Originally from Puerto Rico, the Ñetas began expanding along the eastern coast of the United Stated in the early 1980s. The 1990s were marked by heavy criminality and the involvement of the group in conflicts with other street gangs, including the Latin Kings and the Crips. It was during this period that *La Asociación* was classified as a gang, as much by the public authorities as by the media and its own members.[5] In the mid-90s, despite several internal splits, the Ñetas counted several thousand members all united under the same command, the *Junta Central*. In that period, they encountered the Zero Tolerance policy of the newly elected mayor, Rudolph Giuliani. Targeted as a group, marginalized as Puerto Rican community members and racialized based on the colour of their skin, they faced the type of structural violence and spatial inequalities described by Brotherton and Barrios (2004) and Bourgois (1995) in New York City.

In 1993, following the expulsion from the United States of two Ecuadorian prisoners who were members of the Ñetas, the group expanded to Latin America (especially Peru and Bolivia) from Ecuador, where it remains entrenched. In Guayaquil, the base for the *La Asociación* in South America, the group began a war with the Latin Kings, another gang that followed the same trajectory. Most recently, the group had expanded into Spain through Ecuadorean immigration in the 2000s, planting themselves in Barcelona and Madrid. Once again, conflict was sparked with other groups following the same trajectory from New York, including the Latin

Kings and the Dominicans Don't Play. In the mid-90s, the New York Ñetas began writing a book which became known as the *Liderato*. This text recounted the story of Carlos La Sombra, of *La Asociación*, and outlined the Ñetas' laws.

After getting out of prison in the early 90s, Dips returned to his parents and became involved in the local Ñeta chapter around the corner of his house. He climbed the ranks and eventually became one of its leaders. During this period, Dips remembers the internal struggles for power and the tension between the different chapters. Some wanted to wrest control from the Junta Central; others wanted to perpetuate their business through the sale of drugs and arms. It was a difficult period, and Dips managed to attain high-level positions within the Junta's adminis- tration. Spurred on by former members of the Young Lords Party,[6] and to avoid the pitfalls of disorganization and lethargy among its members, the Junta leaders decided it was time to make a pilgrimage to Puerto Rico and retrace the roots of their founder, Carlos La Sombra. This is why Dips found himself back in Puerto Rico with the other Ñetas. Upon their return home, they launched into writing the *Liderato*. With this, the Ñetas changed their direction in the mid- 90s thanks to a centralization of power within the Junta Central. This "bureaucratic turn" for the gang was marked by a systematic recourse to writing and archiving the group's history and self-produced texts. The focus on writing gave the group a renewed sense of identity as it went through a transformation. In particular, *Le Liderato* provided the Ñetas with a sense of belonging by redrawing their collective profile.

In fact, the Ñetas emerged and transformed at a particular moment in the history of New York City. Violence in the City was sparked as a consequence of the high rate of criminality around the drug trade in the 1980s and 1990s and especially the crack epidemic (Bourgois 1995). Both drug dealers – mostly big owners, or *bichote*, monopolizing the market in New York – and repressive policing policies were factors behind the increased violence in neighbour- hoods at the centre of the drugs trade. According to Curtis (1998), in the aftermath of the war on drugs, gangs – mainly Ñetas and Latin Kings – benefited from the high rates of incarcera- tion within the New York prison system. These groups capitalized on the frustration of many young men and women targeted by the police and the drug *barons*. Simultaneously, as the large corporate-style drug-dealing barons were targeted and dismantled by the police, there was a vacuum in the market to be filled. It is in this critical moment that the Ñetas' evolution took place, as the Junta Central took control, directing the gang away from the initial wars against the Latin Kings but also from drug dealing. As Curtis (1998) notes, Latino gangs during this period were not interested in taking over the drug market and instead reached out to community lead- ers or intellectuals, such as the Young Lords or some non-profit organizations, in search of guid- ance. The Ñetas, and other gangs, gained popularity in the streets of impoverished New York neighbourhoods as a response to the high levels of violence via the war on drugs (Curtis 1998).

The code

The group's laws, like the *Liderato*, are kept secret. For this reason, I have decided to not fully reveal them. The twenty-five rules[7] codify everything from sexuality, including the protection of homosexuals, to safety. The laws are physical and also include stipulations regarding hygiene. They insist on the respect for hierarchy and the family and place particular attention on the dignity and honour of each member. Fourteen of the twenty-five rules are prohibitions, gener- ally of the "do not do this" type.

While the latter half of Chapter 7 of the *Liderato* is dedicated to judgements, the first half records the "basic" rights of all members during a trial. As *La Asociación* is based on democratic rules given in the *Liderato*, the accused has the right to respond to those charges levelled against a member at a *mesa disciplinaria* (i.e., when coming before the disciplinary committee). The accused has the right to call upon a *Capítulo* member to defend them and to provide them with advice. They also have the right to call witnesses and ask for a person present at the hearing to be excluded.

The *Liderato* also outlines the trial process, for example, when notes are to be taken, how much time each speaker has to make their presentation and when sanctions are to be applied. The *Liderato* even contains a sample form for the accused to sign at the end of the judgement that includes whether they accept the sanctions against them and if they would like to appeal. Also written on this sheet is the person's name, the rule they did not obey and the sanctions made against them by the *mesa disciplinaria*. It is signed by the accused, the plaintiff and the moderator.

The last page of Chapter 7 lists the standards and the different sanctions to be taken. Several levels of sanctions are provided, depending on the rule and the number of times it was broken. The death penalty is the highest sanction.

The law

What status should we give to these norms? Are they legal in nature, meaning that they are a form of Ñetas law, a law that runs parallel to Spanish, American and Ecuadorean law? When we look at the words used,[8] we note that the Ñetas use the terms *"normas"* and "rules". Although the word "law" is never used, members are said to have "rights" (*derechos*). Similarly, the word "trial" is never used, but the word "judgement" is. "Punishment" is not used but, "sanctions" (*sanctiones*) and disciplinary hearings (*caso disciplinarios*) are. While the term judge is not used, there is a "moderator" (*moderador*) and "disciplinary hearing" (*mesa disciplinaria*) held against the "accused" (*acusado*), and there is a plaintiff (*acusador*). The accused is held "affected" but not "guilty".

From a lexical perspective, the Ñetas have not fully chosen to use formal legal vocabulary. Does this mean they don't have laws? An epistemological question about our use of analytical categories when dealing with laws seems appropriate, reminiscent of the debate between Max Gluckman and Paul Bohannan. Gluckman defined the methodology for case studies in his 1955 publication *The Judicial Process among the Barotse of Northern Rhodesia*. This work used legal terms for the rules that Barotse judges based their decisions on, including regulations, orders, customs, traditional uses and habits. One of his fiercest critics was Paul Bohannan (1957), who published *Justice and Judgement among the Tiv* in 1957. Bohannan called out Gluckman for having imposed an Anglo-American concept of laws onto the Barotse by applying Western legal categories. According to Bohannan, the Tiv had rules of conduct but these were not considered a "body of rules". He felt that the Tiv had laws but not "the law". To overcome this debate, which, as Mark Goodale says, closed the book on legal anthropology, leaving room for only an epistemological approach, I prefer to apply the non-essentialist approach proposed by Tamanaha (2001: 155 in Pirie 2013: 44) and consider law and the legal system that which people identify and apply through social practices.

Another approach to be taken when looking at the Ñetas' legal system is to analyze the mandatory nature of these regulations. Are these norms considered guidelines that are imposed upon members? Or are they declarative precepts to remind members of their commitment? In a study of Franciscans, philosopher Giorgio Agamben (2011) states that one way of looking at the obligatory nature of regulations is not to study the relationship between rules and precepts but to look at the nature of the obligation itself. Are transgressions *ad culpam*, implying a mortal sin, or *ad poeam*, a transgression involving a penalty? Philosophically speaking, the existence of penal law depends on the capacity of its members to transgress precepts without committing a sin, as long as the offence to be purged is established as a transgression. Only in the case where a rule can be transgressed – that is, if there are established penalties or sanctions – can a regulation be considered a law. For the purposes of our study, the Ñetas' laws are accompanied by a detailed list of sanctions for those who transgress them, which defines a form of penal system or legal order for the Ñetas (Lamotte 2017)

We could say, in fact, that the Ñetas have implemented a penal legal order despite the use of ambiguous legal vocabulary. The punishment received by Dips was a caning, but the punishment was "affected", and he was not found "guilty". The terminology related to affectation is, as we will see later, significant to a particular relationship that the Ñetas maintain between themselves and Carlos La Sombra, their founder. This relationship is part of the initiation process for Ñetas during the *Convivencia* process.

2 La Convivencia: an idealistic approach to legal order

Like all Ñetas, Dips was sworn in after a long *Convivencia* process. The probation period ranges from six months to a year depending on the chapter, culminating in a test. In front of the other members, Dips had to answer a series of questions about Carlos' life, the Ñetas' rules and prayers. He was made to remember their code and history by heart as written in the *Liderato*. Learning holds a central place in the *Convivencia* process.

As Fernanda Pirie explains, rendering justice is not the final goal of the legal system. Rather, it also serves to oversee people and ensure they keep to the duties and obligations of the law. Legal texts provide the rules that guide each member of society, ensuring that they live harmoniously with the community. For the Ñetas, this vision dovetails with the image of Carlos, who is considered more than just the founder but also the ancestor of all members and the promoter of laws.

Convivencia: a shared lineage

Aside from the code of conduct, the Ñetas' writings are primarily concerned with Carlos' story, which appears at the beginning of the Liderato and is read most closely by new initiates. These papers are also the most commonly shared texts between the New York, Barcelona and Ecuadorean chapters. Carlos La Sombra's story is told from his birth to his death and includes the details of his assassination. These pages discuss his life story and his struggles and draw a hagiographical portrait of Carlos as a person.

These texts are read, integrated and ingested by members during *la convivencia* initiation process where applicants go from being a *conviviente* (coexisting with other members) to being a full member. Throughout this companionship phase, the initiate attends spiritual ceremonies and group meetings. This is when the initiate is required to learn Carlos' story, the codes of conduct and Ñetas' philosophy. This learning is done by reading the Liderato but also by repeating the stories that members tell to the *convivientes*. Dates, names and facts – everything is learned by heart. Ñetas are more than warriors or brothers in arms, for they share a history and a common ancestry, and for some, it is a kind of family tree. Dips can trace the member of his lineage back to its origins in Puerto Rico. Each new initiate must be able to identify who started the chapter and who its presidents were. According to some members, "history is what we are made of . . . you can't mess around with it . . . otherwise you are damned".[9]

Being a Ñeta requires a drive to learn about a past that has been lived and recounted by others and that is taken on as one's own. It means learning about an adopted ancestor, being part of a connection and being a transient part of the struggle and its history. It means being part of a lineage and having a kinship. Above all, Ñetas are "brothers" of history. Its members are tied by these stories, and their transmission is a pillar of *La Asociación*. To use Herrou's expression (2008), the Liderato represents "A shared substance that allows them to consider themselves parents".[10] The construction and sharing of a collective history remains one of the Ñetas' central aspects and a condition of its existence. Like Dips, few of the New York members who were active in the 1990s lived through the initial 1980 period in Puerto Rico when the Ñetas grew out of the island's penal system. To be a member, though, you need to know Carlos' life like the back of your hand. Each member is part of a lineage that unfolds from the beginning, making the Ñetas the children of Carlos.

This initiation begins when a chapter president decides to give the *conviviente* the first few pages of the Liderato, detailing the life of Carlos, as well as Chapter 7, which list the laws of *La Asociación*. History is intimately tied to the Liderato, as is the means of transmission, at least in part, between each *conviviente* who enters into the secret circle of knowledge and of learning.

Carlos, an exemplary figure?

The Grito is a spiritual ceremony held on the 30th of each month to honour the death of Carlos La Sombra. It is an important moment in the lives of *La Asociación*. Each commemorative ceremony is an opportunity to re-memorize Carlos' story as a hero and leader of Puerto Rican prisoners. In 1974, Carlos was the leader of one of the major prison strikes in Puerto Rico. Holding hostage the penitentiary administration and demanding rights for the inmates, Carlos asked to meet and be represented by three eminent figures of the independence movement: Carlos Gallisá, who later would became his lawyer; Juan Mari Bras, founder of the Puerto Rican Socialist Party (PSP – Partido Socialista Puertorriqueño); and Ruben Berrios, president of the Puerto Rican Independence Party (PIP). From this time on, Carlos engaged fully within the Puerto Rican independence movement, alongside the PSP, headed by Carlos Gallisá. In and out of prison, Carlos advocated for the Independence cause and suggested that there could be no prisoners' rights as long as Puerto Rico remained a United States colony. He was frequently invited to participate in PSP conferences and its outreach campaigns. The letters Carlos sent from prison to PSP members demonstrate his evolution and importance within Puerto Rican independence movement. Indeed, in the 1970s, he signed as a common law prisoner, whereas before his assassination, on March 30, 1981, his signature evolved as "political prisoner".

Dips is fascinated by Carlos' life path as told by the Ñetas. It is said that Carlos lived among criminals and earned the respect of drug addicts, prostitutes and thieves. He sees himself in Carlos' life, with its violence and darkness, but also because of his ability to organize the poor and face the injustices of the abusive prison administration. He identifies with this "Caribbean Jesus" and his story of redemption and justice. He sees his own future in the path led by his elder. After his initiation, Dips decided that to be a Ñeta, he needed to become a better person and follow Carlos' example.

When described this way, the narrative of Carlos offers the possibility of transformation, with going to prison not seen as the end of the road but rather as a chance for renewal. This transformative vision is tied to Carlos' ability, according to legend, to transcend the space of his cell, start a movement and develop political consciousness. The *convivencia* process proves just how central Carlos is for the Ñetas, with his life described as the model for the *conviviente*, serving as an example of how to reorganize one's own trajectory. For Dips, the essence of Carlos' life is found in the rules.

The initiation period is not the end of the learning process for new members, and Dips remembers long discussions in parks with older Ñetas concerning *La Asociación*'s rules and principles. The rules are based on community living, each member must be able to recite them when asked and they are learnt by heart at first. There is more then just knowing the rules, however. They also must be incorporated into one's own life. Discussing the rules is a means of education that older Ñetas constantly use to train not only the *conviviente* but also junior members. Upon becoming a Ñeta, a second phase of learning is begun. While new initiates know the rules by heart, they also need to understand them and apply them. Spending time with other chapter members on a daily basis, and experiencing different situations, is part of this learning process, for they will always be asked by older members to interpret a situation according to Ñetas rules. What would Carlos do in this type of situation? How can one differentiate good from bad based on the rules of the Liderato? This sort of education continues into a "philosophical training" where the rules are interpreted on a daily basis based on real-life situations. Carlos' life serves as a model that exemplifies the rules in conversations about the text. Each discussion of the rules allows for the development of group knowledge but also of one's own self. Access to this knowledge (the rules and its know-how) *allows for the development of practices and self perfection*,[11] marking a deep investment in the self.

This work of interpreting the rules responds to a core aspect of *La Asociación*: the insistence on transforming the members and working on self-development. Like Carlos, the members enter into a self-improvement and personal transformation process by applying the rules to their own lives. Through discussion about the rules, the lives of members are also discussed, and the rules become both a means of correcting manners and an illustration of a possible perfect life. This self-work is also a means of diluting the individual within the Ñetas collective and can also be a renunciation of the self in favour of a common vision. Renunciation, dilution and transformation through the *conviviente* are all for the benefit of sanctifying Carlos La Sombra and of fostering a collective and individual love of *La Asociación*.

3   A heart filled with love

During his trip to Puerto Rico, Dips tried to retrace the life of Carlos La Sombra. He visited his grave and interviewed his former prison mates. Dips still remembers the love he had for *La Asociación* and his "*Hermanitos* y *Hermanitas*", convinced of the justice of his fight and that he was on the right path. When he returned to New York, he faced the *Mesa Disciplinaria* for having broken the rules by drinking alcohol the night of the Grito. For Dips, Bebo (the junta secretary), was trying to become president and had been plotting against him. He (Bebo), a warlord and political leader, had progressively worked his way up to the top of the Ñetas hierarchy and until then had been Dips' friend only to betray him by organizing his trial. Nonetheless, none of this changed Dips' love for the cause and for Carlos.

"De Corazón"

The heart is commonly used in Ñeta iconography, as a tattoo symbol for the members or as graffiti on walls. The heart represents love for *La Asociación*, for the *Hermanitos* and *Hermanitas*. By saying "*De Corazón*", it implies that the individual is fully behind anything said or done and that it is said with love. This love is performed during one key moment of the Grito, when members take each other in their arms and say "*De Corazón*". This love is tied to an individual's well-being (the love for self) and for the well-being of the collective as a whole (the love for *La Asociación*). "*De Corazón*" is possessive, meaning "with all my heart", and commits the individual to a complete investment. Proclaiming one's love for *La Asociación* and for the *Hermanitos* and *Hermanitas* is encouraged by the Ñetas. It allows them to create a distinction between members who love and respect each other, under a single code of law, and other gangs, the police and even society. In this sense, love is held up as being a distinctive feature of *La Asociación*[12] which has developed a language of love with its own vocabulary – *hermanito, Carlito.*

With this in mind, the *convivencia* process builds a parallel between the experience of commitment in the associative structure of the Ñetas and a commitment to love. At the end of the initiation period, the Ñetas feel that they are in love (*enamorado*) *with La Asociación.* The secrecy surrounding the Liderato, the long *Conviviente* period and the rituals such as the Grito are part of learning to love *La Asociación.* Little by little, the *conviviente* is initiated into the Ñeta world, and on the day they are initiated, their love of the cause and the struggle for the group is tested. It is precisely during the *convivencia* that the initiates are supposed to develop a love for the group and their future *hermanitos.* But there is a distinction between loving "by the book" and "truly", "fairly" loving with honesty and sincerity, between those who learn the rules by heart and those who apply the rules in their lives, making it a lifestyle, allowing themselves to be affected. This discourse aims to make love a way of interacting with the world and with other Ñetas, as new members are taught to make decisions by following their heart. However, this rhetoric is not reserved for gang members, and neither is it new. Other gangs, such as *La Familia* or some Maras, refer to a language of love, expressed between members, even when it is accompanied with a language of war against other members and/or the police. As the quote from Che Guevara in the epigraph shows, this same rhetoric of love is present in the idea of revolution, especially in the Caribbean movement for freedom and independence (in particular the independence of Puerto Rico), where love is expressed toward the nation, the physical place and its people.

A paternal figure and power relationships

This symbiosis that figures so heavily among the Ñetas requires nuance. The rules and their application allow for the potential suppression and exclusion of any protest or internal opposition. In this case, the rules become a means of imposing obedience, dominance and hierarchical power. From this perspective, Ñetas power relations are strictly defined, constituting a system of authority and control through forms of domination. It is a system that is so heavily codified that referring to these groups as informal may not be applicable, as they are, seemingly, both very formal and formalist. As such, this language of love also represents a language of affective control and domination by Ñetas' leaders. This dedication to love can be so total it becomes an abdication, particularly in a context where the members are required to transform themselves and appear to renounce themselves as individuals. This transformation into the image of Carlos hinges on whether the initiate succeeds in the process under the watchful eye of the chapter president and is yet another characteristic of the submission the Ñetas use that could be described as a paternal relationship.

The position of the president is ambiguous. He is elected by the members of the chapter, is in charge of educating the *convivientes* and is the one who gives the initiates the Liderato. He is also the one tasked with establishing the path to be followed and the interpretation of the rules. As mentioned previously, the Liderato is the shared substance that allows members to consider themselves parents, with the historical text creating a form of "lineage". Within this brotherly love, the president replaces the tutelary figure of Carlos and is the one who provides access to the fraternity and the lineage with the group's founder. He (the president) protects and aids the members in their transformation, interprets the rules and is a paternal figure. In other words, presidential authority is more than contractual and hinges solely on its words (Geffray 1995), for its legitimacy comes from a capacity to mobilize love from those being dominated, for whom he is the incarnation of the law. What is specific about this paternal relationship is the form of dependence it instils in those who are subordinate. This language of love is used "on a pseudo-paternal and filial register" (Geffray 1995: 368) and can be applied unequally. In this sense, the Ñetas love for Carlos and *La Asociación* is "viewed and encouraged as a true treasure . . ., serving as a vector for their collective identity" (Geffray 1995: 370).

In essence, the Ñetas have developed a collective aesthetic based on this love which also serves as a means of control and an affective domination. It allows for the development of a discourse that hides the power relationships while deploying collective representations of a loving and brotherly *Asociación*. As such, it is important to replace this type of power relationship within the framework of marginalization, impoverishment, racialization and structural violence that members suffered in New York City. The potential of violence applied against each other within the same gang has to be analyzed as part of the violence continuum theorized by Nancy Scheper-Hughes and Philippe Bourgois (Bourgois 2012, 2010; Scheper-Hughes & Bourgois 2004). Ironically, the Ñetas tolerate and reproduce the same type of violence from which they suffer. As Bourgois notes, the proliferation and trivialization of various forms of violence within the segregated population can generate a common sense that silences the existence of such violence. This can be seen in the Ñetas when the group ignores the violence behind love discourses or produces a law discourse that enables the issuing of a death sentence.

This is what was in part at play in Dips' trial. It was a reminder of: (i) the rule and its proper interpretation, (ii) a power reconfiguration within the group, (iii) a redistribution of hierarchies and (iv) a dispute between Dips and Bebo. As such, if the law is a discourse that gives meaning and shapes the world, it is also a discourse filled with force (see Goodale & Merry 2017); "after all," says Fuller (1994: 11), "law is about repression just as much as imagination". Thus, legal systems that encode asymmetrical power relationships (Collier & Starr 2018), and where presidents such as Dips and Bebo gain respect and have significant authority, are constitutive of the way laws are often used and interpreted within the group.

Conclusion: affection

> You live it any way you can . . .
> Carlito La Sombra was a revolutionary organizer . . .
> When you take on this manner of living
> and you apply it in your life on a daily basis,
> you are a Ñeta from the heart,
> from the *Corazón.*
> Spade, May 15, 2012

Following his return from Puerto Rico, Dips began trying to recover from the mesa Disciplinaria and the betrayal by those close to him. Unable to accept Bebo's power, he began to distance himself from *La Asociación* and became what the Ñetas call a "non-active". It was a difficult decision to make. To excuse (or explain) himself, Dips insists that he still lives in accordance with the Ñetas code and faithfully follows Carlos' life model. "It hurts me" he adds, "when I see what the Ñetas have become today. It is painful to think what we did and having to distance myself."

The rules for the Ñetas are more than a series of sanctions and require more than just learning them off by heart. They are based on a constant interpretation of practice. It is no longer enough to observe the rules of law; they must be lived as an actual lifestyle. This is shown in the interview with Spade. Like Dips, Spade is no longer an active member, and all of the inactive members I spoke with have more or less the same thing to say. They all remain Ñetas even though they no longer participate in group activities, because they continue to follow the rules and philosophy of *La Asociación*. Their lives are guided by these rules. From this perspective, the pledge that *convivientes* make during their initiation is a permanent link, perhaps not with the group, but with a lifestyle and the rules that frame it. The members do not just follow the rules; rather, they follow a lifestyle that is defined for them. The initiation is more ascetic than legal, and this asceticism is part and parcel of a rigorous reflection on one's own life and the move toward self-perfection by reproducing the model presented by Carlos' life narrative. It is a shift from a legal type of obedience – following rules – to an ascetic type of obedience – observing a lifestyle. For the members who are still active, the legal and ascetic forms are superimposed on the learning process by following the rules and through the pursuit of self-perfection. However, for inactive members, only the asceticism remains.

I argue that Ñetas are practising a hermeneutic work around the norms. They implement a dual interpretation of the texts: a deep knowledge of the norms that make up the Ñetas community and a self-awareness to transform the individual. While the norms remain real and material, such as the caning received by Dips, what this hermeneutic work is attempting is not solely to guide members' approach to life but rather to ensure that the group's norms and laws run parallel with life until they become life itself. How does an hermanito live his life? How can they perfect it? How do they enter, once initiated, into the practice of self-perfection? The connection between hermanitos is not just legal in nature. It is more than an oath and an observation of the rules but is a life connection. These rules constitute a community, but also, they produce the conduct that Ñetas are meant to observe, thereby creating their lives. Since they are exercised on a daily basis by the members, whether in prison or not, the rules define the lifestyle. They become so closely tied together in form that they become inseparable. The Ñetas global community is a perfect example of the imagined communities of Benedict Anderson (2015), with its pantheon of prophets, heroes, founders, rules and stories. However, its existence, and the implication of the law, is real within the lives of its members. The hermeneutic work and practice around the text of law, and its implication within the transformation of members, produces a technology of the self that is not very different from the ones produced by the Latino-Caribbean revolution. As Lucia Michelutti (2017) explains, at the heart of revolutionary politics is the making of the New Man. Indeed, "Revolutions are *sui generis* political forms with their own ontologies that set up the coordinates within which people are made who they are" (Michelutti 2017: 233). By this language of love and affection, it is the fabric of a "New Man" with its own lifestyle that Ñetas are trying to develop.

Dips' story also shows us that the rules are part of an affective substance, shaping the lives of members into the idealized lifestyle of Carlos. From this perspective, the *Convivencia*, for Dips, Spade and other inactive members who still observe the rules, remains successful. This process therefore is a veritable emotional education which, as anthropologist Ann Stoler wrote in another context, "shape[s] appropriate and reasoned affect, by directing affective judgements, by severing some affective bonds and establishing others, by adjudicating what constituted moral sentiments – in short, by educating the proper distribution of sentiments and desires" (2004: 5). This art of governance takes the form of "the art of being a Ñeta", of transformation and self-improvement, that cannot be summarized by an abstract internalization process. Indeed, as Stoler stated, affective knowledge is at the core of political rationality.[13]

To understand why the Ñetas bow to these laws and the sanctions that come with them, we cannot simply look at the reasoning behind their joining. We also must consider the entire learning process that forms the affective fabric of the Ñetas community. We also should remember that this is not just about submitting to an irrational or moral failing, either. On the contrary, to understand the hold which law has, and the manner in which the Ñetas are affected by it, there must be a pairing in the analysis of the affective disposition and political control, the art of governance and the importance of love and passion. This is the only way that submission to the law and its consequences can be analyzed politically through its power relations. This relationship to law is part and parcel of a public and collective life as well as a private and individual life.

This form of asceticism and transformation is done through the process of affection and the process of an internal alteration that can take the form of alienation, through the transformation of an oppressed person into another (Garcia 2019). Like all submissive relationships, complicity and agency in self-transformation are required for self-investment to be liberating. This is as much true for the Ñetas as it is for the portion of the poor and racialized Puerto Rican population of New York and is an example of resistance in the face of the social, political and economic oppression that they face. This seeming ambiguity or paradox is at the heart of the Ñetas membership and consists of submitting oneself to a law with its potentially violent sanctions but also freeing oneself from a social situation marked by social, political and economic domination. All this is done by accepting a lifestyle transformation and belonging to a powerful group that bases itself on the life script of its founder.

Notes

1 Carlos La Sombra died on March 30th, 1981, but the Ñetas celebrate the Grito on the 30th of each month. However, the 30th of March is a bigger celebration compared to the other Gritos of the year.
2 To borrow the famous sentence of anthropologist Malinowski: "The hold which life has" 1922: 25.
3 The author notes that domination without submission is domination founded on violence. This relationship is unstable, because when violence is no longer applied, the relationship ceases (pg. 33). As Dips submitted to the violence of the Ñetas' law, he did so without violence and without coercion.
4 "Affection in this sense is a quality, which when followed, can change a person" (Aristotle 1986: 21).
5 The term 'gang' is ambiguous, and there is no agreement within the social science literature on how to define a gang (for a full discussion, see Brotherton 2015). I use the term 'gang' only for the early 1990s period, when Ñeta members themselves agreed that part of their movement was evolving toward a more 'criminal' path.
6 A Puerto Rican grassroots movement organized in New York between 1969 and 1972 around the independence of Puerto Rico, self-determination and social justice issues.
7 The Ñetas use "norms " and "rules" interchangeably. For ease of reading, I do the same.
8 I was only given access to the Spanish version, which is in large part a translation of the English Literado.
9 Interview with Bebo n°2, April 5th, 2012.
10 Herrou, Adeline, 2008, "When the Taoist monks of China 'write themselves into being'" Baptandier, Brigitte, and Giordana Charuty 2008: 43).
11 Adeline Herrou's formulation See Herrou, Adeline. 2008. *Op. Cit.*, 2008.
12 This over-representation of love is not specific to *La Asociación,* however. In the South Bronx and among Barcelona's "Latino community", as well as in the Guayaquil *barrio,* love and its expression are an integral part of social life. It is a common topic of conversation – who loves whom and why and who has fallen out of love. Love expressed in the Puerto Rican community in New York and Latino community in Barcelona is also common and is a sign of belonging. While love isn't specific to the Ñetas, publicly stating the sentiment allows for a distinction to be made between those who love and those who do not love *La Asociación.*
13 This attention allows us to surpass the idea of the great divide, as indicated by D. Puccio Den (2014), which imposes a clear separation between rational society and irrational criminal society.

Martin Lamotte

References

Agamben, G. (2011). *De la très haute pauvreté règles et forme de vie*. Paris, Editions Payot & Rivages.

Agier, M. (2009). *Esquisses d'une anthropologie de la ville: lieux, situations, mouvements*. Louvain-la-Neuve, Academia Bruylant.

Anderson, B. (2015). *L'imaginaire national: réflexions sur l'origine et l'essor du nationalisme*. Paris, La Decouverte.

Aristotle (1986). *La métaphysique*. Paris, J. Vrin (trad. J. Tricot).

Balandier, G. (1951). "La situation coloniale. Approche théorique." *Cahiers internationaux de sociologie*, 11: 44–79.

Baptandier, B., & Charuty, G. (2008). *Du Corps au Texte: Approches Comparatives*. Nanterre, Société d'ethnologie.

Bohannan, P. (1957). *Justice and Judgement Among the Tiv*. London, Published for the International African Institute by Oxford University Press.

Bourgois, P. (1995). *In Search of Respect: Selling Crack in El Barrio*. Cambridge, Cambridge University Press.

Bourgois, P. (2010). "Recognizing Invisible Violence: A Thirty-Year Ethnographic Retrospective." In B. Rylko-Bauer, L. Whiteford, & P. Farmer (eds.), *Global Health in Times of Violence*, Santa Fe (New Mexico), School for Advanced Research Press, 18–40.

Bourgois, P. (2012). "Théoriser la violence en Amérique: retour sur trente ans d'ethnographie." *Anthropologie début de siècle L'homme*: 139–168.

Brotherton, D. (2015). *Youth Street Gangs: A Critical Appraisal*. Abingdon, Routledge.

Brotherton, D., & Barrios, L. (2004). *Street Politics and the Transformation of a New York City Gang*. New York, Columbia University Press.

Collier, J. F., & Starr, J. (2018). *History and Power in the Study of Law: New Directions in Legal Anthropology*. Ithaca, Cornell University Press.

Cooper, F., & Stoler, A. L. (1997). *Tensions of Empire Colonial Cultures in a Bourgeois World*. Berkeley, University of California Press.

Curtis, R. (1998). "The Improbable Transformation of Inner-City Neighborhoods: Crime, Violence, Drugs, and Youth in the 1990s." *Journal of Criminal Law and Criminology*, 88 (4).

Ferguson, J. (2013). "Declarations of Dependence: Labour, Personhood, and Welfare in Southern Africa." *The Journal of the Royal Anthropological Institute*: 223–242.

Fuller, C. 1994. "Legal anthropology". *Anthropology Today*. 10 (3): 9-12.

Foucault, M. (1994). *Dits et écrits: 1954–1988*. Paris, Editions Gallimard.

Garcia, M. (2019). *On ne naît pas soumise, on le devient*. Paris, Flammarion.

Geffray, C. (1995). *Chroniques de la servitude en Amazonie brésilienne: essai sur l'exploitation paternaliste*. Paris, Karthala.

Gluckman, M. (1958). *Analysis of a Social Situation in Modern Zululand*. Manchester, Manchester University Press.

Gluckman, P. D. (1955). *The Judicial Process Among the Barotse of Northern Rhodesia*. Manchester, Manchester University Press for the Rhodes-Livingstone Institute.

Godreau, I. P. (2015). *Scripts of Blackness: Race, Cultural Nationalism, and U.S. Colonialism in Puerto Rico*. Urbana, University of Illinois Press.

Goodale, M., & Merry, S. E. (2017). *Anthropology and Law: A Critical Introduction*. New York, New York University Press.

Herrou, A. (2008). "When the Taoist Monks of China 'Write Themselves into Being'" In Baptandier, B., & Charuty, G. *Du Corps au Texte: Approches Comparatives*. Nanterre, Société d'ethnologie.

Lamotte, M. (2017). "The Ñeta Law, the Ñeta World: Ethics and Imaginaries in Circulation Between the South Bronx, Barcelona and Guayaquil." *Current Sociology*, 65 (2): 302–314.

Massey, D. S., & Denton, N. A. (1993). *American Apartheid: Segregation and the Making of the Underclass*. Cambridge, MA, Harvard University Press.

Michelutti, L. (2017). "'We Are All Chávez' Charisma as an Embodied Experience." *Latin American Perspectives*, 44 (1): 232–250.

Naepels, M. (2011). *Ethnographie, pragmatisme, histoire: un parcours de recherche à Houaïlou (Nouvelle-Calédonie)*. Paris, Publications de la Sorbonne.

Naepels, M. (2019). *Dans la détresse. Une anthropologie de la vulnérabilité.* Paris, Ehess Editions.

Pirie, F. (2013). *The Anthropology of Law.* Oxford, Oxford University Press.

Puccio-Den, D. (2014). "'Dieu vous bénisse et vous protège'. La correspondance secrète du chef de la mafia sicilienne Bernardo Provenzano (1993–2006)." *rhr Revue de l'histoire des religions*, 228: 307–326.

Scheper-Hughes, N., & Bourgois, P. (2004). "Introduction: Making Sense of Violence." In N. Scheper-Hughes & P. Bourgois (eds.), *Violence in War and Peace: An Anthology.* Oxford, Blackwell, 1–27.

Stoler, A. L. (2004). "Affective States." In D. Nugent & J. Vincent (eds.), *A Companion to the Anthropology of Politics.* Malden, MA: Blackwell Pub.

Wacquant, L. (2008). *Urban Outcasts: A Comparative Sociology of Advanced Marginality.* Cambridge, Malden, MA, Polity.

6

The Catholic Church and the gangs
Toward a liberationist critique of gang violence

Benjamin Jonathan Schwab

Introduction

More than a quarter of a century after signing the Peace Accords that ended a long and bloody civil war, El Salvador is still considered one of the most violent countries in the world. The high homicide rates, far above the 10/100,000 inhabitant threshold used by the World Health Organization to diagnose violence as an epidemic, is not new in the smallest country of Central America (Walter, 2018). Even so, the current situation seems to have particular features and new challenges. Throughout the twentieth century, campesinos, indigenous, and communists were the number-one public enemy of Salvadoran society; two decades ago, the gangs took that place (Zilberg, 2007). Every new administration, together with the majority of mass media outlets, has been the main force behind promoting this perception within the public opinion. Without irrefutable data that demonstrates the proportion of homicides for which the gangs are responsible, we are only able to consider two obvious facts. First, the gangs are not the only generators of violence in the country, and, second, even so, the control they exercise in most of the national territory generates terror and fear in addition to producing countless victims. To date, the State has been incapable of finding a solution to this grim problem, and the public security policies of the last two decades have focused almost exclusively on repression, thus increasing the levels of violence.[1]

Cases of successful peace building have come mostly from civil society and particularly from churches. This is not surprising in a society in which 80% of the population confesses the Christian faith (Segura, 2019). The small Pentecostal churches, which have experienced a significant boom over the last decades and are now found in almost all the marginalized neighborhoods and rural communities of the country, have done important work in the rehabilitation and reintegration of former gang members. Very often Evangelical churches abound in the same neighborhoods where gangs enjoy territorial control. This overlap makes the interaction between both groups almost inevitable.

There now exists a vast literature, including ethnographic studies and journalistic research, on the dynamics and variables that make it possible for gang members to convert and to become brothers within the evangelical church, or even evangelical pastors themselves (Brenneman, 2011; Wolseth, 2011). In addition to the previously stated, it is significant to note that in the Catholic sector, these experiences are very rare or almost absent. This is more surprising if we consider that, to date, Catholics represent a little more than half of the Christians in El Salvador and that the Catholic Church, particularly the circles close to liberation theology, has played a crucial role in the defense of human rights and work for peace in El Salvador's recent history.

The intractability of violence in El Salvador has led to much soul searching on how to address its deep roots, while religious leadership has played an important role in the mitigation and mediation of this violence. The absence of the Catholic Church in addressing the country's current violence is a gap in the literature, which this chapter hopes to begin to unpack.

Overall, this chapter seeks to recover and update the legacy of liberation theology on the work for peace and reconciliation and then critically analyze the current commitment of the Catholic Church to the rehabilitation and reintegration of the most marginalized sectors of society. At the heart of this chapter is the question: with a growing literature on the nexus between religion and gangs, why is the Catholic Church absent, and how can the radical tradition of liberation theology inform a new critique of criminal violence and its resolution? First, it is necessary to briefly outline the historical and social context of gangs in El Salvador.

Gangs: a symptom of a discriminatory society

Since colonial times, practices of dispossession, domination, and oppression towards a large majority of the population by a small economic and political elite reveal a continuous pattern and unbroken arc of violence in El Salvador. This is expressed in key historic events such as the elimination of communal lands at the end of the nineteenth century, the massacre of 30,000 campesinos and indigenous people in 1932, the oppression of the popular masses in the 1960s and 1970s, and the civil war (1980–1992). Understanding the current situation of violence as disconnected from this history would be a serious mistake. El Salvador, perhaps more than any other country in Latin America, shows how violence mutates over space and time and how political violence can feed into criminal violence.

As early as the 1980s, the psychologist and Jesuit Ignacio Martín-Baró warned that Salvadoran society suffered from a profound "psychosocial trauma" (Martín-Baró, 1990), a result of war that even today manifests itself as an environment of distrust, fear, and collective hatred; a thirst for revenge; and the recurrent choice of violence to resolve most conflicts. According to the political scientist, José Miguel Cruz, in the postwar period, the "culture of violence" was intensified by the weakness of the judicial branch, the availability of large quantities of small arms, migration, and displacement, as well as the remilitarization of public security (Cruz, 1997).

According to a United Nations report, at the root of this violence is the outrageous economic inequality and the dispossession experienced by a large portion of the population (UNDP El Salvador, 2013). The emergence of the neoliberal model in the 1980s, especially after the end of the civil war, worsened the situation. Currently, wages do not respond to the cost of living but rather the productivity of the workforce. Therefore, the workers are dependent on consumption.[2] During the last decades, this continual process of social and economic degradation has markedly contributed to the evolution and explosion of the gang phenomenon in El Salvador. More than manifestations of common crime or criminal gangs, gangs must be understood as a social phenomenon that responds to a specific historical context, permeated by exclusion, lack of opportunities, and a history of violence.

Gangs, particularly the Mara Salvatrucha (MS-13) and the Barrio 18, were formed in the second half of the last century in marginalized neighborhoods of Los Angeles. They were transplanted to Central America in the 1990s as a product of several waves of mass deportations of gang members from the United States. According to the United Nations, gangs in their current form represent "an extreme result of the inability of the Salvadoran society to provide real opportunities for its people, particularly, for young people."[3] Since the end of the civil war, there are tens of thousands of young Salvadorans who – in the absence of recognition, security and affection – have joined a gang in which they are among equals, experience a strong collective identity, and are embraced and supported to satisfy their emotional and social needs (Savenije, 2009, p. 219).

Unlike street gangs from the 1970s and 1980s, current Salvadoran gangs demand strong commitments from their members. It is no longer just about having a good time and petty delinquency but rather about serious activities that compromise the gang member's life, implicate a long-term commitment, and involve a shared group identity and a new value system.[4] Currently, the three main gangs[5] have a presence in the majority of the neighborhoods and cantons in El Salvador, where there is an ongoing fight between them for territorial control. Many teenagers, especially in marginalized neighborhoods, grow up in this gang environment. Although they are not gang members, they are frequently used by the gang as messengers from an early age. If they show resistance, they are harassed and threatened. Only a few become full-fledged members, but many are socialized into the culture of de facto gang control of the neighborhood.

The lack of employment and education opportunities and the generalized social stigma of being young and poor makes getting "jumped-in" – that is, entering the gang – a relatively attractive option for some young people. Subsequently, the unconditional loyalty to the group and the high level of internal cohesion are the gang members' life insurance. That is why in El Salvador gang membership is for life, with few exceptions for exit. Leaving the gang is usually interpreted as treason to the family and is punishable by death.

In addition to internal solidarity and respect, violence is one of the gang's main qualities, albeit not the only one that defines them. Excluded from the formal labor market, gangs use violence to access informal and, mainly, illegal means of subsistence. The most common method used to obtain money is through extortion. On a weekly or monthly basis, the gang charges a certain amount of money, commonly referred to as "rent," to small or medium-sized businesses such as convenience stores, transportation cooperatives, and informal businesses in exchange for "protection." Not paying the rent puts the owner and business at risk (Bruneau, 2014). The majority of illicit flows for gangs come from charging rents to different bus routes as well as charging large distribution companies, but gangs will also extort small businesses that operate in their territory.

However, the violence that gangs exert on themselves and society is not only for economic ends. Violence has another utility for gangs: it grants them the power to intimidate and produce terror. For many gang members, since they have been rejected by society, the gang is the central entity that gives meaning to their lives. In this sense, the use of violence and threats establishes and maintains an alternative social hierarchy in the community. In a way, the gang reverses the social order established in the neighborhood by imposing a totalitarian regime of the marginalized. The American psychiatrist James Gilligan, who for decades has worked with convicts in maximum-security prisons, says that the use of violence has the psychological utility to restore the aggressor's self-respect to overcome a humiliating situation. The root of shame has not been explored enough in the Salvadoran gang literature, but Gilligan's arguments resonate with what many scholars have observed in the field. Gilligan quotes a young inmate convicted of an armed assault, who says that he had never received "so much respect before in [his] life as [he] did when [he] first pointed a gun at somebody" (1997). For a person who has long lived under a regime of disdain, the temptation to instantly earn respect may be stronger than the risk of going to jail or dying in the attempt. This does not explain the exponential increase in gang recruitment in the mid- and late 90s in El Salvador, but it is part of the puzzle. It is safe to assume that young Salvadoran gang members who rob, extort, and threaten their neighbors experience something similar. As for Gilligan's patient, for Salvadoran gangs, violence has become a legitimate and justified method to recover the power and social space lost by social and economic marginalization.

Gang violence: theological keys for interpretation

Faced with the horror of military dictatorships and popular uprisings in Latin America during the second half of the twentieth century, a significant sector of the Catholic Church, inspired by the Gospel and the documents of the Second Vatican Council (1963–1965), chose to be on the side of the poor and oppressed and to demand social justice. The representatives of this 'Theology of Liberation' and their ideas were harshly attacked by both political and economic elites and by the Vatican itself, since this preferential option for the poor questioned the foundations of established power in society. Many paid for this commitment with their lives, among them the Archbishop of San Salvador, Oscar Arnulfo Romero (recently recognized as a *saint* of the Catholic Church), and the Jesuit and public intellectual Ignacio Ellacuría – both killed by death squads of the Salvadoran army (Peterson, 1997).

Despite the tragic end of their lives, the work and legacy of both substantially contributed to the peace process that ended the civil war. The following section seeks to outline and update these theological reflections in search of humanizing practices, rooted in the Salvadoran Liberationist tradition, that produce more life and less death in today's Salvadoran society.

A liberation theology approach to current violence

Among the ongoing debates about poverty, justice, and development, the issue of violence barged into the Latin American Church. The documents of the Second General Conference of the Latin-American Episcopate, held in the Colombian city of Medellín in 1968, provided an ideal foundation for theologizing on the subject. In Latin America, in an environment of oppression and insurgency, there was a lively regional discussion about the ambivalence of violence, led by the Peruvian theologian Gustavo Gutierrez, the Salvadoran Jesuits Ignacio Ellacuría and Jon Sobrino as well as the then Archbishop of San Salvador, Oscar Arnulfo Romero.

Ignacio Ellacuría spoke of "structural" violence as the "original violence, root, and start of all other social violence" (1988a). In liberation theology, this form of violence, and therefore all forms of violence derived from it, are linked directly to social injustice and, specifically, to poverty. Liberation theologians argued, and continue to do so, that economic exclusion is at the heart of violence and is violence itself.

Gustavo Gutiérrez explicitly positions the dimension of violence within injustice by asserting that, "it is a matter of denial and contempt for human life" (Gutiérrez, 1980). According to him, it is a serious matter, "because we are not facing something occasional or temporary; but a social system built and institutionalized on the death of the poor and for the benefit – and wealth – of a few."[6] Any attack on someone's life is an attack on God's plans, according to theologians of liberation, and therefore the gravest of sins. Thus, institutionalized violence is an expression of what the bishops who gathered in Medellín in 1968 called "structural sin."[7]

However, this structural sin does not simply remain in the structural or bureaucratic spheres but leaves hundreds of millions of human beings in misery and dead throughout the world. Jon Sobrino develops this idea further. According to his position, "poverty is not only the denial of life [on an individual level,] but denial of peace," as it leads to violent conflicts and to a fight for survival (Sobrino, 1988). Liberation theology considers social death – of which the gang is perhaps the most clear modern expression – as part of a larger problem of economic violence, since the gang member represents the lowest rung of the urban poor and working classes. Solidarity with the poor then would also imply, to a certain extent, an accompaniment of gang members, but a theologically rooted discourse and action to confront gang violence has faced many obstacles, not least the title of 'terrorist' afforded gang members by the Salvadoran state and embraced by many.

For years, the violence that gangs have exerted on civil society in El Salvador – including murders, torture, forced disappearances, and mass sexual assaults – have reached brutal dimensions and created a sense of terror among the population. The levels of violence experienced in El Salvador have led many in society to see gang violence through the lens of terrorism. But what people are currently experiencing in marginalized neighborhoods of El Salvador falls short of Oscar Romero's definition of terrorist violence as a "sterile and unjustified bloodshed" (Cardenal et al., 2014). Gang members are officially classified as terrorists under Salvadoran law, and social media has branded them beasts, rats, cockroaches, all but human beings. Those that demand the death penalty for gang members and applaud the cruelties of the extermination groups have great social acceptance across the country.

However, the term 'terrorism' should be understood as a political term, one that is conditioned mainly by the particular political moment, in this case, a post-9/11 securitization lens and source of foreign security funding. By recasting gangs as terrorists, it seamlessly fits into larger international narratives of security. In the Salvadoran case, this term also has many legal implications, which have led to El Salvador's incredibly high incarceration rate, second only to US prisoners per 100,000.

But, returning to Ignacio Ellacuría and the liberationist literature, terrorism is not simply "what those who are called terrorists do, but rather terrorists are those who do terrorism, objectively defined as such" (Ellacuría, 1988b). At first glance, it might seem like a redundancy, but it is not. Terrorism, according to Ellacuría, is "the use of violence, particularly physical violence, against defenseless people, whether they are civilians or not, in order to terrorize" and therefore is "always condemnable."[8] In this sense, there is no doubt that gangs carry out acts that sow terror and that they are reprehensible, but it is quite another thing to call gangs terrorists, a term which says more about the political moment than about those actually committing the violence. Moreover, to brand all gang members, or young non-gang members who live in marginalized neighborhoods in El Salvador, terrorists is a "pre-judgment or prejudice" rooted in the larger history of criminalizing the poor and is, therefore, an injustice. Without the slightest intention to justify the violent and barbaric acts for which the gangs are known, a society cannot condemn a social structure, such as the gang phenomenon, for whose genesis and development it is deeply co-responsible.

It is now more than ever, during times of growing inequality, evident that the institutionalized and structural violence to which the Medellín documents alluded is still a relevant critique today. Since then, the global capitalist system has not ceased to produce new victims. Andre Corten argued that, "Liberation theology will remain, for many years to come, an element of the ethico-political field in Latin America. It has not died. Although it is no longer able to broaden mobilization at the base" (1999). Though liberation theology no longer garners much support and can't mobilize the masses as it did in the 1980s, its critique has always been a part of the ethical opposition to capitalism and exclusionary societies. Though no longer invoked in name, many of these ideas have informed the ideas of the current pope.

Pope Francis, in his apostolic exhortation *Evangelii Gaudium*, expresses this clearly when he affirms that "such an economy kills" (2013). The pope denounces that, in this system, "everything enters into the game of competitiveness and the law of the strongest, where the powerful eats the weakest." The "new and often anonymous kinds of power" reduce the human being to a disposable "consumer good." The people excluded today, the pope resumes, are no longer "exploited" or marginalized in their societies but are left out of them; "the outcast, the 'leftovers'," are left "without work, without possibilities, without any means of escape."[9]

At the origin of this situation, Pope Francis finds a deep anthropological crisis in which denying the primacy of the human being led us to create new idols such as "the idolatry of money" and "the dictatorship of an impersonal economy lacking a truly human purpose."[10] For Christians, denying humanity and denying life – whether by individuals, a government or an economic structure – is by definition a sin. In El Salvador, this social or structural sin is committed daily, under neoliberal budgeting, and affects large swaths of the population. In addition to this "poverty and slow death" (Sobrino, 1997), as Jon Sobrino articulates, capitalism also employs repression to defend its global sovereignty. Unlike the 1970s and 1980s, repression nowadays takes the form of a low-intensity conflict with the help of mass social media, which has created an atmosphere of fear and collective insecurity and which is used to justify the never-ending setbacks to political and civil rights (Falquet, 2002). Stripped of their humanity and anxious to regain their self-respect and dignity, many young people are attracted to the gang life and see it as a way to rebel against this faceless enemy.

From this perspective and from its political dimension, gang violence can also be interpreted, with many reservations, in terms of "revolutionary violence" (Rodgers and Jensen, 2008). Rodgers and Jensen skillfully employ Deleuze and Guattari's concept of the War Machine to describe gang violence, but suffice it to look at Deborah Levenson's book on the history of gangs in Guatemala to see that gangs proliferate precisely in the void left by labor unions and social movements (Levenson, 2013). The violence used by gangs in El Salvador does not employ a radical critique, even if it is born of a similar social exclusion that led to other forms of revolutionary violence.

For the liberationist, this would mean "to affirm the denied life . . . to survive against the empire of the death [and] to free itself from what prevents a minimal fulfillment of the human being himself" (Ellacuría, 1988b), as conceptualized by Ignacio Ellacuría. However, unlike the revolutionary liberating violence of the past era, which found some approval amongst liberation theologians and even in Oscar Romero, gang violence, from an ethical-theological point of view, is absolutely intolerable and incompatible.

This is first because it coincides with the terrorist violence that, according to Ellacuría, is "always condemnable"[11] and second because it does not comply with a concept of revolutionary violence, since it is not strictly violence in self-defense or in defense of the oppressed people, nor does it consist of "radically changing a situation of injustice" (Sobrino, 1997). Gang violence, in other words, has no political-social purpose that seeks the common good. Some might even suspect that gangs were infected, in a way, with the germ of the neoliberal era and thus participate in what Pope Francis calls the "globalization of indifference" which makes us incapable of "weeping for other people's pain."[12] The type of justice that gangs seek is limited to street justice and a devouring justice that, in practice, leads to an even greater injustice by attacking in the most atrocious manner the common good. Gangs are not without their own grievances, which, at times, are eloquently articulated, but their violence is far from ideologically motivated and, on the whole, is predatory.

Even through the forms of rebellion adopted by gangs, the isolation and total destruction against an obviously unjust system, are not tolerable, ethically or theologically, we cannot ignore the primary status of gangs as victims of structural sin. This fact has serious implications for the Church in a theological and pastoral sense, as well as for the social and political nature of society as a whole.

Christian reconciliation

The statement that, above all, gang members are victims of structural sin, far from finding acceptance, instead causes rejection and outrage by a large majority of the Salvadoran society. This sentiment only seems to increase when it is argued that, in order to find a solution to the current crisis of violence, it is necessary to offer future prospects to gang members. "It is unfair that lazy people and murderers benefit, while the vast majority of honest people live in poverty and without opportunities." This can be heard on an almost daily basis in the country.

If, in the 1980s, revolutionary violence was a possibility and, according to many, even a necessity, to free the popular majorities from institutionalized violence, today violence has become the main ill of society, demonstrating its ineffectiveness in eradicating criminal violence. If, during the civil war, the oppressed engaged in an armed uprising against the oppressors, today in El Salvador, there is a war of the poor against the poor, under the yoke of a faceless oppressor – neoliberal and globalized capitalism.

Therefore, the Church must find new ways to overcome violence and humanize the world. This radically informed approach must be, at its core, nonviolent. And the first need to attend to is the reconciliation of a historically divided society.

This is much the case in El Salvador at the end of the civil war, where "nothing was done, and everything was left as it was" (Wade, 2016). Although the agreements signed between the guerrilla forces and the government put an end to twelve years of civil war, there was never a true reconciliation process. That is, political peace never translated into a social peace. This process, though lauded as a success, in reality largely failed due to the absence of the three presuppositions that, according to Jon Sobrino, are essential for a true reconciliation: truth, justice, and forgiveness.

The more than twenty-nine years lost to a hypocritical reconciliation process have resulted in piling social debt. A profound and true reconciliation process in El Salvador is now more urgent than ever, but at the same time, it seems more distant because of a highly polarized society. To talk about truth, justice, and forgiveness in this setting, where victims victimize each other (Goldstein, 2007) and lose sight of the common oppressor, is difficult, delicate, and painful. To actually put into practice what has been discussed can be even more difficult, delicate, and painful. It is true that El Salvador, as a postwar society, is in need of a reconciliation process, but it is also true that this process will need to take on a new dimension, which is the reintegration of gang members. Reconciliation will mean working with gangs but also changing a deeply divided society so that it can create the social conditions for reentry.

(1) Truth

The lack of truth and, in particular, the institutionalization of lies, as previously noted, is one of the determining factors of the current levels of dehumanization and violence. The truth is liberating (John 8:32); however, in the past, many women and men in El Salvador paid the price of that freedom with their lives. Because Oscar Romero, Ignacio Ellacuría, and many more were speaking the truth, they became a threat to the power of the ruling class of that time, a power built on lies and death. Speaking truth and exposing power dynamics are indispensable to real social justice.

In today's neoliberal era, oppression is more subtle, and those in power have turned to other strategies to prevent the truth of their activities from coming to light. Insecurity and fear, which have become a way of life for most Salvadorans (Moodie, 2011), seem to be the ideal mechanism to keep the people in chains. The gangs, which undoubtedly represent a serious threat to society and are responsible for a significant part of the violence, are above all the perfect scapegoat in the current situation. Most media outlets profit from this lie and often link any murder with gangs, even when there is no evidence to back up these claims. The permanent moral panic surrounding gangs helps to maintain the status quo. In that way, they are co-responsible for the environment of terror and fear that exists in society. Telling the truth still requires a lot of courage and audacity in El Salvador. Resolving the intractability of gang violence in the Salvadoran context requires speaking unpopular truths to power.

(2) Justice

The truth, in its function of promoting and cultivating life, always goes hand in hand with justice. If the truth is already a challenge, demanding and doing justice is even more difficult. However, without justice, there can be no reconciliation or peace, since peace is a product of justice. Once the truth is known and articulated and the victims have a voice, it is necessary to seek justice. According to the Liberationist critiques of the stagnated peace of the postwar era, the truth exposes victims' wounds and makes the victims even more vulnerable. Justice closes those wounds, because it heals, repairs, and dignifies.

Preaching justice is easy, especially if it is an historical justice. But seeking justice today is no less dangerous than it was in biblical times. In addition to being dangerous, seeking justice is almost always controversial. How can justice be achieved in a society where the oppressed are also victimizers? Where the orphan becomes a murderer and the widow survives on the collected rents extorted from taxi drivers? This complex and messy reality puts us before new ethical and political challenges.

In short, there are no simple and safe recipes for reconciliation, and all human action is prone to error. Faced with this reality, Comblin stresses the need for a permanent ethical-theological judgment and from there, attending to the need to explore a possible reconciliation project, which will exist within a certain historical context, and the concessions that should be made to the partial injustice to better approach a greater justice (Comblin, 2002).

Specifically, rehabilitating gang members and giving them opportunities for work and self-development seem like unfair actions to many people who consider themselves honest and honorable citizens. However, these actions do not mean, in any way, rewarding gang members for their criminal behavior but rather freeing them from their condition of victims of an unfair system, as well as helping with the rebuilding of a broken social fabric. By humanizing the lowest and most perverse parts of the society, the Kingdom of God is built. By doing this, we do justice to gang members, as victims of structural violence and, at the same time, we manage to eradicate the symptomatic violence they exercise that causes so much pain and suffering in society.

(3) Forgiveness

Even though forgiveness is essential in any reconciliation process, it has also been abused and misrepresented countless times. It should be clear that when we talk about forgiveness, we are not talking about the "forgive and forget" policies and amnesties that have historically obscured the truth and denied access to justice to victims in many countries of the world in order to safeguard the political-economic interests of elites. Forgiveness, certainly, is the most delicate and difficult step of reconciliation, because forgiveness is not possible without justice (Sobrino, 2003).

Certainly, no one can demand or expect that gang members, like those who committed atrocities during the civil war, be blindly forgiven as a blanket solution to violence in El Salvador. This would be naive. On the other hand, if a gang member puts violence aside and seeks to repair the damage caused to his victims, as a society, we should welcome him. Above all, from a liberation theology point of view, the society is urged to meet the needs of the victims of violence and to build up fair and supportive human relations in which the victims can heal and eventually offer their forgiveness. A successful reduction in violence and a successful reconciliation process will be possible, in large part, thanks to a willingness on the part of society to embrace gang members instead of excluding them.

The Catholic Church and the gangs: stances and strategies

Considering the historical leadership of the Catholic Church in El Salvador, personified in the Archbishop Oscar Romero, his successor Arturo Rivera y Damas (Guardado, 2012), and the Jesuit Ignacio Ellacuría, among others, as well as the wealth of theological thought on the subject, it would not be strange to think that Catholics today, who still represent around 50% of the population, remain at the forefront of peace work in El Salvador. However, the reality is quite another. The American Mennonite sociologist and theologian Robert Brenneman, in his study on the role of religion in grappling with gang violence, identifies that as more and more evangelical churches, especially small congregations in poor neighborhoods, approach gang members who seek conversion, the Catholic Church's involvement becomes increasingly minimal in this context (Brenneman, 2011). The Catholic Church, long one of the key political players in Salvadoran society, is not a protagonist when it comes to mitigating gang violence, not even when it comes to the country's religious communities.

It is worth asking when and why the Catholic Church, to a large extent, has renounced its social leadership and commitment to justice, particularly when one considers its long tradition of critical thought when it comes to critiquing power and economic structures. Without a doubt, the main reason is rooted in the Church's internal processes. Although the Second Vatican Council, convened by Pope John XXIII in the early 1960s, constituted the greatest transformation of the Church in centuries and opened the Church to an increasingly globalized and plural world, the ultra-conservative sectors of the Church, during the following decades, went to great lengths to reverse these changes while prioritizing orthodoxy over all types of social and political pastoral work. The papacy of John Paul II (1979–2005) played a key role in this process. Karol Woytila, who later became Pope John Paul II, experienced firsthand the oppression of Soviet communism and the persecution of the Catholic Church. As a pope, he distrusted the progress of the socialist revolutions in Latin America and of priests and bishops who accompanied and encouraged the organization of the people. Liberation theology, which in the late 1960s was experiencing a significant boom in Latin America promoting social justice and human rights, had quickly become a threat both to the interests of the more conservative sectors of the Church and to US foreign policy for its alleged affinity with revolutionary movements. From the 1980s onwards, the Vatican, under the benevolent gaze and auspices of the CIA (Lee, 1983), started to implement a resolute agenda to fight liberation theology. Besides two official notifications signed by Cardinal Joseph Ratzinger, the future Pope Benedict XVI, that in 1984 and 1986 alleged doctrinal deviations of the progressive current and attempted to moderate their aspirations, John Paul II admonished and suspended several Latin American priests and theologians. However, the measure that deeply transformed the Latin American ecclesial landscape and whose impact is apparent even now is the particular policy of appointing bishops during the papacy of John Paul II, which was maintained under his successor, Benedict XVI. Over three decades, the Vatican ensured that the episcopal headquarters throughout the continent were gradually occupied by like-minded candidates, many of them close to ultra-conservative movements such as *Opus Dei* or the Neocatechumenal Way. Among them, the Colombian Cardinal López Trujillo stands out, who became secretary of the Episcopal Conference of Latin American (known by the Spanish acronym as CELAM), and in El Salvador, the Archbishop Fernando Sáenz Lacalle. These strategic bishop appointments had severe consequences with regard to clergy formation, lay participation, and social pastoral work. While Popes John XXIII and Paul VI in the 60s and 70s had fostered a Church open to the world, which encouraged the option for the poor and work for social justice in the spirit of the Second Vatican Council, the following decades were characterized by a relapse and backsliding to ancient privileges and alliances with political-economic elites.

This tendency did not change until the arrival of Pope Francis in 2013, who has stood out for his social and reformist discourse. Reversing the previous trends is extremely difficult; on one hand, there is an environment of growing secularization of society and, on the other, a rise of religious fundamentalism, both in Catholic and Evangelical communities.

To a large extent, these historical dynamics explain the current inertia of the Salvadoran Catholic Church in the face of gang-related violence and social issues more generally. Although it is possible to speak of an inertia on the part of ecclesiastical leaders, theirs was not a total silence, mainly because ignoring the gang phenomenon in El Salvador is almost impossible, as it affects many aspects of every day life. For this reason, the church hierarchy was forced to reckon with the growing violence in several instances. Even if the church struggled to muster a real pastoral response to the crisis of violence, it did release several official positions regarding the issue.

In 2005, the Episcopal Conference of El Salvador published a pastoral letter addressing the violence crisis, entitled "Do not be overcome by evil," in which it declared that "the actions against youth gangs or *maras* [have become] the center strategy of public security authorities" and noted the fact that it seems that "the violent actions [of the State] had generated more violence" (CEDES, 2005). In the same paragraph the bishops asked the authorities to implement "a policy that creates prevention, rehabilitation and social integration programs with sufficient economic investment and other resources to guarantee a solution to the violence suffered by the country."[13] The letter includes a call

> to the members of the youth gangs or *maras*, and to all who have believed and opted for a violent solution for their problems, to change this attitude to benefit social peace by making an effort on their own personal growth with the help from society.

Finally, the bishops exhort the need for "a comprehensive and solidary humanism that can encourage a new social, economic and political order, founded on the dignity and freedom of every human being" and stress "the responsibility of each Salvadoran in building a fraternal, peaceful, just and supportive society in which peace truly reigns."[14]

It wasn't until 2013 that the Episcopal Conference explicitly brought up the issue of violence again in an official document. In this new document, the Episcopal Conference takes a stand on the gang phenomenon, condemns their activity based on the Catechism of the Catholic Church, and creates distance from the so-called "truce between gangs," an issue that had caused tension within the episcopal conference (CEDES, 2013). In November 2014, the bishops issued a new message, "because the phenomenon of violence has become even more serious and complex" (CEDES, 2014). Fundamentally, the document reiterated the position outlined nine years earlier in its pastoral letter and, again, regretted and denounced the situation experienced by the population.

In a quite extraordinary first pastoral letter, the current archbishop of San Salvador, José Luis Escobar Alas, published another official statement at the beginning of 2016, a watershed moment in the country's gang violence at the end of the most violent year in recent history, with a homicide rate of 103 per 100,000 inhabitants. The ninety-page letter stands out for the rigorous socio-historical analysis that occupies the first part, citing several authors of liberation theology and an understanding of the current violence as a structural problem resulting from historical injustices. In the section on pragmatic proposals that seek to eradicate violence, however, the archbishop restricts himself to the spiritual and religious sphere, such as an invitation to participate in the Eucharist and to understand the Virgin Mary as a model of fraternity. The tone in the final exhortation is no less conciliatory and abruptly contrasts the initial analysis when saying, "I beg to those who hold economic power for a more supportive economy."[15] It is noteworthy that in the entire letter there is not a single explicit reference to gangs or *maras* but rather to "criminal groups" or "sheep in the dark," and they are asked with "their conversion, to distance themselves from the paths of violence and crime in which they have taken part."[16]

These statements from the Salvadoran ecclesiastical hierarchy reveal that, although in its social analysis, it maintains a certain degree of critical spirit, the pastoral practice in favor of justice and peace of the Catholic Church in El Salvador is a far cry from the radical option for the poor and the victims that characterized it throughout the second half of the last century. Currently the church does not have any official program that openly and officially works with gang members. This, however, does not mean that there are no reliable and successful programs aimed at prevention, training, and reintegration run by parishes, religious orders, or Catholic charitable organizations in the country. Besides the work of 'Caritas,' which has been done for many years in violence prevention and peacebuilding, it is worth highlighting the efforts of different religious communities, such as the Passionists, the Salesians, the Carmelites, and the 'Fe y Alegría' projects, managed by the Jesuits. These are smaller initiatives that operate mainly under the radar but are nonetheless meaningful interventions.

The way in which these Catholic initiatives work differs fundamentally from the strategy used by the Pentecostal Evangelical churches. While the latter explicitly approaches gang members, seeking their social reintegration through religious conversion, the Catholic approach focuses more on the field of prevention, accompaniment, and development of young people, their families, and communities, and conversion is not a prerequisite for involvement.

Arturo Sánchez,[17] director of the ecclesial work in 'Caritas' in one of the Catholic dioceses of El Salvador, describes their comprehensive approach.[18] His organization has been working with vulnerable youth for years but also with their social environment, that is, with parents and teachers, with the aim of strengthening their resilience and their psycho-emotional skills. "We are working with people in a very fragile condition and we work in" what he calls, "'affective nutrition' to lift their self-esteem. A person with high morale can do anything," explains Sánchez. Simultaneously, the Caritas team works with the youth on their future prospects.

> We accompany the boys and girls who are studying English, who are studying in the university so that they can be ready and create small businesses lead by young people . . . and we also look for companies that have a social conscience and want to support young people in this condition.

The motto of this project is 'Talita kum,' or 'get up!', Jesus's call to Jairus' dead daughter in Mark 5:41. To date, with the support of the organization, twenty micro-businesses have been created with a solidarity economy approach; they produce and sell products such as coffee, dairy products, shoes, and clothing in various departments of El Salvador. Although, by law, the organization cannot directly work with gangs, the director of Caritas admits that on a day-to-day basis, contact with these structures is inevitable: "We need to ask permission for everything in order to work." In El Salvador, it is a fact that any state agency, social organization, or church that wants to work in gang-controlled territories has to negotiate some sort of local agreement for access. But also, this closeness with the population has allowed Caritas to separate numerous young people from the gang through affection, psychosocial accompaniment, and concrete economic alternatives.

Up to a certain point, Sánchez admires the work that many Pentecostal churches do with gang members: "These churches are very present in the country. . . . There are temples everywhere. If a gang member or a young man is going through a tough time and approaches the church, they help him and accompany him in person." On the other hand, he respectfully critiques the strictly spiritualistic and religious approach of evangelicals. Sánchez explains,

> We see the whole. We see people as children of the same father. We think that it is necessary to help them lift their self-esteem to obtain economic outlets afterwards, whether they attend university or create business as a comprehensive response to the problem. That's what the Pentecostal church does not achieve. They convert them and make them believers and they persevere for three or four years and then leave. So, that proposal, in essence, is not comprehensive.

It is a fact that the territorial presence of Catholic initiatives and non-governmental organizations (NGOs) that promote a culture of peace and seek to offer concrete alternatives to young people in a gang context are emerging but do not receive much support from the ecclesiastical hierarchy. They are mostly small projects that rely on the personal commitment of local ecclesiastical leadership, as is the case of Arturo Sánchez, who are often inspired by prophetic voices such as that of Archbishop Oscar Romero. Despite the fact that these initiatives do not enjoy massive and rapid success, they are no less relevant. On the contrary, they are committed to medium- and long-term structural changes by investing in the social capital of young people and the accompaniment of their communities.

Conclusions

Finally, it has been shown that, although its initiatives are neither immediate nor media focused and although its presence is decreasing, the Catholic Church remains a central voice for the eradication of violence in El Salvador's gang context.

The significant theological legacy of the Second Vatican Council (1963–1965), from the Medellin Conference (1968) and liberation theology, updated according to the demands of this time, continues to offer clues to the analysis and transformation of violent and excluding societies, of which gangs are a symptom. This reflective theoretical reach of liberation theology transcends the strictly religious scope, as it provides tools for analysis and political advocacy in support of peace in secular contexts, too. Particularly, it is important to highlight the contributions made to the ethical discourse on power relations in society and the theoretical elaboration on the reconciliation processes that has been reaffirming the victim's historical demands for truth, justice, and reparation. There can be no new criminological imagination without a strong ethical stance.

Regarding practical and territorial work, it becomes clear that the approaches of the Pentecostal and Evangelical churches greatly differ from the way in which Catholic programs work. However, instead of seeing the approaches as opposites and selective, they should be seen as complementary. The Evangelical approach is noteworthy in its reach and its commitment to working directly with gang members in the country's most problematic neighborhoods, but this approach lacks a reconciliatory element that engages directly with society. Evangelizing gang members without bridging the divide that separates them from society, not to mention addressing the economic and political origins of the gang phenomenon, will do little to sustainably reduce violence.

El Salvador's current challenging reality and, especially, the rehabilitation and reintegration work with young people, gang members, and non-gang members in vulnerable situations offers a historical opportunity for a truly ecumenical project. If the different religious denominations were willing to enter into a process of learning and mutual enrichment, they could expand their territorial presence and their results, thus feeding into their common goal, which is a real social peace.

While the strength of the evangelical churches, without a doubt, is the spiritual dimension in terms of individual conversion, massive presence in neighborhoods, and experience in direct work with gangs, the Catholic Church provides a solid theological basis and social scope, specifically a focus on social justice and the transformation of economic structures, which give sustainability and traction to theses processes of violence reduction and social reintegration. As Kevin Lewis O'Neill points out, notions of Christian piety do provide benefits for gang members looking to remake their lives, but this is not substitute for more holistic and political transformations that are needed to deal with issue of gang violence (2015). This is to say, what is needed is a political process that can accompany the work of directly engaging with gangs; otherwise, the conversion approach will be just a drop in the bucket. Individual conversion stories from gang members, such as individual stories of criminal desistance more generally, can provide some needed inspiration and hope to a grim landscape of violence, repression, and incarceration, but the individual conversion narrative only feeds into the neoliberal logic of personal moral failures and does not tackle the systemic roots of violence.

Ignacio Ellacuría precisely emphasizes the importance of integrating the individual scope with the social when he affirms that in order to make salvation a reality within the world, emphasis has to be put on both "the transformation of hearts" and "the creation of new structures" (2000). In this sense, considering the moral and social influence that religion continues to have in El Salvador and in the absence of strong state strategies to foster a culture of peace, the work that churches do for peace is key and a model for society.

Excerpts from this chapter were previously published originally in Spanish in the journals:

- Schwab, Benjamin, "Cultivar la vida, vencer la muerte. Reflexiones sobre pandillas, violencia y paz en El Salvador desde la teología de la liberación," Iglesia Viva, 273 (2018), 113–132.
- Schwab, Benjamin, "Violencia, pandillas y redención en El Salvador. Reflexión desde la teología de la liberación," Revista Latinoamericana de Teología, 96 (2015), 359–395.

Notes

1 The Inter-American Commission on Human Rights has written about El Salvador's sharp increase in extrajudicial killings.
2 *Ibid.*, p. 69.
3 *Ibid.*, p. 214.

4 *Ibid.*, pp. 106–107.
5 A quick note regarding gang affiliation and nomenclature. The Mara Salvatrucha is commonly referred to as, MS-13, while the two factions of the Barrio 18 gangs are referred to as Sureños y Revolucionarios.
6 *Ibid.*
7 "Documento sobre la Paz", n. 1, en: II. Conferencia del Episcopado Latinoamericano, *Documentos finales de Medellín*, 1968.
8 *Ibid.*, p. 93.
9 *Ibid.* (pg. 52–53).
10 *Ibid.* (pg. 55)
11 *Ibid.*, p. 93.
12 *Ibid.*, Evangelii Gaudium, (pg.54)
13 *Ibid.*
14 *Ibid.*, n. 1.
15 *Ibid.* (pg 177)
16 *Ibid.* (pg. 186).
17 For reasons of safety, this is a fake name, upon request of the interviewee.
18 Interviewed by the author on August 21st, 2019.

Bibliography

Brenneman, R., 2011. *Homies and Hermanos: God and Gangs in Central America*. Oxford University Press, Oxford.

Bruneau, T., 2014. Pandillas and Security in Central America. *Latin American Research Review*, 42(2).

Cardenal, R., Martín-Baró, I., and Sobrino, S. (eds.), 2014. *La voz de los sin voz. La palabra viva de Monseñor Oscar Arnulfo Romero*. UCA Editores, San Salvador.

CEDES, 2005. *No te dejes vencer por el mal. Carta pastoral de la Conferencia Episcopal de El Salvador*, San Salvador, 21 de noviembre.

CEDES, 2013. *Posición de la Conferencia Episcopal de El Salvador ante el fenómeno de las pandillas en nuestro país*, San Salvador, 11 de mayo.

CEDES, 2014. *Mensaje de la conferencia Episcopal de El Salvador frente a la grave Situacion de violencia que vivimos*. "Bienaventurados los artesanos de la paz", 21 November, n.1.

Comblin, J., 2002. *Teología de la reconciliación*. Centro de Estudios y Publicaciones, Lima .

Corten, A., 1999. *Pentecostalism in Brazil: Emotion of the Poor and Theological Romanticism*. Palgrave Macmillan, London.

Cruz, J.M., 1997. Los factores posibilitadores y las expresiones de la violencia en los noventa. *Estudios Centroamericanos (ECA)*, 588 (octubre 1997).

Ellacuría, I., 1988a. Violence and Non-Violence in the Struggle for Peace and Liberation. *Concilium*, 195, pp. 69–77.

Ellacuría, I., 1988b. Trabajo no violento por la paz y violencia liberadora. *Concilium*, 215, pp. 85–94.

Ellacuría, I., 2000. Historia de la salvación. In *Escritos teológicos, Vol. 1*, UCA Editores, San Salvador.

Falquet, J., 2002. La violencia doméstica como forma de tortura: reflexiones basadas en la violencia como sistema en El Salvador. *Revista del CESLA*, 3.

Francis, P., 2013. *Apostolic Exhortation: The Joy of the Gospel – Evangelii Gaudium*. United States Conference of Catholic Bishops, Washington, DC.

Gilligan, J., 1997. *Violence. Reflections on a National Epidemic*. Vintage Books, New York.

Goldstein, D.M., 2007. Human Rights as Culprit, Human Rights as Victim: Rights and Security in the State of Exception. In *The Practice of Human Rights: Tracking Law between the Global and the Local*. Cambridge University Press, Cambridge.

Guardado, U.P., 2012. *Pastorale Diplomatie: die Rolle der Katholischen Kirche und des Erzbischofs Arturo Rivera y Damas im Friedensprozess in El Salvador (1980–1992)*. Harrassowitz Verlag, Wiesbaden.

Gutiérrez, G., 1980. A violência de um sistema. *Concilium*, 160, pp. 565–575.

Lee, M.A., 1983. *Their Will Be Done*. [online] Mother Jones. Available at: www.motherjones.com/politics/1983/07/their-will-be-done/.

Benjamin Jonathan Schwab

Levenson, D.T., 2013. *Adiós Niño: The Gangs of Guatemala City and the Politics of Death*. Duke University Press, Durham.

Martín-Baró, I., 1990. La violencia política y la guerra como causas del trauma psicosocial en El Salvador. *Revista de psicología de El Salvador*, 9(35).

Moodie, E., 2011. *El Salvador in the Aftermath of Peace: Crime, Uncertainty, and the Transition to Democracy*. University of Pennsylvania Press, Philadelphia.

O'Neill, K.L., 2015. *Secure the Soul: Christian Piety and Gang Prevention in Guatemala*. University of California Press, Berkeley.

Peterson, A.L., 1997. *Martyrdom and the Politics of Religion: Progressive Catholicism in El Salvador's Civil War*. SUNY Press, Albany.

Rodgers, D., and Jensen, S., 2008. Revolutionaries, Barbarians or War Machines? Gangs in Nicaragua and South Africa. *Socialist Register 2009: Violence Today*, 45, pp. 220–238.

Segura, E., 2019. *El Catolicismo Está A Punto De Dejar De Ser Mayoría En El Salvador*. [online] Noticias de El Salvador – La Prensa Gráfica | Informate con la verdad. Available at: www.laprensagrafica.com/lpgdatos/El-catolicismo-esta-a-punto-de-dejar-de-ser-mayoria-en-El-Salvador-20190415-0550.html [Accessed 17 March 2020].

Sobrino, J., 1988. Injusta y violenta pobreza en América Latina. *Concilium*, 215, p. 72.

Sobrino, J., 1997. La violencia de la injusticia. *Concilium*, 272, pp. 65–74.

Sobrino, J., 2003. El cristianismo y la reconciliación: camino a una utopía. *Concilium: Revista internacional de teología*, 303, pp. 95–106.

UNDP El Salvador, 2013. *Informe sobre Desarrollo Humano El Salvador 2013. Imaginar un nuevo país. Hacerlo posible*. Diagnóstico y propuesta, San Salvador.

Wade, C.J., 2016. *Captured Peace: Elites and Peacebuilding in El Salvador*. Ohio University Press, Athens.

Walter, K., 2018. *La muerte violenta como realidad cotidiana. El Salvador, 1912–2016*. AccesArte, San Salvador.

Wim, S., 2009. *Maras y barras. Pandillas y violencia juvenil en barrios marginales de El Salvador*. FLACSO, San Salvador.

Wolseth, J., 2011. *Jesus and the Gang: Youth Violence and Christianity in Urban Honduras*. University of Arizona Press, Tucson.

Zilberg, E., 2007. Gangster in Guerilla Face: A Transnational Mirror of Production between the USA and El Salvador. *Anthropological Theory*, 7(1), pp. 37–57.

7

Gangs, space and the state

Bringing Henri Lefebvre's spatial theory to critical gang studies[1]

Tilman Schwarze

Introduction

The 'critical turn' in gang research has opened up new avenues in examining the gang phenomenon under neoliberal capitalism and late modernity. Protagonists of critical gang studies argue that gangs need to be analysed against the background of social segregation and marginalisation (Fraser, 2015) in cities in which the state implements a restrictive and penalising policy agenda in marginalised communities. In those areas, "gangs and other groups of armed young men occupy the vacuum created by the retreat of the social welfare policies of the state" (Hagedorn, 2005: 154).

Moreover, critical gang studies suggest that, in order to understand the gang phenomenon, one needs to critically examine the complex relationship between urban space, the state and gangs. The underlying argument here is that "too often, gangs are understood and explained at the level of the individual, with structural and cultural factors relegated" (Fraser, 2015: 38). Building on this argument, I suggest that examinations of the gang phenomenon under neoliberal capitalism would benefit from critically analysing how the urban *space* of gangs is socially produced. The starting point of my argument is that the notion of 'social space' is not as straightforwardly defined as some criminological research on gangs might suggest. Too often, mainstream criminological research has relied on a static conceptualisation of space that only focuses on the territoriality of gang spaces, thereby assuming that space takes the form of a physical container that exists in itself and that needs to be filled with content. Rather, I wish to highlight that space is always socially and politically constructed in certain moments in time. Thus, space is a relational and political concept that is constantly produced and reproduced.

In order to elaborate on these lines of thought, I propose that one theoretical lens through which the complex relationship between gangs, space and the state can be examined is Henri Lefebvre's theory of *The Production of Space*. Lefebvre has been one of the key scholars promoting the idea that any space is socially produced. As argued by Brenner (1997), "according to Lefebvre, space is a crucial dimension of social relations under capitalism, itself historically produced, reconfigured, and transformed" (140) by political and corporate interests. I believe that incorporating Lefebvre's spatial theory into gang studies enables gang scholars to engage with the complex socio-economic and political processes of capitalism which themselves become visible via the transformation of urban space in which gangs exist. Or, as Stanek (2011) has argued in the context of urban studies,

> what makes Lefebvre's theory productive in urban research is its general character, which allows integrating such categories as 'city' and 'space' into an overarching social theory and facilitates an investigation of spatial processes and phenomena from the private to the global level.
>
> *(130)*

By providing examples from my own field research in a minority community on Chicago's South Side – a community with a long history of gang presence – my aim is to demonstrate where his spatial theory might benefit critical gang studies. These examples will demonstrate, first, how his spatial theory can help scholars to understand how gangs appropriate urban social spaces for activities of everyday life and how such appropriation attempts can lead to conflicts with local state agents. Second, these examples will also show how the state-led spatial intervention of the demolition of public housing in Chicago has accelerated gang dynamics and conflicts. The overall aim of this chapter is to make Lefebvre's writings on space and the state fruitful to critical studies on gangs which are concerned with the multi-faceted and complex socio-economic and political structures and processes of neoliberal capitalism.

In order to do so, the next section will briefly outline how the concept of space has already been incorporated into critical research on gangs. Moreover, it will illustrate the definitional challenges that one faces when using such an elusive concept. This is followed by a theoretical examination of Henri Lefebvre's theory of *The Production of Space*. In order to make his theory fruitful to critical gang studies, some suggestions on how his spatial theory can be applied to gang research are also discussed. The last sections deal with Lefebvre's concept of "abstract space", which denotes the space of capitalism and the state. In order to demonstrate the concept's empirical applicability, the demolition of Chicago's public housing estates with the subsequent consequences for gang dynamics in the city is discussed as an example of abstract space.

(Critical) gang research and the question of space

The 'critical turn' in gang scholarship has opened up new avenues for researchers to engage with "issues of power, class and social inequality" (Fraser, 2017: 17). Such engagement has led to an examination of the role of space and urbanisation. As argued by Brotherton (2008),

> all gang subjects both make and are made by historical forces (using a fairly traditional Marxist concept of materialism) and that it is essential to locate our studies in such a historical and political economic framework to understand more fully the contexts of actions, the meaning webs of culture, and the contradictions of institutional settings (e.g. schools, prison).
>
> *(119; see also Hallsworth and Brotherton, 2011)*

The role of urban marginality, social exclusion and gentrification has become an important topic in understanding the gang phenomenon within a post-industrial society (Fraser, 2015; Hagedorn, 2007). In this respect, some scholars (e.g. Hagedorn, 2007, 2008; Young, 2007) have focused on the spatial transformation and peripheralisation within cities in the course of global economic processes. These authors argue that, in the context of post-industrial cities, "capitalism has transformed the opportunity structures in poor neighborhoods where gangs have always been found. Many of the generic-labor jobs – factory work which requires little skill or education – have moved away from inner cities" (Hagedorn, 2001: 43). Or, as stated by Winton (2014),

> the impact of spatial transformation of cities . . . plays a key role in the (re)production of gangs across contexts. In particular, violent spatial processes of segregation, gentrification and forced relocation, and spatial polarization all have a profound effect on social structures. This spatial violence, the dual expulsion-concentration of the socially excluded is compounded by the (symbolically violent) social stigmatization of these spaces.
>
> *(8)*

Moreover, the introduction of Pierre Bourdieu's (1985, 1986, 2010) social theory – particularly his concepts of "habitus", "social field", "symbolic violence" and "capital" – into gang research has spurred critical discussion of spatial processes within the urban environment of gangs, particularly with the aim "to re-engage with structure, agency, and culture in understanding the gang phenomenon" (Fraser, 2015: 32; see also Sandberg, 2008; Sandberg and Fleetwood, 2016).

What this short overview illustrates is that the examination of (urban) *space* and *spatial transformation* processes within cities in order to understand the gang phenomenon in the contemporary globalised world has become a key concern of critical gang research. For John Hagedorn, space – besides race – even constitutes a "good twenty-first-century starting point . . . for a theoretical reconsideration of gangs in the global city" (Hagedorn, 2007: 27).

In prioritising space, critical gang scholarship follows a more general trend towards spatialisation in the social sciences over the last three decades. As argued by Jessop et al. (2008), the concept of space has found its way into the social sciences via several "spatial turns" with each of them attempting "to reveal the unstated, and often problematic, spatial assumptions underpinning social scientific inquiries" (390). Yet this spatialisation of social sciences has not been a linear, conflict-free process, particularly since the question of what actually constitutes space had been a contested one. As succinctly argued by Massey (1992),

> many authors rely heavily on the terms 'space'/'spatial', and each assumes that their meaning is clear and uncontested. Yet in fact the meaning that different authors assume (and therefore – in the case of metaphorical usage – the import of the metaphor) varies greatly. Buried in these unacknowledged disagreements is a debate that never surfaces; and it never surfaces because everyone assumes we already know what these terms mean.
>
> *(66)*

Mainstream criminological research on gangs has arguably amplified rather than clarified the ambiguity about what 'space' means. Such works tends to use the concept of space merely to describe a gang's 'turf' and reduce analysis of turf to an economic one, where territorial control facilitates economic activities, such as drug dealing, and only secondarily as a realm for collective identification (Spergel, 1995: 88; Valasik and Tita, 2018: 841). Critics of the mainstream approach to space-as-turf have argued against its static denotation of space because it focuses predominantly on a fixed territoriality "in which control is exerted over activity and access" (Fraser, 2015: 220). Static spatial conceptualisations do not consider how, for example, gentrification and displacement *relocate* territorial boundaries and how de-industrialisation and ghettoisation *intensify* spatial immobility (ibid.; see also Smith, 1982, 2010 [1984]). In short, 'space-as-turf' presents an unchanging physical reality – a container with pre-defined and fixed structural and territorial demarcations, where space is an *a priori* fact (Reutlinger, 2009: 19), prior to the social relationships and processes that take place inside and outside the territorial boundaries. A long critical tradition in the social sciences has critiqued static spatial concep-tualisations – particularly among geographers – and has instead stressed that space is socially constructed rather than a mere physical entity. Massey (1992) goes even further, arguing that the 'social' in social construction must be applied to spatial relations as well as spatial sites. She points out that

> for, while it is surely correct to argue that space is socially constructed, the one-sideness [sic] of that formulation implied that geographical forms and distributions were simply out-comes, the end point of social explanation. . . . [However] the social is spatially constructed too, and that makes a difference. In other words, and in its broadest formulation, society is necessarily constructed spatially, and that fact – the spatial organization of society – makes a difference to how it works.
>
> *(70)*

A key effect of a move toward social-spatial relationships is that space and the spatial get seen as realms for political struggle:

> if spatial organization makes a difference to how society works and how it changes, then far from being the realm of stasis, space and the spatial are also implicated . . . in the production of history – and thus, potentially, in politics.
>
> *(ibid.)*

In this reading, then, space is an inherently political and ideological concept.

It is at this point where it is useful to turn to Henri Lefebvre's spatial theory and to examine the extent to which it can be fruitfully incorporated into critical gang studies. Critique of a static, container-like definition of space is also the starting point of Lefebvre in *The Production of Space* (Lefebvre, 1991 [1974]). The following statement probably best captures his approach to space: "it seems to be well established that physical space has no 'reality' without the energy that is deployed within it" (13). This observation leads him to conclude that "(social) space is a (social) product" (26)" and to elevate space alongside time as key social concepts. Thus, he calls his theory "a reorientation of human inquiry away from its traditional obsession with time and toward a reconstituted focus on space" (Dear, 1997: 49). Moreover, for Lefebvre, space is always also a political concept in which existing power relations in society unfold: "it [space] is also a political product, a product of administrative and repressive controls, a product of relations of domination and strategies decided at the summit of the State" (Lefebvre, 2009 [1980]: 213p.).

The following sections will examine his spatial theory in more detail, particularly the politi-cal economy of space, in order to further elaborate on the relational character of space and, most importantly, to provide an alternative theoretical lens for critical gang studies to incorporate the concept of space into its research agenda. For Lefebvre, it has always been very clear that capitalism "has succeeded in achieving 'growth'. We cannot calculate at what price, but we do know the means: *by occupying space, by producing space*" (Lefebvre, 1976: 21, italics i.o.). Although his spatial theory has found its way into some studies on gangs already (e.g. Gutiérrez River, 2010; Hagedorn, 2007; Venkatesh, 1997; Zilberg, 2011; Geenen, 2009), I would, nevertheless, argue that the full potential of his spatial theory has not been utilised in gang research yet. This is particularly so because Lefebvre's spatial theory follows a strict dialectics which needs to be considered in its entirety in order to define space. This dialectical thinking about space is mostly absent in those gang studies that have utilised his writings.

In the following sections, I will discuss his dialectics of space and the political nature of space in more detail. For both the dialectics of space and the political nature of space, I will discuss empirical examples of how his spatial theory can be fruitful to gang studies. As stated, the first example deals with the way gangs appropriate urban social spaces and the resulting conflicts with state agents. The second example demonstrates how state-led urban spatial planning in Chicago has contributed to the acceleration of gang dynamics and conflicts in the city, thereby exemplifying that, for Lefebvre, space is always also the scenery for political interventions.

Lefebvre's dialectics of space

"(Social) space is a (social) product" (Lefebvre, 1991 [1974]: 26). The statement, though seemingly clear enough, requires particular clarification with respect to the term "product". Lefebvre (1991 [1974]) acknowledges that "to speak of 'producing space' sounds bizarre, so great is the sway still held by the idea that empty space is prior to whatever ends up filling it" (15). Nevertheless, the idea that space is socially *produced* is important because it signifies the relational character of space. Since space is not an *a priori* fact, existing in and of itself, it is socially *produced*.

For Lefebvre, production means different things at the same time: on the one hand, it signifies "the strictly economic production of things" (Elden, 2004: 94). On the other hand, it also denotes the production of all different aspects of society such as the production of knowledge and of institutions (ibid.). Lefebvre develops his idea of producing space through a critical reading of the various and different traditions of Western philosophy in conceptualising space. Based on this reading, Lefebvre sees the need for a "unitary theory" "between different 'fields' of space which had hitherto been apprehended separately in Western intellectual (Cartesian-Newtonian) practice" (Merrifield, 1993: 523). Lefebvre (1991 [1974]) distinguishes three such "fields" of space: "first, the *physical* – nature, the Cosmos; secondly, the *mental*, including logical and formal abstractions; and, thirdly, the *social*" (11p., italics i.o.). The *physical* field comprises nature and materiality. It is the physical space which is defined by the perception of nature. The *mental* field refers to formal abstractions and knowledge about space. Last, in the context of the *social* field, "we are concerned with logico-epistemological space, the space of social practice, the space occupied by sensory phenomena, including products of the imagination such as projects and projections, symbols and utopias" (ibid.).

This triad of different fields is the starting point for Lefebvre's (1991 [1974]) production of space. For him, space consists of two interrelated triads: the first conceptual triad comprises the distinction between *spatial practice*, *representations of space* and *spaces of representations* (33, 38p.). The second consists of different dimensions of space which he describes as *perceived*, *conceived* and *lived* spaces (40). These two distinct triads together produce space and therefore *cannot be separated from each other* but must be seen and understood together. Schmid (2010) provides a vivid summary of these two triads:

1   The material production which produces *spatial practices* and thereby the *perceptible* aspects of space (*espace perçu*).
2   The production of knowledge which produces *representations of space* and, consequently, a *conceived* space (*espace conçu*).
3   The production of meaning which is connected to *spaces of representation* and which therefore produces a *lived* space (*espace vécu*) (208, my emphasis).

Table 7.1 The moments in the production of space

spatial practice	l'espace perçu	perceived	physical	materialism
representations of space	l'espace conçu	conceived	mental	idealism
spaces of representation	l'espace vécu	lived	social	materialism and idealism

Elden (2007: 110) succinctly visualises these different elements of and moments in the production of space (Table 7.1).

Spatial practices, the perceived dimension of space, comprise the externalised material environment of space (Gottdiener, 1993: 131). They therefore refer to "the material dimension of social activity and interaction", "denot[ing] the system resulting from articulation and connection of elements or activities. In concrete terms, one could think of networks of interaction and communication as they arise in everyday life" (Schmid, 2008: 36; see also Shields, 1991: 52). Within this material dimension of social activity, spatial practices denote the way people experience and live their daily lives within a certain material context. An example of a material context under neo-capitalism, for Lefebvre, are government-subsidised high-rise housing projects (Lefebvre, 1991 [1974]). In this material context, spatial practices signify how residents of these housing projects appropriate the buildings for activities of everyday life via certain daily practices and routines. Such practices and routines, in turn, create "networks of interaction" (Diener et al., 2006: 169), which, for their part, also use and incorporate material objects, such as the streets around the buildings as well as the buildings themselves.

Representations of space, or the conceived space, denote the *discursive* elements in the production of space. They are "conceptualized space, the space of scientists, planners, urbanists, technocratic subdividers and social engineers, as of a certain type of artist with a scientific bent – all of whom identify what is lived and what is perceived with what is conceived" (Lefebvre, 1991 [1974]: 38). In other words, representations of space comprise the knowledge one possesses about a certain space. For example, cartography creates a certain knowledge about a landscape, city or neighbourhood (see also Phillips and Bloch's chapter in this volume). Newspaper discourses on certain neighbourhoods generate certain representations of these areas, portraying them in a certain way. Another example of representations of space are city planners' and architectural projects. According to Stanek (2014), for Lefebvre, "architects produce drawings and models, but in so doing they respond to representations of space produced by other agents, from individual desires and embodied memories to institutionalized images and collectively shared symbols" (265).

This last example already illustrates that the way a certain space is produced also depends on collective and institutionalised interests which define how a certain space should be represented. Here, the role of power and politics in the production of space already manifests itself, which, as I will demonstrate later, is central in understanding Lefebvre's spatial theory. In the context of urban planning, Prigge (2008), therefore, stresses that representations of space

> define how space can be talked about and lend scientific coherence to the spontaneous ideologies of appropriated lived space (thereby ensuring the cohesion of spatial practice). Through their mechanisms of exclusion (who has the right to speak about space?), they formulate the dominant ways of representing and exercising power over space.
>
> *(53)*

For the specific field of gang studies, the question of who has the right to speak about space can become important, for example, in the way media outlets or state representatives portray entire neighbourhoods as "gang-infested" and/or "crime-ridden" (Schwarze, 2021), which, in turn, contributes to their socio-economic, political and cultural marginalisation and stigmatisation. Examining this question of who has the right to speak about space is crucial in understanding the directionalities and presumptuousness of space-knowledge formulations in public discourses on gangs.

The last of the three dimensions of space refers to *spaces of representation*. This is the dimension of *lived* space (*espace vécu*), referring to the "space as directly *lived* through its associated images and symbols, and hence the space of 'inhabitants' and 'users'" (Lefebvre, 1991 [1974]: 39, italics i.o.). Spaces of representation are rooted "in the history of a people as well as in the history of each individual belonging to that people" (ibid.: 41). They comprise the phenomenological space of lived experience (Wilson, 2013: 367). Consequently, spaces of representation are the spaces that are created by activities of everyday life (Lefebvre, 1991 [1974]: 116). At the same time, this space overlays the physical space of spatial practices, "making symbolic use of its objects" (ibid.: 39). Thus, spaces of representation are social inventions, codes, signs, symbols and material constructs such as the built environment of a city or a neighbourhood, seeking "to generate new meanings and possibilities for spatial practices" (Harvey, 1990: 257).

For Lefebvre, these dimensions of space cannot be separated from each other. Space is produced via the simultaneous and linked relationality of all three dimensions. In this production, time is also important, because each spatial dimension is produced by certain temporal processes which, in turn, produce different spaces at different points in time. Thus, "time and space are not separable within a texture so conceived: space implies time, and vice versa" (Lefebvre, 1991 [1974]): 118).

Lefebvre's dialectics of space and the study of gangs

How, then, can Lefebvre's spatial theory be fruitfully applied to critical gang studies? This section is dedicated to a discussion of examples of how his spatial theory can be useful to gang research. In particular, it will focus on the way gangs appropriate urban social spaces for activities of everyday life and how this can create conflictual relationships with local state agents. Moreover, incorporating Lefebvre's spatial theory might also be beneficial to future criminological research on gangs more generally, since it allows mainstream criminology to look beyond its own disciplinary and academic boundaries and to engage more extensively with scholarly work from other schools of thought. This self-referential character of criminological gang research in studying the gang phenomenon has been criticised by Hallsworth and Young (2008), who argue that "given that gang researchers within this tradition . . . only reference other gang researchers while avoiding other non-gang-related studies of youth violence, the end result is that research is solely in the language of gang talk!" (186). Hence, Lefebvre's spatial theory might be one way to broaden criminology's theoretical outlook to the study of gangs. In the following sections, I wish to provide some analytical starting points in how to empirically incorporate his spatial theory into gang studies.

Representations of space – the conceived space of the production of knowledge – have clear relevance to the variety of different visible symbols and place identifiers that do not just demarcate a gang's territory but represent meaning for its members and practices. For example, gang graffiti as a visible and visual form of spatial representations marks territory but also signals collective attachment and in turn structures the identity of the gang (Adams and Winter, 1997). Insights from research on social movements from landless rural workers in Brazil (Garmany, 2008) establish that representations of space can also be addressed through the way outsiders perceive the social space of a social movement or, in the case of gangs, the community in which these groups reside. In this respect, Venkatesh's (2008) descriptions of how community residents of the Robert Taylor homes in Chicago opposed the external representation of their community as a "project" and, instead, argued that they live in a *community* (43) exemplify how a certain representation of space also contributes to the stigmatisation of certain neighbourhoods that are associated with gangs. The dominant discourse on space defined public housing estates as projects, even though the self-representation of their residents defined them as a community with which people identified. Here, Prigge's (2008) remarks that representations of space are always also defined "through their mechanisms of exclusion (who has the right to speak about space?)" and that "they formulate the dominant ways of representing and exercising power over space" (53) become manifest. Similarly, examinations of media discourses on gangs (e.g. Esbensen and Tusinski, 2007; Thompson et al., 2000), particularly how such discourses portray and dismiss entire neighbourhoods as "gang-infested", thereby facilitating the socio-cultural stigmatisation of whole urban communities, can be critically examined using Lefebvre's concept of representations of space. Such hegemonic public discourses and representations might also form part of a gang's collective consciousness and identity.

Spatial practices – the perceived dimension of space – can foreground how gangs appropriate the urban social space of their environment through certain (routinised and improvised) daily practices (see also Fraser, 2015). For Lefebvre, spatial practices refer to the materiality of the elements that constitute space (Diener et al., 2006: 169) and what kind of ritualised practices people use in order to appropriate this materiality. In the context of advanced marginality (Wacquant, 2007), the urban built environment often does not provide many opportunities for gangs to organise activities of everyday life. Regardless of such limitations, the creativity that gangs possess in using material objects in their urban surrounding can be analysed through the lens of spatial practices. In this respect, the way certain objects, such as park benches or playing grounds, are appropriated by gangs as places to "hang out", to meet fellow companions and to execute socio-cultural performances also forms part of such practices (Conquergood, 1991). Such an examination also emphasises the conflictual relationship between representations of space and spatial practices. Oftentimes, certain material objects in the urban built environment of neighbourhoods are created by architects or city planners – actors who are often *external* to a neighbourhood – with a certain purpose in mind which, at the same time, prohibits alternative ways of appropriating them. In other words, their representations – that is, the discursive elements of such objects and their intended purpose (Lefebvre, 1991 [1974]) – can collide with spatial practices by individuals who appropriate these objects in a way contrary to the objects' original purposes.

I want to highlight this conflictual relationship between representations of space and spatial practices by using the example of the social space of a playground in an urban area that has experienced gang activities (see Figure 7.1).

This sign attached to the fence of a playground in a neighbourhood on Chicago's South Side[2] represents and signifies an exclusionary space from which specific social groups – in this case, gangs – are actively excluded via a certain representation of what this playground should *not* be used for. A reading of this sign would be that, as long as someone is not in a gang and does not do any of the things mentioned on the sign, he or she should not experience any difficulties in appropriating the space of the playing ground via certain spatial practices. However, this way of appropriation sounds more straightforward than it actually might be.

An alternative scenario also presents itself: a group of young men meets on a warm summer evening to enjoy a little bit of free time outside of their homes. The nearest and probably one of the few existing public places where this group can meet "in the context of limited space and resources" (Fraser, 2015: 117) in neighbourhoods on Chicago's South Side is a local playground. Without being involved in any of the activities mentioned on the sign, this group of young men

Figure 7.1 Playground sign, Chicago, November 2017

appropriate this playground to talk about the day that has passed. Living in a neighbourhood that frequently has been an area of gang activity and gang violence, the next police officers passing by the playground observe this group of young males sitting in a space that was originally not created for such activities. Moreover, knowing that the large majorities of gang members in this area are young males in their 20s or younger, the police officers approach this group in order to investigate whether any crimes or inappropriate behaviours were committed. Whether the police officers are, then, going to disperse this group, only ask what they are up to or even arrest them for, in their eyes, unlawful conduct is likely to be important to the people involved. Yet, for my examination here, more important is how this example underlines that the way a certain space is socially produced determines the ability of people to appropriate said space. What this imaginary yet plausible scenario communicates is the conflicting relationship between representations of space and spatial practices as described by Lefebvre. The young men's spatial practices created "alternative representations of space" (Garmany, 2008: 321) which were unintended in the original plans of city planners and architects and, because of the discrepancy, reveal a gulf between how the police are also engaged in alternative spatial practices, securitising the alternative use regardless of the activity taking place. Local authorities are thus engaged in the rejection of alternative representations of space. That rejection is not natural or neutral and is itself a routinisation of securitised (counter-)spatial practice that monitors and polices the relationship between bodies and space and is trained to detect and root out community-led spatial practices that do not cohere and coincide with the imaginary original. The fact that the police response is at least as much and likely much more violent and coercive than the young men's spatial practices in this scenario gets lost (Rios, 2011). So, too, does the critical observation that the authoritative projection of an imaginary original onto the playground space is itself a violent spatial practice, marking the space as unsafe in new ways that extend beyond that same imaginary.

From the playground scenario, critical gang researchers are able to examine the (in)ability of gang members or adolescents living in areas with gang presence to appropriate the urban built environment in which they live. This (in)ability signifies that those areas in which gangs exist are often characterised by an abstract space (Lefebvre, 1991 [1974]) in which the state's "presence, control, and surveillance in the most isolated corners" (Lefebvre, 2009d [1978]: 227) of the city or, in this case, a neighbourhood, constitutes a central part of gang members' experiences of everyday life. In other words, the state becomes deeply embedded in gang members' everyday lives through means of punitive social control (Rios, 2011).

This abstract space, therefore, also alters the lived experiences of everyday life in space – Lefebvre's third dimension of *spaces of representations*. In the playground example, the lived spatial experiences and the associated symbols of space for the young men pass from the possibility of equal spatial use to one dominated by emphasis of the proximity of young men not just to gang violence but to the violence of the state. Spatial violence is direct and structural: young men face potential bodily injury, incarceration or harassment from authorities for being engaged in spatial practices that are different from the state's projected imaginaries.

But they are also subjected to normative violence via the sign itself, which marks the playground space and, by extension, all neighbourhood space, as a zone of exclusion. Where do the planners intend young men to hang out? The young men find themselves excluded from the projected imaginary. Being asked what they associate with the lived experiences of everyday life in the social space of their neighbourhood, the young men might emphasise the encounter not just with the police but with the sign itself as stigmatising encounters. Thus, Lefebvre's notion of spaces of representation prioritises the actual *and* lived, the felt, experience of everyday life in the young men's neighbourhood: what do they associate with this life symbolically, socially and culturally? How do they *live* with – not just live in terms of survive or tolerate, but live in the sense of respond to, resist, ignore and adapt to – the advancement of marginality, social stigmatisation and exclusion that is felt to be designed into the lived environment? The examination of the lived experiences of everyday life involves the recognition that the lived environment is marked by the violence and coercion of actors additional to gangs. That recognition insists that the qualities and characteristics of everyday life in the neighbourhood of a gang and of gang life in urban space both be considered. It also insists on seeing how state bureaucracy of social control alters the urban space of gangs and how such alteration, in turn, becomes ingrained in the lived experiences and collective identities of gang members in their social spaces. The playground sign is the graffiti of the state, even as the state continues to *see* only the graffiti of the gang (Conquergood, 1997).

With Lefebvre, and especially the insight that the three dimensions be seen together, a shift occurs where the research view of the critical gang researcher shifts to the complex sociocultural, economic and political processes unfolding in the urban space of gangs. Lefebvre's vision risks abstraction, but its utility lies in anchoring it to individual-centred perceptions, conceptions and lived experiences, where the individual human body must be the subject of study and not the state that has already and over-confidently assumed to know the subject or to be able to box the subject out of or inside its own spatial imaginations. Lefebvre himself emphasised this individual-centred approach, arguing that

> the perceived-conceived-lived triad (in spatial terms: spatial practice, representations of space, representational spaces) loses all force if it is treated as an abstract 'model'. If it cannot grasp the concrete (as distinct from the 'immediate'), then its import is severely limited, amounting to no more than that of one ideological mediation among others.
>
> *(Lefebvre, 1991 [1974]: 40)*

To be concrete means to be anchored to actor-led articulation, to de-centre the spatial perspective and to question whether and how the state conceptualises space to locate, know and contain the gang member. This section emphasised not only the critical opportunities that become possible through such actions but again reiterated how space constitutes an important medium in understanding the gang phenomenon.

That spatial critique emphasises the multiple conflictual relationships between actors also reminds the field of critical gang scholarship that space is political, too, and that the state is inevitable in understanding gang dynamics (Brotherton, 2015). The political nature of space and, more specifically, Lefebvre's notion of abstract space as engendering a political *economy* of space is the subject of the next section.

The abstract space of capitalism and the state

> Capitalism has found itself able to attenuate (if not resolve) its internal contradictions for a century, and . . . it has succeeded in achieving 'growth'. We cannot calculate at what price, but we do know the means: by occupying space, by producing space.
>
> (Lefebvre, 1976: 21)

> There is a politics of space because space is political.
>
> (Lefebvre in Elden, 2004: 93)

These two quotes by Lefebvre illustrate that space is not only a social product but always also hints at the real and political consequences of different perception-conception-lived experiences. In other words, the social production of space is never free of political interests and, where the space of the built urban environment is concerned, political interests are frequently corporate ones. Hence, for Lefebvre (2009b [1970]),

> space is not a *scientific object* removed . . . from ideology or politics; it has always been political and strategic. . . . Space has been fashioned and molded from historical and natural elements, but in a political way. Space is political and ideological. It is a product literally populated with ideologies.
>
> *(170, italics i.o.)*

The production of space is always also influenced by collective interests which aim to appropriate space for their own benefit, usually the generation of value and profit. Lefebvre calls this kind of space "abstract space", denoting the space of capitalism and the state. For him, abstract space "is a reflection of the world of business on both a national and international level, as well as the power of money and the *politique* of the state" (Lefebvre, 2009c [1979]: 186, italics i.o.).

Abstract space encompasses the rise of capital, abstract labour and bureaucracy (Sayer, 1993: 458). There are two characteristics of abstract space which, at first sight, seem contradictory: first, abstract space attempts to *homogenise* space in order to make it fruitful to capital accumulation and the generation of value. Second, abstract space *fragments* space into small parcels, pieces and elements, thereby unveiling its character of a *simultaneous homogenisation and fragmentation* of space.

The aim of homogenising space is to make it useful to the generation of value and profit. Anything that prevents such generation needs to be removed from space. Such removal focuses especially on the removal of difference – of people, objects and structures that stand in the way of capital accumulation (Merrifield, 2000: 176). Thus, space is not only a means of production but also an object of consumption which "is consumed for production just as are industrial buildings and sites, machines, raw materials, and labor power" (Lefebvre, 2009c [1979]: 188).

Meanwhile, the fragmentation of space by powerful agents into small parcels and pieces also forms part of abstract space. Here, the role of the state becomes particularly important because the fragmentation of space is "an instrument of political power; it [the state] divides and separates in order to rule" (Lefebvre, 2009 [1980]: 215). Lefebvre stresses that this tendency to segregate space becomes particularly evident in the context of spatial planning within cities. Bureaucratic and administrative procedures segregate space in order to control it:

> Rendered artificially scare anywhere near a centre so as to increase its 'value', . . . it [space] is literally pulverized and sold off in 'lots' or 'parcels'. This is the way in which space in practice becomes the medium of segregations, of the component elements of society as they are thrust out towards peripheral zones.
>
> *(Lefebvre, 1991 [1974]): 334)*

What such fragmentation of space allows the state to do is "to introduce its presence, control, and surveillance in the most isolated corners" (Lefebvre, 2009d [1978]: 227) of a city or a neighbourhood.

For Lefebvre, the state seeks to manage and administer space in such a way that it promotes capital accumulation and the development of markets (Brenner, 2001: 791; Elden, 2008: 87). The means to do so are large-scale and long-term investments into the urban built environment of cities in order to contribute to industrial production, collective consumption, commodity circulation, transportation and communication. Yet, at the same time, the access to such investments is also regulated and limited by the state (Brenner, 2008: 238): investments into the urban built environment are not distributed equally among different urban spaces but rather centralised in a few spaces. Consequently, "the state . . . operates as the most crucial *institutional mediator of uneven geographical development* under capitalism" (Brenner, 2000: 370, italics i.o.). With this understanding of state spaces, Lefebvre's approach differs from 'the social ecology approach' associated with the Sociology Department of the University of Chicago, which has pioneered gang studies. Protagonists of the social ecology approach, particularly Clifford R. Shaw and Henry D. McKay, understood delinquency as a direct outcome of the social disorganisation of communities. For them, turning towards social processes *within* the community allows to identify the causes for delinquent behaviour. Jon Snodgrass (1976) criticises this approach because it ignores the wider political economy of society and how it contributes to delinquency:

> A most striking aspect of Shaw and McKay's interpretation . . . is the absence of attempts to link business and industrial invasion with the causes of delinquency. The interpretation

stayed at the communal level and turned inward to find the causes of delinquency in inter-nal conditions and process within the socially disorganised area.

(Snodgrass, 1976: 10)

This shortcoming of correlating delinquency with the political economy of society is prob-lematic insofar as it ignores that the state and the capitalist economy are the major drivers in urban redevelopment processes and thereby also fundamental in understanding gang dynamics. The gang is not a social phenomenon that exists outside or independent of socio-economic and political processes within society. Rather, it is always also the *direct* outcome of state spatial and economic interventions into the built environments of urban communities. Thus, scholarship on gangs needs to reorient its focus towards the question of *how* the state and political economy of neoliberal capitalism alter space and how this alteration, in turn, impacts gang dynamics. I believe that Lefebvre's spatial theory provides this reorientation not only because it concep-tualises the social production of space *within* urban communities in which gangs exist and how gangs form part of this spatial production but also because it examines *how* the state and the political economy of neoliberal capitalism alter this production process. The following section will detail possible ways critical gang research can utilise Lefebvre's finding that the production of space is always also political.

The study of gangs via abstract space

What, then, does the concept of abstract space contribute to empirical, conceptual and theo-retical examination of gangs in urban social spaces? With its tendency to make space solely productive to capital accumulation, abstract space produces "a spatial epistemology that restricts the ability of individuals to realize the true productive and collective power of their social space" (Jones and Popke, 2010: 117). For example, individuals are unable to participate in the produc-tion of their urban social spaces in the context of large-scale urban restructuring projects and city planning initiatives. Such urban restructuring projects can also have important implications for gang dynamics in urban spaces, as I will demonstrate subsequently in more detail by discuss-ing the demolition of Chicago's public housing estates.

The destruction of former public housing estates and the relocation of their inhabitants – including gangs – into other neighbourhoods of the city is a key site and practice of abstract space (Jones and Popke, 2010; Venkatesh, 2008). As argued by Hagedorn (2007), "the tearing down of housing projects produce 'abstract spaces' that have utility for the powerful but also have the unintended effect of producing different kinds of 'social spaces' with different modes of gang activity" (26). This tearing down of public housing estates forms part of "an unprec-edented tendency [within urban planning] to merge urban design, architecture and the police apparatus into a single, comprehensive security effort" (Davis, 2006: 224). In the context of Chicago, for example, public housing redevelopment was based on the common beliefs among protagonists of such urban renewal that the "demolition of substandard housing reduces crime" (Vale, 2013: 316). Yet, and not surprisingly,

significant reduction in criminal activity in the neighborhood that coincided with demo-lition and upgrading of the area ought to be expected, but it is not something directly caused by better housing conditions since the presumed criminals (and/or their victims) are no longer present. *In many cases, crime and violence are either displaced to other neighborhoods or simply dispersed.*

(ibid.: 325, my emphasis)

Displacement and dispersion are particularly important in understanding the relationship between abstract space and the gang as a collective actor. The abstract space of public housing redevelopment in Chicago contributed to shifting gang dynamics between different neighbourhoods of the city (Aspholm, 2020; Hagedorn et al., 2019). Instead of an overall reduction of crime, violence and gang activity, the redevelopment project merely redistributed gang activities away from the public housing buildings into other, often nearby, neighbourhoods of the city. I encountered this quality of abstract space in my own field research in a neighbourhood on Chicago's South Side which received a large share of the residents from the vacated public housing blocs. This spatial intervention by the Chicago Housing Authority (CHA) had a severe impact on the social space of this neighbourhood, particularly with respect to the unfolding of new gang dynamics. Two long-term neighbourhood residents described the impact on them and their living space:

> You had gangs from other communities coming in. So you have two different gangs now because those gang members were children and when . . . they move with their mom and dad or whoever they were living with and now they're in this new community. There was existing gangs. So now you have rival gangs living and they're fighting for turfs. So what do you have? You have war. Lot of shooting.
>
> A lot of the people that came out of these projects came up with the same thing they were doing in the projects which they wasn't doing over here. If they did it, it was low key. You didn't know. But once all that took place it just became a battle ground for gangs and drugs.

Lefebvre's notion of abstract space contributes insights to critical gang research in light of these residents' narrated experience "because it calls attention to the ways in which our spatial epistemologies can work to obscure the social relations and political negotiations that produce urban space" (Jones and Popke, 2010: 116). In the context of Chicago's social housing units, the abstract space of state-led urban planning displaced gang members from their homes to other neighbourhoods, which, in turn, created tensions with already existing gangs in those areas. The spatial epistemology of this state-led urban planning intervention considered the social spaces of those neighbourhoods receiving displaced residents from public housing empty and homogenous containers. In such an understanding of space-as-container, one can simply "house objects, people, machines, industrial facilities, flows, and networks" (Lefebvre, 2003 [1970]: 48) into these areas from a top-down position held by state actors, a position that does not consider the lived experiences of the residents or their demands and visions for the socio-spatial constitution of their communities.

Thus, a critical re-orientation towards abstract space shifts attention away from the mere fact of an increase in gang violence and towards the role that planning authorities played in fomenting that violence. Richard Rothstein's (2017) important work on racial segregation in the United States demonstrates in this respect that racial segregation has ever since been a political project in which the state has been the main actor promoting such segregation. According to Rothstein, various state actors, such as the federal and local government, state courts, universities, schools and state real estate commissions, have all actively promoted racial segregation within US cities. This, in turn, has fostered direct and structural forms of violence against African American communities. In the context of Chicago's demolition of social housing estates and the subsequent relocation of their residents, it is telling that state agents showed little to no consideration for the impact that relocation programmes would have. A critical turn towards abstract space helps to centre the experience of re-located and previous residents to emphasise additional forms of violence. In the case of the neighbourhood under consideration in my field research, that violence took the form of the fragmentation and disintegration of pre-existing social and cultural structures and relations of the neighbourhood, which in turn created new tensions between established and new residents (Elias and Scotson, 1965). Established residents considered the newcomers intruders, and residents stressed that the city's decision to relocate individuals was the precipitating cause of the increase in violence, which expands the field of agency in critical gang studies to incorporate actors beyond the young men who are gang members. That the relocation also produced *new* gang dynamics and violence underscores a deep fissure to the entire production of space in the neighbourhood: the representations of space – that is, the conceived space in the form of residents' and outsiders' knowledge about the neighbourhood – were now even more dominated by internal and external labelling of the neighbourhood as "gang-infested", which, in turn, contributed to its further socio-economic and cultural marginalisation. With respect to the lived experiences of people in space, residents of the neighbourhood had to adapt to this new configuration of gang dynamics as well as to new forms of socio-economic precarity in their everyday life routines.

The abstract space of public housing redevelopment had far-reaching consequences for the social space configurations of this particular neighbourhood. Not only did it intensify the level of physical violence due to newly created gang conflicts; it also spurred forms of structural and symbolic violence (Galtung, 1969; Bourdieu, 2010), since it contributed to aggravated socio-economic and cultural marginality through reduced access to health care provision and to fresh, healthy food (wherein the neighbourhood became a 'food desert'). It also entrenched a stigmatising public representation of the neighbourhood as just one more among Chicago's several violent communities. Lefebvre was attuned to the multiple levels of violence of abstract space, writing:

> structural violence is enabled by a symbolic 'violence enthroned in a specific rationality, that of accumulation, that of bureaucracy . . . a unitary, logistical, operational and quantifying rationality' through which social space is discursively homogenized and stripped of qualitative content in order to function as a 'passive receptacle for the planners'.
>
> *(Wilson, 2014: 115)*

Emphasising the redevelopment decision itself as community violence also responds to residents' own lived experience of loss because any decision to tear down existing housing 'projects' ignores the extent to which their building residents identified with the buildings themselves and with the spaces within and around them as forming community. Moreover, it acknowledges the further lived experience of violence of pre-existing residents where the displaced were transferred. The CHA seemed to have not reflected enough about the multiple violences that would result from the relocation of these residents. The abstract space exhibits the simultaneity of capitalism and the state, where both work together harmoniously to homogenise a vision of social space where city planners can superimpose their own spatial agenda without considering the lived experiences of inhabitants. New gang dynamics were one 'side-effect' of such hegemonic spatial intervention programmes in these neighbourhoods, but other forms of violence also rippled out from the initial decision. Abstract space as a critical conceptual site to present and conceptualise lived experience must therefore be an indispensable tool for critical gang theorists.

Conclusion

Although formulated half a century ago, Lefebvre's concept of space is as relevant as it was when it was published for examining the contemporary era of neoliberal urbanisation in which socio-spatial exclusion and marginalisation as well as the production of different forms of vio-lence – structural and symbolic as well as physical – lead to multiple forms of violence that get lost or marginalised in orthodox presentations that presume to site violence only within a gang's own activities. His conceptualisation is therefore of paramount concern to those scholars who wish to study social phenomena, such as gangs, with respect to their spatio-temporal dimen-sions. Although the notion of space has been part of gang scholarship since its origins within the early Chicago School of Sociology, there remains an ambiguity about what scholars mean by the notion of 'space' when used in gang research. That ambiguity has a real impact in repro-ducing problematic knowledge claims and praxis, as can be seen when mainstream criminol-ogy reduces complex socio-spatial processes present under advanced marginality and globalised neoliberal urbanisation to a study only of the violent rationality of some of the most marginal actors located within those processes.

I have argued that Lefebvre's spatial theory – particularly *The Production of Space* (1991 [1974]) – ought to be integral for gang studies to reflect critically upon the relationship between gangs, space and the state. This theory allows for examination of how the urban space of gangs is socially produced, emphasises the multiple roles that gangs themselves play in this produc-tion and insists on a conceptual, empirical and theoretical focus on how collective and political interests contribute to socio-spatial marginalisation processes which are as important in under-standing the gang phenomenon as the gang's recruitment tactics, activities and employment of violence. The chapter has empirically grounded the potential of Lefebvre's spatial concep-tualisation within neighbourhood actors' articulations of the multiplicity and directionality of violence and through a construction of plausible spatial imaginaries that lead with actors' own experiences as objects of state violence. There remains great scope for the empirical, conceptual and theoretical potential of these arguments beyond what this single chapter can do. It has aimed instead to highlight key insights and propose fruitful avenues for future research. A second limitation of this chapter is that it can only introduce a small portion of Lefebvre's work. With almost 70 books published, Lefebvre has been one of the most influential scholars in thinking about everyday life, the urban, space and the state. As a result, I see this chapter as a call for an extended and elaborated exploration of the full body of Lefebvre's philosophical and sociologi-cal work within critical gang studies.

Notes

1 I wish to thank Jaremey McMullin and Jeffrey Murer for their help and invaluable insights, comments and critiques on this chapter.
2 For anonymity purposes, I use this broader denotation and do not specify which neighbourhood is concerned here.

Bibliography

Adams, K.L. and Winter, A. (1997). Gang Graffiti as a Discourse Genre. *Journal of Sociolinguistics* 1(3) (pp. 337–360).
Aspholm, R.R. (2020). *Views from the Streets. The Transformation of Gangs and Violence on Chicago's South Side*. New York and Chichester, West Sussex: Columbia University Press..
Bourdieu, P.F. (1985). The Social Space and the Genesis of Groups. *Theory and Society* 14(6) (pp. 723–744).
Bourdieu, P.F. (1986). The Forms of Capital. In: Richardson, J.G. (ed.). *Handbook of Theory and Research for the Sociology of Education*. New York and London: Greenwood Press (pp. 241–258).
Bourdieu, P.F. (2010). *Distinction*. London and New York: Routledge.
Brenner, N. (1997). Global, Fragmented, Hierarchical: Henri Lefebvre's Geographies of Globalization. *Public Culture* 10(1) (pp. 135–167).

Brenner, N. (2000). The Urban Question as a Scale Question: Reflections on Henri Lefebvre, Urban Theory and the Politics of Scale. *Journal of Urban and Regional Research* 24(2) (pp. 361–378).

Brenner, N. (2001). State Theory in the Political Conjuncture: Henri Lefebvre's "Comments on a New State Form." *Antipode* 33(5) (pp. 783–808).

Brenner, N. (2008). Henri Lefebvre's Critique of State Productivism. In: Goonewardena, K., Kipfer, S., Milgrom, R. and Schmid, C. (eds.). *Space, Difference, Everyday Life. Reading Lefebvre*. New York: Routledge (pp. 231–249).

Brotherton, D.C. (2008). Youth Subcultures, Resistance, and the Street Organization in Late Modern New York. In: Flynn, M. and Brotherton, D.C. (eds.). *Globalizing the Streets. Cross-Cultural Perspectives on Youth, Social Control, and Empowerment*. New York: Columbia University Press (pp. 114–132).

Brotherton, D.C. (2015). *Youth Street Gangs. A Critical Appraisal*. New York: Routledge.

Conquergood, D. (1991). Rethinking Ethnography: Towards a Critical Cultural Politics. *Communication Monographs* 58 (pp. 179–194).

Conquergood, D. (1997). Street Literacy. In: Flood, J., Heath, S.B. and Lapp, D. (eds.). *Handbook of Research on Teaching Literacy through the Communicative and Visual Arts*. Mahwah, NJ: Lawrence Erlbaum Associates, Inc., Publishers (pp. 354–375).

Davis, M. (2006). *City of Quartz. Excavating the Future in Los Angeles*. London and New York: Verso.

Dear, M. (1997). Postmodern Bloodlines. In: Benko, G. and Strohmeyer, U. (eds.). *Space & Social Theory. Interpreting Modernity and Postmodernity*. Oxford and Malden: Blackwell (pp. 49–71).

Diener, R., Herzog, J., Meili, M., de Meuron, P. and Schmid, C. (2006). *Die Schweiz. Ein städtebauliches Portrait*. Basel: Birkhäuser-Verlag für Architektur.

Elden, S. (2004). Between Marx and Heidegger: Politics, Philosophy and Lefebvre's the Production of Space. *Antipode* 36(1) (pp. 86–105).

Elden, S. (2007). There Is a Politics of Space Because Space Is Political. Henri Lefebvre and the Production of Space. *Radical Philosophy Review* 10(2) (pp. 101–116).

Elden, S. (2008). Mondialisation before Globalization. In: Goonewardena, K., Kipfer, S., Milgrom, R. and Schmid, C. (eds.). *Space, Difference, Everyday Life. Reading Lefebvre*. New York: Routledge (pp. 80–91).

Elias, N. and Scotson, J.L. (1965). *The Established and the Outsiders. A Sociological Enquiry into Community Problems*. London: Frank Cass & Co. Ltd.

Esbensen, F.-A. and Tusinski, K.E. (2007). Youth Gangs in the Print Media. *Journal of Criminal Justice and Popular Culture* 14(1) (pp. 21–38).

Fraser, A. (2015). *Urban Legends. Gang Identity in the Post-Industrial City*. Oxford: Oxford University Press.

Fraser, A. (2017). *Gangs & Crime. Critical Alternatives*. Los Angeles: Sage Publications.

Galtung, J. (1969). Violence, Peace, and Peace Research. *Journal of Peace Research* 6(3) (pp. 167–191).

Garmany, J. (2008). The Spaces of Social Movements: A Movimento dos Trabalhadores Rurais Sem Terra from a Socio-Spatial Perspective. *Space and Polity* 12(3) (pp. 311–328).

Geenen, K. (2009). "Sleep Occupies No Space": The Use of Public Space by Street Gangs in Kinshasa. *Africa: Journal of the International African Institute* 79(3) (pp. 347–358).

Gottdiener, M. (1993). A Marx for Our Time: Henri Lefebvre and the Production of Space. *Sociological Theory* 11(1) (pp. 129–134).

Gutiérrez River, L. (2010). Discipline and Punish? Youth Gangs' Response to "Zero-Tolerance" Policies in Honduras. *Bulletin of Latin American Research* 29(2) (pp. 1–13).

Hagedorn, J. (2001). Globalization, Gangs, and Collaborative Research. In: Klein, M., Kerner, H.-J., Maxson, C. and Weitekamp, E. (eds.). *The Eurogang Paradox*. Dordrecht: Springer (pp. 41–58).

Hagedorn, J. (2005). The Global Impact of Gangs. *Journal of Contemporary Criminal Justice* 21(2) (pp. 153–169).

Hagedorn, J. (2007). Gangs, Institutions, Race, and Space. The Chicago School Revisited. In: Hagedorn, J. (ed.). *Gangs in the Global City*. Urbana and Chicago: University of Illinois Press (pp. 13–33).

Hagedorn, J. (2008). *A World of Gangs. Armed Young Men and Gangsta Culture*. Minnesota: University of Minnesota Press.

Hagedorn, J., Aspholm, R., Córdova, T., Papachristos, A. and Williams, L. (2019). *The Fracturing of Gangs and Violence in Chicago: A Research-Based Reorientation of Violence Prevention and Intervention Policy*. Chicago: Great Cities Institute. University of Illinois at Chicago.

Hallsworth, S. and Brotherton, D.C. (2011). *Urban Disorder and Gangs. A Critique and a Warning*. London: Runnymede.

Hallsworth, S. and Young, T. (2008). Gang Talk and Gang Talkers: A Critique. *Crime Media Culture* 4(2) (pp. 175–195).

Harvey, D. (1990). Flexible Accumulation Through Urbanization. Reflections on "Post-Modernism" in the American City. *Perspecta* (pp. 251–272).

Jessop, B., Brenner, N. and Jones, M. (2008). Theorizing Sociospatial Relations. *Environment and Planning D: Society and Space* 26 (pp. 389–401).

Jones, K. and Popke, J. (2010). Re-Envisioning the City: Lefebvre, Hope VI, and the Neoliberalization of Urban Space. *Urban Geography* 31(1) (pp. 114–133).

Lefebvre, H. (1976). *The Survival of Capitalism*. London: Allison & Busby.

Lefebvre, H. (1991 [1974]). *The Production of Space*. Malden: Blackwell Publishing Ltd.

Lefebvre, H. (2003 [1970]). *The Urban Revolution*. Minneapolis and London: University of Minnesota Press.

Lefebvre, H. (2009a [1980]). Space and Mode of Production. In: Brenner, N. and Elden, S. (eds.). *State, Space, World. Selected Essays. Henri Lefebvre*. Minneapolis and London: University of Minnesota Press (pp. 210–222).

Lefebvre, H. (2009b [1970]). Space and the State. In: Brenner, N. and Elden, S. (eds.). *State, Space, World. Selected Essays. Henri Lefebvre*. Minneapolis and London: University of Minnesota Press (pp. 223–253).

Lefebvre, H. (2009c [1979]). Reflections on the Politics of Space. In: Brenner, N. and Elden, S. (eds.). *State, Space, World. Selected Essays. Henri Lefebvre*. Minneapolis and London: University of Minnesota Press (pp. 167–184).

Lefebvre, H. (2009d [1978]). Space. Social Product and Use Value. In: Brenner, N. and Elden, S. (eds.). *State, Space, World. Selected Essays. Henri Lefebvre*. Minneapolis and London: University of Minnesota Press (pp. 185–195).

Massey, D. (1992). Politics and Space/Time. *New Left Review* (pp. 65–84).

Merrifield, A. (1993). Place and Space: A Lefebvrian Reconciliation. *Transactions of the Institute of British Geographers* 18(4) (pp. 516–531).

Merrifield, A. (2000). Henri Lefebvre. A Socialist in Space. In: Crang, M. and Thrift, N. (eds.). *Thinking Space*. London and New York: Routledge (pp. 167–182).

Prigge, W. (2008). Reading The Urban Revolution. Space and Representation. In: Goonewardena, K., Kipfer, S., Milgrom, R. and Schmid, C. (eds.). *Space, Difference, Everyday Life. Reading Lefebvre*. New York and London: Routledge (pp. 46–61).

Reutlinger, C. (2009). Raumdeutungen. Rekonstruktion des Sozialraums "Schule" und mitagierende Erforschung "unsichtbarer Bewältigungskarten" als methodische Felder von Sozialraumforschung. In: Deinet, U. (ed.). *Methodenbuch Sozialraum*. Wiesbaden: VS Verlag für Sozialwissenschaften (pp. 17–32).

Rios, V.M. (2011). *Punished. Policing the Lives of Black and Latino Boys*. New York and London: New York University Press.

Rothstein, R. (2017). *The Color of Law. A Forgotten History of How Our Government Segregated America*. New York and London: Liveright Publishing.

Sandberg, S. (2008). Street Capital. Ethnicity and Violence on the Streets of Oslo. *Theoretical Criminology* 12(2) (pp. 153–171).

Sandberg, S. and Fleetwood, J. (2016). Street Talk and Bourdieusian Criminology: Bringing Narrative to Field Theory. *Criminology & Criminal Justice* 17(4) (pp. 1–17).

Sayer, A. (1993). Review. Henri Lefebvre, the Production of Space. *International Journal of Urban and Regional Research* 17(3) (pp. 358–459).

Schmid, C. (2008). Henri Lefebvre's Theory of the Production of Space. Towards a Three-Dimensional Dialectic. In: Goonewardena, K., Kipfer, S., Milgrom, R. and Schmid, C. (eds.). *Space, Difference, Everyday Life. Reading Henri Lefebvre*. New York: Routledge (pp. 27–45).

Schmid, C. (2010). *Stadt, Raum und Gesellschaft. Henri Lefebvre und die Theorie der Produktion des Raumes*. Stuttgart: Franz Steiner Verlag. 2nd edition.

Schwarze, T. (2021). Discursive practices of territorial stigmatization: how newspapers frame violence and crime in a Chicago community. *Urban Geography*. DOI: 10.1080/02723638.2021.1913015

Shields, R. (1991). *Places on the Margin. Alternative Geographies of Modernity*. London and New York: Routledge.

Smith, N. (1982). Gentrification and Uneven Development. *Economic Geography* 58(2) (pp. 139–155).

Smith, N. (2010 [1984]). *Uneven Development. Mature, Capital and the Production of Space*. London and New York: Verso. 3rd edition.

Snodgrass, J. (1976). Clifford R. Shaw and Henry D. McKay: Chicago Criminologists. *The British Journal of Criminology* 16(1) (pp. 1–19).

Spergel, I.A. (1995). *The Youth Gang Problem*. New York: Oxford University Press.

Stanek, Ł. (2011). *Henri Lefebvre on Space. Architecture, Urban Research, and the Production of Theory*. Minneapolis: University of Minnesota Press.

Stanek, Ł. (2014). Architectural Project and the Agency of Representation: The Case of Nowa Huta, Poland. In: Stanek, Ł., Schmid, C. and Moravánszky, Á. (eds.). *Urban Revolution Now. Henri Lefebvre in Social Research and Architecture*. Surrey and Burlington: Ashgate (pp. 265–281).

Thompson, C.Y., Young, R.L. and Burns, R. (2000). Representing Gangs in the News: Media Construction of Criminal Gangs. *Sociological Spectrum* 20(4) (pp. 409–432).

Valasik, M. and Tita, G.E. (2018). Gangs and Space. In: Bruinsma, G.J.N. and Johnson, S.D. (eds.). *The Oxford Handbook of Environmental Criminology*. New York: Oxford University Press (pp. 839–867).

Vale, L.J. (2013). *Purging the Poorest. Public Housing and the Design Politics of Twice-Cleared Communities*. Chicago and London: University of Chicago Press.

Venkatesh, S.A. (1997). The Social Organization of Street Gang Activity in a Urban Ghetto. *American Journal of Sociology* 103(1) (pp. 82–111).

Venkatesh, S.A. (2008). *Gang Leader for a Day. A Rogue Sociologist Crosses the Line*. London: Penguin.

Wacquant, L. (2007). Territorial Stigmatization in the Age of Advanced Marginality. *Thesis Eleven* 91(1) (pp. 66–77).

Wilson, J. (2013). "The Devastating Conquest of the Lived by the Conceived": The Concept of Abstract Space in the Work of Henri Lefebvre. *Space & Culture* 16(3) (pp. 364–380).

Wilson, J. (2014). Puebla Panama: The Violence of Abstract Space. In: Stanek, Ł., Schmid, C. and Moravánszky, Á. (eds.). *Urban Revolution Now: Henri Lefebvre in Social Research and Architecture*. Farnham: Ashgate Publishing Limited (pp. 113–131).

Winton, A. (2014). Gangs in Global Perspective. *Environment and Urbanization* 26(2) (pp. 1–16).

Young, J. (2007). Globalization and the Social Exclusion. The Sociology of Vindictiveness and the Criminology of Transgression. In: Hagedorn, J. (ed.). *Gangs in the Global City*. Urbana and Chicago: University of Illinois Press (pp. 54–93).

Zilberg, E. (2011). *Spaces of Detention. The Making of a Transnational Gang Crisis Between Los Angeles and San Salvador*. Durham and London: Duke University Press.

Part II
Critical methodologies

Cultural criminology and gangs

Street elitism and politics in late modernity

Elke Van Hellemont and Michael Mills

Introduction

In the words of Roger Matthews, cultural criminology's early development infused an 'increasingly dry and lifeless' discipline with a much-needed 'breath of fresh air' (2014: 204). Although still provocative, it *now* represents an established feature of the intellectual landscape it originally sought to disrupt. In the period of its early development, cultural criminology (CC) emerged in the 1990s as a transatlantic synthesis of two main inspirations: the American interactionist tradition running through subcultural and labelling theories (e.g. Cohen, 1955; Becker, 1963), and the work of the UK Birmingham School (e.g. Hall and Jefferson, 1975; Ferrell and Sanders, 1995; on CC's other influences see Hayward, 2016). At the same time, its reinvention of these paradigms has also been propelled by critical *opposition* to other schools of thought – particularly 'the unimaginative and soul-crushing . . . character' of much so-called 'orthodox' (or administrative) criminology in the late 20th and early 21st century (Muzzatti, 2006: 63). All together, then, CC has come to resemble a sustained attempt to reinvigorate criminology's past, remake its present, and (so long as it does not run out of puff) *keep* breathing new life into the discipline's future development (see Hayward, 2016; Ilan, 2018).

Amidst its varied influences and antagonisms, CC's defining feature is its interest in the intersections between culture, rule-breaking, and rule-making. Consistent with its roots in subcultural theory, CC posits that the motive to commit crime rarely 'springs fully fledged out of certain material predicaments (e.g. poverty, unemployment) or biological characteristics (e.g. youth and masculinity)' (Young, 2011: 100). It emphasises that deviance is, instead, often energised by shared interpretations of, and responses to, social circumstances – meaning that crime can frequently be read as a 'cultural product' (Ferrell et al., 2015: 4). It should be no surprise, then, that much cultural criminological research is united around the ethnographic study of crime's situated meanings, symbolism, and emotions (see Ferrell, 1997). Concerning rule-*making*, and reflecting its overlaps with labelling theory, CC simultanously stresses that categorisations of deviant and criminal behaviour are similarly underpinned by contested cultural meanings, symbolic displays, and interpretations. Cultural criminologists' subject matter therefore includes crime's mediated representation and various campaigns designed to define both crime and its consequences (Ferrell et al., 2015: 3).

Extending beyond its 20th-century influences, CC has made numerous contributions to criminological theory and research. This chapter, though, will provide a brief overview of what these advancements offer to specific the field of gang studies. Among myriad other innovations, four of CC's contributions to its discipline are of particular interest to us here. First, CC's commitment to examining transgression as an emotive and expressive response to regulations, exclusions, and insecurities permeating everyday life in 'late modernity' (see Young, 2007). Building on Katz's (1988) work on the 'seductions' of crime, CC prioritises the 'foreground' of the criminal event. Here, it emphasises that, if we are to fully understand crime, we must appreciate the anger, humiliation, desire, joy, and expressive risk-taking (Lyng, 1990) that undergirds much offending. Second, related to this, is the examination of the so-called 'crime-consumerism nexus' (Hayward, 2004) that sits at the heart of much cultural criminology. Here, cultural criminologists explore the connections between subjectivities that run through both consumerist desires and transgression, also analysing the 'commodification' of crime and security and the use of crime-related imagery in commercial advertising (more on this later). Third, CC takes consideration of the powers and inequalities at play at different layers of society and at a *global* level (Hayward, 2016). Cultural criminologists thus train their attention toward the often locally contested politics of crime control, as well as the international proliferation of late modern neoliberalism that shapes worldwide crime industries and creates widespread social harms (Brotherton, 2004).

Fourth, and running throughout all of this, is CC's attempt to expand and update criminology's engagement with the media. Certainly, CC shares with media and cultural studies a focus on 'the image', in which it recognises the everyday late modern experience as being increasingly saturated with various visual media forms. Against this backdrop, CC proposes new ways of understanding how crime and its representation interact in this context (see Ferrell et al., 2015: 123–157), positing that an endless circulation of images and symbols in, throughout, and across multiple platforms blurs the lines between crime's reality and its mediated representation. Against this backdrop, criminologists must not merely comprehend how certain phenomena may be misrepresented and constructed but also how such representations impact reality 'on the ground' (and other subsequent *re*-representations).

Considering all of this, CC opens fertile ground for multidisciplinary collaboration in criminological work – and offers much that is of particular interest to the field of gang research. This chapter thus clarifies and outlines the central tenets of cultural criminological work around this area (Young and Brotherton, 2014). To do this, we will build on the themes introduced above and start by establishing the ways in which CC's social constructionist perspective on the ontology of gangs diverges from a 'mainstream' approach. Then, we explore its cultural geographic analysis of the gang's natural habitat: 'the streets'. Following this, we consider the complex ways in which representations of the gang are woven throughout numerous media (including consumer advertising). Finally, the chapter addresses the ways in which cultural criminological work situates gangs, and responses to them, in a political context – including a critique of state and economic power.

Chasing a ghost: a gang's ontology in cultural criminology

The beginnings of gang research and CC are notably united by common theoretical roots (the study of 'deviant' youth subcultures by the Birmingham School and US subcultural theory) *and* methodological approaches (ethnography). Many gang ethnographies and CC thus share a 'cultural lens', which (1) views the gang as a cultural practice instead of a criminal group and (2) provides thick descriptions of gang members' lives. The majority of contemporary gang ethnographies also include an analysis of 'the gang' in popular culture, and its impact on everyday reality in a manner that matches CC's interest in crime's mediated representation (Brotherton et al., 2008; Fraser, 2015; Ilan, 2015; Roks, 2017; Van Hellemont, 2018). To begin with, then, the overlap between cultural criminology's interests and the traditional focus of gang research creates a vast collection of existing ethnographies that could arguably be termed cultural criminological gang studies.

Perhaps unsurprisingly, though, there is substantial variation within cultural criminological perspectives on gangs. Like the field of gang research in general, CC's range of gang studies even remains divided over the very *existence* of gangs. Some cultural criminologists claim that, as a concept, 'the gang' should be abandoned altogether (Ilan, 2015), while others advocate a focused understanding of what constitutes a gang (Hallsworth, 2013). As a consequence, various cultural criminological works have understood gangs in divergent ways – be it as political fantasies (Hallsworth and Young, 2011), criminalised (Ilan, 2015) or criminal (Roks, 2016) manifestations of street culture, resistant street organisations (Brotherton, 2008), fluid identities (Garot, 2010), forms of edgework (Garot, 2015), urban legends (Fraser, 2015), and myths (Van Hellemont, 2015). While varied in their arguments, these studies share similar perspectives on gangs' ontology, and a distinct interest in the existential 'foreground' (and thus the phenomenological study) of gangs. In line with CC's social constructionism, cultural criminological studies are thus united in rejecting the view that gangs are objective autonomous entities in the world *out there* (Garot, 2007; Kontos and Brotherton, 2008). At the same time, these works likewise study gangs through an empirical perspective that embeds gang performances, narratives, and discourses in a structural analysis of a late modern capitalism (see Roks, 2016; Fraser, 2015; Ilan, 2015; Brotherton, 2008; Hallsworth, 2013).

Thus, in line with Conquergood's view, CC studies 'the gang' as *a process* as well as *an organisation* (Conquergood and Johnson, 2013). Such a perspective shifts the empirical focus of gang studies away from the conventional cataloguing of group characteristics (e.g. size) and behaviour (e.g. criminal conduct). Thus, while 'orthodox'/administrative and cultural criminologists might study the same 'gangs', their approaches to these groups diverge dramatically. Mainstream research studies gangs through the crime committed by group 'members' and the way group characteristics correlate with criminal behaviour. In this approach, a gang is inherently criminogenic: an organisation whose objective is the facilitation of crime and violence. For cultural criminologists, a gang gains a semi-autonomous existence through its collective cultural practices (Katz, 1988). CC thus acknowledges that meaning-making processes are essential to a gang's survival and crucial in understanding the gang member experience (whereas mainstream gang studies consider a gang's symbolic life largely irrelevant) (Weerman et al., 2009). Consistent with its interest in the phenomenology of transgression, CC also considers an understanding of the 'foreground' of that gang experience to be vital in comprehending gang formation in late modernity (Katz, 1988). In contrast to the administrative focus on crime, CC is thus equipped to expose the distinctive set of positive emotions and valorising experiences that gang life withholds for its members.

Inside the hall of mirrors: gangs as meaning and 'the streets' as a cultural space

Cultural criminologists' attempts to study *representations* of crime often involve an analysis of up-and-downwards meaning-making processes, as well as their impact on life and control 'on the ground'. In this dynamic, gangs are perhaps a quintessential example of what Ferrell (1999: 397) labels 'a bouncing image inside the hall of mirrors'. This hall is a place of 'circulating cultural fluidity that challenges any certain distinction between an event and its representation, a mediated image and its effects, a criminal moment and its ongoing construction within collective meaning' (Ferrell et al., 2015: 130). Within the hall of mirrors, cultural criminologists scrutinise mediated representations of gangs, combining a critical analyses of gang performances in the street (Garot and Katz, 2003) with gang representations in popular culture (Ilan, 2015), 'gang talk' in the media and politics (Hallsworth and Young, 2008), and even gang discourses in academia (Palmas, 2015).

Such analysis dictates that CC goes beyond the mainstream perspective on a gangs' habitat – 'the streets' – as public space (Weerman et al., 2009). In line with Conquergood's (1994) work, CC perceives 'the streets' as an 'embodied space' and 'interlaced network of intercommunal communication' (49–50), within which gangs are 'pre-eminently a communication phenomenon' (52). Conquergood's notion of 'cultural space' (1994) is resonant of the US symbolic interactionist approach and finds transcendent qualities in urban places across the entire planet (Brotherton et al., 2008; Hazen and Rodgers, 2014). Indeed, in ethnographies from inner-city black America (Anderson, 1999), to the post-industrial city of Glasgow (Fraser, 2015), 'la Rue' or 'les banlieus' in Paris (Mohammed and Mucchielli, 2016), South Africa's boroughs in Johannesburg (Glaser, 2000), and even online (Lane, 2018), gangs roam 'the streets'. For cultural criminologists, then, the notion of 'the streets' is one removed from any one urban space and notably represented (and indeed *re*-represented) throughout shared gang cultures and imaginaries.

Moreover, while gangs share public spaces with many other urban dwellers, their reality has, since the beginnings of gang studies (Thrasher, 1927: 3), been described as 'a world distinctly their own – one far removed from the humdrum existence of the average citizen'. For CC, gangs linger in the 'soft' or 'experiential city' (Hayward, 2004): 'a non-place' – in a geographical sense – whose presence is not observed but *felt* (Katz, 1988: 96, 139). Studying 'the streets' from a cultural criminological perspective thus goes beyond merely observing events as they occur in a designated space accessible to us all. It requires a deep criminological *verstehen* that enables a researcher to empathetically sense the space's covert meanings and the distinct emotions this extra layer of meaning generates. Thus, where subway stations might be emotionally numbing spaces for daily commuters, they are revealed by cultural criminology as important 'performative spaces' (Conquergood, 1994) in a gang scene, signalling turf and engendering intense emotions of fear, relief, and excitement (Van Hellemont, 2015).

As alluded to previously, as well as being interested in the ways gang culture constructs, represents, and experiences 'the streets', CC is likewise attentive to 'downward' constructions of gangs in mass media. Of course, interest in media representations of gangs is not new (see, for example, Thrasher, 1927: 102–116, 1949). However, in recent decades, a plethora of platforms have disrupted earlier representations of gangs and the arena of gang performance – and thus the way we ought to *understand* representations of the gang. As explored in the following section, this has complicated the dynamics between gangs and their representation, with CC emerging as a valuable perspective through which we may unpack the complex relationships between the frustrations, communications, representations, and re-representations that surround urban gangs in late modernity.

The digitalisation and commodification of gangs and 'the streets'

In the late modern 'mediascape' (Appadurai, 1996), cultural criminologists draw our attention to ways that gangs resonate throughout news broadcasts, Hollywood movies, advertising, the music industry, and various other media platforms (see Ferrell et al., 2015: 123–157). Even for many far removed from their physical environments, interaction with 'gangs' is thus part of the everyday experience. Meanwhile, for those immersed in the immediate reality of gangs, mediated representations pose something to be responded to, adapted to, or even *created*.

Within varied channels of mediated representation, CC helps us understand how the attractions of 'the gang' may be affected by highly mediated consumer culture. Whereas the Birmingham School celebrated consumption for its oppositional and resisting qualities (Hayward and Smith, 2017), CC assigns a more ambiguous criminogenic role to contemporary consumer culture. In particular, Hayward's 'crime-consumerism nexus' contends that consumerism appears to particularly cultivate 'forms of subjectivity based around desire, individualism, hedonism and impulsivity, which, in many instances, can find expression in transgressive and even criminal behaviour' (Hayward and Smith, 2017: 314). Within this, mass consumerism is argued to have altered the classic Mertonian experience of 'strain'. Much more than feeling deprived of the hierarchical status consumer objects provide, Hayward's (2004) concept of 'hyper-strain' refers to emotions (rage, sadness, anger) associated with the exclusion from more basic consumption-based identity work. Where the inability to consume means *an inability to construct identity*, exclusion from access to consumer items may be nothing less than 'an intense experience' of 'ultimate humiliation' (Young and Brotherton, 2014). Against this backdrop, we may understand the frustrations and desires of many economically excluded gang members as maintaining a relationship with the late modern mediascape through which consumer culture proliferates.

In a separate thread of enquiry, cultural criminologists also consider the ways in which crime has entered into consumer advertising, becoming a 'prime marketing tool for selling products in the youth market' by associating products with edgy identities (Ferrell et al., 2015). Here, there is much to be said about gangs. After all, gang styles and street culture have been identified by the global fashion industry as a tool to add 'street coolness' to affluent consumer identities (Ilan, 2015), while also being co-opted for seductive entertainment produced by multi-national music, video game, and film conglomerates (Metcalf, 2009). Many young consumers today may thus easily enjoy gang dress codes and fashion without 'being' a gang member (Brotherton and Kontos, 2008). Within such a context, gangs are a paradoxical phenomenon: feared by the wider population, they are also objects of consumerist desire.

Thus, while gangs may be regarded as delinquent, oppositional, or resistant subcultures, much of their meaning is complicated by the 'commodification of crime' and 'marketing of transgression' cultural criminologists analyze (Van Hellemont, 2018). Indeed, while the illicit meanings of gangs cements their value to industries selling 'street coolness', processes of commercialisation lead to an increased incorporation of gang representations into mainstream youth or urban culture – thus diluting gangs' criminal meaning while also *giving momentum to continuing criminalising processes* (Ilan, 2015). On this latter point, US gangsta rap, in which artists and record labels portray criminal 'black' street life to pique the imagination of the genre's white suburban audiences, amplifies the illicit meanings of 'the street'. Rap artists and executives become millionaires while marketing and sustaining 'the very discourses political and cultural leaders use to justify their war on crime' (McCann, 2017) – the matter of which we will return to in the next section.

In such dynamics, we witness the complex series of processes described by cultural criminologists as media 'loops' and 'spirals', in which 'the gritty, on-the-ground reality of crime, violence, and everyday criminal justice is dangerously confounded with its own representation' (Ferrell et al., 2015). In such a setting – where 'the street scripts the screen and the screen scripts the street' (Hayward and Young, 2004) – the weak ontological roots of gangs and 'the streets' feed into the a global mediascape and gang glocalising processes. Real-life gangs may be impacted by representation son screen – imitating the styles, discourses, aspirations, and activities of protagonists in popular entertainment – while control agents and the public simultaneously define gangs more on the basis of a media-led imagination (Ricoeur, 1979) than what happens 'on the ground'.

Meanwhile, the inter-connections between gangs and the media continue to evolve. The digital revolution, for instance, has hit the world with immense speed. Giving unprecedented prominence to network perspectives in analysing our contemporary society (Castells, 2011), it has recently prompted scholars to noted the eagerness of gang members to adopt the newest 'communication technologies' (Conquergood, 1994). Whereas in Conquergood's (1994) time, this involved the 'pager-beeper', more recently, the increased use of mobile devices and social media has given way to an 'online gangland' (Van Hellemont, 2012) and the rise of the 'digital street' (Lane, 2018). From 'Twitter Beefs' (Ilan, 2012), to gangs' YouTube performances (Mendoza-Denton, 2015), the controllability of the online environment and the vastness of the worldwide web have had a profound impact on gang communication and thus its constitutive meaning-making process (Urbanik and Haggerty, 2018). In mediating and facilitating their creations – their own *self-made* representations – on a global scale (Hagedorn, 2008), the 'digital streets' now make gang upward representations but 'a swipe away' for multiple audiences. Here, CC's ability to transcend conventional binaries and its sensual understanding of 'the streets' (as outlined earlier) allow gang researchers to surpass the on-and-offline divide experienced in mainstream studies and see 'the streets' as a 'fluid interstitial space' that will continue to be affected by 'online and offline environs' that are 'mutually constituted and evolve in tandem' (Urbanik and Haggerty, 2018: 1358).

The 'politics of meaning' and the 'lost gang'

CC's focus on the representation of crime has drawn criticism from critical strains of realist criminology, in which it has been claimed cultural criminologists run the risk of engaging in 'full-blown social constructionism' (Matthews, 2014: 204; see O'Brien, 2005; Hall and Winlow, 2007). From this view, CC fails to outline a structural analysis, or programme of social and political change, that could productively alter the reality it problematises. Such criticism, however, contrasts with (1) cultural criminologists' view of their perspective as 'an orientation designed especially for critical engagement with the politics of meaning surrounding crime and crime control' (Ferrell, 2013: 258) and (2) the criticisms of state and economic power that run throughout much cultural criminological scholarship. As Jeff Ferrell puts it, 'critical intervention' that can 'repair the damage done by officially imposed understandings' ultimately sits at the *centre* of the cultural criminological project (Ferrell, 2013). While there is no doubt room to expand to CC's political and transformative dimensions (see Matthews, 2014; Hayward, 2016), it *is* fundamentally concerned with identifying conditions that contribute to crime and its control so that they might be disrupted.

This ambition indeed runs throughout several strains of cultural criminological gang research. Among them are areas in which CC's deconstruction of particular gang representations *extends into critiques of those who mobilise them*. In many instances, CC's intent to decode constructions around gangs is ultimately undergirded by an intent to 'problematize their taken-for-granted acceptance and thereby expose their power' (Ferrell, 2013). Throughout history, 'gang talk' (Hallsworth and Young, 2008) on the part of authorities has been widely noted to construct a 'public enemy' and facilitate repressive crackdowns on neighbourhoods 'controlled' or 'plagued' by gangs in many countries – including France (Goaziou and Muchielli, 2013), the United Kingdom (Hallsworth and Lea, 2012), and Belgium (Demart, 2013). In CC, then, an analysis of 'gang talk' is not constructionism for constructionism's sake. Rather, it serves to uncover the ways political power affects the semantics around gangs and the ways these semantics guide responses to a range of social problems (Young and Brotherton, 2014). The importance of deconstructing gang representations is also further reaffirmed where representations of street/gang culture – in the format of music (Ilan, 2012), graffiti (Bloch, 2019), and fashion styles (Hayward and Yar, 2006; Hier et al., 2011) – have even become the focus of gang interventions by agencies of social control (as exemplified by the United Kingdom's recent crackdown on the genre of 'drill' music) (Pinkney and Robinson-Edwards, 2018; Fatsis, 2019).

Outside of national politics, CC's overlapping interest in representation and global capitalism also allows us to unpack the politics and consequences of 'gang talk' across various borders. Take, for instance, the criminalisation of migration flows across Central and Northern America – where such talk serves to justify zero-tolerance policing in the United States and many migrants' countries of origin (Zilberg, 2011). At the time of writing, US Republicans' strategic association of MS-13 with migrant 'caravans' moving through Central America and Mexico attests to the lingering resonance of 'gang talk' in anti-immigrant politics (see Fontes, 2018). Through cultural criminological work, we can trace how the political class's use of mediatised gang meanings thus feeds not only into in the domestic criminalisation of urban disorder and civil protest (Hallsworth and Brotherton, 2011; Goaziou and Muchielli, 2013), crackdowns on the young (Garot, 2007; Durán, 2018), and the working class in general (Brotherton 2008), but also dislocated migrant communities (Brotherton and Barrios, 2004) cast 'adrift' within the instabilities of global capitalism (see Ferrell, 2018).

Beyond this, as Ferrell has emphasised, CC's commitment to exploring the phenomenological foreground of crime is also reflective of a 'methodological politics' (2013: 266) that challenges 'a top-down 'hierarchy of credibility'' imposed by state agencies and administrative criminologists on discussions of crime and crime control. As addressed earlier, in contrast to 'orthodox' approaches to gang research, CC uses ethnography to draw out the often forgotten, or willingly ignored, emotional experience of gangs. This largely 'lost' perspective has seen cultural criminologists criticised as 'zoo-keepers of deviance' presenting 'a gilded invitation to readers to revel pruriently and voyeuristically in the exotica of' deviant subcultures (O'Brien, 2005: 610). Yet, at the same time, such ethnographies serve an important purpose. Bringing forth accounts of gang members sheds valuable light, for instance, on the ways mainstream perspectives overestimate the extent to which 'the gang' can be blamed for the criminal behaviour of those who represent it. Among their various insights, such studies have highlighted how studying the gang through crime glances over the many non- and even anti-criminal aspects of everyday gang life. Concerning gang violence, CC studies have thus shown that gang members fulfil a number of non-violent and non-criminal roles (Fraser and Atkinson, 2014), that many gang members go out of their way to avoid violence (Garot, 2010), and that fear of retaliation is often a much more important driver of conflict than the will to violence (Vandenbogaerde and Van Hellemont, 2016). Herein lies the potential to contest the dominant way the 'gang problem' and 'gang life' is understood and policed.

Likewise, cultural criminological ethnography tends to draw on its 'tales' of those under study to situate gangs in a wider political and structural context. While a great many gang ethnographies capture gangs' valorising emotions of, for instance, honour, power, and respect, CC regularly focus on going beyond description to explore how the gang can be an answer to emotional needs generated by broader social and economic conditions (see Young, 2003). This cultural criminological 'blend' of phenomenology with a 'sociological and structural analysis of late modern culture' builds toward a multilevel explanatory analysis that Hayward labels 'historically contextualised phenomenology' (2015: 3–4). In this vein, for example, Moran (2014) outlines how gangs' 'feelings of pride' counter the shame that arises as a 'by-product of marginalization' within 'bulimic' societies (Young, 1999) that celebrate achievement and consumption against a backdrop of structural exclusion. In isolation, then, 'micro' accounts of the gang experience may lack weight. However, within CC's commitment to situating them in a larger context, they serve to accurately locate the appeals of 'the gang' – and the nature of any subsequent 'gang problem' – in a socio-political context. Rather than being apolitical, then, CC's analysis of the gang phenomena is saturated with critical politics.

Conclusion

This chapter has outlined numerous ways in which the work of cultural criminologists overlaps with existing directions and themes in gang studies, contrasts with others, and has either opened up or broken new ground. CC's position on the ontology and performative nature of the gang has been outlined, as has its cultural perspective on 'the streets' that gangs inhabit across the world. CC's phenomenological approach to study of gang's foreground has also been introduced. So, too, has its attentiveness to the mutating meanings of the gang across the digitalising and globalising gang-media nexus, including the rampant commodification of the gang. Finally, we explored some of the ways cultural criminological work feeds into a critical contestation of 'gang talk', the 'gang problem', and their places in global late modern capitalism.

As we outlined at the start of the chapter, CC is broadly grounded in criminology's past and resembles a significant part of its present. What, then, might it contribute to gang research *going forward*? While we contend that many features of CC's existing contributions to this field will remain relevant for years to come, we will conclude by singling out one issue around which CC is positioned to be of particular future value: the growth of gang culture online. In less than a decade, the online life of gangs has moved to the top of the research agenda in the field of gang research. Within cultural approaches to studying gangs, more narrowly, it has particularly revived interest in studies of gangs as a performance (Conquergood, 1994). It seems here that CC will occupy a prominent place in the continued explication of this evolving dimension of 21st-century gang life. Its empirical tradition enables scholars to fully engage with the online and offline dynamics of the street world combining on-and-offline participant observation with media content analyses, delivering veritable 'multi-layered ethnographies.' Meanwhile, though critical criminology in general has always examined the social construction of crime and control, the labelling of groups, and the role of power and meaning, CC might be different in 'the degree of methodological militancy with which meaning is pursued' in this endeavour (Ferrell, 2013: 264). CC's approach is unique in its degree of immersion in the cultural processes that shape gangs and their control 'on the ground'. As gangs are, in CC's terms, images that bounce between an increasing number of mirrors, at a higher speed than ever before, and across a variety of global borders, this perspective looks set to sustain its increasingly important investigation into the movements of gang representations and their impacts on everyday gang realities.

References

Anderson, E. (1999). *Code of the Street: Decency, Violence, and the Moral Life of the Inner City*. New York, WW Norton.

Appadurai, A. (1996). *Modernity at Large: Cultural Dimensions of Globalization*. Minneapolis, University of Minnesota Press.

Becker, H. S. (1963). *Outsiders: Studies in the Sociology of Deviance*. Glencoe, IL, Free Press of Glencoe.

Bloch, S. (2019). "Broken Windows Ideology and the (Mis) Reading of Graffiti." *Critical Criminology*: 1–18.

Brotherton, D. (2004). "What Happened to the Pathological Gang? Notes from a Case Study of the Latin Kings and Queens in New York." *Cultural Criminology Unleashed*: 263–274.

Brotherton, D. (2008). "Beyond Social Reproduction: Bringing Resistance Back in Gang Theory." *Theoretical Criminology* **12**(1): 55–77.

Brotherton, D. and L. Barrios (2004). *The Almighty Latin King and Queen Nation: Street Politics and the Transformation of a New York City Gang*. New York, Columbia University Press.

Brotherton, D. and L. Kontos (2008). *Encyclopedia of Gangs*. New Haven, CT, Greenwood Press.

Brotherton, D., et al. (Eds.). (2008). *Globalizing the Streets: Cross-Cultural Perspectives on Youth, Social Control, and Empowerment*. New York, Columbia University Press.

Castells, M. (2011). *The Rise of the Network Society*. New York, Wiley.

Cohen, A. K. (1955). *Delinquent Boys: The Culture of the Gang*: Glencoe, IL, Free Press of Glencoe.

Conquergood, D. (1994). Homeboys and Hoods: Gang Communication and Cultural Space. In L. Frey (Ed.), *Group Communication in Context: Studies of Natural Groups*. Hillsdale, NJ, L. Erlbaum: 23–62.

Conquergood, D. and E. P. Johnson (2013). *Cultural Struggles: Performance, Ethnography, Praxis*. Michigan, University of Michigan Press.

Demart, S. (2013). "Riots in Matonge and . . . the Indifference of Public Authority?" *Brussels Studies* (68): 1–9.

Durán, R. J. (2018). *The Gang Paradox: Inequalities and Miracles on the U.S.-Mexico Border*. New York, Columbia University Press.

Fatsis, L. (2019). "Policing the Beats: The Criminalisation of UK Drill and Grime Music by the London Metropolitan Police." *The Sociological Review*. doi: 10.1177/0038026119842480.

Ferrell, J. (1997). "Criminological Verstehen: Inside the Immediacy of Crime." *Justice Quarterly* **14**(1): 3–23.

Ferrell, J. (1999). "Cultural Criminology." *Annual Review of Sociology* **25**(1): 395–418.

Ferrell, J. (2013). "Cultural Criminology and the Politics of Meaning." *Critical Criminology: An International Journal* **21**(3): 257–271.

Ferrell, J. (2018). *Drift: Illicit Mobility and Uncertain Knowledge*, Berkeley, CA, University of California Press.

Ferrell, J. and C. Sanders (1995). *Cultural Criminology*. Boston, Northeastern University Press.

Ferrell, J., et al. (2015). *Cultural Criminology: An Invitation*. London, Sage Publications.

Fontes, A. W. (2018). *Mortal Doubt: Transnational Gangs and Social Order in Guatemala City*, Oakland, CA, University of California Press.

Fraser, A. (2015). *Urban Legends: Gang Identity in the Post-Industrial City*. Oxford, Oxford University Press.

Fraser, A. and C. Atkinson (2014). "Making Up Gangs: Looping, Labelling and the New Politics of Intelligence-Led Policing." *Youth Justice* **14**(2): 154–170.

Garot, R. (2007). "'Where You From!': Gang Identity as Performance." *Journal of Contemporary Ethnography* **36**(1): 50–84.

Garot, R. (2010). *Who You Claim: Performing Gang Identity in School and on the Streets*. New York, NYU Press.

Garot, R. (2015). "Gang-Banging as Edgework." *Dialectical Anthropology* **39**(2): 151–163.

Garot, R. and J. Katz (2003). "Provocative Looks: Gang Appearance and Dress Codes in an Inner-City Alternative School." *Ethnography* **4**(3): 421–454.

Glaser, C. (2000). *Bo-tsotsi: The Youth Gangs of Soweto, 1935–1976*. James Currey.

Goaziou, V. L. E. and L. Muchielli (2013). *Quand les banlieues brûlent . . .: Retour sur les émeutes de novembre 2005*. Paris, La Découverte.

Hagedorn, J. (2008). *A World of Gangs: Armed Young Men and Gangsta Culture*. Minneapolis, University of Minnesota Press.

Hall, S., and T. Jefferson (1975). *Resistance Through Rituals: Youth Sub-Cultures in Post-War Britain*, Teaneck, NJ, Holmes & Meier Publishers, Incorporated.

Hall, S. and S. Winlow (2007). "Cultural Criminology and Primitive Accumulation." *Crime, Media, Culture* 3(1): 82–90.

Hallsworth, S. (2013). *The Gang and Beyond: Interpreting Violent Street Worlds*. London, Palgrave Macmillan.

Hallsworth, S. and D. Brotherton (2011). *Urban Disorder and Gangs: A Critique and a Warning*. London, Runnymede Trust.

Hallsworth, S. and J. Lea (2012). "Understanding the Riots." *Criminal Justice Matters* **87**(1): 30–31.

Hallsworth, S. and T. Young (2008). "Gang Talk and Gang Talkers: A Critique." *Crime, Media, Culture* **4**(2): 175–195.

Hallsworth, S. and T. Young (2011). Gangland Britain? Realities, Fantasies and Industry. In *Youth in Crisis?* London, Routledge: 195–209.

Hayward, K. (2004). *City Limits: Crime, Consumer Culture and the Urban Experience*. London, Glasshouse Press.

Hayward, K. (2016). "Cultural Criminology: Script Rewrites." *Theoretical Criminology* **20**(3): 297–321.

Hayward, K. and O. Smith (2017). "Crime and Consumer Culture." *The Oxford Handbook of Criminology*: 306–328.

Hayward, K. and J. Young (2004). "Cultural Criminology: Some Notes on the Script." *Theoretical Criminology* **8**(3): 259–273.

Hayward, K. and M. Yar (2006). "The 'chav' Phenomenon: Consumption, Media and the Construction of a New Underclass." *Crime, Media, Culture* **2**(1): 9–28.

Hayward, K. J. (2015). "Cultural Criminology: Script Rewrites." *Theoretical Criminology* **20**(3): 297–321.

Hazen, J. M. and D. Rodgers (2014). *Global Gangs: Street Violence Across the World*. Minneapolis, University of Minnesota Press.

Hier, S. P., Lett, D., Walby, K. and A. Smith (2011). "Beyond Folk Devil Resistance: Linking Moral Panic and Moral Regulation." *Criminology & Criminal Justice* **11**(3): 259–276.

Ilan, J. (2012). "'The Industry's the New Road': Crime, Commodification and Street Cultural Tropes in UK Urban Music." *Crime, Media, Culture* **8**(1): 39–55.

Ilan, J. (2015). *Understanding Street Culture: Poverty, Crime, Youth and Cool*. London, Palgrave Macmillan.

Ilan, J. (2018). "Cultural Criminology: The Time is Now." *Critical Criminology* **27**(1): 5–20.

Katz, J. (1988). *Seductions of Crime: Moral and Sensual Attractions in Doing Evil*. New York, Basic Books.

Kontos, L. and D. Brotherton (2008). *Encyclopedia of Gangs*. Greenwood Press.

Lane, J. (2018). *The Digital Street*. Oxford, Oxford University Press.

Lyng, S. (1990). "Edgework: A Social Psychological Analysis of Voluntary Risk Taking." *American Journal of Sociology* **95**: 851.

McCann, B. J. (2017). *The Mark of Criminality: Rhetoric, Race, and Gangsta Rap in the War-on-Crime Era*. Alabama, University of Alabama Press.

Matthews, R. (2014). "Cultural realism?" *Crime, Media, Culture* **10**(3): 203–214.

Mendoza-Denton, N. (2015). *Gangs on YouTube: Localism, Spanish/English Variation, and Music Fandom*. Los Angeles, Working Papers in Urban Language and Literacies.

Metcalf, J. (2009). "From Rage to Rap and Prison to Print." *European Journal of American Studies* 2.

Mohammed, M. and L. Mucchielli (2016). *Les bandes de jeunes: Des "blousons noirs "à nos jours*. Paris, La Découverte.

Moran, K. (2014). "Social Structure and Bonhomie: Emotions in the Youth Street Gang." *British Journal of Criminology* **55**(3): 556–577.

Muzzatti, S. L. (2006). "Cultural Criminology: A Decade and Counting of Criminological Chaos." *Advancing Critical Criminology: Theory and Application*: 63–81.

O'Brien, M. (2005). "What Is Cultural About Cultural Criminology?" *British Journal of Criminoly* **45**(5): 599–612.

Palmas, Q. L. (2015). "The Policies and Policing of Gangs in Contemporary Spain. An Ethnography of a Bureaucratic Field of the State." *Sociologica* **2**: 1–51.

Pinkney, C. and S. Robinson-Edwards (2018). "Gangs, Music and the Mediatisation of Crime: Expressions, Violations and Validations." *Safer Communities* **17**(2): 103–118.

Ricoeur, P. (1979). "The Function of Fiction in Shaping Reality." *Man and World* **12**(2): 123–141.

Roks, R. A. (2016). *In de h200d: een eigentijdse etnografie over de inbedding van criminaliteit en identiteit*. Rotterdam, Erasmus University of Rotterdam Press.

Roks, R. A. (2017). "In the 'h200d': Crips and the Intersection Between Space and Identity in the Netherlands." *Crime, Media, Culture*. doi: 10.1177/1741659017729002.

Thrasher, F. M. (1927). *The Gang: A Study of 1313 Gangs in Chicago*. Chicago, IL, University of Chicago Press.

Thrasher, F. M. (1949). "The Comics and Delinquency: Cause or Scapegoat." *Journal of Educational Sociology* **23**(4): 195–205.

Urbanik, M.-M. and K. D. Haggerty (2018). "'# It's Dangerous': The Online World of Drug Dealers, Rappers and the Street Code." *The British Journal of Criminology* **58**(6): 1343–1360.

Van Hellemont, E. (2012). "Gangland Online: Performing the Real Imaginary World of Gangstas and Ghettos in Brussels." *European Journal of Crime Criminal Law and Criminal Justice* **20**: 165.

Van Hellemont, E. (2015). *The Gang Game: The Myth and Seduction of Gangs.* Leuven, KU Leuven.

Van Hellemont, E. (2018). "Legalization by Commodification: The (Ir)relevance of Fashion Styles and Brands in Street Gangster Performance." *Outlaw Motorcycle Clubs and Street Gangs: Scheming Legality, Resisting Criminalization*: 45–68.

Van Hellemont, E. and J. A. Densley (2018). "Gang Glocalization: How the Global Mediascape Creates and Shapes Local Gang Realities." *Crime, Media, Culture.* doi: 10.1177/1741659018760107.

Vandenbogaerde, E. and E. Van Hellemont (2016). "Fear and Retaliation: Gang Violence in Brussels and Caracas." In C. L. Maxson and F.-A. Esbensen (Eds.), *Gang Transitions and Transformations in an International Context.* Cham, Springer International Publishing: 51–63.

Weerman, F. M., et al. (2009). *Eurogang Program Manual: Background, Development, and Use of the Eurogang Instruments in Multi-Site, Multi-Method Comparative Research.* Missouri, University of Missouri Saint Louis.

Young, J. (1999). *The Exclusive Society: Social Exclusion, Crime and Difference in Late Modernity*, New York: Sage Publications.

Young, J. (2003). "Merton with Energy, Katz with Structure: The Sociology of Vindictiveness and the Criminology of Transgression." *Theoretical Criminology*, **7**(3), 388–414.

Young, J. (2007). *The Vertigo of Late Modernity.* New York, Sage.

Young, J. (2011). *The Criminological Imagination.* Cambridge, Polity Press.

Young, J. and D. C. Brotherton (2014). "Cultural Criminology and Its Practices: A Dialog Between the Theorist and the Street Researcher." *Dialectical Anthropology* 38(2): 117–132.

Zilberg, E. (2011). *Space of Detention: The Making of a Transnational Gang Crisis Between Los Angeles and San Salvador.* Durham, Duke University Press.

9

Interviewing gang members
A note on research design

Kevin Moran

The sociologist's task would be much easier if, when faced with each relationship between an 'independent variable' and a 'dependent variable', he did not have to determine how the perception and appreciation of what is designated by the 'dependent variable' vary according to the classes determined by the 'independent variable'.

Bourdieu, Distinction (100)

Introduction

As gang researchers Decker and Pyrooz note, "Perhaps no substantive area in criminology is as closely tied to a methodology as gangs are to ethnography" (2011, 274). Indeed, the most prominent works in the field employ the methodology: Vigil (1994, 2002, 2007), Brotherton and Barrios (2004), Moore (1980), Jankowski (1991), and Conquergood (1993) as an emic, from-within, description and analysis of the life-world of the gang (see Decker and Pyrooz 2011 for a complete list ranging from the 1890 study by Riis to Garot's 2010 work in Southern California). There are several motivations for employing the ethnographic method when researching gangs. On one hand, it is often a practical necessity in researching this hard-to-access population unamenable to survey approaches, postal, telephone, internet-based, face-to-face, or otherwise. In an observation common to methodological sections in gang research, Sanchez-Jankowski's *Islands in the Street* notes that access to gang life only occurred after "the initial period of suspicion, mistrust, and testing" (1991, 13) which required evidence that he would not cooperate with the police and, in this particular study, having to physically fight with gang members in an assessment of his character akin to an initiation. The ethnographic method is also chosen as a means of studying gangs in by-passing ambient stereotypes of this highly stigmatized group which could potentially distort analysis by casting this group in a pathological light. Such motivations can be found in the methodological section of Brotherton and Barrios's *The Almighty Latin King and Queen Nation* (2004), whose work began during a high point in law enforcement suppression of gang activity in New York City during the mid- to late 1990s, which inevitably was accompanied by maligning depictions in the media as well as scholarly discourses focused on the "criminality" of this urban *bête noire* – to which the work is a conscious riposte. Most importantly, it is perhaps a sense that as a status of ontological import, that is, a way of being-in-the-world, being a gang member requires the fullness of description afforded by qualitative methodologies. This sentiment-cum-epistemology, shared by most ethnographers of the gang, is most clearly expressed in Venkatesh's work on gangs in Chicago's Taylor Homes housing project, where he notes:

> I liked the questions these [survey] researchers were asking, but compared to the vibrant life that I saw on the streets of Chicago, the discussion in these seminars seemed cold and distant, abstract and lifeless. I found it particularly curious that most researchers didn't seem interested in meeting *the people* they wrote about.
>
> *(2008, 3. Emphasis added)*

Despite the prominence of ethnography in research on gangs, there is little express theorization of how the method may be adjusted and applied to researching this population specifically. An exception in this respect is Brotherton's *Youth Street Gangs: A Critical Appraisal*, published in 2015. Arising from two decades of fieldwork with urban gangs, Brotherton's overall argument is that gang research needs to combine the work of 'thick description' developed by modernist traditions in ethnography with a cognizance of how the actors under study are located within wider power asymmetries which constitute their social context and which they reconstitute through praxis that is both unconsciously and self-consciously political (see Brotherton 2015). More specifically, Brotherton offers several methodological principles to guide research in this area. First is an injunction to ethnographic reflexivity in balancing the immersion required for naturalistic *verstehen* with the recognition that the researcher inevitably bears their social position into the research process, most reflected in a tendency to exoticize and pathologize the socially distant. As Brotherton notes, one remedy for the drift into othering is to establish relationships with the researched, contingent on an ethnographic honesty about the identity the researcher both as a means to trust-building (for nothing severs the rapport necessary for ethnographic work more than the researched sensing they are being objectified, i.e. reduced to models or theory frames) but also as a means of reflexively entering the researcher into the round of analysis. Furthermore, Brotherton asserts the empirical advantages of a collaborative approach to research design as well as in seeking the knowledge generated to be recursively beneficial to the group both in challenging wider misconceptions but also internally as a means of consciously reflecting on itself. Brotherton also suggests expanding the ethnographic repertoire through multiple data collection avenues: the sociolinguistics of the group, its location in physical and human geographic space, its visual culture as captured by photography, and the group as a locus of cultural production and performance – reflecting a holistic approach to studying multi-layered gang subculture and its relationship with the city environment.

Ethnography is indeed a family of methods – direct and sustained contact with social actors (Willis and Trondman 2000) – but one which is often also supplemented with field interviews as well as more organized forms of qualitative interview, so too surveys, and indeed, on occasion, statistical analyses. Most gang ethnographies incorporate some version of the qualitative interview, albeit supplementary to the data collected through observation. Resulting from this secondary status within qualitative gang research, even less theoretical energy has been given to interview methods in relation to studying gangs. Overall, in both sociology and criminology (qualitative researchers of offending most obviously straddle the two disciplines), there has been an ambient hesitancy to theorize the interview, as this chapter will argue, most evidently found in the subject of protocol design. This hesitancy in making subject-specific statements or recommendations for protocol design stems from a reluctance to introduce methodological artifacts to data but also a suspicion that this would be a dehumanizing imposition akin to the kind that standardization of survey instruments incurs. Overall – one cannot help feeling – this reluctance additionally derives from a humanist impulse (underlying much motivation to become a qualitative researcher) not to contain or contaminate the purity of the *vox populi* with the *vox dei* of the researcher. So too, an over-sensitivity to power dynamics between researcher and researched can result in reducing the researcher to simply a passive medium of the subject's uncontaminated expression.

Nonetheless, as will be argued subsequently, the repeat questioning that composes the qualitative interview has methodological advantages over other forms of qualitative inquiry in that it can be used to excavate the various layers that make up meaning-making central to qualitatively based research studies. An infrequently explored matter in methodological discussions of qualitative interviewing is how to expressly incorporate layered conceptions of subjectivity into research design. The suggestion here is that in this methodological vacuum, researchers do not respond idiosyncratically; rather, the result is often to introduce theoretical distortions which project the contemplative role of the scholar, that is, a vision of itself, onto the researched in the form of the thinking/reasoning subject as a working ontology. The suggestion that protocol design be more active and focused does run the risk of imputation itself, that is, the misrecognition of artifacts of the interview process as characteristics of interviewee subjectivity, but at least methodological deliberation on the matter affords more reflexive appreciation of such potential distortions than the methodologically tacit, that is, an unconsciously imputed ontology of the merely thinking subject. To this end, this chapter resists now-orthodox conceptions of the interview which stress interviewer passivity both as a methodological critique and in forwarding the necessity of theoretically informed active interviewing. To this analysis, this chapter, in a more practical sense, attempts to expand beyond the most often examined element in interview research – thoughts, reasoning, knowing – to emotions and the pre-reflexive in ways specific to researching the gang.

Interview methods textbooks

A survey of methodological sections contained in the major qualitatively based works on gang life reveals sections on qualitative interviewing which typically discuss, in a general sense, the rationale for conducting interviews with gang members, that is, to capture the subjective view of the actor and, in a specific sense, the matters of access, rapport building, and the sample information local to the study (Brotherton and Barrios 2004; Conquergood 1993; Jankowski 1991; Moore 1980; Vigil 1994, 2002, 2007). What is absent are mid-range methodological principles, that is, principles between general methodological choices and sample specific practicalities which might lead to useful and generalizable methodological practices. This absence is likely in part due to the tendency of publishers to limit – for the sake of readability – detailed technical discussions of methodological practices when publishing book-length studies. So, too, a general sense by researchers that qualitative interviews, like observational work, be approached as a craft which is developed and cultivated via practice over time, that is, the apprenticeship provided by actual research on the ground. In this sense, good research is more a refinement of sensibility which cannot be replaced by methodological training accomplished prior to, and hence abstracted from, research practice itself. The lack of direction at the mid-range often leaves novice gang researchers reliant on more general guides found in the methodological literature. Unfortunately, as this chapter will now argue, most methodological texts in the current moment are strongly influenced by post-structuralist theory refracted through the terminology of social scientific work not likely to provide much in the way of methodological guidance; indeed, this has theoretically relegated guidance in both the learning and application of interview methods to that of anachronism.

Prior to the 1970s, guides to qualitative interviewing stressed the technical aspects of the interview process. Central to this approach was for interviewers to design and conduct interviews in a manner which limited contamination of the data by either the biases of the researcher or the distortions arising from ill-planned or clumsily executed interviews. Latter-day qualitative interview handbooks, however, reflect the ongoing influence of post-structuralist theory on the social sciences and, overall, have seen stress on technical education in interview methods cede way to sprawling discussions of epistemology based on the socially situated nature of the interview interaction. Whilst a step forward in drawing attention to the social nature of the interview exchange, namely the effects differences in social position between the interviewer and interviewee may have on both what is disclosed and how it is disclosed by the interviewee, the remedy has sidelined technical proficiency as an artifact of now-outdated epistemological principles. A recurrent stress in methodological handbooks on interviewing is that former technically based approaches unconsciously framed the interviewee as a passive "vessel for answers" – with the interviewer shaping the interaction to maximize the flow of valid information (Holstein and Gubrium 1995; Weiss 1994). As an alternative, interviewers are encouraged to regard the interview as a site of meaning making, meaning which is co-produced during the interview as a communicative exchange. In this sense, the interviewee is viewed as actively and artfully constructing meaning rather than "passively" verbalizing their internal point of view as elicited by the "activity" of interviewer questioning: "Interview participants are as much constructive practitioners of experiential information as they are of repositories or excavators of experiential knowledge" (Gubrium et al. 2012).

The stress on the "activity" of the research subject as a constructor of knowledge probably reflects less a methodological concern but rather an ethic regarding the democratization of the research process. A subtext to recent critiques of conventional approaches is that emphasis on technically informed direction of the interview by a trained interviewer is disempowering to the interviewee, since it relies on privileging the interviewer as the active party in the exchange. In practical terms: "Empowerment can be gotten by lessening interview control in the interview" (Holstein and Gubrium 1995, 35), which then frees the interviewee to speak with their own voice. In real terms, it is, however, difficult to distinguish this concern with interviewee 'voice' from older concerns about maintaining the integrity of interviewee accounts, except perhaps that it is now expressed with the more high-sounding language of liberation rather than the terminology of empirical validity. More importantly, however, if meaning is constructed during an interview and is, moreover, contingently constructed, then the interview data is logically not even generalizable to the subject themselves, let alone in their function as a sample revealing a variant of more general social processes or perceptions. For if interview data is contingent and ephemeral, as is suggested – unreliable – then the entire enterprise is simply a collection of situationally developed meaning constructs unique to the encounter and hence of little scientific and social use.

Here an acceptance of variability gives way to a sentimentalism of the individualist uniqueness of each research subject, which is simultaneously coupled with a conception that equalizing the interview process serves as a form of compensation for unequal power relations at the group level. It is not clear, however, how granting agency to the interviewee accomplishes much more than recasting interviewer passivity as an ethical act – and hence the interviewer as an ethical actor. The empirical sacrifice is the introduction of a methodological hesitancy to the interview process and pedagogy by endorsing a vague sense of self-doubt as a research orientation. As Roulston recommends,

> Instruction in how to conduct interviews must therefore a) examine epistemological and theoretical assumptions concerning how interviews are used for research purposes, b) encourage interviewers to be reflective and consider reflexivity in the use of qualitative interviews, and c) provide opportunities for researchers to critically observe their practices and analyze interaction methodologically.
>
> *(2012, 61)*

The withdrawal of the interviewer, however, implies a voluntarist conception of the research subject, that is, that behavior stems primarily from conscious processes amenable to spontaneous expression by the interviewee. As will be argued in the following, one significant methodological advantage of the qualitative interview is its capacity to excavate the extra-cognitive components of perception and behavior. This is reliant, however, on conscious exploration and active guidance by the interviewer. As Katz notes, to assume that the experience of being is one which the actor consciously "constructs" is to risk saying:

> something misleading . . . that [the interview subject's] understanding is not sensed as constructed: it is already and naturally there. If our language does not allow us to see people dwelling naturally in the world, we will not be able to set up problems for explaining how different forms of tacit involvement develop.
>
> *(2001, 143)*

Suggested here is that methodological principles find ground beyond that of the craft-apprenticeship approach whereby skillful interviewing is iteratively developed via research experience and the laissez-faire of the post-structuralist interview process, in more explicit methodological practices consciously derivative of theoretically sophisticated understandings of human subjectivity.

Re-conceptualizing the interview

The utility of interview methods is in their capacity to reveal relatively consistent patterns in perception, thought, and feeling, which, based on sampling, have some claim on generalizability. Interviews are artificial in that they are outside ordinary spontaneously occurring talk. Although similar to conversation, they are more akin to therapeutic sessions in that the interviewee is not required to reciprocate attention normally found in conversational turn-taking, nor is the interviewer, except in a parsed and quasi-strategic manner, to mingle their own subjectivity into the exchange. With respect to artificiality, interviews are also *an extended reflection on what is normally simply done*, that is, require a degree of self-consciousness or introspection as a subject, a solicitation to render themselves as an object of contemplation. Interview subjects are asked to take a point of view on themselves, to verbalize or give an account of what may simply be taken for granted or of logics that manifest in doing rather than thinking. In this sense, interviews are akin to a native language speaker trying to give account of their speech in terms of grammatical rules, whose appropriateness is more sensed and intuited during the course of linguistic production than consciously selected. So the interview may be drawing into conscious awareness, that is, giving verbal articulation to, what Bourdieu notes is the fuzzy, practical logic immanent to being-in-the-world, whose logics reside in the sub-cognitive that is the extra-verbal. It is here that the interviewer must reflexively thread a balance between aiding such articulation and the transference or importation to them of logics foreign to those held by the interviewee.

The post-structuralist informed methodological approach outlined previously incorrectly assumes the self-knowledgeability of the research subject. By contrast, a phenomenological approach assumes that in our natural attitude as a being-in-the-world, we are to a large extent caught up in the flow of experience, with much of the logics of action lying beyond conscious awareness of the actor (see Giddens 1984 on practical consciousness). Indeed, natural being-in-the-world is that which is ontologically closest to us and hence for this reason, most invisible to us, as water is to a fish. A phenomenological analysis is thus one which raises to the level of consciousness the elements of being that, for most of the time, we simply are. The rendering into consciousness is accomplished via articulation or naming in language – that is, rigorously undertaken, close description. In this sense, phenomenological sociology is a form of naming to perceive and thus to know. Careful attention must be paid in light of this observation as descriptive categories, as linguistic categories, limit and define what can be perceived: "the eye cannot see, what the mind does not know". A major advantage that interview methods have over other qualitative approaches is that repeat questioning allows for the drawing into verbal articulation by the interviewee of the dynamics contained in their experience. However, this is contingent on the interviewer's own consciousness of these elements, which requires strong pre-theorization and careful selection of questions.

An active approach to interviewing was previously suggested by Merton in his (and others) development of the 'focused interview' (1946). The distinctive qualities of the focus interview are as follows:

1   Respondents are selected for having participated in a particular concrete social situation.
2   The hypothetically significant elements and patterns of this situation have been previously analyzed by the investigator. This content analysis has generated a set of hypotheses concerning the meaning and dynamics of this situation.
3   On the basis of this analysis, the interviewer fashions an interview guide setting forth the major areas of inquiry and the hypotheses which focus interview questioning on areas of pertinence.
4   Whilst the interview itself is focused on subjective experiences, pre-interview work allows for the testing of hypotheses generated by the content analysis and wider theory, whilst remaining open to unanticipated responses which suggest modifications in theory.

Important for the exploration of subjectivity here – which involves rendering into language that which normally operates below or outside of language – pre-theorization allows for the "flow of concrete and detailed reporting of responses", as Merton notes (541). More specifically, summary statements by interviewees indicate avenues of meaning need be given substance by skilled questioning by the interviewer. It is worth quoting Merton here at length:

> It is not enough for the interviewer to learn that the informant regarded a situation as "unpleasant" or "anxiety-provoking" or "stimulating" – summary judgements which . . . are consistent with a wide variety of interpretations. He must discover precisely what "unpleasant" denotes in this context; what further feelings were called into play; what personal associations came to mind, and the like. Failing such details, the data do not lend themselves to adequate analysis . . . a clear picture of the total response.
>
> *(541–542)*

We will now turn to how such a conception of the interview process might be applied to interviewing gang members.

Gang thematic considerations

The centrality of emotions

All methodologies operate with a tacit notion of human ontology. In conventional interview approaches, this is the thinking-acting subject and practically speaking translates to an emphasis on exploring reasons, attitudes, and perceptions with the assumption that behavior progresses based on the logic(s) of cognition to be revealed in the interview process. This orientation derives from the tenets of symbolic interactionism, where the crucial insight as to the interpretative basis for human action and interaction is nonetheless limited to the conscious, selecting, and discerning agent:

> the individual is designating different objects to himself, giving them meaning, judging their suitability to his action, and making decisions based on this judgement.
>
> *(Blumer 1986, 80)*

The ontology implicit here is suggestive of too much agency, the thinking-acting subject gives meaning to objects rather than that meaning may given to the subject – not just in the sense of socialization – but that the status or order of things may be given, if not primarily, through dynamics, beyond consciousness and hence the control of the agent. As Katz notes, emotion is of the subject, yet the subject is also subject to emotions and thus compelling forces that have logics independent of the thinking-willing element of our subjectivity. Rather, as posed here, the ontology to be assumed in designing interview schedules should be the "senti-pensante" (thinking-feeling) subject as recommended as an overall conception of the subject by Brotherton in his synthetical work *Youth Street Gangs: A Critical Appraisal* (2015), in that taxonomies of the mind are always affectively valenced. Indeed, it is likely as Damasio observed in his work *Descartes' Error: Emotion, Reason, and the Human Brain* (2005) that we are continuously emoting, even if in a low-level background sense, between periods of more specific emotional states. Emotions are heavily implicated in action: "cognitions of the themselves are incapable of triggering an instrumental process, unless they first generate an emotion that mobilizes a motivational state capable of recruiting action" (Zajonc 2000, 47).

Above all, gangs are associations and, in a Durkheimian sense, require cohering dynamics, as suggested here, the primary of which are emotions. It was noted as far back by Thrasher that gangs originated in playgroups, that is, friendship groups:

> On a warm summer evening children fairly swarm over areaways and sidewalks, vacant lots and rubbish dumps, streets and alleyways. The buzzing chatter and constant motion remind one of insects which hover in a swamp, yet ceaselessly dart hither and thither within the animated mass. . . . In this ubiquitous crowd of children, spontaneous play-groups are forming everywhere – gangs in embryo.
>
> *(2013, 26)*

Yet few gang researchers since Thrasher have taken seriously the fact that most gangs are friendship groups or expanded versions thereof – whose dynamics can be studied as a version of friendship groups (Pahl 2000). Indeed, most youth join gangs between 12 and 15 years of age, the same time peer groups reach maximum influence (Snyder and Sickmund 2006). This opacity is rendered on both conventional and critical orientations towards gangs, the former by the lexically scientific but distancing term 'peers' and the latter in the phenomenological impoverishment which occurs when relating gangs to macro-social dynamics such as opportunity structures and historical marginalization (see below how this, nonetheless highly salient features, might be accomplished ideographically). Socio-psychological cohering in friendship groups is the capacity for interactions to generate positive affect over time (Dishion et al. 1995; Paterson et al. 2000), which in turn is reliant on congruity of members. Conquergood has perhaps best depicted this feature of gangs, that gangs are, at base, bounded sets of non-instrumental interpersonal relations, and much of rich gang subculture, although declarative and "spectacular", is internally directed, an iteratively and stylistically practiced group bonding. This all points to a psychological explanation not often explored, that is, the pleasures of group belonging, one of the fundamental motivators of human life and practices of thought, action, and association (Baumeister and Leary 1995).

To give an example of the cognitivist bias in interview research on gangs, take Padilla's *The Gang as an American Enterprise* (1992), whereby the meaning chain pursued by the researcher skirts the emotional subtext, one which is not easily articulable but is suggested by the summary judgment 'being cool', as an interpersonal, and hence likely affective, matter:

FELIX: You told me you knew things about the gang when you were in eighth grade. What exactly were your thoughts of the gang at the time?

ELF: It was cool – a bunch of guys who cared for each other and who were having a good time.

FELIX: And that's what cool meant to you then?

ELF: Yeah, it said you were part of a bunch of guys who trusted each other. The gang was cool in that way. There are some guys who don't know how to act cool. They are always showing off . . .

FELIX Are you saying that other youngsters were not cool because they did not belong in the gang?

ELF: . . . but you see, the gang forces you to always be cool, together. You know, this is your homey, and brother, so take care of him. . . . Everybody is a friend and a brother. You treat people like a brother.

(1992, 67)

As noted already, one methodological advantage of interview methods over field interviews or observation more generally (in which the observer would disrupt the scene by prompting an introspection foreign to the naturalistic integrity of the moment) is the capacity to explore the extra-cognitive, granted by the agreement of the researched to participate in the unnatural, that is, artificial, act of subjecting themselves to repeat questioning. Here, Padilla's follow-on question to the introduction of the term 'cool' – defined in moral-emotional terms as 'care', is to request the research subject to repeat their definition of 'being cool'. Here the repetition is misrecognized as elaboration, but along lines of cognitive meaning or definition. An alternative line of questioning, to use a spatial metaphor, could be to 'go down', not across, and into the meaning of 'care':

- What you mean by guys caring for each other?
- How do guys show they care for each other?
- and finally, how does someone being cool with you make you feel?

Here we have the symbolic interactionist fallacy, a misunderstood causal pathway. The fallacy is that the subject (cognitively) defines a situation and then responds (see Blumer, previously). Rather it is the response to the situation that is then (cognitively) labeled. In questioning, the linguistic verbalization comes first, but *not socially or experientially*; it is being and feeling (caring and emoting towards this care) which is later categorized as 'being cool'. Of course, the advantage of an open-ended interview schedule is the capacity for in-the-moment inflexion towards a meaning vista opened by the respondent, but this turning in is little prepared by the underlying thinking-based ontology, the researcher not self-consciously pursuing meaning down into the affective, and thus these dynamics are dormant to the analysis.

As an additional alternative, we might take Katz's recommendation for interviews, which is to ask interviewees to give "a sequential narrative describing a recent instance of a certain kind of emotional experience, and they are pressed for details, especially about what happened at turning points in the events" (2001, 9) – with the aim of bringing the interviewer, and by extension the reader, "there", to the socially situated emotion dynamics. Katz employed this method in exploring the fundamental issues about the nature and contingencies of anger as it emerges and declines in social interaction (18). To this end, Katz drew upon 150 detailed reports based on qualitative interviews asking respondents to recount one or more experiences of becoming pissed off while driving around Los Angeles. Katz uses a three-fold strategy to closely examine the phenomena of anger, indeed, all emotions explored in his *How Emotions Work*. First, he probed for a close description of the distinctive features of the social interaction under examination as described by the respondent. Second, interview schedules examined the embodied qualities of the experience of anger, paying close attention to 'metamorphosis', the sensual transformation in which the body of the person becomes a new vehicle for experience. Third, he also sought to understand how becoming "pissed off" represented not only a negatively defined experience but a positive effort to construct new meaning for the situation. To summarize, Katz proposes that socially situated emotions contain an interactive interpretation, a specific experience of metamorphosis, and a transcendent narrative project. In following from Padilla noted previously, we might suggest a gang respondent:

1   Describe a recent instance of co-presence with another gang member or members, including both time of day and location, as well as when in the arc of the respondent's day this event occurred.
2   Explain thought and feeling prior to the instance, as well as the interactions which give rise to the sense the encounter is positive (being "cool" and having a "good time").
3   Reflect on how interactions like the one described give rise to perceptions of the gang over time. So, too, a speculation on what interactions could occur to render the instance a negative experience.

It is by the repeat questioning that interviews afford that researchers can arrive at a clear picture of the subject's total response in a given, theoretically relevant social situation including both cognitive and affective elements.

A final word on emotions may be added here. Despite attention to the more sensational behavior of gangs, most gang members spend most of their time simply 'hanging out'. Indeed, much of the positive affect generated through friendship interactions is through talk. Surprisingly little attention in gang literature has been given to what is the majority activity of gangs. Much of the attractions of gang membership must, logically, come from what occurs during these periods of low-activity co-presence. Hints of this come from Conquergood, drawing upon Carey's conception of communication as symbolic process by which reality is produced and maintained but, above all, dwelt in:

> Gang youth articulate their experience . . . through imagery of home and family. They name themselves *homeboys, homeys, homz*, and the term of intracommunal address is *bro*, short for brother. Bro is a term of endearment, communitas, an expression of "we feeling," asserting that you are an extension of myself . . . Powerfully significant, this term marks a move to trust and intimacy, and it is not used idly. I moved into Big Red mid-December 1987, but it was June 14, 1988, before anyone addressed me as "bro." It took 6 months of intensely participative fieldwork to earn the trust signified by this relational marker. However, once one has earned this epithet, it is used liberally to lend emotional warmth as well as stylistic rhythm to verbal exchanges: "Hey bro, anybody steal your bicycle, bro, you tell us, bro, we'll get it back for you, bro. Hey bro, we'll even get you a better one."
>
> *(1993, 40)*

Overall, the concept of phatic communication seems central here – communicative interaction more for the purpose of establishing an atmosphere or maintaining social contact than for exchanging information or ideas. As for the content of talk, researchers have suggested that central to the generation of positive affect among "deviant" groups is the recounting of past deviant activity – which is often recounted as a form of humor – but whose retelling may come to form the folklore of the group and, in this sense, provide members with a sense of location within the narrative construction of the group. For a non-gang example, take Jackson-Jacobs' ethnographic study of the world of informal fights in Tucson, Arizona. For the young males, 'brawling' reveals a double thrill. On the one hand, the thrill of self-discovery, namely of their 'strong character', through the demands and risks of the fight. On the other hand, the status attained through successful fighting, which is enjoyed primarily in the recounting and reliving of violent episodes in the folklore of the group. Indeed Jackson-Jacobs argues that a strong motivation for fighting is the enjoyment of reputation as communicated and perpetuated through stories; that is, it is not the 'background' that prompts fighting but *post-factum* reflection that provides the seductions of the 'scrap', upending any simple sense of positivist cause and effect.

Wider social context

The most consistent statistical regularity as concerns gangs is the association between gang formation and high concentrations of urban poverty. Cloward and Olin's formulation held that delinquent subcultures developed from the strain between the aspirations of the American Dream and the lack of opportunities for realizing these aspirations, as well as the availability of illegitimate opportunity structures in a given urban area (2013). More specifically, *conflict subcultures* – of which gangs are an extension – develop when both legitimate and illegitimate sources of status are limited, and, as an alternative, street hierarchies based on the use of violence (a resource for status enhancement democratically available to anyone) thus form. Whilst Cloward and Olin's theory has merits in understanding the displacement of status contest onto violent conflict, the theory has difficulty in accounting for the communitarian content of much of gang subculture. Suggested here is that whilst gang members are cognizant of their low status within wider social structures, it is the ambient parent culture, as translated into perceptual structures, that gives content to gang subculture (see also Hebdige 1981). Although often criticized in recent gang literature, Miller was correct about gang culture as an extension of ambient lower-class cultural milieu but wrong about the specific content, namely he overlooked the strong solidaristic current in working and lower-class cultural life that is transposed onto the gang, suggested here that this is largely one of culture, or is strongly culturally mediated, and thus an avenue for exploration in qualitative interviews.

It was Bourdieu who most clearly traced the relationship between class-experiences and internalized dispositions which serve to orient behavior in the present. According to Bourdieu, class socialization results in the internalization of dispositions and perceptual schema which pre-dispose, in a creative way, holders to generate certain forms of action. Such structures operate spontaneously and function below the level of consciousness as a world-sorting view. Several axes concern the differences between lower- and working-class cultures and the culture of the middle class (see also Willis 1977). On one hand, there is that between the pleasures of the present and a future-oriented asceticism as well as interpersonal warmth and familiarity and individual distinction and taste for novelty – where lower- and working-class cultures stress the former end of such spectra across a wide range of areas, one of which is food:

> The art of eating and drinking remains one of the few areas in which the working classes explicitly challenge the legitimate art of living: In the face of the new ethic of sobriety for the sake of slimness, which is most recognized at the highest levels of the social hierarchy, peasants and especially industrial workers maintain an ethic of convivial indulgence. A bon vivant is not just someone who enjoys eating and drinking; he is someone capable of enter-ing into the generous and familiar – that is, both simple and free – relationship that is en-couraged and symbolized by eating and drinking together, in a conviviality which sweeps away restraints and reticence. The hedonism which seizes day by day the rare satisfactions ('good times') of the immediate present is the only philosophy conceivable to those who 'have no future' and, in any case, little to expect from the future. It becomes clearer why the practical materialism which is particularly manifested in the relation to food is one of the most fundamental components of the popular ethos and even the popular ethic.
>
> *(Bourdieu 1984, 207)*

Bourdieu's point is that patterns of class consumption do not simply reflect differences in incomes, as those with similar incomes may display qualitatively different leisure patterns, rather class-specific orientations or dispositions. The contrast here, which was noted by Conquergood in his critique of "ontological individualism", is characteristic of much academic research on gangs. Arising from the disposition of the middle-class researcher is a stress on the individual as a locus of personhood which reifies in research procedure the individualism of the middle class projected onto research subjects of communally oriented cultural origins (1993) – of which gang members are the most culturally elaborate expressions.

Suggested here is that interview protocols take seriously the dispositional difference between class populations. This might be accomplished in several ways. First is to note that consciousness of class position, as well as racial and ethnic identity, develops as early as six or seven years old, according to the literature on identity development (see Phinney 1989). Furthermore, accord-ing to research on identity development, the sense of identity distinction develops through an awareness of contrast in a process of comparison. Although not a point developed in the lit-erature, it could be speculated that class-identity develops in part through a process of noticing differences in terms of physical dilapidation across neighborhoods. This point is made by Durán in his *Gang Life in Two Cities* in an extract from his field notes (2013):

> In the white neighborhoods there is a quiet serenity that allows residents to stay behind closed doors . . . in a spectacle of space that highlights an aura of elitism. I feel very out of place walking in these white neighborhoods. The birds chirp as I think to myself that the

differences between the barrio and suburbs easily explain whether an individual will be required to make the decision of whether to join a gang.

(119)

Self-definition here is found in terms of contrast with middle-class affluence. In psychological terms, this status placement is the problem, in Albert Cohen's sense, to be dealt with or solved. Lower-class youths, it seems, accomplish this via a form of ethical alchemy. A sense of this can be found in MacLeod's *Ain't No Making It*, in posing a communitarian ethos in contrast to individualist self-interest:

SLICK: What it is, it's a brotherhood down here. We're all fucking brothers . . . we're always here for each other . . . we're not like them up there – rich little boys from the suburbs or whatever. There's a line there. On this side of the line we don't fuck with each other; we're tight.

(1995, 34)

The point here is that the relational basis for identity is not often explicitly explored in gang research; as a result, gang subculture is viewed as being largely self contained rather than existing in dialogue with the wider culture, as suggested by Matza more generally (see 1964). Suggested here is that the sense of gang identity as a resistance (most explicitly explored in Brotherton and Barrios 2004), in large part, stems from more protean defiance of status placement that weaves its way across working-class cultures – challenges to the art of living – stressing the familiar, the convivial, the generous, which finds highest expression in the *espirit de corps* of the gang. Indeed, it is the stress on loyalty – and its moral properties – which in part give substance to the gang as a form of righteous self-assertion, reflecting and revising the communal culture (i.e. the parent culture) specific to their class.

There is an additional sense by which the contrast between class cultures is reflected in the gang, that is, as engendering a moral cynicism toward conventional norms. There is an anti-normative element to gang activity – not simply in the sense of defying status placement, which is common to most working- or lower-class communities – but in the association with gang membership and offending. Such activities reflect a distance from conventional norms prohibiting fighting, dropping out of school, drug-dealing, and so on, an interpretative gloss which renders null these norms as legitimate, morally compelling standards of behavior. What is suggested here is that observations of inequality, as well as racial discrimination, engender a sense of injustice which translates a perception of wider social groups as morally suspect or underhand in that beneath claims of moral conventionality by higher-status groups lies a hypocritical acceptance of the advantages of prejudice and favoritism. It is the betrayal of moral self-presentation by its easy existence with forms of inequality and prejudice (i.e. reflections of self-interest manifested in resource inequities) that renders conventional norms a dismissible hypocrisy – a world view that frees the gang member, in a neutralizing sense, to engage in delinquent behavior with it, thereby challenging a moral sense of self. Arguably, these moral logics are more sensed and enacted than they are the result of rational deduction. In effect, they are powerful perceptual schema central to the relationship of gang membership to inequality but also delinquency and, occasionally, resistance. These logics should be explored intentionally in interview design and implementation.

The discursive

As has been suggested throughout this chapter, most qualitative interview work is limited to cognition. Indeed, there is much to the understanding of social phenomena that necessitates an examination of intended, deliberate, conscious thought. This, however, remains the default level in qualitative interviewing and does not need elaboration here. An additional comment on this subject, however, might be made here. As best expressed by Goffman, actors in a social encounter continually self-monitor and self-adjust to maintain a satisfactory presentation of self. Dramaturgically, actors engage in selective self-disclosure, maintaining some information about themselves in the front-stage, whilst concealing some in the back-stage. We must add to the roster of artificiality of the research process not only the matter of dialogue of some intimacy with a stranger but, and this is especially true of gang research, the awareness of differences in social hierarchies. This is true of class or racial differences between the interviewer and the interviewee, but this is never entirely erased, for inherent in the research encounter is the social fact that the interviewer occupies a relatively privileged role as someone who has the material means to suspend a practical apprehension of the world in order that this world be rendered an object of contemplation rather than action. On the other hand, the interviewee may also reflect on the interview process and may consciously select what is disclosed in order to construct a certain presentation of self. There is much talk in the literature but little that is concrete in terms of social asymmetry effects in interview encounters, but it might be said that an encounter with conventional or 'straight' society may yield exculpatory work, resulting in interview responses having more a character of rationalizations, a product of the dynamics of the encounter, not the true logics of thought and action.

To further explain, there is a selection effect in terms of who comes to be a qualitative researcher. That is to say that the majority of interview studies involve "studying down", typically with the motivation of humanizing the socially stigmatized – a confounding of research empathy, in part, with sympathy for the disadvantaged, which includes gangs. The moral exculpatory motive has sometimes the tendency to seep into the interview process in the following way. Often interviewers, in collaboration with interview subjects, downplay or avoid altogether socially disapproved-of aspects of the interviewee – their thought and behavior. An example of this can be found in Padilla's interview study when interviewing gang members on their conduct in school:

FELIX: What was your "acting up" like?
RAFAEL: We were bad. We didn't listen. We used to fight all the time.
FELIX: What were you hoping to get from acting up?
RAFAEL: Well, it was no big deal. It was my way of getting even. You know, teachers were saying and doing all this nasty shit, and I wasn't going to put up with this anymore . . . just because you're Puerto Rican or Latino, they treat you like dirt.

Padilla's analysis of the disruptive behavior of his respondent is to take at face value the rationalization of this behavior as a form of resistance to generalized negative attitude by teachers towards Puerto Rican culture and behavior. Denied, as Padilla claims, conventional means of carrying out the routines of everyday life, the affectionately termed "youngsters" develop an oppositional system of strategic activities. Suggested here is that suppressed in this analysis are two elements: first is the potential legitimacy of teacher reactions to disruptive, even dangerous behavior. Instead, "discipline" is transmuted as prejudice. Second is the hedonic element of "acting out", which is transmuted as a compelled form "resistance" rather than a harmful response to the boredom and restrictions experienced by those with little investment in education. The issue here is that researcher has a double incentive to suppress unflattering elements of gang member behavior in collaboration with the research subject both in terms of portraying gang members, as members of marginalized and maligned communities, in a sympathetic light but also in terms of maintaining rapport with the research subject during the interview. The point here is that interview data may at points confuse the subject's presentation of self with an objective account of social processes.

The challenges of rapport maintenance make it difficult to go against co-established working definitions of the situation. In practical methodological terms, interviewers need to develop a means for challenging interviewee accounts without sabotaging the sense of trust that the method requires (indeed all qualitative methods) or risk obscuring social processes with a moralizing gloss. It is difficult to give express instructions on how this might be accomplished during an interview. Rather, this point about interviewer naïveté is raised so as to be included in the roster of reflexive mechanisms, one apropos to researching "deviant" populations but which must be tailored to the question sequences in a given study.

End discussion

In sum, this chapter has argued against an intellectual trend toward reducing the authority of the interviewer, which, in large part, reflects a drift towards methodological communism in interview research. Rather, it has suggested that more empirically profitable forms of interview require not only a rigorous pre-theorization but incorporation of theory into interview protocol design and a more active approach to interview questioning. This more active approach capitalizes on the opportunity the interview encounter provides (i.e. repeat questioning allowing for follow-up and clarification) to explore meaning-making and its logics beyond conscious thought and to go "down" into the emotions and the sub-cognitive whose dynamics are more sensed and enacted than deliberated. It only thereby that phenomenologically complete rendering of the social actor and the logics of social action – cognition, sub-cognition, and emotion – can be achieved. With respect to gangs, the framing topic of this chapter, argued here is for interview design and implementation to self-consciously explore – with forms of follow-up questioning – emotions, the submerged logics of class culture, that is, that which "goes without saying" for social actors, as well as a reflexive stance towards the capacity for conscious thought to serve as *post-hoc* rationalizations for socially disproved behavior – expressed in the interview process as a co-produced moral gloss on gang activity. The sequence of sections in this chapter has been deliberately reversed, leaving the most common point of departure, conscious thought, to last. Theoretically grounded interview design as well as theoretically informed active questioning are arguably the means by which a cumulative science of the gang may be accomplished, going against a trend which downplays hypothesis testing and replication and which stresses interviewer passivity and research originality. I argue that this more accepted praxis of gang member interviewing ultimately results in a cacophony of literature on the gang, foreign to the logics of the phenomenon, as, if it were all so complicated, then living and acting would be an impossibility.

References

Baumeister, Roy F., and Mark R. Leary. 1995. "The Need to Belong: Desire for Interpersonal Attachments as a Fundamental Human Motivation." *Psychological Bulletin* 117 (3): 497–529.

Blumer, Herbert. 1986. *Symbolic Interactionism: Perspective and Method*. Berkeley: University of California Press.

Bourdieu, Pierre. 1984. *Distinction: A Social Critique of the Judgement of Taste*. Cambridge: Harvard University Press.

Brotherton, David C. 2015. *Youth Street Gangs: A Critical Appraisal*. 1st edition. Abingdon, Oxon and New York, NY: Routledge.

Brotherton, David C., and Luis Barrios. 2004. *The Almighty Latin King and Queen Nation: Street Politics and the Transformation of a New York City Gang*. New York: Columbia University Press.

Cloward, Richard A., and L. E. Ohlin. 2013. *Delinquency and Opportunity: A Study of Delinquent Gangs*. London: Routledge.

Conquergood, Lorne Dwight. 1993. *Homeboys and Hoods: Gang Communication and Cultural Space*. Evanston: Center for Urban Affairs and Policy Research, Northwestern University.

Damasio, Antonio. 2005. *Descartes' Error: Emotion, Reason, and the Human Brain*. Reprint edition. London: Penguin Books.

Decker, Scott H., and David C. Pyrooz. 2011. "Contemporary Gang Ethnographies." *Handbook of Criminological Theory*. https://asu.pure.elsevier.com/en/publications/contemporary-gang-ethnographies.

Dishion, Thomas J., Deborah Capaldi, Kathleen M. Spracklen, and Fuzhong Li. 1995. "Peer Ecology of Male Adolescent Drug Use." *Development and Psychopathology* 7 (4): 803–824.

Durán, Robert. 2013. *Gang Life in Two Cities: An Insider's Journey*. New York: Columbia University Press.

Giddens, Anthony. 1984. *The Constitution of Society*. Cambridge: Polity Press.

Gubrium, Jaber F., James A. Holstein, Amir B. Marvasti, and Karyn D. McKinney. 2012. *The SAGE Handbook of Interview Research: The Complexity of the Craft*. Los Angeles: SAGE Publications.

Hebdige, Dick. 1981. *Subculture: The Meaning of Style*. London: Routledge.

Holstein, James A., and Jaber F. Gubrium. 1995. *The Active Interview*. 1st edition. Thousand Oaks: SAGE Publications, Inc.

Katz, Jack. 2001. *How Emotions Work*. Chicago: University Of Chicago Press.

Matza, David. 1964. *Delinquency and Drift*. New York: Wiley.

MacLeod, Jay. 1995. *Ain't No Making It: Aspirations & Attainment in a Low-Income Neighborhood*. Colorado: Westview Press.

Merton, Robert K., and Patricia L. Kendall. 1946. "The Focused Interview." *American Journal of Sociology* 51 (6): 541–557.

Moore, Joan. 1980. *Homeboys: Gangs, Drugs, and the Prison in the Barrios of Los Angeles*. Philadelphia: Temple University Press.

Padilla, Felix M. 1992. *The Gang as an American Enterprise*. New Brunswick, NJ: Rutgers University Press.

Pahl, Ray. 2000. *On Friendship*. 1st edition. Cambridge: Polity Press.

Patterson, Gerald R., Thomas J. Dishion, and Karen Yoerger. 2000. "Adolescent Growth in New Forms of Problem Behavior: Macro- and Micro-Peer Dynamics." *Prevention Science* 1 (1): 3–13.

Phinney, Jean S. 1989. "Stages of Ethnic Identity Development in Minority Group Adolescents." *The Journal of Early Adolescence* 9 (1–2): 34–49.

Riis, J. *How the Other Half Lives*. (2004, orig. 1890). New York: Barnes and Noble.

Roulston, Kathryn. 2012. "The Pedagogy of Interviewing." In *The SAGE Handbook of Interview Research: The Complexity of the Craft*. Jaber F. Gubirum, James A. Holstein, Amir B. Marvasti, and Karyn D. McKinney (eds). Los Angeles: SAGE Publications.

Sánchez-Jankowski, Martín. 1991. *Islands in the Street: Gangs and American Urban Society*. Berkeley: University of California Press.

Snyder, Howard N. and Melissa Sickmund. 2006. "Juvenile Offenders and Victims: 2006 National Report: Report Highlights." Accessed March 3, 2019. www.ncjj.org/Publication/Juvenile-Offenders-and-Victims-2006-National-Report-Report-Highlights.aspx.

Thrasher, Frederic Milton. 2013. *The Gang: A Study of 1,313 Gangs in Chicago*. Abridged edition. Chicago, IL: University of Chicago Press.

Venkatesh, Sudhir. 2008. *Gang Leader for a Day: A Rogue Sociologist Takes to the Streets*. Reprint edition. New York: Penguin Books Ltd.

Vigil, James Diego. 1994. *Barrio Gangs: Street Life and Identity in Southern California*. Austin: University of Texas Press.

———. 2002. *A Rainbow of Gangs: Street Cultures in the Mega-City*. 1st edition. Austin: University of Texas Press.

———. 2007. *The Projects: Gang and Non-Gang Families in East Los Angeles*. Austin: University of Texas Press.

Weiss, Robert S. 1994. *Learning from Strangers: The Art and Method of Qualitative Interview Studies*. New York: Free Press.

Willis, Paul. 1977. *Learning to Labour*. Farnborough: Saxon House.

Willis, Paul, and Mats Trondman. 2000. "Manifesto for Ethnography." *Ethnography* 1 (1): 5–16.

Zajonc, Robert B. 2000. "Feeling and Thinking: Closing the Debate Over the Independence of Affect." In *Feeling and Thinking: The Role of Affect in Social Cognition*. Joseph Forgas (ed). Cambridge: Cambridge University Press.

10

New standards for social practice ethics?

Researching processes of gang exit with former gang members

Line Lerche Mørck

Introduction

> The dual focus of social work ethical obligations – ensuring individual rights and freedoms and advocating for social justice and social change – requires consideration of ethical questions for research that transcends questions raised in traditional ethics committees.
>
> (Antle and Regehr, 2003, p. 142)

Discussions of research ethics are mostly focused on the codes prescribing how we as researchers should engage in research practice. Antle and Regehr (2003), quoted previously, discuss the main principles of research ethics and how they are related to prescribed codes of informed consent, anonymization and confidentiality. However, they also help us move beyond traditional discussions of ethics by arguing that social work research should combine traditional ethical guidelines with further considerations, such as whether the research will benefit the group being studied and the broader risks resulting from the group's participation in research and other contexts. They argue the need for a meta-ethical perspective, with an overarching focus on both individual and collective interests, and call for ethical reflections on:

> how to balance highly valued ethical principles that are individually focused, such as self-determination and nonmalfeasance (the obligation to do no harm), with equally important values that have a collective focus, such as justice and beneficence (the obligation to bring about good).
>
> *(Antle and Regehr, 2003, p. 136)*

The same authors (Antle and Regehr, 2003, p. 142) point to traditions of advocacy, participatory (Park, Brydon-Miller, Hall, and Jackson, 1993) and feminist research (Wise, 1987) that combine the social justice principle of representing the interests of oppressed people through our grounded scholarship. Such traditions seek to legitimize the experiences of those who have historically gone unheard or whose experiences have been misunderstood or misrepresented. The goal is to put research capabilities in the hands of deprived and disenfranchised people so they can transform their lives for themselves. In this chapter, I advocate for research methodologies that empower participants, recognize them as experts in their own lives and include them in the research endeavor.

Other researchers within social science or social work have challenged the dominant institutional perspectives on research ethics, arguing that a *situated* point of view is also needed:

> While institutional and professional codes prescribe ethical practice in research, situated ethics recognises that ethical practice is not external to contexts, but emerges within them.
> *(D'Cruz and Gillingham, 2017, p. 437)*

Searching leading social science databases,[1] I only found a few studies exploring or applying such a situated approach to research ethics. One interesting study about situated ethics is D'Cruz and Gillingham (2017), who apply and at the same time reflect on situated research ethics in complex, conflictual and contradictory research practice situations. Except for Deuchar (2015), which I unfold subsequently, I did not find any studies that reflected on research dilemmas as situated ethics within gang (exit) research.[2] In this chapter, in which I reflect on my social practice research with former gang members as co-researchers, and in line with D'Cruz and Gillingham (2017), I will illustrate how to engage in situated researcher reflexivity in relation to specific dilemmas in ongoing research practice:

> Reflexivity is therefore an ongoing process, engaged in throughout the research process. . . . It may manifest as an internal dialogue by the individual, and, as Doel et al. (2010) suggest, through regular and ad-hoc discussions of dilemmas as a form of "ethical engagement". Furthermore, situated ethics through reflexivity engages the researcher in "ethical self-regulation" whereby "conventions [are called] into question" (Lovelock and Powell, 2004, p. 217).
> *(D'Cruz and Gillingham, 2017, p. 438)*

Few gang researchers openly reflect on the many challenges of living up to institutionalized ethical principles. Deuchar, for example, discusses how to "balance between being transparent about . . . research while also accepting the need for subtle forms of deception" (2015, p. 73). As part of the first case, I will touch upon the dilemmas Deuchar (2015) highlights in relation to informed content. There is often no straightforward solution to such dilemmas; instead, we have to reflect, act and reflect again on the practical consequences of our research. This point also applies to principles of anonymization. Taylor (2015), who studied young homeless people over many years, discusses the difficulties in anonymizing a person to such an extent that it is impossible to discover the person's identity. She also points to the fact that some participants might not even want to be anonymized. This is also a dilemma I consider in reference to longitudinal studies of former gang members' identity formation.

As such, this chapter is positioned within ongoing discussions regarding the need for a more contextualized and situated approach to research ethics by discussing research on "gang exit" and "formers" (i.e., former gang members). This focus contrasts with most gang exit research that mainly employs traditional institutionalized standards when discussing research methodology. My goal in this chapter is to encourage the development of practice-oriented ethical standards, which I refer to as 'social practice ethics,' basing my arguments on the ethical dilemmas and action possibilities I have encountered in social practice research conducted with formers as co-researchers, who, during the research process, change in terms of who they are and how they understand and represent themselves in and across contexts.

Social practice ethics are examined through posing a number of questions: What are the dilemmas and possibilities when working with institutional research ethics? How may we move beyond these dilemmas by articulating new situated standards of social practice ethics? How can we produce emancipatory research that expands action possibilities in practice? How can we as researchers support the humanization of formers in a society with severe conflicts? How may common engagement in practice and research contribute to concrete mo(ve)ments[3] beyond marginalization and risk?

In the following, I discuss critical psychological practice research and illustrate how participants are invited to become co-researchers. In this, I show how practice research addresses humanization and how it is an intrinsic aspect of the standards of social practice ethics by including participants as co-researchers, recognizing their contributions and thereby creating movements beyond demonization and alienation. I also discuss specific cases of ethical dilemmas, such as: What can we do when institutionalized ethical standards, such as anonymity, are not possible? And how do we assess risks in a conflictual and rapidly changing environment? This is an especially pertinent question in the aftermath of the recent killing of Nabil, one of my former co-researchers. Finally, I consider how we as critical social (gang) researchers use our reflections on ethical dilemmas and action possibilities in an ongoing effort to (re)formulate situated standards for social practice ethics in and across different social research contexts.

Practice research – negotiations of common interests with co-researchers

In my practice research on gang exit, a primary goal is to understand (dis)engagement processes from formers' first-person perspectives and produce knowledge that contributes to practice development (Mørck, 2000). Within critical psychological practice research, we use the terms 'subjects' and 'co-researchers' when writing about the people we do research with and for:

> the "subjects" whose actions we wish to understand must be "subjects" in the full human sense of that word: that is, not only "objects" and "individuals", but also recognized and realized in our research practices as "agents" and self-reflecting centers of intention and consciousness, as persons with agency. In a word (or two), they must be recruited as participants, as co-researchers. Empirical research, then, (for, with and about humans) is necessarily a kind of cooperative introspection in a flow of action. It is we who investigate how each of us live and act, for what reasons, under which conditions etc., and we have practical reasons for doing so."
>
> *(Nissen, 2000, p. 153)*

Such practice research is conducted in so-called 'joint ventures', organized around a common interest in collaboration and an ongoing dialogue with our co-researchers (Mørck et al., 2013; Nissen, 2012). The process of negotiating meanings and common interests varies from project to project, but in all cases, ongoing dialogue is a way to produce subject-subject relations and thereby trust:

> I have gained a lot of trust in you through this collaboration. It is also the most important thing; I want to praise the way you have done it. Every time, you enter into a dialogue and share it [research, PowerPoints, analysis] – it means a lot. It is difficult, because we are at a

point in time when it is difficult to rely on things like interviews, and the people who do journalism work and research, it is very difficult. I have also been contacted by journalists who want to write books etc., who I have rejected.

(X)

In my joint research venture with co-researcher X, the common interest was to challenge and nuance a highly stigmatized discourse about former gang members becoming Muslims, often equated with risks of radicalization (Christensen and Mørck, 2017; Mørck and Khawaja, in press). In another joint venture, with a co-researcher I call Peter, the common interest concerned the creation of knowledge regarding concrete gang-exit processes and understanding the various possibilities and limitations of exit programs and their impact on participants. A further goal was to contribute to the development of alternative approaches and methodologies; the Life Conduct List is one example (Mørck and Celosse-Andersen, 2016). The mo(ve)ment methodology is another example of such co-production (Mørck and Celosse-Andersen, 2019).

In relation to a third co-researcher, whom I call Nabil, we shared a common interest in establishing a legitimate public space where formers could share their experiences and perspectives on how to improve gang prevention and we both engaged publicly in critical reflections on the Danish government's crime and gang prevention policies. As part of his study to become a pedagogue and social worker, Nabil also interviewed me about the consequences of the latest preventive policy. As was the case in my collaboration with Peter, we exchanged and shared the interview data for use in different projects by both parties.

Participants' backgrounds and different engagements over time

Each of the three co-researchers represented in the cases has a unique life trajectory and exit process. However, at the same time, their mo(ve)ments represent certain general aspects when exploring exit processes from the Danish biker gang milieu. They have between five and ten years of embodied experience within this milieu, including different kinds of leadership experiences. All three were active and engaged in the biker gang milieu until the years of 2013–2014, when they each left the gang environment in different ways. Their life trajectories had both similarities and important differences.

The most actively engaged co-researcher, Peter, experienced a very poor, chaotic and violent childhood. He describes how the lack of a father figure in his life fueled a powerful longing for community and belonging, something he searched for and finally found in the biker gang environment in his late teenage years. For the next 12 years, he fought his way into one of the big international biker gangs in Denmark and ended up becoming a biker gang president and involved in a violent biker gang conflict. His movements beyond the biker gang milieu began while he was still involved in the conflict and continued as he (as leader) dissolved the group and joined the national exit program. Thereafter, he was actively involved in different NGOs while also becoming a research apprentice and a very active and critical voice in public debates surrounding the Danish national exit program (Mørck and Celosse-Andersen, 2019).

X and Nabil both moved to Denmark as sons of young immigrant parents but had very different upbringings. X lived a rather sheltered childhood. As a teenager, X became more actively engaged in the local housing area, was involved in community work and was respected by peers and adults alike. He also pursued a healthy lifestyle as a dedicated boxer. However, one day, some gang members attacked him in a case of mistaken identity, and from that point on, his life changed, and he was drawn into some very violent conflicts with biker and street gangs. In the process of fighting back, he became a prospective gang member and then the leader. After about 4–5 years in this environment, he was arrested. While imprisoned, he dedicated himself to changing his life and became a good Muslim, closing down the street gang for good (Mørck and Khawaja, in press). He also committed himself to 'doing good' at the forensic psychiatric unit where he was placed and became a respected spokesperson. Working with both employees and patients, he produced a 'patient manifesto' outlining how the two groups could help and motivate each other to make a better community at the unit.

Nabil came to Denmark with his parents at the age of four. He grew up watching his mother being beaten by his father. The traumatic events of his childhood made him long for a sense of "family," where "you look after each other" – something he sought out in the gang environment. In his teenage years, Nabil became a member of a street-oriented group in a local housing area, advancing through the ranks to a (co-)leading position of a local subgroup belonging to one of the bigger international biker gangs. At the age of 26, while in prison, he decided to join the national exit program. Later, he took part in public debates about gang prevention and the gang environment, got a job hosting a radio program, started working with conflict resolution in an NGO, and studied to become a social worker. His life ended at the age of 31 when he was fatally shot after a reception celebrating the publication of a book about his life, his time in the biker gang milieu and his exit process.

My ongoing practice research with the different co-researchers has varied in terms of the intensity of exchanges, dialogues and joint projects but has so far lasted up to seven years. During this period, I have continued to deepen my understanding of the complexity of exit processes in practice, including the extreme conflicts, problems and double binds formers have to deal with and their struggles to overcome and move beyond them.

Ethical dilemmas and possibilities for action – analysis of cases

Many of my co-researchers (in and across various research projects) were engaged in 'doing good' by participating in public debates, and some of them also make reference to their participation in and contribution to our common research. As former gang members, they are still to some extent struggling with marginal and stigmatized positions in Danish society, and we have to reflect on how our research may expand their possibilities in life, as well as the possibilities for other formers, when developing emancipatory research ethics. We need to recognize that it is part of their 'life interest' to become 'more of something' while co-creating 'something new' (Mørck and Celosse-Andersen, 2019) and that they want to be more than just anonymized research subjects, presented as just another former gang member.

Case 1: Co-researching with publicly known formers – dialogue about sensitivity of information and development of subject-subject relations

Peter is one of the formers who took the initiative to contact me after reading about my research in the media. At the time, in 2014, he was imprisoned in a high-security psychiatric institution and wrote me a handwritten letter about how he felt his life was going in circles. He wanted to start a new, safe family life with his wife and leave the gang conflicts behind. In the letter, he quoted different psychological theorists, already practicing what later emerged as a telos of becoming an academic (Mørck and Hansen, 2015). When he got out of prison, he was able to communicate via email, and I invited him to take part in an interview about his experiences with the Danish national exit program, which he had joined as part of his exit process. From the start of the first interview, and in an informal chat after, he spoke openly about the conflicts and dilemmas he faced. During this first meeting, he told me how, at the age of five, he had watched his stepfather shoot himself. I listened and initially categorized this as very private and sensitive information that I would not use in my research or share with others. Three years later, Peter mentioned the same traumatic episode again, this time in a public video. I hereby learned that this information did not have to be treated as private, as I had thought to begin with, and that I could also use it to discuss the themes of sensitivity and privacy in this chapter.

Not only did Peter make the initial contact, he continued to take many initiatives in our research joint venture and quickly moved from co-researcher to research apprentice, co-authoring several publications (Mørck and Hansen, 2015; Mørck and Celosse-Andersen, 2016, 2019). Peter was very engaged in the (re)formulation of research methodologies and new research projects. The subject-subject dialogue around the different issues – exchanges via email, text messages or even a handwritten letter – was a critical part of maintaining this co-researcher relationship, a dialogue that challenged the institutionalized standards for the safe storage and exchange of data. To (re)produce subject-subject dialogue, I tend to use my co-researchers' preferred formats for dialogue, for example, whether they prefer to communicate using social media, private text messages, email or an encrypted messaging platform, and I respond via their preferred channel. At the same time, we always reflect on what kinds of knowledge could be shared and on which platforms. Through this, I involved my co-researchers in reflections on the sensitivity of specific information, continuously exploring together what constituted sensitive information only to be shared in private or secure fora.

Researcher codexes and situated dialogue as an alternative to written informed consent

Many former gang members have a relationship to the establishment, whether in the shape of prison or gang-exit programs, marked by experiences of distrust, coercion and a lack of col-laboration. Therefore, if asked to sign a written informed consent document the first time they meet a researcher, it may result in resistance and feelings of alienation (Deuchar, 2015). To avoid alienation and build trust, social practice researchers have to develop dialogical procedures for obtaining informed consent and for exploring the sensitivity of specific data in practice. For each practice research collaboration, we[4] developed a specific researcher codex, which informed the co-researchers about the goal, content and conditions of the research project – conditions that we as researchers had to live up to. The codex included information about who we (the researchers) are and how we share different kinds of data and detailed how we would try to anonymize participants by using a pseudonym. Furthermore, this written document outlined how participants are invited, as co-researchers, to read all empirical analysis concerning them, ensuring that nothing is published that they consider too sensitive or private or to be putting them at risk.

Most importantly, to produce subject-subject relations and trust, we revised the widespread practice of written consent, where it is the principal researcher not the co-researcher who signs the researcher codex.

Standards of informed written consent vary between different fields of study and from country to country. In Scotland, lengthy negotiations were necessary for Professor Ross Deuchar to convince the university ethics board that, as an ethnographic gang researcher, he could not make his informants sign a written consent form the first time they met – which could be on a street corner (Deuchar, 2015). In Denmark, as social practice researchers, we can refer to more flexible ethical principles concerning practice-oriented research for the common good to negotiate the way we practice informed consent in dialogue with our co-researchers.

In my collaboration with Peter, I prepared a researcher codex informing him about the content and goal of the research, as well as how he, for security reasons, would have the opportunity to review quotes and analysis before publication. Every time I or we were about to finish a new research publication, I would send him the PowerPoints or the paper so he could help me ensure his safety would not be jeopardized. This way of working with situated consent as an ongoing concern also interpellated (Nissen, 2012) Peter and the other formers as engaged co-researchers.

Movements beyond anonymity that expand co-researchers' opportunities for agency and recognition

At a very early stage of our collaboration, we (the co-researchers and I) were confronted with the dilemma that anonymity and the secure exchange of data were not always an option and that other parties had a say in the matter. Our agency in this regard could be limited in various ways. Due to Peter's formerly prominent position in the gang environment and placement in a high-security psychiatric institution, it was highly likely that somebody had already read his handwritten letter before I received it. Likewise, I had to consider that he could be under police surveillance during the initial stages of the exit process where he was still in conflict with his former gang. When storing our common empirical data and our exchanges via email and text messages, I had to consider and negotiate the institutional standards of anonymity and secure data storage. Through our collaboration, I learned that what is perceived as sensitive data depends on one's perspective and might change over time due to tragic episodes beyond our control. Sensitive data, as defined by university ethics boards (such as a psychiatric diagnosis or a former position as president of a biker gang), did not seem to be a major concern for Peter. He also seemed very accustomed to being under surveillance, due to his many years in a leading position within the biker gang environment and as a patient in forensic psychiatric treatment. The years spent living under surveillance formed his view of what he considered sensitive knowledge and how it could be safely shared and stored. At the same time, however, as he was in the midst of the exit *process*, his everyday life, considerations, values and ways of thinking (about himself and others) were in transition. This zone of liminality (Stenner, 2018), where old meanings have ceased to exist and new meanings are yet to emerge or settle, is a general condition for former gang members at the beginning of an exit process.

It therefore became a common and continuous task for us to explore what kinds of knowledge could be treated as empirical data and what constituted personally sensitive information, which should be treated as private and not be shared or published. I also had to learn how what Peter considered sensitive information varied between contexts. For example, I learned from Peter that it was okay to mention sensitive data (his full name, former gang affiliation and diagnosis) at a PhD course at the university, which he perceived as a very safe place, but not in other (more or less) public settings outside the university. I learned that his openness and trust differed in relation to various 'people of significance.' I learned that Peter's relationship with the police and other authority figures who were supposed to help him in his exit process, such as his exit coordinator, was very conflicted. I also learned that there were good reasons for his distrust. For example, his exit coordinator was the same police officer who used to investigate him and his gang.

We began to discuss, reflect on and produce new ethical standards, legitimating a form of social practice research, conducted as part of academic discussions during PhD courses in which Peter also participated. Together, we produced a video to be used in teaching about these ethical dilemmas. We called the video "Lived Ethics" to indicate the need to explore the differences between, on the one hand, ethical rules and procedures and, on the other hand, ethical conduct specific to the individual co-researcher, referring to the latter as lived ethics in practice. In the video, we shared dialogues and reflections regarding the potential need to develop new standards of ethics in practice in order to uphold ethics under paradoxical conditions. We also began to combine research with teaching (Nissen and Mørck, 2019), with intervention (Swartz, 2008) and with innovation of social practice ethics in and across the different contexts that we were involved in. In dialogue with (PhD) students and professors, such as Jean Lave and Ross Deuchar (Deuchar, 2015), we began to discuss and question institutional ethical standards, such as anonymity and written informed consent, developing new situated ethics better suited to our common goals of developing subject-subject relations while avoiding placing co-researchers at risk.

From co-researcher to research apprentice and innovative academic

These mo(ve)ments beyond anonymity, where Peter was engaged in teaching and video production discussing ethical standards, also brought about possibilities for recognition and a process of becoming more of an academic – a telos (Lave, 1997) that emerged and was given substance through Peter's participation in the production of teaching, videos and so on. Peter quickly positioned himself as an extraordinarily active co-researcher and a creative academic thinker. On the day of the second (follow-up) interview, he told me that he had started to produce a series of video logs about his exit process. He asked me to help him ensure the empirical material was of a high academic standard because he wanted to produce high-quality empirical data for his future master's thesis. From that moment, he moved beyond just being a co-researcher, becoming a research apprentice – a category that we borrowed from Jean Lave and her book *Apprenticeship in Critical Ethnographic Practice*. We adopted Jean Lave's critical ethnographic telos and way of conducting research: "Becoming an apprentice to one's own changing practice" (Lave, 2011, p. 2). Soon after, we used the video logs as the foundation for our first co-authored scientific article, titled "From Biker to Academic" (Mørck and Hansen, 2015). For security reasons, we published our first article under the pseudonym Peter Hansen, instead of using Peter's real name. During the first year of our collaboration, and the first year of Peter's exit process, he preferred to use the pseudonym Peter Hansen when we made co-presentations at conferences, lectures and seminars. In 2016, we developed a social technology called the Life Conduct List, this time using his real name. We began to teach Life Conduct List courses together and co-authored another scientific article on the subject (Mørck and Celosse-Andersen, 2016). Peter's security situation had changed a lot since 2014, and he was no longer in 'bad standing' in relation to the biker gang environment and longed for public recognition as a co-author and co-developer of the Life Conduct List.

In a practice research case, like ours, where mo(ve)ments beyond anonymity offer Peter possibilities for recognition and for becoming more academic, it is more ethical to carefully reflect on mo(ve)ments beyond anonymity than to attempt to uphold a false and unrealistic research norm of anonymity. In cases like Peter's, where institutional guidelines are in direct opposition to a co-researcher's personal telos, we should rethink the standards of anonymity. Producing these new situated standards of social practice ethics also requires more democratic and dialogical standards of practice-oriented research. Social practice ethics uphold a standard where questions of 'anonymity or recognition' and 'situated informed consent' should always be discussed in relation to each context, each co-researcher and the sensitivity of the concrete topics presented.

As I show in my analysis of the dilemmas in the next case, it is not my intention to reject the principle of anonymity for all. We need to continue to work on identifying topics where it is risky to be quoted as a co-researcher when absolute anonymity cannot be ensured. We need to work out situated procedures to continuously assess risks; the risks can change dramatically and are difficult to assess properly, as demonstrated by tragic events like the killing of Nabil.

Case 2: Dilemmas of how to present the evolving Danish "biker gang environment" without reproducing negatively deviant categorizations or putting co-researchers at risk

Within gang research, there is a widespread tendency to discuss gangs using universal and abstract definitions that feed into dilemmas of abstract dualistic thinking, reproducing categorizations of *them*, 'the criminal, pathological, dangerous', versus *us*, 'the normal, civil people.' Many formers struggle with the dilemma that once you have been categorized as 'gang' (in research, by the police and others), it is very difficult to become 'one of us.'

Within traditions of critical criminology (Brotherton, 2020), it is discussed how "we resist reproducing the dominant culture's pathological, exoticizing, and negatively-deviant categorizations of groups" and how we as critical researchers avoid tendencies to reproduce a "limitless web of assumptions that normalizes 'our difference' from 'them'" (Brotherton, 2020). With Professor David C. Brotherton, we can also ask: How can we develop gang research that supports the humanization of gangs, gang members, and former (biker) gang members?

Dualistic tendencies of othering and demonizing categorizations can be found within the (biker) gang environments themselves and within policies, research and interventions addressing gangs. I also struggle with such dilemmas in my own research, and there is no easy universal solution. Seen from a social practice theoretical perspective, dilemmas cannot be totally resolved. Like the other dilemmas discussed in this chapter, we need to reflect on and understand the meaning of each step as we collectively struggle to identify action possibilities that help us address and move beyond the dilemma (Mørck et al., 2013).

Mo(ve)ments beyond dualistic discursive misrepresentations of the biker gang environment

One action possibility – a first step in the process of trying to move beyond these dualistic tendencies – is to invite the formers to involve themselves in subject-subject relations in research exploring their first-person perspectives (Schraube and Osterkamp, 2013) as they move in and across communities. This includes an exploration of the dialectics of changing involvements and environments. In a research project about 'border jumping' and 'cross-overs' funded by the Danish Ministry of Integration, Tina Wilchen Christensen and I explored concrete mo(ve)ments where formers changed their engagement and involvement in and across specific groups. We also explored the collective practices and ideologies within a group, as well as similarities and differences among different groups that the interviewed formers were moving between (Christensen and Mørck, 2017). However, it remains a very difficult task to describe the Danish biker gang environment from within – partly because the environment has undergone and continues to undergo rapid change in recent years (Mørck et al., 2013) but also because it may put formers at risk if they go into too much detail about their knowledge of this conflict-ridden and changing environment.

Over the last decade, more and more (biker) gangs have been in conflict, and some gangs and chapters have closed down (this includes the groups that were led by X and by Peter). Conflicts and closures tend to leave a growing number of (biker) gang members in situations where they have to consider possibilities for exit or for 'crossing over' to other communities.

Sometimes, due to a lack of good options, they also engage in processes of building new communities, where their embodied experiences and competences are recognized (Christensen and Mørck, 2017) and where they can use their background for something productive. In the next section, I give examples of these productive ways of 'making good' (Mørck, Hartvig, and Bildstedfelt, 2020).

'Making good': public dialogues, giving voice and nuancing misrepresentations

The co-researchers presented in this chapter have also talked and/or written about their way in and out of the gang environment. Some have shared their personal experiences of various gangs in response to how gangs and exit processes are often misrepresented in dominant discourses. They have all contributed with presentations at (closed) seminars. Nabil and Peter have also participated in public radio or television programs in an effort to nuance the general public's perspectives on gangs and see this public speaking and sharing as a way of giving back and 'making good' as penance for all the bad things they did when they were younger. Nabil, for example, talked about how he had tried to correct a common misrepresentation among Danish social workers that attributed his gang membership to his parents' 'other' culture or 'Muslim origins':

> I also tell them that I came to Denmark as a 4-year-old, so they have an idea that this person has not brought anything from his home country. It is because of my upbringing in Denmark that I became a gang member. . . . A lot of people think: "Well that's because he is a Muslim", so I reject that right away: "I came here when I was 4 – my parents – my Dad ate pork and my mother never wore a scarf, so don't use Islam" . . . – that's what I tell them.
>
> *(Nabil)*

Nabil told us that he also tried to nuance people's view that gang members mostly belong to ethnic minorities by talking about his experiences as a member of an ethnically mixed gang, including many white Danes:

> There are many people who think that we grow up in our homes in another way than Danes. There are a lot of people who believe that this is some immigrant thing, gangs. That is incorrect. I have been in the gang environment: the majority of the people I met were white, Christian Danes. And the majority of the most prominent gang members are Danes.
>
> *(Nabil)*

X is more wary of becoming too personally engaged when making presentations. He shared the questions, feelings and experiences that made him stop involving himself in more presentations:

> Perhaps to build a career or to be beneficial? You have to constantly remind yourself. I also ask myself these questions when I sit here with you: Why am I sitting here, and what is the purpose? It's also why I didn't want to do more after that presentation. All of a sudden, I was in it, and I was grabbed by it, when I sit and tell. So many years have passed, and I have never talked about it. Only after six years, I sat for the first time and talked to one of the boys from the old days, after so long. It gave me such a jolt through my body. What

have I done? Such a dirty [feeling], you know, fake environment and fake life I had been in. So, we were just talking about it and exchanging some words. There I could really feel it in my body, you know. It is not beneficial for one [me] to talk about it.

(X)

Even though he enjoyed doing the presentations at Grundtvigs Højskole, where I met him the first time, he also experienced talking about his former life as "a jolt through his body." He felt that it was in conflict with his new telos, his deep engagement in seeking recognition by God. He felt that it was best for him and his process not to think back or talk about his time in the gang environment. Nevertheless, he wanted to contribute to our research in order to help challenge and correct the demonizing misrepresentations of being former gang member and becoming Muslim.

Serious risks when speaking publicly about the biker gang environment

In the last decade, a growing number of formers (many of them my co-researchers) have become public figures through their appearances in the media. Nabil made a presentation at Grundtvigs Højskole back in 2013, which led to an interview published in one of the major Danish newspapers. He shares his belief that his media appearances motivated others to go public, even though it is a very risky affair:

It is only after I got into the exit [program] almost six years ago that I have seen many from my old environment [in the media]. I've seen a lot of people who have started to talk publicly in the media because I'm still out there and showing them: try and listen, I'm still here. Yes, I am threatened every day. Yes, I'm on a death list, but I'm still standing here and I'm not talking shit about people – I'm talking about our children. And if somebody wants to kill me for it – well then, it's not me who gets a bad conscience, it's them. Because it is not because I have gone out and shot one of their brothers, or owe any of them money, or have put any of them in court – not at all: no one is sitting inside a prison due to me. It's because I sit and talk about the need to help the young people [stay away from gangs].

(Nabil)

Nabil did not just receive death threats, he ended up being killed. So the risks we are talking about are very serious. Every time the formers represent and talk about the gang environment in public and in research, we (researchers and journalists) have to think carefully about how to ensure their safety and avoid putting them at unnecessary risk as they present their stories and experiences in ways that others can learn from.

Some formers manage to negotiate representations in ways that allow them to live ordinary everyday lives without (too many) threats. Others have written about their time in the biker gang environment and live in exile outside Denmark due to serious threats.

Nabil went a number of steps further than all the other formers in the public eye. He got a paid job hosting a radio program called 'Police radio' alongside a journalist and a former police officer – something other formers have done without any consequences. However, he also felt a strong sense of belonging to the journalist community, describing the radio station and the other journalists as his "new family" and that it was his longing for family that got him into the gang in the first place. It also seemed that, as part of the journalist community, he thought his new family could protect him, even if his journalism was highly confrontational, overstepping certain boundaries in confronting the gangs:

> they (the gangs) are scared. . . . Now I'm throwing it in the media. . . . So, it is a mechanism I have learned to use . . . they are really afraid of journalists. They also know that if they lay a finger on a journalist, then . . . I got a direct response from my management here. If they lay a finger on me, we break them in the journalist world and they are eaten. . . . So I use that, "Okay, you don't want me talking about [the gang], but do you want to come in and talk to me about why I shouldn't talk about [the gang]?" Right? So, I am trying to approach it as a journalist, right? And then I don't hear from them again.
>
> *(Nabil)*

In the quote, he tells us that he learned certain confrontational repertoires, including a specific mechanism to oppose the gangs, calling for an increased critical and ethical self-awareness in the practice of journalism. Even though Nabil seemed to be reproducing some of his old repertoires from the gang environment, his local journalistic community shared a responsibility to help him as a newcomer to the profession, to critically reflect on and discuss the risks he was facing. We all need to reflect, learn and change after what happened to Nabil.

Risk assessment as situated in and across contexts and time

To avoid exposing anybody to such risks, my co-researchers and I usually try not to place ourselves in such extreme positions. We assess the boundaries we face, viewing them in relationship to the content of our research and to where and how we publish it. We refer to this as a situated reflection on risk. After Nabil's death, my co-researchers and I had to carefully reconsider what is safe and what is a risk. This was a very difficult process, because we did not know the precise motives for and circumstances of his murder. Years later a member from the specific biker gang that Nabil mentioned in the interview was convicted for the murder, but according to the verdict, they were still unsure of the specific motives for the killing. On a more general level, it underscores why ethics and risk analysis in research should not be considered merely static and abstract rules. The borders and boundaries of our research situation can change drastically after specific historical events. We have to learn from and reflect on these changes when researching such conflict-related situations and practices involving gangs and gang exit.

Recent gang policies and emerging risks for researchers and co-researchers

Danish gang policies in the former conservative governmental period have involved an increasing criminalization of gangs. More and more gang members are in jail and being imprisoned for more and minor offences. In addition, laws have been introduced potentially doubling sentences for those affiliated with a gang and allowing prison sentences for gang members for being in a prohibited zone, and latest the Ministry of Justice also won a lawsuit which forcibly disband one of the larger street gangs. As such, in Denmark, you can receive up to two years of prison sentence for wearing the logo of this specific street group.

The prosecutors representing the government in this lawsuit recently tried to call Aydin Soei, who is a journalist, sociologist and author, as a witness. The police demanded that he should be a witness against the gang and provide access to his anonymous sources to also be called upon as witnesses. Aydin, like me, is one of the very few academics talking and writing about gangs in Denmark. Fortunately, the journalists' union and his publisher hired him a lawyer and he did not have to appear as a witness. Episodes like this keep changing the premises and conditions of safety and what we can do to protect our co-researchers if we want to continue to conduct research on the changing gang environment in Denmark.

Conclusion

In this chapter, I have described and analyzed a situated approach to social practice ethics, in line with the emancipatory goals of critical criminology, participatory and social justice research, moving beyond the abstract and institutionalized ethical standards we receive from university ethics boards. I have illustrated how we can develop practice-oriented gang research and dialogue-based methodologies that expand our ethical awareness of the meanings and consequences of research. Expanded awareness is important in this conflictual, changing world, especially when working within a dangerous field such as gang research. I have illustrated how we as researchers can work humanistically, deepening our awareness of the conditions under which studies are performed and increasing our agency in the common interest of ourselves, our co-researchers and society.

I have discussed several empirical cases and the related ethical dilemmas that demonstrate how to practice co-research with publicly known formers when maintaining the principle of anonymity ceases to be a real option. I have also analyzed action possibilities in terms of how to discuss and negotiate the principles of institutionalized ethics of anonymity, data sharing, informed consent and risk assessment when these codes and principles are an integral part of the dilemma. The action possibilities are all based on situated standards and procedures that I call 'social practice ethics' and contribute to more equal subject-subject relations and the overall goal of humanizing our research practices.

I also discussed another dilemma regarding how to present changes in the societal conditions of the Danish "biker gang milieu" without putting co-researchers at risk or reproducing dualistic thinking and problem categorization. As part of establishing situated standards for social practice ethics, I argue for the need to reflect more deeply on the risks facing co-researchers and on the practices of knowledge production in our commitment to nuanced, situated knowledge and to the relentless societal critique as a basis for social change.

We face a serious dilemma of how to avoid putting co-researchers at risk when we (this includes both researchers and journalists) do not know the consequences and meanings produced by the changed repertoires of gangs and the impacts of journalists, prosecutors and gang policies. There is no universal solution to this problem. What we can do, as part of our ongoing practice-oriented research, is continue to critically reflect on the suggested standards of social practice ethics alongside co-researchers, including formers – and thereby develop more principled subject-subject relations with participants, who are subject to the consequences of the research in and on their bodies. We saw how each co-researcher feels differently about discussing the gang environment. We have to carefully examine and acknowledge these differences in our general assessments of risk and of possibilities for recognition and humanization. In that way we can both respect and ensure their ongoing identity formation, and the need of anonymization or blurring of sensitive information.

Notes

1 Such as ProQuest Social Science, Scopus and Web of Science.
2 According to D'Cruz and Gillingham (2017), situated ethics should be understood as a way of thinking about ethical dilemmas within the context in which they emerge "as relationships between participants"

(p. 437), and the researcher's reflexivity should be understood as an awareness of knowledge and power relations and as the ability to respond to situations as they unfold. In this approach to ethics, prescribed codes are understood as unfolding, as "fluid and transitory." Likewise, D'Cruz and Gillingham (2017) argue that it is important to move beyond written consent forms by reflecting upon and reassessing informed consent as the situation unfolds (D'Cruz and Gillingham, 2017).

3 With our so-called mo(ve)ment methodology, we explore significant moments in depth, analyzing the aspects which produce movements in position, identity formation, meanings and telos (Mørck and Celosse-Andersen, 2019).

4 The research project with Peter was conducted in collaboration with a student writing her master's thesis (Lone Maj Sand Clausen), the research with Nabil was conducted with two research apprentices (Cecilie Bildstedfelt and Katja Hartvig) and the research project with X was conducted with Associate Professor Iram Khawaja.

References

Antle, B. J. and Regehr, C. (2003) 'Beyond individual rights and freedoms: Metaethics in social work research', *Social Work*, 48(1), p135–144.

Brotherton, D. (2020) 'Studying the gang through critical ethnography', in Haggerty, K.D. and Bucerius, S. (eds.) *Oxford University Handbook of Ethnographies of Crime and Criminal Justice*. New York: Oxford University Press.

Christensen, T. W. and Mørck, L. L. (2017). *Bevægelser i og på tværs af ekstreme grupper og bande-og rockermiljøet: En kritisk undersøgelse og diskussion af "cross-over" [Movements in and across extremist groups and the"biker gang environment": A critical examination and discussion of cross-over]*. København: DPU, Aarhus Universitet.

D'Cruz, H. and Gillingham, P. (2017) 'Participatory research ideals and practice experience: Reflections and analysis', *Journal of Social Work*, 17(4), p434–452.

Deuchar, R. (2015) 'Dilemmas, deception and ethical decision-making: Insights from a Transatlantic ethnographer', in Bhopal, K. and Deuchar, R. (eds.) *Researching Marginalized Groups*. New York: Routledge, p62–74.

Doel, M., Allmark, P., Conway, P., Cowburn, M., Flynn, M., Nelson, P. and Tod, A. (2010) 'Professional boundaries: Crossing a line or entering the shadows?' *British Journal of Social Work*, 40(6), p1866–1889.

Lave, J. (1997) 'Learning, apprenticeship, social practice', *Nordisk Pedagogik*, 17, p140–152.

Lave, J. (2011) *Apprenticeship in Critical Ethnographic Practice*. Chicago: University of Chicago Press.

Lovelock, R. and Powell, J. (2004) 'Habermas/Foucault for social work: Practices of critical reflection.' In R. Lovelock, K. Lyons and J. Powell (Eds), *Reflecting on social work: Discipline and profession*. Aldershot, England: Ashgate. p181–223.

Miller, W. 1958. Lower Class Culture as a Generating Milieu of Gang Delinquency. *Journal of Social Issues*. 14:5–19.

Mørck, L. L. (2000) 'Practice research and learning resources. A joint venture with the initiative "wild learning"', *Outlines*, 2, p61–84.

Mørck, L. L. and Celosse-Andersen, M. C. (2016) 'Livsførelseslisten: Omfattende identitetsforandring efter bande/rocker-involvering', *Nordiske Udkast*, 44(2), p49–67.

Mørck, L. L. and Celosse-Andersen, M. C. (2019) 'Mo(ve)ment-methodology: Identity formation moving beyond gang involvement', *Annual Review of Critical Psychology*, 16, p634–670.

Mørck, L. L. and Hansen, P. (2015) 'Fra rocker til akademiker', *Psyke & Logos*, 36, p266–298.

Mørck, L. L., Hartvig, K. and Bildstedfelt, C. (2020) 'New meanings, new communities and new identity? Former (biker) gang members' self-representation and self-exposure through dialogical practices', in Melde, C. and Weerman, F. (eds.) *Gangs in the Era of Internet and Social Media*. Cham, Switzerland: Springer, p199–223.

Mørck, L. L., Hussain, K., Møller-Andersen, C., Özüpek, T., Palm, A. and Vorbeck, I. (2013) 'Praxis development in relation to gang conflicts in Copenhagen, Denmark', *Outlines: Critical Practice Studies*, 14(2), p79–105.

Mørck, L. L. and Khawaja, I. (in press) 'Learning to be a good Muslim. Movements beyond gang engagement and radicalization.' In: *Generating Differentiated Equity - A Situated Learning for our Times* (working title), to be send to Cambridge University Press, p1–25.

Nissen, M. (2000) 'Practice research. Critical psychology in and through practices', *Annual Review of Critical Psychology*, 2, p145–179.

Nissen, M. (2012) *Subjectivity of Participation: Articulating Social Work with Youth in Copenhagen.* London: Palgrave Macmillan.

Nissen, M. and Mørck, L. L. (2019) 'Situated generalization with prototypes in dialogical teaching', in Højholt, C. and Schraube, E. (eds.) *Subjectivity and Knowledge – Generalization in the Psychological Study of Everyday Life.* Cham, Switzerland: Springer, p195–220.

Park, P., Brydon-Miller, M., Hall, B. and Jackson, T. (1993) *Voices of Change: Participatory Research in the United States and Canada.* Toronto: OISE Press.

Schraube, E. and Osterkamp, O. (2013) *Psychology from the Standpoint of the Subject. Selected Writings of Klaus Holzkamp.* Basingstoke: Palgrave Macmillan.

Stenner, P. (2018) *Liminality and Experience: A Trans-Disciplinary Approach to the Psycho-Social.* Basingstoke: Palgrave Macmillan.

Swartz, S. (2008) 'Going deep and giving back strategies for exceeding ethical expectations when researching among vulnerable youth', *Qualitative Research*, 11(1), p47–68.

Taylor, R. (2015) 'Beyond anonymity: Temporality and the production of knowledge in a qualitative longitudinal study', *International Journal of Social Research Methodology*, 18(3), p281–292, DOI: 10.1080/13645579.2015.1017901

Wise, S. (1987) 'A framework for discussing ethical issues in feminist research: A review of the literature', *Writing Feminist Biographies: Using Life Histories, Studies in Sexual Politics*, 19(2), p47–88. Manchester, UK: University of Manchester, Department of Sociology.

11

Filming (with) gangs

An essay on visual sociology in Barcelona

Luca Queirolo Palmas

---

1 Can the subaltern film? can the subaltern be filmed?

Buscando Respeto is a documentary about the self-representations generated by those who are represented as dangerous subjects and enemies of the urban order.[1] It is set in Barcelona, where the subjects who appear and take the floor are defined by the media industry through the category of youth gangs. In Spain, as well as elsewhere, this term is often qualified and ethnified – the gang members are in fact Latinos – thus contributing to fueling moral panics around migratory phenomena. In this chapter, I will outline the method and the research trajectory leading to a visual work which combines the language of fiction with that of documentary. I also intend to reflect critically on my research practices in the field of visual sociology around subaltern subjects (Queirolo Palmas, 2017a; Sebag, Durand, Louveau, and Queirolo Palmas, 2018), whose access to word and image is bound by a multiplicity of filters and power relations.

In contemporary societies, the persistence and reproduction of youth groups that are ethnically styled and designated by State thought (Sayad, 1999) as gangs reflect the crisis of the rhetoric of integration applied to the children of migration (Marwan, 2011). The scene[2] within which these forms of youth socialization unfold is also a space of agency, social negotiation and place-making for subalterns, subjects whose ways of life are captured by the institutional gaze only through barbaric and pathological metaphors. Gangs are considered responsible for having brought violence into a society that likes to think of itself as harmonious and civilized. Spivak (1988) adds that the subaltern can only be represented through colonial discourse and archives; they are silent subjects whose resistance does not involve speaking directly but obliquely, through refusal, subtraction, escape and other practices of isolation and self-segregation.

In fact, the marginal youth groups I have observed perform parallel spaces/times (Restrepo, 2007) and produce languages and status systems without being listened to or recognized at the institutional level; what filters through in high social circles is only noise, the production of excess and gratuitous violence, followed by the inevitable penal solution and treatment. In my ethnographic work, I have also come across silent – and silenced – subjects who articulate silent struggles, presences made incomprehensible by the moral panic generated by security entrepreneurs with vested political and economic interests. How can we give voice to these social trajectories? How can we give voice to these resistances? Which images can we construct for these invisible or hyper-visible subjects, depending on what is politically convenient at any given moment? How can we film barbarians?

The documentary *Buscando Respeto* seeks to enable subalterns to have a say, thus escaping the logic of representation by delegating and constructing a space/time in which to reveal, on the one hand, the ability of these subjects to speak for themselves and contest, on the other, the articulated hegemonic discourse around the category of deficit and social danger. To our eyes, the gang scene appears as a crossroads of expressiveness of mixed youth cultures where class conditions and migrant conditions intersect, a territory where young victims of social ostracism invent tactics to produce social, symbolic, cultural, economic and warrior capital[3] (Queirolo Palmas, 2015). I thus approached the object/subject of my research through the classic categories of Bourdieu (1992).[4] Social capital allows one to escape from the loneliness of migration and to articulate youth brotherhood networks; symbolic capital opens up the possibility of accumulating visibility and recognition for marginal subjects; cultural capital generates autonomous patterns of perception and vision from a subaltern condition; economic capital works to extract resources in an informal or illicit manner from the markets of goods and labor, while warrior capital takes the strength of the group and corporeity as sites of production of social respect, reputation and hegemonic masculinity.

Only violence remains in the hegemonic narration of the gang scene. The structural and vertical violence they suffer (poverty, unemployment, exploitation, low wages, benefit cuts, . . .) is permanently concealed, while the personal and horizontal violence they perpetrate is emphasized, thus failing to recognize causality and circularity between the two (Bourdieu, 1998). We can see, for example, the evidence of this regime of truth in these fragments of interviews I did in November 2012 with journalists from two important Catalan newspapers who prefer to remain anonymous:

> If they were saints, they would not make headlines, they are news because they are violent, simple!
>
> *(Journalist of El Periódico)*

> The more violent the event, the more space we have. Since gangs are a problem for cohabitation, my newspaper gives great importance to the topic.
>
> *(Journalist of La Vanguardia)*

How can we tell a different story about the gang scene and the young people passing through it? On the one hand, it is necessary to turn the research object into a subject and then give back part of the power of representation. On the other hand, it is crucial to challenge the positivist epistemology of distance – the science that finds its condition of truth in the distance between the studied object and the subject of enunciation – and to believe in a research tool that is also a common and innovative practice (Queirolo Palmas, 2017a, Back and Puwar, 2012). From this perspective, doing research means creating a place and a long span of time during which subjects with different cultural and economic capital share the production process – in this case, in the making of a sociological and ethnographic film, *Buscando Respeto*. In the following pages, I will retrace three phases of this research path: 1) access to the field; 2) the process of shared writing; 3) objectification in a piece of visual work in order to critically discuss the challenges and potential of filmic ethnography with gangs in Barcelona.

2 Entering the gang scene

For those wishing to explore marginal social spaces, access is always one of the main challenges, one which brings to the fore class and cultural distinctions between researchers and 'researched' (Brotherton, 2015). Suspicion and lack of trust are forms of self-immunization of the subalterns, ways of resisting their lives being made available to another vigilant gaze. After all, what characterizes marginal worlds is the surplus of supervision by different official figures, including anthropologists, sociologists and journalists. How can we overcome these difficulties when visual language removes anonymity, or the guarantee of privacy that the social sciences traditionally offer their interlocutors? In part, by offering the writing process, the soundtrack and the screenplay of the film as places and times of self-representation, limiting our power as authors over the work and its contents and therefore guarding against their usual misrepresentation

Some elements have played in our favor. First, the research subjects' desire to transform the stigma into an emblem, a process that has manifested itself repeatedly in the past, and in the present, whenever a subaltern social group has tried to collectively change its condition.[5] On the one hand, our interlocutors saw their participation in a piece of visual work as an opportunity to make such an inversion possible. On the other hand, the loss of anonymity invited them to become more involved in the symbolic struggle over this piece of visual work, amplifying their request for control over the modes of representation. Moreover, the modes of visual research were implicitly connected with the world of the research subjects – lower-class youths of migrant origin, involved in informal and precarious labor. To them, images spoke, while books were silent. As Scott (1990) and De Certeau (1990) have taught us, written codes are often synonymous with control and power for subalterns. In the case of subjects expelled from the education system, such as the gang scene youths, books and written texts are the codes of a control machine that transforms them, classifying them as culturally handicapped – a tangible sign of their own humiliation and failure. While there were books in the homes of the young people we have had access to during the shooting of *Buscando Respeto*, these were full of screens and images; the only texts they had were religious texts (the Bible) or self-help books about personal achievement (manuals on how to become rich or recover self-esteem). Even the musical texts that the protagonists of the film produced consisted of oral and extemporaneous performances. The very script of the film, which became a written text thanks to our work as researchers, was constantly subverted through acting improvisation. When I approached the young actors to tell them about the outcomes dissemination plan at the end of the project, the book form did not enjoy particular attention, while there was great fascination with the success and the future of the film. Like with the relationship between books and films, in their relations with the subjects of ethnography, researchers are perceived as the bearers of a distant and partly useless intellectual culture, while directors are invested with an acknowledged and sought-after symbolic capital. This interaction can be easily interpreted either through Bourdieu's concept of cultural capital as a vector of inequality or through Bernstein's (1973) work on working-class and middle-class vocabulary, concrete versus abstract languages and restricted and elaborated codes.

Making films and doing visual sociology in subaltern worlds allows me to articulate a more symmetrical common ground and point of access, to capture self-representations that circulate in spaces parallel to the hegemonic space of the written text. None of the young people I met during my research project read the articles by the journalists I interviewed who are experts on gangs, much like none of the texts produced by youths in gangs has sufficient legitimacy to be perceived as a reliable source of information in the production of media discourse on this issue.

In the access phase, we must always consider how the research work and the official figures involved in it are socially perceived in the social environment we seek to explore, as there is no

155

automatic acknowledgement of the usefulness of our work. My experience has highlighted the importance of imagining a common practice between researchers and 'researched', focusing my observation precisely on the relationships and frictions that originated from these encounters. The recurring question that has emerged from the gang scene is a basic and simple one. What is the purpose of this research? What do we need this research for? Taking the common space generated by the desire to know that characterizes research as a field of multiple exchanges and multiple conflicts seems to be the most useful and least hypocritical level of awareness and observation, from which the ethnographer can begin to generate counter-hegemonic knowledge.

3 Learning from friction in the shared film-making process

Access to the field described here was needed to produce a work of filmic and visual sociology. Yet for me, the product was a pretext to observe a process, to articulate a space of relationships and co-presences. To make a film, it was necessary to write and think together, which was why we started a workshop where for 12 months boys and girls from the gang scene[6] met every week and produced a shared narration. The workshop has touched on a variety of themes – migration, prison, work, crisis, police, school, sexuality, music – both through conversation and theatrical techniques (Navone and Oddone, 2015; Cannarella, Lagomarsino, and Oddone, 2018; Kaptani and Yuval Davis, 2008; Erel, Reynolds, and Kaptani, 2017).

For the participants – about twenty – being part of the workshop meant accepting its importance and making it their own. Our role as ethnographers was to document the process. The workshop and the subsequent construction of a collective of authors/interpreters has become the driving force and the field of ethnographic research, a space of exchange in which the researcher had to deliver benefits (legal support to obtain house arrest, economic and material aid, contacts with music producers, social workers or police officers) and from which the research drew a narrative and made underground knowledge available. The workshop also placed the research on a long timescale, forcing the researcher to have a non-contingent relationship and placing him under constant scrutiny regarding the project's modalities, forms and exchanges.

> The participants challenged us on the language we used. David, for example, told us: "if you keep using the term *gang* we're leaving. We're not gangs, we're the street families". So, we started a discursive relationship that made us grow mutually, focusing on new ways of looking and defining. Or they point out that far too often they have worked on cultural projects or as mediators without being paid or having had anything in return from the authorities; they made it clear that it was the same risk they thought they would run in this workshop aimed at producing a collective film. We were only at the beginning of a journey that would last two years . . . as always, the question of trust turned out to be a crucial one in ethnography. They questioned us not only about why and for whom we wanted to do this research, but also about what they could get in return by participating. A real legitimate question . . .
>
> *(notes from the field, Barcelona, December 2011)*

The economic condition of the participants, their social vulnerability, emerged naturally – without the need to use interview techniques – from the stories and the requests that were submitted, revealing their difficulty in participating and keeping a regular commitment for those trapped in precarious and marginal lives – from the fear of taking the underground due not having documents, to the challenge of keeping up with domestic labor (particularly caring for younger brothers) in households with only the mother figure and only one source of income. One day, for instance, Juan sold us a raffle ticket for two euros, for which the prize consisted of a bottle of whiskey bought at the supermarket. On another occasion, Dago asked us for advance payment for the deposit to rent a room after being evicted. The researcher was thus acting as counterpart in an informal negotiation in which participants symbolically bargained about the price for telling a story and/or standing in front of a camera. Our informants in fact had the power to withdraw and make filming impossible, even if the two levels – asking for help/support and participating in the film – were never explicitly tied to one another. On the one hand, the fact that their participation was voluntary and free of charge was reaffirmed. On the other, the relationship built with the researchers created a space for oblique claims based on the code of friendship.

The dynamics of participation fluctuate depending on their appreciation of our ability to make the experience useful, interesting and relevant for the workshop participants. Tensions and conflicts invite us to trade authorial control and resources for their willingness to stay and the possibility of reinventing it. For the young participants, the documentary is the researchers' text, a hetero-representation on the gang scene, while the fiction film – which originates from the theatrical component of the workshop – becomes the privileged site of their self-representation. The documentary is written by us through filmed interviews; the fiction is written by them through a script and improvisation on an open stage. The result combines these two registers. Why does fiction become the main site of autonomous expressiveness in the eyes of the participants? Partly because this code creates a split that makes it possible for them to tell fragments of their real lives in a anonymous way, transfiguring themselves into the characters: thanks to this theatrical artifice, they can speak about prison and violence, love and death, police, loneliness, early pregnancies and drug trafficking, in a condition of protection and immunity guaranteed by the distance of fiction and by the fiction of distance.

Filming *Buscando Respeto* has also brought us into the homes and the other places where our actors-authors live. Walking together in these everyday spaces has allowed us to bring out other stories and other meanings. This forced our interlocutors to grapple with an explanation and description exercise based on questions provided by us as researchers. What does it mean to be in a park and be frequently checked by the police? How do you live in a house with many children and only an intermittent income? How do you deal with early pregnancies or voluntary interruptions of pregnancy in social environments permeated by popular religiosity? How do you feel about school exclusion or about being available to do any kind of work? What needs are satisfied by participating in a religious cult? What does it mean to go around on a subway train from 5am to clean one office after the other? Elements of a subaltern class condition, of an inheritance, that Wilver, former leader of the Mara Salvatrucha gang in Guatemala, challenges: "we are the bill that no one has paid". During this period of urban nomadism next to the young gang members, our authorial intention for the film was challenged, and another narrative became progressively established. What will remain within the film as the fruit of a research and writing process that was both contested and shared?

4 Learning lessons from ambiguity

The gang scene articulates languages and narratives in social spaces distant from the hegemonic ones in which "the press reproduces a stereotypical separation between young Latin Americans and autochthonous young people, favoring the production of a dominant social image that shows them as opposed and irreconcilable" (Cerbino, 2012: 97). But do the subaltern produce images that are different from those that the hegemonic powers project onto them? While I do not claim to answer this question in this chapter, I wish to point out the contradictions inherent in the same non-hegemonic discourse, a discourse subjected to symbolic violence, to the naturalization of domination and its internalization by the dominated. Luis, for instance, a young Latin King just out of prison who took part in the workshop, criticized "the government of journalism that shelters criminals in a tie", while Gonzalo, a chef and former leader of another important 'street family'[7] identifies the police and journalists as responsible for discrimination. Among the young people involved in my ethnographic project, there are no rigid representations or class narratives that structure the reading of their social position. In a precarious and elusive labor market, the figure of the master and exploitation vanish, whereas respect and fame, the police and crime, the press and politicians all remain. When an imminent general strike is discussed during a workshop session, most of the participants confess that they will try to use all the work opportunities that come up on that occasion. Pedro, who until the day before had praised the glorious tradition of struggle of the Bolivian miners, came to the point without feeling too guilty towards his class upbringing: "the strike is for you intellectuals and the local middle class, not for us migrants". The class subjectification is simple and restricts itself to underlining the radical distinction between the way of life of those who have managerial jobs in closed buildings and have the power to speak and classify, and those who break their backs on the streets doing poorly paid strenuous jobs and are reduced to silence. "We are the street families . . . but tie-wearing crooks paint us like criminals" was a recurring topic of our workshop discussions. Let us consider, for example, the following rap text posted on a social network of the Madrid-based Ñeta Association in 2012:

> Do this exercise, go to a police station, communication center or any other institution that defames my ideals, ask why they treat us like criminals? Why can't young people sit in a park? Why can't they dress as they see fit? You can't have tattoos, you can't have your hood on, you can't wear a rosary? Aren't parks for boys? Isn't this a free country? Or am I hurting someone with my lifestyle? Because these politicians, these tie-wearing thugs, these journalists use their power to rule society, to misinform and make people see what they want to see. They take pride in their power, abuse their authority and rule us like puppets.

The young people I met in the gang scene have a profound distrust of the media discourse and steer clear of the media spotlight. We could say that 'they are spoken', but 'they do not speak', or at least they do not speak within that social circle. For the most part, their struggle consists of escape and silence. On the one hand, they do not read the newspapers, they do not publicly contest the language that defines them and they only occasionally seek out information about how their image is constructed to suit public opinion. On the other hand, they produce a parallel space and time where they can circulate their representations, another way of achieving public exposure in relation to youth styles and cultures. On the Facebook page of the film – followed by about one thousand young people from the gang scene in Spain – they discuss music, sport, religion, consumption of alcohol and drugs, internal group organization, motherhood and love. Socio-political issues rarely appear and include the crisis, unemployment, housing and evictions, corruption, struggles and the migrant condition.

Music is another subject I explored in order do understand their imagination and compile the film's soundtrack using music that is popular in the gang scene. A band with whom we interacted during filming, who are affiliated with a powerful chapter of the Latin Kings of Barcelona, put songs with explicit lyrics on YouTube: "Here there's no fear, the fear is all yours, we see it in your face, envy eats you alive, we're the ones who got the street, the money and the women". All of these songs accompanied by a visual narration that simulates the actions of hit men and invokes a burst of "bullets on the enemies to send them straight to the cemetery".[8] What is interesting about these lyrics, as Osvaldo (the young leader of a gang who participated in the workshop) told me, is the fact that they are fictional, a form of magical realism:

> They're just fantasies, they represent what they're not and things they don't do, maybe not even what they were. Just like all the gangsta rap with billionaires going on about and exalting the violence of the ghetto from their Miami villas. They only do it to recruit kids.

Our interlocutors are not assassins; they do not spend their time playing shootings with their enemies, they do not have weapons, they do not control the streets from which they are permanently expelled by urban authorities (Giliberti and Queirolo Palmas, 2014), they have no money, they hardly ever have credit on their mobile phones and they used ours repeatedly. The crime they produce is of the lowest quality and, as nomadic gatherers, they take from the streets what is useful to get them through the day. However, some of them love to represent themselves publicly, through lyrics and videos, following this gangsta imagery, which is basically the barbaric imagery through which the hegemonic discourse labels them. When we discussed the opportunity of using those lyrics for a film that seeks to challenge the pathological code of the hegemonic narration, they offered us the following reflections:

> We use gangsta aesthetics to send a message. It's just a code to be heard. It's what we have. In our neighborhoods the most famous people are thieves. We have many talents. Look at the Puerto Rican gangstas who have become billionaires. We talk about bullets because this is what the street kids want to hear, but then we put in other contents. We talk about bullets because the other groups must know that if they do not respect us, we're able to settle the score.

As the lyrics of these songs as well as many testimonies collected during the ethnography remind us, the *tropos* conveyed by the hegemonic narration can certainly rely on elements of truth. However, they are also documented mechanisms of a self-fulfilling prophecy, of gang production through the media, in which young people end up looking like a bad copy of how they were painted and finally give life to what had existed in the first place in the language of power.

In the gang scene, fame and respect are often gained through the inferiorization of an Other that is basically an identical Other, a double, that is, a lower-class young man of migrant origin.[9] However, searching for fame and respect can also create spaces to claim and question the existing symbolic order infused by stigma and discrimination. For example, during the writing of the soundtrack of *Buscando Respeto*, an inversion of hegemonic representations appeared; like in many other documented cases, exiting the groups will open up religious scenarios (Castellani, Lagomarsino, and Queirolo Palmas, 2014). The following lyrics were discussed and generated during the workshop and are performed by a group of Dominican origin called Kitasellos (those who free themselves from labels).

> I'm looking for respect. Treat me like I treat you, don't judge me, don't ignore me, please
>   You don't know how many times I cried in my bed, you don't imagine the hunger I suffered
>   Nobody gave me a glass of water when I was thirsty, no one congratulated me when I passed my exams

Now don't tell me what I have to do, if I've killed, if I'm a criminal, it's the fault of the system, get it into your head

If I'm sitting down, the police tell me to go away and get suspicious right away, and if I say something, I get a slap, and you want me to respect the system?

My life was in danger for problems on the streets, I saw my friend's enemy die

The police were tracking me down, but I ran away and got lucky, and a couple of times I even escaped death

Tell me if you know what it feels like when they look at you with disgust and spite, people that you know well don't smell better than you and aren't worth more than you are

Respect me and I'll respect you. If you humiliate me, I won't humiliate you, in fact I'll show you that respect is earned with respect.

It's the crisis . . . there's no work, problems at home. Many end up in drugs and others in the Bible. And where do I go? I don't know, but I'm with God. Whenever I can I pray, and I say thanks for what I have. But I'm not settling for this and I want more. I imagine myself with a lot of money to help my people and the whole world . . .

This narrative does not exclude that biographies can be marked by crime and violence, but it places responsibility on the social conditions of exclusion affecting young people of migrant origin. A short circuit is thus generated in the hegemonic discourse, projecting something that belongs to the society in which they are settled on the outside. As Conquergood (1994, 2002) has already noted, the violence attributed to gangs is nothing but the deformed reflection of a similar violence which is typical of the way the most normal and legitimate social institutions function, such as family, work, school, sexism, authoritarianism, classism. The construction of a color line (Du Bois, 1903), culturalized and racialized, places these young people in a condition of even deeper estrangement. The hegemonic media spread *appropriate* narratives, either defining gangs as public enemies, forgetting their existence or invoking punishment or rehabilitation. The self-representations of the young people I have encountered during this visual ethnography play with the stigma, reflecting its modalities and languages while trying to articulate a public discourse of an 'Other Us' that has been discriminated against – youth, poor, migrants – or to protect itself from the regime of visibility and surveillance, hiding under in plain sight (Hebdige, 1988). The workshop for *Buscando Respeto* produced an end for the film in which the obvious destiny for these young gangs is to be forcefully pushed towards drug trafficking. Let us consider the final lines of the film in which the protagonists discuss the future:

- We must traffic (in drugs) and that's it! Let's organize the traffic! Come on let's go!
- You're out, bro!
- I don't know, guys, but what I know for sure is that if you don't have money, you get no respect from people.
- But if we get involved in trafficking, we'll pile up money . . . yes, we can!
- Because, as the saying goes: "If you have nothing, you're worth nothing"

These words describe a realistic destiny that they would like to deny and which is a source of collective fear. The screenplay, written through fiction and improvisation, lets out a cry that evokes how it is precisely this place and this role in petty crime, drugs, and theft that they will have to deal with unless the social disinvestment on young lower-class people is reversed. The thread of the narrative that came out of the workshop and was written by a leader of the Ñeta association depicts the loneliness of a young migrant who finds in the gangs – the street families – a symbolic refuge from institutional exclusion. The youth scene of the gangs is thus shown as a natural product of a host society, rather than some kind of exotic import.

> Here, if it weren't for my friends in the group, I'd have no one. At least with them I have something in common. My classmates mock me, they ask me if we eat with our hands . . . among us Latinos we're doing well . . . but I hate it when they start calling me monkey about anything. They don't even imagine that all they're doing is making my identity and my hate grow, not towards them, but towards their ignorance. . . . Today my soul is strong, today the Lord is great! The humble will be the first and the oppressed will enter the kingdom of heaven. That's how I feel and that's how I see my friends in the group, we all have a something in common among the thousands of things that set us apart. They taught me this in yesterday's meeting . . . we must come together with the others who accept us and come together with those who don't accept us but live the same life as us and struggle to prove it. We must unite the street families, seeking respect for everyone. This is the mission, I no longer feel aimless, at least I have a concrete direction in this city. It's time to get out of my room and win respect at home . . . God help me.

Buscando Respeto is an ambiguous work precisely because it carries within it the sign of the multiplicity of registers that subaltern discourses can produce, and it unfolds them onto a field that intersects with the point of view of the researchers-directors. The outcome of the authorial struggle between documentary codes and fiction codes, between researchers and 'researched', stabilizes the narrative line of the film around the scenes that were imagined and improvised by the actors/authors in the workshop. Consequently, in the film, as a young Latin King named Spartaco puts it, "there is no moral, there is no solution, there is no lesson". After all, the visual product is only a pretext, and it was precisely this unstable objectification that we were looking for: observing the process of production and crystallization of images, using the film as a vector that penetrates a social and symbolic space, leaving behind a trail, a microphysical opening for relationships and possible futures. *Buscando Respeto* spreads through the rhizomatic channels of social networks, through informal presentations in which for us, the researchers, dissemination is an opportunity to produce new knowledge, through the tens of thousands of views on YouTube. What remains is the attempt by a group of young people of migrant origin to live through the crisis starting from their generational, class and gender condition, exposing what they have, not only what they lack, revealing, with all its contradictions and temporariness, their ability to act and resist, producing a language and a horizon of meaning in the face of the conditions of material, symbolic, legal and cultural exclusion to which they are subjected.

Conclusion

It is important to highlight some of the dynamics at work in the practice of filmic sociology. First, using an ethnographic workshop as one of the possible strategies in the field of filmic sociology helps to situate the research as the kind of activity and concrete production that researchers and research subjects are meant to perform together. Second, sharing research activities can create a special relationship with time and space, deepening aspects such as trust and amity. The participation and involvement of gang youths in the visual workshop lays the foundations for a co-production of knowledge that is then transferred to the narrative and to the film-making and editing processes. Third, images can be used as a form of writing once participants master certain types of knowledge and techniques. This means that training is one of the main conditions to run and build the workshop. Fourth, as Jean Rouch said about shared anthropology, to be crystallized as objects, films need to be looked at from three perspectives, that is, not only from the points of view of researchers and actors-subjects but also from a third, combined perspective (one that does, however, have its own tensions). Finally, the process is as important as the product. Film production workshops bring up constant conflicts caused by the tensions due to the fact that narratives, texts, codes and dialogues arise from people's lives. What emerges then are social worlds that researchers will want to describe and interpret. What films and filmic sociology highlight are those challenges and tensions that would have remained unseen and unheard had the sociological research been undertaken without the film.

What was the usefulness of a visual approach to ethnography? It allowed me not only to better reveal the logic behind the functioning of a social world – the gang scene in Spain between 2010 and 2014 – by cultivating a more symmetrical common ground between those who do research and those who are being researched but also to contaminate the symbolic positions and places of enunciation of each side. Fragments of our discourses have penetrated among the youth of the street families like no sociology book or essay could have ever done, while fragments of their points of view and positions have pervaded our narration and our gaze. Who is the author and what is the work?

Notes

1 This chapter comes from my experience leading the YOUGANG project (Gangs Policies: Youth and Migration in Local Contexts, Marie Curie Intra-European Fellowship – 7th European Community Framework Program, 2011–2013). The film *Buscando Respeto* (2014) has been made by Jose González Morandi in the context of a broader ethnographic research project: www.youtube.com/watch?v=kSMHicXO7F0 (full version). The overall results of the research have been published in: Queirolo Palmas, 2017b. I'm grateful to Elena Boschi for her editing work on this text.

2 The concept of *scene* (Hallsworth, 2013) – which differs from Anderson's perspective (2000), a somewhat rigid *street code* – better represents the concrete functioning of these social spaces, highlighting the fluid and turbulent character of belonging and practices. The term 'gang' does not correspond with the language of the young members of these groups, who instead prefer the terms 'chorus', 'group', 'nation', 'association', 'organization', 'family'. Having acknowledged its limitations, from now on, the term gang will be used without inverted commas.

3 According to Sauvadet (2006), warrior capital is based on physical strength, and it is accrued and established on the streets. The horizontal violence produced in the gang scene questions the state monopoly on physical violence and contributes to the accrual of respect, like a form of symbolic capital.

4 For a Bourdieusian approach to gangs as lower-class style, see Mauger (2006).

5 A step towards building trust in and gaining access to the underground world of gangs has been interviewing King Tone, a charismatic former leader of the Latin Kings in New York (see: www.youtube.com/watch?v=w1BZCDO2g4k). The interview, which highlighted the importance of having a public voice and getting out from the shadows, received thousands of views and comments once it was posted on YouTube, contributing to building our reputation and position among Spanish gangs. This also accounts for the transnational quality of the gang worlds (Queirolo Palmas, 2016).

6 Young people from the following street gangs in Barcelona and Madrid took part in the project of *Buscando Respeto*: Latin Kings, Ñetas, Mara Salvatrucha, Kitasellos.

7 This is a term used in order to transform the stigma of gangs into an emblem.

8 See: www.youtube.com/watch?v=FDIPNzjm5mA and www.youtube.com/watch?v=wfFUKNMMpGA

9 For the most part, the violence is endogenous, suicidal, one could say; it is aimed towards subjects of a similar class and ethnic origin, but it does not affect local people or the upper-middle classes (Conte, 2011).

References

Anderson E. (2000), *Code of the Street: Decency, Violence, and the Moral Life of the Inner City*, New York: Norton & Company.

Back L., Puwar N. (eds) (2012), *Live Methods*, London: Wiley-Blackwell.

Bernstein B. (1973), *Class, Codes and Control. Theoretical Studies Towards a Sociology of Language*, St. Albans: Paladins.

Bourdieu P. (1992), *Réponses. Pour une anthropologie réflexive*, Paris: Editions du Seuil.

Bourdieu P. (1998), *Contre-feux. Propos pour servir à la résistance contre l'invasion néo-libérale*, Paris: Raisons d'Agir.

Brotherton D. (2015), *Youth Street Gangs. A Critical Appraisal*, London-New York: Routledge.

Cannarella M., Lagomarsino F., Oddone C. (2018), Documentare la prigione: riflessioni a partire da un laboratorio video-etnografico, in Sebag J., Durand J.P., Louveau C., Queirolo Palmas L. (eds), *Sociologie visuelle et filmique. Le point de vue dans la vie quotidienne*, Genova: GUP.

Castellani S., Lagomarsino F., e Queirolo Palmas L. (2014), *La banda y la iglesia. Transiciones y espacios de subjetivización de la juventud latina en Barcelona y Genova*. Actas del XIII Congreso de Antropología de la Federación de Asociaciones de Antropología del Estado Español, Tarragona: Universidad Rovira i Virgili, http://digital.publicationsurv.cat/index.php/purv/catalog/book/123.

Cerbino M. (2012), *El lugar de la violencia. Perspectivas críticas sobre pandillerismo juvenil*, Quito: Taurus-Flacso.

Conquergood D. (1994), How street gangs problematize patriotism, in Herbert S.H., Billig M. (eds) *After Post-Modernism. Reconstructing Ideology Critique*, London: Sage Publications.

Conquergood D. (2002), Performance studies. Interventions and radical research, in *The Drama Review*, 46(2).

Conte M. (2011), Le qualità eccedenti dell'omicidio. La violenza e la morte nei gruppi di strada latino-americani a Milano, in *Rassegna di criminologia*, 3.

De Certeau M. (1990), *L'invention du cotidien*, Paris: Gallimard.

Du Bois W.E.B. (1903), *The Souls of the Black Folk*, Chicago: McLurg & Co.

Erel U., Reynolds T., Kaptani U. (2017), Participatory theatre for transformative social research, in *Qualitative Research*, 17(3), 302–312.

Giliberti L., Queirolo Palmas L. (2014), Le bande e la città. Conflitti e spazio pubblico nella Spagna contemporanea, in *Etnografia e Ricerca Qualitativa*, 2, 423–444.

Hallsworth S. (2013), *The Gang and Beyond: Interpreting Violent Street Worlds*, London: Palgrave Macmillan.

Hebdige D. (1988), *Hiding in the Light. On Images and Things*, London-New York: Routledge.

Kaptani E., Yuval-Davis N. (2008), Participatory theatre as a research methodology: Identity, performance and social action among refugees, in *Sociological Research Online*, 13(5), 1–12.

Marwan M. (2011), *La formation des bandes. Entre la famille, l'école et la rue*, Paris: PUF.

Mauger M. (2006), *Les bandes, le milieu et la bohème populaire*, Paris: Belin.

Navone L., Oddone C. (2015), Fare ricerca nelle istituzioni: la formula del laboratorio video-etnografico, in Queirolo Palmas L., Stagi L. (eds), *Fare Sociologia Visuale*, Trento: Professional Dreamers, www.professionaldreamers.net/_prowp/wp-content/uploads/Fare-sociologia-visuale.pdf.

Queirolo Palmas L. (2015), The policies and policing of gangs in contemporary Spain. An ethnography of a bureaucratic field of the state, in *Sociologica*, 1.

Queirolo Palmas L. (2016), Gangs in the Latino Atlantic: La Raza Latina, transnationalism and generations, in Carles Feixa, Carmen Leccardi, Pam Nilan (eds) *Youth, Space, Time. Agoras and Chronotopes in the Global City*, New York: Brill.

Queirolo Palmas L. (2017a), Scrivere e fare sociologia con le immagini. La prospettiva delle etnografie filmiche, in Tota A., Serpieri R. (eds) *Quali culture per altre educazioni possibili?* Milano: Angeli.

Queirolo Palmas L. (2017b), *Come se construye un enemigo publico, La "bandas latinas"*, Madrid: traficantes de suenos.

Restrepo C. (2007), *Con el diablo adentro: pandillas, tiempo paralelo y poder*, México: Siglo XXI.

Sauvadet T. (2006), *Le capital guerrier. Concurrence et solidarité entre jeunes de cité*, Paris: Arman Colin.

Sayad A. (1999), *La double absence. Des illusions aux souffrances de l'immigré*, Paris: Seuil.

Scott J. (1990), *Domination and the Arts of Resistance: Hidden Transcripts*, Yale: Yale University Press.

Sebag J., Durand J.P., Louveau C., Queirolo Palmas L. (2018), *Sociologie visuelle et filmique. Le point de vue dans la vie quotidienne*, Genova: GUP, http://gup.unige.it/sites/gup.unige.it/files/pagine/SOCIOLOGIE%20VISUELLE%20ET%20FILMIQUE%20Le%20point%20de%20vue%20dans%20la%20vie%20quotidienne.pdf.

Spivak G.C. (1988), *Can the Subaltern Speak?* Basingstoke: Palgrave Macmillan.

12

Why gang members are dehumanized in court

John M. Hagedorn

Consider Roget's Thesaurus' synonyms for "gang member"

> bad person, evil person, no saint, sinner, hardened sinner, *LIMB OF SATAN, ANTI-CHRIST*, evildoer, fallen angel, backslider, recidivist, lost sheep, lost soul . . . *ONE WITHOUT MORALS*, immoralist reprobate, scapegrace, good-for-nothing, ne'er-do-well, black sheep, scallywag, scamp, rake . . . profligate, libertine, wanton, hussy, *LOOSE WOMAN* . . ., outcast, dregs, riffraff, trash, white trash, SCUM, object of scorn . . .

Over the top? Here is what prosecutors said at sentencing about Jacqueline Montañez, a 15-year-old girl convicted of shooting two rival gang members:

> *Jacqueline Montañez is a COLD, CALCULATING, VICIOUS MURDERER full of hate beyond her years.* She showed *NO REMORSE* at the trial and I believe today shows no remorse about what happened. [She] *EXECUTED Hector Reyes and Jimmie Cruz IN A MANNER THAT AL CAPONE WOULD BE PROUD OF.* Jacqueline Montañez, Judge, has become *THE TEEN QUEEN OF CRIMINALS.* She stands 15 years old, but by her actions, SHE'S A SEASONED VETERAN, A *COLD-BLOODED ASSASSIN.*
> *(Montañez v. Illinois 1993, p. E-146)*

Well, at least she wasn't accused of being the Antichrist. All this about a 15-year-old Puerto Rican girl, who it turns out, was physically and sexually abused beginning at age 8 by her Latin King step father. She repeatedly ran away and was regularly returned by police to her abusive home. Finally she escaped and joined the rival Maniac Latin Disciples and violently displaced her anger toward her father onto two members of his gang. When I asked her in prison to close her eyes and recount the shooting, she began the story and then broke down and cried, "It wasn't them I wanted to shoot it was my stepfather." No surprise to anyone familiar with the child abuse that typically characterizes "women who kill" someone other than their child or spouse (Jones 1996).

This chapter aims to explain why patently false stereotypes about gangs are so persuasive in court. Rather than look at *demonizing* as what "they" do, I examine the social psychological roots of humankind's "us vs. them" mindset. The social cognition, communication, and neuroscience literatures are incredibly vast and complex, but I'll pick out a few seminal concepts like "prototypes," "frames," and "priming" to explain how our hard-wired proclivity to think in categories is kindled into a raging fire by prosecutors' demonizing rhetoric. Then I'll explain why dehumanizing gang members is psychologically necessary to get juries and judges to hand out long sentences or the death penalty. I'll illustrate these ideas with examples from my court cases, which I expand on in my book, *Gangs on Trial: Challenging Stereotypes and Demonization in Court* (Hagedorn forthcoming)

The way we deal with gangs is similar to our current "war on terror." Indeed, many states' basic laws concerning gangs are some version of "The California Street Terrorism Enforcement and Protection (S.T.E.P.) Act," melding anti-gang and anti-terrorism policy. Edward Said's *Orientalism* (1979, 207) is a masterpiece of the social construction of Islamophobic stereotypes. He could have been talking about gangs when he said

> Orientals were . . . seen through, analyzed not as citizens, or even people, but as problems to be solved or confined.

Inflammatory and dehumanizing rhetoric by prosecutors, like a recurrent nightmare, haunts the courtroom in one form or another whenever a "gang member" is accused of a crime. Such rhetoric permeated our criminal justice system long before Donald Trump called the Central American gang MS-13 "animals." And the president actually added at a Nashville rally: "They're not human beings! They're not human beings!" (Schwartz 2018).

The reckless use by prosecutors, politicians, and the media of stereotypes and sensationalist rhetoric can railroad the innocent. The classic example is the "wolf pack" designation of the Central Park Five in 1989, where a "gang" of five minority teenagers were wrongfully convicted of the brutal rape of a jogger in what is now recognized as a moral panic (Burns 2011). Only a handful of my 81 gang-related court cases are of the falsely accused. In those cases, I've had great satisfaction to see "justice done" – though sadly only after the defendant spent months or even years in jail awaiting trial or served time for a wrongful conviction.

But note: *this chapter is not about the actually innocent but more about the actually guilty*. Nearly every gang member in the 60 homicide cases I consulted in was actually guilty of murder. Seventeen faced the death penalty. Since my first book, *People & Folks*, I've argued gang members are rebels but often destructively. Violence is a rare event among gang members – who hang out more than anything else. However, violence occurs much too often and has devastating consequences for victims, their families, and their loved ones, as well as the offender.

One of the assumptions of my work is that I don't believe anyone should get away with murder. However, what goes on in court is a far cry from jurors rationally considering "evidence and argument so that the cause may be decided on the basis of law" (Center for Professional Responsibility 2016; see also Lippman 2014). I'll show how in court, "implicit stereotypes," like those you've just read from Roget's Thesaurus (1995), mean gang members are in effect guilty until proven innocent, making a mockery of any notion of a "fair trial." Through stories from my 25 years of expert witness work in court, I point out the "dangerous frames" (Winter 2008) that shape juries' and judges' thinking about gangs and subvert the process of justice.

My expert witness work is not aimed at getting defendants off. That is the defense attorney's job. I see my role as countering stereotypes and sensationalism with research, insisting on, or rather begging for, a trial by reason and evidence. Alas, I'll use concepts from linguistics to explain why reason and evidence alone are not enough. My "successes" are often painfully measured by only a year or two taken off an already unbearably long sentence. Most often, I fear I have not had any effect at all.

I've based my work on two other assumptions, which are not universally shared. First, I believe we need to affirm the humanity of even those who kill. Gang members are human beings, no matter what Donald Trump says. Second, I believe our sentences are much too long and unduly punitive, even for murder. Our current criminal justice system exemplifies what is called the "fundamental attributional error" (Fiske and Taylor 1991, 67): that evil deeds come from an evil nature more than circumstances. White jurors particularly have come to believe most Black and Hispanic offenders are unredeemable (e.g. Pickett and Chiricos 2012). In short, I'm arguing the critical study of gangs should not just be about them but about us as well.

Categories, stereotypes, and prejudice

In court, I use the gang research literature to dispel stereotypes that are typically unchallenged in court. However, this chapter introduces the social psychological literature on stereotyping rather than reiterating another synopsis of research on gangs.

The contemporary study of stereotyping really begins with the most evil event of the 20th century. Sociologists and philosophers were trying to explain the Nazis and the horrors of the Holocaust as well as the Germans who went along with Hitler (Horkheimer and Adorno 1944). They posited a special type of person, the "authoritarian personality," who was characterized by "blind submission to authority, strict adherence to middle-class conventions, aggression against those who do not live conventionally, and the tendency to think in rigid categories" (Fiske 358). In other words, stereotyping and prejudice were the product of backward elements – the *deplorables* of that age. Liberal thought insisted: *they* are prejudiced, but *we* are enlightened.

Gordon Allport challenged that idea in *The Nature of Prejudice (1954)*. Allport argued that we all think in categories – in other words, stereotyping is normal, not deviant. Using stereotypes or "cognitive shortcuts" is necessary so we don't have to think through each situation every time. We sit on chairs and put cups on tables and don't need to think about which one to do. "Open mindedness is considered to be a virtue," Allport says with startling implications for criminal trials. "But strictly speaking it cannot occur. A new experience must be redacted into old categories. We cannot handle each event freshly in its own right" (20).

Allport extended his notion of categorization to group stereotypes and prejudice. He pointed out people are also automatically categorized into in-groups and out-groups. These in-groups include kinship, city, country, gender, and race. As Rudyard Kipling cleverly put it long ago:

> All good people agree,
> and all good people say,
> all nice people, like us are We
> and everyone else is They.

Some out-groups are especially stigmatized. There is a mountain of research evidence that white people see black people in a negative, fearful light. Susan Fiske summarizes the literature: "the content of whites' generic stereotypes of blacks as lazy, ignorant, loud, musical, rhythmic, poor, stupid, dirty, and physically skilled (e.g., athletic). More recent historical context contributes to white views of blacks as militant, violent, criminal, and hostile" (1978, 379; see also Entman and Rojecki 2000; Devine 1989).

Winter explains that pre-existing gender and racial schema are stable patterns of thought and belief that have developed over centuries. He argues that "racial schema" are "both close to the surface and positioned cognitively for easy assimilation to political matters" and operate to "subconsciously influence decision-making" (2008, 80). This is the psychological root of Derrick Bell's (1992) notion of the permanence of racism.

Gangs are an example of an especially stigmatized outgroup, and we have research evidence that merely the mention that a defendant is a gang member increases the likelihood of conviction (e.g. Eisen et al 2014; Moore et al 2012). The very appearance of a dark-skinned threatening young man prompts jurors to place him in a "gang frame." Frames are central to understanding how jurors' or judges' minds work when a defendant is labeled a "gang member." Frames are compilations of generalizations that shape how we see a person or phenomenon.

The concept of frames comes from a variety of literatures, including sociology (Goffman 1974), communication (Entman 1993), linguistics (Lakoff 1987), and social movements (Benford 1997). For our purposes, this definition fits best: A frame provides "a central organizing idea . . . for making sense of relevant events, suggesting what is at issue" (Gamson and Modigliani 1989, 3).

A trial can be seen as a "frames contest." Prosecutors tell the facts that fit their "frame" or story of the crime. The defense counters with an alternative story or frame. One strand of research on juror decision-making finds jurors "organize trial evidence into a plausible story. Jurors then attempt to match the story to available verdict categories, selecting the verdict that provides the best fit" (MacCoun 1989, 1047).

Prosecutors argue with the voice of authority, speaking for "the people." This is effective particularly when police experts claim a crime is "gang related." Druckman (2001, 1059) concurs, saying "Framing works when the statements are attributed to a credible source." In most cases, there are no competing frames on gangs even presented by the defense, thus entirely yielding the field (Sniderman and Theriault 2004; Entman 1993). In many of my cases of ineffective counsel, one of the major issues is the lack of any rebuttal by the defense of gang-related allegations.

To reinforce the power of stereotypes, using a reference to the courtroom, two leading social psychologists say

> Stereotypes do not take special effort to acquire. Quite the opposite – they are acquired effortlessly, and take special effort to discount. . . . Yet if we were to think of our minds as court rooms in which trials are held to decide on guilt or innocence one of the downsides of stereotypes is that they compromise due process. By relying on them our minds indict before a prosecutor arrives on the scene.
>
> *(Banaji and Greenwald 2013, 109)*

In court, this means jurors process "facts" in a distinctly biased manner.

> When examining evidence relevant to a given belief, people are inclined to see what they expect to see, and conclude what they expect to conclude. Information that is consistent with our pre-existing beliefs is often accepted at face value, whereas evidence that contradicts them is critically scrutinized and discounted.
>
> *(Gilovich 1991, 50)*

I could summarize the social psychological literature on the power of stereotypes for a hundred pages (e.g. McDonald 2016), but I think even this brief review makes the point. Gang members in court are assumed guilty because they fit the stereotypes we hold of violent young minority males. Trials typically are exercises in confirmation bias more than objective judgment. To make matters worse, Michael Shermer points out brain research

> consistently shows that once people have established what they think is the cause of an event they just observed – (in other words, they have formed a link between A and B) – they will then continue to gather information to support that causal link over other possibilities – if they can even think of alternatives once the first causal link is established, which they usually cannot.
>
> *(Shermer 2011)*

"Cause of an event" is what trials are all about – did "x" murder "y"? Stereotypes undermine the presumption of innocence. Allport (1954, 189) anticipated this problem long ago when he said "it is possible for a stereotype to grow in defiance of all evidence, developing where no real correlations exist." This is really the challenge of my work in court.

Examples of stereotypes in court

One common stereotype of gangs is "blood in blood out," or the gang is lifelong and to leave it means you have to undergo a violent ritual which may be fatal. Though there are important differences between leaving a gang in prison and in the community, I consistently hear police "gang experts" claim that so-and-so is still a gang member because he was not "jumped out." Police gang squad officers regularly testify about gangs as if they are all alike and share common practices like "violating" members if they try to leave the gang. Rather than look at an individual, a specific gang or the situation, the gang defendant is seen as a representative of a stigmatized, uniform category, "gang member."

One illustration of the power of the "blood in blood out" stereotype was in a Milwaukee courtroom in 2002. "Sammy Garcia" was a member of a small Mexican gang that split off from the Latin Kings. He was on probation for an earlier offense and had a court hearing. He told the judge he was no longer a gang member, had a job, and was raising a family. When Sammy said he was not jumped out but had just walked away, the judge exploded. He said it was "common knowledge" you couldn't just walk away from a gang, ordered his probation revoked, and sent him to prison.

His public defender, Patricia Cornwall, appealed the revocation and asked me to address the issue of whether it was necessary to be "violated" to leave a gang. My affidavit, citing my own Milwaukee research, stated that most people leave gangs not by being "jumped out" but by walking away and getting on with their life. The judge's "common knowledge" in this case was simply a euphemism for stereotypes. When the Appeals Court overturned the judge's ruling, Sammy was released. He was ecstatic, but I also got some personal satisfaction. You see, this particular judge had been the manager of my son's Little League baseball team. The judge's comparative appraisal of his kid's and my son's baseball ability had already raised questions in my mind about his objectivity.

Few cases get decided on the basis of research, like Sammy's. In 2012, the US Supreme Court in *Miller v Alabama* overturned automatic life sentences for juveniles convicted of murder. This means nationally more than 2500 juveniles had to be re-sentenced. In Illinois, a juvenile who committed a double homicide or killed a police officer had been automatically sentenced to life without parole (JLWOP), and more than a hundred youthful offenders had to be re-sentenced.

In the case of Jacqueline Montañez, the Miller decision didn't sit well with prosecutors. Jackie's original judge had complained at her sentencing that because she was two weeks away from her 16th birthday at the time of her offense, he was prohibited from giving her the death penalty. Prosecutors later chimed in at clemency hearings: one said she was "lucky" that she "only" received life without parole. Since the Miller decision, individual states varied in their JLWOP re-sentencing policies, but in Illinois, prosecutors reacted with a vengeance.

The first JLWOP case in Illinois was Adolpho Davis, and the strategy to keep this former Gangster Disciple in jail for life was clear: argue that he had not left the gang while incarcerated and therefore was a continuing threat to society. It worked, and Adolpho, who had become something of a model prisoner, was re-sentenced to life without parole. He claimed he had broken ties with the Gangster Disciples while in prison, but the prosecutor scoffed at such a notion, and his gang membership was one of the main reasons an angry judged re-sentenced him to life without parole.[1]

This sent attorneys for other JLWOP clients to scurry about looking for someone who could counter the notion that gang membership in prison is evidence of what Miller calls "irretrievable depravity." One such inmate was Kentrell Stoutmire, an African American member of the Latin Kings. He was raised in the gang – his uncle was a major leader and his family is peppered with LK members. After a police raid in 1997 that arrested the entire "Crown Council" or leadership of his local LK branch, his gang (in Kentrell's words) "was left in the hands of kids 12 to 20 years old." This included 17-year-old Kentrell, who was on patrol of their housing project when he shot and killed two Gangster Disciples. This earned him a mandatory life without parole sentence, which was the reason he was to be re-sentenced due to Miller.

I was retained by Randolph Stone, fabled University of Chicago attorney, at their Mandel Clinic. Randolph is an incredibly smart, impeccably dressed, bow-tied attorney. His background included heading the Cook County Public Defenders office. His calm demeanor reflected his meticulous preparation but belied his passionate drive for justice. I was asked to explain to the judge Kentrell's gang membership in prison and why it should not be held against him.

The facts matter. Like all gang members who go into the Illinois Department of Corrections (IDOC), being in a gang is both functional and necessary for survival. Kentrell told me:

> As soon as I came in they (LKs) gave me clothes, food, cosmetics, radio, the whole care package. It was dangerous in general population. Guys were getting stabbed and it was safer with the Kings. You could get put in a cell with a GD and get raped if the guy was bigger than you. I saw guys get raped. The Kings made sure I was in a cell with friends. I was 19 and skinny. I was scared to death, petrified. The Kings were a survival mechanism.

Like most teenaged inmates, prison strengthens gang identity, but as they age, most see gang banging as kid stuff and try to move on with their lives. It is not so easy in prison, where even the Illinois courts (*People v Puffer* 2017) recognize young people need to be gang affiliated for protection. Kentrell was raised in the gang, and the Latin Kings were an indelible part of his identity. My private interviews with him were stormy, as I challenged him to explain how he "distanced himself" from the gang while remaining a member. At one point he yelled at me, "What do I have to do to convince them I'm not involved!" I wrote an intense report describing his internal torments and "multiple conflicting identities." I argued he distanced himself from the gang while maintaining enough ties to keep himself alive.

At sentencing, the State put on a Gang Intelligence officer who explained to the court that Kentrell could not have left the LKs because he was never beaten out and in fact, is still alive. They played audio tapes of Kentrell's phone calls to other gang members that they claimed proved he was still a member. That set the stage for my two hours of testimony and cross-examination.

Testifying is typically more than contrasting research with stereotypes, like with Sammy's case. George Lakoff (2004, 115) said of confronting "hard frames" like gang stereotypes: "You cannot win just by setting the true facts and showing they contradict your opponent's claims. Frames trump facts. His frames will stay and the facts will bounce off." Actually, it's even worse than Lakoff claims. When frames or stereotypes of gangs are strong, stating research or "the facts" can have a "backfire effect" (Nyhan and Reifler 2011). This psychological process results when strong beliefs, stereotyped or not, are challenged; people sometimes reject "discrepant information" and strengthen their support of their original stance. I've watched with extreme anxiety when judges' or jurors' eyes glaze over when I tried to simply recite research to challenge gang stereotypes.

Lakoff's advice is "Always reframe. *Once your frame is accepted into the discourse, everything you say is just commonsense.*" Complicating matters, the stereotype of "blood in blood out" had some surface validity in Illinois prisons, where it is not possible to openly quit the gang without severe consequences. The IDOC has a formal procedure for renouncing the gang which entails debriefing to Gang Intelligence and telling them who has what position within the gang and spilling any secrets. To renounce always means going into protective custody or transferring out of state to keep the inmate from retaliatory violence by his gang. Some stereotypes are true.

But what this means in practice, I argued, is inmates do not formally quit the gang but "distance themselves" from it while "staying on the count" or keeping nominal membership. Thus, I could give evidence that "distancing" meant avoiding fights, not having gang literature confiscated from your cell, and enrollment in education or religious programming. But I knew just presenting the "facts" would not dent the gang frame.

Leaving a gang is a process that is alien to judges and juries, and the "blood in blood out" stereotype is reinforced by law enforcement "experts." I needed to make the process of leaving an institution like the gang familiar. Like Lakoff, I believe the mind works in metaphors and images. Walter Lippmann (1922) famously said a stereotype is a "picture in your head." If you've seen the movie *American Me*, I'm sure you remember the rape scene.

The judge in this case paid close attention to my testimony, especially since it contradicted the central point of the Assistant States Attorney (ASA) that Kentrell was a life-long Latin King. I cited the research on identity replacement (Maruna 2001) and my own research on the life course of gang members (Hagedorn 1998). He listened, but he really focused in when I said leaving the gang was like leaving the Catholic Church.

My wife, Mary Devitt, was in the courtroom, and I told the judge she had been raised a Catholic. She didn't leave the church through some sudden decision but began to attend less regularly, monthly, then only on Christmas and Easter, and finally stopped altogether. She has since become a Unitarian, but when she meets friends or acquaintances who were Catholic, they talk about sister so-and-so, fish on Fridays, and the latest exposé. The imprint of Catholicism is life-long, though Mary has since stopped following Church rituals and dogma. So it is with the Latin Kings.

The evidence I presented of Kentrell "distancing himself" from the gang, I argued, is how it works, how gang members in prison move on without endangering their lives. They never lose the identity, but once they are released from prison, they can drop the organizational affiliation. The ASA vigorously cross-examined me, confronting me with testimony by "confidential informants" and prison documents that continued to label Kentrell a Latin King. However, I had "reframed" the issue in Lakoff's terms. After the ASA was done with her cross examination, the judge jumped in and asked questions himself, zeroing in on Kentrell's sincerity. I think I scored.

Kentrell was resentenced to a total of 26 actual years (he's been locked up since 1997). He will be released in 2021. As he told me, when he is out, he will be able to "free up his inner yuppie." He got the shortest sentence of any of my six JLWOP cases. Jackie Montañez got the longest, 31 1/2 years, which means she will be released in 2023. Jackie had described her prison cell as a "tomb." She told me correctional officers sometimes would cruelly tell her that she would die in her cell, that a "life sentence" really meant death. They were wrong.

The prosecution never rests . . . when it comes to demonizing gangs

Stereotypes need to be "primed" for jurors and judges, and incendiary language is standard fare for prosecutors. Demonization is a conscious strategy. Consider these words from a manual on how to prosecute gang cases.

> Faced with the prospect of defending a case involving gang evidence, defense attorneys cower. Understanding the power of such evidence, the defense bar will try almost anything to prevent a prosecutor from admitting gang evidence against their client. The first and most clamorous cry is always the same: "Objection! Gang evidence is prejudicial." The prosecutor's response should be equally strident: "Of course it is! That's the point!"
>
> *(Jackson 2004, 8)*

Prosecutors understand the impact, if not the social psychology, of what is called the "proto-type" of a gang member (Rosch 1978). Lakoff (2004) argues we have folk theories of categories, like "gang member." We have an "idealized cognitive model" of what we think a gang member is, and it is more likely to be similar to Roget's Thesaurus than the real-life kid on the corner. With that folk model in mind, the prosecutor "primes" the jury with lurid tales of gang violence.

In one Atlanta case of mine, the local police gang expert presented a slide show of gang crimes across the city, none of them related to the defendant or his neighborhood. The jury was suitably "primed" to fit the defendant into the stereotype of violent gangs. In social science, this is called the "ecological fallacy." In law, it is guilt by association (US v Roark 1991).

The problem is these racialized prototypes of gangs are deeply rooted in our upbringing, and changing them is a long-term process, a significant problem for juries who must make decisions over a matter of hours or days. We apply these stereotypes through a process of "cognitive short-cuts" or, as Kahneman (2011) terms it, "thinking fast." Fiske summarizes that "people normally engage in cognitive shortcuts, unless motivated to go beyond them" (1978, 363).

Priming a stereotype is a simple matter. Claude Steele's (2010) description of *New York Times* columnist Brent Staples running down a Hyde Park street in Chicago shortly after he moved there is instructive. As a young black man in a running suit, Staples fit the "street thug" stereo-type and residents crossed the street and looked warily at him. That is until he whistled a tune from Vivaldi, signaling he was "one of them," someone familiar with classic European culture. However, it is not easy for a black man in an orange jumpsuit to whistle Vivaldi in a courtroom.

Prosecutors recognize the power of priming juries to cue in juror's minds a Roget's Thesaurus-like stereotype of a gang member. The prosecutor's manual gives this lesson:

> Without question, one of the most dramatic and powerful moments in trial occurs when the prosecutor asks the judge to instruct the defendant to stand and remove his shirt, expos-ing a large, gothic script tattoo across his stomach, reading, "BLOOD KILLER."
>
> *(Jackson 2004, 16)*

This actually happened in the trial of Patrick Stout. Stout was on trial for murder, and to cement his case, the prosecutor wanted to imprint on the jury's mind that Patrick was a hard-core Gangster Disciple. At sentencing, Patrick was ordered by the judge to take off his shirt and display for the jury his tattoos, a scene Patrick described to me as evoking a slave auction. The effect on the jury: Patrick got the death penalty.

Brad MacClean of the Tennessee Office of the Post-Conviction Defender claimed Patrick had "ineffective counsel" at trial, in part because the defense attorney did not rebut prejudicial gang testimony, especially the tattoos. In testimony to the Tennessee Court of Appeals, I pointed out that the crudely drawn tattoos were evidence that Patrick had very little idea of the Gangster Disciples or their symbology. I put into evidence a statement by a member of the Gangster Disciples National Board who said that if Patrick had showed up in Chicago with a tattoo like his, he would "get his ass kicked," if not worse. The tattoo, I argued, showed the opposite of what the prosecutor claimed: Patrick was not a hard-core gang member but had been a teenage wannabe drawing on his arm an inaccurate, uniformed idea of a gang tattoo.

This tale has a somewhat happy ending. While Patrick's conviction was not reversed, his death penalty was overturned. Last I heard from him, he was a mentor in a prison program for young gang members. He is serving life without parole.

Dehumanization works

Why do prosecutors go to such great lengths to dehumanize a gang member? In many cases, such demonizing words are overkill. There is a literature on prosecutors' drive to win at all costs (Davis 2001; Godsey 2017; Butler 2017). The most egregious example in my work was the capital trials of Robert Butts and Marion Wilson, who it was claimed were members of Georgia's FOLKS gang. They killed a man whose car they stole, though it was never clear which one of them did the shooting. Their trials contained more examples of scaring a jury with false, sensationalist gang testimony than in any of my cases.

The "prototype" of prosecutor demonization of gangs occurred during direct examination by the Baldwin County district attorney, Fred Bright. In his appeals to the jury to put Marion and Robert to death, Bright asked the local Gang Squad officer, Ricky Horn, what "FOLKS" stood for. "Followers of Our Lord King Satan" Horn told the all-white jury from Millidgeville, Georgia, a small city whose main claim to fame was that it was the capitol of the Confederacy. It apparently still is. While at the ineffective counsel hearing, I presented considerable evidence of the actual, prosaic meaning of "FOLKS," both Butts' and Wilson's death sentences were allowed to stand.

Butts and Wilson were sentenced to death, and both were subsequently executed by lethal injection. Stereotypes indeed can kill.

David Livingstone Smith (2012, 250) has written a history of dehumanization dating back to even before Aristotle's concept of barbarians. His long history of warfare, genocide, and ethnic violence is a worthwhile, if gruesome, read. His argument is:

> On one hand, we are disposed to carve the world into them and us and take a hostile stance toward outsiders. On the other hand, we think of all people as members of the human community and have a powerful aversion to harming them. Dehumanization offered an escape from this bind. By a feat of mental prestidigitation we discovered a method for counteracting inhibitions against lethal violence by excluding our victims from the human community.

In other words, dehumanization allows us to do violence, to kill other human beings since they aren't *really* human beings. I think this argument extends beyond the death penalty.

If Trump is right and gang members are animals, what better place for them than in cages? This is why in another of my death penalty cases, the prosecutor described the defendant as "unstoppable evil." It is why in the Rodney King case, police officers wrote "NHI" on the police report: "No Humans Involved" (Wynter 1994). Experimental research has found whites tend to make implicit connections between black people and apes (Goff et al 2008). The authors of this study coldly conclude "Dehumanization is a method by which individuals and social groups are targeted for cruelty, social degradation, and state-sanctioned violence."

In short, dehumanization gives us a license to kill.

Conclusion: back to critical gang studies

I've taken us far afield from the typical analysis of critical gang studies. My drift from sociology to social psychology parallels an earlier drift in my discipline from social disorganization to labeling theory (Becker 1963; and, as applied to gangs, Moore 1985). Our theoretical tasks, I've argued, include not just understanding "them" but understanding "us" as well.

My studies on social cognition and practice in the courtroom have not caused me to give up my life-long commitment to fundamental change. Now retired, I go to fewer demonstrations, but I've never faltered in my belief that the key to change is activism. From my first book (Hagedorn 1988) to my last (Hagedorn 2015), I've argued that our principal approach to gangs is to draw them into social movements, not jail them or chill them out with "midnight basketball." My twenty-two years teaching and researching gangs in Chicago, however, taught me not to romanticize them. While gangs have been at times a pro-social force, on the whole, they have been destructive of neighborhoods. Chicago gangs have been persistently involved with violence, some of it drug related, lately a relentless cycle of retaliation in neighborhoods of concentrated poverty (Hagedorn et al 2019). The death of a human being leaves permanent scars, and we need to realize prosecution of gang members often has widespread local support. We should never put ourselves in a position of excusing violence.

Neither should we lose sight of the extreme punitiveness of our society (e.g. Garland 1990; Alexander 2010; Rios 2011). The demonizing of gang members I've described here contributes to filling our prisons with people who will grow old and perhaps die behind bars, never having a chance to redeem themselves with productive lives. While I join in movements against mass incarceration, as a white academic, I have felt compelled to stand up for the demonized, as frustrating and at times personally demoralizing as my efforts may be.

For me, the courtroom is an important arena of struggle against the inhumane values of the mass incarceration society. I agree with the words of Father Greg Boyle (2018) at Pepperdine University.

> Stand with the demonized so that the demonizing will stop, stand with the disposable so that the day will come when we stop throwing people away, and you stand with those whose dignity has been denied, and you stand with those whose burdens are more than they can bear, and you stand with the poor and the powerless and the voiceless. Make those voices heard!

For gang researchers, it may be best to return to Edward Said (1979, 327) to remind us

> Perhaps if we remember that the study of human experience usually has an ethical, to say nothing of a political consequence in either the best or worst sense, we will not be indifferent to what we do as scholars.

John M. Hagedorn

Over the past two decades, I have found myself regularly working in the court system, trying to act on several of my core values: 1) the essential humanity of everyone, including gang members; 2) the belief that even those guilty of murder should be tried based on evidence and reason, not stereotypes and demonization; and 3) our sentencing policy needs to reincorporate rehabilitation and sharply curtail overly long, unnecessarily punitive sentences.

For me, the struggle for justice in court is an essential component of critical gang studies.

Note

1 Note: This injustice was addressed on appeal, and Mr. Davis has been re-sentenced a second time and is scheduled was released in 2020.

References

Alexander, Michelle. 2010. *The New Jim Crow: Mass Incarceration in the Age of Colorblindness*. New York: The New Press.
Allport, Gordon W. 1954. *The Nature of Prejudice*. Reading, MA: Addison-Wesley.
Banaji, Mahzarin R., and Anthony G. Greenwald. 2013. *Blindspot: Hidden Biases of Good People*. New York: Random House.
Becker, Howard. 1963. *Outsiders*. New York: The Free Press.
Bell, Derrick. 1992. *Faces at the Bottom of the Well: The Permanence of Racism*. New York: Basic Books.
Benford, Robert D. 1997. "An Insider's Critique of the Social Movement Framing Perspective." *Sociological Inquiry* 67(4):409–430.
Boyle, Fr. Greg. 2018. "Gang Members Taught Me All I Know." Retrieved February 3, 2019. https://www.facebook.com/dailygoalcast/videos/2239895862965005/UzpfSTEwODAxOTg3NDU6MTAyMTUxOTQ1NjI0NzIyOTg/.
Burns, Sarah. 2011. *The Central Park Five*, Kindle Edition. New York: Random House.
Butler, Paul. 2017. *Chokehold: Policing Black Men*. New York: The New Press. February 3, 2019.
Center for Professional Responsibility. 2016. *Model Rules of Professional Conduct*. Chicago, IL: American Bar Association.
Davis, Angela. 2001. "The American Prosecutor: Independence, Power, and the Threat of Tyranny." *Iowa Law Review* 86:393–465.
Devine, Patricia G. 1989. "Stereotypes and Prejudice: Their Automatic and Controlled Component." *Journal of Personality and Social Psychology*, 56(1):5–18.
Druckman, James A. 2001. "On the Limits of Framing Effects: Who Can Frame?" *Journal of Politics* 63(November):1041–1066.
Eisen, Mitchell L., Brenna Dotson, and Alma Olaguez 2014. "Practitioner: Exploring the Prejudicial Effect of Gang Evidence: Under What Conditions Will Jurors Ignore Reasonable Doubt." *American University Washington College of Law Review Brief* 41.
Entman, Robert A. 1993. "Framing: Toward Clarification of a Fractured Paradigm." *Journal of Communications* 43(4):51–58.
Entman, Robert M., and Andrew Rojecki. 2000. *The Black Image in the White Mind: Media and Race in America*. Chicago, IL: University of Chicago Press.
Fiske, Susan T. 1978 (1954). "Stereotyping, Prejudice, and Discrimination." Pp. 357–411 in *The Handbook of Social Psychology*, edited by D. T. Gilbert, Susan T. Fiske, Gardner Lindzey. Boston, MA: The McGraw-Hill Companies, Inc.
Fiske, Susan T., and Shelley E. Taylor. 1991. *Social Cognition*. New York: McGraw-Hill Companies, Inc.
Gamson, William A., and Amedeo Modigliani. 1989. "Media Discourse and Public Opinion on Nuclear Power: A Constructionist Approach." *American Journal of Sociology* 95(1):1–37.
Garland, David. 1990. *Punishment and Modern Society: A Study in Social Theory*. Oxford: Oxford University Press.

Gilovich, Thomas. 1991. *How We Know It Isn't So: The Fallibility of Reason in Everyday Life*. New York: The Free Press.

Godsey, Mark. 2017. *Blind Justice: A Former Prosecutor Exposes the Psychology and Politics of Wrongful Convictions*. Oakland, CA: University of California Press.

Goff, Phillip Atiba, Jennifer L. Eberhardt, Melissa J. Williams, and Matthew Christian Jackson. 2008. "Not Yet Human: Implicit Knowledge, Historical Dehumanization, and Contemporary Consequences." *Journal of Personality and Social Psychology* 94(2):292–306.

Goffman, Erving. 1974. *Frame Analysis: An Essay on the Organization of Experience*. Cambridge, MA: Harvard University Press.

Hagedorn, John M. 1988/1998. *People and Folks: Gangs, Crime, and the Underclass in a Rustbelt City*, 2nd Edition. Chicago: Lakeview Press.

———. 2015. *The In$ane Chicago Way: The Daring Plan by Chicago Gangs to Create a Spanish Mafia*. Chicago, IL: University of Chicago Press.

———. Forthcoming. *Gangs on Trial: Challenging Stereotypes and Demonization in Court*. Philadelphia: Temple University Press.

Hagedorn, John, Teresa Córdova, Roberto Aspholm, Andrew Papachristos, Lance Williams. 2019. *The Fracturing of Gangs and Violence in Chicago: A Research Based Reorientation of Violence Prevention and Intervention Policy*. Chicago, IL: Great Cities Institute. Retrieved February 3, 2019. https://greatcities.uic.edu/2019/01/29/the-fracturing-of-gangs-and-violence-in-chicago-a-research-based-reorientation-of-violence-prevention-and-intervention-policy/

Horkheimer, Max, and Theodor W. Adorno. 1944/1998. *Dialectic of Enlightenment*. New York: Continuum.

Jackson, Alan. 2004. *Prosecuting Gang Cases: What Local Prosecutors Need to Know*. Alexandria, VA: American Prosecutors Research Institute. www.ndaa.org/pdf/gang_cases.pdf.

Jones, Ann. 1996. *Women Who Kill*. Boston: Beacon Press.

Kahneman, Daniel. 2011. *Thinking Fast and Slow*. New York: Farrar, Strauss and Giroux.

Lakoff, George. 1987. *Women, Fire, and Dangerous Things: What Categories Reveal About the Mind*. Chicago: University of Chicago Press.

———. 2004. *Don't Think of an Elephant! Know Your Values and Frame the Debate: The Essential Guide for Progressives*. White River Junction, VT: Chelsea Green Pub. Co.

Lippman, Matthew Ross. 2014. *Criminal Procedure*. Los Angeles: Sage.

Lippmann, Walter. 1922. *Public Opinion*. New York: Harcourt.

MacCoun, Robert. 1989. "Experimental Research on Jury Decision-Making." *Science* 244(4908):1046–1050.

Maruna, Shadd. 2001. *Making Good: How Ex-Convicts Reform and Rebuild Their Lives*. Washington, DC: American Psychological Association.

McDonald, Aubri F. 2016. "Framing in Criminal Trials: The Murder Case of Jacqueline Montañez." Ph.D. Thesis, Criminology, Law and Justice, University of Illinois–Chicago, Chicago.

Miller v. Alabama, 2012.10–9646. Supreme Court of the United States.

Montañez v Illinois, 92-CR–13088, Tr. of Aug 5–6 (Cir. Ct. 1993). [First Trial]

Moore, Joan W. 1985. "Isolation and Stigmatization in the Development of an Underclass: The Case of Chicano Gangs in East Los Angeles." *Social Problems* 33(1):1–10.

Moore, Sarah G, David T. Neal, and Gavan J. Fitzsimons Baba Shiv. 2012. "Wolves in Sheep's Clothing: How and When Hypothetical Questions Influence Behavior." *Organizational Behavior and Human Decision Processes* 117:168–178.

Nyhan, Brendan, and Jason Reifler. 2011. "When Corrections Fail: The Persistence of Political Misperceptions." *Political Behavior* 32(2):303–330.

People v. Buffer, 2017. IL App (1st) 142931. Appellate Court of Illinois, First District, Third Division.

Pickett, Justin P., and Ted Chiricos. 2012. "Controlling Other People's Children: Racialized Views of Delinquency and Whites' Punitive Attitudes toward Juvenile Offenders." *Criminology* 50(3):673–710.

Rios, Victor. 2011. *Punished: Policing the Lives of Black and Latino Boyd*. New York: New York University Press.

Roget's Thesaurus. "Gang Member." Microsoft Bookshelf Edition, 1995.

Rosch, Eleanor. 1978. "Principles of Categorization." Pp. 27–48 in *Cognition and Categorization*, edited by E. B. B. L. Rosch. Hillsdale, NJ: Eribaum.

Said, Edward W. 1979/1994. *Orientalism*. New York: Vintage.

Schwartz, Raft. 2018. "Trump Leads Supporters in Racist 'Animals' Chant at Nashville Rally." *Splinter News*. June 6, 2018. Retrieved January 26, 2019 https://splinternews.com/trump-leads-supporters-in-racist-animals-chant-at-nashv-1826415832?utm_source=splinter_newsletter&utm_medium=email&utm_campaign=2018-06-03

Shermer, Michael. 2011. *The Believing Brain: From Ghosts and Gods to Politics and Conspiracies – How We Construct Beliefs and Reinforce Them as Truths*. New York: Henry Holt & Company.

Smith, David Livingstone. 2012. *Less Than Human: Why We Demean, Enslave, and Exterminate Others*. New York: St. Martins Griffin.

Sniderman, Paul M., and Sean M. Theriault. 2004. "The Structure of Political Argument and the Logic of Issue Framing." *Studies in Public Opinion: Attitudes, Nonattitudes, Measurement Error, and Change*:133–165.

Steele, Claude. 2010. *Whistling Vivaldi: And Other Clues to How Stereotypes Affect Us*. New York: W.W. Norton & Company.

US v Roark. 1991. United States Court of Appeals, 8th Circuit. No. 90–1334WM.

Winter, Nicolas J. G. 2008. *Dangerous Frames: How Ideas About Race and Gender Shape Public Opinion*. Chicago, IL: University of Chicago Press.

Wynter, Sylvia. 1994. "No Humans Involved: An Open Letter to My Colleagues." *Institute NHI* 1(1):42–73.

13

Gang narratives and race-based policing and prosecution in New York City

Babe Howell

Introduction

This chapter examines the recent history of gang policing and prosecution in New York City. In 2012, despite crime rates that had reached historic lows (including violent crime and homicide), the New York City Police Department (NYPD) announced a new era of gang policing christened "Operation Crew Cut" (Beekman 2012; Esposito 2012; Parascandola 2012). In addition to low crime rates, the NYPD's statistics on gang crime indicated that gangs were responsible for far less than 1% of all crimes (Howell 2015) and were last in the list of causes of homicides in New York City (NYPD Murder in New York City 2011 & 2012 Reports). Gangs were not a big problem in New York City, and this was thanks, in part, to using non-law enforcement outreach workers to defuse gang conflict in the 1960s (Greene & Pranis 2007).

Nonetheless, under the newly announced Operation Crew Cut, the NYPD quadrupled[1] the officers assigned to its gang units and told newspapers that informal "crews" were responsible for over 30% of crime in New York City (Goldstein & Goodman 2013). These announcements were followed by numerous "gang takedowns" and multi-defendant prosecutions in both the state and federal courts. In 2016 through July of 2017 alone, the NYPD reported 81 "gang takedowns" (Goodman 2017). These prosecutions relied on conspiracy charges to link together the acts of individuals in mass indictments that covered years. In one of the largest of these indictments, 103 individuals were charged in relation to conspiracies that involved only two homicides (one of which had been long solved) over a period of nearly five years (Goodman 2014; Mays 2014). In a 2016 Bronx "takedown", 120 individuals were indicted in cases that purported to link together six homicides between 2009 and 2016 (Howell & Bustamante 2019). Here, too, some of the homicides had been previously prosecuted. Moreover, the vast majority of defendants were not alleged to have been involved in violent behavior (Howell & Bustamante 2019). Indeed, nearly half of the 120 defendants in the largest "gang takedown" on record were not even alleged by the prosecution itself to be gang members (Howell & Bustamante 2019).

The recent trend in policing and prosecution of "gangs" in New York City makes little to no sense without an understanding that the exaggerated gang narrative is used to insulate policing from critique and to generate support for oppressive race-based profiling. Like loitering laws, the war on drugs, "Broken Windows" policing, and stop-and-frisk policing, gang policing allows for aggressive surveillance, policing, prosecutions, and control of people of color based on discretionary enforcement and non-enforcement of the law. Discretion in enforcing each of these policing strategies has hinged primarily on appearance and geography. Unlike previous iterations of oppressive, race-based policing, "gang policing" has yet to fall into disrepute because the gang label triggers fear.

Although gang policing in New York City in the last decade is somewhat unique in the extreme law enforcement responses in a city with very little gang violence, the exaggeration of gang problems to create moral panic and shore up support for police is not new and has precedents across the country (Archbold & Meyer 1999; Beale 2006; Hagedorn 1998; McCorkle & Miethe 1998; Scott & Steinberg 2008; Zatz 1985, 1987).

It is worthwhile examining gang policing and prosecution in New York to understand what makes the use and abuse of the gang label so appealing to law enforcement in the United States and so dangerous to civil society. In short, gang policing allows law enforcement to engage in intensive surveillance and policing of suspect racial groups with no oversight. It also leads to conspiracy cases that are so difficult to defend that there is virtually no check on gang policing and prosecutions in the form of trials.

This chapter will briefly describe some of the mechanisms of gang policing and prosecution in New York City. Though there are variations in the law from jurisdiction to jurisdiction, the labeling, policing, and prosecution of gangs across the United States is generally very similar to that seen in New York. The gang label allows near-limitless surveillance and data collection and justifies harsh policing and prosecution.

Defining gangs and gang members

How to define a "gang" is a question that has engaged gang researchers from the earliest days of gang research. What makes a group a gang? When does a group become a gang? Is criminal conduct required? Organization? Hierarchy? A common symbol? Researchers have come up with many definitions. For law enforcement, however, the definition of a gang has routinely been stripped of nearly every requirement that would constrain law enforcement from identifying any group that it chooses a gang. Thus, typical law enforcement gang definitions require no more than a common sense of identity and that some members engage in some crime. More importantly, law enforcement itself determines whether a group is a gang and whom to tag as a gang member or associate.

The NYPD's definition of a gang is fairly typical of gang definitions adopted by states and law enforcement agencies across the country:

> GANG – Any ongoing organization, association, or group of three or more persons, whether formal or informal, having as one of its primary activities, the commission of one or more criminal acts, having a common name or common identifying sign or symbol, and whose members individually or collectively engage in or have engaged in a pattern of criminal gang activity.
>
> *(NYPD Patrol Guide, 212–13. Revised 8/1/13)*

Although the NYPD's definition of a gang states that a gang should have "as one of its primary activities" the commission of criminal acts, it goes on to state that the "members" may have engaged in criminal activity individually or collectively. While NYPD's gang definition has never been subjected to legal scrutiny, similar language regarding "one of the primary activities" (California STEP Act 1988) and "a pattern of criminal activity" (RICO Act 1970) has been satisfied in other jurisdictions by proof or two or more crimes committed in the course of a decade. Certainly, crime need not be *the* primary activity of a group designated as a gang. Moreover, no one outside the NYPD reviews these designations.

The NYPD Patrol Guide does not define a "gang member," but the NYPD can certify individuals as gang members without any proof of criminality. The requirements for activation in the NYPD's Enterprise Case Management System "Criminal Group" list provide three bases to certify an individual as a gang member.

Option "A" pick one

- This individual is being activate [sic] onto a group list by admitting membership during debriefing or post[ing] on their personal social media site information such as language, symbols, picture, colors, etc. that are affiliated with a criminal group
- Through the course of an investigation an individual is believed to belong to a criminal group and is identified as such by 2 independent sources (ex. Pct., Personnel, Intel, School Safety, Dep't of Correction, or Outside Agency)

Option "B" pick two

- Known groups [sic] location
- Groups [sic] Related Documents
- Association with known group members
- Social Media site associated with criminal group including pictures
- Scars/Tattoos Associated with groups
- Colors Associated with groups
- Hand signs associated with groups
- Other

None of these criteria require any criminal conduct. This, too, is typical of criteria for identifying gang members in other states and cities (Jacobs 2009).

As with gang databases across the country, there is no notice provided by the NYPD to those certified as gang members and no opportunity to appeal or challenge this designation.[2] (Wright 2005). Similarly, groups that are deemed gangs, including "crews" based on peer groups and referred to some police officers as "block gangs," (because the "crew" are individuals who grew up on a particular block) are not notified by the NYPD that these groups are being identified as gangs and targeted for surveillance. There are currently no external checks on what groups and what individuals are certified by the NYPD as gang members.

Data on alleged gang members

Fewer than 1% of the individuals in the NYPD's Gang Database (officially named the Criminal Group Database) are white. Between December 2013 and February 2018, the NYPD certified

17,452 people in its gang database, and only 140 of these individuals were white.[3] The following table shows the breakdown of those added to the database by race during this period.

Race	Individuals added to database	Percentage of total (17,452)
American-Indian/Native American	5	0.03%
Asian Pacific Islander	72	0.41%
Black	11,456	65.64%
Hispanic Total	5,690	32.6%
Unknown	89	0.51%
White	140	0.80%
Total	17,452	

Over 98% of the gang database is Black or Latinx, nearly 8% were added to the gang database prior to their 18th birthday, and about 3% of the individuals in the gang database were females. While the media portrays gang membership in racialized terms, gang researchers using self-reports by teenagers find that gang membership is rare among all groups (Esbensen and Huizinga 1993; Thornberry et al. 2003). Additionally, whites make up a substantial portion (40%) of gang members in absolute numbers (Greene and Pranis 2007). Although the NYPD's definition of a gang could include every marching band, fraternity, sorority, and youth group one could think of, and certainly should include organized crime and hate groups, the database apparently omits the Mafia, white supremacist groups, the Proud Boys, and other organized criminal groups.

The database has been insulated from review thus far because, unlike stop-and-frisks and quality-of-life arrests, the database and related data-gathering are largely unknown to the public and are not subject to judicial review. Additionally, there are no constitutional safeguards to prevent the police (or anyone else) from collecting data that is publicly available. Even when information is not intended to be "public" – texts, private messages, snapchats, and privately shared social media posts, to name a few – the Fourth Amendment affords no protection. Because we know that our private messages can be shared by the recipient, no "reasonable expectation of privacy" exists in communications with others, and no successful legal challenge can be made. The NYPD has hundreds of officers, both gang detectives and those from the Social Media Analysis and Research Team, scouring social media for posts that they interpret as gang related. Moreover, NYPD officers have used fake profiles (usually of attractive young women) to friend suspected and actual gang and crew members and to obtain access to communications (Goldstein and Goodman 2013).

The secrecy of the data collection and the use of social media allows the NYPD to amass potentially limitless information on those it chooses to add to its database and organize that database in relation to entire social networks. Once a person is activated as a gang member in the Criminal Group Database, the NYPD's Gang Investigation Division Information Management System (GIDIMS) automatically associates all activity related to an individual to a gang folder for the broader gang. The GIDIMS system also contains information about non-gang members, or "Person LITE" who are associated with alleged gang or crew members. We know, based on NYPD responses to Freedom of Information Law requests, that the NYPD has certified 17,452 as "members" in its Criminal Group Database. There may well be thousands more in databases, including "Person LITE", who merely associate with alleged gang members. Additionally, there are other databases and intelligence systems that have garnered less attention. For example, the NYPD claims not to share its gang database with anyone, but the Manhattan District Attorney's

Office has stated that it has collaborated with the NYPD to create its own intelligence systems for tracking alleged gang members or other high priority subjects (Brown 2014). The Criminal Group Database/Gang Database is only a visible tip of the iceberg. As the flaws in this system are exposed, the NYPD will likely pivot to other data systems to avoid critique.

Policing gangs and gang members

The policing of gang members and suspected gang members in New York City is aggressive and pervasive. Because a major goal of gang policing is gathering "intelligence" and mapping social networks, policing extends to non-criminal conduct. The NYPD tracks individuals on social media, it trains NYPD's "School Resource Officers" to identify gang members, it engages in street policing and arrests to detain and question individuals, and it aggressively tracks individuals through special programs.

SMART program and social media surveillance

The NYPD now employs over a thousand officers in the Social Media Analysis and Research Team (SMART) unit. These officers do nothing but track social media postings. According to the NYPD website, Gang Squad detectives also "closely monitor social media to identify members of gangs and crews, and dismantle these organized criminal groups through actionable intelligence, targeted enforcement, and coordinated federal and local prosecutions." As mentioned previously, the NYPD has admitted to creating fake profiles and making friend requests to get access to social media. They also ask individuals who are stopped, detained, or arrested for log-in information for phones and social media accounts. "Evidence" collected in this way is used to certify gang members and to build gang conspiracy cases.

NYPD school safety agents

NYPD school safety agents (SSAs) are NYPD officers placed in schools. There are more NYPD employed and trained SSAs in New York City Public Schools than there are guidance counselors. NYPD trains these officers to "recognize" signs of gang membership, including colors, brand-name clothing, unexplained wealth, and "changes in behavior." Presumably, if the SSAs are trained to recognize signs of gang membership, they are encouraged to report this information to the NYPD. School safety personnel are certainly among the "independent" sources listed for verifying criminal groups to the NYPD's Enterprise Case Management System. The extent to which SSAs or Department of Education personnel contribute "intelligence" to the NYPD is unknown, but this is one potential route for data collection.

Street interactions, arrests, and debriefings

In addition to surveillance on social media and through SSAs, the most dangerous and demeaning aspect of NYPD's gang policing is what it refers to as "targeted" policing. The NYPD aggressively polices those that it considers or suspects to be crew members in the streets. They stop and detain suspected crew members to gather information about crews. In some cases, they will get names, nicknames, and affiliations through street questioning. In others, they will make arrests and take arrestees into interrogation rooms for "debriefings." In debriefings, they ask arrested individuals about neighborhood crews and unsolved crimes. The NYPD and prosecutors avoid "debriefing" in relation to serious arrests, as responses to custodial interrogation could be subject to Fifth Amendment exclusion at trial. However, where the arrest is for a minor offense, the NYPD takes advantage of detention to persuade arrestees to provide information about their peers.

At hearings of the City Council's Public Safety Committee in June of 2018, Police Chief Dermot Shea (now NYPD Commissioner) testified that, on average, the individuals in the Gang Database have about 11 arrests, 5 of which are felony arrests.[4] When asked how many convictions those in the Gang Database had, Chief Shea had no response. The gulf between the number and nature of arrests and the number of convictions is a sign of overly aggressive policing. To amass five felony arrests in New York and not be in prison is strong evidence that the bulk of such arrests must be artificially inflated. To accumulate 11 arrests and not be incarcerated means the arrests are for minor misconduct. The information that we have, from the NYPD's own statements and from defendants, confirms that arrests are used to demonstrate control and to troll for information. Young people alleged to be gang members report arrests for jay-walking, bicycles on sidewalks, loitering for the purpose of gambling, and other conduct that is generally ignored when engaged in by others in New York City. This type of intensive policing is part of the NYPD's approach to "gang" policing, as the NYPD reported to the *New York Times* (Goodman 2015):

> Veteran officers keep lists of teenagers believed to be affiliated with crews – 178 in Brownsville alone, by last count. On the street, the officers might pick them up for truancy or issue summonses for biking on the sidewalk, to reinforce the notion that the police are watching.
>
> "These are not hardened criminals," said Deputy Chief Michael Harrington, who oversees the program. "You lock one kid up, he's going to tell you about everybody."

Policing and surveillance are not limited to individuals who are gang members or even to individuals or groups identified as gangs. According to the NYPD Patrol Guide, as of 2014, gang-related intelligence includes information about suspected gangs and suspected gang members and about activities such as "protests, marches, and other public events" (NYPD Patrol Guide 212–13).[5]

The policing of gang members reaches deep into the personal and social lives of those suspected of crew associations, extends to the streets where alleged gang members are consistently arrested and ticketed for minor conduct, and even results in felony arrests that are not supported by substantial evidence.

Because of the power of the "gang" label, the NYPD's policing of the private lives of young people of color in New York City has drawn admiration from the press. For example, the *New York Times* covered the story of a 19-year-old who denied being in a gang and had been arrested more than a dozen times, beginning at age 11 (Goodman 2015). The reporter seemed to attribute the dismissals of the cases to the notion that witnesses were unwilling to testify against crews rather than even suggesting that the charges might be the product of police harassment. While the "witness fear" explanation comports with the fear of gangs, the particular arrests of the youth included multiple arrests for weapons and jaywalking. A weapon arrest rarely hinges on civilian testimony. A typical weapon arrest in NYC involves a police stop or search and the vouchering of the weapon. Cases will be dismissed if the stop or search violates the Fourth Amendment, if the "weapon" is not a "weapon" within the meaning of the law (e.g. a screwdriver, a pocket knife, etc.), or if the officer's credibility and record are such that the prosecutor believes he cannot go forward with the case. Weapons arrests, jaywalking, and bikes on sidewalks are cases and arrests that do not depend on civilian witnesses. They are the product of police discretion and are supported by police testimony. Repeat arrests that are dismissed are more likely an indication of police harassment and selective enforcement than of serious criminality.

There is additional support for the notion that the aggressive policing of alleged gang and crew members is the product of harassment and not criminality. NYPD officers in the Gang Division have higher numbers of complaints for civil rights violations (including excessive use of force, wrongful arrest, malicious prosecution, and the like) than ordinary NYPD patrol officers (Winston 2019). Research on bias in gang unit officers has also suggested that gang unit officers have higher levels of racial bias than non-gang unit officers (Sim, Correll, & Sadler 2013). Gang units across the country have been loci of corruption and violence. The vilification of their "targets" provides a narrative framework in which racially diverse police units justify aggressive enforcement because they see themselves as fighting "groups of evil perpetrators" (Katz & Webb 2006).

There is a very real danger that the gang or crew label drives both police and targeted individuals to interactions that increase the likelihood of illegality from both sides. Targeted individuals will have a hard time completing school, getting and holding jobs, and staying out of trouble. Targeting officers may stretch or even break the law in pursuit of the "gang." Gang units may see every arrest as an opportunity to build a larger conspiracy case or an opportunity to communicate to targets that they are being watched.

Prosecution of gangs and crews in New York

"Gang" prosecutions are the troubling product of intensive policing of gangs. Individual cases against crew members may be dismissed, prosecuted and resolved by plea bargain, or prosecuted to a trial and conviction or acquittal. Later, the NYPD and prosecutors in New York City collaborate to compile broader conspiracy cases, linking entire groups to the conduct of members. In these broader conspiracy cases, prosecutors will often point to conduct that was previously adjudicated (whether there was a conviction or not) as proof of membership in the conspiracy and as proof of intent to advance the conspiracy's goals. In an essay laying out a step-by-step application of the New Orleans Strategy to Combat Violent Street Crews, the United States Attorney for the Central District of Illinois urges prosecution teams to pull every incident involving the targets whether "suspects, witnesses, or victims. No exceptions. . . . Convictions, acquittals, dismissals, no charges – they all should be pulled" (Chambers 2014). Non-convictions and even acquittals can be relitigated or used to demonstrate association or presence in the so-called gang territory in a case.

Conspiracy indictments

The first step in turning the sprawling gang or crew investigation into a conspiracy case is obtaining a criminal indictment that ties together the conduct of everyone in a crew or gang and, sometimes, those merely associated with it. An indictment is a felony charge or set of charges that is voted on by a grand jury (typically a majority of 23 ordinary citizens). It is notoriously easy to obtain an indictment; indeed, former Chief Judge of New York Sol Wachtler has been frequently quoted for saying a grand jury would indict a ham sandwich. Grand jury proceedings are secret. Neither judge nor defense attorney is present during grand jury proceedings. Prosecutors alone lay out the evidence using informants, police officers, as principal witnesses, and then instructing the grand jurors on the law, reminding them that it is not the job of the grand jury to determine guilt but only if there is probable cause to bring the charges.

In the gang conspiracy case, the evidence must seem particularly overwhelming to the grand jurors. In order to obtain an indictment, the prosecution works with police gang detectives and informants. The informants are typically individuals who have been arrested and charged with serious offenses and against whom the evidence is very strong. The informants enter cooperation agreements and, in exchange for what they hope and expect will be very lenient sentences, they testify before the grand jury in order to draw the picture of the entire conspiracy. The informants prepare with police and prosecutors to identify all the members and associates of the crew, to explain their crimes to the grand jury, and, most importantly, to explain the workings of the crew in a manner that emphasizes criminality. The prosecution totes in boards of photos. The informant admits their own crimes and explains that they did those crimes as part of the crew. They claim that committing violence is critical to being a crew member or associate.

The witnesses and gang unit officers lay out the contours of the alleged "gang war." Informants give the overarching narrative. Prior criminal histories show the criminality of the alleged gang members. Selected social media posts, videos, and rap lyrics show the group hanging out and communicating in ways that seem to glorify violence or their local neighborhood clique.

In these sprawling gang cases, it is difficult to imagine that the grand jurors (who are regular citizens with no expertise) would not assume that each alleged crew or gang member might have committed some offense. Moreover, where a conspiracy is charged, the individual defendant does not have to commit an offense or even be present or aware of that an offense was taking place. The basic elements of a conspiracy are an agreement to commit one or more target offenses and the intent that those offenses should occur. Evidence of an actual agreement is not needed; the agreement can be proven circumstantially. The agreement can be inferred from conduct, including tweets and social media posts. The informant cooperator tells the grand jury that members of the crew engage in violence to dominate their turf, that they sell drugs to buy guns, and that they swear to have each others' backs. As a result, membership in the crew may be enough to satisfy the grand jurors that individuals belonging to a crew agree to a conspiracy with goals of violence, narcotics trafficking, and weapon possession.

Pre-dawn militarized raids

The conspiracy indictment is made public on the same day that law enforcement executes pre-dawn raids to arrest indicted defendants. Hundreds of armed law enforcement officers in raid gear descend on the targeted area to break down doors and arrest those named in the mass indictment. These raids involve battering rams, flash-bang grenades, tanks, and helicopters. Law enforcement rounds up individuals who have been surveilled in communities and on social media for months or years. They parade the accused in front of the media in shackles. Headlines and local news anchors announce yet another "gang" takedown. They broadcast images of law enforcement in raid gear herding shackled men of color into vans.

The impact of these raids on family members and communities is hard to justify. All family members – from infants to the elderly – are typically ordered to the floor at gunpoint and may be held for hours by invading forces. In the 2016 raids of Eastchester Gardens in the Bronx, a man who feared that he was a target of the raids plunged to his death (Alcorn et al. 2016). He was not a target. Across the country, similar raids have led to the deaths of non-targets, targets, pets, and law enforcement officers.

These raids are theater, designed to sell a narrative that exaggerates the actual danger posed by the crews. Law enforcement has been waiting and watching, allowing individuals to remain in the communities for months and even years under surveillance. Those who are in the community are typically not alleged to have engaged in the most serious misconduct. They could easily be arrested outside their homes to minimize danger, trauma, and property destruction.

Arrests in Prisons and Jails

Individuals facing more serious charges are often arrested in jail or in prison. Thus, in the June 2014 Harlem raids that followed indictments of 103 individuals, the police were looking for about 60 individual defendants. A significant number of the defendants were already in prison or jail. In that case, the indictments related to two homicides. One of the homicides had been prosecuted long before the indictments, and those who committed it were serving sentences of 25 to life. Some of these defendants are brought from jails or prisons to be arraigned on conspiracy charges. Often the conspiracy charge is based on the same conduct for which they are already serving time. It is not uncommon that individuals who have served a sentence and are expecting to be released are re-arrested and re-detained based on the same conduct for which they are already serving time.

Pre-Trial Detention

Prosecutors in gang cases argue for pre-trial detention. Judges tend to respond to gang allegations by setting high bail or remanding[6] defendants during the pendency of the case. For example, in the 2016 federal "gang takedown" in the Bronx, 101 of the 120 defendants were remanded – subjected to pre-trial incarceration without the possibility of pre-trial release – in accordance with the prosecution's recommendation. Of the 19 who were released, only 4 were released over the prosecution's objection.[7] Fifteen of those "released" were released on condition that they remain under house arrests These "lucky" released individuals lost their jobs, were not allowed to walk their children to school, could not sit in the local park on a beautiful day.

The "Bronx 120" (as the April 2016 twin indictments have come to be known) cases provide a perfect example of the power of the gang narrative to subvert even the Eighth Amendment's prohibition on excessive bail. On the morning of April 27, 2016, the Bronx 120 indictments were unsealed. Over 700 local and federal officers descended on two Bronx neighborhoods, with helicopters and tanks providing backup. At a press conference, Preet Bharara, then United States Attorney of the Southern District of New York, made the following announcement:

> Today we announce what is believed to be the largest gang takedown in New York City History. We have charged *120 defendants in two rival Bronx Street gangs* with racketeering, narcotics, and firearms offenses. In addition, the charges include allegations of multiple murders, attempted murders, shootings, stabbings, and beatings, committed in furtherance of federal racketeering conspiracies.[8]

A review of all publicly available government filings in the Bronx 120 cases reveals that, according to the government itself, nearly 60 of the Bronx 120 were not members of the two rival street gangs and that two-thirds had no felony criminal history. At the close of the case, only about 20 defendants were even convicted of possession of a gun (and the prosecution insisted on a plea to this charge where they thought it could be proven). For each individual convicted for involvement in one of the five homicides referenced in the indictment, 20 people had been swept up and prosecuted as violent gang members.

The judges for the Bronx 120 relied on the prosecution's allegations and held nearly all in pre-trial detention. Judges would not normally hold individuals with little to no criminal record in jail pre-trial. The narrative of rival street gangs terrorizing neighborhoods for years and the broad indictment caused just this result. The Bronx 120 case is larger than most gang takedowns, but surveys of defense attorneys (Howell 2011) and observations in other cases demonstrate that the gang allegation is often accepted without question and used as a basis to deny individuals pre-trial release.

Plea bargaining in the gang takedown case

The American criminal system is a system of plea bargains (Bibas 2004; Roberts 2013). These "bargains" are marked by extreme disparities in both power and access to information. The system could be better characterized as one of plea coercion than bargaining. The typical defendant can accept the best offer the prosecution is willing to make or face many more years or decades or even capital punishment if he is convicted after trial. In 1978, in the case of *Bordenkircher v. Hayes*, the Supreme Court held that a prosecutor who tells a defendant that refusal to plead guilty will result in reindictment on additional charges and a life sentence does not violate due process or engage in unlawful coercion.

There are few prosecutions where the disparities in power and information are more extreme than in the mass gang prosecution.

In mass gang prosecutions, individuals face conspiracy charges that typically carry maximum sentences of either 20 years or life. They may also face multiple charges that can result in consecutive sentences (e.g. 20 years, followed by 15 years, followed by 5 years). Federal law allows courts to sentence individuals involved in narcotics conspiracy based on the aggregate weight of all the drugs that any member of the conspiracy sold during the course of the conspiracy. In the Bronx 120 case, individuals who sold $5 and $10 bags of marijuana (a misdemeanor under New York State law) faced maximum sentences based on estimates that their crews would have sold 25 or even 50 kilos over the course of the 9 1/2 years of the alleged conspiracy. Moreover, as in *Bordenkircher*, those who refused to plead guilty on the terms offered by the prosecution were re-indicted and often faced additional charges as a result of superseding indictments.

In terms of information, the prosecution and police have years of surveillance and debriefing materials, subpoenaed Facebook records for the defendants, grand jury testimony, transcripts of wiretaps and jail calls, and notes from numerous meetings with informants and other witnesses. As an initial matter, they provide none of these materials to defendants. Citing the complexity and size of the case, they seek and obtain long adjournments during which they can organize these materials and provide some of these materials to defendants (but not the critical statements of witnesses and informants that would implicate the defendant). When the first round of materials is provided to the defendant, it is communicated electronically through the defense attorney. These early materials may include thousands of pages of social media posts. Defendants can only look at these electronic files when they are given limited access to computers. These materials are covered by protective orders. Only the defendant and his defense attorney can look at the materials. Neither the typical defense attorney nor the defendant is in a good position to identify which of the thousands of entries will be used should the defendant refuse a plea deal. More importantly, the prosecution is not required by federal law to provide previous statements and testimony of witnesses it intends to call at trial until the jury is sworn in. At best, some of this material is provided a few weeks before trial, but it is provided at a point when the option to plead guilty has been taken off the table.

Thus, the typical defendant has little to no information about the prosecution's case during the first several months of the case. When he receives information, he receives a deluge of materials, much of it irrelevant and difficult to access or analyze. The critical information about the actual charges against an individual may also be in flux, since the prosecution seeks new indictments against the rare individual who refuses to take a plea.

Such individuals are rare indeed. Of the Bronx 120, only 2 individuals went to trial. Three cases were dismissed by the prosecution, and the other 115 defendants pleaded guilty. One hundred thirteen of them pleaded guilty to felonies. Because two-thirds of these individuals did not have prior felony convictions, the prosecution created over 70 new felons. These individuals, young men of color, who grew up in a heavily policed and under-resourced neighborhood in the Bronx, had grown to adulthood without getting into serious trouble. The mass gang indictment creates pressure such that those who are barely involved or are innocent are held in jail or on house arrest. They can fight the case for years, facing sentences that may involve decades in prison, or they can accept plea offers for felonies that allow for short sentences or even sentences of time served. Twenty-two of the Bronx 120 took pleas and were sentenced to time served. Another 18 were sentenced to less than 2 years after pleading guilty. Although the sentences may not be long for those who are marginally involved, a felony conviction with or without a prison sentence will likely burden the defendant and by extension the defendant's family and community for life. Moreover, the pleas carry with them a period of "supervised release" (typically 5 years), during which they are subjected to criminal justice supervision and may face incarceration for technical violations. The relatively short sentences are convincing evidence that the gang prosecution reached non-violent individuals, but they should not be taken to suggest that the sentences were fair or that the impact on the lives of these vulnerable individuals was anything less than catastrophic.

Gang conspiracy trials: the procedural and evidentiary advantages

Conspiracy was famously dubbed "the darling of the federal prosecutor's nursery." The procedural and evidentiary advantages for the prosecution of the conspiracy charge are enormous. As Supreme Court Justice Jackson wrote in 1949:

> When the trial starts, the accused feels the full impact of the conspiracy strategy. Strictly, the prosecution should first establish *prima facie* the conspiracy and identify the conspirators, after which evidence of acts and declarations of each in the course of its execution are admissible against all. But the order of proof of so sprawling a charge is difficult for a judge to control. *As a practical matter, the accused often is confronted with a hodgepodge of acts and statements by others which he may never have authorized or intended or even known about, but which help to persuade the jury of existence of the conspiracy itself.* In other words, a conspiracy often is proved by evidence that is admissible only upon assumption that conspiracy existed.
>
> A co-defendant in a conspiracy trial occupies an uneasy seat. There generally will be evidence of wrongdoing by somebody. It is difficult for the individual to make his own case stand on its own merits in the midst of jurors who are ready to believe that birds of a feather are flocked together.
>
> *Krulewitch v. United States, 336 U.S. 440, 453–454 (1949) (Jackson, J. concurring)*

In a typical criminal trial, the prosecutor must prove beyond a reasonable doubt that the defendant committed a particular crime on a particular date. Evidence that he committed some other crime on some other date is excluded as irrelevant and prejudicial. The more similar the previous crime, the more prejudicial. Evidence about crimes that other people committed – irrelevant. Evidence that his friends are criminals – irrelevant and prejudicial. The defendant has clear notice from the day he is arraigned about what he is alleged to have done and when. He and his attorney can begin to prepare for trial from the beginning. If he can prove he was not there, or that he took no part in the offense, if he can even raise a reasonable doubt, he should be acquitted.

In a conspiracy case, one can be convicted of a conspiracy to commit a crime without taking any role in the crime, without being present for the crime, or even knowing of the crime's commission. Proving that you were at your best friend's wedding, at work, or at a local bar nowhere near the scene of the crime is not a defense. The rules of evidence allow in all the prejudicial evidence of other crimes and awareness to prove circumstantially that the individual agreed to the conspiracy to commit a crime. Statements of all alleged co-conspirators "in furtherance of the conspiracy" are also admissible. The trial of a conspiracy case allows the prosecution to bring in a limitless array of evidence, over a vast span of time. Because the prior crimes of individuals within the conspiracy may be offered to prove the agreement to commit crimes and the intent to commit crimes, the evidence facing a defendant in a gang conspiracy may include a mountain of unrelated criminal acts of others or of the defendant himself, even if he has already served time for his prior crimes.

Gang conspiracy trials – the evidence

As suggested in the opinion of Justice Jackson penned 70 years ago, much of the evidence in the conspiracy trial is about proving association and criminality in general. In this final section, I will briefly lay out the common elements that can be observed in the cases of the few individuals who resisted the pressure to plead guilty and went to trial. While I have certainly not reviewed all or even most gang conspiracy trial records in New York, the cases of the 2 defendants who went to trial in the Bronx 120 cases, the 6 who went to trial in the 2014 Harlem takedown of 103 individuals, and a recent trial case of 3 in a 2017 "takedown" in the Bronx have common features that raise compelling concerns. A systematic review of these cases to determine whether our system should continue to permit prosecutors to obtain convictions on conspiracy charges in this manner is in order.

The key types of evidence that have been presented in trial cases of the dozen defendants I have reviewed are 1) cooperator testimony; 2) social media posts, videos, chats, photos, and correspondence; 3) prior arrests and convictions; 4) police officers with significant credibility issues that are not disclosed to juries; 5) missing forensic evidence to corroborate the accusations, and 6) gang "experts" who explain how the gang works.

1   Cooperator testimony

The key testimony in gang conspiracy cases is the testimony of one or more cooperating witnesses. As mentioned earlier, the typical cooperating witness faces serious charges, strong evidence, and decades in prison. These witnesses enter guilty pleas to a laundry list of crimes (including RICO conspiracy), and sentencing is postponed until after they have satisfied the prosecution with their cooperation. These cooperating witnesses are often implicated in far more crime and more violent crime than the individuals they testify against. Nonetheless, at the close of the case, they often get light sentences (federal cooperators in the Bronx 120 case got time served) and are released into society. The cooperators in these gang cases generally will claim to be eye-witnesses to a particular serious crime the prosecution wants to prove. Some cooperators who cannot plausibly claim to be an eyewitness to an incident will testify that the defendant confessed to them.

2   Social media posts

Social media posts, YouTube videos, Facebook chats, photos with friends – all these are used to corroborate the association among and between defendants with others in the crew.

Particularly damaging are rap videos and lyrics that are treated to prove association, criminality, and as confession of actual crimes. Even when social media posts and photos show mere association, the gang allegation has significant biasing effects on jurors (Eisen 2013) and can lead to conviction, even where evidence is insufficient to prove charges beyond a reasonable doubt (Eisen 2014).

3 Bad NYPD testimony

If the conspiracy cases relied on cooperators alone, they might result in acquittals. However, in the few cases from the mass indictments that have gone to trial, cooperator testimony is bolstered in very important ways by NYPD testimony of questionable reliability. In the Bronx 120 case, two cases went to trial. In each trial, an NYPD officer testified that he recovered a loaded gun from the defendant. In one case, the jury had no idea that the officer who claimed to have recovered the gun had been sued for civil rights violations seven times since 2015. They had no idea that New York City attorneys had settled six of these cases and paid out over $200,000 without admitting misconduct. The jury had no idea that both the Internal Affairs Bureau and the Civilian Complaint Review Board had substantiated claims of misconduct against the detective. These jurors, who gave up weeks of their time to determine whether the case was proven beyond a reasonable doubt, were missing critical information to evaluate the testimony of this officer. In the other Bronx 120 trial, the jurors did not know that the officer who testified that he had recovered a gun from a place he claimed to see the defendant stash it used the twitter handle @obamahater55. Both his tweets and twitter handle suggested a high level of bias that might be relevant to credibility. In another recent gang trial, the NYPD officer who claimed to have recovered a gun from the defendant's car had seven civil rights cases settle for over $240,000 (three cases settled for undisclosed amounts), including the one involving the defendant. The jurors did not know that the Bronx District Attorney had dismissed the case or that the City Law Department had paid damages to settle a lawsuit stemming from this alleged gun seizure. They were unaware of allegations of a prolonged campaign of NYPD harassment aimed at the defendant on trial.

4 Missing forensic evidence

What has been conspicuously absent from these cases is forensic evidence. In the cases mentioned previously, the guns the police officers with credibility issues claimed to have recovered were not tested for fingerprints or DNA. The word of the cooperators on critical crimes was bolstered by police officers but not by forensic evidence that one might expect.

5 Prior convictions and arrests

A final type of evidence that is no doubt very damning is evidence of prior convictions and arrests (even those leading to acquittals). As mentioned previously, those who are identified as alleged gang members are aggressively policed and have a high number of arrests. The criminal justice system is a system of pleas. Some of these arrests will result in guilty pleas. Others may be dismissed by prosecutors because of concerns about the sufficiency of the evidence. Pleas may be accurate or inaccurate, dismissals may be accurate or inaccurate, but, given the Sixth Amendment's apparent bar on double jeopardy, most people expect to be prosecuted only once for any particular conduct. In conspiracy cases, prior arrests and convictions are used to prove parts of the cases and to provide support for new convictions based on the same conduct. Thus, in the

Bronx 120 marijuana seller trial, though the defendant did not deny selling marijuana and the government agreed he was not a member of the targeted "gang," the prosecution introduced evidence of prior marijuana arrests that were years old and already adjudicated in state court, giving these cases a second life. Particularly where a defendant has pleaded guilty and done a day of community service, paid a fee, or served some time in jail, there is no way that he can challenge the prior conviction. The use of prior convictions does not violate double jeopardy because the conspiracy charge has different elements from the original arrest crime. Nonetheless, the conspiracy charge allows a defendant to be convicted, at least in part, for offenses that were previously adjudicated.

6 Gang "experts"

Gang Unit police officers are often introduced as experts in gang cases, despite the fact that their only training is typically received in a few days from other gang unit police officers. These "experts" are often the very investigators who put the case together. Like the cooperators, they may provide the entire narrative for how the gang operates. In the New York cases reviewed, gang "experts" were used in the state cases but not in the federal cases.

Conclusion

The policing and prosecution of alleged gang members in New York is just one of many permutations of gang policing and prosecution in the United States. Across the country, gang policing and prosecution have become increasingly aggressive, even in eras of historically low violent crime and in tandem with anti-immigrant and racist rhetoric. Some jurisdictions have additional tools for policing gangs, including civil injunctions and loitering laws. Others may have more formal gang databases and different criteria for certification of gang membership, though generally there is no requirement of criminality. Some states use criminal gang statutes (which New York State lacks) rather than general conspiracy and RICO charges. New York City, however, is particularly instructive because it enjoys low levels of gang violence, with prosecutors collaborating with police to bring mass gang prosecutions based on vast troves of surveillance data related to social networks of vulnerable young people of color. Gang policing and gang prosecutions sweep up the good with the not so good and deprive all defendants of any semblance of individualized justice. Criminal procedure and due process are undermined by the gang label, with prosecutors abusing the power that the fear of the gang war narrative generates. The right to bail, notice of charges, time and information to prepare a defense, and protection from re-prosecution are all denied. All of these practices have been upheld as constitutional, but an honest look at these cases suggest that many of these decisions fail to adequately protect due process. These prosecutors claim to be progressive and to work in the interest of the communities they are targeting but coordinate militarized raids and overbroad cases. New York City shows how pernicious and powerful the moral panic relating to gang violence can be. The policing and prosecution of these cases subverts the rights of suspect communities. This creates another all-encompassing method for criminalizing young people, particularly young men of color in New York City.

In the broader context, exaggerated narratives of gang violence and televised raids of mass takedowns perpetuate narratives and stereotypes that equate violence with young men of color and feed larger racist and anti-immigrant sentiments in our society (Beale 2006; Lane 2002; Pimental 2013). Repeat punishment and punishment of multiple individuals for the conduct of peer group members promises to feed mass incarceration even as crime reaches historic lows. Militarized raids, mass surveillance, secret databases, and intensive policing are expensive tactics which have given rise to more gangs and more gang violence in cities such as Los Angeles and Chicago (Greene & Pranis 2007). Put another way, the choices that New York is currently making to track and target suspected gang and crew members for prosecution rather than to invest in anti-violence measures (jobs, cure violence programs, mental health, substance abuse treatment, etc.) that can help vulnerable young people may increase gang violence over time.

Notes

1 The Gang Division was doubled with the announcement of Operation Crew Cut in 2012 and then doubled again in 2013, according to the *New York Times*. The Gang Division may well have grown since these announcements.
2 California has recently passed legislation requiring notice of inclusion be provided for a shared gang database (Cal. Penal Code 186.34 2018), but it is nearly alone in this regard. Moreover, a recent state audit (California State Auditor 2016) of the CalGang Database revealed a failure to comply with the notice requirements for juveniles and failure to perform self-audits. Not surprisingly, the audit showed that the database was rife with errors.
3 This data was provided to the author by the NYPD's legal department, in response to a Freedom of Information Act request in March of 2018.
4 Statement of Chief Dermot Shea to the Committee on Public Safety, June 13, 2018, available at https://legistar. council.nyc.gov/LegislationDetail.aspx?ID=3506401&GUID=43D779AF-FAC6-4122-9886-87F19E AE5CC6&Options=&Search=
5 Perhaps recognizing that that this language goes to the core of protected First Amendment rights to protest, this phrase was revised in 2015 to exclude protests and marches but to cover such events anyway. As of 12/31/15, gang intelligence includes "plans by persons affiliated with a gang to organize or take part in public events, 'community' events (as defined by gang)."
6 A judge "remands" a defendant upon a determination that no amount of bail or other conditions will permit a defendant's release and incarcerates the defendant pre-trial without the possibility of release.
7 Perhaps recognizing the futility of requesting pre-trial release given the gang indictment, the majority of defendants did not even challenge their detention.
8 USAOSDNY, *120 Members of Street Gangs in the Bronx Charged in Manhattan Federal Court*, YouTube (Apr. 29, 2016), https://bit.ly/2UD1hh4 [https://perma.cc/7LNR-9PJC].

References

Alcorn, Chauncey, Tracy, Thomas & Rayman, Graham, *Robbery Suspect Falls to His Death While Running from Cops During Bronx Gang Raids,* New York Daily News (Apr. 27, 2016). https://www.nydailynews.com/new-york/man-falls-death-running-cops-bronx-gang-raids-article-1.2616559

Archbold, Carol. A. & Meyer, Michael, *Anatomy of a Gang Suppression Unit: The Social Construction of an Organizational Response to Gang Problems*, 2 Police Quarterly 184 (1999).

Beale, Sara Sun, *The News Media's Influence in Criminal Justice Policy: How Market-Driven News Promotes Punitiveness*, 48 William & Mary Law Review 397 (2006).

Beekman, Daniel, *Bronx Community Leaders Praise New NYPD Anti-Gang Initiative, Argue More Youth Programs Are Also Needed: NYPD Gang Division to Double in Size in Intensive Effort to Stem Shootings*, New York Daily News (Oct. 3, 2012).

Bibas, Stephanos, *Plea Bargaining in the Shadow of Trial*, 117 Harvard International Law Journal 2463 (2004).

Brown, Chip, *Cyrus Vance Jr.'s "Moneyball" Approach to Crime*, New York Times Magazine (Dec. 7, 2014).

California State Auditor, *The CalGang Criminal Intelligence System: As a Result of Its Weak Oversight Structure, It Contains Questionable Information That May Violate Individuals' Privacy Rights*, Report 2015–130 (Aug. 2016).

Chambers, K. Tate, *Developing a Step-by-Step Application of the New Orleans Strategy to Combat Violent Street Crews in a Focused Deterrence Strategy*, Central District of Illinois, United States Attorney Bulletin, Vol. 62, issue 3, 90–95 (May 2014). Available at www.justice.gov/sites/default/files/usao/legacy/2014/06/03/usab6203.pdf

Eisen, Mitchell, L. et al., *Examining the Prejudicial Effects of Gang Evidence on Jurors*, 13 Journal of Forensic Psychology Practice 1 (2013).

Eisen, Mitchell, L. et al., *Probative or Prejudicial: Can Gang Evidence Trump Reasonable Doubt?* 62 University of California, Los Angeles Law Review Disc 2 (2014).

Esbensen, Finn-Aage & Huizinga, D., *Gangs, Drugs and Delinquency in a Survey of Urban Youth*, 31 Criminology 565 (1993).

Esposito, Richard, *New York's Kelly Plans "Crew Cut" for Gang Members*, ABC News (Oct. 2, 2012). Available at https://abcnews.go.com/Blotter/nypd-plans-crew-cut-gang-members/story?id=17370903

Goldstein, J. & Goodman, J. D., *Frisking Tactic Yields to Focus on Youth Gangs*, New York Times (Sept. 18, 2013).

Goodman, J. David, *Dozens of Gang Suspects Held in Raids in Manhattan*, New York Times (June 4, 2014).

Goodman, J. David, *As Shootings Rise in New York, Police Focus on a Small Number of Young Men*, New York Times (July 21, 2015).

Goodman, J. David, *Trump Takes Aim at 'Pathetic Mayor.' De Blasio Thinks He Knows Who He Means*, New York Times (July 28, 2017.)

Greene, Judith & Pranis, Kevin, *Gang Wars: The Failure of Enforcement Tactics and the Need for Effective Public Safety Strategies*, Justice Policy Institute Report (2007).

Hagedorn, John M., *Gang Violence in the Postindustrial Era*, 24 Crime & Justice 365 (1998).

Howell, K. Babe, *Fear Itself: The Impact of Allegations of Gang Affiliation on Pre-Trial Detention*, 23 St. Thomas Law Review 620–659 (2011).

Howell, K. Babe, *Gang Policing: The Post-Stop-and-Frisk Justification for Profile-Based Policing*, 5 University of Denver Criminal Law Review 1 (2015).

Howell, K. Babe & Bustamante, Priscilla, *Report on the Bronx 120 Mass "Gang" Prosecution* (2019). Available at www.bronx120.report

Jacobs, James B, *Gang Databases: Context and Questions*, 8 Criminology & Public Policy 705 (2009).

Katz, Charles M. & Webb, Vincent J., *Policing Gangs in America*, Cambridge University Press (2006).

Lane, Jodi, *Fear of Gang Crime: A Qualitative Examination of Why Fear of the Four Perspectives*, 39 Journal of Research on Crime & Delinquency, 4, 437–471 (2002).

Mays, Jeff, *District Attorney Cast Too Wide a Net in Harlem Gang Crackdown, Critics Say*, DNAInfo (Oct. 6, 2014).

McCorkle, Richard C. & Miethe, Terance, *The Political and Organizational Response to Gangs: An Examination of a "Moral Panic" in Nevada*, 15 Justice Quarterly 41 (1998).

Parascandola, Rocco, *NYPD to Double Gang Division to Combat Street Violence*, New York Daily News (Oct. 1, 2012).

Pimental, David, *The Widening Maturity Gap: Trying and Punishing Juveniles as Adults in an Era of Extended Adolescence*, 46 Texas Tech Law Review 71 (2013).

Roberts, Jenny, *Effective Plea Bargaining Counsel*, 122 The Yale Law Journal 2650 (2013).

Scott, Elizabeth S. & Steinberg, Laurence, *Rethinking Juvenile Justice*, Harvard University Press (2008).

Sim, Jessica J., Correll, Joshua & Sadler, Melody, *Understanding Police and Expert Performance: When Training Attenuates (vs. Exacerbates) Stereotypic Bias in the Decision to Shoot*, 39 Personality and Social Psychology Bulletin 291–304 (2013).

Thornberry, Terence P. et al., *Gangs and Delinquency in Developmental Perspective*, Cambridge University Press (2003).

Winston, Ali, *Looking for Details on Rogue N.Y. Police Officers? This Database Might Help*, New York Times (Mar. 6, 2019).

Wright, Joshua D. *The Constitutional Failure of Gang Databases*, 2 Stanly Journal Civil Rights Law Journal Liberties 115 (2005).

Zatz, Marjorie, *Los Cholos: Legal Processing of Chicano Gang Members*, 33 Social Problems 13 (1985).

Zatz, Marjorie, *Chicano Youth Gangs and Crime: The Creation of a Moral Panic*, 11 Contemporary Crises 129 (1987).

Cases

Bordenkircher v. Hayes, 434 U.S. 357 (1978).
Krulewitch v. United States, 336 U.S. 440, 453–454 (1949)(Jackson, J. concurring).

Statutes

California Penal Code section 186.34.
The Racketeering Influenced Corrupt Organization Act, 18 U.S.C. §§ 1961–1968 (1970).
The Street Terrorism Enforcement and Prevention (STEP) Act, Ca. Penal Code § 182.22 (1988).

Part III
Policies and repressive models

Policies and repression model

14

Securitization and the transnational governing of Central American gangs

Markus-Michael Müller

Introduction

In his first State of the Union Address on January 30, 2018, United States (US) President Donald Trump frequently referred to the security threats that Central American street gangs, called *maras* or *pandillas*, such as Mara Salvatrucha or 18th Street Gang, would represent for US communities: 'Tonight', he stated, by linking Central American gangs to the alleged weakness of the US-Mexican border, 'I am calling on the Congress to finally close the deadly loopholes that have allowed MS-13, and other criminal gangs, to break into our country'. 'For decades', he went on 'open borders have allowed drugs and gangs to pour into our most vulnerable communities. . . . Most tragically, they have caused the loss of many innocent lives'. Later in his speech, President Trump introduced Homeland Security Investigations (HSI) Special Agent Celestino Martinez. After having served 15 years in the US Air Force, Martinez joined the US Immigration and Customs Enforcement (ICE), which was created in 2003. It was part of the revamping of the US national security infrastructure in the aftermath of the attacks of September 11, 2001 (9/11). Following the enacting of the Homeland Security Act by Congress in November 2002 and the resulting creation of the Department of Homeland Security (DHS), which united 22 federal security agencies under one bureaucratic superstructure, ICE was established – through a merger of the US Customs Service and the Immigration and Naturalization Service (INS)[1] – as another branch of the DHS. In his speech, Donald Trump praised ICE's role in the fight against Central American gangs, particularly for having 'sent thousands and thousands of MS-13 horrible people out of this country or into our prisons' (quoted in *The Atlantic* 2018).

As this episode makes clear, Central American street gangs have not just been perceived as a threat to their own countries, where governments have responded with overly repressive policies 'to the extent that it is no exaggeration to talk of Central American governments having declared a veritable "war on gangs"' (Rodgers and Hazen 2014: 1). Rather, and due to the transnational aspects of Central American gangs, this threat perception and resulting repressive postures also capture US anti-gang policies that are increasingly influenced by post-9/11 security framings, notably counterterrorism and counterinsurgency discourses. This can be seen, for instance, in the fact that a few months before Donald Trump's speech, Attorney General Jeff Sessions suggested designating MS-13 as a terrorist organization.[2] As US anti-gang policies, moreover, often directly influence Central American anti-gang efforts, for instance, through security assistance programs, this post-9/11 framing of gangs is also taking hold in Central America, thereby pushing the local war on gangs towards a new level.

The assessment of these interlinked policy responses and derived efforts of governing transnational Central American gangs in the post-9/11 context stands at the center of this chapter. It will particularly highlight the role of 'securitization' processes in aligning post-9/11 Central American politics and US geopolitical interests in governing Central American gangs. With securitization, I refer to efforts of 'the staging of existential issues in politics to lift them above politics'. In doing so, 'an issue is dramatized and presented as an issue of supreme priority; thus, by labelling it as security, an agent claims a need for and a right to treat it by extraordinary means' (Buzan el al. 1998: 26). Stated in other terms, securitization describes 'successful political speech act(s) transforming the decision-making process and generating a politics of exception, often favoring coercive options' (Bigo and Tsoukala 2008: 5).

The remainder of this chapter will trace the genealogy of interlinked securitization efforts targeting Central American street gangs. It starts with a brief contextualization regarding the origins, scope and developments of transnational Central American gangs. Next, the trajectory of the punitive efforts of governing Central American gangs, as well as their underlying securitization efforts, will be assessed by following the development of Central American security policies targeting street gangs from zero tolerance-inspired policing efforts to more militarized, counterinsurgency and counter-terrorism driven approaches within the Global War on Terror (GWOT). The conclusion will summarize the main findings of this chapter and highlight their implications for future research on the topic.

Mapping the context

Despite the fact that contemporary US and Central American security bureaucracies as well as politicians tend to agree that Central American gangs, first and foremost MS-13 and 18th Street – which will be the focus of this chapter – have become a 'transnational concern that demands a coordinated, multi-national response to effectively combat increasingly sophisticated criminal gang networks' (USAID 2006: 5), and a burgeoning global academic interest in Central American street gangs notwithstanding (e.g. Bruneau et al. 2011; ERIC et al. 2004–2006; Faux 2006; Rodgers 2009), our knowledge about this phenomenon is still very limited. As a recent contribution to the United Nations International Children's Emergency Fund (UNICEF)'s Evidence for Action blog summed it up:

> Basic data on gangs in the Latin American region is largely unavailable. We know from existing data that adolescents of the region are disproportionately the main victims of violent crime, although to what extent gang members are victims is largely unknown. Data that would allow for a better understanding of gangs' contribution to violent crime as well as to allow comparisons across countries of the region is also still largely unavailable, including figures on the prevalence of gangs (how widespread they are) as well as the nature of offending of gang members (delinquent acts they engage in).

These 'data gaps', the contribution highlighted, also include the issue of the actual size and geographic scope of Central American street gangs – with membership estimates ranging from

69,000 to up to 500,000 – as well as their social composition, including their age structure and members' motivation to join a gang (Chávez 2018).

While knowledge about Central American gangs remains limited, at least three features regarding their origins and later development are well established and undisputed: First, gangs are not a new phenomenon to the countries of the region. In fact, local gangs can be traced back, at least, to the late 1950s and early 1960s (e.g. Levenson 2013; Smutt and Miranda 1998: 30–31; WOLA 2006: 1). Second, there is a clear correlation between marginality and gang formation. In fact, while no single factor seems to explain people's decision to join a gang, gangs are a particularly pronounced phenomenon in Central American settings marked by the intersection of 'poverty, the existence of poor-quality formal education, the lack of career education, and the ubiquity of violence' (Cruz 2014: 137). Third, the 'new quality', of the gangs of the Isthmus. This refers to their transnationality, as well as their involvement in crime. In contrast to mediatized images of hyper-violent street gangs, or portrayals of these gangs as 'organized' criminal actors, such involvement can be attributed to 'a tiny hard-core' of gang members who, in the case of MS-13, amount to about 5 percent of its members who are engaged in a plethora of criminal activities, 'mainly extortion, robbery, and drug dealing' (Ward 2013: 196–170). This 'new quality', notably with regard to MS-13 and 18th Street, is the product of US deportation policies during the 1990s.

A key event in this regard were the Rodney King riots in Los Angeles in 1991 (for an analysis of the riots, see Cannon 1999; Gooding-Williams 1993). Following the videotaped beating of African American car driver Rodney King by members of the Los Angeles Police Department, and their later acquittal in court, between April 30 and May 5, Los Angeles witnessed massive riots and lootings, which led to the death of 52 persons. While African American gangs were initially identified as a key factor behind the riots, this perception changed in the riots' aftermath, when it was discovered that most of the rioting and looting happened in neighborhoods with a predominant Mexican and Central American population. The subsequent 'Latinization' of the riots, which is their entanglement in public discourse with the issues of illegal Latino immigration, and urban violence embodied in the trope of the 'Latino looter' in turn, triggered a toughening anti-gang and immigration laws (Zilberg 2011: 59–63).

Leading to a wave of new legal and policing measures, the immediate aftermath of the riots contributed to a revamping of urban security policies that, in many ways, predated the rise of 'revanchist' urban governance models (Smith 1998) and the more general turn towards a 'new military urbanism' (Graham 2010), affecting increasingly polarized cities around the globe. Amongst the newly designed legal and policing tools targeting Latino gangs (for an overview, see Müller 2015), the Illegal Immigration Reform and Immigrant Responsibility Act as well as the Antiterrorism and Effective Death Penalty Act, both enacted in 1996, stand out. In enhancing the legal definition of 'aggravated felony', by including crimes often associated with gang membership, such as theft, gambling offenses or violence, these laws opened the door for deporting gang members 'back home': 'Notwithstanding blistering criticism on constitutional and human rights grounds, and on-going legal and legislative disputes, these laws were implemented, and the number of annual deportations skyrocketed' (Matei 2011: 198).

In fact, deportation became the means of choice for 'solving' the domestic gang problem by sending Central American gang members – many of whom were undocumented immigrants whose parents fled from the violence of the US-backed military regimes in El Salvador, Guatemala and Honduras during the 1970s and 1980s – particularly from MS-13 and 18th street (on the origins of MS-13 and 18th street, see Váldez 2011; Vigil 2002: 130–147; Ward 2013: 73–111) back to their war-torn 'home countries' of the Northern Triangle of Central America, which comprises the countries of El Salvador, Guatemala and Honduras.[3] After deportation, many gang members embraced their US gang experiences as a means of coping with the precarious living conditions they encountered in these countries. Moreover, the imported gang culture also seemed particularly attractive for local marginalized youth, who, in turn, started to join them (Diaz 2011: 34; Jütersonke et al. 2009: 379–380). As Sonja Wolf has summed up in a paradigmatic way for the case of El Salvador:

> Deported youths, separated from their families and with few memories of their countries of origin, often felt disoriented and alienated by the humble surroundings they encountered. Although many expected to make a fresh start, disaffection and continued marginalization prompted some to continue the gang lifestyle they knew best. The gang members' comparatively smarter dress, money, and romanticized descriptions of gang life held a fascination that local adolescents found hard to resist.
>
> *(Wolf 2017: 10)*

As a consequence of these developments, from the mid-1990s onwards, MS-13 and 18th Street expanded their presence throughout the Northern Triangle. This process was accompanied by a spread of violence, often tied to gang-related illegal activities, mostly 'small-scale, localized crime and delinquency such as petty theft and muggings (although these can often result in murder)' (Rodgers et al. 2009: 9). The securitization-driven political response to the expanding gang presence in the Northern Triangle, and the violence associated with gang expansion, eventually contributed to a qualitative transformation of the criminal and violent quality of Central American gangs, as well as their transnational scope.

Securitizing the gangs of Central America

The 'home countries' of the deported gang members, El Salvador, Guatemala and Honduras, were – and continue to be – some of the most unequal societies of the region. They have historically been ruled by small oligarchies, keen on preserving the status quo, if necessary through violent means and military rule. In this regard, a recent publication by the United Nations Economic Commission for Latin America and the Caribbean (ECLAC) identified a prevailing 'culture of privilege that normalizes social hierarchies and highly unequal access to the fruits of progress, political participation and production assets' as a key contributing factor to the fact that 'Latin America and the Caribbean is not only the most unequal region in the world, but also the most violent' (ECLAC 2018: 213, 16). This correlation between inequality and violence is particularly pronounced in the Northern Triangle. As another recent publication by the World Economic Forum put it: 'The more unequal a setting, the higher the rates of violence'. As the report continues to elaborate:

> Latin America's cities are the most unequal on the planet: roughly 111 of the region's 588 million inhabitants live in slums. Although poverty reduction was prioritized by many governments, Latin America is home to 10 of the 15 most unequal countries in the world. What's more, in 2015, the region was home to 47 of the 50 most murderous cities on earth. Cities in El Salvador, Honduras, Mexico and Guatemala were at the top of the charts.[4]

The social upheavals and insurgencies that shaped each of these Central American countries' (El Salvador, Honduras and Guatemala) Cold War experiences were directly related to this outcome. With the end of the Civil Wars in the 1990s, the countries of the Northern Triangle returned to civilian rule but continued to be governed by what William I. Robinson (2003) called parties of the 'New Right'. These parties, while seeking to modernize their countries' political and economic systems, were keen on maintaining the privileges of comparatively small elite segments and the socio-political status quo.

After the return to civilian rule, this implied that local elites and their governing projects needed to secure the legitimacy of the local populations in and through democratic elections. As post-Civil War El Salvador, Guatemala and Honduras were all affected by growing 'poverty, marginalization, and a pandemic of crime, drug abuse, and interpersonal violence' (Robinson 2003: 1–2), local politicians increasingly resorted to punitive populist agendas that claimed to promote the 'security of law-abiding "ordinary people"' while 'punishing those whose crimes jeopardize this' (Pratt 2007: 12). In so doing, political elites aimed at boosting the legitimacy of their political projects by channeling multiple local grievances towards the issues of crime and insecurity. Thereby, they sought to politically capitalize on voters' security concerns by appearing to be committed to public security issues without having to address many of the structural factors – such as socio-economic inequality and marginalization – that substantially contributed to growing levels of crime and violence in the first place (Wolf 2017: 4). And, as elsewhere in Latin America, part and parcel of these efforts has been a growing securitization of crime by declaring it an 'existential' threat to local societies, requiring 'extraordinary' *tough* law enforcement measures in response (Müller 2012, 2016). In Central America, the main targets of this securitization process were street gangs. In fact:

> The specific Central American 'twist' of this trend was that it evolved around a widely shared common sense, underpinned by moral narratives about choice, character and self-discipline – in many cases supported by neo-evangelical religious ideas, – that nearly exclusively blamed street gangs as the ultimate 'evil' urban other and as the root cause of crime, violence, and insecurity. As a result of this, the countries mostly affected by the presence of MS-13 and 18th Street, El Salvador, Guatemala, and Honduras, all witnessed the unleashing of lawfare and the implementation of tough on crime (*mano dura*) anti-gang policing strategies, frequently inspired – in ideational as well as in practical terms – by New York City-style zero-tolerance policing.
>
> *(Müller 2015: 709)*

Such policy responses (for a regional overview, see Cruz 2010; Jütersonke et al. 2009; Müller 2015), whose political appeal is evidenced by the successful presidential campaigns of right-wing politicians, such as Antonio Saca of El Salvador (2004) and Otto Pérez Molina in Guatemala (2011), who 'were elected presidents after promising *mano dura* approaches to gangs and crime' (ICG 2017: 7–8), ultimately aggravated the gang problem. In turn, this allowed politicians to continue to resort to tough-on-crime policies in order to 'solve' the gang issue, which their very same policies helped to expand and exacerbate.

Two processes are particularly relevant in this regard: First, Central American tough-on-crime agendas implied a trend towards more, and increasingly repressive, *mano dura* policing of marginalized urban neighborhoods – often through joint military-police patrols. This, in turn, was accompanied by the toughening of local penal codes, implying new and longer sentencing possibilities for gang-related activities. Both developments, second, produced a massive prisoner intake throughout the 2000s, creating some of the highest levels of prison overcrowding worldwide. In El Salvador, for instance, overcrowding levels – driven by the country's anti-gang policies – reached '310.4 per cent of capacity in 2016, and 567 Salvadorans out of every 100,000 are imprisoned' (ICG 2017: 7). During the same year, prison-overcrowding rates reached 200 percent in Honduras and 'only' 125 percent in Guatemala, according to the *World Prison Brief*.[5]

The overall growth of the prison population throughout the Northern Triangle transformed the Central American prison system into a veritable 'cradle for the expanded territorial organization of the gangs' by enabling them to 'debate, make pacts, and decide on structures, strategies, and ways to operate' (Cruz 2010: 392). Anthony W. Fontes aptly described the underlying processes for the case of Guatemala:

> By the early 2000s, prisons in Guatemala, as in Honduras and El Salvador, were packed full of mareros alongside young men who became easy fodder for gang recruitment as they took on the group identity foisted upon them by police profiling. . . . Imprisoned gang leaders formed the first 'Wheel of the Barrio' (Rueda del Barrio), through which the most powerful ramfleros met and coordinated trade in weapons, soldiers and territorial claims on the outside. Surviving leaders even claim to have ordered homies on the street to intentionally get arrested. Through miscalculated misbehavior and disruption, they sought to have marero prisoners be transferred to select facilities in order to gain numerical dominance. Such strategies helped make the maras a force to be reckoned throughout the prison system.
>
> *(Fontes 2018: 105–106)*

In fact, and in addition to facilitating MS-13 and 18th Street to strengthen their internal cohesion (Gutierrez Rivera 2012; Levenson 2013: 113), gangs' ability to navigate the region's prisons to their advantage also enabled them to act 'nationwide as well as internationally, insofar as foreigners also served sentences inside the jails', thereby contributing substantially to the transnational quality of MS-13 and 18th Street as well as to the gangs' ability to engage in more sophisticated criminal activities (Cruz 2010: 395–396).

The securitization agendas of Central American politicians (and security bureaucracies) that contributed to this exacerbation of the local gang problem, however, were not only inward looking, in terms of trying to win local elections and maintain political legitimacy. Rather, these developments were accompanied by a securitization-driven 'internationalization strategy', through which local actors 'seek to use foreign capital, such as resources, degrees, contacts, legitimacy, and expertise . . . to build their power at home' (Dezalay and Garth 2002: 7). And the audience for this strategy was the US foreign policy and security establishment. Reproducing a historical pattern of what has been termed 'intervention by invitation' (Müller 2015; Müller and Hochmüler 2017; Tickner 2007) in and through which Latin American actors perform their weakness vis-à-vis 'extraordinary' domestic security threats – such as insurgent groups during the Cold War – to a political audience in Washington in order to 'invite' for a US engagement that is expected to provide local actors with otherwise unavailable resources, Central American governments early on tried to 'sell' the gang threat to the US – which, after the end of the Cold War, has substantially downscaled its security assistance for Central America.

A first related effort took place at a 2003 summit of the region's heads of state when Central American presidents declared that gangs are 'a destabilizing menace, more immediate than any conventional war or guerrilla' (quoted in Jütersonke et al. 2009: 383). As the US did not immediately respond to this discursive move, securitization efforts were pushed to a new level. In 2004, Central American governments started placing the region's gangs in the post-9/11 global threat scenario. They achieved this by openly speculating, but without providing credible evidence, about possible connections between Central American gangs and transnational Islamist terrorist groups, such as Al-Qaida – and the implicit threat potentials of such alliances for the US (ibid., see also Müller 2015, 2019). This time, the invitation was successful, as it sparked new rounds of security assistance for the gang-affected Central American countries. In turn, the latter enabled local politicians and military actors to deepen their 'tough on crime' efforts through a re-militarization of domestic security governance, a move that could be justi-fied by claiming that a deeper engagement of the military forces in domestic security affairs would be an essential precondition for successfully countering gangs, and, ultimately, *insurgency* and *terrorism*.

Of gangs, insurgents and terrorists

The post-9/11 context, and the ensuing GWOT, provided new global framings regarding the threat potentials of so-called 'non-state armed actors' roaming freely in the 'ungoverned' spaces of 'failed' or 'failing' states around the world (Clunan and Trinkunas 2010; Rabasa et al. 2007; Rotberg 2003). From the mid-2000s onwards, these framings traveled beyond the major thea-tres of the GWOT and enveloped Latin America (Kruijt and Koonings 2004; Müller 2020; Prevost et al. 2014). As a consequence of this, armed and violent criminal actors throughout the region, including Central American gangs, have increasingly been framed through a counter-terrorism lens that early on converged with counterinsurgency (Hochmüller and Müller 2016, 2017; Levenson 2013; Vanden 2014; Zilberg 2011). An important contributing factor to this development was the conceptual work of a group of US-based security scholars, policy analysts and practitioners, who were capable of adapting a GWOT vocabulary to the analysis of street gangs in the region. In turn, the latter have been presented as the 'new urban insurgency' (Man-waring 2005) or 'criminal insurgents' (Sullivan and Elkus 2008), whose activities, and alleged connections to terrorists, are said to weave together '[c]rime, terrorism and insurgency' in 'ways that threaten not just the welfare but also the security of societies in the western hemisphere' (Killebrew and Bernal 2010: 6; for details, see Müller 2020).

Two interrelated processes contributed to the resulting incorporation of such framings into anti-gang policies – with serious implications for the Central American 'war on gangs'. First, there has been a growing cross-fertilization between domestic and foreign US security efforts within the GWOT. With police officers and soldiers rotating back and forth between the US and the major theatres of post-9/11 counterterrorism and counterinsurgency operations, such as Afghanistan and Iraq, security practitioners and analysts started drawing practical parallels between gangs and insurgents, as well as between methods of countering them. As, for instance, a Special Operations Forces 'mentor' to the Afghan National Police, who previously worked 'with the Federal Bureau of Investigations Safe Streets Task Force, dismantling organized nar-cotics gangs using Racketeering Influenced Corrupt Organizations (RICO)' summed up:

> Organized gangs are into drugs, human trafficking, selling stolen cars, and other criminal activities to make money for the criminal organization. Insurgent groups will also deal in illegal activities. There are a lot of similarities between the organized gangs of urban American and insurgent and criminal organizations in Afghan communities.
>
> *(Martin 2018)*

Such discoveries not only meant that anti-gang policing efforts, such as community-oriented policing, were seen as crucial elements for a successful fight against insurgents abroad (Müller and Steinke 2020). On the flipside, this also meant that homecoming GWOT veterans, many of whom joined US police departments, brought their counterinsurgency experience back home and applied it to the fight against local gangs (Hochmüller and Müller 2017). This development was exacerbated by the general hype surrounding counterinsurgency's revival, which, in turn, implied that counterinsurgency tools were seen as useful, and legitimate, means of countering 'unconventional' domestic security threats, in particular gangs. In the words of Mike Katone, a police officer who implemented a counterinsurgency strategy to confront the local gang problem in Springfield, Massachusetts:

> Insurgents and gang members both want to operate in a failed area – a failed community or a failed state. . . . They know they can live off the passive support of the community, where the local community is not going to call or engage the local police. . . . If the government is not going to do it, and individuals are not going to do it, why can't police partner up with the community and say, 'Hey, here's a plan. This is what we want to do to help. Because the status quo of traditional policing, it just ain't gonna work.'
>
> *(quoted in The Washington Times 2013)*

While it might be a stretch to say that Springfield was actually turned into a 'laboratory' for the growing domestic application of counterinsurgency-inspired policing practices, as envisioned by Harvard professor and Afghanistan veteran Kevin Kit Parker (quoted in *The Boston Globe* 2012), such reasoning and derived practices, indeed, did spread.

Probably the most well known case is Salinas, in Monterey County, CA, whose counterinsurgency-policing ventures even predate the Springfield 'experiment'. In a collaborative effort of developing a 'new approach to the fight against the domestic terror wrought by street gangs which might be applied across the nation', the Salinas Police Department teamed up with the Naval Postgraduate School with the goal of 'applying lessons learned by the military in combating insurgent groups around the world to combating gang violence in Salinas' (MCCVPISRF 2010: 44–45). Likewise, the related 'fight against the criminal gang insurgency in Salinas' (SPD 2009) is driven by the assumption that 'counterinsurgency provides a useful focus from which to approach the question of how to effectively combat the instability street gangs bring to an environment' (Arnold et a. 2010: 37).

Through so-called 'police diplomacy' efforts, as well as underlying forms of knowledge production that led to the creation of a new, *generic insurgency concept*, that of 'criminal insurgencies' – paradigmatically personified by Central American street gangs – but also through security assistance programs, such as the Central America Regional Security Initiative (CARSI), such reasoning, which portrays counterinsurgency as a promising counter-gang strategy, has been exported to Central America. In turn, the fight against local street gangs has increasingly taken a counterinsurgency outlook (Hochmüller and Müller 2016; see Müller 2019; 2020 for related developments throughout the region).

Part and parcel of this process is the build-up, training and financial support for special police units with a strong counterinsurgency outlook. A case in point is the Special Response Team and Intelligence Troop (*Tropa de Inteligencia y Grupos de Respuesta Especial de Seguridad* TIGRES), an elite unit of the Honduran National Police. Set up in 2013 with the support of the US and Colombia, and trained by US Special Forces – and their Colombian counterparts – the unit's 500 members are often deployed in joint operations with the anti-gang inter-agency task force National Inter-institutional Security Force (*Fuerza Nacional de Seguridad Interinstitutional*, FUSINA), which has also been trained by US civilian and military personnel in 'rapid response' tactics.[6] As one FUSINA member put it:

> In the operations or raids we carry out at the national level against drug trafficking, organized crime, gangs, or high-impact operations benefitting from military-police training, the participation of TIGRES, which can easily adapt due to its training, is always crucial.[7]

The creation of, and external support for, militarized special police units, like TIGRES or FUSINA, is clearly inspired by 'a counterinsurgency policing model [that] the U.S. implemented in Iraq and Afghanistan and is trying to apply to Central America' (*Telesur* 2016). In this regard, such developments, which deepen the previously discussed militarization of domestic anti-gang policing, are not exclusive to Honduras. They started to proliferate across the Isthmus. As one report summed up the most recent developments in this regard:

> In May 2015, the Salvadoran government created three battalions to help police in anti-gang efforts; at that time, some 7,000 soldiers were already involved in public security efforts. In March 2016, Salvadoran President Sánchez Cerén deployed hundreds of military reservists. Since taking office in January, Guatemalan President Jimmy Morales has extended the mandate of some 4,500 soldiers organized in nine groups that were involved in domestic security efforts during the previous government.
>
> *(Ribando Seelke 2016: 12–13)*

As a consequence of this, the militaries of the Isthmus are now at the forefront of the fight against gangs, often in direct collaboration with increasingly militarized police forces. For example, in El Salvador, 'The Salvadoran Armed Forces (FAES) are leading the country's fight against the violent Mara Salvatrucha (MS-13) and Barrio 18 (M-18) street gangs, playing a key role in the "Nuevo Amanecer" [New Dawn] plan'. The latter 'provides a framework for joint operations with the National Civil Police to improve public safety', under which 'the FAES are deploying their most accomplished and experienced Army service members to take on the gangs'.[8]

Such developments can draw upon the appropriation of the criminal insurgency narrative by local actors (e.g. Gómez Hecht 2017; Murillo Zamora 2017) and the closely related recycling of (counter)terrorism discourses (Müller 2020). Both narratives, it should be recalled, were already heavily used during the Cold War. During these years, as the Guatemalan Human Rights Commission (2013) has put it, such framings 'endorsed the violent repression against anyone who challenged existing structures of racism, or economic and political exclusion, labeling them "subversives", "guerrillas", "terrorists", and "internal enemies".'

The GWOT and the local appropriation of globally circulating security discourses contributed to a revival of these framings in the Central American context by substituting the 'old' *internal* enemy in the guise of 'subversion' for the new '*transnational* threat' posed by street gangs. In turn, this pushed previous securitization efforts towards a new level. When framed through contemporary post-9/11 security discourses, gangs are no longer seen as having only *potential* links to transnational terrorists. Rather, Central American gangs themselves are portrayed as insurgent/terrorist actors. Accordingly, the existential threat gangs are said to represent for the affected countries increased. To counter this threat, a new set of extraordinary measures is needed. In addition to the export of counterinsurgency policing, the most recent development in this regard has been the return of counterterrorism legislation throughout the Northern Triangle.

The first country to classify gangs as terrorists, was El Salvador, where, in 2015, the country's Supreme Court 'officially designated MS-13 as a terrorist organization', with the consequence that terrorism charges now 'carry maximum penalties of up to 60 years, compared to up to 20 years for homicide or up to 50 years for aggravated homicide' (Blake 2017: 42–43). Following the Salvadoran example, in 2017, the Honduran parliament approved a reform of the country's penal code in regard to terrorism. In order to confront the local gang problem, gang-related activities, such as extortion or the intimidation of the local population, are now classified as acts of terrorism, punishable by up to 50 years in prison (*Prensa Libre* 2017). Reformed paragraph 335 of the penal code defines terrorists as people who 'are part of illegal associations and develop activities whose aim is, by committing or threatening to commit violent crimes, to undermine [*alterar*] the public peace, terrorize or intimidate the population, or a part of it' (Poder Judicial de Honduras 2017: 110). And about one year on, in January 2018, Guatemala's government was proposing a similar law to the parliament that classifies gang members as terrorists (*El Nuevo Diario* 2018).

Conclusion: de-securitizing gangs

As this chapter has shown, political efforts of governing the street gangs of Central America's Northern Triangle, in particular MS-13 and 18th Street, have been driven by an escalating transnational securitization process. This development has been sustained by the convergence of US and Central American elites and security bureaucracies regarding the punitive containment of gangs – from initial *mano dura* policing approaches towards an increasing reliance on heavily militarized and GWOT-related counterinsurgency as well as counterterrorism means. In light of the previous analysis, the success of such measures for a sustainable solution of the gang problem remains doubtful. In fact, as this chapter has demonstrated, the unintended consequences of securitization – in the US and Central America – were key in creating and worsening the gang problem. While securitization allows politicians to continue promoting politically motivated penal populist agendas and security bureaucracies, in particular the military, to benefit, in symbolic and material terms, from their new role as legitimate domestic security providers, as long as the underlying structural root causes of the gang problem, namely marginalization and socio-political exclusion, will not be tackled, a sustainable solution to the gang problem won't be found. As Wolf (207: 4) has put it for the case of El Salvador: 'Reductions in gang violence and crime will come only by ending the social marginalization that leads youth into gangs, and this, in turn, demands a restructuring of Salvadoran society, including its power relations and socio-economic inequalities'. In this regard, it is important to stress that securitization is not a one-way street. Securitization processes can be undone through *desecuritization* efforts that move particular topics 'out of emergency mode and into the normal bargaining process of the political sphere' (Buzan et al. 1998: 4). In this regard, the main implication of this chapter's findings is that by acknowledging that gangs and gang-related violence in the Northern Triangle, as well as in the US, are inseparable from persisting social inequalities, such a desecuritization agenda can be pursued by prioritizing the *social question* that lies at the center of the gang problem over the so-far-dominant security framings of the issue – particularly as the latter have tended to exacerbate the problem they promised to solve.

Notes

1 See www.ice.gov/about
2 https://thehill.com/homenews/administration/329435-sessions-says-ms-13-gang-could-qualify-as-terrorist-organization
3 The underlying topography of this migration-deportation pattern explains why Costa Rica and Nicaragua have been relatively spared from the spread of MS-13 and 18th Street. See Rodgers et al. (2009: 23–24); Ranum (2001: 108).
4 www.weforum.org/agenda/2016/06/latin-america-s-cities-unequal-dangerous-and-fragile-but-that-can-change/
5 www.prisonstudies.org/map/central-america
6 www.wola.org/analysis/which-central-american-military-and-police-units-get-the-most-u-s-aid/

7 https://dialogo-americas.com/en/articles/southcom-donation-strengthens-honduran-elite-police-force
8 https://dialogo-americas.com/en/articles/specially-trained-salvadoran-troops-take-violent-street-gangs

References

Arnold, L. H., C. W. O'Gwin, and J. S. Vickers (2010) *Small Town Insurgency: The Struggle for Information Dominance to Reduce Gang Violence.* Monterrey, CA: Naval Postgraduate School.

The Atlantic (2018) 'The Transcript of Trump's State of the Union Address', January 31.

Bigo, D. and A. Tsoukala (2008) 'Understanding (In)Security', in D. Bigo and A. Tsoukala (eds.) *Terror, Insecurity and Liberty. Illiberal Practices of Liberal Regimes after 9/11.* London: Routledge, pp. 1–9.

Blake, J. (2017) 'MS-13 as a Terrorist Organization: Risks for Central American Asylum Seekers', *Michigan Law Review* 116: 39–49.

The Boston Globe (2012) 'To counter gangs, Springfield adopts tactics from war zones', August 20.

Bruneau, T., L. Dammert, and E. Skinner (eds.) (2011) *Maras. Gang Violence and Security in Central America.* Austin, TX: Texas University Press.

Buzan, B., O. Waever, and J. de Wilde (1998) *Security: A New Framework for Analysis.* Boulder, CO: Lynne Rienner.

Cannon, L. (1999) Official Negligence: How Rodney King and the Riots Changed Los Angeles and the LAPD. Boulder, CO: Westview.

Chávez, C. (2018) 'What We Know and What We Don't Know about Youth Gangs in Latin America,' United Nations United Nations International Children's Emergency Fund (UNICEF)'s Evidence for Action Blog, September 27, 2018. https://blogs.unicef.org/evidence-for-action/know-dont-know-youth-gangs-latin-america/

Clunan, A. L. and H. A. Trinkunas (eds.) (2010) *Ungoverned Spaces: Alternatives to State Authority in an Era of Softened Sovereignty.* Stanford, CA: Stanford Security Studies.

Cruz, J. M. (2010) 'Central American Maras: From Youth Street Gangs to Transnational Protection Rackets', *Global Crime,* 11 (4): 379–398.

Cruz, J. M. (2014) 'Government Responses and the Dark Side of Gang Suppression in Central America', in T. Bruneau, L. Dammert and E. Skinner (eds.) *Maras. Gang Violence and Security in Central America.* Austin, TX: University of Texas Press, pp. 137–158.

Dezalay, Y. and B. Garth (2002) *The Internationalization of Palace Wars: Lawyers, Economists, and the Contest to Transform Latin American States.* Chicago, IL: University of Chicago Press.

Diaz, T. (2011) *No Boundaries. Transnational Latino Gangs and American Law Enforcement.* Ann Arbor, MI: University of Michigan Press.

Economic Commission for Latin America and the Caribbean (ECLAC) (2018) *The Inefficiency of Inequality.* Santiago: United Nations, ECLAC.

El Nuevo Diario (2018) 'Gobierno Guatemala pedirá que Congreso declare a las maras como terroristas', January 30.

Equipo de Reflexión, Investogación y Comunicación (ERIC), Instituto de Encuestas y Sondeos de Opinión (IDESO), Instituto de Investigaciónes Económicos y Sociales (IDIES) and Instituto Universitario de Opinión Pública (IUDOP) (eds.) (2004–2006) *Maras y pandillas en Centroamérica,* vol. 4. El Salvador: UCA Editores.

Faux, F. (2006) Les maras, gangs d'enfants: Violences urbaines en Amérique centrale. Paris: Editions Autrement.

Fontes, A. W. (2018) *Mortal Doubt. Transnational Gangs and Social Order in Guatemala City.* Oakland: CA: University of California Press.

Gómez Hecht, J. R. (2017) 'Gangs in El Salvador: A New Type of Insurgency?', *Small Wars Journal.* https://smallwarsjournal.com/jrnl/art/gangs-in-el-salvador-a-new-type-of-insurgency

Gooding-Williams, R. (ed.) (1993) *Reading Rodney King/Reading Urban Uprising.* London: Routledge.

Graham, S. (2010) *Cities under Siege. The New Military Urbanism.* London: Verso.

Guatemalan Human Rights Commission (2013) *Rethinking the Drug War in Central America and Mexico: Guatemala Section.* http://www.ghrc-usa.org/resources/other-publications/rethinking-the-drug-war-in-central-america-and-mexico-guatemala-section/

Gutierrez Rivera, L. (2012) 'Geografías de Violencia y Exclusión. Pandillas encarceladas en Honduras', *Latin American Research Review* 47 (2): 167–179.

Hochmüller, M. and M.-M. Müller (2016) 'Locating Guatemala in Global Counterinsurgency', *Globalizations* 13 (1): 94–109.

Hochmüller, M. and M.-M. Müller (2017) 'Countering Criminal Insurgencies: Fighting Gangs and Building Resilient Communities in Post-War Guatemala', in L. W. Moe and M.-M. Müller (eds.) *Reconfiguring Intervention: Complexity, Resilience and the "Local Turn" in Counterinsurgent Warfare*. Basingstoke: Palgrave Macmillan, pp. 163–186.

International Crisis Group (2017) *Mafia of the Poor: Gang Violence and Extortion in Central America*. Brussels: ICG.

Jütersonke, O., R. Muggah, and D. Rodgers (2009) 'Gangs, Urban Violence, and Security Interventions in Central America', *Security Dialogue* 40 (4–5): 373–397.

Killebrew, B. and J. Bernal (2010) *Crime Wars: Gangs, Cartels and US National Security*. Washington, DC: Center for a New American Security.

Kruijt, D. and K. Koonings (eds.) (2004) *Armed Actors. Organised Violence and State Failure in Latin America*. London: Zed Books.

Levenson, D. T. (2013) *Adiós Niño: The Gangs of Guatemala City and the Politics of Death*. Durham, NC: Duke University Press.

Manwaring, M. G. (2005) *Street Gangs: The New Urban Insurgency*. Carlisle, PA: U.S. Army War College.

Matei, F. C. (2011) 'The Impact of U.S. Anti-Gang Policies in Central America: Quo Vadis?' in T. Bruneau, L. Dammert, and E. Skinner (eds.) *Maras. Gang Violence and Security in Central America*. Austin, TX: Texas University Press, pp. 197–210.

Martin, C. (2018) 'Community Oriented Policing in a Counter Insurgency Environment', *SOF News*, April 26, 2018. www.sof.news/afghanistan/community-oriented-policing/

Monterrey County's Comprehensive Violence Prevention, Intervention, Suppression, and Reentry Framework (MCCVPISRF) (2010) 'A Framework for Safety and Peace', Salinas, CA.

Müller, M.-M. (2012) 'The Rise of the Penal State in Latin America', *Contemporary Justice Review* 15 (1): 57–76.

Müller, M.-M. (2015) 'Punitive Entanglements: The "War on Gangs" and the Making of a Transnational Penal Apparatus in the Americas', *Geopolitics* 20 (3): 696–727.

Müller, M.-M. (2016) *The Punitive City. Privatised Protection and Policing in Neoliberal Mexico*. London: Zed Books.

Müller, M.-M. (2019) 'Terrorism and Insurgency in Post-9/11 Latin America,' in D. M. Jones, P. Schulte, C. Ungerer, and M. L. R. Smith (eds.) *Handbook of Terrorism and Counter Terrorism Post-9–11*. Cheltenham: Edward Elgar, pp. 361–370.

Müller, M.-M. (2020) 'Enter 9/11: Latin America and the Global War on Terror', *Journal of Latin American Studies* 52 (3): 545–573.

Müller, M.-M. and M. Hochmüler (2017) 'From Regime Protection to Urban Resilience? Assessing Continuity and Change in Transnational Security Governance Rationales in Guatemala', *Geoforum* 84: 389–400.

Müller, M.-M. and A. Steinke (2020) 'Community Policing's Extended Military History: Brazilian Pacification from the Global Cold War to the Global War on Terror', *Policing and Society*, DOI: 10.1080/10439463.2020.1772256

Murillo Zamora, C. (2017) 'Transnational Organized Crime as Policy without Insurgency: The Experience of Central America', *Desafíos* 28 (2): 177–211.

Poder Judicial de Honduras (2017) *Decreto 144–83 Código Penal*. Tegucigalpa: Poder Judicial.

Pratt, J. (2007) *Penal Populism*. London: Routledge.

Prensa Libre (2017) 'Honduras aprueba ley que califica de 'terroristas' a pandilleros y manifestantes', February 22.

Prevost, G., H. Vanden, C. Campos, and L. F. Ayerbe (eds.) (2014) *US National Security Concerns in Latin America and the Caribbean. The Concept of Ungoverned Spaces and Failed States*. Basingstoke: Palgrave Macmillan.

Rabasa, A., S. Boraz, P. Chalk, K. Cragin, T. W. Karasik, J. D. P. Moroney, K. A. O'Brien, and J. E. Peters (eds.) (2007) *Ungoverned Territories. Understanding and Reducing Terrorism Risks*. Santa Monica, CA: RAND Corporation.

Ranum, E. C. (2001) 'Street Gangs of Nicaragua', in T. Bruneau, L. Dammert, and E. Skinner (eds.) *Maras. Gang Violence and Security in Central America*. Austin, TX: Texas University Press.

Ribando Seelke, C. (2016) *Gangs in Central America*. Washington, DC: Congressional Research Service.

Robinson, William I. (2003) *Transnational Conflicts. Central America, Social Change and Globalization*. London: Verso.

Rodgers, D. (2009) 'Slum Wars of the 21st Century: Gangs, *Mano Dura* and the New Urban Geography of Conflict in Central America', *Development & Change* 40 (5): 949–976.

Rodgers, D. and J. M. Hazen (2014) 'Introduction: Gangs in a Global Comparative Perspective', in J. M. Hazen and D. Rodgers (eds.) *Global Gangs. Street Violence Across the World*. Minnesota, MN: University of Minnesota Press, pp. 1–25.

Rodgers, D., R. Muggah, and C. Stevenson (2009). *Gangs of Central America: Causes, Costs, and Interventions*. Geneva: Small Arms Survey Occasional Paper 23.

Rotberg, R. I. (ed.) (2003) *When States Fail Causes and Consequences*. Princeton, NJ: Princeton University Press.

Salinas Police Department (SPD) (2009) *Louise Fetherlof, Chief of Police. 180-day Report to the Community*. Salinas, CA: SAPD.

Smith, N. (1998) 'Giuliani Time: The Revanchist 1990s', *Social Text* 16 (4): 1–20.

Smutt, M. and J. L. Miranda (1998) *El fenómeno de las pandillas en El Salvador*. San Salvador: UNICEF/FLACSO.

Sullivan, J. P. and A. Elkus (2008) 'State of Siege: Mexico's Criminal Insurgency', *Small Wars Journal*. http://smallwarsjournal.com/jrnl/art/state-of-siege-mexicos-criminal-insurgency

Telesur (2016) 'US Counterinsurgency Tactics Ravage Honduras', 12 April 2016.

Tickner, A. B. (2007) 'Intervención por invitación. Claves de la política exterior Colombiana y de sus debilidades principales', *Colombia Internacional* 65: 90–111.

United States Agency for International Development (USAID) (2006) *Central American Gang Assesment*. Washington, DC: USAID.

Valdez, A. (2011) 'The Origins of Southern California Latino Gangs', in T. Bruneau, L. Dammert, and E. Skinner (eds.) *Maras. Gang Violence and Security in Central America*. Austin, TX: University of Texas Press, pp. 23–42.

Vanden, H. E. (2014) 'Maras, Contragoverned Spaces and Sovereignty', in G. Prevost, H. Vanden, C. Campos, and L. F. Ayerbe (eds.) *US National Security Concerns in Latin America and the Caribbean. The Concept of Ungoverned Spaces and Failed States*. Basingstoke: Palgrave Macmillan, pp. 81–92.

Vigil, J. D. (2002) *A Rainbow of Gangs. Street Cultures in the Mega-City*. Austin, TX: University of Texas Press.

Ward, T. W. (2013) *Gangsters Without Borders. An Ethnography of A Salvadoran Street Gang*. Oxford: Oxford University Press.

Washington Office on Latin America (WOLA) (2006) *Youth Gangs in Central America. Issues in Human Rights, Effective Policing and Prevention*. Washington, DC: WOLA.

The Washington Times (2013) 'Massachusetts Police Take Iraq Counterinsurgency Tactics to Streets to Fight Gangs', May 6, 2013.

Wolf, S. (2017) *Mano Dura. The Politics of Gang Control in El Salvador*. Austin, TX: Texas University Press.

Zilberg, E. (2011) *Space of Detention. The Making of a Transnational Gang Crisis Between Los Angeles and El Salvador*. Durham, NC: Duke University Press.

15

Gangs and the garrison state

(In)security politics and democracy in Latin America

Katherine Saunders-Hastings

Home to just 8 percent of the world's population, but over 33 percent of its murders, violent crime indisputably presents a challenge to the security of Latin America's states and citizens. High levels of public anxiety over real and perceived crises of criminal violence have brought electoral success to politicians across the region vowing to rein in urban insecurity and take city streets back from gangs. Rarely, though, have these promises or the policies that followed translated into meaningful, sustained reductions in levels of gang violence. What they have done is ushered in new forms of state securitization in poor urban communities while raising the profile of security politics and security forces in everyday life.

Through recent gang suppression campaigns in Guatemala and Brazil, this chapter examines two distinct, if often intersecting, strains of contemporary Latin American urban policing. The first is an increasing recourse to the militarization of internal security and crime control, which can be observed both in direct military involvement in policing operations and in the militarization of police organizations through the adoption of command structures, arsenals, and institutional cultures traditionally associated with armed forces. The second is a rise in territorially-focused offshoots of community-oriented policing, which embed security forces in the physical and social spaces of marginal urban communities as never before.

The analysis presented here draws on my own ethnographic fieldwork in Guatemala City and comparative reference to literature on Rio de Janeiro. Both cities have seen recent public security programmes that embody the previously mentioned trends: the task forces that installed military barracks in some of Guatemala City's most high-risk neighbourhoods and the Police Pacification Units (UPPs) that purported to bring a new model of security to Rio's *favelas*. Following an introduction to the militarization and territorialization of urban gang policing, I consider its impact on the implementation and outcomes of the two case studies. The aim is not to present an exhaustive account or evaluation of these programmes but rather to explore how they illuminate important challenges for and concerns raised by state responses to urban insecurity.

In both cases, I concentrate on local assessments of the efficacy and legitimacy of territorially-focused gang policing. Emphasizing the perspective of residents of targeted neighbourhoods addresses a gap in the emerging literature on policing in the context of a 'new military urbanism' (Graham 2010, 2012), which is lacking in fine-grained observations of specific security interventions rooted in the 'socio-spatial contexts' in which they take place (Fahlberg 2018: 307).

Focusing precisely on those socio-spatial contexts and local experiences also illustrates the dynamics that play out on the ground when gangs and state forces press overlapping claims on urban space, territorial power, and the means of violence. Although they are typically treated as problems for and challenges to state governance, gangs, crime, and violence can also be 'resources for governance' (Müller 2018: 178). I ask, therefore, not only what urban 'wars on crime' do to (and for) gangs and residents of gang territories but also what they do for (and to) the states that wage them. Adapting Herbert Lasswell's (1941, 1962) concept of the 'garrison state' to contemporary Latin America illuminates the currents of political capital that circulate through anti-gang operations and how certain factions of the state stand to gain – and to lose – from the ascendency of insecurity politics.

I. Urban gang suppression strategies

I focus on responses to armed gangs in Guatemala City and Rio de Janeiro because of my familiarity with the former and the international prominence of the latter. However, trends of police militarization and territorialization are certainly not limited to these two settings, nor indeed to Latin America. To take but a few recent examples: El Salvador's Special Reaction Forces united army and police personnel to 'liberate' neighbourhoods seen to be *mara* strongholds (Callamard 2018; Wolf 2017), temporary joint military and police occupations in designated 'Zones of Special Operation' (ZOSOs) have been continuously extended by the Jamaican legislature since their introduction (Asman 2017; Eldemire 2018), and the South African Police Service and Defence Force have combined to 'take back communities from criminals and to re-assert the authority of the state' (Lamb 2018: 947). These gang-suppression efforts all demonstrate the same 'growing overlap between military and criminal justice complexes' that Kraska (2007: 505) identified in 21st-century US policing. They also all target the most notorious, high-risk urban neighbourhoods – neighbourhoods which are typically also socially, economically, and politically marginal. They are expressions of a 'new military urbanism' (Graham 2010, 2012) in which cities and their inhabitants have supplanted hostile states as the central source of perceived threats.

The programmes I describe in this chapter participate in a certain 'police-military role convergence' in which the 'traditional distinctions between military/police, war/law enforcement, and internal/external security are rapidly blurring' (Rantatalo 2012: 57; Kraska 2007: 501). The prevailing concern in the criminological literature from North America and Western Europe has been with the militarization of police – the diffusion of material, cultural, organizational, and operational elements of the military model to civilian forces (see Rantatalo 2012). Rather less attention has been paid to the obverse of that role convergence: the 'policization' of the military (cf. Kraska 2007). Yet this expanded deployment of the military into what were once understood as realms of police action and authority is an especially important trend in gang suppression campaigns and urban policing generally in many parts of Latin America.

The second development is an ongoing boom in 'Community-Oriented Policing (COP) reforms' that initially seems to offer a counterweight to police militarization and *mano dura* (iron fist) strategies (Magaloni et al. 2018: 2). However, it important to note that despite its more progressive aura, community policing is not synonymous with community empowerment in matters of local security or order-making. Scholars of both North and South American community policing distinguish two basic 'strands' (Kraska 2007) or 'models' (Ungar and Arias 2012). The first of these does aim to substantively improve police-community relations and typically includes prevention-focused elements (Frühling 2012). But the second, stressing aggressive policing *of* local space rather than collaborative policing *with* local people, shares its heritage and worldview with broken-windows and zero-tolerance policing models and 'emphasizes taking back the neighbourhood, creating a climate of order' (Kraska 2007: 510). In Latin America, this genre of community policing typically 'focuses on homicide control efforts, mainly in particularly violent and dangerous urban communities and [is] centered on a specialised police unit' (Ungar and Arias 2012: 10).

This territorially-oriented, homicide-focused mode of policing in violent urban gang territories unites the Guatemalan and Brazilian programmes I detail in the following, both of which installed new security units in some of these cities' most notorious neighbourhoods. Both were presented as being about the state retaking territory from criminals who have usurped it; they were about claiming and performing state control and state competence over unruly urban spaces using military forces and militarized police. These initiatives – joint military-police task forces in the former case and police pacification units in the latter – represented a new form of government engagement in Guatemala City's mara-dominated barrios and Rio de Janeiro's trafficker-dominated favelas. The prevailing anti-gang strategy in both places had long been periodically to stage big, spectacular raids that would shut down neighbourhoods, sweep up dozens of real and imagined delinquents, produce crowing media headlines proclaiming gang defeats or contraband seizures, and have virtually no impact on local criminal economies or violent governance once state forces withdrew. The new units marked a transition to a strategy of territorial reclamation and control based on sustained presence and state penetration into the everyday spaces and lives of targeted neighbourhoods.

Both Guatemala City and Rio de Janeiro underwent a transition from spectacular and sporadic interventions to a strategy of gang suppression and crime control based on constant proximity and vigilance. These new models, however, did not change the terms of the relationship between the state and these neighbourhoods. State security forces' presence and engagement – while now permeating the everyday spaces of targeted barrios and favelas as never before – remained rooted in the understanding of these places as criminal margins and enemy territories.

★★★

The Guatemalan term for the most infamous gang neighbourhoods – *zona roja*, red zone – makes their status as a locus of threat particularly clear: it originates from the counterinsurgency-era practice of labelling areas of guerrilla control red on military maps, designating the territory of the internal enemy. The criminal enemy inhabiting contemporary red zones are transnational street gangs called *maras*. They appeared in northern Central American cities in the early 1990s, hybridizing an imported Californian gang culture with existing local forms and traditions of street gangs. Their violence and criminal economy – centred on the extortion of households, businesses, and transportation in their territories – expanded significantly over the following years. By 2003, a summit of Central American heads of state declared *maras* 'a destabilizing menace, more immediate than any conventional war or guerrilla' (Rodgers 2009: 968). The joint military-police task forces introduced in 2012 represented a newly intensified effort to combat this menace in urban territories where gang violence and power concentrate.

Fuerza de Tarea Maya (Task Force Maya) was the first of these to be implemented, deployed in several of the most notorious barrios of zone 18, the largest, poorest, and by most measures most violent of the capital's 22 sub-divisions. Among its targets was Colonia el Romero,[1] a neighbourhood often said by residents and outsiders alike to be among the 'reddest' of Guatemala's so-called 'red zones'. Zone 18 in general, and El Romero in particular, were thus emblematic places to unfurl a programme that was promoted as an operation to reclaim and redeem urban territories under the power of armed gangs. The model was subsequently extended to 28 other 'red zones' throughout the capital and the country.

In a speech on the first morning of Task Force Maya's operations, then-President Otto Pérez Molina, whose *mano dura* policies were an essential part of his campaign, explained that zone 18 had been chosen because it registered more homicides and violent assaults than any other part of the capital (Government of Guatemala 2012). Minister of the Interior[2] Mauricio López Bonilla declared that zone 18's residents 'have lived as captives of the gangs' and that the task force was being implemented because they 'should not have to be under the yoke of these people' (Government of Guatemala 2012). The task force's objectives were, therefore, to bring down homicide statistics, to disrupt gang control, and to entrench state presence within their sphere of operations.

That same morning, roughly 300 soldiers – one detachment of the larger task force – arrived in Colonia el Romero. They claimed its community hall for their barracks, and although their initial mandate was for just four months, they would spend nearly six years there until Task Force Maya was disbanded in April 2018. Much of the task force's daily activity focused on deterring violence by maintaining a highly visible presence throughout the barrio at all times. Military and police trucks, some mounted with artillery, constantly circulated the neighbourhood's handful of navigable roads, foot patrols walked its alleys and staircases, and soldiers were stationed on street corners and at fortified look-out points. State security was imposed through a saturation of local space with hyper-visible military presence. This was hardly the first time the military was deployed to combat gangs. Indeed, at almost no point since the 1996 end of Guatemala's long-running civil war have its armed forces *not* been involved in combating crime. Nevertheless, the task forces vastly expanded the intensity and duration of military involvement in policing and controlling sectors of the capital.

The task forces were consistently advertised as 'joint operations' of the Ministry of Defence and the Ministry of the Interior, responsible for the military and the police respectively. But these were rather skewed partnerships: 1300 military personnel were initially assigned to Task Force Maya and only 120 police (Government of Guatemala 2012). Task Force Maya was coordinated out of a military base, not police stations. In El Romero, no additional agents were assigned to the small National Civilian Police (PNC) outpost, but scores of soldiers operated out the community hall-cum-barracks. Due to such disparities, the UN High Commissioner for Human Rights expressed concern that the extent of Guatemala's militarization of public security was being masked through the use of joint operations involving civilian police but 'made up of majority military personnel' (UN 2015: 11 §41). Residents of targeted neighbourhoods certainly perceived this as a military operation and a military occupation.

Task Force Maya was hailed as a promising model for suppressing gang violence and proof of the Pérez administration's ability to deliver on its *mano dura* platform. While its achievements were often promoted in government press conferences, media reports, and on the presidential Twitter feed, not everyone on the ground was as fulsome. One high-ranking member of the PNC told me that violence and criminality were merely being displaced, claiming that the military's deployment in zone 18 coincided with a dramatic rise in the number of bodies of homicide victims discovered in neighbouring districts.

Not all murders moved, either. Although there was an important drop from the average of four daily murders previously registered in zone 18, only 12 days out of the operation's first 286 could be declared '24–0': without homicides (Gámez 2013). In 2013, the first full year of task force operations, zone 18 'succeeded' in recording a total of 77 days without a murder. Task Force Maya also encountered difficulty in sustaining violence reduction over time. By 2015, attempted murders and homicides in zone 18 had risen to 5 percent higher than 2012 levels (UN 2015: 11 §42).

Throughout my time in El Romero, however, it was not homicides but almost always gang extortion that residents put at the top of their lists of the most disruptive and distressing forms of insecurity in their community. For reasons I return to subsequently, the task force had very little success in interrupting this practice. The fetishization of the homicide rate in policy responses to gangs and urban insecurity in northern Central America (and Latin America more broadly) risks enshrining a myopic view that misses much of what is most important about violence to the people living closest to it. Extortion is the heart of the *maras'* criminal economy, and it has devastated the economic and social capital of many of Guatemala's most vulnerable urban communities. By leaving intact the gang's power to continue its coercive extraction of local resources, Task Force Maya would inevitably prove a disappointment to many residents within the territories it occupied.

After years occupying El Romero and other red zone neighbourhoods, Guatemala City's task forces were disbanded in 2018 as – in a move interpreted in some quarters as a sop to the international community amid mounting corruption scandals – President Jimmy Morales transitioned the military out of its most visible public security and policing roles. Reflecting the occupation's perceived inefficacy against local violence and insecurity, I found many residents rather indifferent to the pull-out of the soldiers and the return of (nominal) control of the neighbourhood to the police. However, with now-President Alejandro Giammettei vowing in the 2019 election campaign to confront gangs 'with testosterone,' militarized *mano dura* policing seems to have a bright future in Guatemala.

★★★

Afflicted by powerful armed gangs competing for market share in the city's cocaine trade, Rio de Janeiro has recorded high levels of violence and criminal territorial power in its poorer informal districts over several decades. Drug-trafficking factions regulate many facets of life in the favelas they control, violently enforcing a social order that protects their business interests. Adding to the vulnerability favela residents experience as a result of gang presence in their communities, Rio state's Military Police force has long operated with a great deal of violence in these districts.[3] As Rio approached hosting the 2014 World Cup and the 2016 Olympics, addressing these twinned issues of non-state and state violence became more pressing. In November 2008, then-governor of the state of Rio de Janeiro Sergio Cabral established the Police Pacification Units (Unidades de Polícia Pacificadora) as new kind of force 'in charge of policing the favelas, taking control of their streets, and developing community policing programmes in them' (Frühling 2012: 82).

Much like Guatemala's joint task forces, the UPPs' main objectives were to reduce armed confrontations and violent deaths and to 'wrest the control of territory from drug gangs, and directly substitute criminal authority for that of the state' (Wolf 2017: 562). One important point of difference from the reliance on the military in Guatemala's territorial model was that the UPPs were meant to shift longstanding patterns of militarized, violent, and corrupt policing of Rio's favelas. It was a programme initiated under a banner of reform and rapprochement rather than *mano dura* repression. And although the extent of police reform secured is debatable, the UPPs' early successes soon made the programme the 'new darling of state securitization' at home and abroad (Larkins 2015: 58).

The pacification model prescribed an initial invasion and occupation by elite police squadrons like Police Special Operations Battalion (BOPE) or, in some cases, the armed forces.

The timeline varied across targeted favelas, but after some weeks or months of 'stabilization,' the territory would receive its deployment of UPP officers. These were all meant to be recruits fresh out of police training, theoretically untainted by the institutional culture of the Military Police. As the programme expanded over the years, personnel pressures led to the reassignment of older officers to UPP units, diluting their distinct identity. Another progressive element that rapidly faded was the so-called *UPP social*, which had promised infrastructure upgrades and expanded social services but shrivelled due to lack of funds and political will (Magaloni et al. 2018: 7).

The idea 'proximity policing' that became a UPP hallmark was not initially so prominent. The units were 'sold as a community policing model' until criticism that they lacked 'elemental principles of community policing' led to a shift in labelling by the Cabral administration (Wolf 2017: 564). Proximity policing is a prime example of the second, territorial strand of community-oriented policing in Latin America. It relies not so much on decentralized decision-making or democratized participation in policing but on a spatial intensification of security forces to insert the state as a 'permanent presence in occupied *favelas*' (Fahlberg 2018: 308; Wolf 2017; Salem 2017). The 'proximity' to be established was not so much between police and favela residents but between state forces and urban spaces suborned by illicit authorities; they are designed to secure insecure physical territories, not vulnerable social milieus.

A particular territorial logic shaped the deployment of UPPs, which – especially at first – clustered in the south-zone favelas adjacent to Rio's wealthier residential and tourist neighbourhoods and thus appeared to prioritize the interests of 'the business and economic elite, as well as protecting the profits from tourism' (Magaloni et al. 2015: 15). Furthermore, although the UPPs at their height covered nearly a quarter of the population living in Rio's 700-odd favelas, only 2.5% of targeted districts were *milicia* territories, despite the fact that these bands (whose members often have ties to security forces) control many of the city's most violent districts (Magaloni et al. 2018: 22; Franco 2018).

Examining outcomes from the first several years of UPP operations, a number of scholars found treated favelas recorded fewer incidents of violence and greater integration into the formal city in terms of new business openings and increased tourism, as well as residents reporting high levels of support and improvements to local safety (see Oosterbaan and van Wijk 2015; Wolff 2017). Early surveys claimed homicide numbers in UPP districts dropped by up to 75% (Wolff 2017: 565). However, comprehensive quantitative analyses of how the UPPs affected violence suggest a more complicated picture. Magaloni et al. (2015, 2018) argue that while the programme did reduce murders, it was by decreasing police killings of civilians – not gang killings – that the UPPs had a measurable effect. Controlling for improving socio-economic factors and a generalized city-wide decline in murder rates, UPP presence produced no additional reduction in lethal inter-personal violence but, between 2008 and 2013, did produce a 45% reduction in police killings (2015: 42, 2018: 4). Favela residents were perhaps not significantly less likely to kill each other or be killed by gangs under UPPs than they would have been without them, but they were for a time much less likely to be murdered by police. The effect of the UPPs on drug gangs' operations is harder to measure. In at least some cases, the drug trade continued more or less unaffected in UPP districts (Larkins 2015: 143). While armed confrontations declined for a period in targeted favelas, this may – as in Guatemala – have resulted more from displacement than suppression, and the UPPs appear to be have led to a diffusion of crime and violence throughout the city (Magaloni et al. 2015: 43, 2018: 24).

From 2013, and particularly after the end of Rio's cycle of sporting mega-events, the UPP programme received increasing criticism as the 'fragile "armed peace"' (Salem 2017: 300) it was credited with securing appeared to shatter. The 'Amarildo scandal' of 2013, in which UPP officers were revealed to be involved in the torture and murder of a resident of the Rocinha favela, marked one turning point in public opinion. But as early as 2010, when then-President Lula da Silva authorized a nearly 18-month army occupation of the Alemão favela complex as a precursor to a pacification that never came, there were concerns that this police reform was coinciding with a return to military involvement in domestic security unseen since the 1985 end of Brazil's dictatorship (Passos 2018).

Before her 2018 assassination, politician and activist Marielle Franco was an outspoken critic of this re-militarization of favela policing. She argued that the notion of the UPP programme as a distinct form of policing evaporated in the wake of the mega-events, as evidenced by the subordination of the previously autonomous UPPs to local Military Police Battalions in 2017 (Franco 2018: 190). At the same time, UPP officers on the ground were turning ever more towards 'classic military tactics more appropriate for securing control of territory than preventing crime' (Smilde 2017: 306). The units increasingly retreated to heavily fortified outposts in the favelas, while patrol officers were trained in urban warfare techniques (Salem 2017: 301). This period also marked a return to more violent policing in the favelas. By 2017, police killings, which had declined so dramatically in the UPPs' early years, were back to nearly pre-reform levels (Magaloni et al. 2018: 8).

Waning political will, slashed budgets, and reduced personnel allocations to UPPs further marked this retreat from reform, and during the 2018 federal intervention that placed Rio's public security under military tutelage, a number of pacification units were shut, absorbed, or redeployed (Fenizola 2019; Soares 2018). Following that military intervention, according to ex-commander of the UPP's coordinating body Robson Rodrigues, the traditional model of military policing in the favelas has been fully restored and 'the UPPs remain in name only' (Soares 2019).

II. States, gangs, and security seen from the urban margins

To understand better how Guatemala City's task forces and Rio de Janeiro's UPPs operated on the ground, I turn here to the perspectives of residents of the urban territories these programmes targeted and how they evaluated their efficacy and legitimacy. Both interventions introduced new kinds of 'security encounters' (Harriott and Jaffe 2018) between residents of targeted neighbourhoods and state forces. The concept of security encounters captures both 'how security providers assert their authority over populations and territories' and how inhabitants of insecure spaces negotiate citizenship in face of these authorities, their actions, and their claims (Harriott and Jaffe 2018: 82). These encounters can take multiple forms across a single community, varying with factors such as residents' age and gender, most notably, but also race, employment status, household composition, and religious affiliation, among others (Harriott and Jaffe 2018; Fahlberg 2018). All of these facets of residents' (real or attributed) identities shaped what they anticipated and experienced from militarized territorial policing in their communities.

UPPs appeared to generate initially high levels of support in targeted communities. In 2009, 60 percent of household heads surveyed in the first two favelas occupied believed 'security had improved' because of the intervention; in 2010, 93 percent of respondents in another survey of 'pacified' favelas agreed that their neighbourhoods had become safer (Fahlberg 2018: 308). However, available research from Rio de Janeiro suggests that, despite promising a transformed relationship between state forces and the favelas they policed, not everyone's encounters with the new security providers were positive. By 2013, complaints of mistreatment or abuse had been filed against officers in 76 percent of Rio's UPPs (Franco 2018: 190). Knowledge of abuses, however, does not necessarily disrupt the local legitimacy of these forces for those less directly affected. Fahlberg, for instance, found that although residents of the City of God UPP district were critical of the treatment darker-skinned friends and neighbours received, of officers' high-handed searches of homes, and of the persistence of petty crime under their purview, virtually every person she met 'believed that the City of God improved after the UPP occupation' (2018: 314).

Most people I spoke with in El Romero also supported the military's presence there, although (as many inhabitants of UPP-treated areas did) they refrained from actively co-operating or engaging with soldiers out of fear of gang reprisals. The most significant positive change that residents attributed to the task force, particularly in the first few years, was an improvement in how safe they felt moving around the neighbourhood. The pastor of a local church said that 'the extortions continue, but the streets are much safer, and people feel safer, too.' The omnipresent surveillance of rotating patrols and strategic armed posts seemed for many residents to lessen the degree of unpredictable risk they faced in public space and to provide a reassuring visual structure of order and control in their environment.

Yet despite this enhanced appearance of state-imposed order, El Romero's gang continued to collect extortion as residents remained convinced of their capacity to exact harsh punishment for refusal. One woman explained that 'there are places in which the soldiers cannot be. So you keep paying them.' The chilling effect of military vigilance was confined to the most public and visible manifestations of violence. And so, a friend assured me, 'that subterranean world that exists in the barrio stays intact. They do not touch the daily life of criminality.' These sentiments persisted through the years of military occupation that followed; residents told me in 2017 that the *mara*'s grip on the neighbourhood was widely viewed as unshaken, with people reporting that the gang remained 'the shadow power of the community' and that 'the clique's control is hegemonic, it's total.'

Nor was everyone in the neighbourhood moving more freely in the streets with the military present. Young men, adolescents, and boys as young as seven or eight had to start carrying identification papers with them at all times or risk very rough treatment during the multiple daily stops and searches they could expect from military patrols. Some male adolescents of my acquaintance took to limiting their time in public spaces after a number of unpleasant run-ins featuring verbal and physical abuse, and young people were generally less likely than older adults to view the task force positively.

Military personnel were unresponsive to concerns regarding abuses or excessive force. When a young community activist brought up the need for soldiers to respect residents' human rights at a public meeting, he was interrupted by the task force's spokesman. 'You don't understand anything,' he was told. 'Human rights have nothing to do with this. We're in charge here now, and we'll do what we need to do.' This blunt statement diverged sharply from the message delivered by the president in inaugurating the capital's second task force, when he assured residents that the military 'is coming to take care of you and to respect you' (*Prensa Libre* 2012).

In spite of variations across generational or demographic profiles, significant portions of occupied communities in both Rio and Guatemala wanted security forces to remain and often to be intensified. To understand why, it is important to disaggregate the state and its security forces as seen from the urban margins and to attend to the conditions under which military or militarized interventions in local space could seem acceptable or even desirable.

In Rio, the initial military or BOPE invasion was frequently the phase of the UPP process seen to be most effective. Residents in a number of favelas reported preferring 'the deployment of military forces over police even though it meant the application of a war-like device along the urban landscape' (Passos 2018: 316). I also found a clear preference for military over police intervention in El Romero. An older woman explained that 'people believe in the army's security – they don't believe in police.' Her analysis appears apt: while one survey found only 10 percent of respondents trusted the police, the Guatemalan armed forces regularly record much higher levels of public trust than other state organs (Sanford 2008: 11; PNUD 2012: 24). In the urban neighbourhoods most vulnerable to gang violence and extortion, experiences of police abuse, corruption, and inefficacy mean that the police are 'not a resource to turn to in times of trouble; they themselves *are* trouble' (Godoy 2006: 56). Soldiers, seen as much less corrupt and less likely to be infiltrated by gangs, are often compared favourably to police officers by local residents.

Gang violence and urban insecurity in Latin America have often led to vocal support for repressive state and para-state responses, including by those sectors of the population most likely to be harmed by such measures (for instance, Caldeira 2000; Scheper-Hughes 2004; Goldstein 2007, 2012). Moreover, these demands often coexist with profound (and typically well-earned) distrust in the efficacy and good intentions of the state and its agents. How, then, to explain why groups with histories of exclusion and victimization at the hands of the state appear to be asking for more of same?

Studies from Rio and my own ethnographic research in Guatemala City suggest that support for repressive state security policies is tied to the destabilizing and debilitating effects on local social cohesion and order generated by certain forms of gang governance. Perceptions of the pre-existing local order were highly influential in shaping people's assessments of UPPs. In territories that had been under the relatively stable control of one drug-trafficking gang, people were much less likely to want the UPP to continue than where criminal governance had been either more predatory or more disorderly. In Comando Vermelho stronghold Rocinha, only 27 percent of residents wanted the UPP to stay on, compared to 75 percent in *milicia*-held Batan (Magaloni et al. 2018: 38).

In El Romero, people often spoke of a decline of local social and normative order as a result of the gang's elaboration of a predatory extortion economy (see Saunders-Hastings 2019). The 'devastated toolkit' of collective action (Godoy 2006: 35) that can result from violently parasitic criminal governance is an important factor in explaining tolerance for military occupation of local space. It leads people to turn to external providers of order as they attempt to find new coping strategies amid insecure environments. As one woman explained to me, El Romero needed the military because 'they have to send others to look after us now; we cannot do it ourselves anymore.'

Residents might have hoped militarized policing would help to secure local space, but they were unconvinced that it could truly penetrate and transform criminal power over them and in their neighbourhoods. Even those who were most supportive of the task force's presence and mission kept them at arm's length. An older man who consistently expressed positive views of the soldiers nevertheless warned that 'you cannot be friendly with them. How could they understand what goes on here?'

The wariness that some residents felt regarding the soldiers was returned in kind by military personnel viewing El Romero and its inhabitants through the filter of its notoriety as a 'red zone' gang stronghold. An officer commanding the neighbourhood's detachment several years into the occupation told me that taking up his post there had felt like 'putting oneself in the jaws of the wolf.' This opinion and the many others like it that I heard over the years from soldiers deployed to El Romero left no doubt that it was and remained enemy territory in their imagination.

★★★

Contrary to the promises of their political backers, neither Guatemala City's task forces nor Rio de Janeiro's pacification units presented insuperable obstacles to gangs in the urban territories in which they operated. The military presence in El Romero affected some aspects of how the *mara* and its collaborators operated – with a reduction in visible displays of gang violence – but it did not significantly impede the operation of the gang's extortion-based criminal economy. While state forces patrolled the streets and performed their control of local space through actions such as building fortified guard posts and interrupting the movement of young men around the neighbourhood, the gang still charged extortion throughout its turf, and residents remained convinced that they could and would be violently disciplined for refusing or reporting gang demands.

Although the soldiers' presence made many feel somewhat safer in the street, it did not substantially change their calculus of risk where the gang's extortion economy was concerned. Initially, inhabitants explained this with reference to their fear that the task force would withdraw after a matter of months, leaving them exposed to gang reprisals. However, the force's apparently indefinite presence in the neighbourhood never seemed to shift local concern over the gang's power or augment confidence in the state. Five years into El Romero's military occupation, residents reported that 'extortions in El Romero go on the same, or worse.' Meanwhile, the neighbourhood's soldiers and gang members were said to 'manage a coexistence' governed by 'an unspoken peace agreement.'

Similarly, ethnographic research in Rio's City of God favela complex found that its UPP 'managed to co-exist with drug traffickers without exacerbating armed conflict' and that the two forces appeared to have arrived at some agreement 'about who controlled which spots at which times' (Fahlberg 2018: 316–317). In Rocinha, meanwhile, many residents reported that rather than disrupting corrupt police-trafficker relations, the pacification process 'had actually *enhanced* the power sharing between police and traffickers in an almost farcical fashion' (Larkins 2015: 145). While UPP officers continued to manifest a visible presence and perform state control in the lower half of Rocinha, which lies closer to the formal city, they had retreated from the upper half, reclaimed as trafficker territory. A 2018 survey carried out by the Military Police itself appears to confirm the geographical division of power, finding that Rocinha's UPP officers were no longer patrolling at least 51 percent of their assigned district (Soares 2018).

In both Guatemala City and Rio de Janeiro, security programmes that had trumpeted their determination to reclaim the urban margins from gangs ultimately appeared to be more occupied with manipulating the geography and visibility of violence than with permanently disrupting or diminishing criminal power over those territories and their residents. A prevailing concern with the optics rather than realities of territorial control has been identified in the UPP programme, where successful state presence and penetration 'was defined by virtue of authority, preventing criminals from disposing guns in an ostensive way outside favela perimeters, but not necessarily disarming them permanently' (Passos 2018: 319).

The importance of controlling the public visibility of gang violence to El Romero's task force was made strikingly clear when one of its commanding officers explained in a moment of candid condescension: 'Sweetheart, we're here to change the image of this place. Its *image*, not its reality.' This amounted to a blunt confession that he and his men were there to project an image of control that was useful to the state and profitable for the government. Not primarily for its effects in the red zones like El Romero but for its communicative power beyond them. The state (or a faction of it) is making a claim to legitimacy through its occupation of the neighbourhood, but this claim is directed elsewhere and does not ultimately depend on displacing the other source of organized coercion in the territory. Indeed, in some ways, it depends on their continuing presence. The final section of this chapter explores the logic and consequences of this mode of gang policing.

III. Gang policing, security politics, and the garrison state

The trends of militarized and territorialized policing that I identified at the outset of this chapter may represent shifts in the direction of the 'garrison state' (Lasswell 1941, 1962). Coined in the 1930s to describe the rise of militarized nationalism in East Asia and Europe, the term refers to a situation in which 'specialists on violence are the most powerful group in society' (Lasswell 1941: 455). Basing their claims to authority on their (purported) capacity to secure the nation and defeat its enemies, these specialists on violence increasingly acquire management of traditionally civilian purviews (Lasswell 1941: 458). The effect of this militarization or 'garrisoning' of the state is to concentrate power 'in the hands of a loosely knit elite of civilianized military officers and militarized civilians' (Fitch 1985: 32).

Like the subversive that obsessed the counter-insurgency states covering much of Latin America in the late twentieth century, the criminal enemy is an internal one rather than the external enemy Lasswell originally envisaged. Nevertheless, across the region, contemporary specialists on violence are – often successfully – pressing claims to be in the best position to defend a frightened citizenry from the evils that threaten them. The perpetual recourse to war metaphors in modern politics and policy – pitting governments and good citizens against a panoply of human and non-human forces in 'wars' on crime, drugs, terror, poverty, and so on – works to further entrench this securitization by bolstering 'authoritarian and militarized notions of the state's role in maintaining order' (Graham 2010: 23). Such discursive practices not only shape public understanding of what threatens them but also 'guide problem-solving processes' (Kraska 2007:505): if there is a war on crime, gangs, or drugs to be waged, the logic of turning to society's designated warmakers to wage it appears irrefutable.

The post-Cold War decline of (threats of) state-on-state violence seemed to some to mark a clear trend away from the relevance of the garrison state construct (Stanley and Segal 1989). However, the rise of non-state actors as violent contenders on the world stage led others to reformulate rather than abandon the concept. Morgan's (2004) 'terror-focused garrison state' is one modification accounting for the contemporary persistence of social and political militarization. He emphasizes that the garrison state is defined not by the nature of the enemy but by the identification and construction of threats that appear to 'necessitate the garrisoning of society and enhance the role of military and police organizations' (2004: 6). The perceived intensity of threat matters more than the nature or origin of the enemy in an era of state securitization defined by 'the cross-fertilization and blurring between the traditional military imperatives of war, external to the state, and those of policing internal to it' (Graham 2010: 73).

I suggest it is worth considering the possibility of a 'gang-focused' garrison state, which may account for both the political currency and apparent futility of wars on crime as exemplified by the militarized territorial policing programmes examined in this chapter. Across the Americas, the external non-state threat of the terrorist and the internal non-state threat of the criminal gang are coming together to fuel the fusion of war and policing, military and civilian functions that are critical features of both Graham's new military urbanism and Lasswell's garrison state.

In his study of the 'protection racket state' in wartime El Salvador, Stanley (1996: 7) argues that the military's hold on the country derived from its capacity to corner the market in violence as a 'currency of relations between state and non-state elites.' The military and its allies used their capacity for violence, coercion, and repression to leverage power from economic elites fearful of social and political disorder. Security states are in this sense a kind of 'violent entrepreneur' (Volkov 2002), dependent upon the use and display of force – much like the criminal and/or terrorist organizations they perennially confront. And for the violent entrepreneurs in the powerful military-aligned faction of the Guatemalan state, the fear elicited by *maras* and their violence presents an opportunity. As an officer of El Romero's task force explained, when the country's long internal conflict finally limped to a close in the 1990s, 'people didn't want, didn't like the army. But now, with the insecurity, those same people are asking the army to come back to the streets to bring order.'

Nearly 20 years ago, Agamben tied the rise of security politics to neoliberal retrenchment: amidst a 'progressive surrender of traditional tasks of the state, security imposes itself as the basic principle of state activity . . . [and] becomes the sole criterion of political legitimation' (2001). The search for legitimation through securitization may prove especially tempting where the state's effective territorial penetration is uneven, weak, or contested. In these conditions of compromised or attenuated governance,

> law enforcement may provide a privileged site for staging efforts . . . to summon the active presence of the state into being, to render it perceptible to the public eye, to produce both rulers and subjects who recognize its legitimacy.
>
> *(Comaroff and Comaroff 2006: 280)*

Efforts in this direction by the military-aligned faction of the Guatemalan state appear to have met with some success. Despite provisions in both the country's constitution and the 1996 peace accords restricting its role to defence of the nation from external threats, in recent years, the Guatemalan military has been more involved in internal security and policing, more politically prestigious, and more visible in daily life than at any time since the war's end. Much of this currency is gained through the military's status for the Guatemalan public as the most credible institution confronting gang violence and urban disorder – a claim deployed and reinforced through the kind of security theatre the task forces staged daily in the streets of the capital's red zones. Similarly, through their hyper-violent professional performances in notorious favelas, Rio's elite military police force BOPE 'embodies a different face of an otherwise beleaguered state' (Larkins 2013: 555).

The profitability – indeed indispensability – of that security theatre goes some way towards explaining the territorial co-existence of gangs and security forces observed in both Guatemala City and Rio de Janeiro. The state that derives its legitimacy from governing insecurity requires threats to security to justify itself, leading to 'the development of a clandestine complicity of opponents' (Agamben 2001). By purporting to reclaim urban gang territories, the state is 'dramatizing its capacity to rule over the problem populations and quarters of the big city' (Wacquant 2008: 71). But if the threat that justifies garrisoning was ever truly defeated – if that enemy territory was ever truly redeemed – the political power of the specialists on violence would lose its legitimating basis. One El Romero resident pointed to this five years into the task force's occupation of his neighbourhood, alleging that 'the gang serves one purpose: justifying militarization.'

IV. Conclusion

In both Guatemala City and Rio de Janeiro, the past decade has seen intensive and long-running security operations aimed at displacing armed gangs from urban neighbourhoods under their control in order to (re)incorporate these territories into the state's zone of efficacy, authority, and legitimacy. Two prominent trends in twenty-first-century urban policing generally, and Latin American anti-gang policing particularly, intersect in the joint military-police task forces deployed in Guatemala City's 'red zones' and the pacification units stationed in dozens of Rio's favelas. The first of these is militarization, which can take the form of either direct military involvement in urban policing operations (as in El Romero's Task Force Maya) or a reshaping of civilian police cultures, command structures, and modes of operation and engagement along military lines (as seen in the Brazilian case). The second is an increasing use of the kind of territorially-oriented security programming embodied by the idea of 'proximity policing' made famous by the UPPs.

Although descended from the community-oriented policing tradition, there is in fact nothing inherently progressive or inclusive about the territorial intensification of policing; it fits quite well with the outlook and strategies characteristic of the new military urbanism. The security programmes this chapter examines embedded state agents in the quotidian space of the urban margins as never before. It did not follow, however, that the needs and priorities of these territories' residents achieved a similar degree of prominence in state security policy. Neither Guatemala's task forces nor Rio's pacification units marked a meaningful change in state–citizen relations in their zones of operations. Instead, over years of occupation by security forces, targeted neighbourhoods were continuously constructed as enemy territories.

Although both programmes began with high levels of public support, optimism that this new presence of the state would mark a transformation of local social orders was short lived for many residents. If the security encounters residents expected and experienced with police and military forces remained largely stable, so too did the kinds and degrees of gang power in these urban territories. While both cities recorded short-term reductions in violence, gang structures, enterprises, coercive capacity, and territorial integrity ultimately went largely undiminished. Perhaps the most significant effect on the security landscape for residents of occupied zones was that they faced not one but two 'violent entrepreneurs' in their daily environment.

Both programmes reveal a disjuncture between the places and populations on which security is performed and the audiences for whom security is staged. Militarized and territorialized gang policing in these cases contributes to a garrison-state politics of urban insecurity. These wars on crime do little to disrupt patterns of gang power and predation in vulnerable neighbourhoods. But they do serve to normalize and legitimize an increasingly intensive if uneven securitization of urban space. By analysing militarized urban policing through the lens of Lasswell's garrison state concept, I am not suggesting a tidy isomorphism between contemporary Latin American governments and the brutal fascist regimes of the 1930s. Rather, what the garrison state construct asks us to consider are the consequences of handing over to specialists on violence the governance of the social ills of the contemporary city, of issues of gangs, criminal violence, and illicit markets that have deep systemic and structural roots.

Notes

1 A pseudonym. I have conducted ethnographic research in this neighbourhood in 2011–2013, 2015, 2017, and 2019. Unless otherwise cited, all observations and quotations are from interview transcripts or detailed fieldnotes. I omit interlocutors' names, identifying details, and interview dates to protect their anonymity.
2 *Ministro de Gobernación*: responsible for public security, including oversight of police forces.
3 Brazil's police forces are organized at state level and divided into the Military Police, responsible for maintaining public order and preventing and deterring crimes, and the Civil Police, who are charged with the investigation of crimes.

References

Agamben, G. (2001) Security and Terror, trans. C. Emcke. *Theory and Event* 5(4): 1–2.
Asman, P. (2017) Jamaica to Initiate Security Crackdown as Murders Surge. *InSight Crime*, 26 July. Retrieved from www.insightcrime.org/new/brief/jamaica-initiate-security-crackdown-as-murders-surge/

Caldeira, T.P.R. (2000) *City of Walls: Crime, Segregation, and Citizenship in São Paulo*. Berkeley: University of California Press.

Callamard, A. (2018) El Salvador End of Mission Statement, United Nations Special Rapporteur for Extrajudicial, Summary or Arbitrary Executions. Retrieved from www.ohchr.org/en/NewsEvents/Pages/DisplayNews.aspx?NewsID=22634&LangID=E.

Comaroff, J. and J.L. Comaroff (2006) *Law and Disorder in the Postcolony*. Chicago: University of Chicago Press.

Eldemire, S. (2018) Welcome Sight: Why Some Jamaicans Want the Army to Stay. *BBC News*, 17 November. Retrieved from www.bbc.c.uk/new/world-latin-america-46139175.

Fahlberg, A.N. (2018) 'It Was Totally Different Than What We Had Before': Perceptions of Urban Militarism under Rio de Janeiro's Pacifying Policing Units. *Qualitative Sociology* 41: 303–324.

Fenizola, L. (2019) If This UPP Were Mine: With an End to Pacification, Residents Dream of Reoccupying Public Spaces. *Rio on Watch*, 11 March. Retrieved from www.rionwatch.org/?p=51582.

Fitch, J.S. (1985) The Garrison State in America: A Content Analysis of Trends in the Expectation of Violence. *Journal of Peace Research* 22(1): 31–45.

Franco, M. (2018) 'Pacification' for Whom? trans. B. Whiteoak. *Sur: International Journal on Human Rights* 27: 187–192.

Frühling, H. (2012) A Realistic Look at Latin American Community Policing Programmes. *Policing & Society* 22(1): 76–88.

Gámez, D. (2013) Zona 18, un año después de instalada de la Fuerza de Tarea Maya. *Agencia Guatemalteca de Noticias*, 10 August. Retrieved from www.agn.com.gt/index/php/component/k2/item/7374-zona-18-un-año-después-de-instalada-la-fuerza-de-tarea-maya.

Godoy, A.S. (2006) *Popular Injustice: Violence, Community, and Law in Latin America*. Stanford: Stanford University Press.

Goldstein, D.M. (2007) Human Rights as Culprit, Human Rights as Victim: Rights and Security in the State of Exception. In M. Goodale and S. Merry (eds.) *The Practice of Human Rights: Tracking Law between the Global and the Local*. Cambridge: Cambridge University Press, pp. 49–77.

Goldstein, D.M. (2012) *Outlawed: Between Security and Rights in a Bolivian City*. Durham: Duke University Press.

Government of Guatemala (2012) Presidente inaugura Fuerza de Tarea Maya en zona 18. 22 September. Retrieved from www.guatemala.gob.gt/index.php/2011-08-04-18-06-26/item/1576-presidente-inaugura-fuerza-de-tarea-maya-en-zona-18.

Graham, S. (2010) *Cities under Siege: The New Military Urbanism*. London: Verso.

Graham, S. (2012) When Life Itself Is War: On the Urbanization of Military and Security Doctrine. *International Journal of Urban and Regional Research* 36(1): 136–155.

Harriott, A. and R. Jaffe (2018) Security Encounters: Negotiating Authority and Citizenship during the Tivoli 'Incursion'. *Small Axe: A Caribbean Journal of Criticism* 22(3): 81–89.

Kraska, P.B. (2007) Militarization and Policing – Its Relevance to 21st Century Police. *Policing* 1(4): 501–513.

Lamb, G. (2018) Police Militarisation and the 'War on Crime' in South Africa. *Journal of Southern African Studies* 44(5): 933–949.

Larkins, E.R. (2013) Performances of Police Legitimacy in Rio's Hyper-Favela. *Law & Social Inquiry* 38(3): 555–578.

Larkins, E.R. (2015) *The Spectacular Favela: Violence in Modern Brazil*. Berkeley: University of California Press.

Lasswell, H.D. (1941) The Garrison State. *American Journal of Sociology* 46(4): 455–468.

Lasswell, H.D. (1962) The Garrison-State Hypothesis Today. In S. Huntington (ed.) *Changing Patterns of Military Politics*. New York: Free Press, pp. 51–70.

Magaloni, B., E. Franco, and V. Melo (2015) Killing in the Slums: An Impact Evaluation of Police Reform in Rio de Janeiro, Stanford Center for International Development Working Paper No. 556. Retrieved from http://globalpoverty.stanford.edu/sites/default/files/publications/556wp.pdf.

Magaloni, B., E. F. Vivanco, and V. Melo (2018) *Killing in the Slums: Social Order, Criminal Governance, and Police Violence in Rio de Janeiro*. http://dx.doi.org/10.2139/ssrn.3010013.

Morgan, M.J. (2004) The Garrison State Revisited: Civil-Military Implications of Terrorism and Security. *Contemporary Politics* 10(1): 5–19.

Müller, M. (2018) Governing Crime and Violence in Latin America. *Global Crime* 19(3–4): 171–191.

Oosterbaan, S. and J. van Wijk (2015) Pacifying and Integrating the Favelas of Rio de Janeiro: An Evaluation of the Impact of the UPP Programme on Favela Residents. *International Journal of Comparative and Applied Criminal Justice* 39(3): 179–198.

Passos, A.M. (2018) Fighting Crime and Maintaining Order: Shared Worldviews of Civilian and Military Elites in Brazil and Mexico. *Third World Quarterly* 39(2): 314–330.

PNUD (2012) *Resumen – Guatemala ¿Un país de oportunidades para la juventud? Informe nacional de desarrollo humano 2011–2012.* Guatemala City: Programa de las Naciones Unidas para el Desarrollo.

Prensa Libre (2012) Presidente Otto Pérez Molina instala Fuerza de Tarea Kaminal, 5 November. Retrieved from www.prensalibre.com/noticias/Presidente-Molina-Fuerza-Tarea-Kaminal_0_805119726.html.

Rantatalo, O. (2012) The Miscellany of Militaristic Policing. *Journal of Policing, Intelligence and Counter Terrorism* 7(1): 51–65.

Rodgers, D. (2009) Slum Wars of the 21st Century: Gangs, Mano Dura and the New Urban Geography of Conflict in Central America. *Development and Change* 4(5): 949–976.

Salem, T. (2017) Diplomats or Warriors? The Failure of Rio's Pacification Project. *NACLA Report on the Americas* 49(3): 298–302.

Sanford, V. (2008) From Genocide to Femicide: Impunity and Human Rights in Twenty-First Century Guatemala. *Journal of Human Rights* 7(2): 104–122.

Saunders-Hastings, K. (2019) Red Zone Blues: Violence and Nostalgia in Guatemala City. *Ethnography* 20(3): 359–378.

Scheper-Hughes, N. (2004) Bodies, Death, and Silence. In N. Scheper-Hughes and P. Bourgois (eds.) *Violence in War and Peace.* Oxford: Blackwell, pp. 175–185.

Smilde, D. (2017) Crime and Revolution in Venezuela. *NACLA Report on the Americas* 49(3): 303–308.

Soares, R. (2018) Intervenção anuncia o fim de 12 UPPs e mudanças em outras sete. *O Globo*, 26 April. Retrieved from www.oglobo.globo.com/rio/intervencao-anuncia-fim-de-12-upps-mudancas-em-outras-sete-unidades-22631936.

Soares, R. (2019) Operações frequentes 'mini-Bope' e 15 mortes em um mês: a nova fase das UPPs. *Extra*, 16 June. Retrieved from www.extra.globo.com/casos-de-policia/operacoes-frequentes-mini-bope-15-mortes-em-um-mes-nova-fase-das-upps-23742933.html.

Stanley, J. and D.R. Segal (1989) The Garrison State. *Defense Analysis* 5(1): 83–86.

Stanley, W. (1996) *The Protection Racket State: Elite Politics, Military Extortion, and Civil War in El Salvador.* Philadelphia: Temple University Press.

Ungar, M. and E.D. Arias (2012) Reassessing Community-Oriented Policing in Latin America. *Policing & Society* 22(1): 1–13.

UN, United Nations General Assembly, Human Rights Council (2015) Report of the United Nations High Commissioner for Human Rights, Addendum: Report of the United Nations High Commissioner for Human Rights on the Activities of his Office in Guatemala, A/HRC/28/3/Add.1, 12 January. Retrieved from www.insightcrime.org/images/2015/March-2015/UNGuatemalaReport.pdf.

Volkov, V. (2002) *Violent Entrepreneurs: The Use of Force in the Making of Russian Capitalism.* Ithaca: Cornell University Press.

Wacquant, L. (2008) The Militarization of Urban Marginality: Lessons from the Brazilian Metropolis. *International Political Sociology* 2: 56–74.

Wolf, S. (2017) Pacification or Escalation in El Salvador's Gang Territories? *NACLA Report on the Americas* 49(3): 290–297.

Wolff, M.J. (2017) Policing and the Logics of Violence: A Comparative Analysis of Public Security Reform in Brazil. *Policing & Society* 27(5): 560–574.

16

Misguided strategy

New York City's decision to criminalize gangs

Josmar Trujillo and Alex S. Vitale

New York City has long had a complex relationship with "gangs." Historically, New York City avoided some of the more severe gang suppression tactics in other cities. In the 1950s and 60s, the City's Youth Board deployed large numbers of street workers to try to connect with young people involved in gangs to try to encourage them to reduce violent conflicts and steer them towards education and employment.[1] By the 1970s, the city established a "Roundtable of Youth" under Mayor Lindsay that met regularly at Gracie Mansion to express youth concerns and attempt to integrate street-involved youth into productive problem solving discussions.[2]

At the same time, youth who became involved in more radical politics were regularly subjected to intense criminalization. In the 1960s and 1970s, youth involved with the Black Panther Party, the Young Lords, and the Chinatown-based I Wor Kuen were all subjected to local police surveillance, harassment, and criminalization. Similarly, the Latin Kings were subjected to intense criminalization under the Giuliani administration in the 1990s.[3]

Despite these attacks against politically oriented youth, the city largely avoided framing the problems of youth crime and violence as a "gang issue." As recently as 2008, the Public Advocate's office recommended that the City "shift resources to alternatives to detention programs . . . encourage youth programming that meets the specific needs of the community it serves through the Request for Proposals (RFP) process" and involve young people directly in anti-violence initiatives.[4] By avoiding strategies that relied primarily on criminalization and the labeling of youth as gang members, New York did not develop the kind of multi-generational gang violence seen in Los Angeles and Chicago.

Over the last 25 years, New York City has also experienced dramatic reductions in serious crime across categories. And while many people report the existence of gangs in their communities, they were not the focus of policing-based interventions. Instead, the city relied on widespread "stop and frisk" practices, intensive "broken-window"-oriented enforcement, and targeted "hot spot" policing.

These forms of policing, however, were coming under intensive pressure from communities and legal advocates concerned about the widespread criminalization of youth of color and civil rights violations. A series of lawsuits, legislative changes, and political mobilizations undermined the NYPD's ability to continue these practices with the same intensity.

In response, the NYPD initiated a major change in how it deals with issues of youth violence beginning in 2012. That year, then-Commissioner Ray Kelly announced "Operation Crew Cut," which would double the number of officers in the gang unit from 150 to 300. Kelly made it clear that this new operation was intended to target "loosely affiliated groups of teens" who often "identify themselves by the blocks where they live and are responsible for much of the violence in public housing."[5]

In addition, the NYPD recreated its "Criminal Group Database" to track alleged gang members and wipe out alleged gang violence through large-scale conspiracy cases. The result has been thousands of juveniles and adults arrested and charged in gang conspiracy cases; tens of thousands placed into a secretive gang database; and many more subjected to harassment, intimidation, surveillance, and threats.

The new focus on loose associations of young people came just as political and legal challenges to widespread "stop, question, and frisk" practices increased.[6] It appears that the NYPD is merely substituting one set of techniques to tightly manage the lives of young people of color for another and uses the "gang" label to mute public opposition.[7] The NYPD has taken the term "gang" and turned it into a marker of violence and lawlessness.

Almost every person targeted by these initiatives has been Black or Latinx. This kind of law enforcement relies on the same logic that has driven much of the enormous increase in incarceration over the last 40 years. Gang suppression policies wrongly assume that deterrence and incapacitation are the only ways to reduce violence. Cities like Oakland, Los Angeles, and Chicago have spent decades trying to "suppress" gangs through intensive surveillance, harassment, and criminalization. These efforts, however, have done nothing to reduce the presence of gangs in these cities. In fact, some research shows that these tactics actually enhance young people's identification with gang life, and make these gangs more violent.[8]

When specialized gang units are created, they have a tendency to become insulated from oversight from within their departments and from the public. Historically, gang suppression units have been notoriously corrupt and brutal. The Los Angeles Police Department's CRASH Unit, for example, was responsible for widespread human and civil rights abuses, and officers in the unit were later found to be dealing drugs, using excessive force, and falsifying arrests.[9]

During the 1960s and 70s, the gang intelligence unit of the Chicago Police Department was directly involved in infiltrating and disrupting the Black Panther Party. They shared information with the FBI's COINTEL Program and coordinated with the State's Attorney Office that orchestrated the assassination of Black Panther leader Fred Hampton.[10] More recently, officers in Chicago's gang unit were involved in torturing suspects to extract confessions and faking evidence.[11] And just last year, an FBI investigation found members of the Area Central gang team were involved in robbing drug dealers.[12] In Portland, Oregon, the local police disbanded their Gang Enforcement Team after an outside review by the portland city auditor showed that their proactive enforcement efforts had no positive effect on crime rates, utilized high numbers of improper pretextual traffic stops, and were racially skewed.[13]

This chapter will look at the NYPD's use of gang suppression policing and the consequences this has for young people of color in some of the city's poorest and most underserved communities. We rely on public statements and documents from police officials and interviews with young people targeted by police, as well as their families and other community members, and insights from layers defending young people subjected to NYPD gang policing practices.

Gang raids

In 2014, the NYPD, in collaboration with the Manhattan District Attorney's Office, launched a massive gang raid in West Harlem. Hundreds of armed police officers swarmed the Manhattanville and Grant Houses, as well as surrounding buildings, in a coordinated pre-dawn operation. The West Harlem sweep was the largest gang takedown in New York City's history at the time and led to two indictments of 103 mostly young Black and Latinx individuals.[14] After the raid, several parents from the developments and neighboring apartment buildings that were raided held a protest outside the Harlem State Office Building. Several mothers said that police pointed guns at them, their children, and some senior citizens living in the buildings. One mother described how her son, who was arrested during the operation, was physically assaulted:

> They came to my house, raided my house and then they assaulted my son. They kicked him in the scrotum – when he was handcuffed. And he's already sick. Just came out the hospital, they raided my house the next day on June 4th and they kicked him in the scrotum when he was down.[15]

Taylonn "Bam" Murphy, Jr., was one of those indicted. Murphy's sister, Tayshana "Chicken" Murphy, was one of the people killed in the feud that law enforcement officials used as a rationale for the raid. District Attorney Cyrus Vance made the connection between Chicken's death and the gang raid.[16] Chicken's father, Taylonn Murphy, Sr., however, criticized the takedowns, pointing out that the two people who killed his daughter were already in prison:

> So, I think the narrative they were trying to spin was that we did these raids because these two individuals got killed. And you know my daughter was one of the individuals that got killed. And I found that to be very troubling because you know you're trying to pin a whole neighborhood against me and my family.
>
> Saying that you're the reason for 400 police officers coming in to our neighborhood and kidnapping individuals or arresting individuals or detaining individuals and I had to immediately speak out about that. I had to immediately say "hey listen, the two individuals that killed my daughter were already arrested."
>
> You can't be vilifying a whole neighborhood saying they had something to do with my daughter's death because that's not true.

Murphy's death is also striking because her family has contended that she did not have to die. The family alleges, and the trial of her convicted killers partly revealed, that a police officer watching live security monitors as part of the Video Interactive Patrol Enhanced Response (VIPER) unit failed to intervene or summon help when he saw Murphy being chased by the armed men who took her life. The suggestion that the police department would not intervene in Murphy's death obviously raises serious concerns – but perhaps points to a larger pattern of disturbing actions. Murphy's father described instances in which police in West Harlem would stay in their patrol cars as rival youth from neighboring housing developments fought on the street.

> They were looking and watching what these young people were doing. They were allowing them to hurt one another. I know that for a fact because 15 minutes before my daughter was killed, we had a VIPER room officer in the VIPER room looking at these cameras and he watched the young man come out of a totally different building across the street

with a firearm, menace a group of other individuals and there was no calling, no intervention. He said in the trials that, he said in the trial of *The People of New York vs. Robert Cartagena* . . . he witnessed that. He showed the jury that you could see the gun on camera. And the main question that the defense attorney said to him was "well why didn't you stop him?" And the DA did not allow him to answer that question.

On April 27th, 2016, the NYPD and several federal law enforcement agencies executed another large gang takedown operation in the Bronx. The raid, which led to 120 indictments, saw residents and media describe an even larger military-like show of force than West Harlem and surpass West Harlem to become the biggest gang raid in New York City history. Instead of local prosecutors, the Department of Justice's South District Office partnered with the NYPD to bring Racketeer Influenced and Corrupt Organizations (RICO) conspiracy charges. Being charged under the 1970 RICO Act presented a significantly more difficult legal challenge for the Bronx 120 defendants, including the prospect of being judged by a federal Southern District jury, which can generally be a higher-earning and whiter jury pool than a Bronx jury pool (which are also believed to be less friendly to law enforcement).

The effect on the ground was, as some residents have described it, like "they were arresting [Osama] bin Laden." Helicopters circled over the Eastchester Gardens housing development, and a Homeland Security armored vehicle, which neighbors described as a tank, was driven into the middle of the development's courtyard. A 21-year old man, who mistakenly thought he was a target of the raid, ran from police, climbed out of a window and fell to his death.[17] In a 2019 report from the CUNY School of Law, Prof. Babe Howell and Priscilla Bustamante (see also this volume) showed that two thirds of those indicted weren't convicted of violence, a third were convicted of marijuana-related crimes, and about half of those indicted weren't even alleged to be gang members by prosecutors themselves.[18]

NYPD gang database

CUNY School of Law Professor Babe Howell received data from the NYPD in March of 2018 indicating that over 17,000 people were added to the NYPD's Criminal Group database from December 2013 through February 2018. Of those added, over 98% were identified as either Black or Hispanic. While almost no one outside of the police department knows who, by name, is on the database, we do know some of the criteria that the police say they use for database inclusion:

1   An individual will be entered if he/she admits to membership during debriefing

     OR

2   Through the course of an investigation an individual is reasonably believed to belong to a gang and is identified as such by two independent sources (e.g. Police Precinct Personnel, Police Intelligence, Personnel from School Safety, Department of Corrections, or an Outside Agency)

     OR

3   Meets any two of the following criteria:
     1   Known gang location
     2   Scars/Tattoos Associated with gangs

3   Gang related documents
4   Colors Associated with gangs
5   Association with known gang members
6   Hand signs associated with gangs

During testimony to the New York City Council on June 13th, 2018, NYPD Chief of Detectives Dermot Shea added "social media post admitting to membership in a gang" to the criteria. Police interpretation, or perhaps willful misinterpretation, of gang admission on social media can include emojis, hashtags, or other forms of communication. There is also the question of how police can authenticate who is posting or operating a social media account. Claiming membership in a gang can also be based less on reality and more on a fictional projection for those who seek value in street culture. Self-admission can also be influenced by the disproportionate power imbalance between an individual, especially a minor, and a police officer.

Most "independent sources" are not independent. Precinct personnel (Pct. Personnel), the NYPD Intelligence Division (Intell) and School Safety Division are all part of the NYPD. The Department of Corrections (DOC) has its own internal gang tracking system, the Gang Intelligence Unit (GIU). Because DOC oversees a confined population that often has to associate with gangs and others for safety, gang designations can be more overreaching – and follow individuals after they leave jail.

Another potential source for gang labeling are neighborhood coordination officers (NCOs) from the "neighborhood policing" efforts that have expanded in recent years. After a high-profile killing of a teenager in the Bronx by alleged gang members, it was local NCOs who led public meetings encouraging community members to watch out for gang activity. According to the NYPD patrol guide, NCOs have access to schools and watch for "problematic conditions, violent crime, and gang/crew activity."

The third pathway into the gang database lays out six options, two of which need to be included. "Known gang location" and "associate with known gang members" are likely to be affected by housing segregation and offer considerable overlap in public housing developments, where families share common space and build friendships from childhood. Since most of the areas marked as gang territories by the NYPD are areas with higher concentrations of Black and Latinx populations, a "known gang location" (fulfilling half of the criteria towards gang designation) can serve as a proxy for race. So-called associations might mean shaking hands, talking to, or being connected on social media. And, as the city has expanded surveillance of public housing, adding over 4,000 cameras in NYCHA since 2014, such residential spaces are further magnified.[19]

Other options for fulfilling the third criteria include "scars/tattoos associated with gangs" and "colors associated with gangs." While people can age out of gang involvement, few can do the same with gang tattoos, making them problematic signifiers of gang activity. In other states, federal law enforcement use of tattoos in making gang designations have been the subject of lawsuits.[20]

Gang database analysis

At a 2018 City Council hearing, top NYPD officials invoked the language of mass incarceration, even tying gangs to the opiate epidemic, as they provided insight into how police label and catalogue gang members.

> Criminal groups that operate on our streets are drivers of a significant portion of violent crime in the city, and some are prime peddlers of narcotics which drive the subsequent increase in opiate overdoses plaguing our city.

> While New York City is the safest big city in the nation. In some cases, criminal groups hold pockets of our city hostage, inhibiting mothers from letting their children play outside, or preventing the elderly from taking walks in the neighborhoods.
>
> *(Dermot Shea, NYPD chief of detectives)*

The NYPD has claimed that people in the gang database are not chosen for frivolous reasons and have extensive criminal histories and many arrests. They do not say whether those arrests resulted in convictions or are indicative of harassment precisely because of their gang designation. On the other hand, the police department has said that the white nationalist group Proud Boys, who describe themselves as a gang, are not in the database and refuse to acknowledge whether traditional Mafia organizations are included. The NYPD doesn't appear to differentiate between a local "crew" of mostly young men of color from the Mafia when they work to bring conspiracy charges devised precisely for those traditional organized crime syndicates.

Investigations into gang databases elsewhere have uncovered wildly inaccurate information, racial bias, and abusive and illegal practices. A recent report by the Chicago Office of the Inspector General found that the Chicago Police Department's database was filled with inaccuracies, was shared with immigration officials, and "potentially undermines public confidence in the Department's legitimacy and effectiveness in the service of its public safety mission."[21] An audit of the Cal Gang database by the California State Auditor found wild inaccuracies in the database, including the presence of infant children, and raised concerns regarding fundamental privacy protections.[22] A review of the United Kingdom's Gangs Matrix system by Amnesty International found similar privacy issues based on evidence that data was shared with other government agencies, affecting people's access to basic government services and employment. Like the NYPD's gang database, the majority of those in the UK's Gangs Matrix were people of color with little or no criminal history.[23] In Portland, OR, police decided to end the use of their database in 2017 rather than reveal its inner workings when requested to do so by local journalists.[24]

Gang-policing personnel are also a concern. Studies show gang unit cops exhibit "extreme bias" regardless of bias training, and a *New York Times* article says police misconduct data shows NYPD gang cops have been "sued for misconduct more frequently than most patrol officers."[25]

The NYPD, however, says its database is a part of its "precision policing" efforts that allows it to narrowly target those most likely to be involved in serious and ongoing criminal activity. Instead, the constant surveillance, inclusion in conspiracy cases, enhanced criminal penalties, and other consequences that relate to the database outline a strategy of racialized suppression that undermines safety for the communities that police claim they are working to serve.

Inventing gangs

The "Oww Oww Gang" was classified as an inactive Brooklyn gang by the NYPD Intelligence Division in 2015. The supposed "gang" was at the center of a trial in 2016 where two Brooklyn residents were convicted and sentenced to 100 years in prison each. However, residents of Brooklyn's Gowanus Houses, where the gang is said to be based, say that the "gang" doesn't exist.[26] "Oww Oww" was the name of an amateur hip-hop song and video popular in the Gowanus and Wyckoff Houses.[27] Ronnie Williams was one of the young men from Gowanus who was convicted and alleged to be in the gang. His mother explained how that gang label was affixed to her son:

> As far as I remember, as soon as it started happening, they tried to paint him as a gang member. They started saying outwardly [inaudible] referring to him as a "gang member". When he would hang out with his close friends at the time Dante and one of his other really close friends named Nunu, and he was a rapper. . . . So, he [Nunu] wrote the song about Gowanus and called it Oww Oww. So, they [police] used that to say, like, that was an anthem for their gang.

Williams' sister disputed her brother being in a gang as well as "Oww Oww" being an actual gang:

> That song became really popular in the community and people would walk by each other and say Oww Oww just because it was Gowanus' song. But they took that and said that all of those guys who would rep the song, that was a gang. And the name of the gang was Oww Oww. . . . But that would only come from people who weren't from Gowanus.

Music, hip-hop in particular, has been used by law enforcement as evidence and markers of gang violence, but not without controversy. Hip-hop lyrics were at the basis of the 2014 federal trial of alleged Brooklyn gang leader Ronald Herron, also from Gowanus, whose lawyers argued, on first amendment grounds, that his rap lyrics should not be used as evidence.[28] A federal judge disagreed.

Chico gang

In February of 2019, a dozen young men in East Harlem were arrested and charged with gang conspiracy, among other allegations. They were alleged to be members of the "Chico Gang" by police and several media outlets. According to police and Manhattan District Attorney Cyrus Vance, the "gang" was based in the Wagner Houses and formed after the shooting death of Juwan "Chico" Tavarez in 2016.[29]

However, several residents of the Wagner Houses said they weren't aware of such a gang. Some were familiar with the sayings "Chico Gang" or "Chico World" that became popular in Wagner amongst friends and classmates of Tavarez, but they weren't aware of it as a gang. There is also no public record of the gang in media articles before the arrest or even in the most recently available NYPD gang map.

In a statement from Vance's office, authorities referred to the defendants discussing criminal activity on social media as part of the case against them.[30] However, the mining of social media posts, an arena where adolescents and young adults may not understand the implications of what they post and where law enforcement is free to infer whatever meaning helps a criminal case, is a recipe for abuse. In New York City, police even use emojis to decipher gang identities and threats of gang violence.[31]

A social media search on any given day can find hundreds, if not thousands, of posts referencing a gang, most of which are clearly not related to organized crime. In fact, while there is a growing amount of research dedicated to deciphering how social media relates to gang violence, little, if any, has sought to separate public expressions of "gangs" to actual violence. Amongst youth, words are fluid and meant to be accessible to many. Police can, however, wittingly or unwittingly take dangerous liberties by ascribing criminality or violence to these expressions. One recent report found that police "massively overestimated the direct linkage between what someone does online and what someone does offline."[32]

What is clear in interviews with residents of Wagner Houses is that the community was hurt by the loss of Chico Tavarez. While his classmates wore lanyards with large pictures of Chico after his death, this could have been an indicator, to police, of involvement in the dubious "Chico Gang." In one Manhattan courtroom, NYPD detectives on a different case testified that they looked at people wearing similar commemorative pictures "more closely" when looking for retaliatory gang violence. Notably, some of the charges against those alleged to be in the Chico Gang went back as far as 2015 – before Chico was killed and the gang could have existed.

Consequences of being gang labeled

Harassment and hyper-policing

One of the primary consequences of being labeled a member of a gang by the NYPD, whether formally in the gang database or even informally amongst gang unit and precinct officers, is heightened *harassment and hyper-policing*. Police interactions, despite an overall decrease in reported stops in New York City in recent years, continue to have a disproportionate impact on communities of color – and this could be more pronounced for alleged gang members. Street-level contact with police has been a constant theme amongst community residents who were interviewed for this report, specifically mothers and grandmothers. In one interview, a 61-year-old woman from East Harlem's Jefferson Houses described prior harassment of her grandson by police officers from the local housing police unit, PSA 5:

> They start gathering the information of how old you are around 14 or 15. They start stopping you – now they can't stop you anymore – I don't know what they gon' do. But they stop you. "How old are you?" take you to the precinct – your mother gotta come and get you – you know, stuff like that.

With more policing and more arrests came deeper forms of harassment. Police officers would search for her grandson in her apartment, she said. He was arrested several times, including once, she alleged, over a robbery simply because he and his friends were in the vicinity of the incident. That arrest would derail his education, preventing him from graduating high school because he was sent to Rikers Island just before his final Regents high school exam, she said. Ironically, in Rikers, he was continuously assaulted because he didn't belong to a gang.

> So . . . they unfairly label us – them – as gang members. You know I told them he's not a gang member. He hangs out with friends he grew up with. How's that a gang? You have 5 people sitting right here – what are you? A gang? They know each other. They known each other all their lives. You know? Those are the same ones that are with him. . . . They're all – I went to court yesterday. And the whole courtroom was full with either everybody from here or their parents. Including me and my daughter because they have my grandson.

In a 2015 *New York Times* article, the focus by police on individuals they deemed gang involved was described through the story of a young man from the Brownsville section of Brooklyn named Alexander Williams.[33] Mr. Williams had been arrested numerous times, according to the *Times*, and was part of a "few hundred" individuals across the city that police were now targeting to combat violence. Mr. Williams' story was an example of a new trend by police to dedicate efforts towards high-priority targets, including the policing of smaller offenses, like jaywalking.

> Their names and faces are distributed to precincts across the city. Their gang affiliations and Instagram postings are studied by officers. They are repeatedly arrested, stopped or given tickets, including violations for minor offenses like jaywalking.
>
> Mr. Williams, in an interview, described a smothering police presence in his life that "does not stop." Twice, he said, he has been cited for jaywalking. He denied that he was a member of a gang or that he committed the crimes the police have alleged.

Williams and his friends, the article says, were often arrested. However, charges were almost just as often dismissed. In an interview, Williams detailed some of the policing that seemed to follow him everywhere, including instances when officers would call out his name as he walked down the street. Though Williams was reportedly not included, the *Times* described the police department's use of the Intelligence Violence Assessment Reduction Plan, which lists the top five most violent people or locations in the city's 15 most violent precincts.

This approach is consistent with the NYPD testimony at the City Council that those in the gang database had an average of over 11 arrests, 5 of which are felonies. In New York, sentences for even a second felony are typically severe under the predicate felony law. Multiple felony arrests are more likely a sign of harassment and police pressure than of criminality.

For another Brooklyn resident, hyper-policing preceded a serious gang charge. Ronnie Williams, an alleged member of the "Oww Oww" gang, was convicted and sentenced for what prosecutors said was his role in a shooting. In interviews, however, Williams' mother, Diana, and sister, Shaniqua, say that he was not a gang member and was unfairly swept into the indictment by officers from the 76th precinct who targeted him for years after his first arrest at age 12. His sister explained how her brother felt the need to run from police from an early age:

> He told me on one Halloween he was probably 14 or 15 he and his friends were out trick or treating and they started throwing eggs at each other [inaudible] and he said that the cops came and he did like the whoop sound as a warning signal to let people know that they were there and they just kept playing and whatnot and eventually they started to walk away because the cops didn't leave and he said that he looked back and that they were still following him and he just started to run and he said he ran for a long time. They just kept chasing him. Finally, he had to stop because he has asthma. He couldn't breathe. So, he just set in between 2 cars on the curb and he said that the cops came up to him with their guns out telling him to put his hands up for no reason.

That arrest, she says, marked a pattern of unwarranted attention from cops that began to become more personalized:

> They would take him in and just ask him questions about how fast he is like it was a game to them like "Oh so you're pretty fast? Like, why do you gotta make us chase you all the time." Harassing him and bringing him down to the precinct and ask him about how and why he's so fast . . .
>
> He has also told me that they would sit in their car and talk on the speaker and call him out by name, his full name and ask him what are you doing out here? Just taunting him. And he's just hanging out in the neighborhood that he lives in. Crazy stuff like that, psychological stuff, as well as the physical and trying to lock him up in or get him locked up.

While it is not clear at what age the NYPD may have tagged Williams a gang member, their gang database includes hundreds of minors. As Williams got older, his mother said, his interactions with police become more serious, including once when officers assaulted him in the hallway of their building. She described probing visits from police when Williams was 16 or 17 years old.

> They would come and knock on my door and say that somebody said my son had guns in my apartment. And I was like why do you want to come in my apartment? And they would say that somebody said that he had guns and I would say no there are no guns. So, I didn't allow them in my apartment, and I knew there were no guns but I'm not going to allow you to come in based on what somebody else said.

On the day he was arrested for the charges he'd face in 2016, she said, police knocked on her door and she asked to see a warrant, wary of riot gear-clad cops standing in her hallway. One officer insisted on showing her the warrant – inside. When she opened the door, the entire group of cops stormed in and ransacked the apartment. They arrested her son. She never saw the warrant. Williams was eventually convicted despite the lack of a weapon or physical evidence tying him to the shooting.

Gang labeling by agencies outside of the police department can also escalate relatively routine encounters with police, a car stop. Victor Dempsey, community organizer with the Legal Aid Society, left the Bloods gang in 2014 when he was 19 years old after serving time for attempted robbery. In 2017, however, after being pulled over for failure to signal, a minor infraction, NYPD officers handcuffed him and put him in their squad car.[34] From the backseat of the police car, Dempsey says he saw "security risk group" on the police computer next to his old mugshot. Security risk groups are gangs tracked throughout the jail system by the Department of Corrections Gang Intelligence Unit.[35] The NYPD's access to Dempsey's DOC gang designation (which suggests his gang status hadn't changed in 13 years) dramatically altered the encounter.

Enhanced bail

The problems presented by hyper-policing are compounded when community members labeled as "gang" affiliated reach the court system. In New York, accused persons must be brought before a judge for a bail hearing within 24 hours of their arrest. Judges are only permitted to set bail to ensure that a person returns to court. Historically, in New York, courts have been permitted to consider an accused person's "character, reputation, habits and mental condition" when determining how much bail to set. This provision of the bail law allows prosecutors to take the NYPD's gang designation and bring it into the courtroom. When a prosecutor alleges that someone has gang affiliations, it often results in judges setting high bail, far higher than would be necessary to merely ensure a community member's return to court. Judges frequently assume "gang member" to mean a person is dangerous or regularly engages in criminal activity. It could also suggest willingness to intimidate, tamper, or harm witnesses, particularly where someone has been harmed as a result of the alleged crime. While judges are not supposed to factor in these considerations under the law, in reality they are very concerned about releasing someone they perceive to be dangerous. As one defense lawyer who took part in a survey for the report explained, just alleging gang affiliation can change the bail decision for people they represent:

> The simple allegation that a person is affiliated with a gang, even when it is merely asserted by a prosecutor and even when it is disputed by a defense lawyer, greatly increases the chance that bail will be set and the amount of bail.

Another attorney put it more succinctly, "Judges freak out when they hear it," while another stated, "it's extremely harmful and difficult to refute." One attorney reported asking a judge to lower the bail amount for a 17-year-old because her client's family could not afford the amount. After calling the prosecutor and defense lawyer to the bench, the judge commented off the record in a concerned tone that the previous judge had written "Trinitario" on the court file. The judge denied the request to lower bail.

The NYPD "gang" designation follows people into the criminal legal system, disadvantaging them from the initial bail decision onward. By using a gang affiliation to request high bail, prosecutors ensure that a person is deprived of their liberty pre-trial. Judges and prosecutors know that people subject to the violence of incarceration are more desperate to secure their release through cooperation with an investigation. For example, Afrika, a young woman from Harlem, had bail set in a gang conspiracy case. When supporters from her church community attempted to pay the bail, the judge would not approve the bond.

> Their idea was that I was gonna get locked up, I was gonna be facing this bail issue and then because I was gonna be under pressure I would cooperate, and the case would be done.

Beginning January 1st, 2020, consideration of an accused person's "character, reputation, habits and mental condition" has been removed from the bail law. Though the new law does not prohibit prosecutors from raising this via an alleged gang affiliation or judges from considering it, defense lawyers have strong arguments that the legislature removed this language precisely because of the discriminatory manner in which it was being used. In reality, it is likely that prosecutors will continue to use an NYPD gang designation in bail arguments and judges will continue to be biased by it. With high or no bail, defendants are further pressured to take plea deals, become cooperating witnesses, or both.

Indictments, trials, and plea deals

In a survey we carried out among New York defense attorneys and public defenders, they were asked about the influence of gang allegations in courtrooms:

> In many cases, an allegation of gang membership is not an element of a charged crime. In bail applications, prosecutors will simply assert that they have information that a person is a gang member without revealing their sources. We are left to fight blindfolded against the gang allegations. Police can also get young people to admit to "gang affiliation" if they know anyone who is in a gang even when they aren't in gangs themselves.
>
> Because many teenagers in the Bronx know SOMEONE in a gang or have some family member in a gang, it's very easy for police and prosecutors to claim that they are "gang affiliated." Teens are then treated as guilty by association without the prosecution needing to prove that they have done anything wrong. Young people in poor black and brown communities specifically end up being targeted and harmed by this practice.

Few terms can color a courtroom like the word "gang." As another defense lawyer put it, "being in a picture with friends from your neighborhood sometimes seems like sufficient [probable cause] for an indictment." The power of a gang allegation also affects plea offers from prosecutors, according to another defense attorney:

> In the Bronx, cases that involve allegations of gang affiliation often go to the same courtroom/same judge – this courtroom and judge are notoriously pro-prosecution, speedy

trial and discovery rights are completely ignored, and clients get bullied into cooperating or taking unfavorable pleas.

Trials present more problems. Indictments are obtained by offering cooperation agreements to individuals who have already been charged with serious violent offenses if they tie other alleged members of the group to various crimes. Defendants are then often brought up on "conspiracy" charges as a way to admit evidence that is excessive, irrelevant, and not from a credible source in order to inflate sentencing and charges. As one juror on a gang trial put it, "conspiracy charges were wide enough to drive a bus through," referring to the expansive definition of what constitutes "conspiracy. In this context, juries may wind up finding someone guilty without agreeing on what exact crime they are guilty of committing."

In the trial of a 36-year-old father from the Bronx whose family says he had long been harassed by cops from the 47th precinct, federal racketeering charges were brought largely because of his relationship with a co-defendant, who was also a childhood friend. Hearsay testimony and old arrests, including some that were dismissed, were presented as evidence. The jury, on the other hand, was not allowed to hear the full misconduct history of one of the detectives whose testimony proved vital to the prosecution. This detective who made the arrest had at least eight federal civil rights lawsuits filed against him, four totaling about $235,000 and three for undisclosed sums. The jury was only told about one.

This man's mother believes the local precinct put her son on the gang indictment because of his past complaints and lawsuits against some of these officers. She was also frustrated by testimony from government witnesses:

> So they all get to use that RICO conspiracy to tie them into making this a bigger case. But what I'm seeing is that what they want people to do is they use other people who are un-credible . . . on another case that could be, uh, incarcerated somewhere. So, they're going to use them, and they bring them like "Hey, do you know these young men? Gimme something on them, work with us." They could say whatever they want to say. I mean, they're in a situation to say, "You know what, I'm going to get a sweet deal to get home."

To juries, accusations of gang membership can be confused with the crime of conspiracy – a major problem that threatens freedom of association. Since conspiracy charges need to prove the element of agreement to commit a crime, prosecutors may try to prove this agreement by emphasizing that by associating, defendants are tacitly "agreeing" to criminal acts. However, association is not a crime and does not prove an agreement or intention or even gang membership: gang members and non-gang members are part of the same communities, neighborhoods, and families.

In practice, prosecutors often succeed in proving that defendants are part of a conspiracy by introducing evidence that should merely prove that they know each other; the jury is shown countless social media posts and messages. Prosecutors intentionally blur the line between conspiracy and association. After presenting posts and private messages, their content is often "translated" either by gang experts (police officers involved in gang policing, not necessarily with any education or background) or by police cooperators and informants.

Posts can contain rap lyrics and quotes, which are then presented to the jury as matter-of-fact statements made by the co-defendants. Additionally, gang experts may say that they understand the slang used by defendants, but there's no protocol in place to ensure that evidence is interpreted correctly. In one interview for this report, a mother described how a picture her son posted of himself holding money was presented in court to suggest he was a drug dealer:

> They took that and said, OH, he's a big-time drug dealer. They criminalize him in any photograph that he had. Not knowing the story where that came from that known what that meant to him and to be able to hold his son to say, I have a son, you know, I'm able to support my family, you know, um, how they pose in pictures and whatever to the message is misconstrued in that sense.

Jury members have to endure weeks or months of this. What results is a general atmosphere of criminality, built by prosecutors, that serves to convince juries less of what crime the defendants are accused of and more that they are associated with a criminal world and therefore must be guilty of something. Individualized justice is not afforded to people who are connected to gangs and to the alleged behaviors of their co-defendants – who are oftentimes friends and peers but, in some cases, can even be virtual strangers. In this context, along with the pressures of being incarcerated often without bail, many feel compelled to plead out, boosting conviction rates and creating the impression that collective punishment is in fact producing justice.

Conclusion

Gang policing is dangerous and discriminatory and contributes to the ongoing hyper-criminalization and mass incarceration of young men of color in high-need neighborhoods. These tactics place youth at risk of police harassment, incarceration, and even increased levels of communal violence.

Many young people turn to life on the streets because of problems at home. Their parents are overwhelmed by poverty and the problems that often go with it, such as unstable housing, substance abuse, hunger, and mental illness. Instead of gang takedowns, the city could support parents so that they can better support their children by looking at the structure of working hours and the high costs of childcare, as well as direct financial support of families that has been undermined by welfare reforms over the last 30 years.[36]

Still, with more support services in place, the number-one challenge young people face is access to stable incomes – even while in school. Expansion of summer employment is an important part of that, but young people also need jobs during the school year to deal with personal and family expenses. Many young people involved in violence also suffer from unstable housing and homelessness. While increased income can help, increases in the stock of truly affordable and public housing (as opposed to banning so-called offenders from housing) is also essential to creating stability for young people.

In schools, education officials need to replace school resource officers (SROs are sworn law enforcement officers responsible for crime prevention and school safety) with counselors, restorative justice programs, and resources to help students navigate home lives and communities that may be severely disordered and dangerous. Using teachers and SROs to inform on them and criminalize them[37] will serve to undermine their attachment to schooling and drive them out onto the streets, towards violence and/or into the criminal justice system.

One of the primary predictors of violence is past trauma. Youth and adult-aged people involved in violence have almost always been the victims of violence either in the community or at home. Even when they may not have personally been the victim, they have witnessed the victimization of friends and family members, often repeatedly. The city should provide services to deal with trauma – including mental health and substance abuse services as well as improved educational and recreational services.

New York City has created a new emergency trauma response capability called Mobile Trauma Units that can respond to shootings and provide immediate interventions and referrals to ongoing care as available. But there is a lack of adequate services to refer people to, so that capacity must be expanded. These services need to be culturally appropriate and linked to wrap-around health and social services support for young people and their families. Those who have experienced trauma and other adverse childhood experiences (ACEs) are also more likely to have substance abuse and mental health challenges. So, in addition to trauma services, they and their families need access to high-quality mental health and substance abuse services on demand.

The city already supports programs designed to reduce shootings and violence by relying on community-based "violence interrupters" or "credible messengers" who work with young people. These "messengers" come from the neighborhoods where violence is a problem and have a reputation on the streets that makes them appropriate for peer-to-peer outreach, mentoring, and counseling designed to break the cycle of violence.[38] These programs operate on the understanding that violence can operate like a disease, spreading from one victim to another.

The John Jay College of Criminal Justice reported that neighborhoods with credible messenger programs had significant crime reductions compared with similar control areas without them. In the East New York site run by the anti-violence community group Man Up!, gun injury rates fell by 50 percent over four years; the control site in East Flatbush fell by only 5 percent. Similarly, shootings were down by 63 percent in the Save Our Streets South Bronx area but only 17 percent in the East Harlem control neighborhood. New York City should expand the number of credible messenger programs and equip them with more resources to help young people and their families.[39]

Rather than vilifying and criminalizing "gangs," we should include young people and the groups they form into the community process in ways that do not force them to renounce the close connections they form with others in the community. This can be done through "social inclusion" strategies that give these social groupings a legitimate voice in shaping the affairs of their communities and the city. Recent work in Latin America by John Jay College's David C. Brotherton has shown that these strategies can substantially reduce violence rates.[40]

Using police to solve the problems of young people is a misguided strategy. We need to defund police-led interventions and reinvest that money in the kinds of services that will create healthier and more resilient individuals, families, and communities.

Notes

1 Judith Green and Kevin Pranis, "Gang Wars: The Failure of Enforcement Tactics and the Need for Effective Public Safety Strategies," Justice Policy Institute, 2007.

2 David C. Brotherton, "Education in the Reform of Street Organizations in New York," in Louis Kontos et al eds., *Gangs and Society: Alternative Perspectives*. New York: Columbia University Press, 2003; David C. Brotherton, *Youth Street Gangs*. New York: Routledge, 2015.

3 David C. Brotherton and Luis Barrios, *The Almighty Latin King and Queen Nation: Street Politics and the Transformation of a New York City Gang*. New York: Columbia University Press, 2004.

4 Betsy Gottbaum, "Old Problem, New Eyes: Youth Insights on Gangs in New York City," Office of the Public Advocate, 2008, www.nyc.gov/html/records/pdf/govpub/moved/pubadvocate/gangs-recs-comboreportfinal.pdf.

5 Associated Press, "NYPD Plans to Double Size of Gang Unit," *USA Today*, October 10, 2012, www.usatoday.com/story/news/nation/2012/10/02/nypd-gangs-social-media/1607799/.

6 K. Babe Howell, "Gang Policing: The Post Stop-and-Frisk Justification for Profile-Based Policing," *University of Denver Criminal Law Review*, 5(1), 2015; Joseph Goldstein and J. David Goodman,

"Frisking Tactic Yields to Focus on Youth Gangs," *New York Times*, September 18, 2013, www.nytimes.com/2013/09/19/nyregion/frisking-tactic-yields-to-a-focus-on-youth-gangs.html.

7 K. Babe Howell, "Gang Policing: The Post Stop-and-Frisk Justification for Profile-Based Policing," *University of Denver Criminal Law Review*, 5(1), 2015; Stephon Johnson, "Stop-and-Frisk Makes Way for Operation Crew Cut," *Amsterdam News,* September 26, 2013, http://amsterdamnews.com/news/2013/sep/26/stop-and-frisk-makes-way-operation-crew-cut/.

8 David C. Brotherton, *Youth Street Gangs*. New York: Routledge. 2015. Malcolm W. Klein, *Gang Cop*. New York: AltaMira Press, 2004; Judith Green and Kevin Pranis, "Gang Wars: The Failure of Enforcement Tactics and the Need for Effective Public Safety Strategies," Justice Policy Institute, 2007.

9 Joe Domanick, *Blue: The LAPD and the Battle to Redeem American Policing*. New York: Simon and Schuster, 2015; Max Felker-Kantor, *Policing Los Angeles*. Chapel Hill: UNC Press, 2019.

10 Simon Balto, *Occupied Territory: Policing Black Chicago from Red Summer to Black Power*. Chapel Hill: UNC Press, 2019, pp. 201–204.

11 Spencer Ackerman and Zach Stafford, "Chicago Police Detained Thousands of Black Americans at Interrogation Facility," *The Guardian*, August 5, 2015, www.theguardian.com/us-news/2015/aug/05/homan-square-chicago-thousands-detained.

12 Jason Meisner et al, "Chicago Cops Stripped of Powers as FBI probes Ripoffs of Drug Dealers," *The Chicago Tribune*, February 1, 2018, www.chicagotribune.com/news/breaking/ct-met-chicago-cops-stripped-fbi-sting-20180131-story.html.

13 Portland City Auditor, "Gang Enforcement Patrol," Portland City Auditor, Audit Services Division, 2017, www.portlandoregon.gov/auditservices/article/677598.

14 J. David Goodman, "Dozens of Gang Suspects Held in Raids in Manhattan," *New York Times*, June 4, 2014, www.nytimes.com/2014/06/05/nyregion/dozens-of-suspected-gang-members-arrested-in-raid-of-2-harlem-housing-projects.html.

15 Josmar Trujillo, "Harlem Mom Speaks Out Against NYPD, Daily News After Gang Raids," *Youtube*, June 14, 2014, www.youtube.com/watch?v=uyi3tKJthm8.

16 Christina Santucci, "Vance Says Gang Bust Tied to 'Chicken' Murphy Slay." *QNS*, June 14, 2014.

17 Chauncey Alcorn et al., "Robbery Suspect Falls to His Death While Running from Cops During Bronx Gang Raids," *Daily News,* April 27, 2016.

18 Babe Howell and Priscilla Bustamante, "Report on the Bronx 120 Mass 'Gang Prosecution,'" April 2019, www.bronx120.report.

19 New York City, "De Blasio Administration Announces Completion of Camera Installation at 22 NYCHA Developments," New York City, June 7, 2017, https://www1.nyc.gov/office-of-the-mayor/news/396-17/de-blasio-administration-completion-camera-installation-22-nycha-developments.

20 Derek Hawkins, "Bad News for the Juggalos: The FBI's Gang Label Could Be Here to Stay," *Washington Post*, December 19, 2017, www.washingtonpost.com/news/morning-mix/wp/2017/12/19/bad-news-for-the-juggalos-the-fbis-gang-label-could-be-here-to-stay/?noredirect=on.

21 Office of the Inspector General, "Review of the Chicago Police Department's 'Gang Database," City of Chicago Office of Inspector General, April 2019, www.documentcloud.org/documents/5816977-OIG-CPD-Gang-Database-Review.html.

22 California State Auditor, "The CalGang Criminal Intelligence System," California State Auditor, August 2016, www.voiceofsandiego.org/wp-content/uploads/2016/08/CalGangs-audit.pdf.

23 Amnesty International, "Met Police Using 'Racially Discriminatory' Gangs Matrix Database," Amnesty International, May 9, 2018, www.amnesty.org.uk/press-releases/met-police-using-racially-discriminatory-gangs-matrix-database.

24 Carimah Townes, "Portland is Saying Goodbye to its Controversial Gang Database," *The Appeal*, September 12, 2017, https://theappeal.org/portland-is-saying-goodbye-to-its-controversial-gang-database-e88e6c05262c/.

25 Ali Winston, "Looking for Details on Rogue N.Y. Police Officers? This Database Might Help," *New York Times*, March 6, 2019, www.nytimes.com/2019/03/06/nyregion/nypd-capstat-legal-aid-society.html.

26 Josmar Trujillo, "Brooklyn's Wrongful Convictions Persist With 'Gang' Cases," *Huffington Post,* February 17, 2018, www.huffpost.com/entry/brooklyns-wrongful-convictions-persist-with-gang_b_59610852e4b085e766b5131d?guccounter=1.

27 Ill Flo, "nu Money – nu nu – oww oww Official Video," *YouTube,* July 5, 2011, www.youtube.com/watch?v=1rHUgIF1T3M.

28 Stephanie Clifford, "Artist or Gang Leader? Rapper's Trial Begins," *New York Times,* May 27, 2014, www.nytimes.com/2014/05/28/nyregion/rappers-federal-racketeering-trial-begins.html.

29 Noah Remnick, "A 16-Year-Old Boy Killed, and an East Harlem Neighborhood's Grief," *New York Times*, March 28, 2016, www.nytimes.com/2016/03/29/nyregion/juwan-tavarez-16-killed-an-east-harlem-neighborhoods-grief.html.

30 Manhattan District Attorney, "DA Vance and Police Commissioner O'Neill Announce Indictment of 12 Members of East Harlem 'Chico Gang'," Manhattan DA's Office, February 8, 2019, www.manhattanda.org/da-vance-and-police-commissioner-oneill-announce-indictment-of-12-members-of-east-harlem-chico-gang/.

31 Sara Dorn, "New York Gangs Are Using Emojis as a Secret Language to Plan Crimes," *New York Post*, August 3, 2019, https://nypost.com/2019/08/03/new-york-gangs-are-using-emojis-as-a-secret-language-to-plan-crimes/.

32 Chip Mitchell, "Study: Cops Overstate Effects Of Social Media On Chicago Gang Violence," *WBEZ*, May 10, 2019, www.wbez.org/shows/wbez-news/study-cops-overstate-effects-of-social-media-on-chicago-gang-violence/7f3e77f9-ba83-429b-98b2-2df1bd4ade49.

33 J. David Goodman, "As Shootings Rise in New York, Police Focus on a Small Number of Young Men," *New York Times*, July 21, 2015, www.nytimes.com/2015/07/22/nyregion/as-shootings-rise-in-new-york-police-focus-on-a-small-number-of-young-men.html.

34 The Takeaway, "'All This Time Went by and I'm Still in a Database': Questions Arise Regarding Police Gang Databases," *WNYC*, July 10, 2018.

35 Shelly Feuer Domash, "Working Gangs from Inside Prison," *Police: The Law Enforcement Magazine*, May 1, 1999, www.policemag.com/338700/working-gangs-from-inside-prison.

36 Elizabeth Palley and Corey S. Shdaimah, *In Our Hands: The Struggle for U.S. Childcare Policy*. New York: NYU Press, 2014.

37 David C. Brotherton, "The Contradictions of Suppression: Notes from a Study of Approaches to Gangs in Three Public High Schools," *Urban Review*, 28(2), pp. 95–120, 1996.

38 The Credible Messenger Justice Center, https://cmjcenter.org/.

39 Sheyla A. Delgado, Laila Alsabahi, Kevin Wolff, Nicole Alexander, Patricia Cobar, and Jeffrey A. Butts, "The Effects of Cure Violence in the South Bronx and East New York, Brooklyn," John Jay College Research and Evaluation Center, October 2017.

40 David C. Brotherton and Rafael Jose Gude, "Social Inclusion from Below: The Perspectives of Street Gangs and Their Possible Effects on Declining Homicide Rates in Ecuador," Inter-American Development Bank, March 2018.

References

Ackerman, Spencer and Zach Stafford. "Chicago Police Detained Thousands of Black Americans at Interrogation Facility. *The Guardian*. August 5, 2015. www.theguardian.com/us-news/2015/aug/05/homan-square-chicago-thousands-detained.

Alcorn, Chauncey et al. "Robbery Suspect Falls to His Death While Running from Cops During Bronx Gang Raids." *Daily News*. April 27, 2016.

Amnesty International. "Met Police Using 'Racially Discriminatory' Gangs Matrix Database." *Amnesty International*. May 9, 2018. www.amnesty.org.uk/press-releases/met-police-using-racially-discriminatory-gangs-matrix-database.

Associated Press. "NYPD Plans to Double Size of Gang Unit." *USA Today*. October 10, 2012. www.usatoday.com/story/news/nation/2012/10/02/nypd-gangs-social-media/1607799/.

Balto, Simon. *Occupied Territory: Policing Black Chicago from Red Summer to Black Power*. Chapel Hill: UNC Press, 2019, pp. 201–204.

Brotherton, David C. "Education in the Reform of Street Organizations in New York." In Louis Kontos et al. eds., *Gangs and Society: Alternative Perspectives*. New York: Columbia University Press, 2003.

———. *Youth Street Gangs*. New York: Routledge, 2015.

Brotherton, David C. and Luis Barrios. *The Almighty Latin King and Queen Nation: Street Politics and the Transformation of a New York City Gang*. New York: Columbia University Press, 2004.

Brotherton, David and Rafael Gude. "Social Inclusion from Below: The Perspectives of Street Gangs and Their Possible Effects on Declining Homicide Rates in Ecuador." Inter-American Development Bank. March 2018.

California State Auditor. "The CalGang Criminal Intelligence System." California State Auditor. August 2016. www.voiceofsandiego.org/wp-content/uploads/2016/08/CalGangs-audit.pdf.

Clifford, Stephanie. "Artist or Gang Leader? Rapper's Trial Begins." *New York Times.* May 27, 2014. www.nytimes.com/2014/05/28/nyregion/rappers-federal-racketeering-trial-begins.html.

The Credible Messenger Justice Center. https://cmjcenter.org/.

Delgado, Sheyla A., Laila Alsabahi, Kevin Wolff, Nicole Alexander, Patricia Cobar, and Jeffrey A. Butts. "The Effects of Cure Violence in the South Bronx and East New York, Brooklyn." John Jay College Research and Evaluation Center. October 2017.

Domanick, Joe. *Blue: The LAPD and the Battle to Redeem American Policing.* New York: Simon and Schuster. 2015.

Domash, Shelly Feuer. "Working Gangs from Inside Prison." *Police: The Law Enforcement Magazine.* May 1, 1999. www.policemag.com/338700/working-gangs-from-inside-prison.

Dorn, Sara. "New York Gangs Are Using Emojis as a Secret Language to Plan Crimes." *New York Post.* August 3, 2019. https://nypost.com/2019/08/03/new-york-gangs-are-using-emojis-as-a-secret-language-to-plan-crimes/.

Felker-Kantor, Max. *Policing Los Angeles.* Chapel Hill: UNC Press, 2019.

Goldstein, Joseph and J. David Goodman. "Frisking Tactic Yields to Focus on Youth Gangs." *New York Times.* September 18, 2013.

Goodman, J. David. "Dozens of Gang Suspects Held in Raids in Manhattan." *New York Times.* June 4, 2014. www.nytimes.com/2014/06/05/nyregion/dozens-of-suspected-gang-members-arrested-in-raid-of-2-harlem-housing-projects.html.

———. "As Shootings Rise in New York, Police Focus on a Small Number of Young Men." *New York Times.* July 21, 2015. www.nytimes.com/2015/07/22/nyregion/as-shootings-rise-in-new-york-police-focus-on-a-small-number-of-young-men.html.

Gottbaum, Betsy. "Old Problem, New Eyes: Youth Insights on Gangs in New York City." Office of the Public Advocate. 2008. www.nyc.gov/html/records/pdf/govpub/moved/pubadvocate/gangs-recs-comboreportfinal.pdf.

Green, Judith and Kevin Pranis. "Gang Wars: The Failure of Enforcement Tactics and the Need for Effective Public Safety Strategies." Justice Policy Institute. 2007

Hawkins, Derek. "Bad News for the Juggalos: The FBI's Gang Label Could Be Here to Stay." *Washington Post.* December 19, 2017. www.washingtonpost.com/news/morning-mix/wp/2017/12/19/bad-news-for-the-juggalos-the-fbis-gang-label-could-be-here-to-stay/?noredirect=on.

Howell, K. Babe. "Gang Policing: The Post Stop-and-Frisk Justification for Profile-Based Policing." *University of Denver Criminal Law Review,* 5(1), 2015.

Howell, K. Babe and Priscilla Bustamante. "Report on the Bronx 120 Mass 'Gang Prosecution.'" April 2019. www.bronx120.report.

Ill Flo. "nu Money – nu nu – oww oww Official Video." *YouTube.* July 5, 2011. www.youtube.com/watch?v=1rHUgIF1T3M.

Klein, Malcolm W. *Gang Cop.* New York: AltaMira Press. 2004.

Manhattan District Attorney. "DA Vance and Police Commissioner O'Neill Announce Indictment of 12 Members of East Harlem 'Chico Gang'." Manhattan DA's Office. February 8, 2019. www.manhattanda.org/da-vance-and-police-commissioner-oneill-announce-indictment-of-12-members-of-east-harlem-chico-gang/.

Meisner, Jason et al. "Chicago Cops Stripped of Powers as FBI Probes Ripoffs of Drug Dealers." *The Chicago Tribune.* February 1, 2018. www.chicagotribune.com/news/breaking/ct-met-chicago-cops-stripped-fbi-sting-20180131-story.html.

Mitchell, Chip. "Study: Cops Overstate Effects of Social Media on Chicago Gang Violence." *WBEZ.* May 10, 2019. www.wbez.org/shows/wbez-news/study-cops-overstate-effects-of-social-media-on-chicago-gang-violence/7f3e77f9-ba83–429b-98b2–2df1bd4ade49.

New York City. "De Blasio Administration Announces Completion of Camera Installation at 22 NYCHA Developments." New York City. June 7, 2017. https://www1.nyc.gov/office-of-the-mayor/news/396-17/de-blasio-administration-completion-camera-installation-22-nycha-developments.

Office of the Inspector General. "Review of the Chicago Police Department's 'Gang Database.'" City of Chicago Office of Inspector General. April 2019.www.documentcloud.org/documents/5816977-OIG-CPD-Gang-Database-Review.html.

Palley, Elizabeth and Corey S. Shdaimah. *In Our Hands: The Struggle for U.S. Childcare Policy*. New York: NYU Press, 2014.

Portland City Auditor. "Gang Enforcement Patrol." Portland City Auditor, Audit Services Division. 2017. www.portlandoregon.gov/auditservices/article/677598.

Remnick, Noah. "A 16-Year-Old Boy Killed, and an East Harlem Neighborhood's Grief." *New York Times*. March 28, 2016. www.nytimes.com/2016/03/29/nyregion/juwan-tavarez-16-killed-an-east-harlem-neighborhoods-grief.html.

Santucci, Christina. "Vance Says Gang Bust Tied to 'Chicken' Murphy Slay." *QNS*. June 14, 2014.

The Takeaway. "'All This Time Went by and I'm Still in a Database': Questions Arise Regarding Police Gang Databases." *WNYC*. July 10, 2018.

Townes, Carimah. "Portland Is Saying Goodbye to Its Controversial Gang Database." *The Appeal*. September 12, 2017. https://theappeal.org/portland-is-saying-goodbye-to-its-controversial-gang-database-e88e6c05262c/.

Trujillo, Josmar. "Harlem Mom Speaks Out against NYPD, Daily News after Gang Raids." *YouTube*. June 14, 2014. www.youtube.com/watch?v=uyi3tKJthm8.

———. "Brooklyn's Wrongful Convictions Persist With 'Gang' Cases." *Huffington Post*. February 17, 2018. www.huffpost.com/entry/brooklyns-wrongful-convictions-persist-with-gang_b_59610852e4b085e766b5131d?guccounter=1.

Winston, Ali. "Looking for Details on Rogue N.Y. Police Officers? This Database Might Help." *New York Times*. March 6, 2019. www.nytimes.com/2019/03/06/nyregion/nypd-capstat-legal-aid-society.html.

17

Off the books and off the blocks

The dual economic marginalization of black gang members in Chicago

Roberto R. Aspholm

Introduction

Chicago's street gangs have long occupied a central place in both scholarship and public discourse on gangs and violence. For decades, the city's major traditional African American street gangs, including the Black Disciples, Black P Stones, Four Corner Hustlers, Gangster Disciples, Mickey Cobras, and Vice Lords, were among the largest, most organized, and most infamous gangs in the country. The most recently documented chapter in the collective history of these gangs involves their post-1960s reconfiguration as vertically organized outlaw-capitalist drug organizations. Prominent within this canon is sociologist Sudhir Venkatesh's (2006) *Off the Books*, a study of a corporate-style gang's drug enterprise in and around the notorious and now-demolished Robert Taylor Homes on Chicago's South Side during the 1990s. Borrowing from the title of Venkatesh's book, this chapter explores the demise of these traditional corporate-style gangs during the first two decades of the twenty-first century, making the argument that today's gang members are marginalized in not only the formal economy but in the informal economy as well. In other words, they are both off the books of conventional employment *and* off the blocks that once functioned as *ad hoc* workplaces in the illicit drug trade.

The findings presented here are based primarily on in-depth, semi-structured qualitative interviews with a purposive sample of thirty-five African American gang members from ten communities on Chicago's South Side (Aspholm 2020). This research grew out of my community work with gang members and other at-risk young people on the South Side of Chicago as a community-based social worker. These formal interviews were supplemented by a number of additional sources of data, including countless informal interviews and conversations, both with many of these study participants as well as with other gang members, their families, community workers, and others; fieldnotes and memos detailing my experiences in the field conducting this research; and my broader experiences living and working on the South Side, which provided an invaluable relational foundation from which to undertake this research and enriched the analysis through experiential contextualization. Additional data were also derived from a conference I helped convene on gang fracturing and violence at the University of Illinois at Chicago's Great Cities Institute in April 2018 (Hagedorn et al. 2019).

Deindustrialization and street gang corporatization in Chicago

Chicago's major black street gangs were all founded between the late 1950s and early 1970s on the city's South and West Sides. Up through the 1990s, these gangs were organized as cross-neighborhood federations that members referred to as "street organizations" and/or "nations" (e.g., the Almighty Black P Stone Nation) composed of a number of neighborhood-based chapters, or sets, each with its own local leadership hierarchy and collectively organized under the control of a central leadership body. Most of Chicago's major gangs had at least a dozen sets, and many gangs had substantially more than that: The Gangster Disciples, long the largest gang in Chicago, had upwards of 100 sets throughout the city during their peak. Membership at the neighborhood level – that is, within each set – was typically rather large, often numbering in the dozens, with members' ages often spanning multiple generations. Leadership structures were relatively rigid and hierarchical, with divisions of labor that often included various committees as well as demarcated roles for women and younger members. Central leadership formalized and coordinated instrumental relationships and mediated disputes between their gangs' various chapters. Organizational "literature" detailing each gang's history, values, symbols, laws, practices, and prayers served to legitimize these leadership hierarchies, delineate prescriptions for behavior, and socialize members by providing a comprehensive framework for collective identity, values, and action. Gang scholars refer to groups with complex, durable forms of organization like these as "institutionalized gangs" (Hagedorn 2008, 4).

Following an intense period of initial formation, explosive growth, and involvement with social movements and community activism, beginning in the mid-1970s, Chicago's black street gangs embarked on a path of "corporatization" in which they reoriented themselves around the underground economy. A number of dynamics contributed to this process, including the decline of social movements after the 1960s, a suppressive "war on gangs" waged by former mayor – and former gang chief – Richard J. Daley that preceded the broader explosion of the carceral state in the final two decades of the twenty-first century, and, beginning in the mid-1980s, the crack cocaine epidemic (Dawley 1992; Hagedorn 2006, 2008; Jacobs 1977; Venkatesh and Levitt 2000). Perhaps the most crucial factor in this transformation, however, was the deindustrialization taking place in Chicago and other industry-heavy northern cities like Detroit, St. Louis, Baltimore, and Philadelphia. In Chicago, this process and its catastrophic effects on the city's black communities were documented in widely circulated works like William Julius Wilson's (1987, 1996) *The Truly Disadvantaged* and *When Work Disappears*. In particular, Chicago lost a staggering 326,000 manufacturing jobs in just two decades from 1967 to 1987, 60 percent of all such positions. African American workers were heavily overrepresented in these industries, and their disappearance sent levels of joblessness and poverty soaring in Chicago's black neighborhoods, with official rates exceeding 75 percent and 60 percent, respectively, in the most devastated areas of the South and West Sides (Wilson 1996, 12, 19).

Within this context, John Hagedorn (2006, 204) argues that "the gang became the new hiring hall for young men" in Chicago's working-class African American communities. Black gangs had forcibly taken over control of retail-level drug distribution in black neighborhoods from the Outfit, the city's mafia organization, during the late 1960s, although at that time the illicit drug trade was a relatively small-scale business (Cooley 2011; Hagedorn 2015, 36–39). The transition from clandestine to open-air markets for heroin and other drugs over the following decade or so and the explosion of crack cocaine use in the mid-1980s, however, created new business opportunities for these gangs, whose control of neighborhood territories provided a basis for the establishment and control of these emerging public drug markets. Gang leaders, many of whom had been incarcerated since the early 1970s, perceived the economic possibilities at hand and began reorienting their organizations more intentionally around the illicit drug trade. Where drug crews and organizations emerged in New York and other cities independently of street gangs, in Chicago, the street gangs themselves essentially became the drug organizations (Curtis 2003; Venkatesh and Levitt 2000). Following from their hierarchical structures, gang leaders reaped a disproportionate amount of the profits from these economic endeavors, autocratically dictated gang policy, and waged wars over control of drug markets that drove levels of violence in Chicago to unprecedented heights in the early 1990s (Hagedorn 2015; Levitt and Venkatesh 2000).

By that time, Chicago's black street gangs had become some of the largest, most organized, and infamous gangs in the country. They embodied the archetype of the hierarchical outlaw-capitalist drug organization that increasingly pervaded the national imagination and discourse on street gangs (for example, see Dawsey 1990; Faison 1994; Fedarko 1997; *NBC News* 1989). For a number of reasons, however, the dynamics that shaped Chicago's gang landscape during the 1980s and 1990s ultimately could not be sustained. Beginning around the dawn of the millennium, the black street gangs on Chicago's South Side underwent a process of destabilization that culminated in their eventual shattering. Among the principal factors in this process was the decline and transformation of open-air urban drug markets in the early twenty-first century.

Transforming drug markets and diminishing underground mobility

As the 1990s came to a close, the crack cocaine epidemic that had seized dispossessed urban communities across the United States beginning in the mid-1980s was in major decline, and consumer demand for crack was in freefall (Contreras 2013; Johnson, Golub, and Dunlap 2000; Venkatesh 2006; Zelenko 2014). This trend has continued unabated into the twenty-first century: While more than half of Chicago arrestees tested positive for cocaine in 2000, less than one-fifth did so by 2012 (Office of National Drug Control Policy 2014). Law enforcement agencies have claimed credit for these declines, framing them as the result of their successful disruption of cocaine supply chains in South and Central America. Yet diminished demand is clearly responsible for reduced crack use, as cocaine prices have fallen by nearly 75 percent since the mid-1980s. A reduced supply in the face of consistent demand, on the other hand, would have sent prices skyrocketing (Zelenko 2014).

As children during the late 1980s and 1990s, most of the study participants recalled growing up during the height of Chicago's crack era, and a number of them reported that their mothers and fathers had been addicted to crack cocaine. By the time they had come of age and became involved in gang life, however, the market for crack had drastically diminished. People had seen the effects that crack addiction had on families and communities, and the drug was increasingly shunned, particularly by the young people who sold it on the streets and their peers. "Crack-head" entered the urban lexicon as a derisive term denoting a desperate, impulsive, fanatical person who lacked self-control and failed to maintain basic personal care (Furst et al. 1999). Crack was officially "wack" in the eyes of urban youth, who increasingly turned to marijuana as a safer, less destructive alternative. Data from the National Institute for Drug Abuse, for example, indicate that among a probability sample of male arrestees in Chicago from 2000 to 2010, two-thirds of those born before 1970 tested positive for recent cocaine use, while only 10 percent of those born after 1989 tested positive. On the other hand, approximately three-fourths of this younger group tested positive for marijuana, compared with less than one in four members of the older cohort (Golub, Brownstein, and Dunlap 2012). These statistical trends are reflected in the following firsthand account of evolving patterns of drug use on the South Side of Chicago provided by Cassius, a twenty-year-old Outlaw Gangster Disciple.

CASSIUS: People sell crack, but these days, people work off they phone. They don't just be outside talkin' 'bout, "What's up? Rocks and blow!" People work off they phone, so if you want some crack, you gon' call a mu'fucka like, "Bring me one down."

RRA: So it's not like it was in the nineties?

CASSIUS: Like, the *nineties*? Nah. Hell nah! It was scorchin' hot for crack. Now it's, like, calmed down. It's just the basic addicts every day who call the phone and shit. . . . But weed is – shit, I don't think that's never gon' fade out, shit. If you smoke weed, you smoke weed [you're dedicated to it].

RRA: So weed is more popular nowadays?

CASSIUS: Yeah, the weed is more popular. It's more, like, a friendly-zone drug. So it's a lot of more people do it.

Cassius's statements also lend insight into another dynamic that has reshaped the nature of the illicit drug trade in the early years of the twenty-first century, namely, the transformation of drug markets themselves. The open-air drug markets that dominated public housing developments, street corners, and other public space in dispossessed urban communities in the 1980s and 1990s have increasingly disappeared from these neighborhoods in recent years. Like their brick-and-mortar retail counterparts in the formal economy that have been devastated by the rise of online shopping, technological developments have rendered drug markets rooted in stable, physical public spaces increasingly unnecessary, irrelevant, and unprofitable. In this case, this transformation is largely a result of the ubiquity of cell phones. Gang members today no longer have to stand on a street corner to sell drugs, waiting for customers that may or may not be coming, subjecting themselves to potential arrest and prison time, and exposing themselves to attacks by their opposition. Instead, they can conduct business from their cell phones and make drop-offs to familiar customers as necessary. Indeed, while made possible by the ubiquity of cell phones in the twenty-first century, this switch was also precipitated by the declining profitability of fixed, open-air drug markets driven by the decline of the crack era: In a mobile drug delivery model, fewer people are needed to serve as retail-level drug dealers, and the need for lookouts, security, runners, and other ancillary positions (read: jobs and attendant operating costs) associated with open-air markets are largely eliminated. The realities of rampant gang conflicts and police occupation, moreover, make selling drugs on a street corner a rather unattractive proposition in the face of a viable alternative.

The rise of cell phones and, more recently, the internet as tools for conducting drug sales, moreover, has served to shift retail-level drug distribution points away from their traditional inner-city locales more broadly, as suburbanites and other outsiders are no longer forced to depend on the reliability of these public urban markets to purchase drugs. Instead of sojourning to the inner-city to buy drugs on a street corner, suburban drug users can just call or text their local dealer – typically a white suburban peer – to set up transactions locally. "Use of mobile devices has quietly revolutionized drug dealing. . . . Low-income black and Latino communities are no longer needed as drug super-markets," as the authors of a 2017 article on suburban heroin addiction conclude (Bowser, Fullilove, and Word 2017, 29, 30; see also Jacques and Wright 2015). Indeed, by 2013, less than one in five Chicago arrestees who tested positive for or who described using cocaine reported buying crack cocaine outdoors, and nearly three-quarters purchased these drugs from a "regular source," that is, someone they knew and patronized often (Office of National Drug Control Policy 2014).

What these changes in drug consumption and markets meant for black street gangs on Chicago's South Side was a dramatic reduction in drug revenues, which had served as the gangs' primary economic lifeblood since the 1980s. The higher cost of cocaine as well as the shorter, more intense high of crack and its higher level of addictiveness make the potential profit margins associated with selling crack substantially higher than those for selling marijuana. The proliferation of mobile, clientele-specific drug dealing, moreover, has drained clients from Chicago's once-prominent, gang-controlled open-air drug markets. Combined with these groups' corporate organizational structures that funneled the bulk of drug profits to gang leaders, drastically declining drug revenues meant that gangs could no longer sustain their status as populist employers of their respective memberships. Chicago gangs' involvement in the illicit drug trade during the crack epidemic of the 1980s and 1990s had allowed them to employ thousands of young black men facing "the irresistible tide of joblessness" wrought by deindustrialization (Hagedorn 2006, 203). If the crack trade had once brought about new employment opportunities, however, then the end of the crack epidemic was akin to the loss of yet another major industry, and its workers – in this case, gang members – likewise suffered widespread occupational displacement.

Another significant factor that contributed to the declining profitability of Chicago's drug markets was the near-wholesale demolition of the city's public housing projects. Between 1995 and 2010, the Chicago Housing Authority (CHA) razed more than 21,000 public housing units, with clearance efforts ramping up in earnest in 1999 with the release of the CHA's ten-year *Plan for Transformation*. Chicago's public housing projects had long housed many of the city's most lucrative, defensible, and violently contested drug markets (Hagedorn 2008; Popkin et al. 2000; Venkatesh 2000). Their demolition effectively eradicated these markets, further undermining the economic foothold of the city's black street gangs in the underground drug economy.

As gang leaders struggled to maintain their own earnings in the face of plummeting drug profits, youthful gang members were increasingly marginalized within and even excluded entirely from the gang-controlled drug-selling operations in their neighborhoods. The drug trade, then, increasingly failed to ensure even basic subsistence – or pocket change, for that matter – for growing numbers of gang members. The economic benefits that had served as a cornerstone of gang membership during the 1980s and 1990s did not apply to the generation of members coming of age in the early twenty-first century. Moreover, opportunities for mobility within the gangs' organizational structures, which had existed to some degree in previous decades and had once constituted a common aspiration among young gang members, were likewise evaporating alongside profit margins. Despite these considerable shifts in the gang landscape, however, youthful gang members were still expected to conform to their gangs' leadership hierarchies and follow the directives of their superiors. Yet the lack of even meager wages, diminishing avenues for and aspirations of organizational mobility, and declining moral support from gang higher-ups compromised the control that gang leaders were able to exercise over their rank-and-file members and fostered rebelliousness among young gang members. Terrence, a twenty-two-year-old Mickey Cobra, explains these dynamics as they played out in his neighborhood during his teenage years in the first decade of the twenty-first century:

TERRENCE: They [older gang members] was gettin' money, [but] they didn't used to help us with nothing. They used to leave us out there stranded. . . . They didn't give us no guidance, no nothing . . .

RRA: Why do you think that they didn't provide the type of leadership for you all that they got when they were comin' up?

Roberto R. Aspholm

TERRENCE: On the South Side of Chicago, it's not too much drug dealin' goin' on. . . . When the older generation was doin' they drug dealin', it was on the decline, so they wasn't makin' as much money as the [generation before them]. So they couldn't provide for us like they was provided for – like, people who had bought them drugs, guns, and all that. They couldn't do that for us. 'Cause the lil money they made off [selling drugs] was just for them to survive . . .

[When] we was in age about fourteen, fifteen, sixteen, we start gettin' into it with them hard 'cause they wanted us to stop fightin', stop gangbangin' more. They was older than us, so they was more about money – gettin' they money outside. We was younger, we was fightin' every day, makin' it hot [increasing police scrutiny], and they didn't want – they didn't like that. . . . They said we used to gangbang for no reason 'cause we wasn't doin' it for no money.

In addition to the declining profitability of open-air drug markets on Chicago's South Side, at least two other factors simultaneously fueled internal tensions and undermined existing gang hierarchies during the early twenty-first century. The first of these was the disruption of long-standing gang neighborhoods associated with the demolition of the city's public housing projects. The disruptive effect of these demolitions was twofold, as they effectively disbanded some of the most organized gang sets in the city that had been rooted in public housing and simultaneously displaced thousands of gang members from these sets into existing gang territories in other communities. Indeed, despite political rhetoric justifying public housing demolition as a vehicle for "deconcentrating poverty," the realities of entrenched racial and class segregation in Chicago meant that the majority of displaced project tenants moved to neighborhoods on the South and West Sides that were among the poorest and most racially segregated in the city (Chicago Housing Authority 2011; Oakley and Burchfield 2009; Sink and Ceh 2011). These neighborhoods were often already home to established gangs. The influx of unprecedented numbers of gang members displaced from public housing, then, created conflicts and violence in many of these areas over gang rivalries, control of local drug markets, neighborhood "ownership," and various interpersonal issues. These transitions, however, did not always – or at least did not *permanently* – result in violence. Gang members from the projects were often integrated into established gangs in their new communities via existing relationships, increasing neighborly familiarity, and/or flat-out necessity. These individuals were increasingly able to – and did – retain their original gang identities even as they were integrated into gang life in their new neighborhoods through developing and/or strengthening relationships.

Part of what facilitated this dynamic of intergang integration, and the second factor alluded to previously, was the incarceration of increasing numbers of gang leaders in the Federal Bureau of Prisons via large-scale federal drug and organized crime prosecutions. While most of Chicago's gang chiefs had run their organizations from the confines of various Illinois state prisons since the 1970s, their dispersal to federal facilities throughout the country and their routine placement in solitary confinement or other "supermax" custodial conditions dramatically weakened their capacity to provide leadership and dictate policy to their members on the streets. The loss of many of the most talented gang leaders to federal correctional institutions produced a crisis of leadership, and the gang leaders who remained on – or at least close to – the streets began to lose control of their organizations both at the neighborhood level and, even more definitively, at the broader, cross-neighborhood level. Lacking leaders who possessed the authority and legitimacy to mediate disputes between sets, gangs increasingly lost their capacity to maintain organizational cohesion across neighborhoods, and internal conflicts, whether based on money, power, or personal animosities, spun out of control and fueled further organizational erosion (see also Hagedorn 2015; Moore and Williams 2011).

Rank-and-file gang members grew increasingly disillusioned with and resistant to their subordinate position within their respective organizations, which these dynamics collectively threw into sharp relief. In particular, the notion that gang soldiers might be able to attain mobility within their organization's drug/leadership hierarchies – while always more of an illusion than a realistic possibility for most – had evaporated along with the golden age of drug profits brought about by the crack epidemic. By the close of the first decade of the twenty-first century, gang leaders had lost control of their organizations, as disillusionment within the gang rank and file found expression in internal rebellion. These uprisings, which played out idiosyncratically and somewhat unevenly across neighborhoods and across gangs, nonetheless affected all of the major South Side gangs in strikingly similar ways. In the end, these once-formidable corporate-style gang organizations were left effectively shattered.

Dual marginalization in the conventional and underground economies

The dynamics described previously have fundamentally reshaped the contemporary landscape among African American gangs on Chicago's South Side. Youthful gang members have refashioned their gangs in radically new ways that often stand in direct contrast to the traditional hierarchical, outlaw-capitalist organizations that they supplanted. These groups operate independently at the neighborhood level, governing themselves, and lack formal oversight or accountability to any type of central leadership structure. Indeed, today's gangs have emphatically rejected the culture of obedience that long defined Chicago's traditional black street gangs in favor of an intense culture of personal autonomy and egalitarianism, and nearly all of these groups are horizontally organized and formally leaderless. These gangs are increasingly composed of members with rival traditional gang identities, as personal relationships have superseded such affiliations as the primary basis for contemporary gang solidarity. Individuals who identify as Gangster Disciples, Mickey Cobras, and Black P Stones, for example, may all live in the same neighborhood and claim the same gang. Increasingly popular renegade identities, moreover, which are denoted by the addition of "Outlaw," "Nolaw," "Insane," or "Renegade" in front of the name of a traditional street gang, serve as a symbolic repudiation of the ideologies and hierarchies of these traditional gangs.

The transformed drug trade continues to shape gang life in important ways as well. The increasing marginalization and exclusion of rank-and-file gang members from the underground drug economy wrought by the consumer shift from cocaine to marijuana and the retail shift from open-air markets to mobile sales practices has only intensified in recent years as these dynamics have further congealed. Thus, while selling drugs represented the focal point of gang life in Chicago during the 1980s and 1990s, the findings from this study emphatically indicate that, in the early twenty-first century on the city's South Side, this is no longer the case. To the extent that participants in this study discussed selling drugs, it was often to highlight its decline within their communities and gangs.

While I had been keenly aware of these realities from my pre-research days working with young people on the South Side of Chicago, they came into even sharper focus during the course of my research. On one occasion in the field, for example, I was hanging out with some guys outside of a corner store on a busy thoroughfare near the large apartment building where most of them live and that serves as their collective home base. A balmy, eighty-degree summer day, the streets were full of both car and pedestrian traffic, the latter driven in part by two nearby public train stations. The group of guys on the block grew from four or five to about a dozen or so as the afternoon wore on, and I eventually pulled a few of them away individually to conduct interviews. During one of these interviews, Memphis, a twenty-two-year-old Black Disciple, told me that he was the only one of his comrades on the block actively selling drugs. One of his peers later verified the veracity of this claim, which was also seemingly supported by the various phone calls that Memphis fielded from his friend whom he had left in charge of selling his drugs and who was attempting to make a sale to a haggling customer during our interview. That this was the dynamic in a neighborhood with a good amount of both car and foot traffic and proximity to both major public transportation and the Dan Ryan Expressway betrays the extent to which selling drugs has become a marginal part of daily gang life on Chicago's South Side. In the following passage, Memphis describes these dynamics as well as the bleak realities he and his peers face in trying to survive on the streets and their desperate and escapist attempts to cope through their own substance abuse.

MEMPHIS: Like, right now – okay, you just seen . . .

RRA: Like, ten guys on the block.

MEMPHIS: And who you think hustlin'?

RRA: You tell me!

MEMPHIS: Me. Out of ten niggas! This what I'm sayin', everybody else just out there. It's just a typical day. And they only out there 'cause ain't no mu'fucka wanna be in no crib [house]! They ain't got no job, and a mu'fucka ain't got no money, so they just out there. Why you think everybody tryin' to jump on this [interview]? They broke – everybody broke. You know what I'm sayin'?

After you brought up in something for so long, you know, you gon' become condemned to shit. You gon' fall right in line with however the usual routine you been doin' every day. Most niggas wake up every day broke, tryin' to find a high, B. You know, that's fucked up, but it's the truth. . . . You ain't even buy yourself a fuckin' meal to eat! I'm sayin' this 'cause I witness – I done did this shit a couple of times. I done grew out the shit now, but it's fucked up that I know that's what's goin' on.

Those participants who reported selling drugs, moreover, admitted that their earnings from these activities were generally far below a basic subsistence wage. Indeed, as discussed briefly earlier, even during the height of the crack epidemic, when the earnings potential for retail-level drug dealers was likely at its peak, wages for these dealers rarely cracked the legal minimum wage (Bourgois 1995; Levitt and Venkatesh 2000). Marijuana's displacement of crack as the substance of choice among urban drug consumers, then, has only served to further erode these meager earnings. In practical terms, many gang members today have difficulty earning enough money to ensure that they are able to feed themselves, indulge in their minor vices, and occasionally purchase a new outfit or pair of fashionable shoes. In short, although selling drugs was never very lucrative for the vast majority of Chicago gang members, contemporary patterns of drug consumption and distribution have intensified this harsh reality. As Marco, a twenty-one-year-old Black Disciple, succinctly put it, "A'ight, I sell drugs, I got twenty dollars in my pocket. But this my life savings, you feel me?"

As highlighted in routine media coverage and countless investigations and reports nationwide, heroin has experienced a major resurgence in popularity in recent years, making heroin dealing an often-lucrative endeavor. Indeed, the few participants in this study who talked about selling heroin and what I know from conversations with other individuals whom I know to sell heroin but did not interview formally indicate that they tend to earn substantially more money than their counterparts who sell weed. Yet this renewed consumer demand for heroin has had little impact on illicit drug markets on Chicago's South Side, as the city's heroin trade remains firmly rooted in the West Side, which has been home to Chicago's premiere heroin markets for decades (Kane-Willis and Metzger 2016; Main 2017; Ralph 2014). The demand for heroin on Chicago's South Side, then, simply does not appear high enough to make this an industry with anything but severely limited employment opportunities for gang members on that side of town. Most gang members involved in the drug game on the South Side, therefore, are stuck peddling marijuana, a drug with relatively low levels of potential profitability. The economic precarity of weed-selling gang members is further exacerbated by their own routine use of the drug as a means of coping with their everyday experiences of marginality and despair, as described by Memphis in the previous passage. This dynamic has the effect of sending whatever meager profit margins these individuals might enjoy from their drug sales quite literally up in smoke. In the following passage, James, a twenty-year-old Black P Stone, explains the near impossibility of effectively sustaining oneself as a retail-level marijuana dealer. Both the financial struggles associated with low-wage, menial – and, in this case, illegal – work, as well as a reliance on substance abuse as a coping mechanism in the face of such struggles, are apparent in his account.

> It's a slight struggle, because you gotta understand – say if you buyin' weed. Okay, I'm finna buy a zip [an ounce] for $300, you know? I'm finna bag up $550, so I'm finna bag up fifty-five bags, all sawbucks [ten-dollar bags of marijuana for resale]. So I just spent $300. And I smoke weed, so now I'm finna smoke at least, by the time I been done sold the whole thing, if I ain't got a good line [a high demand], I done smoked $100 worth already. So now I'm goin' back to the store [mid-level drug supplier] with my $300, 'cause I'm puttin' $150 up [saving $150]. But, really, I ain't even put $150 up 'cause I'm smoking, so that mean I gotta buy Swishers. And they two for a dollar or seventy-five cents. So that's another thirty dollars gone. You know, and I'm smokin' cigarettes, and now they, what, twelve seventy-five a pack, thirteen dollars a pack. . . . And that depends on how many packs I go through a day. Then I'm buyin' food all day 'cause I'm high and I'm hungry. Then I gotta pay my phone bill, it's fifty dollars a month, you know?
>
> So, really, it be hard to maintain. . . . You still gotta buy the weed, you gotta buy sandwich bags, you gotta buy a scale to weigh your weed, make sure they gave you the exact amount – the right amount for your money's worth. All that. It's a lot [of hassle], man. It's a lot.

The eradication of the organizational hierarchies of Chicago's traditional black street gangs, moreover, means that the precious few remaining opportunities to make decent money and pursue mobility in the drug business are no longer attainable via traditional standards for advancement, such as "putting in work" for the gang as an effective salesperson or obedient soldier or being the beneficiary of internal gang politics. Instead, such opportunities are increasingly dependent upon key personal, and frequently familial, relationships with individuals in prominent positions within drug distribution networks. Many of these individuals are former gang leaders or older gang members who have been heavily involved in the drug trade for many years. Crucially, however, these networks are no longer synonymous with the city's street gangs: Drugs are sold readily across gang lines, and drug networks, like today's gangs, often include members from a variety of traditional street gangs who are not beholden to customary gang leadership structures. A Black Disciple from a predominantly Mickey Cobra gang might sell drugs for a Gangster Disciple. While Latino gangs with connections to Central American drug cartels control the upper echelons of the drug game, among black gangs on Chicago's South Side, the old model of street-gang-as-drug-organization is largely, if not entirely, defunct. In the following passage, Floyd, a twenty-eight-year-old Black Disciple, emphasizes the scarcity of opportunities for substantive entrée into and mobility within the drug trade, comparing these dynamics to the exclusivity and nepotism associated with restrictive craft unions, and distinguishes the relative positions of black and Latino gangs within the city's drug hierarchy.

FLOYD: [You] had to already been sellin' drugs to be in the drug game. It's kinda like a union, you gotta be grandfathered in now. So if you ain't already in it, you ain't gon' be in it. 'Cause you ain't got the clientele – you ain't known by nobody. You gotta *know somebody*, know somebody. You have to be grandfathered in to what they got goin' on and be gettin' on through they clientele.

RRA: But it ain't no gang-type shit that's runnin' the drug shit at this point, right?

FLOYD: Not on the black perspective. Maybe the Latinos. You know, the Latinos still got access to the cartels and stuff. But on the black side? You had to have already been doin' this for twenty – you have to already be plugged in, you feel me? . . .

RRA: Like, Tito's big brother was kinda in play with that, too, right?

FLOYD: Oh, yeah. Like him, he another person – he grandfathered in from the early 2000s, late '90s. He been gettin' money, so he was able to come home [from prison], and he still seein' – he makin' a lot of money. And Tito, he was able to get put on by his big brother. But, you know, for the next person [they don't have that opportunity].

Taken together, these findings reveal the increasing marginality of African American gang members in the underground drug economy on Chicago's South Side. Most gang members do not sell drugs, those that do tend to make very little money in these endeavors, and opportunities to increase earnings or climb the illicit occupational ladder are nearly nonexistent. Such opportunities, moreover, are often based on factors beyond the control of any individual gang member: These opportunities are either available to them or they are not, and there is little they might do to alter this reality. The study participants, in the throes of the desperate struggle for daily subsistence associated with selling – or, even worse, not selling – marijuana and occasionally other drugs at the retail level, were acutely aware of these dynamics. They harbored no illusions about the fallacy of "fast money" so often linked to gangs and drugs in the public imagination and popular discourse. The ambitions of gang and drug mobility that held sway in an earlier era have given way to the sober recognition among today's gang members that gang-banging and selling drugs no longer constitute a viable career path.

Given the lack of profitability and essentially nonexistent potential for advancement associated with selling drugs on the South Side of Chicago today, the continued, if marginal, participation of the city's African American gang members in the underground drug economy can only be understood within the broader context of acute exclusion from the conventional job market. A 2016 report from the University of Illinois at Chicago's Great Cities Institute, for example, reveals that nearly 90 percent of working-age black teenagers in Chicago are jobless, as well as nearly 60 percent of young black adults ages twenty to twenty-four (both of these rates are even higher on the South and West Sides; Córdova and Wilson 2016; Ross and Svajlenka 2016). These are the highest rates for black youth among the nation's ten largest metropolitan areas. The overall official unemployment rate in the ten communities from which participants hail averages a staggering 25 percent, which is at least twice Chicago's citywide unemployment rate and more than six times the national rate. To situate this figure in another way, the national unemployment rate during the Great Depression peaked at 25 percent in 1933, meaning that levels of unemployment on par with the nadir of the Great Depression exist as a daily fact of life in many of Chicago's African American neighborhoods. Of perhaps even greater consequence, the actual rate of joblessness in participants' communities is 68 percent, meaning that *more than two in three working-age residents of these communities lack even part-time formal employment*. Unsurprisingly, the average poverty rate for these communities is 37 percent, more than three times the national poverty rate (Farooqui 2017).

When presented with opportunities for conventional employment, no matter how menial and precarious, participants reported that they and their peers took advantage of such opportunities virtually without exception. The "guaranteed check" associated with standard employment was preferable to the inadequacy and instability of "hustling." These perspectives are consistent with my experiences running a half-dozen state- and city-funded youth employment programs that collectively employed hundreds of young people during my time working on Chicago's South Side. It would be difficult to overstate the demand among young people in these communities for these jobs, which are temporary, part-time, and typically pay just above the state's minimum wage for youth workers ages fourteen to twenty-four. In particular, I recall my surprise during my first summer running these programs, as young gang members with big reputations on the streets, whom I had assumed would scoff at such menial job opportunities, desperately scrambled to secure the paperwork they needed to render them eligible for the program. *Why on earth would these guys want these jobs?* I wondered. The answer, I soon learned, was simple: They were not making much money on the streets. More generally, navigating the blitz of young people eager for work as they sought to claim slots for these programs was an unenviable challenge that, based on basic numerical realities, inevitably left many desperate youth on the outside of these programs looking in. Indeed, recent reports for the city's One Summer Chicago, a joint public-private youth employment initiative, show that the city turned down more than 160,000 young job seekers between 2014 and 2017 alone, nearly 60 percent of the program's total applicants, due to inadequate funding (Mayor Rahm Emanuel's One Summer Chicago 2018).

In the end, black youth on Chicago's South Side today find themselves on the margins of both the conventional and underground economies, where they exist not only off the books but off the blocks as well.

Conclusion

Throughout US history, African Americans have disproportionately been relegated to the most marginalized and exploited segments of the nation's collective workforce. This remains so today, particularly for blacks living in segregated urban communities that have been devastated by deindustrialization and public retrenchment. Despite a relatively low national unemployment rate, black communities on Chicago's South and West Sides today suffer from Depression-era levels of official unemployment – as well as overall levels of joblessness likely much higher than those of the Great Depression. Black youth in these communities, in particular, are excluded with near totality from conventional employment opportunities. Moreover, those who can find employment – youth and adults alike – typically work part-time or as temporary workers in menial jobs for pitiful wages. Unsurprisingly, poverty in these communities is pervasive and manifest in widespread blight and crumbling infrastructure.

With the advent of the crack cocaine epidemic in the mid-1980s, Chicago's black street gangs refashioned themselves as outlaw-capitalist drug organizations, providing employment opportunities in the underground economy for thousands of young people who had been shut out of the conventional economy via urban deindustrialization. By the early years of the twenty-first century, however, the crack epidemic was in steep decline, and cell phones rendered open-air urban drug markets increasingly obsolete. In combination with the demolition of public housing and the incarceration of scores of gang leaders in federal prisons, the end of the crack epidemic dramatically eroded gang revenues, weakened organizational structures, and produced a crisis of leadership on the streets. Increasingly excluded and marginalized from their gangs' drug operations, young rank-and-file gang members waged rebellions against remaining gang leaders that eventually shattered these once-formidable street organizations.

Gang members on the South Side of Chicago today, then, are mostly stuck "petty hustling" in an attempt to fulfill their basic needs and desires – food, bus and train fare, cigarettes, marijuana, and the occasional new outfit or pair of shoes. Their marginalization in the formal economy, in other words, now increasingly characterizes their experiences within the underground economy as well. While rank-and-file gang members during previous decades also faced long odds of actually making a decent living in the drug game, the crack era provided an abundance of opportunities for low-level income generation, and gang hierarchies provided at least the illusion of potential mobility. Indeed, the erosion of this illusion was among the chief factors that brought about the internal rebellions that shattered these hierarchies in the first place. While a repudiation of the coercion and exploitation that often characterized the gang leadership of yesteryear has clearly shaped today's egalitarian gang ideologies and structures, the sober recognition that precious few tangible opportunities for advancement in the underground economy remain for present-day gang members has likely informed these developments as well: Within a context of near-ubiquitous dispossession, hierarchies make little sense.

These research findings challenge a number of popular stereotypes and common misconceptions, including that gangs function primarily as drug enterprises and that gang members are synonymous with drug dealers. Perhaps most importantly, however, this research lays waste to the notion that gang members earn large sums of money selling drugs and therefore have no interest in conventional employment. This narrative often serves as a tacit, if not overt, explanation for the appalling rates of unemployment in urban African American communities and as a justification for disinvestment from those communities. The findings from this study refute these stereotypes and make the case that meaningful employment opportunities should be made available to those on the margins of society as part of a concerted effort to restore the vitality of communities that have suffered from decades of abandonment. Such interventions will almost certainly necessitate the marshalling of vast public resources. While real opportunities for intervention to address gangs and reduce violence exist today in Chicago, the real question is whether the political will to move on these opportunities exists as well.

References

Aspholm, Roberto R. 2020. *Views from the Streets: The Transformation of Gangs and Violence on Chicago's South Side*. New York: Columbia University Press.

Bourgois, Philippe. 1995. *In Search of Respect: Selling Crack in El Barrio*. Cambridge: Cambridge University Press.

Bowser, Benjamin, Robert Fullilove, and Carl Word. 2017. "Is the New Heroin Epidemic Really New? Racializing Heroin." *Journal of the National Medical Association* 109, no. 1: 28–32.

Chicago Housing Authority. 2011. *The Plan for Transformation: An Update on Relocation*. Chicago: Chicago Housing Authority.

Contreras, Randol. 2013. *The Stickup Kids: Race, Drugs, Violence, and the American Dream*. Berkeley: University of California Press.

Cooley, Will. 2011. "'Stones Run It': Taking Back Control of Organized Crime in Chicago, 1940–1975." *Journal of Urban History* 37, no. 6: 911–932.

Córdova, Teresa L., and Matthew D. Wilson. 2016. *Lost: The Crisis of Jobless and Out of School Teens and Young Adults in Chicago Illinois and the U.S.* Chicago: Great Cities Institute, University of Illinois at Chicago.

Curtis, Ric. 2003. "The Negligible Role of Gangs in Drug Distribution in New York City in the 1990s." In *Gangs and Society: Alternative Perspectives*, edited by Louis Kontos, David C. Brotherton, and Luis Barrios, 41–61. New York: Columbia University Press.

Dawley, David. 1992. *A Nation of Lords: The Autobiography of the Vice Lords*. 2nd ed. Prospect Heights, IL: Waveland Press.

Dawsey, Darrell. 1990. "Gangs Targeted in Federal Sweep." *Los Angeles Times*, June 16. www.latimes.com/archives/la-xpm-1990-06-16-mn-327-story.html.

Faison, Seth. 1994. "Arrests in New York Are Said to Cripple a Huge Drug Gang." *New York Times*, September 9. www.nytimes.com/1994/09/09/nyregion/arrests-in-new-york-are-said-to-cripple-a-huge-drug-gang.html.

Farooqui, Suniya. 2017. *Chicago Community Area Indicators, 2015*. Chicago: Social Impact Research Center, Heartland Alliance.

Fedarko, Kevin. 1997. "Long Arm of the Outlaw." *Time Magazine*, May 19. http://content.time.com/time/magazine/article/0,9171,986344,00.html.

Furst, R. Terry, Bruce D. Johnson, Eloise Dunlap, and Richard Curtis. 1999. "The Stigmatized Image of the 'Crack Head': A Sociocultural Exploration of a Barrier to Cocaine Smoking Among a Cohort of Youth in New York City." *Deviant Behavior* 20, no. 2: 153–181.

Golub, Andrew, Henry Brownstein, and Eloise Dunlap. 2012. *Monitoring Drug Epidemics and the Markets That Sustain Them Using ADAM II: Final Technical Report*. Washington, DC: U.S. Department of Justice.

Hagedorn, John M. 2006. "Race Not Space: A Revisionist History of Gangs in Chicago." *Journal of African American History* 91, no. 2: 194–208.

Hagedorn, John M. 2008. *A World of Gangs: Armed Young Men and Gangsta Culture*. Minneapolis: University of Minnesota Press.

Hagedorn, John M. 2015. *The In$ane Chicago Way: The Daring Plan by Chicago Gangs to Create a Spanish Mafia*. Chicago: University of Chicago Press.

Hagedorn, John M., Roberto Aspholm, Teresa Córdova, Andrew Papachristos, and Lance Williams. 2019. *The Fracturing of Gangs and Violence in Chicago: A Research-Based Reorientation of Violence Prevention Policy*. Chicago: Great Cities Institute, University of Illinois at Chicago.

Jacobs, James B. 1977. *Stateville: The Penitentiary in Mass Society*. Chicago: University of Chicago Press.

Jacques, Scott, and Richard Wright. 2015. *Code of the Suburb: Inside the World of Young Middle-Class Drug Dealers*. Chicago: University of Chicago Press.

Johnson, Bruce, Andrew Golub, and Eloise Dunlap. 2000. "The Rise and Decline of Hard Drugs, Drug Markets, and Violence in Inner-City New York." In *The Crime Drop in America*, edited by Alfred Blumstein and Joel Wallman, 164–206. Cambridge: Cambridge University Press.

Kane-Willis, Kathleen, and Scott Metzger. 2016. *Hidden in Plain Sight: Heroin's Impact on Chicago's West Side*. Chicago: Illinois Consortium on Drug Policy at Roosevelt University.

Levitt, Steven D., and Sudhir Alladi Venkatesh. 2000. "An Economic Analysis of a Drug-Selling Gang's Finances." *Quarterly Journal of Economics* 115, no. 3: 755–789.

Main, Frank. 2017. "On the West Side, Maps Show Heroin ODs, Shootings Go Hand in Hand." *Chicago Sun-Times*, March 24. https://chicago.suntimes.com/crime/on-the-west-side-maps-show-heroin-ods-shootings-go-hand-in-hand/.

Mayor Rahm Emanuel's One Summer Chicago. 2018. "Newsroom." www.onesummerchicago.org/Newsroom/.

Moore, Natalie Y., and Lance Williams. 2011. *The Almighty Black P Stone Nation: The Rise, Fall, and Resurgence of an American Gang*. Chicago: Lawrence Hill Books.

NBC News. 1989. "Gangs, Cops & Drugs." Directed by Wayne Ewing and Kyle Good, featuring Tom Brokaw. Aired August 15, on NBC.

Oakley, Deirdre, and Keri Burchfield. 2009. "Out of the Projects, Still in the Hood: The Spatial Constraints on Public-Housing Residents' Relocation in Chicago." *Journal of Urban Affairs* 31, no. 5: 589–614.

Roberto R. Aspholm

Office of National Drug Control Policy. 2014. *2013 Annual Report, Arrestee Drug Abuse Monitoring Program II*. Washington, DC: Executive Office of the President.

Popkin, Susan J., Victoria E. Gwiasda, Lynn M. Olson, Dennis P. Rosenbaum, and Larry Buron. 2000. *The Hidden War: Crime and the Tragedy of Public Housing in Chicago*. New Brunswick, NJ: Rutgers University Press.

Ralph, Laurence. 2014. *Renegade Dreams: Living Through Injury in Gangland Chicago*. Chicago: University of Chicago Press.

Ross, Martha, and Nicole Prchal Svajlenka. 2016. *Employment and Disconnection Among Teens and Young Adults: The Role of Place, Race, and Education*. Washington, DC: Brookings Institution.

Sink, Todd, and Brian Ceh. 2011. "Relocation of Urban Poor in Chicago: HOPE IV Policy Outcomes." *Geoforum* 42, no. 1: 71–82.

Venkatesh, Sudhir Alladi. 2000. *American Project: The Rise and Fall of a Modern Ghetto*. Cambridge, MA: Harvard University Press.

Venkatesh, Sudhir Alladi. 2006. *Off the Books: The Underground Economy of the Urban Poor*. Cambridge, MA: Harvard University Press.

Venkatesh, Sudhir Alladi, and Steven D. Levitt. 2000. "'Are We a Family or a Business?' History and Disjuncture in the Urban American Street Gang." *Theory and Society* 29, no. 4: 427–462.

Wilson, William Julius. 1987. *The Truly Disadvantaged: The Inner City, the Underclass, and Public Policy*. Chicago: University of Chicago Press.

Wilson, William Julius. 1996. *When Work Disappears: The World of the New Urban Poor*. New York: Alfred A. Knopf.

Zelenko, Michael. 2014. "If the Drug War Is Failing, Where'd All the Cocaine Go?" *Vice*, January 24. www.vice.com/read/if-the-drug-war-is-failing-whered-all-the-cocaine-go.

18

Responding to exclusion in Hartford

Albert DiChiara

Introduction

Gangs formed in Hartford's public housing projects in the 1950s as a response to structural racism, segregation and oppression, and while some gangs developed a political consciousness, others took a different route over the ensuing decades. By the 1980s, the gangs had become drug organizations, and gang wars plagued the city during the 1990s. Structural racism, spatial and economic segregation and deindustrialization are at the center of the story of gang formation in Hartford, while attempts to control the gang problems of the 1990s included inclusionary programs created by liberal social welfare groups and organizations that also contained a range of pathologizing frameworks and programs complementing the dominant paradigm and tactics of law enforcement, especially during the era of zero tolerance.

In response to police pressure, the largest of these gangs, the Solids, attempted to transform itself during the 90s with a process supported by a variety of social service and education professionals who provided funds for educational and work-based programs. This transformation hinged on the Solids adopting a self-pathologizing and assimilationist stance in contrast to Hartford's first wave of gang formation in the 1960s that resisted this adaptation to marginalization and powerlessness. This chapter explores the cycles of gang formation in Hartford within the context of structural racism and the roles played by those "progressive" individuals and organizations dedicated to gang violence reduction that shaped gang development with unintended and often problematic outcomes.

Hartford's history of gang formation set within the context of segregated public housing projects illustrates the complexity of developing a genealogy of gang and radical youth group formation. In this chapter, drawing on my experiences and reflections from this period, I analyze and describe the competing cultural, ideological and oppositional forces at play and how subcultural groups adapted under changing social and historical economic conditions (Brotherton and Barrios, 2004; Dawley, 1992; Hagedorn, 2007; Jankowski, 2003). My analysis makes use of interviews, observations and other engagements with the Solids and other gangs over the past 25 years. For the historical parts of my analysis, I also interviewed members of the Hartford Black Panther Party and Blackstone Rangers, augmenting this with documents and films belonging to the Hartford Panther's founder, the late Butch Lewis. I also studied the FBI's

COINTELPRO files on these groups held at the National Archives and other literature on the history of Hartford.

Gang formation in Hartford

Gang formation is typically conceptualized as the product of social and spatial marginality, status frustration and fatalistic and antisocial attitudes (Thrasher, 1927; Cohen, 1955; Yablonsky, 1959; Vigil, 1988). While these approaches have yielded important insights, they imply an uncomplicated movement toward greater alienation, deviance and pathology. The large national drug gangs' self-definition as "nations" contributed to a re-thinking of gang theory and gang research since the 1970s and moved gang theory in new directions (Coughlin and Venkatesh, 2003). In these new approaches, there is an appreciation that gangs know where they are in society and history, with gangs viewed as collective responses to globalization, deindustrialization, cultural and economic oppression, pathologized othering and the pressures of living in modern control states. Compared to the past, some gangs are now more entrepreneurial and violent, with a number composed of older and female members in powerful and important roles. Today, some gangs are resisting oppression by reorganizing into cultural and political movements that respond to structural changes in the economy and other pressures to realize their potential for change in whatever configurations they choose (Bourgois, 1995; Brotherton and Barrios, 2004).

Hartford's gang structure developed among teenagers in newly erected public housing projects built in the early stages of Hartford's deindustrialization. The gangs formed naturally as street-corner groups identified by the jackets they wore. In no way did residents or the police view these gangs as criminal. Former Police Chief Daryl K. Roberts, who grew up in the North End, put it this way, "Ten guys on the block, let's all put on red jackets, and now we're a gang" (Hartford Courant, 2009). The larger gangs were the Magnificent 20s, Emperors, Hustlers and the Imperial Pimps, along with two gangs, the Savage Nomads and the Ghetto Brothers, that merged to form the Solids in the late 1980s. Some of the jacket gang organized themselves as activist youth groups to force the city to solve problems and create opportunities for youth. They were involved in positive activities in the community, more so than others. The Magnificent 20s in Bellevue Square were the exemplar of these positive gangs, giving away Thanksgiving turkeys; hosting Halloween parties for children; sponsoring camping trips, dances and events for the elderly and mentally challenged. Meanwhile, Eddie Perez, who would become the nation's first Puerto Rican mayor, was a former member of one of these gangs, the Ghetto Brothers.

Several of these jacket gangs moved toward Black radicalism and gained wide support in the community. At age 16, Mike, who would become a leader of the Hartford Black Panther Party in the 1970s, was typical of the leadership of these pro-social subcultures. He organized his friends to create the Youth Council in the Bellevue Square housing project, Hartford's "Black-only" public housing project, and began work with South Arsenal Neighborhood Development (SAND) corporation to create a voice for youth. Their first task was to improve recreation in the projects which, in turn, spread to other public housing projects. SAND went on to oppose many of the city's elite-driven North End redevelopment plans and was materially supportive of the Panthers, providing a venue for more radical agitation. An architect working with SAND explained its radical democratic threat to the established powers:

> because we are talking about government and the only people who in a sense seem to put us down, say that if we get together and become an entity unto ourselves that we will set

a pattern for all the other neighborhoods, and I think the city manager's afraid that he's gonna wind up with sixteen sort of little countries under him, each one self-governed.

(Hartford Public Library, 2014)

The Panthers and the Blackstone Rangers also promoted an organic model of resistance through direct political action, a focus on self-defense, social protests, community organizing, neighborhood improvements, street education and monitoring the police in a performance of confrontation and radicalism – complete with sunglasses, black leather jackets, berets and military-style regimentation. Two transgressive acts illustrate the resistance of the Panthers and Rangers and the threat they posed. First, the Panthers came to the attention of the FBI by organizing with the residents of public housing to protest dangerous conditions by blocking a major street during afternoon rush hour. Second, in the riots of 1969, the Panthers and the Rangers used the occasion to exact street justice through committing acts of arson against a few North End businesses that overcharged or were discriminatory.

Thus, the Panthers and the Blackstone Rangers blurred the lines between a gang and a political movement. The Panthers kept large caches of legal weapons for self-defense as required in the "10 Point Program" and raised funds selling the Black Panther newspaper on the streets. The FBI suggested the Rangers were more involved in drug sales than the Panthers, but no one I spoke with said that this was the case, apart for small-scale sales of marijuana. However, the Rangers were generally younger and were said to be more volatile. Each group remained true to the philosophy espoused by their national leadership. The common thread of this hybridization is that members found inspiration from the angry residents of public housing, particularly the highly segregated Bellevue Square project.

Racial control in public housing: a major social source of Black radicalism

The North End is the most neglected and troubled part of the city and was developed to house Blacks and Puerto Ricans who were moved from their homes for new city developments. Redlining and real-estate interests promoted a white exodus from Hartford, thereby initiating apartheid, while the undeveloped North End was designated as a holding area of unwanted people (Wacquant, 2007). After 1945, city leaders envisioned a new Hartford and began to redevelop the areas around downtown while, at the same time, jobs were moving to the suburbs. The city demolished the neighborhood called the Bottoms, a poor and working-class neighborhood that contained the city's largest concentration of Blacks (Radcliffe, 1998), forcing residents to move to eight new public housing projects in undeveloped land north and south of downtown. Moving to public housing was a great improvement for many because these were newer apartments, but the multi-generational families from the Bottoms felt cramped, and, importantly, there was nothing for the kids to do. Meanwhile, the city did not plan for playgrounds, nor did it improve schools in the area.

The four neighborhoods in the North End were further segregated from the rest of the city by the placement of the interstate highway that established *de facto* apartheid while opening the North End to the formation of a broad informal economy that became dominated by drug sales in the 1980s. Later, Hartford's business and political growth machine (Molotch, 1976), known as The Bishops, planned a local diaspora. Showing no regard for history or culture, they considered moving all the people out of the North End to the fresh air of a planned community 20 miles away, known as the infamous Greater Hartford Process

(American City Corporation, 1972). One resident described this development Hartford as follows:

> They're building a wall . . . because these Black people are getting too close to the insurance companies.
>
> *(Hartford Public Library, 2014)*

Meanwhile, local law enforcement helped this process. For example, in 1967, during the housing riots, they allowed the North End to burn, while they prevented these same riots from spreading to the white South End. One person describes this in the following terms:

> All right now, when the rock throwing and the, you know, all the harassment and rioting was taking place in the North End of town, the police didn't do anything about it they let them tear it up. OK, there was a movement. All right, somebody said in the crowd, 'OK, let's go downtown.' So now what happened, we [get] to Morgan Street, this is where the cordon sets up. We've got every policeman in the city of Hartford there now, making sure nobody does anything.
>
> *(Hartford Public Library, 2014)*

Another resident expressed the outrage typical felt among the community:

> After the '67 disturbances, which was the first one, there was great, great concern on the part of the establishment. We had all kinds of meetings, getting together and planning and we told what we wanted, what we thought needed to be done. Still, no movement and very frankly, a lot of us are tired of talking.
>
> *(Hartford Public Library, 2014)*

The massive movement of poor people into public housing caught the city flatfooted. Affirming the racist foundations of city development plans, the Bellevue Square project was designated for only Black residents, while other projects offered housing for African Americans on a limited basis through a policy called "controlled integration." Essentially, the city was not ready to deal with the demands of Black residents, since their demands had been ignored for decades, causing mounting and accumulated inequalities in education, housing and jobs. There was nothing for kids to do in Bellevue Square – no functional basketball or tennis courts, no baseball fields, nothing for girls and no clubs or organized activities. Public housing developments in Hartford were *projects* in the truest sense. They were inchoate processes, experiments in human housing, and every year city researchers arrived to study the projects, collect data and propose changes for the coming years, mostly to ensure white cultural dominance in public housing. The projects and the plan to move residents from the North End to the countryside illustrate Hartford's historic inability to deal with minority populations that migrated to the city after 1850 and its focus on downtown development at the expense of neighborhoods.

Organic radicals in public housing

If the previous explains the source of the developing radicalism, what or who was promoting it? Radicalism had been simmering in the North End since the 1950s. Visits by prominent militant civil rights leaders mobilized the North End. Malcolm X visited the city regularly starting in 1955 and spoke every Thursday evening in Bellevue Square in the summer of 1963 (Close, 2001).

Radical church-based activist groups challenged the older Black churches, the NAACP and the Urban League and produced the Black Caucus, a radical coalition whose march in 1967 led to two days of riots. Radical groups, including the Panthers, moved away from the usual sources of leadership and created the Black Citizens Review Board to patrol the police and investigate police brutality (Fernandez, 2018). From 1967 to 1972, Hartford struggled to deal with these expressive riots that began as housing protests and the spread of street radicalism in the form of political education and the public recruitment of residents into radical groups. In response to the riots, officials in Hartford's North and South End conflated youthful crime and political protest, demonstrated by Connecticut's US Senator Thomas Dodd, who insisted that the city was on the brink of civil war, "with black extremists preparing for action against the white community" (Close, 2001: 250).

In 1969, a series of meetings at Bellevue Square, organized by the Panthers and SAND, were recorded on film now archived in Hartford's public library. The films show meetings between city leaders and representatives of businesses and other civic groups and the displays of anger about the racism, the school system, poor housing, poor police-community relations and the sell-out Black leadership. Residents are seen criticizing the "Toms" who run community organizations and social service agencies. One city council member was chastised by a resident who said, "I've known you all my life and you've been 'Tomming' for Charlie for years." Another Hartford resident and a member of the National Conference on Black Power stated: "Hartford is saturated with black Uncle Toms – no real leadership. . . . Where are your real black voices, your black leaders?" He goes on to argue that John Bailey (the state Democratic chairman and the most powerful politician in the state) "just doesn't want black people to have this power" (Close, 2013: 248). Meanwhile, others complained that an "Establishment" of business-friendly liberals "buys off" the most qualified activists from the streets in a "divide and conquer" strategy.

The Chamber of Commerce and the Toms became the establishments that "control our very destiny." A grandmother with ten children expressed her contempt for whites and those Blacks who tried to fit into white society in her demand for equality.

> I think that white people . . . no, they don't spend a lot of time hating black people because they act like we're not even here. . . . They've tried bleaching and it don't work. Whites have tried sun-tanning and that don't work. They've got to come up with something new. Equality is about the newest thing there is because we haven't had any of it.
>
> *(Hartford Public Library, 2014)*

Mr. Johnson said,

> For the first time in the city of Hartford, black folks went to their city hall and (unintelligible) and were heard over all TV stations. First time because the kids threw bottles and bricks. Never seen so many crows in one meeting. And they got up there and they told them how they felt loud and clear and were heard.
>
> *(Hartford Public Library, 2014)*

Then, this wonderfully clear expression of transgressive resistance follows,

MR. CARTER: That's the way the establishment looks at it though. You only hurt yourself by disturbances. You're only hurting yourself and I don't think that's true. That's the only way we gain anything.

MR. JOHNSON: You have nothing.

MR. CARTER: Right. Nothing to lose. Everything to gain.

So far, I have described the radical background to these gangs in Harford prior to the 1990s. What happens during the next phase of gang formation with the emergence of the Solids is instructive, demonstrating how the political radicalism of the previous gang generations was controlled and neutralized with the expanding new drug economy playing a major role.[1]

The arrival of the Solids

In its official handbook written in the late 1980s, the Solids were presented as a duality. It was primarily a drug business that included "laboratories" with specific instructions on selling "product," while it was also an alternative support system for those preyed upon by other gangs and disconnected Puerto Rican youth. Elements of the handbook reflected the social welfare/pathology model of deviance and made recommendations as to how the Solids could rejoin the community. I refer to this as their manifesto. As one member of the Solids wrote,

> The actual thought of a future with more trust in our surroundings and each other was what encouraged us to start really setting our needs and goals in place. . . . What we would do to help our young members in school was to make sure that if they needed help (sic) we would provide the necessary assistance [and] to make sure that our members would keep a C average or higher.
>
> *(Unknown, 1994)*

According to one member, "When people say we're a gang, I guess in a way it's true, but I find it disrespectful. We're a family. We go out together; we stick by each other." Brotherhood and the *jíbaro* ideal were stressed as the basis of a new community of young Puerto Ricans who stand against economic oppression and cultural domination. The Solids' manifesto sets out this oppositional, yet conservative and assimilationist orientation. The gang was composed of four relatively well-articulated initiatives: (i) economic survival through drug sales, (ii) family support, (iii) community development, and (iv) movement into the legitimate community. The manifesto embraced core themes of the pathology and personal deficit:

> The family and friends you grew up with are now addicted to drugs. . . . The majority of young males in our communities today don't have any family. That's why they're out running around and acting all crazy and foolish.
>
> *(Los Solidos Handbook, no date)*

While the manifesto explains the "*Solido* Achievement Plan":

> As a Nation of Solid Brothers, our plans for the future are to have a chain of stores, have Brothers as lawyers, doctors, and politicians, and have our families be well off (sic). . . . Our main objective at this point is to expand our Family into the mainstream of society.
>
> *(Los Solidos Handbook, no date)*

An essay by an unknown Solid written in the early 1990s encourages members to give up the streets, fit into conventional society and achieve success:

> The majority of gang members sooner or later, if they survive the street, end up settling to exchange dollars for hours. Yet there is another hustle, the hustle with contractor, electrician, plumbers, etc. They soon find a need to learn skills.
>
> *(in possession of the author)*

The Solids qualify as a "street organization" that offered its members protection on the streets, a resistant identity, empowerment and a spiritual family (Brotherton, 2008). What accounts for their movement toward social reproduction is primarily historical. The first wave of Puerto Ricans was working class and business oriented. By the 1980s, it had achieved some level of electoral power in the city, and Puerto Rican activists worked to end their cultural and economic marginality (Cruz, 1998). Perhaps reflecting this, the Solids organized primarily as an ethnic enterprise (Padilla, 1992) that offered emotional support but also the opportunity to do crime as a source of income. The manifesto localized their complaints to bad actors and bad conditions in Hartford. They did not consider systematic discrimination, loss of jobs and repression as anything other than their bad luck and their parents' fault. Meanwhile, their criminal response was presented as a logical, anomic response rather than a class-based quest for economic opportunity and radical resistance to oppression. Thus, their vision of the future was limited to the individual success of the members, with the ideal presented in the manifesto as the creation of a cadre of *Solido* lawyers and workers who would "hustle" as plumbers to "exchange dollars for hours."

But there was a conflict between the lure of the informal economy and the mainstream life of the *jibaro*. Factions in the Solids put pressure on leaders and the collective identity of the gang. Some of the gang's leaders led the pro-social transformation, and younger gang members pushed for a large slice of the pie while the ruling leadership managed the drug gang with an iron fist. Protecting drug turf and compliance were the major motivations of the leadership.

The Solids transformation

Waves of serious gang violence from 1992 to 1994 brought national attention to Hartford's gang problems, and by 1996, the gang was decimated by federal indictments. After years of working with jacket gangs and then ignoring the emergence of drug markets in public housing in the 1980s, the police were forced to respond to fearful conditions in the city.

This brazen behavior and other transgressions were featured in the media and got the attention of the police and the Clinton Administration that funded a number of anti-gang initiatives in the city. Meanwhile, they crashed the annual Puerto Rican Day parade, making aggressive taunts, saying they were disrespected by being left out of the ceremonies. On another occasion, they clogged the streets for miles in a long funeral procession for a murdered leader; still, on a separate occasion, they were organized by a Black contractor and occupied a construction site demanding jobs. At this point, two competing strands of thinking had emerged which structured gang change: the assimilationist approach of the gangs' mentors and a more radical approach linked to Puerto Rican independence and the transformation model of the New York City Latin Kings.

Three respected individuals helped to frame the Solids' complaint and shepherded their transformation and social reproduction. A series of meetings between supporters and the Solids constructed a new public image that would emphasize the idea that the gang was a family and economic lifeline for rejected youth and young adults. Most important among the mentors was Roberto, a drug treatment specialist and a member of the Young Lords. Roberto stressed the need for more ameliorative programs and the leadership of experts and street workers. He crafted a message that the gang was an adaptation of the traditional Puerto Rican institution of extended families to neoliberal times. He argued that the Puerto Rican gangs developed out of the conditions of recession and the effects of neoliberal policies as the inner city became abandoned. Carl was a former Black Panther and a long-time community activist. He was a city youth employment specialist, and his reputation and legitimacy as a street-wise activist gave him the opportunity to testify before the US Senate and meet with President Reagan. He had associations with local politicians and was well connected to the foundations which provided funding opportunities. Last, the dean of the University of Connecticut School of Social Work, who formed the Institute for Violence Reduction (IVR) with the goal of addressing gang problems, also became an important advisor. These three individuals organized the social ser-vice infrastructure to engage the gang by creating programs and entry points into official circles of government and civic society. They formed a group that met weekly for a year or so with the Solids, Latin Kings and 20 Love, brainstorming ways to move the gangs in new directions.

The leadership authorized a group of representatives to work on improving the gang's image in response to pressure from the police and the media's quest for interviews. In one glar-ing example of where such publicity went wrong, the President of the Solids, Peking, gave an interview on national TV in which he admitted to controlling the Hartford drug trade, bringing more local and federal police attention. To try to limit the damage, he chose three of his lieutenants to become the face of the gang. Geanie, the leader of about 50 female Solids, who held a high leadership rank; Big Bird, the leader of the junior Solids, called the Original Family Organization; and Smurf, the "Speaker" of the Solids. These individuals became the link between the gang's supporters and its leadership. Smurf worked the media, relations with the police and social service agencies, while Geanie kept the female members involved and active in positive initiatives, and she also worked with members of the clergy. Last, Big Bird tried to ensure the junior members were involved in their alternative schools project that they had designed. The three worked with supporters on professional development-style day-long conferences at the University of Connecticut and the University of Hartford, traveled the state speaking to various audiences and all found employment in the funded programs in education created by the gang's mentors. It is of note that Geanie and Smurf were the only Solids to be hired by the patrons during this time and today still have employment in gang and violence prevention programs.

The narrative of the gang as an alternative family was endorsed by the gang's patrons and became the center of the gang's new public image, not least because it was easy to understand and did not indict the social system. The Hartford Housing Authority bought into this frame and hired Smurf to monitor violence in public housing, where much of the drug dealing and violence was happening. A Housing Authority official stated:

> Gangs are a family, protection. They take care of each other. If someone in the family died and needed a stone for a grave or to ship a body, they'd sell drugs to raise the money. If they only sold candy or did car washes, they'd be wonderful organizations.
>
> *(Radcliffe, 1998)*

The Solids received national media attention when CBS sent Dan Rather to Hartford for a story about the gang. The story focused on the gang's drugs sales and its image as a refuge for victimized youth. This elevated the gang's image as a new force in city life, and Smurf was booked to represent the gang in TV and radio interviews. In 1994, some of the Solids traveled to New York City to meet with leaders of the New York City Latin Kings, where they found ideological support for a more politicized future direction. Big Bird was especially enthralled with this development and said the Solids were now becoming a Puerto Rican resistance group. He said, "we used to be like the mafia, now we are like *Los Macheteros*. We're political." At this time, the Solids began a dialogue with factions of the Latin Kings and 20 Love about their shared problems and concerns. But this potential transformative event was undercut by imme-diate events related to more police aggression in the face of increased violence. The accidental killing of a seven-year old girl unleashed an aggressive anti-gang effort by the city and federal police. The hope that the Solids would move toward political transformation was foreclosed by the decisions of the leadership to move further underground until mass arrests decimated the leadership. The Solids fell apart in the fall of 1994. The top three leaders were "terminated" (expelled from the gang) and physically beaten by lower-ranking members. At the same time, a joint task force intercepted a call from the gang's "godfather" LB, suggesting that a civil war was underway, and this promptly led to the arrest of 17 Solids. After the arrests, the Solids fragmented into a dozen factions of mostly younger members.

The role of the pastoral state and the social welfare system at work

A core of service providers that worked with the Solids included the Urban League, the Capital Region Conference of Churches, Community Renewal Team, Hartford Workforce Development and the Capital Region Education Council (CREC). Their chief goal was to integrate the group into mainstream society. This assimilationist engagement was dominated by a Puerto Rican academic who created the Institute for Violence Reduction to work with the Solids to end intra-gang violence related to beat downs and infractions of gang rules and, later with Roberto and Carl, brokered a peace between the Solids and the Latin Kings. Three Solids, Smurf, Geanie, and Big Bird, were authorized by the leadership to work with supportive groups and individuals.

The Institute for Violence Reduction had the closest relationship with the gang leadership. The IVR produced a video made by members of the Solids and 20 Love called *From the Heart* to present their story of abandonment. As a way to counter negative publicity, IVR organized a speaker's bureau that sent gang members across the state to educate suburbanites about the gangs. IVR and the Solids organized a cleanup of the Frog Hollow neighborhood and rebuilt a derelict boat landing on the Connecticut River as gestures of good will to the community. The charismatic Smurf became the most prominent gang member in the media. His task was to explain the relationship of gang crime and alienation, and his personal story became the official story of gang member marginalization. He is the son of frequently incarcerated, drug-addicted and violent parents, and he and his older brother joined the Solids for survival. He skillfully built relationships with civic leaders, the news media and the chief of police to manage the gang's image and apologized for its crimes.

Education and business were the focus of the Solids' supporters. The IVR and CREC, the educational foundation, established an alternative school for gang members. These schools were envisioned with input from the Solids and 20 Love, and some found employment as "community coaches" to work the streets for participants and keep order at school. Later, the IVR taught gang members to write business plans to submit to lenders, but none did. Many Solids I knew were interested in job skills that would lead to jobs suitable for men. Laundry work was not what they wanted; they wanted jobs as welders and carpenters: the kind of work that was associated with the *jibaro*[2] ideal.

The schools became the hallmark of the Solids' attempt at assimilation. Gang leaders were hired as street-wise "community coaches" who would manage the participation of unruly gang members; however, the needs and daily problems of gang life made instruction difficult. For example, one day, a car full of Latin Kings drove in a threatening manner past the students waiting to enter the building, leading to a confrontation that caused the cancellation of the day's classes. Meanwhile, there were problems of drug use that were ignored by the coaches, with discipline a constant concern, as was the apparent lack of commitment to this type of schooling among many of the students. In addition, there was no consistency in the instruction provided, with students left on their own to work on lessons while the teachers often hid in the office. I sent college interns to these schools to help and did observations of their work, but it seemed that the interns did more with the students than the teachers. Most students (it was reported) left after being served lunch.[3]

The lead agency, CREC, hired a few teachers to teach basic courses leading to reentry into public school or the GED. The teachers and interns were unprepared for their students' needs and behaviors and did little to engage them. At least one was fired for incompetence. The schools operated for two years in several locations but did not achieve much. Super Dave, a high-ranking Solid, said there was elitism in these projects. To populate the project, it was decided that students who were not in gangs would be allowed to participate, and they drew most of the teacher's attention because they were working on structured programs for high school equivalency or to return to school after expulsion. The reality from my vantage point was that the gang's supporters and some gang members used the project to build their résumés and to find better jobs. An evaluation written by one of my interns (Smith, 1997) showed that the students thought the curriculum was not focused on their immediate employment needs and was built to conform to the skills of the teachers who could be hired for that particular job. There was unhappiness among many of the participants in the school because the programming was not focused on job skill development and did not address transportation and childcare needs. Despite the planning provided by the Solids, they were not involved in any process evaluations, with CREC making all decisions based on its needs.

Conclusion

New approaches to gangs recognize the ambiguous nature of opposition and resistance within gangs as well as gangs as local institutions. The vital importance of race and ethnicity as a core dynamic of gang formation is highlighted in the Hartford gang experience, along with the creation of an exclusionary public housing system. The prison experiences of gang members and the formation of prison gangs are relevant in understanding gang violence on the streets. There is a new appreciation of the interstitial nature of gangs that implicate spatial segregation, cultural domination and marginalization. Hartford politics and urban development centered on racial and ethnic segregation. The city created the structural foundation for gang formation by concentrating the poor in public housing with inadequate services. This spatial control is fundamentally implicated in gang formation. Gangs began to develop an ideological consciousness and forged relationships with other movements, for example, the Blackstone Rangers and Gangster Disciples in Chicago and the Latin Kings in New York City. The relationship between the Black Panthers and the Blackstone Rangers can be explored further to see where the line was drawn between gangs and political radicalism and how these types of organizations cooperate as well as cross-pollinate with ideas over space and time during their development.

Thoughtful transgressions and conscious attempts at direct action now characterize many gang ideologies. Opposition, resistance and transgressions serve to inform the gang's sense of agency. Acts of resistance by the Solids attempted meaningful opposition to authority in a political as well as cultural way. They used crime and intimidating transgressive public displays as their principal forms of resistance, but in the end, this was unproductive. The precarious life of the Solids made realizing their transformational collective activities an organizational impossibility. The leadership's response created a dualism in the gang, a violent drug faction and a reintegration faction, with each group working toward the *Solido* Achievement Plan.

The city of Hartford offers some insights about gang development, organization and functions in smaller cities with established neighborhoods. The overbearing role of community patrons was a significant factor in Hartford's response to the Solids. Those offering ideologies of liberal inclusion institutionalized the processes of Othering (Young, 2011). Their project proposals and outcome evaluations essentialize deviance and legitimatize the existing structures of moral, spatial and economic boundaries, offering only social reproduction. There was a synergy between the strategies of liberal inclusion offered by the social service complex that surrounded the Solids and their efforts to realize their achievement plan. This eventuated in the school and other projects but became exercises in self-pathologizing and loss of agency. The different relationships between gangs, radicalized residents and social service professionals' stand out as an important aspect of the Hartford gang experience.

The early gang experience in Hartford suggests that at one time, members had an open-ended understanding of their potential as political entities and oppositional movements. But the transformation of Hartford subcultures into criminal drug gangs in the 1980s interrupted this movement, as the adoption of carceral logics and the prison experiences of gang members created a more defensive worldview that moved to the streets and only increased the level of danger in gang life and in the community. Gang colors and styles, large rallies, media appearances and aggressive othering by the police and the media alienated the community from the Solids. Together, the rise of national gang identities and the appropriation of these identities by local movements led to increased fear and hyper-demonization in the media.

I argue that the Solids did not reject the hegemony of the pathological view but instead embraced it as the best option available. It was through the lens of the Puerto Rican experience of success that the Solids viewed their efforts for inclusion. I concluded that they were a self-centered, conservative movement focused on personal change, finding work and joining the community, with their opposition neither directed beyond their own troubles nor aimed at challenging power structures. The Solids, in understanding their situation, failed to appreciate Hartford's decline due to globalization and instead held onto the slim hope that self-improvement would lead to good jobs.

It is true that individual Solids did benefit from their work with social welfare patrons. The two most active Solids during the transformation, Geanie and Smurf, found paid work while in the gang and went on to develop successful careers in gang and violence prevention. Geanie moved to Washington, DC, and today works for a national community development organization, while Smurf is the founder and CEO of the Peace Center of Connecticut. However, the divisions within the Solids thwarted their attempts at order maintenance. Eventually, one of the main leaders, Big Bird, was convicted of manslaughter and tragically died soon after his release from prison. Essentially, the group's responses to address pressure from police investigations together with the efforts of their social service supporters to intervene only conspired to move the group's entrepreneurial aspects underground. In the end, having witnessed the group's evolution over more than a decade, I saw the most positive and promising members of the group adopt stances that in certain historical moments appeared to be forms of resistance but eventually only supported the social reproduction of their oppression. It was a lost opportunity for renewal, not unlike the contradictory journey of street gangs or street organizations that we have witnessed in other social contexts.

Notes

1 A similar dynamic can be seen in the evolution of the Los Angeles Bloods (see the documentary "Bastards of the Party").

2 A *jíbaro* is generally understood as a typical country-dwelling, self-subsistence farmer who was iconic in representing Puerto Rican culture and the importance of people's ties to the land and nature.
3 These observations are all based on my field research at the time.

References

American City Corporation. 1972. *The Greater Hartford Process*. American City Corporation. Columbia, MD.

Bourgois, Philippe. 1995. *In Search of Respect: Selling Crack in El Barrio*. Cambridge University Press. Cambridge.

Brotherton, David C. 2008. "Beyond Social Reproduction: Bringing Resistance Back in Gang Theory." *Theoretical Criminology*. Vol. 12, No. 1, pp. 55–77.

Brotherton, David C. and Luis Barrios. 2004. *The Almighty Latin King and Queen Nation: Street Politics and the Transformation of a New York City Gang*. Columbia University Press. New York.

Close, Stacy. 2001. "Fire in the Bones: Hartford's NAACP, Civil Rights and Militancy, 1943–1969." *Journal of Negro History*. Vol. 86, No. 3 (Summer), pp. 228–263.

Close, Stacy. 2013. "Southern Blacks Transform Connecticut." *Connecticut Explored*. Fall. www.ctexplored.org/southern-blacks-transform-connecticut/

Cohen, Albert. 1955. *Delinquent Boys: The Culture of the Gang*. Free Press. New York.

Coughlin, Brenda C. and Sudhir Alladi Venkatesh. 2003. "The Urban Street Gang After 1970." *Annual Review of Sociology*. Vol. 29, pp. 41–64.

Cruz, José E. 1998. "A Decade of Change: Puerto Rican Politics in Hartford, 1969–1979." *Journal of American Ethnic History* (Spring), pp. 45–80.

Dawley, David. 1992. *A Nation of Lords*. Waveland Press. Long Grove, IL.

Fernandez, Maritza. 2018. "Hartford, Connecticut Riot (1969)." *Black Past*. March 1, 2018. www.blackpast.org/african-american-history/hartford-connecticut-riot-1969/.

Hagedorn, John M. 2007. "Gangs, Institutions, Race and Space: The Chicago School Revisited." Pp. 13–33 in *Gangs in the Global City*. Edited by John M. Hagedorn. University of Illinois Press. Urbana and Chicago.

The Hartford Courant. 2009. "Police: Gangs in Schools." October 16.

Hartford Public Library. 2014. *Butch Lewis Video Collection Documenting Civil Rights Era, Hartford*. Hartford History Center.

LB. *Los Solido Handbook (written by LB)*. No date.

Jankowski, Martin. 2003. "Gangs and Social Change." *Theoretical Criminology*. Vol. 7m, (May), pp. 191–216.

Molotch, Harvey. 1976. "The City as a Growth Machine: Toward a Political Economy of Place." *American Journal of Sociology*. Vol. 82, No. 2 (September), pp. 309–332.

Nieves, Evelyn. 1994. "Hartford Becomes A Test Case in Fighting Menace of Gangs." *New York Times*, December 26.

Padilla, Felix. 1992. *The Gang as an American Enterprise*. Rutgers University Press. New Brunswick, NJ.

Radcliffe, David. 1998. *Charter Oak Terrace: Life, Death and Rebirth of a Public Housing Project*. Southside Media, Hartford, CT.

Smith, Laura. 1997. *Evaluation: Hartford Neighborhood Learning Centers*. Department of Sociology. University of Hartford. Unpublished.

Thrasher, Fredric M. 1927. *The Gang: A Study of 1,313 Gangs in Chicago*. University of Chicago Press. Chicago.

Unknown. 1994. "Statement on The Solids." Unpublished Essay in Possession of the Author.

Vigil, James. 1988. *Barrio Gangs: Street Life and Identity in Southern California*. University of Texas Press. Austin.

Wacquant, Loic. 2007. "Three Pernicious Premises in the Study of the American Ghetto." Pp. 34–53 in *Gangs in the Global City*. Edited by John M. Hagedorn. University of Illinois Press. Urbana and Chicago.

Yablonsky, Lewis. 1959. "The Delinquent Gang as a Near Group." *Social Problems*. Vol. 7, No. 2, pp. 108–117.

Young, Jock. 2011. *The Criminological Imagination*. Polity Press. Cambridge, Oxford, Boston and New York.

Part IV
Global case studies

19

The war on gangs and gangsters

The Latino/a experience with settler colonialism

Robert J. Durán and Jason A. Campos

The gang literature has primarily framed gang members as more criminal, delinquent, drug involved, risk involved, and violent than non-gang members (Klein and Maxson 2006; Maxson et al. 2014; Thornberry 1998; Valdez 2007). These "facts" were even considered "one of the most robust and consistent observations in criminological research" (Thornberry 1998, p. 147). After receiving such a dangerous appraisal by researchers, we may then ask, who are these gang members? Why are they considered so dangerous? According to the National Gang Center's (NGC 2018) National Youth Gang Survey, the largest proportion of gang members based on law enforcement reports were Latino from 1996 to 2011. Law enforcement officers reported that 46.2% of the estimated 782,5000 gang members were Latino, followed by 35.3% of Blacks, 11.5% of Whites, and 7% other. Moreover, it was estimated 92% to 94% of gang members were male. Conversely, these numbers differed from population estimates offered by the United States Census Bureau (2019), which have Latinos at 18.5% of the population, Blacks at 13.4%, and Non-Hispanic Whites at 60.1%. The NGC numbers differ from several surveys, which have found a greater proportion of Whites and females in gangs (Esbensen and Winfree 1998; Estrada et al. 2014). The racialized image of gangs has coincided with minority group threats and moral panics (Chavez 2013; Cohen 1972; Jackson 1992; McCorkle and Miethe 2002; Shelden, Tracy, and Brown 2001). Jackson (1992) defines minority group threat as the mobilization of policing resources during a fear of crime and fear of a loss of dominance by the majority group. Thus, the civil rights movement and racial unrest encouraged the White majority to perceive this advocacy for improved treatment and inclusion as provoking hostility. Cohen (1972) defined moral panics as a disjuncture between a perceived and real threat. Moreover, Chavez (2013) explains in his concept of Latino Threat how Latinos have been socially constructed as a threat to US interests. Socially constructing paranoia sparks fear in the general public and provides a racialized ideology that allows public officials to increasingly push for policies and practices that institutionalize second-class citizenship for Latinos and Blacks (Bonilla-Silva 2018; Durán 2013; Lopez-Aguado 2018; Rios 2011; Romero 2001).

The racialized ideology for each historical time period has been reflective of its leadership. In the United States, the 73-year-old president, Donald J. Trump, has been verbally and institutionally attacking the Latino community, specifically those of Mexican origin. During his 2015 presidential announcement, Trump addressed the nation to reiterate the dangers that illegal immigration posed on society by claiming that the root of criminal activity on American soil lies in undocumented chain migration from Mexico. His speech, televised on every major news network, was embedded with false precautionary messages and stereotypes of Latino/a immigrants as criminals. He claimed Mexican nationals and their government were not "sending their best" in the waves of migrants crossing the international border. He furthered his argument by stating Mexican immigrants were drug dealers and "rapists" who have decided to settle in the United States. The narrative centered on elevating immigration as the most important US problem has become increasingly popular based on political rhetoric (The Associated Press-NORC Center for Public Affairs Research 2018; Chavez 2013). Latinos from El Salvador, Guatemala, and Honduras have encountered numerous difficulties in seeking asylum in the United States, and many of these men, women, and children have been held at federal immigration detention centers. MS-13, a gang formed in Los Angeles by Salvadoran immigrants and then, due to deportation, relocated to El Salvador (Ward 2013), has also been a popular target for Trump to incite fear. The combined propaganda of "threat" and "invasion" were used to manufacture a national emergency declaration to "build a wall" between the United States and Mexico. Prior to Trump's presidency, several scholars had already reported the US-Mexico border as a militarized zone based on the numbers of border patrol, unmanned planes, technology, and fences that continued to maintain the greatest economic divide between two countries (Andreas 2000; Dunn 1996; Heyman 2008; Massey, Durand, and Malone 2002). Residents of the US territory Puerto Rico lacked national support after Hurricane Maria in 2017. Although Trump falls in line with much of the confrontational approaches to the politically constructed US-Mexico border and the hostile policies and practices against Latinos (Chavez 2013; Meier and Ribera 1996; Navarro 2005), he has intensified a level of rhetoric and propaganda that has not been seen since the reign of the Ku Klux Klan in the 1920s (McVeigh and Estep 2019). Trump's racial ideology was put into action when a White man drove 10 hours to the city of El Paso to kill "Mexicans." Since 2014, border enforcement alongside minority group threats and moral panics have resulted in a deadly combination specifically targeting Latinos/as.

This chapter highlights how the term "Latino/a gang" has become politicized and criminalized to the point to where the focus is not gangs per se but rather Latinos as a racialized ethnic group targeted for elimination. The fear of Latinos, socially constructed historically and maintained through contemporary myths, allows for sustained moral panics regarding a changing society (Chavez 2013), a change brought about by demographic fluctuations involving an undercounted population, an overall younger average age, higher birthrates, and higher rates of immigration compared to the White majority, which has become older, has fewer children, and receives lower levels of immigrants compared to the past (Vespa, Armstrong, and Medina 2018). These narratives have placed Latinos at the margins of society in the way they were permanently labeled with a foreign status despite living in a country where the border had shifted 500,000 square miles after the US-Mexican War. Incorporating a broader array of the scholarly literature, one which merges the inclusion of race and ethnicity with the topic of gangs, allows for an opportunity to develop a more nuanced understanding of the reasons for Latino/a gang origination, belonging, and activities and the importance of cultivating grassroots forms of resistance to state control. Brotherton (2015) emphasized the symbolic Othering of gangs and gang members as part of various moral crusades against poor and minority communities to maintain social and class domination

Sociologist Patricia Hill Collins (2000) emphasized the value of subordinate groups creating knowledge that fostered both empowerment and social justice. She provided a compelling argument for the uniqueness of the standpoint of Black women. Thus, the authors of this chapter also believe in the value of standpoint for situating an analysis of the experience of Latinos and gangs. By incorporating storytelling, advocated by critical race theory (Bell 1992; Delgado and Stefancic 2017), the authors situate their backgrounds and how they first came to learn about gangs:

> As a young teenager, the first author, Durán, was captivated by movies such as American Me, Blood In, Blood Out, Mi Familia, and Mi Vida Loca. In the small sized city of Ogden, Utah, the Mexican American population and increasing immigrant population from Mexico lacked representation in professional occupations. Most social institutions were White dominated with the exception of gangs: a historical institution created in response to local discrimination. After initiation into a gang, Durán felt a sense of comradery. He and his friends dressed cool, drove cool cars, spoke cool slang, and marked themselves with tattoos. Homies stuck up for one another and became closer through opposition with the police, rival gangs, cowboys, and overall White institutions. Public officials demonized gangs in the community and over time, arrests, jail, incarceration, and deportation altered these young lives to have less opportunities than their White peers.

The question became, were gangs the problem or the level of social inequality established and maintained by the state? Eleven years later, the second author was a product of similar circumstances:

> Growing up in public government housing, Campos, the second author, gained and fostered an insider perspective on gang life, crime, and the ramifications of what occurs when these two worlds collide. Gang traditions offered protection, respect, and social capital that carried weight in a society that did not value the way the culture or language was practiced at home. Police sirens were all too common in the lives of Brown and Black youth in the Santa Maria Valley, and seeing friend and relative lives taken due to gang affiliation, immigration status, or simply the vilification of residing in these communities became a reoccurring theme. Over time, these odds become unbeatable, and making use of communal resources resulted in outside consequences. The perils of being brown, resisting, and growing up in the era of mass incarceration fueled the misinformed narratives of what really occurs when confined to these spaces of exclusion.

The authors' stories situate the theoretical angle utilized in the writing of this chapter: settler colonialism. Historian Kelly Hernández (2017), in her book City of Inmates, described settler colonialism as different from colonialism because it was not organized around resource extraction or labor exploitation but primarily on acquiring land and working to remove indigenous populations. Even indigenous labor was never expected to provide full inclusion into society. Glenn (2015) emphasized how it was important to recognize settler colonialism as an ongoing structure rather than a past historical event for analyzing US race and gender formation. Glenn described how Mexicans primarily experienced four types of control: "(a) containment (separation and segregation), (b) erasure (cultural assimilation), (c) terrorism (violence, lynching), and (d) removal (expulsion, deportation)" (p. 62). Thus, the stories of Durán and Campos reflect the lives of many Latino youth growing up in the Southwest where there was never a nationwide plan for inclusion. It is towards this exclusion that the authors work to explain the process of linking gangs and Latinos to justify the conquest of indigenous lands.

Socially constructing a fear of gangs and Latinos

Although reasons for the origination of Latino gangs in Denver, El Paso, Los Angeles, and San Antonio have been covered by previous research studies (Durán 2013, 2018; Moore 1978; Tapia 2017; Vigil 1988), the predominant description of gangs of the 1920s to 1940s was marked by Eastern European ancestry and the struggle for residents to fit into an unwelcoming society (Thrasher 1927; Whyte 1943). In contrast, several gang researchers have emphasized how the response to gangs, in particular Latino gangs, has been driven by fear and the use of media by officials to enhance panic in the general public (Durán 2013, 2018; Mirandé 1987; Moore 1978; Romero 2001; Vigil 1988; Zatz 1987). Sociologist Alfredo Mirandé (1987) stated the view of Chicanos as criminals has its origins in the bandido image of the 19th century, but it was not until the 1940s that it began to be associated with youth gangs and drugs. In the early 1940s, the general public increased its negative images of first- and second-generation Mexican Americans whose parents migrated to the United States to answer the call for the country's growing labor demand in agriculture and the service sector. Soldiers of Mexican descent were dying on the battlefields at the height of World War II, while their younger brothers at home were being targeted and labeled as criminal gang members. Alarmist concerns regarding their flamboyant style became a major highlight as *pachucos* began to fashion their long-tailed coats and tailored baggy slacks. In 1943, a violent confrontation between *pachucos* and American soldiers on military leave started what later became known as the "zoot suit riots" (Escobar 1999; McWilliams 1948). This event increased police targeting, roundups, and discriminatory policies to make young Latinos and Latinas conform in mainstream society and maintain the expectation to remain hidden from public view (Durán 2013, 2018; Escobar 1999; Moore 1978).

Sociologist Marjorie Zatz (1987) reported how the image of gangs, especially those who identified as Chicano, became targets for organizations (i.e. the media, courts, and law enforcement) to secure funding for specialized functions that worked in their own interest. Zatz stated, "I suggest that the *social imagery* of Chicano youth gangs, rather than their actual *behavior*, lay at the root of the 'gang problem' in Phoenix" (p. 130). Zatz documented how Mexican and Chicano gangs were labeled as "different" from other gangs, and their perceived growth was a cause for alarmist concern: a "moral panic" version of "social dynamite" that could explode at any minute. However, she found that the police department's assessment of the city's "gang problem" could not be supported empirically. Law enforcement officials had estimated that the number of gangs in Phoenix went from 5 or 6 in 1978 to 35 gangs in 18 months. Three months later, those 35 gangs became 50 or 60 and later jumped to somewhere between 100 and 120. According to these findings by police officials, that would mean that one quarter of Phoenix's Spanish-origin males were identified by police as gang members. A general conclusion from the increasing number of gangs included a perception of increased levels of crime. However, Zatz found incidents of violent crime in Phoenix only increased slightly in the late 1970s and then decreased in the early 1980s. To further her argument, it was determined that there were conflicting views from police officers, social workers, and city residents. Each group had different definitions of gangs and the seriousness of the issue. Court documents also countered the claim regarding an increase in gang membership and criminality. She suggested that the socially accepted stereotypical characteristics of Chicano youth gangs were at the root of this moral panic but that it was also tied to national law-and-order campaigns targeting youthful offenders, rising nationalism, and xenophobia.

From the 1940s to the 21st century, vilified conceptions of gangs continued. In 2001, sociologist Mary Romero stated, "The most widely distributed representation of Latino youth today is as a gang member" (p. 1095). She explored how the construction of Latino criminality justified and obscured the history of state violence against Mexican Americans. No matter what portrayal was used by media and public officials over the last 150 years, bandit to gang member, the end result was always one of a criminal. Concerns regarding a rising Latino threat were evident in several additional cities for which researchers recognized a presence of gangs but a level of involvement and illegal activity far less than what was alleged by law enforcement officials (Durán 2013, 2018; McCorkle and Miethe 2002). Criminologist Jodi Lane (2002) conducted focus groups with White and Latino residents in six different neighborhoods in Santa Ana, California. She reported how respondents stated a belief in recent Latinos being culturally different from Whites and long-term Mexican and Mexican American residents. These respondents reported how new Latinos were bringing negative changes to the community. Middle- and upper-income White residents reported a fear of gangs and Latinos encroaching into their neighborhoods, but they used their social capital to work with city officials. Latino respondents primarily lived in lower-income neighborhoods, and they too reported fear but took precautions to prevent victimization. Lane described how residents shared a similar belief regarding the environmental causes of their fears, yet neither group lived in neighborhoods where gang crime was a serious threat. She emphasized how such fears may be more reflective of the collateral consequences of the media and public officials to pursue more punishment-oriented policies reflective of a moral panic.

The state's use of gangs to enhance criminalization

Moral panics have not remained dormant without an outlet. Public officials have utilized social constructions of fear regarding gangs and Latinos to create new legislation and policies to target gangs, gang members, and perceived associates. These tactics began with the creation of specialized gang units that aggressively targeted perceived gangs and gang members with an increased level of community-police contact. In addition to suppression, gang units gathered "intelligence" composed of creating a list of suspected gang members. As documented by the National Gang Center, law enforcement perceptions of gang members primarily included Latino and Black residents. These lists were created during police stops with suspected gang members, seizures of property (i.e., pictures, notebooks, clothing, etc.), and even monitoring social media. Officers then utilized a gang evaluation form where a simple collection of points could easily convert individuals from higher-crime neighborhoods, peer groups, and families into validated gang members. Residents listed as gang members remained in a database for at least five years to indefinitely, and getting on this list never required a delinquent act or crime (Baker 2013; Durán 2013, 2018). Determining gang membership did not require alerting an individual of the entry into the gang database, and there was no adversarial process to provide any form of critique to the officers' decision-making in reaching this conclusion. These lists were later used for gang injunctions; vertical prosecution; gang enhancements; and the increased monitoring of suspected gang members in schools, probation, and incarceration (Durán 2013; Lopez-Aguado 2018; Rios 2017).

Criminologist Mike Tapia (2011a) analyzed the National Longitudinal Survey of Youth, which surveyed 3,881 youth between the ages of 12 to 18 years of age and found gang membership increased the levels of arrest for youth, regardless of socioeconomic status. Utilizing the same data set, Tapia (2011b) found support for undue arrest risk experienced by Blacks and Hispanics, much greater than what was experienced by Whites who were not in gangs and those who were in gangs. Complicating the already active involvement of law enforcement officers maintained with monitoring gang members, gang injunctions made it possible to arrest labeled gang members for non-criminal behavior such as being out past curfew or associating with other labeled gang members, including family members (Baker 2013; Barajas 2007). Barajas' (2007) examination of a gang injunction in Oxnard, California, compared such tactics to an invading army. As a historian, he noted the historic marginalization of Chicanas/os within this community as early as 1900. The injunction symbolized to many residents a level of privileged adjacency wherein gangs were targeted in areas with goals toward real estate development and revitalization to bring in more affluent residents. Baker (2013) critiqued a gang injunction later found unconstitutional in Ogden, Utah, on several grounds: removal of due process, rights to assemble and associate with family members, and being overly vague and open to excessive interpretation. She questioned the practice of criminalizing lawful activity in an effort to decrease crime and how instead this injunction created artificial crime and a false sense of security for residents. Baker reported, "Violating the rights of persons who have not been convicted of a crime is an unacceptable answer to the gang problem" (p. 257).

Although there remains a scholarly established critique of law enforcement practices involving gangs, the courts do not appear to be a panacea for justice. The adversarial process of prosecution and defense often experiences a level of difficulties leading the courtroom work group to simply push cases through regardless of innocence or guilt (Van Cleve 2016). In gang cases, merged with heightened stigmatization, it was often difficult to shake these images for jurors or to sway the opinions established by law enforcement gang experts (Hagedorn and MacLean 2012; Klein 2004; Rios and Navarro 2010). Additional themes such as the abuse of rights deserve increased study in the targeting of gangs with immigration enforcement and the lack of due process in addition to the experiences of jail and prison inmates during incarceration (Kassel 2003).

Malcolm Klein (2004), a researcher who had studied gangs for 40 years, cautioned about the approach of primarily responding to gangs with suppression because there was a disjuncture between perception and actual research evidence. Although Klein did not use the concept of moral panic, his description fits that definition. He emphasized the importance of recognizing that most gang crime is minor, most gang activity is noncriminal, gangs are social groups, street life becomes a part of a gang culture, and understanding gangs requires insight into the neighborhood or community context. Gang crime primarily involved drinking, graffiti, loitering, and petty theft.

Gangs as institutions cultivating resistance

A critical problem with the gang literature is aligning gangs as synonymous with crime. Even the topic of leaving gangs has become consumed by a literature focusing on crime desistance (Carson and Vecchio 2015; Pyrooz and Decker 2011; Pyrooz, Decker, and Webb 2014). Most studies of gangs have not viewed gangs from the lens of settler colonialism to the point where the state has secured power for a foreign population which has primarily sought to conquer and eliminate indigenous groups. The United States has formalized whiteness as foundational since the beginning of its existence and then maintained exclusion, elimination, and second-class status for people of color (Feagin 2013; Hernández 2017). Most researchers will remain colorblind in making any connection to the problems inherent in gang research involving White researchers and Black and Brown gang members and their obsession with criminality (Bonilla-Silva 2018). In the traditional "gangs as criminal" view, leaving gangs results in reducing the level of criminal offending, but very little of the research literature has explored how leaving gangs does not remove state violence, the slow dehumanizing process of second-class treatment, and actions leading to the genocide of Black and Brown people.

According to the historian Robert Rosenbaum (1981), after conquest, Mexicanos responded with four basic tactics: withdrawal, accommodation, assimilation, and resistance. The response selected was often based on efforts of self-preservation that included physical survival, an attempt to preserve a traditional way of life, and adapting to a new way of living while attempting to hold onto some traditions. As rural Mexicanos began adapting to increasingly urbanized areas such as Albuquerque, Denver, El Paso, Los Angeles, and San Antonio, it required new forms of self-protection. From the 1920s to the 1990s, gangs became one source of refuge for a Latino population stigmatized for elimination (Durán 2013, 2018; Moore 1978; Tapia 2017; Vigil 1988). For inclusion purposes, some Mexican American organizations and leaders were pursuing full political integration by using an ideology based on proving whiteness (Haney López 2003). The success of such assimilation and accommodation usually benefitted those higher in socio-economic class. The lower economic and service class had to pursue different options. The gang became one form of resistance to settler colonialism, yet members often moved towards other types of adaptations over time, as highlighted in Figure 19.1.

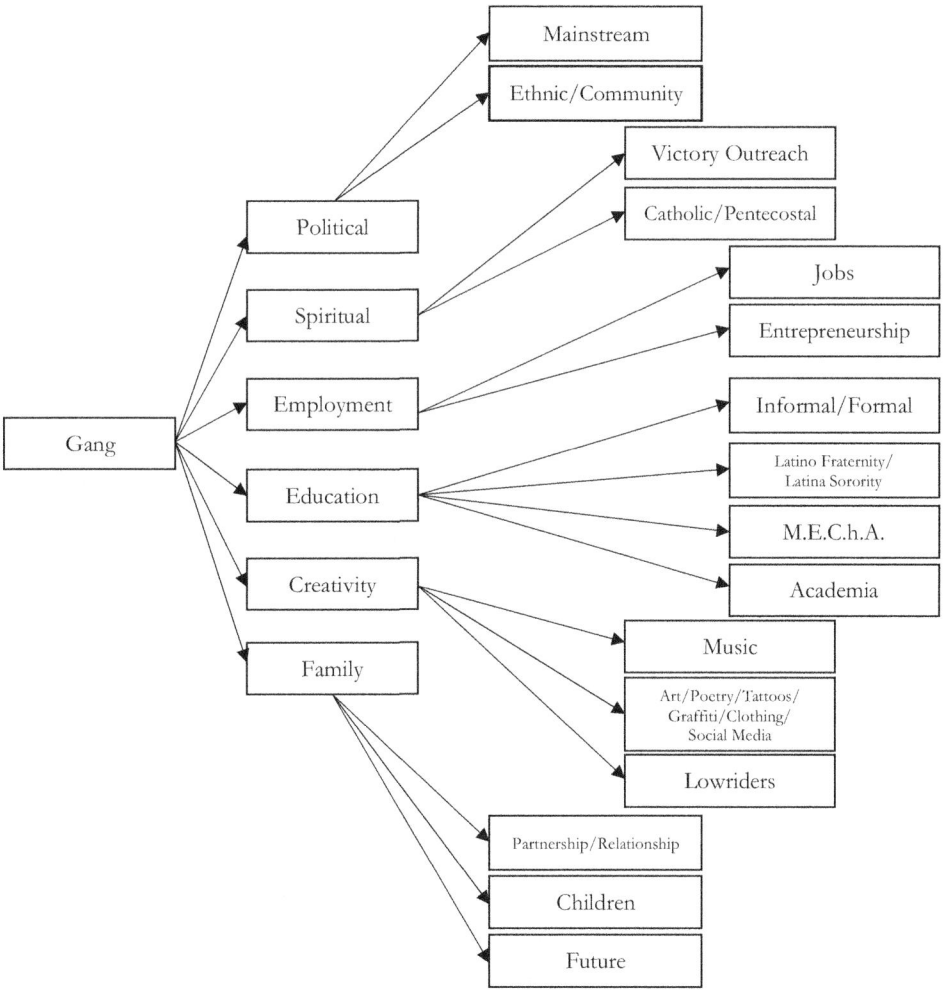

Figure 19.1 A diagrammed example of gangster adaptations of resistance. Note that each of these pathways is an individual avenue that gang members have taken. While these are the current adaptations that have been documented, alternative adaptations are developing and being incorporated into the literature on resistance.

As highlighted by Figure 19.1, the gang can provide an organizing consciousness that can be helpful to a wide variety of other social institutions. We primarily explored how the gang contributed to creativity, education, employment, family, political, and spiritual institutions of resistance. These categories are not exhaustive or mutually exclusive, and the categories below demonstrate a lot of overlap, but they do provide an opportunity to move beyond explanations of crime desistance and a perception of failure for members who leave behind their active level of gang involvement. Instead of thinking about reducing levels of criminal involvement, let's think about ways Latino residents survived attempts to deport, incarcerate, and eliminate their existence from the United States. We begin by reviewing the gangster adaptations of resistance covered more thoroughly in the literature and then move to less developed adaptations.

Political forms of resistance as a result of gangs were focused on becoming a part of traditional Democratic or Republican parties or aligning themselves with community-created organizations. According to political scientist Armando Navarro (2005), strategies of resistance were reflected in various time periods. Navarro grouped these time periods from 1848 to 2003. Of these time periods, probably the time frame called "The Epoch of Militant Protest Politics (1966–1974)" was the most reflective of how Chicano/a mobilization began incorporating previously gang-involved young men and women. In the 1960s, militant groups such as the Black and Brown Berets were created to fight discrimination against Chicanas/os while remaining politically active in their formation. These were among the first grassroots coalitions to draw in former gang members to challenge discrimination in schools and law enforcement (Vigil 1999). Montejano (2010) found that from the mid-1950s to the mid-1960s, gang warfare had broken out in San Antonio's neighborhoods every two years, but starting in 1969, such incidents ceased for nearly a decade due to the activities of the Chicano Movement. A similar finding was reported by Vigil (1999) in Denver. Flood (2003) reported how the Latin Kings and Queens began as an informal social club in Chicago during the late 1940s with the goal of helping ease the transition of Puerto Ricans migrating to the mainland. The goal was to offer protection against racial violence and police suppression. It was noted that the Latin King social movement spread into the Mexican barrios of Chicago through aligning socio-political views which had their theoretical underpinning in building community coalitions towards an activist pathology.

Sociologist Alfredo Mirandé's (1987) chapter titled "Gangs or Barrio Warriors?", in his book *Gringo Justice*, critiques the gang literature focusing on Chicano youth and how it reinforced an image of Chicanos as criminal or deviant and blamed this population for their own subordination. Instead of cultivating this perspective, Mirandé pointed out some of the positive functions of neighborhood-based groups involving "barrios" and "homeboys." Key was the opportunity to build on street organizing and re-organize these efforts into political activism.

Esteva Martínez (2003) documented the journey of gang member street activists in Los Angeles: from a reckless underclass to politically engaged agents of social change. Based on interviews and participant observations conducted by the author and members of the Street Organization Project, they found that gang activists were successful at coalescing with other leaders in the broader community due to their previous roles in the gang and respect earned from the host community. In turn, this produced greater results for the group overall. Much of what urban street activism worked to develop was political consciousness among its membership, stressing the link between global capitalism and the criminalization of youth. Ironically, many gang activists had their first experiences as activists in prison, suggesting that the spillover of a past carceral identity helped to conjure up the necessary knowledge to navigate a turbulent climate. Thus, street activists, often with gang, drug, criminal, and prison histories, developed a level of cultural capital not available to traditional experts (Durán 2013; Flores 2018; Lopez-Aguado 2012; Moore 1978).

Ethnographic fieldwork has documented how some local coalitions in two southwestern cities dedicated a portion of their time to record the interactions between police and civilian contacts (Durán 2013). The goal of the group was to ensure that the rights of citizens were not being violated, as well as capturing the current state of differential policing among Black, Brown, and White residents. Many of these activist groups become successful at gaining traction as advocates for their respective communities. Although these organizations were working to equip gang members with skill-based learning and other self-help programs, they also functioned as centers of transformation for many repatriated gang members and ex-convicts (Durán 2013; Flores 2018; Lopez-Aguado 2012).

Spiritual forms of resistance went beyond traditional versions of religion as highlighted in the work of David C. Brotherton, Luis Barrios, and Ed Flores. Sociologist David C. Brotherton and psychologist Luis Barrios's (2004) research on the Almighty Latin King and Queen Nation in New York City indicated how gang members developed a collective identity based on the Latinization of identity, identity and hope, and identity of the spirit. These identities helped members to challenge colonial subjugation and work to socially transform the gang into a street organization that could help provide for the needs of its members who also encounter external and internal adversaries. Despite such social transformation among members, the street organization continued to experience high levels of criminal justice oversight in the life of its members and leadership. Flores's (2018) study of ex-gang members and prisoners in Los Angeles and Chicago described efforts to reintegrate "felons" back into society upon release, but they were consistently denied jobs. The ex-prisoners and former gang members began working with faith-based organizations to change legislation and employer policies that restricted certain occupations from hiring felons. These efforts helped to transform members' stigmatized identities into a more socially accepted and admired role of community organizers.

Although using spirituality as a framework for all his devotion to the community, Father Greg Boyle and Homeboy Industries reflect the importance of obtaining employment. For example, when their motto states "Nothing Stops a Bullet Like a Job." Book publications about (Fremon 1995) and by Father Gregory Boyle (2010) highlight the importance of having the opportunity to work and obtaining money legitimately as an important pathway for staying away from crime and gang involvement.

Although the dismal rates of formal education have been noted in previous research (Pyrooz 2014), less explored has been the importance given by community members, including current and former gang members, to believing in education as a strategy for giving back and advocating on behalf of the community. David C. Brotherton's (2003) research on the Almighty Latin King and Queen Nation and the Asociación Ñeta for a period of three years (1997–2000) found a commitment to education to help develop consciousness. These groups endorsed formal and informal education to transform themselves socially, spiritually, and intellectually; to lead productive lives and become role models; and to continually develop the organization towards social upliftment. Although the number of current or former gang members who have since become doctoral trained researchers remains small, these individuals continue to play an important role in changing how society thinks about gangs and gang members.

Two additional forms of resistance were cultivated by gang membership and have been less explored (i.e., creativity, and family) but continue to serve as important markers for future researchers and community groups working to provide alternatives to gangs. Creativity exists in various forms, including but not limited to art; music; poetry; and social clubs built on modes of transportation such as lowriders, motorcycles, and other customized vehicles. The creative side of gang life has also been one of the most targeted and criminalized aspects of gangs, as it has provided authority figures a visual and symbolic target to pursue. Such a pattern of targeting and criminalization has existed since the zoot suit riots. However, cultural expression allows members and former members an outlet and a way to express culture, identity, history, neighborhood, and sense of self in a way that often goes beyond what can be spoken in words. Finally, the importance of family in the Latina/o culture extends to non-gang and gang members alike. The major difference for gang members compared to non-gang members probably entails a sense of understanding that life and the lived moment can be short due to all the negative structural outcomes, including death, deportation, and incarceration. Rather than a sense of fatalism, it becomes a way to survive and strategize into the future. Previous research has found both gang-involved mothers and fathers have been impacted by parenthood and for looking at pathways of resistance that need to go beyond a traditional gang.

Conclusion

Creating an ideology of fear for the Latino/a population developed from the settler colonialism model of elimination of the indigenous population. In the process, a White foreign population adopted a White racial frame, creating a belief of being rightful heirs to North America based on the divine sanctions of manifest destiny (Feagin 2013; Navarro 2005). Despite Native American genocide, the colonizing countries such as Spain, Portugal, and France were unable to eliminate indigenous populations, as they were using them for resource extraction and labor. The United States' history and experience with colonization, however, has been different wherein the Mexican, Mexican American, and Latin American populations struggle to exist in a space where the colonizing group has no intention of leaving (Glenn 2015; Hernández 2017).

As Latinos have become the largest numerical minority group, Donald Trump, the former president of the United States, has realized his motto of "Make America Great Again" cannot occur when the mestizo population remains a counter-historical presence against such propaganda. Trump's targeting of gangs, immigrants, and criminals allowed for a level of fear to generate wherein the vilification of the most marginalized in society allowed for the demonization of an entire population of Latinos. According to the Bureau of Justice Statistics, we have begun to witness major changes in federal law enforcement. Immigration has become the primary offense for arrest and incarceration. Non-citizens have become arrested more than citizens. Deportations have increased. Latinos/as have become the racialized group arrested more frequently, even more than the majority group (Whites) in this country. The media upholds the distancing of Latinos and posits them as being a threat to the nation due to the reproduction of media imagery, citizenship discourse, and long practice of excluding foreigners from becoming part of the country. The ramifications of these notions have given way for new stereotypes of Latinos to emerge: unwilling to assimilate, politically inactive, and dependent on government benefits (Chavez 2013). It has become more difficult for Latinos – citizens and immigrants alike – to evade the objectifying force that these tactics employ.

Gangs have been maintained as but one additional form of vilification for the Latino/a community. In the eyes of the state, resistance to elimination requires enhanced punishment and social control. In such a climate, groups cannot organize to protect family and friends from violent victimization. Gangs can be used to incite moral panics and minority group threats that legitimize the targeting of entire Latino/a communities for enhanced oversight, criminalization, and exclusion from constitutional rights. Despite the negative stigma attached to gangs and gang members, activists should realize the importance of one of the most marginalized organizations in our society that has already decided they are willing to give everything to survive settler colonialism. The authors of this chapter have defied many statistical odds to have the opportunity to write this chapter. They have grown up during a period of US history where to be a Latino is to experience heightened tactics for criminalization. Defying these odds, the authors now have the responsibility of exposing settler colonialism and cultivating a level of resistance found in decolonizing, or at the least supporting, efforts to change these structural conditions.

References

Andreas, Peter. 2000. *Border Games: Policing the U.S.–Mexico Divide*. Ithaca, NY: Cornell University Press.

The Associated Press-NORC Center for Public Affairs Research. 2018. "2019: The Public's Priorities and Expectations." Retrieved December 27, 2018 (www.apnorc.org/projects/Pages/2019-The-Public%27s-Priorities-and-Expectations.aspx).

Baker, Megan K. 2013. "Removing the Presumption of Innocence: A Constitutional Analysis of the Ogden Trece Gang Injunction." *Utah Law Review OnLaw* 22:240–257.

Barajas, Frank P. 2007. "An Invading Army: A Civil Gang Injunction in a Southern California Chicana/o Community." *Latino Studies* 5:393–417.

Bell, Derrick. 1992. *Faces at the Bottom of the Well: The Permanence of Racism*. New York: Basic Books.

Bonilla-Silva, Eduardo. 2018. *Racism without Racists: Color-Blind Racism and the Persistence of Racial Inequality in America*. New York: Rowman and Littlefield.

Boyle, Gregory. 2010. *Tattoos on the Heart: The Power of Boundless Compassion*. New York: Free Press.

Brotherton, David C. 2003. "Education in the Reform of Street Organizations in New York City." Pp. 136–157 in *Gangs and Society: Alternative Perspectives*, edited by L. Kontos, D. Brotherton, and L. Barrios. New York: Columbia University Press.

Brotherton, David C. 2015. *Youth Street Gangs: A Critical Appraisal*. New York: Routledge.

Brotherton, David C. and Luis Barrios. 2004. *The Almighty Latin King and Queen Nation: Street Politics and the Transformation of a New York City Gang*. New York: Columbia University Press.

Carson, Dena C. and J. Michael Vecchio. 2015. "Leaving the Gang: A Review and Thoughts on Future Research." Pp. 257–275 in *The Handbook of Gangs*, edited by S. H. Decker and D. C. Pyrooz. Malden, MA: John Wiley & Sons.

Chavez, Leo R. 2013. *The Latino Threat: Constructing Immigrants, Citizens, and the Nation*. Stanford, CA: Stanford University Press.

Cohen, Stanley. [1972] 2002. *Folk Devils and Moral Panics*. New York: Routledge.

Collins, Patricia Hill. 2000. *Black Feminist Thought: Knowledge, Consciousness, and the Politics of Empowerment*. New York: Routledge.

Delgado, Richard, and Jean Stefancic. [2001] 2017. *Critical Race Theory: An Introduction*. New York: New York University Press.

Dunn, Timothy J. 1996. *The Militarization of the U.S.-Mexico Border 1978–1992: Low-Intensity Conflict Doctrine Comes Home*. Austin, TX: University of Texas Press.

Durán, Robert J. 2013. *Gang Life in Two Cities: An Insider's Journey*. New York: Columbia University Press.

Durán, Robert J. 2018. *The Gang Paradox: Inequalities and Miracles on the U.S.-Mexico Border*. New York: Columbia University Press.

Esbensen, Finn-Aage and L. Tom Winfree. 1998. "Race and Gender Differences Between Gang and Non-gang Youths: Results from a Multisite Survey." *Justice Quarterly* 15(3):505–526.

Escobar, Edward J. 1999. *Race, Police, and the Making of a Political Identity: Mexican Americans and the Los Angeles Police Department 1900–1945*. Los Angeles: University of California Press.

Esteva Martínez, Juan Francisco. 2003. "Urban Street Activists: Gang and Community Efforts to Bring Peace and Justice to Los Angeles Neighborhoods." Pp. 95–115 in *Gangs and Society: Alternative Perspectives*, edited by L. Kontos, D. Brotherton, and L. Barrios. New York: Columbia University Press.

Estrada, Joey N., Tamika D. Gilreath, Ron Avi Astor, and Rami Benbenishty. 2014. "Gang Membership, School Violence, and the Mediating Effects of Risk and Protective Behaviors in California High Schools." *Journal of School Violence* 13:228–251.

Feagin, Joe R. 2013. *The White Racial Frame: Centuries of Racial Framing and Counter-Framing*. New York: Routledge.

Flood, Richard M. 2003. "Towards a Theory of Revolutionizing Street Nations." *Socialism and Democracy* 17(1):245–253.

Flores, Edward O. 2018. *"Jesus Saved an Ex-Con": Political Activism and Redemption After Incarceration*. New York: New York University Press.

Fremon, Celeste. 1995. *Father Greg and the Homeboys: The Extraordinary Journey of Father Greg Boyle and His Work with the Latino Gangs of East L.A.* New York: Hyperion.

Glenn, Evelyn Nakano. 2015. "Settler Colonialism as Structure: A Framework for Comparative Studies of U.S. Race and Gender Formation." *Sociology of Race and Ethnicity* 1(1):52–72.

Hagedorn John M. and Bradley A. MacLean. 2012. "Breaking the Frame: Responding to Gang Stereotyping in Capital Cases." *University of Memphis Law Review* 42:1027–1060.

Haney-López, Ian F. 2003. *Racism on Trial: The Chicano Fight for Justice*. Cambridge, MA: The Belknap Press of Harvard University Press.

Hernández, Kelly L. 2017. *City of Inmates: Conquest, Rebellion, and the Rise of Human Caging in Los Angeles, 1771–1965*. Chapel Hill, NC: The University of North Carolina Press.

Heyman, Josiah McC. 2008. "Constructing a Virtual Wall: Race and Citizenship in U.S.-Mexico Border Policing." *Journal of the Southwest* 50(3):305–334.

Jackson, Pamela Irving. 1992. "Minority Group Threat, Social Context, and Policing." Pp. 89–101 in *Social Threat and Social Control*, edited by A. E. Liska. Albany, NY: State University of New York Press.

Kassel, Phillip. 2003. "The Gang Crackdown in the Prisons of Massachusetts: Arbitrary and Harsh Treatment Can Only Make Matters Worse." Pp. 228–252 in *Gangs and Society: Alternative Perspectives*, edited by L. Kontos, D. Brotherton, and L. Barrios. New York: Columbia University Press.

Klein, Malcolm W. 2004. *Gang Cop: The Words and Ways of Officer Paco Domingo*. Walnut Creek, CA: AltaMira Press.

Klein, Malcolm W. and Cheryl L. Maxson. 2006. *Street Gang Patterns and Policies*. New York: Oxford University Press.

Lane, Jodi. 2002. "Fear of Gang Crime: A Qualitative Examination of the Four Perspectives." *Journal of Research in Crime and Delinquency* 39(4):437–471.

Lopez-Aguado, Patrick. 2012. "Working Between Two Worlds: Gang Intervention and Street Liminality." *Ethnography* 14(2):186–206.

Lopez-Aguado, Patrick. 2018. *Stick Together and Come Back Home: Racial Sorting and the Spillover of Carceral Identity*. Oakland, CA: University of California Press.

Massey, Douglas S., Jorge Durand, and Nolan J. Malone. 2002. *Beyond Smoke and Mirrors: Mexican Immigration in an Era of Economic Integration*. New York: Russell Sage Foundation.

Maxson, Cheryl L., Arlen Egley, Jody Miller, and Malcolm W. Klein, eds. 2014. *The Modern Gang Reader*. 4th ed. New York: Oxford University Press.

McCorkle, Richard C. and Terance D. Miethe. 2002. *Panic: The Social Construction of the Street Gang Problem*. Upper Saddle River, NJ: Prentice Hall.

McVeigh, Rory and Kevin Estep. 2019. *The Politics of Losing: Trump, the Klan, and the Mainstreaming of Resentment*. New York: Columbia University Press.

McWilliams, Carey. 1948 (repr. 1990). *North from Mexico: The Spanish-Speaking People of the United States*. Westport, CT: Praeger.

Meier, Matt S. and Feliciano Ribera. 1996. *Mexican Americans/American Mexicans: From Conquistadors to Chicanos*. New York: Hill and Wang.

Mirandé, Alfredo. 1987. *Gringo Justice*. Notre Dame, IN: University of Notre Dame Press.

Montejano, David. 2010. *Quixote's Soldiers: A Local History of the Chicano Movement, 1966-1981*. Austin, TX: University of Texas Press.

Moore, Joan W. 1978. *Homeboys: Gangs, Drugs and Prison in the Barrios of Los Angeles*. Philadelphia, PA: Temple University Press.

National Gang Center. "National Youth Gang Survey Analysis." December 27, 2018 (www.nationalgang-center.gov/Survey-Analysis).

Navarro, Armando. 2005. *Mexicano Political Experience in Occupied Aztlán*. Lanham, MD: AltaMira Press.

Pyrooz, David C. 2014. "From Colors and Guns to Caps and Gowns? The Effects of Gang Membership on Educational Attainment." *Journal of Research in Crime and Delinquency* 51(1):56–87.

Pyrooz, David C. and Scott H. Decker. 2011. "Motives and Methods for Leaving the Gang: Understanding the Process of Gang Desistance." *Journal of Criminal Justice* 39:417–425.

Pyrooz, David C., Scott H. Decker, and Vincent J. Webb. 2014. "The Ties That Bind: Desistance from Gangs." *Crime and Delinquency* 60(4):491–516.

Rios, Victor M. 2011. *Punished: Policing the Lives of Black and Latino Boys*. New York: New York University Press.

Rios, Victor M. 2017. *Human Targets: Schools, Police, and the Criminalization of Latino Youth*. Chicago: University of Chicago Press.

Rios, Victor M. and Karlene Navarro. 2010. "Insider Gang Knowledge: The Case for Non-Police Gang Experts in the Courtroom." *Critical Criminology* 18:21–39.

Romero, Mary. 2001. "State Violence, and the Social and Legal Construction of Latino Criminality: From El Bandido to Gang Member." *Denver University Law Review* 78(4):1081–1118.

Rosenbaum, Robert J. [1981] 1998. *Mexicano Resistance in the Southwest*. Dallas, TX: Southern Methodist University.

Shelden, Randall G., Sharon K. Tracy, and William B. Brown. 2001. *Youth Gangs in American Society*. Belmont, CA: Wadsworth-Thomson Learning.

Tapia, Mike. 2011a. "U.S. Juvenile Arrests: Gang Membership, Social Class, and Labeling Effects." *Youth and Society* 43(4):1407–1432.

Tapia, Mike. 2011b. "Gang Membership and Race as Risk Factors for Juvenile Arrest." *Journal of Research in Crime and Delinquency* 48(3):364–395.

Tapia, Mike. 2017. *The Barrio Gangs of San Antonio: 1915–2015*. Fort Worth, TX: TCU Press.

Thornberry, Terence P. 1998. "Membership in Youth Gangs and Involvement in Serious and Violent Offending." Pp. 147–166 in *Serious and Violent Juvenile Offenders*, edited by R. Loeber and D. P. Farrington. Thousand Oaks, CA: Sage.

Thrasher, Frederic M. [1927] 1963. *The Gang: A Study of 1,313 Gangs in Chicago*. Chicago: University of Chicago.

United States Census Bureau. 2019. *QuickFacts: United States*. Washington, DC: Government Printing Office. (www.census.gov/quickfacts/fact/table/US/PST045218).

Valdez, Avelardo. 2007. *Mexican American Girls and Gang Violence*. New York: Palgrave Macmillan.

Van Cleve, Nicole Gonzalez. 2016. *Crook County: Racism and Injustice in America's Largest Criminal Court*. Stanford, CA: Stanford University Press.

Vespa, Jonathan, David Armstrong, and Lauren Medina. 2018. "Demographic Turning Points for the United States: Population Projections for 2020 to 2060." in *U.S. Department of Commerce, Economics and Statistics Administration*. Washington, DC: U.S. Bureau of the Census.

Vigil, Ernesto B. 1999. *The Crusade for Justice: Chicano Militancy and the Government's War on Dissent*. Madison, WI: University of Wisconsin Press.

Vigil, James Diego. 1988. *Barrio Gangs: Street Life and Identity in Southern California*. Austin TX: University of Texas Press.

Ward, T. W. 2013. *Gangsters Without Borders: An Ethnography of a Salvadoran Street Gang*. New York: Oxford University Press.

Whyte, William F. [1943] (1993). *Street Corner Society: The Social Structure of an Italian Slum*. Chicago: University of Chicago Press.

Zatz, Marjorie S. 1987. "Chicano Youth Gangs and Crime: The Creation of a Moral Panic." *Contemporary Crises* 11:129–158.

20

Indigenous gangs in Western Canada

Sandra M. Bucerius, Daniel J. Jones and Kevin D. Haggerty

Introduction

There is a constantly evolving gang landscape in Canada. The Hamilton Police service reported in March of 2018 that there are 430 active gangs in Canada, some of which are prominently publicized in the media. The "Quebec Biker War," for example, which took place between the Rock Machine and the Hells Angels between 1994 and 2004 and left 162 dead, was a constant point of reference for the media (Parker and Vronsky 2015). Other gangs and gang wars, like the constant battling between the Redd Alert, Alberta Warriors, and the Indian Posse in Edmonton in the late 90s, garnered notably less attention from local media. While gangs in Canada differ with respect to their ethnic composition, intentions, symbolism, and engagement in crime and violence, the most stereotypical form of "street gangs" in Canada are Indigenous based. These groups are turf based and operate in a manner that allegedly poses the greatest threat of violence to the general public (Johnston 2018). This chapter focuses on the origins and contemporary features of Canada's Indigenous gangs, in a context where these groups are under-researched and their impact on both gang members and the broader community is not well understood.

Indigenous people in Canada have been, and continue to be, overrepresented in the criminal justice system as both offenders and victims (Boyce 2016; Brzozowski, Taylor-Butts, and Johnson 2006). While Indigenous people constitute only 4% of the overall Canadian population, they account for 23.2% of federal inmates, 27% of the provincial and territorial inmate population, and 13.5% of offenders supervised in the community (Maleakieh 2018; Dauvergne 2012; Office of the Correctional Investigator 2012). Indigenous people are 10 times more likely to be incarcerated than the average Canadian, an over-representation that is significantly starker than for African Americans in the United States. The disproportionate number of Indigenous people in custody is consistent across Canada, although this overrepresentation is especially acute in the Canadian Prairie region (Alberta, Saskatchewan, and Manitoba). For example, while Indigenous people represented 15.5% of Manitoba's population in 2013, they accounted for 69% of admissions to provincial correctional facilities (Owusu-Bempah and Wortley 2013). Indigenous people are "twice as likely to report being the victim of a violent assault . . . about six times more likely to be the victims of homicide . . . [and] at a higher risk of being victimized multiple times" (Monchalin 2016, p. 145). Indigenous women are the most victimized group in Canada

(Brennan 2009, 2011), being subjected to more state and interpersonal violence than any other demographic group (Combs 2018).

Perhaps most shockingly, Indigenous youth make up close to 50% of all admission to youth correctional facilities across the country (Statistics Canada 2018). A considerable proportion of these admissions are related to gang activity and membership.

The emergence of self-identified Indigenous gangs in Canada has been a comparatively recent development. This chapter provides a brief overview of some factors related to the emergence and development of these gangs. Unlike discussions of racialized gangs in the United States – where one can assume a readership familiar with the broad historical backgrounds of the groups being discussed – that is typically not the case with Canadian Indigenous gangs. Consequently, we commence with an overview of the somewhat longer history of Indigenous/settler relations. Any understanding of Indigenous street and prison gangs in Canada must situate these groups in the context of Canada's settler colonial history – something that has profoundly affected all aspects of the lives of Canada's Indigenous people.

History

Prior to the arrival of European settlers, Indigenous people lived in kinship groups and were governed by decentralized, regionally specific kinship systems that regulated interactions both within and between groups (Ray 2016, pp. 25–38). While each Indigenous group followed and celebrated its own unique traditions and possessed distinctive skills and livelihoods, these groups shared a number of mutual values such as "respect, harmony, and the maintenance of balance" (Monchalin 2016, p. 53). Important to these shared principles was the fact that Indigenous concepts of justice and social harmony were intrinsically connected to a form of spirituality grounded in a respect for, and veneration of, the Earth and all facets of nature understood as equal creations (Hendry et al. 2018). It is a worldview that fostered a sense of equality and reciprocity among various groups and which allowed for successful and expansive trade network across the country. These arrangements were often solidified in peace and friendship treaties that were "recorded orally and represented through the exchange of sacred items" (Monchalin 2016, p. 81).

When European settlers arrived, many Indigenous groups entered into similar peace and friendship arrangements with the newcomers. Dating back to the 1600s, these early agreements clarified the rights pertaining to European settlers and Indigenous people with respect to land usage and related responsibilities. Perhaps most importantly, they clearly outlined Indigenous people's original land titles. As trade networks expanded throughout the 16th and 17th centuries, the Canadian government, under the authority of the British Crown, legislated the government's entitlement to sovereignty over the land and people of Canada in the Royal Proclamation of 1763 (Monchalin 2016, p. 82). This legislation had profound consequences for the relationship between European settlers and Indigenous communities, as it solidified the view that Indigenous individuals and communities would no longer be viewed as equal partners. As the British Crown worked to expand land ownership and economic development, Indigenous communities came to be seen as an obstacle to the Euro-Canadian vision of land acquisition (Ray 2016). Consequently, Indigenous people were relegated to reserves and settlements through the numbered treaties,[1] which limited Indigenous use of land for hunting and farming. The passing of the Indian Act in 1876 further limited the abilities of Indigenous individuals and communities to live in accordance with traditional ways of life (Ray 2016). Such colonization and assimilation were not just apparent in Canada, as the cultural genocide of the American Indian occurred all across the United States (Churchill 1997), and the desire to rid colonized countries of Indigenous populations was also manifest elsewhere, including Australia, South Africa, and New Zealand (Reyhner and Singh 2010; Hixson 2013; Byrd 2011; Coombes 2006).

Moving to more recent history, during the 20th century, the Canadian government instituted a number of explicitly assimilationist projects. Perhaps the most infamous and consequential was the creation of the residential school system, which sought to "kill the Indian in the child."[2] Initiated in the 1880s, but reaching their height in the 1930s, residential schools were a central plank in the Canadian government's efforts to assimilate Indigenous people and have been likened to a form of cultural genocide (MacDonald and Hudson 2012). Educational officials removed Indigenous children from their homes and families as part of an effort to strip them of their culture and language and assimilate them into the white settler population. Many children housed in the residential schools suffered physical, sexual, psychological, and emotional abuse from school staff (Regan 2010; Stout and Kipling 2003). The last residential school only closed in 1996, leaving many families suffering from long-term and intergenerational trauma (Regan 2010; TRC 2015). In 2008, Prime Minister Stephen Harper issued an official apology on behalf of the federal government of Canada for this policy.

The educational system worked in conjunction with other efforts by the Canadian government to distance Indigenous children from their biological families. The Sixties Scoop (Johnston 1983), for example, saw child welfare authorities placing Indigenous children up for adoption, preferably with white middle-class families. Beginning in the late 1950s, and running until the 1980s, this program resulted in approximate 20,000 Indigenous children being removed from their biological families (TRC 2015). Today, many see the operation of the contemporary foster care system as a *de facto* continuation of the Sixties Scoop and the residential school system (Sinclair 2016). In 2011, for example, 48% of foster care children younger than 14 in Canada were First Nations, Métis, or Inuit, despite representing just 7% of that age group. In the Western provinces of Manitoba and Saskatchewan, 85% or more of foster children were Indigenous (Turner 2016).

Other notable assimilationist policies included criminalizing a series of traditional cultural practices, including the gift-giving feast known as the Potlatch, and the Sun Dances and Thirst Dances, as practiced by different Indigenous groups. Perhaps the most pointed of these efforts, however, was the 1969 White Paper which was tabled in the House of Commons. This legislation essentially sought to extinguish any dedicated rights for Indigenous people, eliminating Indian status and reserve status and terminating all programming that had been specifically focused on First Nations communities under previous legislation (Ray 2016). Although it was ultimately withdrawn in the face of public opposition, the White Paper represents a stark and relatively recent effort to extinguish any and all special rights and recognitions of Canadian Indigenous people.

Today, the displacement and marginalization of Indigenous people continues, something that is particularly pronounced in the criminal justice system. As a democracy, legal processes in Canada work on the assumption that justice should be distributed equally among Canadians and that punishment should be related exclusively to criminal conduct. The legacies of colonialism and structural racism, however, have culminated in disproportionately high arrest, prosecution, and sentencing rates for Indigenous people. Parliament and the Supreme Court of Canada have introduced measures to try and rectify this situation. For example, section 718.2(e) of the Criminal Code and the "Gladue" ruling by the Supreme Court instruct judges at the time of sentencing to seriously consider the unique background and structural factors impacting Indigenous people. Judges are expected to seek "all available sanctions other than imprisonment" in an explicit effort to reduce Indigenous overrepresentation in Canadian correctional institutions.

Despite these measures, this over-representation has further increased in the last decade (Bucerius and Urbanik 2015; Statistics Canada 2018).

Indigenous communities face a litany of other disadvantages. For example, they are under- and unemployed at higher rates than other Canadians and have lower than average rates of educational achievement in both cities and on reserves (Monchalin 2016: 145; TRC 2015). Compared to non-Indigenous Canadians, Indigenous individuals suffer from poorer health outcomes, higher rates of alcoholism, higher residential mobility, and worse living conditions and are more likely to live with a single parent or in the custody of child welfare (Monchalin 2016, pp. 154–170). Young Indigenous people are also experiencing an epidemic of suicides (Mihychuk 2017).

A growing political and public recognition of the extent to which Indigenous people have suffered at the hands of the settler colonial project, especially the lingering legacy of the residential school system (which was most pronounced in Alberta), culminated in the creation of the Truth and Reconciliation Commission (TRC) in 2008. The goals of the TRC included "documenting and promoting the extent and impact of residential school experiences; providing a safe setting for former students to share their stories; and producing a report to the federal government on the legacy of the residential school system" (TRC 2015). While the TRC produced a series of "calls to action," and halting first steps towards reconciliation are being made, the intergenerational trauma inflicted on Indigenous people, the ongoing refusal by many Canadians to acknowledge their complicity in this situation, and the ongoing discrimination in the criminal justice system, among other hardships, continue to shape the life experiences of Canada's Indigenous people.

This brief overview does not do justice to the full scope of the atrocities committed against Indigenous people in Canada. Nor can it adequately convey a sense of the continued intergenerational trauma and suffering of Canada's Indigenous people. It does, however, provide a starting point for understanding the historical legacies and contextual conditions in which Indigenous street and prison gangs have formed.

Indigenous gangs

While the media occasionally highlights sensational instances of Indigenous gang violence in Western Canada (Sinclair and Grekul 2012), there are few empirical academic studies on this topic and only a smattering of government-initiated reports (Totten 2009). Generally speaking, these works show that Indigenous gang membership has been increasing in the Prairie region since the 1990s, particularly in the cities of Winnipeg, Regina, Saskatoon, and Edmonton (Preston, Carr-Stewart, and Bruno 2012). While Indigenous gangs have now existed for more than 20 years, they remain comparatively disorganized and have not reached the same level of sophistication found in more organized crime groups – notwithstanding the fact that the police have begun to refer to them as Aboriginal-based organized crime (ABOC). These groups have gained a noticeable presence in both prisons and on the streets but are still largely seen as "wannabe" groups, "known for their violence, their structure based on African American gangs (e.g., tattoos, hand symbols, chains of command), and their conflict with other groups" (Dunbar 2017). This includes a notable incorporation of Indigenous terms and symbols in gang names and tattoos, as well as an embrace of the concept of the 'warrior.' Indigenous gangs are known to have a strong intergenerational component, with the majority of members being over 18 but with one study showing that children as young as 8 are being recruited (Comack et al. 2013).

Both Indigenous and non-Indigenous scholars have argued that Indigenous gangs evolved as a consequence of living conditions characterized by "inequity, racism, dislocation, marginalization, and cultural and spiritual alienation" (Comack et al. 2013, p. 17). While Kathleen Buddle (2011, p. 176) suggests that Indigenous gangs probably first emerged as survival and resistance groups in the residential school system, to our knowledge, there are no scholarly accounts of anything that could conventionally be recognized as "gangs" existing within residential schools. Instead, the concept of "Indigenous streets gangs" first enters the lexicon in the 1980s. A key institutional context for the creation and reproduction of such gangs appears to have been prisons and young offender facilities. As Comack puts it, "[y]oung Aboriginal people came to realize that they could assert themselves if they were in organized groups . . . [i]n many cases, this realization came while young Aboriginal friends were locked up together in one institution or another" (Comack et al. 2013, p. 59). Independently of whether gangs existed in the residential school system, it is widely understood that Indigenous gangs can be seen as an empowered, albeit anti-social, rejection of colonial conditions of poverty and social subjugation.

The remainder of this chapter relies heavily on our own interview material to briefly describe the origins and evolution of Indigenous gangs across Western Canada.

Methodology and setting

The data presented in his chapter are part of the University of Alberta Prison Project (UAPP). Over a period of two years, we interviewed 587 prisoners and 136 correctional officers across four prisons in one province in Western Canada. We entered into a research agreement with the correctional ministry of that province, providing us unrestricted access to interview prisoners in these four prisons, including those on gang units, maximum security units, solitary confinement units, and protective custody units. We also interviewed on general population units and boot camp units. Two of the four prisons were remand facilities, housing those who have not yet been charged but are awaiting trial. One was a sentenced facility, and one housed a mix of remand and sentenced prisoners. All four facilities were part of the provincial system which holds all remanded prisoners as well as prisoners who have received a sentence up to two years. The remand facilities house prisoners who are incarcerated for crimes ranging from non-payment of fines all the way to those who have committed multiple homicides. The two remand prisons were characterized by significant overcrowding, with one housing close to double the number of inmates for which it was originally designed.

Our data consist of both surveys (not used in this chapter) as well as 587 in-depth interviews with prisoners (495 male, 92 female). The topics of discussion ranged widely, and, taking a 'life history' approach, touched upon incarceration, victimization (Jones, Bucerius, and Haggerty 2019), religiosity, race (Tetrault, Bucerius, and Haggerty 2019), opioids and fentanyl (Bucerius and Haggerty 2019), and relations with the police. While the focus of our study was not on Indigenous gangs per se, by virtue of talking to prisoners about their general experiences in Western Canadian prisons, and the fact that Indigenous gangs have a large presence in these institutions, we learned a great deal about this phenomenon.

The following sections provide an overview of some key insights into the origins and evolution of Indigenous gangs in our research context.

Origins of Indigenous gangs in Canada

For the longest time, Canada seemed to have little gang activity, and local law enforcement did not concentrate on gang-related violence or operations. Police agencies did not create dedicated gang units until about 15 to 20 years ago. For example, the Calgary Police Service first officially acknowledged that the city had a "gang problem" in 2003, following a public outcry after a series of drive-by shootings (Mathews, 2005, p. 205). A few years earlier, in 1999, the Edmonton Police Service had created its own gang unit. In other words, concerns about and attention to gangs came to Canada much later than was the case in the United States.

The earliest Indigenous street gangs appear to have emerged in Winnipeg, Manitoba, around 1988, with the first being the Indian Posse. At its inception, the Indian Posse was composed of disenfranchised Indigenous youth who mainly operated on the street level in the inner city of Winnipeg, wearing gang colors, marking turf with paint tags, and selling drugs. They were also involved in a series of assaults and break and enters (Grekul and Laboucane-Benson 2006). Seen by the authorities as marginalized kids, their activities did not spark much police attention.

As gangs can require an "enemy" in order to forge their own group identity, it is perhaps not surprising that about a year later, another Indigenous gang emerged in Winnipeg: the Manitoba Warriors. In contrast to the Indian Posse, the Manitoba Warriors modeled themselves after motorcycle gangs. While not typically riding motorcycles, they wore vests reminiscent of such gangs, and their slogan "Warriors Forever, Forever Warriors," also clearly mimicked that of the Hell's Angels: "Angels Forever, Forever Angels." Both the Manitoba Warriors and the Indian Posse dealt drugs. For the Warriors, this involved a connection with local motorcycle gangs, whereas the Indian Posse – who at the time positioned themselves against the motorcycle gangs – received their drugs through organized crime circles connected to Asian crime groups.

Expansion across the prairies

While for the first five years of their existence the Indian Posse and Manitoba Warriors repeatedly – and often viciously – battled each other, they still drew relatively little police attention. This neglect may be attributable to the fact that their violence was inter-group, targeting other Indigenous individuals but not aimed at the general public. According to our interviews, two events in the 1990s happened in short succession which attracted the attention of both the public and law enforcement. Most conspicuously was the murder of 13-year-old Joseph Spence, known as "Beeper." Although he was not a member of a gang, he was shot in the back and killed after he proclaimed a gang connection when confronted by members of the Deuce gang:

> there was an incident where a young kid . . ., he was about 13 years old . . . was walking down the street in North Winnipeg where the gangs were heavy. He had some family members that were Indian Posse and they told him, "If you ever get jammed up, and anyone ever asked, you say you're down with IP." He says it and they level a shotgun and they blow him away. They killed this 13 year-old kid. So that becomes a massive political issue and this 13 year-old Indigenous kid gets killed in the streets of Winnipeg and the police aren't really responding. Second thing that happens, there is a house party and the Indian Posse have a house party and at this house party, a young lady, she just . . . after having a baby . . . a newborn and it becomes a real crack, big party . . . she gets high and puts the baby on the floor and no one pays attention that the baby is there, and the baby ends up being killed at the party with multiple skull fractures, multiple bone fractures, lungs punctured. The baby was trampled to death. So as a result of those two things, and obviously, a plethora of other shitty, shitty things, um, it was actually the coroner [who] came out and said, "the police need to do something about the gang problem in Winnipeg."

Increased public and media attention pressured law enforcement to focus on the "gang problem" and related violence in Winnipeg. As a consequence, our participants told us that the police had a "typical law enforcement response" and started to "incarcerate, incarcerate,

incarcerate." Most of these gang members were sent to Stoney Mountain prison, outside of Winnipeg. However, it became difficult to manage the two opposing groups within a single institution. Consequently, Correctional Service Canada (CSC) – the federal correctional system – started to disperse gang members across the Prairie Region in Western Canada. Thus, members of the Indian Posse and the Manitoba Warriors were moved to provinces outside of Manitoba, such as Saskatchewan and Alberta.

It was each groups' respective allegiance (or non-allegiance) to motorcycle gangs, especially the Hell's Angels, which shaped much of the Indian Posse's and Manitoba Warrior's position both in prisons and on the streets, as each group started to grow in reputation and numbers. While the Indian Posse remained hostile towards motorcycle gangs and are known to be "incompatible" with members of such groups while in prison, the Manitoba Warriors continue to be aligned with motorcycle gangs. The motorcycle gangs are particularly well organized and involved in high-level crimes, but in the prairie provinces their number are comparatively low, so they consequently often rely on Warriors (and newer groups, such as Redd Alert) for protection while incarcerated.

From the streets to the prisons

Within prison, both Indigenous groups quickly gained power and recruited new members, with the Manitoba Warriors creating an off-shoot called the Alberta Warriors. At the time, most prisons had segregated gang units, with affiliates of different gangs being housed on separate prison units. One unintended consequence of this (now abandoned) system was that it allowed the respective gangs a comparatively easy means to recruit non-aligned individuals who were also housed on their unit, growing in numbers without having to compete against another gang on the same living unit. As one of our interview participants noted: "The two places that recruiting really occurs is in the jails and at powwows." In their study of gang involvement among prisoners in Alberta, Chalas and Grekul (2017) found that 42% of their 175 participants (both male and female) first became gang involved in prison.

One might expect Indigenous gangs to provide their membership with a sense of cultural connection, similar to how the Almighty Latin King and Queen Nation in the United States connect their members to Latinx culture (see Brotherton and Barrios 2004). Within prison, the Indigenous gangs certainly did claim a racialized space designed to foster solidarity and entice fellow Indigenous prisoners to join their groups. As Comack reports, one sign on the wall in Stoney Mountain Penitentiary reads "Tread softly, Whitey. You're in Indian Country now" (Comack et al. 2013, p. 95). However, our data clearly show that connections to Indigenous culture are secondary or tertiary to other appeals of gang membership. Many members joined these gangs in prison for protection. Alternatively, the gang provided a sense of belonging that was only thinly connected to Indigenous culture or history. As many other scholars have shown, for young disenfranchised men, the streets and prisons can become spaces for major identity formation (see, for example, Bucerius 2014; Garot 2010), as they offer group solidarity and profitability for both individual members and the group as a whole. The gang can be a substitute for family and other forms of brotherhood. When asked by an interviewer why he first joined a gang, for example, one of our participants expressed his desire for family, independent of Indigenous aspects, a sentiment that was common to many participants:

> I don't know. Okay, well, mostly because, I had nobody to show me family, right? And . . . growing up, I wanted a family. I wanted that fucking, you know, somebody that actually had my back, through thick and thin. And . . . that's the whole reason why I joined Redd Alert. Was because of that.

Gang research in the United States has consistently shown that gangs in prison "exhibit higher levels of racial and ethnic homogeneity [than street gangs]" (Decker and Pyrooz 2011, p 13). In contrast, while many of the gangs in our research setting were racialized, even the "Indigenous" gangs tended to have members of diverse ethnic and racial backgrounds. Our participants typically explained this situation with nods to Canadian multiculturalism ("It's Canada. We all get along here" – see Tetrault, Bucerius, and Haggerty 2019). The business aspects of prison gangs also played a significant role in this cultural heterogeneity. As one participant succinctly put it "prison gangs are a numbers game," and higher membership numbers often translated into a stronger and more powerful presence in the prisons, something that can lead to more profitable connections in the prison drug trade. Both in prison and on the streets, trafficking drugs provides gang members with some relative economic independence, and incorporating non-Indigenous members can be a way to further those economic ambitions. This is in line with previous research by Grekul and LaBoucane-Benson (2006), who observed that membership and alliances among street gangs in Edmonton are determined rationally, rather than on the basis of race or ethnicity, as "the best partners are those who may best enhance and increase the wealth and power of the gang" (19).

However, gang leaders certainly made connections to Indigenous culture to enhance the group's attractiveness to marginalized Indigenous people in prison or on the street. As several of our participants told us, the gangs draw upon a hybrid mixture of American ghetto (Mukherjee 2006) and Indigenous cultural referents to appeal to potential Indigenous recruits:

> It was how you become a warrior now, it was the new style of warrior, the ghetto soldiers. [There was a] phenomenal artist [a gang leader] who drew a picture, and the picture was a head in half, and one half was an Indigenous leader wearing a headdress with a pipe, and the pipe turns into a handgun and the other half of the head – it becomes this perversion of Indigenous culture to recruit individuals to become gang members.

And while decisions regarding recruitment and the general direction of the gangs seem to be dominated by business concerns, we also found that senior figures in the gang hierarchy tended to have an appreciation for their own cultural history and can speak knowledgably about Indigenous issues. One participant, for example, informed us that: "The Manitoba Warriors literally used to go to the AIM conference every year. So, the American Indian Movement conference." Likewise, one of the staff participants commented about the leader of the Indian Posse:

> The leader of the Indian Posse knows more about colonization, residential schools, 60s scoop, the lack of payment of indigenous soldiers of their benefits when they returned from World War I and World War II, than anyone I know. He 100% knows it, and at one point in time in a conversation that he and I had, had said, "my goal is one day to turn the Indian Posse into the PLO," The Palestinian Liberation Organization. He said, because, "45 years ago in Israel the Jewish people said they were nothing more than a bunch of rock throwing heathens and now they're the greatest, um, you know, liberation force in the world."

In contrast, most of our participants who were lower-level gang members had little knowledge about, or connection to, their cultural heritage. This is perhaps not surprising, given that many of them grew up in the foster care system and were raised by non-Indigenous caregivers. Those more senior gang members who actually were conscious of Indigenous traditions seemed to do little to educate younger Indigenous members about their culture and traditions beyond impressing on them the importance of being a "warrior." As one participant told us: "they talk about Indigenous culture enough to talk about a culture that has been persecuted and in order to win back your pride, you needed to be a gangster." Another gang member accentuated the same point: "They taught almost nothing about the Indigenous culture other than to be a Warrior. You had to fight everything that was white, including the cops." In other words, the cultural knowledge of those members at the top of the gang hierarchy does not seem to be being conveyed to younger or more junior members. As another participant observed: "So, at the highest level, that's where the mindsets were, it [Indigenous cultural knowledge] never filtered down. And they never took the time to teach that. They just thought it and talked about it in small circles, and it was the street and drugs and the sex trade and the violence that they concentrated on."

As the concept of an "Indigenous gang" filtered out into the wider community a procession of new groups emerged, drawn to the prospect of excitement, money, and women (Chalas and Grekul 2017). Undergirding it all, however, was still a clear desire for a sense of belonging:

> Trying to belong to something because they don't belong to anything else. They don't fit into other places and that's really common, like these kids don't have places to fit in. They don't fit in at school, they don't fit in at home, they usually are in the system because of, usually, the young offender system or whether it's the child welfare system. It's these kids that just don't have anything else so they need to belong to something.

The consequence has been a constantly evolving Indigenous gang scene, with groups expanding beyond the cities into smaller rural communities and reserves. The transient nature of many of these groups can make it hard to compile an accurate inventory, but some notable gangs include the Native Syndicate, Indian Posse, ASAP (Always Strive, Always Prosper), Crips, West End Boys, Death Do Us Part, Wolf Pack, Mixed Blood, and Deuce. A correctional officer in our sample highlighted the transitory nature of many such Indigenous gangs in prison:

> [ASAP is] small potatoes – but in the jail, they're recruiting like it's going out of style. But it's kind of like being recruited into a book club. If you don't show up, who cares? . . . It's like, oh, you want to be in my gang? You're 18? Yeah, sure! You're getting out in a week? OK! . . . Native gangs, they fall apart like crackers.

From the prisons back to the streets

Federal Canadian prisons house inmates who are serving a sentence of two years or more. These institutions are spread across the country, and federal inmates are often transferred from prison to prison, many of which are hundreds of miles from their home communities. This is particularly true for gang-involved inmates. As is common in Canada, prisoners who have served their sentence are released into the city adjacent to where the prison is located, even if that is far from their home community. One unintended consequence of this practice was that Correctional Service Canada inadvertently contributed to the spread of Indigenous gang members throughout the Prairie Region, even introducing members to adjacent provinces. As David Maze, former head of the Criminal Intelligence Service of Alberta (CISA) put it, "What they did was educate other local criminals that were incarcerated . . . and build new gangs" (as quoted in Henton 2011). Edmonton, the capital of Alberta, for example, is home to the "Edmonton Max" – a maximum security prison that houses many of the most violent criminals in the Prairie Region. As prisoners were released, a good number of Indigenous gang members simply gravitated to the local gang scene, something that helped to make Edmonton a hub for much of the Western Canadian's gang activity.

As this was happening (in approximately 1995), a third Indigenous gang formed in Edmonton which was to become prominent. Originally a rap group speaking out against drugs and violence, Redd Alert soon became involved in gang activity, initially working closely with the Indian Posse. For several years, the Redd Alert and the Indian Posse wore the same colors (red) and united against the Alberta Warriors (blue), before Redd Alert started collaborating with motorcycle gangs themselves.

> You saw this very close connection with them, up until there was a rip off between, an alleged or apparent non-payment for drugs to the Indian Posse from the Redd Alert, so they started to be at war. The war really started heavily in'98. Home invasions were happening on a daily basis, guys were getting their arms cut off . . . we had multiple shootings, um, multiple um, violent attacks, stabbings in prison, stabbings on the street.

As is common in gang wars, our gang member participants demonstrated highly variable understandings of the history of such conflicts. When we asked younger members in the prison system why gangs were "at war," we regularly received starkly different answers. Participants often stated that they did not really know the origins of a conflict or that it was just part of being in their gang to fight against another specified gang. Higher-ranked members would often know the specifics, but they were also conscious that passing along the details in order to justify the conflict was unnecessary, as members will simply follow orders.

I: Do you think that most of the ones who were involved then knew what this was about originally?
P: It becomes a tale of lore, and it just becomes a war. It just becomes, it's like if you go back, it's funny. If you go back really into history and into what happened with the Indian Posse and the Manitoba Warriors . . . now I guarantee you probably no one will know this anymore, but I know this because, I've lived this for so long. There is a lady . . . a very, very pretty woman who was sleeping with a Manitoba Warrior and cheated on him with an Indian Posse. The entire war, between the Indian Posse and the Manitoba Warriors, is over a girl. That's what started the entire thing.

Contemporary state

> The stupid thing that they don't understand was that they were bringing drugs to their own people and killing their own people, right? It became very, very much like the black experience and the Latino experience in the US, right? Marginalized people killing marginalized people.

As noted previously, and much in contrast to what research in the United States has shown, Indigenous gang membership is not exclusively tied to one's ethnic background. Instead, membership is typically fluid. Members often switch allegiances multiple times in their lives, a process known as "crew hopping," something that is, again, quite distinct as compared to the American situation, where such practices are not generally tolerated:

> You get this kid, he doesn't like that kid in RA [Redd Alert] anymore, then he'll jump over to Alberta Warriors. Yeah. They're crew-hoppers. They'll jump from crew to crew to crew to crew. I've experienced that my whole life. When I first joined, I was Alberta Warrior, then – and that was, it wasn't for long at all, it was like a couple months.

Such fluidity means that these groups tend to be less stable and organized than comparable gangs or organized crime groups (Bolden 2012). Unfortunately, there is very little gang research in the Canadian context, which makes it impossible for us to determine whether crew hopping is a Western Canadian or Indigenous phenomenon only or also common among other Canadian gangs in Pacific, Atlantic or Central Canada. Thus, much of Canadian gang knowledge relies on the information released by law enforcement or anecdotal knowledge from stakeholders, many of whom characterize Indigenous gangs as fluid and unstable. During our prison research, for example, the presence of the Indian Posse and Alberta Warriors had declined precipitously in the provincial system. In their place were Redd Alert and a newer group called ASAP. Both, however, lacked a clearly defined leadership, making it hard for them to organize and equally difficult to try to predict how they might evolve. As one of our police officer participants observed, "There is literally no direction in these groups." In reality, perhaps the key organizational dynamic for Indigenous gangs is that they continue to be subordinate to outlaw motorcycle gangs, serving as soldiers on their behalf, selling their drugs, and helping them access illegal markets that would otherwise be inaccessible to motorcycle gangs, such as reserves. As one of our participants notes:

So we've actually seen people that have gone from the Redd Alert to actually being members or hang arounds for the HA [Hell's Angels]. So there is some progression there, and you also see Redd Alert, strong Redd Alert ties to places that have Hells Angels. Like you'll see Redd Alert in Kelowna, you'll see Redd Alert in Vancouver, you'll see Redd Alert in places that you wouldn't expect to see them because they are an Edmonton-based street gang. That's where they started but they've kind of sprung out because they've become that dirty, street, reserve sellers, they can go to the reserves and sell dope where a biker can't go onto Maskwacis or Enoch [reserves in Alberta] or anywhere and sell drugs, but these guys can.

Conclusion

We have provided a brief outline of some aspects of the evolution of Indigenous gangs in Western Canada. This gang situation demands public and political attention, given their growing size and disconcerting levels of violence and homicide associated with these groups. In 2017, for example, the Canadian police reported 163 gang-related homicides, which account for one-quarter of all homicides in the country. The prairie provinces of Alberta and Saskatchewan – where Indigenous gangs are most pronounced – account for almost half (47%) of all gang homicides in Canada (Statistics Canada 2017). At the same time, the topic of "Indigenous gangs" can also be easily sensationalized, with commentators able to draw upon longstanding derogatory caricatures of dysfunctional Indigenous communities. Researchers, politicians, and journalists consequently need to sensitively attend to the realities of a complex and occasionally exaggerated situation – bearing in mind lingering histories of colonization and marginalization – so as to avoid recourse to lazy stereotypes and unwarranted vilification.

One challenge in distinguishing the real from the embellishments concerns our limited knowledge base on this topic. Whereas the United States has a vibrant research tradition on gangs that goes back decades and which provide an often-nuanced picture of the myriad forms of variability both within and between gangs, things are entirely different in Canada. With some notable exceptions, there is little independent empirical scholarship on gangs or Indigenous gangs more specifically. The factors contributing to this situation are legion. With a national population that is smaller than that of California, Canada does not have anything approaching an academic research infrastructure comparable to that of the United States. Only a few research-focused criminology departments exist in Western Canada, and perhaps only a handful of researchers are actively studying gang issues.

Given the tendency for the social sciences in the United States to become hegemonic, Canadian scholars need to work to develop our own knowledge base. We also need to forge our own theories of Indigenous gang formation that do not simply transplant conceptual frameworks from the United States. Instead, what is needed are approaches to gang involvement and gang activity that can incorporate an appreciation for the unique aspects of Canada's settler-colonial situation and the ongoing struggles of Canada's Indigenous peoples.

On top of that are the familiar challenges of conducting research on gangs, something that is compounded when working with Indigenous communities where a researcher might not share a cultural background with their participants and where extra effort is required to build trusting relations and nurture ongoing collaborations with Elders and key community organizations. Accessing gang members in Canadian prisons presents its own challenges given that both provincial and federal correctional officials have been notoriously reluctant to provide research access to individual academic researchers, which is particularly the case when that research is more qualitative, critical, or ethnographic.

While it is customary to conclude by pointing to potential fruitful avenues for future research that could fill existing knowledge gaps, the reality is that almost *any* empirical research on the lived experiences of Indigenous gangs and gang members in Canada would be an important contribution, given the current paucity of knowledge on this topic.

Notes

1 Also referred to as the Post-Confederation Treaties, these 11 treaties were signed between First Nations groups and the Government of Canada (1871–1921). They affirmed assorted rights of the First Nations signatories and allowed the Government of Canada to undertake resource extraction in what are modern-day British Columbia, Alberta, Saskatchewan, Manitoba, Ontario, and the Northwest Territories.
2 This phrase is commonly attributed to Duncan Campbell Scott, the Canadian bureaucrat who oversaw the residential school system, but was actually uttered by an American military officer (Abley 2013).

References

Abley, M. (2013). *Conversations with a Dead Man: The Legacy of Duncan Campbell Scott*. Madeira Park, BC: D & M Publishers.

Bolden, C. L. (2012). Liquid Soldiers: Fluidity and Gang Membership. *Deviant Behavior, 33*(3), 207–222.

Boyce, J. (2016). *Victimization of Aboriginal People in Canada, 2014*. Juristat, 36(1). Ottawa, ON: Canadian Centre for Justice Statistics, Statistics Canada.

Brennan, S. (2009). Juristat: Canadian Centre for Justice Statistics. Retrieved from: https://www150.stat-can.gc.ca/n1/en/pub/85-002-x/2011001/article/11439-eng.pdf?st=sP61ccEy.

Brennan, S. (2011). *Violent Victimization of Aboriginal Women in the Canadian Provinces*. Ottawa: Statistics Canada.

Brotherton, D., and Barrios, L. (2004). *The Almighty Latin King and Queen Nation – Street Politics and the Transformation of a New York City Gang*. New York: Columbia University Press.

Brzozowski, J., Taylor-Butts, A., and Johnson, S. (2006). *Victimization and Offending Among the Aboriginal Population in Canada*. Juristat: Canadian Centre for Justice Statistics, 26(3). Retrieved from: https://www150.statcan.gc.ca/n1/en/pub/85-002-x/85-002-x2006003 eng.pdf?st=zOat-6gr.

Bucerius, S. (2014). *Unwanted – Muslim Immigrants, Dignity, and Drug Dealing*. New York: Oxford University Press.

Bucerius, S., and Haggerty, K. D. (2019). Fentanyl Behind Bars: The Implications of Synthetic Opiates for Prisoners and Correctional Officers. *International Journal of Drug Policy*. doi: 10.1016/j.drugpo.2019.05.018.

Bucerius, S., and Urbanik, M. (2015). Crime and Punishment in Canada. In *The Encyclopedia of Crime and Punishment*, W. G. Jennings (Ed.). doi:10.1002/9781118519639.wbecpx233

Buddle, K., Proulx, C., and Howard, H. A. (2011). *Aboriginal Peoples in Canadian Cities: Transformations and Continuities.* Waterloo: Wilfrid Laurier University Press.

Byrd, J. A. (2011). *The Transit of Empire: Indigenous Critiques of Colonialism.* Minneapois: University of Minnesota Press.

Chalas, D. M., and Grekul, J. (2017). I've Had Enough: Exploring Gang Life from the Perspective of (Ex) Members in Alberta. *The Prison Journal, 97*(3), 364–386.

Churchill, W. (1997). *A Little Matter of Genocide: Holocaust and Denial in the Americas 1492 to the Present.* San Francisco: City Lights Books.

Comack, E., Lawrence, D., Morrissette, L., and Silver, J. (2013). *"Indians Wear Red": Colonialism, Resistance, and Aboriginal Street Gangs.* Halifax and Winnipeg: Fernwood Publishing.

Combs, L. (2018). Healing Ourselves: Interrogating the Underutilization of Sections 81 & 84 of the Corrections and Conditional Release Act. *Manitoba Law Journal, 41*(3), 163–189.

Coombes, A. E. (2006). *Rethinking Settler Colonialism: History and Memory in Australia, Canada, New Zealand and South Africa.* Manchester: Manchester University Press.

Dauvergne, M. (2012). *Adult Correctional Statistics in Canada, 2010/2011.* Juristat. Statistics Canada Catalogue no. 85-002-X. Ottawa, ON: statistics Canada.

Dunbar, L. (2017). *Youth Gangs in Canada: A Review of Current Topics and Issues.* Ottawa, ON: Public Safety Canada Research Report: 2017 – R001.

Garot, R. (2010). *Who You Claim: Performing Gang Identity in School and on the Streets.* New York: New York University Press.

Grekul, J., and Laboucane-Benson, P. (2006). *An Investigation into the Formation and Recruitment Processes of Aboriginal Gangs in Western Canada.* (Aboriginal Peoples Collection No. 25). Ottawa, ON: Public Safety Canada: Aboriginal Corrections Policy Unit.

Hendry, J., Tatum, M. L., Jorgensen, M., and Howard-Wagner, D. (2018). *Indigenous Justice: New Tools, Approaches, and Spaces.* London: Springer.

Henton, D. (2011). Thug Life; Alberta's Response to Gangs. *Alberta Views*, June.

Hixson, W. (2013). *American Settler Colonialism: A History.* London: Springer.

Johnston, P. (1983). *Native Children and the Child Welfare System.* Ottawa, ON: Canadian Council on Social Development.

Johnston, S. (2018). Edmonton's Downtown Business Association Worried About 'Blatant Drug Use' Along Jasper Avenue. *Global News*, June 7, 2018.

Jones, D., Bucerius, S., and Haggerty, K. (2019). Remanded Women in Western Canada: A Qualitative Analysis. *Journal of Community Safety and Well Being, 4*(3), 44–53.

MacDonald, D. B., and Hudson, G. (2012). The Genocide Question and Indian Residential Schools in Canada. *Canadian Journal of Political Science/Revue Canadienne de Science Politique, 45*(2), 427–449.

Maleakieh, J. (2018). *Adult and Youth Correctional Statistics in Canada 2016/17.* Ottawa, ON: Statistics Canada.

Mathews, F. (2005). *"Youth Gangs" in Issues and Perspectives on Young Offenders in Canada.* Edited by John A. Winterdyk, 3rd Edition. Toronto: Thomson Nelson.

Mihychuk, M. (2017). *Breaking Point: The Suicide Crisis in Indigenous Communities.* Report of the Standing Committee on Indigenous and Northern Affairs. Ottawa, ON: Government of Canada.

Monchalin, L. (2016). *The Colonial Problem: An Indigenous Perspective on Crime and Injustice in Canada.* Toronto: University of Toronto Press.

Mukherjee, R. (2006). The Ghetto Fabulous Aesthetic in Contemporary Black Culture. *Cultural Studies, 20*(6), 599–629.

Office of the Correctional Investigator. (2012). *Spirit Matters: Aboriginal People and the Corrections and Conditional Release Act.* Catalogue no.PS104–6/2013E-PDF. Ottawa, ON: Government of Canada.

Owusu-Bempah, A., and Wortley, S. (2013). Race, Crime, and Criminal Justice in Canada. In *The Oxford Handbook of Ethnicity, Crime, and Immigration*, S. M. Bucerius and M. Tonry (Eds.). Oxford: University Press, 281–320.

Parker, R., and Vronsky, P. (2015). *Hell's Angels Biker Wars: True Story of The Rock Machine and Bandido Massacres*. RJ Parker Publishing.

Preston, J. P., Carr-Stewart, S., and Bruno, C. (2012). The Growth of Aboriginal Youth Gangs in Canada. *The Canadian Journal of Native Studies*, *32*(2), 193–207.

Pyrooz, D, Decker, S. and Fleisher, M. 2011. "From the Street to the Prison, from the Prison to the Street: Understanding and Responding to Prison Gangs," Journal of Agression, Conflict and Peace Research, 3(1), 12-24.

Ray, A. J. (2016). *An Illustrated History of Canada's Native People*. Montreal and Kingston: McGill-Queen's University Press.

Regan, P. (2010). *Unsettling the Settler within: Indian Residential Schools, Truth Telling, and Reconciliation in Canada*. Vancouver: UBC Press.

Reyhner, J., and Singh, N. K. (2010). Cultural Genocide in Australia, Canada, New Zealand, and the United States. *Indigenous Policy Journal*, *21*(4).

Sinclair, R. (2016). The Indigenous Child Removal System in Canada: An Examination of Legal Decision-Making and Racial Bias. *First Peoples Child & Family Review*, *11*(2), 8–18.

Sinclair, R., and Grekul, J. (2012). Aboriginal Youth Gangs in Canada:(de) Constructing an Epidemic. *First Peoples Child & Family Review*, *7*(1).

Statistics Canada. (2017). Homicide in Canada, 2017. *The Daily*, Ottawa.

Statistics Canada. (2018). *Adult and Youth Correctional Statistics in Canada*, 2016/2017. Ottawa: Juristat.

Stout, M. D., and Kipling, G. D. (2003). *Aboriginal People, Resilience and the Residential School Legacy*. Ottawa, ON: Aboriginal Healing Foundation.

Tetrault, J., Bucerius S., and Haggerty, K. (2019). Multiculturalism Under Confinement: Prisoner Race Relations Inside Western Canadian Prisons. *Sociology*, *54*(3), 534–555.

Totten, M. (2009). Aboriginal Youth and Violent Gang Involvement in Canada: Quality Prevention Strategies. *IPC Review*, *3*(March), 135–156.

TRC (2015). *Honoring the Truth, Reconciling for the Future. Summary of the Final Report of the Truth and Reconciliation Commission of Canada*. Ottawa: Governemnet of Canada.

Turner, A. (2016). *Living Arrangements of Aboriginal Children Aged 14 and Under*. Ottawa, ON: Statistics Canada.

21

Transnationalism and postnational identities

The three lives of a Latin King

Carles Feixa

César Andrade, a.k.a. King Manaba, born in Manabí, Ecuador, in 1976, has lived three lives in three different nations. The first life was in Ecuador, from his birth until he turned 27 in 2003, when he decided to emigrate to Spain. He was following the exodus of people fleeing the economic and political crisis that then affected the Andean country, looking for the "promised paradise" in a "mother country" undergoing a time of prosperity. The second life started from this date, as a migrant experiencing the boom and crisis of the Hispanic immigration process, until 2009, when he was convicted of crimes against public health and went to prison for the first time. The third life started when he received the letter of his release from prison in 2013, returning to civil life in his new country and rising up again like the "phoenix". In these three lives, he felt part of three different "nations": in addition to his country of origin and his country of destination, which in this case is also binational, as it mixes Spanish and Catalan identities, King Manaba has also been part of a third "transnational nation" since he was crowned as a Latin King in Santo Domingo, Ecuador, at age 19, becoming part of the Almighty Latin Kings and Queens Nation (ALKQN). Since then, he has gone through three other stages in his life that correspond to those prescribed by the *King's Constitution Manifesto*: the "Primitive King" stage in his initiation and expansion phase; the "Conservative King" stage in his time of imprisonment and introspection; and finally the "New King" stage, in his phase of rebirth and maturation. Three stages that correspond to the same number of "homelands": Chicago – the "mother earth" – Santo Domingo – the "original father" – and Barcelona – the adoptive family. Thanks to this threefold experience – biographical, transnational and gang – King Manaba currently lives in a "nation of nations" – according to his own words – and thanks to the Internet, he connects daily with "*hermanitos*" and "*hermanitas*" of the ALKQN from Spain, Italy, Ecuador, almost all of Latin America and the United States. Based on King Manaba's life story, collected in multiple conversations from over the past 15 years, this text addresses the relationship between transnational migration processes and post-national identities.

Introduction: one Sunday at a youth centre

It's been almost 15 years since, shortly after meeting him, I promised César Gustavo Andrade Arteaga, a.k.a. King Manaba, that I would write a book about his life. I still haven't kept my promise, despite his insistence every time we meet. Looking back, I remember the experiences we have had together and which coincide with the birth, expansion, growth, fall and resurrection of the Almighty Latin King and Queen Nation, popularly known as the Latin Kings in Barcelona and beyond. I have now set myself the task of compiling the more than twenty recorded conversations – and many others that weren't recorded – that we have had over these years, aiming to put into practice the autobiographical imagination that I have always advocated.[1]

It's been almost 15 years since I first spoke with King Manaba, but I remember it as if it were yesterday. It was the first Sunday of June 2005. At around mid-morning, I received a call at my house in Vilafranca del Penedès (a city near Barcelona) from the director of the Transformadors Youth Centre in Barcelona. Her voice was shaky because she was in the middle of a delicate situation: the youth centre was surrounded by more than a hundred national policemen. They had come to record and file the identities of the two hundred young people of Latin American origin, mostly Ecuadorian and a dozen other nationalities. These included adolescents, children and mothers with babies, mainly dressed in baggy black clothes (with hints of yellow), who had a meeting at the youth centre that morning. We knew that they were Latin Kings, although neither she nor I knew then what lay behind this label. A year and a half ago, this name had been in all the newspapers, associating it with a dangerous youth gang similar to the terrifying Central American *Maras*. It had risen to fame in the wake of the tragic death of a young Colombian, Ronny Tapias, at the doors of a high school in Barcelona at the end of 2003 (in this case, the Latin Kings were not victimizers but victims, although the press treated them like they were the bad guys in a movie).

A few weeks before that Sunday, I had given the director of the youth centre a letter for the Latin Kings, requesting an interview with the backing of Luis Barrios, David C. Brotherton and Marcia Esparza, professors at the City University of New York who had been working with this group for years and who had just published the most important book on the organization (Brotherton and Barrios, 2003). It was the first time that I had used such a formal procedure to approach a youth subculture, but after reading the aforementioned book and other texts about this group, and due to my previous experiences with youth gangs in Catalonia and Mexico (Feixa, 1998), I sensed that it was a more complex group than a simple street gang. Until that day, the letter had not received an answer. In fact, no one officially knew that this group of people were Latin Kings, but when they asked the director to meet at the house on behalf of an association called STAE Nation, the City Council informed the local police, who made inquiries and discovered that the acronym stood for the *Sagrada Tribu Atahualpa Ecuador* (Sacred Tribe Atahualpa Ecuador), a group linked to the Latin Kings. Their first reaction to this discovery was to expel them from the premises, although their behaviour had been extremely correct and they had religiously paid the fee for using the facilities. Luckily, the City Council Prevention Services had commissioned me at the beginning of the year to carry out a study on young people of Latin American origin in Barcelona, motivated by the death of Ronny Tapias. The main objective of the study was to analyse what was myth and what was real in the problem of the so-called "Latino gangs". The director of this service, Josep Maria Lahosa, rightly understood that it was time to try to get in touch with them, to include them in our study and in the process explore the possibility of initiating a mediation. The intervention of the Barcelona Youth Council, which managed the premises and whose board of directors stated that they could not expel a group that had not done anything wrong or illegal, was also a crucial element.

On the Sunday in question, the director of the youth centre told me in a trembling voice that the leader of the group, feeling harassed by the police presence, had asked to speak with me. She immediately handed him the phone and I heard the voice of a person I would come to know as King Manaba. His voice seemed irritated but firm. I volunteered to mediate in the conflict and explained our study's objectives and the possibility of contacting the authorities if they agreed. We arranged to meet the next day in the centre to speak calmly. After a while, the director called me again to tell me that the call had had a positive effect. The leader had remained very calm after talking to me, and the police had left after recording the identities of all the young people. Later, these files would be used at press conferences to show that the Latin Kings were known and monitored and would not be allowed to expand in Spain.

The next day I arrived in good time at the appointment, along with my son Santiago, who was then eight years old. He had been born in Rionegro, Colombia (the hometown of the leader of the most famous gang in the world, although for other reasons: Pablo Escobar. I had recently learned from a Chicago Latin King to whom Manaba introduced me that the Narco par excellence used gang members and bought police officers to enter the United States through Puerto Rico). As it was school holidays, I had my son with me, but my motive for taking him to the meeting was to show that I was not afraid and that they could trust me. Manaba and two other young people attended the meeting: an Ecuadorian, King Plocky (who was eventually deported to Guayaquil), and a Catalan, King Baby White (who would become famous for leading a faction of the Latin Kings opposed to Manaba and who is now serving a jail sentence). We talked for a while. Manaba confessed to me later that he hadn't been completely sure about me, suspecting that I was a policeman or, worse still, a journalist. However, they had ventured to trust me. The way the letter was written and the mention of Luis Barrios, whom they knew not from his books but from the HBO documentary about the Latin Kings of New York, *Black and Gold*, made them think that maybe I was someone they could trust. The meeting confirmed my earlier intuitions about the group and that it was not a criminal organization but rather a youth street group, like those I had been studying since the eighties. However, it was a type of group that was very different from those I had known until then. Its transnational character, organizational level and symbolic elaboration were far more sophisticated than the gangs that I had previously studied (including Catalan *quinquis* formed by young gypsies and Mexican *Mierdas Punks* and *chavos banda* groups; see Feixa, 1998). At some point, I feared that the enemies of the legalization process that began later would use that initial meeting against me, as happened in New York and then in San Salvador, where the mediators ended up becoming the accused. This happened to the aforementioned Father Barrios and Father Toño, a Spanish priest who was involved in the truce between the Salvadoran government and the *Maras*, with whom I met later in their neighbourhood of Mexicanos in San Salvador, just before of the killing of Christian Poveda, the filmmaker of *La Vida Loca*. But, since I had a clear conscience, and I never offered anything that was outside the law, nor could I commit myself or them, I threw caution to the wind.

From criminal gang to cultural organization

The year that followed that meeting was hectic. We finished our study and presented it at the Centre of Contemporary Culture of Barcelona in November 2005, at a conference attended by two hundred researchers and professionals and a hundred Latin Kings & Queens and members of the alleged rival gang: the Ñetas. The book resulting from the study appeared the following year and had a large impact, although it did not focus on studying gangs but rather on the processes of migration and reception of young Latinos in Barcelona (Feixa, Porzio, and Recio, 2006). Later I promoted a research project on youth street groups at the time that the legalization process of the Latin Kings and Ñetas began, with the support of entities like Fedelatina (a federation of Latin American associations in Barcelona) and the Catalan Institute of Human Rights. This culminated in August 2006 with the constitution of the Cultural Organization of

Latin Kings and Queens of Catalonia, which was presented at the same Transformadors Youth Centre at a press conference attended by a hundred journalists (including the *Chicago Tribune* and *Los Angeles Times*, and Spanish and Ecuadorian television stations, which reported the event in the prime time news). The Ñetas Sociocultural, Musical and Sports Association was constituted the following year

The next two years were intense: concerts; meetings; the United for the Flow project at the Roquetes Youth Centre in Nou Barris, a neighbourhood populated mainly by emigrants (Unidos por el Flow, 2008); the photography project with the MACBA (Museum of Contemporary Art of Barcelona) (Schoellkopf, 2008); the soccer tournament between the twenty Latin King chapters of Barcelona and its metropolitan area (the Champion's Kings); trips to Madrid, Genoa and New York; countless meetings with *hermanitos* and *hermanitas* (brothers and sisters), educators, politicians, police, journalists, religious people, neighbourhood leaders and even with the CNI (National Intelligence Centre), who invited me to its headquarters in Madrid to give a talk on the subject. King Manaba and Queen Melody – his partner at the time, president of the association and key person in the process – were even invited to solemnly intervene in the youth commission of the Catalan Parliament. As several police officers have pointed out, the violence did not disappear during those years; however, the fights did significantly decrease, and most importantly, a network of mediators was created – including police and group leaders like King Manaba – who tried to mediate in the conflicts. Nevertheless, there were also hard times: tensions with sensationalist journalists, disagreements with the City Council and other institutions, internal conflicts within the Latin Kings and also the research team caused by impostors who took advantage of me and the young people and even accusations in a police conference in Rubí that all of this was done so an anthropologist could get rich by publishing a book about the experiment (which other police officers confirmed was doomed to failure even before it began).

In 2011, without the situation inside the gangs having changed, the new Home Minister of the Catalan government, Ramon Espadaler,[2] publicly announced – first on *Catalunya Radio* [the public regional radio] and then in parliamentary headquarters – that the "*do-goodism*" was over and a "hard hand" (*mano dura*) stage would begin (he said this after denying the corruption accusations that had begun to stalk the party in government). The team of police (*Mossos d'Esquadra*), who had worked on the subject with great professionalism and a preventive perspective, linked to the intelligence unit, received new managers, who had a strictly police view of the phenomenon and who depended on the criminal organizations unit (focused then and now on jihadist terrorism and drug trafficking). As one of the agents who had acted as a mediator said to me: "When you have a hammer, all you see are nails". Thus, all gang members were considered criminals, including minors who were still in school and for whom the cultural organization had been an effective alternative to the street. He ended the process and began a phase of raids, persecution and imprisonment. This coincided with the worst of the economic crisis, during which many of my former informants lost their jobs, returned to their countries of origin or served jail sentences. I temporarily left my field work, keeping the numerous and rich ethnographic data collected for another, better occasion, while others who had barely been on the periphery of the process made a career with much more superficial data, sometimes obtained through trickery.[3] Of course, I did not publish the book that should have made me rich, which Manaba did not cease to reproach me for.

As I begin to prepare to deal with this issue, César Andrade is now part of our research team at the Pompeu Fabra University and no longer the 29-year-old I met in 2005. In that time, he has matured, now almost 44 with many adventures but still requesting the book I promised him at our first meeting. In 2017, I obtained an Advanced Grant from the European Research

Council – the institution that finances the most cutting-edge research in all scientific fields – to research transnational gangs as mediation agents.[4] One of my ideas was to start the project by publishing the life story of King Manaba, using it as an excellent example of gangs as mediators, without idealizing or stigmatizing them but locating them between resistance and resilience. The TRANSGANG project began in January 2018 and during the first year focused on constituting the research team of more than thirty researchers, who will study the phenomenon in twelve cities in southern Europe, North Africa and America, including Chicago, the "motherland" of the Latin Kings and also of gang studies, as well as various places where this group is present – Medellín, San Salvador, Santiago de Cuba, Milan, Madrid, Barcelona, Casablanca, Tunisia and Algiers.

The three homelands of the Latin Kings

There are several legends about the origin of the Latin Kings. All agree that they emerged in Chicago, the same place where the first serious study on the subject was published: *The Gang*, by Frederick M. Thrasher (Thrasher, 1927/2021),[5] but disagree about the time and circumstances. Some versions maintain that the Latin Kings emerged in the 1940s as a defence of the second-generation Latino immigrants against the dominance of African American gangs. Others claim that they emerged in the 1960s, within the civil rights and minority defence movements (giving rise to groups like the Black Panthers and the Young Lords). Wikipedia gives the official founding date as 1954, and the official constitution of the group, the KMC (King's Manifesto Constitution), known as the Latin King Bible, says that the group was born in 1962. However, one of the current American referents of the group claims that it was founded in 1963 (Mission, 2008). As we were told recently by some brothers from Chicago whom King Manaba brought to the university, it seems that the Latin Kings first emerged as a street gang in the Latin neighbourhood of Chicago (around Humboldt Park) and was then officially formed in prison, where some of the leaders who drafted the aforementioned KMC were serving sentences.[6] In the 1970s, the Latin Kings expanded among the Latino community in other cities in the United States, mainly on the eastern coast, where Puerto Rican and Caribbean emigration was predominant. In the years of 1980 and 1990, the New York tribe underwent a process of politicization and community commitment thanks to new leadership and the support of intellectuals and religious people. This resulted in a fragmentation among followers of the Chicago doctrine (more traditionalist and hermetic) and those of New York (more reformist and open to contact with external agents). As part of this process, hip-hop was introduced, coming together in the concept of *nation* (drawing inspiration from the Zulu nation founded in 1973 by Kevin Donovan, a.k.a. Africa Bambaataa), around a *mestiza* nation – the *brown coffee* nation in the heart of the wasp nation. A female branch (the Queens, led by Queen Zulma) was also incorporated. This resulted in the official creation of the Almighty Latin Kings and Queens Nation.[7] The process, however, ended abruptly in 1996, when Rudolph Giuliani, the mayor of New York, launched Operation Corona, resulting in the incarceration of the most combative leaders of ALKQN.[8]

A few years before, in 1994, an Ecuadorian member of the New York tribe, King Boy Gean, was deported to his home country, where he re-founded the Nation, under the name of *Sagrada Tribe Atahualpa Ecuador* (STAE). It grew rapidly in the neighbourhoods of Guayaquil and Quito and began the transnationalization of the Latin Kings. In 2000, another Ecuadorian Latin King, King Wolverine, emigrated to Spain and planted the flag of a the new nation, the *Sagrada Tribu América Spain* (STAS). In 2004, after appearing on the TV talk show "Patricia's Diary", he was arrested and convicted of rape. During the same years, which coincided with a profound economic and political crisis in Ecuador and the economic boom in Spain, other Ecuadorian Latin Kings and Queens emigrated to Madrid and then to Barcelona and Murcia and re-founded the other branch of the Latin Kings (STAE). In 2006, the Catalan branch was officially constituted as the Cultural Organization of Latin Kings and Queens of Catalonia, with the support of the Barcelona City Council, the Catalan government and the regional police (Mossos d'Esquadra). This process was replicated in other regions such as Alicante, Mallorca and Navarra, although it failed in Madrid due to the opposition of the community president, Esperanza Aguirre (today accused of corruption), who opposed the efforts of Pedro Núñez Morgades, a child advocate named by the ruling conservative party, Popular Party (PP), to begin a dialogue. In 2007, the Madrid faction of the Latin Kings (STAS) was put on trial for unlawful association, in which I participated as an expert. The Spanish military police (*Guardia Civil*) had promoted *Operation Pañuelo* against this group, based on wiretapping and statements by former members (some of whom were linked to relatives of police agents). However, since there were no serious crimes and the evidence was very weak, the Supreme Court overturned the sentence and forced a retrial. In 2012, they reached a definitive conviction, although the arguments and evidence were almost identical. Nonetheless, the defendants chose not to appeal, since they had been waiting for years and the social climate had now become punitive, with the penal code in 2010 adding new criminal types (criminal group, criminal organization) and simplifying the probative criteria. The State Attorney General's Office, during the term of the PP government, promoted the idea that gangs (identified *de facto* with Latino gangs, despite the discriminatory nature of this equalization) should be followed and monitored, which meant that the majority of groups were subject to raids and criminal proceedings (while other gangs, such as extreme right groups or those of other ethnic backgrounds, were treated differently). In 2011, the Mossos d'Esquadra (Catalan police) replaced their more reformist leaders with those who believed in a more punitive criminal justice approach. This coincided with the increasing economic crisis among Latin American emigrants, some of whom chose to the return to their country, while others lost their jobs and started criminal careers.[9]

In 2007, the Rafael Correa Ecuadorian government, following the path opened up in Barcelona, legalized the Latin Kings as the Latin Kings and Queens Corporation of Ecuador, initiating a mediation process, which significantly reduced crime (Brotherton and Gude, 2018). Today, Latin Kings are present in most Latin American countries and in many European and even Asian countries. At the international level, there is no single leadership due to the persistent rivalries between Chicago and New York. In Ecuador, they are still legal (and even have a deputy in the parliament: Ronny Aleaga), while in Catalonia, where they have still not been declared illegal, they are not very active. In Madrid, by contrast, the STAS is an illegal association. The evolution of this group in different contexts and settings reflects the group's different pathways, be it criminal, legal or transnational.[10]

A Google search of the "Latin Kings" produces thousands of entries. The vast majority are news stories based almost always on police sources (mainly from the FBI), which highlight their link to organized crime. Academic studies on this group are inversely proportional to their fame. In the United States, we must cite the classic study by Conquergood (1994) on the Chicago tribe, focusing on its forms of verbal and nonverbal communication, as well as the complete ethnography on the New York tribe (Brotherton and Barrios, 2003). In Spain, the only book on the Latin Kings was published by two sensationalist journalists based on what the police confiscated from King Wolverine (Botello and Moya, 2005). Other books on Latin gangs have been promoted by police or security entities and never offer the viewpoint of the members themselves (Aparicio and Tornos, 2009; Association of Chiefs and Commands of the Local Police – Valencian Community, 2010). It is also worth mentioning the book resulting from our study on young Latinos in Barcelona (Feixa, Porzio, and Recio, 2006) and the essay by Queirolo (2017) which compares the situation of Latin gangs in Barcelona and Madrid. There is also an autobiographical account (*My Bloody Life*) of a former Latin King of Chicago in the witness protection programme. It was translated into Spanish a few years ago (Sánchez, 2000) and seems to be an apocryphal text prepared by the police from several testimonies without being clear what is true, fiction or exaggeration, as it agrees completely with the black-and-white portrait painted by the police.

The three lives of King Manaba

César Andrade was born twice. The first time was in Manabí, in the interior of Ecuador, in 1976, in a working-class family. The second time was in Santo Domingo, Ecuador, at age 20, in 1996, when he was crowned a Latin King, adding to his name King Manaba. After a few years of commitment to the Ecuadorian branch of the Nation, known as STAE, the conflict with other gangs – especially with the Ñetas – motivated him to emigrate. He arrived in Madrid in 2003, where 3 years earlier, the first European branch of the Latin Kings, known as STAS, had been founded. In early 2005, he arrived in Barcelona with the aim of expanding the Nation, and in June of that year, we met and began our collaboration. After three intense years in which he became involved in countless cultural projects, he was then imprisoned and sentenced to five years for a public health crime. After serving his sentence he returned to civilian life and took multiple jobs in the underground economy (during his prison stay, he was unable to renew his papers and is currently completing his second regularization process). In 2015, he was arrested again in a macro-raid with the explicit aim of dismantling the legal sector of the Latin Kings. Although there were no serious crimes behind the accusations, the objective of the new Mossos d'Esquadra leaders and the Prosecutor's Office was to set a precedent and condemn the group as a criminal organization. This had been facilitated by the reform of the Spanish penal code in 2010. What they wanted was to prove that Manaba was a leader, although there was no material evidence of who was involved in crimes and the evidence was based on contradictory statements by former members (some were allegedly threatened with deportation if they did not cooperate).[11] The trial took place in December 2018, and I acted again as an expert (as I did in the trial against STAS in 2007 and 2009, although this time a professional judge listened carefully to my intervention). As I write this chapter, we are waiting for the sentence.

Nowadays César / Manaba works as a research assistant in the TRANSGANG project. He comes every morning to his office at the university to do his work. He is a great conversationalist with a great sense of irony. At lunchtime he eats his home-cooked meal with his Tabasco sauce from his lunchbox with the research team in the university staff dining room and is never disrespectful to any of us (as we are not to him). Now he is single, although his Latin lover fame endures, and is waiting for his son Aaron, now 18 years old, to be able to reunite with him and his ex-wife, Queen Melody, with whom he has a cordial relationship.

My work on the life story of King Manaba (contained in the book referred to previously) is based on a total of twelve conversations over these last 15 years. The first is a focus group interview with the protagonist and two other Latin Kings, which took place in September 2005, at the headquarters of the Ombudsman for Children of Catalonia. There are four in-depth interviews (three individual and one with his partner at the time, Queen Melody) from 2006, in the middle of the legalization process and our action research. There are two other follow-up interviews in 2008, two interviews on leaving prison in 2012 and three interviews between 2016 and 2019. Another dozen recorded interviews and many other informal conversations that took place over the years have also been compiled.

In the book, I have divided his life story into three parts, each of which corresponds to a colour and a state through which a Latin King passes, as defined in the KMC, the ideological basis of *kingism* (the religion of the Kings and Queens). These parts contain the twelve chapters (called Conversations), which follow the chronological order of the interviews. Part I is the Colour Gold, allusion to royalty and corresponding to the status of Primitive King, the first phase in which the Latin King seeks the light of knowledge. It contains seven conversations that took place in the initial stage of the study, between 2005 and 2008, focused on the biographical itinerary and the legalization process. Part II is the Colour Black, an allusion to the pain and sacrifice of the Kings and corresponding to the state of Conservative King, the second phase in which the Latin King matures and regresses. It contains two deep and emotional interviews about Manaba's prison experience. Part III is Colour Coffee Brown, the brown fruit of the union of gold and black, an allusion to the miscegenation of the Latin Race, and corresponds to the State of New King or King Reborn, who is able to overcome death in life. This section contains three interviews conducted in recent years, from the last arrest to his phoenix-like resurrection, and focuses on his and the Nation's present and future. In the epilogue, César Andrade provides his vision of King Manaba, based on a classroom conversation entirely rewritten by the protagonist. In this concluding chapter, the protagonist summarizes the three lives of a Latin King in this way:

> Now I'm here as César Andrade, but I want to see King Manaba the way I knew him in Ecuador. In all this time he has matured, he no longer feels involved one hundred percent in the organization, he directly or indirectly helps many young people who follow and continue in the organization but in a way that in my time they did not help me. Because in my times maybe I didn't have a person who was older than me who could tell me this is good and this is bad. When you are a teenager you do things because you think they are good, but later it turns out that they are bad. So, I see that the evolution has been good. Time makes you evolve, it makes you more mature. I see that César Andrade sees King Manaba as a Latin King within the three stages of the king, as the New King, as the one who has evolved, as the one who now wants to see different things because he no longer wants problems in the streets. He doesn't want problems of any kind, he is just focused on his family environment and closest friends, his work on his studies, which is what all young people really should have and do. But of course, young people are also crazy, it's part of the process of this life, of each of us as a person. This has to be the mentality of every Latin King and Queen, to help all young people to prepare, educate them together with the values of the Nation and the values of our parents. This will reinforce the idea much more that every young person who wants to be part of the Nation has to be a King or a Queen of good for their community and society.
>
> In all this time many things have changed. Before, maybe, we had the wrong idea of what the organization was, we were younger, crazier. But when you grow up, as you get older, well you also start to see life differently and the way of behaving with society, with people, you start to experience it differently. Change is always for the good, never think it's bad, even though during all this time all you see are obstacles, whether you're young or old you'll always stumble and make mistakes, because life is made of stumbling and mistakes, and that is what will make you stronger and smarter. In my personal life, I'm a responsible person, in the sense that now with my work, with my personal life, with people, I suppose before I had other worries, I was not thinking much, I'm a bit more intelligent now. The street makes you smart too, the experiences that you live in the streets of Ecuador, and here in Barcelona and the journey that I've made over almost all of Spain visiting the different groups of

brothers, of friends that I have, are things that in the end make you mature and make you be a little more cautious and a little smarter in this life. Because as you get older you get smarter. You have to show that the years have not passed in vain and that they have served to change and so that your values and sacred five points come first before everything else.

What has not changed? Well I have not stopped being a Latin King, I have not retired because, as many people enter the group, they stay for a while and then they decide to sign the letter of expulsion (symbolically speaking), one of the things that has not changed over this time, and I've been part of the Latin Kings for almost 25 years, are my feelings towards the organization: every day that passes I have a feeling that is different and deeper, a bigger feeling. I'm not going to lie: at the beginning it looked like something different, like we had to get respect in the streets, in the neighbourhood, that nobody comes into our territory because we're going to take them out any way we have to, that was the mentality when I was young. But over time my mentality is that young people have to study, to prepare themselves to be someone in life. I know that many young people have their parents to give them the necessary advice, but many of the young people who look for these groups do not see their parents' support, so they are looking for a different lifestyle in us, they are looking for an identity that gives them the self-esteem that maybe in their homes they don't find. Then we give them self-esteem, we give them a power both inside and outside so they enjoy the gift of a leader, which is what we try to put into the heads of young people, who are leaders in their lives and that of people who ask for help, only then can they be an example of help for other young people, the community and society.

(King Manaba)

The three stages of the King – primitive, conservative, reborn – correspond to the three colours of the Nation, personified in the *bandana*:

The bandana for me is an amulet: I usually wear several colours, but in many cases, when I have to talk about my personal life as a Latin King, I wear the yellow and black bandana, it gives me inner strength to express myself in front of people, sometimes I keep it inside my pocket. Its meaning: gold represents the fabulous bright sun in its highest gaze, the radiance of hope in the oppressed people, the brilliance of the mind and the unity in strength, love and sacrifice; the black represents the dominant colour of the universe, the brave and courageous, the darkness of the immense night, it represents people of an idea, a body and mind and soul, the alpha and the omega. They are our primary colours in our organization. The gold and black unite to form the colour of coffee, which is the strength of our skin, of the Latinos and for which we must fight, "coffee strength" we call ourselves.

(King Manaba)

Throughout the entire research process, we have adhered to the general ethical protocols of ethnographic research with only one exception: anonymization is not total but rather partial. The names of César Andrade and Erika Jaramillo are their real names for obvious reasons and by their own decision, the same as those of the aforementioned adult professionals and public persons. The names of kings and queens appear with their a.k.a., the way they are known within the Nation. The place names are also real, except in those cases in which compromising situations are explained, in which case we have used generic names. Sometimes it is not easy to find the balance between describing the facts realistically without falling into sensationalism. Although we always try to respect all the people who appear in the story (young people, police officers, officials, etc.), we do not necessarily agree with their actions or opinions. The central chapters of the book refer to conflicts inside and outside the Nation at various levels. These involve conflicts over leadership; conflicts and crossed alliances between the North American, Ecuadorian and European tribes; and conflicts between the researchers that accompany the process in New York, Barcelona, Madrid, Genoa and Quito. I have met and interviewed the majority of the leaders (except King Boy Gean and King Wolverine, who agreed to meet with me in the prison; however, the prison services did not authorize it in time). The legalization process also caused tensions, and King Manaba's assessment of this process changes throughout the interviews, as he was more enthusiastic at the beginning (when all sectors seemed to support it) and more critical later (when a faction of the Latin Kings withdrew from the process and the City Council and the Mossos d'Esquadra decreased their support). Now the successes and failures of the process can be evaluated in perspective, and his assessment is more nuanced. Someone said that the "Latin King curse" had fallen on the people involved in the process (that of having opened Pandora's box, by projecting light on the darkness of the Nation and the nation, which mummified Tutankhamen). But deep down, these conflicts are about power and counterpower struggles similar to the "segmental opposition" processes which Sahlins (1968/1972) defined as a central feature of primitive tribal societies (and apparently also modern tribal societies).[12]

Reading keys

What are the reading keys to interpret the life story of King Manaba? I highlight three possible keys: (i) the life story as a *vertical synthesis* of social history and as a *horizontal synthesis* of social structure, (ii) the life story as a *chronotope* and (iii) the life story as a *subaltern story* (see Feixa, 2018).

The objective of the first reading key is to "read a society through a biography" (Ferrarotti, 1981, p. 43). According to this, Ferraotti says

> every human life is revealed, even in its less generalizable aspects, as the vertical synthesis of a social history. Each behaviour or individual act appears in its most singular forms as a horizontal synthesis of a social structure . . . our social system is entirely present in each of our actions, in each of our dreams, delusions, works, behaviours, and the history of this system is found whole in the history of our individual lives.
>
> *(1981, p. 41, my translation)*

In the case of King Manaba's story, it is about reading contemporary society (Barcelona, Catalan, Spanish, Ecuadorian, transnational) through the biography of a young gang member, initiated as a Primitive King in a coastal town of Ecuador, who emigrated to Madrid and then Barcelona, where he reached the category of Inka, and who after going through prison in his time as Conservative King was later reborn as New King. On one hand, King Manaba's story can be read as the vertical synthesis of a social history and that of the Latin American exodus to Europe (the crisis in Ecuador, dollarization, emigration to Spain, arrival in times of plenty, the crisis in Spain, voluntary return versus permanence, clandestinity versus regularization). On the other hand, his story can also be read as the horizontal synthesis of a social structure that originates, maintains and persecutes gangs such as youth street groups (originating in the North American ghettos, re-founded in Latin America as an effect of the deportation policy, transnationalization towards Europe, social segregation of emigration, "zero tolerance" versus "inclusive" policies, the influence of media representations, xenophobic discourses, expansion of the neoliberal criminal state, etc.). But far from being a puppet trapped between the two coordinates (horizontal and vertical), King Manaba shows himself to be a conscious and thoughtful actor, able to face his destiny and take charge of his life.

Second, although the autobiographical narrative can be read as an "open work" that is subject to different readings, so the reader becomes (co)author and the interpretation is polysemic and polyphonic (Eco, 1962/1984), our reading key is inspired by the "dialogic imagination" proposed by Bakhtin (1994), more specifically by the concept of *chronotope*, which we have tried elsewhere to apply in the study of youth cultures (Feixa, Leccardi, and Nilan, 2016). In *The Dialogic Imagination*, Bakhtin showed that the understanding of the space and time of a novel (which can also be applied to autobiography) depends on the *heteroglossic* ability (that is, on the ability to make other voices echo, to interpret not only depending on the text but also on the context). This capacity arises from a double dialogue: the "internal dialogue", fruit of the interaction of the subject with their own memory, and the "external dialogue", fruit of the interaction with the social environment represented by the audience (or by the researcher who asks, transcribes and interprets what is spoken):

> The lived statement, having taken meaning and form at a particular historical moment in a specific social environment, cannot avoid undoing hundreds of vivid dialogic threads, woven by socio-ideological consciences around the very object of the declaration; they cannot avoid actively participating in social dialogue.
>
> *(Bakhtin, 1994, p. 276, my translation)*

From this perspective, the spaces and times of King Manaba's life can be summarized in seven central chronotopes: the Nation, the nation, the border, the corner, the gold, the black and the coffee brown force. The first, the Nation (capitalized), is the space-time of the Almighty Latin King and Queen Nation, with their myths of origin, their rites of passage, their three states (Primitive King, Conservative King, New King), their four phases (Observation, Five alive, Probatory and Coronation), their five points (Love, Honour, Obedience, Sacrifice, Rectitude), their formal organization in chapters, sectors and tribes, and their informal organization in factions, clans and generations, their annual calendar of local and universal meetings, and their culmination in the 360 (the hermeneutic and social circle of the imagined community, which some interpret as the circle of pain where neophytes must bear the blows of the initiated). The second, the nation (lowercase), is the transnational space-time that connects the identity of origin (Ecuador) and the identity of destination, also binational (Spain-Catalonia), which is expressed in the concept of "Nation of nations" and is a constant in the story. The third, the border, refers to the physical, legal and symbolic barriers that separate continents, countries, neighbourhoods and rival gangs, as well as the instances (political, police, media) that build walls and justify exclusion. The fourth, the corner, refers to the connections and alliances that allow these borders to be crossed or mitigated, as well as the refuge-places (parks, youth centres, parishes, discos, etc.) where fraternal and friendship ties can be made. The fifth, gold, refers to both the first phase of the protagonist's life (that of the Primitive King) and the luminous and creative moments experienced inside and outside the Nation. The sixth, black, refers both to the second phase of the protagonist's life (that of the Conservative King) and to the dark and depressive time in prison or in spaces of seclusion and failure. Finally, the seventh, the brown coffee force, refers both to the third phase in the protagonist's biography (that of the New King) and to the experiences of cultural hybridization and mediation in which he has participated, from his commitment to the process of constituting the association to his interaction with researchers of the TRANSGANG project, including his task as a "peacemaker" between different factions of the group and between rival groups. The coffee brown force is the magic potion that allows you to be reborn as a republican king, according to the classic phoenix metaphor that resurfaces from its own ashes.[13]

Third, King Manaba's life story represents giving a voice to subaltern cultures, as Antonio Gramsci observed in his *Prison Notebooks* (1975). In one of the notebooks written during his imprisonment by Mussolini, between 1932 and 1935, the Italian politician and thinker reflects on the value of autobiographies:

> It is true that autobiography has great historical value, since it shows life in action and not only as it should be according to written laws or dominant moral principles. . . . However, history, in general, is made on the written law: when new facts that reverse the situation come to light afterwards, vain questions arise, or there is a need to document how the mutation has been prepared 'molecularly' before exploding.
>
> *(Gramsci, 1975, pp. 1718–1724, my translation)*

Jail is one of the autobiographical territories par excellence because from this incarcerated space reflecting on one's past and identity arise spontaneously and by different forms of writing (letter, memory, graffiti, tattoo). Gramsci was one of the first Marxist authors who promoted the biographical genre as a fundamental instrument in social research, compensating for the difficulties of the subaltern culture to make itself heard and become hegemonic. Only through biographies is it possible to see the "mechanism" in action and embodied in real individuals. Autobiography can be conceived "politically"; although one life is similar to many other lives, it always contains original entries. History and life are complementary poles in the construction of a type of humanistic *materialism* that allows us to understand not only how structures work but also how specific people react to historical changes or, in the author's words, how these changes are prepared in an invisible way "molecularly" before exploding. Gramsci himself, in the letters he wrote from prison to his wife and children, shows the fruitfulness of biographical writing and the dialogic nature of all vital reflection. In another jail notebook, the author refers to folklore in these terms:

> It could be said that until today folklore has been studied primarily as a 'picturesque' element. . . . It should be studied, instead, as the 'conception of life and the world', largely implicit, of certain strata (determined in time and space) of society, in contrast (also in general implicit, mechanical, objective) with the 'official' conceptions of the world (or, in a broader sense, of the cultured parts of historically determined societies) that have happened in historical development. . . . Folklore can only be understood as a reflection of the conditions of people's cultural life, although some conceptions of folklore can be prolonged after the conditions are (or seem) modified or give rise to strange combinations.
>
> *(Gramsci, 1975, vol. III, pp. 2,311–2,317, my translation)*[14]

From this perspective, the Latin King subculture, and all the cosmovision contained in the KMC and kingism, fit with the characteristics of the popular culture of the subaltern classes (generating a "strange combination" that could be called ganglore or kinglore). On the one hand, it reflects a social structure based on unequal access to resources and power, reproduces traditional values, alludes to the past as something sacred and immutable (as survival) and reproduces ethnocentrism and sometimes sexism. However, on the other hand, it also has a progressive force as an experience of community and resistance, as a channel to express the voice of the oppressed. Ernesto de Martino analysed this two-fold character of the subaltern culture in his works on progressive folklore (De Martino and Feixa, 2008). The Latin Kings can be considered a variant of those "contemporary subalterns" that Gramsci, De Martino and Pasolini identified in Italy before and after World War II as seeds of social change. This implies not giving up a class analysis or a political reading of autobiographies, combining resistance and resilience (see Feixa *et al.*, 2019).

Conclusion

Somewhere between the criminal gang and the musical band,[15] my book aspires to narrate in first person the life of a King. It is conceived as the first part of a trilogy, whose second part (*Is It Possible to Legalize a Gang?*) envisages analysing the process of "constituting an association" in Catalonia and whose third part (*The Golden Nation*) is conceived as a transnational ethnography of the Latin Kings & Queens. This first part of the trilogy is inspired by the life of King Manaba, although its resemblance to reality could be pure coincidence. The *leit motif* is the personal memory of the protagonist, always selective: the exercise of introspection, narrated by a gang member who sometimes reminds us of Tony Soprano but who has not committed his misdeeds, conversing with an anthropologist who sometimes acts like Dr. Melfi without being a psycho-therapist. From the Italian-American mafia to the Latino gangs – passing through *The Wire* and *Peaky Blinders* – reality sometimes mimics fiction. King Manaba's life seems like a movie, at times in the form of a hagiographic biopic, at other times in the form of anti-biographic flash-backs, a comedy or a tragedy. If a filmmaker turns it into a television series – soap opera, police series, epic story or situation comedy – they will find ample material.

Postscripts

Postscript 1. On the day I began to review for the first time the Spanish version of this text, 22 July 2019, when I arrived home, I watched the television summary of the investiture session of Pedro Sánchez as president of the Spanish government and was surprised to hear several references to the term "gang" (in Spanish "*banda*"). The leader of the Ciudadanos party (centre-right), Albert Rivera (whom Queen Melody and I met in a meeting on youth policies in Brasilia when he was just beginning his political career in 2009) accused the socialist candidate and his possible political and nationalist allies of being a dangerous "gang" and addressed Sánchez in the following terms:

> With whom is he going to carry out his plan? With his gang, and what a gang! With Otegui (Basque pro-independence left) celebrating with the nationalists in Navarra, with those of Més [nationalist left] in the Balearic Islands, with the nationalists in the Valencian community, with Podemos (left) leading the economy of Spain. Those are his partners and he has a plan and he has a gang. And the question is: Has the gang just got together for this investiture in the next room? No, they have been together for a long time. . . . You have Mr. Torra (Catalan pro-independence president) and his company in the gang. Sánchez has a plan, and he has a gang, those who want to liquidate Spain and those who do not believe in the free market or free trade. You have perpetrated his plan with this gang. The Sanchez plan is underway, the gang already knows who it is and now he wants to put it in the national government (sic).

As the use of the term is a clear allusion to the terrorist "gang" (*banda*) ETA, Aitor Esteban, a spokesman for the Basque Nationalist Party (PNV), replied ironically:

> Let's get to the heart of the matter. How ironic! So patriotic in the chamber that he fills his mouth with the word Spain . . . Well, I also imagine him in a band, but in this case a musical band, setting the note from the podium and the serenade from his seat (resic)].

Postscript 2. In October 2019, when the book was finished, the *hermanitos* from Ecuador sent a video to King Manaba with a speech by President Lenin Moreno, who, to calm the anger of the indigenous people protesting against the economic austerity measures taken on the insistence of the IMF, addresses them with the words:

> Citizens, everything is completely clear and it is also advantageous for our indigenous brothers: It is the drug traffickers, the criminal Latin Kings, it is the Correistas who do these acts of vandalism. Luckily the indigenous people have detected them and are separating them from their ranks (sic).

The reference is not trivial: one of the leaders of the Latin Kings and Queens Corporation of Ecuador, Ronny Aleaga, is a deputy in the National Assembly of the party of former President Correa, a division of the government Alianza País.

Postscript 3. On 14 October, 2019, while I am with Manaba in Catalunya Square in Barcelona, the day the sentence was published against the Catalan independence leaders, we learn that Moreno has backed down and has withdrawn the decree. Manaba comments: "The protesters in Ecuador are like the protestors here, but with *ponchos*". And I answered. "I'm sure they won't take long to start talking about the protesters as 'organized gangs'". On 17 October, after several days of protests in Catalonia, I woke up listening to the morning talk on *Catalunya Radio*. A speaker close to the Ciudadanos party refers to the Maras by saying: "Those of the Democratic Tsunami (Catalan pro independence movement) are a violent gang, like the *kale borroka* (street violence in the Basque Country during the era of terrorism)". To which another speaker responds "there are gangs, but the most dangerous are the fascist gangs". The "gang", then, as a throwing weapon, stigma and metaphor of political combat.

Postscript 4: In recent times, the three politicians who promoted "heavy hand" polices against the Latin Kings and carried out raids and processes accusing them of being a "criminal organization" – Rudolph Giuliani in New York, Esperanza Aguirre (ex-leader of PP right-wing ruling party) in Madrid and several politicians of the CiU, a (conservative nationalist) party in the Catalan government in 2012 in Barcelona – have been charged with corruption. In all three cases, large amounts of money allegedly stolen from the public treasury are at stake. All of them have expensive private lawyers; none have served pretrial detention, nor have they been convicted so far (with the exception of some second-level CiU politicians); neither have the political parties to which they belonged, which endorsed or turned a blind eye to these practices, been made illegal. During the same period, the majority of "Latino gangs" in Spain have been prosecuted for "illegal association", "criminal group" or "criminal organization". Although there have been some serious cases – whose victims are usually the gang members themselves – in general, the crimes allegedly committed are of little economic entity, linked to small drug trafficking, fights or simply group membership. The majority of the defendants went through pretrial detention, were defended by ex officio lawyers – who acted with great professionalism despite the low pay and the many pages of the file that had to be reviewed – and have served or are currently serving sentences. Almost all the groups to which they belong have been made illegal at some point, although their members continue to act openly.

Postscript 5. When the book was completed, I had access to the sentences of the trials for unlawful association against the Latin Kings in Spain, with surprising findings. In the first trial of 2007, the Provincial Court of Madrid published the sentence in record time (barely 15 days after the end of the trial!), which leads us to suspect a presumption of guilt. In 2009, it was overturned by the Supreme Court, due to insufficient justification: one of the speakers was Luciano Varela (progressive member, who has been part of the trial for the Catalan referendum). In 2010, the trial was repeated, again with a conviction, although the arguments were similar but more refined. In 2011, after the reform of the penal code, a new punitive climate and a government of the conservative PP party, the Supreme Court ratified the sentence. One of the speakers was a judge who has recently become famous for presiding over the trial for the Catalan referendum and whom politicians of the PP proposed to chair the General Council of the Power of Attorney because they felt they could control him from behind: Manuel Marchena.

Postscript 6. On 27 January 2020, one day after sending the corrections of the second proofs of the book and one day before sending it to print, when the two authors of the same were in a practical seminar on the subject of crime and communication media, part of the criminology degree of the UPF, while the students commented in groups on the news items about Latin gangs that appear in the book, we received a whatsapp from César's lawyer, with an attached document that included another long text of 190 pages: judgment 10/2020, issued by section 21 of the Provincial Court of Barcelona, by the procedure of summary 11/2017, for the crimes of "CRIMINAL ORGANIZATION, THREATS, OBSTRUCTION OF JUSTICE, MURDER, AGAINST PUBLIC HEALTH, ILLEGAL DETENTION, ABUSE OF WORKSITES AND THEFT" against 23 defendants, presumably members of the Latin Kings legal sector, including César Gustavo Andrade Arteaga as principal accused, for whom the prosecution requested a sentence of 28 years in jail as leader of the criminal organization, whose detention, preventive detention and trial is described in great detail in the last two conversations of the book. The decision of the three judges who drafted the sentence is conclusive: they condemn six of those accused for minor offences, but César Andrade and the remaining defendants are acquitted of all charges. When we read the news, we jumped for joy. The students, to whom we had just explained the complex relations of the Latin Kings with the press, the police and the judicial system, observed us with surprise. We explained that when King Manaba was arrested, it was prominent news on the radio, television and in the press (who, despite the secrecy of the operation, were present at 6am on June 2015 at the house of Santa Coloma de Gramanet where the raid began). In the days following the acquittal, no important media reported the news, with the sole exception of a small digital medium – www.metropoliabierta.com – with the heading "The Latin Kings win a great judicial battle". When we said goodbye after six consecutive hours of class and seminars, we agreed that sometimes there is justice in life. We could not imagine a better ending to this book!

Postscript 7. On 25 March 2021, when I proofread this text, we launched *El Rey* for the umpteenth time since it was published a year ago, and for the first lauch of *La Banda*, the classic Thrasher's book that we have just translated into Spanish. We do it by zoom and by youtube, in front of a transnational audience. Only the first lauch was live (at the Ecuadorian food restaurant *El Manaba* in Barcelona). The rest have been virtual, since the pandemic in which we continue to live arrived. During this time, Cesar's acquittal was confirmed, who was finally able to regularize his situation in Spain for the second time and was able to be hired as a TRANSGANG research assistant. Our intention in the coming months is to be able to present the book in Ecuador and, who knows, also in Chicago. To be continued.

Acknowledgments

This chapter is an outcome of the TRANSGANG project: Transnational Gangs as Agents of Mediation: Experiences of Conflict Resolution In Youth Street Organization in Southern Europe, North Africa and the Americas (www.upf.edu/web/transgang). This project has received funding from the European Research Council (ERC) under the European Union's HORIZON 2020 research and innovation programme under grant agreement No 742705.

Notes

1 The book was finally completed and published in Spanish with the title *El Rey. Diario de un Latin King* (Feixa and Andrade, 2020).
2 Catalan politician, between 2012 and 2015, he was the interior minister. On that date, he was a member of the UDC, a Christian democratic party; In the most recent elections to the Catalan Parliament of 2017, he appeared on the lists of the PSC, a socialist party.
3 This process can be seen in three articles published in the leading Spanish journal *El País* (Feixa and Muñoz, 2004; Feixa, Cervino *et al.*, 2006; Feixa, 2014).
4 *El Pais Semanal* published a report entitled "Professor Punk's Millionaire Scholarship: Hip-Hop Against Youth Gangs" (1–10–2017).
5 In the framework of the TRANSGANG project, we have recently translated and published the Spanish version of *The Gang*, with an introductory study (Thrasher, 1927/2021).
6 On the Latin Kings of Chicago, see the works of Conquergood (1994) and the documentary promoted by the same researcher: *The Heart Broken in Half* (Siegel and Conquergood, 1990).
7 When we use *Nation* with a capital letter, we are referring to the ALKQN; *nation* with a lowercase letter refers to any other nation.
8 See Brotherton and Barrios, 2003; Kontos, 2003; Latin Kings, 2019; ALKQN, 2019. The reform phase of the ALKQN in New York is explained in the documentary *Black and Gold,* produced by HBO (Rowley and Soohen, 2000).
9 For an analysis of this period, see Feixa, Porzio, and Recio (2006), Feixa *et al.*, 2008, 2011). The first part of this process – legalization – is reported in the documentary films *Vida Real: Latin Kings en Cataluña* (Casals and Martínez, 2006), and Unidos por el Flow (2008); The second part – the crisis – is reported in the documentary film *Buscando Respeto* (González Morandi, Palmas, and Feixa, 2012).
10 The Ecuadorian legal branch of the Latin Kings recently starred in a documentary film on TVE: *Amor de Rey* (En Portada, 2019).
11 Although the prosecution requested prison without bail, the judge considered the reasons given insufficient and that the defendant should be released.
12 In addition to the internal segmentation in each city, there is a nationwide segmentation between Chicago and New York, Quito and Guayaquil, Madrid and Barcelona.
13 Brazilian researcher Joao Gabriel Almeida showed me some parallels between the colours and rituals of the Latin Kings and those of the Afro-Caribbean santeria. The rule of ifá uses as its foundation the opposition of two colours, yellow and green in the Cuban tradition and orange and green in the Nigerian tradition, to place life and death in opposition. In addition, the necklace is the symbol of entering a religion, while necklaces with a mallet represent an initiate with higher rank, who already has the approval of the leader in some of the orishas. There is a coincidence in the use of necklaces as a ritualistic element of entry to the group and visual recognition of status, as well as the reference to the idea that being part of the group leads to a pact between death and life, represented by the opposition of two colours. The idea of gold as a reference to light and beauty corresponds to the worship of the goddess Oshun, while the cult to Iku, death, uses a black and white necklace, in which the black represents death in this opposition logic.
14 See De Martino and Feixa (2008). In his book on the meaning of life, Joan Prat shows how autobiographies written under the model of social marginalization or exclusion can lead to the dissolution of the subaltern self (Prat, 2007).
15 In Spanish Gang is *Banda*, a word that has two meanings: criminal group and music group.

References

Aparicio, R., & Tornos, A. (2009). *Aproximación al estudio de las Bandas Latinas de Madrid*. Madrid: Gobierno de España: Ministerio de Trabajo e Inmigración.

Asociación de Jefes y Mandos de la Policía Local-Comunidad Valenciana. (2010). *Grafitis y Bandas Latinas*. Valencia: Mad.

Bakhtin, M. (1994). *The Dialogic imagination*. Austin: University of Texas Press.

Botello, S., & Moya, A. (2005). *Reyes Latinos: Los Códigos Secretos de los Latin Kings en España*. Madrid: Ediciones Temas de Hoy.

Brotherton, D. C., & Barrios, L. (2003). *The Almighty Latin King and Queen Nation. Street politics and the transformation of a New York City gang*. New York: Columbia University Press.

Brotherton, D. C., & Gude, R. (2018). *Social inclusion from below: The perspectives of street gangs and their possible effects on declining homicide rates in Ecuador*. Washington, DC: BID. http://dx.doi.org/10.18235/0001057.

Conquergood, D. (1994). How street gangs problematize patriotism. In H. W. Simons & M. Billing (Eds.), *After postmodernism. Reconstructing ideology critique* (pp. 200–221). London: Sage.

De Martino, E., & Feixa, C. (Eds.). (2008) *El foklore progresivo y otros ensayos*. Barcelona: MACBA.

Eco, U. (1962/1984). *Obra abierta*. Barcelona: Planeta.

Feixa, C. (1998). *De jóvenes bandas y tribus*. Barcelona: Ariel.

Feixa, C. (2014, Abril, 16). 'The Wire' en el Born. *El País*, La Cuarta Página.

Feixa, C. (2018). *La imaginación autobiográfica*. Barcelona: Gedisa.

Feixa, C., & Andrade, C. (2020). *El Rey: Diario de un Latin King*. Barcelona: NED.

Feixa, C., Canelles, N., Porzio, L., Recio, C., & Giliberti, L. (2008). Latin Kings in Barcelona. In F. van Gemert, D. Peterson, & I.-L. Lien (Eds.), *Street gangs, migration and ethnicity* (pp. 63–78). Devon, UK: Willan Publishing.

Feixa, C., Cervino, M., Palmas, L., & Barrios, L. (2006, Junio, 6). El fantasma de las bandas. *El País*, Tribuna.

Feixa, C., Leccardi, C., & Nilan, P. (Eds.). (2016). *Youth, space & time. Agoras and chronotopes in the global city*. Leiden and Boston: Brill.

Feixa, C., & Muñoz, G. (2004, April 12). ¿Reyes Latinos? Pistas para superar los estereotipos. *El País*, 12/12/04. Reproducido en *El Universal*, Quito.

Feixa, C. (Dir.), Porzio, L., & Recio, C. (Coords.). (2006). *Jóvenes latinos en Barcelona. Espacio público y cultura urbana*. Barcelona: Anthropos-Ajuntament de Barcelona.

Feixa, C. (Dir.), Sánchez García, J. (Coord.), Ballesté, E., Cano-Hila, A. B., Masanet, M.-J., Mecca, M., & Oliver, M. (2019). *The (Trans)Gang: Notes and queries on youth street group research*. Barcelona: Universitat Pompeu Fabra & European Research Council. http://dx.doi.org/10.31009/transgang.2019.wp02.1

Feixa, C., Scandroglio, B., López, J., & Ferrándiz, F. (2011). ¿Organización cultural o asociación ilícita? Reyes y reinas latinos entre Madrid y Barcelona. *Papers: Revista de Sociología*, 96(1), 145–163.

Ferrarotti, F. (1981). *Storia e storie di vita*. Bari: Laterza.

Gramsci, A. [1932–35] (1975). *Quaderni del carcere*. Torino: Einaudi.

Kontos, L. (2003). Between criminal and political deviance: A sociological analysis of the New York chapter of the Almighty Latin King and Queen Nation. In D. Muggleton & R. Weinzierl (Eds.), *The postsubcultures reader* (pp. 133–150). London: Berg.

Mission, K. (2008). *The official globalization of ALKQN/La globalización oficial de ALKQN*. New York: Self edition.

Prat, J. (2007). *Los sentidos de la vida*. Barcelona: Bellaterra.

Queirolo Palmas, L. (2017). ¿*Cómo se construye un enemigo público? Las 'bandas latinas'*. Madrid: Traficantes de Sueños.

Sahlins, M. (1968/1972). *Las sociedades tribales*. Barcelona: Labor [*Tribesmen*. New York: Prentice Hall].

Sánchez, R. (2000). *My bloody life: the making of a Latin King*. Chicago: Chicago Review Press.

Schoellkopf, J-L. (2008). Altres xarxes socials: els Latin kings. En *Imatges metropolitanes de la nova Barcelona*. Barcelona: Macba-El Periódico.

Thrasher, F. M. (1927/2021). *The gang. A study of 1313 gangs of Chicago*. Chicago: University of Chicago Press. [*La Banda. Un estudio sobre 1313 bandas de Chicago*. Barcelona: NED].

Unidos por el Flow. (2008). *Latin Kings, Ñetas y otros jóvenes de Barcelona . . . Unidos por el Flow*. Barcelona: K. Industria Cultural.

Filmography

Casals, M., & Martínez, J. C. (Dirs.), Feixa, C. (Guión). (2006). *La vida real. Latin Kings en Cataluña*. España: Jolines Producciones-UdL. (40').

En Portada. (2019). *Amor de Rey*. España: TVE. (39').

González Morandi, J. (Dir.), Palmas, L., & Feixa, C. (2012). *Buscando respeto*. España: UdL–UE (Marie Curie).

Rowley, R., & Soohen, S. (2000). *Black and gold*. Big Noises Film. (75').

Siegel, T., & Conquergood, D. (1990). *The heart broken in half*. Collective Eye Films. (60').

Unidos por el Flow. (2009). *Latin kings, Ñetas y otros jóvenes de Barcelona . . . Unidos por el Flow*. España: K Industrial Cultural. (60').

Webography

ALKQN. (2019). Almighty Latin King and Queen Nation. Official Web. Consulted: 28 September, 2019 at www.alkqn.org.

Latin Kings. (2019, 6 September). Wikipedia, Free Encyclopaedia. Consulted: 28 September, 2019 at https://es.wikipedia.org/w/index.php?title=Latin_Kings&oldid=118974569.

22

Race and youth gangs in France

Denial, ambiguity, and recognition

Marwan Mohammed and Akim Oualhaci

In France, the oft-used concept of "ethnic gangs" refers mainly to groups consisting of young Arab and Black men who live in poor urban neighborhoods. The concept appears first in the beginning of the 1980s, peaks in the 1990s, and then comes back and forth in the news through the issue of collective confrontations. The concept postulates the racial overdetermination of a phenomenon that, until the end of the 1970s, remains mainly associated with the racially neutral working-class youth, that is to say white youth. Through this prism, the gang is primarily described and explained by the origin or the skin color of its members. Membership, unity, and collective action are supposed to take root in ethno-racial identities. This omission of race fuels a burning and passionate debate which is situated at the intersection of immigration, the *banlieues*, and insecurity, three major ingredients of a recurrent discourse on immigration, national identity, and presumed challenges to the Republic in neighborhoods where the poorest postcolonial minorities are concentrated. The social and political pressure, therefore, is very powerful when broaching this topic, even though it has not been sufficiently addressed by French sociologists. For half a century, the number of studies on gangs in France has been few, especially on gangs in rural areas and in mid-sized cities.

The sociological studies on gangs in the United States and in France are very heterogeneous. Early on, US researchers paid some attention to the question of race in contrast to their French counterparts, and we would broadly argue that the cultural, political, and administrative approaches of the two countries have been quite different. In the United States, race is an administrative category used by the Census Bureau for the survey of the population as well as a category of practice, that is, a category that people use to explain and orient their everyday experiences and their vision of the social world. In France, race is not an administrative category, and it is even legally forbidden to produce so-called "ethnic" statistics. Few French people use the category of race on an everyday basis. It does not mean that there is no structural and ongoing racialization in French society, or racism, or even that individuals do not see the social world and social relations through a racial prism. On the contrary, the long-standing denial of the racialization processes partakes of a deliberate ignorance of the way French society operates and also contributes to the production of racism in France. It is therefore crucial for sociologists to pay much greater attention to the issue of race, articulating it with class and gender,[1] all the more so when one studies gangs. To take up that epistemological prism is essential for two main reasons: on the one hand, racial minorities are commonly associated with gangs and are targeted by the police who use anti-gang laws in the United States. On the other hand, the common representations about gangs are often caricatural and tend to associate them with criminality and young men from racial minorities. The recurrent uses of a blurred definition of the gang and the association of these words with young men of color from disadvantaged urban neighborhoods makes the sociological study of these phenomena and race a major issue.

The social relations based on race structuring are now widely studied in US academia, even if some continue to defend a long-standing hegemonic colorblindness paradigm,[2] which is largely dominant in France. We are reminded of this by the unanimous vote of the members of the Parliament, on July 12th, 2018, that suppressed the word "race" from the 1st article of the constitution. Before this vote, the 1st article stipulated that France "ensures equality before the law of all citizens without distinction of origin, race or religion." After the vote, the text stipulates that France "ensures equality before the law of all citizens without distinction of sex, origin or religion." The word "race" appeared in the preamble of the 1946 Constitution before being taken out in 1958, in the context of the end of Nazism, in order to reject the biological racism theorized in the 19th century and implemented in the French colonies. The argument that was put forward for this suppression is based on natural science. The human species is one and indivisible and, therefore, there are no different human races. This limited conception of race has been adopted by leftist members of parliament for some time and supported by several members of Parliament from the French overseas territories. Officially, the legitimacy of the vote should be scientific and not political. Yet the suppression of the word "race" fits perfectly with the dominant republican doxa based on the idea of the abstract universalism of values and the indivisibility of the human being. Individuals are free and equal before the law with the Republic blind to differences. For the State and most of the French elites, racism, when it is recognized, is grasped in terms of individual prejudice rather than a system of power. It is, therefore, not surprising that knowledge on the issue of race produced by autonomous scholars in the social sciences is rejected as a whole and subjected to intense, and sometimes hysterical, campaigns of disqualification in the public sphere.

Yet this denial of race is related to the trivialization of racism in French society and in the operating systems of public administrations and the State. Through these statements of its representatives and through government policies and the functioning of some administrations, the State contributes to the racialization of social phenomena, although it cannot be discussed in these terms. It (the state) participates in the criminalization of minorities through penal targeting which escapes statistical scrutiny by making the origin or skin color of the criminalized invisible in its databases. The same is true for many of the country's elites who are quick to denounce any reference to whiteness,[3] while at the same time giving great credence to studies explaining transgressive behavior based on cultural origin.[4] The same is also true of the debates on the alleged over-representation of certain non-white minorities from disadvantaged families in the criminal justice system and in prison. In France, the dominant political interpretation of criminal involvement is racist because it derives crime and its punishment from the cultural characteristics and origins of the convicted only when they belong to minorities.

This selective denial of the issue of race has not spared the institution in charge of producing knowledge about the social world. This denial remains vivacious even as research on the racial dynamics of French society and its articulation with economic, cultural, and political issues would constructively contribute to redefining the terms of the theoretical and academic debate. Therefore, it is not surprising to see the invisibility of these issues in scholarly work, particularly in the sociology of youth gangs. For this reason, we are focusing our attention on the links between gangs and race through a diachronic examination of French academic production and its political context.

From the "Black Jackets" to the youths from the *banlieues*: gangs caught up by immigration

From the beginning of the 20th century, the media coverage of gangs in France ignored the racial issue until the end of the 1970s. At the start of the 1960s, skin color was absent from press articles that dealt with gangs. This is evidenced by the media treatment of the "Black Jackets," gangs that were influenced by the rock'n'roll wave that popularized North American movies, clothing, and music. Journalists described these groups' members as young, working-class white people wearing black jackets.[5] According to the studies in question, these young individuals had little or no experience of racial plurality. Following this group, ten years later, a new generation of gangs emerged called the "Loubards." They marked a decisive transition from the "world of the working class" to the "world of the housing projects." Yet, as early as the 1960s, observations by a number of researchers revealed a different racial reality, although they never gave rise to in-depth and extensive analyses.

Paul-Henry Chombart de Lauwe, in one of the first empirical studies in social housing districts, noted in 1963 that "ethnic segregation has not yet been studied in France" and that the "problem is nevertheless of importance in certain sectors."[6] In addition to this, he focuses mainly on the demarcation logics that structured "the division of groups and . . . categories of perception"[7] in the large newly delivered social housing complexes that initially provided accommodation for the working and middle classes. Paul-Henry Chombart de Lauwe did elaborate on this "ethnic segregation" observation but restricted his analysis to the polarizations between "social outcasts," at the lower fringes of the working class and the rising middle and upper classes. Although the racial question is latent, it is not part of the issues addressed. In another major study conducted in the 1960s and published in 1970, Jean-Claude Chamboredon and Madeleine Lemaire made little reference to racial dynamics as they analyzed the mistrust and distance, the stigmatization of certain behavior, the experiences of education, and the conflicts that permeate life in high-rise buildings. Here again, class and intra-class divides were the preferred prism of analysis.

Ethnographic studies during this period reveal more of the reality. For example, it was the ethnologist Jean Monod – one of the few researchers to observe gangs directly and durably – who provided more accurate accounts, describing the Black Jackets in Paris with young immigrants among its ranks, together with insights into racial differences in the mid-1960s:

> I had had many opportunities to see the racism of thugs. I had explained it to myself with economic reasons. Marginal like the thug, the '*crouilles*',[8] a derogatory word for "Arabs", constitute a sub-proletarian mass that contributes to the devaluation of the wages of other youth. But this was a rationalization since, on the whole, these young people refused all work. Their contempt for the *crouilles* was then only the logical extension of their (general) contempt for workers. In addition, there was also very pervading virulent racism in working-class circles. . . . Solidarity in the gangs was an ideal that was too often flouted. Like the North Africans, they only gave the impression of being united because they were rejected *en masse* by society.

This racism and contempt of non-white youth did not prevent some North Africans from becoming gang leaders or playing an important role in gangs that came at a cost:

> Fascinated by what they hate, thugs quickly turned into exceptions those who, adorned with the prestige of caricature, come to them to do the same thing as them and more easily.[9]

Jean Monod even observes a limited number of predominantly foreign gangs on the Paris outskirts:

> In Sarcelles, I met a gang that limited their membership to thirty. . . . They were all work-
> ing class with a large number of foreign origin; they work in the suburbs, either in factories
> or alongside craftsmen (mirror makers, locksmiths); they do not live in the new projects,
> but in the surrounding countryside, in isolated slums or low-income housing; they all have
> a moped to get around; they only find themselves at the end of the week in the snack bar
> adjacent to the project's only cinema.[10]

In general, media coverage of the time ignored these descriptions.[11] Monod's remarks remind us that even when they are workers, and contrary to visions that boast an ideal past coexist-ence between North African and native proletarians, foreigners are stigmatized but tolerated in some gangs as long as they are fully committed. However, given the sociological and historical research of the period, class divisions and moral demarcations were privileged over other forms of differentiation in the public eye.[12]

Paradoxically, during the 1970s, the racial question disappeared again, situated at the margins as a form of urban decorum. For Michel Fize, it was described as a decade of transition moving from "monoethnicity" to "multiethnicity."[13] Meanwhile, ethnologist Colette Pétonnet pointed out that there was no "ethnic hierarchy" in the neighborhoods and that only interpersonal hierarchies counted.[14] Despite a considerable increase in the number of young Arabs or Blacks among the working class and within the world of gangs, the racial dimension nevertheless remains secondary when it is not made invisible.[15] Sociologist Gérard Mauger even admits to having "frenchized" the first names of several of the Maghrebi[16] respondents in his studies and considered only social origin and class important.

While it is undeniable that economic and urban issues have always played a role in gang for-mation, the refusal to consider the place and role of the minorities' experience with racism and discrimination is puzzling, especially since during the 1970s, the social environment of gangs and their members were deeply affected by the continuous deterioration of living conditions, the reinforcement of segregation, and discrimination. These changes were the result of major economic and political transformations. It was the end of the period of growth that followed the Second World War, highlighted by a rise in unemployment that reactivated an already well-established nationalism.[17] The year 1974 was marked by a sudden halt in labor immigra-tion. With social and economic degradation, immigration became an important political prob-lem, first addressed from a health perspective with reference to living conditions and housing problems, then through the prism of identity and insecurity. These developments can be seen, among other things, in the tightening of immigration legislation during President Valery Gis-card d'Estaing's seven-year term, the development of incentives to return to the home country ("Stoléru law"), and the deterioration of relations between foreigners and the police in the front line of migration flow management.[18] Another striking sign was that high-rise buildings were becoming the scene of recurrent tensions between the police and young people, particularly those of North African origin.[19] Collective revolts were on the increase, which in turn contrib-uted to a profound change in the public image of the descendants of immigrants.

1980s: gangs, the economic crisis and the national question

After the "Black Jackets" wave and to a lesser extent, the "Loubard" generation, the issue of gangs in the news was gradually linked to postcolonial immigration. The image of the young white, rebellious, and virile worker regularly presented in the news media at the beginning of the 1980s disappeared, giving way to an emphasis on ethno-racial otherness, sometimes articulated with socio-economic otherness. To illustrate this transition, we can cite the right-wing daily newspaper *Le Figaro* of July 7th, 1981, in which it was stated that the "housing projects" were now complying with "the law of Maghrebi gangs." Fear of gangs, fear of foreigners, and fear of housing projects therefore were seen to forge an intimate and reciprocal relationship. This combination of immigration and insecurity was a powerful political and ideological medium. The *banlieues* and their housing projects became the – postcolonial – setting for an alleged opposition between the "Republic" as a normalized (and civilized) territory and the "*banlieues*" as the object of "reconquest." Éric Macé summed up this new media consensus by showing that

> the question of insecurity passes . . . from the register of "social violence" to that of "immigration," with a semantic shift: by "malaise of the *banlieues*," we must no longer understand "stress of high-rise buildings," but "problems of integration of immigrants and their children into the French nation.[20]

During the 1980s, this rhetoric first flourished on the political right. Anti-racist doctrine remained dominant within the political left, in a context where the opposition between repression and social prevention still structured political divisions in the field of security.[21] The newly elected socialist government was not insensitive to the social situation in the poor neighborhoods, the demands of stigmatized minorities, and the progress of the far-right National Front. The Minguettes revolts in 1981 and the March for Equality against Racism in 1983 pushed senior officials to take urgent action through social and cultural activities. Under the leadership of the State, social intervention practices were organized around a dual targeting of priority territories and populations.

The relational economy in housing projects was also changing, particularly with regard to racial demarcations. Claire Calogirou observed that even if the interpersonal networks crossed racial boundaries, certain racial tensions still appeared. She also underlined that there was a latent hierarchy of non-white populations, with a "positive pole" ("Asian") and a negative pole ("Africans," "West Indians," and "Arabs").[22] The Maghrebins, absent in the text of Chamboredon and Lemaire, become, in the "exile districts,"[23] dominated and stigmatized minorities, local symbols of a more general degradation.[24]

Concerning youth gangs, the scientific consensus was breaking down. Questioning the existence of an ethnicized version of marginalized youth, François Dubet and his team identified two important elements: (i) there were no gangs of young immigrants, and (ii) if there were any racial specificity with French gangs, it was in a double accentuation. In his research, he concluded that while immigrant youth were more frequently in trouble with the authorities than their French counterparts, both their support system was stronger and their opportunities to reverse this trajectory were better defined for them.[25] In her doctoral research, Maryse Esterle-Hédibel, in contrast, observed two gangs of young people of Algerian origin and insisted on the racial dimension of their experience. She presented the homogeneity of origins as the result of stigmatization and exclusion, that is, a defensive and compensatory form of communalization.[26] She also highlighted the dysfunctions of traditional Algerian family education. She concluded that the gang's subculture is a compromise between the values of the culture of origin and those of the society where the parents settled. For these reasons, the ethnic segregation experienced since childhood appeared to Esterle-Hédibel as a powerful factor behind gang grouping.[27] During the same period, J.-C. Lagrée and P. Lew-Fai studied young people between 15 and 20 years of age who were excluded from both school and work. The authors recall that the gang represents a privileged form of sociability and that it is first and foremost cosmopolitan . . . except for a gang of young West Indians in conflict with another group composed of Maghrebians. The researchers note that the unity of the former is achieved "in the name of the capacities, culture and mentality of the Black people of Reunion Island and the West Indies," with myths first expressed in the "exclusion and demarcation relationships" that shape the group's experiences.[28] Race acted as a resource and energy for some and as a collective crutch for others. Differentiated functions of the racial experience that question but do not erase the fact that all the protagonists shared the same social origin and often the same difficulties at school. Other research continues in parallel, deliberately ignoring racial dimensions, in accordance with some tenets of Marxism and/or republicanism, leading to the same rigid blindness.

The emergence of "ethnic gangs"

We argue that gradually, the denial of racial dynamics is giving way to an ambiguous consideration, already initiated in the previous decade. If identity assertions are so important, it is because the working class and its supervisory institutions are disappearing or because the model of republican integration that should lead to assimilation is not working. This double unconsciousness of ethnocentrism and "worker-centrism" is powerfully present in social science research on the *banlieues* and youth gangs. The issue is not to deny the possible compensatory mechanisms at work through the use of this or that element of identity but rather to highlight the questionable assumptions that lead to these analyses. In the early 1990s, the idea emerged that racial or religious self-identification responded to the social and identity uncertainties of children of immigrants, even more so since their demographic weight is constantly increasing, while their social situation is continuously deteriorating. For Michel Kokoreff,

> in a context marked by the indeterminacy of collective references and a process of urban desocialization, it is important to describe how these young people try to tinker with references, to build an identity, a "we" in order to combine this feeling of exclusion or virtual oblivion that threatens them.[29]

As a result, a few years after denying their existence, François Dubet admits the existence of a compensatory ethnicity in the gangs:

> Everything happens as if these young people, unable to call upon social status, social class, profession, ideology, were calling upon the only identity that remains available to them, that of the territory, a mixture of neighborhood and race.[30]

Not only is he reassessing the question of gang membership, Gérard Mauger also revisits his theory based on the centrality of virile and warlike identities by recognizing at the margin a vague "ethnicity" that he associates with such bodily properties (skin color, curly hair, slanted eyes . . .) an *ad hoc* culture made of bric-a-brac, decontextualized elements (black, "Islamic"), serving as an identity resource for the most deprived agents of economic and cultural resources. But two other logics thwart this "ethnic" logic: affinity logic, the unity of the socio-cultural condition, and "warrior" logic, the unity of the gang world."[31] Political scientist Olivier Roy tries to clarify the fragile and shifting contours of these gang affiliations:

> *Beurs* and Blacks are not transplants of an ethnic group that would have brought with it traditions and lifestyles, they are reinventions, the creation of new identities, with fragments of

memories borrowed from the previous and lost generation, fantasies, features of modernity, and forms of perfectly modern and urban structures, such as the gang that existed before them.[32]

From the early 1990s, a consensus seems to have emerged on the role of race in the gangs, thanks to the coming into play of the "Zulus" generation.[33] Between skepticism and excitement, the state of mind prevailing in academic circles at the beginning of the 1990s can be summarized by this quote from Michel Fize: "Ethnic gangs exist: we have met them. Let us note on this subject the media erasing of the *Beurs* gangs in favor of the Black gangs!"[34]

Thus, the "Zulus" generation emerged in a gloomy economic context, marked by the ghettoization of working-class neighborhoods, when public concerns about urban revolts and violence on the margins of high school demonstrations increased. If this period marks a turning point, it is because some of these new gangs, discreetly smoldering since the mid-1980s, were the first to advertise their racial identifications, particularly the gangs of young blacks in the Paris region.[35] This new symbolic economy of the gangs is the product of three distinct dynamics.

First of all, the "Zulu" phenomenon derives from the "Zulu nation" movement imported from the United States, structured around the organization created by Africa Bambaataa. This movement promoted a positive ethic of fraternity and solidarity, while rejecting drugs and violence, importing the symbolic and cultural repertoire of the Black American ghettos through the hip hop movement and responding to a latent demand for cultural references from a segment of the youth. As an organization, it was structured by a hierarchical system, requiring its members to strictly respect its rules of conduct and obedience. In addition, a number of other groups, gangs, and cliques emerged whose practices did not incorporate the principles and goals of Africa Bambaataa but were characterized by their delinquent activities.

Second, the period was marked by significant growth of activity by white supremacist groups, especially in Paris and its suburbs. These groups increased attacks on immigrants and their children, directly contributing to the emergence of defense groups, with some linked to the extreme anti-fascist left and the Punk movement and others composed mainly of young black men[36] or mixed mainly non-white gangs. It should be noted that despite their racism, the skinhead gang was not considered an "ethnic" gang at the time, unlike the gangs that formed in response to their violence, a form of white privilege in the French context. These supremacist gangs based their recruitment, functioning, ideology, and targets on racial criteria. However, it was the gangs of young Blacks whose anti-racist ideology was explicit that primarily embodied the racial turn of the gang phenomenon. The fact that some of these gangs clashed fiercely with each other facilitated this development.

Finally, the specific situation of young Blacks in large social housing projects in France has to be considered. Such youth are concentrated in the Paris region, where they occupy a minority position.[37] Their relatively low numbers led some of them to join forces, forming a few large Parisian gangs that have brought them to the public's attention.[38] The rupture they created at the level of social representation was largely due to the emergence of new police expertise in the field of "urban violence."

In 1991, the Intelligence Service (*Renseignements Généraux* or RG) created a specialized section ("Cities and *Banlieues*") to monitor urban disorders. Its first report is entitled "Zulus, *Banlieues* Gangs and Rioters." The RG's investment in the theme of gangs is as much about addressing public concerns[39] as it is about questioning these gangs' legitimacy; that is, did they emerge simply to take advantage of the context to "demonstrate their performance in terms of collective violence"?[40] As they rushed to fill the vacuum in knowledge, the RG gradually established itself as the main source of information on the gangs for journalists and public authorities. Each report on the subject was widely distributed in the press. The large Parisian gangs captured much of the public attention at that time, becoming canonical. The publicized RG notes generally focus on a handful of themes (aggravation of violence, drug trafficking, ethnicization, rejuvenation, etc.) but rarely defined what was meant by gang and thus contributed to freezing the phenomenon, obscuring its diversity, and endorsing the dominant media representation. Consequently, the typical gang was very violent and racially homogeneous and constituted of members drawn from minority groups. The centrality of the large Parisian gangs is due to their specific characteristics: significant memberships, located in busy commercial and touristic places, and some distinguished by an explicit black identity. In the early 1990s, these groups, although very much in the minority at the national level, provided a perfect illustration of the theses of the domestic threat and the risk of "American-style drift" in a context where insecurity concerns were emerging.[41] Since that time, concerns about black youth gangs have cyclically picked up again. In 1998, just before the soccer World Cup, Intelligence Services published an alarming note entitled "Black Gangs, a Worrying Community Withdrawal." This document, which coincided with the inauguration of the *Stade de France* in Saint-Denis, revealed concerns related to the upcoming soccer world cup. Then, in a 2007 note, the Intelligence Service Headquarters again alerted public opinion of "a significant return of the phenomenon of ethnic gangs composed mainly of individuals of sub-Saharan origin, bearing a name, codes or clothing signs inspired by black American groups."[42]

The 2000s and the return of race

The media resonance of these few Parisian gangs foreshadows future developments. Until the mid-1990s, the racial question was integrated, if not diluted, into the social question; minorities were in the minority and above all "victims" of segregation, inequality, and racism. But gradually, racist theses have gained momentum in the public debate. In a culturalist reading of the phenomenon within the rhetoric of "common sense," the collective behaviors of minorities are presented as the product of their "origin."[43] What is new is not the content of the discourses but the status of their promoters, who claim to defend republican orthodoxy. Highly selective in its targets, this new rhetorical regime "moves from the most dogmatic universalism to the least controlled differentialism."[44]

These developments raise once again the question of the persistence of the negative mention of the origins of the populations from Africa and the West Indies and only them. Admittedly, rural and then European migration has faced rejection, vexation, and discrimination.[45] But this did not prevent rural workers, whether Polish, Hungarian, Belgian, Italian, Spanish, or Portuguese, from taking their place and above all from gaining access to a form of legitimacy or less indifference, while discrimination and rejection persist and have even intensified for postcolonial migrants and their children, especially Muslims. As Robert Castel summarizes it, "a Western immigration has been able to merge into a French national identity without the return to the origins of the first settlers being constantly repeated." The analysis of representations, grids of interpretation, and cognitive patterns buried in national history (but first and foremost in the recent colonial past) is essential to a raced understanding of the gang phenomenon.

Contemporary social sciences now offer a more detailed knowledge of the experience of poverty and racial condition in France.[46] Many studies are pointing to the inversion of demographic power relations in some areas where minorities become "visible majorities." Regarding spatial segregation and racial concentration, Tanter and Toubon write that

> population policies as defined . . . have aggravated the ethnic specialization of the areas
> they were supposed to combat. By delegitimizing immigrant families where they were

welcomed, these practices have contributed to ensuring that they are not welcomed elsewhere, particularly in the new social estate, which is located on a more or less peripheral location, thus reinforcing their concentration in stigmatized areas.[47]

The racial experience of young people with modest backgrounds is particularly studied from the education perspective through the impact of origins on the quality of the schools as well as classes attended[48] or from the perspective of school performance and orientation.[49] Following the literature on schools, other work has focused on racist discrimination in the workplace.[50] Ethnicity also plays a direct role in the level of exposure to the police,[51] the strained relationships that result, the types of judicial treatment,[52] and the likelihood of experiencing prison. In different forms, discrimination and racism also affect university graduates,[53] as well as managers and executives from poor neighborhoods who are nonetheless protected from precariousness. More recently, this issue has returned to the theme of the ghetto. According to Didier Lapeyronnie, "the ethnic and racial dimension of the ghetto is now evident to all its inhabitants, the latter almost never having recourse to a representation in terms of social class."[54]

Recent research on gangs has also reflected these developments. While a number of scholars persist in not taking racial dynamics[55] into account, others, such as Benjamin Moignard, observe that the

> high visibility of allochtonous adolescents is . . . nothing more than a reflection of a highly segregated neighborhood on the one hand, and the mark of an ethnicity that is constructed in opposition to the labelling and designation processes carried by traditional society on the other hand.

He adds that the school "greatly reinforces . . . the construction of this proud and demanding ethnicity that is found particularly among gang members."[56] This work also shows that the expressions of ethnicity among young people are not reduced to an opposition between the majority and the minorities,[57] between the established and the outsiders,[58] but that they also permeate relations between minority groups through informal and subtle games of demarcation. Thomas Sauvadet argues that the social relations of "young people in the projects" are dominated by a widespread form of "xenophobia" and source of conflict, even if we do not find in the author's *Warrior Capital* any in-depth study on the forms and contexts of expression of this "xenophobia."[59]

In an attempt to overcome the denials or partial aspect of some analyses, the first author (Marwan Mohammed) has attempted to address this serious gap in the French literature by focusing on the different ways in which race is at the intersection of dynamics of domination reflecting the social, economic, spatial, and minority statuses of individuals and communities. It is in this context that race is actively mobilized by some of the gangs, both within the group and in their relationships with institutions and the outside world. Through an ethnographic approach to youth gangs, linking social and symbolic practices as well as various othering phenomena, Mohammed concluded that gangs were a reflection of segregation, domination, and power relations between hegemonic and minority populations. Alongside identities defined by domination, we see gangs in relationship to the experience of discrimination, urban segregation, and inequality. It this experience combined with the lack of positive recognition and clear opportunities for self-realization that prompt individuals to form groups and develop their own communities.[60] Any critical approach to the study of gangs must include the issue of race both historically and as it is experienced in everyday life. Our goal in this chapter was to demonstrate the need for such a turn in French social science and our commitment to the dynamic growth of a field that includes this sensibility in its founding principles.

Notes

1 On this topic, see the special issue on intersectionality edited by Abdellali Hajjat and Silyane Larcher: http://mouvements.info/category/intersectionnalite/.
2 It is especially against the obscuring of the issue of race in law teaching and research that critical race theory has developed; see, for example, the synthesis proposed by Richard Delgado and Jean Stefancic (Delgado R., Stefancic J., 2017, *Critical Race Theory. An Introduction* (3rd Edition), New York, NYU Press.
3 Cervulle M., 2013, *Dans le blanc des yeux. Diversité, racisme et médias*, Paris, Éditions Amsterdam.
4 See the journalistic reception of the book by Hugues Lagrange, 2010, *Le déni des cultures*, Paris, Seuil.
5 Robert Ph., Lascoumes P., 1974, *Les bandes d'adolescents*, Paris, Les Éditions ouvrières.
6 Chombart de Lauwe, P.-H., 1963, "Introduction au livre de Kaes, R." *Vivre ensemble dans les grands ensembles*, Paris, les Éditions ouvrières.
7 "Relations between Heterogeneous Groups Are Dominated by the Petty-Bourgeois Moral Opposition to the Working-Class Condition." Chamboredon J.-C., Lemaire M., 1970, "Proximité spatiale et distance sociale. Les grands ensembles et leur peuplement", *Revue française de sociologie*, 1, pp. 3–33, 23.
8 Derogatory word for "Arabs."
9 Monod J. 1968, *Les Barjots*, Paris, Julliard, 374.
10 Monod J. 1968, *Les Barjots*, Paris, Julliard, 295.
11 Bacher C., 2000, "Le phénomène Blousons noirs vu par la presse", Master thesis, University of Clermont-Ferrand II. However, in a 1964 video, the head of the services of the Lyon Child Protection Brigade, when asked about the "Black Jackets" phenomenon, stated that "assaults are not committed by minors but by North Africans": www.ina.fr/video/LXF99005028/les-blousons-noirs-et-la-securite.fr.html.
12 Tétard F., 1988, "Le phénomène blousons noirs en France fin des années 1950 – début des années 1960, in Collectif", *Révolte et société: tome 2*, Paris, Colloque d'histoire au présent, pp. 205–214.
13 Fize M., 2008, *Les bandes. De l' "entre soi adolescent" à l' "autre-ennemi"*, Paris, Desclée de Brouwer.
14 Pétonnet C., 1979, *On est tous dans le brouillard*, Paris, Galilée, p. 224.
15 Mauger G., 1977, *La vie buissonnière, marginalité petite-bourgeoise et marginalité populaire*, Paris, Maspéro; Mauger G., Fossé-Poliak C., 1983, "Les Loubards", *Actes de la recherche en sciences sociales*, 50, pp. 49–67.
16 The Maghreb is the Arabic term that refers to the region of Africa north of the Sahara Desert and west of the Nile – specifically, coinciding with the Atlas Mountains.
17 Noiriel G., 2004, *Gens d'ici venus d'ailleurs*, Paris, Éditions du Chêne.
18 The logic of hardening was reflected in the Bonnet Law of 1980.
19 Hajjat A., 2013, *La Marche pour l'égalité et contre le racisme*, Paris, Amsterdam Editions.
20 Macé É., 2002, "Le traitement médiatique de l'insécurité", in Mucchielli L., Robert Ph. (dir.), *Crime et sécurité, l'état des savoirs*, Paris, La Découverte, pp. 33–42, 36.
21 Body-gendrot S., Duprez D., 2001, "Les politiques de sécurité et de prévention dans les années 1990 en France. Les villes en France et la sécurité", *Déviance et Société*, 4(25), pp. 377–402.
22 Calogirou C., 1990, *Sauver son honneur, rapports sociaux en milieu urbain défavorisé*, Paris, L'Harmattan, p. 26.
23 Dubet F., Lapeyronnie D., 1992, *Les quartiers d'exil*, Paris, Seuil.
24 Villechaise-Dupont A., 2000, *Amère banlieue*, Paris, Le Monde-Grasset.
25 Dubet F., 1987, *La galère. Jeunes en survie*, Paris, Fayard, p. 130.
26 Weber M., 1995, *Économie et Société*, Paris, Press Pocket, 2 tomes.
27 Esterle-Hédibel M., 1995, "Le rite et le risque, la culture du risque dans les bandes de jeunes de milieu populaire à travers la conduite routière", PhD dissertation, La Sorbonne, Paris V, p. 203. Two years later, she would specify that the "hostility and mutual mistrust" of which Robert speaks is that of adults towards young people and of the French towards Arabs and vice versa, Esterle-Hedibel M., 1997, *La bande, le risque et l'accident*, Paris, L'Harmattan, p. 73.
28 Lagrée J.-C., Lew-Faï P., 1985, *La galère. Marginalisation juvénile et collectivités locales*, Paris, Éditions du CNRS, pp. 100–111.
29 Kokoreff M., 1991, "Tags et zoulous: une nouvelle violence urbaine", *Esprit*, 2, pp. 23–36, 25.

30 Dubet F., 1991, "Sur les bandes de jeunes", *Les Cahiers de la Sécurité Intérieure*, 5, pp. 83–94, p. 92.

31 Mauger G., 1998, "Bandes et valeurs de virilité", *Regards sur l'actualité*, Paris, La documentation française, pp. 29–39, 34, 243.

32 Roy O., 1991, "Ethnicité, bandes et communautarisme", *Esprit*, 69, pp. 37–47.

33 With the exception of Olivier Roy's attempt, the study of the content and modalities of expression of the ethnicity of the gangs has remained rudimentary.

34 Fize M., 1993, *Les bandes*, Paris, Desclée De Brouwer, p. 120.

35 Madzou L., 2008, *J'étais un chef de gang*, Paris, La Découverte. Additional insights/sociological contextualization found additional insights at the end of the book with the chapter "Voyage dans le monde des bandes" written by Marie-Hélène Bacqué.

36 It was the case for the "Black Dragons."

37 Madzou L., op. cit.

38 At that time, we should note the particular case of the "Mendy Boys" gang formed by young people belonging to the Mendy and Gomis families, originally from Guinea-Bissau, many of whom settled in the Yvelines (Achères, Mantes-la-Jolie, Les Mureaux, etc.). The "Mendy Boys" are to our knowledge the only "diasporic" gang, in which family and ethnic origins are claimed.

39 This announcement comes after a series of riots that began in Vaulx-en-Velin in October 1990 and continued between March and July 1991 in the Paris region.

40 Bonelli L., 2001, "Renseignements généraux et violences urbaines", *Actes de la recherche en sciences sociales weird that these authors are not quoted in the text itself*, 1–2, pp. 136–137, 95–103, 98.

41 Robert Ph., 2002, *L'insécurité en France*, Paris, La Découverte.

42 Le Monde, 5 September 2007.

43 As Etienne Balibar notes, "perhaps more than ever the principle of race or 'racialization' is socially and culturally imperative, in particular as a *genealogical* principle, and of representations that relate to the origin and descent of supposed 'mentalities' or individual and collective "aptitudes." Balibar E., 2007, "Le retour de la race", *Mouvements*, mars 2007, URL: www.mouvements.info/Le-retour-de-la-race.html.

44 Fassin D., Fassin É. (dir.), 2006, *De la question sociale à la question raciale ? Représenter la société française*, Paris, La Découverte, p. 9.

45 Noiriel G., 2006 "'*Color blindness*' et construction des identités dans l'espace public français", in Didier Fassin et Éric Fassin (dir), *De la question sociale à la question raciale. Représenter la société française,* Paris, La Découverte, pp. 158–174.

46 Maurin É., 2004, *Le ghetto français. Enquête sur le séparatisme social*, Paris, Seuil.

47 Tanter A., Toubon J.-C., 1999, "Mixité sociale et politiques de peuplement: genèse de l'ethnicisation des opérations de réhabilitation", *Sociétés contemporaines*, pp. 33–34, 59–86, 83.

48 "It Is Ethnic Segregation That Creates Ethnicity and Not the Other Way Around." Felouzis G., Liot F., Perroton J., 2005, *L'apartheid scolaire. Enquête sur la ségrégation ethnique dans les collèges*, Paris, Seuil, p. 92; Lorcerie F., 2003, *L'école et le défi ethnique. Éducation et intégration*, Paris, INRP-ESF.

49 Baudelot C., Establet R., 2009, *L'élitisme républicain – L'école française à l'épreuve des comparaisons internationales*, Paris, Seuil, la République des idées; Brinbaum Y., Kieffer A., 2009, "Les scolarités des enfants d'immigrés de la sixième au baccalauréat: différenciation et polarisation des parcours", *Population, INED*, 64(3), pp. 561–610.

50 De Rudder V., Vourc'h F., 2007, "Les discriminations dans le monde du travail", in Fassin D., Fassin E. (dir), *De la question sociale à la question raciale?*, Paris, La Découverte, pp. 175–194.

51 Levy R., Jobard F., 2009, *Profiling Minorities: A Study of Stop-and-Search Practices in Paris*. New York: Open Society Institute.

52 Jobard F., 2007, "La couleur du jugement. Discriminations dans les décisions judiciaires en matière d'infractions à agents de la force publique (1965–2005)", *Revue Française de Sociologie*, 48(2), pp. 243–272.

53 Simon P., 2000, *Les discriminations ethniques dans la société française*, Paris, IHESI, Etudes et recherches.

54 Lapeyronnie D., 2008, *Ghetto urbain, Ségrégation, violence, pauvreté en France aujourd'hui*, Paris, Robert Laffont, p. 335.

55 Boucher M., 2007, "Le retour des 'bandes' de jeunes: Regards croisés sur les regroupements juvéniles dans les quartiers populaires", *Pensée plurielle*, 14(1), pp. 111–124.

56 Moignard B., 2007, "Bandes d'adolescents de la France au Brésil: comparer l'incomparable ?" in Mucchielli L., Mohammed M. (dir), *Les bandes de jeunes des Blousons Noirs à nos jours*, Paris, La Découverte, pp. 351–377, 363.

57 Bertheleu H., "Sens et usages de 'l'ethnicisation'. Le regard majoritaire sur les rapports sociaux ethniques", *Revue Européenne des Migrations internationales*, 23(2), pp. 7–28.

58 Élias N., Scotson J.-L., 1994, *The Established and the Outsiders. A Sociological Enquiry into Community Problems*, London, F Cass.

59 Sauvadet T., 2006, *Le capital guerrier: solidarité et concurrence entre jeunes de cité*, Paris, Armand Colin.

60 Cf. chapter 5 of his book. Mohammed M., 2011, *La formation des bandes. Entre la famille, l'école et la rue*, Paris, PUF.

23

Performing "gang-ness"

The transformative "realness" of gang violence in the Netherlands

Robert A. Roks

Introduction

Since the late 1980s, there have been reports of gang members in Europe influenced both by fictional American gangster movies and factual, albeit mythologized, American street gangs (Van Gemert 2001; Van Gemert et al. 2016; Van Hellemont and Densley 2019; Roks and Densley 2020). Global flows of gang and street styles – or gang glocalization (Van Hellemont and Densley 2019) or transnationalism (Baird 2019) – brought on the dissemination of gang cultures and symbolism, resulting in European "gang franchises" that could be seen as a simulacrum (Baudrillard 1983) of the infamous American street gangs. They display standardized signals or symbols, including infamous gang names such as Crips and Bloods and the colors, clothes, and vernacular (stereo)typically associated with these gangs, and have offered individuals across the globe the potential to create a fiction of their gang that, over time, can become accepted as fact (Densley 2012; Gambetta 2009; Baird 2019; Roks and Densley 2020).

No other topic in criminology is so powerfully influenced and distorted by its stereotypical representation as gangs (Katz and Jackson-Jacobs 2004). In their seminal text *The Criminologists' Gang*, Katz and Jackson-Jacobs (2004: 92) argue that gang life for the most part consists of "recounting history-making events, celebrating resonant symbols, and posturing defiance against morally hostile forces". These "rituals professing commitments" are seen by Katz and Jackson-Jacobs (2004: 92) as necessary due to "the lack of any independent, objective reality of the gang". In fact, Katz and Jackson-Jacobs (2004) take their analysis a step further by stating that the central myth is that gangs exist. The absence of an ontological reality of the gang haunts research on gangs in gang-ridden areas of the world. However, as the lines between the "realistic and the fictional landscape" are becoming blurred because of the distance of audiences from direct experiences of the signifier, as Appadurai (1996: 35) argues, "the more likely they are to construct imagined worlds that are chimerical, aesthetic, even fantastic objects" (Appadurai 1996: 35). Therefore, studying the world of gangs outside the realms of so-called intergang environments (Lauger 2012), like in Europe, might be even more complex.

This chapter will deal with the mythmaking practices of the Rollin 200 Crips, a Dutch gang from the city of The Hague. The empirical material underlying this chapter was collected during an ethnographic study on the embeddedness of crime and identity in a small neighborhood in The Hague that has been the home base of the Dutch Crips since the late 1980s (Roks 2016). Three years of fieldwork resulted in a network of 150 informants, consisting of (former) members of the Crips, residents, youngsters hanging around the neighborhood and a Youth Center, social workers, and local police officials. The usage of interviews, informal conversations, and observations resulted in collecting in-depth information about the lives and/or criminal careers of 60 of these informants (see also Roks and Densley 2020). A defining moment during the fieldwork, and the history of the Dutch Crips in general, was the murder of Quincy "Sin" Soetosenojo, a well-respected member, in the city of Amsterdam during the summer of 2012. This violent incident, and especially the ways these Dutch gang members made sense of this murder, will be used throughout this chapter to illuminate some of the mythmaking practices of the Dutch Crips.

"Real" gangs in Europe?

Traditionally, the perspective on gangs has been framed by "understanding them as 'corner groups' of youth from the same neighborhood" (Hagedorn 1988: 134). Nowadays, however, the contextual orbit of gangs has changed, with gang cultures becoming global and transnational (Brotherton 2007: 63). Gangs have "become globally recognized and consumed, mediated through film, popular culture and 'real-life' TV" (Fraser and Hagedorn 2018: 42–43). According to Hayward (2004: 170), this has made it "very difficult to tell whether 'gangster rap' imagery and styling is shaping street gang culture in the US or vice versa". These "media loops and spirals" (Ferrell et al. 2008: 129–139) are at the heart of why the topic of gangs is so powerfully influenced and distorted by its stereotypical representation (Katz and Jackson-Jacobs 2004).

Although these feedback loops between fact and fiction have impacted American gang life, this influence is mostly referenced when addressing the phenomenon of American-styled gangs outside of the confines of the Americas. This is exemplified by framing the presence of gangs in Europe as the "Eurogang paradox", the title of the first publication of the Eurogang research network (Klein et al. 2001). Aside from the apparent socio-structural differences between Europe and the United States, Klein (2001: 7) argues that research on European gangs is complicated by the so-called "Eurogang paradox": "the denial that there are street gangs in Europe, because the gang patterns do not fit the American pattern of highly structured, cohesive, violent gangs". However, one might wonder whether (most) American gangs do indeed fit these patterns and, more in general, what constitutes a "real" American gang.

Discussions about the true nature of gang life are not just an academic enterprise, as the work of Lauger (2012) shows. Also, amongst the boys and men who are labeled as gangs and gang members by outsiders, there are struggles for legitimacy and "realness". In his ethnographic research in the city of Indianapolis, Lauger (2012: 3) examines how complex intergang interactions influence gang members' behavior. A gang member's definition of being "real", as Lauger shows throughout the book, is a carefully socially constructed project through his or her experiences and interactions within the intergang environment: "each gang formed a collective identity that was embraced and enacted by members and then publicly displayed to peers" (Lauger 2012: 4). However, these self-defined real gang member identities often are scrutinized and challenged by other gangs and gang members, resulting in a constant struggle to gain and maintain legitimacy as "real" gangs and gang members. In this process, Lauger (2012: 99) signals a paradox of legitimacy because of the lack of "clear agreed-upon standards for establishing and maintaining legitimacy". Gang members, therefore, tend to be "unable to demonstrate objectively to peers that they belong to the intergang field" (Lauger 2012: 99).

What follows from the work of Lauger (2012) is that instead of "the gang being an entity that is part of the world of things" (Van Hellemont 2015: 6), "nothing in the world of the gang is ever quite where it ought to be" (Hallsworth 2013: 131). This echoes the critical perspective set out by Katz and Jackson-Jacobs (2004), who take their analysis a step further by stating that the central myth is that gangs exist. More in general, Hallsworth notes that these contemporary studies show the "inherent propensity of gang members to myth-make", that gang members are part of "life-world in which their fictional representations of themselves carry as much significance as, and sometimes even more than, their embodied material selves (whatever they are)", and that in this process "facts and fictions interweave" (Hallsworth 2013: 132).

In light of the interwoven nature of fact and fiction, it is noteworthy to address the ways gangs in Europe, and especially the presence of Crip and Blood gangs, have been accounted for in some of the academic literature. No transnational linkages between Crip or Blood gangs, like the global branches Brotherton (2007: 372–373) describes in the case of the Latin Kings and Queens, have been reported for gangs in Europe. Alternatively, Decker et al. (2009), argue that culture, and especially the role of popular culture, should be seen as the "chief explanation" as to why Crip gangs are found in Europe. In particular because of the differing nature of the root causes of gangs Decker et al. (2009) conclude that any comparison between Crips in the United States and Europe rests primarily on style and identity. In addition, the authors note that the Dutch Crips "are far less organized, are not organized around drug sales, are not territorial, and engage in much lower levels of violence" (Decker et al. 2009: 401).

These assumptions can be traced back to an analysis of the police and justice reports on three Dutch Crip gangs by Van Gemert (2001). Although Decker et al. (2009) stress the importance of identity and style in the dissemination of the Crip gang culture and symbolism to Europe, they make use of the rather stereotypical gang elements of involvement in criminal activities, territoriality, and violence to draw their comparison between the US and European Crips. Notwithstanding the evident global influences on the stylistic features of the Southside First Tray Crips and the Eastside Crips in Van Gemert (2001) study, there are also clear references to the local surroundings of these groups: the Southside of Rotterdam and the Eastside of The Hague. Limiting our understanding of territoriality as "exerting violent territorial supremacy for the purposes of economic gain" (Fraser 2015: 130) would obfuscate noticing spatial practices as acts of territoriality, for instance, as a means of creating space and differentiating identity (Fraser 2015: 121; Conquergood 1994: 39–40; Ilan 2015: 74–75).

These street spatial practices illustrate how local spaces are intertwined with identity and space becomes an important "badge of selfhood" (Fraser 2015: 118). Van Hellemont's (2012, 2015) research on youth from the Belgium capital of Brussels serves as a prime example of the ways global street and youth styles influence local identities and spatial practices. By referring to their city as "Bronxelles", mixing Bruxelles with The Bronx, these youth portray their local surroundings as a "ghetto" or "hood" to provide a believable context for Belgium gang life (Van Hellemont 2012: 176). Furthermore, the work of Van Hellemont (2012, 2015) is one of the few studies to date to fully unpack the gang's mythmaking activities. Van Hellemont and Densley (2019: 170) define mythmaking as a process of impression management, interacting with "socially shared narratives in 'upward and downwards' construction of reality". Central in this process of mythmaking is Garot's (2007, 2010) notion of (gang) identity as performance. Rather than essentializing gang identity as a fixed characteristic, Garot (2007: 50) argues that gang identity is a dynamic, strategically, and contextually determined resource, thereby highlighting the importance of the construction and communication of identity.

Making sense of the murder of Sin

In the remainder of this chapter, I will zoom in on the acts of mythmaking of the Dutch Crips. The mannerisms central to these mythmaking practices, which I will refer to as the performance of "gang-ness" (cf. Van Hellemont 2015: 31), were noticeable throughout the course of my fieldwork, but became particularly apparent in the aftermath of the murder of a well-respected member of the Dutch Crips. This defining moment during my fieldwork will be used to illustrate these mythmaking practices but also to shed light on how my informants made sense of this violent incident.

In the late hours of August 19th 2012, Quincy "Sin" Soetosenojo was shot several times at close range in his home town of Amsterdam. Later that night, he passed away in the hospital, succumbing to his severe injuries. Over the years, I met Sin several times in the vicinity of other members of the Crips, but our contact never went beyond a greeting or a quick exchange of pleasantries. In fact, I got to know Sin through the stories members of the Crips told about him. People spoke highly of Sin, especially because of his unscrupulous way of composing himself on the street and during criminal activities.

Sin embodied the second generation of Crip members in the set. Historically, the Dutch Crips were a group of brothers, relatives, and friends from a local neighborhood in The Hague. Over the years, the composition of the gang changed: friends of friends joined the set, and prison became a place where new members were recruited. This has resulted in a gang that no longer consisted of just local gang members but saw members from different parts of The Hague and in some cases even from different cities (Roks and Densley 2020). Sin – originally from the Dutch capital of Amsterdam – got in touch with members of the Crips through mutual acquaintances and soon earned the respect of the older generation of gang members. He founded an Amsterdam branch of the Crips whilst simultaneously remaining part of the set of the Crips that were located in The Hague. In the months leading up to his death, he also joined Satudarah MC, a Dutch outlaw motorcycle gang, as a prospect.

Three days after Sin was shot and killed, I met up with several members of the Crips. Most of the evening was spent discussing the circumstances surrounding the murder of Sin. Members of the Crips emphatically discussed the motives behind the violent incident but also focused their attention on the possible shooter(s). On several occasions that night, I was struck by the detailed manner in which they carried out their investigation. Mirroring the methods used by law enforcement officials, they had spoken to friends and acquaintances of Sin about whom he had spent time with recently and whether he had any ongoing conflicts. As both a member of the chapter of the Crips in Amsterdam and The Hague, and because he recently joined Satudarah MC, Sin moved in different circles, prompting a long list of potential suspects, various rather vague suspicions, and a heap of conspiracies surrounding his death. Additionally, eyewitness reports and photographs of the crime scene that were published in the print and electronic media were studied meticulously. It was argued that the shooter had to have been a friend of Sin because of the way cars were parked on the lot where he was shot, also taking into account the position of the other vehicles on the photographs and the location of Sin's house. Also the (type of) firearm and the ammunition used to murder Sin were the subject of a lively discussion. More information about the gun, the caliber, and the bullets that killed Sin would give the members of the Crips more insight into possible culprits.

In the process of reconstructing the murder, I could notice that Sin's death had an emotional impact on members of the Crips. During the first days after his death, I observed a mixture of disbelief, sadness, and anger. Simultaneously, however, this violent incident was also used to reiterate the informal rules of Dutch gang life:

> That's why I always say: let me know your whereabouts. That shit can keep you alive. Let me know where you are and let me know when you've made it home. I know it sounds childish, but that shit can keep you alive. It's fucked up, but this has to be a lesson for the young homies. This is not a joke, this shit is serious. Fucked up that a homie like Sin has to be the example.
>
> *(August 23 2012, excerpt from fieldwork notes)*

This comment offers a window into the daily practices of the Dutch Crips and the ways they navigate their street surroundings. For their own safety, gang members were obliged to give an update about their whereabouts. The leader of the gang argued that if Sin had operated according to this "code", this might have prevented the violent incident he fell victim to. The ambiguities surrounding the death of Sin are obfuscated by depicting Dutch gang life as an environment with clear-cut rules of conduct. However, instead of seeing this specific "code" as a hard determinant of behaviour, the central argument put forth by Copes et al. (2013) is that "telling the code" (Wieder 1974) illustrates how Dutch gang members give meaning to the world around them, explaining their behaviour both to themselves and to others.

The transformative "realness" of the death of Sin

In the months following Sin's untimely demise, the term "real" was used verbatim by members of the Dutch Crips to refer to his murder. However, the question of what is or should be considered "real" in the Dutch gang context is not easy to answer. In "Real Gangstas" (2012: 77), Lauger points to a so-called "dilution narrative": "a collective, though fragmented attempt by those invested in street life and street gangs to ascribe meaning to various collectivities that inhabit their surroundings". Because many young people have embraced symbols of street and gang life, the word "gang" is used by and applied to different groups in the urban context "that are clearly different from the pure, ideal, or intended conceptualization of 'gang'" (Lauger 2012: 76). This is true in Indianapolis, where Lauger carried out his fieldwork and where an "intergang environment" is present (Lauger 2012: 3–5), but perhaps more emphatically so in (European) countries, where the image of what should be considered a "real gang" is mostly fed by the stereotypical representations of gangs in popular culture (Hayward 2004: 170; Ferrell et al. 2008: 129). In the latter case, simulacra and simulacrum (Baudrillard 1983) have become intricately entangled to the point that a distinction between the "real" and a diluted copy of the original can no longer be made. However, the terms "real" and "fake" are used verbatim in Dutch street culture as "boundary work" (Lauger 2012: 99), not just by members of the Dutch Crips.

The "realness" of Sin's murder brought about distinctive "narratives of interpretations" (Presser 2009: 182; Presser and Sandberg 2015) that illuminated three specific mythmaking practices by the Rollin 200 Crips. First, the murder of Sin was used to discipline members of the Crips, calling on them to behave as "real gangstas in the h200d". Second, the "realness" of Sin's violent death was also used to explain changes in the composition of the gang in the months that followed his death. Last, the "realness" of the murder of Sin functioned as an affirmation of the collective violent performances by the Rollin 200 Crips.

"Keeping it real" in the h200d

The home base of the Dutch Crips is a small neighborhood in The Hague that they refer to as the "h200d". With this term, the Crips specify a square in the neighborhood of approximately the size of a football field, which is situated behind a youth center and is surrounded by blocks of low-rise houses. More so than with the generic "hood", a sense of territoriality is communicated with "h200d". By mixing the number 200 with "hood", the Rollin 200 Crips follow the example of American styled black gangs like the Rollin 40 Crips from Los Angeles who use "h40d" to distinguish their "hood" from other "hoods". "H200d", thereby, holds both a reference to the name of the set or gang – the Rollin 200 Crips – but also to the house number (252) of the youth center (Roks 2017b). For members of the Dutch Crips, especially those members who have been around since the late 1980s or early 1990s, the h200d is considered a sacred place: it is a place to relax, to kick back, to meet up with fellow gang members: a space where the Crips feel safe and protected. "Keep the h200d clean" was a phrase that was uttered (verbatim) on several occasions during my fieldwork and reflected one of the unwritten codes of conduct of the Rollin 200 Crips: crime and nuisance were to be kept to bare minimum whilst within the boundaries of the "h200d".

In the aftermath of the murder of Sin, members of the Crips seem to be in a "hidden state of emergency" (Green 1994: 228) in the h200d. Although knives were considered part of the standard apparel of these Dutch Crips members, and in addition many informants claimed to be "always strapped", there was a noticeable increase in (personal) security in the h200d. The first weeks after the death of Sin, several different weapons, varying from a baseball bat to a small handgun, were hidden in the nearby bushes. Moreover, the violent death of one of their homies brought about an intensification of a practice the Crips referred to as "h200d patrol" (Roks 2017b). This street spatial practice consisted of several gang members positioning themselves around the various entry points between blocks of houses to "guard" and protect the h200d – but especially older gang members – from potential enemies. Several accidental passers-by, often just passing through the neighborhood, would be watched closely, followed if they acted "suspiciously", and on occasion even told to take their hands out of their pockets.

Before the death of Sin, a lack of commitment in executing h200d patrol could be observed, a product of days and even weeks passing by without any noteworthy activities in the neighborhood. During these moments, especially in the absence of the OGs, younger Crips openly started questioning the function of "h200d patrol". As a consequence of these emerging doubts, patrolling the block and surveillance were carried out in a less strict way. After Sin's murder, the heightened sense of security in the h200d seemed to gradually diminish, although several members would still actively engage in speculations about the perpetrators and their motives. Contrary to the attentiveness that could be noticed in the preceding weeks, most of the Crips on h200d patrol no longer seemed bothered with unknown persons in the neighborhood. Instead, they would talk aloud, laugh, exchange cigarettes, and listen to music coming out of the speakers of their mobile phones.

On an evening about two weeks after Sin had passed, a couple of gang member were assigned h200d patrol. Increasingly, however, it became apparent that the impact of the death of Sin, in terms of the effect this had on their sense of safety and security within the confines of the h200d, had started to fade. When none of the members assigned to h200d patrol reacted or even budged when a scooter passed a pedestrian-only area, the gang leader, clearly annoyed by the diminished alertness amongst the Crip members, shouted out, "the homie is dead man, please keep it real!"

In this case, the phrase "keeping it real" refers to representing and defending their "turf", the h200d. This "strip of reality" (Appadurai 1996: 35) – since gangs do engage in defensive localism (Adamson 2000) – forms a base "out of which scripts can be formed of imagined lives". However, the transformative realness of the murder on Sin led to different interpretative schemes. From the perspective of the gang leader and some of the other members who had been part of the Dutch Crips since the late 1980s, claiming a hood and defending one's territory is something "real gangstas" do (Lauger 2012), especially following the death of a fellow gang member. This, however, was not how the murder of Sin, and the following intensification of h200d patrol, was experienced by the younger and new gang members. For them, especially during the days and weeks after Sin's death when nothing went down in the neighborhood, the h200d was on the verge of becoming a boring space. Instead of this violent event leading to a (re)affirmation of the realness of Dutch gang life, it translated into growing doubts about the function and necessity of defending a hood.

When things get too real? Gang disengagement and the role of violence

Although all of the members of the Dutch Crips seemed to be affected by his death, this was expressed in different ways. During informal conversations, several older members of the Crips noted that this was not the first time they had lost a homie or relative to gun violence. In fact, a few of them explicitly stated that they "were used to it". Some, however, shared that the murder of Sin had such a profound impact that they had trouble sleeping and regularly cried. In his pioneering work on gangs, Thrasher (1927) describes conflicts with other gangs but also comments that conflicts with invisible or imagined adversaries can help the process of gang integration: an "integration through conflict" (Thrasher 1927: 46). In the aftermath of Sin's death, a similar integration took place, particularly because the violent event brought an amplification of several existing (personal) conflicts within the gang, most of which related to a general disillusionment with Dutch gang life.

Just like their US counterparts, the Dutch Crips have embedded in their subcultural repertoire the claim that gang membership is "for life". Drawing on the "blood in, blood out" mantra surrounding leaving gangs in the United States, most members of the Dutch Crips have tattoos that reflect the "till death" gang loyalty in the form of phrases like "Crip for Life", "Tru Blu To The Casket", "200 Gang or Die", and "Crip or Die". Moreover, this "Crip or Die" narrative is fed by Dutch gang members drawing on comparisons with stereotypical depicting of gang life in parts of Northern or Latin America featured in popular films, series, or videos on YouTube but also by telling stories about former members getting "kicked out" of the gang. For some members, this "Crip or Die" narrative limited actual disengagement. Yet research in the United States has shown that gang membership is transitory and that most members can and do leave gangs (Decker and Lauritsen 2002; Brotherton and Barrios 2004; Pyrooz and Decker 2011: 419; Bolden 2013). The Netherlands, however, lack an actual gang environment or gang culture to debunk the powerful myth surrounding leaving the gang captured by the "Crip or Die" narrative. Nonetheless, most members who have left these Dutch Crips since the formation of the gang in the late 1980s have done so without suffering the consequences the "Crip or Die" narrative might call forth.

Starting some months before the murder of Sin, the composition of the gang changed drastically. Several members left the gang after becoming disillusioned with the gang life experience. Younger members in particular encountered a lack of financial compensation for the work they put in for the gang, which in the long run outweighed the benefits associated with being part of the Rollin 200 Crips (Roks 2017a). During 2013, I met and interviewed most of the members who had left the gang. Next to talking to the former members, I also kept in touch with the active members of the Rollin 200 Crips. In general, the rapid decline in members frequently came up during conversations in the h200d. Rick, one of the OGs, framed the departure in a certain way:

> After. . . . After Sin, after Sin was killed, the shit became too real for them. Then they couldn't bang anymore, because they suddenly had a job or something. But you know, the police also knows this. That's why they see us as the core members. But many have left, man.
> *(20/12/2012, conversation with Rick)*

Just like Rick, most of the older members made sense of the sudden departure by claiming that gang life became "too real" when Sin was shot and killed.

However, during the interviews with the informants who left the gang, the murder of Sin was seldom referenced as a deciding factor in their processes of gang disengagement. During the long and often emotional conversations, they addressed several problems that all could be summarized as disillusionment with the gang experience. First, for most, the nature of the gang activities did not match their expectations about Dutch gang life. Most former members were drawn to the imagery surrounding the Rollin 200 Crips either because of the media coverage or their reputation on the street of The Hague. They had certain ideas and expectations about Dutch gang life, in part inspired by the imagery of the Rollin 200 Crips in the Dutch media but also influenced by the more stereotypical representation of American gang life in popular culture, or contemporary documentaries and (rap) videos on YouTube.

However, as Klein (1995: 78) observes for (American) street gangs, the most common gang activity is inactivity. A similar thing seemed to hold true for these Dutch Crips: the anticipation of being part of a gang was trumped by a day-to-day reality that meant spending time hanging around the h200d, waiting, and doing nothing. The murder of Sin had a transformative real-ness in this respect. According to the remaining Crip members, the murder of Sin separated the "real" from the "fake" gang members. However, none of the members who left explicitly pointed to the role of Sin's death their decision to leave the gang.

The transcendental "realness" of the murder of Sin

Nevertheless, for some members of the Crips, this violent episode might have triggered their first doubts about their role as gang members. Although violence was at the center of the Rollin 200 Crips' presentation of self, the actual levels of (gang) violence in the Netherlands are low. For instance, the analysis of several gangs in different countries by Klein et al. (2006: 41) indicates that both the patterns of violent behavior and the levels of violence of European gangs are, in general, less serious than in the United States. Klein et al. (2006) attribute these differences to the recent nature of gangs in Europe, the overall lower availability of firearms, and lower levels of gang territoriality in Europe. Zooming in on the Dutch context, Ganpat and Liem (2012: 329) show that between 1992 and 2009, on average 223 persons per year died due to a homicide. The majority of these homicide cases could be traced back to an argument or a domestic dispute. Criminal homicides made up 12% of all homicide cases, with incidents varying from "drugs addicts killing on another, drug users who killed dealers, and dealers who killed one another during a bad deal" (Ganpat and Liem 2012: 333). None of the homicides in this period were labeled as gang related. Since 2009, the murder rate has been declining in the Netherlands. The most recent statistics show that a total of 158 persons were murdered in 2017, which meant an increase of 50 compared to 2016. The murder of Sin was one of 157 murders in 2012, translating into a homicide rate of 0.94 per 100,000 inhabitants (CBS 2017).

These statistics are noteworthy to contextualize the violent performances of the Dutch Crips during their media presences. Over the years, the case of Dutch Crips is well documented in local and national media: they feature in articles in popular magazines (Viering 1994; Van Stapele 1998, 2003, 2009), their members have appeared on various Dutch national television programs, and the gang was the focus of a book (Van Stapele 2003) and the 90-minute documentary film *Strapped 'N Strong* (Van der Valk 2009). During the first scene of the documentary – of which the title in itself is symbolic of their violent and powerful presentation of self – the gang leader, who has acted like the gang's spokesperson in the media – enters a house. Looking at the blood stains that are spread out over the living room floor, he says: "Look, I think it is clear what happened here, right? This is a deal that went bad, you know? And this type of shit happens every day, but this is the kind of shit people don't see". In addition to emphasizing their familiarity with violence and death, the Dutch Crips have on several occasions during their media coverage alluded to their hyperreal will to violence (Schinkel 2004: 23–24). For example, during an interview with the Dutch glossy magazine *Panorama*, the gang's leader told the interviewer: "If I want you dead tomorrow, then you'll be dead tomorrow. If I want you to die in one year, you'll be dead in a year" (Viering 1994: 41).

However, these violent performances by the Dutch Crips have been met with a considerable degree of scepticism by people outside of the gang. During conversations with residents from the local neighborhood, some trivialized and even ridiculed the presence and activities of the Crips in the h200d, referring to them as "fake gangsters" or "smurfs" because of their predilection for the color blue. Additionally, journalists also openly questioned the "realness" of the violent claims of the Dutch Crips. For instance, when the gang's leader spoke about the violent nature of Dutch gang life, the interviewer asked to what extent the Dutch Crips were imitating the Los Angeles Crips. The gang leader responded with: "Don't mistake our lives for a game or romance, the life of a Crip is hard. If we would live in America, in LA, several of us would have been arrested or killed a long time ago" (Viering 1994: 41). In this statement, violence was offered as a rebuttal to statements questioning the authenticity or credibility of the violent performances of the Dutch Crips. The same narrative could be discerned more than ten years later, during an episode of the show "Moccah" on a local television channel in 2005, when the gang's leader stated: "You know, I mean, you hear a lot of people saying we are copying the United States, imitating America, but European bullets kill people too".

The murder of Sin in 2012 had, in additional to a transformative "realness", also a transcendental significance for the Rollin 200 Crips as a gang. Every year, various social media accounts featured commemorative posts for Sin. On the website of Caloh Wagoh Main Triad MC, a recently established outlaw motorcycle gang that features some of prominent members of the Dutch Crips (Roks and Densley 2020) a page is dedicated to all the "cuzzos that we lost over the years. They will never be forgotten". The caption beneath a picture of Sin reads "Triad in Peace Sin Locc". These digital artifacts all transmute Sin's well-respected status within the gang and, simultaneously, as Conquergood's (1994: 51–52) analysis of physical death murals for gang members attests, activate "the cultural memory of the group" and "[become] a generative source of strengthening cohesion and commitment". Throughout these communicative and mythmaking practices, the murder of Sin is woven into the gang mythology of the Dutch Rollin 200 Crips.

Conclusion: the performance of gang-ness

This chapter was organized around three specific mythmaking practices of the Rollin 200 Crips: the acts of territoriality central to h200d patrol, the Crip or Die narrative surrounding leaving the gang, and their (collective) violent presentation of self. Central to these practices, as is shown throughout this chapter, is "a credible, dramatic, socially constructed representation of perceived realities that people accept as permanent, fixed knowledge of reality while forgetting (if they were ever aware of it) its tentative, imaginative, created and perhaps fictional qualities" (Van Hellemont and Densley 2019: 170). These three particular mythmaking practices provide powerful examples of the ways American gang stereotypes and myths are (re)constructed and (re)produced in modern mediascapes (cf. Fraser 2017: 219).

Both individually and collectively, these mythmaking acts illustrate the performance of "gang-ness". Building on the work of Van Hellemont (2015), I take this concept to refer to the ways individuals and groups use symbols and engage in both verbal and nonverbal performativity to declare their group identity as a gang (Esbensen and Tusinski 2007: 23), something that the bulk of gang research tends to include as part of the definition of a gang (see Van Hellemont 2015: 6–21). More specifically, the concept of "gang-ness" refers to the amalgamation of global symbols and stylistic examples from US gang and street cultures that has influenced youth outside of the usual "intergang environments" (Lauger 2012). To better match the circumstances surrounding gang life in Europe, the notion of the performance of gang-ness captures both the mythmaking practices (Van Hellemont 2015; Van Hellemont and Densley 2019), the role of stereotypical depictions of US gang and street life in this process (Hayward 2004: 170; Van Hellemont and Densley 2019), and also the glocal identities that result from the interplay between these global flows and local experiences.

Throughout this chapter, I have used the violent death of one of the members of the Rollin 200 Crips to illustrate the mythmaking acts. However, the rhetoric central to the narratives of interpretation that came to the fore in making sense of the death of Sin also warrants further attention. In the reaction to the death of Sin, there seemed to be what Cintron (1997: 152–153) refers to as a logic of violence apparent: "a tight knot of emotion, reality, and ideological interpretation. It makes sense of 'the way things are' and are expected to be". The murder of Sin seems to work in two contrary ways. For some members, the violent event provided them with an understanding of what and who were "real". In these instance, the murder of Sin had a "transformative magic" that brought "comic-book symbolism" to life (Katz 1988: 129–131; Van Hellemont 2015: 191–224), (re)affirming the "realness" of the Rollin 200 Crips. For others, however, the murder of Sin seemed the start or the crystallization of emerging doubts about the reality of being in a gang in the Netherlands, testing "the participant's identity as well as their understanding of gangs as a fictional concept and as a fantasy" (Van Hellemont 2015: 324).

References

Adamson C (2000) "Defensive Localism in White and Black: A Comparative History of European-American and African-American Youth Gangs." *Ethnic and Racial Studies*, 23(2): 272–298.

Appadurai A (1996) *Modernity at Large: Cultural dimensions of Globalization.* Minneapolis: University of Minnesota Press.

Baird A (2019) "Man a Kill a Man for Nutin': Gang Transnationalism, Masculinities, and Violence in Belize City." *Men and Masculinities.* doi: 1097184X19872787.

Baudrillard J (1983) *Simulations.* New York: Semiotext(e).

Bolden C (2013) "Tales from the Hood an Emic Perspective on Gang Joining and Gang Desistance." Criminal Justice Review, 38: 473–490.

Brotherton DC (2007) "Proceedings from the Transnational Street Gang/Organization Seminar." *Crime, Media and Culture,* 3(3): 372–381.

Brotherton DC and Barrios L (2004) *The Almighty Latin King and Queen Nation. Street Politics and the Transformation of a New York City Gang.* New York: Columbia University Press.

CBS (2017) "More Murder and Manslaughter Victims in 2017." www.cbs.nl/en-gb/news/2018/36/more-murder-and-manslaughter-victims-in-2017 (accessed January 31, 2019).

Cintron R (1997) *Angels' Town: Chero Ways, Gang Life, and Rhetorics of the Everyday*. Boston: Beacon Press.

Copes H, Brookman F and Brown A (2013) "Accounting for Violations of the Convict Code." *Deviant Behavior*, *34*(10): 841–858.

Conquergood D (1994) "Homeboys and Hoods: Gang Communication and Cultural Space." In Frey LR (ed.) *Groups Communication in Context: Studies of Natural Groups*. Hillsdale, NJ: Lawrence Erlbaum Associates, pp. 23–55.

Decker S, van Gemert F and Pyrooz D (2009) "Gangs, Migration, and Crime: The Changing Landscape in Europe and the United States." *Journal of International Migration and Integration*, 10: 393–408.

Decker SH and Lauritsen J (2002) "Leaving the Gang." In Huff CR. (ed.) *Gangs in America*. Thousand Oaks: Sage, pp. 51–67.

Densley J. (2012) "The Organization of London's Street Gangs." *Global Crime*, 13: 42–64.

Esbensen FA and Tusinski K (2007) "Youth Gangs in the Print Media." *Journal of Criminal Justice and Popular Culture*, 14(1): 21–38.

Ferrell J, Hayward K and Young J (2008) *Cultural Criminology*. London: Sage.

Fraser A (2015) *Urban Legends: Gang Identity in the Post-Industrial City*. Oxford: Oxford University Press.

Fraser A (2017) *Gangs & Crime: Critical Alternatives*. London: Sage.

Fraser A and Hagedorn JM (2018) "Gangs and a Global Sociological Imagination." *Theoretical Criminology*, 22(1): 42–62.

Gambetta D (2009) *Codes of the Underworld*. Princeton, NJ: Princeton University Press.

Ganpat SM and Liem MC. (2012) "Homicide in the Netherlands." In *Handbook of European Homicide Research*. New York, NY: Springer, pp. 329–341.

Garot R (2007) "Where You From! Gang Identity as Performance." *Journal of Contemporary Ethnography*, 36(1): 50–84.

Garot R (2010) *Who You Claim: Performing Gang Identity in School and on the Streets*. New York, NY: New York University Press.

Green L (1994) "Fear as a Way of Life." *Cultural Anthropology*, *9*(2): 227–256.

Hagedorn J (1988) *People and Folks. Gangs, Crime and the Underclass in a Rustbelt City*. Chicago: Lake View.

Hallsworth S (2013) *The Gang and Beyond: Interpreting Violent Street Worlds*. Basingstoke: Palgrave Macmillan.

Hayward K (2004) *City Limits: Crime, Consumer Culture and the Urban Experience*. London: Routledge-Cavendish.

Ilan J (2015) *Understanding Street Culture. Poverty, Crime, Youth and Cool*. London: Palgrave Macmillan.

Katz J (1988) *Seductions of Crime. Moral and Sensual Attractions in Doing Evil*. New York, NY: Basic Books.

Katz J and Jackson-Jacobs C (2004). The Criminologists' Gang. In Sumner C (ed.). *The Blackwell Companion to Criminology*. New York, NY: John Wiley & Sons, pp. 91–124.

Klein MW (1995) *The American Street Gang: Its Nature, Prevalence, and Control*. New York/Oxford: Oxford University Press.

Klein MW (2001) Resolving the Eurogang Paradox. In Klein MW, Kerner HJ, Maxson CL and Weitekamp EGM (eds.) *The Eurogang Paradox: Street Gangs and Youth Groups in the U.S. and Europe*. Dordrecht: Kluwer Academic Publishers, pp. 7–19.

Klein MW, Kerner HJ, Maxson CJ and Weitekamp EGM (2001) *The Eurogang Paradox. Street Gangs and Youth Groups in the U.S. and Europe*. Dordrecht: Kluwer Academic Publishers.

Klein MW, Weerman F and Thornberry T (2006) "Street Gang Violence in Europe." *European Journal of Criminology*, 3: 413–437.

Lauger TR (2012) *Real Gangstas: Legitimacy, Reputation, and Violence in the Intergang Environment*. New Brunswick: Rutgers University Press.

Presser, L (2009) "The Narratives of Offenders." *Theoretical Criminology*, 13(2): 177–200.

Presser, L and Sandberg S (2015) *Narrative Criminology: Understanding Stories of Crime*. New York: NYU Press.

Pyrooz DC and Decker SH (2011) "Motives and Methods for Leaving the Gang: Understanding the Process of Gang Desistance." *Journal of Criminal Justice*, 39: 417–425.

Roks RA (2016) "In de h200d. Een eigentijdse etnografie over de inbedding van criminaliteit en identiteit. [In the h200d. A Contemporary Ethnography on the Embeddedness of Crime and Identity]." Unpublished PhD dissertation, Department of Criminology, Erasmus University Rotterdam.

Roks RA (2017a) "Crip or Die? Gang Disengagement in the Netherlands." *Journal of Contemporary Ethnography*. doi.org/10.1177/0891241617725786.

Roks RA (2017b) "In the 'h200d': Crips and the Intersection between Space and Identity in the Netherlands." *Crime, Media, Culture*. doi: 10.1177/1741659017729002.

Roks RA and Densley J A (2020) "From Breakers to Bikers: The Evolution of the Dutch Crips 'gang'." *Deviant Behavior*, *41*(4): 525–542.

Schinkel W (2004) "The Will to Violence." *Theoretical Criminology*, *8*(1): 5–31.

Thrasher F (1927) *The Gang*. Chicago, IL: University of Chicago Press.

Van der Valk J (2009) "Strapped'n Strong." www.documentairenet.nl/review/crips-strapped-n-strong/ (accessed January 31, 2019).

Van Gemert F (2001) "Crips in Orange; Gangs and Groups in the Netherlands." In Klein M, Kerner H, Maxson C and Weitekamp E. (eds.) *The Eurogang Paradox*. Dordrecht: Springer, pp. 145–152.

Van Gemert F, Roks RA and Drogt M (2016) "Dutch Crips Run Dry in Liquid Society." In Maxson C and Esbensen F. (eds.) *Gang Transitions and Transformations in an International Context*. Switzerland: Springer, pp. 157–172.

Van Hellemont, E (2012) "Gangland Online: Performing the Real Imaginary World of Gangstas and Ghettos in Brussels." *European Journal of Crime, Criminal Law and Criminal Justice*, 20: 159–173.

Van Hellemont E (2015) "The Gang Game: The Myth and Seduction of Gangs." PhD Dissertation, Koninklijke Universiteit van Leuven, Leuven.

Van Hellemont, E and Densley J (2019) "Gang Glocalization: How a Global Mediascape Creates and Shapes Local Gang Realities." *Crime, Media, Culture*: 1–21. doi: 10.1177/1741659018760107.

Van Stapele S (1998) "Crips." *Nieuwe Revu*: 43–47.

Van Stapele S (2003) *Crips.nl: 15 jaar Gangcultuur in Nederland* [*Crips.nl: 15 Years of Gang Culture in the Netherlands*]. Amsterdam: Vassalucci.

Van Stapele S (2009) "Papa is een Crip [*Daddy is a Crip*]." *Revu*, 45(14): 22–28.

Viering, P (1994) "Straatroof, inbraak, doodslag [Street Robbery, Burglary, and Manslaughter]." *Panorama:* 37–42.

Wieder DL (1974) *Language and Social Reality: The Case of Telling the Convict Code*. Den Haag: Mouton 1974.

24

Stuck in between

A former *marero* in the "European capital" of Salvadoran gangs

Paolo Grassi

---

1 Searching *mareros* in Milan

The very first time I saw Oscar, it was on a crowded subway car in March 2019.[1] I had been doing my fieldwork on youth gangs in Milan since January 2019, strenuously trying to build up a network of contacts who could help me understand what was going on in the city that some journalists, just three years earlier, had called "the European capital of Salvadoran gangs" (Valencia 2016b).[2] Despite this sensationalistic tone, none of my earliest interlocutors had contacts with any active member living in Milan. This explains my surprise when, clinging onto a handle on the green line of the subway, I found myself gazing at this man with an old, badly cancelled – but still legible – tattoo on his forehead: an M and a S, obviously the initials of Mara Salvatrucha, one of the two main and infamous Central American gangs. The man was sitting next to a woman, making small talk with her and playing on his phone. On his right hand, I recognized another *mara* "marker", a tattoo with three points: the hospital, the prison, and the cemetery – the three certainties in la *vida loca*, according to *marero* mythology (see Demoscopía 2007). I observed the man for a while, wondering if I could try to start a conversation with him: "Come on Paolo, you have an authentic *marero* in front of you!", I thought. However, I did not. After two or three stops, I just got off the train.

During my first months of research, a journalist and two social researchers who were working on Milanese street groups had talked to me about a former Salvadoran gang member called Oscar, who was living in Milan and who was willing to talk about his experiences. After a couple of attempts, I got his telephone number and called him. We met at Porta Genova, one of the main train stations in the city. While approaching him, I immediately noticed the old badly cancelled tattoo on his forehead. He was Oscar, the same man I had seen on the subway.

Oscar and I arranged an interview. After some days, we were sitting at a table in an office at my current place of work, the Polytechnic University of Milan. I closed the door and turned on a small recorder. Oscar started to speak, retracing what seemed to be a well-known script – I do not mean fictional but structured in a coherent narration, repeated on several occasions, as will be shown in the following. He focused on the reasons so many youngsters like him had joined the *maras* in Central America from the beginning of the 1990s (see Grassi 2018).

2 Becoming a *marero* in El Salvador

Oscar's account started from his family and the more general social conditions of his country at the beginning of 1980s, when he was born:

> I grew up with my two grannies [*abuelitas*]. My parents got divorced when I was three months old. My mother went to Guatemala, my father was an alcoholic and a drug addict. I grew up in a humble family, man. We were poor, very poor, because my country was poor in those days.

In this story, family disintegration and poverty are two of the pivotal issues that justify and signify Oscar's experience. The third is the most important in his opinion. It is the war:

> I experienced a war, a civil war. I remember, on one side were the guerrillas, on the other was the army. My childhood . . . what can I say? I got used to seeing corpses everywhere. *Maras* are a product of the civil war. Why? Because young people escaped from the country looking for a better future. They went to the US, but they were affected by this like any other migrant, or any person without documents: without a job, without anything, alone, without a family. For these reasons, they joined gangs.[3]

Oscar continued with his narrative, describing the processes that culminated in the proliferation of his gang, the Mara Salvatrucha, together with its most ferocious enemy, the Barrio 18. He spoke of the arrests and deportations of Central American citizens suspected of gang membership from the United States to their home countries at the beginning of the 1990s, leading to the replication – thanks to the actual deportation of gang members – of the *maras* in Central America throughout the 1990s. He talked of a parallel development between those two main groups, which increased the level of violence, ensuring that countries such as El Salvador, Honduras, and Guatemala attained the world's highest premeditated homicide rates during the 2000s (see UNODC 2007; Arias & Goldstein 2010). He went on, "Two guys [gang members] came to my neighbourhood from the US. All the young people of the neighbourhood – the children of the neighbourhood, because I was a child, I was 11 years old – started to meet up with them. So, I joined the gang, the MS13, in 1992."

The rest of Oscar's Salvadoran life is prototypical of a *marero* "deviant" career (see Becker 1963). Progressing from a simple lookout to – according to Oscar's words – being the leader of a gang clique which, over the years, succeeded in assembling about 60 members. Oscar described some of the "missions" he had carried out against members of the rival gang. However, as was the case with many young gang members around the world (see Decker & Lauritsen 1990), a critical event led Oscar to change his mind:

> When I was 19 years old . . . I got married to a Salvadoran woman. I got to know her, and she got pregnant. From that moment, I started to see things from a different perspective. . . . Wow, a baby! I didn't want this crazy life for her. So, in 2001, when my daughter was born, I remember I met all these boys and said: "I am going to calm down, you know."

While today such a decision would be impossible (Oscar would probably be killed by his own homeboys), in those days, it was still an available option (see O'Neill 2015). However, even though Oscar strove to make a new life with his wife and his daughter, things got inexorably worse. While he did not have too many problems with his old clique, members of another gang made an attempt on his life. He started to manage a small business, selling bootlegged CDs and DVDs and earning money in a street market in San Salvador. However, other vendors – according to Oscar – plotted a sort of "conspiracy", reporting him to the police. Oscar was arrested and charged with extortion and only got out of various Salvadoran prisons in 2009. A year later, he got a flight to Milan, thanks to a fellow countryman, and bid farewell to San Salvador for the very last time.

3 Meanwhile, in Milan

While Oscar was calming down, Latin American gangs were starting to spread in Italy. In fact, at the beginning of 2000s, small groups of young Latin Americans – especially, but not only, coming from Ecuador, Peru, El Salvador, and the Dominican Republic – started to meet on street corners, in public parks, and at discos in certain cities (initially in Genova and Milan) and were joined by Italian adolescent men and women. These groups were different from the Italian baby gangs associated with the Mafia or Camorra or from others in the Italian past, such as those described by Pier Paolo Pasolini in his famous novel *Ragazzi di vita* (Pasolini 1955). These "new" gangs had some peculiarities: they were a contemporary phenomenon, the result of recent migration dynamics connected to transnational practices and globalized imaginaries. While the names of the groups at that time included the Latin Kings, Ñetas, and Comandos, Mara Salvatrucha and Barrio 18 appeared some years later.

In parallel, a group of Italian sociologists started to research these gangs, trying to understand what was going on. In 2005, the first book on Latin American gangs in Italy appeared. It was edited by Luca Queirolo Palmas and Andrea Torre and described what happened in Genova from the end of the 1990s, when Latin Americans became the biggest community of migrants living in the capital of the Liguria region. This increase brought growing numbers of boys and girls into the public spaces of the city. The comfortable image of the Latin American "maid" – many Latin American women got jobs as housekeepers or caretakers in Italy during these years – was quickly replaced with the image of gangs. Using ethnography and participatory methodologies, the authors tried to depict the first "thick" description of this social phenomenon (Queirolo Palmas & Torre 2005).

During these years, Latin American gangs also began to appear in Milan, leading a group of researchers to start working on the same issue using a participatory perspective. The group was related to an independent research agency called Codici. The man in charge of the group was Massimo Conte. Together with the non-profit organization Comunità Nuova, its members began to work on the streets of Milan, trying to bring about a mediation process between the gangs and the Milanese institutions. A similar process was taking place in Genova with a group coordinated by Queirolo-Palmas. These two experiences remained the most important mediation processes between gangs and institutions in Italy.

In the meantime, Milanese police started to investigate the phenomenon. Arrests soon began to take place. The first police operation dated back to 2005 and was called "Street fighter". The main gangs involved were the Latin Kings and Comandos, largely composed of young Ecuadorian and Peruvian citizens.[4] Massimo Conte described how this operation affected the work of his team:

> In June 2006, Milanese newspapers reported headlines such as "Baby gangs of Latinos, super raids in Milan", or "Gangs: raids against Latinos". The news concerned the arrests of some young members of the Latin Kings and Comandos, two juvenile groups which, since 2004, had been in conflict in the streets of Milan. . . . The police operation had a big

media impact, especially as it came after a similar operation executed in Genova a month earlier, involving the Latin Kings and Ñetas. The arrests seriously affected the action and mediation process we had been carrying out in Milan and in Genova.

(Conte 2007: 1)

Both the Genovese group and the Codici used terms "street organization" (see Brotherton & Barrios 2004) or "street groups" (Bugli & Conte 2010) when referring to these youngsters, preferring not to use the term "gang". This was first to avoid discriminating and criminalizing them and second because their structures were often (though not always) quite blurred,[5] or at least more blurred than those developed in Latin America.

According to Massimo Conte, in Milan gangs were the result of a process of interaction between two groups of young Latin Americans: those coming to Italy through family reunification procedures and those in a more marginal condition, escaping from street life in their home countries and looking for a better life. Gangs became a way of dealing with their frustrations and a means of inventing a new identity to counter their marginalization (Conte 2007). In the same way as the Central American gangs described by Oscar, the Milanese Latin gangs negotiated, through their practices, a new provisory identity in search of a "better future" and social emancipation. This identity was constructed in opposition to other groups, at a symbolic level, and also through violent conflicts.

However, the relationship between these Milanese *pandilleros* and their urban territory was something new. Conte and his colleague Valentina Bugli indicated, in another article, that it was not about a sense of belonging to the city of Milan, but rather, it was about "precariousness" and "crossing" a specific time and space (Conte & Bugli 2008). A "Latin American Milan" was inscribed in the urban space through specific imaginaries and practices, such as hanging around in the public parks, drawing tags or graffiti, or meeting at certain discos and in private houses. This reinvention of the city was a form of resisting the process of exclusion, contrasting their social marginalization at a symbolical level (see Conte, Meola & Milanesi 2008). The existence of gangs in Milan was interpreted as an experience of "defensive re-socialization" carried out by young migrants rather than a criminal phenomenon. Gangs in Milan did not control territory, drug trafficking, or prostitution. Instead, they offered accessible and understandable codes to these youngsters to signify their replacement (Bugli 2009).

This specific relationship between Latin American gangs and the urban space of Milan was also apparent to Oscar, when he understood that in Italy he should have to deal with them:

> Here [in Milan] there are gangs [*pandillas*], but the difference is that they don't have a base, a neighbourhood [*barrio*]. One lives in Loreto, one in Lodi, one in Cadorna [different areas of Milan]. There is no building controlled by them, for example, where they can say: "Here we are, here we were born". This is the difference, man.

4 Landing at another gangland?

Oscar arrived in Milan in 2010:

> I landed in Malpensa [the main airport of Milan] in 2010. I remember I arrived and didn't know anyone. I took a bus that took me to the central station. Then I remember I took the number 91 bus. The bus circled round and round. Then I got off and took the number 12 tram. I got off. There was a park. I said to myself: "Well, it's my turn". I stopped there. I had come from a hot country. I remember it was April and for me it was cold. These were my first movements in Italy.

With no relatives or friends, Oscar spent around two months homeless.

In 2010, there were around 350,000 foreign residents in the metropolitan area of Milan (11.2% of the population). Most of them came from Egypt (10.9%), the Philippines (10.6%) and Romania (10.2%). The primary Latin American nationalities (Peru and Ecuador) occupied the fourth and fifth places. There were only around 4,000 Salvadorans.[6] Milan was already the richest city of Italy[7] and governed by a right-wing majority, but soon, in June 2011, Giuliano Pisapia would mark the beginning of the left-wing administrations that would govern the city until the present day.

As with many other poor people in Milan, Oscar found shelter with the Catholic Church. Oscar described, in Messianic tones, the moment he met the priest who would help him over the next few years:

> One day – I remember – I was walking near this church. I said to God: "Father, I am your son. Please let the priest come here and speak to me". I remember I was walking, and I stopped in front of this church. The doors opened and a priest came out. He said to me: "Ciao". I remember I answered, and I started to weep.

The priest helped Oscar to find accommodation and to start the legal process for an application as an asylum seeker.[8] As a Salvadoran citizen, Oscar could go to Italy without a visa but needed documents to stay there legally after three months.[9] One of the few possibilities for obtaining these documents was to seek international protection by demonstrating that he was escaping from his country because of a well-founded fear of being persecuted or of suffering serious harm (Perruchoud & Redpath-Cross 2011). I asked Oscar if he had known about the asylum application since his arrival: "Yes, I knew. The truth is that I don't want to go back to my country. I am afraid. I was traumatized by the *pandillas.*"

The spectre of the *maras* continued to haunt Oscar, even when he was thousands of kilometres away from his home:

> The shadow of my past never let me alone. It never left me in peace, because as soon as I came here, I noticed that there were *pandillas*. The first time two guys came to me. They were the Latin Kings. They asked me: "What are you?" "I am nothing, man", I said. However, they were drunk, and I was drunk, too. When one of them pulled out a knife, I reacted. I broke a bottle and I cut him. I defended myself. Probably I made a mistake. I made a lot of mistakes when I arrived here. I didn't want to, but it was because of the trauma I suffered in El Salvador. I was traumatised; I thought that this [Milan] was the jungle of El Salvador: you live, or you kill. This is the true: live or kill, you know man? You have to kill to survive there.

During these years, Oscar only managed to find temporary and low-paid jobs. He also supplemented his income by doing tattoos with a rudimentary machine that he had made himself. At the same time, his misadventures with the Milanese Latin American gangs continued:

> I had many problems with *pandillas* and I still have. The problem is that, in their opinion, I never left my old life. For example, I remember one day, while I was on the 56 bus, two guys from the Barrio 18 got on. They said: "*Que pedo?*" [What's the problem?], something like that. And they wanted to lift up my shirt [to check his tattoos]. It was the same at the discos, too.

While Oscar was struggling with "the shadow of his past", Latin American gangs seemed to disappear from the Italian academic literature. The research of the Genovese team and Codici stopped around 2010. Luca Queirolo Palmas investigated similar topics in Spain (Queirolo Palmas 2017). Codici continued to work on street groups, thanks to another project, but only for a year.[10]

I asked Oscar what he thought about the organization of the Latin American gangs he had met in Italy. His interpretation was similar to that elaborated by Massimo Conte and his research team some years earlier. Even if he spoke about "gangs", rather than "street groups", he perceived that their structure was very different from the Central American one:

> There is not a tight structure here, and I hope it will never come to that. Compare it to my country, where they are more than *pandillas*. They are "mafias": money laundering, extortions, guns, drugs. Here [in Milan] gangs never developed, never got power.

In "evolutionary" terms, he compared the current Milanese groups to the old Salvadorian ones:

> Milano is like San Salvador was in 1992. There are boys and girls who come from there; many of them come here fleeing from their home countries, not only from El Salvador. However, they come here, and they get "sick": "*mara* here, *mara* there" [*que la mara aquí, que la mara allá*]. Why don't they want to live in peace?

In 2013, the shadow of Oscar's past caught up with his present:

> I was there, in Padova Street. I took a beer in a small shop managed by a Chinese man. It was Monday morning and I had to work from 10:00 pm. I was working for a cleaning service. I had my beer. It was around 12:30 am. I went out and into the street where there were five men. When they saw me, they started to hit me. They broke one of my ribs. They were *pandilleros*. I broke the bottle and I cut one of them. I said: "I'm going to kill you". The police came and arrested me.

Oscar was taken to San Vittore, the old prison of Milan. After the sentence, he spent 25 months in several cells, passing through three penitentiaries. He was released in June 2015, just as a new wave of moral panic was emerging in the Latin American communities of Milan (see Cohen 1972).

5 Out of the Italian prison system

In June 2015, while Oscar was trying to pick up the pieces of his life once again, the World Exposition of Milan had just started, guaranteeing a billion-dollar investment flow. Giuseppe Sala, the commissioner of the public company in charge of its management, is today the mayor of the city. Since then, Milan has focused on the redevelopment of vast urban areas and on the implementation of mega-regeneration projects. New squares, skyscrapers, and infrastructures have sprung up. Milan has established itself as a metropolitan city capable of competing with other major European capitals (Bolocan Goldstein 2009). However, social polarization also grew (Comune di Milano e Assolombarda 2018). Within this urban setting, the Latin American gangs of the city experienced an escalation of violence. New groups were added to the old ones with the Central American Mara Salvatrucha (MS-13) and Barrio 18 appearing.

For the very first time, gang violence was directed outside those groups. Two events marked this stage. On 11 June 2015, a supposed clique of Mara Salvatrucha attacked a ticket inspector at Milano Villa Pizzone train station. One of the boys pulled a machete out and severely injured the inspector, who almost lost his arm in the attack (Galli & Giuzzi 2015). A year later, on 3 July 2016, an Albanian citizen aged 18 became embroiled in a fight between two street groups on tram number 15, in front of the Lime Light, a disco frequented by Latin American boys and girls, especially on Sunday afternoons. A 21-year-old member of a local clique of Mara Salvatrucha stabbed him, and he died 11 days later (Berni 2016).

Sensationalist headlines were published in several newspapers. Massimo Conte and other social workers who were in contact with the imprisoned boys gave some interviews. More and more people got to know also Oscar's story – an "authentic" Central American *marero* in Milan! – and started to ask his opinions about what was going on. Oscar, despite having no knowledge of this, became a privileged interlocutor for journalists, video makers, and researchers.[11] In this way, he structured his coherent narration that he would also share with me.

On 22 April 2016, Roberto Valencia published a long article on Elfaro.net, entitled "Mareros en Milan" (Valencia 2016a). On 24 April, the article was translated into Italian and published in *Internazionale*, one of the most famous Italian weekly magazines, with the title "Milan is the European Capital of Salvadorian Gangs". Valencia focused his attention on Mara Salvatrucha and Barrio 18, starting his narration from 2006. He mapped some of the "hot spots" frequented by the two gangs, following a man called Tiger, a member of Barrio 18, who had escaped from El Salvador. He mixed this narrative with several interviews with the following: Massimo Conte again; another ex *marero* called Cholo; an elderly leader of the "Monsignor Romero" Catholic group, one of the reference points for the Salvadorians of Milan; two policemen, members of a special gang unit of the flying squad of the city; and a representative of the Salvadorian consulate of Milan. Valencia indicated a precise starting point of the war between these two gangs: 13 July 2008, when Necio and Pirata, members of Mara Salvatrucha, attacked Ricardo, a member of Barrio 18, with a bunch of other boys. During the fight, Ricardo lost an eye. Valencia affirmed that in this period, there were other Latin American gangs in Milan, both local (Comandos, Trébol, and Latin Forever) and transnational (the Latin Kings, Ñetas, Bloods e Trinitarios). However, since 2008, only Mara Salvatrucha and Barrio 18 have been of particular concern to Italian police (Valencia 2016b).

Mara Salvatrucha and Barrio 18 also began to be of interest to Italian academia but at a more criminological level. In 2016, Tommaso Comunale started a PhD in criminology at the Catholic University of Milan within the Transcrime research group. We spoke in January 2019, and he directed me to Oscar as a potential interlocutor. Another research group of the same university started to study the gang phenomenon within the city. The group is called ITSTIME: Italian Team for Security, Terroristic Issues & Managing Emergencies. This group continues to map the phenomenon nowadays, especially working on social networks.

In the meantime, between 2012 and 2015, police repression grew intensely. Four police operations almost put an end to all the Latin American gangs, or at least to their leaders. These four operations, plus the earlier one of 2005, investigated around 200 people on charges of organized crime, attempted murder, and grand larceny, as well as drug trafficking, illegal possession of firearms, extortion, and rape.[12]

After these police operations, Latin American gangs in Milan seemed weaker and more fragmented than they had been in previous years. A policeman who wished to remain anonymous (a member of the flying squad of Milan) confirmed this during an interview in April 2019. I asked him:

> "So, we're talking about teenagers or youngsters coming from Latin American countries who were not gang members in their home countries, right? "

"Some were already members there. Others started here," he replied.

"Do you know the numbers? How many people are we talking about? I imagine a few dozen people."

"About 30."

"The Latin Kings, MS13, Barrio 18: all together!?"

"Well, the Latin Kings is a somewhat out-dated phenomenon. We are following those [gangs] that are more active, even if the 'active' adjective is not appropriate, because they probably continue to meet, but fundamentally the phenomenon of reactivation that occurred some years ago does not exist today. We are talking about 20, 30 people between MS13 and Barrio18. They are constantly monitored."

Certainly, it is difficult to understand the size of the gang phenomenon in Milan today, depending on the definition we use, that is, the way we frame it (see Hazen & Rodgers 2014). However, it is possible to argue that understanding gang space in Milan means interpreting it as an extremely dynamic matter. Any photography of the Milanese situation can be only provisional, temporary, and transitory. The policeman confirmed this:

"They change, they move around," he said.

"Is it a very fluid phenomenon?" I asked him.

"Yes, it's very fluid. Look at the discos: some are frequented mainly by Latin Americans, but others may be frequented more by Barrio18 rather than by MS13, and so on. In short, they are variable; we're not talking about entire neighbourhoods or areas dominated by specific groups. Especially nowadays, because the numbers are very small."

Also, the ethnic composition of these groups seems to be very changeable. Mara Salvatrucha and Barrio 18 were initially formed by Salvadorians, Ñetas by Puerto Ricans, Trinitarios by Dominicans, and the Latin Kings by Ecuadorians. However, this division is not strict. Peruvians and Colombians, as well as Filipinos, Sri Lankans, Africans, and some Italians joined the two *maras* and the Latin Kings. Other gangs were formed in Italy (for example, Latin Forever and Trébol).

It is also worth considering that, for some of my interlocutors, the socialization dynamics of the Milanese youngsters have deeply changed over the last 15 years. For example, during an interview in July 2019, a manager of a social cooperative that has implemented several street education projects explained to me – probably in too-peremptory but significant tones – that today, the public space of the city does not provide stable meeting points for groups of adolescents and young boys and girls: "They use Whatsapp; they don't hang out around," she stated.

Despite this very fluctuating and changing dynamics, at least two recent events have shown that gangs still exist in Milan. The first event dates back to March 2019, when a Salvadorian citizen of 34 years was stabbed to death in an abandoned farmhouse in San Giuliano Milanese, in the outskirts of the city. Three compatriots were arrested some days afterwards. Police talked about an internal fight among members of Mara Salvatrucha (Il Giorno 2019). The second event dates back to June 2019, when a Peruvian citizen was killed by two members of Barrio 18 as a result of an attempted robbery (Carra 2019).

6 No way to change

While I was turning off my recorder, Oscar explained to me that he would have liked to do volunteering activities with adolescents in Milan: "You know, man, I would like to work with adolescents. A good thing I can get from my experience – the only good thing – is giving an example to other people." Some months before this, I had made contact with a social worker who had visited some former gang members in Milan. He said to me that he wanted to organize outreach activities in schools, to prevent adolescents from getting close to this social phenomenon. I told Oscar about this opportunity, thinking that he would be a perfect fit for the social worker's plan. Oscar reacted with enthusiasm, so I arranged a meeting.

Some days later, we were sitting around a table in the office of the social worker's organization: Oscar, the social worker himself, one of his colleagues, and me. However, the talk lasted only few minutes. The social worker asked Oscar if he had any documents – he said he needed it to justify his presence within the project as a volunteer – and Oscar answered no. After being in prison, due to his legal problems, he was still awaiting a definitive response to his application as a refugee seeker and had not received a temporary receipt for his request.[13] We got up and shook hands. My attempt to help Oscar miserably failed. I walked Oscar to the closest subway station. He did not say a word. He seemed frustrated, annoyed, and sad. I said goodbye and sorry. I did not know that the social worker would have asked him for his documents, though I should probably have made some inquiries beforehand.

Some months later, I was at home, sitting at my desk, when a social researcher friend of mine sent me a message with a link to an article. I clicked on it and read the title. It said something like: "The crazy day of an ex *marero*." It was easy to understand that the *marero* was Oscar himself. The journalist described him as a violent migrant member of the "ferocious" Mara Salvatrucha: no mercy, no explanation. Just an ex *pandillero* and his "crazy day": Oscar got drunk and hit his partner, then he went out, took a subway and began to harass other passengers. The police arrived and Oscar started a fight, punching and hurting some of them. Oscar was imprisoned for resisting arrest and was investigated for abuse.

The shadow of Oscar's past had caught up with his present again, causing his biographic trajectory to come to an end. Stuck between a dreadful past and a too-precarious present, Oscar did not manage to negotiate a different future, or, rather, he did not get an opportunity to ensure it. Oscar became a reluctant witness of the spread of Central American *maras* in Milan, or at least of their "brands", which were adopted by small groups of young Latin Americans wandering in the public space of the city.

Although Oscar experienced a very different phenomenon in his home country (far more structured, pervasive, and violent than that present in Milan today), he was trapped in what Anthony Fontes has called "liminal redemption", struggling "within the severely delimited space of possibility in which the radical transformation from a *marero* into something else might take place' (Fontes 2018: 211) – a redemption that is always incomplete, because it is threatened by a precariousness, stigmatization, and inequality, and in Italy, in its richest city.

Notes

1 This chapter draws on ongoing ethnographic research being conducted in Milan since January 2019 and funded by the TRANSGANG Project, coordinated by the Universitat Pompeu Fabra of Barcelona. The TRANSGANG project has received funding from the European Research Council (ERC) under the European Union's HORIZON 2020 research and innovation programme under grant agreement no 74270. All names have been changed to protect the subjects' privacy and security.
2 All translations from Spanish and Italian into English are my own.
3 See InSight Crime and CLALS (2018) for a brief history of Mara Salvatrucha and Central American gangs.
4 Interview with Tommaso Comunale (January 2019), PhD candidate in criminology at the Catholic University of Milan, Transcrime research group (see section 5).

5 For example, the Latin Kings had quite a structured organization in Milan.

6 In eight years, there would be around 460,000 foreigners (14% of the population), with Chinese residents occupying the fourth place before the Peruvians and Ecuadorians. There would be around 8,300 Salvadorans (National Institute of Statistics – ISTAT – 2010 & 2018, elaborated by Tuttitalia.it). The estimated number Salvadorans, as of 1 July 2018, together with a like share of "illegal" immigrants, is around 19,000 (GMIES, ISMU 2019).

7 Milan, with 1,300,000 residents, produces about 10% of the national GDP. The unemployment rate is at 6.2% (against a national average of around 10%), and the per capita income is the highest in the country (€30,156 in 2014 – Camera di Commercio Metropolitana 2017).

8 In Italy, the number of asylum applications made by Salvadorans was 1,691 in 2018 (GMIES, ISMU 2019).

9 El Salvador is among the countries whose citizens are exempt from visas for a stay of a maximum duration of 90 days (for tourism).

10 The project was called "Latinos" and was funded by the Ministry of the Interior and the European Union (Integration Fund).

11 To protect the privacy of my interlocutors, I have chosen not to quote any of them.

12 Interview with Tommaso Comunale, January 2019.

13 While refugee seekers are waiting for their "permit of stay" [*Permesso di soggiorno*], they receive from police a receipt that attests their applications, and this can be used as a temporary identification document.

References

Arias, E. D. and D. M. Goldstein (2010). *Violent Democracies in Latin America*. Durham, NC: Duke University Press.

Becker, H. S. (1963). *Outsiders. Studies in the Sociology of Deviance*. New York: The Free Press.

Berni, F. (2016). Rissa in via Castelbarco, morto il 18enne accoltellato domenica. In *Corriere della Sera*, 15 July.

Bolocan Goldstein, M. (2009). *Geografie milanesi*. Rimini: Maggioli Editore.

Brotherton, D. C. and L. Barrios (2004). *The Almighty Latin King and Queen Nation. Street Politics and the Transformation of a New York City Gang*. New York: Columbia University Press.

Bugli, V. (2009). Diventare latinos e latinas a Milano. In L. M. Visconti and E. M. Napolitano (eds.), *Cross Generation Marketing*. Milano: Egea, pp. 303–325.

Bugli, V. and M. Conte (2010). Giovani latinos e gruppi di strada nella metropoli Milanese. In L. Queirolo Palmas (ed.), *Atlantico latino. Gang giovanili e culture transnazionali*. Roma: Carocci, pp. 85–102.

Camera di Commercio Metropolitana (2017). *Milano, l'Europa. Città metropolitane a confronto*. Milano: Camera di Commercio Metropolitana: Milano, Monza-Brianza, Lodi.

Carra, I. (2019). Milano, cadavere nel Lambro: due uomini fermati per omicidio. In *Repubblica*, 14 June.

Cohen, S. (1972). *Folk, Devils and Moral Panics. The Creation of the Mods and Rockers*. London: McGibbon & Kee.

Comune di Milano e Assolombarda (2018). *Osservatorio Milano 2018*. Milano: Comune di Milano e Assolombarda.

Conte, M. (2007). Latinos metropolitani. In *Contest*, 2(4), pp. 22–28.

Conte, M. and V. Bugli (2008). Latin Kings a Milano. Dagli scontri alla costituzione in associazione. In C. Cannarella, F. Lagomarsino, and L. Queirolo Palmas (eds.), *Messi al bando. Una ricerca-azione tra i giovani migranti e le loro organizzazioni della strada*. Roma: Carta, pp. 40–63.

Conte, M., L. Meola, and M. Milanesi (2008). Milano. Giovani latinoamericani alla prova della metropolis. In C. Cannarella, F. Lagomarsino, and L. Queirolo Palmas (eds.). *Messi al bando. Una ricerca-azione tra i giovani migranti e le loro organizzazioni della strada*. Roma: Carta, pp. 102–121.

Decker, S. H. and J. Lauritsen (1990). Breaking the bonds of membership. Leaving the gang. In C. R. Huff (eds.), *Gangs in America III*. Thousand Oaks, CA: Sage, pp. 51–70.

Demoscopía, S. A. (2007). *Maras y pandillas. Comunidad y policía en Centroamérica*. Guatemala: ASDI, BCIE.

Fontes, A. W. (2018). *Mortal Doubt. Transnational Gangs and Social Order in Guatemala City*. Oakland: University of California Press.

Galli, A. and C. Giuzzi (2015). Milano, capotreno ferito col machete, Intervento di 8 ore per salvare l'arto. Due fermati, membri di gang latinos. In *Corriere della Sera*, 11 June.

GMIES, ISMU (ed.) (2019). *Da El Salvador all'Italia (e ritorno): analisi di un fenomeno migratorio*. Milan: Soleterre, project report.

Grassi, P. (2018). Deux périphéries, trois jeunes, un imaginaire partagé. Note comparative sur la violence et l'adolescence entre un barrio de Guatemala-ville et un quartier d'habitat populaire de Milan. In *Cultures & Conflits*, 110, pp. 77–97.

Hazen, J. M. and D. Rodgers (eds.) (2014). *Global Gangs. Street Violence across the World*. Minneapolis: University of Minnesota Press.

Il Giorno (2019). San Giuliano Milanese, accoltellato e sepolto in un campo: vendetta dei latinos. In *Il Giorno*, 15 March.

InSight Crime and CLALS (2018). MS13 in the Americas. How the world's most notorious gang defies logic, resists destruction. www.insightcrime.org/wp-content/uploads/2018/02/MS13-in-the-Americas-InSight-Crime-English.pdf.

O'Neill, K. L. (2015). *Secure the Soul. Christian Piety and Gang Prevention in Guatemala*. Oakland, CA: University of California Press.

Pasolini, P. P. (1955). *Ragazzi di vita*. Milano: Garzanti.

Perruchoud, R. and J. Redpath-Cross (eds.) (2011). *Glossary on Migration* (2nd edition), International Migration Law, no. 25. Geneve: IOM.

Queirolo Palmas, L. (2017). *Cómo se construye un enemigo público: las «bandas latinas» Una etnografía del Estado*. Madrid. Traficantes de sueños.

Queirolo Palmas, L. and A. Torre (eds.) (2005). *Il fantasma delle bande. Genova e i latinos*. Genova: Fratelli Frilli.

UNODC (United Nations Office on Drugs and Crime) (2007). *Crime and Development in Central America: Caught in the Crossfire*. Vienna: United Nations.

Valencia, R. (2016a). Mareros en Milán. In *El Faro*, 22 April.

Valencia, R. (2016b). Milano è la capitale europea delle gang salvadoregne. In *Internazionale*, 24 April.

25

A genealogy of gangs in Hong Kong

Alistair Fraser, Karen Laidler and Helen Leung

Introduction

In recent years, the field of criminology has become slowly attuned to the intellectual and political legacies of colonialism. As a growing number of scholars attest, despite claims to 'global' criminology, there remain uncomfortable convergences of geo-political and intellectual power in the construction of contemporary criminological knowledge (Franko-Aas, 2012). Like the Mercator world map, shown to underestimate the scale of less-developed nations, criminology's world map remains overwhelmingly skewed toward North America and Europe (Cain, 2000). Against this backdrop, criminologists have started to develop new theoretical and methodological tools with which to interrogate these epistemological and ontological assumptions (Lee and Laidler, 2013; Carrington et al., 2016). Mirroring these trends, while the field of gang research has to date been premised on definitions and concepts emanating from American and European field sites (Fraser and Hagedorn, 2018), critical gang scholars have increasingly sought to disrupt and decentre the production of global gang research (Winton, 2014).

In this chapter, we respond to calls for gang research to critically engage with colonialism and urban history (Brotherton, 2015) through a historical case study of gangs in colonial-era Hong Kong. The chapter will be set out in four sections. In the first, we briefly situate our argument through a dialogue between recent discussions in 'Southern criminology' (Carrington et al., 2016) and critical gang studies. In the second, focusing on the 1845 Triad Ordinance, we discuss the United Kingdom's annexation of Hong Kong and subsequent criminalisation of Triad gangs as an instance of colonial statecraft akin to territorial gang activity (Rodgers, 2006). The third contrasts the construction of the 1932 Juvenile Crime Ordinance with the statistical picture of youth crime at the time, suggesting an administrative fiat grafted from British law. In the fourth, we suggest that major policy reforms of the 1970s – including the institution of the Independent Commission Against Corruption in 1974 – had the unintended consequence of creating a youth gang 'problem' where none had previously existed. Departing from the imaginary of gangs as youthful, depoliticised and distinct from organised crime, we present the genealogy of gangs in Hong Kong as embedded in cultural history, colonial statecraft and the criminal-political nexus.

Recentring the world of gangs

Following in the wake of debates across the social sciences (Bhambra and Santos, 2016), there is growing recognition of the complex legacies of colonialism within criminology. Like sociology, criminology has had a clear tendency to "read from the centre" (Connell, 2007: 45). Indeed, for Agozino, criminology is an "imperialist science" with embedded colonial assumptions, complicit in the exportation of criminal justice policies to colonised nations (Agozino, 2003). As processes of globalisation confound and disrupt the traditional dualisms of East/West and North/South, there is a pressing need for an expansion of criminology's world map and a reckoning of the intersections between colonialism and criminology. Postcolonial, decolonial and anti-colonial perspectives have the potential to enlarge and decentre the world map of criminology in a way that is sensitised to the hierarchies of power embedded in global knowledge-production, creating new spaces for intellectual exchange and dialogue. As Cunneen notes, "[c]olonization and the postcolonial are not historical events but continuing social, political, economic, and cultural processes . . . an aftermath of colonialism and it manifests itself in a range of areas" (2011: 249).

In this context, a growing seam of scholars seek to decentre criminological knowledge. There are a range of voices and agendas for those moving beyond the Northern paradigm, from those in Europe, South America and Australia/New Zealand to Asia. Through movements towards a counter-colonial criminology (Agozino, 2003), Asian criminology (Lee and Laidler, 2013), cultural criminology of Asia (Fraser et al., 2017) and Southern criminology (Carrington et al., 2016), scholars have sought to build the foundations for a wide-ranging critical criminology that privileges field sites and forms of knowledge outside the global North (Connell, 2007). Across these perspectives, there is broad agreement that the Northern paradigm has been too easily "imported". Instead, it is suggested that differing notions of crime and justice exist in different cultural and geopolitical spaces, making clear that the fit between the "North" and the "South" is incongruous (Laidler, 2018). For Southern and Asian criminologies, there has been an attempt to decolonise the discipline, problematising the production and unidirectional flow of knowledge, yet there are fundamental differences within, as Moosavi (2018) has observed, and there is a need for reflexivity and dialogue.

These arguments have started to take root in the field of critical gang studies, which seeks out insights and experiences from the global South alongside those in the global North. Winton (2014), for example, critiques the dominance of American gang tropes in the field. As she notes, "US-style gangs and gang-research have for a long time defined thinking" (Winton, 2014: 49). Instead, Winton emphasises the importance of relational and organisational aspects of gangs, arguing for a shift of emphasis from individual-level violence to structural violence. For Winton, gangs are best understood on a continuum of survivalism to expansion, and she suggests that "making sense of contemporary gangs requires the development of more open, flexible approaches" (2014: 414). This scholarship suggests that gangs are a changeable social form that responds to matrices of oppression, including those relating to civil war (Hagedorn, 2009), colonialism (Brotherton, 2015), global inequality (Venkatesh and Kassimir, 2007) and international development (Hazen and Rodgers, 2014). What was once a field of study dominated by the study of young men living in the urban peripheries of Europe and the United States has become gradually more critical, global and reflexive in orientation.

Despite the growth of critical scholarship in the United States and Europe, there have been few meaningful efforts to engage with the complex legacies of colonialism on gang scholarship. In what follows, we seek to respond to Brotherton's (2015) call for greater engagement with history and colonialism in understanding gangs in a global context. There is a pressing need to root understandings of gangs in the situated historical relations and path dependencies within specific urban contexts. Hong Kong is a unique site of research, as although its residents are "predominantly of Chinese descendent practicing traditional Chinese cultures and norms", the newer generation are also "substantially influenced by Western cultural values" (Chui and Chan, 2012: 382). As such, existing theory can only operate at a "high level of generality" and rarely takes into account the cultural variations and processes underlying delinquent behaviour (Cheung and Ng, 1988). In this genealogical approach, the city becomes a lens through which global and national forces become refracted and articulated at a local level (Fraser and Hagedorn, 2018). A genealogical approach to gangs in the urban context seeks out the historical, political and social levers that have resulted in contemporary configurations of gangs in that specific context while seeking out vectors of difference with similar groups elsewhere (Hagedorn, 2009).

A genealogy of gangs in Hong Kong

Hong Kong's history of gangs is intimately connected with its status as an instance of "collaborative colonialism" (Law, 2009), an economic colony as opposed to a settlement (Cunneen, 2011: 250). In the 19th century, European nations sought to establish strategic bases through which to control preferential shipping routes in a pattern that has since been described as "state-organised crime" (Chambliss, 1989). Hong Kong was founded during the Opium Wars (1839–1860), in which British naval strength was deployed to force the importation of opium into China (Carroll, 2007). Hong Kong was established as a British treaty port, while Canton, Xia'men and Shanghai were divided up between a number of European nations. The British government of the time was scathing about its prospects, with Lord Palmerston famously describing the territory as a "barren rock with nary a house upon it". Established as a colony in 1841, with further cessation of land in 1898, the territory was for the majority of the 21st century governed according to English law, administrative bureaucracy and custom.

In what follows, we present a history of gangs which seeks to understand their inter-relation with historical, cultural and economic dynamics across time and space. Our approach is to examine the key turning points and the formation of official responses, as the latter has been integral to the definition and public understanding of triad gangs. As we illuminate, Hong Kong's long history with gangs – originally part of an underground political movement in China – emerged centre stage in Hong Kong largely as adult male criminal groups involved in crime and corruption. The link between triads, gangs and young people emerged decades later and remained largely defined and responded to as an adult affair.

The 1845 ordinance: triads, territory and control

Triads have a long history, with historians noting the rise of secret societies attempting to preserve or restore Chinese rule as early as the Han Dynasty (1–6 AD) and later with the Ming Dynasty (1368 to 1644 AD) (Morgan, 2000). More often, however, their origins are dated to around the 1670s (Chan, 1979; see also Bolton et al., 1996). The term "Triad", also known as the "Three United Society" (Chu, 2000), originated at Tiandihui around the Three Rivers. The term "Triad" came from the three forces of Heaven, Earth and Man (Chu, 2000). Gradually, as Triad activities – often involving organised crime – spread among Chinese communities overseas, the English word 'triad' became widespread as a "generic term for the *Tiandihui*" and its "offshoot overseas Chinese communities in Southeast Asia" (Bolton et al., 1996). From the start, the British colonial government, in discussions with Chinese authorities, was well aware of the influx of men associated with a "secret agency" into Hong Kong. Through their triad associations, these men were understood to be plotting the overthrow of the Manchurian Empire (Bickley, 2005).

Triad gangs have long been associated with a distinct argot, rituals and codes. Initiation ceremonies tended to be elaborate ceremonies, with tests and rituals symbolising the initiates' "rebirth" and the organisation's "new social order" and oath-taking with pledges to the brotherhood with respect to equality, mutual help, secrecy, honesty and integrity and loyalty (including no betrayals to the police) (Yue, 1993: 34–37). The organisation was hierarchical, including the use of names such as "Dragon Head" or "First Route Marshall" as the head of the society, "White Paper Fan" as the administrative manager and "Straw Sandal" as the chief messenger/liaison officer, among many other names for other positions (Bolton et al., 1996: 263). As Chan (1979) elaborates, Chinese triads stemmed from patriotic secret societies that were "closely guarded", and members were "punished for breaking an oath of silence" through cruel punishment and even the risk of death.

Although there were triad members in Hong Kong prior to British colonisation, almost all triads who had migrated to Hong Kong had joined a society in China and, importantly, attached themselves to certain clan or district organisations (Chu, 2000). As historians have noted, there were at least three distinct types of triads in Hong Kong's early colonial days, formed around ethnicity or trade or as a local territorial gang (Yue, 1993). Triads had strong political origins and anti-government sentiment, with an original desire to overthrow the Ch'ing government in an environment of rising political discontent (Chan, 1979: 24). The activities included "printing inflammatory literature", resorting to "offensive mannerisms" and "flagrant misconduct" to "instigate the people".

The colonial government recognised the threat posed by this form of political collectivism. Early in the annexation of the territory, civil servants indicated that "the Mandarins persuaded Governor Sir John Davis into passing an Ordinance (Number 1 of 1845)" (Bickley, 2005: 60), with the "preamble" noting the organised threat to public order from triad organisations. The Ordinance states that "these associations have objects in View which are incompatible with the Maintenance of good order and constituted authority, and with the security of life and property, and afford, by means of a secret agency, increased facilities for the commission of crime and for the escape of offenders". As such, the first iteration of the Ordinance proscribed "branding" as part of the punishment. As a magistrate at the time observed, upon expulsion, branded Triad members would be returned to China, where they would be met with further punishment (Bickley, 2005). As is noted in the Ordinance:

> Be it enacted and ordained . . . that . . . if any person or persons being of Chinese origin in the said Island or its dependencies shall be a member or members of the Triad society or other secret societies . . . shall in consequence thereof be guilty of felony and being duly convicted thereof shall be liable to be imprisoned for any term not exceeding three years with or without hard labor and at the expiration of such term of imprisonment that such person shall be *marked on the right cheek* in the manner usual in the case of military deserters and be expelled from the said Island.

Soon after, administrators objected to branding the cheek as a stigmatising mark of "permanent infamy", and the ordinance was amended slightly (branding under the arm, discretionary deportation and restriction to only those involved in Triads rather than other secret societies).

The passage of the Triad Ordinance might be read as a legitimate effort to maintain order and reduce crime within the territory. Against a backdrop of racialised stratification of local Chinese populations, however, such policies can be viewed as a political strategy to suppress

Chinese collective action. The 1888 European District Ordinance, for example, outlawed the building of "Chinese tenements" in European enclaves of Hong Kong, while the 1895 Light and Pass Ordinance required Chinese nationals to carry a lamp and identification at night. Despite the creation of this new law and the difficulties of enforcement, the colonial government admitted that triads:

> flourished unchecked, Hong Kong having become its headquarters for the South of China, and three fourths of the Chinese population were believed to have been enrolled as members . . . and with a Police ignorant not only of the habits and haunts of the most active and dangerous of its members, but unable to converse with those who did know them, it was not at all wonderful that crime should have been on the increase and its detection become every day more difficult.
>
> *(cited in Morgan, 2000: 61)*

In subsequent years, Triad associations made use of Hong Kong's population influx and growing economic prosperity, acting as workers' unions and hiring their own fighting forces, while "individual groups strived to control and expand 'territories' and lucrative rackets in labor market monopolies, for gambling, prostitution, loan-sharking, and protection" (Chu, 2000). The political and social environment at the time proved conducive to the success of Triads. Drawing upon the "long term resentment" against the colonial government, Triads took an "antagonistic position" towards the government (Chu, 2000). By the 1880s, triad societies had taken control of the labour market – a lucrative enterprise, as increasing numbers of coolies were needed for Hong Kong's growing infrastructure and at the docks of trading companies.

Throughout this period, Triad organisations were also engaged in politics. Government inquiries found that triads had infiltrated the civil service, leading to amendments to the 1845 ordinance (Yue, 1993). By 1909, distinct triad organisations had formed alliances so as to avoid competitive, sometimes violent, clashes and the unwanted aftermath of police intervention (Yue, 1993). While much of their activities revolved around vice and extortion, they were recruited for patriotic rebellions from the 1890s through to the 1911 revolution (Morgan, 2000). During the Japanese occupation of Hong Kong during World War II, triads were understood to have worked for the Japanese and allowed to continue their vice-related activities (Liu, 2001). Triads were implicated in political unrest in the 1956 Shek Kip Mei incident, when the influential Triad group, the 14K (associated with the KMT), rioted after the Nationalist flag was destroyed, resulting in the deaths of a consulate and his spouse. This event led authorities to create a police division to focus solely on controlling triads, who were subsequently reported to have arrested over 10,000 triad members and deported 500 leaders. Colonial administrators further amended the Triad and Secret Societies Ordinance to include activities related to rituals, paraphernalia or claiming membership.

From the start, colonial authorities were aware of triads, whom they perceived as politically volatile and a threat to law and order. The 1845 ordinance was, as with other legislation at the time, likely part of a broader colonial strategy to suppress potential collective action, whether politically or criminally oriented. Remarkably, despite the phenomenal growth and social change experienced in Hong Kong, the Triads Ordinance, even with amendments, has remained in place throughout periods of both British and Chinese sovereignty. While the imaginary of gangs from the global North has largely cast gangs as a youth phenomenon, it is clear from the case of Hong Kong that triads, including "localized gangs", were largely understood and defined as an adult phenomenon. This may be related to the cultural specificities of Triads, but it also connected to conceptions of youth in the colony.

The 1932 Ordinance: youth, Occidentalism and disciplinary welfare

Up until 1932, there was no formal recognition of youth as a legal category in Hong Kong. The system was initially one of indifference to the needs of young people. When arrested for trivial offenses like hawking and related street obstruction and public health violations, young people were tried in adult courts (Lee, 1989). In the 1930s, however, the colonial government "imported" the rehabilitation model of the United Kingdom with the founding of the Juvenile Offenders Ordinance in 1932 (Lee, 1989). Transplantation of the British model, with its emphasis on "care and protection" for children, adopted the frame of children as "weak and malleable beings entitled to special care in their own right" and led to the emergence of a penal welfare model of juvenile justice (Lee, 1989: 43), including the establishment of a juvenile court and probation service.

Over the next 30 years, the Ordinance was used infrequently. One explanation is that authorities had few concerns about youth delinquency, as there seemed to be little of it (Jones and Vagg, 2007), with the exception of "groups of troublesome youth called 'ah feis' or 'teddy boys' comparable to the mods and rockers in the UK" who caused few problems for authorities (Adorjan and Chui, 2014). A second explanation, however, is that "youth" as a distinctive stage of the life-course was not readily apparent in Hong Kong. As Jephcott (1971: 34) put it, "Hong Kong is essentially a society that as yet has little use for the pleasurable aspects of leisure. It believes in hard work and makes few concessions to childhood or youth." Hours of employment were long, with children aged 14 working for up to eight hours a day, six days a week (Jephcott, 1971).

Reflecting on her experiences of teaching criminology in the West Indies, Cain (2000) discerns two parallel problems in the relationship between criminological research and the global South. The first, rooted in Edward Said's classic work *Orientalism* (1978), is a tendency to exoticise the 'Other' of unknown or foreign cultural contexts – as Comaroff and Comaroff (2012: 1) note, representing such contexts as sites of "parochial wisdom, or antiquarian traditions, of exotic ways and means". The other, rooted in an unreflective colonial sensibility, is what Cain terms "Occidentalism", or the assumption of sameness. She notes further that street-based groups of men "were not age-stratified" (Cain, 2000: 242), and therefore that "claims that the relationship between age and crime is a cultural universal should be regarded with astonishment" (Cain, 2000: 253).

The introduction of the 1932 Ordinance can be said to represent an instance of Occidentalism (Cain, 2000). Grafted onto Hong Kong law by administrative fiat, the Juvenile Crime Ordinance was premised on an assumption of sameness in a British climate bedevilled with popular fears and moral panics over youth (Pearson, 1983; Brown, 2005). Latterly, in the early 1960s, a series of reforms to divert young persons from incarceration emerged, including the 1962 enactment of the Police Superintendent's Discretionary Scheme. Chan (1988: 21) argues that these reforms were an attempt to "imitate" the "sovereign state rather than a response to juvenile delinquency or child welfare". This imitation had important consequences as the colonial government in the aftermath of what has been termed Hong Kong's "watershed" (Cheung, 2009): the 1966/67 riots.

Against a backdrop of unrest during the Cultural Revolution in China, anti-colonial sentiment in Hong Kong became increasingly evident. These sentiments emerged from extreme inequalities of wealth alongside a lack of social provision, weakness of trade unions a 60–70-hour working week (Cheung, 2009). The first of the riots involved largely poor youth voicing discontent over labour conditions, wages and living standards. The colonial administration's inquiry and subsequent response depoliticised the riots, finding growing alienation among youth and the corresponding need for discipline and moral training (Jones and Vagg, 2007; Adorjan and Chui, 2014). In 1967, the second riot, over labour disputes, was led by emerging leftists, with authorities believing some youth had been naively misled. The colonial administration's inquiry framed this second riot as relating less to political disruptions and more squarely on youth economic disadvantage.

These events prompted a step-change in Hong Kong's approach to young people (Cheung, 2009). In the aftermath of the riots, a series of reforms were introduced, in the form of the 'Four Pillars' of housing, education, health and social services (McLaughlin, 1993; Adorjan and Chui, 2013). Compulsory education was introduced at both the primary and secondary level and a systematic improvement of housing, health and welfare. Alongside these reforms, the juvenile courts and probation service began to be used more systematically as a means of responding to youth crime. These apparently bifurcatory reforms have been conceptualised as a form of "disciplinary welfare" (Gray, 1991), involving welfarist policies with a strong basis in moral guidance, which reverberates to this day. As Vagg (1998: 260) argues, there remains little tolerance for even relatively minor forms of non-conformism, and as a result, "harsh strategies are used with a comparatively large proportion of minor and first offenders, unless they are prepared to demonstrate openly a level of remorse, contrition, and respect for authority". The techniques of social control deployed on the youthful population during this period therefore reflected the use of both punitive and welfarist policies to control youthful activities and ensure economic productivity. As Gray (1996: 320) summarises:

> We may be over-emphasising the seriousness of juvenile crime in Hong Kong, dealing with it in an unnecessarily harsh manner, and unjustifiably interfering in young people's lives. Juveniles are also part of the community, and greater attention should be given to protecting their rights and reducing segregation by developing more community-based alternatives to tackle their criminal behaviour.
>
> *(Gray, 1996: 320)*

Brown (2005) argues that the so-called 'discovery' of juvenile delinquency in the late nineteenth century in the United Kingdom was related less to increased rates of crime and more to the desire to control and regulate working-class youth in a period of low economic productivity. For Brown, the category of 'delinquency' developed amid broader ideas of child-saving and class-based moral education, coinciding with an economic need for factory workers and a public zeal for reform. Brown also makes a clear connection between colonialism and imperialist constructions of youth, with similar logics applied to young people in the processes of colonisation. In Hong Kong, it is notable that these shifts in policy took place amid a change in economic production mode, towards an increasing demand for flexible, short-term labour. The move toward compulsory education resulted in a twin-track educational system in which those who were less educated were denied access to economic opportunity (Groves et al., 2011). This, all together, contributes to high youth unemployment and ultimately the fragmentation of the life route of many young people (Chiu, 2005).

From the 1930s through to the 1970s, then, young people increasingly came under the watchful eye of colonial authorities. Despite young people's initial legal invisibility, this gradually shifted with Hong Kong's rapid social and economic changes and political discomfort at youth-led political protests. The juvenile courts, initially transplanted from the British model, came to adopt a distinct paternalistic approach, guided by the principles of discipline and control. At the same time, triad presence continued and became embedded within Hong Kong's informal economy, for which its members were recruited among the growing population of unemployed youth. There was, however, no reference to youth street gangs as they have been commonly understood in the United States and Europe.

The 1974 foundation: corruption, reform and the problem of gangs

By the 1970s, it became clear that Hong Kong's social ecosystem was buttressed by a criminal and political equilibrium in which palms were greased and blind eyes turned. This structured system of bribery represented a microcosm of the broader system of 'collaborative colonialism' at play in Hong Kong society at large (Law, 2009). Alongside the sweeping reforms in housing, education, health and social services (Adorjan and Chui, 2013), Governor Murray McLehose founded the Independent Commission Against Corruption (ICAC). The establishment of ICAC was the direct result of the public exposure and condemnation of the symbiotic relationship and syndicated corruption that had developed between Triads (and their vice activities) and strategically placed police officers (Yue, 1993). Lo (1999) argues that the concentration of power in the hands of a small number of elite colonial officials rendered the system uniquely open to corrupt practices. In this context, civil servants were "not accountable . . . [and] had the power to manipulate their positions for private gain, whereas criminals used money in exchange for protection and administrative fixes" (Lo, 1999: 76). By 1960, it was estimated that there were 600,000 triad members in Hong Kong – one in every seven of the Hong Kong Chinese population of 6 million (Lo, 1999). Lui Lok, a powerful detective staff sergeant, said that "law did exist, police enforcing did not" (Lo, 1999: 67).

It is notable that during this period, Triad gangs began to emerge elsewhere. The passage of the US Immigration and Naturalization Act of 1965 resulted in Chinese, particularly from the southern region and Hong Kong, migrating for family reunification during the late 1960s and early 1970s. It was at this time that Chinese gangs, often affiliated with martial arts clubs and Tongs (Chinese mutual aid societies), came to be a fixture of New York's and San Francisco's Chinatowns (Joe, 1994; Zhang and Chin, 2003). In Southeast Asia, North America and Europe, Chinese 'Tongs' emerged as mutual aid societies to provide welfare, support and social control for local Chinese residents (Chu, 2000; Chan, 1979). Today, although triad members have distinct affiliations to a particular society, they nevertheless believe they are part of the "universal triad brotherhood" who are "under the same roof of the Hung Family" in protection of each other (Chu, 2000). This suggests that whereas gangs are, generally, territorially rooted on a neighbourhood level, triads hold a broader sense of diasporic identity.

One consequence of these internal and external processes was a diffusion of ritual and symbolism within Triad organisations. While certain traditions remained, such as participation in the lion dance, martial arts dojos and the existence of hand signs and poems, other traditions were discarded. Chan notes a "gradual loosening of the hierarchical structure" coupled with "diminishing central power and control", leading to an increase in splinter groups (1979: 45). The Triad Ordinance was amended to reflect these alterations, such that 'claiming' Triad membership became a crime in itself. As Bolton et al. (1996) note:

> It was argued by the authorities that the triads, as a result of police pressure, had ceased to conform to the model of triad societies presented in the colonial literature on triads . . . and enshrined in the law. They had, for instance, largely ceased to hold set-piece initiation ceremonies, since these had been the target of police raids. In most cases the ritual has been reduced to a simple verbal exchange, sometimes accompanied by the gift of a so-called 'lucky money' envelope in the form of a 'red packet' ('lai see' or 'lai sze', leih sih) containing HK $36 or $36.6 (approximately US $4.50) or even HK $3.60 (US 50¢).

These changes were significant in relation to the development of youth gang formations. Given the symbolism of rituals to "excite the feelings of individuals", allowing the secret societies to "claim them totally" (Chan, 1979: 35), the loss of rituals had important implications. With the loss of the initiation ceremony, recruitment and vetting practices were weakened and the experience of socialisation into Triad norms diminished (Chan, 1979: 117). One consequence was the rise of localised factions that are more akin to youth gangs. As Chan notes, "young, strong armed elements form[ed] their own splinter groups to operate rackets whilst still younger delinquent gangs terrorise neighbourhood 'turf'" (Chan, 1979: 34). Chan notes that the primary reason for joining a Triad was to seek protection and security (1979). For example, one claimed that he joined the Triad because "I feel obliged to join the Triad because I owed them, I was protected from them when I needed it". One claimed that his *dai lo*, or big brother, also provided him with a place to stay overnight when he was involved in a family conflict and left home (Chan, 1979). Therefore, in addition to exclusive gang and/or Triad activities that the *dai lo* might involve one with, the institution also represents a source of refuge outside of home when many become adrift.

By the 1980s, it was clear that triad businesses continued, particularly in sex work, drug trafficking, gambling and extortion (Yue, 1993). At the same time, the government's earlier pillars of reform resulted in the full-fledged emergence of social work, with a particular focus on outreach to youth, who were increasingly perceived as "latch-key" and "at risk." Social workers of the time recount their experiences in working with "boy gangs" whom they understood from traditional theories of youth gangs from the United States (Kwok, 1988; Wong, 1989). Kwok (1988: 56–57) observed that many troublesome youngsters were likely to join the triads and concurred with the government's view:

> Triad activities are of a menace in two main ways: gang activity, the threatening behavior, the assaults, the intimidation and the blackmail, and deep involvement in organized crimes like drugs, protection rackets, vice and gambling. . . . A discussion document [from the government] also outlined a typical progression of a delinquent's involvement in organized crime. It states that a boy may join a youth gang involved in juvenile delinquent behaviors. If he agrees to follow the leader who is a triad member, he will gradually be involved in gang fights, settlement talks and other organized crime. Of course, not all the boys joining youth gangs will become involved in triad related activities and will take a criminal career.

Similarly, Lo (2011) has addressed the process through which such youth gang formations relate to adult Triad groups. Basing his findings on several tranches of data collection from the 1980s onward, Lo argues that young people in marginalised housing estates undergo a process of "triadization" as they grow up. This process represents a slower and more diffuse process of street socialisation, in which alienated, street-based youth "gradually inherit and adapt triad norms and values through interaction with their friends in youth gangs under the umbrella of triad societies" (Lo, 2011: 560).

By the 1990s, youth involvement in street-based groups became a focus of the government's attention. Terms introduced into public debate include "yeh ching" 夜青 or "young night drifters" (Groves et al., 2011); "gai tong" 街童, meaning 'street children'; "cheun tong" 村童, meaning 'children in public estates'; "tong dong" 童党, meaning 'youth gang', 'at-risk youth' (Lee, 2011); "fei zai" 飛仔, meaning youth with behaviour that is not socially acceptable (Lee, 2011); "B boys" for those with a passion for breakdancing (Groves et al., 2011); and "gu wak zai" 蠱惑仔, meaning 'young and dangerous youth'. All together, a majority of the labels associated with gangs and triads hold a negative connotation in society. Such popular fears featured in legislative council discussions on the proposed organised crime bill. As Eric Li, from the Hong Kong Legislative Council, stated:

> Many of our youth are attracted by curiosity to the mysterious rules and organization of triad societies. They are falsely led to believe that triad societies are gatherings of "heroes" who will fend for each other out of a sense of brotherhood and that triad membership is something to be proud of; so they join the societies voluntarily. There are also innocent young people who are intimidated by triad members into joining. There are still others who would fall pretty to the temptation of material gain and become triads and engage in illegal activities.
>
> *(18 December 1991)*

From the 1970s through the 1980s, Hong Kong witnessed rapid population growth and economic development. The impact of these changes on triads and youth gangs was twofold. First, it clearly impacted and disrupted the symbiotic relations between triads and authorities, resulting in the formation of ICAC. In doing so, triad groups became more flexible, accommodating and reconfiguring their organisations, businesses and relationships, including a more active engagement with young people. As Triad gangs became more diffuse, they came to resemble street-based youth gangs. As Kwok notes: "since triads are disorganised, it is more appropriate to name them gangs. They are opportunists; you can find their footsteps wherever the money lies" (2017: 19). Second, the changes felt in Hong Kong included a growing visibility of a youth population perceived as "at risk" with their "latchkey" status and in need of structure, guidance and supervision. These "needs" could be addressed through compulsory education and social work intervention, informed by British social work traditions. The subsequent 'discovery' of the problem of youth gangs in the territory therefore emerged both from changes within Triad organisations, youth unemployment and the growth of social work services.

Conclusion

It would be fair to say that the distinct organisation of Hong Kong's triad gangs has been shaped through colonial statecraft. Policies that were intended to control political and criminal mobilisations gave way to a more symbiotic relationship. Ironically, Hong Kong was a lucrative and entrepreneurial entrepot for both British governments and Triads. Historical reflections remind us of the shifts, turns and accommodations the colonial authorities made in their relations with Triads. Importantly, it is also worth noting that the undercurrent of Triads involvement in politics has also surfaced at various points in Hong Kong's history. From local labour disputes to the Shek Kip Mei riots and the Japanese occupation, Triad gangs have mobilised as non-state actors with political power. These historical antecedents help illuminate the contemporary political moment. Formerly known as a centre of laissez-faire economics (Chiu and Lui, 2009) and low rates of crime (Broadhurst et al., 2017), today Hong Kong is increasingly a byword for mass protest, civil disobedience and police brutality, and Triad gangs have once again played a part. In the current wake of a series of mass protests against a new Extradition Bill, protesters were assaulted by a masked group of attackers. Dressed in white and wielding metal poles, the group attacked members of the public at random as they travelled home to Yuen Long, in the northern territories of Hong Kong. At least 45 were injured. There is clear evidence that the attackers were triad affiliated and widespread speculation that the attack was politically motivated, with the triad gangs acting as 'thugs-for-hire' for political forces (Varese and Wong, 2018). It is widely speculated that Triad groups have forged allegiances with mainland China, reflecting the shifting sands of 'collaborative colonialism' at play in the territory (Law, 2009).

How do "youth gangs", so fundamental to the criminology of the United States and Europe, fit into the Hong Kong context? Historical analysis suggests that despite the transplantation of the juvenile court in the 1930s, the notion of "youth" was not fully recognised as a legal and social entity until the 1970s, when political concerns over youth unrest prompted wide-ranging interventions. The ramifications of these changes were significant, in effect constituting the conditions for street-based youth gangs to develop. In effect, then, the youth gang phenomenon in Hong Kong can be said to be a consequence of colonialism.

References

Adorjan, M. and Chui, W.-H. (2013). Colonial responses to youth crime in Hong Kong: Penal elitism, legitimacy and citizenship. *Theoretical Criminology*, 17(2), 159–177.

Adorjan, M. and Chui, W.-H. (2014). *Responding to youth crime in Hong Kong: Penal elitism, legitimacy and citizenship*. New York: Routledge.

Agozino, B. (2003). *Counter-colonial criminology: A critique of imperialist reason*. London: Pluto.

Bhambra, G. K. and Santos, B. D. S. (2016). Global futures and epistemologies of the South: New challenges for sociology [Special issue]. *Sociology*, 51(1).

Bickley, G. (Ed.). (2005). *A magistrate's court: Nineteenth century Hong Kong*. Hong Kong: Proverse Hong Kong and Bickley.

Bolton, K., Hutton, C. and Pau-Fuk, P. I. (1996). The speech-act offence: Claiming and professing membership of a triad society in Hong Kong. *Language & Communications*, 16(3), 261–290.

Broadhurst, R, Lee, K. and Chan, C. (2017). Crime Trends. In W. H. Chui and T. Wing Lo (Eds.), *Understanding criminal justice in Hong Kong* (2nd ed., pp. 57–79). New York: Routledge.

Brotherton, D. (2015). *Youth street gangs: A critical appraisal*. London: Routledge.

Brown, S. (2005). *Understanding youth and crime: Listening to youth?* Maidenhead: Open University Press.

Cain, M. (2000). Orientalism, Occidentalism and the study of crime. *British Journal of Criminology*, 40(2), 239–260.

Carrington, K., Hogg, R. and Sozzo, M. (2016). Southern criminology. *British Journal of Criminology*, 56(1), 1–20.

Carroll, J. M. (2007). *A concise history of Hong Kong*. Hong Kong: Rowman & Littlefield.

Chambliss, W. (1989). State-organised crime. *Criminology*, 17(2): 183–208.

Chan, P. Y. (1988). The juvenile justice system in Hong Kong: Helpful or punitive? MSS Criminology Thesis, Sociology, University of Hong Kong. Unpublished thesis, Hong Kong.

Chan, W. S. (1979). Becoming a triad: A naturalistic study on secret society recruitment in Hong Kong. Unpublished doctoral dissertation, University of San Francisco, San Francisco, CA.

Cheung, G. K.-W. (2009). *Hong Kong's watershed: The 1967 riots*. Hong Kong: University of Hong Kong Press.

Cheung, Y. W. and Ng, A. M. (1988). Social factors in adolescent deviant behaviour in Hong Kong: An integrated theoretical approach. *International Journal of Comparative and Applied Criminal Justice*, 12(1–2), 27–45.

Chiu, S. W. (2005). Rethinking youth problems in a risk society: Some reflections on working with "youth-at-risk" in Hong Kong. In F. W. Lee (Ed.), *Working with youth-at-risk in Hong Kong* (pp. 99–112). Hong Kong: Hong Kong University Press.

Chiu, S. W. and Lui, T.-L. (2009). *Hong Kong: Becoming a Chinese global city*. London and New York: Routledge.

Chu, Y. K. (2000). *The triads as business*. London: Routledge.

Chui, W. H. and Chan, H. C. O. (2012). Outreach social workers for at-risk youth: A test of their attitudes towards crime and young offenders in Hong Kong. *Children and Youth Services Review*, 34(12), 2273–2279.

Comaroff, J. and Comaroff, J. (2012). *Theory from the South: Or, how Euro-America is evolving toward Africa*. Boulder, CO and London: Paradigm Publishers.

Connell, R. (2007). *Southern theory: The global dynamics of knowledge in social science.* Cambridge and Malden, MA: Polity Press.

Cunneen, C. (2011). Postcolonial perspectives for criminology. In M. Bosworth and C. Hoyle (Eds.), *What is criminology?* Oxford: Oxford University Press.

Fraser, A. and Hagedorn, J. M. (2018). Gangs and a global sociological imagination. *Theoretical Criminology*, 22(1), 42–62.

Franko-Aas, K. (2012). 'The Earth is one but the world is not': Criminological theory and its geopolitical divisions. *Theoretical Criminology*, 16(1), 5–20.

Fraser, A., Lee, M. and Tang, D. (2017) Crime, media, culture: Asia-style. Special Issue of *Crime, Media, Culture*, 13(2), 131–134.

Gray, P. (1991). Juvenile crime and disciplinary welfare. In H. Traver and J. Vagg (Eds.), *Crime and justice in Hong Kong* (pp. 25–41). Oxford: Oxford University Press.

Gray, P. (1996). The struggle for juvenile justice in Hong Kong 1932–1995. *Hong Kong Law Journal*, 26(3), 301–320.

Groves, J. M., Ho, W. Y. and Siu, K. (2011). Youth studies and timescapes: Insights from an ethnographic study of "young night drifters" in Hong Kong's public housing estates. *Youth & Society*, 20(10), 1–19.

Hagedorn, J. M. (2009). *A world of gangs.* Minnesota: University of Minnesota Press.

Hazen, J. M. and Rodgers, D. (Eds.). (2014). *Global gangs: Street violence across the world.* Minnesota: University of Minnesota Press.

Hong Kong Legislative Council. (1991, December 18). Legislative discussion on White Bill on Organized Crime.

Jephcott, P. (1971). *The situation of children and youth in Hong Kong: A study undertaken for UNICEF in conjunction with the social welfare department, Hong Kong.* Hong Kong: UNICEF.

Joe, K. (1994). The new criminal conspiracy? Asian gangs and organized crime in San Francisco. *Journal of Research in Crime and Delinquency*, 31(4), 390–415.

Jones, C. and Vagg, J. (2007). *Criminal justice in Hong Kong.* New York: Routledge-Cavendish.

Kwok, N. Y. (1988). Social structure and delinquent patterns: An exploration of boy gangs in the public housing estates of Hong Kong. MSS (Criminology) University of Hong Kong. Unpublished thesis, Hong Kong.

Kwok, S. I. (2017). *Triad society in Hong Kong: The hierarchical approach and criminal's collaborations.* PhD, City University of Hong Kong. Unpublished thesis, Hong Kong.

Laidler, K. (2018). Broadening the criminological terrain: Public criminology meets southern criminology. Paper presented at the annual meetings of the Australian and New Zealand Society of Criminology. Melbourne, December.

Law, W. S. (2009). *Collaborative colonial power: The making of the Hong Kong Chinese* (Vol. 1). Hong Kong: Hong Kong University Press.

Lee, F. (2011). *Nurturing pillars of society: Understanding and working with the young generation in Hong Kong.* Hong Kong: Hong Kong University Press.

Lee, M. (1989). Care and control of juvenile delinquents in Hong Kong. M.Phil. Sociology, University of Hong Kong. Unpublished thesis.

Lee, M. and Laidler, K. J. (2013). Doing criminology from the periphery: Crime and punishment in Asia. *Theoretical Criminology*, 17(2), 141–157.

Liu, B. (2001). *The Hong Kong triad societies: Before and after the 1997 changeover.* Hong Kong: Net e-Publishing.

Lo, T. W. (1999). The political-criminal nexus: The Hong Kong experience: Minimizing crime and corruption. *Trends in Organized Crime*, 4(3), 60–80.

Lo, T. W. (2011). Triadization of youth gangs in Hong Kong. *British Journal of Criminology*, 52, 556–576.

McLaughlin, E. (1993). Hong Kong: A residual welfare regime. *Comparing Welfare States: Britain in International Context*, 105–140.

Moosavi, L. (2018). A friendly critique of 'Asian criminology' and 'southern criminology'. *The British Journal of Criminology*, 59(2), 257–275.

Morgan, W. P. (2000). *Triad societies: Triad societies in Hong Kong* (Vol. 6). London: Taylor & Francis.

Pearson, G. (1983). *Hooligan: A history of respectable fears*. London: Palgrave Macmillan.

Rodgers, D. (2006). Living in the shadow of death: Gangs, violence and social order in urban Nicaragua, 1996–2002. *Journal of Latin American Studies*, 38(2), 267–292.

Said, E. (1978). *Orientalism*. London: Routledge & Kegan Paul.

Vagg, J. (1998). Delinquency and shame: Data from Hong Kong. *British Journal of Criminology*, 38(2): 247–264.

Varese, F. and Wong, R. (2018). Resurgent triads? Democratic mobilization and organized crime in Hong Kong. *Australian & New Zealand Journal of Criminology*, 51(1), 23–39.

Venkatesh, S. A. and Kassimir, R. (2007). *Youth, Globalization, and the Law*. Stanford: Stanford University Press.

Winton, A. (2014). Gangs in global perspective. *Environment and Urbanization*, 26(2), 401–416.

Wong, Y. C. (1989). Youth subculture n Hong Kong: Case studies of young deviants. MSS (Criminology) thesis. University of Hong Kong, Hong Kong.

Yue, T. W. (1993). Triad society in Hong Kong and organized crime. MSc dissertation. University of Cardiff, Cardiff.

Zhang, S. and Chin, K. (2003). The declining significance of triad societies in transnational illegal activities. *British Journal of Criminology*, 43, 469–488.

26

Reimagining the landscape of gangs

Reflections from Bangladesh and China

Sally Atkinson-Sheppard

Introduction

For over 100 years, gangs, and the crime they commit, have been of interest: to academics, policy makers and wider society. Thrasher's (1927) seminal work in Chicago was arguably the first robust analysis of gangs, and since then, there has been a consistent effort to understand gang-related crime in the global North. However, gangs operate in virtually every country in the world and in many places in the global South (Hazen and Rodgers, 2014). Zilberg (2011) for example, considers the transnational nature of gangs between the United States and El Salvador, while Hagedorn (2008) illustrates the competitivity of 'global gangs'. Brotherton and Barrios (2004) illuminate the factors that contribute to understanding the emergence and behaviour of gangs, moving away from stereotypical images of 'gangs' and into a more complex and comprehensive domain. They demonstrate how gangs (the Latin Kings and Queens) develop as a form of resistance and are a proactive, and in many cases positive, social movement (Brotherton and Barrios, 2004). It is important to do, as Brotherton (2015) advises, and see gangs a multi-faceted, complex social institutions, which help to form and shape identities and effect social change rather than just a vehicle of committing crime. Thus, the role of 'the gang' is multi-faceted, often associated with violence but not exclusively so; gang members play pivotal and at times positive roles in communities (ibid.) – often in the global South.

Despite this, a paradoxical landscape still permeates the discourse. Most theories that underpin research into gangs derive from Anglo-American research. Extant literature which frames understandings of gangs does so through a lens which, in many ways, remains unchallenged by research conducted in the global South. Questions arise, including how can we move away from global North conceptualisations and into global understandings of gangs, the crimes they commit but also the lives gang members lead, and the context in which their involvement in gangs develops and evolves over time? How might we approach critical, comparative research to explore these issues further in the global South and beyond?

By drawing on two large-scale studies conducted in Dhaka, Bangladesh, and mainland China, this chapter explores the nature and the dynamics of gangs and how these criminal groups operate in each country, often in alliance with the state. The chapter considers gangs through the lens of critical and Southern criminology and in doing so deliberates extant gang research largely derived from the global North. The chapter concludes by reflecting on the need to re-imagine the landscape of gangs and organised crime, to expand awareness of the fluidity and variety of gangs, particularly those that operate as the lower echelons of organised crime groups.

It is important to note that the fluidity of gangs remains a pertinent and well-discussed issue. Moore et al. (1978), for example, argued that gangs are a continuum of youth groups and subcultures, something also proposed by a variety of other scholars (i.e. Hallsworth and Young, 2006; Harris et al., 2012). There have been extensive critiques of 'orthodox criminology' that sees gangs predominantly in relation to their involvement in crime (Young, 2011) and thus misses wider aspects of the fluidity debate, that is, wider social connections and social mobility as well as the hybrid nature of gangs (Brotherton and Barrios, 2004). A pervasive lacuna still permeates the discourse. Gangs are repeatedly considered distinctively *different* to organised crime. I argue that it is imperative we move away from this dichotomy and into an expansive arena that allows for an understanding of gangs as part of established crime groups, including mafias. The implications for theoretical explanations of gangs, Southern criminology and the development of global understandings of gangs and organised crime are discussed.

Gangs and Southern criminology

The development of research into gangs in the global North, notably the United States and United Kingdom, has progressed through various stages, beginning with Thrasher and his Chicago School colleagues in the 1920s and moving on to 'post-war' reflections which included an increased focus on the context in which youth crime occurs, gang dynamics, debate about 'race' and ethnicity and the relationship between gangs and organised crime (Fraser, 2017). However, there have been some important critiques of the Chicago School. Questions have been raised about the validity of some of the Chicago School's findings (i.e. (Snodgrass, 1983; Moore et al., 1978). Morris (2017) for example, draws our attention to the ways in which Du Bois's work, which discussed many of the issues addressed by Thrasher, Park and colleagues, was largely dismissed and marginalised, something Morris argues was based on racism and discrimination among the 'Chicago School ranks', thus raising questions about the applicability of the Chicago School's revelations and the very underpinning of the discipline and wider origins of criminology overall. There have been wider discussions about the conflict between 'orthodox criminology', which aligns gangs with violence and crime, and more critical stances, which develop a 'criminological imagination' (Young, 2011) and seek to see the gang amid its wider social function, structures and society. The 1970s saw great developments with regard to the latter. Chambliss's (1973) classic text *Saints and Roughnecks* was one of the first to demonstrate how social class and labelling lead to some young people being labelled delinquent and others, largely based on social class, 'saints' engaging in normal peer-related behaviour.

The Birmingham School's seminal text *Resistance Through Rituals* (Hall and Jefferson, 1976) illuminated the importance of resistance in understanding youth subcultures and helped to demonstrate the ways in which young people, largely marginalised from society, form and develop mechanisms to protect their identities and dignity, as well as ways in which to earn income and access social structures and acquire mobility. Hebdige's 1979 book *Subculture: The Meaning of Style* explored youth subcultures, consumption and discrimination and the homology between groups of young people rather than their differences.

This means that research into gangs is extensive but largely situated within the context of Anglo-America theory, epistemology and empirical data. This poses several issues, particularly in light of gangs in a global sphere. Questions arise, including 'How can we understand gangs that operate in places outside of the global North? And how far are extant theoretical explanations useful when considering gangs in places such as Bangladesh and China?' This speaks to a wider debate and the development of the new and emergent discourse of Southern criminology, which argues that criminology as a whole requires 'rebalancing; to better reflect crime that occurs – and is experienced – in the global South, where most of the world's population live' (Carrington et al., 2016).

It is widely acknowledged that defining the 'gang' is an arduous task (see Harris et al., 2012; Fraser, 2017), yet despite challenges, global North definitions of the gang are well established, embedded in policy and remain largely unopposed by research derived from the global South. Global North definitions often 'operate as the archetype' (Fraser and Hagedorn, 2016), leaving little room to consider where these definitions might *not* apply. In addition, comparative research often arises from quantitative epistemologies, leading to a 'static view of gang membership that neglects the localized meanings, historical antecedents and cultural contexts of gangs' (ibid.: 2).

One of the most pervasive definitions associates gangs and the streets. For example, Klein and Maxson (2006) argue that gangs are generally made up of young people who engage with the streets and conduct crime collectively, in alliance with other gang members. This relates to the development of the group's identity and criminal activity. This definition is ubiquitous in research in America and increasingly in Europe and has helped shape the Eurogang Forum's (a group of over 100 academics and practitioners who specialise in gangs in Europe and wider afield) definition of the gang, which states that gangs are: 'any durable street-oriented youth group whose group involvement in illegal activity is part of their group activity' (van Gemert, 2005: 148). There are various scholars who are aligned with this perspective, for example, van Gemert and Fleisher's (2005) work on Moroccan gangs in The Hague, Weerman's (2005) research, also in the Netherlands, and Gatti et al.'s (2005) research into gangs in Genoa. This 'version' of gangs tends to closely align conceptualisations of gangs with violence and separates discussions of gangs from other forms of group-related criminality, including organised crime.

There is a counter-argument. Various scholars point to the notion of different types of gangs (McLean et al., 2018). Others argue that global North definitions of gangs are narrow and restricted (Hagedorn, 2008) and do not adequately reflect the fluid nature of gangs and the ability of some gangs to develop into more established forms of organised crime (Fraser and Hagedorn, 2016). Winton (2014), drawing on her work with gangs in Latin America, suggests that our consideration of gangs should move away from a focus on the individual and towards a greater understanding of the structural drivers for violence. Others argue that the distinction between gangs and organised crime is more complex than Anglo-American definitions depict. Densley (2012) makes a compounding case related to the developing organisation of gangs, and Hallsworth and Young (2006) consider the ways in which group-related offending – including gangs and organised crime – are often closely interlinked. Other scholars argue that gangs operate amid organised crime groups and exist as the lower echelons of these criminal entities (Levitt and Venkatesh, 2000; Atkinson-Sheppard, 2016). For the purpose of this chapter, organised crime is defined as 'group attempts to regulate and control the production and distribution of a given commodity or service unlawfully' (Varese, 2011: 15). Mafias are organised crime groups that monopolise markets but also engage in a market for protection (Varese, 2011; Gambetta, 1993). This distinguishes organised crime from criminal groups that are organised (Varese, 2011) and opens up discussions about the role that gangs play in these criminal hierarchies.

For centuries, the task of the Anglo-American criminologist has been to consider crime and violence but also how criminal groups, including gangs, organise themselves for recreation and solidarity and to commit crime (Decker and Pyrooz, 2014). In fact, the organisation of a group often depicts more than just its structure but also its likelihood of survival and how it colludes with other criminal groups and the state (ibid.). Gangs are argued to exist on a spectrum of organisation (ibid.; Densley, 2012). However, these perspectives are arguably aligned with 'orthodox criminology' (Young, 2011), and because of this, scant attention has been paid to the organisation and evolution of gangs (McLean et al., 2018) and their potential association with organised crime in the global South, particularly in Bangladesh and China.

Bangladesh and China

The topic of gangs in Bangladesh has received little international attention. However, Shafi (2010) argues that *mastaans* are organised crime groups that exist in Dhaka and operate in some of the city's most impoverished areas, often in collusion with corrupt politicians and the state. Zafarullah and Rahman (2002: 1021) describe how organised crime groups operate 'under the shelter of godfathers, who are mainly ministers, members of parliament and business leaders'. Lewis (2012) proposes that mastaan work to secure votes for corrupt politicians and that their activity often spans a plethora of criminal activity. Jackman's (2018) recent study in Dhaka supports this notion and argues that 'gang-like' behaviour occurs under the direct control of politicians. In one of the few studies to specifically consider gangs in Bangladesh, Atkinson-Sheppard (2016) argues that *mastaans* are organised crime groups that engage in a variety of crime and violence, operate in hierarchies and engage gangs to conduct their activities on the streets; young people form the lowest echelon of these criminal groups and engage in what Atkinson-Sheppard (2016) argues is 'illicit child labour'.

In China, research into gangs is also limited (Webb et al., 2011). Current discourse is based largely on quantitative data, meaning that the nature and dynamics of gangs remain largely unknown (Atkinson-Sheppard, 2018). Nevertheless, research that does exist suggests that gangs are often transient entities that rarely exist for lengthy periods (Zhang et al., 1997), but group members do engage in violence more than non-gang-affiliated peers (Pyrooz and Decker, 2013). In addition, vulnerable children, including those 'left behind' in villages while their parents migrate to urban areas to find work, are particularly vulnerable to joining and forming gangs for solidarity and protection and as a way to develop income generation via pro-criminal means (Tao, 2016). This relates closely to a variety of scholarship which argues that migrant children engage in higher levels of violence than their non-migrant peers (Li and Cai, 2009; Wei at al., 2014).

Research regarding Chinese organised crime is more established. Wing Lo's (2012) extensive discourse considers the Triads in Hong Kong, and Wang (2017) describes how organised crime groups illustrate mafia-type characteristics across mainland China. Similar to the situation in Bangladesh, corrupt politicians provide protection to organised crime groups in return for financial profit and the opportunity to run illegal businesses (Lo and Kwok, 2013). Atkinson-Sheppard and Hayward (2019) argue that gangs in China largely fall within the remit of organised crime groups, something discussed in more depth as this chapter progresses.

In both instances, an understanding of the context in which gang crime occurs is imperative, particularly in light of the state and governance in each country. In Bangladesh, the state is weak, with partisan politics and widespread violence underpinning the political landscape (Moniruzzaman, 2009). In China, the opposite is apparent; authoritarian governance means that the political landscape is one of control and, at times, oppression. Despite this, there are similarities. In the 1970s, both countries experienced vast social change. Bangladesh emerged as a nation in 1971, following a War of Independence with Pakistan. In China, the 1970s marked the end of the Cultural Revolution and Mao's regime. Both countries also face social issues, including vast rural-urban migration and the marginalisation of vulnerable citizens. In Bangladesh, millions of children live on the streets, struggling to survive (UNICEF, 2012); in China, the numbers of street children are on the decline (Gao et al., 2018), but millions of children are involved in the country's migration trajectory (Chinese National Bureau of Statistics, 2017). This means that in both instances, large numbers of children are vulnerable – and thus potentially susceptible to the threat of gangs and organised crime. Yet questions arise as to how we might compare these seemingly different countries and how the impact of context – in a political, historical, economic and social sense – affects the emergence and establishment of gangs today.

Research methods

The research methods discussed in this chapter arise from two separate but closely interlinked case studies. Case study methodology was specifically chosen for each study to allow for a plethora of data to be collected over a lengthy time period (Yin, 2014). This collection of data from a variety of sources helps to provide context to a study and supports the triangulation of data sources, leading to robust and reliable findings (Bowling, 2010). The qualitative case study method has been used in criminological studies, that is, to consider policing (Bowling, 2010) and the Chinese mafia (Wang, 2017). However, this is the first study to develop a comparative lens through which to consider both China and Bangladesh.

The data collection for both studies consisted of participant observation (including a media analysis); interviews with adult practitioners; and engagement with young people, street children in Bangladesh and young people with experience of, or existing on the periphery of, gang crime in China.

The specific research methods for each site included three years of participant observation of the criminal justice system in Bangladesh (including a media analysis); 80 interviews (42 semi-structured and 38 unstructured) with criminal justice practitioners, NGO workers and community members; and a year-long embedded case study with a group of 22 street children and the organisation that housed and supported them. In China, I acted as the principal investigator and initiated a collaborative research team of British and Chinese academics; together we carried out extensive observation of Chinese society, a media analysis (of Chinese and English-speaking press) of reports of gangs across the country (including available statistics, of which there were few) and an in-depth review of available literature related to gangs and organised crime in both Chinese and English. Ninety-nine qualitative interviews (of both semi-structured [52] and unstructured [47] formats) were conducted with police officers; prison officers; social workers; NGO workers; academics; journalists; diplomats; and community members from a variety of location across China, including Beijing, Shanghai, Hong Kong, Wuhan, Kunming, Xi'an, Shenzhen, Hubei, Shandong and Tianjin. The participants also included one ex-gang member and young people with friends or associates in gangs, 12 of whom were incarcerated in a young offenders' institution in Shanghai, the majority for offences committed in groups.

Access proved one of the more challenging aspects of the research but was supported by local 'gatekeepers'. I lived and worked in both countries during the duration of each study. This supported the process of accessing local knowledge and developing an understanding of context and helped to develop contacts to provide access to participants. This also meant that 'snow-balling sampling' underpinned the research, and the data collection progressed in line with the development of new contacts. Informed consent was gained from all participants (via the use of an information sheet and consent form). There were nuanced differences between the research sites. In China, verbal as opposed to written consent was favoured – taking into consideration the objections many people have about signing their name in China (see Wang, 2017, for more details). In Bangladesh, both written and verbal consent was gained. A specific child protection process was initiated for both studies and designed to address issues of informed consent among the young people, ensure their anonymity and ensure safe guarding mechanisms should they disclose information related to a criminal offence. Interpreters supported the data collection at both research sites, assisted by my basic grasp of Mandarin.

The research methods for each study were designed with comparative analysis in mind. The processes and methods of data collection were similar at each site. Analysis of the data of Bangladesh was conducted first, in line with the chronological order of the data collection. The research in China was then completed, including analysis of the data. Comparative analysis was then carried out and considered the similarities and differences between the data sets in light of one another and in light of extant research from around the world. The proceeding discussions within this chapter are the results of this analysis.

It is important to note that it is outside of the boundaries of this chapter to discuss the empirical data gathered in each study in great depth. Rather, the chapter aims to summarise the research findings and draw on and discuss the parallels between the data, particularly with regard to defining gangs, the organisation of gangs and the ways in which these studies can help us to reflect – critically – on extant research into gangs and organised crime. For a more in-depth discussion of the data, including the participant's views, please see (Atkinson-Sheppard, 2016; Atkinson-Sheppard and Hayward, 2019).

Gangs in Bangladesh

The data from both Bangladesh depicted a complex picture of gangs, the landscape in which they operate and their relationship with the state. First, it is important to note that for some criminal groups, the Anglo-American definition of a gang as 'any durable street-oriented youth group whose group involvement in illegal activity is part of their group activity' (Van Gemert, 2005: 148) was relevant. For example, the data demonstrated a variety of gangs described by the participants in Bangladesh as the 'Gulshan boys' to depict groups of young people who come from a relatively affluent area of Dhaka, Gulshan. These groups are made up of predominantly young men who engage in low-level offending (drug taking, reckless driving, hanging out together, graffiti), often as part of a group (Atkinson-Sheppard, 2018). The Gulshan boys, and those like them, provide members with solidarity; crime is largely expressive and fuelled by the frustrations the young people feel towards wider Bangladeshi society (ibid.). The nature of the 'Gulshan boys' illustrates 'peer group'-related behaviour (Hallsworth and Young, 2006: 4) and, on some occasions, gangs.

However, these gangs were seen as secondary to those that exist as the lower echelons of organised crime groups, criminal groups that 'attempt to regulate and control the production and distribution of a given commodity or service unlawfully' (Varese, 2011: 5). The data illustrated the pervasive presence of mastaans, organised crime groups that operate in a market for protection, crime and violence. These groups aim to monopolise markets: drugs, weapons, extortion and social protection (Atkinson-Sheppard, 2017), thus aligning these groups with definitions of mafias, largely considered organised crime groups that operate in a market for protection (Gambetta, 1993; Varese, 2011).

Mastaans require group members to conduct their activities on the streets and thus engage gangs to do so. These gangs engage in a wide variety of crime and violence on behalf of their mastaan bosses, including drug dealing, weapon carrying, extortion, political violence, 'land-grabbing' and contract killings (Atkinson-Sheppard, 2016). It is also important to note that the data illustrated a fluidity that pervades these criminal groups. The highest echelon of mastaan groups are well established, but lower down the ranks, more variability occurs. For example, mastaan groups may have established gangs that work amid their middle echelon; however, the data also showed instances in which gangs, or individuals, are hired to conduct specific tasks (such as contract killings, often fuelled by revenge). Gangs operate in alliance and in collaboration with mastaan groups, imperative to their survival, but they can also exist as separate entities, engaged at times in mastaan-related behaviour but at other times involved in activities to maintain group cohesion and earn an income via pro-criminal pursuits (ibid.).

The context of the state is imperative to these discussions. Within the boundaries of a weak state, mastaan groups have emerged and flourished, particularly within some of the country's most impoverished areas. In slums, mastaan bosses engage in the delivery of services such as gas, water and electricity, which they charge inflated prices for; alongside this, mastaan groups collect informal taxes from slum residents (Atkinson-Sheppard, 2017), demonstrating a form of 'concurrent governance' (Sergi, 2015) and mafia-like behaviour.

The data also demonstrated a variety of other 'gangs', some involved in organised begging and others in politics. The 'student groups' were described by the participants as the 'youth factions' of Bangladesh's two main political parties, the Awami League (AL) and the Bangladesh National Party (BNP). Violence between the two parties is well known (Moniruzzaman, 2009), and the participants described how each political party operates via different echelons that is, the AL has the *Chatra league* (student league), the *jubo league* (youth league) and the *Chatra sabok league*. The BNP has the *chatra dol* (student league), the *jubo dohl* (youth league) and the *chatra sabok dohl*. Although the nature of these groups is distinctively political, the participants described instances where members of the student leagues became involved in political violence and a variety of other forms of criminality, often driven by income generation (Atkinson-Sheppard, 2018). Thus, it is difficult to distinguish where politics ends and crime begins, particularly in light of the collaboration between mastaans and politics discussed earlier but also because of the similarities between the student factions of the political parties and notions of gangs as criminal entities that engage in crime collectively.

Overall, the landscape is complex and multifaceted. Gangs operate as separate entities but largely within the context of organised crime which has associated with politics. It is thus imperative to understand gangs in the context in which they occur: a weak state with a corrupt political system, endemic poverty and a wide range of parties that distribute human services and thus engage in the delivery of social protection – including organised crime groups. It is also important to move away from any single notion of a gang and to explore the variety and complexity of gangs in Bangladesh today.

Gangs in China

In China, an analogous picture appeared. First, the data demonstrated a wide array of terms used in legislation, in the media and by the participants to describe gangs and organised crime, painting an ambiguous picture of how gangs are conceptualised and understood in mainland China (Atkinson-Sheppard and Hayward, 2019). However, in similarity to Bangladesh, there were some criminal groups for whom the Anglo-American definition of the street gang was both useful and relevant. The participants discussed relatively small groups of 5–6 who engage in crime collectively, groups of migrants in cities where association with a gang is linked to their home town and disputes arise because of conflict between areas, towns or cities (ibid.). Young street children and 'left-behind' children also form groups for solidarity and in some instances engage in crime collectively, often for financial profit. Other gangs are involved in drug dealing, theft and robbery (ibid.).

However, these gangs were seen as secondary to gangs that exist as part of organised crime groups that 'aim to monopolize markets' (Varese, 2011). The data illustrated gang members or 'thugs' (Ong, 2018) who can be hired (often by corrupt members of the state) to engage in a variety of crime and violence and who also engage in the collection of protection fees, aligning their behaviour with definitions of mafia groups, organised crime groups that aim to monopolise markets, including protection (Varese, 2011; Gambetta, 1993). Gangs also monopolise transportation markets and drug dealing, and in Shanghai, they operate as the lower echelons of organised crime groups that engage in a variety of crime and violence (Atkinson-Sheppard and Hayward, 2019). The data showed how these groups in Shanghai often mirror the characteristics of the Triads in Hong Kong, which, as Wing Lo (2012) argues, are hierarchically based and have been an endemic presence in Hong Kong for many years.

The context in which gangs occur in China is imperative for understanding their nature, dynamics and engagement with the state. State control is imperative in this context. Within a context of strict authoritarian governance, 'street gangs' are less likely to thrive. In fact, the landscape of government control means that groups 'hanging around on street corners' are largely prohibited in China – in line with government control of any group of people congregating in a public place. This means that the alliance and association with the streets, as seen in a multitude of studies into gangs in the global North, is not necessarily relevant in China (Atkinson-Sheppard and Hayward, 2019). The streets are places of control rather than areas for exhibitions of violence based on territory and respect.

Developing a new landscape of gangs

The data from Bangladesh and China suggests that it is necessary to develop a new landscape of gangs, one which includes a larger focus on a variety of gangs, moving away from the dichotomy of gang or non-gang member and into a more fluid terrain. The data from both studies discussed illustrates a wide variety of gangs, some of which could be aligned with the global North definition of a 'street gang' but others less so. Scholars such as Rodgers and Baird (2015) discuss gangs in Latin America and urge us to be cautious when considering gangs amid organised crime, yet, in the instances of Bangladesh and China, the majority of gangs exist not as street-based entities but rather as significant players within hierarchies of organised crime. Anglo-American definitions of the gang are thus narrow, limited and of limited relevance outside of the global North (Hagedorn, 2008). We need a new way to conceptualise gangs in the global South. The parallels between data arising from two distinctively different countries in terms of society, culture, history and politics are what make these findings relevant in Asia but potentially wider afield.

The drivers behind the emergence and expansion of these gangs are closely associated with the context in which they occur. In both China and Bangladesh, organised crime groups that exist – and succeed – are generally those that operate in alliance with the state and engage, at some level, in 'concurrent governance' (Sergi, 2015). The groups that operate at the middle echelon of organised crime groups in Bangladesh and China consist of youth who persist over time and for whom 'illegal activity constitutes part of group identity' (Klein and Maxson, 2006), but these gangs also have another, wider function: to operate as part of an organised criminal group, engaged in monopolisation of markets and, in some instances, protection.

There are nuanced differences between Bangladesh and China. In China, authoritarian governance and strict control of the streets mean that rather than being a place where gangs congregate, the streets are some of the most controlled areas of the country (Atkinson-Sheppard and Hayward, 2019). In Bangladesh, endemic poverty means that the presence of gangs 'hanging around' on the streets is largely considered a 'middle-class youth' pursuit. Gang members who operate in the slums and poor areas of Bangladesh do more than 'hang around on the street'; they live there, a stark contrast to the ways in which gang membership is understood in extant, largely Anglo-America data. The domain of the streets is different, its function wider than global North definitions allow. The nature of gangs in Bangladesh and China is different to the street gangs of LA, London or New York, less about respect and more about money and more of a focus on social inclusion rather than subculture.

There are theoretical implications associated with the development of a new landscape of gangs. First, it is important to reflect upon the epistemological underpinning of extant theories into gangs. As mentioned previously, gang research is largely derived from the global North, but there is more to the debate than locale. Current gang research is ethnocentric in its development but also in its theoretical base. The starting point from which we explore and conceptualise these criminal entities is based, largely at least, on the assumption that these groups are 'subcultures' – something witnessed in Thrasher's (1927) early research and something which permeates gang research today.

The research discussed in this chapter provides an alternative viewpoint. Gangs in China and Bangladesh are not solely subcultures but rather entwined with and influenced by the dominant culture; they exist as a wider spectrum of organised crime groups that engage with wider society and the state. In many ways, research into gangs ignores the role of the state; something questioned by the data from both Bangladesh and China. In both research sites, it is the relationship between gangs *and* the state that helps to frame understandings of criminal groups. Questions thus arise as to how we might conceptualise these gangs from the perspective of theory. Should they be subsumed into literature on organised crime, which itself is an ambiguous concept (Von Lampe 2006)? Or perhaps it is time to re-consider gangs from the perspective of the global South and reflect on what this means for extant criminological theory today and in the future.

Conclusion

The chapter has discussed gangs in Bangladesh and China in light of theory and from the perspective of Southern criminology; in doing so, it has reflected on the issues of applying extant criminological theory, largely derived from the global North to places in the global South. The chapter has considered the nature of gangs in China and Bangladesh and demonstrated the plethora of criminal groups that operate in both countries, often in alliance with the state. Anglo-American definitions of 'street gangs' have limited relevance in these contexts.

The nature of gangs and their ability to exist among most of the world's cultures today suggests that we need not only a 'southern' way of understanding these criminal entities but also a global one. A new landscape of gangs should be developed to reflect this, to represent the diversity of the world today and the impact this has on criminality, particularly among groups. A more fluid, expansive landscape is necessary to understand global gangs but also to tackle the crime and violence they commit – but one that recognises difference among gang members, the groups they engage with, the context in which their behaviour occurs and the varying impact of these groups around the world today (Fraser and Hagedorn, 2016). However, the variants in the nature of gangs in China and Bangladesh and the context in which they occur should be acknowledged and better understood. In fact, it is the context which defines the gangs discussed in this chapter; their associations with the state that help to frame understandings of gangs; the ways in which they exist and operate, flourish or desist.

Fraser and Hagedorn (2016: 1) argue that 'our search for similarity has resulted in a failure to recognize and understand difference', meaning that a search for a universal definition of a gang has played further into the stereotypical – and Anglo-American – notion of the gang.

This ethnocentrism should be considered and addressed; drawing on a 'global exchange' (ibid.) is both necessary and timely; however, this exchange must be couched in global perspectives if we have any hope of developing a conceptual framework suitable for explaining international gangs. It is not as easy as countering northern research with data from the south. Southern criminology must be considered in light of Asian criminology (Moosavi, 2018) and the complexity of criminology arising from different places in Asia better understood. Issues of comparison are complex, and methods for analysis require greater thought and consideration. Comparisons between countries in the global South are rare, particularly those drawing on similar research methods, as discussed in this chapter. More studies should be designed concurrently to assist in both data collection and comparative analysis. Finally, we must be cautious in our categorisations; developing a dichotomy of 'north' and 'south' feeds into ethnocentric research from both perspectives.

But questions remain: How is it possible to conduct comparative research across countries, continents and globally? Which methods and analysis are the most suitable for doing so? How can we remain critical in our approach while at the same time identifying what is the same but also what differs? The task is to move away from global North conceptualisations or even Southern discourse and into critical, global narratives of gangs and organised crime. But what steps might be taken to do so? How might we develop a conceptual landscape suitable for considering gangs on a global scale?

Bibliography

Atkinson-Sheppard, S. (2017) Mastaans and the market for social protection: Exploring mafia groups in Dhaka, Bangladesh. *Asian Journal of Criminology*, 12(4): 235–253.

Atkinson-Sheppard, S. (2018) Organised crime, gangs and the complexity of group offending in Dhaka, Bangladesh. In *Handbook of South Asian Criminology*. Florida: Routledge.

Atkinson-Sheppard, S. (2016) The gangs of Bangladesh: Exploring organised crime, street gangs and 'illicit child labourers' in Dhaka. *Criminology and Criminal Justice*, 16 (2): 233–249.

Atkinson-Sheppard, S. and Hayward, H. (2019) Conceptual similarities; distinct difference: Exploring 'the gang' in mainland China. *British Journal of Criminology*, 59 (3): 614–633.

Bowling, B. (2010) *Policing the Caribbean: Transnational Security Cooperation in Practice*. London: Oxford University Press.

Brotherton, D.C. (2015) *Youth Street Gangs: A Critical Appraisal*. New York: Routledge Press.

Brotherton, D.C. and Barrios, L. (2004) *The Almighty Latin King and Queens Nation*. New York: Colombia University Press.

Chambliss, W.J. (1973) The Saints and the Roughnecks. *Society*, 11 (1): 24–31.

Decker, S. and Pyrooz, D.C. (2014) Gangs: Another form of organised crime? In L. Paoli (ed) *The Oxford Handbook of Organised Crime*. Oxford: Oxford University Press.

Carrington, K., Hogg, R. and Sozzo, M. (2016) Southern criminology. *British Journal of Criminology*, 56 (1): 1–20.

Densley, J.A. (2012) 'It's a gang life but not as we know it': The evolution of gang business. *Crime and Delinquency*, 1–30.

Fraser, A. (2017) *Gangs and Crime: Critical Alternatives*. London: Sage.

Fraser, A. and Hagedorn, J. (2016) Gangs and a global sociological imagination. *Theoretical Criminology*, 22 (1): 42–62.

Gao, Y., Atkinson-Sheppard, S. and Yu, Y. (2018) A review of the national policies on street children in China. *Children and Youth Services Review*, 93: 79–87.

Gambetta, D. (1993) *The Sicilian Mafia*. London: Harvard University Press.

Gatti, U., Francesca, A., Marengo, G., Melchiorre, N. and Sasso, M. (2005) An old-fashioned youth gang in Genoa. In S. Decker and F Weerman (eds) *European Street Gangs and Troublesome Youth Groups*. Oxford: AltaMira Press.

Hagedorn, J. (2008) *A World of Gangs: Armed Young Men and Gangsta Culture*. Minneapolis: University of Minnesota Press.

Hall, S. and Jefferson, T. (1976) *Resistance through Rituals: Youth Subcultures in Post-War Britain*. London: Hutchinson.

Hallsworth, S. and Young, T. (2006) *Urban Collectives: Gangs and Other Groups*. A report prepared for the Metropolitan Police Service and Government Office for London. London: Metropolitan Police Service.

Harris, D., Turner, R., Garrett, I. and Atkinson, S. (2012) *Understanding the Psychology of Gang Violence: Implications for Designing Effective Violence Reduction Interventions*. London: Ministry of Justice.

Hazen, J.M. and Rodgers, D. (2014) *Global Gangs*. Minnesota: University of Minnesota Press.

Hebdige, D. (1979) *Subculture: The Meaning of Style*. London: Routledge.

Jackman, D. (2018) The decline of gangsters and politicization of violence in urban Bangladesh. *Development and Change*, 1–25. DOI: 10.1111/dech.12428.

Lewis, D. (2012) *Bangladesh: Politics, Economy and Civil Society*. Cambridge: Cambridge University Press.

Levitt, S.D. and Venkatesh, S.A. (2000) An economic analysis of a drug selling gang's finances. *Quarterly Journal of Economics*, 115: 755–789.

Li, X F. and Cai, J. (2009) A study on the living situations and organizational assistance of problematic street children. *Hubei Social Sciences*, 8: 53–56.

Lo, T.W., and Kwok, S.I. (2013) Triads and tongs. In G. Bruinsma and D. Weisburd (eds) *Encyclopedia of Criminology and Criminal Justice*. New York: Springer, 5332–5343.

McLean, R., Deuchar, R., Harding, S. and Densley, J. (2018) Putting the 'street' in gang: Place and space in the organization of Scotland's drug-selling gangs. *British Journal of Criminology*. https://doi.org/10.1093/bjc/azy015.

Morris, A. (2017) *The Scholar Denied: W. E. B. Du Bois and the Birth of Modern Sociology*. Berkeley, CA: University of California Press.

Moniruzzaman, M. (2009) Party politics and political violence in Bangladesh: Issues, manifestation and consequences. *South Asian Survey*, 16 (1): 81–99.

Moore, J.W., Garcia, R., Cerda, L. and Valencia, F. (1978) *Homeboys: Gangs, Drugs, and Prisons in the Barrios of Los Angeles*. Philadelphia: Temple University Press.

Moosavi, L. (2018) A friendly critique of 'Asian criminology' and 'southern criminology'. *The British Journal of Criminology*. https://doi.org/10.1093/bjc/azy045.

National Bureau of Statistics of China (2017) Statistical bulletin of the People's Republic of China on national economic and social development in 2016. Available online at www.stats.gov.cn/tjsj/zxfb/201702/t20170228_1467424.html (accessed 11 September 2018).

Ong, L.H. (2018) Thugs abd outsourcing of state repression in China. *The China Journal*, 80. https://doi.org/10.1086/696156

Pyrooz, D.C. and Decker, S.H. (2013) Delinquent behavior, violence, and gang involvement in China. *Journal of Quantitative Criminology*, 29: 251.

Rodgers, D. and Baird, A. (2015) Understanding gangs in contemporary Latin America. In H. Scott, S.H. Decker, and D.C. Pyrooz (eds) *Handbook of Gangs and Gang Responses*. New York: Wiley.

Sergi, A. (2015) Mafia and politics as concurrent governance actors. Revisiting political power and crime in Southern Italy. In P. C. van Duyne, A. Maljević, G. A. Antonopoulos, J. Harvey, and K. von Lampe (eds) *The Relativity of Wrongdoing: Corruption, Organised Crime, Fraud and Money Laundering in Perspective*. Oisterwijk: Wolf Legal Publishers.

Shafi, S.A. (2010) *Urban Crime and Violence in Dhaka*. Dhaka: The University Press.

Snodgrass, J. (1983) The Jack-Roller: A fifty-year follow-up. *Urban Life*, 11 (4): 440–459.

Tao, L. (2016) Q&A with Sociologist Li Tao on Youth Gangs in Rural China. Available online at http://www.sixthtone.com/news/723/qa-sociologist-li-tao-youth-gangs-rural-china (accessed 15 June 2019).

Thrasher, F.M. (1927) *The Gang*. Chicago: University of Chicago Press.

UNICEF (2012) Child rights Bangladesh: UNICEF. Available online at: www.unicef.org/bangladesh/children_4878.htm (Accessed 12 September 2018).

van Gemert, F. (2005) Youth groups and gangs in Amsterdam: A pretest of the Eurogang expert survey. In S. Decker and F Weerman (eds) *European Street gangs and Troublesome Youth Groups*. Oxford: AltaMira Press.

van Gemert and M. Fleisher (2005) In the grip of the group: Ethnography of a Moroccan street gang in the Netherlands. In S.H. Decker and F. Weerman (eds) *European Street Gangs and Troublesome Youth Groups: Findings from the Eurogang Research Program*. Walnut Creek, CA: Altamira Press, pp. 11–30.

Varese, F. (2011) *Mafias on the Move: How Organised Crime Conquers New Territories*. Princeton, NJ: Princeton University Press.

von Lampe, K. (2006) The interdisciplinary dimensions of the study of organized crime. *Trends in Organized Crime*, 9 (3), 77–95.

Wang, P. (2017) *The Chinese mafia: Organized crime, corruption, and extra-legal protection*. Oxford: Oxford University Press.

Weerman, F. (2005) Identification and self-identification: Using a survey to study gangs in the Netherlands In S. Decker and F Weerman (eds) *European Street gangs and Troublesome Youth Groups*. Oxford: AltaMira Press.

Webb, V.J., Ren, L., Zhao, J., He, N. and Marshall, I. (2011) A comparative study of youth gangs in China and the united states: Definition, offending, and victimization. *International Criminal Justice Review*, 21: 225–242.

Wei, Y.H., Zhu, M.H. and Ning, L.Y. (2014) A study on penal policies applied to handle rural left-behind children. *Journal of Heilongjiang Administrative Cadre College of Politics and Law*, 2: 61–64.

Wing, Lo, T. (2012) Triadization of youth gangs in Hong Kong. *The British Journal of Criminology*, 52 (3): 556–576.

Winton, A. (2014) Gangs in global perspective. *Environment and Urbanisation* 26 (2): 401–416.

Young, J. (2011) *The Criminological Imagination*. Cambridge: Polity Press.

Yin, R.K. (2014) *Case Study Research: Design and Methods*. (5th Edition). London: Sage.

Zafarullah, H. and Rahman, M.H. (2002) Human rights, civil society and non–government organisation: The nexus in Bangladesh. *Human Rights Quarterly*, 24 (4): 1011–1034.

Zilberg, E. (2011) *Space of Detention: The Making of a Transnational Gang Crisis between Los Angeles and San Salvador*. Durham: Duke University Press.

Zhang, L., Messner, S., Lu, Z. and Deng, X. (1997) Gang crime and its punishment in China. *Journal of Criminal Justice*, 25: 289–302.

27

Russian street gangs, their social construction and political use-value

Svetlana Stephenson

The discourse about Russian gangs represents a deviation from the dominant view of gangs that has taken hold across the Western world (Brotherton 2015; Hallsworth and Young 2008; Hallsworth 2013), in which the gang is presented as the manifestation of archetypical evil; the bane of the city; a force that seduces and corrupts vulnerable youth, stands behind most urban disorder and crime and has to be fought off with the full power of the repressive apparatus of the state. In Russia, while anxieties about street youth do resurface from time to time, this demonic vision of the gang has been largely absent. Consequently, Russia lacks gang suppression strategies, gang injunctions or gang antisocial behavior orders, all the measures of gang control that are currently deployed in Europe and the United States. Youth street organizations tend to be seen not as pernicious entities and collections of parasites that are born in urban "badlands" and then grow and multiply to feed on the social body but as a traditional form of youth social association. Street life, and male socialization within it, is normalized in Russian society and is largely perceived as an organic cultural form. Although anxieties about youth do periodically resurface, the discourse of a "dangerous gang" is absent. In fact, past membership of a gang is sometimes drawn on as positive reputational capital by members of the political class.

In this chapter, I address some of the key features of Russian gangs, discuss their social construction and reflect on the ideological uses of the gang that may explain the strange non-existence of a "dangerous gang" discourse.

The Russian street gang as a form of traditional male socialization

Territorial youth groups exist across the former Soviet Union. Historical and anthropological research shows that young people (especially men) have been culturally expected to spend much of their time on the streets, in the company of their peers, only to leave their groups when they become adults. (Stephenson 2012; Shchepanskaia 2001; Morozov and Sleptsova 2004). Evidence collected in Bishkek (Nasritdinov and Schröder 2016), Moscow, Kazan (Ageeva 1991; Stephenson 2008, 2012, 2015) and other cities across the Russian Federation (Gromov 2009; Karbainov 2009; Golovin and Lurie 2008) shows that these quasi-kin groups tend to unite young male residents aged around 10–18 living in peripheral areas of large cities and most of the youth in medium-sized cities and small towns, as well as the capital cities of Yerevan (Ponomareva 2014, 2015) and Tbilisi (Zakharova 2010, 2012, 2016).

In Russia, members of these groups are far from being marginalized or socially excluded. In fact, one might say they are "over-included" in the local networks (often at the expense of their education). Not only do they sustain close relationships with their fellow group members, but they also actively socialize with their classmates and young people from other areas (Stephenson 2012).

Many have strong identifications with football teams and participate in football-related violence. Their predominant identities and concerns are, however, territorial, linked to the "defense" of their local turf (Pilkington 2002; Stephenson 2012). Although members of some groups can be involved in street crime (stealing, shoplifting or extortion of money and mobile phones from their peers), the nature of these crimes is primarily social rather than economic – any money "earned" through delinquency is quickly spent at gaming arcades and on beer, alcohol and marijuana, consumed together with friends. Street crime, if it happens at all, is inseparable from the overall goal of reaffirmation of the group as collective masters of the street. Young men use it to confirm their power in their area, demonstrating the right to dictate the rules of behavior to other participants of the street space. Street victimization is only partially oriented towards material gain, being an instrument for sustaining the group's territorial domination (see also Dowdney 2005; Rodgers 2009).

Group members are deeply attached to their neighborhoods, where they spend most of their lives, and see it as their duty to defend them. Their attempts to achieve control over their neighborhoods include intimidation of young people who do not belong to their street groups and warfare aimed to "protect" their territories and prove their elite status on the streets. In many urban areas across Russia, the strength of the group is determined in a key ritual of youth collective life called a *strelka* (arranged fight). Some researchers see this ritual as transposed into cities from rural communities, where these practices formed a core part of village life (Morozov and Sleptsova 2004; Bernshtam 1988; Kabanov 1928) and may reflect a particular feature of Russian urban development which involved the rapidly expanding cities incorporating neighboring villages.

Rather than being collections of marginalized and stigmatized delinquents (Anderson 1990; Sánchez-Jankowski 1991; Whyte 1993), the street groups are neighborhood organizations. They can be seen as a classic case of Turner's *communitas*, a society of equal members linked by unmediated social bonds (Turner 1995). Although some of the groups have informal leaders, they do not tend to have a hierarchical structure of command and subordination or strict discipline.

Russian street organizations are typically multi-ethnic, and they unite the young residents of the territory irrespective of their social backgrounds, with major distinctions drawn between those young people who participate in the street lifestyle and those who withdraw into the space of home. Their social composition reflects the specific character of Soviet urbanization that was associated with relatively low residential social differentiation, the legacy of which still remains in many urban areas. The groups differ in the extent of their use of violence and criminal activities, inclusion of girls and young women, the presence or absence of leaders, style of clothes and group insignia (Gromov 2009).

The groups are commonly regarded, by adults and young people alike, as "schools of life" for young men. Here they remove themselves from the sphere of school control and parental discipline, at least for the time that they spend outdoors. In individual conflicts and ritual fights with "enemies" from neighboring streets, they learn to be "real men". Here they become fearless warriors, defenders of the local space and loyal friends. In other words, they acquire qualities relating to conceptions of hegemonic masculinity (Messerschmidt 2012). Rather than anomic social actors lashing out at a world in which they have no stake, or members of deprived ethnic and racial minorities, young people see themselves as the key local reputational group that upholds social order in the community (Collins 2008, p. 229; Suttles 1968).

The groups tend to have a street conduct code, a set of implicit instructions that create cultural unity in the group and establish their social order. Interviews with members of street organizations across the post-Soviet urban space show that the key principles are very similar (Stephenson 2015; Gromov and Stephenson 2008). They should behave as representatives of the street elite, as honorable warriors, who never lose face or let down their group. If challenged, they should respond violently to any perceived assault on their dignity and defend the honor of their group in street altercations. They should refrain from assaulting women, young children and elderly people. They are expected to demonstrate control and integrity, refrain from making empty threats or accusations and behave confidently and decisively in any street interaction. They should be able to present themselves as masters of the street (while placing non-street young men in positions of inferiority) and act as experts in its rules.

During the post-communist transition and its conditions of poverty, unemployment and the collapse of law and order, many of the street organizations in Russia began to engage in extortion and protection rackets. They expanded to form larger units with cohort structures and systems of leadership and forced local businessmen, street traders, street drug traders and sex workers to pay "protection" money (Stephenson 2015). The top echelons of these gangs penetrated into state structures, invested their money into large businesses and eventually became legal entrepreneurs. However, the core members, those who grew up in street peer groups and later formed the "little families", "teams" and other primary social units of organized crime structures, retained their ethos of street brotherhood. Like members of "*cosca*", the basic social unit of the Italian mafia, they were not corporate units but social organizations linked by trust, loyalty, solidarity and control (Paoli 2003).

The social construction of a street gang

As already mentioned, participation in street organizations has been a culturally prescribed form of transition to adulthood for young Russian men. The dominant attitude to youth participation in street organizations as part of normal social reproduction, as an organic cultural mode, was only problematized in media and expert discourse during periods of rapid social change. Whenever steady youth transitions to adulthood were no longer viable, a moral panic would emerge about youth, its supposed resistance to social and political authority and its drift towards criminality. Even then, the criminogenic properties of youth street organizations did not emerge as a key focus of concern. Rather than the dangerous gang, it was the figure of the "hooligan", defined by involvement in senseless violence, that was at the center of public anxieties throughout the 20th century, a figure that has now morphed into that of a *gopnik*, the representative of street culture populated by members of the urban underclass.

As in other European countries (Pearson 1983), rapid urbanization and industrialization in late imperial Russia gave rise to anxieties over the disruption of social order and control over public space. These anxieties focused on working-class youth and their street associations. Neuberger's research into portrayals of delinquent youth in the boulevard-press in St Petersburg at the end of the 19th to the beginning of the 20th century revealed considerable moral panic about violent and uncontrollable groups of young "hooligans" (Neuberger 1993). These hooligans were involved in what seemed like bacchanalia of senseless violence. This was despite the fact that, as some of the publications demonstrated, the groups followed strict codes of honor and fought each other for specific, well-defined reasons, largely to do with protection of turf.

After the 1917 revolution and the civil war, the street groups of *besprizornye*, orphaned and neglected children, became the subject of the next moral panic (Goldman 1993). Anxieties about youth dislocation, and fears that the members of the young generation were actively resisting calls to join socialist youth organizations and failed to conform to the new socialist ideals, were reflected in the resurgence of fears about street hooligans (Furst 2010; Gorsuch 2000). Further on, the social and economic devastation of the Second World War, and the increase in crime (partly produced by the mass amnesty for the criminal inmates of the gulag in 1953), gave a new lease on life to fears about young people, now seen as vulnerable to being lured into gangs organized by recidivists (Dobson 2009).

Generally, however, despite the extreme punitiveness of the Soviet regime, street youth groups were viewed through a normalizing lens. While antisocial and violent behavior in the street context was readily labeled as "hooliganism", youthful territorial associations and networks themselves were not seen as criminogenic. For the Soviet authorities, the social construction of the "dangerous street gang" would not have served any useful ideological purpose. On the contrary, they were reluctant to admit the existence of any organized criminality within the socialist state. In addition, youth street groups and gangs were not seen as problematic, as the class or ethnic divisions that might lead to delinquent responses were not seen as a part of the Soviet social structure. The same was true of concentrations of socially problematic behaviors in particular spatial zones, in light of the fact that, as already discussed, there was no stark residential segregation in Soviet urban areas. (cf.: Thrasher 1963; Anderson 1990; Shaw and Mckay 1942). Soviet criminologists did not see social background or ecological factors as having any bearing on delinquency. Instead, youth delinquency was explained by the psychological problems of transition to adulthood, susceptibility to peer pressure, family dysfunction, and insufficient oversight of youth by the school and political authorities (Connor 1972; Stephenson 2001).

Only towards the end of the Soviet regime in the 1980s, with the sudden emergence of a plethora of youth subcultural groups that refused to conform to the expectations of the Soviet educators and political authorities (Pilkington 1994), did deviant and oppositional youth practices become the focus of attention. Although far from all groups were street based, "dangerous gang" discourse finally emerged – albeit not for mass consumption. Researchers from the Ministry of Interior and the General Prosecution Office identified the presence of "informal street groups with a cult of force, protecting their territory" across the country (Sibiriakov 1990, pp. 170–171). The groups were not only seen as responsible for street crime but were also blamed for territorial fights where, it was claimed, they used knives and guns. Soviet criminologists even wrote that that group members were not afraid of law enforcement and attacked police officers (Prozumentov and Sheksler 1990; Baal 1990; Kashelkin 1990). Although much of the criminological literature was classified at the time, some of the groups, such as *liubery*, young body-builders from the Moscow suburbs who were involved in fights and acquisitive crime, and the Kazan racketeering gang Tiap-Liap, became subject of a handful of press publications (Pilkington 1994). But even then, public discourse about the gang as a dangerous organization that acts as vehicle for crime and violence was absent. Young people were seen as drawn towards antisocial behavior because of the weakness of adult social control, that is, the absence of youth clubs and sports facilities, and weak oversight of youth by the Komsomol, schools and local authorities (Baal 1990; Ovchinskii 1990).

In the 1990s, with the collapse of the Soviet socialist system, new anxieties emerged, focusing largely on street and homeless children, as well as on the rise of violent youth crime (Stephenson 2001). During this period, many of the street groups across Russia transformed into racketeering gangs. Nevertheless, the phenomenon of territorial groups as progenitors of organized crime remained strangely invisible. With rare exceptions (Salagaev 2001; Salagaev and Shashkin 2005), scholars analyzed the rise of racketeering gangs and mafias, seeing them as products of the Soviet legacies of corruption and alliance between former Communist officials and the criminal underworld of "thieves-in-law", professional criminals (Cheloukhine 2008; Serio and Razinkin 1995; Gurov 1990). When the practices of criminal gangs were discussed, the attention of researchers was largely directed at penetration into the structures of legal power and its role in compensating for the weakness of institutional regulation of economic activities (for example, Varese 2001; Volkov 2002; Sokolov 2004; Kupatadze 2013). Wherever young people were concerned, they became commonly seen as sportsmen (athletes), with origins in Soviet youth sports or professional athletes, who had fallen on hard times and decided to sell their services as enforcers in new illegal markets (Volkov 2002; Konstantinov 2004). Scholars of Russian organized crime, if they considered young people at all, regarded them mainly as bands of hoodlums who assembled to engage in primitive extortion, or as fodder for the bosses of organized crime, but not as independent agents. Territorial youth groups operating in the criminal economy were largely neglected.

New concerns about youth dislocation surfaced at the end of the 2000s and were largely linked to young people living in areas with high unemployment. It is now claimed by policy-makers and journalists that there is active "grooming" of young people by criminal organizations. There are reports of young people from many areas across Russia but particularly in Zabaikalie, a poor area in Siberia with a high concentration of penal colonies, who are forced to commit crime in order to make contributions to adult criminal gangs and send money to incarcerated criminals. A new criminal movement, AUE, has been accused of recruiting teenagers. AUE is typically seen as an abbreviation for "*Arestantskoe Urkaganskoe Edinstvo*" ("The Prisoners' and Gangsters' Union") or "*Arestansky Uklad Edin*" ("the Prisoners' Lifestyle Is Unified") (Petelin 2016). No research has yet been published that confirms the actual existence of this movement. AUE subculture, although popular among teenagers, is mostly an Internet phenomenon. The moral panic about AUE seems to encapsulate the anxieties and fears about social reproduction in an increasingly unequal society.

These days, the hooligans have transmogrified into low-class gopniks, seen as belonging to a violent youth subculture heavily influenced by prison culture (Kosterina 2006). The gopniks' style of clothing (often cheap tracksuits), their slang that borrows heavily from criminal culture and their manner of walking the streets in groups or "aggressively" occupying street corners all seem to signify their presumed social and cultural inferiority. Being transformed into "folk devils", some of these young people have begun to use the same scripts to embrace subcultural styles and symbolism (Cohen 1972). Although many reject the derogatory name of "gopnik", preferring to call themselves *obychnye*, *normalnye* or *mestnye patsany* ("normal", "ordinary" or "local" lads) (Stephenson 2012), others have boldly embraced this denomination. There are now numerous websites where self-identified gopniks place photos of themselves in characteristic working-class attire, upload videos of group fights and drinking sessions and present stories about their "role models" from the criminal underworld. They also provide links to their favorite music. These are invariably "prison songs", a traditional Russian genre of romantic, sentimental songs relating the travails and sorrows of criminal "outlaws". The gopnik culture is both reviled and celebrated in modern Russia. In its parochial stubbornness, it seems to represent resistance to late modernity and to an increasingly individualized, diverse and consumer-oriented way of life. Ironically, the consumer industry increasingly seeks to commodify street style and appropriate the symbols of subcultural resistance (Frank 1998). For example, the international designer Gosha Rybchinskiy developed his post-Soviet aesthetics by borrowing heavily from the gopnik style: black leather jackets, cloth caps and thick sweaters tucked into tracksuit bottoms.

Political uses of the street gang

Although gopniks have become a demonized figure in modern-day Russia, street culture is also used to give added legitimacy to the political regime. Across Russian society, references to one's street upbringing, use of slang and evocation of the rules of the street permeate public discourse, with the cultural knowledge of the street world being widely seen as a marker of being a "real man" (Yusupova 2015). Members of the political class have also started using street cultural repertoires to boost their image and confirm their populist credentials.

Russia's President Vladimir Putin often refers to his youth spent on the streets of Leningrad (now St Petersburg) and to the invaluable life lessons he learned in this formative environment. He told the journalists who interviewed him for his first biography, "I was a hooligan, not a young pioneer . . . I really was a bad boy" (Putin 2000, p. 18). Later on, in his speech to an audience of international journalists and experts at the Valdai Forum on 22 October 2015, Putin made the following remark in relation to Russia's intervention in Syria. "Fifty years ago, the streets of Leningrad taught me that if a fight is inevitable, you have to hit first". Following Putin, some of the highest-ranking members of the civil and military apparatus, members of the Russian economic elite, as well as state TV presenters, have begun to use street slang in their public pronouncements, using it to show readiness for confrontation with their political adversaries, the capacity to respond immediately to perceived or real slights and, above all, to demonstrate authenticity, showing that they are men of the people rather than faceless bureaucrats or greedy oligarchs. One recent example was a YouTube address by General Victor Zolotov, the head of the Russian National Guard, in which he challenged the leader of the opposition Alexei Navalny to a "duel" as retaliation for Navalny's videos that exposed alleged corruption in Zolotov's organization. "[I] would like to say why all this is happening. It is because nobody has given you, Mr. Navalny, payback [*otvetka*, a street term – SS]", said Zolotov to Navalny (Zolotov 2018).

A former member of Yeltsin's government, Oleg Sysuev, noted in a radio interview that:

> We have this culture, so to speak, street culture; it has now moved to the screens of state TV, into the apparatus of the Russian representatives in the UN, and this, of course, is very scary. It's this aesthetics. It dominates all artistic production on our TV, in the popular series. All this half-bandit, so to speak, street, aesthetics.
>
> *(Sysuev 2017)*

The journalist Irina Petrovskaya commented on the language of political shows:

> there is a new population of TV presenters, who can be called gopniks, or "serious" or "real" lads. . . . [street swear words] – all these words have now become part of the every-day speech of the presenters and participants of political shows, who say them without any shame and even feel proud of their unbelievable bravery and coolness.
>
> *(Petrovskaya 2017)*

Although it is perhaps ironic that people who have state power and resources at their disposal present themselves as street warriors and outlaws, this arguably serves an important political purpose. Street culture, with its romanticism of male camaraderie and poetry of violence, is used – alongside nationalist and militaristic tropes – as a resource that helps the dominant elite to consolidate its ideological hegemony. I see the members of the Russian dominant class as following the traditions of European romanticism in a search for suitable cultural forms that would provide spiritual sustenance for a deracinated world of bourgeois calculation.

Unlike in modern Western society, where street culture is seen as something that needs to be repressed, in Russia, it became a highly important cultural form during the rise of capitalism. Here we can see parallels with the emergence of romanticism late 18th–early 19th-century England. Developing the ideas of Mill and Gramsci, Eagleton argued that romanticism emerged when a pragmatic "visionless" bourgeoisie needed to connect to organic cultural modes in order to consolidate its ideological hegemony (Mill, cited in Eagleton 1975, p. 82; Gramsci 1971, p. 18). Romanticism emphasized the primacy of imagination over calculation, of collective destiny over utilitarian concerns and of nation over state. While naked economism and utilitarianism were the main discursive forms of state and economic institutions, romantic ideas were, to use Miller's term (Miller 1997), "sutured" onto the cold logic of capitalist accumulation. The Russian street arguably represents such an organic social mode, where aspects of *Gemeinschaft*, collective bonds of male brotherhood, are used to animate cold bureaucratic and corporate logics. Street culture helps to fill the gaps in the system of signification, performing important repair work.

Conclusion

In conclusion, the "gang" should not be stereotyped as a falsely monolithic and ahistorical construction. Its organizational forms reflect local cultural traditions, and it can – as has indeed been the case in Russia – be seen as a part of traditional male socialization. The youth street gang as some intrinsically violent and criminogenic entity has largely been absent from public discourse. During periods when concerns about orderly social reproduction led to panic about youth, it was expressed as fetishistic displacement of social problems onto individual hate figures such as "hooligans", as well as constructions of youth practices as resulting from the "grooming" of innocent young people by adult criminals. The Soviet authorities denied the existence of the gang in the socialist society at all; post-Soviet representations of the gang focused on adult criminals rather than on street youth. With the development of capitalism, street culture has become commodified, as well as used as a source of added legitimacy by members of the dominant class.

The strange non-existence of the "dangerous gang" discourse in Russia – in contrast to Anglo-American and increasingly continental European representations of the gang (Klein 2001) – can be explained by the fact that the youth street organization is still largely seen as a traditional form of male socialization. The social construction of the gang as a form of organized resistance from below, especially by members of a racialized underclass, is not in evidence. Instead it is the irrational (hooligan) violence, and the efforts of adult criminals to disrupt orderly transitions to adulthood, that are seen as the social evil. With capitalism creating new chasms and divisions, the Russian ruling elite, which in reality is rapidly becoming part of the global capitalist class, attempts to reclaim what it sees as organic cultural modes to demonstrate its local authenticity. The gang, a street brotherhood grounded in ancient traditions of warrior masculinity, is presented as a force of male vitality and social solidarity rather than the source of delinquency and disruption. Ultimately, as we have seen, the gang as a cultural and social phenomenon can be subject to alternative interpretations and responses. From a cross-cultural perspective, then, the use-value of a gang, just as the use-value of crime (Christie 2004) is changeable and flexible, and the gang itself can be reviled, accommodated or indeed celebrated, depending on cultural traditions and political needs.

References

Ageeva, L. V. 1991. *Kazanskii Fenomen: Mif i Real'nost*. Kazan: Tatarskoe Knizhnoe Izdatel'stvo.
Anderson, Elijah. 1990. *Streetwise : Race, Class, and Change in an Urban Community*. Chicago and London: University of Chicago Press.

Baal, E. G. 1990. "Problemy Kriminologicheskogo Izucheniia Neformalnykh Grupp, Ob'edinenii, Dvizhenii." In *Kriminologi o Neformalnykh Molodezhnykh Ob'edineniiakh*, edited by I. I. Karpets, 130–143. Moscow: Iuridicheskaia Literatura.

Bernshtam, T. A. 1988. *Molodezh v Obriadovoi Zhisni Russkoi Obshchiny XIX – Nachala XX Veka: Polovozrastnoi Aspekt Traditsionnoi Kultury*. Leningrad: Nauka.

Brotherton, David. 2015. *Youth Street Gangs: A Critical Appraisal*. New Directions in Critical Criminology 10. London: Routledge.

Cheloukhine, Serguei. 2008. "The Roots of Russian Organized Crime: The Old-Fashioned Professionals to the Organized Criminal Groups of Today." *Crime, Law and Social Change* 50: 353–374.

Christie, Nils. 2004. *A Suitable Amount of Crime*. 1st ed. London and New York: Routledge.

Cohen, Stanley. 1972. *Folk Devils and Moral Panics : The Creation of the Mods and Rockers*. London: MacGibbon & Kee.

Collins, Randall. 2008. *Violence: A Micro-Sociological Theory*. Princeton, NJ; Woodstock: Princeton University Press.

Connor, Walter D. 1972. *Deviance in Soviet Society. Crime, Deliquency and Alcoholism*. New York and London: Columbia University Press.

Dobson, Miriam. 2009. *Khrushchev's Cold Summer: Gulag Returnees, Crime, and the Fate of Reform after Stalin*. Ithaca, NY and London: Cornell University Press.

Dowdney, Luke T. 2005. *Neither War nor Peace: International Comparisons of Children and Youth in Organised Armed Violence*. Rio de Janeiro: Viva Rio / ISER / IANSA, 7Letras.

Eagleton, Terry. 1975. "Ideology and Literary Form." *New Left Review* 90: 81–109.

Frank, Thomas. 1998. *The Conquest of Cool: Business Culture, Counterculture, and the Rise of Hip Consumerism*. Chicago: University of Chicago Press.

Furst, Juliane. 2010. *Stalin's Last Generation : Soviet Post-War Youth and the Emergence of Mature Socialism*. Oxford: Oxford University Press.

Goldman, Wendy Z. 1993. *Women, the State, and Revolution: Soviet Family Policy and Social Life, 1917–1936*. Cambridge: Cambridge University Press.

Golovin, V. V., and M. L. Lurie. 2008. "Ideologicheskie i Territorialnie Soobshchestva Molodeozhi: Megapolis, Provintsialnii Gorod, Selo." *Etnograficheskoe Obozrenie* 1: 56–70.

Gorsuch, Anne E. 2000. *Youth in Revolutionary Russia: Enthusiasts, Bohemians and Delinquents*. Bloomington and Indianapolis: Indiana University Press.

Gramsci, Antonio. 1971. "The Intellectuals." In *Selections from the Prison Notebooks*, edited by A. Gramsci, Q. Hoare, and G. N. Smith, 3–23. New York: International Publishers.

Gromov, D. V. 2009. "Podrostkovo-Molodeozhnye Ulichnie Gruppirovki Kak Ob'ekt Etnograficheskogo Issledovaniia." In *Molodeozhnie Ulichnye Gruppirovki: Vvedenie v Problematiku*, edited by D. V. Gromov, 8–72. Moscow: IEA RAN.

Gromov, D. V., and S. Stephenson. 2008. "Patsanskie Pravila: Normirovanie Povedeniia v Ulichnikh Gruppirovkakh." In *Molodie Moskvichi. Krosskulturnoe Issledovanie*, edited by M. Iu Lebedeva N. M. Martynova, 427–456. Moscow: RUDN.

Gurov, A. 1990. *Professionalnaia Prestupnost'*. Moscow: Iuridicheskaia Literatura.

Hallsworth, Simon. 2013. *The Gang and Beyond. Interpreting Violent Street Worlds*. Basingstoke: Palgrave Macmillan.

Hallsworth, Simon, and Tara Young. 2008. "Gang Talk and Gang Talkers: A Critique." *Crime, Media, Culture* 4 (2): 175–195. https://doi.org/10.1177/1741659008092327.

Kabanov, S. F. 1928. *Bor'ba s Ugolovnoi Prestupnost'iu v Derevne*. Moscow: Izdatel'stvo NKVD RSFSR.

Karbainov, N. I. 2009. "'Ei, Khunkhuz, Kuda Idiosh? Zdes' Bratva, i Ty Umriosh!': 'Ulichnie Voiny' v Ulan-Ude." In *Molodezhnie Ulichnie Gruppirovki: Vvedenie v Problematiku*, edited by D. V. Gromov, 132–148. Moscow: IEA RAN.

Kashelkin, A. 1990. "Nasilie Kak Forma Antiobshchestvennogo Povedeniia Molodezhnikh Gruppirovok." In *Kriminologi o Neformalnykh Molodezhnykh Ob'edineniiakh*, edited by I. I. Karpets, 232–238. Moscow: Iuridicheskaia Literatura.

Klein, Malcolm Ward. 2001. *The Eurogang Paradox : Street Gangs and Youth Groups in the U.S. and Europe*. Dordrecht and London: Kluwer Academic Publishers.

Klein, Malcolm Ward, and Cheryl Lee Maxson. 2006. *Street Gang Patterns and Policies*. Oxford: Oxford University Press.

Konstantinov, Andrei. 2004. *Banditskii Peterburg. Dokumental'nie Ocherki*. Vol. 1. St.Petersburg: Neva.

Kosterina, I. V. 2006. "Skinkhedy i Gopniki: Raznie Liki Agressivnoi Maskulinnosti." In *Konstruirovanie Maskulinnosti Na Zapade i v Rossii*, edited by I. A. Shkolnikov and A. V. Shnyrova, 21–37. Ivanovo: Ivanovskii tsentr gendernikh issledovanii.

Kupatadze, Alexander. 2012. *Organized Crime, Political Transitions, and State Formation in Post-Soviet Eurasia*. Houndmills, Basingstoke, Hampshire; New York, NY: Palgrave Macmillan.

Messerschmidt, James. 2012. "Engendering Gendered Knowledge: Assessing the Academic Appropriation of Hegemonic Masculinity." *Men and Masculinities* 15 (1): 56–76.

Miller, Jacques-Alain. 1997. "Suture (Elements of the Logic of the Signifier), Trans. Jacqueline Rose." *Screen* 18 (4): 24–34.

Morozov, Igor Aleksandrovich, and Irina Semionovna Sleptsova. 2004. *Krug Igry: Prazdnik i Igra v Zhisni Severorusskogo Krest'ianina*, XIX–XX Vv. Moscow: INDRIK.

Nasritdinov, Emil, and Philipp Schröder. 2016. "From Frunze to Bishkek: Soviet Territorial Youth Formations and Their Decline in the 1990s and 2000s." *Central Asian Affairs* 3: 1–28. doi: http://dx.doi.org/10.1163/22142290-00301001.

Neuberger, Joan. 1993. *Hooliganism: Crime, Culture, and Power in St. Petersburg, 1900–1914*. Berkeley: University of California Press.

Ovchinskii, V. S. 1990. "Gastrolnie Poezdki Antiobshestvennykh Gruppirovok Podrostkov i Molodezhi – Novii Fenomen." In *Kriminologi o Neformalnykh Molodezhnykh Ob'edineniiakh*, edited by I. I. Karpets, 192–196. Moscow: Iuridicheskaia Literatura.

Paoli, Letizia. 2003. *Mafia Brotherhoods: Organized Crime, Italian Style*. Oxford: Oxford University Press.

Pearson, Geoffrey. 1983. *Hooligan : A History of Respectable Fears*. London: Palgrave Macmillan.

Petelin, G. 2016. "Urkagany Vsiali Shkoly pod Kontrol". February 2. www.gazeta.ru/social/2016/02/02/8053655.shtml.

Petrovskaya, Irina. 2017. "Govorit i Pokazyvaet Podvorotnia." *Novaya gazeta – Novayagazeta.ru*, April 13, 2017. www.novayagazeta.ru/articles/2017/04/13/72144-govorit-i-pokazyvaet-podvorotnya.

Pilkington, Hilary. 1994. *Russia's Youth and Its Culture : A Nation's Constructors and Constructed*. London and New York: Routledge. www.loc.gov/catdir/enhancements/fy0648/93026766-d.html.

———. 2002. *Looking West?: Cultural Globalization and Russian Youth Cultures*. University Park, PA: Pennsylvania State University Press. www.h-net.org/review/hrev-a0d0t4-aa.

Ponomareva, E.Ya. 2014. "Konstrukty i Praktiki Maskulinnosti v Ulichnykh Podrostkovo-molodyozhnykh Soobschestvakh g.Yerevana (Armeniia)." In *Antropologiia goroda: Materialy konferentsii molodykh uchenykh. Moscow, 4–6 December 2013*, 116–125. Moscow: IEA RAN.

———. 2015. "Dramaturgiia Konflikta v Erevanskoi Ulichnoi Kul'ture." In Lavrovskii Sbornik: Materialy XXXVIII и XXXIX Sredneaziatsko-Kavkazskikh chtenii 2014-2015 g.g.: Etnologiia, Istoriia, Arkheologiia, Kul'turologiia, 472–476. St. Petersburg: MAE RAN.

Prozumentov, L. M., and A. V. Sheksler. 1990. "Tipologiia Prestupnykh Grupp Nesovershennoletnikh." In *Kriminologi o Neformalnykh Molodezhnykh Ob'edineniiakh*, edited by I. I. Karpets, 196–205. Moscow: Iuridicheskaia Literatura.

Putin, Vladimir Vladimirovich. 2000. *First Person: An Astonishingly Frank Self-Portrait by Russia's President Vladimir Putin*. London: Hutchinson.

Rodgers, Dennis. 2009. "Living in the Shadow of Death: Gangs, Violence and Social Order in Urban Nicaragua, 1996–2002." In *Youth Violence in Latin America*, edited by D. Rodgers and G. A. Jones, 25–44. New York: Palgrave Macmillan.

Salagaev, Alexander. 2001. "Evolution of Delinquent Gangs in Russia." In *The Eurogang Paradox: Street Gangs and Youth Groups in the U.S. and Europe*, edited by Malcolm Ward Klein, H. Yu. Kerner, Cheryl Lee Maxson, and E. Weitekamp, 195–202. Dordrecht Boston: Kluwer Academic Publishers.

Salagaev, Alexander, and Alexander Shashkin. 2005. "After-Effects of the Transition: Youth Criminal Careers in Russia." In *Youth – Similarities, Differences, Inequalities. Reports of the Carelian Institute*, edited by Vesa Puuronen, Jarna Soilevuo-Grønnerød, and Jatta Herranen, 154–172. Joensuu: University of Joensuu.

Sánchez-Jankowski, Martín. 1991. *Islands in the Street : Gangs and American Urban Society*. Berkeley: University of California Press.

Serio, Joseph D., and Vyacheslav Razinkin. 1995. "Thieves Professing the Code: The Traditional Role of Vory v Zakone in Russia's Criminal World and Adaptations to New Social Reality." *Low Intensity Conflict and Law Enforcement* 4 (1): 72–88.

Shaw, Clifford Robe, and Henry Donald Mckay. 1942. *Juvenile Delinquency and Urban Areas*. Chicago: University of Chicago Press.

Shchepanskaia, T. B. 2001. "Zony Nasiliia (Po Materialam Russkoi Sel'skoi i Sovremennikh Subkulturnikh Traditsii)." In *Antropologiia Nasiliia*, edited by V. V. Bocharov and V. A. Tishkov, 115–177. St. Petersburg: Nauka.

Sibiriakov, S. L. 1990. "Ulichnie Gruppirovki Molodiozhi v g. Volgograde." In *Kriminologi o Neformalnykh Molodezhnykh Ob'edineniiakh*, 168–176. Moscow: Iuridicheskaia Literatura.

Sokolov, Vsevolod. 2004. "From Guns to Briefcases: The Evolution of Russian Organized Crime." *World Policy Journal* 21 (1): 68–74.

Stephenson, Svetlana. 2001. "The Abandoned Children of Russia: From 'Privileged Class' to 'Underclass.'" In *Education and Civic Culture in Post-Communist Countries*, edited by S. Webber and I. Liikanen, 187–203. Basingstoke: Palgrave Macmillan.

———. 2008. "Searching for Home. Street Youth and Organized Crime in Russia." In *Globalizing the Streets. Cross- cultural Perspectives on Youth, Social Control, and Empowerment*, edited by Dave Brotherton and Michael Flynn, 78–92. New York: Columbia University Press.

———. 2012. "The Violent Practices of Youth Territorial Groups in Moscow." *Europe-Asia Studies* 64 (1): 69–90.

———. 2015. *Gangs of Russia : From the Streets to the Corridors of Power*. Ithaca, NY: Cornell University Press.

Suttles, Gerald Dale. 1968. *The Social Order of the Slum. Ethnicity and Territory in the Inner City*. Chicago and London: University of Chicago Press.

Sysuev, Oleg. 2017. "Interview with Oleg Sysuev." *Echo Moskvy*. https://echo.msk.ru/programs/personalnovash/1961842-echo/.

Thrasher, Frederic Milton. 1963. *The Gang. A Study of 1,313 Gangs in Chicago*. London and Chicago: The University of Chicago Press.

Turner, Victor Witter. 1995. *The Ritual Process : Structure and Anti-Structure*. New York: Aldine de Gruyter.

Varese, Federico. 2001. *The Russian Mafia : Private Protection in a New Market Economy*. Oxford, England and New York: Oxford University Press. www.loc.gov/catdir/enhancements/fy0612/2001016333-t. htmlwww.loc.gov/catdir/enhancements/fy0612/2001016333-d.html.

Volkov, Vadim. 2002. *Violent Entrepreneurs: The Use of Force in the Making of Russian Capitalism*. Ithaca, NY: Cornell University Press.

Whyte, William Foote. 1993. *Street Corner Society: The Social Structure of an Italian Slum*. Vol. 4. Chicago and London: University of Chicago Press.

Yusupova, Marina. 2015. "Masculinity, Criminality, and Russian Men." *Sextures* 3 (3): 46–61.

Zakharova, Ye.Yu. 2010. "Tbilisskaia Ulitsa kak Sreda Muzhskoi Sotsializatsii." *Laboratorium. Zhurnal Sotsialnykh Issledovanii* (1): 182–204.

———. 2012. "Tbilisskaia Ulitsa kak Iavleniie Pravovoi i Politicheskoi Zhisni Gruzii." In *Obshchestvo kak Ob'ekt i Sub'ekt Vlasti. Ocherki Politicheskoi Antropologii Kavkaza.*, edited by Yu.Yu. Karpov, 111–130. St Petersburg: MAE RAN.

Zakharova, Evgeniia. 2016. "The Tbilisi 'Street' as a Legal and Political Phenomenon in Georgia." In *State and Legal Practice in the Caucasus: Anthropological Perspectives on Law and Politics*, edited by Stéphane Voell and Iwona Kaliszewska, 69–82. Routledge: London and New York.

Zolotov, Viktor. 2018. "Obrashchenie Direktora Rosgvardii." www.youtube.com/watch?v=lZd1yUZD30g.

28

The fourth corner of the triangle

Gang transnationalism, fragmentation and evolution in Belize City

Adam Baird

Introduction

Belize has one of the highest homicide rates in the world; however, the gangs at the heart of this violence have rarely been studied. This chapter uses empirical data to explore how Blood and Crip 'gang transnationalism' from the United States flourished in Belize City beginning in the early 1980s. It is argued that gang transnationalism makes cultural connections between local settings of urban exclusion between origin and destination countries. Terrains of exclusion in Southside Belize City made the foreign gang appealing as an identity package, driving poor black and brown youths to join up. The establishment of gang practices then led to a marked rise of street violence. Counterintuitively, homicide rates rose most dramatically as violence became *less* organised when the Blood and Crip structures began to fragment at the turn of the millennium, and a new generation of gangs emerged. The new gang identities were a culturally syncretic evolution of the Bloods and Crips, 'Creolising' over time, demonstrating the fluidity of post-transnational gang life.

Belize is a small country of 350,000 people on the Caribbean Sea best known as a tourist idyll. It shares borders with Mexico and Guatemala and is unique, being both Central American and Caribbean. Belize is also a young nation, formerly British Honduras, only gaining full independence in 1981. Below the Haulover Creek that bisects Belize City and its 65,000 inhabitants, Southside is composed of some reasonably constructed and many dilapidated neighbourhoods located on unforgiving marshlands. Southside, and one notorious downtown street called Majestic Alley, have played host to gang violence since the 1980s. National murder rates reached 45 per 100,000 in 2017, making Belize one of the most violent nations in the world, comparable to its country neighbours (Peirce 2017), and Gayle et al. have argued that violence and trauma are higher amongst boys in Belize City than anywhere else in the Caribbean (Gayle and Mortis 2010). Murders are driven by gangs in Southside, popularised by Ross Kemp's documentary on gangs in 2008. Belize is a country characterised by elitism and inequality, and residents south of the creek have long been at the bottom of the country's socio-economic strata. Thirty-one percent of households across Belize are poor, and on Southside, over half of the heads of household do not have a job (UNICEF Belize 2011: 37). The country has a decidedly mixed heritage, with sizeable Mayan, Spanish, Mestizo and Garifuna (Afro-Indigenous) populations. The Creole minority of African descent makes up 15% of the national population but accounts for the majority of Southside's residents. It is therefore unsurprising, as Gayle says, that most gang members there are black and brown (Gayle et al. 2016, p. 192). The overwhelming weight of academic attention to gangs in the region is focused on the Northern Triangle countries of El Salvador, Guatemala and Honduras. Belize is the forgotten fourth corner of the triangle.

Baird (2019) and Gayle (Gayle and Mortis 2010; Gayle et al. 2016) are the only international scholars to publish on violence in Belize using primary data with gang members themselves, and only Baird has focused on Blood and Crip transnationalism per se. The transnationalism literature tends to refer to US–*mara* deportation experiences to Central America during the 1990s (e.g. Berg and Carranza 2018; Cruz 2014; Zilberg 2011). Gangs are generally seen as socio-cultural forms of street-level youth associations lacking any clear transnational criminal structure (Brotherton and Gude 2018; Cerbino and Rodríguez 2008; Roks and Densley 2019). Critically, transnational gangs depend upon vulnerable terrains to insert themselves into. They tend to arise as a diaspora in marginalised contexts organised by transnational gang members or local disaffected youths who aspire to gang membership (Rodgers and Baird 2015). Literature on Blood and Crip transnationalism is particularly sparse. Exceptions in the Americas include include (Flores 2009; Gemert 2001; Hagedorn 2008, 2014), Roks and Densley in Europe (Roks 2017; Roks and Densley 2019) and Johns in Australia (2014). In the Belizean case, only Miller Matthei and Smith (1998) have considered Bloods and Crips specifically, although this research occured before the dramatic rise in gang violence.

This chapter divided into four sections. A methodological overview is followed by three analytical sections on gang transnationalism, gang fragmentation and gang evolution in Belize City.

Methodology

The fieldwork was built cumulatively by layering together three- to four-week ethnographic revisits to Belize between 2011 and 2018.[1] This is not an unusual approach to fieldwork for post-PhD academics with numerous commitments. However, the author's prior experience of designing the Southside Youth Success Programme in 2011, a gang intervention project run in collaboration with UNDP and a national ministry (Baird 2011), created a bedrock of relationships with individuals across institutions and Southside communities, which were crucial in gaining the access and trust from respondents that are essential to researching sensitive issues around gangs, crime and violence.

Interviews were conducted with 12 gang members, 8 participants in gang intervention programs, a local rapper and dancehall singer, the wife of a murdered gang leader, an individual from a powerful drug trafficking family, four focus groups on Southside and numerous informal conversations with local inhabitants. Beyond the streets, over 50 expert interviews were conducted across national and international institutions (see also Baird 2019b).

The methodology included time spent on the streets with gangs, in youth detention centres and in Belize Central Prison, called 'da pisshouse' by locals. Whilst potentially hazardous, this was mitigated through the use of gatekeepers, including a local iman to enter the prison, a well-liked youth worker who helped conduct impromptu interviews on Southside, and a politician conducting ceasefire negotiations with gangs who arranged meetings with them at her office. The author's experience of gang research in the region also provided a foundation of 'ethnographic safety', an intuitive understanding of the rules of the game around street violence which helped mitigate risks (Baird 2009, 2018b). However, risks cannot be assuaged entirely;

I witnessed an attempted murder/suicide, was questioned about my business on the streets by a boy I was later told was an informant for the local gang, and was told not to ask questions about drug trafficking in one costal town, as someone was recently disappeared – bar a severed finger with the wedding ring still attached – for doing something similar.

Gang transnationalism as cultural transfer

First Bloods and Crips

In 1961, Hurricane Hattie flattened Belize City, prompting a significant exodus north. By the year 2000, approximately 30% of the entire population resided in the United States (Vernon 2000). This newfound diaspora stateside provided the populace for later deportations of Blood and Crip gang members back to Belize City and the genesis point of a national gang culture.

Whilst Belize reflects the *mara* deportation experience of gang transnationalism, this process intuitively coalesces along ethnic and language lines. The black and brown Creole and Garifuna migrants that joined gangs in the United States understandably gravitated towards the English-speaking African American Bloods and Crips, not the Latino *maras*. Of note, the Bloods and Crips arrived in Belize as early as 1981, arguably making them the first experience of gang transnationalism in the entire region. There are no figures for 1980s deportations, but over the decade between 1992–2002, there were 1,122 deportees, many of these coming back to Southside (Warnecke-Berger 2019).

The first wave of Bloods and Crips encountered a nascent democracy with limited institutional capacity to enforce the Rule of Law. Angel, who was deported from Los Angeles in 1981, was due to serve the remainder of his sentence in Belize; he went on to become the first leader of the Majestic Alley Crips. His narrative reflects the early days of Americanised gang culture on the streets (20/05/2016):[2]

> I cum home. I have my aunty here in Belize City . . . in Majestic Alley. Firs' we were selling weed, crack-cocaine hadn't even touched Belize. I started selling and jus doin hustling, whateva, just to mek a buck. Dere weren't gangs den, jus' guys who hang out and try to hustle. Dere weren't really any guns, we use to chase our enemies wid stick and machete, you know. Only lik de big people would have guns. Da cocaine came in lik di 85. Da firs man dat talk big, I shoot in his chest.
>
> Yeah, more money, more bigger you get. Den man come to trade gun for crack, gun for weed. So, ah sell weed, but if ah have no army, man tek it away. Ah used to pack a 9mm and a 357, that's a barrel gun, it sound like a bomb explode, so everybody respec' you. *Dat's a Big Man gun y'know!* My friend he started acting real gangster, de way America does it, you know. He's de one dat decide dat Majestic Alley would be blue [Crip], and anyting over swing bridge, dat's Red [Blood], yeah, in 87, 88. We use to fight at da local disco, if you from over the bridge, we pick a fight with you, wid knife and machete. Dey were serious fights, but not really wid guns. . . . We go an kidnap the watchman, and took his 16 [gauge shotgun] and cut di barrel shaft, we call it *sawdaff* [sawn-off], you could stick it in your side, you run up into your enemy and you jus bus it and run off.

Marijuana has been smoked on Southside for generations, long before the Bloods and Crips emerged. 'Base Boys' used to sell it on the streets, and whilst they were 'hustlers', they were not known for violence and had no guns. However, the new colours gangs quickly absorbed the Base Boys as two principal factions developed: the Majestic Alley Crips and the George Street Bloods. Early Bloods and Crips quickly gained influence beyond the Base Boys, and numerous young men began to pledge allegiance to them. Carlos (11/05/2016), a former gang member from the late 1980s, explained that the new gang leaders were proactive, distributing Blue or Red rags and bandanas and handing out money and weapons to 'protect' gang members from the rivals that, ironically, they had discursively created on the streets.

Successful gang leaders rapidly embedded on Southside. George 'Junie Balls' McKenzie, a Crip from Majestic Alley, and later 'Shiney' from George Street Bloods (Muhammad 2015, p. 169) became folkloric characters known as *Generals* in their communities. The meteoric rise of the Blood and Crip prototypes became the masculine standard bearer for young Creole success on the streets, where the Generals and their gunmen – *shottas* – became iconic, hyper-visible and aspirational figures (Baird 2019).

Whilst this chapter does not go into depth about role of politics in the development of Belizean gangs, clientelist practices facilitated the growth of gang structures in the urban periphery. Bolland and Shoman (Bolland 1997; Shoman 2011) highlight the role of clientelism in the emergence of the two major parties in Belize; the United Democratic Party (UDP) and the People's National Party (PNP). Many locals, experts and gang members themselves referred to historical and contemporary clientelist relationships across Southside during the fieldwork. Political parties used Generals from the two main factions, the George Street Bloods and the Majestic Alley Crips, to provide them with authority and legitimacy on the streets (Bill 15/11/2017; Muhammad 2015, p. 71). Furthermore, whilst early George Street and Majestic Alley violence clearly existed, the leadership, structure and discipline of these factions largely kept a lid on homicidal gang violence, which reached a relatively low 17:100,000 in 2000 (UNODC 2019). This will become relevant later in the chapter, when the homicide boom is explained as 'disorganised violence'.

Cultural transfer

'Cultural vulnerability' as outlined and critiqued by Tomlinson suggests that

> Cultures in the West, specifically, the United States saw a standardized version of their cultures exported worldwide, the "weaker" cultures of the developing world that have been most threatened. Thus, the economic vulnerability of these non-western cultures is assumed to be matched by a cultural vulnerability.
>
> *(2003)*

Furthermore, Tomlinson (2003), Espagne (1999) and Greenblatt (2009) state that whilst some are more hegemonic than others, cultures do not actually obliterate each other; rather, forms of 'cultural transfer' occur where they morph and change in complex ways. Certainly, the modern identity of Belize has been moulded by colonialism and migration. One local academic lamented, "We have been taught to embrace and value the foreign more than our own history. Even Jesus is foreign!" (Raul 15/11/2017). A confluence of historic, cultural and socio-economic circumstances on Southside contributed to a propensity amongst a number of youths to "embrace that [US] ghetto culture . . . because Creole culture is not held sacred. Young gang members have no recollection of history" (Raul 15/11/2017).

Evoking Espange's notion of 'cultural transfer' (1999), US gangs represented a rebellious black youth identity that transposed fluidly into Belize City's urban margins. This was observed by local scholar Nuri Muhammad, who stated that the media images of the *Boys 'n the Hood* gangsters from Los Angeles became the cultural signifier for Belizean gang activity:

> We were trying to imitate what we saw at the street level. To get their money, have parties, bring all the money out, all the girls out . . . it would imitate those aspects of the culture, because it was what was in front of us.
>
> *(2015, p. 16)*

The social terrain into which gangs insert themselves has deliberately been termed 'vulnerable' (see the concept of 'chronic vulnerabilily', Baird, 2020). This is not to justify consequent acts of gang violence; rather, this serves in part as an explanation as to why young men did not join gangs from the wealthier neighbourhoods on Northside. It also points to the critical role that recipient social terrains play in gang transnationalism. One government worker stated bluntly that on Southside, "People feel that destitution is their fate, they don't have hope, they don't trust governance, they can't find the motivation to escape" (Papa 05/11/2016). This was reflected by a Southside youth worker, who angrily lamented when asked why young people join gangs that "Dere ain't nutin' fa yout to do roun' here, jus smoke, drink an' fuck" (10/10/2016). Two young men struggling to get out of Southside poverty said that in their music videos they

> show the real gutter on Southside, people livin' in the street, garbage, homeless people. . . . We just show what's the general feeling of shit. This is still a beautiful country when you go out of the city, but it's crazy here, so we show what is real of most people's everyday life.
>
> *(16/11/2016)*

Vulnerable terrains are also gendered. Belizean 'gang transnationalism' can be understood as a 'transnational masculinity' that makes cultural connections between local settings of urban exclusion, that is, from South Central to Southside (Baird 2019). Multiple and historic marginality in Belize City generated masculine vulnerabilities to the foreign gang as an identity package with the power to reconfigure positions of subordination. The intersection of gender, class and race allowed *OGs* and *Homeboys* to transpose with cultural fluidity into Belize's urban margins precisely because their departure and destination social terrains share subordinations. Therefore, understanding the terrains into which Bloods and Crips inserted themselves is pivotal to understanding how gangs relocated from the United States. The iconic figure of the disenfranchised young black man striking back at structural violence was a compelling symbol in a postcolonial Belize with a tendency to venerate US culture.

Gang fragmentation and the disorganisation of violence

JK: It's not like when [gangs] first came to Belize, in past years you can be on da same block, now they're beefin'.

MESSIAH: People still say I'm Red or I'm Blue, but I'm not Red to a point that when I see a nigga that's Blue I'm about to spray that nigga [with bullets]. It is to an extent about territory, but it's not too much about you moving into my territory and taking my money.

Some niggas be killin' niggas over a bitch and shit. An' then the two niggas that was fightin' over dis girl just end up havin' a bunch of niggas – that's their squad – you see what I mean, and when they see them niggaz (punches fist into hand to indicate a fight). And that goes on for years and years and years, until the origin of the beef is even unknown. . . . And the guns that is out there is big guns, nigga.

JK and Messiah, a rapper and dancehall singer, respectively, from Southside (08/11/2016)

By the early 1990s, gangs were being taken seriously by authorities. In 1991, a Crimes Commission was set up to create legislation responding to growing public concern around the gang phenomenon. Responses included *mano dura*–type crackdowns, representing clear dissonance with clientelist forms of gang engagement, and for the first time in the country's history, the Belizean Defence Force was deployed to the streets (Miller Matthei and Smith 1998), although present-day responses are led by the notorious Gang Suppression Unit.

By the mid-2000s, some two decades after the Bloods and Crips first appeared in Belize, one might assume that the increasing gang organisation and disputes over drug turf would drive the homicide rate. However, unlike the progressive institutionalisation of the Shower Posse in Jamaica, *maras* in Central America, *pandillas* Medellin or *comandos* in Rio de Janeiro or Sao Paulo, Belizean gangs actually went through a process of rapid fragmentation at the turn of the millennium. Certainly, the gang suppression strategy of the 1990s had destabilised gangs by dislodging the Generals, contributing to the splintering and the George Street–Majestic Alley duopoly in the city. As Jabaar said

> Back in de day, dey [police] started killing off de heads [Generals] because dey wuz able to be identified. So, widout heads de gang situation basically jus' got outta hand, cuz de killers are now 17 and 18 years old. New leaders fight for dis position.
>
> *(11/05/2016)*

The following field diary entry highlights gang factions:

> With my two gatekeepers, we stopped by Majestic Alley. The wife of a murdered Crip leader said that gang truces don't work because there's always disrespect between gang members on opposite turfs, so it escalates, and all kicks off again. She had a demeanour about her that was overwhelmingly sad, of a woman in mourning. Her husband was murdered in 2007, and they just killed her son. 'They killed my baby' she said, only three months ago as he took over the Majestic Alley gang. She said the police let the rival gang through so they could get rid of him. The rival gang was called 'Jungle' . . . *yet another new gang splinter*. The sad thing was that she was taking care of her one-year old granddaughter, right there on the street in a little push-bike for babies. That was her son's daughter. My gatekeeper got nervous as people started asking questions about me, so we wrapped up the conversation and jumped back in the van. My gatekeeper then said that George Street [gang] was splitting apart too.
>
> *(field diary, 16/11/2016)*

The structural fragmentation of gangs galvanised a 'disorganised violence' of the streets, to the extent that the very notion of 'turf' has become blurred. One civil servant working in a youth programme said that young people on Southside are increasingly confused about gang territories (Shirley 18/05/2016), and Vartas the leader of the PIV gang (People in Violence, a.k.a. Peace in the Village) confirmed this, saying, remarkably, that he wasn't even sure who the leader of the neighbouring George Street gang was (18/05/2016). A senior police officer on Southside (15/11/2016) said:

> George Street has at least eight subsidiaries to it, and each have their own leader. They fight under George Street still, but not everything they do is under control of the leader of George Street. The inter-gang rivalries are the most difficult to police, you never know who is who, and because of the small geographical area in which they operate it is difficult to police them. Most of the gangs begin to fragment after the main leader die.

AUTHOR: George Street was Pinky then Shiney [Generals, both murdered]?

POLICE OFFICER: So, after Shiney dead, there is a fight over who will be the next leader. Others [names three] are proclaiming to be leaders of George Street. . . . After Pinky died, George Street disputes started and some went with Shiney and some with X [another gang leader].

AUTHOR: What's the violence about?

POLICE OFFICER: Most of them don't know what they are fighting for. It's just that they grow up in an area, and they know that this area have an issue with that area. We have also found that much of the violence is driven by hate and anger. They hate this man because of this or that. And we find that they get upset very easily. They think that the easiest way to resolve a conflict is with the use of a gun.

AUTHOR: So how organised are gangs?

POLICE OFFICER: Structurally, I don't think that they're properly organised, but they are to the extent that they can become effective [lethal violence]. Weapons come in from Guatemala, the same routes as marijuana. Gang members [aren't rich] like Jamaica! Belizean gangs are poor. The money that they make from the sale of drugs, it's like day-to-day.

In short, gang violence has risen, whilst gang institutionalisation has gone backwards over the last two decades. Despite spanning some four decades, gangs in Belize are currently very much at the margins of organised crime and transnational drug trafficking networks. Although gangs sold crack cocaine in the late 1980s, Shorty, a jailed gang leader, said nowadays cocaine only ended up on Southside when someone found a bale jettisoned by traffickers washed up at the beach and that a gang member probably averaged US$15 income on a good day (19/11/2016). This was corroborated during an interview with a member of a significant drug trafficking family from the coast, who said their clandestine networks deliberately avoided street gangs (interview, 22/05/2016). This is not to say that gangs do not sell drugs on the streets but that they are not international traffickers and that turf wars over drugs are considerably less than in other gang-affected cities in the region.

Whilst gangs themselves are not embedded in organised crime, and transnational drug trafficking largely passes them by, they have become increasingly well armed with weapons filtering across the border through Belizeans with family members in Guatemala. During the fieldwork, it became clear that murders between gang members were predominantly small-scale beefs. Belize City is a small town, and rapidly splintering gangs have meant that there are numerous micro-level beefs that drive the homicide rate.

Murder rates rose from 9 per 100,000 in 1995, to 17 in 2000, to 30 in 2006 and 45 in 2017 (Peirce 2017; UNODC 2019). In the Belize District (Belize City and environs), the homicide rate in 2018 was 78 (Belize Crime Observatory 2019). By 2008, there were over 30 gangs in Belize City with 500 youth members, and in 2015, gang membership had tripled to 1,500 as gang territories packed closer together (Haylock 2013, p. 46; Peirce 2017, p. 21). One gang member said that in his neighbourhood alone, there were four gangs: Peace in the Village, Bacalan (Back-of-land) Crips, the Complex City Crips and the Third World Bloods, estimating that

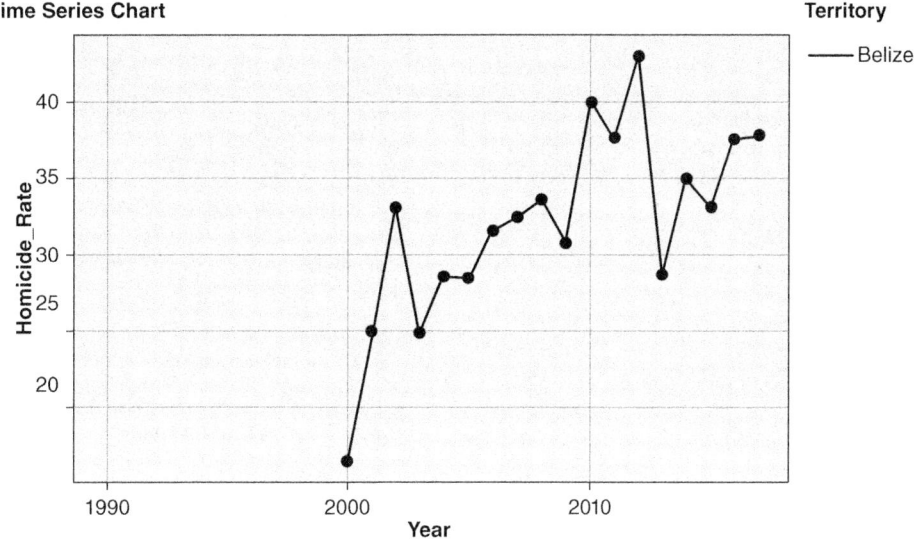

Time Series Chart

Territory

——— Belize

Figure 28.1 Time series chart
Source: https://dataunodc.un.org/GSH_app, cited 07/10/2019

half of all young males in the area were in gangs (Smalls 12/05/2016). Even gangs in tiny territories suffer from internecine conflict. Shorty, a jailed gang member, said "Now Vartas and Driver [both from PIV] hate each other, like I said, it's a dog-eat-dog world" (19/11/2016). As one civil servant stated, violence has become so splintered and anomic that he refers to it as "interpersonal violence at a gang level" (9/11/2017). A 2019 report by the IDB lists a myriad of new gangs.

Gangs are now broadly acknowledged to be disorganised, with fast-flowing ephemeral membership, a far cry from the early days of the Generals, when civil servant Shirley said tellingly, "gangs used to be more social, now dey jus' crazy" (18/05/2016).

Gang evolution

Messiah and JK were two young men from Southside. They were aspiring musicians but still flitted in and out of gangs and hustled on the corner. JK had recently been involved in a shoot-out, but he said that the police let him off the hook because they knew he was trying to get out of gang life and into music. For a poor Southsider, JK had the latest smart phone, which raised questions. Only after the voice-recorded interview had finished did he admit that a wealthy older lady had 'given' it to him, euphemistically referring to sex work. That morning, I asked Messiah if he could fix a meeting with some Southside gang members, and he later left me a WhatsApp message (15/11/2016) saying (verbatim):

> Yo! We're right over here chillin' nigga. Let me see if I could fuckin' get them niggaz [gang members] together probably for Thursday [for an interview]. I'll see, I'm not sure I could do it. We'll see wud'up, and if everyting come tru I'm gonna holla at'you, and then we'll scoop you up and then, you just put gas in the car, and I'll take you over there.

Though it is hard to translate forms of speech to the page, Messiah, a born and bred Southsider, used a strong US gangsta lexicon and accent undoubtedly key to his rapper persona and

Gang name	Age			Membership	
	Youngest	Oldest	Average	Low	High
Peace in the Valley Bloods	12	40	26	100	200
South Side Gang (Crips)	12	40	26	90	100
Gaza New Generation Bloods	11	19	15	70	90
Ghost Town/Banak Crips	11	45	28	60	70
George Street Bloods	18	45	31.5	40	50
Majestic Ally Crip	12	45	28.5	25	50
Jane Usher Bloods	12	40	26	35	45
Supal Street Bloods	12	40	26	30	40
Jungle Bloods	12	40	26	20	40
West-Molan (Taylors Alley) Bloods	12	35	23.5	30	40
Louise Bevans Crips	14	35	24.5	30	40
Antelope Street Bloods	14	40	27	20	35
Victoria Street Bloods	12	40	26	18	35
Jump Street Crips	14	40	27	15	35
Lacroix Blvd Bloods	12	39	25.5	20	35
Back-a-Town Bloods	14	45	29.5	20	30
Back-a-Lands Crips	14	45	29.5	20	30
Kelly Street Crips	12	40	26	20	30
Kraal Road Crips	13	40	26.5	20	30
Police Street Crips	14	38	26	30	30
Conch Shell Bloods	14	35	24.5	25	30
Gill Street Bloods	**13**	35	24	20	30
Plum Tree Bloods	14	35	24.5	20	25
Amara Street Bloods	14	35	24.5	20	25
Kings Park Crips	18	40	29	15	20
Rocky Road Crips	17	35	26	15	20
103 New Road Bloods	12	30	21	15	20
Riverside Boys	12	20	16	15	20
Jerusalem Crips	12	45	28.5	10	15
Afghanistan Bloods	14	35	24.5	10	15
102 (Parham) Crips	18	35	26.5	10	15
Belama (Riverside Bloods)	15	35	25	10	15
Simon Lamb Street Crips	20	35	27.5	10	15
Neals Penn Road (Gaza) Bloods	15	35	25	10	15
Sunset Crips	14	35	24.5	10	15
Horse and Carriage Blood	12	35	23.5	10	15
Average	**13.6**	**37.4**	Total	**938**	**1,365**

Figure 28.2   Active gangs in Belize City by age and membership
Source: Conscious Youth Development Programme

in much of his public life. It was striking the way he absorbed US gangsta identity so readily, whilst JK had done the same but had taken on a 'dancehall' Jamaican persona. This cultural transfer of highly regarded gangsta and dancehall identities was a way of resisting the pernicious effects of multiple marginality and the threat of emasculation through the emphatic assertion of an Americanised or Jamaican black masculinity.

This is dissimilar to Johns's depiction of the 'blackness' of Pacific Islander gangs in Australia as a rebellion against white male hegemony (Johns 2014: 301). Rather, in Belize, the male Creole population curiously represents society's extremes; the nation's political and business elites are Creole men. Ergo, the assertion of gang masculinity was an accessible way for these youths to establish an identity and self-esteem in response to structural constraints on Southside (for an extended debate on gangs and male inclusion in Belize, see Gayle et al. 2016, and Baird 2019).

However, gang transnationalism in Belize did not represent the wholesale transfer of a cultural template. It has been a process of local adaptation. This is an empirical inflection in Nayak's (2003) reasoning that flows of global culture produce hybrid youth identities. Gang members in Belize do not simply imitate foreign gang culture; rather, they absorb and interpret it to negotiate the harsh realities of everyday life.

Given the complexity of overlapping cultures in Belize, which Beske states is hybridised, Creolised and Mestizoised (2016, p. 64), when Blood and Crip gang culture arrived, it immediately began a dialectic process of cultural negotiation, whereby gang identities became creolised. Syncretic gang identities have been detailed in other contexts in the evolution of cultural-linguistic differentiation between English and Spanish-speaking Latina gangs in California by Mendoza-Denton (2008), and Brotherton and Barrios (2004) have charted the profound change of Latin King and Queen gangs from violent gang to social movement in New York City. Messiah and JK, previously, are expressions of this type of malleability and cultural hybridity on the streets. Muhammad (2015, pp. 16–17) states:

> Gangs are both foreign and local in origin at the same time. Foreign in the sense that media images of the gangster in the 1980s and 1990s were the black youth of Los Angeles. . . . Whilst these images were foreign in style, there were socio-economic and historical conditions for our own crop of gang activity. In Belize today we see more than the imitation of a foreign culture, we see the creations of [gang members] with their own set of values and definitions of what society is about and what means they will use to survive in a social environment they view as increasingly hostile and unfair. They lost hope and as a result became rebellious to the status quo.

Blood and Crip identities adopted on the streets in the 1980s have gone through culturally syncretic processes. Although present-day gangs still bear remnants of US gangsta culture seen in the ongoing use of red or blue 'rags' and imported Dickies trousers, the influence of the Bloods and Crips as an organisational structure has been eroded over the last two decades. As Vartas, the leader of PIV, said, "Bloods and Crips don' matter no more" (18/05/2016).

Belizean gang identities not only conflate with local culture, they continue to draw upon foreign influences. Now street culture looks less to US gangsta iconography and more to Jamaican rude boy identities and music. As JK said,

> LA go first, den it change to da new modern set up. You know da youths they change a lot, dey wearin' different clothes, you know da Jamaica mix. So dey still wear some American clothes, but dey have a Jamaican mix, Jamaican stylin', you know.
>
> *(08/11/2016)*

Gang names are now copied from Kingston:

TIGER: People look up to George Street as de main gang, 'coz dey get de name Gaza from de gang in Jamaica.

AUTHOR: So, George Street just took the name Gaza from Jamaica?

TIGER: Gaza! Dey jus' tek da name from Jamaica. Dey just call the gang Gaza. So, everybody look up to Gaza as de main gang, dey got the most gang members, dey're de biggest gang down dere, dey got more weapons.

(Tiger 11/11/2016)

It is interesting to note Southside gangs are not only territorially fluid and in constant flux, they are also culturally morphic. Despite this fluidity, however, original Blood and Crip structures in Belize City established a lasting set of social practices perceivable in contemporary gangs: the aesthetics of language, the pose, the cars or gold chains, the symbolic *shotta* notoriety and fear, sexual access to women, street parties, drinking and drug-taking and, of course, propensity to use violence. This has been observed in previous gang research as a form of street 'capital', performed to a ghetto audience to acquire meaning (Baird 2018a; Fraser 2013; Sandberg 2008). These displays are a version of hegemonic masculine localism, a set of socially and culturally adaptable and relational notions, practices and displays, performed under specific social and economic conditions. It has been argued that despite the fluidity of contemporary gangs in Belize City, there is continuity to the hegemonic masculine language of their social practices, including violence (Baird 2019). Here, the iconic male Generals have been replicated intergenerationally by *Big Men*, *Boss Men*, *Shottas*, *Killer Men* and *Strike Men* who picked up the mantle as the new gangsta personas driving the localised hegemonic masculine ideal. Or, as Muhammed said in more prosaic terms, on the streets of Southside, 'a cyclical drama is being played out' (Muhammad 2015, p. 139).

Conclusions

This chapter has charted the rise of gang culture in Belize in recent history. Importantly, the arrival of the Bloods and Crips in the 1980s as a form of gang transnationalism is also a form of cultural transfer and transnational masculinity that connects local settings of exclusion in different global settings. Social terrains are crucial for gang transnationalism to flourish, and vulnerability in these terrains should be understood as both an ethnic and gendered phenomenon, where the African American gangsta identity appealed to disenfranchised Creole male youths as a way of re-codifying multiple subordinations. Unfortunately, these conditions of vulnerability show little sign of abating. When walking around conversing with a local youth worker, he said:

Dese guys [gangs] are nothing to play wid, but notin' has changed in two and a half decades. If you go to dese areas like George Street, de only ting dat has changed is dat de structures have gone from board to cement. No industries have been set up, or no real change has taken place to mek an impact on de community.

(07/11/2016)

Whilst the arrival of the Bloods and Crips in Belize City led to a rise in violence, epidemic levels of homicide were only reached when gangs fragmented at the turn of the millennium. Hence, counterintuitively, gang violence peaked through disorganisation, as opposed to gangs becoming more institutionalised. Clearly, this capacity for disorganised violence was enhanced by the flow of weapons into gangs across the Guatemalan border.

This chapter has also highlighted that gang transnationalism should not be understood as a template being imposed in a foreign setting; rather, host communities adapt foreign gang identities locally, and on Southside, gang culture has proved culturally syncretic over time, evolving its own Belizean identity that continually draws upon local and foreign influences that reflect its subordinations along racial and class lines. Nonetheless, despite the constant evolution of gangs on Southside, their violence is stubbornly consistent, driving homicidal violence in the country to this day.

Notes

1 The author acknowledges the important role played by the British Academy, Leverhulme Trust and Coventry University in funding the research; further thanks UNDP Belize and the University of Belize for sponsoring a Masculinities and Violence conference held in Belmopan, March 2018, to disseminate and discuss the research findings.
2 Quotations from interviews have been written phonetically where the interviewees spoke with a pronounced Creole accent. These tended to be young people and gang members, whilst expert interviewees would typically 'lighten their tongue' or 'speak American' for the benefit of foreigners.

References

Baird, Adam. 2009. 'Methodological Dilemmas: Researching Violent Young Men in Medellín, Colombia'. *IDS Bulletin* 40(3).

Baird, Adam. 2011. *Southside Youth Success: Pathways to Employment for Young Men at-Risk of Joining Gangs in Belize City*. Belize City: UNDP.

Baird, Adam. 2018a. 'Becoming the Baddest: Masculine Trajectories of Gang Violence in Medellín'. *Journal of Latin American Studies* 5(1):183–210.

Baird, Adam. 2018b. 'Dancing with Danger: Ethnographic Safety, Male Bravado and Gang Research in Colombia'. *Qualitative Research* 18(3).

Baird, Adam. 2019. 'Man a Kill a Man for Nutin': Gang Transnationalism, Masculinities, and Violence in Belize City'. *Men & Masculinities*. Published online first.

Baird, A. 2020. 'From Vulnerability to Violence: Gangs and "homicide booms" in Trinidad and Belize', *Urban Crime – An International Journal* 1(2):76–97.

Belize Crime Observatory. 2019. *Belize Crime Statistics*. Belmopan. http://crimeobservatory.bz/templates/custom_template/crimedata.html

Berg, Louis-Alexandre and Marlon Carranza. 2018. 'Organized Criminal Violence and Territorial Control'. *Journal of Peace Research* 55(5):566–581.

Beske, M. 2016. *Intimate Partner Violence and Advocate Response: Redefining Love in Western Belize*. Lanham, MD: Rowman & Littlefield. https://rowman.com/ISBN/9781498503600/Intimate-Partner-Violence-and-Advocate-Response-Redefining-Love-in-Western-Belize#

Bolland, Nigel. 1997. *Struggles for Freedom: Essays on Slavery, Colonialism and Culture in the Caribbean and Central America*. Belize City: The Angelus Press Limited.

Brotherton, D. C., & Barrios, L. 2004. *The Almighty Latin King and Queen Nation Street Politics and the Transformation of a New York City Gang*. New York, NY: Columbia University Press.

Brotherton, David and Raphael Gude. 2018. *Social Inclusion from Below: The Perspectives of Street Gangs and Their Possible Effects on Declining Homicide Rates in Ecuador*. Washington, DC: Interamerican Development Bank.

Cerbino, M. and Ana Rodríguez. 2008. 'La Nación Imaginada de Los Latin Kings: Criminología Cultural y La Banda Transnacional'. in *Otras Naciones: Jóvenes, transnacionalismo y exclusón*, edited by M. Cerbino and L. Barrios. Quito.

Cruz, Jose Miguel. 2014. 'Maras and the Politics of Violence in El Salvador'. Pp. 123–144 in *Global Gangs: Street Violence Across the World*, edited by J. Hazen and D. Rodgers. Minnesota: University of Minnesota Press.

Espagne, Michele. 1999. *Les Transferts Culturels*. Paris: Press Universitaires e France.

Flores, Juan. 2009. *The Diaspora Strikes Back Caribeño Tales of Learning and Turning*. New York: Routledge.

Fraser, Alistair. 2013. 'Street Habitus: Gangs, Territorialism and Social Change in Glasgow'. *Journal of Youth Studies* 16(8):970–985.

Gayle, H., V. Hampton, and N. Mortis. 2016. *Like Bush Fire: A Study on Male Participation and Violence in Urban Belize*. Belize City: Cubola Productions.

Gayle, H. and Mortis, N. 2010. *Male Social Participation and Violence in Urban Belize: An Examination of Their Experience with Goals, Guns, Gangs, Gender, God, and Governance*. Ministry of Education, Belmopan.

Gemert, F. V. 2001. 'Crips in Orange: Gangs and Groups in the Netherlands'. in *The Eurogang Paradox: Street Gangs and Youth Groups in the U.S. and Europe*, edited by E. G. M. Weitekamp, M. W. Klein, H. J. Kerner, and C. L. Maxson. Dordrecht: Springer.

Greenblatt, S. 2009. *Cultural Mobility: A Manifesto*. Cambridge: Cambridge University Press. http://www.cambridge.org/us/academic/subjects/anthropology/anthropology-general-interest/cultural-mobility-manifesto?format=HB&isbn=9780521863568

Hagedorn, John. 2008. *A World of Gangs*. London: University of Minnesota Press.

Haylock, Nicole. 2013. *National Public Policy Proposal: Prevention of Youth-Involved Violence in Belize 2012–2022*. Belmopan: Interpeace Belize.

Johns, Amelia. 2014. 'Bloods, Crips and Southern Cross Soldiers: Gang Identities in Australia'. *A Critical Youth Studies for the 21st Century*: 299–316.

Mendoza-Denton, N. 2008. *Homegirls: Language and Cultural Practice Among Latina Youth Gangs*. Malden, MA: Wiley-Blackwell.

Miller Matthei, Linda and David Smith. 1998. 'Belizean 'Boyz 'n the "Hood"? Garifuna Labor Migration and Transnational'. Pp. 270–290 in *Identity in Transnationalism from Below*, edited by M. P. Guarnizo and L. E. Smith. NewBrunswick, NJ: Transaction Publishers.

Muhammad, Nuri. 2015. *Insights into Gang Culture in Belize: Essays on Youth, Crime, and Violence*. Belize City: Reynolds Desktop Publishing.

Nayak, A. 2003. *Race, Place and Globalization: Youth Culture in a Changing World*. Oxford, UK, and New York, NY: Berg Publishers.

Peirce, Jennifer. 2017. *Gap Analysis Report: Citizen Security in Belize*. Washington, DC: Interamerican Development Bank.

Rodgers, Dennis and Adam Baird. 2015. 'Understanding Gangs in Contemporary Latin America'. in *The Handbook of Gangs*, edited by S. H. Decker and D. C. Pyrooz. New York: Wiley.

Roks, Robert A. 2017. 'In the "H200d": Crips and the Intersection between Space and Identity in the Netherlands'. *Crime, Media, Culture: An International Journal*. doi: 10.1177/174165901772900.

Roks, Robert A. and James A. Densley. 2019. 'From Breakers to Bikers: The Evolution of the Dutch Crips "Gang"'. *Deviant Behavior*:1–18.

Sandberg, S. 2008. 'Street Capital: Ethnicity and Violence on the Streets of Oslo'. *Theoretical Criminology* 12(2):153–171.

Shoman, Assad. 2011. *A History of Belize in 13 Chapters*. 2nd ed. Belize City: The Angelus Press Limited.

Tomlinson, J. 2003. 'Globalization and Cultural Identity.' *The Global Transformations Reader*, 2, 269–277.

UNICEF Belize. 2011. *The Situation Analysis of Children and Women in Belize 2011 An Ecological Review*. Belize City: UNICEF.

UNODC. 2019. *Global Study on Homicide 2019: Homicide: Extent, Patterns, Trends and Criminal Justice Response*. Vienna: UNODC. https://www.unodc.org/documents/data-and-analysis/gsh/Booklet2.pdf

Vernon, Sadie. 2000. *In-Transit: The Story of a Journey*. Belize City: The Angelus Press Limited.

Warnecke-Berger, H. 2019. *Politics & Violence in Central America & the Caribbean*. New York and London: Palgrave Macmillan. https://doi.org/10.1007/978-3-319-89782-0

Zilberg, Elana. 2011. *Space of Detention: The Making of a Transnational Gang Crisis between Los Angeles and San Salvador*. Durham, NC: Duke University Press.

29

Gang governance in the tropics

The political economy of violence and social order in contemporary Nicaragua

Dennis Rodgers

Introduction

Visions of gangs as embodiments of anarchic violence and disorder are commonplace, whether in policy-making circles, among law enforcement officials, or the general public at large. At the same time, however, there also exists a long-standing tradition of gang research highlighting how they can be institutional vectors for the imposition and promotion of particular forms of local social structuration, or what might be termed "gang governance". The means through which gangs achieve and implement such forms of governance can vary significantly, however, both between and within specific contexts, as well as over time. Drawing on over 20 years of longitudinal ethnographic research in *barrio* Luis Fanor Hernández,[1] a poor neighbourhood in Managua, the capital city of Nicaragua, this chapter traces the way that different local gang iterations have emerged, transformed, and disappeared over time in order to explore the varying underlying nature of the governance that these have provided. In particular, it highlights the volatility of gang governance, as well as its inherent susceptibility to broader structural processes.

Gangs and governance

Numerous studies have highlighted how gangs can emerge institutionally as organising mediums for local collective life, particularly in the slums and poor neighbourhoods of cities, providing micro-regimes of order as well as communal forms of belonging to definite, albeit bounded, collective entities (see e.g. Arias, 2006; Brotherton and Barrios, 2004; Jensen, 2008; Mohammed, 2011; Rodgers, 2006a; Stephenson, 2015). Still among the most detailed, however, is Gerald Suttles's (1968: 224) pioneering study of the "the social order of the slum", where he describes how gangs in the Addams slum area of Chicago contributed to maintaining a system of "ordered segmentation" between different ethnic groups, based on "control over land usage and population movements", achieved through particular patterns of territorial occupation and conflict, as well as the upholding of a particular "moral order . . . provid[ing] a decent world within which people can live" (Suttles, 1968: 234).

One way of thinking about such patterns of behaviour is through the conceptual trope of what might be termed "gang governance". The notion of governance relates to the act of governing, which in turn, at its most basic, is concerned with the imposition of a sense of order and regularity onto a given social reality, context, or process. In other words, it is a concept that relates to how "operational rules shape specific outcomes" (Hyden *et al.*, 2004: 4). Governance is obviously something generally associated with states and their particular modes of action, or regimes – for example a "welfare state", a "neo-liberal state", a "republican state", and so on (see e.g. Silver, 1994; Wood *et al.*, 2004) – and the forms of citizenship that this provides (Kostakopoulou, 2008). There is no reason, however, other institutions cannot play the same role, including gangs.

Indeed, Jaffe (2013) has explicitly described gangs as providing localised forms of "hybrid citizenship" in inner-city Kingston, Jamaica, taking on a range of governmental functions that the Jamaican state fails to provide, including the provision of public services such as welfare, employment, and security, providing jobs, financial loans, protection, and even health care. Arias (2006) describes a similar situation in Rio de Janeiro, Brazil, where drug gangs resolve disputes and maintain "rough" justice in the city's *favelas*. At the same time, Arias highlights how there are often intimate connections between the state and drug gangs, and often it is not so much that the state is absent but rather that it has chosen to withdraw and has "outsourced" service provision to gangs (see also Buur, 2005). Gang governance can also emerge as a form of opposition to the state, as Jensen and Rodgers (2008) have highlighted in relation to South African gangs (see also Brotherton, 2015).

One key question about "gang governance" is why this kind of non-state governance regime might emerge rather than one based on another social institution, such as for example, in Latin America, "religious governance", considering the long-standing importance of the Catholic Church and ever-growing plethora of evangelical churches in the region (Levine, 2012). In this respect, it is potentially illuminating to turn to Simone's (2004: 407) concept of "people as infrastructure", which he developed in order to emphasise how in many cities in the so-called "Global South", where the state is not the primary vector of social organisation – whether by choice or due to lack of resources – it is individual city-dwellers who often constitute the basis for the "modes of provisioning and articulation" that allow life to exist in the city. More specifically, cities, according to Simone (2004: 408), are characterised by incessant "intersections" of city-dwellers that depend on their ability to "engage complex combinations of objects, spaces, persons, and practices. These conjunctions become an infrastructure – a platform providing for and reproducing life in the city". He traces in particular how different types of city-dwellers in inner-city Johannesburg, South Africa, provide regularities that anchor the livelihoods and transactions of other urban residents, thereby making urban life work. His examples include postal workers, garbage collectors, and small shopkeepers, as well as drug dealers and gang members, all of whom he qualifies as "human infrastructure" through which a sense of everyday order and regularity is constituted in inner-city Johannesburg.

One unanswered question in Simone's analysis, however, is why certain types of individual social agents might become infrastructurally more important than others and what it is that allows them to "deter or determine how individuals interact with others" (Simone, 2004: 428) or, in other words, establish a form of governance. In this respect, gangs and their members arguably constitute particularly powerful forms of governance infrastructure for several reasons. First, most gang members are youth, and as the Lebanese film-maker Ziad Doueiri (1998) – maker of the powerful film *West Beyrouth* – has pointed out, youth generally "have a stronger instinct for survival than adults[,] . . . no doubt . . . because [they] adapt better and faster to exceptional circumstances". Seen from this perspective, gangs can be said to emerge organically as vanguard protagonists in circumstances of oppression, intensified competition, or neglect by broader authorities, offering alternative forms of organisation both for their members but also for others in the communities within which they originate.

A second, more instrumental reason why gangs might emerge as potent governance infrastructure relates to the fact that within local communities, gang members are often sources of what Geffray (2002: 89) has termed "manna", that is to say of resources – both financial and otherwise – which they distribute in ways that cannot be reciprocated, meaning that they become inherent sources of debt and obligation. In contexts of acute scarcity and limited opportunities, this over-determines gangs and gang members within their local socio-economic fields and provides them with an enhanced social status and added infrastructural "weight" from a governance perspective.

Having said this, however, as Hagedorn (2008: xxv) has highlighted, gangs are highly volatile social institutions, and "today's youth gang might become a drug posse tomorrow, even transform into an ethnic militia or a vigilante group the next day" (see also Matza, 1964). This volatility means that any exploration of the nature of gang governance must inevitably approach "the question of what accounts for the emergence, decline, spread and evolution" of gangs in a fundamentally dynamic and longitudinal manner (Ayling, 2011: 2). The next section consequently considers the evolution of gang dynamics in *barrio* Luis Fanor Hernández, a poor neighbourhood in Managua, the capital city of Nicaragua, in order to trace the different iterations of gang governance that have emerged and how these have changed over time.

A gang history of barrio Luis Fanor Hernández

Barrio Luis Fanor Hernández is a neighbourhood of approximately 3,000 inhabitants located in southeast Managua, the capital city of Nicaragua. The locality was originally founded as an illegal squatter community by rural-urban migrants in the early 1960s, one of many such informal settlements that mushroomed on the edge of Managua at that time. Due to its inhabitants' extreme poverty, the settlement was initially known as *La Sobrevivencia* (Survival) but was completely rebuilt during the early 1980s as part of the *Sandinista* revolution's (1979–1990) housing development programme and renamed "*barrio* Luis Fanor Hernández" (after a local "martyr of the Revolution"), although socio-economically it remained in the lowest quartile of Managua neighbourhoods. The settlement has always been infamous for its high levels of crime and delinquency but became extremely notorious in the post-revolutionary period due to the emergence of a very brutal local gang. This bad reputation has persisted into the present, although the gang has changed significantly over the past two decades, even disappearing completely during the latter half of the 2000s.

Although there were gangs in *La Sobrevivencia* during the 1960s and 1970s, these were mainly spontaneous groups of youths that emerged organically, hung around neighbourhood street corners drinking and smoking, and only lasted as long as the specific peer group underpinning them. A qualitatively different gang culture developed in the post-revolutionary period, which can broadly be divided into seven distinct phases: an "emergent" phase (1989–1992), a "Golden Era" phase (1993–1998), a "drug dealing" phase (1999–2005), a "pacified" phase (2006–2011), a "revival" phase (2012–2015), a "*Combo*" phase (2016–18), and finally, a "Post-April 2018" phase. The gang's structure has evolved over these phases, both in terms of its size, organisation, and the spread and median age of members, but beyond such arguably superficial mutations, it is the way that the different phases of the *barrio* Luis Fanor Hernández gang's evolution can each be associated with distinct types of gang governance that is most significant and which will now be analysed phase by phase.

1989–1992: emergent phase

The first post-war gang emerged in *barrio* Luis Fanor Hernández in 1989 and lasted until 1992. The core was a group of eight youths between 18 and 20 years old who were former *Sandinista* Popular Army conscripts and who had demobilised more or less simultaneously in 1989. They began hanging out together on a neighbourhood street corner, along with four slightly older youths between 20 and 23 years old who had also been conscripts, as well as two younger individuals 9 and 10 years old who gravitated to the group for idiosyncratic reasons. This group of 14 began to engage regularly in a range of violent activities, including beating up individuals who robbed, attacked, or threatened their friends or family, something that happened frequently in the post-war context of heightened flux and uncertainty that characterised Nicaragua in the early 1990s due to the discombobulation of the *Sandinista* state.

The impulse for this particular pattern of vigilante violence was clearly related to the ex-conscript nature of gang members, both in relation to their military training as well as an ideological commitment. These systematically mentioned three basic reasons for joining a gang. First, the change of regime in 1990 led to an abrupt devaluation of their social status, which as conscripts "defending the Revolution" had previously been very high within the local community, and becoming gang members had seemed a means of reaffirming themselves vis-à-vis a wider society that seemed to rapidly forget them. Second, becoming gang members had been a way of recapturing some of the dramatic, yet marking and almost addictive, adrenaline-charged experiences of war, danger, and death, as well as of comradeship and solidarity which they had lived through as conscripts and which were rapidly becoming scarce commodities in post-war Nicaragua. But perhaps most importantly, becoming gang members had seemed to many a natural continuation of their previous role as soldiers. The early 1990s were highly uncertain times, marked by political polarisation, violence, and spiralling insecurity, and these youths talked about how they felt they could "serve" and "protect" their friends and families more effectively as members of a gang than as individuals. Drawing on their military training, as well as the historical "*pandilla*" ("gang") culture that in many ways was the traditional institutional vehicle for youth organisation in poor neighbourhoods prior to the *Sandinista* revolution, they formed gangs in order to better defend their social networks.

This first generation of post-conflict *barrio* Luis Fanor Hernández gang members had in other words clearly been collectively 'pre-socialized' into their distinct pattern of violence due to the group's experience of conscription, as well as, more indirectly, their general experience of *Sandinista* revolutionary ideology (see Rodgers, 2006a, 2017a). Partly because of this socialisation grounded in a prior individual experience, the gang governance regime that the gang promulgated was limited in scope, based very much on kinship and friendship networks, and aimed principally at providing a measure of protection and security.

1993–1998: 'Golden Era' phase

From 1992 onwards, however, the ex-conscript members of the first post-war iteration of the *barrio* Luis Fanor Hernández gang began to 'mature out' of the gang. Over a period of a couple of years, they were all replaced by new members who had no military background or significant personal experiences of *Sandinismo*. The vigilante norms and practices of previous gang members nevertheless continued to influence new ones due to a transformation in the way that factors such as revolutionary ideology were internalised by gang members. Rather than being based on individual gang members' ideological experience of "defending the Revolution", the *barrio* Luis Fanor Hernández gang's vigilante impulse became based on an intense sense of local territoriality, linked to the broader shrinking of the collective social imaginary in post-revolutionary Nicaragua that Núñez (1996) has described as involving an ontological shift "from the nation to the neighbourhood".[2] This in turn allowed for an institutionalisation of the conscript-derived vigilante ethos of the first iteration of the *barrio* Luis Fanor Hernández gang, despite it having derived from personal experiences which the new generation of gang members did not share.

Certainly, the new gang's territorial identification was evident in the fact that members began to call themselves "*Los Sobrevivientes*", in reference to the neighbourhood's pre-revolutionary name, as well as the fact that members did not necessarily have direct personal connections to each other, except that they all lived in *barrio* Luis Fanor Hernández. This move from a peer group-based gang to a more territorialised gang also meant that the 'Golden Era' gang was bigger and more organised than previously, growing to having about 100 members at its greatest height, albeit divided up into three spatially distinct sub-groups that operated separately but never fought each other and collaborated in gang wars (see Rodgers, 2006a).

This institutionalisation also affected the nature of gang governance, something that was well exemplified in a transformation in the gang's violent practices. The first gang's vigilante violence had been rather *ad hoc* in nature and principally aimed against individuals perceived as threatening to gang members' families and friends. The *barrio* Luis Fanor Hernández gangs in the mid-1990s aimed at imposing a form of spatial order rather than just protecting friends and family, in order to constitute the whole neighbourhood as a "safe haven". Gang members never targeted local community members and actively engaged in a range of activities to mitigate the unpredictability of violence in the neighbourhood, including providing "bodyguard" services to inhabitants when they ran errands outside the neighbourhood as well as regularly patrolling the neighbourhood's borders. Such actions were widely recognised and indeed appreciated by local inhabitants, who not only frequently talked very approvingly about the local gang but also often provided assistance to local gang members, for example, hiding them if they were chased into the neighbourhood by other gang members or private security guards whilst engaging in the delinquent activities outside the neighbourhood.

1999–2005: drug-dealing phase

Gang dynamics in *barrio* Luis Fanor Hernández changed dramatically around the turn of the century due to the spread of crack cocaine from 1999–2000.[3] This led to the gang moving from displaying a sense of solidarity with the local community to becoming a more predatory organisation. On the one hand, this was due to the fact that gang members became crack consumers. This made them very aggressive and unpredictable, and they began to regularly attack, steal from, burgle, and threaten local neighbourhood inhabitants. On the other hand, the breakdown of the gang's relationship with the *barrio* Luis Fanor Hernández community was also due to the group becoming involved in drug dealing.

In this regard, due to somewhat idiosyncratic reasons, *barrio* Luis Fanor Hernández was one of a handful of neighbourhoods through which cocaine arrived into Managua from the Caribbean coast of Nicaragua (*en route* from Colombia) and from which it was then distributed (see Rodgers, 2018). Drug dealing was centred around a single individual known as *el Indio Viejo* (the Old Indian), who had been a member of the first iteration of the *barrio* Luis Fanor Hernández gang and who organically integrated current gang members into his emergent business as individual street dealers but also collectively, as a security apparatus. The gang as a group would guard drug shipments whenever they came in or went out of the neighbourhood, enforce contracts, and more generally, engage in a campaign of terror to intimidate local inhabitants, to prevent denunciations, and ensure that drug dealing occurred unimpeded and that potential clients were not challenged.

Contrarily to the past, then, when the gang's governance sought to explicitly control the territory of the neighbourhood, it now aimed at controlling its population in order to violently underpin a process of exclusive (primitive) economic capital accumulation that enabled a small group of drug dealers to make it good within a broader context of poverty and limited alternative opportunities for capital accumulation (see Rodgers, 2017b). This change in gang governance dynamics meant that the *barrio* Luis Fanor Hernández gang evolved structurally, becoming smaller, reducing to between 18–20 members, and its membership older. While gang members in the 1990s had been 7–22 years old, during the early 2000s, they were between 16 and 25 years old. This trend was partly due to crack consumption becoming a major element of gang culture, as its negative health consequences are magnified the younger one is, but it was also linked to the fact that it is necessary to be of a certain size and strength in order to be an effective street dealer. Another reason was the fact that because the *barrio* Luis Fanor Hernández gang became the security apparatus of the drugs trade, it functionally needed to be a well-coordinated and tight-knit group, which its 100-person previous incarnation would not have been able to be. The gang also took on a new, non-territorialised name, *Los Dragones* (the Dragons).

The rise of the drugs trade in Managua led to violence no longer remaining contained within poor neighbourhoods such as *barrio* Luis Fanor Hernández but spreading throughout the city (see Rodgers, 2006b). Following over a decade during which the police had effectively withdrawn from poor neighbourhoods and informal settlements, a new trend emerged during this period involving the police implementing a policy of "spectacular" policing, regularly entering poor neighbourhoods in an arbitrary and intimidating manner, heavily armed, wearing riot gear, and specifically targeting young men. Such new forms of policing occurred in tandem with a spatial isolation of poor neighbourhoods through major infrastructural transformations, which led to violence being very much "pushed back" into poor neighbourhoods and slums, particularly in Managua (see Rodgers, 2004, 2012, 2019). This new security approach had two consequences. On the one hand, it led to frequent violent exchanges between the police and the local gang. On the other hand, it also led to increasing engagement between the police and drug-dealing gangs. In *barrio* Luis Fanor Hernández, while this was initially confrontational, it rapidly became accommodating – perhaps not surprisingly, considering that the Nicaraguan police is the least well paid in Central America (Dudley, 2012) – to the extent that within a few years collusion became systematised.

2006–2011: pacification phase

Partly as a result of this systematic collusion between the authorities and drug dealers, the *barrio* Luis Fanor Hernández gang underwent a "pacification" phase from mid-2006 onwards. This was also linked to the professionalisation of *el Indio Viejo*'s drug dealing activities. In particular, he became more selective in his choice of business partners, partly because crack consumption made gang members unreliable but also because of their fundamentally amateur nature as drug dealers and as a security apparatus. *El Indio Viejo* consequently constituted a group that came to be known locally as the "*cartelito*" ("little cartel"), which excluded local *barrio* Luis Fanor Hernández gang members. This rapidly led to a series of confrontations that left several gang members critically injured and one killed, after which the gang effectively ceased to exist as a collective unit. Although individuals who had been gang members continued to hang out in the neighbourhood streets, they did so alone or in small groups of twos or threes as the *cartelito* consolidated its domination of *barrio* Luis Fanor Hernández through regular, unpredictable patrolling of the neighbourhood that actively targeted any local youth congregating on street corners. In this way, the *cartelito* sought to impede the emergence of a new gang that might potentially have coalesced as a rival, and consolidated a very different form of governance over *barrio* Luis Fanor Hernández.

As it professionalised, the *cartelito* also fought against other equivalent organisations located both in Managua and beyond in order to secure an increased share in the drug market and develop drug-trafficking activities (which were much more profitable than dealing). Shoot-outs in and around the neighbourhood became commonplace, albeit unpredictable, occurrences, although the *cartelito* also sometimes employed the police as a proxy in its conflicts with rival organisations. At the height of its success, the *barrio* Luis Fanor Hernández *cartelito* was by all accounts one of the four most important native drug-trafficking organisations in Nicaragua, but in 2011, *el Indio Viejo* was arrested along with most other members of the *cartelito*, reportedly at the behest of a rival *cartelito* based in another Managua neighbourhood that had developed close links to certain members of the Nicaraguan government. By 2012, however, the last Nicaragua *cartelito* was disbanded by the Nicaraguan state, which took over monopoly control of the country's narcotics trade, to the extent that we can plausibly talk of Nicaragua now being a "narco-state" (see Rodgers, 2018).

2012–2015: revival phase

El Indio Viejo's arrest and the demise of the *cartelito* fundamentally changed dynamics in *barrio* Luis Fanor Hernández, allowing for the emergence of a new youth gang in 2012, made up of a group of twelve 14–15-year olds who began regularly hanging out together as a group on neighbourhood street corners. All were involved individually in a variety of petty criminal activities, although most local inhabitants considered them more or less innocuous, as these were generally low level and they did not carry out their delinquent activities in the neighbourhood.[4] To this extent, any form of gang governance that could be associated with this new gang iteration in *barrio* Luis Fanor Hernández was rather tenuous insofar as it did not really have any major impact on the local community.

In July 2012, however, this new *barrio* Luis Fanor Hernández gang attacked the gang in a nearby neighbourhood, and although they were repelled with several being injured, this instance of collective violence by the group was seen as the beginning of a cycle of gang warfare by *barrio* Luis Fanor Hernández inhabitants, one of whom called *Doña* Yolanda exclaimed rather gleefully during an interview just after the event that "the gang is back!", clearly because she saw the new gang as beginning to engage in activities reminiscent of gang dynamics during the 'Golden Era'. At the same time, though, the "Revival" gang phase was characterised by high member turnover and institutional ephemerality, with a succession of short-lived, unrelated groups following each other, some engaging in stronger forms of gang governance than others. These groups were all very similar, involving between 6 and 12 individuals, generally between 13 and 17 years of age. To this extent, the gangs of the "revival" phase can be said to very much organically approximate the classic social formation of a "street corner gang" (see Whyte, 1943).

The situation in *barrio* Luis Fanor Hernández was mirrored at the wider city level and marked a general resurgence in gang activity – see also Rocha (2013) and Rodgers and Rocha (2013) – that, by 2014, meant that gangs came to be perceived by the Nicaraguan authorities as a social nuisance, particularly as their increasing ubiquity constituted a visible contradiction of the government's tourist- and FDI-friendly discourse about the country being "safe" and "crime-free" (see Weegels, 2018a, 2018b). This led to a new change in the predominant forms of urban policing, as poor neighbourhoods came to be patrolled by a new, purposefully created police unit known as *Los Dantos*. These were heavily armed, motorised units, dressed in anonymous black uniforms, who from 2015 onwards began to engage in targeted campaigns of intimidation against urban youth. In *barrio* Luis Fanor Hernández, collective patrols of up to 20 motorcycles, each with a driver and a passenger carrying a shotgun or an AK-47, would be a regular intimidating presence, often "corralling" male youth in public spaces before strip-searching them, beating them, confiscating money and mobile phones, arresting anybody with drugs, and then arbitrarily loading one or two individuals into pick-up trucks that would drive to the other side of Managua and leave them there naked, something profoundly humiliating in Nicaragua's *machista* social context.

2016–2018: combo phase

This new form of policing successfully stymied the spread of male gangs, both in *barrio* Luis Fanor Hernández and more widely but had the (unintentional) consequence of leading to the unprecedented emergence of female gangs. Known locally as "*combos*" – a term that seems to have been borrowed from a popular Colombian telenovela shown on Nicaraguan TV – these female gangs displayed very different dynamics to the male gangs of previous eras, however. In *barrio* Luis Fanor Hernández, the first *combo* came to the fore in late 2015 and was made up of 15 young women between 16 and 21 years old, not all of whom were from the neighbourhood – although most had been to school together – but interacted mainly via Facebook, although they would also collectively meet in person "to party every Saturday" at neighbourhood *fiestas* or nightclubs. At the latter, individual *comberas* would get into fights with other young women – who were often members of other *combos* – for reasons linked to *macho* pride – "I saw a girl dissing me and when I went over to ask her what her problem was, she started mouthing off, so I got angry and I challenged her to a fight" – but most frequently over young men – "she was dancing with a guy I liked, so I went up to him and told him that he should be with me, not her, and she got angry and challenged me to a fight".

These fights were generally extremely violent one-on-one encounters, sometimes resulting in death – a 17-year-old girl from *barrio* Luis Fanor Hernández was killed during my visit in November 2016 – although most of the time they stopped when one of the combatants was seriously injured, ran away, or asked for mercy. These conflicts were prolonged on social media, however, as fights were often recorded and uploaded on Facebook, and the virtual platform was also used for rival *comberas* to trash talk – both individually and collectively – with each other about the fights, throw out personal or group insults, or else to upload scantily-clad photos of themselves on the Facebook timeline/walls of young men that they liked, telling them to dump their current girlfriend with come-ons such as: "this is what you're missing", "I'm more beautiful than her", or "I'm a better fuck than her", and so on. Due to the semi-public nature of such communications, they would often lead to rival *comberas* challenging each other virtually and then agreeing to meet and fight in person.

This particular behaviour pattern can be directly related to the new tactics of the *Dantos* special police forces and their impact on the territorial presence of young males in *barrio* Luis Fanor Hernández. Indeed, the marked absence of the latter on the streets was striking in 2016 compared to my visits in 2012 and 2014. Several youths – both male and female – explained how this had completely upset the local sexual economy. Previously, young men and young women had met each other and flirted in streets, before then pairing off to court semi-privately in the neighbourhood parks, squares, and patios. By 2016, this had ceased almost entirely as a result of police repression. The main space for flirtation and courtship between young men and women in *barrio* Luis Fanor Hernández were a couple of local night clubs and the occasional neighbourhood *fiesta* where the dynamics of social interaction were completely different: these are eminently collective, public, heated, loud, and hugely performative spaces, characterised by strutting, preening, and aggressive dance-offs, and so on. The sense of competition is extreme, and as a *combera* called Olga told me, "girls who have developed reputations for being good fighters have a better chance of getting the boys they want without being challenged", and she argued that the whole logic of the *combo* was about "getting a man". Certainly, young women tended to "retire" from their *combo* once they had done so – as Olga put it, "now that I've got my husband, I've distanced myself from the *combo* and don't involve myself like I used to". From a gang governance perspective, it could be argued that this corresponded to a more involuted form of governance, one which had retreated from the public sphere and had become more intimate in nature.

Post-April 2018

In April 2018, Nicaragua was the theatre of a mass popular uprising against the current government. Now only revolutionary in name, representing an elite oligarchy rather than the poor majority of the population, the *Sandinista* regime that returned to power in 2007 had become increasingly unpopular over the previous years as the end of Venezuelan aid following the death of Hugo Chavez in 2013 undermined the social redistribution programmes that had underpinned its clientelist political system for a decade (see Collombon and Rodgers, 2018). These were replaced by increasing repression and social control, in a broader context of increasing levels of impoverishment, rising inequality, and fiscal imbalance (see Rocha, 2018). The government's attempt to implement huge pension cuts and tax increases were the spark that led to mass demonstrations across the country. Caught unprepared, the government violently repressed the protests, breaking up demonstrations, taking apart barricades, and instituting a reign of fear and terror through arbitrary acts of violence and the imposing of curfews in poor neighbourhoods. Over 600 people were killed, hundreds more "disappeared", thousands arrested, while over 80,000 Nicaraguans fled across the border to Costa Rica. This "pacification" process took place over the course of several months and involved the police as well as what were termed "*parapoliciales*", or "parapolice", that is to say armed groups of civilians deputised by the police (see Collombon and Rodgers, 2018).

The events since April 2018 arguably marked a new phase in Nicaragua's gang history. On the one hand, just as had been the case of gangs in the late 1970s during the original *Sandinista* revolutionary insurrection, the *combos* effectively dissipated in the face of more violent (and better-armed) actors. On the other hand, many of those recruited into the *parapoliciales* were former (male) gang members. The recruitment of gang members by the *Sandinista* government in order to disrupt opposition is not new (see Rocha, 2008; Rodgers and Young, 2017) and responds to a clear logic of recruiting violence "experts", but it has occurred on a much larger scale than previously, with the number of *parapoliciales* estimated to be around 10,000 in total. Military veterans, former policemen, and *Sandinista* party activists have also been recruited, but former gang members are widely thought to make up a significant proportion. This included at least two individuals in *barrio* Luis Fanor Hernández whom I interviewed in 2020. One was a gang member in the early 2000s and the other a gang member in the early 2010s. Both were recruited through the *Sandinista* party's youth organisation in late 2018 and were provided with weapons and paid 300 *córdobas* (approximately 10 US dollars) a day to regularly enter other neighbourhoods at night and randomly shoot off to intimidate people during the whole of 2019. The government initially paid the *parapoliciales* out of the country's foreign reserves, but when these ran out in December 2018, they switched to offering immunity from prosecution instead, which has led to levels of crime and delinquency spiralling. Considering how the current Nicaraguan government drew the drugs trade into its orbit in the late 2000s, its current *rapprochement* with gangsterism is not surprising. From a gang governance perspective, however, it arguably effectively signals a nationalisation of gang governance, from the local to the national . . .

The political economy of gang governance

Understanding how and why gangs change and evolve over time is obviously a complex and multifaceted matter (see Rodgers and Hazen, 2014), but the overview of the evolution of the *barrio* Luis Fanor Hernández gang presented above clearly suggests that two issues are particularly important to take into account. The overarching trajectory of the *barrio* Luis Fanor Hernández gang is one of a transformation from a vigilante gang organised around ex-conscripts in the immediate post-war period in the early 1990s, to an institutionalisation of this vigilante ethos around local territorial identity, to a predatory drug dealing gang, to the elimination of the gang as a result of the professionalisation of the drugs trade and the rise of a more powerful local violence actor in the form of the *cartelito*, to the organic re-emergence of "classic" adolescent street corner gangs following the fall of the *cartelito*, to these street corner gangs' repression due to new forms of policing in the mid-2010s and their replacement by de-territorialised female gangs, and finally to a nationalisation of gang governance with the repression following the April 2018 uprising.

Each iteration of the *barrio* Luis Fanor Hernández gang can be associated with distinct types of gang governance, associated with different violent practices. How are we to understand the move from one form of gang governance to another? What triggers transformation from one phase to another? At one level, there is obviously repetition of different types of violent practices between different phases of the *barrio* Luis Fanor Hernández gang's evolution. This is not necessarily surprising. While gangs are highly variable and contradictory social institutions (see Rodgers and Hazen, 2014), part of what makes all the different iterations of the *barrio* Luis Fanor Hernández gang, 'gangs', is their common activities and behaviours, and so it should not be unexpected that there are similarities between different phases. For example, the continuities between forms of gang governance promulgated in the 'Emergent' and 'Revival' phases could be read as illustrating what might be considered basic originating processes through which gangs come to the fore as a social phenomenon, reminiscent of Frederick Thrasher's (1927: 57) classic foundational observation concerning 1920s Chicago gangs that these "originally formed spontaneously, and then integrated through conflict. . . . The result of this collective behavior [was] the development of tradition, unreflective internal structure, *esprit de corps*, solidarity, morale, group awareness, and attachment to a local territory."

But while there are a number of continuities across phases, there also exist clear shifts in the nature of gang governance, which can be directly related to the influence of factors exogenous to the local context within which the gang operates and originates. For example, the move from the 'Golden Era' to the 'Drug dealing' phase and the concomitant transformation of the nature of gang governance was clearly precipitated by the arrival of cocaine in the neighbourhood. The shift from 'Pacification' to the 'Revival' phase was directly linked to the fall of the *cartelito*, while the change from the 'Revival' to the 'Combo' phase can be connected to the transformation of policing patterns and the rise of the *Dantos*. In and of themselves, these transformations are relatively easy to understand – for example, the shift towards a focus on capital accumulation between the 'Golden Era' and the 'Drug dealing' phase makes logical economic sense (see Rodgers, 2006a), while the repressive targeting of males by the police in the 'Revival' phase clearly opened up a space for female gangs to emerge. However, it is less obvious why exogenous factors systematically seem to create disjuncture. While this could potentially be linked to a question of scale, insofar as external processes are likely to be more wide ranging than local ones, it is arguably more likely due to the way that exogenous factors impact the internal neighbourhood political economy.

Certainly, the last three phases of the *barrio* Luis Fanor Hernández gang evolutionary arc raise a broader issue, which is the relationship of the gang to other local violent actors. In this regard, there is arguably a clear process at work, insofar as the gang's transformation in its first three phases is one of increasing hegemonic domination over the *barrio* Luis Fanor Hernández territory and community that is not significantly impacted by external actors. The exogenous introduction of drugs disrupted this trajectory by ultimately introducing a new actor, the *cartelito*, which did more than simply impose itself hegemonically but rather sought and achieved a monopoly over violence, thereby excluding the gang from its "sociological (street) space". Its grip tightened further in collusion with the Nicaraguan state, until the latter turned against it. The fall of the *cartelito* opened up a new space for the gang to re-emerge in the 'Revival' phase but in a form that was clearly struggling to establish any local hegemony and had to moreover face the introduction of a new exogenous actor in the form of the *Dantos* Police units before being able to institutionalise in any meaningful manner. The rise of *Combos* as a result is a testament to this lack of institutionalisation and sociologically speaking constitutes an attempt to develop an alternative gang form that might circumvent the police hegemony. The outlier here is the post-April 2018 trajectory, which has seen gangs return to the fore in collaboration with a weakened Nicaraguan state, now contributing to imposing a regime of gang governance that goes beyond the local but encompasses the whole country. This marks a major scalar shift in gang governance, but considering that the current political crisis in Nicaragua is still unfolding, it is unclear how this development will affect the future evolution of the country's gangsterism.

Conclusion

Gangs can frequently be said to promulgate forms of local-level governance that are highly variable in nature, as the example of gang dynamics in *barrio* Luis Fanor Hernández in Managua, Nicaragua, highlights well. At the same time, however, the evolution of gang dynamics in *barrio* Luis Fanor Hernández also underscores how "gang governance" can be highly volatile, changing frequently and often quite radically. Understanding the political economy of the nature of the violence and social order associated with different iterations of gang governance is clearly a critical question. In this respect, two key issues can be identified. First, while gangs are clearly autonomous social phenomena, with complex internal logics and dynamics, they are simultaneously also epiphenomena, fundamentally reflecting – and shaped by – broader social structures. This is to a certain extent normal insofar as gangs are fundamentally embedded social phenomena, but it also raises critical questions regarding both the nature and the scale of gang governance, especially in comparison to state governance. Partly because gang governance necessarily emerges as a local phenomenon, it does not intrinsically imply the development of an encompassing interest in the same way that the governance of a state does, as least conceptually (see Spinoza (1951 [1883])). Indeed, gang governance inherently involves the differential treatment of different segments of the population. This raises broader questions concerning the nature of violence and social order, as well as the nature of governance more generally. In this regard, however, the epiphenomenal nature of gangs can plausibly be said to constitute them as insightful "bellwether" institutions, with the evolution of their governance trajectories revealing of deeper underlying social trends, as the current evolution of gang dynamics in Nicaragua highlights well.

Notes

1 This name is a pseudonym, as are the names of all the individuals and places mentioned in this chapter.
2 It can also be related to Dwight Conquergood's (2013: 226–227) notion that gang members are fundamentally "bonded communitarians".
3 Although drugs were by no means unknown to gang members in the neighbourhood during the early and mid-1990s, the main drugs of choice at the time were marijuana and glue (for sniffing).
4 Albeit less due to any consideration for the neighbourhood and more for reasons related to preserving their anonymity when carrying out delinquent acts, as well as former gang members coming together to "explain" to these new gang members that they were not to target local inhabitants following an "unfortunate mistake" shortly after the new gang began to coalesce as a group. .

References

Arias, E. D., (2006), *Drugs & Democracy in Rio de Janeiro: Trafficking, Social Networks, & Public Security*, Chapel Hill: University of North Carolina Press.

Ayling, J., (2011), "Gang change and evolutionary theory", *Crime, Law and Social Change*, 56(1): 1–26.

Brotherton, D. C., and L. Barrios, (2004), *The Almighty Latin King and Queen Nation: Street Politics and the Transformation of a New York Gang*, New York: Columbia University Press.

Brotherton, D. C., (2015), *Youth Street Gangs: A Critical Appraisal*, New York: Routledge.

Buur, L., (2005), "The sovereign outsourced: Local justice and violence in Port Elizabeth", in T. B. Hansen and F. Stepputat (eds.), *Sovereign Bodies: Citizens, Migrants, and States in the Postcolonial World*, Oxford: Princeton University Press, pp. 192–217.

Collombon, M., and D. Rodgers, (2018), "*Sandinismo* 2.0: Reconfigurations autoritaires du politique, nouvel ordre économique, et conflit social", *Cahiers des Amériques*, 87(1): 13–36.

Conquergood, D., (2013), *Cultural Struggles: Performance, Ethnography, Praxis*, Ann Arbor: University of Michigan Press.

Doueiri, Z., (1998), *West Beyrouth (Information Sheet)*, Versoix: Trigon-film.

Dudley, S., (2012), "Folk Singer's Death Shines Light on Nicaragua Police Corruption", *InSight Crime*, 9 July, available online at: www.insightcrime.org/nicaragua-a-paradise-lost/folk-singers-death-shines-light-on-nicaragua-police-corruption.

Geffray, C., (2002), "State, wealth, and criminals", *Lusotopie*, 9: 83–106.

Hagedorn, J. M., (2008), *A World of Gangs: Armed Young Men and Gangsta Culture*, Minneapolis: University of Minnesota Press.

Hyden, G., J. Court, and K. Mease, (2004), *Making Sense of Governance: Empirical Evidence from 16 Developing Countries*, Boulder: Lynne Rienner.

Jaffe, R., (2013), "The hybrid state: Crime and citizenship in urban Jamaica", *American Ethnologist*, 40(4): 734–748.

Jensen, S., (2008), *Gangs, Politics and Dignity in Cape Town*, Chicago: University of Chicago Press.

Jensen, S., and D. Rodgers, (2008), "Revolutionaries, barbarians, or war machines? Gangs in Nicaragua and South Africa", in C. Leys and L. Panitch (eds.), *Socialist Register 2009: Violence Today – Actually Existing Barbarism*, London: Merlin.

Kostakopoulou, D., (2008), *The Future Governance of Citizenship*, Cambridge: Cambridge University Press.

Levine, D. H., (2012), *Politics, Religion, and Society in Latin America*, Boulder: Lynne Rienner.

Matza, D., (1964), *Delinquency and Drift*, New York: Wiley.

Mohammed, M., (2011), *La formation des bandes: Entre la famille, l'école et la rue*, Paris: Presses Universitaires de France.

Núñez, J. C., (1996), *De la Ciudad al Barrio: Redes y Tejidos Urbanos en Guatemala, El Salvador y Nicaragua*, Ciudad de Guatemala, Universidad Rafael Landívar/PROFASR.

Rocha, J.-L., (2008), "La Mara 19 tras las huellas de las pandillas políticas", *Envío*, 321, https://www.envio.org.ni/articulo/3902.

Rocha, J.-L., (2013), *Violencia Juvenil y Orden Social en el Reparto Schick: Juventud Marginada y Relación con el Estado*, IADB discussion paper No. IDB-DP-308, Washington, DC: Inter-American Development Bank, available online at: http://publications.iadb.org/bitstream/handle/11319/5772/IDB-DP-308_Violencia_Juvenil_y_Orden_Social_en_el_Reparto_Schick.pdf.

Rocha, J.-L., (2018), "El tigre nica en la rebelión de abril", *Envío*, 434, www.envio.org.ni/articulo/5480.

Rodgers, D., (2004), "Disembedding the city: Crime, insecurity, and spatial organisation in Managua, Nicaragua", *Environment and Urbanization*, 16(2): 113–124.

Rodgers, D., (2006a), "Living in the shadow of death: Gangs, violence, and social order in urban Nicaragua, 1996–2002", *Journal of Latin American Studies*, 38(2): 267–292.

Rodgers, D., (2006b), "The state as a gang: Conceptualising the governmentality of violence in contemporary Nicaragua", *Critique of Anthropology*, 26(3): 315–330.

Rodgers, D., (2012), "Haussmannization in the tropics: Abject urbanism and infrastructural violence in Nicaragua", *Ethnography*, 13(4): 411–436.

Rodgers, D., (2017a), "*Bróderes* in arms: Gangs and the socialization of violence in Nicaragua", *Journal of Peace Research* 54(5): 648–660.

Rodgers, D., (2017b), "Why do drug dealers live with their moms? Contrasting views from Chicago and Managua", *Focaal: Journal of Global and Historical Anthropology*, 78: 102–114.

Rodgers, D., (2018), "Drug booms and busts: Poverty and prosperity in a Nicaraguan narco-*barrio*", *Third World Quarterly*, 39(2): 261–276.

Rodgers, D., (2019), "Urban anti-politics and the enigma of revolt: Confinement, segregation, and (the lack of) political action in contemporary Nicaragua", *Ethnos*, 84(1): 56–73.

Rodgers, D., and J. M. Hazen, (2014), "Introduction: Gangs in a global comparative perspective", in J. M. Hazen and D. Rodgers (eds.), *Global Gangs: Street Violence across the World*, Minneapolis: University of Minnesota Press, pp. 1–25.

Rodgers, D., and Rocha, J.-L. (2013) The evolution of gang violence in post-revolutionary Nicaragua. In *Small Arms Survey 2013: Everyday Dangers*. Cambridge: Cambridge University Press, pp. 46–73.

Rodgers, D., and S. Young, (2017), "From a politics of conviction to a politics of interest: The changing ontologics of youth politics in India and Nicaragua", *Antipode*, 49(1): 193–211.

Silver, H., (1994), "Social exclusion and social solidarity: Three paradigms", *International Labour Review*, 133(5–6): 531–578.

Simone, A., (2004), "People as infrastructure: Intersecting fragments in Johannesburg", *Public Culture*, 16(3): 407–429.

Spinoza, Benedict, (1951 [1883]), *A Theologico-Political Treatise and A Political Treatise*. New York: Dover.

Stephenson, S., (2015), *Gangs of Russia: From the Streets to the Corridors of Power*, Ithaca: Cornell University Press.

Suttles, G. D., (1968), *The Social Order of the Slum: Ethnicity and Territory in the Inner City*, Chicago: University of Chicago Press.

Thrasher, F., (1927), *The Gang: A Study of 1,313 Gangs in Chicago*, Chicago: University of Chicago Press.

Weegels, J., (2018a), "Implementing social policy through the criminal justice system: Youth, prisons, and community-oriented policing in Nicaragua", *Oxford Development Studies*, 46(1): 57–70.

Weegels, J., (2018b), "'The terror and scourge of the barrio': Representations of youth crime and policing on Nicaraguan television news", *Journal of Latin American Studies*, 50(4): 861–887.

Whyte, W. F., (1943), *Street Corner Society: The Structure of an Italian Slum*, Chicago: University of Chicago Press.

Wood, G., I. Gough, A. Barrientos, P. Bevan, P. Davis, and G. Room, (2004), *Insecurity and welfare regimes in Asia, Africa and Latin America: Social policy in development contexts*, Cambridge: Cambridge University Press.

30

Understanding the dynamics and functions of gang violence

The case of El Salvador

Chris van der Borgh

Introduction

Over the past decades, homicide rates in the northern triangle of Central America countries – Guatemala, El Salvador and Honduras – have been among the highest in the world.[1] While gang violence is one of the important causes of the elevated homicide rates, the nature of the violence used by gangs is still poorly understood. Gangs are often portrayed as criminals that use violence without pursuing a political agenda, but this overlooks the fact that over the past decades, gangs have come to play a political role in Salvadoran society, which is essentially based on the shown capacity and willingness to use violence. This chapter makes two connected arguments. First, street gangs have become a 'perverse' or 'informal' institution, which is capable of using violence strategically, on the basis of which gangs play a political role in society. Second, it is stressed that the evolution of gangs, and the ways in which the nexus between gang violence and gang power evolved, has to be understood in its historical and societal context. In other words, gangs and gang violence have become more intense and complex in a context that was already (and still is) characterized by different forms of violence. In this context, gangs developed a capacity to use violence vis-à-vis different types of actors. A better understanding of these different relations in which violence is used can improve our understanding of the logic of gang violence and inform discussions about the ways to contain that violence and to deal with gangs effectively.

The chapter is structured as follows. The next section explains that gang violence will be analyzed as a form of strategic and goal-driven violence, while stressing the importance of the historical and contemporary context in which gangs emerged and which contributed to the transformation of gangs and their use of violence. The following section provides an analysis of the evolution of gangs in El Salvador over the past three decades. It shows that gang structures have become stronger and more complex over time and have come to use violence towards a growing number of societal actors. It is argued that the gang phenomenon, the violence used by gangs and the intensity of violence should be understood in light of developments at the transnational, national and local levels, while the intensity of violence varies and changes depending on developments at these levels. The following section takes a more fine-grained look at the gang as institution, zooming in on the different functions of gang violence. It is argued that gang violence is not a uniform phenomenon but serves different goals vis-à-vis different actors. It maps and explores the different connections between gang violence and gang power in each of these relations. A distinction between these different types of power relations of gangs, and the functions of violence in each relation, brings to light the multiple and changing sub-dynamics and logics of violence. The chapter ends with a conclusion that summarizes the main arguments made and reflects on the challenges to deal with gang violence and gang power.

The chapter illustrates the arguments referring to the case of Nueva Concepción (a rural town) and 22 de Abril, Soyapango, which is part of the Metropolitan Area of San Salvador (Area Metropolitana de San Salvador, AMSS). The evidence presented is based on a literature review and on fieldwork of the author.[2] The study of Wim Savenije (1997) about social organizations and the emergence of gangs in the neighbourhood 22 de Abril (Soyapango) was used to illustrate developments there.[3]

Gang violence, functions and context

While the assumption of this chapter is that the violence used by gangs is at least in part strategic and goal driven (Eisner, 2009), it has to be stressed that violence is a complex and multi-faceted phenomenon (Achterhuis, 2002, 2008; Tilly, 2003). Indeed, gang violence is only one dimension of a much more complex and protracted constellation of 'violences' in Salvadoran society (Moser and Winton, 2002; Savenije and Andrade-Eekhoff, 2003). The next paragraph briefly discusses some of the main social and historical features of violence in Salvadoran society that are essential to understand the evolution of the street gangs into a social phenomenon that institutionalized violence in new ways. The rest of the section argues that gangs can be seen as (perverse) institutions, whose organized and collective use of violence has provided them a power position in Salvadoran society.

Salvadoran gangs and gang violence have evolved in a context of widespread social, political and structural violence which has had a profound impact on the development of the gang phenomenon. First, it is widely recognized that a number of structural or risk factors – that are clearly not of the making of gang members – may lead youth to join gangs, including social exclusion and lacking economic opportunities, a culture of violence, community disorganization and family disorganization (Cruz, 2007; Savenije and van der Borgh, 2004; Savenije and Andrade-Eekhoff, 2003; Savenije, 2009). Second, gang violence should be understood in the context of historical forms of violence (of state and non-state groups or intrafamilial). While there is discussion about the characteristics and nature of this relation, organized violence and war are dynamic and complex phenomena that can transform over time rather than simply disappear (Krause, 2012; Lemarchand, 2009). Thus, the possible connections between contemporary violence and 'old violence' (not least violence used by the state during and before the war) have to be taken into account when looking at contemporary gang violence (Bourgois, 2001; Levenson, 2013; Savenije and van der Borgh, 2004; Walter, 2016). Third, changes in the national political economy have an impact on the dynamics of societal violence and the opportunities for gangs to build up local power positions (Stephenson, 2013). This includes the more 'unintended' outcomes of political and economic liberalization (Paris, 2004), as well as the elite resistance against security sector reform (Cruz, 2011; Silva, 2014; Wade, 2016).

From this, it becomes clear that the context in which gangs emerge and have become a major security threat, is characterized by multiple insecurities and vulnerabilities that reflect a broader societal crisis. These insecurities are further hampered by the existence of gang structures, which have taken the shape of informal institutions[4] with a capacity to organize the use of violence and to use violence strategically in its interactions with other actors (Eisner, 2009).

Gangs can be seen as 'specialists in violence' (Tilly's, 2003, 36), who deploy organized violence or threats of violence so that others comply with their demands.[5] The organizational structures created by specialists in violence have their own needs, such as the survival of the entity they belong to, recruitment of new members and resources to sustain them (e.g. through taxation) (ibid., 40). In addition, these structures also produce normative behaviour and can 'selectively cultivate or contain the personality characteristics and abilities associated with violence' (Eisner, 2009, 48).

Gang power is partly based on (the threat of) violence, but violence is not the only and not necessarily the most efficient way to relate to other actors. Indeed, the capacity to use violence has to be seen in relation to other sources of power (e.g. ideological, familial, economic) (Shaw, 2009, 105). Gangs have a capacity to use other means, such as negotiation, coordination and cooptation, both vis-à-vis actors with a capacity to use violence (like other gangs, organized crime, police and military), as well as non-armed actors (local governments, local organizations, residents). Arias (2017, 248) reminds us that criminal activity should not simply be analyzed as an expression of conflict and violence, since these groups are involved in 'substantial efforts at cooperation, governance, and exchange that underlie these activities'. These relations (both of a more cooperative or more conflictive nature) differ from place to place, can be subject to (abrupt) change and do not necessarily lead to stability (Arias, 2013, 2017; Pansters, 2015).

Thus, rather than seeing the use of violence as at odds with power, violence and the threat of violence are the key instruments to build and maintain the power of gangs. Gangs are capable of organizing the use of violence, and their ability to manipulate power is based on the capacity and willingness to employ such violence. While the use of violence is a key attribute of gang power, gangs can act strategically, although violence is not always considered a necessary means or 'a promising strategy' (Eisner, 2009, 46). The intensity of violence is therefore always context specific, and 'understanding how, when and why illicit enterprises employ violence is of vital importance' (Shirk and Wallman, 2015, 1350). It is through the use of violence that gangs have developed a power position, which includes influence over government officials (political power), control over territory and people (social and political power) and a capacity to extract resources (economic power). But violence is not the only instrument to expand or maintain that power position, as gangs need to maintain different power relations that they have developed over time, and it would be far too costly to do so by violent means alone. The next section shows how the relations of gangs with other actors in society diversified over the past three decades, and the section thereafter discusses the functions of violence in each of these relations.

Transformations of gang violence

This section discusses the changes in the gang phenomenon in El Salvador and the consequences of these changes on the use of violence by gangs. It first discusses how, in the period after the civil war, gangs quickly grew and how the use of violence within and between gangs intensified. Next it shows how the more repressive government responses led to reorganization of gangs and the more frequent use of violence vis-à-vis residents and, at a later stage, towards government officials.

Post-war growth of gangs and gang violence

The phenomenon of street gangs dates back to the years before the civil war, and while the phenomenon survived the war years, it quickly expanded in the post-settlement context (Savenije, 2009). In the early years, street gangs (or 'maras') were smaller groups of friends, with a strong identity and their own signs and symbols, who claimed to protect or control a territory (neighbourhood or part thereof). Youth joining gangs had a certain fascination with violence, but it would be mistaken to argue that violence was the only reason of being in the gang. Gangs also provided status to young men, as well as a sense of protection and belonging. One gang member in 22 de Abril argued that boys found 'peace and tranquillity' in the gang, something they often didn't find at home (Savenije, 1997, 38). Nevertheless, the animosity with other gangs is and has remained extremely important in the identity and internal cohesion of gangs. This animosity is based on a strong 'us vs. them' divide that is violently cultivated and re-created by gangs. Attacks against the other gangs and the protection against aggression of other gangs strengthens the group and deepens the boundary between the gangs.

In the mid-1990s, clashes between gangs and the number of casualties increased. This was, in part, the result of an 'arms race' between the gangs leading to more dangerous and even mortal fights (Savenije, 1997, 44) but even more due to the incapacity of the government to deal with such escalation. The gangs were not a new phenomenon to the police. A former gang member from a neighbourhood in San Salvador remembered that when there were problems with the gang, the police arrived and just talked to them.[6] A former member of the National Police in Nueva Concepción reported that in 1991 – before the signing of the peace agreements – he arrested gang members for shooting in the air.[7] While during the period of the armed conflict, gangs maintained a lower profile, the post-settlement demilitarization of political life and of society gave more space to the gangs to flourish. It is fair to say that the reform of the security sector (from military police to a civilian police), a process with many deficiencies, also hampered the capacity of the government to deal with this new phenomenon. Although the central government discussed measures to stop the violence attributed to gangs, it was not able to come up with an adequate response (Savenije, 1997). Thus, in the early phase, weak state presence and inadequate responses gave gangs almost free reign in 'their' territories.

The growth of Salvadoran gangs was deeply influenced by the massive deportation of Salvadoran youth with experience in the US (mostly Southern Californian) gang culture. Thousands of returning youth 'imported' US gang culture back into El Salvador. The US policy of deporting immigrants with criminal records to their country of origin (adopted in 1996) led to a growing influx of gang members and influence from the US gang experience (DeCesare, 1998; ICG, 2017, 5). In this period, alleged gang members were actively targeted by the Los Angeles Police Department for deportation (Zilberg, 2004). Thus, the United States not only exported its social problems to El Salvador but indirectly contributed to the transformation of Salvadoran gangs (ibid., 761). As a result, the American gang structures, Mara Salvatrucha (MS13) and the 18th Street Gang (Barrio 18), came to dominate the gang world in El Salvador. Smaller maras aligned with one of the two structures, as the pressure to join either of the gang structures increased, and by the end of the 1990s, most maras had become part of one of these two structures.

There were hardly any relations between gangs and former warring parties (the army and the guerrillas), who had reached a peace agreement in 1992. But although gangs were a new type of institution, it is fair to say that they were influenced and affected by older patterns of local animosity and violence, and – in a context of weak state power – partly reproduced these. The flow of internally displaced persons (IDPs) to cities led to new settlements of densely populated and marginalized neighbourhoods. For example, in the 22 de Abril barrio, IDPs settled in the lower part of the neighbourhood, while some 10 years earlier, groups of non IDPs had settled in the upper parts. Tensions between the upper and lower parts that had existed previously were to some extent reproduced by the gangs (Savenije, 1997, 35). Similar tensions between older and newer neighbourhoods seemed to exist in Nueva Concepcion, which also had received large numbers of internally displaced people during the war years.[8] Rather than reproducing the 'civil war', gangs reproduced certain daily practices and violent forms of conflict resolution that already prevailed in households and neighbourhoods, for example, by settling interpersonal conflicts with weaponry such as the machete (Savenije, 1997, 51). Interestingly, in the case of Nueva Concepción, some local residents compared the extortion practices of street gangs with those of local military and paramilitary during the war years.[9]

In sum, in the early period, in the 1980s and 1990s, gangs were a sub-cultural phenomenon that quickly grew and transformed during the post-war years. The national context of rapid demilitarization and problematic security sector reform, in combination with the massive deportations of Salvadoran youth from the United States, provided a fertile space for the gang phenomenon to grow exponentially and allowed for a hardening and escalation of inter-gang violence. The use of violence thus became a key characteristic of gangs, both internally, and in particular vis-à-vis other gangs. While gangs still provided a deep sense of belonging to members and also had possibilities to contain the violence and its escalation, nevertheless, they continued to increase their local power positions through violence and intimidation.

Diversification of violence and institutionalization of gangs

In the first decade of this century, major changes in gang structures and their use of violence took hold. Such transformation was largely an adaptation to the increasingly repressive response to gangs by the Salvadoran government. For example, in 2003 and 2004, a series of zero-tolerance policies (called Mano Dura and Mano Super Dura) were introduced aimed at solving the gang problem by locking up more and more of the gangs' members (Savenije and van der Borgh, 2015; Wolf, 2017). Between 2004 and 2009, the number of imprisoned gang members increased from 2,963 to 7,555 (Gomez Hecht, 2013, 144, 149).[10] This was accompanied by a policy to segregate the members of different gangs in separate prisons, which had the unintended effect of strengthening the gangs' internal cohesion and allowed them to take de facto control over 'their' respective facilities (ibid., 144). Not only did prisons serve as a meeting ground for members of different cliques that had not been in touch with each other before (becoming a kind of 'headquarters'), but non-gang detainees and gang members also came in touch with each other (ibid., 145, 146).

These repressive policies led to different and more complex gang structures. Gang members changed their style (different dresses and no tattoos) and left their neighbourhoods when necessary (Gomez Hecht, 2013, 148). While in the 1990s, 'maras' had integrated into larger gang structures, these gang structures became more integrated and hierarchical, with prison leaderships playing a key role and exerting a degree of control over local groups (cliques) and programs (a number of cliques in a certain sector) (ibid., 139). This phenomenon also implied that decision-making became more complex and communication with gang members outside of prison had to be secured (mobile phones playing an important role). Importantly, the internal use of violence (to punish) was no longer only a matter of relations within the smallest unit of the gang (the clique), but higher levels could now also be involved. And although the relations between cliques and prison leaderships varied, the knowledge that at some point gang members could end up in prison very likely influenced their conduct.[11]

One of the major changes in this period was the development of extortion regimes, often carried over from within the prison system. While before 2003, gangs were involved in extortion on a more ad hoc basis, in the following years, extortion became the most important way for gangs to finance themselves. It is estimated that in 2010, almost 10 million dollars had been collected (ibid., 153), with the most important targets businesses, bus companies, the self-employed and in a number of cases individual households (ICG, 2017, 15). A great deal of the extortion is organized from within the prisons, but the practice of extortion requires operational structures with gang members outside of prison who have a presence on the ground to identify victims, collect money and punish those who do not pay.

The extortion practices have had a profoundly perverse impact on local communities, leading – at least in the short term – to more violence. For example, in the period between 2011 and 2016, an appalling 692 transportation workers were killed in El Salvador (ICG, 2017, 16). The widespread use of violence also has had profound consequences on local social capital and cohesion (INCIDE, 2016). This was clearly the case in the municipality of Nueva Concepcion. In this case, we saw that by 2003, local bus owners had filed complaints of extortion against local gang members[12] but to no avail. In the subsequent years, the targeted use of violence against those not willing to pay, including respected prominent local businessmen, instilled a deep fear.[13] The violence had a clear message to the rest of the community and a profound impact on the local social fabric. 'Those who did not want to pay, [sic] were killed.'[14] Thus, the selective and visible use of violence had a demonstrable effect on the broader community, ensuring that residents remained silent over what they heard and saw.

However, the relations between gang members and local residents differed from place to place. The growth of the gang phenomenon led to the formation of a kind of 'social base' of gangs: a group of residents who were not members of gangs but were 'close to the gangs' – such as family members, sympathizers with gangs or residents of neighbourhoods with a historically high gang presence. There are estimates of some 600,000 people who would belong to the 'social base' of gangs, which (if correct) would amount to 10% of the Salvadoran population. Indeed, it is hard to check these data and to analyze whether those considered to belong to the 'social base' support the gang or are rather forced into obedience. But there can be little doubt that there exist relations and dependencies between gang members and local residents. For example, family members of gangs (wives, children) may depend on money from their imprisoned father. Family members are also deeply concerned and upset about the situation in the prisons of family members. In an interview in 2017, a religious leader in the barrio 22 de Abril remarked that mothers of imprisoned gang members were extremely concerned about the health of their children in prison and the fact they were no longer allowed to visit them.[15]

In their day-to-day interactions with government staff, gangs have developed a marked capacity to put pressure on and, when necessary, to co-opt officials both inside and outside of prisons. There are no academic studies about the gang influence on government staff, but a scan of newspaper articles and research reports shows that gangs have developed a considerable capacity to exert such influence, using violence as a 'last resort'. Reportedly, a large number of prison guards have been involved in smuggling telephones, phone chips, drugs and so on. (Gomez Hecht, 2013, 141). It is not clear whether these staff have been forced or bribed to cooperate, but given the capacity and willingness to strategically use violence by gangs and the low wages of the prison guards, it is likely that those who receive a 'request' of gangs will simply not refuse (or quit and look for another job). As to the relations with government staff outside of prisons, there have been reports of police and judges who have been threatened by gangs to not arrest or try gang members.[16] A large number of schools also seem to suffer under gang influence and intimidation,[17] and there is evidence that local government staff have to deal with the demands of gangs for a range of services, including employment, influence on appointments and funds (van der Borgh and Abello Colak, 2018).

The growing presence and the unabatedly high homicide rates in El Salvador have led to a continuous search for effective responses by the Salvadoran government. In this regard, in the period after 2012, the government first tried a more accommodating approach only to be followed by a 'war on gangs'. In 2012, the minister of justice and public security facilitated a truce signed between leaders of the two major gangs (in a high-security prison). Among other things, the gangs promised to reduce the homicide rates, and the government promised to improve prison conditions and to invest in socio-economic projects for gang members. The truce was relatively short lived and unravelled in the course of 2013, but it led to a temporary drop in homicide rates, and it made clear that gangs were able to contain violence.

However, when the truce unravelled, a new series of different government measures (both formal and informal) led to a full crackdown on gangs (van der Borgh, 2019). The consequences of these policies were twofold: the tougher approach – which included an increase in summary executions – led to the debilitation of the gangs. In the case of Nueva Concepción, residents openly talked about the police who were now 'killing the gangs', although they didn't have evidence. One argued that: 'They don't do that in town, but in the countryside they kill them'.[18] On the other hand, it led to reorganizations of gangs and to an increasing number of gang attacks and retaliations against police and military – at a scale that was unprecedented (ICG, 2017).

These changing policies not only affected the relations with the government but also had profound consequences on the internal relations of gangs. During the truce, the prison gang leadership gave orders to contain at least some of the violence that gangs used. This was not always understood, nor obeyed at the lower levels, leading to the punishment and violent retaliations against those not obeying. However, the end of the truce weakened the position of the gang leadership that had supported the truce and also led to questions about their role during the truce and to conflicts within the gangs. For example, the imprisoned gang leadership of MS13 that had been involved in the truce process was accused by members of the Fulton Locos Salvadoreños (FLS) of self-enrichment, leading to deteriorating retaliations with the Hollywood Locos inside and outside prisons and resulting in the killing of four Fulton leaders and subsequent revenge killings (Goi, 2017).[19] This conflict was also felt in the case of Nueva Concepción, where the new wave of repression led to a call of the FLS cliques to the inactive gang members (including veterans and young boys who had joined evangelical churches) to 'remobilize'.[20] Reportedly, this was a reason for several veterans and their families to leave town.[21]

The new wave of repression not only led to more pressure on gangs but also on residents living in neighbourhoods controlled by gangs. In this regard, there is a marked difference between the neighbourhood of 22 de Abril and the town of Nueva Concepción. In the latter, residents generally welcomed the new repressive policies (Van der Borgh, 2019). However, many young men who were not aligned to the gangs were treated harshly by the police and military. In the case of 22 de Abril, repression not only affected local gang members but the local population in general, who are – given the strong presence of gangs in the neighbourhood – suspected of relations with gangs and often treated badly.[22] In a number of cases, this seemed to strengthen the bond between local residents and gangs.[23]

In sum, the introduction of more repressive approaches in the beginning of the century changed (or accelerated the changes in) gang structures and the functions of gang violence. Gangs became better organized and had a greater capacity to coordinate between cliques, and established violence was used towards local society in a more systematic way, while clashes between gangs continued, and it was not uncommon for gangs to target residents from neighbourhoods under control of the enemy gang. After a relatively short period of 'strategic' containment of violence (the truce), repression increased and led to growing gang violence vis-à-vis police and the military. The escalation of violence between gangs and government also had repercussions on the relations within gangs, between gangs and between gangs and society.

Functions of gang violence

The previous section sketched how the use of gang violence changed over the past three decades. This section focuses on the functions of gang violence. Categorizations of different types of violence are distinguished by types, functions and actors.[24] Several authors have argued that categorizations of violence tend to be 'misleading', as violent practices do not necessarily fit neatly into the proposed boxes (Cramer, 2006, 84; Krause, 2012: 43). The Geneva Declaration (2008, 3) even questioned the possibility of making distinctions between different types of violence, stating that

> the blurring of the line between political and non-political violence, the growth of transnational gangs, the expansion of non-state armed groups, and persistently high levels of insecurity in most post-conflict situations – makes drawing clear distinctions between different forms of armed violence practically and analytically impossible.

However, the fact that armed violence is complex should not stop us from trying to better understand it (Cramer, 2006, 85; Eisner, 2009, 44; Durán-Martínez, 2015).

The categorization presented here focuses exclusively on the violence used by gangs and distinguishes between the different relations in which violence is used. A limitation of such an analysis is that it does not make linkages to other armed actors and types of armed violence in society, while it also leaves out the context in which gang violence emerges. However, the strength of this more limited focus is that it enables us to map and to link different types and manifestations of violence of one particular actor, while taking into account the power relations with other relevant actors. The framework bears some similarities to the one developed by Berg and Carranza (2018, 569), which distinguishes between three main functions of organized criminal violence (competitive, coercive and exploitative) found in different types of targets (criminal groups, state officials and the population).[25] Rather than using the proposed distinction between three broad functions of violence,[26] the categorization presented here makes a more fine-grained distinction between the broader strategic objectives of the use of violence in certain relations and the more immediate and more tangible short-term functions of violence (e.g. to punish, attack or retaliate).

Box 30.1 presents the four types of power relations in which gangs can use violence: within the gang, between gangs, between gangs and governments and between gang and society. For each of these relations, it points at the main targets of violence, as well as the principal strategic objectives of violence in that relation (e.g. protection of the organization, turf). Last, the box mentions some of the more immediate functions of violence, as it can serve to maintain or change the status quo or order in the given relationship (such as retaliation, punishment, recruitment). Subsequently, the different types are discussed.

The first two rows in Box 30.1 deal with violence used between and within gangs. In both cases, violence is extremely important in the clashes with (and the defence against) other gangs. The animosity between gangs is cultivated internally and has turned extremely violent over the past decades, with deadly attacks becoming much more frequent. Gang violence not only serves for protection of the own gang and its turf against the other gang but also gives gang members the opportunity to show their courage and the feeling to belong to a group. Although relations between gang members can be extremely hostile, there also exists a capacity to contain violence between gang leaders of opposing gangs, which can have serious repercussions on the everyday relations at the neighbourhood level. For example, in the period after the truce, when confrontations between state and gangs led to high levels of 'state–gang' violence, inter-gang

Chris van der Borgh

Box 30.1 Relationships, targets, objectives and functions of gang violence

Relationship	Targets	Strategic objective	Immediate function
Intra-gang	Members of own gang	Maintain or challenge the internal order or hierarchy.	Punish ('homies' by leaders/chiefs) and challenge (leaders by 'homies') Revenge (e.g. conflicts over money, women) Reaffirm (to show courage towards group or reaffirm leadership)
Inter-gang	Members of other gangs	Protect the organization, the turf and the honour of the gang against other gangs.	Retaliate ('homies' of other gangs) Take back control (over turf)
Gang–government	Government officials and staff	Protect organization and turf against government interference. Extract resources from the state.	Retaliate (e.g. police or staff who are mistrusted) To threaten or terrorize (e.g. local government staff)
Gang–society	Residents, businesses, other illicit groups	Protect and maintain organization. Foster local gang control and gang-based order. Extract resources from society.	Retaliate (those who cooperate with 'enemies') Threaten or terrorize (those who do not pay or do not want to cooperate)

violence was lower. The violence between gangs thus has the function to shape and protect the organization, the turf and the honour of the gang against other gangs. Attacks and retaliation are the most important forms of violence.

While solidarity is a key attribute of gangs, and the strong bonds with other homies and the strong sense of belonging are important reasons to join a gang, violence also has a number of internal functions. Arguably, the fact that a gang uses violence vis-à-vis other persons and groups is key to its attractiveness (in most cases, new members become part of the gang through a ritualized beating – 'el brinco'). Violence is also important in the maintenance and challenges of order. Within gangs, there is frequent competition for status and power, and the succession of the leadership (e.g. after an arrest) can turn violent. Moreover, homies who have misbehaved or broken rules of the gang – for example, breaking the existing rules about (non)extortion of local residents – can for instance be beaten up as a punishment (Carballo, 2014). Thus, violence has the function of maintaining (and challenging) the internal order of gangs and takes the form of revenge, recruitment and punishment.

Third, violence can be used against government staff, such as police, local government representatives and so on. Lessing (2015) points to the fact that violence of criminal organizations is used with a view to constrain state behaviour and influence their policies instead of conquering the state. However, violence is not the only means to secure cooperation with the state. Penglase (2009, 50) points out the option to deal with – and circumvent – state power and to establish 'dangerous liaisons' with corrupt politicians and policemen, providing them with selective protection of the state (Penglase, 2009, 50). Arias (2017, 247) stresses the importance of these governance arrangements, arguing that 'the puzzle of armed violence in Latin America is better comprehended as a system of governance than as a war'. In the Salvadoran case, relations with government officials differ from place to place. There have been reports of cooperation between police and gangs, but over the past years, the renewed repression against gangs also led to seeing the police as a legitimate target of violence. With regard to local government staff, different types of liaisons exist. In many cases, government officials need to deal with (and can be forced into) cooperation with gangs (van der Borgh and Abello Colak, 2018). Thus, violence vis-à-vis government staff can take different forms. It can be a means to retaliate (vis-à-vis police) but also a means to secure compliance, by setting examples and thus instilling fear. Last, as will be discussed further on, threats of violence vis-à-vis government staff in prisons and municipalities can also provide access to resources.

Fourth, the importance of the relations of armed actors with civilians has been increasingly emphasized in the academic literature (Kalyvas, 2006; Shaw, 2009). In this regard, the linkages of street gangs with society have increased and multiplied over the past decades. Gangs claim to control territories and residents working in these territories in order to protect their organization, the retail of drugs in these territories and extortion of local residents and/or businesses. Violence is used to retaliate (those who are accused of cooperation with the police or other gangs) or to threaten (e.g. those not willing to pay tributes). However, local residents can also become targets of conflicts between and within gangs when family members of gang members that are not involved in gang life are targeted by other gang members to take revenge or to intimidate.

While gang violence can be related to one of the strategic objectives, there is obviously also some blurring. Residents can be attacked by an adversary gang from a different neighbourhood out of revenge (inter-gang) and/or to show the courage of a gang member towards peers (e.g. intra-gang initiation ritual). Violence used towards the police can also instil fear among local residents or have a backlash on local residents who are targeted by police. This does not imply that all gang violence is intentional and matched by a broader plan or strategy of the gang. As mentioned before, the use of violence is not necessarily intentional or strategic and can also be more emotional, 'uncontrolled' or 'spontaneous'. The categorizations in Box 30.1 highlight the everyday and immediate functions of gang violence in different social relations, while the accumulation of the different immediate functions provides gangs with a power position vis-à-vis local society and local and national government representatives.

Conclusions

This chapter discussed how and why gang power and gang violence have transformed over the past three decades in El Salvador, making a distinction between different types of power relations of gangs and the functions of violence therein. It combines an explanation of the gang phenomenon that stresses structural factors leading to the growth of an extremely violent gang phenomenon with the analysis of the outcome of this development: a gang structure that has become embedded in society on the basis of its capacity to use violence. What can this chapter teach us about more effective responses to gang violence and gang power?

The analysis of three decades of gang violence in El Salvador shows that gang structures became more complex and violent in a context of problematic implementation of the peace agreements (in particular security sector reform), changes in the national political economy leading to further social exclusion, the deportation of youth from the United States and the focus of the Salvadoran government on zero-tolerance policies. These factors contributed to the violent development of the gang phenomenon and also complicated the possible solutions to deal with gangs. In addition, the measures of the US government (to deport youth) and of the Salvadoran government (to wage war on gangs) did not lead to the containment of gangs but rather to their transformation into a more violent type of gang. Finding a way out of this situation will not be an easy task. But the recognition that the gang phenomenon is a societal problem is and remains of utmost importance. To say that gang members are the products (and oftentimes victims) of structural violence and social exclusion should not be seen as a justification of the violence used by gangs and of the fear and pain in society for which they are responsible. It simply should remind us of the fact that the gangs are the product of a society in crisis and that the containment of gangs and gang violence is not the responsibility of gangs alone. To stem this violence, a viable alternative to the current policies must be made a priority.

Gang structures, in the absence of effective and holistic gang policy, became more complex over time, and gangs use violence towards a growing number of societal actors, as shown in Box 30.1. Violence is an important means that can be used by gangs, but in each relationship, gangs have a capacity to contain violence and to liaise with other actors as well. Within gangs, a fascination with violence and the capacity and willingness to use it are part of the very identity of the group. However, gangs also provide friendship and stability. Relations between enemy gangs can be extremely tense, but at different levels (not least the elite level), a capacity to act together and to make truces has come into existence. In relations with residents and other societal actors, the capacity and willingness to use violence provide gangs with a power position, but – depending on local context and juncture – gangs have an ability to coexist with local residents. In relation to government actors, gangs have been reluctant to use (high levels of) violence, but, faced with quick changes in government policies and extrajudicial killings, violence has been used towards police and military as well.

A recognition of the different functions of gang violence and of the capacities at different levels to contain violence should inform government strategies to deal with gang power. Indeed, government responses can have repercussions on the use of violence in the four domains, not in the last place the relations of gangs with local residents and local government staff. For example, the war on gangs by the central government can hamper a more effective presence of the local government, which usually requires some form of communication of local municipal staff with local gangs. It can also lead to police targeting local residents of neighbourhoods with a strong gang presence, as police find it hard to tell gangs and local residents apart, resulting in a growing distrust of residents vis-à-vis the police. Thus, the efforts to contain gang power and gang violence requires at least a recognition of the potential repercussions on local residents and government staff.

Notes

1 *The Economist*, Shining Light on Latin America's Homicide Epidemic. Latin America's Violent Crime, and Ways of Dealing with It, Have Lessons for the Rest of the World, 5 April 2018.

2 The material that is particularly relevant for this chapter is: interviews from a research visit in February 2014 to several municipalities involved in the local truce process (10 interviews in total); five research visits to San Salvador and Nueva Concepción in the period between February 2015 and July 2017 (40 interviews in total); and interviews in San Salvador with experts, policy makers and local residents about local and national gang policies (20 interviews in total). In addition, a two-week research visit was made in November 2017 and a one-week visit in November 2018 to the AMSS, conducting interviews at the grassroots level with local government representatives, residents, representatives of civil society organizations and gangs (35 interviews total).

3 In addition, I conducted a few interviews in and around 22 de Abril in 2017 and 2018. The other work of Savenije, especially Savenije (2009), as well as the many private conversations with him, have been of great importance for my knowledge about the development of gangs in El Salvador.

4 Institutions are defined as 'the relatively permanent arrangements of behaviours, roles, norms, and values that structure aspects of human activity in patterned ways' (Eisner, 2009, 48).

5 In this chapter, we both refer to violence and other forms of coercion that are based on the threat of violence. Eisner (2009, 42) notes that violence can be seen as a subcategory of a much broader class of coercive acts. Collective violence takes place when damage is inflicted 'on persons and/or objects, [involving] at least two perpetrators of damage, [resulting] at least in part from coordination among persons who perform the damaging act' (Tilly, 2003, 3).

6 Fieldnotes, neighbourhood La Dina, San Salvador, July 2017.

7 Author's interview with interviewee #8, Nueva Concepción, February 2015.

8 Author's interviews, Nueva Concepción, add #19, April 2016.

9 Author's interviews, Nueva Concepción (2014–2017). Also see Schroeder's (1996) discussion of the changes and continuities in the organization of organized violence (political and criminal) in Nicaragua in the 1920s and 1930s.

10 In the period between 2002 and 2010, the prison population in El Salvador quadrupled from 6,000 to 23,800 (Gomez Hecht, 2013, 143).

11 Author's interview with NGO worker Soyapango, November 2017.

12 See *La clica FLS habría asesinado a ganadero de Nueva Concepción*, in elsalvador.com, 16 January 2009, online available at http://archivo.elsalvador.com/mwedh/nota/nota_completa.asp?idCat=6364&idArt=3239371

13 Fieldwork notes, Nueva Concepción, February 2017.

14 Ibid.

15 Interview religious leader, neighbourhood 22 de Abril, Soyapango, November 2017.

16 Fieldwork notes.

17 Private correspondence with Wim Savenije.

18 Author's interview with interviewee #22, Nueva Concepción, February 2017.

19 Allegedly, the leaders who had agreed to sign a truce had received government funds.

20 Author's interview with interviewee #1, Nueva Concepción, February 2017.

21 Ibid.

22 Author's interview, 22 de Abril, November 2017. This was also reported in other neighbourhoods with a high gang presence in AMSS, for example, in Mejicanos (source).

23 This is particularly the case in neighbourhoods with a more stable and better-organized gang presence, where gang members (have to) respect local residents.

24 For example, Moser and Winton, 2002 (who distinguish between economic, social, political and institutional violence) and Krause, Gilgen, and Muggah, eds. (2011, in Krause, 2012, 43) who distinguish between organized and interpersonal violence, each with its own subdivisions.

25 Furthermore, the authors differentiate between the type of violence used vis-à-vis each group (from homicides, to intimidation and extortion) and how the violence is used (selective or indiscriminate, visible or invisible).

26 Berg and Carranza (2018) look at the functions of violence that can explain the logic of 'territorial control': competitive violence vis-à-vis other armed groups to protect their turf; coercive violence, directed at residents of a territory or state officials to influence their behaviour; and exploitative violence to extract resources from the population (p. 569). However, as argued in the introduction of this chapter, categorizing violence on the basis of broader functions is problematic as the different functions can blur; for example, coercive violence also serves the objective to control turf. I therefore propose to distinguish between immediate functions of violent acts and strategic objectives of actors that have a capacity to use violence.

References

Achterhuis, H., 2002, 'Violent Utopias', *Peace Review* 14(2): 157–164.

Achterhuis, H., 2008, *Met Alle Geweld*, Rotterdam: Lemniscaat.

Arias, E., 2013, 'The Impacts of Differential Armed Dominance of Politics in Rio de Janeiro, Brazil', *Studies in Comparative International Development* 48: 263–284.

Arias, E., 2017, *Criminal Enterprises and Governance in Latin America and the Caribbean*, Cambridge: Cambridge University Press.

Berg, L. A. and Carranza, M., 2018, 'Organized Criminal Violence and Territorial Control: Evidence from Northern Honduras', *Journal of Peace Research* 55(5): 566–581.

Bourgois, P., 2001, 'The Power of Violence in War and Peace: Post-Cold War Lessons from El Salvador', *Ethnography* 2(1): 5–34.

Carballo, W. C., 2014, *The Truce and Everyday Life in a Violence-Free Municipality: The Case of Santa Tecla in El Salvador*, Violence Research and Development Papers 11, Bielefeld: University of Bielefeld, www.uni-bielefeld.de/icvr/docs/carballo.pdf.

Cramer, C., 2006, *Civil War Is Not a Stupid Thing: Accounting for Violence in Developing Countries*, London: Hurst & Company.

Cruz, M., 2011, 'Criminal Violence and Democratization in Central America: The Survival of the Violent State', *Latin American Politics and Society* 53(4): 1–33.

Cruz, M., et al, 2007, *Street Gangs in Central America*, San Salvador: Universidad Centroamericana.

Decesare, D., 1998, 'The Children of War: Street Gangs in El Salvador', *NACLA Report on the Americas* 32(1): 21–29.

Durán-Martínez, A., 2015, 'To Kill and Tell? State Power, Criminal Competition, and Drug Violence', *Journal of Conflict Resolution* 59(8): 1377–1402.

Eisner, M. 2009, 'The Uses of Violence: An Examination of Some Cross-Cutting Issues', *International Journal of Conflict and Violence* 3(1): 40–59.

Geneva Declaration, 2008, *Global Burden of Armed Violence*. Geneva: Geneva Declaration Secretariat.

Goi, L., 2017, 'Tensions Rise over Dissident MS13 Faction in El Salvador', *Insight Crime*, 28 April, www.insightcrime.org/news-briefs/tensions-rise-over-dissident-ms13-faction-in-el-salvador.

Gomez Hecht, J., 2013, 'El Crimen Organizado en las Cárceles: Las Extorsioines desde los Centros Penales en El Salvador (2008–2009)', *Revista Policía y Seguridad Publica* 3(1).

INCIDE, 2016, *El Salvador: Nuevo patrón de violencia, afectáación territorial y respuesta de las comunidades (2010–2015)*, San Salvador: Instituto Centroamericano de Investigaciones para el Desarrollo y el Cambio Social (INCIDE).

International Crisis Group (ICG), 2017, *Mafia of the Poor. Gang Violence and Extortion in Central America*, Latin America Report 62, 6 April 2017, Brussels: International Crisis Group.

Kalyvas, S., 2006, *The Logic of Violence in Civil War*, Cambridge: Cambridge University Press.

Krause, K., 2012, 'Hybrid Violence: Locating the Use of Force in Postconflict Settings', *Global Governance* 18: 39–56.

Krause, G. E. and Muggah, R. (eds.), 2011, *Global Burden of Armed Violence 2011: Lethal Encounters*, Cambridge: Cambridge University Press.

Lemarchand, R., 2009, *The Dynamics of Violence in Central Africa*, Philadelphia, PA: University of Pennsylvania Press.

Lessing, B., 2015, 'Logics of Violence in Criminal War', *Journal of Conflict Resolution* 59(8): 1486–1516.

Levenson, D., 2013, *Adiós Niño. The Gangs of Guatemala City and the Politics of Death*, Durham: Duke University Press.

Moser, C. and Winton, A., 2002, *Violence in the Central American Region: Towards an Integrated Framework for Violence Reduction*, Working Paper 171, London: Overseas Development Institute.

Pansters, W. G., 2015, '"We Had to Pay to Live!" Competing Sovereignties in Violent Mexico', *Conflict and Society* 1: 144–164.

Paris, R., 2004, *At War's End*, Cambridge: Cambridge University Press.

Penglase, B., 2009, 'States of Insecurity: Everyday Emergencies, Public Secrets and Drug Trafficker Power in a Brazilian *Favela*', *PoLAR* 32(1): 47–63.

Savenije, W., 1997, *22 de Abril. Collectief handelen en conflicten in een Salvadoraanse wijk*. MA thesis, Utrecht University, mimeo.

Savenije, W., 2009, *Maras y Barras. Pandillas y violencia juvenil en los barrios marginales de Centroamérica*, San Salvador: FLACSO.

Savenije, W. and van der Borgh, C., 2004, 'Youth Gangs, Social Exclusion and the Transformation of Violence in El Salvador', in Koonings, K. and Kruijt, D. (eds.), *Armed Actors: Organised Violence and State Failure in Latin America* (pp. x–x), London: Zed Books.

Savenije, W. and Andrade-Eekhoff, K., 2003, *Conviviendo en la orilla: exclusion social y violencia en el area metropolitan de San Salvador*, San Salvador: FLACSO.

Savenije, W. and van der Borgh, C., 2015, 'San Salvador: Violence and Resilience in Gangland – Coping with the Code of the Street', in Koonings, K. and Kruijt, D. (eds.), *Violence and Resilience in Latin American Cities* (pp. 90–107), London: Zed Book.

Schroeder, M., 1996, 'Horse Thieves to Dogs: Political Gang Violence and the State in the Western Segovias, Nicarague, in the Time of Sandino, 1926–1934', *Journal of Latin American Studies* 28(2): 383–434.

Shaw, M., 2009, 'Conceptual and Theoretical Frameworks for Organised Violence', *International Journal of Conflict and Violence* 3(1): 97–106.

Shirk, D. and Wallman, J., 2015, 'Understanding Mexico's Drug Violence', *Journal of Conflict Resolution* 59(8): 1348–1376.

Silva, H., 2014, *Infiltrados. Crónica de la corrupción de la PNC (1992–2013)*, San Salvador: UCA editores.

Stephenson, S., 2013, 'The Kazan Leviathan: Russian Street Gangs as Agents of Social Order', *The Sociological Review* 59(2): 324–347. DOI: 10.1111/j.1467–954X.2011.02007.x

Tilly, C., 2003, *The Politics of Collective Violence*, Cambridge: Cambridge University Press.

Van der Borgh, C., 2019, 'Government Responses to Gang Power. From Truce to War on Gangs in El Salvador', *European Review of Latin American and Caribbean Studies* 107: 1–25.

Van der Borgh, C. and Abello Colak, A., 2018, 'Everyday (In)Security in Contexts of Hybrid Governance: Lessons from Medellin and San Salvador, Research Brief, LSE and Utrecht University', www.lse.ac.uk/lacc/publications/PDFs/ResearchBriefing-FINAL.pdf.

Wade, C. J., 2016, *Captured Peace. Elites and Peacebuilding in El Salvador*, Athens, OH: Ohio University Research in International Studies.

Walter, K., 2016, *La Muerte Violenta Como Realidad Cotidiana. El Salvador, 1912–2016*, San Salvador: AccessArte.

Wolf, S., 2017, *Mano Dura. The Politics of Gang Control in El Salvador*, Austin: University of Texas Press.

Zilberg, E., 2004, 'Fools Banished from the Kingdom: Remapping Geographies of Gang Violence between the Americas (Los Angeles and San Salvador)', *American Quarterly* 56(3): 759–779.

31

The making of Central America's street gangs

Sonja Wolf

Mara Salvatrucha (MS-13) and the Eighteenth Street Gang are associated with much of the contemporary violence in northern Central America. Both groups, however, originated in the United States, where they are considered two of the country's major Latino gangs (Diaz, 2009). Both gangs emerged in marginal neighbourhoods of Los Angeles where Mexican immigrant labourers and Central American refugees settled. Faced with everyday struggles of survival and integration, the children of some of these low-income families ended up joining a gang. In the United States, MS-13 has developed a reputation for spectacular violence, a notoriety that has been fanned by the media (Martínez, 2019). Gang suppression and deportations have helped spread MS-13 and the Eighteenth Street Gang across the United States and northern Central America (Müller, 2015). In El Salvador, Honduras, and Guatemala, *mano dura* (iron fist) policies fuelled gang growth and violence. Gang violence now contributes to the forced migration of Central Americans to the United States, where many of them hope to seek asylum. Increasingly, however, asylum-seekers are discouraged from even crossing the US-Mexico border (HRF, 2017), and undocumented immigrant youth are falsely labelled as gang members in order to render them deportable (Hlass and Prandini, 2018).

This chapter analyses how MS-13 and the Eighteenth Street Gang emerged and evolved, particularly in Central America. I argue that the "gang problem" did not undergo an inevitable transformation, but was manufactured through the intersection of three kinds of policies: US foreign policy; US immigration and refugee policy; and US and Central American gang policy. The chapter is divided into four substantive parts. The first examines the evolution of MS-13 and the Eighteenth Street Gang in Los Angeles and Central America. The second section analyses the political nature of the *mano dura* gang policies and their effects. The third part discusses the implementation and aftermath of a gang truce implemented in El Salvador between 2012 and 2013. The fourth section explores the gangs' territorial control and their relationship with state institutions and political parties. I conclude with some reflections on street gangs as a symptom of social problems and as a form of resistance against the conditions of social oppression that give rise to gangs.

The roots of Central America's "transnational" gangs

The social and political exclusion that, for decades, had marked Central America culminated in civil wars (Guatemala, El Salvador, and Nicaragua) and military rule (Honduras). The conflicts were prolonged partly because, at the height of the Cold War, the United States propped up ultraconservative, reactionary governments in the region in an attempt to thwart a perceived communist takeover in the Western Hemisphere. US administrations delivered essential economic and military aid to Guatemala and El Salvador, and maintained a military presence in Honduras to support the Contras counter-revolutionary forces in unseating Nicaragua's Sandinista government and to prevent El Salvador's Farabundo Martí National Liberation Front (FMLN) from taking power. During the war, El Salvador alone received $4.5 billion in military and other aid from the United States, as well as military training at the notorious School of the Americas (Gill, 2004; Hayner, 2011, p. 49). People hit hard by the protracted political violence fled north, in many cases to California, including an estimated one million Guatemalan and Salvadoran refugees (Coutin, 2011, p. 576). But they struggled to obtain asylum in a country that partnered with Central American regimes in suppressing guerrilla movements. The sanctuary movement, a network of congregations that formed in response to the United States' restrictive asylum policy, provided shelter and protection to Central American refugees (Perla and Coutin, 2010). Nevertheless, many families in exile were essentially compelled to live clandestine lives. In Los Angeles, the birthplace of Mara Salvatrucha (MS-13) and the Barrio Dieciocho (Eighteenth Street Gang), these refugees had little choice but to settle in impoverished, overcrowded neighbourhoods rife with crime and gang activity. In addition to encountering racial discrimination, culture shock, and language barriers, parents had to work long hours for paltry wages. The strains of undocumented immigrant life often gave rise to domestic abuse and child neglect, and youth experiencing this multiple marginality (Vigil, 2002) became affiliated with groups such as the Eighteenth Street Gang or formed their own gang, MS-13.

The United States has a long history of street gangs that dates back to the early 1820s (Howell, 2015). The aftermath of the American Revolution saw the arrival of large groups of European immigrants in New York City, then the principal port of entry to the country. The young metropolis received these low-skilled, low-wage labourers with woefully inadequate housing stock and public services, and the ensuing conditions of marginalisation gradually gave rise to crime and gangs (Howell, 2015). Over the coming decades, street gangs developed and expanded in the Northeast and other regions of the United States. Law enforcement, policy, and media narratives recurrently cast gang activity as a problem of immigrants. Indeed, the Chicago School, which pioneered gang studies in that country, supported this idea (Thrasher, 1927). Since the early days, however, gangs have been a marker of the socio-economic and demographic changes that American society has undergone (Hagedorn, 2008; Hayden, 2005). These transformations include not only economic restructuring, racial inequality, segregation, underfunded schools, and poverty (and the despair it produces) but also the impacts of ineffective immigration and criminal justice policies (Garland, 2009; Massey and Pren, 2012). This was no different when the major Latino gangs began to take shape.

From the 1920s onwards, Southern California's economic boom sparked an increase in Mexican immigration to the Southwest of the United States. The first Chicano (Mexican-American) gangs emerged in the 1930s in the Boyle Heights and Pico Gardens areas of Los Angeles (Howell, 2015). But the growth of Chicano gangs really picked up in the following decade. The controversial Sleepy Lagoon murder trial fostered resentment against Mexican-Americans and ended up unleashing a media-fanned moral panic about rising Mexican-American juvenile delinquency. The subsequent Zoot Suit Riots, prompted by racially motivated attacks on Mexican-American youth, led many young Chicano men to idolise the gang members who fought in the uprising (Delaney, 2006, pp. 53–56). The emergence of the Eighteenth Street Gang in the 1960s was followed, in the 1980s, by the formation of Mara Salvatrucha in the Pico-Union area of Central Los Angeles (Fogelbach, 2010–2011). Like earlier generations of street gangs, both groups developed in response to the discrimination and victimisation of marginalised immigrant youth (Ward, 2013). Both gangs have since spread throughout the United States and the Northern Triangle of Central America. Law enforcement estimates once put their numbers at tens of thousands of members worldwide. But the US National Gang Intelligence Centre, which last published its *National Gang Report* in 2015 (NGIC, 2015), has, for unknown reasons, stopped providing disaggregated gang membership figures. In the past, these estimates had been questioned, since states may rely on different definitions of gangs and gang members (Finklea, 2018). The criteria for gang definition and gang member identification vary widely, making gang membership notoriously hard to track. There is a striking difference, for example, between critical social science research that sees gangs as amorphous youth groups adapting to changing socio-economic conditions and law enforcement agencies, concerned with arrests and sentencing enhancements, which statically define gangs as intentional and cohesive delinquent groups (Hagedorn, 2008). The absence of transparent data makes it difficult to determine the size and scope of the gangs.

Domestically the United States has sought to tackle major Latino gangs predominantly through suppression (Greene and Pranis, 2007). For more than a decade, federal law enforcement has even been pushing for the application of federal organised crime statutes to street gang operations, notably the Racketeer Influenced and Corrupt Organisations (RICO) Act (Diaz, 2009). Such legislation provides for extended criminal penalties and targets gang leaders for arrest in order to induce the dissolution of the entire gang. To date, gang prevention and intervention programmes remain few and far between. They are typically carried out by non-profit organisations, such as Homies Unidos (Los Angeles) and Barrios Unidos (Santa Cruz), both run by former gang members (Guerra Vásquez, 2005; Hurtado and Sinha, 2016), and Homeboy Industries (Los Angeles), led by Father Greg Boyle (Freemon, 2008). Rare are government-supported comprehensive gang strategies, such as the Gang Reduction and Youth Development (GRYD) programme, implemented by the Los Angeles Mayor's Office (Urban Institute, 2015), and the Montgomery County (Maryland) Department of Health and Human Services' Positive Youth Development Initiative, which is administered by a former gang member and Barrios Unidos leader.

The United States' regional approach to street gangs is not much different. Law enforcement views the Eighteenth Street Gang and MS-13 as transnational organised crime groups with a presence as well as communication and financial ties spanning several countries (Finklea, 2018). The perception of gang networks embedded in immigrant communities and responding to a centralised command structure echoing the hierarchical structure of police organisations (Hallsworth, 2013), rather than of autonomous, loosely connected groups claiming a symbolic allegiance, informs the mistaken belief that the gang problem can somehow be uprooted with deportations (Zilberg, 2011). In addition to repatriations of foreign citizens, the United States provides security assistance to the Northern Triangle countries that is meant to improve information sharing and gang enforcement operations (Meyer, 2019).

The deportations since the late 1980s were stepped up after the 1996 Illegal Immigration Reform and Immigrant Responsibility Act (IIRIRA), which made crimes retroactively applicable for deportable subjects (Brotherton, 2018). These expulsions returned gang members to countries they barely knew and whose language they barely spoke. The street gang subculture they brought with them became a source of fascination for media hitherto unaccustomed to tattooed, flamboyantly dressed strangers, especially for local youth in search of identity and belonging. *Barrio* gangs existed in Central America since the 1960s (Levenson, 2013; Wolf, 2011). These territorial crews brought together disaffected adolescents who lingered at street corners, dabbled in drugs, and liked to party. But while they may have been a neighbourly nuisance, they never constituted a public security threat. The political violence focused everyone's attention on the armed actors. When the transitions to democracy began, the Central American countries directed their energies and resources toward rebuilding shattered infrastructure and economies, not toward what was then an incipient social problem. The peace accords that ended the wars in El Salvador and Guatemala mandated a series of institutional and socio-economic reforms that met with elite resistance and were only partially, if at all, implemented. Security sector reforms, which required the military to hand over public security responsibilities to newly created civilian police forces, coincided with spiralling violent crime. Back then, the mainstream press virtually glamorised the gang lifestyle, noting how the deportees embodied power and status for alienated teenagers (Valencia, 2018, p. 36). Lacking desperately needed reinsertion opportunities, the returning gang members fell back on the social support networks they were familiar with. Existing gangs dissolved or were absorbed by the Eighteenth Street Gang and Mara Salvatrucha, which both began to grow and, in the following decade, to develop in unintended ways. In 2005, the Eighteenth Street Gang in El Salvador split into two rival factions, Sureños and Revolucionarios (Martínez and Sanz, 2014).

Gang members initially fought their rivals with knives and homemade weapons. Gradually they moved to using commercial firearms capable of inflicting more lethal violence, and both the use and sale of drugs became more habitual. In the socially disorganised neighbourhoods of the capital cities and other major urban centres where the gangs were concentrated, they became a growing source of insecurity for local residents. As the gang presence became more perceptible, interest in gang studies grew. The University Institute of Public Opinion (IUDOP) at San Salvador's Jesuit University spearheaded much of this research. This included, notably, a gang survey that employed gang members as co-investigators and the *Maras and pandillas in Central America* series that examined gang development, social capital deficits in gang-affected communities, and responses to gangs in the region (ERIC, IDESO, IDIES, IUDOP, 2001, 2004; ERIC, IDIES, IUDOP, NITLAPAN-DIRINPRO, 2004; Cruz, 2006). These studies began a tradition of gang research that, at least in the case of El Salvador, continues to this day (Rosen and Cruz, 2019). Police responded to gang activity through standard law enforcement. Their chief concern at the time was not street gangs but criminal groups, often comprising demobilised fighters, which carried out armed robberies and kidnappings. It was abundantly clear from these developments that Central American countries had long lacked a coherent gang policy that saw the gang not just as a crime problem but as a social problem emerging from a specific socio-historical context.

Mano dura: the politics of violence

In the early 2000s, the Northern Triangle governments launched *mano dura* (iron fist) policies, ostensibly to crack down on street gangs and homicides. The strategies entailed graffiti removal, joint police/military anti-gang squad patrols, and neighbourhood sweeps to round up suspected gang members, often in the presence of journalists who filmed and photographed this display of force. Honduras and El Salvador even adopted anti-gang legislation that criminalised gang membership and permitted the police to arrest gang youth based on symbolic identifiers, such as tattoos or clothing (Jütersonke et al., 2009). Many of the arrested were released for lack of evidence of a criminal offense, but even so, gang-related mass arrests exacerbated the overcrowding of Central America's decaying and poorly managed prisons. The *mano dura* policies, launched largely with electoral objectives in mind, were penal populist strategies that offered seemingly simple solutions (arrest and incarceration) to a complex problem (gangs as a symptom of social exclusion). The policies enjoyed widespread popular backing, at least as long as the public could be convinced that gang suppression was essential and effective (Wolf, 2017).

Media coverage was instrumental in raising the visibility of gang enforcement operations and in shoring up public support for an abusive, and ultimately counterproductive, approach to gang violence reduction (Wolf, 2017). With their ties to Central America's economic elites, mainstream media companies are mostly unsympathetic to investigative journalism and make the news a for-profit business that relies heavily on routinised reporting and official sources (Wolf, 2019). Media coverage of gangs and gang policy dehumanised gang members, depicting them as categorically criminal and relentlessly violent individuals who were out to terrorise local communities. Gang development was portrayed as stemming from individual character deficiencies rather than structural dislocations. Gang prevention and intervention were dismissed in favour of a punitive strategy (Wolf, 2017). Unsurprisingly, these understandings of gangs, and of the factors contributing to their growth, made some policy interventions seem more sensible than others. Surveys of security perceptions, most systematically conducted in El Salvador, showed that media messages were critical in shaping public opinion on the subject. Media content influenced people to think that street gangs had become a national problem and that *mano dura* policies were successfully diminishing gang violence, even when evidence to the contrary was mounting (Wolf, 2017).

Gang suppression was accompanied by a notable spike not only in homicides but also in extortion (Cruz, 2010). Gang youth abandoned the practice of soliciting voluntary contributions in their neighbourhoods and began demanding large, regular payments, initially only from transport companies, in order to support imprisoned gang members and their families. The groups toughened their recruitment process and asked their members to avoid visible tattoos and dress more conventionally (Aguilar Villamariona, 2006). Women's roles shifted from gang members to one of girlfriends, mothers, or nannies, or to one of gang collaborators who help collect extortion fees or smuggle drugs and firearms (Santacruz Giralt and Ranum, 2010, pp. 206–211). The detention of gang members in segregated prisons, a decision that was meant to reduce inter-gang conflict, allowed gang members to connect and socialise more than in the past. This helped the groups become more cohesive and strengthen their leadership structures. Crimes, often planned and ordered from behind bars, were committed by street-based gang youth with increasingly indiscriminate and brutal violence.

The *mano dura* strategy provoked resistance from political opposition parties and civil society groups which condemned the human rights violations and criticised the lack of a comprehensive gang policy. Some NGOs pushed for gang policy reform; others modelled gang prevention and intervention programmes they felt governments ought to implement. Homies Unidos-El Salvador was, until a lack of funding forced its closure in 2012, the only organisation run by and for gang members in the country. It worked to defend the human rights of gang members and also pioneered the idea of helping them access jobs and social services in order to encourage their desistance from active gang life (Wolf, 2017). Gang members and their families periodically protested the adoption of anti-gang legislation and especially the abysmal prison conditions (Aguilar, 2010). In addition to severe overloading and a crumbling infrastructure, these included unpalatable food, inadequate hygiene and medical services, and the glaring absence of genuine rehabilitation programmes. By 2006, the *mano dura* strategy was abandoned in name, but not in practice, when the violence it kindled incurred a political cost that governments were, for some time, unprepared to assume (Cruz, 2011). Despite continuing high rates of violence, much of it related to the presence of gangs (UNODC, 2019), in Honduras and Guatemala, street gangs have since been displaced from the public agenda by issues such as electoral fraud, the killings of human rights defenders, public corruption, and the fight against impunity. Not so in El Salvador. There gang violence remains a major concern, as does the war on gangs that was unleashed, paradoxically, by ostensibly leftist FMLN governments in power between 2009 and 2019.

El Salvador's gang truce (2012–2013)

The Northern Triangle countries have, over the years, seen a series of inchoate attempts to nego-tiate gang truces. The most advanced ceasefire, and the one with the most potential to achieve a sustainable reduction in gang violence, was approved by the Mauricio Funes administration (2009–2014). Funes, a former television journalist, ran on the FMLN ticket and helped secure that party its first presidential victory. Acknowledging the adverse effects of *mano dura* policies, his government pledged to take a radically different approach to crime and gangs with a National Policy of Justice, Public Security, and Coexistence (MJSP, 2010). But financing problems of this plan, an unexpected homicide spike in late 2009, and charges of incompetence by the media and the private sector intensified pressures to resume a punitive strategy. The mid-2010 Mejicanos massacre, which saw Dieciocho members riddle one bus with bullets and set fire to another and injure and kill almost two dozen passengers (Wolf, 2010), added to the government's hardening stance on gangs. That same year, new anti-gang legislation was adopted. Amid growing differences between Funes and the FMLN, in late 2011, the president replaced Security Minister Manuel Melgar with General David Munguía Payés, hitherto the defence minister. Melgar, a former guerrilla commander whom the United States considers responsible for a war-time attack that killed US military personnel, had delivered disappointing results. Munguía Payés was given a free hand to reduce homicides by any means necessary and spoke of stamping out the gangs (Sanz and Martínez, 2012). But El Salvador's cycle of violence was temporarily disrupted by a gang truce.

In March 2012, *El Faro*, a digital newspaper committed to investigating issues such as organ-ised crime and public corruption, published the first of a series of pieces on the ceasefire (Martínez et al., 2012). *El Faro* claimed that the government had negotiated the agreement to lower the murder rate, a deal which reportedly included generous cash payments to gang lead-ers. But the exposé came at a time when the truce mediators had yet to create strong political leadership and a communication strategy to connect with the public. In 2011, the Organisa-tion of American States (OAS) had conducted a security sector assessment and concluded that, without a different approach to street gangs, El Salvador would not find peace. After discussing its review with the government later that year, the OAS was invited to observe and verify the gang mediation process (Blackwell, 2015). Working alongside local mediators, the team saw a pause in the violence as a necessary first step toward dialogue and social opportunities for gang members and communities.

As part of this process, incarcerated historical gang leaders were transferred to lower-security prisons. Communications between these leaders and street-based gang members had been cur-tailed by the *mano dura* policies, and restoring these links was deemed vital to encouraging adherence to the truce. Gang leaders recognised that the violence had been hurting families and communities and hoped to return the gangs to their identity-based origins.[1] They asked for a repeal of the anti-gang law, an end to police harassment, improved prison conditions, and social opportunities (Cruz, 2019). In return, the gangs carried out symbolic disarmaments and com-mitted to ceasing violence and recruitment and to disclose the location of clandestine graves. The Delegation of the European Union supported the process, but the United States Embassy boycotted it (Van der Borgh and Savenije, 2019). Federal law enforcement agencies worried about the consequences of a truce, and the United States Department of the Treasury (USDT, 2012) even designated MS-13 a significant transnational criminal organisation. This designation makes it illegal for US citizens to deal with its members and hampers the implementation of US grant-reliant reinsertion projects.

The truce coincided with a sharp decline in homicides, from a daily average of 14 to 5 mur-ders (Martínez, 2013). In the communities where the ceasefire was implemented, the respite in violence allowed people to slowly start to live again.[2] The gangs, however, maintained their territorial control and refused to give up extortion in the absence of alternative sources of income. Salvadoran society remained sceptical of the truce, partly because of its perceived lack of transparency (IUDOP, 2013) and partly because of generalised distrust toward both the gangs and the FMLN. After about a year, the mediation process crumbled amid ongoing difficulties to build the required political and public support. President Funes endorsed the truce and claimed credit for a lowered homicide rate. But he consistently distanced himself from the dialogue with the gangs and did not help make it work.[3] The truce provoked disagreements in the FMLN, which thought the initiative constituted a weak electoral platform and had always viewed the gangs favourably as allies in its own electoral strategy but not as autonomous territorial groups.[4] These internal conflicts meant that Funes lacked the support of much of his security cabinet and FMLN-controlled ministries. In addition, party-connected sources in police intelligence provided *El Faro* with misleading information in order to sabotage the process.[5]

The ceasefire broke down amid difficulties to help gang members access education and job opportunities and faltering government support for gang integration once Munguía Payés, whose appointment as security minister was declared unconstitutional, had returned to the Defence Ministry. In the 2014 presidential elections, the Nationalist Republican Alliance (ARENA), the elite party whose administrations had launched the earlier *mano dura* policies, proposed to militarise public security and rejected negotiations with perceived criminal groups. This prompted the FMLN to also discard a gang truce. Soon after the main political parties had turned their back on a mediation process, the homicide rate spiralled to a daily average of 18 killings or an annual per capita murder rate of 103 per 100,000 inhabitants (Rentería, 2016), making 2015 the bloodiest year in the post-war period. Luis Martínez, the attorney general at the time, considered the gangs terrorist groups and began prosecuting individuals who had played an active role in the truce. *El Faro*, whose reporting may have contributed to the demise of the ceasefire, has since made the need for one a central part of its writings on violence and security. The current lack of political and public support for a gang truce, however, makes a restart of the earlier initiative unlikely in the foreseeable future. Nonetheless, engaging with gang members on how they can be part of society without resorting to violence not only permits a more nuanced understanding of their subjective experiences but is indispensable for the creation of alternative restorative justice and security policies that could allow communities to come together and heal.

The government of President Salvador Sánchez Cerén (2014–2019) committed, at least on paper, to the same comprehensive security policy as his predecessor (CNSCC, 2015). It carried out some limited social prevention (ICG, 2017) and continued previous efforts at improved prison management and prisoner rehabilitation and social reintegration (ICG, 2017). Mostly, however, the Sánchez Cerén government struggled with the complexities of the post-truce context. Police officers and soldiers not only have had to contain rising violence but have themselves been the targets of ambushes. Catching the victims off guard, the attacks are ostensibly carried out by gang members to resist suppression. The Sánchez Cerén administration responded to these attacks by declaring a war on gangs (Rauda Zablah, 2016). This latest offensive has seen police officers perpetrate abuses against youth in gang-affected communities (SSPAS, 2019). The most egregious human rights violations have been occurring in connection with "confrontations" between police officers and gang members, events that tend to cause few casualties among the former but a high number of fatalities among the latter. According to the official account, the law enforcement agents merely repel attacks. Human rights investigations (PDDH, 2019), however, point to a pattern of extrajudicial executions of gang-affiliated and non-affiliated persons, followed by crime scene cover-ups. The United Nations Special

Rapporteur for Extrajudicial, Summary or Arbitrary Executions found a six-fold increase in such killings between 2014 and 2016 (OHCHR, 2018). This state-sponsored aggression drives much of the violence but has done nothing to diminish the power of the gangs it has tried so hard to break.

Local power brokers

Over the years, the gangs have not only tightened their territorial controls but also transformed their relationship with state and government institutions and with political parties. In order to deter rival gang infiltration and attacks, gang members have established stricter controls over neighbourhoods and the access routes to them, for example, questioning people and checking their identity cards, thus restricting the mobility of those not from the area. These barriers obstruct merchandise deliveries, the undertaking of surveys, studies, NGO projects, and even the provision of government services. Students attending school in rival gang territories are vulnerable to threats or physical harm and often drop out of education. In the absence of the state, gangs have created alternative spaces of governance. In some communities, their members have sponsored parties, helped build sports fields and carry out cleaning and health campaigns, or even mediated conflicts (Murcía, 2015, pp. 24–25).

Increasingly, the gang presence is a factor for internal displacement and forced migration (Cantor, 2016). Those who refuse gang demands, such as recruitment, extortion payments, or romantic relationships, and work in or with law enforcement have little choice but to flee from their homes. This drop-by-drop displacement of individuals or families, but rarely of entire communities, has remained relatively invisible. Its magnitude has not been systematically measured (IDMC, 2019), nor have adequate victim assistance and protection programmes been put in place (Cristosal, 2019). The governments of El Salvador and Guatemala have been loath to acknowledge that forced displacement due to violence is even occurring (Fundación Heinrich Böll, 2019), for admitting as much would be a tacit acknowledgement that the state has lost much of its territorial control and ability to safeguard the population. Civil society activism, particularly strategic litigation (Cristosal, 2018), has raised the media visibility of the issue. But this advocacy has yet to help achieve the implementation of more effective policies addressing the security-development-migration nexus.

The direct or indirect influence of gangs in state institutions, especially the security sector as well as the criminal justice and prison system, has become a growing concern. Gang members have been found to be working in the police academy, the police, and the Armed Forces. But state agents, who often live in gang-affected neighbourhoods, are also threatened or bribed into collaborating with gang members. Such ties permit gang members to get training, acquire uniforms, firearms and ammunition, and obtain intelligence, expose protected witnesses and sabotage law enforcement operations. In Honduras, police, prosecutors, and judges have colluded with gang members (*El Heraldo*, 2016), whereas in Guatemala, mid- and senior-level police and military officers have been arrested for leaking information to gang members or laundering money for them (Puerta, 2018). El Salvador's former police chief Ricardo Menesses was dismissed for gang and drug trafficking ties (Silva Ávalos, 2018). Although the scale of the problem is unclear, it was reported that the El Salvadoran Armed Forces expelled 638 of its members due to gang ties between 2010 (when such cases were first registered) and 2018 (Hernández, 2018). In 2018 alone, 547 officers resigned from that country's police force due to death threats and violence (Flores, 2019). While background checks seek to prevent the recruitment of gang members, they may inadvertently bar people from certain jobs simply for living in gang-affected communities or having gang members in their extended family.

The gangs have also developed relationships with local governments (across the political spectrum) and with political parties (particularly during election times). For example, in Aguilares, a town north of San Salvador, the local gang approached successive mayors to request access to workshops and jobs and to extort a monthly sum of several hundreds of dollars. Feeling they had little choice but to comply, the mayors diverted funds from construction projects and gave gang members jobs in public works.[6] In Apopa, one of the Salvadoran municipalities that participated in the gang truce, the ARENA mayor at the time permitted the local gang to use official vehicles to transport drugs and firearms and to spend public funds on gasoline and drug-fuelled parties (Huerta et al., 2017). Elías Hernández has since been convicted for illicit association and is considered an illustrative case of how politicians and gangs have collaborated for mutual benefit. For the gangs, this relationship brought money and jobs; for the mayor, it brought votes and a hold on power. Few cases have been as well documented as that of Hernández, but it is safe to assume that it is not an isolated one.

Since the demise of the gang truce, El Salvador's main political parties have adamantly rejected a return to any form of dialogue with the street gangs. In private, however, these same parties have negotiated access to gang-affected communities for electoral campaigning, most recently in the 2019 presidential poll. Moreover, since at least the 2014 presidential election, the main political parties have secretly paid off the gangs in return for their voter mobilisation (Lemus and Martínez, 2018). These agreements show that the parties are well aware of the influence the gangs wield through persuasion or intimidation and have understood how to use it to their advantage. At the same time, it is clear that the gangs have become inevitable social actors. Governments and political parties may be loath to acknowledge the gangs, yet the private meetings and pacts afford the gangs the very legitimacy they have been publicly denied. The fact that any involvement with the gangs is illegal under the current gang law, yet is in practice unavoidable, underscores the absurdity of the entire approach to gangs. The persistent denial of rights and opportunities will, in the end, be met with defiance and resistance, violently if necessary. Gang members' interests, abilities, and potential contributions might be put to better use if they were brought into the licit space.

Conclusion

The official narrative in both the United States and Central America has painted MS-13 and the Eighteenth Street Gang as criminal structures. This depiction makes gang suppression seem the necessary and only viable response. Yet, although the gangs have security ramifications, they are essentially a symptom of structural social problems that successive governments have failed to address. The reluctance to do so contributes, along with political and electoral interests in short-term security improvements, to the enduring preference for *mano dura* policies. Street gangs arise in communities marked by protracted exclusion, and some youth, if deprived of the means to live a dignified life, respond to these conditions by joining a gang. This is not to justify the injuries gang members inflict. Problematically, however, they tend to be seen foremost as perpetrators, when it is also essential to understand them as victims of structural and state violence. Directing the analytical gaze towards the reasons for gang membership helps recognise that responses that do not enable young people to heal and to integrate into society will never effectively reduce the violence and transform gang-spawning communities.

Former gang members have for many years been working for gang violence prevention. In California, Homies Unidos and Barrios Unidos are positive examples of efforts to heal community violence. In Central America, where there is less openness to gang peace-making and intervention, there have been few such organisations. In El Salvador, the local chapter of

Homies Unidos closed due to lack of funding, and OPERA's work came to a halt when its director was arrested in 2016 under a multi-country law enforcement operation targeting MS-13. Dany Romero, himself a former MS-13 member, had denounced extrajudicial killings of suspected gang members and was accused of using the NGO to attack the state (Mackey, 2016). As activists, former gang members face not only the stigma of past gang membership but also the suspicion that they remain involved in crime and violence. Both in human rights advocacy and in truces, gang members have important contributions to make yet often find it difficult to convince society that they are genuine about change. Truces are meant to reduce the violence so that safe spaces for dialogue can be created. They are meaningful initiatives, provided they incorporate legitimate social and economic opportunities for gang members. Those wielding political power have readily used the gangs for their own purposes but have been much less receptive to the idea of sharing resources with historically marginalised populations. Creating and maintaining spaces for dialogue about alternatives to gang suppression will remain challenging. But without such spaces, the violence will continue. Surely, this is not in any society's interest.

Notes

1 Interview with Paolo Luers, former truce mediator, San Salvador, 13 July 2016.
2 Interview with Adam Blackwell, former Secretary for Multidimensional Security, OAS, Washington, DC, 10 October 2017.
3 *Ibid.*
4 Interviews with Adam Blackwell, former Secretary for Multidimensional Security, OAS, Washington, DC, 10 October 2017; Paolo Luers, former truce mediator, San Salvador, 13 July 2016.
5 Interview with Paolo Luers, former truce mediator, San Salvador, 13 July 2016.
6 Conversation with Mario Girón, advisor to the mayor of Aguilares, 29 July 2016.

References

Aguilar, D. (2010) 'Pandilleros piden mejores tratos en las cárceles'. *Contrapunto*, 4 March. Available at: www.archivoscp.net/2008-2012/index.php/sociedad/75-categoria-sociedad-civil/2496-noticias-de-el-salvador-contrapunto.

Aguilar Villamariona, J. (2006) 'Los efectos contraproducentes de los planes mano dura'. *Quórum, Revista de pensamiento iberoamericano* 16, pp. 81–94.

Blackwell, A. (2015) *If the War on Drugs Is Over . . . Now What? Security without Easy Answers*. Victoria: Friesen Press.

Brotherton, D.C. (2018) 'Social Banishment and the US "Criminal Alien": Norms of Violence in the Deportation Regime'. *L'Année sociologique* 68(1), pp. 185–210.

Cantor, D.J. (2016) 'Gang Violence as a Cause of Forced Migration in the Northern Triangle of Central America'. In Cantor, D. and Rodríguez Serna, N. (eds.) *The New Refugees: Crime and Forced Displacement in Latin America*. London: University of London, pp. 27–45.

CNSCC (Consejo Nacional de Seguridad Ciudadana y Convivencia). (2015) *Plan El Salvador Seguro*. San Salvador: CNSCC.

Coutin, S. (2011) 'Falling Outside: Excavating the History of Central American Asylum Seekers'. *Law & Social Inquiry* 36(3), pp. 569–596.

Cristosal. (2018) *Visibilizar lo invisible. Huellas ocultas de la violencia. Informe sobre desplazamiento interno forzado por violencia en El Salvador en 2017*. San Salvador: Cristosal.

Cristosal. (2019) *Señales de una crisis: desplazamiento forzado interno por violencia en El Salvador, Guatemala y Honduras, 2018*. San Salvador: Cristosal.

Cruz, J.M. (ed.) (2006) *Maras y pandillas en Centroamérica: Las respuestas de la sociedad civil organizada*. Vol. IV. San Salvador: UCA Editores.

Cruz, J.M. (2010) 'Central American *maras*: From youth street gangs to transnational protection rackets'. *Global Crime* 11(4), pp. 379–398.

Cruz, J.M. (2011) 'Government Responses and the Dark Side of Gang Suppression in Central America'. In Bruneau, T., Dammert, L. and Skinner, E. (eds.) *Maras: Gang Violence and Security in Central America*. Austin, TX: University of Texas Press, pp. 137–157.

Cruz, J.M. (2019) 'The Politics of Negotiating with Gangs: The Case of El Salvador'. *Bulletin of Latin American Research* 38(5), pp. 547–562.

Delaney, T. (2006) *American Street Gangs*, 1st ed. Upper Saddle River, NJ: Pearson Prentice Hall.

Diaz, T. (2009) *No Boundaries: Transnational Latino Gangs and American Law Enforcement*. Ann Arbor, MI: University of Michigan Press.

El Heraldo. (2016) 'Investigan a cuatro jueces por nexos con la MS-13'. 1 March. Available at: www.elheraldo.hn/pais/935440-466/honduras-investigan-a-cuatro-jueces-por-nexos-con-la-ms-13.

ERIC (Equipo de Reflexión, Investigación y Comunicación), IDESO (Instituto de Encuestas y Sondeos de Opinión), IDIES (Instituto de Investigaciones Económicas y Sociales), IUDOP (Instituto Universitario de Opinión Pública) (eds.) (2001) *Maras y pandillas en Centroamérica*. Vol. I. Managua: UCA Publicaciones.

ERIC (Equipo de Reflexión, Investigación y Comunicación), IDESO (Instituto de Encuestas y Sondeos de Opinión), IDIES (Instituto de Investigaciones Económicas y Sociales), IUDOP (Instituto Universitario de Opinión Pública) (eds.) (2004) *Maras y pandillas en Centroamérica: Pandillas y capital social*. Vol. II. San Salvador: UCA Editores.

ERIC (Equipo de Reflexión, Investigación y Comunicación), IDIES (Instituto de Investigaciones Económicas y Sociales), IUDOP (Instituto Universitario de Opinión Pública), NITLAPAN-DIRINPRO (Instituto de Investigación y Desarrollo-Dirección de Investigación y Proyección Social) (eds.) (2004) *Maras y pandillas en Centroamérica: Políticas juveniles y rehabilitación*. Vol. III. Managua: UCA Publicaciones.

Finklea, K. (2018) *MS-13 in the United States and Federal Law Enforcement Efforts*. Congressional Research Service Report R45292. Washington, DC: Congressional Research Service.

Flores, R. (2019) 'Masiva renuncia de policías durante 2018'. *La Prensa Gráfica*, 11 February. Available at: www.laprensagrafica.com/elsalvador/Masiva-renuncia-de-policias-durante-2018-20190210-0300.html.

Fogelbach, J.J. (2010–2011) 'Gangs, Violence, and Victims in El Salvador, Guatemala, and Honduras'. *San Diego International Law Journal* 12, pp. 417–462.

Freemon, C. (2008) *G-Dog and the Homeboys: Father Greg Boyle and the Gangs of East Los Angeles*. Albuquerque, NM: University of New Mexico Press.

Fundación Heinrich Böll. (2019) *Políticas de Estado, desplazamiento forzado y migración: una mirada regional al norte de Centroamérica*. San Salvador: Fundación Heinrich Böll.

Garland, S. (2009) *Gangs in Garden City: How Immigration, Segregation, and Youth Violence Are Changing America's Suburbs*. New York: Nation Books.

Gill, L. (2004) *The School of the Americas: Military Training and Political Violence in the Americas*. Durham, NC: Duke University Press.

Greene, J. and Pranis, K. (2007) *Gang Wars: The Failure of Enforcement Tactics and the Need for Effective Public Safety Strategies*. Washington, DC: Justice Policy Institute.

Guerra Vásquez, G.A. (2005) 'Homies Unidos: International Barrio warriors waging peace on two fronts'. In Maira, S. and Soep, E. (eds.) *Youthscapes: The Popular, the National, the Global*. Philadelphia, PA: University of Pennsylvania Press, pp. 103–118.

Hagedorn, J. (2008) *A World of Gangs: Armed Young Men and Gangsta Culture*. Minneapolis, MN: The University of Minnesota Press.

Hallsworth, S. (2013) *The Gang and Beyond: Interpreting Violent Street Worlds*. New York: Palgrave Macmillan.

Hayden, T. (2005) *Street Wars: Gangs and the Future of Violence*. New York: The New Press.

Hayner, P.B. (2011) *Unspeakable Truths: Transitional Justice and the Challenge of Truth Commissions*. 2nd ed. New York: Routledge.

Hernández, F. (2018) 'Ejército separó a 638 militares por vínculos con pandillas desde 2010'. *La Prensa Gráfica*, 29 November. Available at: www.laprensagrafica.com/elsalvador/Ejercito-separo-a-638-militares-por-vinculos-con-pandillas-desde-2010-20181128-0098.html.

Hlass, L.L. and Prandini, R. (2018) *Deportation by Any Means Necessary: How Immigration Officials are Labeling Immigrant Youth as Gang Members*. San Francisco: Immigrant Legal Resource Center.

Howell, J.C. (2015) *The History of Street Gangs in the United States: Their Origins and Transformations*. Lanham, MD: Lexington Books.

HRF (Human Rights First). (2017) *Crossing the Line: U.S. Border Agents Illegally Reject Asylum Seekers*. New York: HRF.

Huerta, F., Silva, H. and Dudley, S. (2017) *Symbiosis: Gangs and Municipal Power in Apopa, El Salvador*. Washington, DC: *InsightCrime*.

Hurtado, A. and Sinha, M. (2016) *Beyond Machismo: Intersectional Latino Masculinities*, Austin, TX: University of Texas Press.

ICG (International Crisis Group). (2017) *El Salvador's Politics of Perpetual Violence*. Brussels: International Crisis Group.

IDMC (Internal Displacement Monitoring Centre). (2019) *Painting the full picture: Persistent data gaps on internal displacement associated with violence in El Salvador, Guatemala and Honduras*. Geneva: IDMC.

IUDOP (Instituto Universitario de Opinión Pública). (2013) *Los salvadoreños y salvadoreñas evalúan el cuarto año de gobierno de Mauricio Funes. Boletín de prensa Año XXVII, No. 1*. San Salvador: IUDOP.

Jütersonke, O., Muggah, R. and Rodgers, D. (2009) 'Gangs, Urban Violence, and Security Interventions in Central America'. *Security Dialogue* 40(4–5), pp. 373–397.

Lemus, E. and Martínez, C. (2018) 'Testigo de Operación Cuscatlán: la MS-13 compró cocaína con el dinero que entregó Neto Muyshondt'. *El Faro*, 28 February. Available at: https://elfaro.net/es/201802/salanegra/21521/Testigo-de-Operación-Cuscatlán-la-MS-13-compró-cocaína-con-dinero-que-entregó-Neto-Muyshondt.htm.

Levenson, D.T. (2013) *Adiós Niño: The Gangs of Guatemala City and the Politics of Death*. Durham, NC: Duke University Press.

Mackey, D.M. (2016) 'The U.S. government accused a Salvadorian human rights activist of gang activity. Now he's in jail'. *The Intercept*, 8 August. Available at: https://theintercept.com/2016/08/08/the-u-s-government-accused-a-salvadorian-human-rights-activist-of-gang-activity-now-hes-in-jail.

Martínez, C. (2013) 'El gobierno da la espalda a la tregua'. *El Faro*, 9 December. Available at: https://elfaro.net/es/201312/noticias/14157/El-gobierno-da-la-espalda-a-la-tregua.htm.

Martínez, C. and Sanz, J.L. (2014) 'El Barrio roto'. In Sala Negra de El Faro (ed.) *Crónicas negras desde una región que no cuenta*. Mexico City: Aguilar, pp. 28–86.

Martínez, Ó. (2019) 'La Mara Salvatrucha derrota a Trump en Long Island'. In Sala Negra de El Faro (ed.) *Crónicas desde la región más violenta*. Mexico City: Debate, pp. 227–250.

Martínez, Ó., Martínez, C., Arauz, S. and Lemus, E. (2012) 'Gobierno negoció con pandillas reducción de homicidios'. *El Faro*, 14 March. Available at: https://elfaro.net/es/201203/noticias/7985/Gobierno-negoció-con-pandillas-reducción-de-homicidios.htm.

Massey, D.S. and Pren, K.A. (2012) 'Unintended Consequences of US Immigration Policy: Explaining the Post-1965 Surge from Latin America'. *Population and Development Review* 38(1), pp. 1–29.

Meyer, P.M. (2019) *U.S. Strategy for Engagement in Central America: Policy Issues for Congress*. Congressional Research Service Report R44812. Washington, DC: Congressional Research Service.

MJSP (Ministerio de Justicia y Seguridad Pública). (2010) *Política Nacional de Justicia, Seguridad Pública y Convivencia*. San Salvador: MJSP.

Müller, M.M. (2015) 'Punitive Entanglements: The "War on Gangs" and the Making of a Transnational Penal Apparatus in the Americas'. *Geopolitics* 20(3), pp. 696–727.

Murcía, W. (2015) *Las pandillas en El Salvador: Propuestas y desafíos para la inclusión social juvenil en contextos de violencia urbana*. Santiago de Chile: Comisión Económica para América Latina y el Caribe.

NGIC (National Gang Intelligence Center). (2015) *National Gang Report 2015*. Washington, DC: Federal Bureau of Investigation.

OHCHR (Office of the High Commissioner for Human Rights). (2018) *Agnes Callamard, United Nations Special Rapporteur for Extrajudicial, Summary or Arbitrary Executions*. El Salvador End of Mission Statement, 5 February. Available at: www.ohchr.org/EN/NewsEvents/Pages/DisplayNews.aspx?NewsID=22634&LangID=E.

PDDH (Procuraduría para la Defensa de los Derechos Humanos). (2019) *Informe especial sobre las ejecuciones extralegales atribuidas a la Policía Nacional Civil en El Salvador, período 2014–2018*. San Salvador: PDDH.

Perla, H. and Coutin, S. (2010) 'Legacies and Origins of the 1980s US-Central American Sanctuary Movement'. *Refuge* 26(1), pp. 7–19.

Puerta, F. (2018) 'Arrest of colonel with MS-13 ties reveals sophisticated gang tactics,' *Insight Crime*, 24 April. Available at: www.insightcrime.org/news/brief/arrest-colonel-ms13-ties-reveals-sophisticated-gang-tactics/.

Rauda Zablah, N. (2016) 'Sánchez Cerén: "Aunque algunos digan que estamos en una guerra, no queda otro camino"'. *El Faro*, 7 March. Available at: https://elfaro.net/es/201603/el_salvador/18180/Sánchez-Cerén-Aunque-algunos-digan-que-estamos-en-una-guerra-no-queda-otro-camino.htm.

Rentería, N. (2016) 'Gang warfare in El Salvador pushes death rate to record'. *Reuters*, 21 January. Available at: www.reuters.com/article/us-el-salvador-violence-widerimage/gang-warfare-in-el-salvador-pushes-death-rate-to-record-idUSKCN0UZ1FK.

Rosen, J.D. and Cruz, J.M. (2019) 'Rethinking the Mechanisms of Gang Desistance in a Developing Country'. *Deviant Behavior* 40(12), pp. 1493–1507.

Sanz, J.L. and Martínez, C. (2012) 'Aplicaremos el método de pacificación que se usa en las favelas de Río'. *El Faro*, 26 January. Available at: www.salanegra.elfaro.net/es/201201/entrevistas/7374/.

Santacruz Giralt, M.L. and Ranum, E.C. (2010) *"Seconds in the Air": Women Gang-Members and their Prisons*. San Salvador: IUDOP.

Silva Ávalos, H. (2018) 'La depuración policial malograda por la administración Funes'. *Revista Factum*, 5 January. Available at: http://revistafactum.com/la-depuracion-policial-malograda-por-la-administracion-funes/.

SSPAS (Servicio Social Pasionista). (2019) *Informe de violaciones a derechos humanos 2018*. Mejicanos: SSPAS.

Thrasher, F. (1927) *The Gang: A Study of 1,313 Gangs in Chicago*. Chicago: University of Chicago Press.

UNODC (United Nations Office on Drugs and Crime). (2019) *Global Study on Homicide*. Vienna: UNODC.

Urban Institute. (2015) *Evaluation of the Los Angeles Gang Reduction and Youth Development Program*. Washington, DC: Urban Institute.

USDT (United States Department of the Treasury). (2012) *Treasury Sanctions Latin American Criminal Organization*. Washington, DC: USDT. Available at: www.treasury.gov/press-center/press-releases/Pages/tg1733.aspx.

Valencia, R. (2018) *Carta desde Zacatraz*. Madrid: Libros del K.O.

Van der Borgh, C. and Savenije, W. (2019) 'The Politics of Violence Reduction: Making and Unmaking the Salvadorean Gang Truce'. *Journal of Latin American Studies* 51(4), pp. 905–928.

Vigil, J.D. (2002) *A Rainbow of Street Gangs: Street Cultures in the Mega-City*. Austin, TX: University of Texas Press.

Ward, T.W. (2013) *Gangsters Without Borders: An Ethnography of a Salvadoran Street Gang*. New York: Oxford University Press.

Wolf, S. (2010) 'Public Security Challenges for El Salvador's First Leftist Government'. *NACLA Report on the Americas*, 7 July. Available at: https://nacla.org/news/public-security-challenges-el-salvador's-first-leftist-government.

Wolf, S. (2011) 'Street Gangs of El Salvador'. In Bruneau, T., Dammert, L. and Skinner, E. (eds.) *Maras: Gang Violence and Security in Central America*. Austin, TX: University of Texas Press, pp. 43–69.

Wolf, S. (2017) *Mano Dura: The Politics of Gang Control in El Salvador*. Austin, TX: University of Texas Press.

Wolf, S. (2019) 'Spoilers of the Peace: Elites and the News Media in El Salvador (1992–2019)'. *Estudios Interdisciplinarios de América Latina y el Caribe* 30(2), pp. 14–39.

Zilberg, E. (2011) *Space of Detention: The Making of a Transnational Gang Crisis between Los Angeles and San Salvador*. Durham, NC: Duke University Press.

32

A critical criminology of gangs and organized crime in Brazil*

Marcos Burgos

Between 2010 and 2016, ominous rumblings coming from the peripheries of Brazil's gang world should have been taken more seriously,[1] but the country and much of the world was fixated on developments in Rio de Janeiro, even more than usual. During this period, a timely expansion and territorial reconfiguration of Brazilian gangs was underway[2], mostly in the country's northern[3] regions. These shifts occurred under the radar until the drawn-out era of international sporting events ended in Rio. By this point, enmity triggered by a series of overstepped boundaries, power flexes, disses, betrayals, and other offenses had been festering for several months in the shadows of Brazil's criminal world. This led to Brazil's two largest gangs declaring war on each other in late 2016 after more than twenty years of non-adversarial relations. The rupture between Rio's *Comando Vermelho* (Red Command, CV) and São Paulo's *Primeiro Comando da Capital* (First Capital Command, PCC) should have sounded blaring alarms within Brazil's expansive public security apparatus, prison system, and the media, but hostilities peaked when all attention was geared towards the 2016 Olympic Games in Rio. The consequences of the split quickly became evident. Between October and November 2016, minimally reported prison massacres left nineteen inmates dead in the Amazon states of Acre and Rondônia. Then, on New Year's Day 2017, only a few months after the Closing Ceremony of the 2016 Olympics, simmering tensions erupted in a ghastly show of violence at an overcrowded prison (known as COMPAJ)[4] in Manaus, the capital of Amazonas, Brazil's largest state, located thousands of miles northwest of Rio. A then little-known gang called the *Família do Norte* (Northern Family, FDN) instigated a massacre that resulted in the deaths of fifty-six members of São Paulo's PCC, Brazil's largest and most powerful gang. Reprisal killings broke out between rival groups in northern prisons, resulting in almost 200 inmate deaths during the first three weeks of 2017 alone. During all of the massacres, widely circulated footage showed decapitated and dismembered inmates, as well as dozens more left charred beyond recognition.

Shocking displays of violence are nothing new to the world of crime and public security in Brazil. But the massacres and gang-related violence have become even more gruesome and geographically dispersed in reality and virtually, though digital technologies that now deliver horrifying media to a much wider audience than ever before[5], especially via WhatsApp[6], a ubiquitous messaging service in Brazil. Pirated DVDs of the carnage still sell out quickly on the streets of northern Brazil. Footage of dismemberments and grisly massacres and their widespread dissemination on social media have become emblematic of Brazilian prison-*favela*[7] gang life (Paiva 2019: 173–174)[8], similar to trends in narco-cultures elsewhere in Latin America, particularly Mexico. These incidents sent shockwaves through Brazil, where few had heard of the FDN and had no idea the PCC, headquartered 2000 miles southeast in São Paulo, were active in Amazonas state. Confusion and curiosity increased after news emerged that the nascent FDN was aligned with Brazil's oldest prison-*favela* gang, Rio's CV, leading to more questions on the poorly understood presence of criminal groups from Rio and São Paulo in northern Brazil.

The January 2017 COMPAJ massacre and ensuing violence alerted Brazilians, especially those in the more prosperous Southeast, to the new social and geographic structure of gang violence in their country and to the more dispersed security challenges Brazil now faces. The levels of violence in northern Brazil have become so intense that 2017 went down as the most violent year on record[9] despite homicide rates decreasing in São Paulo and Minas Gerais,[10] which together contain one third of Brazil's entire population.

The Southeastern states of Rio de Janeiro, São Paulo, and to a lesser degree Minas Gerais and the Federal District of Brasília hold political economic and cultural hegemony over the rest of Brazil. This regional dominance extends to the world of gangs and is one of the reasons that in recent years, smaller neighborhood and street gangs (often known as *quadrilhas* or *gangues*) have been consolidating into new statewide and regional *facções* (large gang collectives) to push back against *forasteiro* (outsider) gangs from São Paulo and Rio.

Since 2017, a flurry of mostly Portuguese-language publications have analyzed and attempted to explain the recent developments occurring in less familiar areas outside of Brazil's financial, media, and tourism-dominant Southeast region. Hardly anything has been published in English on the aspiring prison-street *facções* proliferating throughout northern Brazil during the last few years, and to date (early 2021), there has not yet been a proper critical examination of these momentous changes. This chapter provides a timely overview for English readers of the contemporary but evolving socio-spatial landscape of gangs in Brazil.[11]

Intense corruption, inequality, racism, and class struggles lie at the core of the current crime wars that every year destroy the lives of tens of thousands of poor mostly young black and brown men in Latin America and the Caribbean. This is clearly the case in Brazil, where historically entrenched racism, classism, and a notoriously violent and corrupt police, along with other powerful local, regional, and international forces, shape the world of gangs and public security responses to them. While the root causes are structural and to be properly understood need to be historically situated, this chapter affords little room for this type of critical analysis.[12] Thus, the following work is mostly descriptive, with an emphasis on the criminal groups and regions currently most affected by gang violence in Brazil.

In view of this, a main objective of this chapter is to shed some much-needed light on the large gangs (*facções*) active in northern states, where the highest levels of *facção*-related violence in Brazil now occur (IPEA 2019: 6–7). Northern prisons, *favelas*, and urban hinterlands, as well as hotspots in the Amazon forest and certain flashpoints along thousands of miles of mostly watery international borders, are now more relevant to understanding the challenges of gangs, crime wars, gun violence, and public security in Brazil than the *favelas* of Rio de Janeiro. In short, any contemporary study of Brazilian gangs and organized criminal groups (OCGs) should take the recent changes into account. For these reasons, this chapter focuses as much on gang activity in northern Brazil as in Rio and São Paulo, where the overwhelming majority of attention has been centered since Brazilian gang studies emerged in the mid-1980s (Zilli and Beato 2015: 77).

In the following, I discuss three aspects of contemporary Brazilian gang culture essential to an appreciation of their history and ongoing development: (i) translation and cultural contexts of the gang, (ii) a primer on Brazilian gangs, and (iii) the recent social reconfiguration and changing landscapes of gang violence.

I Translations and cultural contexts

The issue of translation relates to the considerable linguistic and cultural challenges in capturing the shades of meaning that develop out of the contexts and spaces where gang discourses are spoken. The history of Brazilian gangs and the mutable social geographies they inhabit are vastly different culturally and politically to those of their analogous counterparts in the United States, where the academic study of gangs originated, proliferated, and became the prevailing model of gang studies worldwide. The following examples illustrate simple but highly relevant distinctions.

In Brazilian Portuguese, *gangue* is adopted from the word "gang", as in US street or prison gangs, but is generally associated with smaller loosely organized criminal or delinquent groups (Zilli 2015: 466–467), as opposed to a *facção* (faction), which is a larger moderately to highly organized criminal group that often unites a collective or network of smaller groups (Paiva 2019), for instance, the title of a 2019 journal article by UFC[13] sociologist Luiz Paiva, "'There's No Gang Here, Only a Faction': The Social Transformations of Crime in Fortaleza, Brazil".[14] Variants of the quote, "There's no gang here, only a faction" are often iterated by members of the *Guardiões do Estado* (State Guardians, GDE), a prison-street gang in Ceará. Paiva adds that an interviewee in his GDE research emphasized the idea behind the catchphrase, the "days of *gangues* in Fortaleza are over, it's all *facção* now and everyone better show respect" (Paiva 2019: 170). Such a comment would make little sense in the United States, where gangs like the Crips, MS-13 (and its much larger rival Barrio 18), or the Latin Kings have tens of thousands of members each and exist within vast networks of criminal organizations, often operating transnationally in multiple countries. Aside from this issue of language, which is somewhat particular to Brazilian gangs, it is important to also consider the cultural setting in which Brazilian gangs emerge. I briefly underscore three related points: the absorption of small gangs into larger gangs, the specific Brazilian nature of the gang, and the role of toxic masculinity in gang formations.

My living experience and fieldwork across Brazil since 2000 indicate that small US-style neighborhood or street-corner gangs no longer exist on a significant scale in Brazil. Such gangs in Brazil have been, in large part, absorbed or swiftly crushed by more powerful groups like the PCC, FDN, or *milícia* gangs and the police. In recent years, particularly in northern Brazil, smaller street gangs have consolidated into new gang collectives (*facções*) to defend themselves against outsider gangs. Therefore, in the current context of Brazilian gangs, it makes more sense to speak of what Hagedorn refers to as institutionalized gangs (2008: 7–10), because there is no clear or convenient distinction between the large institutionalized gangs and OCGs. Hagedorn clarifies that if there is any constant in today's gangs around the world, it is their changing forms: how they can be categorized at one point in one way and then a few months or years later adapt or transform into something quite different (2008: 31).

There should also be more emphasis on studying gangs in locations where they have not been significantly influenced by back-and-forth migration to the United States. In Brazil, there is a need for research in places where active gangs were not formed in the United States and exported (or deported) and have not been strongly shaped by US prison and gang cultures. In other words, Brazil is a prime example of a country that has been minimally shaped by US gang culture and where most US-European gang theories do not neatly fit. While social class and state or regional identity are important, race, ethnicity, and national identity mean very little to Brazilian gangs.

Last, according to the United Nations, Brazil has the world's fifth-highest femicide rate.[15] Thus, Brazilian gangs exist in a violent world of toxic masculinity where the misogyny of larger Brazilian society is magnified. The few females who join male-dominated gangs almost always serve in subordinate roles. While female gangs exist (mostly in prisons), they are generally small, ephemeral, and not well known throughout Brazil. More research on female gangs and female gang members is much needed.

II A primer on Brazilian gangs

The history and numerous changes that transpired recently within the socio-spatial world of Brazilian gangs are impossible to fully cover in this short chapter. The following section briefly describes the four most dominant prison-street gangs in Brazil, including *milícia* gangs, which are briefly introduced as the most powerful and socially injurious (Chambliss 2010: 15–16) criminal organizations in Brazil. *Milícias* have often been considered sui generis groups in contrast to other prison-*favela* gangs, a position this work will suggest is now outdated.

i Comando Vermelho – the quintessential Brazilian gang

The Comando Vermelho (CV) is the quintessential Brazilian gang. With seeds planted in the late 1970s and rapid growth during the early 1980s, the CV was the first bona fide prison-street gang in Brazil (Leeds 1996: 52–57). More than other *facções*, the CV exemplifies Brazil's 1960s to 1980s military dictatorship from which it was born, in brutality, authoritarianism, and heavily armed structure. The CV also embodies the hedonism and bacchanal spirit stereotypical of Rio's Carnaval culture. The CV love to party, and the packed gatherings they host also increase their drug sale profits. When the CV lost control of Rocinha[16] to the ADA gang in 2004, it did not take long for many young people to complain that the parties were better before. When it won Rocinha back in 2017, the wild parties resumed, despite the presence of the impotent UPP.[17] Members of the CV and young residents of the *favela* communities they dominate invented a gang-oriented subgenre of *funk*[18] known as *proibidão* in the early 1990s.[19] *Proibidão* is the bedrock of Rio's famous all-night *favela* funk parties and serves as a source of *facção* and community news, propaganda, and memorial to departed *amigos* and to threaten and *esculachar* (diss) rivals. *Proibidão* is an integral part of *facção* life in all parts of Brazil, even among Rio's *milícia* gangs.

The CV is important for being Brazil's first organized drug-trafficking gang and for remaining the largest gang in Rio since its formation. Rio is also home to the *Terceiro Comando Puro* (Pure Third Command, TCP) and the *Amigos dos Amigos* (ADA) gangs. Both groups are significantly weaker than the CV, with the TCP regularly combining forces with *milícia* gangs and the PCC to combat the CV in Rio and beyond. Since late 2017, after losing Rocinha, the ADA has all but vanished from Rio's gang scene.[20] Both the TCP and the ADA are historically important gangs, with the former still a relevant *facção*.

In the early days, the CV did not have a name set in stone. According to André Torres, one of the core founders, in the beginning, the group called itself the Union Group (*Grupo União*), or just the Union (*União*). William Silva, the professor, claims at first it was called *os da Lei* or just *os Lei*, after the newly modified National Security Law (*Lei de Segurança Nacional*, LSN) that landed the members behind bars on a tropical island in the same section as recently arriving political prisoners.

Some important questions remain unanswered concerning the CV's origin and initial expansion. Accounts of the organization's history abound, some more rigorous than others, but most scholars agree on certain key points regarding the rise of the CV, emphasizing the fact that the group first emerged on *Ilha Grande* (an island off the coast of southern Rio de Janeiro) at the

Devil's Cauldron penitentiary (Cândido Mendes Penal Institution) in the late 1970s. On other details, however, such as how the CV was *really* founded and by whom; why the *Grupo União* (Unity Group), established evidently on collectivist principles dedicated to "Peace, Justice, and Liberty" for prisoners and the oppressed, quickly converted into the hyper-violent, highly capitalist *Comando Vermelho*; why the name of early CV member Rogério Lemgruber, who apparently was not among the core founders, was later included in the gang's official title (CVRL); when and under what circumstances the TCP (originally known as the *Terceiro Comando,* TC) emerged; how the ADA gang organized; and so on.

Until recently, the CV was Brazil's largest and most powerful prison-street gang. But by 2010, the CV had been engaged in a multifront war[21] and had sustained years of territorial losses, which, according to Feltran[22] and others, had always been the basis of the CV's power. The biggest loss came in 2004, when the CV lost Rocinha, the single most lucrative drug market territory in Brazil. When Rocinha switched from the CV to the rival ADA, it was a major financial loss for the CV. The ADA[23] and the TCP continued chipping away at the near hegemony the CV enjoyed from the 1980s through the early 2000s. By 2007, intense and sustained police operations from governor Sergio Cabral and José Beltrame's public security forces targeted Rio's gangs, with particular ire towards the CV and its stronghold, Complexo do Alemão. By 2009, after notable *favela* massacres and international outcry, Cabral's government shifted more towards the budding UPP community policing program. On the third front, the CV was also defending territories and often losing them to the rapidly expanding *milícia* gangs, particularly in Rio de Janeiro's West Zone.

The situation was quite different 275 miles southeast in São Paulo, with the PCC enjoying monopoly control of the state's prisons and streets by 2002. The CV might have set the "this ain't no *gangue*, we're a *facção*" standard that virtually all of Brazil's subsequent gangs aspire to, but by around 2010, they had been surpassed by São Paulo's PCC as the country's most powerful gang. While the truth likely lies in the depths of Brazil's underworld, one of the most common explanations for the CV-PCC rupture dates to 2013, when the CV prohibited the PCC from baptizing new members in the prisons of Mato Grosso, a mammoth state sharing a 560-mile border with Bolivia that is strategic to drug trafficking.

Both the CV and PCC operate nationally and transnationally in Colombia, Bolivia, and Paraguay, with the PCC also trying to make inroads into Argentina's criminal underworld. The PCC has become the largest criminal organization in South America, which says a lot about the steady decline of the once-dominant and hierarchical Colombian drug cartels. Both the CV and the PCC do business with drug trafficking organizations (DTOs) in Colombia that might or might not be linked to the FARC but are consistently labeled FARC by Brazilian authorities. The PCC also deals with Italy's 'Ndrangheta (among the most powerful OCGs in the world) and *supposedly* with Hezbollah.[24]

Members of these groups never hid their organized crime ambitions, but for years, certain influential scholars of Brazilian *favelas*, crime, and urban issues in general, as well as some dissident voices at high levels in law enforcement,[25] argued that the CV and the PCC operated like loose networks of prison-*favela* relationships centered around drug trafficking. They asserted that their structure was too amorphous and decentralized and lacked clear *facção*-wide leaders or the upper-level hierarchy necessary to be classified as organized criminal groups.[26]

However, gangs and OCGs have never been static categories, even if they have been defined as such. Rather, they come in various sizes, scales of power, and types of governing structures. Second, while the PCC has a larger reach and more money and, according to Lessing and Willis (2019: 1), is the most powerful prison gang in the world, no gang in Brazil, and probably no gang anywhere in the world, possesses as many soldiers with military-grade weaponry or is engaged in more frequent urban warfare than Rio's *Comando Vermelho*.

ii Primeiro Comando da Capital – São Paulo's criminal secret society

In *Neither War Nor Peace,* Dowdney (2005: 33–35) suggests that throughout the world, organized armed groups vary structurally, from the "militarized command structure" of Rio's drug factions, to the "corporate structures" of Chicago's institutionalized gangs, to the informal horizontal structure of Cape Town's Hard Livings gang. Combine these three formidable types of criminal organizations and then add to the mix the structure of a secret society (Feltran 2018), and one can begin to understand how São Paulo's PCC is organized.[27]

Since the late 1990s, sociologist and urban ethnographer Gabriel Feltran has closely studied the PCC and São Paulo's urban peripheries they control. Today he is one of the leading experts on the group. Feltran makes a convincing argument that the PCC is notably different from other gangs and OCGs in a number of important ways. For one, and in contrast to Rio's CV, the PCC is far more concerned with dominating markets (drug, arms, large-scale robberies) than controlling physical territories (Feltran 2018). Second, the PCC is notable for being the first Brazilian gang born in the era of liberal democracy (or neo-liberal, depending on one's perspective), in Latin America's largest city and most important financial center. It is not surprising that the PCC, while maintaining its prison-street gang presence and credibility, also operates like a multifaceted corporation (Feltran 2018). Third, the PCC is the only prison-*favela* gang still involved in large-scale armed robberies of banks, armored cars, jewelry stores, gold deliveries, and other valuable cargo. A sound argument could be made that the PCC and its *Novo Cangaço* affiliates constitute the most intense and sophisticated armed robbery gangs in the world.[28] Fourth, and one of the PCC's most important strategic characteristics according to Feltran, is how the PCC operates like a decentralized secret society, similar to a criminal version of the Freemasons in structure and thus impenetrable to outsiders (Feltran 2018).

Feltran's original description of the PCC's hidden and horizontal composition conjures up other cryptic nonhierarchical OCGs, like the *Camorra*, headquartered in Naples, Italy. The Camorra is among the world's best-known criminal secret societies, with an organizational structure notorious for being highly decentralized and horizontal, traits that have made it difficult to take down, unlike the severely weakened (since the 1990s) Sicilian Mafia (*Cosa Nostra*), with its traditionally hierarchical configuration. While the PCC and the Camorra are obviously distinct organizations headquartered in vastly different political economic, social, and cultural settings, they are also strikingly similar in certain key features. Feltran is correct to say the PCC are truly unique among Brazilian gangs, so future research on the PCC might benefit from comparison and contrast with the Camorra or other secretive OCGs outside of Brazil.

A final point worth mentioning: Biondi, Feltran, and others depict the informal social control exerted by the PCC in São Paulo similarly to how Skarbek describes the ways gangs provide informal governance in prisons in *Social Order of the Underworld*. For instance, the PCC is credited by Feltran and others[29] as responsible for "a radical reduction" of São Paulo's homicide rate by 70% since the late 1999s (Feltran 2020: 26). The PCC still has crime in Brazil's largest city on lockdown. For the last couple of years, São Paulo, which was one of the country's most violent cities and states in the 1990s, has had the lowest homicide rate in Brazil.

iii Família do Norte – the Amazon crime family

The *Família do Norte* is one of the most important gangs in the recent socio-spatial reconfiguration of OCGs in Brazil. Manso and Dias date the origin of the FDN to around 2006. At that time, the gang's future kingpins (then leaders of smaller, less organized Amazon gangs) were incarcerated in the Catanduvas Federal Penitentiary in the Southern state of Paraná, alongside

PCC inmates from São Paulo.[30] Manso and Dias[31] also suggest that inmates from Amazonas state, and other gang leaders throughout Brazil, who were incarcerated in remote federal prisons alongside longtime PCC and CV leaders, acquired specialized knowledge on organized crime from their São Paulo and Rio de Janeiro counterparts.

Still, the group's precise origins are obscure and even controversial.[32] What is known is that key FDN founders started out in a drug trafficking gang called the *Primeiro Comando do Norte* (PCN) or the First Command of the North.[33] The PCN was formed sometime around 2008, when groups of neighborhood drug dealers in Manaus joined forces. Until roughly 2015, the PCN was aligned with the PCC in Amazonas. That year, the dissenting PCN openly broke ties with the Sao Paulo–based gang because the PCC continued baptizing new members in Amazonas state despite warnings not to.[34] It was likely around this time that the PCN became known as the FDN, possibly because the *Primeiro Comando* part of PCN was too similar to the name of its former partners-turned-new rivals. From the start, the FDN had strong ties to the Rio's CV, and initially, it was known as the FDN-CV, but a glance at the recent local (Manaus) crime news online indicates that at some point during 2019, the FDN and the CV severed their relationship and are currently engaged in a bloody war in northern prisons, *favelas*, and working-class neighborhoods.

By 2014, Amazonas state had become a major battleground for Brazil's most powerful prison-street gangs. Early on, the FDN became known for its extreme violence, even among other violent *facções*. Over one weekend in July 2015, the FDN killed 38 members of two rival gangs, the PCC and a much smaller group known as the *Família Esparta 300*. Since its start, the FDN has executed more inmates in prison massacres than any other Brazilian *facção*. The FDN was able to grow powerful quickly mainly because of its strategic geographic location within the international drug trade. Amazonas state borders Peru, Colombia, and Venezuela, and the immensely important route of the *Rio Solimões* (the local name of the Amazon River) runs through the entirety of the behemoth state, from the triple border with Peru and Colombia to the confluence with the Rio Negro. The *Rio Solimões* is one of South America's key drug trafficking routes from the cocaine-producing countries of Colombia and Peru. The FDN is the main Brazilian gang that controls drug trafficking along the Amazon River.

Milícias

Hagedorn, who is wary of the traditional US-Eurocentric criminological typologies that tend to pigeonhole gangs into convenient classifications, offers an "amorphous" (2008: 31–34), more inclusive explanation of gangs, describing them (part of his broader definition on page 34) as "vigilante bands or violent tools of those holding state power" and stating that "no matter where gangs are located, they often change from one form to another, as they are influenced by other armed groups, causing the boundaries between formerly distinct criminal organizations to often fade away" (2008: 34). This certainly applies to Rio's *milícia* gangs, which have origins in Brazil's paramilitary death squads and vigilante extortion groups but today are no more paramilitary than the Zetas Cartel in Mexico.

Present-day *milícia* gangs operate like multifaceted cartels composed of powerful networks of corrupt former and current members of Brazil's security apparatus, along with an increasing number of former members of prison-*favela* drug-trafficking gangs. Critical gang studies would benefit from including groups like Brazil's *milícias* within the context of institutionalized gang and OCGs rather than continuing, as certain authorities do, to consider them paramilitary groups, a label that carries a more benign or semi-official–sounding undertone. *Milícias* are extremely corrupt, brutally violent OCGs that prey on poor marginalized communities and should not be confused in any way with the controversial but constitutionally legal US-style militias.

According to Benjamin Lessing, an expert on criminal conflict and organized armed violence in Latin America, in a recent interview in *O Povo* newspaper, the vast network of more structured and institutionally connected OCGs known as *milícias* represents a more serious threat to public security in Brazil than other prison-*favela facções* because, unlike the CV, FDN, or even PCC, the *milícias* tend to be more politically oriented criminal enterprises (Lessing and Willis 2019).[35]

Milícia-type gangs have operated as criminal organizations since the 1960s throughout Brazil, though until the early twenty-first century, most groups were much smaller and called by various names, such as *polícia mineira* in Rio de Janeiro (Zaluar and Conceição 2007: 91–95). Known as *milícias* since roughly 2006 (Misse 2018: 139), the term paramilitary or "parapolice" (Misse) is often used to describe *milícia* gangs because of the large proportion of their early members who came from careers in law enforcement, prison security, or fire fighting. Since *milícia* gangs exploded onto the scene in the early 2000s, there has been a strong tendency to view them as distinctly unique forms of underground organizations. But, according to Rafael Estrela of the Rio de Janeiro State Attorney's Office,[36] as well as several participants interviewed for my research, including a current CV member, the *milícias* in Rio should be viewed as *facções* or highly organized gangs. In Rio de Janeiro, the state most famous for *milícia* gang activity, Estrela argues that the paramilitary label is outdated, because the latest public security data shows that the majority of *milícia* members now come from drug-trafficking organizations.[37] Even Sergio Moro, Brazil's well-known conservative (and politically polarizing) former minister of justice and former *Lava Jato* federal judge (2014–2018), recently stated that *milícias* should be considered *facções criminosas* alongside the CV and PCC.

III Spatial reconfigurations and the current landscape of gang violence

New *facções* have proliferated in northern Brazil. This rapid increase has been in part because of the aggressive encroachments of São Paulo's PCC, and to a lesser extent Rio's CV, into northern prisons and working-class neighborhoods. Large northern gangs have also mushroomed because of the profits, or potential profits, from drug trafficking.

There was another unintended key factor that contributed to the significant sociospatial changes within Brazilian gangs and OCGs during the last several years, namely the 2006 creation of Brazil's Federal Penitentiary System (SPF).[38] Ironically, the federal prison system, which as of 2020 consisted of six maximum security facilities, was intended to distance Rio and São Paulo gang leaders from their communities and home state *facções* by isolating them in distant states, such as Paraná, Rondônia, Mao Grosso do Sul, and Rio Grande do Norte. Instead, the SPF functioned like a school for the leaders of smaller gangs from mostly northern states, where they learned *facção* organizational structure from PCC and CV kingpins.[39]

Northern *quadrilhas* and *gangues* consolidate into *facções*

With 14 murders a day in 2017, the homicide rate in the Northeastern state of Ceará more than quadrupled from 1998 to 2017[40] (and increased 545% in absolute homicide numbers from 941 to 5,134), with only 28% population growth for the same period. This dramatic rise in violence was caused by constant fighting among dozens of small drug-trafficking gangs in the early 2000s and later, as Luiz Fábio Paiva explains, due to gang wars that erupted after the PCC and CV split in 2016 (Paiva 2019: 176). Around early 2016, small gangs (*gangues* and *quadrilhas*) in Fortaleza consolidated into the *Guardiões do Estado*, now a large prison-*favela facção* with over 25,000 members in less than five years.[41]

There are five rather unusual aspects of the GDE worth noting. First, it is foremost a combatant gang like the CV. Second, its approach to war is political. Interviewed by Aquino and Sá, GDE members spoke of a kind of anti-colonialist movement toward the domination of the *forasteiro* (outsider) gangs. The very name Guardians of the State suggests protection of a local criminal dynamic against the threats of powerful crime *facções* of the Southeast, which, if not defended against, could end up appealing to criminally involved youth in Ceará. Third, like other new-era northern gangs, the GDE is composed of a proportionally larger number of teens and children than the CV or PCC, with the latter adopting official rules against baptizing minors.

As the name suggests, the GDE defends itself against the CV, which has had a presence in Ceará since the early 1990s. In 2019, the GDE ordered large-scale attacks on public property throughout Fortaleza, including firebombing buses, cars, and stores, in order to protest miserable prison conditions. The group increased its ranks after a GDE faction emerged from the PCC, when some former PCC members no longer wanted to pay the faction's monthly fee and felt that the PCC had too many rules. By contrast, the GDE understands crime as freedom, that is, doing what is prohibited by law, and therefore it makes no sense to be in a life bound by the rules of crime itself. The GDE is known for its revolt against established norms, including those of criminal subcultures.

In Rio Grande do Norte, the *Sindicato do Crime* (Crime Syndicate, SDC) was formed in 2013 in a struggle against the PCC and to protest against inhumane prison conditions (Melo and Rodrigues 2017: 52). The SDC is aligned with the CV. As has become a pattern, the SDC only became known outside of the region after a prison massacre in January 2017, a PCC reprisal attack for the killings in Manaus a couple of days earlier. State authorities knew an attack was coming but did nothing, allowing armed PCC members to slaughter rival SDC inmates, decapitating 15 of the victims. The result was 26 *official* deaths, though victims were removed in wheelbarrows in an assortment of mutilated and charred pieces. The state conducted no DNA testing, and families complain that many inmates remain missing (Melo and Rodrigues 2017: 50, 55).

One of the most curious developments of the new generation of Brazilian gangs is a group called *Okaida* (the Brazilianized pronunciation of Al-Qaeda) that hails from the Northeastern state of Paraíba and was engaged in a war with rival Paraíba gang *Estados Unidos* (United States) that began around 2011. Okaida (OKD) emerged in the years following the 2001 terrorist attacks in New York City and, like many of the new northern gangs, was initially aligned with the PCC in order to have access to the guns and drugs that it needed in order to grow. But as was the case in other northern states, the PCC's expansionist program eventually made it unwelcome. Okaida is among the new generation of Brazilian gangs that recruited new members and grew quickly by singling out *forasteiro* gangs as their most serious threat and CV and Estados Unidos backed by the PCC. Terrorism-inspired nicknames and themes are common in Brazilian *favela* culture, especially in *funk proibidão*.

Bahia and the Bonde do Maluco

Throughout Brazil, the "factionalization" of smaller Brazilian gangs into larger, longer-lasting, and better-organized prison-street *facções*[42] has been taking place over the last several years. But Arias and Barnes are correct to suggest that ultimately, criminal governance is distinct to each prison and community as well as the local-level social and political processes (2017: 13). For instance, as of late 2019, the state of Bahia was run mainly by six prison-street gangs from Bahia, the most powerful being the *Bonde do Maluco* (BDM), which is also active in Sergipe, Alagoas, and Goiás. The *Comando da Paz*, is the oldest gang in Bahia, and along with the *Kaitara* gang, is among the most prominent gangs in Bahia.

The Brazilian South

The South, often idealized within and outside of Brazil as the most *developed* and safest of the country's five official geopolitical regions, has seen a significant rise in violence, incarceration rates, and police killings in recent years.[43] Smaller street gangs merged into large *facção*-type organizations and into groups like the *Primeiro Grupo Catarinense* (First Catarinense Group – PGC) in the state of Santa Catarina[44] and *os Manos* (the Bros), *os Brasas*, *Bala na Cara* (Bullet to the Face), and *Falange Gaúcha* in Brazil's most southern state, Rio Grande do Sul.[45]

In recent years, important changes also occurred in Brazil's Southeast. Consequently, this chapter ends back in Rio, where I write from Rocinha, an *officially* "pacified" *favela* controlled by the Comando Vermelho.[46] From September 2017 until mid-2018, there was prolonged (on and off) war in Rocinha. The gang that had controlled the community since 2004 (the ADA) lost control to the CV after 13 years of dominating Rio's most lucrative drug market. Between September 2017 and March 2018, there were two people killed every week in relation to Rocinha's most recent drug gang war, and this is not counting the related deaths not reported that took place during the same period. Once among the largest gangs in Brazil, the formerly powerful ADA is now on the brink of extinction. Both the TCP and especially the CV have expanded in the wake of the ADA's rapid decline, but over the last several years, no Rio de Janeiro–based gang has expanded as rapidly as the *milícias*. By 2019, *milícia* gangs controlled illegal businesses in more *favelas* and working-class neighborhoods in Rio than either the CV or the TCP.

Conclusion

Today, Brazilian gangs exist in an era of globalized capital, continuously changing technologies, soaring inequality, political economic instability, porous borders, and displaced people and within increasingly transnational criminal networks. Dogmatic typologies, cultural assumptions, and US-European hegemonic academic generalizations are not constructive to researching and analyzing gangs around the world. In the past, scholars often drew clear lines between gangs and organized crime groups,[47] though Hagedorn cautions that underestimating gangs as disorganized local groups ignores the history of their diversity as institutionalized gangs, politically active or politically manipulated gangs, or, in the Brazilian case, the frequent transformations gangs make from groups of juvenile delinquents to organized criminals (2008: 24).

Thus, in Brazil, there are no clear boundaries between relevant street gangs and organized crime groups. Smaller street-corner gangs of the conventional US model that are restricted to individual neighborhoods or communities have been taken over by or morphed into larger *facções*. In addition, the long US tradition of street-prison gangs based on race and ethnicity is highly unprecedented in Brazil. Since roughly 2010, the powerful Rio de Janeiro– and São Paulo–based *facções* have made major inroads into the poorer, more isolated states of the Brazilian North and Northeast. Shortly after the Olympic Games ended in late 2016, the bloodiest gang war in Brazilian history erupted in the prisons, streets, and urban peripheries of northern states. While São Paulo and Rio de Janeiro are where the most influential and relevant gangs in Brazil emerged, is it now essential for scholars and policy-makers to better understand and focus greater attention and resources on the country's northern states, where a large portion of contraband enters and exits the country and where Brazil's highest levels of gang violence are currently located. Also crucial, in recent years, no gang has expanded as alarmingly as the politically connected and hidden in plain sight *milícia* gangs.

Notes

* This chapter is part of a larger ongoing study of inequality, corruption, crime, and violence in Brazil. Except for minor edits, it was completed between late 2019 and early 2020, before COVID-19 devastated Brazil. A proper analysis of the ways the global pandemic has affected gangs, OCGs, and public security in Brazil is beyond the time constraints of this work.

1 *Anuário Brasileiro de Segurança Pública: Edição Especial 2018*. Dias and Manso. 2018: 6–7. Fórum Brasileiro de Segurança Nacional.

2 See Manso, Bruno Paes and Camila Nunes. 2018. *A Guerra: a ascensão do PCC e o mundo do crime no Brasil*. Chapter 1, 5 paragraphs from the end, beginning with, "Pelas sombras, sem publicidade . . . ".

3 In this work, "northern" is a generic umbrella term referring to Brazil's official North and Northeast regions combined.

4 *Complexo Penitenciário Anísio Jobim* (Anísio Jobim Penitentiary Complex, COMPAJ).

5 See Manso, Bruno Paes and Camila Nunes. 2018. *A Guerra: a ascensão do PCC e o mundo do crime no Brasil*. Chapter 2, paragraphs 1–12.

6 See Feltran, Gabriel. 2018. *Irmãos: Uma Historia do P.C.C.* Chapter 6, paragraph 6, in section titled, "O SEGURO E AS POLÍTICAS DO CRIME".

7 Concisely, favelas are low-income historically oppressed informal urban communities, often referred to generically in English as slums.

8 The dehumanization permitted to take place in Brazilian prisons has created a form of banality of violence throughout Brazil. Since late 2016, amid prison riots, gang members have been filmed on multiple occasions playing soccer with victims' heads.

9 IPEA. 2019. *Atlas da Violência*. Page 5.

10 IPEA. 2019. *Atlas da Violência*. See chart on page 23.

11 Since 2001, several hundred recorded interviews have been conducted with gang members, the police, prison guards, politicians, bureaucrats, public security experts, investigative journalists, and other everyday citizens caught in the middle. Ethnographic data is bolstered by a long-running review of the literature and official documents and a systematic monitoring of relevant issues in the media.

12 A larger ongoing research project accentuates political economic corruption and inequality as elements fundamental to the world of gangs and crime in Brazil.

13 Federal University of Ceará.

14 *"Aqui não tem gangue, tem facção": as transformações social do crime em Fortaleza, Brasil*, translation by the author and slightly altered to more accurately reflect meaning than a literal word-for-word translation of the original title (Paiva 2019).

15 Located in Rio's South Zone and with a population of roughly 150 thousand, Rocinha is one of Brazil's largest favelas and the community where I have lived intermittently (approx. 14 years) since 2001.

16 The acronym (UPP) stands for *Unidade de Polícia Pacificadora*, or Police Pacification Unit. Though they have largely failed to meet their stated objectives, the UPPs, which were ostensibly intended to be a type of community policing program, are to date the most important public security intervention implemented in Rio's favelas.

17 Retrievable from < https://nacoesunidas.org/onu-feminicidio-brasil-quinto-maior-mundo-diretrizes-nacionais-buscam-solucao/ >. Last accessed Sept. 8, 2019.

18 Funk, which is minimally influenced by and very different than the US genre typified by James Brown or the Meters, is a uniquely Brazilian type of Miami bass and freestyle and the most popular type of music among young Brazilians. There are several subgenres of *funk*, such as *ostentação* (ostentatious), *funk carioca* or *favela funk* (Rio *favela* style), and *proibidão*.

19 For more on *favela funk* and its subgenre of *proibidão*, see Paul Sneed. 2019. *Machine Gun Voices. Favelas and Utopia I Brazilian Gangster Funk*. Seoul National University Press. Seoul, Republic of Korea. Chapter 1 of the Kindle version.

20 See "Death of a Rio Cartel", an in-depth investigative report by Cecília Oliveira and Yuri Eiras in *The Intercept*. 2018, December 13. Article retrievable from https://projects.theintercept.com/death-of-a-rio-cartel/. Link last accessed March 2021.

21 See Manso, Bruno Paes and Camila Nunes. 2018. *A Guerra: a ascensão do PCC e o mundo do crime no Brasil*. Chapter 8, paragraph 20, beginning with "As peças foram se movimentando . . . "

22 Feltran, Gabriel. 2018. *Irmãos: Uma Historia do P.C.C.* E-book, about one-third of the way through Chapter 3.

23 See "Death of a Rio Cartel", an in-depth investigative report by Cecília Oliveira and Yuri Eiras in *The Intercept*. 2018, December 13. Article retrievable from https://projects.theintercept.com/death-of-a-rio-cartel/. Link last accessed March 2021.

24 The PCC–Hezbollah link espoused by US and Brazilian authorities should be taken with a grain of salt considering the long history of both countries exaggerating or completely fabricating these types of stories for political purposes.

25 Most notably Hélio Luz, a left-leaning former chief of Rio's Civil Police.

26 See Alvito 2001: 80–85; Penglase 2008: 122–123.

27 PCC research has become an almost distinct subfield of urban studies and criminology in Brazil, and in the last few years, there has been a marked growth in the amount of scholarly attention this group has received. Ironically, the PCC was decried as a myth by the media from 1993 until 2002 (Manso and Dias 2018).

28 See de Aquino 2019. "Pioneers: The PCC and Specialization in the Market of Major Bank Robberies."

29 See Biondi (2016: 3), Feltran (2018: Chapter 7, section titled "A QUEDA DOS HOMICÍDIOS EM SÃO PAULO"), and Biderman et al. (2019: 576, 599–601).

30 See Manso, Bruno Paes and Camila Nunes. 2018. *A Guerra: a ascensão do PCC e o mundo do crime no Brasil*. Middle of Chapter 2, paragraph beginning with "A sementes da Família do Norte".

31 See Manso, Bruno Paes and Camila Nunes. 2018. *A Guerra: a ascensão do PCC e o mundo do crime no Brasil*. First third of Chapter 8, paragraphs 1–23.

32 Siqueira and Paiva 2017: 9.

33 Candotti, Cunha, and Siqueira 2017: 35–47.

34 See Manso, Bruno Paes and Camila Nunes. 2018. *A Guerra: a ascensão do PCC e o mundo do crime no Brasil*. Middle of Chapter 2, paragraph beginning with "As sementes da Família do Norte . . . ". Middle of Chapter 2, paragraph beginning with "A partir de 2010, a FDN deu".

35 Interview with Benjamin Lessing in *O Povo* by Carlos Holanda. See Holanda, Carlos in References.

36 Vara de Execuções Penais do Tribunal de Justiça do Estado do *Rio de Janeiro* (TJ-RJ)

37 Interview with Rio de Janeiro magistrate Rafael Estrada for *O Globo* (2019) six-part docuseries, "Violência Encarcerada." From video #2, beginning at the 5:47 mark.
   https://infograficos.oglobo.globo.com/brasil/violencia-encarcerada.html#video2. Link last verified on Feb. 15, 2020.

38 See Manso, Bruno Paes and Camila Nunes. 2018. *A Guerra: a ascensão do PCC e o mundo do crime no Brasil*. First third of Chapter 8, paragraphs 1–23.

39 See Manso, Bruno Paes and Camila Nunes. 2018. *A Guerra: a ascensão do PCC e o mundo do crime no Brasil*. Chapter 8, paragraphs 18–23.

40 See data from the Institute for Applied Economic (IPEA) 2018 Atlas de Violência. Data available at the following link, www.ipea.gov.br/atlasviolencia/dados-series/20. Last verified Feb. 10, 2020.

41 Freitas, Cadu. 2021, January 18. *Diário do Nordeste*.

42 Dias and Manso (2018: 6) in the *Anuário Brasileiro de Segurança Pública*. Fórum Brasileiro de Segurança Nacional.

43 See *Edição Especial 2018, Anuário Brasileiro de Segurança Pública*. 2018: 111–113, 126–128. Fórum Brasileiro de Segurança Nacional. Paraná (pp. 86–88) is the only state in the South that has seen a slight drop in violent crime in recent years, but this has occurred, as in much of Brazil, with a sharp rise in police killings (not classified as homicides).

44 See Manso and Dias (2018). *A Guerra: a ascensão do PCC e o mundo do crime no Brasil*. Middle of Chapter. Third Section of Chapter 1, second paragraph, beginning with "Encurralado na mesma cela de Carlos . . . ".

45 See Azevedo and Cipriano 2015; Cipriani 2016

46 Those familiar know there are often significant risks involved with fieldwork, particularly ethnographic research in conflict zones or high-crime areas. These dangers are multiplied when the ethnographer lives in the community where the study is taking place. Experience has taught me it is better not to enter into much detail concerning the criminal activities of the community I call home.

47 Hagedorn 2008: 30–31.

References

Alvito, Marcos. 2001. *As Cores do Acari: Uma Favela Carioca.* Editora FGV. Rio de Janeiro.

Arias, Enrique Desmond and Nicholas Barnes. 2017. "Crime and Plural Orders in Rio de Janeiro, Brazil." *Current Sociology,* 65(3), pp. 448–465.

Biderman, Ciro *et al.* "*Pax Monopolista* and Crime: The Case of the Emergence of the *Primeiro Comando da Capital* in São Paulo." *Journal of Quantitative Criminology* 35, 573–605 (2019). https://doi.org/10.1007/s10940-018-9393-x.

Biondi, Karina. 2016. *Sharing This Walk: An Ethnography of Prison Life and the PCC in Brazil.* The University of North Carolina Press, Chapel Hill.

Candotti, Fabio, Flávia Cunha and Italo Siqueira. 2017. "A Grande Narrativa do Norte: considerações na fronteira entre crime e Estado." In *BR 111: A Rota das Prisões Brasileiras.* Edited by F. Mallart, R. Godoi, pp. 35–47. Veneta/Le Monde Diplomatique, São Paulo.

Chambliss, William J., Raymond Michalowski, and Ronald C. Kramer. 2010. *State Crime in the Global Age.* Willan Publishing, Portland, OR.

Cipriani, Marcelli. 2016. "Da 'Falange Gaúcha' aos 'Bala nos Bala': A emergência das 'facções criminais' em Porto Alegre/RS e sua manifestação atual." *Direito e Democracia,* 17(1), pp. 105–130.

de Aquino, JPD. 2019. "Pioneers: The PCC and Specialization in the Market of Major Robberies." *Journal of Illicit Economies and Development,* 1(2), pp. 193–203. Article. https://doi.org/10.31389/jied.34. Link last verified March 2021.

de Azevedo, Rodrigo Ghiringhelli and Marcelli Cipriano. 2018. "Um estudo comparativo entre facções: O cenário de Porto Alegre e o de São Paulo." *Sistema Penal & Violência,* 7(2), pp. 160–174, July–December 2015.

de Sá Leonardo Damasceno and Jania Perla Diógenes de Aquino. 2019. "A 'guerra das facções' no Ceará (2013-2018): socialidade armada e disposição viril para matar ou morrer." 42nd Annual Meeting of Anpocs. GT35 – Violência, punição e desvio: reflexões e investigações empíricas. Article retrievable from https://www.anpocs.com/index.php/papers-40-encontro-3/gt-31/gt35-10. Link last verified March 2021.

Dias, Camila Nunes and Bruno Paes Manso. 2018. "Tecendo redes criminais: as políticas de encarceramento e a nacionalização das facções prisionais." *Edição Especial 2018, Anuário Brasileiro de Segurança Pública.* Fórum Brasileiro de Segurança Nacional.

Dowdney, Luke. 2005. "Neither War nor Peace. International Comparisons of Children and Youth in Organised Armed Violence." Report sponsored by Save the Children Sweden, Ford Foundation, DFID and World Vision, and coordinated by Viva Rio, ISER, IANSA, and COAV. Accessible from https://resourcecentre.savethechildren.net/library/neither-war-nor-peace-international-comparisons-children-and-youth-organised-armed-violence. Last verified March 2021.

Feltran, Gabriel. 2018. *Irmãos: Uma Historia do P.C.C.* Companhia das Letras. São Paulo. Apple Books.

Feltran, Gabriel. 2020. *The Entangled City. Crime as Urban Fabric in São Paulo.* Manchester University Press, Manchester, UK.

Freitas, Cadu. 2021, January 18. "GDE tem mais de 25 mil membros e domina maioria dos bairros de Fortaleza, diz PC." In *Diário do Nordeste* newspaper. Accessible from https://diariodonordeste.verdesmares.com.br/seguranca/gde-tem-mais-de-25-mil-membros-e-domina-maioria-dos-bairros-de-fortaleza-diz-pc-1.3034221. Link Verified Mach 2021.

Hagedorn, John M. 2008. *A World of Gangs. Armed Young Men and Gangsta Culture.* University of Minnesota Press, Minneapolis, MN.

Holanda, Carlos. 2019, August 21. Interview with Benjamin Lessing, "Facções não têm Projeto político claro; milícias, sim, de acordo com pesquisador." *O Povo.* Paywall free version retrievable from Benjamin Lessing's website. Accessible from https://drive.google.com/file/d/1X_2H3WavZagqoVYpXKTAMHO2xUg9sgBW/view. Last verified March 2021.

Instituto de Pesquisa Econômica Aplicada (IPEA). 2019. "Atlas da Violência." Accessible from www.ipea.gov.br/atlasviolencia. Last verified March 2020.

Leeds, Elizabeth. 1996. "Cocaine and Parelle Polities in the Brazilian Urban Periphery." *Latin American Research Review,* 31(3), pp. 47–83.

Lessing, Benjamin and Graham Denyer Willis. 2019. "Legitimacy in Criminal Governance: Managing a Drug Empire from Behind Bars." *American Political Science Review*, 113(2), pp. 584–606.

Manso, Bruno Paes and Camila Nunes Dias. 2018. *A Guerra: a ascensão do PCC e o mundo do crime no Brasil*. Todavia, 1st Edition. Apple Books version, São Paulo.

Melo, Juliana and Raul Rodrigues. 2017. "Notícias de um massacre anunciado e em andamento: o poder de matar e deixar morrer à luz do Massacre no Presídio de Alcaçuz, RN." *Revista Brasileira de Segurança Pública*, 11(2), pp. 48–62.

Misse, Michel. 2018. "Between Death Squads and Drug Dealers: Political Merchandise, Criminal Subjection, and the Social Accumulation of Violence in Rio de Janeiro." *The Global South*, 12(2), pp. 131–147.

O Globo. September 2019. "Special Report and Six-Part Docuseries, Violência Encarcerada." Accessible from https://infograficos.oglobo.globo.com/brasil/violencia-encarcerada.html. Last verified February 15, 2020.

Paiva, Luís Fábio S. 2019. "'Aqui Não Tem Gangue, Tem Facção': as Transformações Sociais do Crime em Fortaleza, Brasil." *Caderno CRH*, 32(85).

Penglase, Ben. 2008. "The Bastard Child of the Dictatorship: The Comando Vermelho and the Birth of 'Narco-Culture' in Rio de Janeiro." *Luso-Brazilian Review*, 45(1), pp. 118–145

Siqueira, Ítalo Barbosa Lima and Luiz Fábio Silva Paiva. 2017. ""No Norte Tem Comando": As Contradições e os Efeitos Políticos do Encarceramento em Massa." *18th Congresso Brasileiro De Sociologia* (Congress of Brazilian Sociology). July 26–29, Brasília. Group 32, Violência, Crime e Punição (Violence, Crime and Punishment).

Siqueira, Ítalo Barbosa Lima and Luiz Fábio Silva Paiva. 2019. "'No Norte, tem Comando': as maneiras de fazer o crime, a guerra e o domínio das prisões do Amazonas." *Revista Brasileira De Sociologia*, SBS, 07(17), pp. 125–154.

Zaluar, Alba and Isabel Siqueira Conceição. 2007. "Favelas sob o controle das Milícias no Rio de Janeiro: que paz?" *São Paulo em Perspectiva*, 21(2), pp. 89–101, July/December.

Zilli, Luís Felipe. 2015. *O "mundo do crime" e a "lei da favela": aspectos simbólicos da violência de gangues na região metropolitana de Belo Horizonte*.

Zilli, Luís Felipe and Cláudio Beato. 2015. "Gangues juvenis, grupos armados e estruturação de atividades criminosas na Região Metropolitana de Belo Horizonte." *DILEMAS – Edição Especial*, 1, pp. 73–110.

33

The legalization of the Latin Kings in Ecuador

The two hands of the state, from the production of marginalization to policies of inclusion

Ana Rodríguez and Mauro Cerbino

In the 1990s, a group of young Ecuadorian kids who had been deported from the United States, where they had belonged to the Almighty Latin Kings and Queens Nation (ALKQN), went on to found the Latin King nation in the cities of Quito and Guayaquil in Ecuador. These young people sought to form and preserve an organization in which music, aesthetics and a sense of belonging and protection could replace family and the state as forms of community and social bond. In the 2000s, as part of a massive labor migration phenomenon due to the economic crisis in Ecuador, several of these young people traveled to Europe, where they founded the nation in a number of Spanish and Italian cities. In 2006 and 2007, they would obtain legal status in Barcelona (Spain) and Quito (Ecuador), followed later by other groups in different cities. That formal recognition, inscribed in the framework of inclusion and pacification, marked the beginning of a process that would have interesting effects and that today we can evaluate and project as a real alternative to the "heavy handed" policies deeply installed in the Latin American region.

After fifteen years of quasi-clandestinity, the process of rapprochement with authorities in Spain, Italy and Ecuador resulted in the formal recognition of the organization, not only granting it formal legal status but also the capacity to make agreements with the state and other institutions. In Ecuador, this happened within the framework of a government that summoned society as a whole to a constituent process in which rights, social inclusion and the recognition of cultural diversity were to become cornerstones. The transnational dimension of the organization, as well as the symbolic order parallel to the nation-state, both represent conceptual keys better enabling us to understand the reproduction of gangs in times of globalization and capitalist pressure on daily life, work and social ties. The forms of community that these organizations exhibit offer alternative visions of social and political organization with respect to evaluating the scope of "legalization" and the relationship between State and society.

This chapter deals with the problems and history of this organization from five fundamental perspectives on the Latin Kings process in Ecuador: the political and social context in which the organization arises; its history and memory; the conditions of its transnationalization

(US-Ecuador-Spain/Europe relations); its formal recognition and attainment of legal status (the legal process of creating the Corporation of Latin Kings and Latin Queens in Ecuador); and, finally, the current situation, nearly twelve years after the creation of the Corporation. The process is evaluated from a political and reflexive perspective and considers potential advances and challenges in the future.

The forms of its existence then and later would depend on the place it occupied and occupies in an Ecuadorian society characterized by the political action of its successive governments. On the other hand, the chronological reconstruction of the appearance of the organization and the description of some of its key events enables us to rescue the meaning within the very fabric of society – against the backdrop of deviant interpretations – which turns out to be a necessary task for the writing of a history that was subsumed in the folds of a national narrative that portrayed the youth experiences concentrated in the "margins" of the ordinary as residual. The thesis here is that the symbolic and material modes of organization of the LK nation are constituted as a parallel order to that other order that has sought to keep it on the sidelines by treating it as if it were something accidental. Accidental and without history, one might say. Thus, the writing of the past and present history of the LK nation acquires heuristic and political relevance, revealing that which has been produced as absent by the unattainable and fictional presence of the hegemonic discourse about the Ecuadorian nation.

Context of the rise of the Latin Kings in Ecuador: the 90s

It was in 1997 when we first heard about the Latin Kings during an investigation into youth cultures in Guayaquil. Young informants from marginalized social sectors spoke of the existence of a youth organization called "the nation of the Latin Kings". It was differentiated from common youth gangs in being a very numerous organization: "of a few thousand," they said. Some said that it had absorbed several dozen gangs, rescuing them from the difficult life of the street.

Whatever the true version of events, the existence of the "Latin kings" was enveloped in a mythical atmosphere that, with spectacular bias, became one of the most exploited dimensions of its representation in the media. Certain violent events that occurred during those years in Quito and Guayaquil began to be attributed to the Latin Kings; in particular, a series of taxi driver murders unleashed an initial wave of speculation about the violent intentions of the gang, which was subsequently projected as a criminal youth organization. It is important to note that one of those responsible for these murders became a "king"[1] inside the prison once convicted. As in most of the ethnographies we have conducted, this was a response to the search for protection and part of an effort to guarantee a relative "respect" (safeguard) which are fundamental conditions for survival inside any prison.

In sociological terms, the emergence of the organization should be located, among other factors, within the framework of Ecuadorian youth gang culture, a phenomenon first mentioned in the second half of the 1980s. Andrade's research (1990, 1994) frames this phenomenon in the political and social violence characterizing the national landscape from the second half of the 80s, which deeply penetrated the daily life of different sectors of society. The gang phenomenon should be situated amongst a growing militarization of society that increased levels of repression, particularly amongst sectors of the working classes, together with an escalating change in attitudes leading to forms of domestic, work and street violence. Beginning from a vision pathologizing the formation of gangs, the official discourse consequently adopted apocalyptic positions in the face of the phenomenon.

Police authorities established a direct association between gang violence, drug consumption and drug trafficking, which in 1987 (considered the peak year of gang activity according to data provided by the Guayaquil police force, which estimated the presence of more than 1,000 gangs located in suburban neighborhoods) led to the creation of the Special Anti-Gang Group (Grupo Especial Antipandillas, GEA), with the explicit purpose of combating gangs (Andrade 1994:145).

The press played an influential role in those years, fanning the flames of social alarmism. In some cases, there was even talk of urban guerrilla clashes, as the following headlines report: "War to death against gang members" or "authorities versus gangs", "Youth gangs invade Guayaquil", "This is the 10th in a month: Killer gangs take another victim", "Killer hordes take another victim" (Andrade op. cit.: passim). Andrade reminds us, however, of the need to analyze forms of gang affiliation in relation to other forms of power, either "to impose by force the legitimacy of certain actors in spheres of intra-institutional politics" or to sustain the "political clientelism of certain populist *caciques* (local chieftains) from Guayaquil" (op. cit. 152). Our research confirms the presence of this factor, clearly showing how gangs can be re-purposed by the establishment so as to act with quasi-legal ends, taking advantage of the moral panic (Cohen 1972) of which they would be the bearers.

The condition of the neighborhoods is another central factor: their historical constitution, the degree of infrastructure provision making possible the reproduction of social life, the presence (or absence) of the State and local authorities and the organization of leisure and recreation are all, among other aspects, useful indications for thinking about the city as a whole. This is what Caldeira (2007) indicates when stating that

> the rules that organize urban space are basically patterns of social differentiation and separation. These rules vary culturally and historically, they reveal the principles that structure public life and indicate how social groups interrelate in the space of the city.
>
> *(257)*

In Guayaquil, the working-class neighborhoods indistinctly occupy the majority of the city's inhabited territory in a somewhat disordered fashion, alternating between working-class neighborhoods, luxury urbanizations, middle-class neighborhoods and commercial and industrial sectors. There are physical and symbolic barriers between them, however, which make the city appear fragmented and differentiated, with the wealthiest "citadels" being places of fortification and evidently separated from the rest, similar to what Caldeira (op. cit.) calls "fortified enclaves" or what, before her, David Sibley (1995) defined as geographies of exclusion. In our case, we conceive of slums as spaces unfit for life (Cerbino 2016).

The failure to comply with urban planning in Quito added to the topography of the city that is configured as a long alley bordered by mountains and crossed by ravines, making the "south" and the "north" appear as two distant poles broken by a historic colonial center and a financial hypercenter located between the two. Unlike the north – where the city has grown since the 1930s and which has monopolized administrative centrality and visibility – the southern neighborhoods – formerly agricultural and cattle ranches and later an industrial development zone with many working-class neighborhoods – began to be built in the 1960s through forms of popular organization, worker cooperatives and mechanisms to resolve housing issues.

In this sense, it is not possible to talk about the existence of ghettos in Ecuador in the sense of a precise spatial and above all racial delimitation, developed over a concentric city – as they are known in the United States, for example (Wacquant 2007). Quito is a city whose slums are dispersed, many of them informal settlements that were regularized over the years, so they do not always have even the minimum of basic services. Many of the neighborhoods in southern

Quito, where most members of the organization live, are neighborhoods that were or still are "informal".

So how are marginality and exclusion constituted in Ecuador? The conditions are diffuse, crossing physical and symbolic spaces, although they are also concentrated in certain places and involve certain social sectors that remain impoverished, violated and precarious due to the constant absence of adequate public policies capable of sustaining economic redistribution and social justice. This brief description by King Charly (2005) of the neighborhood in Guayaquil where he lived before leaving for Spain is a good illustration of how he perceived his social space:

> Things in Ecuador were ugly. I live in a very ugly neighborhood, very hot, I live in *South Guasmo* in Guayaquil, you understand me? It's not a matter of what life is like, but of what life is like in my neighborhood: traffickers, robberies, you go out to the corner and they rob you, if someone looks at you bad they stab you, if you do not rise well, in the end they consider you a nothing, they don't just steal from your house, if you have sisters you have to take care of them, if you have your mother you have to go see her on the bus so that nothing happens. That's to say that the security that you need there you cannot have. At least here (in Madrid) you have it, you can walk calmly. If you buy some new shoes – there – you cannot even take them out to the corner because they steal them. It is a neighborhood where you cannot sleep peacefully, because every night there are shots.

When the LK nation was founded in the 1990s, there were some historical events that revealed contradictions denoting the incoherent but functional nature of incipient state policy. The economic crisis that began in 1995 as a consequence of the neoliberal structural reforms would have a high social cost, especially among the poorest classes. The armed conflict with Peru that same year further aggravated the crisis, the enormous armament expenses causing an imbalance in precarious economic "stability". Between 1996 and 2005, Ecuador bore witness to ousted presidents (1997, 2000, 2005), interim governments (1997–98), the worst financial crisis of the modern era (1998), the dollarization of the economy (1999) and the subsequent wave of migration to Spain. These events, here just briefly outlined, thwarted the pale attempts to set up a new nation-state project that could be envisioned with the return to democracy in 1979. It is in a context of this nature that the reproduction and updating of the nation of the Latin Kings of Ecuador must be situated.

The beginnings of the Nation in Ecuador

The Latin Kings nation in Ecuador was founded on November 11, 1992. The act is registered almost simultaneously in Quito and Guayaquil, although at that time there was no connection between the two. The place chosen for this baptism of the future organization, with certain characteristics worthy of the act, was the *Plaza de la Ciudadela Primero de Mayo* located to the south of the city. In effect, it consists of the square itself and a double staircase that borders the houses of the neighborhood, at a height that affords a view of much of southern Quito.

Graffiti denoting the Latin Kings is still visible on the wall that divides the double staircase. It is a young Ecuadorian who returned every year to Ecuador for vacations from New Jersey, a city where he lived with his emigrant parents who is credited with the appearance of the nation in Ecuador. "King Juice" (his pseudonym) took the first steps to spread the worldview and type of organization he had learned of during his time in the American city. We are not aware of the connections that this young man had with the Latin Kings of the north or how he came into contact with them before bringing to Ecuador the experience of an organization that was in full development in New York under a historical leader called King Blood (Brotherton and Barrios 2004:14). It should be noted that it was a year earlier, in 1991, when the group, which had been consolidating itself inside American prisons, began to spread on the streets of neighborhoods in New York (op. cit.). Nor has it been possible to establish if King Juice brought with him some of the texts of the LK literature or the set of canonical texts of the organization, which had originally been drawn up in Chicago before subsequently being updated in New York and other cities in the United States. These texts make up the so-called LK Bible.

King Juice brought with him a prodigious idea from the United States, weaving together various strands, and managed to articulate a discourse that undoubtedly made a lot of sense to the first people with whom he met up with during his summer stays. He spoke of a "nation of Latin Kings and Latin Queens" that fought against the injustice and discrimination suffered by its members in the country in which they lived, that acted to defend and uphold the name of the "Latin race." He spoke of an organization with laws and purposes and with a strictly conceived hierarchical order. He talked about brotherhood, about a community or *pueblo* of brothers who protect each other reciprocally. He told stories of an organization that was becoming more powerful every day, capable of arousing "respect" in the territories in which it acted.

In some corner of "la Primero de Mayo", King Juice dreamt of having a group of young people gathered around a common mission, of belonging, of self-defense, of togetherness and cohesion, in an urban space that was often hostile due to the presence of similar groupings that made it impossible for a young person to even conceive of their existence and social reproduction outside of belonging to one or other of them. It brought with it an idea of organization that could guarantee recreation, the organization of dances and fun. In addition, King Juice brought this idea in *English*, which aroused its own special attraction for being a language of prestige, deemed to open paths that projected outwards, to contribute to alleviating the symbolic misery installed in everyday life and as a language which marked overwhelming differences by permitting secrecy and representing an element of distinction from *other* groups that could not understand it.

Planting the flag

While we have stated it was King Juice, an Ecuadorian from New York, who founded the Almighty Nation of the Latin Kings in Ecuador in 1992, it was not he who "planted the flag". According to the testimony of King M (the current leader of the nation), the act of planting a flag occurs when the mission of organizational expansion is clearly established. Thus conceived, that act occurs for the first time with King Boy Gean, another son of a family who had emigrated to the United States who had met some kings of the Nation in a New York jail where he had been confined. Boy Gean planted the flag in Guayaquil in 1994, two years later than in Quito and a year before Antonio Fernández (a.k.a. King Tone), head of Brooklyn, would go on to ascend to the Supreme and Inca Crown of the Almighty Latin Kings and Queens Nation in New York and New Jersey. King Tone is blessed (a kind of "sacred authorization") by King Blood to assume the leadership of the nation. The new leader seeks to make changes in the leadership, proposing a renunciation of the violent past in order to survive, and initiates a campaign to reform the organization and turn it into a community movement (Brotherton and Barrios op. cit.). We don't know if King Tone's change of direction had any influence on the kind of leadership Boy Gean contemplated for the group in Ecuador, but according to testimonies, it followed a similar direction.

The act of planting a flag tells us of the intense symbolic vocation that characterizes the Nation. Despite the multiple identity crises it went through and the fact that it was on the verge of being undone on several occasions, the founding act of "planting the flag" has served as a referential anchor each time it has been necessary to rethink the existence of the nation or cement its deep roots.

Because planting a flag is a "sacred act", a foundational rite, it places those unforgettable kings who have achieved it on "Olympus." They will always occupy a special place on the scale of the kings; their names will appear in the manifestos (updated texts of the nation's literature) and some, those considered the most important leaders, will be remembered in the rituals held in the universals – periodic mass meetings – in which to name certain dates is akin to celebrating patriotic national holidays.

1992 is the date stamped on all the yellow and black t-shirts (the colors of the nation) that young people use in their meetings and at parties. Those early years are described this way:

> there is a big difference between those years and now because we were few, and among the few that we were we all knew each other, and the Nation was very rigid then. There were little brothers who had control . . . and the nation had total and absolute respect.
>
> *(King M. 2006)*

The two periods: primitive and conservative

The previous testimony shows that control of the organization was crucial from the very beginning and, as the number of members increases, it becomes more difficult to exert the control and discipline necessary to maintain order. In addition, the members of the nation recognize the articulation of two periods marking the pace and development of the organization as a fundamental part of its history. King M (2006) characterizes them as such:

> There are two periods, the primitive and the conservative: the primitive is when it was founded until 2001. There is the change – from 2001 onwards is the conservative phase – when we think about things before doing them. When we have to think about everyone behind us to talk about things. It is no longer as with the primitive: because he threw a stone at me I threw a bullet at him. Now you throw a stone, what do we do? in conjunction with the supreme we think, or perhaps it is what I call the (move from) conservative to maturity.

Along the same lines, King Chino Ice (2006) expresses:

> The primitive stage deals with a king who as a king is in a period in which he commits all kinds of atrocities. The conservative stage is a stage that I tell you is over. For what reason? since there started to be problems, people started to walk with a low profile, so obviously you covered yourself, yes, it's called the conservative stage because when you're like a mummy because obviously you wrap a mummy around something and what happens, it's conserved, no? and now what? – it's the stage of the new king – we still need to reach the stage of the new king . . . individually, but more generally in the nation, there is a long way to go for that.
>
> *(2006)*

If one takes into account that this articulation of the two phases (and a third, that of the new king, which was yet to occur) seems to be a characteristic trait of the functioning of the nation at a general level, it can be inferred that one would not be thinkable without the other, that is, the conservative without the primitive (see also Brotherton and Barrios 2004).

King Boy Gean convenes the first meetings of the newly formed organization in a small park near a shopping center in the city of Guayaquil called Garzocentro. It was a place where groups of young people influenced by urban culture would meet up to practice rap and hiphop.

King Boy Gean, who as we have said came from New York as a deportee, could plant a flag in Ecuador (according to the rules of the Nation) only by having written permission from the leader of the city that empowered him to open a new chapter. It has never been possible to verify whether this permission really existed. During the following years, this issue of permission was the subject of heated discussions and open conflicts within the organization, which would further demonstrate the importance of matters of symbolic order in its operation.

In fact, it was another young Ecuadorian from Chicago, King Lucky, who appears in 1996 claiming for himself the leadership of the nation constituted two years previously. He does this under the same rule stating that if a king comes from the "motherland" (Chicago), it was not necessary to have any permission to plant a flag in another country (not so for the kings of New York). It was the sign of Chicago's supremacy over any other city in the world and its undisputed recognition as being the motherland of the Latin King nation. That recognition granted a special "blessing" (this is the expression used in the testimonies) to someone like King Lucky, who, arriving in Ecuador, perceives himself as the one with the power to lead the nation.

This explains the conflict between King Boy Gean and King Lucky over the leadership of the nation, which culminated in a public confrontation between the two, conducted in English. This fact takes on an almost mythical dimension since many of those present – other kings – fail to understand the contents of the discussion. The confrontation results in a virtuous arrangement: the division of the Nation, with the north of Guayaquil led by Boy Gean and the south by Lucky.

Lucky's appearance represents the moment in which changes begin to take place in the very conception of the organization and consequently in its actions. Indeed, the two leaders represented two different ways of thinking about the nation.

Boy Gean, belonging to the New York tradition, intended to form an organization based around the creation of leisure and entertainment spaces, with musical activities predominant. In fact, the intentions of Boy Gean were that the "Latin Kings" should be the name of a musical group or record label that promoted young, upcoming singers. Several testimonies report how young people approached this new organization to participate in the parties and dances organized by its members. These encounters were a chance to exhibit the lifestyles linked to rap, the musical genre of the moment, and to show off the baggy, branded clothes and break dance skills. All these were constituent elements of most youth groups but came with the addition of a special stamp representing the name of the Latin Kings, whose affiliation was to an organization in the United States, birthplace of those lifestyles.

The testimony of a former leader and member of another youth organization that existed during those same years in Guayaquil confirms the memories that the former members of the Latin Kings have of that initial period:

> I was a member of the gang of Los Alemanes which was born in the Aguirre Abad school. In 1994 I was part of one of the largest organizations of that time, the Iron Nation (Nacion de Hierro). There was still no gang war, we all got along well: "The Five-pointed Star", "Latin Kings", ours. . . . People competed in the clubs, danced break dance in the clubs. I am one of the first of all these organizations. The founder of the "Latin Kings" was a singer and sang in the discos. "Master", which is one of the oldest organizations in Ecua-

dor, more so than the "Latin Kings", began as a musical group, with an ideology from here, although it has foreign roots, they're one hundred percent Ecuadorian. The other four organizations all came at once: "Kings", "Ñetas", "Big Klein" and Hierro. They shared the stage, they got along well. The Ñetas were even the ones who organized meetings between the five organizations, because it had been decided that no one else would be allowed to leave because it damaged the image. At that time everything was peace. Once, however I remember there was a war against the rockers in Garzocentro, because there were two different genres of music, some hip-hop and others rock. It was a big fight, one of the first. Then they closed a nightclub, the organizations no longer had the same coexistence as before, and began to grow.

(George Asanza 2006)

Two elements can be highlighted in this story. The first is that street youth organizations were able to coexist, act or compete in the field of music. The first problems linked to violent conflict arise from the closure of the nightclub where coexistence was possible and competition was channeled in the form of a confrontation between different musical styles, and with it disappeared the possibility of having appropriate spaces for peaceful coexistence. The second is that it was in one of the largest schools in Guayaquil ("Aguirre Abad") where the gang of the "Germans" was formed. In other words, the vulnerability experienced by young people in educational institutions is in addition to the precariousness they experience in their neighborhoods.

During Boy Gean's tenure, former members report how the leadership made it possible to carry out activities considered useful to the community. Lucky on the other hand, who was linked to the Chicago tradition, was more oriented towards the protection of its members with a markedly "primitive" vision: to the development of defense (and sometimes attack) capabilities necessary to survive in the streets and in hostile territories, or in any case spaces marked by very intense conflict. King Chino Ice (2006) discusses these two different ways of conceiving of the nation:

Gean's people weren't used to using weapons. When the Latin Kings started there was no custom of weapons, no custom of carrying knives. That was the Chicago way that was learned by Lucky, who taught you the tricks of where to carry knives so that if the police checked you, they wouldn't find them. It was the Chicago law.

Although the testimonies present the primitive and the conservative as two distinct periods of development of the Nation, in reality, they're not merely two different chronological moments (that occur at the level of the transnational organization) but rather represent certain conditions (or souls) that coexist and are co-present in the organization. When situations of extreme conflict arise, such as street confrontations with adverse groups, or the protection of attacked siblings, it acts in a primitive way (the testimonies say it is inevitable). When it comes to fine-tuning negotiation measures or approaching government institutions in order to bring about transformative processes and other changes with respect to the past, it acts more conservatively, or even as a "new king".

In any case, as mentioned earlier, from 1997 the Nation begins to be the object of a stigmatizing media gaze and consequently public opinion that starts to associate it with gangsterism, holding it responsible for numerous acts of violence. During that same year, Boy Gean was arrested and held in the Litoral Penitentiary, where he remained for a few months.[2] Chino Ice reports that the police initially believed that he was a member of the rebel group Alfaro Vive Carajo (an anti-systemic group), which was still active in those years. Thus begins a difficult period for the nation because Lucky also decides to return to the United States, where he would die a few years later. The leadership is assumed by King Moonface, who was Boy Gean's man.

At this point, there was a new rupture inside the organization, the most significant since that first important confrontation between the leaderships of Lucky and Boy Gean. In an (2006) interview, the latter explains the reasons that pushed him to take the decision to leave the Nation:

> The experience of prison – being located in a maximum security section – had produced an enormous state of anxiety and fear in me, and above all I realized that when I was behind bars the Nation did nothing for me, rather it had abandoned me. I only had the personal support of a few siblings and my parents. This fact made me very angry and I thought that the Nation as it was heading . . . it wasn't going anywhere. . . . But I have never broken my necklaces, because I was a king and I will always be a king.

Moonface was at the head of the Nation for just a few months during a period defined as transitional, after which he was replaced by Eric, someone from Lucky's school who had accompanied him to the end. His leadership lasted until 1999, when he decided to emigrate to Spain. In 2000, Eric founded the Nation in Madrid, giving rise to a new chapter called STAS (Sacred Tribe Atahualpa Spain) separated from the organization of Ecuador STAE (Sacred Tribe Atahualpa Ecuador), and assumed the pseudonym of King Wolverine. Eric would be replaced in Ecuador by King M, who had also been trained by Lucky and who remains the leader of the Nation today.

The situation created through the conflicts described previously contributed to the Nation beginning a process of immersion and quasi-clandestinity in 1997 that would last until 2005 when, first in Barcelona and then at the beginning of 2006 in Quito, a series of initiatives were launched to facilitate the emergence, recognition and search for social legitimacy of the organization.

The transnational nation: diaspora and translocality

Linked to the intensification of migratory flows from Ecuador to Spain and Italy at the end of the 90s, and due to reasons directly or indirectly related to the multiple economic crises that the country experienced in those years, many adolescents and young people embarked on the same path. Most of them did so under the dynamics of family reunification, which in the early 2000s was triggered by the immigration policies of the destination countries. It is important to point out that the majority of adolescents who migrate do so against their will, exposing them to multiple and greater difficulties in perceiving the advantages of living in a new country and consequently complicating their adaptation (Suárez-Orozco 2000). It is in a context of this nature that some of the reasons behind the reactivation and reconstitution of the LK nation in Spain appear more viable.

According to several testimonies gathered during field work carried out in Madrid, Barcelona, Valencia and Murcia between 2005 and 2006, the LK Nation was founded in February 2000 in Galapagar, a village near Madrid, Spain. It is King Eric, with the pseudonym of King Wolverine, and King Baby Black who take the initial steps in creating the organization they name Sacred Tribe America Spain (STAS). It is clear that the new organization wants to distinguish itself from the Ecuadorian version of the Nation and project itself as autonomous, in spite of its Ecuadorian origin and the original STAE affiliation of its members. Two distinct positions were adopted within the organization in this regard. There were those who believed that the Nation in Spain, although it should maintain a single constitution ensuring a unitary conception, must nevertheless build an independent course to that in Ecuador because the problems and opportunities in Spain shaped a distinct context. On the other side were those who vindicated that the nation of Ecuador was akin to a new "motherland", without prejudice toward the unquestionable recognition of Chicago as the Nation's one and only true birthplace. Those who supported this thesis recognized the affiliation with the nation of Ecuador and deemed that the entire organization could be kept united despite the distance between the different chapters and, on the contrary, that the foundation of an autonomous, uniquely Spanish chapter would endanger the necessary unity to fulfill the primary functions of the nation: that of offering its members protection and opportunities for progress. The divisions produced through these different perspectives deepened with the passage of time and gave rise to a deep internal fragmentation within the nation.

In any case, the role played by the LK nation beyond its anchorage to the Ecuadorian reality – that of projecting itself as a transnational organization despite the racial foundation of "the Latin" or precisely because of the performative use of this signifier – was clearly evident. This was also due to the derivations of the condition of "race", which Queirolo Palmas (2009) associates with the idea of a "Latin Atlantic" (paraphrasing Gilroy) to account for a "set of opportunities and practices of youth and generational transnationalism" (2009:129). For this reason, "Latin", more than being merely a condition of ethnogenesis, functions as a space of youth construction practices – for example, of musical styles – and, being globalized could, and in fact did, attract other non-Latin youth subjects.

These practices, carried out by young Ecuadorians as they rebuilt the LK nation on the edges of cities in Spain and Italy, can be interpreted in terms of diaspora. Hobsbawm (1990) reflects that one of the conditions of the construction of the modern nation is the process of the cultural identification of nationals in a diaspora situation at its time of origin. According to Clifford (1997), one can speak of diaspora in a contemporary sense according to certain key features: "a history of dispersion, myths/memories of the homeland, alienation in the country that receives them (badly?), the desire for return, the sustained support of the homeland and a collective identity defined in an important way by this relationship" (1999:303). The diaspora can also be understood as a way of inhabiting several places at the same time, even virtually, under diverse influences and multiple identities. For Appadurai (1999), "human mobility in the context of the crisis of the nation-state stimulates the emergence of translocality". In this case, translocality refers to the fact that the nation in Ecuador provides the elements enabling the empowerment of young migrants in the context of the exclusionary conditions they suffer in Spanish society. A bridge is created between knowledge of the Ecuadorian *barrio* or neighborhood and the process of re-territorialization in Spain that passes neither through the symbolic or imaginary dimensions of the Ecuadorian Nation-State, nor that of the Spanish. It is a translocalization of an antagonistic attitude-strategy with respect to the immediate environment of rejection, an awareness of the paradoxical reality lived and experienced by migrants. Faced with the de-citizenization of migrants, re-subjectivation in an organizational sense is, in cultural and social terms, a strategic form of survival. It cannot be said that there existed an organizational consciousness such as that found in social or political movements or other politically active youth groups; however, we do note a series of strategies enabling the configuration of a movement of visibilization of their own social and cultural practices. It is a collective action in the most literal sense: a strategic aesthetic performance, including bodily practices, in Spanish public space. We could say, based on the scant academic orthodoxy and scriptural formality of Michel De Certeau (1995), treated as an organizational "tactic", that emphasizing that oxymoron allows us to emphasize the precarious character of approaches to language and cultural practices at once youthful and marginal. Instead of thinking that one "no longer belongs" to the world that is left behind (Ecuador-neighborhood-home) and "does not yet belong" to the world arrived at (Spain-work-immigration) (Grinberg 1984), we could say that the migrant subject can be collectively reconstructed to the extent that they never belonged to the world left behind and will never belong to the world they came to . . . which is to say that these are not simply two different worlds but are variations of the same situation of exclusion repeated in both Ecuador and Spain.

Formal recognition and legal status

In the preceding pages, we have traced the history of the organization, moving from the United States to Ecuador, and from Ecuador to Spain, showing on a small scale the complex conditions found at the global geopolitical level. Faced with this reality, we are obliged to look no longer towards the center of the metropolis but towards the margins of national states which do not include migrants as citizens but instead serve as corridors of exclusionary labor migration. Marginalities, border zones and small wars here characterize the emergence of youth organizations and groups. States have failed to recognize these realities, perhaps because they are part of a greater and more complex reality that they do not control, be it regional, continental or global, so it has largely been academia that has assumed the task of describing and understanding them. Social movements have been strengthened to different degrees in different countries and regions in an effort to confront these realities. Meanwhile, the general trend continues to be for governments to criminalize these vulnerable groups in order to minimize political burdens such as insecurity or unemployment.

When a government *does* decide to make a difference and ask questions previously only asked by academia or social movements, then it is safe to assume that it is different to most, something akin to a political laboratory. That was Ecuador in 2007: the creation of a reflective space in which to think about other capitalist alternatives to capitalism and a place of confluence for the rehearsal and construction of short-lived sovereign policies. The Ecuador that dreamed of piecing together the basic agreements, of instigating a democracy of high intensity, the Ecuador of the constituent promise and the turn towards sovereignty. In 2007, with the momentum of a majority consensus, Ecuadorians came together in a massive and organized fashion to participate in a national process of drawing up a new framework of rights: the constitution of Montecristi.

Only a public policy that reflects and addresses the specific geopolitical condition of capitalist flows and migratory movements can hope to develop recognition processes of national migrations, marginal organizations and those who have been criminalized. In this context, the Latin Kings is constituted as an organization that brings together young immigrants returned from the United States and later mobilized in other countries such as Spain. It is not only a matter of a policy of recognition toward a youth organization in a situation of marginality – which is already enormous – but also about recognizing the constitutive character of the Ecuadorian identity as a migrant identity; as a society built on a culture of exchanges.

From that point, recognizing the Latin King Nation means beginning to develop a translation that enables us to better understand how youth practices in the north adapt to Ecuadorian realities and how they then travel and are translated into European societies.

A process of public policy construction took place in Barcelona in 2005 that stemmed from a new vision of security that promised the integration of street youth organizations and organized young migrants, replacing traditional "heavy-handed" policies. With the support of the CIIMU (Institute of Children and the Urban World) and a group of researchers committed to the youth process, an Association of Latin Kings and Queens of Catalonia was created. From that first experience, approaches to other groups were made, initiating the beginnings of a trustful relationship between leaders of the organization and researchers. A process of recognition had been instigated in Ecuador in 2004, with a police colonel leading a dialogue process between the largest gangs in Guayaquil. When we (Mauro Cerbino and Ana Rodríguez) met with the leaders of the Nation in Quito on our return from Barcelona, we considered the possibility of formal recognition among several other ideas, which necessarily implied establishing a direct relationship with the government of that time. The "corporation", based on the legal status deemed most suitable for that purpose, is the fruit of a translation of the nation's existing structure, constituted of three powers: legislative, government and control. The exercise (carried out among a group of LK leaders, lawyers and us as researchers) concluded that the structure of the organization should be reflected in the nascent statute of the corporation, based on a translation of its rules into juridical language.[3] The creation of the corporation marked a milestone in the history of the LK nation, enabling it to manage projects and resources and to win recognition and rights.

On August 2, 2007, the President of the Republic of Ecuador, Rafael Correa, presented the statutes to the youth at an official lunch at the Carondelet Palace. It was a memorable day that set a precedent for the LK nation and for the history of street youth organizations in Ecuador.

A number of rights concerning public space, meeting spaces and the right to wear (gang) colors have been won since legalization in 2007. Thus began a new stage enabling previous clandestinity to be left behind and affording a new legitimacy to relations with institutions and other youth or neighborhood organizations.

One of the flagship projects of the Corporation was the CETOJ (Technological Center of Youth Organizations), which alongside FLACSO Ecuador developed a non-formal education program that responded to the wishes of the organization's members. Some of the proposed courses included sound, design, locution, photography and video, none of which had any prerequisites, and were adapted to the needs of young people who had dropped out of formal education.[4] Several other processes developed in those early years of the corporation, including concerts such as "Paz Urbana" (Urban Peace) and projects such as "Taxi Solidario" (Solidarity Taxi) that together instigated news reports about LK to shift from being framed in the "Judicial" section of newspapers to being found under Culture or Society.

2007–2017: Reflections on the ten years of the corporation of Latin Kings and Latin Queens of Ecuador

2017 marked 10 years of "legalization". The nation found itself recast in a new scenario in 2018 when the corporation, which had been the institutional and officially recognized arm, suffered a crisis of legitimacy due to accusations of corruption that paralleled Ecuador's political scene writ large, in which the current government is accusing the previous government of corruption, breaking with the political continuity it supposedly represented.

The context of the LK nation in destination countries has also changed in recent years: the last wave of Ecuadorian labor migration in the 2000s began to recede with the return of many Ecuadorians, victims of the global real estate and financial crisis that began in 2008. There was a kind of autonomization of the LK organization in these countries and a radical independence on the part of chapters in Spain that had initially reported to Ecuador, calling it the "mother earth of Spain". New forms of relationship and articulation have been born in recent years between the transnational chapters.

Ten years after legalization, and after thirteen years accompanying the process, we as researchers are trying to piece together a joint reflection. Updating (or deconstructing) Gramsci's thought, Luca Palmas provides some keys to further interpretation. What do the gangs consist of? Organic intellectuals, subaltern classes, street groups in contemporary post-migratory societies or post-migrant proletarian youth? All this is in a society where basic rights and the State have receded in light of the ground gained by the exclusion generated by transnational capitalism, regional wars and violence.

In a 2017 workshop held in Quito to evaluate the previous ten years and draw up strategies for the future, three distinct moments of the process clearly emerged in retrospect: the recognition to walk together (the organization, academia, the State and society), walking alone (no longer hand in hand with institutions or academia) and walking together and with autonomy (without political uses, without institutions but together with other youth organizations with which a common agenda is defined).

The following conclusions emerged when reflecting on the path traveled during the workshop:

The most significant victories or achievements:

- The right to the city and public space, the right to assembly
- The right to our identity and to wear our colors
- The right to negotiate our positions with the social state (the left arm of the State) in an upfront manner and not only with the repressive state (the right arm, in matters of weapons and clandestine territorial trafficking).

The first moment of legalization and hope:

- The process of recognition (new forms of clandestinity but above all of visibility) and new forms of relationship with institutions, which appear as opportunities
- Legalization as a hope for a new identity
- Agreements with organizations reduce violence in the streets

The major problem of capitalist exclusion:

- Legalization as a limit: it does not solve the problem of exclusion and inequality
- Politics and realpolitik: we don't want to be used anymore
- Political reproduction in the mirror: we cannot avoid following the mandate of the people, condemning corrupt subjects and common enemies

The main conclusions of the workshop pointed to the need to understand the global nature of the reproduction of marginality in cities, driven by the movement of capitalist flows and the pressure exerted on young and excluded migrants in cities with rights that are unevenly exercised.

Some maxims that were manifested:

"We are a youth organization first of all and our values, history and identity unite us".
"We want to continue being a gang and an organization".
"We (also) want to be a political movement someday without ceasing to be who we are".

The gang and *the political movement* were defined in the same workshop, emphasizing that they do not contradict each other: "the former recognizes us and protects us from within. The latter seeks to transform society by exercising power or pressuring power".

From our first theoretical inquiries, the character of the organization was interpreted as a symbolic order parallel to that of the hegemonic order, as a reproduction of the macho, patriarchal, militarized and hierarchical society. The conclusions of this reflective exercise bring us back to that parallel symbolic order in which not only do the rigid and disintegrating values of society draw the excluded youths together but so too does the contemporary global crisis of democracy and representation. Taken together, these factors appear as a clear sign for young people to take other initiatives and, for the first time since the experience of negotiating with power as a corporation, to call into question the capacity of the state and to bet instead on the organization of a political platform that is an end in itself, seen as an alternative means of making demands and seeking transformation.[5]

Epilogue

As we go through this chapter in August 2019, we are bombarded with further questions. How does the LK youth see the process today? A former member who was part of the process says:

> There was something positive in being legalized, to reach agreements. Looking at it today, I think we were very inexperienced in political issues. More important things could have been achieved than we imagined. We were able to have a headquarters (to put) more brothers in politics, inserted in work, etc. It could have been bigger. More learned and demonstrated to society. It was a good decision. If it had only been repression we would have had more violence in the streets. It has been 12 years in which the LK, Ñeta, Master organizations have understood things. Today the gang no longer attracts so much attention. The membership of the kids dropped, it was positive for society and the government. Many people were saved. It changed their lifestyle, their opportunities, many saw a way out, change, through the few opportunities that were given. There were supports that were opportunities.

The feeling that it was positive but insufficient is a constant. All interviewees agree that it was a positive step and a precedent of some form, but they also have the feeling that more could have been done, that an opportunity for a more sustained change was lost. They fear being used politically and feel that their internal efforts and demands have not been understood in an institutional way and that they depend on a certain political lobby that deprives them of hope because it doesn't transform their contexts in any real or integral sense. Amongst both those young people who left and those who remain in the organization, a constant concern arises: they are repeatedly victims of a justice system that does not work, and their ranks continue to grow inside the prisons because many young people need protection against a reality of mafia and drug trafficking networks that overflow the prisons of Ecuador. The leader of the LK, King M, tells us:

> a country that does not invest in its prisons and its youth is not thinking about the future. We could help and conduct projects, there is experience amongst our leaders, but the authorities don't call us, they don't understand how serious it is.

(2019)

An IDB report (Brotherton and Gude 2018) concludes that the legalization and pacification of street youth organizations, as well as a comprehensive security policy,[6] would have led to a reduction in Ecuador's homicide rates. What are the necessary conditions to continue this reduction? How can we continue the process of the pacification of gangs? What is the situation of these young people today? The answer is somewhat hopeless. Young people feel that they are left to their fate, their ranks are growing in prisons and they are not being heard or understood in a world in which unemployment, school drop-out rates and social decomposition in many neighborhoods are all on the rise, making them feel that a new era, more primitive than conservative, more exclusionary than democratic or egalitarian, is once again approaching.

Demonstrating the urgency and showing a maturity that is the fruit of a long and complex process leaves some hope in the midst of contradictions. The organization's leader says: "For now, we are rebuilding what was started in 2007 and starting again but this time with experience. We will not surrender, and well, in the end, we will do what our people ask" (King M. 2018). Now more than ever, it is vital to understand the lack of effectiveness of heavy-handed policies in the United States, Central America and Spain, and above all that in the experiences of organized youth can be found insights into thinking about the future, drug trafficking, arms and prisons, as well as about the integrity of security policies, with professional police institutions, infrastructure and spaces for coexistence, which will not necessarily be guaranteed by states but implemented instead through new models of governance that we must collectively construct.

Notes

1 A hierarchical position within the structure of the nation, which after a trial period culminates with a coronation.
2 King Boy Gean was charged with the illegal possession of weapons and murder. The latter was not proven, leaving the accusations of illicit association and the illegal possession of weapons.
3 The Legal Clinic of the Universidad San Francisco, Quito, sponsored this process.
4 To delve deeper into CETOJ, see Cerbino M., Panchi M., Voirol J. (2019)
5 The Latin Kings of Ecuador themselves witness the effects of this turn: they state that the Assemblyman Ronny Aleaga, self-defined as a Latin King of a dissident faction of the LK nation, is one of the results of this long process. Likewise, the fact that the Ñetas organization has one of its members, Fabricio, elected as a councilor in the Mayor's Office of Guayaquil demonstrates the effect of this movement in which gang and politics seek to exercise direct political influence through the ballot box.
6 It is essential to understand that these are comprehensive policies, which include improvements, professionalization and decent salaries in the police force, for example.

Bibliography

Andrade, Xavier (1990). "Culture as stereotype: Public use in Ecuador". Disponible en: www.flacsoandes.org/antropologia . . . /public_uses_of_culture.pdf.
Andrade, Xavier (1994). "La dimensión cotidiana: violencia y vida cotidiana en el Ecuador". En: Julio Echeverría y Amparo Menéndez-Carrión (Eds.), *Violencia en la región Andina. El caso de Ecuador*. Quito: FLACSO-Sede Ecuador.
Appadurai, Arjun (1999). "Soberanía sin territorialidad. Notas para una geografía posnacional". En *Nueva Sociedad*, N° 163. Buenos Aires: FES, pp. 109–125, además. Disponible en: www.nuso.org/upload/articulos/2799_1.pdf.
Brotherton, David y Barrios Luis (2004). *The Almighty Latin King and Queen Nation. Street Politics and the Transformation of a New City Gang*. New York: Columbia University Press.
Brotherton, David y Rafael Gude (2018). *Inclusión social desde abajo: Las pandillas callejeras y sus posibles efectos en la reducción de la tasa de homicidios en el Ecuador*. Quito: Inter-American Development Bank.
Caldeira, Teresa (2007). *Ciudad de muros*. Barcelona: Gedisa.
Cerbino, Mauro (2012). *El lugar de la violencia. Perspectivas críticas sobre pandillerismo juvenil*. Quito: Taurus/Flacso.

Cerbino, Mauro et allí (2019). "Marginal Images: Youth and Critical Subjectivities from Art as a Resource". In H. Cuervo and A. Miranda (Eds.), *Youth, Inequality and Social Change in the Global South. Perspectives on Children and Young People*, vol 6. Singapore: Springer Nature.

Cohen, Stanley (1972). *Folk Devils and Moral Panics. The Creation of the Mods and Rockers*. London and New York: Routledge.

Clifford, James (1997). *Itinerarios transculturales*. Barcelona: Gedisa.

De Certeau, Michel (1995). *La invención de lo cotidiano 1. Artes de hacer*. México: Universidad Iberoamericana.

Grinberg, León (1984). *Psicoanálisis de la migración y del exilio*. Madrid: Alianza Editorial.

Hobsbawm, Eric (2000 [1990]). *Naciones y nacionalismo desde 1780*. Barcelona: Crítica.

Queirolo Palmas, Luca. (2009). "Pandillas en el Atlántico latino: Identidad, transnacionalismo y generaciones". En *Íconos: revista de ciencias sociales*. Quito: FLACSO sede Ecuador, n.34, mayo.

Sibley, David (1995). *Geographies of Exclusion: Society and Difference in the West*. London: Burns and Oates.

Suárez-Orozco, C. (2000). "Identities under siege. Immigration stress and social mirroring among the children of immigrants". En A. Robben y M. Suárez-Orozco (Eds.), *Cultures Under Siege. Social Violence & Trauma*. Nueva York: Cambridge University Press.

Wacquant, Loïc (2007). *Los condenados de la Ciudad: gueto, periferias y Estado*. Buenos Aires: Siglo XXI.

34

Peace processes in Ecuador

Fabricio José García Díaz

In the following brief discussion of his role in the inter-gang peace process in Ecuador, a leader of the Masters of the Street provides an important analysis of the failure and success of this policy. Bearing in mind that Ecuador is one of the few countries in the world ever to embark on an anti-violence strategy that involved engaging directly with street gangs as part of the government's commitment to the goals and principles of universal social citizenship. This radical rethinking of gang social control occurred between 2007 and 2017, contributing to the nation's remarkable drop in homicide rates from 21.8:100,000 in 2008 to 5.6:100,000 in 2016.

This chapter presents my point of view on the peace process in Ecuador. I believe that this process resulted in a decrease in violence and homicide rates in certain communities but may only be temporary if other serious problems in poor neighborhoods are not resolved.

Personal introduction

I've been a member of the organization Masters of the Street (MOS) since 2003 in the city of Montecristi, Ecuador. I became a leader in 2006 and was eventually elected secretary of the organization in the city of Manta. I was also a delegate in the peace negotiations in 2008 with Mario Guillén, president of the organization at that time. Throughout my leadership roles in the MOS, I have been particularly involved in organizing youth and their development.

Outside of the Masters of the Street, I've played a part in labor struggles and Communist Party politics. I was involved in organizing unions in the lumber and tuna processing industries where I worked for several years. The earthquake that occurred in the province of Manabí on April 16, 2016, caused me to leave the factories and help direct volunteer aid work for several months in the region.

After doing militant political work within the Communist Party, I was chosen to participate in the 2017 national elections as an alternate to the Andean Parliament.[1] This was part of an agreement between the governing Alianza País party and the Communist party in which two elected positions were granted to communist militants. We won these positions thanks to the support of the MOS and the workers' movements that supported me. I took a non-salaried position as an alternate in the Andean Parliament representing my country, Ecuador.

Introduction to the organization

Masters of the Street is one of the three major organizations that entered into the gang peace process in Ecuador and is a well-known and respected group found in working-class neighborhoods throughout the country. Its full name is Organización Master Of the Street Ecuador (OMOSE), but is also known as the "Masters of the Street" or just as the "Masters." The organization emerged in Guayaquil in the '90s under the leadership of its founder Henry López with cultural influences from the hip-hop culture of that period. They adopted the shield symbol of the Wu-Tang Clan because of the influence that that rap group had on López, who had spent some time in New York City. A constitution was created to govern the organization, establishing rules to maintain its organic structure in the future.

The first generation of Masters that grew from a few smaller groups within a few years already had cells in the provinces of Manabí, Esmeraldas, El Oro, and Los Ríos. Cells later formed in the rest of the country as well as outside of Ecuador. The organization maintains provincial leaders who set the rules as to how to run the group in their sectors in line with the founding constitution. Then there are also the chapter leaders in charge of recruitment and as well as providing leadership. Generally there are one or two chapters in each neighborhood, and the organization has managed to maintain a unified structure without a national leader. Provincial leaders exist in some provinces but not in others, with the neighborhood and chapter leadership controlling the direction of the organization as necessary.

The Masters of the Street organization and its involvement in violence in the country

Ecuador is a relatively peaceful country in comparison with other countries in Latin America, but it still maintains high levels of violence in specific regions. For example, the city of Manta in 2009 saw about 120 homicides in a population of 210,000, making it one of the most dangerous places in Ecuador. The MOS, as the largest such organization in Manta, was inevitably involved in these bloody statistics.

In cities like Guayaquil, which also had high homicide rates, our organization had to hold its own in specific neighborhoods. The policy of the organization at the time was zero alliances, which basically meant a war with everyone. This position was also shared by the Ñetas, Latin Kings, and all the big organizations at the time. It was understood that if you were part of one organization, directly or indirectly, then you were the enemy of all the others.

The MOS, however, maintained a brotherhood alliance with the Blood Masters and later with the Wu-Tang, organizations that emerged mainly in Quito and the interior highlands. There were also organizations such as the Hausers that, although they had been influenced by the MOS, over time became our sworn enemies (I should mention that these problems between us would come to an end after the peace processes). Nonetheless, prior to the peace, violence was widespread, with different chapters dealing with the other organizations closest to them mainly in places of mutual confluence between the groups.[2]

Beginnings of the peace process

There were already peace processes taking place between the organizations before the arrival of outside actors. For example, there were meetings between leaders, respected truces on certain days, and tolerance of rivals in various areas to avoid conflict. The first official attempt at peace that had a lot of publicity was known as Ser Paz,[3] which brought together various street leaders. Ser Paz's proposal was to reintegrate young people from the organizations through training, sports, and cultural activities, as well as helping to stimulate employment through financing small productive businesses. This initiative was based on the idea that generating activities would help to insert young people into society. However, little attention was given to the actual structures of the organizations and, therefore, this initiative was destined to be a resounding failure. The only thing that was rescued from this process was the approach to conflict resolution through mediation, and this served to stimulate the successful peace process that followed.

The external actors who were involved in trying to solve the violence problem showed weaknesses in Ser Paz. Many of these actors were activists who had to account for and justify their projects and needed to demonstrate certain accomplishments. This led them to disguise the truth in order to show achievements that in fact were not achieved. For example, after the departure of the larger organizations from the initiative, they opted to involve smaller organizations that did not play a role in the high rates of violence.

Second attempt at pacification

The second attempt, which finally achieved success, had as a starting point the meeting between leaders of all the organizations and the then-president, Rafael Correa, and his ministers. In that meeting, where I represented MOS, all the organizational leaders criticized the approach taken by Ser Paz, and we were given the opportunity to prioritize ideas that we developed ourselves to carry out the process.

Since the organizational leadership MOS didn't – and still doesn't – have absolute control of all its structures, the signed peace agreement remained a mostly symbolic act displayed for mainly for the media. Our organization never lent itself to these types of mediatic showcasing, except in Esmeraldas, where a faction closely aligned with Ser Paz handed over their weapons in a highly publicized event.

Leaders cannot order a simple cease-fire and freeze all conflicts overnight. Our leadership role in the second peace effort was as activists directing a process of internal pacification. The table where legitimate leaders of each organization sat down and decided that they would no longer be at war created a superior command structure and established a solid base upon which to plan a peace that could be respected by all the actors. This process had not only to do with the internal affairs of the organizations but also with formulating public policy, reforming policing practices (whether institutional or the result of custom), and raising the cultural consciousness in the society at large.

The government's promises were varied. Central to the agreement was the political recognition given to the organizations. That is to say the government gave legitimacy to the leaders to carry out our planning, unlike Ser Paz, which gave this legitimacy only to their activists who negotiated and later handed over agreements to the leadership. This new context forced the leaders of our organization to take on other roles and capacities, including negotiating with the government, project development, and a greater understanding of local and national political life.

One of the things that was proposed was training within the ranks of the police, which significantly improved the general relationship between the police force and the street organizations. But among the proposals for economic development, few real contributions were made. There were no loans to the organizations to maintain real economic projects. There was mistrust on the part of the government's security forces, who feared that the organizations would succeed in monopolizing resources that would be invested in arms and drug trafficking.

When the Secretaría del Pueblo took over the peace process in 2008, we were able to hold national meetings with the help of their resources. The activists of this secretariat sponsored leaders for travel and even helped in the political formation of many cadres, within which I also participated. The work by the Secretaría del Pueblo was an attempt to bridge the gap between the street organizations and the government, but this unfortunately had its problems. Each ministry had its own interests and channels to each street organization through the Secretaría. So while this entity was slowly falling apart, our relationships with other ministries were also affected. Developments were slow, creating constant frustrations among the leadership. Later on, we had to engage politically with each ministry separately, requiring more time and effort. Several years after the meeting with the president, doors began to close.

However, the peace process bore fruit over time. Politically, the organizations demonstrated their strength and maturity on issues such as the attempted coup against Correa by the police force, where the youth of the organizations mobilized to support him. The conflict was resolved in one day as we demonstrated our capacity to organize far surpassed any other youth organization and was on a par with large leftist activist groups that had far more experience in street protest.

Not continuing with the formal political process did not mean failure for the peace process. Authorities such as police officers began to understand the problems better, while young people in the organizations began to follow the example of their leaders. The new generations were no longer interested in wars and violence but were rather focused on social or cultural issues, which in itself meant peace. This still failed to tackle other social problems such as drug addiction and petty crime, but the leadership still continues to strive towards structures capable of guiding youth away from drug addiction and toward the gradual elimination of the culture of violence.

At present, our organization does not have any problems with any other street organization. Even inside the prisons, the gangs' colors and spaces are respected. There are channels of communication where the most serious problems (which have not come up in years) are brought to attention and are usually swiftly resolved.

Notes

1 The Andean Parliament is based in Bogotá, Colombia, and is made up of five Andean countries: Bolivia, Colombia, Ecuador, Perú and Chile. The main role of the Andean parliament is to foster regional integration between the member states.
2 When the author mentions, "places of mutual confluence," he is referring to public parks and, in particular, to nightclubs. As the gang phenomenon in Ecuador took off in the 90s, nightclubs played a central role in the early years in the expansion of gang culture in coastal cities. Though inter-gang violence played out in different urban spaces, nightclubs and parks were the main sites of confrontation.
3 For a good overview of the Ser Paz gang initiative run by Nelsa Curbelo, please see Chapter 8 of: Geneva Small Arms Survey, 2010. *Small Arms Survey 2010: Gangs, Groups, and Guns*. Cambridge: Cambridge University Press.

   Though Ser Paz played an important role in normalizing gang intervention in Guayaquil, this approach was later rejected by the gangs as overly paternalistic. Gang leaders argued that the Ser Paz approach was rooted in a traditional desistance model that did not recognize the agency of gangs to transform themselves collectively.

35

Gangs in the post-Chávez Bolivarian revolution

How *mano dura* policies and political pacts have organized crime in Venezuela[1]

Verónica Zubillaga,[2] Rebecca Hanson[3] and Andrés Antillano[4]

Introduction

On July 13, 2015, "La Piedad", a populous poor neighborhood situated in the south periphery of Caracas, awoke at dawn under siege due to a spectacular and unexpected militarized invasion in which 14 people died and more than 200 were detained by the Bolivarian National Guard. Hours later, President Nicolás Maduro announced the new militarized operation – it was the fourth in the last five years. The military intervention was called *Operación de Liberación y Protección del Pueblo* (OLP; People's Liberation and Protection Operation). President Maduro said in the afternoon: "With these four operations taking off . . . we have elements in hand to prove that Colombian paramilitarism, Colombian drug trafficking and all that conspirators have come to seize, to control and to establish [their] model".[5]

One year and eight months after having launched and systematically deployed the OLP throughout much of the country, on March 31, 2017, Attorney General of the Republic Luisa Ortega announced that the year before, 21,752 people were murdered in Venezuela. Of these, she said, 4,667 people died at the hands of various state security forces. That day, the attorney general revealed that the Venezuelan state was responsible for 21% of the violent deaths that occurred in 2016 in our country. In short, our law enforcement agencies had turned into the most lethal in the world.

This chapter contributes to a critical approach to the study of gangs by highlighting the deleterious effects of *mano dura* policies, such as the ones exemplified by the OLP, on criminal groups. First, using the case of Caracas, we want to show how such policies encourage gangs to adapt in different ways, in some cases adopting a warfare mode. These policies have contributed to the transformation of gangs into organized criminal groups, which has been widely discussed in the literature (Cruz, 2010; Lessing, 2017). Second, we want to illustrate how these policies in Venezuela have contributed to the reorganization of gangs, turning them into informal political actors of importance with whom the State, in periods of contested legitimacy and high political instability, is compelled to negotiate. This is especially so given the highly disruptive power of armed violence acquired by the criminal groups and their internal cohesion developed during confrontations with the police (Hagerdorn, 2005; Cruz, 2016; Barnes, 2017; Cruz and Durán

Martínez, 2016). One of the main goals of this chapter is to tackle the diversity of the relationships between the Bolivarian state and armed actors. We understand the state not as a unitary and coherent set of institutions but as "congeries of institutions, agencies and agendas at different levels that are not necessarily connected with each other" (Gupta, 2012:56).[6] By analyzing how some gangs evolve into organized criminal groups in response to state policies – from persecution to pacts, from pacts to declarations of war and back to pacts – we aim to enrich the literature on violence, organized crime and politics (Arias, 2013; Wennmann, 2014; Durán Martínez, 2015; Lessing, 2015; Barnes, 2017; Cruz, 2018). A third goal of this chapter is to contribute to an understanding of why Venezuela has seen such an increase in violence despite the fact that it has not experienced the civil wars that have occurred in countries with similar homicide rates through a focus on *mano dura* policies (Cruz, 2010; Jütersonke, Muggah and Rodgers, 2009; Antillano y Avila, 2017; Wolf, 2017).

In this analytical project, we build on the concept of *criminal politics*, which Barnes (2017:973) describes as

> interactions between states and violent organizations that are motivated more by the accumulation of wealth and informal power and which seldom have formal political ambitions pertaining to the state itself; however have become increasingly engaged in politics of the state through the accumulation of the means of violence itself.

(see also Lessing, 2015). Furthermore, different authors propose a typology of state and organized crime group relations ranging from zero tolerance and eradication to attempts at transformation and integration into the political and social life (see Wennmann, 2014).[7]

While acknowledging that the militarization of citizen security is historically rooted in Venezuelan democracy (Hernández, 1986; Avila, 2017), we argue that we must analyze militarization in distinct phases in the Chávez era (Zubillaga and Hanson, 2018). In 2009, massive incarceration was the dominant security logic, one that contributed to the alliance of gangs and their transformation into criminal organizations. Later, in 2013, while continuing to imprison, the government experimented with a policy of integration referred to as the *Zonas de Paz* (Peace Zones). This failed integration attempt allowed gangs in some spaces to consolidate their territorial sovereignty. In response, the government declared a war on criminal groups, launching the spectacular military operation called "Operativo de Liberación del Pueblo." In some places, criminal gangs have responded to this initiative with impressive lethal power, using weapons such as hand grenades that can only be obtained through the state security forces attacking these organizations, though, as we note subsequently, the effects of the OLP and *mano dura* approaches are far from homogeneous. Finally, there was a return to negotiations between high-ranking government officials and the leaders of criminal groups as the government sought stability and support in the face of a contested electoral process. Thus, we identify four strategies that were developed and juxtaposed with each other at distinct but also overlapping time periods: violent enforcement, failed negotiation and integration, confrontation and instrumental negotiation.

This research is based on ethnographic and interview data we have collected since 2017. Two years after the launching of "Operativo de Liberación del Pueblo", we started to visit La Piedad, once or twice a week, to register the impact of "this war for territorial sovereignty" declared by the government in this urban poor community.[8] From the beginning, we were astounded by the devastation caused in the community by the police forces; later on, we were impressed by the visibility of guns and hand grenades in public spaces in the barrio. From August 2017 to August 2018, a fieldwork diary of each visit was kept. For safety reasons, not all interviews were recorded, though many were. Seven group discussions and 16 individual interviews were conducted with women. We also had the opportunity to interview young men, mostly about their experiences during the military interventions. The leader of the criminal group we focus on in this chapter (whom we will call here Doni) was usually around; we were able to speak with him four times about his life, a recent pact with high-ranking officials, his family and the transformation of his business. We also spoke with local drug traffickers.

Between March and July of 2018, we conducted 90 interviews with officers from various security forces, including the National Police, Venezuela's forensic police (CICPC) and municipal and state police forces. Our sample contained men and women officers between the ages of 23 and 47 from different rankings in the police hierarchy and different lengths of time on the job. While some officers were completing their first year in the forces, others had over 20 years' experience. All the group discussions and interviews recorded were transcribed and coded following the main principles of grounded theory in qualitative data analysis (Charmaz, 2006).

Violence and street gangs before the OLP

In 2016, Venezuela became the second most violent country in the region, behind El Salvador, with a rate of 70 homicides per 100,000 residents. Like patterns throughout the region, those who are dying are mostly young poor men of color. The persistent exclusion of young poor men from popular sectors, the collapse of prisons due to the sudden massive incarceration of these youths – discussed in the next section – and the deepening of the economic crisis associated with the collapse of oil prices correlate with the strengthening of criminal networks and more visible crimes such as kidnapping and homicides (See Wacquant, 2001, 2008; Antillano and Avila, 2017).

This substantial increase in violence can only be explained by a multiplicity of interrelated factors and processes occurring within the frame of what is known as the Bolivarian Revolution (see Smilde, Hanson, and Zubillaga, forthcoming).[9] Although we cannot review this complex phenomenon in full here, we argue that state fragmentation and inner struggles contributed significantly to an inability to develop sustained citizen security policies – such as police reform and gun control policies – and to the deterioration of the systems of justice administration and the police, with the latter overtly involved in killings and organized crime. Intense state fragmentation and progressive militarization of the Bolivarian government can be noted as well in the frequent rotation of ministers in the sphere of citizen security truncating the continuity of any public policy. From 1999 to 2019, 20 years of the Bolivarian Revolution, 15 ministers have been designated and removed – 12 of them have been from the military. Concerns over the potential threats posed by internal and external opposition have motivated an important increase in the purchase of weapons during the first decade of the 21st century in Venezuela. According to reporting by El Nacional, by 2009, Venezuela dedicated more resources to the purchase of weapons than any other country in the region. The country ranked eighth worldwide in this category.[10] These legal purchases feed illegal weapons circuits (Cano, 2001).

Here we use the recent history of the territory of La Piedad in Caracas to consider gang modes of operation and transformation across the four security strategies identified previously, placing special emphasis on the process of militarization that has characterized the Maduro administration.

La Piedad, where the OLP was launched in 2015, is a popular neighborhood that is part of the territorial extension of slums, subject to a pathological imagination (Brotherton, 2015), especially of police officers and the media. As if to justify the cruelty and killing of the population, the conglomeration of slums began to be called "the Death Corridors" (*Corredores de la Muerte*) months after the OLP.[11]

Located on the south-central periphery of the city, the neighborhood is closely connected with a variety of other middle-class neighborhoods and commercial areas. Its location plays an important role in criminal activity in the area. The difficult terrain of the mountain the neighborhood is built on provides a degree of safety to groups operating in the barrio. The close proximity of a large number of poor neighborhoods provides important opportunities for collaboration, such as hiding stolen cars and kidnapping victims, and the clandestine movement of weapons across rough terrain that has a series of paths connecting different parts of the city. The neighbors describe their community as a labyrinth. Furthermore, the height of the mountain also provides strategic advantages. It is a lookout, and criminal groups with their surveillance crews can always detect when police agents are coming.

Gangs made their presence evident in La Piedad long before the network of organized crime groups we describe here developed. Previous to 2015, these gangs were the result of various characteristic conditions of poor and excluded neighborhoods, described in the literature on gangs of American urban sociology, incorporating other conditions of the Latin American context such as the chronic absence of justice, the abundance of uncontrolled weapons and high levels of police brutality and repression (Briceño-Leon and Zubillaga, 2002; Rodgers and Muggah, 2009; Rodgers and Baird, 2015).

Groups of young people, organically formed with a group identity, were attached to their specific territory. In fact, the gangs assumed the names of their neighborhood sector. They were involved in recurring armed confrontations with gangs of neighboring sectors. These armed conflicts, known as *culebras* (snakes), were unleashed for multiple reasons, for example, territorial invasions and robberies into neighboring sectors. *Culebras* entail the revenge for deaths of relatives or peers, thus constituting a network of obligations. The duty to avenge and respond on behalf of the *"dolientes"* (mourners) by family and friends has produced numerous deaths (see Zubillaga, 2008). One of the members of a gang that we interviewed explained that shootings he engaged in before were "for *culebras* we had with [other gangs]! I am involved with these faggots because they killed a friend, or a friend of a friend of mine. And that has been a chain; a chain that started when I was a child and extends to the present".

These were gangs without formal hierarchies (Dubet, 1987), deploying expressive violence as a means of performing their masculine identities and defending their neighborhood from robberies and attacks by other gangs.[12] Excluded from the formal job market, they engaged in micro-trafficking to accumulate resources for the gang. This micro-trafficking was irregular and unstructured, oriented around profit but also individual consumption (see Decker and Van Winkle (1996) on this form of trafficking).

The participation in the micro-trafficking of drugs caused frequent clashes with the police. A police officer assigned to La Piedad in the past that contrasted the time he spent working in the area with the present:

> La Piedad, *Tucusito, Cien Caminos* [we have changed the barrios' names]. There is an alley [that connects all these neighborhoods] and they all communicate with each other. I used to pass through all those alleys with five officials, running around, shooting up criminals! Now that cannot be done, you have to go in with three hundred other officers, and even then it's likely that you will be killed.

Militarization, violent enforcement, persecution and imprisonment

Despite a civilian-led police reform initiated in 2006, a new phase of military operations was inaugurated in 2009 (Hanson, 2013a, 2013b, 2017) with the launch of the *Dispositivo Bicentenario de la Seguridad* (Bicentennial Security Device operative), followed by the *Madrugonazo al hampa* operative in 2011 and *Plan Patria Segura* in 2012. These plans consisted of massive invasions of neighborhoods and the intensive detention of poor young men.

A large increase in the prison population quickly became evident, with the prison population doubling between 2009 and 2011 from 30,483 to 50,000. In fact, Minister of Interior and Justice Tareck El Aissami commented on Twitter: "The situation is complex, during 2010, the prison system reached the largest population deprived of liberty in history", revealing the strides made in incarceration during the socialist revolution.[13]

Most of those imprisoned were young men from popular sectors held for minor crimes such as drug trafficking. In the only prison survey published by the government, it was noted that 90.5% of those deprived of liberty are men, and almost half of them were young people, with 45% between 18 and 25 years old (88% under 40 years old). The vast majority were poor, with 56% from stratum IV and 11.6% from V, and almost a quarter of those were held for drug trafficking and distribution.[14] The rapid increase of the prison population led to a critical prison situation, evidencing a loss of state control over some but not all of the prisons. In these spaces developed autonomous and sophisticated internal organizing of those deprived of liberty (see PROVEA, 2013; Antillano et al., 2015).[15] This political prison order simulates a sort of state, with a government directed by leaders, a military branch and even mechanisms for capturing rent used to buy weapons and ammunition.

In La Piedad, many men were imprisoned and were socialized in this hierarchical prison order. The men involved in the illicit economies, aware that they would likely be imprisoned at some point, knew it would be advantageous to have acquaintances or contacts in prisons to ensure their own protection and survival. In some spaces, previously incarcerated youth, upon returning to their neighborhoods, reproduced a new order with clear hierarchies, headquarters and an army of vigilantes, prepared to respond to the official declaration of war.

The massive imprisonment and gathering of young men with knowledge and experience in illicit economies favored the creation of social networks in the world of crime. A policeman commented precisely on this porosity between the world of jail, the world of the neighborhood and the importance of social networks among criminals when explaining why Doni, the leader of La Piedad criminal gang, could not have been arrested:

> He takes shelter, more than everything in prison, in Tocorón. He is hidden there. He goes there and stays several months and does not leave, and when he leaves, he goes to La Piedad and walks with several riflemen. We have tried to catch him, but he has friends everywhere. So when the police are already in civilian clothes and hidden in cars in the lower part of the neighborhood, they tell him and then he doesn't leave, he goes to another place.

It is important to clarify that the prison–gang connection in Venezuela operates at a much smaller scale than those found in places like São Paulo and Rio de Janeiro. The degree to which prison hierarchies and social structures have influenced gangs in Caracas is more limited than in other places in Latin America. However, these connections are becoming increasingly important in understanding the modus operandi of criminal groups in the country.

A failed integration attempt: Las Zonas de Paz and the strengthening of the gangs

By 2013, it became clear that mass incarceration was not an effective solution to crime. Homicide rates had increased from 49 in 2009 to 53 homicides per 100,000 inhabitants in 2012. It seemed to a sector of the Ministry of Interior and Justice that it was time to try other policies.

The "Peace Territories" were an initiative developed by the vice minister of internal policy and legal security, José Vicente Rangel Ávalos, in the framework of the Misión a Toda Vida Venezuela (Mission to All Life Venezuela).[16] The goal of this plan was to establish meetings with heads of gangs in the country and convince them to agree to ceasefire pacts and turn over their weapons. In exchange, they would gain relief from police repression and resources and loans that would be provided by the government in order to create cooperatives and motivate agricultural development and construction within the gangs' communities (see Gómez and Hanson, forthcoming). In 2013, Rangel announced that the plan would be piloted in the Valles del Tuy; Barlovento; and sectors in the states of Aragua, Falcón and Guárico, where the well-known gang of El Picure operated. The vice minister visited the identified areas in person and negotiated directly with the young members of the gangs.

Gómez and Hanson (forthcoming) write that the experiment, implemented with little planning and without trained experts and the support of local institutions, ended in complete disaster. Rather than establishing peace, the plan strengthened gangs in key territories. With no oversight or support to create cooperatives or engage in economic development, gangs in some places used the money intended for these purposes to buy high-caliber weapons and grenades from state security forces. In the interviews with police officers we conducted, one agent commented:

> Since it was not fully planned, there was no supervision plan, or a control plan, or a follow-up plan. When they gave the money, what did criminals who have never had a micro-enterprise do? Upon receiving the money, they say: "What are we going to do with this money?" and they say: "We are going to buy more weapons then!", they took it and invested the money in guns.

The transition to Peace Zones resulted in an unprecedented change in certain gangs, who grew in size and became increasingly capable of engaging in large-scale kidnappings, extortion, bribery, vehicle robbery and other lucrative illicit activities that were coordinated from within the Peace Zones. Indeed, by 2014, the collapse of oil prices had begun to affect both the redistributive capacity of the state as well as illicit economies. Traditional activities, like the micro-trafficking of drugs, were no longer sufficient, and gangs had to turn to other activities.

The vice minister claimed that the experiment was novel, without precedent. In an interview with the vice minister, while defending himself against "attacks" on his program, he commented: "First, it was not something we planned. This came out alone, and then nothing is written down. This is unique in the world. A Vice Minister who talks from you to you, with gangs totally armed."

Yet El Salvador was already 16 months into a gang truce that had been initially negotiated between gangs and certain political actors. The truce consisted of a non-aggression pact between the two main Salvadoran gangs, the Mara Salvatrucha 13 and the Eighteenth Street Gang, as a first stage. During the second stage, "Violence Free Territories" were to be created. Unlike the Venezuelan experiment, the truce eventually involved church representatives, business leaders and local and international organizations such as the Organization of American States (OAS) (see Táger and Aguilar Umaña, 2013; Aguilar Umaña, Arévalo de León, and Táger, 2014; Cruz, 2018).

In a talk show on August 25, 2013, the vice minister spoke, using the same vocabulary as in El Salvador, "Violence Free Territories" and "Peace Territories", to describe the initiative he led. But, unlike the inter-institutional coordination of El Salvador and the later great visibility that the experience gained, in Venezuela, the improvisation of the program, lack of opacity and institutional linkages were evident.

In La Piedad, after years of official persecution and imprisonment, an alliance between gangs with long-standing rivalries began to form. As one youth said, this was seen as a strategy to confront the common enemy – the police. The Peace Territories experiment allowed space for these alliances to form. One of the drug dealers we interviewed told us:

> In Ocumare del Tuy, José Vicente Rangel Ávalos, that fuck went and started talking to the gangsters there! Then, later, Doni, you know that Doni knows everyone! Then, [Doni] brought a guy from [Ocumare del Tuy, where the Peace Territories started], then they started with the thugs like "Look, the peace!" And now we are all calm. Because before we were enemies, and they killed people here and we killed people there too! But we reached a friendship. Totally serious.

The alliance of the different gangs and the relative peace established between them allowed the strengthening and expansion of this criminal network. Increasingly, gangs were organized by sector and had recognized leadership and defined positions. This new alliance later allowed for a common front against the police and the state's *mano dura* policies (see Antillano and Avila, 2017). A young member of the gang, when recounting how his gang had organized, said:

> By sectors, and each guy leads his sector. Doni takes his sector, Niki takes his sector, another guy leads his sector, there are thirty-six sectors, but there are sectors that are dominated by the same guy, so, I am the head here, here are ten *panas* of mine. Here I am the first, he is the second and he, the third. It is a hard safety ring to get there. To get to where they are, you have to go through like ten *alcabalas*. "*Gariteros*". It is the structure they have in the neighborhood.

This structure is homologous to the prison, where the term "*garitero*" refers to the guards located at strategic points.

According to the interview we conducted with the leader of the La Piedad gang, the gang had about 100 members. According to both police officers and a young member interviewed, if all gangs in La Piedad and the neighboring sectors of the chain of barrios were added up, there would be about 300 members.

The visibility of criminal activities was astounding. Several neighbors reported with intense discomfort how common it was in their community to see kidnapped persons being held, and some reported hearing and seeing the blows and threats in phone calls with the kidnapped family members to negotiate terms. In a conversation with Doni, the leader of the band, he was quite sure of himself and the returns on kidnapping: "It is the activity in which you have a reward that you are going to charge. You have a victim, you negotiate with someone in the family to solve. It always goes well."

A young man who belonged to the same gang remembered the period in the following way:

> You had to sweat every day to kidnap or steal someone! You know that you can make twenty thousand dollars with a kidnapping, and you go and buy two rifles for ten thousand each. And if you want, tomorrow you sell [the rifle] and buy a smaller gun. But mostly, that AR-15 [a type of rifle], you buy from the National Guard.

Despite the fact that La Piedad was established as a Peace Zone, in which the police were formally prohibited from entering, some officers continued to "*cobrar su multa*", as some youths described to us in interviews. A part of the gang's earnings ended up in the hands of the police.

Thus, intermittent confrontations between the police and gangs and regular police extortion continued in La Piedad.

And, with the economic crisis deepening month by month, officers began to "adjust" agreements and unilaterally increase "their fines." As one young drug dealer told us: "Doni has been seized a thousand times; he is basically a money maker for the police". But there came a point that gang members said it was unacceptable:

> then from there we ended up with that *vaina* of the peace zones. The issue was turned around. It became the Zones of Peace against the government, against the police! . . . Then that created a war. I don't want any more "*pacos*" [police agents] here in my neighborhood! A "*paco*" that comes up the hill, we'll hit him! It was then when the thugs got bloodthirsty, that, that was never seen in Venezuela!

This continued bribery would unleash a confrontation with the police agents that would culminate with the declaration of "the frontal war" with the OLP. On June 5, 2015, the gangs' declaration of war on the police erupted in a spectacular expression: in a confrontation, the gangs of La Piedad burned nine police motorcycles (*Policaracas*), threw grenades and wounded at least six officials. The event was widely reviewed in the press: "Mega-Bands: violent groups, at Piedad"; "Camp battle! With rifles and grenades they attack policemen in La Piedad". Neighbors remember the battle very well; they commented that this time "the thugs turned on and burned the police motorcycles with grenades." An old lady added that the "*malandros*" were tired of the extortion, resorting instead to throwing grenades.

A little over a month after the attack on police, the People's Liberation Operation began. Now the state had declared war on the gangs.

Confrontation and instrumental negotiation: a war declared on organized crime and the resulting pact

Officers pointed out that initially OLP raids were carried out in areas where the Peace Territories had been implemented. In other words, from their perspective, the OLP was a response created by the state to deal with the outcomes of a public policy over which they had lost control. While officers blamed the OLP for the reorganization and strengthening of gangs in certain sectors, many responded that it was policies like the Peace Territories that catalyzed these changes. With free rein, as officers described it, gangs were able to work together and strengthen their organizations, as well as invest in better weapons, such as grenades and tear gas. When we asked a member of the PNB's special tactical unit (the FAES) about the Peace Territories he told us:

> Look, these *zonas de paz* have been a disaster, they are the root of why delinquency has increased so much in the country. In those sectors gangs were able to gain more strength. The government gave them money, a credit to start a business or something, but what did they do with that money? They bought guns.

Gang members we interviewed corroborated these accounts. José, one of the young members of the gang we interviewed, commented:

> the People's Liberation Operation was our fault! We were living too fast and furious! We were at high speed all the time! The kidnappings, the car stealing. When they got into La

Piedad [the police officers in the OLP first intervention], there were eighty cars! Up there they took out ambulances, how are you going to have eighty cars here! And they were all from different gangs! Different *panas*! At that time the peace zones that had been created with Rangel Ávalos were destroyed.

Doni himself agreed with this statement; in a conversation, he told us: "We made mistakes. But here you don't mess with people. They gave us the peace zone, but we made mistakes. We continued with kidnappings, stolen cars, we burned cars to the police." A policeman also pointed out that visibility of crimes as "noise": "noise began to be generated regarding what is kidnapping, homicide, in those sectors that were benefited with special terms, in those sectors called peace zones". Another one said: "La Piedad was sounding [*sonando*] too much". Different media kept on defining Zonas de Paz as zones of impunity.[17]

It is perhaps unsurprising, then, that the *Operación de Liberación del Pueblo* (People's Liberation and Protection Operation) was initiated in La Piedad, "the Caracas sector with the most active criminal gangs". Very soon, the abuse of force that occurred within various security forces marked the beginning of a new phase of systematic killing (see Zubillaga and Hanson, 2018).

Conversations with the women we interviewed in La Piedad made evident the systematic armed harassment they lived through two years under the OLP. In fact, we can grasp the systematic pattern of invasion in the narrative of a mother whose son was killed in one of the invasions:

> Well, as I say, they enter the houses without even knocking. They burst in and enter violently. They steal what they have to steal. They kill who they have to kill. Do you understand? Then they do, we can say, their "show". They set up the spectacle. "There was a confrontation!" they say. Shots in the air, everything! This reaches the ears of the highest [referring to highly ranked functionaries] and they believe everything they say. They have just to justify their operation. They have to take ten, fifteen dead bodies with them. Innocent [*sano*] or not. . . . It's a successful operation for them, they came to the neighborhood, they "cleaned it" and left.

La Piedad was indeed a barrio where the warfare was very intense. Now, post-Peace Territory, criminal groups were both willing and able to respond to the declaration of war with high-caliber weapons to which they had access through the military.[18]

We noticed that it was in 2015, the year *Operativo de Liberación del Pueblo* was launched, that the press started to report killings by hand grenades during confrontations between the police and criminal groups in Caracas. In 2015, 15 killings by grenades were reported in this city, three occurring in *La Piedad*. The next year, a similar number was reported: 16 killings in Caracas, 4 of them in La Piedad.[19]

The military superiority of the criminal group was notorious, both because of the strategic geographical location – the altitude of the hill that allowed them to observe the movements of the agents – the high caliber of weapons and the organization of the men in arms at points in defense (the *Gariteros*). Furthermore, this superiority of the criminal group contrasts with the contradictions in the orders and counter-orders between the director of the National Police and the minister; in an account of the asymmetrical confrontation, a policeman who had to go to La Piedad told us:

> The first time I went up I was scared! Because we were with guns and they, the Gariteros, [the gunmen] fired from a hill at a distance with rifles! And the bullets came close! Then

the director sent us down, go down! Descend! Descend! We cannot! Until finally the Minister: Go up there! And, well, do what you can do!

What we were witnessing was a "criminal war", a notion used by Lessing (2015) to untangle the logics underlying conflict and confrontations between the state and criminal cartels (Lessing, 2015). In criminal wars, as Lessing points out, criminal cartels do not want to seize the state but rather seek alternative arrangements with the state in order to continue their illicit businesses. These are wars of coercion that seek to achieve prerogatives in terms of state practices or policies in order to continue in the illicit economies and its benefits.[20] In this type of war, the warring parties seek to change the opponent's behavior with violence following a logic of coercive bargaining (Lessing, 2015).

The fierce response of criminal groups in La Piedad had the effect the groups had hoped for – an end to war. By mid-2017, Maduro's administration was going through a tough period: four months of widespread anti-government protests, where at least 130 persons were killed, and an upcoming elections to elect a New Assembly – considered illegitimate by a majority of the population – created by the administration and parallel to the National Assembly elected in universal elections in 2015, formed with a majority of deputies from the opposition. By July 2017, the government decided to back down from the war it had declared.

According to gang leaders who took part in the negotiations, the government needed calm in the streets to guarantee there would be no sabotage to the elections and to drop "criminal indexes", as the gang leader we interviewed put it. After phone conversations, high-ranking officials went to La Piedad and participated in talks with the leader of the criminal group. "There was a Word . . . a recognition between faces" (*Hubo una palabra un reconocimiento entre caras*), meaning there was a serious agreement: no more police invasions and raids if the criminals stopped killings and kidnapping – even though the Guardia Nacional could patrol the area, while drug trafficking would be tolerated. The government also committed to "improve social policies, the re-establishment of sports fields in the neighborhood, programs for young people and the repair of houses damaged by the military interventions".

Different neighbors related that the relevant authorities visited La Piedad and had conversations with criminal leaders. When we started fieldwork in La Piedad, women related that it "has been a month" since the raids had stopped. Then, we started to hear about the pact, and in the weeks following, we started to see many young armed men near the community kitchen together with a crowd of children that were always playing in the area.

The agreement was not a secret. Media outlets reported on the pact, saying that thanks to the agreement, La Piedad "again" became a Peace Zone where no police agents could penetrate. Police officers corroborated these reports, claiming that the police could not enter La Piedad. A return to the pact suggests that at least one criminal group in La Piedad had become something of a political actor during a moment of political instability, wielding sufficient political capital to negotiate with the government. The ability to offer a cessation in violence was a resource that was used to manage de facto state policy (see as well in El Salvador, Cruz, 2018).

The pact then, was an instrumental alliance needed by the government in a perilous political period and in light of losing the war. As the Salvadoran sociologist Jose Miguel Cruz points out about the Truce in El Salvador, this pact did not aim to recover territorial sovereignty (as was declared the objective of the OLP) nor to disarm the criminal group. The government needed the armed group to impose legitimacy through coercion if required (Pansters, 2012). The alliance between government officials and armed parastatal actors for the sake of political domination and imposed legitimacy has a long history in the region (Pansters, 2012; Knight,

2012; Snyder and Durán Martínez, 2009; Cruz and Durán Martínez, 2016). Precisely, Cruz (2016) points out that

> in contemporary post transition Latin America, states extend the limits of legal force, trespass their own legal restrictions on the use of force, and tolerate, even seek criminal involvement as part of the strategies of their representatives to claim legitimacy.
>
> *(288)*

In this direction, one police officer stated that it has been the state's revolutionary politics in general that have strengthened gangs in the country:

> Me, as a police officer, I think that the government has to do with all of this, it is a part of all this. Why? Because we cannot explain how there are so many high caliber weapons in the streets . . . how a group of people that don't even have the training, that have never stepped foot in a police academy . . . the government has facilitated access . . . with the goal of intimidating all those who stand against [the revolution].

Thus, two years after the pact, on July 26, there was again a notable confrontation between police agents – specifically the CICPC – and gangs in La Piedad that lasted three hours. After this long combat, police officers had to withdraw, following the minister of justice's order, which contradicted orders from CICPC leaders. The balance: four officers were injured. Media reaction was critical of the withdrawal, accusing the government the weakness in the face of the armed preponderance of the criminal groups. The event is significant, revealing once more the lack of cohesion in the state security apparatus and the degree of coordination among the criminal groups to confront the state.

Conclusion

The impacts of militarized policing on gangs: zooming out from La Piedad

In this chapter, we have analyzed how different strategies deployed by the Maduro government have contributed to cycles of violence in Caracas. We have been particularly interested in demonstrating how *mano dura* policing strategies have contributed to gangs evolving into more organized criminal groups as they confront systematic killing and police impunity.

Militarized operations in La Piedad and Caracas more broadly have made the city more, not less, insecure. While this point has been made in previous scholarship on *mano dura* policies, here we want to conclude by highlighting how the highly fragmented condition of the Venezuelan state has exacerbated *mano dura*'s lethal impacts. In contrast to militarized operations before the Bolivarian Revolution, the OLP was implemented by state institutions – including but not limited to the National Guard, municipal and state police forces and the CICPC – that have become increasingly fractured and pitted against one another during the revolution. Inconsistent and contradictory policies that are poorly implemented, like the Peace Zones followed by the OLP and a return to pacts between the state and criminal organizations, only reinforce gang members' commitment to organized crime and violence, because it is never clear what the future might hold. The fact that some police forces abide by pacts while others do not require that gangs always be prepared to return to war with at least some state institutions.

As Durán-Martínez has noted, criminal actors' incentives to employ violence are not constant. These vacillate according to the cohesion of the state security apparatus, and competition in the illegal market determines traffickers' incentives to employ violence. According to Durán-Martínez (2015:7):

> A cohesive security apparatus is likely to reduce the visibility of violence because it makes state protection more reliable or enforcement more efficient. By contrast, a fragmented security apparatus is likely to increase the visibility of violence because it makes protection less predictable or enforcement less effective.

Cruz and Durán Martínez (2016), when comparing truces and criminal pacts in El Salvador and Medellín, point out that "truces and pacts can reduce homicides when (a) they involve the state as an administrator of violence reduction incentives and (b) criminal groups have achieved group cohesion and leadership that facilitate territorial control and strategic dependability" (2).

Where state security is incredibly fragmented, as in the case of Venezuela, neither state nor criminal actors can trust that today's agreements will hold tomorrow. With state security forces unable and unwilling to coordinate and de facto policy changing according to short-term political ends, the Venezuelan state is unable to credibly commit to protection or prosecution of criminals.

That gangs and more organized groups all depend on the complicity of police and military agents for weapons capable of responding to militarized interventions like the OLP speaks to this fragmentation and incoherence. Despite the war declared on the "criminal groups and paramilitarism", as President Maduro said, the use of grenades by criminal groups discussed previously reveals this collaboration between military officials and the criminal groups (see Arias, 2017). It is this corrupt collaboration that leads to such extraordinary levels of violence when pacts fall apart.

However, it is important to note that the impact of militarized policing on criminal groups is not homogeneous. La Piedád is an example of how *mano dura* strategies can produce more organized groups, a process identified in much of the previous scholarship. But the ways in which *mano dura* policies shape these groups depend on the local history of the neighborhood in which the gang operates, previous relationships between gangs and the police and the geographic location of the neighborhood where the raids occur (urban, peri-urban and rural, for example).

In our interviews, all officers agreed that gangs in the country were much better organized and armed and more violent than those in the past. Some of the officers identified the OLP as the main catalyst. According to one PNB officer, although the intention of the OLP was a good one, that is, to eliminate leaders of the gangs, once this mission was accomplished and the OLP moved to another sector, gangs returned with even more force than before. Neighbors, he reported, were more likely to collaborate with the gang members when they returned due to the resentment and anger that police repression had generated in the community.

This resentment also had implications for officers' sense of security. According to one officer from the PNB, this plan had increased violence against the police:

> The number of police officers killed has increased, for different reasons. . . . the OLP. was a cleansing, let's put it that way. So, delinquents become filled with even more hate for the police. They don't care what color your uniform is, what rank you are, if they were a friend in the past. . . . Since it was the police who participated in the OLP, now the delinquent says "Ok, now it's our turn to fuck the police. . . . After the implementation of the OLP, it has become more dangerous to be a police officer.

Yet in some sectors of the city, like La Vega and El Valle, officers reported that the OLP had successfully wiped gangs out. In other places, officers critiqued the OLP for dislocating gangs, forcing them to move to other sectors. It is important to note here that the OLP most likely contributed to gang violence not only by incentivizing increased cooperation between gangs but also by uprooting gangs from their territory and forcing them to establish control over gangs in another area. By disrupting illicit markets and relocating illicit actors, the plan exacerbated a key motivator of gang conflict.

In describing this process, one PNB officer told us that killing off gang leaders and/or wiping out gangs in some places only opened up space for new gangs to emerge, which generated new conflicts:

> Those spaces that were without leaders, new delinquents appeared to take control over these spaces. So, they start off, they start committing crimes, they start killing, they start to rob. . . . And this generates conflict between these groups, armed confrontation between gangs, things that previous gangs did not allow. Because the gangs that left or were taken out, they had a long time operating in the area, they had learned to bring together the gang and community members, and they co-existed with residents and generated new security measures with them.

The OLP, according to the officer, eviscerated these ties and introduced new armed actors into communities who had no historical connection to the communities they took over.

What remains a constant throughout these reflections is the way in which the fracturing of state institutions and linkages between some state security forces and criminal groups feeds into varied forms of violence in the country, whether that be the increasing organization of gangs or whole gangs being wiped out during raids. Indeed, even ceasefire pacts do not put an end to this violence due to this fragmentation. While some police forces abide by the pacts, others do not. Conflict and competition between state security institutions themselves make peace under pacts short term and intermittent.

Notes

1 This chapter is based on three research projects carried out between 2018 and 2016 supported by the Latin American Project of the Open Society Foundations and CAF-Banco de Desarrollo de América Latina. We would like to express special gratitude to Caracas Mi Convive, who supported us as we conducted fieldwork.

  This chapter benefited from Verónica Zubillaga's stay as visiting fellow at the Kellogg Institute for International Studies, Notre Dame University, Indiana, US, in the academic year 2018–2019.

2 Universidad Simón Bolívar, Departamento de Ciencias y Tecnología del Comportamiento. Caracas. Red de Activismo e Investigación por la Convivencia REACIN. www.reacin.org/

3 University of Florida, Department of Sociology and Criminology and Law and the Center for Latin American Studies

4 Universidad Central de Venezuela, Instituto de Ciencias Penales.

5 The community name has been changed. All news and digital media articles that could identify the particular community have been explicitly changed. We only use digital media articles that refer to this vast popular sector area but do not allow any specific identification of the community.

6 A. Gupta's theoretical image of the state, in his ethnographic study about poverty and structural violence in India, is pertinent to what we are grasping and studying in Caracas: "a disaggregated view of the state makes it possible to open up the black box of unintended outcomes by showing how they are systematically produced by the friction between agendas, bureaus, level and spaces that make the State" (Gupta, 2012:47).

7 Wennmann proposes confrontation, accommodation and transformation (2014) whereas Barnes introduces the terms confrontation, enforcement, evasion, alliance and integration (2017). These typologies will be useful for our analytical purposes to track the type and chronology of the relationships between

the Bolivarian government and gangs that became criminal organizations in Caracas with significant lethal power.

8 The official document entitled: "Protocolo de actuación de los cuerpos de seguridad del estado en la operación de liberación humanista del pueblo" explicitly declares that the OLP was launched with an objective to liberate Venezuelan territory and the protection of the people from common and organized crime (2017).

9 The year 1998 marks the onset of a period of accelerated transformations and conflict escalation known in Venezuela as the Bolivarian Revolution with the beginning of Hugo Chávez's government. In the frame of this process, Venezuela was renamed República Bolivariana de Venezuela.

10 Diario El Nacional 03 de Agosto de 2009

11 See http://contrapunto.com/mobile/noticia/corredores-de-la-muerte-en-caracas-68397/ Consultado el 15 de marzo 2018

12 In contrast with hierarchies described in American urban sociology (Sanchez Jankowski, 1991).

13 Declarations made by the interior minister, Tareck El Aissami, on his Twitter account, @TareckPSUV, Feb. 8th 2011. Consulted on 10 March, 2012.

14 Consejo Superior Penitenciario. Diagnóstico Sociodemográfico de la población penitenciaria en la República Bolivariana de Venezuela. Caracas, 2011.

15 In other work on the formation of prison gangs as forms of internal governance, administered by prisoners themselves with a sophisticated hierarchy (see Antillano, 2015; Antillano et al., 2015). Similar self-rule regimes of prisoners have been reported in Latin America (in Brazil: Biondi, 2008; Nunes, 2011; Lessing, 2017; in El Salvador: Cruz, 2010).

16 The Misión a Toda Vida Venezuela was conceived during the era of Hugo Chavez as a comprehensive public security policy. During its first year under the presidency of Nicolás Maduro, the "Movement for Peace and Life" was created, "an initiative to promote culture, sports, healthy recreation and the incorporation of youth in socio-productive activities, especially in popular areas".

17 www.bbc.com/mundo/noticias/2015/07/150727_venezuela_zonas_de_paz_dp; https://issuu.com/eltiempovenezuela/docs/0718054001433701268/11; https://runrun.es/nacional/venezuela-2/212961/10-claves-para-entender-las-zonas-de-paz/

18 Precisely, Arias points out: "Indeed the metaphor of war [war on drugs; war on Maras; war to paramilitaries, like President Maduro said when launching the Operación de Liberación del Pueblo] reinforces the worst tendencies of state actors, justifying a combat posture against the poor areas where crime is concentrated, while sweeping under the rug the corruption and complicity that make chronic violence sustainable over the long term" (2017:11).

19 In their study "Trafficking and Criminal Use of Grenades in Latin America and the Caribbean", Godnick, Quagliaro, and Bustamante (2015) conclude that except for artisanal grenades, the only sources of grenades are from military arsenals. The study, which included media monitoring between January 2013 and March 2015, showed that Venezuela, Colombia and Mexico, all countries with high levels of internal conflict, are the countries that present a concentrated use of hand grenades. Venezuela was the country with the most fatal victims of grenade outbreaks – 18, followed by 8 in Colombia and 7 in Mexico. In the follow-up to national press reports that we carried out between 2016 and August 2018 in the frame of our research, we recorded double this number: 36 dead and 24 injured due to the manipulation of grenades in Venezuela.

20 In contrast, for example, with an insurgency, which seeks to seize the state or a territory completely. In these wars of coercion, the belligerent parties seek to constrain the opponent in order to change their behavior. Lessing identifies two main strategies: violent lobbying, where criminals aim to influence public policy and address it to high-ranking officers, such as the war declared by Pablo Escobar concerning extradition policies, and violent corruption that aims to influence enforcers (police officers, judges) in order to change repressive actions.

References

Aguilar Umaña, I., B. Arévalo de León, and A. G. Táger. (2014). "El Salvador: Negotiating with Gangs." In: A. Ramsbotham and A. Wennmann (eds.) *Legitimacy and Peace Processes: From Coercion to Consent.* London: Conciliation Resources.

Antillano, Andrés. (2015). "Cuando los presos mandan: control informal dentro de la cárcel venezolana." *Espacio Abierto*, 24(4): 16–39.

Antillano, Andrés and Keymer Avila. (2017). "¿La Mano Dura y la Violencia Policial Disminuyen los Homicidios?" *Revista CIDOB d'Afers Internacionals*, 116: 77–100.

Antillano, Andrés, Iván Pojomovsky, Verónica Zubillaga, Chelina Sepúlveda and Rebecca Hanson. (2015). "The Venezuelan Prison: From Neoliberalism to the Bolivarian Revolution." *Crime, Law and Social Change*, 65: 195–211.

Arias Desmond. (2017). *Criminal Enterprises and Governance in Latin America and the Caribbean.* New York: Cambridge University Press.

Arias, Desmond. (2013). "The Impact of Organized Crime on Governance: A Desk Study of Jamaica." In: Camino Kavanagh (ed.) *Getting Smart and Shaping Up: Responding to the Impact of Drug Trafficking in Developing Countries.* New York: NYU Center on International Cooperation.

Ávila, Keymer. (2017). "Las Operaciones de Liberación del Pueblo (Olp): Entre Las Ausencias y los Excesos del Sistema Penal en Venezuela." *Crítica Penal y Poder*, 12: 55–86.

Barnes, Nicolas. (2017). "Criminal Politics: An Integrated Approach to the Study of Organized Crime, Politics, and Violence." *Perspectives on Politics*, 15(4): 967–987.

Biondi, K. (2008). *A etica evangelica e o espirito de crime Trabajo presentado en la 26va.* Bahia, Brazil: Reunión Brasileña de Antropología.

Briceño-Leon, Roberto and Zubillaga, Verónica (2002). "Violence and Globalisation in Latin America." *Current Sociology* 50(1): 19–37.

Brotherton, David. (1997). "Socially Constructing the Nomads. Part One." *Humanity and Society*, 21(2), May.

Brotherton, David. (2015). *Youth Street Gangs: A Critical Appraisal.* New York: Routledge.

Cano, Ignacio (2001). *La importancia del microdesarme en la prevención de la violencia.* Río de Janeiro: ISER y Universidad Estadual de Río de Janeiro.

Charmaz, Kathy. (2006). *Constructing Grounded Theory: A Practical Guide Through Qualitative Analysis.* London: Sage Publications.

Cruz, José Miguel. (2018). "The Politics of Negotiating with Gangs. The Case of El Salvador." *Bulletin of Latin American Research*: 1–16.

Cruz, José Miguel. (2016). "State and Criminal Violence in Latin America." *Crime, Law and Social Change*, 66(4): 375–396.

Cruz, José Miguel. (2010). "Central American Maras: From Youth Street Gangs to Transnational Protection Rackets." *Global Crime*, 11(4): 379–398.

Cruz, José Miguel and Angélica Durán-Martínez. (2016). "Hiding violence to deal with the state: Criminal pacts in El Salvador and Medellin." *Journal of Peace Research*, 53(2): 197–210.

Decker, Scott H. and Barrik Van Winkle. (1996). *Life in the Gang. Family, Friends, and Violence.* Cambridge, UK: Cambridge University Press.

Dubet, Francois. (1987). *La Galère: jeunes en survie*, París: Points Actuels.

Durán-Martínez, Angélica. (2015). "To Kill and Tell? State Power, Criminal Competition, and Drug Violence." *Journal of Conflict Resolution*: 1–27.

Godnick, William, Celine Quagliaro and Julián Bustamante. (2015). "Tráfico y uso criminal de granadas en América Latina y el Caribe." Centro Regional de las Naciones Unidas para la Paz, el Desarme y el Desarrollo. 13 Reunión del Observatorio del Crimen Organizado en América Latina y el Caribe. Medellín, Colombia. 11–12 de mayo.

Gómez, Leonard and Rebecca Hanson. (Forthcoming). "The Pressure to Bring in a Body: How Systematic Killing Transformed Police Raids and Gangs in Post-Chávez Venezuela." In David Smilde, Rebecca Hanson, and Verónica Zubillaga (eds.) *The Paradox of Violence in Venezuela.* Pittsburgh: University of Pittsburgh Press.

Gupta, Akhil. (2012). *Red Tape: Bureaucracy, Structural Violence, and Poverty in India.* Durham, NC: Duke University Press.

Hagerdorn, John M. (2005). "The Global Impact of Gangs." *Journal of Contemporary Criminal Justice*, 21(2): 153–169.

Hanson, Rebecca. (2017). "Civilian Policing, Socialist Revolution, and Violent Pluralism in Venezuela." Dissertation. Department of Sociology, University of Georgia, Athens, GA.

Hanson, Rebecca. (2013a). "The Impact of Plan Patria Segura on Police Reform in Venezuela." *Venezuelan Politics and Human Rights*, May 19. https://www.venezuelablog.org/the-impact-of-plan-patria-segura-on-police-reform/

Hanson, Rebecca. (2013b). "Police Reform on a Political Tightrope: Citizen Security and Public Perceptions, Part 3." *Venezuelan Politics and Human Rights*, November 21.

Hernández, Tosca. (1986). "Los operativos policiales extraordinarios en Venezuela: dos acercamientos reflexivos al problema." *Capítulo Criminológico*, 14: 1–25.

Jütersonke, Oliver, Robert Muggah and Dennis Rodgers. (2009). "Gangs, Urban Violence, and Security Interventions in Central America." *Security Dialogue*, 40(4/5), Special Issue on Urban Insecurities: 373–397.

Knight, Alan. (2012). "Narco-Violence and the State in Modern Mexico." In: Wil G Pansters (ed.) *Violence, Coercion, and State Making in Twentieth-Century Mexico*. Stanford, CA: Stanford University Press, 115–134.

Lessing Benjamin. (2015). "Logics of Violence in Criminal War." *Journal of Conflict Resolution*, 59(8): 1486–1516.

Lessing, Benjamin. (2017). *Making Peace in Drug Wars: Crackdowns and Cartels in Latin America*. Cambridge: Cambridge University Press.

Nunes Dias, C. (2011). "Estado e PCC em meio às tramas do poder arbitrário nas prisões." *Tempo Social*, 23: 213–233.

Pansters, Wil. (2012). *Violence, Coercion, and State-Making in Twentieth-Century Mexico: The Other Half of the Centaur*. Redwood City, CA: Stanford University Press.

PROVEA. (2013). *Situación de los Derechos Humanos. Informe Anual*. Caracas: Programa Venezolano de Educación-Acción en Derechos Humanos, PROVEA.

Rodgers, Dennis and Adam Baird. (2015). "Understanding Gangs in Contemporary Latin America." In: Scott H. Decker and David C. Pyrooz (eds.) *Handbook of Gangs and Gang Responses*. New York: Wiley.

Rodgers, Dennis and Robert Muggah. (2009). "Gangs as Non-State Armed Groups: The Central American Case." *Contemporary Security Policy*, 30(2): 301–317.

Sanchez Jankowski. (1991). Islands in the Street:Gangs and Urban American Society. Berkeley, Ca: University of California Press.

Smilde, David, Rebecca Hanson, and Verónica Zubillaga (eds.) (Forthcoming). *The Paradox of Violence in Venezuela*. Pittsburgh: University of Pittsburgh Press.

Snyder, Richard and Angélica Durán-Martinez. (2009). "Does Illegality Breed Violence? Drug Trafficking and State-Sponsored Protection Rackets." *Crime Law and Social Change*, 52: 253–273.

Táger, A. G. and I. Aguilar Umaña. (2013). *La tregua entre pandillas salvadoreñas hacia un proceso de construcción de paz social*. Guatemala City: Interpeace.

Wacquant, Loic. (2008). "The Militarization of Urban Marginality: Lessons from the Brazilian Metropolis." *International Political Sociology*, 2(1): 56–74.

Wacquant, Loic. (2001). "The Penalisation of Poverty and the Rise of Neo-Liberalism." *European Journal on Criminal Policy and Research*, 9(4): 401–412.

Wennmann, A. (2014). "Negotiated Exits from Organized Crime? Building Peace in Conflict and Crime-affected Contexts." *Negotiation Journal*, 30(3): 255–273.

Wolf, Sonja Mano Dura. (2017). *The Politics of Gang Control in El Salvador*. Austin: University of Texas Press, p. 320.

Zubillaga, Verónica. (2008). "La culebra: una mirada etnográfica a la trama de antagonismo masculino entre jóvenes de vida violenta en Caracas." *AKADEMOS*, 9(2): 179–207.

Zubillaga, Verónica and Rebecca Hanson. (2018). "Del punitivismo carcelario a la matanza sistemática: El avance de los operativos militarizados en la era post-Chávez." *REVISTA M. Estudos sobre a Morte, os Mortos e o Morrer*, 3(5): 32–52.

36

Gangs in Kenya

Work, manhood and security

Naomi van Stapele

Introduction

This chapter is about working gangs in Kenya and aims to move away from the current association of gangs in Kenya with violence and 'ethnic' politics – that is, gang members as 'thugs for
hire' (Van Stapele, 2016). Based on 14 years of ethnographic research with gangs in Nairobi and
4 years with gangs on the South Coast of Kenya. I argue that to understand gangs in Kenya,
work and gender are at least as important as 'ethnic' politics to grasp processes of gang formation, especially if one wants to understand the gangs from the young men's own perspective.
Gangs are vital to many poor young urban men in Kenya, because they offer work and, as such,
a chance to realise respectable masculinities (Ocobock, 2017). In this sense, gangs can also be
instrumental in realising community development. However, there are enormous barriers in
the underserviced and highly surveyed urban environments, popularly referred to as 'ghettos' in
Kenya, to achieving masculinities and development (Kabiru, Mojola, Beguy, & Okigbo, 2013).
This explains why the gangs under consideration here are so fluid in their existence and why
membership is always fraught with ambiguities.

What I describe as working gangs in Kenya have received very little academic attention,
although they are powerful entities. The focus on more political gangs such as Mungiki (Rasmussen, 2010, see more subsequently) in media and academic representations has overshadowed
working gangs. Yet the more political groups did not operate in isolation but always worked in
conjunction, and in competition, with local working gangs. In contrast to the dominant view of
gangs in Kenya as ethnically and politically motivated and operating in networks that encompass
different neighbourhoods (Wabala, 2013), most gangs are in fact highly local, and, instead of
ethnicity, they are based on popular notions of work, manhood and belonging. These working
gangs are primarily organised around particular income-generating activities such as distilling
alcohol and selling stolen goods and drugs, and they operate in specific, albeit ever-shifting,
turfs within low-income neighbourhoods. They thus differ from ethnic-based groups like the
Mungiki gangs in terms of locality and power, as well as with respect to ethnic and political
identification (or a lack thereof).

Moreover, the working gangs appeared in Nairobi 'ghettos' years before the Mungiki gangs
rose to power, and they continue to exist today. The gangs that feature in this chapter are

generally referred to as bazes (Nairobi) or maskani (the South Coast); they have around 25 members, and they are mainly located at street corners or near places of work (where members produce alcohol, sell drugs, manage toilets or a carwash and organise other types of work together). They commonly provide security through their presence and threat of violence, which is typically geared towards reducing theft and house robbery in the surrounding area of their hang-out. Most thieves operating in their area of influence are perceived to come from outside *mtaa* (a Swahili term baze members use to refer to their part of a neighbourhood) and risk being killed when caught by baze members – 'mob-justice' is quite common in some of these locations. The role of bazes as local non-state security providers is widely accepted by other residents in their neighbourhoods and villages and in some locations even by several police stations that work hand in hand with these groups to reduce crime (such as in Ukunda on the South Coast and in Kiamaiko in Nairobi). Zooming in on the everyday roles of working gangs in local settings, I set out to demonstrate that starting from this point of view enables the reader to acquire a different understanding of their functions in relation to wider social, political and economic developments in Kenya.

Gangs in Kenya

Gangs in Kenya, and elsewhere, are part and parcel of society; hence, it is crucial to explore their identities and their functions from such an embedded position and the concomitant relationalities that may emerge as a result. In doing so, connections can be made between individual motives and cultural, political and social positioning, while also acknowledging the role of power, domination and inequality in societal responses to gangs (Fraser, 2017, p. 38). In colloquial use, the term gang has myriad connotations in Kenya, used often interchangeably with criminal organisations, political gangs, terrorists, militias and vigilantes. As such, gangs are associated with (ethnic) politics, violence and criminality. This obscures their role in community-led development, social justice activism, security and other important social events and processes. Top-down approaches to understanding gangs in Kenya (Schuberth, 2014) have led to rather thin descriptions which reproduce common stereotypes about these groups and contribute very little to understanding of their roles within communities and society as at large. Indeed, these groups take themselves as community-based groups but not as community-based *armed* groups (Schuberth, 2015). The fact that many members have (access to) arms, such as long knives, machetes and guns, has to be considered in the wider context of everyday violence and criminal use of arms, including by the police (MSJC, 2017). To illustrate, different gangs often join hands in securing their neighbourhood during conflict, such as during the 2017 election-related violence, often assisted by other residents who supply them with weapons, food and medicine (personal observations of nine separate short- and long-term conflicts involving gangs between 2007 and 2019).

Many of the conflicts I observed concerned a fight between gangs and police during which the gangs attempted to secure their neighbourhood and fellow neighbours from police raids (such as during two conflicts in Mathare, in Nairobi, in August 2018 and in April 2019). The Kenyan police are extremely criminal and violent, and police killings of alleged gang members are a weekly occurrence in most low-income neighbourhoods in Nairobi and Mombasa (Diphoorn, Van Stapele, & Kimari, 2019; Lind, Mutahi, & Oosterom, 2017). Such killings engender temporal and spatial borders not only around but also within such neighbourhoods, effectively creating micro-spaces of confinement for especially poor young urban men. Following from the criminalisation of poverty, young men specifically are widely taken as 'thugs' and/or 'terrorists' in dominant discourse (Van Stapele, 2016), and killing them is generally considered an effective strategy to reduce crime or thwart terror attacks.[1] To exemplify the extent of such killings, in the week of 23–27 September 2019, eight young men were killed, shot in the back by police, in Kayole, a low-income neighbourhood in Nairobi (discussion with local activists on 27 September 2019), just one of over 100 low-income neighbourhoods in Nairobi. In the context of such widespread police killings that target gangs, many young men in these neighbourhoods told me they more and more seek refuge in the space of such groups. At first glance, this may seem counterintuitive, but police generally read all bodies of poor young men as belonging to a gang and thus as criminal, and they are frequently arrested and killed just for walking outside in the emerging dark of the early evening. A woman in Huruma told me in July 2019 that every evening she picks up her son from the bus stop when he comes home from his work in the city centre to avoid his arbitrary arrest, or worse, murder, by police who manage a road block near their house. She and other parents often expressed to me that it is much harder to raise a son in the 'ghetto' than a daughter. Following this level of unlawful police violence, many young men do not feel safe to work outside their neighbourhoods and thus rely on the gang for income.

As noted, the role of gangs to organise work for young poor urban men in Kenyan cities is underexplored; however, numerous studies have studied gangs in the context of political violence, such as during the 2007/2008 post-election violence (Klopp & Kamungi, 2008; HRW, 2008; Smedt, 2009; Okoth-Okombo & Sana, 2010; Ndung'u & Wepundi, 2012). The role of such groups as security has also been studied in some depth (Heald, 2007; Price, Albrecht, Colona, Denney, & Kimari, 2016). Yet no movement or organisation has captured the public imaginary on gangs like the Mungiki movement (Rasmussen, 2010). The Mungiki movement was allegedly founded during the late 1980s and was believed to organise protection of rural squatter communities (mostly with Kikuyu backgrounds) during clashes in the Rift Valley Province that were instigated by the Moi government during the 1990s. The Mungiki movement purportedly had ties to politicians (mainly with Kikuyu backgrounds), and earned money through revenues from the many Mungiki groups operating in Nairobi's low-income neighbourhoods, along certain public transport routes and later also in a few rural areas. Mungiki attracted much media and academic attention, partly because of the dazzling speed with which these groups took over parts of Nairobi and the transport industry between 1998 and 2001. From the 2002 elections onwards, the Mungiki groups became increasingly and more visibly involved in national politics. The skewed media and academic attention on Mungiki has, at times, fostered the perception that these groups entered seemingly virgin territory inside the Nairobi's low-income neighbourhoods during the late 1990s and were highly unique in their operations and services (Henningsen & Jones, 2013). This is inaccurate. Indeed, long before the Mungiki gangs emerged, local working gangs provided jobs and acted as security agents; some of which were later popularly dubbed vigilante groups (Anderson, 2002). The Mungiki gangs did have unique features in that they had very specific (albeit constantly changing) religious and political ideologies, and their power and scale of organisation were unrivalled. Accordingly, these gangs were able to provide services to a much wider network of people (Wamue, 2001).

Before the emergence of Mungiki gangs in Nairobi 'ghettos', the dominant and later only political party in Kenya, the Kenya African National Union (KANU), deployed youth wingers to provide security in many low-income neighbourhoods. Their job was to arrest and to discipline petty thieves and drugs and alcohol peddlers – and to report cases of domestic violence and other neighbourhood disturbances to the local chief. Also, these groups claimed control of bus stations and routes in the poorer parts of Kenyan cities. Hence, the youth wingers exacted fees for security from drivers and conductors years before Mungiki groups took over this industry between 2002 and 2007 (Rasmussen, 2012). Many KANU youth wingers were also involved in illegal activities, blurring an already thin line between state authority and criminal activities in Kenyan 'ghettos'. A more recent phenomenon, branded 'vigilantism' in dominant discourse, saw the rise of groups – including both young men and women – that were in charge of security, for a fee, and who often worked in conjunction with the local government authorities – be it the local branch of the main political party or the local chief. These security groups were often also involved in so-called illegal economic activities in 'ghettos' such as stealing, dealing drugs and brokering stolen goods.

In earlier times, all these groups mostly had multiple ethnic backgrounds, yet during the 1990s, similar vigilante-cum-political groups emerged that had particular ethnic profiles. The return of multi-party politics, from 1991 onwards, opened up a political space marked by intense electoral competition. Local political leaders of emerging oppositional political parties followed KANU's example and also established youth wings in Kenyan 'ghettos' – or 'armies', *jeshi* in Kiswahili, as they were dubbed locally. Many of these 'armies' had members who had ethnic backgrounds similar to that of the politician with whom they were affiliated. These groups assisted their godfathers – 'Big Man or Woman' in local terms – in politics by mobilising crowds at rallies, disrupting rallies of opponents and using general intimidation tactics during elections. Many also established themselves as vigilantes for a fee (Mutahi, 2011; Ogada & Mue, 2010). Similar to their predecessors, these groups were also involved in hijacking cars, armed robbery, dealing drugs, distilling illegal alcohol and brokering stolen goods.

Interestingly, working gangs are key to understanding the rise and demise of these larger organisations and movements, including Mungiki – which also often had strong components of work in the way they were organised locally. The type of work the working gangs are engaged in often has deep historical roots that hark back to the inception of particular neighbourhoods and ensuing rural-urban migration patterns over the years.

A history of working gangs in the illegal alcohol industry

In Nairobi working gangs are referred to as 'baze', which means a rather fluid network of friends – generally male age-mates who live in the same neighbourhood – and to the particular site where they regularly hang out (Githinji, 2006). Such groups and spaces are termed maskani at the coast. Bazes and maskani mostly manifest in lower-income neighbourhoods in bigger cities and towns, although they can be found in some rural regions. These groups are often depicted as gangs in dominant public discourse (Mwakio & Mwahanga, 2013; Wamucii & Idwasi, 2011). However, while some bazes (with which I also include maskani in this chapter) are engaged in illegal activities – such as dealing drugs, robbery and the sale of stolen goods – they are more often involved in non-criminal economic activities – such as working as motorbike taxi drivers – and seek to help their 'community'. Some work is organised collectively as a baze, such as illegal alcohol distilling, whereas other types of work, such as selling coffee or driving a motorbike taxi, are more individual endeavours. At the baze, friends chat, smoke, drink, chew khat, gamble (using cards) and organise access to work together, and each baze has a particular name. Most bazes are dominated by young men, though mixed bazes and exclusively female bazes also exist. In dominant views, concepts such as baze and 'gang' have become conflated and epitomised by the popular imaginary of 'the thug', making all of them targets for police brutality (Van Stapele, 2016). Yet the rather fluid groups belonging to the bazes can perhaps best be understood as organisations of work within a context of urban precarity (Van Stapele, 2015; Thieme, 2013, 2017). Unknown to many Kenyans who do not live in these 'ghettos', most bazes also have football teams in local leagues; some are registered as youth groups and many also engage in community service – such as garbage collection – and in collective income-generating activities – such as selling water, organising bus stations and managing a toilet or a car wash together. Apart from income generation, such activities can also help build social capital as individuals and groups. Accordingly, bazes do not differ that much from local women's groups or other self-help organisations and can thus also be considered as local development actors. The type of work and particular organisation of bazes in a specific neighbourhood are connected to broader historical, political and economic processes, as is the case of bazes involved in the production of illegal alcohol, locally dubbed *chang'aa*, in Mathare, Nairobi.

As early as the 1930s, women who settled in abandoned parts of the quarry that later came to be known as Mathare earned money through sex work and selling home-distilled alcohol such as *chang'aa* (White, 1990a). The colonial capital Nairobi only allowed a limited number of 'native' ('African') men living in designated housing facilities (Hake, 1977; White, 1990a) while working in the city, whereas 'native' women were forced to seek housing and work opportunities in illegalised settlements nearby. The settlement area that later came to be known as Mathare was near such a housing facility and was also wedged in by the Royal Airforce Eastleigh Base (currently known as Moi Air Base), a local 'soldiers and guards' barrack and a transit camp for the Kings African Rifles. Other police barracks and army bases further away from Mathare also had close ties to sex workers in Pumwani, Pangani and Mathare. The massive influx of soldiers and prisoners of war (Italian prisoners of war) during 1940–45 further attracted a growing number of female sex workers, who increasingly settled in Mathare, where rent was cheaper than in Pumwani (White, 1990a). These women were among the many young people who were forced to leave their increasingly overcrowded homesteads in the rural 'Native Reserves' in the pre-WWII colonial period in search of work for cash to pay for hut tax, among other things (Kanogo, 1987). Even if women made up the majority of residents in Mathare from the onset, men also increasingly came to live here, and some worked for these women as alcohol distillers. They can be regarded as the predecessors of the alcohol working gangs that emerged in this neighbourhood during the late 1980s and early 1990s.

From the late 1930s until the late 1950s, a new wave of rural-urban migrants in Mathare came from illegalised squatter communities in the Rift Valley, where former farm workers had been displaced from European farms as a result of the gradual mechanisation of farm work (Kanogo, 1987). Following these and other developments, Mathare became the bedrock of urban resistance against the colonial government (White, 1990b) and formed an important node in the Kenya Land and Freedom Armies (KLFAs) – also known as 'Mau Mau' (Elkins, 2005). The colonial government detained large sections of what it considered the 'Kikuyu' population and transformed many 'Native Reserves' into 'emergency villages', which functioned as concentration camps during the 'state of emergency' (between 1952–56 – Elkins, 2005, p. 308; Anderson, 2005, p. 90). Close to a million people were locked inside these camps, and tens of thousands of people, suspected of being freedom fighters, were imprisoned in makeshift prison camps scattered all over Kenya. Upon their release, many of these ex-detainees could not return to the 'Native Reserves', as most of these areas were by now perilously overpopulated, while other available lands had been confiscated by the different authorities that had collaborated with the colonial government, with local chiefs being an example (Rutten & Owuor, 2009; Anderson, 2005). As a consequence, released from prison, these men and women had no choice but to join illegalised squatter communities in either rural or urban areas, such as Mathare (Nelson, 2002, p. 238). The influx of these residents boosted the local alcohol economy in this upcoming low-income neighbourhood and informed a local climate of political resistance that would eventually shape the role of worker gangs in activism against police violence in recent years (interviews with Mathare baze members in July 2018).

After independence in 1963, alcohol production and distribution mostly remained a home-based economy in Mathare, and houses often doubled as bars where alcohol and sexual services were sold by women. It was not until the late 1980s and early 1990s that parts of Mathare gradually became the epicentre of the large-scale production and distribution in Nairobi of *chang'aa*. According to several baze members and their bosses, that is, the mostly female bar owners, the influx of rural-urban migrants during this more recent period of accelerated rural-urban migration boosted the sale of *chang'aa* to unprecedented levels. Demographic records and academic estimates vary greatly (MuST, 2012), but it is safe to say that the population in Mathare rose from a few thousand during the colonial era to many tens of thousands between the 1960s and 1980s (Kabagambe & Moughtin, 1983; Ross, 1973; Stren, 1972). The trend of rapid urbanisation, especially in low-income neighbourhoods (Macharia, 1992), that took off after independence in 1963 accelerated during the 1990s (Muganzi, 1996; Syagga, Mitullah, & Gitau, 2001; Muganzi, 1996; Ominde, 1968). Population growth in Mathare only declined slightly during the late 1990s and early 2000s, when even more low-income neighbourhoods came up to absorb the bulk of rural-urban migrants.[2] The recent rise in Mathare's population led to the unparalleled growth of the local alcohol economy and firmly established the role of working gangs in the production side of alcohol whereas (mostly) female bar owners expanded their distribution networks far beyond the boundaries of this neighbourhood. Still today, Mathare is known as the 'head quarter of *chang'aa*' in Nairobi.

The rapid growth of the *chang'aa* production and distribution during the 1990s was supported by local politicians and by officials within government and police who were (and still are) on the take (interviews with bar owners, distillers and police and personal observations, between July 2010 and July 2019). A government decree banned *chang'aa* production in 1983 (Nelson, 2002), but the incoming MP of Mathare at the time allowed the continuation of home-based *chang'aa* production in return for electoral support (interview with Shosho Kingi, 3 November 2005). Soon, the Mathare river saw multiple distilling sites, called 'kitchens', along its banks, which almost 30 years later still continue production today. Each 'kitchen' is managed by a working gang (i.e. baze), and alongside the production and distribution of illegal alcohol most of these groups were (and still are) involved in dealing drugs, brokering stolen goods and sometimes street muggings. Unfortunately, the profit margins have fallen significantly since the late 1990s, following a convergence of rising food prices (especially a type of molasses called *ngutu*) and increasing demands for police bribes since the 2000s. Still, the local alcohol economy sustains thousands of people in Mathare directly and is fundamental to most other economic activities located here. Thousands more depend indirectly on the alcohol economy in Mathare. For example, shortage of firewood plagues adjacent neighbourhoods but not Mathare. Every other small business on Mau Mau Avenue in Bondeni, one of the 13 'villages' in Mathare (MuST, 2012), sells large quantities of firewood. These firewood sellers have arrangements with construction companies for frequent early morning deliveries. Old wood from scaffolding at construction sites is transported to the area in large trucks. Every day, these trucks drop off mountains of firewood intended to fuel the widespread and constant distillation of alcohol at the sites near the river. At the same time, young men, often aspirant alcohol baze members, in search of work hang around these businesses from sunrise to midday to help offload the bulks of firewood and chop them into smaller pieces in return for a small stipend.

Working gangs, manhood and politics

In 'ghettos' such as Mathare, young male baze members often shift back and forth between their role as the diligent worker and the violent adversary in their relationships with their bosses.

Such shifts are tied, in large part, to their desire to achieve respect and, ultimately, a position of male efficacy. In turn, these young men sometimes engage in violence to force a shift in what they view as anomalous and oppressive gender relations, for instance, when working for female bosses or when kept in a position of servitude vis-á-vis male elders, and reverse what they consider their growing redundancy in society and their community. For example, plundering the houses of female alcohol bosses during the 2007/08 post-election violence in Mathare enabled some of these men to invest the profits of their loot in private businesses and to establish themselves as providers of their families (van Stapele, 2015). These men were part of groups that were organised, paid and armed by opposition leaders, but they used their engagement in violence to try to reverse local gender roles and improve their own positions. Moreover, while gender struggles have acquired historically influenced and nuanced variations in other 'ghettos' – such as those with a large Muslim population – young and poor men in other areas also recounted their fears of becoming redundant in the eyes of their wives, family and neighbourhood and in society at large. These men explained that violence was often a last resort to them – a means to force access to economic opportunities and become providers themselves.

This draws attention to a particular significance of the function of bazes, as these groups help in structuring the processes of becoming men by providing networks that young and poor men can use to access income-generating activities, skills development and other opportunities. These processes are popularly imagined as following the gradual attainment of specific social, cultural and economic capital (Bourdieu, 1986). Most young men move out of their family's one-room house after circumcision at the age of 16 to begin life as a junior man. Bazes allow young men to cater to and garner adequate capital with which to eventually establish themselves as senior men. These groups also enable these young men to maintain meaningful relationships with their families by working for close female relatives and performing security and other forms of community service in their neighbourhood area. When they need young men for work – including security provision – local business and property owners (for example, the mostly female alcohol bosses in Mathare) can visit a baze and negotiate a deal. Likewise, politicians and NGOs make similar use of bazes, though all such opportunities often turn out to constitute little more than short-term menial labour. Despite the fact that bazes offer work opportunities to young men, they are expected to leave the working gang and establish themselves as independent providers around the age of 30 at the latest. This puts enormous pressures on young men in economic contexts marked by extreme poverty and uncertainty.

In the context of economic destitution and brutal policing, the baze does wield some power due to their numbers and perceived readiness to engage in violence, which it may leverage in times of heightened crisis and ensuing potential for change. As noted, bazes often work as security providers for political aspirants. In contrast to dominant views, bazes are not just 'thugs for hire' (Kagwanja, 2009, p. 366), but their temporal engagement in politics is often part of longer processes of formation that are deeply embedded in local power configurations, with sometimes surprising outcomes. In early 2016, a local baze member called Chalo in Korogocho, an urban settlement in Nairobi, explained the type of security provided as follows: "These politicians, they can't come to our neighbourhood without us as security. They need to give us that opportunity. If they don't, then we make sure they can't come" (interview, January 28, 2016). Not only politicians but also businessmen and women, and even NGO staff, regularly required a security detail made up of members from the local bazes of young men to protect them, in essence, from these same groups. Similarly, in the run-up to the 2013 elections, I observed a number of bazes that denied politicians access to the Nairobi dumping site by throwing stones at them. Such action was taken because the pay offered by different political aspirants for security was deemed too low, so formerly rival bazes joined forces in opposition. These groups later formed a committee to negotiate with the aspirants and avoid conflict among the rival groups during the election period. In fact, this became a model for several rival bazes in Korogocho and Mathare during the 2017 elections, which helped such groups to increase their leverage vis-à-vis political candidates and earn more money while simultaneously avoiding bloodshed between them.

'Ethnic' politics in Kenya, as elsewhere, is not self-evident, for coalitions by elite politicians on either side of political divides may include individuals with diverse ethnic backgrounds, even those that are popularly imagined as antagonistic. Bazes, too, often have members with multiple ethnic backgrounds; hence, ethnicity may not always determine political affiliation. However, when particular ethnic narratives acquire meaning through locally felt grievances, bazes may display a stronger political and 'ethnic' profile. For instance, Kwale and Mombasa bazes mostly have members who are born in the same area where they join a particular baze, and they not only protect the boundaries of their areas of control from encroaching bazes nearby but also from people who are not considered coastal people, locally dubbed *watu wa Bara* ('people from upcountry') but who migrated to the coast in search of work. Most baze members that I conducted research with have Mijikenda (Digo) backgrounds and identify as 'natives and Muslim'. Many residents in Likoni (in Mombasa) and Ukunda/Bongwe (in Kwale) can trace their family lineage back to the villages in the forest nearby. The proximity of 'home' to these residential and business centres reinforces their claim of belonging and entitlement to this strip of land.

During the election period in 2017, the opposition rhetoric invoked secessionist politics, which resonated deeply with a majority of the Muslim members from the bazes I conducted research with. Particularly at the coast, the secessionist politics of the opposition fell unto fertile soil following the history of such ideologies here. The south coast where Mombasa and Kwale are located is home to a movement called the Mombasa Republican Council (MRC), which has the political aim to secede from Kenya and draws massive support from the many bazes located here. The MRC argues it has a legal basis for its call for secession. The coast was never a British colony but a protectorate, while simultaneously belonging to the Sultanate of Zanzibar. Prior to independence in 1963, as a protectorate and under the Sultan of Zanzibar, the area had largely been self administered (Brennan, 2008). With its incorporation into a newly independent Kenya, it became just one of many majimbo (regions) within Kenya. MRC is firmly embedded in highly local dynamics in Kwale and Mombasa county and at the same time also speaks to similar political aspirations along the entire coast and the more northern parts of Kenya, while also chiming in with grievances of Muslims living in Nairobi.

The MRC is a self-described social movement with political objectives (Willis & Gona, 2013), and members contest the different government frames that label it sometimes a political party or an NGO (supported by foreign funds) and sometimes an armed gang or a terrorist organisation (supposedly aligned to Al Shabaab). MRC came to prominence in 2008, although it has existed in some form since early 1999. While it's hard to ascertain the exact extent of its following and support in the region, the historical and contemporary grievances it raises are believed to resonate with the majority of the coastal people. In fact, the primary causes of the 2007–2008 election violence, land, economic equality and youth unemployment, are also the central grievances of the MRC. Thus, even if people along the coast do not necessarily share the MRC's secessionist vision, many may agree with the grievances it is raising. Together with 32 other groups, MRC was banned in 2008, again in 2010 and again in 2016 (Ombati, 2016). The state repeatedly declared that the MRC was involved in oath taking and was planning to violently attack people 'from upcountry' (interview with a researcher from Amnesty East Africa, on 7 October 2019). There is no evidence that MRC was involved in any (planning of) attacks, but bazes that affiliated themselves with MRC, or more indirectly with its ideology, have conducted attacks against 'newcomers' in recent years, as some baze members shared with me during field-work between January 2017 and August 2018. Yet these acts of violence were mostly directed at informers and police. Informers and police are widely imagined by bazes as 'newcomers', but many baze members shared with me that their attacks did not target 'newcomers' in general. Such attacks thus have to be understood not just as part of alleged ethnic tensions but perhaps even more so in the context of a historical struggle against state oppression by the hands of the police, which also contributed to the emergence of Al Shabaab in this region.

Working gangs and security

When Al Shabaab activity increased in Kenya, especially in Nairobi, North Eastern Province and the South Coast (Mkutu & Opondo, 2019), existing local bazes related in different ways to its recruiters, cells and other types of activity (for instance trade or attacks), varying from partnership to antagonism. Most bazes in my research lost a significant number of members to Al Shabaab, who went to fight in Somalia or elsewhere in Kenya. Many of these members died in battle or were killed by Kenyan police when returning to Kenya (MUHURI & OSI, 2013); other returnees are still hiding (for instance, in the forest in Kwale or in Nairobi settlements). At the same time, the increased Al Shabaab presence in their neighbourhoods and villages attracted intensified police surveillance, which resulted in the killing of many baze members who had no direct affiliation to Al Shabaab (KNHRC, 2015.). Some even at times tried to resist Al Shabaab activities in their neighbourhoods but were perceived as 'terrorists' anyway by local authorities. Several baze members shared with me that the loss and death of members prompted some of these groups to resist Al Shabaab activities by giving information to police. However, this was an extremely dangerous endeavour. First, Al Shabaab members did not hesitate to kill baze members who told on them, and second, police could take such informers as Al Shabaab for the sheer fact of having details to share; thus, they risked execution when doing so. Still, several bazes continued to use different tactics, including informing to police, to get rid of Al Shabaab activities in their neighbourhoods or villages, with the main aim to reduce police brutality and as such improve local security.

Their role as security providers with regard to crime is recognised by most residents and a few local police, whereas their role in resisting Al Shabaab presence remains rather opaque, probably because this is conducted in extreme secrecy for fear of repercussions from Al Shabaab. Sharing information with the police is just one way some of these groups try to oust Al Shabaab in their areas of influence. Other local security groups have secretly killed Al Shabaab recruiters and members (for instance, in Kia Maiko in Nairobi and Bongwe in Kwale). It is, however, quite rare for these groups to engage in open confrontation with Al Shabaab, which stands in contrast to the openly violent ways in which these groups punish (groups of) criminals in their neigh-bourhood. Several reasons underlie the different approach to expel Al Shabaab and other violent jihadi activities (such as Al Qaeda and IS) from their neighbourhoods and villages. Most bazes are afraid of Al Shabaab, because, as noted, Al Shabaab is believed to strike back with a venge-ance. Also, many group members sympathise with Al Shabaab to some extent and understand why some of their members became what they term 'warriors'. In addition to this, some groups work together with Al Shabaab in trade or by hiding Al Shabaab members or their weaponry from the police for money. Open confrontation would jeopardise such lucrative ties. Last, many baze members explained to me that they resist Al Shabaab presence mainly because of the police attention it attracts to the neighbourhood, which also brings them in danger, given that police often take individual members and entire bazes of particular localities as part of such violent jihadi groups (such as in Majengo in Nairobi, in Likoni in Mombasa and in Bongwe in Kwale).

Strikingly, bazes are the only non-state security groups in Kenya that at times deliberately act to counter Al Shabaab activities in low-income localities in Nairobi and on the South Coast. This is notwithstanding other organisations (such as several NGO initiatives and religious elder groups) that try to resist Al Shabaab, but these mainly operate through dialogue and information rather than strict security provision. Similar bazes operate in Lamu, Garissa and other towns near the Kenyan-Somali border, and in more rural areas, these groups are more mobile and often more heavily armed than in the more urban areas. Other non-state security groups, such as Sungu Sungu (at the coast, this term refers to a neighbourhood watch paid by residents), are far and few between, and where they operate, such as in Ukunda, they only focus on crime prevention. When faced with Al Shabaab activity in their streets, they rely on support from baze and police. A Sungu Sungu member in Ukunda shared with me in August 2018 that they generally do not face Al Shabaab head on but will first gather intel from a baze nearby. In one instance, the baze agreed with the Sungu Sungu chair to share such information with a police officer they worked closely with, but as it turned out, another police officer at the station worked together with Al Shabaab, and later this police officer shot one baze member dead and the other baze members went into hiding. Sungu Sungu was left untouched because their involvement was unknown. The officer who was suspected of selling the intel to Al Shabaab was later transferred after complaints from residents. This poignantly reveals the entanglement and complexities involved in shifting positions and relationships between baze, Sungu Sungu, police and Al Shabaab.

Sungu Sungu complicates local security relationships given that Sungu Sungu work directly with police (even if they were taken as non-state by members and residents), while most bazes are frequently targeted as spaces for crime and terror activities by police. As a result, some bazes have closer ties to Sungu Sungu and some to Al Shabaab, while others predominantly focus solely on securing their neighbourhood or village and try to lay low with respect to all the other actors of violence. Sungu Sungu and bazes (for instance, in Ukunda in Kwale) are both non-state security groups with the same main focus, namely crime prevention, but they also differ significantly. The distinction is that Sungu Sungu are selected and paid by residents and work under supervision of the village chairman (or woman), who is accountable to the local chief. Sungu Sungu groups have been declared illegal but have been brought back in some areas (such as in Ukunda). The same part of the neighbourhood under their watch also has bazes, and some baze members work for Sungu Sungu, but a Sungu Sungu does not have the same social depth as a baze. Sungu Sungu patrol the street at night, while baze members hang at their spot. Sungu Sungu work directly with police, whereas bazes may work with individual officers but have no formal partnership with police. When Sungu Sungu catch a suspected thief, they usually will bring him or her to the police station; baze will most likely fight the suspect and even kill him or her. Security provision is the only objective of Sungu Sungu, whereas it is considered an integral part of a variety of baze activities, and members describe their group usually in terms of work and gendered belonging. Security provision in the local neighbourhood is taken by bazes as a part of being a young man and connected to their male responsibility with regard to what they consider their community.

Conclusions

In this chapter, I launched the term 'working gang' for groups that form around notions of belonging to a particular (part of) a neighbourhood and notions of work, including illegal and criminal activities. Referring to illegal practices in this way is not uncommon among groups that are engaged in them. The young baze members are acutely aware of its illegal status, but they imagined it as reputable, as it enabled them to perform (young) male duties and earn respect from community residents. In contrast to the prevailing views on gangs operating in Kenya, working gangs are multi-ethnic, organised in terms of specific income-generating activities (e.g. distilling alcohol, dealing drugs, managing bus stations, brokering stolen goods) and tied to small localities within particular neighbourhoods. Especially striking is the role of working gangs in structuring the processes of becoming men, access to income-generating activities and providing security in low-income neighbourhoods that are beleaguered with criminal police violence and Al Shabaab activity.

Interestingly, notions of work, respectability and community service are not generally associated with gangs in the dominant discourses, whether in Kenya or worldwide. I, however, focused on the everyday role of gangs, and studying these groups from local viewpoints revealed the fluidity and overlap between gangs and between gangs and other social groups of young men such as football teams, youth groups and even CBOs. This view thus helped me to go beyond representations that prevail in both the media and academia. Accordingly, this perspective highlighted the quite different roles of gangs and gang members in the local setting. I hope I have added to the global gang studies by focusing on gangs in East Africa, which is a region that is notably underexplored in gang studies. This helped to nuance the prevailing perception that considers all gangs in sub-Saharan Africa through the lens of religious and political rebellion, casting these groups as somehow different from gangs in other regions of the world. Working gangs in Kenya share many commonalities with gangs worldwide in that they can be regarded as groups that organise access to (illegal/informal) work and other socio-economic opportunities for young, poor and urban men (in this case) who live in dire contexts that are marked by very few legal work prospects. As a consequence, it is imperative to include gangs in sub-Saharan African cities in the emerging global agenda of comparative gang studies. The blurring boundaries between legality and illegality in this chapter may also point gang research, particularly in Kenya, in new directions. As well as suggestions to analyse gangs from local viewpoints and through notions of work and gender, and instead of just looking at political affiliations and ethnic identifications, this study also highlighted the role of gangs in community development and service delivery. This is illustrated by their volunteer work in security provision. Kenya is known for its high crime rates and a volatile political climate. The country's security crisis is painfully exposed by recent attacks (allegedly by Al Shabaab); other junctures of violence between groups; and the disorganised, controversial and corrupt official response to these events. The process of security sector reform that commenced in 2003, and which became ever more urgent after the 2007/8 post-election violence, has still not translated into tangible results on the ground, as the unlawful killings of young and poor men continue to persist.

Notes

1 Focus group discussion with (different types of) community policing members and baze members in Shauri Moyo and Majengo, 18 January 2019. Interviews with residents in different wealthy and marginalized neighborhoods in Nairobi between January 2016 and February 2019.

2 Current estimates are deeply contested based on different ideas on boundaries and 'villages' that together constitute Mathare. For instance, government statistics exclude Mathare 4A, Mathare 4B and Mathare North but include Huruma and Kiamaiko, whereas some NGOs working in Mathare exclude areas with private land ownership.

References

Anderson, D. (2002). Vigilantes, violence and the politics of public order in Kenya. *African Affairs*, *101*(405), 531–555.

Anderson, D. (2005). *Histories of the hanged: The dirty war in Kenya and the end of empire.* New York: W.W. Norton & Company.

Bourdieu, P. (1986). The forms of capital. In J. Richardson (Ed.), *Handbook of theory and research for the sociology of education* (pp. 241–258). New York: Greenwood.

Brennan, J. (2008). Lowering the sultan's flag: Sovereignty and decolonization in coastal Kenya. *Comparative Studies in Society and History, 50*(4), 831–861.

Diphoorn, T., Van Stapele, N., & Kimari, W. (2019). Policing for the community? The mismatch between reform and everyday policing in Nairobi, Kenya. In S. Howell (Eds.), *Policing the urban periphery in Africa. Developing safety for the marginal* (pp. 24–40). Capetown: APCOF.

Elkins, C. (2005). *Imperial Reckoning: The untold story of Britain's gulag in Kenya.* New York: Henry Holt & Company Inc.

Fraser, A. (2017). *Gangs & crime: Critical alternatives.* London: Sage.

Githinji, P. (2006). Bazes and their shibboleths: Variation and Sheng speakers' identity in Nairobi. *Lexical Nordic Journal of African Studies, 15*(4), 443–472.

Hake, A. (1977). *African metropolis: Nairobi's self-help city.* New York: St. Martin's Press.

Heald, S. (2007). Controlling crime and corruption from below: Sungusungu in Kenya. *International Relations, 21*(2), 183–199.

Henningsen, E., & Jones, P. (2013). 'What kind of hell is this!' Understanding the Mungiki movement's power of mobilisation. *Journal of Eastern African Studies, 7*(3), 371–388.

HRW. (2008). *Ballots to bullets: Organized political violence and Kenya's crisis of governance.* Nairobi: Human Rights Watch.

Kabagambe, D., & Moughtin, C. (1983). Housing the poor: A case study in Nairobi. *Third World Planning Review, 5*(3), 227–248.

Kabiru, C. W., Mojola, S. A., Beguy, D., & Okigbo, C. (2013). Growing up at the "margins": Concerns, aspirations, and expectations of young people living in Nairobi's slums. *Journal of Research on Adolescence, 23*(1), 81–94.

Kagwanja, P. (2009). Courting genocide: Populism, ethno-nationalism and the informalisation of violence in Kenya's 2008 post-election crisis. *Journal of Contemporary African Studies, 27*(3), 365–387.

Kanogo, T. (1987). *Squatters & the roots of mau-mau 1905–1963.* London: James Currey.

Klopp, J., & Kamungi, P. (2008). Violence and elections: Will Kenya collapse? *World Policy Institute, Winter,* 11–19.

KNHRC. (2015.). *The error of fighting terror. Preliminary report of KNHRC investigations on human rights abuses in the ongoing crackdown against terrorism.* Nairobi: KNHRC.

Lind, J., Mutahi, P., & Oosterom, M. (2017). 'Killing a mosquito with a hammer': Al-Shabaab violence and state security responses in Kenya. *Peacebuilding, 5*(2), 118–135.

Macharia, K. (1992). Slum clearance and the informal economy in Nairobi. *Journal of Modern African Studies, 30*(3), 221–236.

Mkutu, K., & Opondo, V. (2019). The complexity of radicalization and recruitment in Kwale, Kenya. *Terrorism and Political Violence.* doi:10.1080/09546553.2018.1520700

MSJC. (2017). *Who's next? A participatory action research report against the normalization of extrajudicial killings in Mathare.* Nairobi: MSJC.

Muganzi, Z. (1996). Migration, urbanization and development. In *Population studies research series* (Vol. V). Nairobi: University of Nairobi.

MUHURI & OSI. (2013). *We're tired of taking you to court: Human rights abuses by Kenya's anti-terrorism police unit.* Nairobi: OSI.

MuST. (2012). *Mathare Zonal Plan, Nairobi, Kenya. Collaborative plan for informal settlement upgrading.* Nairobi: MuST.

Mutahi, P. (2011). Between illegality and legality: (In)security, crime and gangs in Nairobi informal settlements. *South African Crime Quarterly, 37,* 11–18.

Mwakio, P., & Mwahanga, S. (2013). MRC, tribal gangs target police at coast. *Standard Media.* Retrieved from www.standardmedia.co.ke/?articleID=2000080427&story_title=-MRC,-tribal-gangs-target-police-at-Coast.

Ndung'u, J., & Wepundi, M. (2012). *Transition and reform: People's peacemaking perspectives on Kenya's post-2008 political crisis and lessons for the future.* London and Nairobi: Saferworld.

Nelson, N. (2002). Surviving in the city: Coping strategies of female migrants in Nairobi, Kenya I. In G. Gmelch & W. Zenner (Eds.), *Urban life: Readings in the anthropology of the city* (4th ed.). Long Grove, IL: Waveland Press, Inc.

Ocobock, P. (2017). *An uncertain age: The politics of manhood in Kenya.* Athens, OH: Ohio University Press.

Ogada, M., & Mue, N. (2010). *Security sector reform and transitional justice in Kenya.* Nairobi: International Center for Transitional Justice.

Okoth-Okombo, D., & Sana, O. (2010). *Balaa Mitaani: The challenge of mending ethnic relations in Nairobi slums.* Nairobi: Friedrich Ebert Stiftung:.

Ombati, C. (2016, December 30). Interior cabinet secretary Joseph Nkaissery reveals 90 deadly criminal gangs in Kenya. *Standard Media.*

Ominde, S. (1968). *Land and population movements in Kenya.* London: Heinnemann.

Price, M., Albrecht, P., Colona, F., Denney, L., & Kimari, W. (2016). *Hustling for security: Managing plural security in Nairobi's poor urban settlements.* The Hague: Clingendael Conflict Research Unit.

Rasmussen, J. (2010). Mungiki as youth movement: Revolution, gender and generational politics in Nairobi, Kenya. *Young, 18*(3), 301–319.

Rasmussen, J. (2012). Inside the system, outside the law: Operating the Matatu sector in Nairobi. *Urban Forum, 23*(4), 415–432.

Ross, M. H. (1973). Community formation in an urban squatter settlement. *Comparative Political Studies, 6*(3), 296–328.

Rutten, M., & Owuor, S. (2009). Weapons of mass destruction: Land, ethnicity and the 2007 elections in Kenya. *Journal of Contemporary African Studies, 27*(3), 305–324.

Schuberth, M. (2014). The impact of drug trafficking on informal security actors in Kenya. *Africa Spectrum, 49*(3), 55–81.

Schuberth, M. (2015). The challenge of community-based armed groups: Towards a conceptualization of militias, gangs, and vigilantes. *Contemporary Security Policy,* 296–320.

Smedt, J. D. (2009). No Raila, no peace! Big man politics and election violence at the Kibera grassroots. *African Affairs, 108*(433), 581–598.

Stren, R. (1972). Urban policy in Africa: A political analysis. *African Studies Review, 15*(3), 489–516.

Syagga, P., Mitullah, W., & Gitau, S. (2001). *Nairobi situation analysis: Consultative report.* Nairobi: GOK/UNCHS (Habitat): Collaborative Nairobi Slum Upgrading Initiative.

Thieme, T. (2013). The "hustle" amongst youth entrepreneurs in Mathare's informal waste economy. *Journal of Eastern African Studies, 7*(3), 389–412.

Thieme, T. (2017). The hustle economy. *Progress in Human Geography,* 1–20.

Van Stapele, N. (2015). *'Respectable 'illegality': Gangs, masculinities and belonging in a Nairobi Ghetto.* Amsterdam: Amsterdam University (Dissertations).

Van Stapele, N. (2016). 'We are not Kenyans': Extra-judicial killings, manhood and citizenship in Mathare, a Nairobi ghetto. *Conflict, Security & Development, 16*(4), 301–325.

Wabala, D. (2013, August 31). Kenya: Country has 46 criminal gangs, report reveals. *The Star.*

Wamucii, P., & Idwasi, P. (2011). Social security, youth, and development situations in Kenya. In K. Kondlo & C. Ejiogu (Eds.), *Governance in the 21st century. Africa in focus* (pp. 188–199). Cape Town: HSRC Press.

Wamue, G. N. (2001). Revisiting our indigenous shrines though Mungiki. *African Affairs, 100*(400), 453–467.

White, L. (1990a). *The comforts of home. Prostitution in colonial Nairobi.* Chicago: The University of Chicago Press.

White, L. (1990b). Separating the men from the boys: Constructions of gender, sexuality, and terrorism in central Kenya, 1939–1959. *The International Journal of African Historical Studies, 23,* 1–25.

Willis, J., & Gona, G. (2013). Pwani C Kenya? Memory, documents and secessionist politics in Coastal Kenya. *African Affairs, 112*(446), 48–71.

Part V
Culture and the gang

Identity and collective resistance among the Almighty Latin King and Queen Nation (New York)

David C. Brotherton and Luis Barrios

It is possible that we are facing a new diaspora of collective action? What happened to the analysis in this quarter century? Why have we become aware only recently of the new diversity of action? Are we dealing with new actors and the new social practices or, rather, with old actors utilizing new practices? Perhaps these questions are too limiting to permit an answer, except in the most ambivalent terms. But we cannot overlook the fact that the social movement of twenty-five years ago had strong state/political orientations and that, in contrast, many of today's actors are searching for their own cultural identities and spaces for social expression, political and otherwise.

(Calderón, Piscitelli, & Reyna 1992:23)

Why should I deny who I am and what I believe in? We've gone back to an era of McCarthyism in the United States.

(King R., 10/05/98)

Introduction

In the process of liberation, all social movements in some way have the ability to claim, deconstruct, construct and reconstruct their identity. According to the literature, there is some consensus that a relationship exists between the construction of identity and collective action (Melucci 1989; Calhoun 1991; Calderón, Piscitelli, & Reyna 1992; Escobar 1992; Castells 1997; Della Porta & Diani 1999). This finding accords with our own analysis of the Almighty Latin King and Queen Nation (ALKQN) and distinguishes our work from that in the tradition of mainstream psychology or those who limit their analysis of identity issues to the causal properties of individual and to deviance.

In contrast to the prominent analytical position that identity occupies in the social movements literature, there is little such attention paid to this aspect of group process in the gang literature. Quite the contrary, for the most part, the importance of identity is restricted to the contemporary notion of "risk factors" (Branch 1997), especially since gangs have increasingly been perceived and defined as socially pathological. As Branch (1997) states, for all the gang's multifunctional qualities, it has never been viewed as a "protective factor" in any marginal youth's path of social and/or psychological development; that is, it has never been seen as the kind of support system that would foster a gang member's transition to mainstream life.

The primary focus in this chapter takes up the question which Branch and others have posed: can a collective identity emerge from a street subculture that makes possible their social transformation? Our approach to this question approximates to the work of social movement students when they declare that identity is a process of meaning construction, both for individuals and for collectivities, by which certain "sources of meaning" (Castells 1997:6) are prioritized over others and eventually become internalized; and which leads to:"the formation of communes, or communities [and] . . . forms of collective resistance against otherwise unbearable oppression" (Castells 1997:8).

In the following, we apply this concept of identity as collective resistance to respondents' narratives and to the various texts and observations that emerged from our participation in the group's day-to-day endeavors. Based on these data, we have developed three identity-related themes to guide the analysis:

1   The Latinization of identity
2   Identity and hope, and
3   Identity of the spirit

1 The Latinization of identity

> I'm always gonna be Boricua no matter what. American or no American, that's my heritage. That's where I was born at. If they think that because Puerto Rico is a part of the States – that they control some of that . . . I'm still one hundred percent Boricua, I would never say, I'm American. No, cuz I know where I come from.
>
> (Queen H. 10/25/97)

As Queen H. describes, Latino identity is of paramount importance to both the members' and the organization's world view and helps to shape many of their everyday organizational practices. Yet the claims to their ethnic identity are not simple and straightforward but emerge out of the specific experiences of their own personal, collective and subcultural histories. This process is dynamic and not at all mechanistic, as might be construed when one first hears expressions of cultural affiliation that appear to be essentialistic. In the following, we organize the analysis of the ALKQN's ethnic reclamation into two sub-themes: (i) the affirmation of Latino heritage and (ii) against invisibility.

i Appropriation of Latino heritage

The respondents in our sample were very much social agents struggling to recognize what liberation theologists describe as their own "*realidad humana.*" In so doing, as we have seen throughout this book, they became increasingly aware that they were struggling against a dominant culture that sought to both neutralize them politically and assimilate them culturally. Many respondents, particularly those of the second generation, discussed the quest for their own ethnicity with reference to the traditions and struggles of their parents:

> I tried actually not to assimilate to American culture because I'm proud of my Puerto Rican and Dominican heritage. I'm proud of all Latinos and I try to keep that in mind.

I know that I live in America and I should get used to the way they do things, but some of my family is very strong when it comes to their culture and they like it. They're proud of it and they try to instill that in me and I try not to forget that. You know I may not be from the islands, but I still have that in me. It's in my blood and I try not to forget where my family came form.

(Queen J. 6/20/98)

These assertions of ethnic self-affirmation and continuity, while they reflect efforts to resolve identity issues at the level of the individual, are carried out in conjunction with the entire membership and form an integral part of the group's collective agency. This point is crucial and, in many ways, distinguishes the ethno-political development of this group from other street subcultures that, while also claiming their members' ethnic solidarity, leave it undeveloped, parochial and particularistic (see, for example, the notions of "mi barrio," or "cholismo" among West Coast Chicano gangs). In the following, King C. discusses what happens when the group and the individual start to get other ideas about their ethnic trajectory:

Well, my own personal opinion is that the white people don't agree with what the Latin Kings are doing because they notice that Latins are getting along with Latins and together they're helping each other in all ways – in school, education, neighborhoods, and we are reaching our goal of uplifting Latino communities, and I think they really mad at us. But deep down they really fear us because we are rising to power and we are doing what we said we were gonna do, which is protect the weak and uplift the Latino community.

(King C)

In King C.'s experience, ethnicity is fine until it calls into question the distribution of power in a city that is famed for its cultural pluralism at the bottom and its highly concentrated and homogeneous hold on wealth (and decision-making) among the white elite at the top. King C., in fact, underscores three important points that are consistent with the group's approach to identity issues. First, the struggle for identity, if it is taken to its logical conclusion in a racially divided society, must always involve a breach of the ethnic status quo, leaving no resolution or accommodation at the individual level. Second, he is part of a group that, while appearing to be peripheral to the city's power matrix, actually exposes the deep cleavages in the fabric of class and ethnic life (Touraine 1988). Third, the audacity of the group along with its ethnic claims to represent the community contradicts the tendency, so rampant in the popular discourse on American social justice, that human and political rights are essentially a Black and White "thing" (Muñoz 1989).[4]

Thus, it was in this contentious manner that respondents spoke of promoting those cultural values that are related to their Latino/a heritage and, in particular, to their Puerto Rican/ Dominican backgrounds. This orientation was prevalent not only in the life history narratives and beliefs of the individuals but also in the rituals present throughout the group's organizational and written practices.

For example, in monthly Universal Meetings, the stage was often decorated with two Puerto Rican flags: the *Grito de Lares,* which is the flag associated with the Puerto Rican independence movement, and the official flag of the colonized present. Toward the end of the research period, however, the staging for the meeting was decorated with a third flag, that of the Dominican Republic. This move toward a more conspicuous ethnic pluralism within the group reflected both the leadership's recognition of the increasing importance of the Dominican membership and its claim that the ALKQN was obscuring its presence, just like the dominant society.

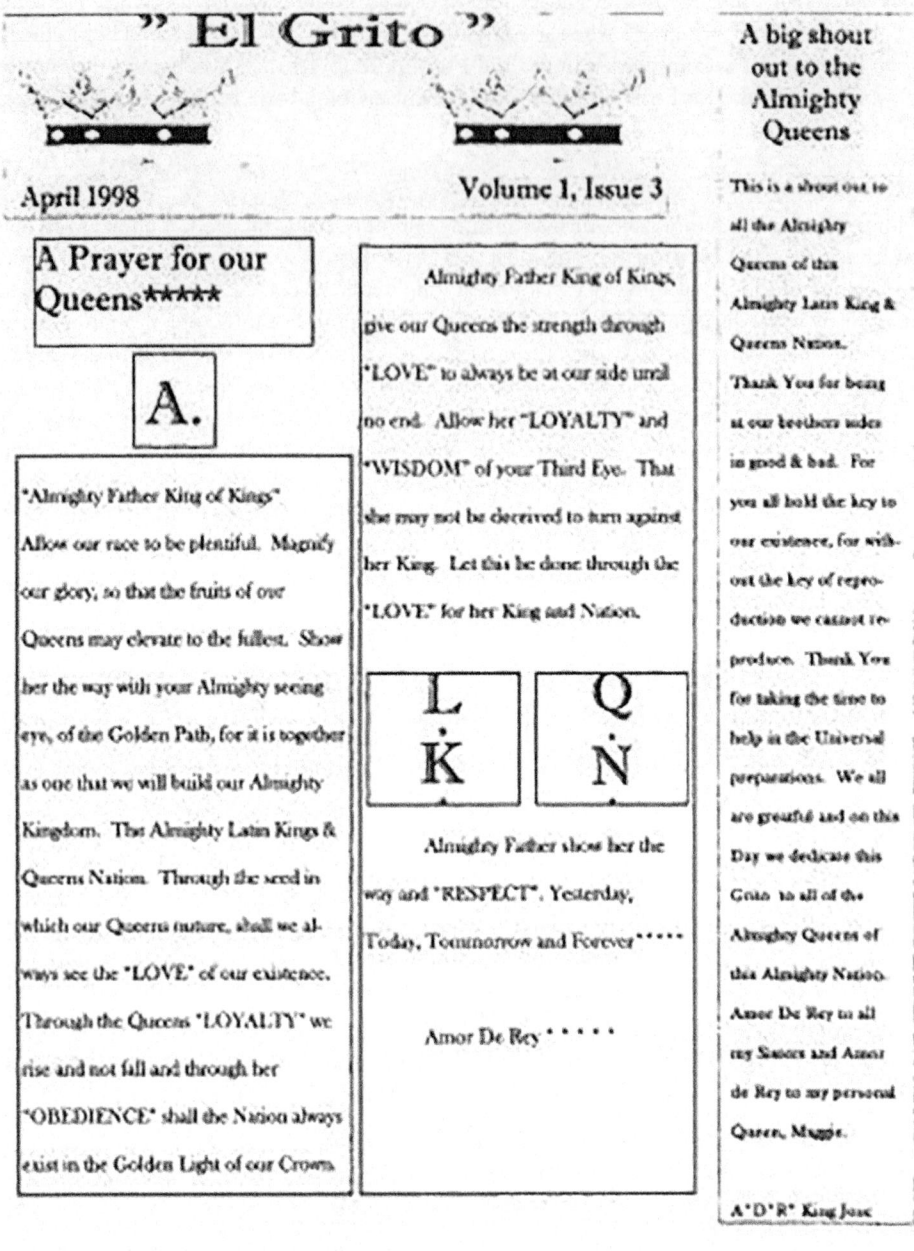

Figure 37.1 Front page from *El Grito*

Further, in *El Grito*, the official newsletter of the ALKQN (1996–1999), many articles were dedicated to memorializaing and promoting Latino culture, with numerous articles reporting on the conditions and circumstances of Puerto Rican political prisoners and highlighting grass-roots movements (see also Moore & García 1978).

Therefore, the group encourages members to discover the source of their Latinness through a variety of means that are relevant to the building, rebuilding and preservation of their community. In addition, the group itself is the vehicle through which members' Latino heritage is recognized and affirmed, becoming a repository for ethnic memory and ethnic innovation. This search for meaning in everyday life inevitably involves them not only in the development of their Latino/a identity but in a search for role models against whom they can measure their own and their community's evolution. However, as many members reported, this thirst for ethnic knowledge is not quenched by the city's school curriculum, which leaves many of the younger members grateful for the group's weekly culture clubs (see Chapter 7):

> they (the culture classes) just show you a little bit more about yourself, about things they don't teach you in school, which is about Latinos, how they came about, how Latinos created a lot of things.
>
> *(Queen A. 6/12/98)*

ii Against invisibility

On a range of ideological, organizational and cultural levels, the ALKQN was dedicated to resisting and ending processes of social-psychological subjugation that is the modus operandi of colonial social control (Fanon 1965). One important facet of this resistance orientation was the commitment of the group's members to: (i) make themselves and "their people" visible again and (ii) reject all attempts by the dominant culture to successfully label the group as criminal and pathological. These tasks were extremely difficult, given the history of political and economic subordination of most Latinos in New York City, the number of members returning to civil society from incarcerated settings and the past actions of the group which haunted its every move.

KING B: When we go out there and find out that we got a felony, well, we can't work. When you go out there to get a job, you have to stand there all day busting your ass working, excuse my language, busting, you know, doing your thing. For what? For five dollars an hour?

I: Five dollars twenty five.

KING B: Yeah, five twenty five. And you realize you're cleaning your life away for 5.25 an hour. Where could you go with that in a week? Not rent, there's nothing out there. And if there is, they're not giving is to us, you know because we're Latin Kings. We're criminals, you know. I see a lot of youth in our Nation that want something out of life. But no, you see a cop, you see the FBI and everybody just assumes that we're doing something wrong.

We haven't completed our goals yet. We haven't yet arrived to where we want to arrive. It's that we are not accepted how we are . . . we are not accepted because we were in jail, because we robbed before, because we used to use drugs, because before we did this and that and the other bad. But accept us now because we changed. Leave our pasts in the past. Don't bother with the past because we don't bother with yours, you understand me? We don't go in the street to say, "Oh, look! Fulana was a crook before and she is an artist now", you know? Don't look at our past, look at us now and we don't do anything bad. We defend ourselves because everybody is putting us down. That's it.

(Queen D. 11/21/97)

The response of the leadership to such experiences of King B. and Queen D. was that rescuing one's identity had to be a primary goal of the group and that the struggle to do so was essentially one of life and death:

> They want to destroy us by taking away our identity. We will demonstrate that we are Latinos/Latinas, and not only that, we will fight against anyone who has the intention to make us invisible by giving us another identity.
>
> *(King Tone)*

QUEEN M: We know how it is to live without. We are survivors. This is what we have [the Nation]; no one can take that away! I don't want to use a messed up past as an excuse, but as a motivation to keep on going. If we don't fight for Latinos, who is going to do it?

QUEEN Z: My history is my inspiration. You got to know where we come from to fight. History repeats itself. Without the knowledge we are destined to commit the same mistakes.

For Tone, as for many Kings and Queens, the pride that one feels for one's ethnic culture can only be achieved by being a member of the ALKQN; such is the level of mistrust for the mainstream institutions of their community who have failed to protect their interests both

Figure 37.2 Photo: A young Latin King with his son, both wearing the group's colors

Source: Photo by Steve Hart

economically and culturally. In effect, the ALKQN, members are "coming out" as Latino/as, unafraid to represent who they are in any social gathering. This is done in various ways, but in particular, it is carried out through their cultural style (Hebdige 1979), including their:

i   attire (e.g. black and gold bandanas; black, gold and sometimes red beads; yellow/gold shirts, sometimes with black ribbing; yellow leather boots, sometimes with black laces etc.);
ii   demonstrative hand gestures, greeting rituals and prayer performances; and
iii verbal self-identifications; for example, "Amor de Rey" or "ADR."

The members' refusal to be coy and camouflaged about their public selves, although they strategically chose to keep their identity concealed at different times, is their way of refusing to be content with an annual celebration of ethnic pride, such as the Puerto Rican and Dominican Day Parades, which mostly reject them in any case. This struggle waged by the ALKQN against the invisibility of Latinos, pitting the group against technicians of the dominant culture and those collaborators within their own community, was not lost on the younger members of the organization. Listen, for example, to the resilient words of King F.:

> My life is . . . it's not all good, but I maintain my life as a man that I feel that I am. My name is King F. . . . I'm 16 years old. I'm a Latin King and that's it.
>
> *(King F., 7/3/98)*

King F.'s simple statement echoes what the younger generations of the subjugated classes have consistently recognized when actively searching for respect in this exclusionary and colonizing society (Flores 2000; Young 1999; Bourgois 1995): claiming one's identity, despite its negative connotations, is an act of social and political defiance. In King F.'s case, he is proclaiming himself to be: (i) a man, despite the enormous structural pressures denying him his (gendered) role in the political economy; (ii) a youth, in a world that is afraid of his kind of generation (Males 1996); and (iii) a Latin King, one of the most "spoiled" identities in any subculture.

King F.'s defiance is part of the general recognition among the ALKQN that, consciously or unconsciously, Latinos have the power to resist and even to change the rules of an oppressive socio-political system.

> The Latino can draw additional strength from another force too, if he has the will and the faith. Anonymous millions of brown man and women have given their life in the fight for liberation. They have fought against colonialism, hunger and ignorance and for the human dignity of our people. They have drawn from one another, through unity, a force of fortitude – brown force – the force which provides the splendor and grow of hope in oppressed people. The seed they cast into the founding of a Nation – The Almighty Latin King/Queen Nation – has withstood the trials of time. Drawing upon the endurance and fortitude of brown force, we continue our quest to unify and insure free political and cultural expression among third world people and among the commonwealth of individuals. We are the people's liberating force – brown force – the foundation of the Nation.
>
> *(ALKQN Manifesto p. 15)*

In this late capitalist society, for the most part, power is increasingly measured not only by access to economic but also to symbolic resources (Bourdieu 1984), particularly in the form of validated knowledge and self-serving imagery. However, there are other ways to demonstrate power which the ALKQN continually promote, for example, indigenous knowledge, self-organization and group spirituality. Previously, the notion of a "brown force" is a metaphor for the potential solidarity of Latinos, much like "black" has been an empowering signifier for the social and cultural aspirations of African Americans. But the process of "becoming" requires a combination of energy, persistence and consistency, as King H. reminds us:

> it took 500 years to get my people to this type of sickness here, it ain't gonna take five years or even three years to bring us out of that sickness. So, for every two steps we take forward, you know, sometimes we take three back, sometimes we take two back, but we keep goin' forward, we keep tryin' to go forward, except now we're like that hamster in that little hamster cage – just doin a lot of energy like when you hustlin', but stayin' in the same spot, you know?
>
> *(1/30/98)*

Thus, for the ALKQN, becoming visible, while it involves striking out against "the system" through a collective embrace of one's neighborhood and community allies, also involves tackling and engaging the many different processes of institutional socialization, particularly schooling (Brotherton 2003). This repossession of oneself and one's culture is not only the power to say "who I am" but "who I am not." According to many members, this recognition and validation of distinctiveness needs to be heard, first as they re-affirm to themselves who they are within the group, and then as they aim their words and actions at the "oppressors".

But the quest for identity is not met solely by affirming who one is within and through one's subculture, even though such activity is an important first step. Neither can the search be satisfied simply by taking advantage of the representational spaces provided by corporate media channels. Rather, being a Latin King/Queen immediately raises one's status, a "social fact" that has often been difficult for them to achieve in the mainstream. This is done through the notion of royalty in the belief system of the organization.

Thus, in the King's Manifesto, they are "the Yahweh Latin American Tribe" and the Latino and Latina children of God. In this construction, this makes them Kings and Queens and the "chosen ones," a direct contradiction of the designation they receive under the gaze of the criminal justice system and through their collective label as "minorities" by the dominant society. In short, while the ruling classes have been telling them and treating them as colonized subjects for generations, they are magically transformed into royalty through their own system of status provision.

Finally, another important feature of their quest for visibility demands that they pay attention to tradition. In this they have not only their ethnic but also their subcultural traditions (as described in Chapters 3, 4 and 5) to help undergird their presence. Below, King M. is describing how he understands the ritual of the circle, one of the most important ways the group demonstrates its solidarity to itself and to the outside world:

> they made a circle, they kept it tight, you know, and the leader would go in the middle and address the circle, so there's a lot of traditions that we follow that we don't even – I don't even know where – that they're ancestral. It just seems to happen, you know, just like the color of our hair, just like our mannerisms, you know? It's like part of our DNA, and, uh, the 360, again, that is one of our – it's holy to us. The circle, the whole circle, is always holy to us. Forever we protect the lives inside of the circle, but now we're becoming aware of the other side of the circle, which is the outside of the circle, so sometimes we could be facin' it, at each other, but sometimes the circle is still there but we must face out.
>
> *(King M. 1/30/98)*

2 Identity and hope

> I love being a Queen. It gives me hope, it makes me proud to say that I've got family
> that I know I can always count on and no matter what happens in my life, I know
> they'll always be there for me and they may not physically be there, but I know them
> spiritually and I know they will be there. You know, I've been in gangs, I've been
> in other nations, I've been in a lot of things, and I've never felt so at home as I have
> when I joined the Queens.
>
> (Queen J. 6/20/1998)

Queen J. expresses a sentiment that ran through many of the respondents' narratives: declaring
one's identity as a King or Queen, by fully embracing one's ethnicity and humanity, cleared the
psychological and cognitive paths to feelings of hope and spirituality. Consequently, reclaiming
one's identity through the group was a powerful riposte to the deep feelings of fatalism that
many of the members' felt prior to joining the organization. In other words, as we have seen
in Chapter 8, members who had weathered such experiences as racial prejudice, physical and
sexual abuse, imprisonment, drug addiction, educational failure, poverty and/or menial labor
had come to expect this daily barrage of negativity to be their lot in life. Nonetheless, with the
adoption of a new self, the feeling of status that comes with being baptized into an organization
of street royalty, or the solidarity that is felt among hundreds of other similarly motivated members of the Latino community, a new era for the individual is announced and, probably for the
first time, the subject looks toward to the future based on a demonstrated level of self-control
and a socially valued place in the world.

In the work of the critical pedagogue Paulo Freire, recognition of the inter-relationship
between identity and hope is of paramount importance and is viewed as the cornerstone to a
politics of liberation aimed at bringing previously alienated and highly marginalized individuals
into the struggle for a more inclusive democracy. As Freire (1970: 186) states:

> It would be horrible if we were sensible to pain, hunger, injustice, and violence without
> perceiving the reasons for all this negativity. It would be horrible if we could feel the
> oppression but could not imagine a different world. It would be horrible if we could dream
> about a different world as a project but not commit ourselves to the fight for its construc-
> tion. We have made ourselves men and women by experimenting in the dynamic of these
> understandings. Freedom cannot be gained as a present. One becomes richer in the fight
> for it, in the permanent search for it, even if there can be no life without the presence,
> however, minimal, of it. In spite of that, we cannot acquire freedom for free. The enemies
> of life threaten it all the time. We must fight to maintain it, recover it, and expand it.

What Freire and Queen J. have in common is their recognition that critically engaging the historical context of one's life is the starting point for a consciousness bound to action and aimed
at both self and social transformation.

> The Queens start talking; these are short parts of their monologues.
> "We know how it is to live without. We are survivors. This is what we have (the
> Nation); no one can take that away! I don't want to use a messed up passed as an excuse, but
> as a motivation to keep on going. If we don't fight for Latinos, who is going to do it. My
> history is my inspiration. You got to know where we come from to fight. History repeats
> itself. Without the knowledge we are destined to commit the same mistakes.

Such an orientation to everyday life, Freire claims, requires an "imagination" and the capacity to dream beyond the boundaries of our enforced social, economic and cultural location. This impetus is captured in the following by King S. and Queen A., who have begun envisioning their "own people" in top decision-making positions which, in reality, is almost unthinkable given the socio-cultural impediments facing most poor Latinos/as:

> I: What sort of government would you like to see?
>
> King S: I would like to see my brothers and sisters well educated, to see one of my brothers and sisters become the Federal Justice, which is the biggest court in the White House. I wanna see my sisters work down in 1 Federal Plaza, you know? Be the next Mary Jo White [the Federal District Attorney for the New York area].
>
> Instead of the media tryin' to discriminate against us, we become the media. Instead of actually like lawyers prosecuting us . . . we could become one of them . . . after some of them has their degrees and things like that they can become part of it. But we can't because of what the Nation was about before. But we go to school now, we do what we have to do in order to get to that stage. When they see a lot of strong people, Latinos, they'll have no other choice. They cannot deny us no more.
>
> *(Queen A.)*

For the most part, however, "hope" by members was expressed in terms of achieving the "American Dream": moving out of the projects, sending their children to decent schools, getting an education for themselves (i.e., finishing their general education diploma, aspiring to college or finishing college), having a government (usually at the city level) that is accountable to the people and surviving the rigors of debilitating and sometimes fatal diseases:

> I: How would you describe your life up to now?
>
> KING D: Great. I mean, you gotta remember I'm HIV positive but today I'm a positive person. I would not let nobody tell me, no doctor tell me, I'm gonna die, cuz I ain't gonna die, see? . . . as long as I keep the positive mind . . . and talk to people freely, let people know how I fell and don't be shy because I'm HIV positive and you cannot get it unless you did the things that I did. You know, I could relate back to the days when I couldn't relate to people. That's when I used drugs, because drugs made me feel comfortable. Today, I feel comfortable with myself and with people. I like people today.

Thus, "hope" was not particularly utopian, even though the rhetoric of the group was relatively grandiose. Rather, it was related to accomplishing goals in members' everyday life – small, incremental achievements that would make their existence that much more comfortable and assured. Sometimes, the leadership would grow impatient with these limited ideals, and might charge the rank-and-file with complacency:

> What is Kingism? Why are we here? What's . . . the whole point other than just, you know, a term like unity. Unity for what sake? You know, unity for the sake of political power, economic empowerment! We lack a collective vision . . . there's one guy that has a dream which is not a vision, and there's another guy who just talks about this. But when you have a vision, you have to have a plan of action.
>
> *(King H. 1/30/98)*

Nonetheless, to habitually approach the world from a position of optimism instead of defeat-ist resignation, or to harbor a set of expectations in which the individual member routinely sees him or herself as an agent in the creation of the everyday (Flacks 1992), was still an extraordinary psycho-social development for most members and, as we observed, infected the entire organization with an upbeat mood during the first two years of the study. But there is a third aspect to this analysis of identity that has to be addressed and helps to further explain how the political animus of the group was maintained over time.

3 Identity and spirituality

> And the movement took on. And I started, you know, putting in religion. I started using King's lessons and using the Bible as a concordant. So everything I learned in Kingism I would match a story from the Bible, I would preach it to the kids and break it down in knowledge and it started working on them. They started getting a sense of spirituality; they got a sense of belonging. They got a sense that I didn't want them, like the pastor, to be Jesus. I just wanted them to try and walk like he did.
>
> (King Tone 10/21/97)

In the construction of their identity, the ALKQN does not restrict its spiritual praxis to mere contemplation or a series of internal abstractions, but rather it very consciously uses this aspect of its identity construction to urge members to reflect on their *realidad humana* through rituals and ceremonies which highlight the daily experiences of poverty, unemployment, police brutality, and racism. This approach to cementing the group's identity on the members' religio-cultural histories (see Chapter 4) played an important role in the reform process and helped to reinforce key tenets of the group's doctrine:

I: Can you describe some of your spiritual and religious practices?

QUEEN C: Um, I personally, I'm a Christian. Well, that's from the religion of my family. Kingism is a mix of Catholic, Born-Again Christians, and . . . we read the Bible. But we're not a cult like people say we are! We all have our different religions . . . it really has nothing to do with it. The main fact of Kingism is that we emphasize our humility, we are one and we're supposed to be there for each other no matter what.

For King Tone, the group's leader and former street preacher, the discourse and rhetorical style used to expand this politicization are often borrowed from standard religious practices, and they became his stock-in-trade as an innovative promoter of the group's ethno-spiritual project:

> I pray that You make these few many and that You bless them with the power of knowledge and the word that you have given us. Give us no limitations. Teach us not to send boundaries and walls that'll keep us from achieving the goal of eternal life. Give us the power to teach our children how to believe in one's self and the things that can be accomplished if one believes in his brother more than he believes in himself. Give us the examples to teach our children how to stand with each other. Even when society says "abandon", we say, "take in". Let us not be the judge of this world, but people who serve it in a righteous way.
>
> *(A prayer offered by King Tone during a Sunday church mass at which both Latin Kings and Queens and the lay congregation of Father Barrios' Latino/a ministry were present)*

515

In meeting after meeting, Tone provided countless renditions of biblical narratives in the form of prayers, anecdotes and parables to refer indirectly to some of the tensions facing the group internally, to illuminate challenges to the group from external sources and to emphasize the need of the organization to keep focused on its possibilities for growth and regeneration. This process of linking the group's collective and individualized identity to the pursuit of a radical and action-oriented spirituality was a determining characteristic of the organization and proved an effective strategy for solidifying the identity of members and helping the group to withstand the pressures of the struggle.

Thus, in our analysis, spirituality is one of the main driving forces behind the group's collective identity, encouraging members to engage in an ongoing reflexive relationship with the structures of their everyday life through a *human reencuentro* with the creation of God. How is this carried out? First, by giving members permission to seek an alternative consciousness; second, by convincing them of the moral need to subvert the present social order; and third, by making them responsible for dismantling their *realidad humana*: for example, their political oppression, helplessness, exploitation and exclusion. In other words, the foundation of the group's spirituality is always manifested in a specific time and space and grounded in the struggle for dignity, justice and respect in daily life. Spirituality, therefore, is an integral part of the meaning systems through which a resistance identity is constructed and regenerated and functions as a powerful bulwark to the pressures of the dominant society's ideological penetrations and corrupting moralities.

In liberation theological terms (Barrios 2003), this spirituality is seen as: (i) not limited to the practice of a formal religion and (ii) encouraging a radical form of solidarity where people change through their psychological and material engagement in a liberation movement. The ALKQN's spirituality, therefore, is an experience of empowerment solidarity in which the group on the one hand is urging its members toward a critical class consciousness and on the other hand is prompting the socio-political transformation of the organization through subverting oppressive circumstances despite the overwhelming odds against doing so (Barrios 2000, 2003). The manifesto of the ALKQN is fairly unequivocal about the need of members to engage this contest:

> The new King recognizes that the day of resurrection is here. A time for the appearance of a new manifestation of truth. The rising of the dead means the spiritual awakening of those who have been sleeping in the graveyard of ignorance. The day of the oppressor must now be judged by the oppressed.
>
> *(The King's Manifesto, p. 10)*

Conclusion

In the previous, we have seen the multiple forms that identity construction in the ALKQN can take. A substantial part of our data show that both the collective and individual identities that emerge out of members' commitment to the group are embedded in a resistance project that Castells has begun to highlight, but no one has yet applied to the case of gangs. These findings point again to significant gaps in the gang research literature where identity formation is largely considered a window into group and/or individual acculturation processes rather than a novel psycho-social pathway into communal levels of empowerment. Based on our research with the ALKQN, and in direct contrast to received wisdom, we have observed socially labeled deviants: (i) engage in endlessly ingenious ways to plumb their ethnicity, transforming themselves into culturally competent social agents; (ii) launch a frontal attack on cynicism and fatalism over time, as part of an effort to change members' self-perception and convince themselves of their unfulfilled and potential agency; (iii) embrace unabashedly their spirituality through reacquainting themselves with their own religio-political biographies; and (iv) experience a collective "we-ness" that inspires individuals to transcend the semblance of their material limitations by reviewing and renewing their commitment to a new morality.

References

Barrios, Luis. 2000. *Josconiando: Dimensiones sociales y políticas de la espiritualidad.* Santo Domingo, República Dominicana: Editora Aguiar, S.A.

Barrios, Luis. 2003. "Spirituality and Resistance in the Latin Kings and Queens." In L. Kontos, D. Brotherton, and L. Barrios, eds., *Gangs and Society: Alternative Perspectives.* New York: Columbia University Press.

Brotherton, David. 2003. "The Role of Education in the Reform of Street Organizations in New York City." In L. Kontos, D. Brotherton and L. Barrios, eds., *Gangs and Society: Alternative Perspectives.* New York: Columbia University Press.

Bourdieu, Pierre. 1984. *Distinction: A Social Critique of the Judgement of Taste.* London: Routledge.

Bourgois, Philippe. 1995. *In Search of Respect: Selling Crack in El Barrio.* New York: Cambridge University Press.

Branch, Curtis. 1997. *Clinical Interventions with Gang Adolescents and Their Families.* Boulder, CO: Westview Press.

Calderón, Fernando, Alejandro Piscitelli, and José Luis Reyna. 1992. "Social Movements: Actors, Theories, Expectations," In Arturo Escobar and Sonia E. Álvarez, eds., *The Making of Social Movement in Latin America: Identity, Strategy and Democracy*, pp. 19–36. San Francisco: Westview Press.

Calhoun, Craig. 1991. "The Problem of Identity in Collective Action." In J. Huber, ed., Macro-Micro Linkages in Sociology, pp. 51–75, London and Beverly Hills, CA: Sage.

Castells, Manuel. 1997. The Power of Identity. New York: Blackwell.

Della Porta, Donatella and Mario Diani. 1999. Social Movements: An Introduction. Malden, MA: Blackwell Publishers.

Escobar, Alberto. 1992. "Culture, Economics, and Politics in Latin American Social Movements Theory and Research." In A. Escobar and S.E. Alvarez, eds., *The Making of Social Movements in Latin America: Identity, Strategy and Democracy*, pp. 62–85. Boulder, CO: Westview Press.

Fanon, Franz. 1965. *Wretched of the Earth.* New York: Grove Press.

Flacks, Richard. 1992. *Making History: The American Left and the American Mind.* New York: Columbia University Press.

Flores, Juan. 2000. *From Bomba to Hip-Hop: Puerto Rican Culture and Latino Identity.* New York: Columbia University Press.

Freire, Paulo. 1970. *Pedagogy of the Oppressed.* New York: Seabury Press.

Hebdige, Dick. 1979. *Subculture: The Meaning of Style.* London: Methuen.

Males, Michael. 1996. *The Scapegoat Generation: America's War on Adolescents.* Monroe, Maine: Common Courage Press.

Melucci, Alberto. 1989. *Nomads of the Present.* Philadelphia: Temple University Press.

Moore, Joan and Robert García. 1978. *Homeboys: Gangs, Drugs and Prison in the Barrios of Los Angeles.* Philadelphia: Temple University Press.

Muñoz, Carlos. 1989. *Youth, Identity, Power: The Chicano Movement.* New York: Verso.

Touraine, Alain. 1988. *Return of the Actor.* Minnesota: University of Minnesota Press.

Young, Jock. 1999. *The Exclusive Society: Social Exclusion, Crime and Difference in Late Modernity.* London: Sage.

38

"They treat us like criminals in front of our kids"

Gang-affiliated Chicanas and *trails of violence* in the barrio

Katherine L. Maldonado-Fabela

Years pass by, and you go through something [violent and painful] again and it's like, why? Why does this happen to me again? First, it happens as a child, then as a teenager, then it happens again as an adult. It's like, why? It's something you already experienced, but then you go through it again. It's a big ol' scar that I'm always gonna have, and I don't know if I will ever, ever, have an answer for that. . . . But honestly, nothing would hurt me more than getting separated from my kids. I would go crazy. It's something that not even rape did to me.

(Mayra, age 30, mother of 5)

Introduction

Mayra's experiences with the streets, drugs and gangs began at age eight. During her interview, she shared experiences of interpersonal and psychological violence, such as the time she was chased and beaten by rival gang affiliates[1] in an alley and lost consciousness, and the trauma she experienced when she was beaten by her partner during her second pregnancy and after giving birth. While her experiences with violence were hair-raising, Mayra's demeanor did not fit many of the social groups or theories I had observed in mainstream criminological thought. Her humor, vocalness and sociological imagination were not what the social science literature describes regarding poor, immigrant, gang-affiliated mothers. She was not destitute, on drugs or living in an abusive setting. Mayra was in fact surrounded by love. She lived in a small one-bedroom house, adorned with elephant ornaments and other portraits bought in local yard sales. Her living room was furnished with a small wooden kitchen table and an inflatable bed. On any given day, one could hear her five kids laughing with each other, crying and asking eagerly, "What's for dinner?" as they did on the day I interviewed her.

Mayra's disposition, however, changed radically when she began talking about a form of violence typically overlooked by sociologists and criminologists: the kind she faced at the hands of the state. She became visually upset and cried out loud as she discussed the termination of her public government assistance (CalWORKs), which left her with the inability to access food for three months in 2015. Mayra questioned why her contact with state agencies shaped her life so dramatically. From the law enforcement teams breaking into her home when she was just a child, to the lack of support she experienced by the criminal justice system after surviving rape as an adult, Mayra always felt alone, poorly supported and discriminated against by public institutions. Although it had been twelve years since she had been active in her neighborhood gang, the impact of this affiliation on her life trajectory persisted as she continued to experience violence and criminalization from institutions that were supposed to support and nurture people like her.

This chapter examines the concept of *trails of violence*: the forms of state structural violence that follow the lives of women even after they leave gang life, in this case, formerly[2] gang-affiliated Chicana mothers. Most longitudinal empirical research on gangs has focused on the immediate correlates of gang membership, such as risk factors, delinquency and victimization (Chesney-Lind and Hagedorn 1999). Yet scant scholarly attention has been given to the violence experienced by gang involved people *after* becoming inactive in a gang. Even less research examines the experiences of women. In other words, there is limited understanding of the forms of institutional violence that gang-involved women experience due to the stigma and criminalization that former gang status brings. In this chapter, I focus on formerly gang-affiliated mothers' experiences with violence at the hands of the criminal justice and child welfare systems, on the role having a history of gang involvement plays in that violence. To echo Beth Richie, a fundamental question in this study is: what happens to Chicana mothers who

> experience violence in a climate that gives way to the buildup of a prison nation – a climate where the broader social agenda is shaped by mean-spirited public policies designed to create intolerance of difference, to erode public services, and to increase social inequality.
>
> *(2012:17)*

To shed light on the everyday social dimensions of this form of violence in the age of hyper-criminalization (Rios 2011) – and I would argue, romanticization of – gang-involved people, I rely on life-history interviews based on photo elicitation, collected over the course of six months in South Central Los Angeles, United States. As a city at the forefront of studies on gangs, South Central is a strategic site for understanding the interplay between carceral control, gangs, violence, motherhood and legal and social relations. I respond to the following questions: First, how do formerly gang-involved Chicana mothers experience institutional violence after exiting the gang? Second, in what ways does institutional violence impact the ways their mothering is viewed and practiced? I provide one of the first studies of how gang affiliation for Chicanas produces and perpetuates institutional violence, or what I call *trails of violence:* a form of violence that is not bound to the period of gang involvement but that is fluid and follows and shapes the lives of gang-affiliated women.

Women in gangs

For almost a century, sociologists and criminologists have produced scholarly work on gangs (Thrasher 1927; Moore 1991; Brotherton 2015), feminist analyses of gendered effects of gang involvement (Chesney-Lind and Irwin 2008; Miller 2001; Mendoza-Denton 2008; Campbell 1991) and structural and individual explanations for the labeling and marginalization of gang members (Vigil 1988, 2002; Brotherton 1996). The gang research agenda has focused on, among other things, how to prevent both boys and girls from joining gangs (Chesney-Lind 2004), how to reduce transnational gang violence and how to implement comprehensive gang control (Wolf

2017). In other words, this research has influenced the development of interventions, laws and policies that strive to end gangs and the violence associated with them (Muñiz 2015). However, less is known about the consequences of gang affiliation – specifically, the experiences of gang-involved people upon exiting gangs and throughout the rest of the life course. Few researchers have investigated the long-term effects "that cascade throughout the person's later development" (Thornberry et al. 2003), focusing instead on the short-term dynamics – that is, effects *during* gang involvement. While the broader literature on crime desistance in gang studies offers some conceptual guidance on this front, one cannot simply assume that desistance simply occurs (Pyrooz et al. 2017), that it comes to an end when factors such as parenthood, and specifically in the case women, motherhood, take place or that the violence that impacts gang members – especially the one at the hands of the state – merely ceases.

The research on women in gangs has been traditionally one dimensional: for many decades, it has focused on the sexual role women allegedly play to the inside of gangs (the title of Thrasher's 1927 "Sex in the Gang" constitutes a lurid example). Over time, feminist criminologists have pushed for studies that explore the multi-dimensional experiences of young women's gang involvement so to understand how to best describe their participation and the kinds of violence they experience. This has led to work that highlights through the lens of gender variations across ethnicity (Quicker 1983), forms of victimization (Miller 2001) and the dimensions of sexuality (Campbell 1990). Feminism-informed explanations concerning women's involvement in gangs of the kind articulated by scholars like Chesney-Lind (2002) have argued that because young women experience abuse at home and victimization in the streets, the forms of crime they engage in constitute a form of resistance, enabling them to better navigate and overcome the violence they experience. When young women join gangs to resist violence, however, their efforts to escape and resist abuse are criminalized and punished, often along racial, ethnic and class lines (López and Chesney-Lind 2014).

> While the good, innocent, virginal girl continues to be an idealized image of womanhood, it is often associated to white women, a characterization that in turn remains largely unattainable for young women of color, who are often labeled as hypersexual, manipulative, violent and sexually dangerous.
>
> *(Stephens and Phillips 2003; Garcia 2009)*

Studies have not paid much attention to the ways that gang-involved women navigate stigma as Women of Color or to how they contend with the multiple layers of marginalization that come together and shape their personal identities and their specific contexts, such as motherhood (Campbell 1991, Fleisher 1998).

Furthermore, the experiences and responses to the criminalization that gang-affiliated mothers face once they leave the gangs have been paid limited attention. In particular, scant research has examined the role institutions like the criminal justice and child welfare systems play in shaping the forms of criminalization that are specific to women and which, as this chapter shows, are often rooted in stigma. To understand how stigma plays out in the lives of gang-affiliated mothers, it is essential to understand it as a process. "Stigmatization," as Link and Phelan state (2001, p. 367),

> is entirely contingent on access to social, economic, and political power that allows the identification of differentness, the construction of stereotypes, the separation of labeled persons into distinct categories, and the full execution of disapproval, rejection, exclusion, and discrimination.

For the gang-affiliated mothers in this study, their interactions with state agencies following their exit from gangs involve financial and social costs that impact their daily life, family, work and community. Despite all of these factors, gang-affiliated mothers continue to constitute a hidden sub-group within the study of gangs and violence and remain grossly underrepresented in research.

(Re)conceptualizing violence in the life course

Scholars have documented the economic, educational, familial and social conditions of women in gangs face (Chesney-Lind and Hagedorn 1999), identifying how sociocultural and environmental contexts explain the relationship between gender and violence (Hunt and Joe-Laidler 1997). Here the performance of violence by women within gangs and women's involvement in other forms of street crime (Miller 2001; Davis 2017) have been described as women's resistance to victimization, a protective measure in response to the vulnerabilities they encounter. Physical and sexual abuse by and of family members is also common in the experience of women in gangs (Miller 2001; Valdez 2007), and in fact, research on violence experienced by female gang members heavily focuses on physical and sexual violence perpetrated by male partners or other gang members (Hunt and Joe-Laidler 2001). Exposure to gang and community violence contributes to the risk of early pregnancy (Miller et al. 2011) and negatively impacts women's health (Varriale 2008). Yet the violence women experience outside of interpersonal and community forms of violence is not largely discussed in gang scholarship. In other words, the narrow scholarly focus on mostly interpersonal violence provides only an incomplete illustration of the wide array of injuries that women in gangs find consequential (Jackman 2002). Scholarly examinations of violence have ignored violence that occurs "gradually (rather than instantaneously), out of sight (i.e., delayed destruction), and across time and space" (Nixon 2011). The present chapter therefore seeks to expand how we think of violence, showing how different forms of violence coexist in specific contexts. As Menjivar (2008: 111) argues, structural, political, symbolic and everyday interpersonal forms of violence are mutually constituted and unravel the interrelated strands of violence that shape the life of women. It moves away from individual-focused explanations to reveal instead the incidence of violence by institutions of power and invivsible forms of violence that maintains exploitative power structures (Bourgois 2010; Farmer 2004). Echoing Galtung in recognizing direct violence as an event yet structural violence as a process (1969) the focus of this study is on violence as a process embedded in the everyday lives of gang-affiliated Chicana mothers through their interactions with institutions, and so in what follows, I focus on the everyday interactions with institutions that amplify not only the various forms of (interpersonal and community) violence in people's lives but also the number of victims, as entire families across generations suffer the impact of punitive institutions.

Theoretically approaching violence in *barrio*[3] South Central

In this study, I use a feminist abolitionist approach, with an effort to continue the collective struggle towards radical freedom (Davis 2003) while placing Chicanas[4] at the center of this chapter. Here, I use the term Chicana to integrate varying indentitaruan positionalities as mothers who identify as Chicana, Xicana-Indigena, Chicana/x Latina and Afro Xicana (Caballero et al., 2017). Chicanas as women of Mexican origin whose experiences are rooted in Mexican-American history, which carries a long legacy of colonialism, violence and discrimination (Arredondo et al. 2003). Given their upbringing in the United States as Mexican Americans, Chicanas' worldview is not confined to the US border, but it is instead transnational. Chicanas

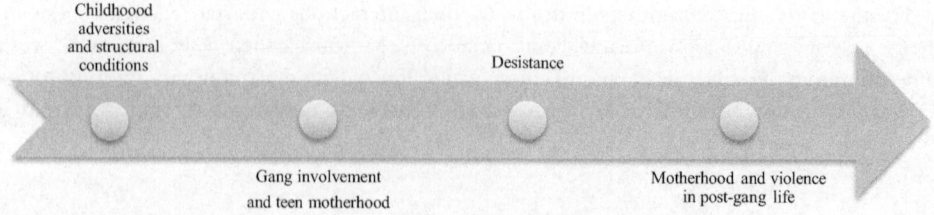

Childhoood adversities and structural conditions

Desistance

Gang involvement and teen motherhood

Motherhood and violence in post-gang life

Figure 38.1 Life course theoretical application on gang-affiliated mothers[6]

physically and symbolically navigate the borderlands, their lived realities and standpoint epistemologies embodying US-México political, economic and familial relations and processes (Anzaldúa 1987). The *testimonios*[5] of Chicana gang-involved women in this study highlight how "discourses, institutional forms of violence and practices themselves migrate between countries, and how features of the security state are imbricated with political subjectivities and spatializing practices" (Zilberg 2011:3).

To understand the complex lives of formerly gang-involved Chicana mothers, I bring together two theoretical frameworks: on the one hand, life course theory to assess the fluidity and transformation of criminalized behaviors rather than criminal careers. On the other, I rely on intersectionality, a conceptual tool which makes visible race, class and gender as interlocking systems of oppression that Chicana gang-affiliated mothers experience along with the stigmatizing label of gang affiliate and the complexity of navigating institutions while embodying – physically and emotionally – that label.

Sampson and Laub's (1990) life course theory suggests that criminal behaviors explain the life-course outcomes of people involved in crime. Life course theory examines continuity and change in behavior as people age and how events shape future events. It acknowledges multiple factors, like historical and geographical context, social networks, agency and timing. The theory has been utilized in the past by other gang researchers to understand the process of and reasons for exiting gang life (Pyrooz et al., 2017). Here, rather than viewing the women as "criminals," which suggests a choice, I view them as criminalized, which acknowledges circumstances outside of their women's control but also as capable of exercising resistance.

The life trajectories of mothers involve not only developmental changes associated with biological age but also the institutional changes that emerge from women's changing experiences with formal and informal forms of social control across their life spans (Sampson and Laub 2016). This theory identifies events associated with alterations to the life-course, such as marriage, parenthood and incarceration, which can be influenced by structures and markers of gang involvement, making institutional violence and mechanisms of resistance persistent.

Intersectionality helps explains women's experiences of violence. Women in this study are marginalized by their race, class, gender and other identities, such as gang affiliation. Intersectionality is inextricably linked to an analysis of power. It exposes how single-axis (i.e., non-intersectional) thinking shapes legal thought, disciplinary knowledge production and women's struggles for social justice. It delineates the "multilayered and routinized forms of domination" (Crenshaw 1991:1245) women face in specific contexts. The analysis of overlapping structures of subordination reveals how women – in this case, gang-affiliated mothers – are made vulnerable to abuse by institutions and unmasks the interventions that further social inequalities (Crenshaw 1991; Richie 2012). Bridging life course theory with intersectionality theory helps explain the forms of violence that results from the interactions between institutions (in this case, the US criminal justice and child welfare systems) and people who have been made marginal. Combined, the two theories offer a perspective that acknowledges not only the complex interaction of identities and institutions and how these interactions take shape across time but also how the political apparatus shapes carceral identities for marginalized Women of Color (Richie 2012; Gurusami 2019).

Methods, setting and context

The study took place in South Central Los Angeles, California. Often referred to as the gang capital of the world, Los Angeles has been a frequent setting for gang research (Vigil 1988, 2002). It is estimated that in the United States, there are 30,700 gangs encompassing 850,000 gang members (Eggley, Howell and Harris 2014). Roughly one in eight active gang members living in America is in Los Angeles (Vigil 2002). South Central Los Angeles is a unique setting to study the immediate and long-term consequences of gang-involvement, as street gangs dominate the social scene. The Million Dollar Hoods Project shows how Los Angeles is a place that operates the largest jail system on earth, incarcerating and arresting more people than anywhere else in the world (Lee et al. 2019). Specifically, it highlights how the East Side and West Side of South Central, where these mothers reside, encompass the largest cost of incarceration across all of Los Angeles County. This is a critical setting and stigmatized place (Contreras 2017) that brings to light the carceral and violent experiences of People of Color.

I am myself a gang-affiliated mother, and my awareness of the world of gangs and gang-involved people comes from my personal background. I grew up in South Central, attending schools and walking streets where I learned about the tensions between Black and Brown gangs. I also learned about gang and prison politics through my brother's direct involvement in one of the largest Latino gangs of the world. My father knew many gang-involved, undocumented people from Central America, while my mother – an undocumented migrant from Mexico, who had a small business at the local swap meet in Pico Union – had to pay piso, a sort of a tax to a local gang that would protect her. I also joined a female gang at the age of 13.

My status afforded me crucial knowledge for recruiting and understanding my participants, a much-hidden population of Chicanas (Durán 2013). I was able to draw on my personal

Table 38.1 Sample characteristics (*N* = 13)

Participant	Age	Number of children	Years since gang exit
Estefania	21	3	2
Mariela	22	1	6
Monica	23	2	5
Lorena	2–1	3	7
Beatrix	25	2	S
Cristal	26	2	8
Patricia	27	3	7
Leticia	29	4	10
Mavra	31	5	12
Jasmine	32	2	14
Susana	40	4	24
Margarita	44	11	25
Rocto	45	3	27

networks and experiences for this project. Three key partners who were also participants helped me gain access to additional interviewees. Like other scholars working with gang-affiliated women (Valdez 2007), I maintained high visibility in the neighborhood and frequent social contacts with participants. The sample included 13 participants who self-identified as formerly gang-involved Chicanas in the South Central Los Angeles area. They were mothers of one or more children. Their ages ranged from 22 to 45 years, with an average age of 29.6 years. The average number children participants had was three. Participants had ceased active gang involvement, on average, 12 years prior to the interview. All the participants were system-impacted. They all had direct experiences with child welfare whether through removal or referrals, or families' threats by CWS. All mothers shared knowledge about navigating the criminal legal system such as directly through incarceration or victimization (DV cases), or indirectly with partners/families' incarceration. All of them indirectly had impacts of immigration system via their parents' migration status, and one of the participants is undocumented. Mothers all had experiences of navigating social welfare agencies as well.

To collect data, I conducted photo elicitation life history interviews (Clark-Ibañez 2004). This methodology, based on participatory, photographic and visual techniques, involves a collaborative process of using photos and images such as drawings and photographs to encourage respondents to tell their life stories. The photos guide the interview and analysis, which are "auto driven" (Clark 1999): I asked participants to bring to the interview photographs of their lives, anything meaningful to them as Chicana mothers, specifically after exiting the gang. Participants gathered as many or as few photos as they wanted, and they had the option to present the photos physically or electronically. Some women presented photos of their children or family. Others showed locations, such as the streets on which they grew up and places they visited (e.g., car shows, prisons, and parks). Still others brought artwork, such as drawings by people who were incarcerated or by children; documents, such as from the courts; or books, such as poetry or the bible. The goal was to understand the participants' perceptions of the photos in terms of their life histories. Visual images can capture moments in life and specific events, and life history interviews can supplement details of experiences that photos may not convey. Thus, while the mothers had conversations about the photos in the interviews, I also asked open-ended questions on childhood, gang affiliation, violence and motherhood. Due to constraints in gaining authorization, these images are not included here, but I hope to exhibit in the future.

I interacted with participants on more than one occasion, before and after data collection. The interviews occurred either over a single or several meetings, usually two or three. Throughout the data collection period, I was invited to family gatherings, where the mothers shared updates with me, such as a job promotion, graduation and familial hardship (e.g., hospitalization, incarceration). I often drove participants by car to help them with their errands. In some cases, their children had play dates with my own children. There was intimacy and trust, despite the presence of street gang rules, such as not being able to talk about specific actors of gang violence. From my first conversations with participants, it was clear they would never have shared their stories with me if I did not actively cultivate trust and comfort and provide understanding and support. We often interacted via late-night phone calls and messages. I provided logistical help with institutional bureaucracies; referrals to community resources; and aid in the form of money or food, advice, and, most often, merely a sympathetic ear. Interviews were audio recorded, and each participant was assigned a pseudonym.

I employed grounded theory for analytical purposes (Corbin and Strauss 1990). Grounded theory involves inductive analysis which means that the themes that emerge solely from the data (Patton 1980: 306). This process involved identification of recurrent patterns or themes, where I constructed cohesive representation of data. The interviews were coded for themes related to institutional violence, interactions with institutions, mothering practices and strategies for resistance to institutional violence. As an insider and qualitative researcher of inequality, my analysis was also shaped by moving through existing theories and frameworks on race, class gender, violence and life course. This follows a process of abductive analysis which involves entering the interviews with a broad theoretical base and developing a theoretical repertoire throughout the research process (Timmerman and Iddo 2012). Grabbing from a critical race methodological toolbox, however, by remaining reflexive throughout the research process, I am "able to 'ground' this study in the life experiences of Mothers of Color."

A brief note on reflexivity

Being reflexive is a key action to take as researchers, to connect our positionalities and experiences with research processes (Zavella 1993; Taylor and White 2001). As I have indicated earlier, I am an insider to this population because I am a Chicana, mother of three and gang-affiliated, raised in South Central, Los Angeles. I am also an outsider in that I am now a graduate student conducting research and I no longer reside in the study area but also remain closely tied to my neighborhood. Thus, as part of my reflexive praxis, I must not only consider my privilege relative to the participants but also my responsibility to my community and in academia to bring awareness to an academic audience about the fine line between being an insider and an outsider. The interactions and constant conversations I have with loved ones from the barrio remind me that while I am knowledgeable insider of the street life and barrio life, I am also an outsider because I am a researcher. Thus, I must make wise decisions about my research, such as choosing appropriate methods and theory and conducting rigorous analysis that can contribute to public sociology and anti-violence policy-oriented work.

VI. Institutional violence and trails of violence

On a Thursday night, I received a text message from Susana, a single mother of four who is known in the streets of South Central as *Prieta*, an endearing nickname in Spanish for women of dark skin. Prieta said in a worried yet determined tone of voice, "Hey, Kat, can you help me do a flyer with this picture of a missing person, please? I already contacted hospitals and jails and . . . nothing." Susana desperately wanted support to find Sandy, her 24-year-old daughter and one of my closest friends growing up. At the time of her disappearance, Sandy had been dealing with methamphetamine use and gang violence.

Sandy's disappearance hit me to the core. I was unable to sleep, and I paced back and forth in my room for several hours, thinking about her situation. I had flashbacks of us getting tattooed together and our many sleepovers. I paused to think about how to best respond to Susana's pain and worry. While I spent the night creating the flyer for Susana's daughter, I could not help but question how Susana's own former gang affiliation was related to Sandy's disappearance, how it shaped her interactions with institutions which, in turn, had direct and indirect impacts on her and her children, including Sandy. Mothering in South Central has been difficult for Susana. It has entailed enduring welfare sanctions, being on Section 8 housing waitlists, visiting Sandy in drug rehabilitation centers and in prison, praying and hoping that her children do not suffer and struggling with poverty and a lack of resources to parent under strained and violent conditions.

Remnants of gang affiliation, such as tattoos of gang symbols, relationships with active gang members and criminal records, lead to greater contact with institutions in the criminal justice and child welfare systems. Despite having no current gang involvement, institutional agents criminalize the women and exert control over them. Regulation of the women's space, time,

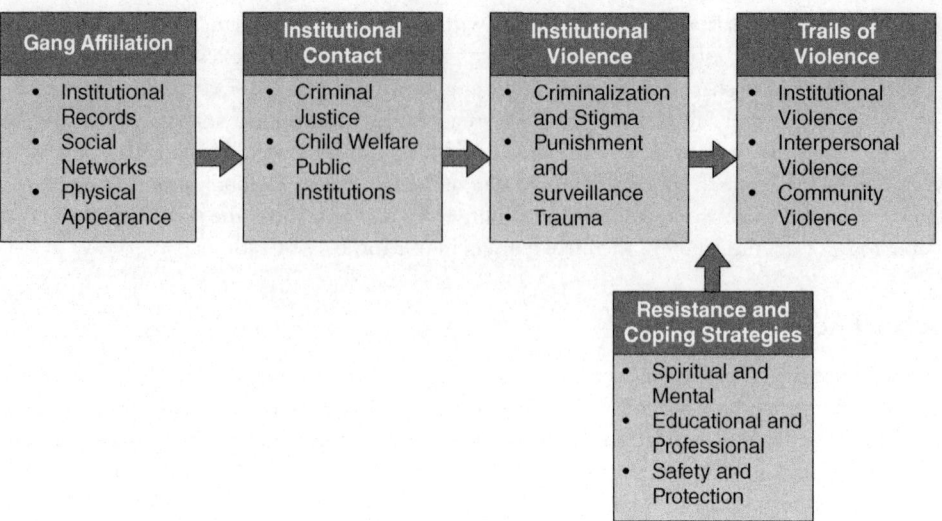

Figure 38.2   Conceptual model of gang affiliation under carceral control, trails of violence and resistance

daily activities and behaviors makes the women feel that they live in a "disciplinary society" (Foucault 1977). These interactions may entail the administration of punitive action, such as removal of a child from the home; the denial of supportive resources, such as mental health services for traumas; or interference with the women's efforts to improve her lot, such as requiring attendance at institutional meetings that interfere with taking classes to continue one's education. To avoid these outcomes, the women ultimately internalize the institutional rules and engage in self-regulation (Foucault 1977; Flores et al. 2017). These interactions and resulting conditions harm the women rather than help them, constituting forms of institutional violence. This in turn makes them and their children vulnerable to other forms of violence, such as interpersonal, community and additional institutional violence. Women also exercise resistance strategies to intervene in intergenerational violence, but this chapter does not focus on those, and they will be addressed in another publication.

Because social inequalities are normalized and institutionalized, states can ignore violence against women (Menjívar and Walsh 2017). Stigma against certain social groups is embedded within various institutions and shapes the actions of state agents (i.e. institutional actors). These agents are street-level bureaucrats (e.g., teachers, police officers and other law enforcement personnel, social workers, judges, public lawyers and court officials, health workers) (Lipsky 2010). They work for institutions that run government programs that provide needed services and benefits and/or sanctions. Their decisions powerfully determine people's life chances. Street level bureaucrats' direct and indirect control of, and failure to support, formerly gang-affiliated mothers constitutes institutional violence and produces *trails of violence*: that is, despite women's exit from gangs, they continue to be labeled gang members and are stigmatized accordingly. The stigma is multiplied by the women's other marginalized statuses – being teen mothers, welfare recipients, residents of crime-ridden neighborhoods, people with limited levels of formal education, Women of Color and low-income women. Their formal and informal interactions with criminal justice and child welfare institutions do not constitute forms of protection but rather of surveillance. As a result, women are exposed to ongoing threats of or actual acts of interpersonal, community and subsequent institutional violence at the hands of state agents. The trails of violence affect not only the women themselves but also their children and families.

A child welfare case in the hood

One of the main perpetrators for institutional violence reported by respondents was Child Protective Services (CPS) – that is, the child welfare system. In the United States, the number of families involved with CPS has increased in recent years. More than 427,000 children were in foster care in the United States in 2015 (Children's Bureau 2018). Latinx children represent a large percentage – about 20 percent – of children in foster care in states with a large Latino population, such as California (Ayon 2015), the site of the present study. Mothers of Color involved with child welfare face institutional racism that contributes to the removal of their children at disproportionately higher rates than White mothers (Roberts 2002). While many scholars have shown that immigration status, race and class contribute to "catching a case" and the removal of Latinx children from families by the system (Lee 2016), my findings show that gang affiliation is also conducive to involvement in the child welfare system and removal of children from parents, specifically from single mothers.

Ten out of the 13 mothers interviewed in this study reported having some form of contact with CPS after exiting the gang. One reported that CPS removed her daughter from the home and the daughter was subsequently adopted by another family. Four mothers reported temporary removal of their children. Five others reported being referred to CPS, although their children were not removed. The rest of the mothers were hyper-aware of the possibility that their children could be removed by CPS. All respondents felt that even minor things could result in the removal of their children. For these mothers, the possibility or actual termination of parental rights undermined their mental health and led several to label it as conveying feelings of death or "dying."

Direct and indirect contact with CPS and the possibility of or the actual removal of their children shaped how the participants navigated their everyday lives and the ways they mothered. Potential or continuous involvement in the system created stress and fear, and many characterized as traumatic their interaction with state agents such as social workers who would often threaten to place the women's children into adoption for no apparent reason. This also led the women to police their personal appearance and to pay close attention to the way they dressed whenever they interacted with their children in public. Respondents indicated they would wear long sleeves to hide their tattoos or gang affiliation and this way prevent unjustified or unexpected interactions with CPS.

Estefania, a 21-year-old mother of three, had the most recent involvement with gangs of all women in the sample. CPS removed her children following allegations of neglect by her family and social workers in the period that followed her husband's violent death. She was no longer active in the gang, but her deceased partner's affiliation and her appearance – she has long black hair and tattoos on her chest conveying gang affiliation – affected her contact and interactions with police agents, social workers, medical doctors, teachers and other street bureaucrats. She felt that her interactions with CPS disrupted her ability to pursue her life goals, including going to college. During our interview, she asked me for help with an application to the local community college. She then changed her mind and said, "Never mind. I don't know why I ask. The parenting classes I have to go to will make it hard to do this" (CPS required that Estefania attend parenting classes to regain custody of her daughter who had been removed from the home).

Estefania shared a photograph showing her daughter at the cemetery visiting her father's grave. Estefania's facial expressions, when discussing the photo, communicated the guilt she felt for what CPS had put her daughter through – experiences that, she felt, a little girl should never go through.

> Damn. . . . It brings tears to my eyes because in that picture she was asking a lot of questions about her dad. 'Til this day she wishes so much how she could hear his voice. It's so sad that all I tried for her I am trying to do for her baby sister. It's not the same because she (her elder daughter) should be with her mom and not adopted. This hurts so much. I feel like my story gets deeper and worst.

Months before our interview, Estefania had several mental breakdowns. ("I don't wanna' talk about windows that I'm trying to close, but all this shit fuckin' hurts a lot," she said). This had led her to have not only a criminal record that documented her former gang affiliation but also a hospital file documenting a prior drug overdose. Although she tried to stay sober, was drug tested weekly, took parenting classes and abided by the court orders, she was not able to regain custody of her daughter.

Some gang scholars who employ life course theory refer to the longitudinal sequence of crimes by individual offenders as "criminal careers" (Piquero et al. 2003). However, Estefania's narrative suggests that a more apt term would be life-course criminalization, because although the behaviors associated with the gang career have ceased, the criminal label persists and shapes life outcomes as if the behaviors had persisted, too. The mothers in this study have to make decisions about how they respond to institutions within the contexts of poverty, substance use, violence and institutional racism. This leaves mothers often questioning what to prioritize when every decision is scrutinized by a system they experience as oppressive and hypercritical (Dunkerely 2017). Their efforts to comply most often do not yield results because the institutions focus on their former gang involvement rather than on their current life contexts. In the case of Estefania, she had just experienced a major trauma associated with community violence (the loss of her husband through homicide). She was poor; not college educated; living in a high-crime, low-income neighborhood. The child welfare system focused on her gang affiliation rather than on examining the ways her multiple marginalizations intersected. As a result, the outcome of the institutional intervention was the loss of custody of her daughter.

Lorena was 24 years old at the time of her interview. She was known as "Dimples," a nickname reflective of her beautiful smile. Her story provides further evidence of the life-course criminalization Chicana mothers face – that is, the kind of criminalization that continues after exiting the gang. She stated during a phone call on a Wednesday before midnight: "my fears started when I was 12. . . . It's crazy to think that today, I am still having those same feelings of fear. I believe that one day, it won't be like that." As a teenager, Lorena walked down the streets of South Central and experienced interpersonal and community violence, such as physical fights and riots linked to her gang involvement. While Lorena moved out of the *barrio* to disaffiliate with the gang and provide a safer life for her children, she continued to face multiple forms of violence, but at the hands of the state.

Lorena tied her experiences with violence as a teenager to her current life as a mother of three children: she described how her past encounters with interpersonal and community violence were similar to her current experiences with street-level bureaucrats. Using photographs and family court paperwork, Lorena detailed her contact with CPS. The father of her daughter, who was physically abusive, reported Lorena to CPS for child abuse, leading to the child's temporarily removal from the home. Given this event and her prior gang involvement and drug use, Lorena feared CPS and the possibility of a repeat removal of her child. She described a picture of herself and children and shared how she felt during the period in which her daughter was removed from her custody:

> Every time her father would abuse me, like, he would hit me, I would take it off on her. She was small, probably, like, 4 months and I would take it off on her. So I mean I came to the point where I hurted her and she ended up in the hospital. They took her away from me probably for, like, 4 months, but it wasn't because I wanted to do it. It's something [I did] because he would do it to me. So I would do it to her. I mean I wasn't on drugs regardless, but they came to the conclusion that it was probably because of that, because they didn't know that I was the one going through it. So I was taking it off on her. I had to fight through a lot to and I had to go through it by myself because I ended up getting out of the relationship that I was in. I ended up leaving her father. I ended up leaving that place. And you know, all those 4 months I ended up being homeless.

Lorena explained that she wished that instead of having her daughter removed, she would have received counseling to address the intimate partner violence. While this aspect has since been solved, she still worries that her prior life as a gang member and CPS history could be used against her. She stated, "I hope my past doesn't creep back, [CPS] took my daughter away once, and now [that] I have three it would be worst." She fears a judge or social worker could use her past as evidence of her being seen as a "bad mother," despite the fact that she is now away from the barrio, working full time and successfully raising three children. Participants show how surveillance in the community by the child welfare system mirror the surveillance of Black and Brown boys and men by bureaucrats in the criminal punishment system (Meyerson 2018; Maldonado 2017).

"They treat us like criminals in front of our kids"

Participants reported experiencing what Flores (2016) calls "wraparound incarceration": a multidimensional surveillance of behavior that works outside of formal institutions of confinement with the constant presence of police officers.

Patricia – whose nickname is "Kutie" – is a 27-year-old mother of three children. Her soft voice, light skin and thin body do not evoke the stereotypical images of gang-involved women, but her style of dress, tattoos, criminal record and social networks with gang members made her vulnerable to surveillance. Her gang involvement began when she was 13 years old. Most of her family (her uncles, aunts, cousins and partner) was gang involved, so she was always familiar with the lifestyle. Patricia was herself at one point a leader of a female gang in South Central. Her involvement resulted in her having a criminal record as a juvenile.

Immediately after exiting the gang, Patricia attempted but struggled to secure housing. She was unable to live in her father's home because her partner was gang involved, and her father feared that her partner's presence would result in unwanted contact with child welfare or police officers, negatively affecting his youngest children. Patricia then rented a room in her mother-in-law's home where two of her brothers-in-law and their wives lived. Other members of the household were active gang members and kept drugs and weapons in the home. Shortly after moving in, Patricia was arrested and investigated for crimes of her brothers-in-law. She was also charged with neglect for "choosing" to raise her daughter in that home – her daughter was temporarily placed in foster care. The state failed to recognize Patricia's limited options, and her living conditions in addition to her past gang affiliation led her to be placed back under surveillance.

All participants in this study had some form of contact with the criminal justice system during, but more specifically after, they had left the gang. These contacts were often the result of their former gang involvement, but often it was the consequence of that of their romantic partners, family members and children. Their interactions with police post-gang involvement show the persistent effects of criminalization. For example, Mayra, a 31-year-old undocumented mother of five children, described how stressful mothering can be under state surveillance, more specifically under police contact. To illustrate her experience, she shared two photographs documenting the criminalization in her day-to-day life. One depicted an incident that occurred long after she had exited the gang: a meeting involving school administrators and police officers as she was trying to enroll her daughter Deja in school:

> When we had that meeting at the office before [Deja] started school, they asked me if I was a gang member, when they already knew I was an ex-gang member. [I told them:] 'You already have it in record. Why are you asking me?' I didn't like that. It irritated me. But I did tell them, "if it wasn't for me getting pregnant with her, I would have been out there doing stuff. But since I had her, I changed my life."

Mayra's quote reveals how the label of gang involvement followed her even after what she had considered a successful departure from gang life. These kinds of contacts with state institutions and agents made Mayra feel that she could not parent freely, that she was judged for her past and was "always on check" – that is, under constant surveillance and punishment by law enforcement and now also under the public education system. She experienced an intense and constant fear that her children – her reason for leaving the gang – would be removed from her custody.

Leticia, also known as Morena, is a mother of four children. At the time of the interview, she was pregnant with her fifth child. She also described similar experiences of institutional violence at the hands of the criminal justice system. Leticia also shared a photo of herself from "back in the day" when she was actively involved in the gang. It shows her wearing clothing characteristic of gang members and wielding a gun which was used for gang activity.

> I left the 'hood long time ago, but they (law enforcement) never stop seeing you like this picture . . . they think we stay doing this all our lives or something, you think I'm gonna carry guns like this nowadays? Hell no, pero this follow you all the time that's why I keep it away. . . . I've had many times where I have to deal with them, when they use to raid the house because they were looking for my brother and for drugs they use to line us up outside in front of our kids like we were criminals and there was no reason because it had nothing to do with us.

Leticia described this form of contact with law enforcement not solely because of how it stood as an example of the forms of violence she endured but also because of how it sought to extend the feeling of intimidation and humiliation to her family, specifically to her children. Interactions of this kind were often shared by participants and were indicative of the ways in which law enforcement communicates and makes patent to the women and their families their devalued social status vis-à-vis that of police. In addition to Mayra and Leticia, other participants shared photographs of their former gang lifestyle. When they did, they always made sure to highlight how the image represented a time was from "in the past, not the present," reflecting their aspiration to be seen for where they stood at today but also the complexities of their current gang affiliations. Combined, the mothers' experiences reflect how their past is "always creeping back" and shaping their encounters with state institutions.

Conclusions

The forms of institutional violence experienced by formerly gang-involved Chicana mothers leads to further violence (institutional, interpersonal and community-based) and create additional victims (primarily the mothers' children). Respondents were labeled by the state as guilty and held responsible for their "bad choices" rather than their actions being understood as "bad circumstances" (Hunt et al. 2011: 2). The stigma they carried as mothers with former gang affiliations was also applied to their children.

Although researchers and policy makers have highlighted the impact of gang membership and worked for decades strategizing gang interventions worldwide (Pyrooz et al. 2017), few empirical studies have investigated the experiences and effects post-gang affiliation of mothers and their children (Hunt et al. 2011). This study examined such among Chicana mothers. They experience institutional violence at the hands of actors in the child welfare and criminal justice systems after exiting the gang, creating long-lasting trails of violence. The data show that institutional violence through interactions with law enforcement, child welfare and public education institutions follows the women years after they have exited the gang. Similar to the collateral consequences of mass incarceration and the "sorting [of] individuals into criminalized collective identities" (Lopez-Aguado 2018), this study found that markers of gang affiliation lead to forms of violence that were often unanticipated by the women and which harm them and their children. While mothers also resist criminalization by employing strategies that reduce contact with institutions and cope through spiritual practices, the post-gang experience is not struggle free. This chapter does not present extended examples of resistance strategies and the ways they learned to navigate the institutions that exposed them to negative experiences, but there are data, and I will address this issue in a further publication.

In fact, despite "doing the right thing" by exiting the gang as mainstream prescriptions establish, the stigma of gang affiliation is persistent and has gendered implications, shaping gang-affiliated women's life chances and mothering. Researchers have largely ignored the significance of gang membership in formerly gang-involved mother's life trajectory, thus ignoring the impacts that gang-affiliation-related stigma have on women and their children. Consistent with prior stigma research showing that stigma affects life chances, low self-esteem, unemployment and income loss (Link and Phelan 2001), this study shows how gang affiliation results in stigmatization that intervenes in their personal, social and professional lives. I ask that we further problematize the (meaning-making) processes and stigmatized labels of gang affiliates, especially when being grounded in the barrio lifestyle – one that should not be punished or devalued.

Similar to the way in which family separation, fear and trauma are built into legal policies afflicting migrant families (Abrego 2014), institutions and their surveillance practices shape the outcomes of the lives of families embedded in gang-affiliated networks. Yet it is important to also emphasize the ways "children allow mothers to transcend psychologically and symbolically the limitations of economic and social disadvantage" (Edin and Kefalas 2005:185). Arguably, better understandings of the experiences of motherhood after gang involvement can inform anti-violence gang prevention and intervention.

The findings show the limitations of current life course theory and suggest a modified conceptualization that accounts for the role of institutions. Thus, a life course, intersectional approach highlights the consequences of gang involvement for gang-involved Chicana mothers and their children. *Life course criminalization* challenges the life course criminal career paradigm in a way that acknowledges individuals' turning points and institutions' failure to provide adequate support. Future researchers and anti-violence practitioners should pay attention to the life course punishment the carceral systems brings. As Michelle Alexander argued,

> many of the current reform efforts contain the seeds of the next generation of racial and social control, a system of 'e-carceration' that may prove more dangerous and more difficult to challenge than the one we hope to leave behind.
>
> *(2018)*

As we take part in decarceration as a movement, we should be aware that the US economy will not "loosen its hold on the bodies that feed its growth so easily" (Michalsen 2019), and this "neutrality will command capitalism's respect" (Fanon 1963:39). Thus, it is crucial to examine the roots and intersections of racism, capitalism and sexism in the criminal punishment system that are used as tools of domination. This study is a call to acknowledge how institutions that are meant to nurture and protect can instead do untold levels of harm. Law enforcement and child welfare agencies play a punitive rather than supportive role in the lives of gang-affiliated Chicana mothers, failing to acknowledge the complexities of their post-gang life. I argue that leaving a gang cannot merely translate into leaving relationships with family and friends who may be gang involved, moving out of high-crime and under-resourced neighborhoods or escaping from conditions of poverty. Rather, this study shows how invisible forms of violence follow these women in structural ways as they navigate raced, classed, gendered inequalities, a process that cannot be left behind. Documentation of this maintenance of exploitative power structures is necessary (Bourgois 2010).

While most research on gangs focuses on highlighting interventions for active gang members, policy makers and practitioners should aim at supporting formerly gang-involved and currently gang affiliated people. "Through everyday acts or tactics of collective resistance against institutional violence, we are establishing an ethos of collective resistance. These acts over time can help produce change that supplements the policy changes for which institutions should be held accountable" (Caballero et al. 2017:61). As a mother, scholar and gang affiliate, I urge for attention to the issues of gang-affiliated mothers. Social scientists, policy makers, activists and street bureaucrats should identify the needs of mothers and find new ways to meet them with transformative justice models and cross-movement collaboration. As panelist Andrea Smith argued, prison abolition is "not simply about tearing down prison walls, but it's about building alternative formations that actually protect people from violence, that crowd out the criminalization regime" (Critical Resistance 2008a:5). If we do not place attention on the violence they experience, specifically on those institutions that are meant to prevent violence, who will protect the next generation of children from falling into cycles of trauma, incarceration and trails of violence?

Acknowledgments

I wish to thank Dr. Tanya Nieri and Dr. Gabriella Sanchez for providing extensive edits to earlier drafts of this manuscript; your mentorship and guidance during these times is highly appreciated. Also, to the mothers in this study for trusting me with their stories, and my children for their patience while conducting this research.

Disclosure statement

No potential conflict of interest was reported by the author.

Notes

1 Gang affiliation and gang involvement will be used interchangeably. Gang involvement refers to being involved in a gang through formal participation. Gang affiliation refers to direct and indirect affiliation and involvement with the gang and social networks (Valdez 2007).
2 I use former/formerly to highlight the "gang member" label as nuanced, one that is applied to by law enforcement and its branches for punishment purposes. The [former] indicates a status that is not a *major status*; rather, it is seen as a *de facto status crime* where "others' perceptions that a person of certain status is certain to commit future crimes" (Cacho 2012). While most women are currently gang affiliated, that is, still in the networks and lifestyles of barrio life, this does not mean the label can be used to mark them as criminals. I say former not to diminish the barrio lifestyle but rather place attention on the consequences of the label.
3 Barrios (neighborhoods), "symbolized the cultural lineage of Chicana/o social and political history. . . . the *barrio* was transformed into both a spatially defined location and, just as importantly an essential resource of cultural memory, identity and pride" (Díaz 2005: 56)
4 I replaced Latina with Chicana as the ethnic identification of participants because it brings a political orientation to this study. I am also committed to contributing to Chicana motherwork scholarship, which focuses on issues pertaining to Chicana mothers, which is a call to action for transformative labor and justice within and outside of academia (Cabellero et al. 2017).
5 Testimonios moves us into a realm of knowledge creation that is grounded in lived experience; it is a method that Women of Color use to "expose brutality, disrupt silence and build solidarity" (Delgado Bernal et al. 2012; Maldonado 2019).
6 This theoretical model is not intended to highlight linear experiences, instead, a theoretical narrative that shows failure of institutions in several stages of women's lives.

References

Abrego, L. J. 2014. *Sacrificing Families: Navigating Laws, Labor, and Love Across Borders.* Stanford CA: Stanford University Press.

Alexander, M. 2018. The Newest Jim Crow. *The New York Times.* Retrieved from www.nytimes. com/2018/11/08/opinion/sunday/criminal -justice-reforms-race-technology.html.

Anzaldúa, Gloria. 1987. *Borderlands La Frontera: The New Mestiza.* San Francisco: Aunte Lute Books.

Arredondo, G., Hurtado, A., Klahn, N., Najera-Ramirez, O. and Zavella, P. 2003 (Eds.) *Chicana Feminisms: A Critical Reader.* Durham: Duke University Press.

Ayón, C. 2011. Latino families and the public child welfare system: Examining the role of social support networks. *Children and Youth Services Review* 33 (10), 2061-2066

Bourgois, P. 2010. Recognizing Invisible Violence: A Thirty Year Ethnographic Retrospective. In *Global Health in Times of Violence.* Santa Fe: School for Advanced Research.

Brotherton, D. 1996. "Smartness," "Toughness," and "Autonomy": Drug use in the Context of Gang Female Delinquency. *Journal of Drug Issues*, 26: 261–227.

Brotherton, D. 2015. *Youth Street Gangs.* New York, NY: Routledge.

Caballero, C., Martinez-Vu, Y., Perez-Torres, J., Telez, M., and Vega, C. 2017. Our Labor is Our Prayer, Our Mothering is Our Offending: A Chicana M(other)work Framework for Collective Resistance. *Chicana/Latina Studies*, 16: 2.

Cacho, L. 2012. *Social Death: Racialized Rightlessness and the Criminalization of the Unprotected.* New York, NY: New York University Press.

Campbell, A. 1990. Female Participation in Gangs. In C.R. Huff (Ed.) *Gangs in America.* Newbury Park, CA: SAGE Publications.

Campbell, A. 1991. *The Girls in the Gang* (2nd ed.). Cambridge, MA: Blackwell Publishers

Chesney-Lind, M. and Hagedorn, J. M. (Eds.). (1999). *Female Gangs in America: Essays on Gender and Gangs*. Chicago: Lakeview Press.

Chesney-Lind, M. 2002. Criminalizing Victimization: The Unintended Consequences of Pro-Arrest Policies for Girls and Women. *Criminology and Public Policy*, 2(1): 81–91.

Chesney-Lind, M. 2004. "Girls and Violence: Is the Gender Gap Closing?" National Electronic Network on Violence Against Women. (August). http;//www.vawnet.org/DomesticViolence/Research/V A WnetDocs/AR GirlsViolence.php.

Chesney-Lind, M. and Irwin, K. 2008. *Beyond Bad Girls: Gender, Violence, and Hype*. New York, NY: Routledge.

Children's Bureau. 2018. Retrieved 4/26/21 https://www.childwelfare.gov/pubPDFs/foster.pdf.

Clark, C. D. 1999. The Autodriven Interview: A Photographic Viewfinder into Children's Experiences. *Visual Sociology*, 14, 39–50.

Clark-Ibañez, M. 2004. Framing the Social World with Photo-Elicitation Interviews. *American Behavioral Scientist*, 47(12), 1507–1527.

Corbin, J. and Strauss, A. 1990. Grounded Theory Research: Procedures, Canons, and Evaluative Criteria. *Qualitative Sociology*, 13(3–21).

Crenshaw, K. 1991. Mapping the Margins: Intersectionality, Identity Politics, and Violence Against Women of Color. *Stanford Law Review*, 43(6): 1241.

Critical Resistance. 2008a. *Abolition Now! Ten Years of Strategy and Struggle Against the Prison Industrial Complex*. Oakland: AK Press.

Contreras, R. 2017. There's no Sunshine: Spatial Anguish, Deflections, and Intersectionality in Compton and South Central. *Environment and Planning: Society and Space*, 35(4): 656–673.

Davis, A., 2003. *Are Prisons Obsolete?* New York, NY: Seven Stories.

Davis, C. 2017. *Girls and Juvenile Justice: Power, Status, and the Social Construction of Delinquency*. Cham: Springer International.

Delgado Bernal, D., Burciaga, R. and Flores, Carmona J. 2012. Chicana/Latina Testimonios: Mapping the Methodological, Pedagogical, and Political. *Equity and Excellence in Education*, 45(3): 363–372.

Díáz, R.D. 2005. *Barrio Urbanism: Chicanos, Planning and American Cities*. London: Routledge.

Dunkerley, S. 2017. Mothers Matter: A Feminist Perspective on Child Welfare-Involved Women. *Journal of Family Social Work,* 20(3): 251–265.

Durán, R. 2013. *Gang Life in Two Cities: An Insiders Journey*. New York, NY: Columbia University Press.

Edin, K. and Kefalas, M. 2005. How Motherhood Changed my Life. In *Promises I Can Keep: Why Poor Women Put Motherhood Before Marriage*. Berkeley: University of California Press.

Fanon, F. 1963. *Wretched of the Earth*. New York: Grove Press.

Farmer, P. 2004. An Anthropology of Structural Violence. *Current Anthropology*, 45(3): 305.

Fleisher, M. 1998. *Dead End Kids: Gang Girls and the Boys They Know*. Madison: University of Wisconsin.

Flores, J. 2016. *Caught Up: Girls, Surveillance, and the Wraparound Incarceration*. Oakland, CA: University of California Press.

Flores, J, Camacho, A. O. and Santos, X. 2017. Gender on the Run: Wanted Latinas in Southern California Barrio. *Feminist Criminology*, 12(3): 248–268.

Foucault, M. 1977. *Discipline and Punish: The Birth of the Prison*. New York, NY: Vintage Books.

Galtung, J. 1969. Violence, Peace and Peace Research. *Journal of Peace Research*, 6(3): 167–191.

Garcia, L. 2009. Now Why Do You Want to Know about That? Heteronormativity, Sexism, and Racism in the Sexual (Mis)Education of Latina Youth. *Gender and Society,* 23(4): 520–541.

Gurusami, S. 2019. Motherwork Under the State: The Maternal Labor of Formerly Incarcerated Black Women. *Social Problems*, 66(1): 128–143.

Hunt, G. and Joe-Laidler, K. 1997. Violence and Social Organization in Female Gangs. *Social Justice*, 24(4): 70. (Losing a Generation: Probing the Myths & Reality of Youth & Violence), 148–169.

Hunt, G. and Joe-Laidler, K. 2001. Accomplishing Femininity Among the Girls in the Gang. *British Journal of Criminology*, 41(4): 656–678. doi:10.1093/bjc/41.4.656.

Hunt, G., Moloney, M., Joe-Laidler, K. and Mackenzie, K. 2011. Young Mother (in the) Hood: Gang Girls' Negotiation of New Identities. *Journal of Youth Studies*, 14(1): 1–19.

Jackman, M. 2002. Violence in Social Life. *Annual Review of Sociology,* 28(1): 387–415.

Joe-Laidler, K. and Chesney-Lind, M. 1995. "Just Every Mother's Angel": An Analysis of Gender and Ethnic Variations in Youth Gang Membership. *Gender & Society,* 9(4): 408–431.

Lee, T. 2016. *Catching a Case: Inequality and Fear in the New York's City's Child Welfare System.* New Brunswick, NJ.: Rutgers University Press.

Link, B. G. and Phelan, J. C. 2001. Conceptualizing Stigma. *Annual Review of Sociology,* 27(1).

Lipsky, M. 2010. *Street-Level Bureaucracy: Dilemmas of the Individual in Public Services.* New York: Russell Sage Foundation.

López, V. and Chesney-Lind, M. 2014. Latina Girls Speak Out: Stereotypes, Gender and Relationship Dynamics. *Latino Studies,* 12(4): 527–549.

Lopez-Aguado, P. 2018. *Stick Together and Come Back Home: Racial Sorting and the Spillover of Carceral Identity.* Berkeley, Ca.: University of California Press.

Maldonado, K. 2017. Review of *Catching a Case: Inequality and Fear in New York City's Child Welfare System* by Tina Lee. *InterActions: UCLA Journal of Education and Information Studies,* 13(1).

Maldonado, K. 2019. Gang Affiliated Chicana Teen Momma Against Systemic Violence: A Testimonio Challenging Dominant Discourse through Academic Bravery. In Cecilia Caballero, Yvette Martínez-Vu, Judith Perez-Torres, Michelle Tellez and Christine Vega (Eds.), *The Chicana Motherwork Anthology Porque sin Madres no hay Revolución* (pp. 24–37). Arizona: Arizona Press.

Mendoza-Denton, N. 2008. *Homegirls: Language and Cultural Practice among Latina Youth Gangs.* Malden, MA: Blackwell Publishing.

Menjivar, C. 2008. Violence and Women's Lives in Eastern Guatemala: A Conceptual Framework. *Latin American Research Review,* 43(3): 109–136.

Menjívar, C. and Walsh, S. D. 2017. The Architecture of Feminicide: The State, Inequalities, and Everyday Gender Violence in Honduras. *Latin American Research Review,* 52(2).

Meyerson, C. 2018, May 24. For Women of Color, the Child-Welfare System Functions Like the Criminal-Justice System. *The Nation.* Retrieved from www.thenation.com/article/for-women-of-color-the-child-welfare-system-functions-like-the-criminal-justice-system/.

Miller, E. 2001. *One of the Guys: Girls, Gangs, and Gender.* New York, NY: Oxford University.

Miller, E., Levenson, R., Herrera, L., Kurek, L., Stofflet, M. and Marin, L. 2011. Exposure to Partner, Family, and Community Violence: Gang-Affiliated Latina Women and Risk of Unintended Pregnancy. *Journal of Urban Health,* 89(1): 74–86.

Michalsen, V. 2019. Abolitionist Feminism as Prisons Close: Fighting the Racist and Misogynist Surveillance in the "Child Welfare" System. *The Prison Journal,* 99(4): 504–511.

Moore, J. W. 1991. *Homeboys and Homegirls in Change.* Philadelphia: Temple University Press.

Muñiz, A. 2015. *Police, Power, and the Production of Racial Boundaries.* New Brunshwick, NJ: Rutgers University Press.

Nixon, R. 2011. *Slow Violence and the Environmentalism of the Poor.* Cambridge, MA: Harvard University Press.

Eggley, A., J. Howell and M. Harris. 2014. Highlights of the 2012 National Youth Gang Survey. Washington, D.C.: Office of Juvenile Justice and Delinquecy Prevention.

Patton, M.Q. 1980. Qualitiative Evaluation Methods. Thousand Oaks, Ca.: Sage.

Piquero, A. R., David P. F. and Alfred B. 2003. The Criminal Career Paradigm: Background and Recent Developments. In Michael Tonry (Ed.), *Crime and Justice: A Review of Research* (Vol. 30, pp. 359–506). Chicago: University of Chicago Press.

Pyrooz, D., Turanovic, J. J., Decker, S. H. and McGloin, J. M. 2017. Parenthood as a Turning Point in the Life Course for Male and Female Gang Members: A Study of within-Individual Changes in Gang Membership and Criminal Behavior. *Criminology,* 55(4): 869–899.

Quicker, J. C. 1983. *Homegirls: Characterizing Chicana Gangs.* San Pedro, CA: International Universities Press.

Richie, Beth E. 2012. *Arrested Justice: Black Women, Violence, and America's Prison Nation.* New York, NY: New York University Press.

Rios, V. 2011. *Punished: Policing the Lives of Black and Latino Boys.* New York, NY: New York University Press.

Roberts, D. 2002. *Shattered bonds: The Color of Child Welfare*. New York: Basic Books.

Sampson, R. and Laub, John H. 1990. Crime and Deviance Over the Life Course: The Salience of Adult Social Bonds. *American Sociological Review*, 55: 609–627.

Sampson, R., and Laub, John H. 2016. Turning Points and the Future of Life-Course Criminology: Reflections on the 1986 Criminal Careers Report. *Journal of Research in Crime and Delinquency*, 53: 321–335.

Stephens, D. P. and L. Phillips. 2003. Freaks, Gold Diggers, Divas and Dykes: The Sociohistorical Development of African American Adolescent Females' Sexual Scripts. *Sexuality and Culture*, 7(1): 3–47.

Taylor, C. and White, S. 2001. Knowledge, Truth, and Reflexivity. *Journal of Social Work*, 1: 37–59.

Thrasher, F. M. 1927. *The Gang: A Study of 1,313 Gangs in Chicago*. Chicago, IL: The University of Chicago Press.

Thornberry, T. P., Krohn, M. D., Lizotte, A. J., Smith, C. A. and Tobin, K. 2003. *Gangs and Delinquency in Developmental Perspective*. New York: Cambridge University Press.

Timmermans, S. and Iddo T., 2012. Theory Construction in Qualitative Research from Grounded Theory to Abductive Analysis. *Sociological Theory*, 30(3): 167–186.

Valdez, A. 2007. *Mexican American Girls and Gang Violence*. New York: Palgrave Macmillan.

Varriale, J. A. 2008. Female Gang Members and Desistance: Pregnancy as a Possible Exit Strategy. *Journal of Gang Research*, 15: 35–64.

Vigil, J. D. 1988. *Barrio Gangs: Street Life and Identity in Southern California*. Austin, TX: University of Texas Press.

Vigil, J. D. 2002. Introduction. In *A Rainbow of Gangs: Street Cultures in the Mega-City*. Austin: University of Texas Press.

Wolf, S. 2017. *Mano Dura: The Politics of Gang Control in El Salvador*. Austin: University of Texas Press.

Zavella, P. 1993. Feminist Insider Dilemmas: Constructing Ethnic Identity with Chicana Informants. *Frontiers: A Journal of Women's Studies*, 13, 53–76.

Zilberg, Elana., 2011. *Spaces of Detention: The Making of a Transnational Gang Crisis between Los Angeles and San Salvador*. Durham: Duke University Press.

39

"The city got my back so the city on my back"

Prisoner's negation of the states' claims of prisoner's humanity

Amy Andrea Martinez

Introduction

In 2010, I worked as the lead research assistant for the Santa Barbara Gang Project at the University of California, Santa Barbara (UCSB). The purpose of this study was to gain an understanding of how small-town institutions treat Mexican/Chicano "gang associated" boys and young men and how these young people respond to cross-cultural conflict. One early afternoon, as I was sitting in the lead investigator's office organizing papers and inputting data, I met a young man who at the time seemed to be in a state of angst and desperation.

JORDAN: "Hi, is Dr. Cabral here?"[1] the young man in the doorway nervously asked.
AM: "No, he's not here right now; how can I help you?" I bade in my usual bubbly voice.
JORDAN: "Do you know when he'll be here?" he asked with a sense of urgency.
AM: "He's not here today, what's your name?" I asked curiously.
JORDAN: "My name is Jordan."

My immediate impression of Jordan was that he was a typical skater college student. He was light skinned – almost white passing, even though I would later learn that Mexican/Chicano was his ethno-racial background. He was 5 feet 8 inches tall. At that time, he wore a black Volcom t-shirt with blue TRU religion fitted jeans, Vans sneakers. His hair was jet-black and spiky. His ears were gauged, a common ear-stretch type of piercing and dress style wore amongst most skaters and punkers.[2] Jordan also had a few visible tattoos on his forearms. I was quickly drawn, however, to a small letter "K" on his left eye. "Where you from?!"[3] I half-jokingly asked him. Although Jordan looked like any other young college student, I understood that the "K" on his face located him as a "gang affiliate" from the Eastside of Santa Barbara. I had been working almost a year in the Santa Barbara Gang Project and had met many boys and young men from the *barrios* of the Eastside but never heard of Jordan. This was probably due to the fact Jordan was spending much of his time as a student at the Santa Barbara City College (SBCC).

At this time, Jordan was 20 years old, and through the community college, he had met students from UCSB that were part of the Latino/a Business Association (LBA) that networked with the community college. Jordan mentioned to me that he had been personally invited by the then-LBA President Mel Figueroa to share his story about the challenges in his life changes and prior involvement with the gang with other student members of the UCSB LBA community at a weekly meeting. After hearing his story, one member suggested that Jordan contact Dr. Cabral for mentorship and guidance. That is how he ended up at the office.

When people typically think about "gangsters" or "gang bangers," most do not think about someone with Jordan's appearance or social status as a college student. While the approach in the social sciences to study gangs has been varied and along a continuum, literature trends within the past couple of decades (particularly in sociology and criminology) have privileged positivism as the governing methodology[4] that continues to categorize self-and/or state-identified gang-affiliated young people within absolute categories; they are portrayed as either pathological "super predators" or romanticized as social rebels (Maxson, Matsuda, & Hennigan, 2011; Venkatesh, 2008; Yablonsky, 1998; Decker, Decker, & Van Winkle, 1996). As a response, counter-trends in the field have resulted in the emergence of critical and radical sociology and criminology that challenge these mainstream narratives of gang members and gang studies from various perspectives by demonstrating the complexities surrounding "gangs" and how individuals who claim gang membership are multifaceted people filled with many contradictions. Thus, Jordan's life presents alternative ways of thinking about young "gang affiliated" people and their experiences with carceral-colonial apparatuses.

In his recent work on African American gang members in Los Angeles, George Barganier (2011) provides a subaltern reading of the origins of the Crips and Bloods and their experiences with processes of racialized dehumanization and challenges radical materialist analyses of Black criminality. For Barganier, although these analyses make crucial contributions to understanding the political economic conditions that have given rise to Black street gangs, they also pathologize Black behaviors in their overreliance on economic conditions. Barganier calls for a decolonial reading of these conditions to push beyond the "methodological eurocentrism" of economic reductionist claims and urges us to develop subaltern perspectives that critically engage the co-constitutive processes of capital accumulation and racialized dehumanization. To accomplish this, Barganier frames his analysis of the history of Crips and Bloods in the historical project of coloniality and lays out how the historical practices of racialized dehumanization continue to play a defining role in the social historical experiences of young Black people. This analysis challenges radical materialist explanations of gang life to more fully account for the role of race in class relations.

Answering Barganier's call for a decolonial reading in understanding the social and material conditions that racialized "gang affiliated" young people navigate, my work investigates how self- and/or state-identified Mexican/Chicano gang-associated boys and men in Santa Barbara embody these similar tensions of state sanctioned violence and racialized dehumanization. In particular, I engage both the life and tattooed body of Jordan to demonstrate how intersectional forces (e.g. coloniality, settler-colonialism, and carcerality) have shaped Jordan and his responses to his criminalization through that act of tattooing practices (in and outside of prison). While criminological scholarship has interpreted tattooing practices among Latino males in the U.S. through a lens of "self-damnation" and "self-defeating" resistance (Phillips, 2001; Solorzano & Bernal, 2001), for the Mexican/Chicano community, these scholars argue, tattooing represents a marker of criminality and gang affiliation, which shapes and reinforces the public imaginary of Mexican/Chicano young people as deviant (Santos, 2009; Vigil, 2007). Although this tradition highlights the ways in which structures of domination are reified through the cultural practices of racialized young people, it fails to account for how these practices constitute forms of resistance to experiences of racialized dehumanization. It is important to problematize stereotypical conceptualizations of how academics, law enforcement, and society at large view tattoos inscribed on racialized bodies through a binary of solely symbolizing gang affiliation and/or reflective of a criminal lifestyle. If the issue of racialized dehumanization is to ever be addressed within gang studies, we must provide an alternative framework that allows for the understanding of the contradictions embedded in racialized young peoples' acts of agency that assert their human dignity as non-pathological. Focusing on Jordan's life experiences and intimate relationship with the colonial-carceral state allows for a close examination and explanation of how state-sanctioned violence and structures of power manifest at the micro level and how young people (like Jordan) explore resistance against it, even if it may lead them to self-defeat or additional carceral punishment.

Drawing on the work of Fanon (1967), particularly his conceptualization of the epidemiology of oppression, he offers a sophisticated lens to unpack these contradictions found in the dialectical relationship between Mexican/Chicano prisoners' agency through tattooing practices and how their expression of agency also reifies the very same structures of oppression they are resisting against. Fanon opens up *Black Skin, White Masks* offering us an intimate preview of the devastating consequences of Black peoples' frustration over not being able to achieve whiteness as a means to establish a level of humanity. It is here in Black peoples' yearning for whiteness where we find the contradictions inherent in their attempts to re-humanize themselves to assert their human dignity by negating their blackness. Fanon demonstrates how internalized oppression amongst Black peoples' leads them to occupy "a zone of nonbeing, an extraordinary sterile and arid region" that, as a result, pushes them to undergo an insidious cycle of self damning resistance. Their internalized oppression consequently leads to the perpetuation of psychological trauma as they continuously find themselves "digging [deep] into [their] own flesh to find meaning" in their existence to assert some claim to humanity to be legible by white society (Fanon, 1967, p. 3). In other words, their expression of resistance results in a hatred of themselves and their black skin all in their attempts to (re)humanize themselves.

Here I see some parallels between Black peoples' struggle to establish a legibility of their humanity through achieving whiteness with Mexican/Chicano boys and men's choices in defying the State's mechanisms of social control over their personhood and human dignity (in and outside of prison) through their tattooing practices to (re)claim their humanity and human dignity. That these boys and young men would risk further positioning themselves as vulnerable to state-sanctioned violence through the colonial-carceral apparatus by choosing to tattoo themselves reveals that they have some understanding that the choice in inscribing their flesh with ink is also a form of striking back against the carceral-colonial apparatus. In other words, even if it costs these boys and men their freedom, their choice to tattoo themselves (in and outside of prison) reveals how invaluable their choices of expressing their resistance (e.g. vis-à-vis the act of inscribing their bodies with tattoos) is to them. As such, tattooing is a political act of reclaiming their humanity and human dignity.

In addition, I borrow from Solorzano and Delgado-Bernal's (2001) conceptualizations of resistance to describe how hegemonic interpretations of young Mexican/Chicano's choice in getting tattooed is typically viewed as "self-defeating". Employing a qualitative methods approach and counter storytelling to examine the construct of student resistance, Solorzano and Delgado-Bernal's research focused on two major historical events within the Chicana/o community – the 1968 East Los Angeles school walkouts and the 1993 UCLA student strike for Chicana/o studies. They extended their understanding of resistance to encompass its transformative and transgressive potential and challenge conventional conceptualizations of student resistance, which typically have focused on using a deficit lens to understand student agency. Student agency here refers to students who may have some critique of their oppressive social conditions but are not motivated by an interest in social justice. As a result, these students engage in behavior that is not transformational and in fact helps to re-create the oppressive conditions from which they originated. I understand how the public imaginary would and does tend to view Mexican/Chicano gang-affiliated prisoners' choice of tattooing practices as self-defeating, as it does further position them as vulnerable targets of carceral punishment. However, I call for an approach that further complicates our understanding of tattooing practices in and outside of prison that goes beyond binary logics that views the choice of tattooing among this population as either "self-damning" resistance, self-harm, psychopathology, reflective of an individual's criminal lifestyle (Phillips, 2001; Rozycki Lozano, Morgan, Murray, & Varghese, 2011; Jennings et al., 2014), and/or a romanticized viewing of the tattooed body as an archival site of resistance and cultural preservation (Clawson, 1995; Olguin, 2010).

Using a decolonial framework to examine young peoples' choice of getting tattooed allows for an appreciation of the dialectic relationship between resistance and oppression through young peoples' ways of coping and negotiating oppressive structures that attempt to strip them of their humanity under a colonial-carceral state. It begins with the assertion that the central logic of coloniality is the racial dehumanization of the "Other" – in this case, Mexican/Chicano self-and/or state-identified gang-associated boys and young men. It contests the binary approach of "good" and "bad" and fixed categories while taking a closer look at the ambiguities in identity construction, the fluid nature of social action, and the range of approaches to daily life from adaptation to resistance and provides a glimpse into the lives of young people's complexity and contradictoriness. Within these contradictions is a dynamism that has potential to produce revolutionary change in how we work through tension and contestations. Instead of questioning why young gang affiliates in and outside of prison (continue) to get tattoos, we can explore how tattooing within this subculture is a material manifestation of the dialectic between the simultaneous internalization and resistance to racial ontological subordination.[5] In this way, a decolonial framework allows for the tattooing practices of Mexican/Chicano self- and/or state-identified gang-associated young people to be seen as a political act of self-preservation, a claim to human dignity, and a form of resistance against "non-being" both inside and outside of prison.

Jordan's background

Jordan was born and raised in the city of Santa Barbara, California. Although not typically associated with street gangs and violence, Santa Barbara serves as a unique site to investigate how self- and/or state-identified Mexican/Chicano gang-associated boys and men engage in their own agency (e.g. tattooing practices inside/outside of carceral institutions) against structural violence to self-represent their belonging and stake a claim for their humanity in an era of hyper-militarized and racially hostile policing practices. Due to its brutal zero-tolerance policing policy, the Mexican/Chicano[6] community commonly refers to Santa Barbara[7] as "Santa Bruta".[8] "Santa Bruta" literally translates to "Brutal Santa Barbara" – a reference to how the Mexican community at large understand the hostile racial tensions between law enforcement and Mexican/Chicano boys and men as deeply rooted in the settler colonial history and racial order of the community.

Jordan is a third-generation non-Spanish-speaking Mexican/Chicano, as his family has strong roots in the city, having also been born and raised there themselves. His mother, Yoli, gave birth to him in 1989. As for as his biological father, he was absent in Jordan's life before he was even born. His father had been in and out of prison and at one point was deported. Jordan's mother remarried and gave birth to two more children; her second-oldest son Gabriel in 1992 and her youngest daughter Tay in 1999. Gus, Yoli's new partner, was the only stable father figure Jordan ever knew.

Like many young people who grew up in Santa Bruta, who belonged either to the East-side or Westside of the town, Jordan grew up on the Eastside from the town of Goleta. Jordan attended Saint Raphael's School, a preschool through eighth grade private Catholic school located in Goleta. When he graduated, Jordan attended Goleta Valley Junior High and after that attended Dos Pueblos and Santa Barbara High School. After living in Goleta for some years, his family decided to move back to the Eastside. Around this time, Jordan was 15 years old and had made new friendships with other young people, many of whom he had met from playing in the community American Youth Soccer Organization (AYSO) and Youth Football League (YFL).

Jordan was constantly suspected of being a "gang member" simply based on his "gang" aesthetics[9] and whom he hung out with, much like other young Mexican/Chicanos in the settler city. Eventually this would prove to be detrimental in Jordan's ability to move freely throughout Santa Barbara without constantly being surveilled by policing forces. After a few curfew violations and encounters with the Santa Barbara Police Department (SBPD), Jordan quickly became legally ensnared by the local Santa Barbara court system at a young age. On one particular occasion, then-15-year-old Jordan had to appear in court for assault charges on a police officer. There was a hostile confrontation between Jordan and a white police officer named Kenneth Kushner from the SBPD that resulted in Jordan spitting at the officer – his spit landing about a foot from where the officer was standing. Jordan recalled the officer slamming him to the ground and yelling "If I see you on the street and you try and spit at me again, I will knock your fucking teeth out!" Jordan was found guilty and was sentenced to a year in Santa Barbara Juvenile Hall.

Jordan's experience reveals how law enforcement in Santa Bruta neglect to recognize the adolescence and humanity of Mexican/Chicano boys and young men within a colonial-carceral apparatus and to what violent heights interactions between the two can escalate to. If coloniality understands the origins of colonialism as having established a social hierarchy informed by the logic of race onto the minds of those subjected to colonial power, then central to its under-standing is the idea that modern racism has established a structure of superiority and inferiority that continues to be the foundation of race as a structure of domination. Thus, today's modern police officers are no different than their colonialist forbearers or the self-appointed vigilantes in the southwest of California whose aim was to put Mexicans/Chicanos "in their place" through racialized dehumanization and public emasculation (Webb, 1965; Carrigan & Webb, 2003; Edwards, 2004). Police officers' primary function in the United States is to serve as an extension of the punitive arm of the state – to protect and uphold a colonial-carceral apparatus.

However, the levels of hostility and toxic hyper-masculine violence that are usually deployed by officers towards boys and teenagers (like Jordan) who are identified as gang members (thus enemies to the state) also stem from a culture of militarized training that is embedded in the "professionalization" of police officers. Police officers have been trained to believe that in order to successfully "serve and protect" the public from these "super predators", they must embody a "warrior mentality" against them. Since they see themselves as soldiers in a battle, with the primary aim to dominate, submit, and/or eradicate their "enemies", it is no surprise, then, that is especially true in their interactions with "gang affiliated" young people (Vitale, 2017). In addition, as Barganier and Rodriguez[10] eloquently stated, it is "law enforcement [who] has been at the front line of the systemic violence that has continued to uphold coloniality. This structural violence functions to enforce racial dehumanization, a dehumanization whose roots lie in the bifurcation of the modern world into what Fanon (1967) identified as the 'zones of being and non-being'."

To further unpack Jordan's interaction with Officer Kushner, I borrow from Third-World feminist scholars' conceptualizations of violence and the body to examine how gendered forms of policing play a role in furthering processes of racialized dehumanization.[11] In her analysis of gendered forms of sexual violence bestowed upon the Black male body, Patricia Hill Collins argues that white violence against Black men, "symbolize(d) the most egregious expressions of racism," in that they were ritualized and public in nature (2004, p. 217). As social scientists we are interested in meaning-making, the mediation of oppressive structures, and people's engagement with how they experience structural violence in real time on the ground. I look at Jordan's encounter with Officer Kushner as an opportunity to interrogate why a full-grown white man would respond to a Mexican/Chicano male teenager spitting at them with this level of excessive force. Simultaneously, I wonder about Jordan's thought processes and emotions he was feeling that prompted him to spit at the officer – perhaps not realizing to what lengths the Santa Barbara courts would go to punish his act of resistance against an already hostile civilian-police encounter.

However, the use of aggressive and hostile policing tactics like this are not new; they have become deeply entrenched in the social fabric of the lives of both Black and Latino boys and men in the ways in which law enforcement polices racialized bodies. Young people are moving in the social world with the expectation that the kinds of interactions they are going to face when confronted by law enforcement will always begin with hostility. The fact that racialized youth have learned to adapt to how they are policed without instruction speaks to the larger issue of how "regular routines" have become a normal function of living in poor communities with concentrated populations of marginalized people (Jones, 2014). Thus, it comes as no surprise that Mexican/Chicano young boys and men like Jordan are already walking into police-civilian encounters ready to assert their claim to their human dignity (no matter the consequence), to resist against their racialized dehumanization. This also challenges how they are constantly depicted as being a threat to the well-being of the Santa Barbara community – a social construction which in turn justifies how Santa Barbara police "handle" its most undesirable youth populations. I read Officer Kushner's use of excessive force and verbal abuse as a public manifestation of gendered toxic hypermasculinity expressed through his ego and performance of male bravado to establish and assert his understanding of himself as absolute law and authority. Juxtaposing law enforcement's dramatic, excessive, and often unnecessary use of force in relation to weaponless young 15-year-old teenagers like Jordan poses the question of whether it is not police who embody the very same violent pathologies that are scripted for boys and young men of color in the United States.

While most people would reduce Jordan's choice of spitting at the officer (which can be read as an act of disrespect and defiance warranting discipline and punishment) as a form of "self-defeating" resistance (because it cost him serving time in juvenile hall), I argue that it can also be seen as Jordan highly valuing his human right to exercise his agency to assert his human dignity. Given the historical racial tensions between white and Brown boys and men in Santa Bruta (Camarillo, 1979), there is no denying that the tensions underlying Jordan and Officer Kushner's interaction could only be amplified due to the convergence of their differences in gender and age and the power dynamics at play (i.e. a full-grown man who has the power of the badge and his white race and a brown male teenager who has been labeled a gang member). I argue that these intersectional forces predetermined how Officer Kushner chose to use emasculation as a mechanism in which to publicly discipline and punish Jordan so as to assert his own masculinity and power. I argue that margins of subalternity provide a space for critical reflection for interpreting the complexities of racialized forms of social control, Mexican/Chicano male subjectivity and resistance, and structural violence.

The following year of Jordan's life consisted of him going in and out of the Santa Barbara Juvenile Hall and Los Prietos Boys Camp[12] (LPBC), a program that is located on 17 acres in the Los Padres National Forest. The facility claims to provide a local commitment option for legally entangled boys between the ages of 14 and 18, offering a 120- or 180-day program. Young people must "earn their way out" of the program based on their participation and behavior. While serving time at LPBC, Jordan was diagnosed with persistent depressive disorder (PDP), also commonly known as "dysthymia," which is a continuous long-term chronic form of depression. Due to it chronic nature, coping with its symptoms of depression can often times be challenging, but with a combination of psychotherapy and medication, the condition is treatable.

After his diagnosis, Jordan was prescribed medication at LPBC. Despite this, Jordan was still struggling being committed at LPBC – he had even made a successful escape from the camp. After that incident, Yoli fought to have him released. After having numerous sessions with the camp counselor, Yoli and the camp counselor came to an agreement that Jordan would not be able to successfully graduate from the program and was able to get him released. Jordan's release was contingent upon him wearing an ankle monitor bracelet so that he could finish his sentence on house arrest. Upon his release, Yoli was finally able to get him into counseling. When speaking to Jordan about this period of his life, particularly about being diagnosed with PDP, he stated "everyone [at LPBC] was getting diagnosed with something – they just wanted to keep us drugged."[13]

Upon his reentry, Jordan sought to be on a different life journey by enrolling himself at the local Santa Barbara City College. Jordan was aspiring to be an attorney, to be of service to young people who shared similar experiences of being legally entangled in the legal system like himself. Jordan got well acquainted with Noel Gomez, a community college counselor and one of the co-founders of the Transitions Program, which was creating a prison to college pipeline at SBCC. Jordan had also been attending the LBA meetings hosted at SBCC – which is how he got connected to LBA student members from UCSB. Jordan was doing well for himself; he had become excited about going to school. The carceral state, however, would pose serious challenges to his new passion for education and college. The carceral state was always looming over Jordan's head.

In 2008, Operation Gator Roll, a sting operation run by the Santa Barbara Police and County Sheriff's Department, joined with federal and state agencies to remove all "identified gang members." Conservative journalist Chris Meagher (2010, August 26) reported in the *Santa Barbara Independent Press*, "Santa Bruta: How the Eastside Gang Was Gator Rolled," that law enforcement "hit the Eastside of Santa Barbara unexpectedly." On the early morning of October 15, more than 400 law enforcement officers "cracked down" on 71 homes ranging from Los Angeles County all the way up to Santa Maria – a stretch covering 176 miles. Nearly 60 young people were "rounded up" and brought to the Earl Warren Showgrounds in Santa Barbara, where law enforcement taskforces had set up their command headquarters. Jordan's and his family's home were one of the homes raided by law enforcement that day. Yoli had no idea what the officers were looking for – they just handed her a search warrant. She overheard an officer state that they were not going to leave her home empty handed. Eventually, the only thing officers were able to confiscate was a pair of nunchucks that were hanging on a Bruce Lee poster in Jordan's room; Jordan had been a fan of Bruce Lee since he was 13 years old. They also seized his laptop, which had contained a school project he had completed showing his personal transformation from a street gang-affiliated young man to becoming a college student. The police and the prosecution would later use his school presentation to validate his gang membership in the Santa Barbara courtroom so as to enhance further prison-time punishment on Jordan. The nunchucks taken that day were the only evidence law enforcement had and used to file charges against Jordan in the federal RICO[14] case of Operation Gator Roll. Jordan's family hired an attorney and were able to get Jordan released, though he was placed on probation for a year. Just one month shy of completing his probation successfully, another knock came at his family's door one early morning. Yoli was handed another search warrant, and Jordan was hauled off in the back of a police car. She would later receive a phone call from him that afternoon. "Mom, they arrested me for attempted murder, I don't know what they are talking about, and you need to help me," Jordan pleaded to his mom. Jordan had been identified by another young person as having been involved in the case of four Eastsiders who had participated in the stabbing of a young Mexican/Chicano from the Westside in 2007. Jordan had been pulled into the case because another young man who had been identified as being involved had "snitched" on Jordan to negotiate a plea bargain. Though the victim had survived,[15] Jordan was facing a 25-years-to-life sentence, while his 19-year-old co-defendant, ChiKo, was looking at 60 years in prison.

Jordan's family posted bail and hired an attorney to "[start] the battle for [their] son's life." Jordan continued to attend school and was working at SBCC; he had begun engaging in motivational speaking gigs at schools, talking to children about his life story, and began to mentor young people. Jordan had also been going to Father Gregory Boyle's Homeboys Industries in Los Angeles to take advantage of their free tattoo removal services; he wanted to remove the small "K" from his face to evade any negative predispositions the judge, prosecutor, and jurors might have against him during court appearances. He was already looking at 25 years to life in prison without any gang enhancements. He did not want his tattoos to be used as a way to add any more time to whatever sentence he might receive.

Despite all his efforts, including over 100 community members – professors, counselors, college students, community activists – showing up to support Jordan on his court sentencing day, on April 25, 2011, then-22-year-old Jordan was sentenced to 15 years in prison by (now-retired) Judge Frank Ochoa. At the time, Ochoa was one of two Latino judges out of a total of 27 judges in the Santa Barbara county. He was also a lecturer in the Chicano/a Studies and Political Science Departments at UCSB. As a young college student, myself, it was hard to believe that a Mexican/Chicano educator and judge could give someone from his own community such an unforgiving sentence.

Jordan was given five years for the stabbing (which he had pleaded no contest to), with an additional ten years due to then-prosecutor Hans Almgren having used photos of Jordan and his friends throwing up gang signs from the college project Jordan had created to demonstrate his personal transformation. These photos were taken from his confiscated laptop during Operation Gator Roll. In addition, Almgren had used an old mugshot of Jordan's body tattoos as evidence of Jordan's *ongoing* gang membership.

Six months prior to Jordan and ChiKo's case, a "gang brawl" took place in downtown Santa Barbara. A then 14-year-old, Ricardo Juarez, participated in the stabbing of 15-year-old Luis Angel Linares, a "rival gang member," which resulted in his death. The then-District Attorney Christie Stanley made the decision to charge Juarez as an adult for murder – despite the fact that he was only 14. On October 15, 2008, a then-15-year-old Ricardo Juarez was found guilty of voluntary manslaughter by a jury at the Santa Barbara Superior Courthouse. The 12-member jury also convicted Juarez of assault with a deadly weapon and of committing the felony for the benefit of a criminal street gang, which added ten years to his original seven-year sentence due to California's Proposition 21.[16] On January 16, 2009, Judge Brian Hill sentenced Juarez to a total of 17 years in prison.

Juarez was the youngest person in the Santa Barbara County and state of California to receive such a sentence at the time. Prop 21 coupled with Santa Barbara's zero tolerance of gang violence facilitated the process of "adultification" of Mexican/Chicano boys and young men in the state of California like Juarez (Giroux, 2003). Juarez's case serves as an important illustration of the settler city's commitment to make examples out of Mexican/Chicano boys and men who are either self- and/or state-identified as "gang associated" and are legally entangled in the court system. Jordan heavily contemplated whether to take his case to trial, especially after the high-profile case of Ricardo Juarez. There was a high probability that if he were to be found guilty, he would be serving a minimum of 25 years in prison or at worst a life sentence. Having also been validated as a gang member, Jordan would have received an additional 10 years added to his minimum sentence of 25 years – extending his sentence to a minimum of 35 years. Thus, Jordan pleaded no contest. Jordan was given five years for a crime that he may or may not have committed but received ten years for having been "proven" to be an active gang member through photos of himself and his tattoos that had been taken long before his case.

Tattoos as manifestations or articulations of contradictory consciousness

Tattoos offer an intriguing opportunity to engage hegemonic assumptions about the functionality of tattoos for a young person involved in the street and/or prison life. For example, Phillips (2001) claims that tattoos serve as visual markers of identity that help gang affiliates "*survive* violent social realms such as the street or prison" (emphasis mine, p. 361). Phillips also claims that tattoos inscribed on the bodies of gang affiliates can result in powerful political semiotic symbols of gang subculture, as some tattoos *are* personal markers of identification (e.g. rank) *or* signifiers of gang affiliation. Even among urban theorists, there has been recognition that tattoos play an important role in the social and semiotic landscape of urban life and situate individuals embedded in the culture to abide by certain rules and/or code of the streets;[17] the tattoo allows a young person to always remain symbolically connected and affiliated in a way that serves as a cloak of protection even when not physically surrounded by their "homies" (Wirth, 1938; Conquergood, 1998, Schildkrout, 2004; Garot, 2010).

In addition, young people who are gang affiliated must navigate precarious terrains that are made hostile by either rival gang affiliates or different ethno-racial groups in and/or outside of prison. However, missing from the discussion is how gang affiliates use the visual power of tattoos to resist against and navigate hostile interactions with law enforcement (i.e. police/prison guards) in and/or outside of prison. Based on my observations of young people in Santa Bruta who are tattooed who are self and/or state identified as gang affiliated, their tattoos not only serve to maintain a sense of who they are (among many other things) but are also strategically used to subvert the colonial-racist-carceral lens in which law enforcement persistently polices their brown bodies. In other words, tattoos among gang affiliates in the "hood" also demonstrate a Mexican/Chicano street double consciousness that reveals their understandings of the prejudiced and oftentimes racist constructions in which law enforcement view and interpret tattoos on their brown body.

I argue that young people are very much aware that any image or symbol that is inked on their already negatively racialized body is always going to be "doubly mark[ed]" because even if not all the tattoos inscribed on their bodies indicate gang affiliation, they will be interpreted as such (Perez, 2002, p. 50). However, for police and/or the community to only and always interpolate the tattoos on these young people's bodies as "evidence" of gang affiliation speaks to the larger issue of the settler city's racial anxieties of Mexican/Chicano boys and men – who, at the

Figure 39.1 An affiliate of the Eastside Traviesos with an "éS" tattooed on his neck; éS is a skateboard footwear company in the Unites States.

Source: Photograph taken by author

same time, may or may not even be gang affiliated. In other words, the ongoing legacies of settler colonialism continues to shape the geopolitical landscape of Santa Bruta in such a way that already predetermines how law enforcement and society "reads" the etched ink on the brown skin of these Mexican/Chicano boys and men as indicative of an active gang membership status.

In Figure 39.1, for example, a then-teenager, Lil Scrappy, from the Eastside *Traviesos* has a tattoo on his neck which reads "éS." At first glance, one *might* automatically associate this tattoo as a symbol representative of the "Eastside" – recognized by the SBPD as the largest gang in the settler city, which houses four sub-cliques: Krazies, *Traviesos*, *La Familia*, and The Gang. The tattoo can communicate different meanings to four different audiences: his peers from his clique, rival gang affiliates, law enforcement, and regular community members, depending on who is doing the viewing. As Perez (2002) has pointed out, just because tattoos have become mainstream and socially acceptable, it does not negate that tattoos remain seen as a symbol reflective of criminality or a criminal lifestyle on racialized bodies. The public imaginary still views the tattooed Mexican/Chicano as deviant.

When I interviewed Lil Scrappy about this tattoo, he shared how the tattoo was actually the brand moniker of a global skateboarding footwear company that has been in existence since 1995. He was tired of being harassed by SBPD for his tattoos, so he decided that he was going to "mess with them" by tattooing "éS" on his neck, *knowing* that the police would automatically read the tattoo as gang affiliated. I found Scrappy's choice of tattooing a skateboarding company's logo on his neck amusing because he found a creative way to not only extrapolate a multi-purpose use out of the skateboarding logo tattooed on his body, but he also created an opportunity to expose law enforcement's prejudices against tattooed Mexican/

Chicano boys and young men like himself. In fact, he was eager to be confronted by police because in his mind, if police officers tried to allege that the tattoo was a marker of his gang affiliation, he could contest it by proving that the tattoo was merely a skateboarding footwear company.

Some scholars, police officers, and/or community members may look at Lil Scrappy's choice of tattoo as a form of "self-defeating" or "self-damning" resistance because the tattoo still had the potential of further antagonizing law enforcement in a potentially already hostile police-civilian interaction and/or heightening his surveillance in the future. Would officers even give him the opportunity to "prove" that his tattoo was not gang affiliated? Would they then assume that Lil Scrappy was appropriating the logo to symbolize his affiliation with the *Traviesos* set? In the larger scheme of things, a young person's choice in tattooing their bodies with any image/symbol (which may or may not be gang affiliated but will still be read as so) can be seen as what I call a self-preserving form of resistance. This self-preserving form of resistance allows a young person like Lil Scrappy to maintain a sense of his humanity and human dignity while claiming a stake of personal freedom amidst the necropolitical terrain of Santa Bruta.

Resistance as self-preservation: green ink therapy in prison

Over the course of Jordan's first years of incarceration, Jordan went through periods of time where he would get "blasted up" with new prison tattoos. As an outsider, I was curious as to how Jordan was getting away with getting tattoos while in prison. I would quickly learn that due to the extreme conditions of deprivation and attempts of dehumanization in institutions of colonial captivity (i.e. prisons), prisoners have come up with creative ways to circumvent their dehumanization. One of the ways to do so has been through acquiring prison ink. These tattooing practices have been described by some scholars as an act of resistance against and response to the State's attempts to have absolute control over their bodies and personhood (Holland, 2017). However, in the case of California prisons, prisoners' choice in tattooing their bodies has been criminalized as it is seen as a violation of the California code of regulations for rulings for adult prisons, which states "inmates shall not intentionally destroy, damage, or deface, state property" (California Code of Regulation for Adult Institutions, Title 15, Article 1, Behavior 3011). Since "inmates" are considered wards of the state, the act of tattooing whiling in prison is a violation of Title 15, Article 1, Behavior 3011; therefore, prisoners are subject to further discipline.

I found myself asking, despite running the risk of having time added to their original sentences and/or or receive institutional charges, why do Mexican/Chicano prisoners[18] choose to get ink done while serving time in prison? How does tattooing serve as a way for Mexican/Chicano prisoners to (re)claim their dignity and humanity? How does this, then, speak to the overall significance of getting tattooed and tattooing in prison? With vast studies on tattoos and tattooing practices, we still know very little on the significance of tattoos and how the act of tattooing among Mexican/Chicano[19] gang affiliates inside and outside of prison functions as a form of self-preservation and resistance against prisonization,[20] racial dehumanization, and a colonial-carceral apparatus.

When I met Jordan, he had approximately eight tattoos spread on his body. He had a small Times New Roman–style "K" tatted next to his right eye – symbolizing the set he claimed and "Fuck my enemies" and "Krazies" written in cursive that hung around his neck. Covering his chest was an "East" and "Side" in old English script. On the back of his head, he had a "KSB." On his left forearm, he had an ambigram tattoo that said "life" and, if you read it upside down, "death." His legs were covered with an "E" and "S," representing the "Eastside," the side of town

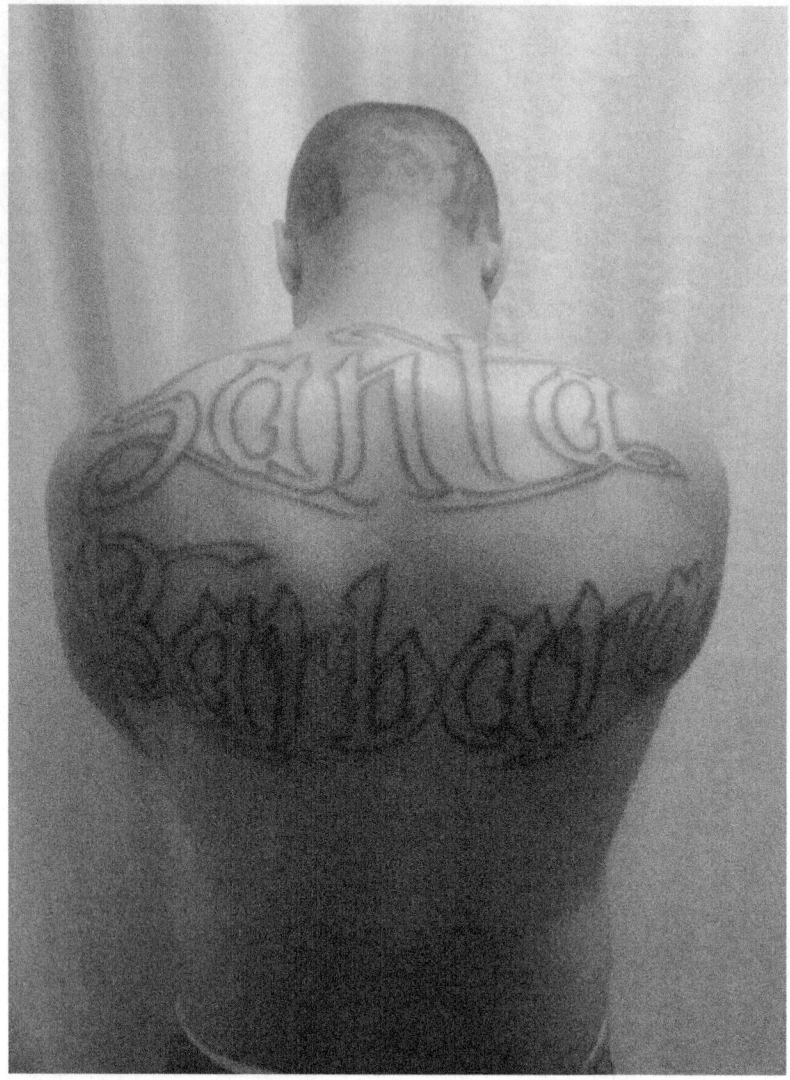

Figure 39.2 The city got my back so the city on my back. #SantaBarbara. #ForMyRealOnes. #reppinHard. #OneShotCauseWeDontTapOut. #SB. #NoPlaceLikeIt.

Source: Photograph taken by another prisoner

he grew up in. All of these tattoos were done outside of carceral institutions in professional tattoo shops.

After Jordan was sentenced, his first stop was Wasco State Prison (WSP), a reception center three hours up north from Santa Barbara. The primary goal of Wasco is to provide short-term housing in order for an "inmate" to get processed and classified and get a physical and mental evaluation before the state determines their security level, program requirements, and appropriate institutional placement.[21] Jordan spent about a month at Wasco before he was sent to Pleasant Valley State Prison (PVSP), also a three-hour drive up north from Santa Barbara. His stay was short lived before he was sent to High Desert State Prison (HDSP), a nine-and-a-half-hour drive up north from Santa Barbara, where he spent roughly a year and a half. Due to the over-crowding in California State prisons at the time, in a "random draw," Jordan was then chosen to be sent off to Tallahatchie County Correctional Facility (TCCF), a privately owned prison for men in Tallahatchie County, Mississippi. At best, this was a twenty-eight-hour drive away from Santa Barbara. Prior to making the long trek, Jordan, alongside other prisoners, were stationed at La Palma Correctional Facility (LPCF), a privately owned prison in Eloy, Arizona – an eight-and-a-half-hour drive away from Santa Barbara. Every time Jordan was shipped off to another prison, he was further removed from his friends and family in Santa Barbara. Here we can see the linkages between African chattel slavery and natal alienation as a modern technology of state violence that has used institutional captivity to subjugate Mexican/Chicano prisoners like Jordan to a state of social death through physical displacement.[22]

On one occasion, Jordan sent me a photo of a new tattoo that had been posted on his social media account; one of his homies had tattooed "Santa Barbara" covering his back (see Figure 39.2). I was curious as to why Jordan did not wait to get such an elaborate tattoo when he was released from prison (as he does have a release date). When I asked him about it, he explained how covering his back with "Santa Barbara" was a way to let others (within the prison and his followers on his social media accounts) know where he was from and that he was "still holding it down" for his community. "Still holding it down" refers to the fact that he has chosen to remain in general population, thus maintaining a status of being "good" (i.e. not being a snitch and/or not going into protective custody due to a desire to relinquish an active gang membership status). The tattoo, then, is a nonverbal form of communication that signifies who he is, where he is from, his status, and what history he carries – literally on his back.

A close analysis of Figure 39.2 offers a glimpse into Jordan's urgency to hold onto the last pieces of home and showcase his pride of where he represents and comes from, even if symboli-cally. Given how far away he has been from home (e.g. being outsourced to a private prison in Mississippi), his choice in tattooing "Santa Barbara" on his back, whether it is aesthetically pleasing or not, speaks to the lengths he is willing to go to represent his community and main-tain a sense of belonging and existence. This is reified through the hashtags on his social media caption: "The city got my back so the city on my back."

Although young people may not have control over a lot of things while incarcerated – they still have power over their body and what they place/mark on it. Their body becomes a vessel, a medium with which to reclaim their humanity and human dignity. It also speaks to the risks prisoners are willing to take to manage getting ink done while in prison. After all, getting prison tattoos often poses health risks and is a painful process due to the lack of proper resources that can result in the ripping and/or scaring of the skin (Holland, 2017; Bonnycastle, 2011; Hellard, Aitken, & Hocking, 2007). Simultaneously, their tattoos can serve as a permanent form of their counterhegemonic agency; a personal tool for survival. While the tattoos Jordan got prior to his incarceration extended his original sentence and have the potential to increase his current sentence, Jordan still chooses to tattoo his body as a form of self-preservation of his dignity, humanity, and existence. The contradictions embedded in Mexican/Chicano boys and men's choices of tattooing themselves are important to explore because it is in these moments we can understand the sense of urgency amongst these young people to resist against state-sanctioned violence (through colonial-carceral apparatuses), even if it means additional carceral punish-ment. As Rios and Lopez-Aguado (2012) argued, "in this struggle, Chicano males reclaim their bodies by inscribing their own meanings, performance and resistance onto themselves" (p. 417). Their *tatuajes* are not simply a decoration; they are a structure, discipline, affirmation, and love for their hood, family, and peers.

Conclusion

Through Jordan's life history and choices in getting tattooed inside of prison, I have deeply reflected about the layered contradictions, meanings, and significance embedded in Mexican/ Chicano prisoners' choices of acquiring prison ink (despite the threat of additional carceral punishment). By looking at the dialectical relationship between Jordan's oppression and his agency (through tattooing practices), I have come to understand and appreciate Jordan's choices of inking his body as a way to maintain a sense of dignified humanity in a space that essentially works to dehumanize racialized bodies like himself and those who are serving time with him – even if his resistance is not completely liberatory.

In Figure 39.3, Jordan is standing in his cell, his arms crossed, head tilted, and head raised looking straight at the camera. The lighting is directly hitting his tattoos on his chest, which says, "Fuck my enemies. Krazies. East Side." Through one of our personal

Figure 39.3   Jordan posing for the camera in his prison cell in a private prison.
Source: Photograph taken by another prisoner

correspondences, I asked Jordan how tattoos have helped him cope with his prison conditions. He shared with me

> It's not what you can give but what you can endure. To me prison tattoos are like a write [rite] of passage. I earned this shyt. Every homie who ever tatted on my body was a gee [gangster] just like me. You put your pain on your body so that it travels with you forever, so that others can read your story and character on your skin.

Using the art of tattooing in prison is a way for Jordan to achieve this dignified posture in this photograph. Even though he is masculine presenting (clearly Jordan is flexing all of his muscles on his fit body), he is also showcasing all his vulnerabilities and pain. He is proactively fighting to communicate to those who are keeping up with him from back home that no matter what carceral institutions he is caged in (or how far), the institution has not and cannot break him. I met Jordan during a pivotal moment in his life where he was making strides towards "phasing out" of an active gang lifestyle. Ironically enough, the tattoos that were used to validate his gang membership and substantively increase his original sentencing of 5 years to 15 years (for a crime he may or may have not committed) in conjunction with Jordan's choice to continue using ink as a form of what he refers to as "green ink therapy" while in prison speak volumes to his will, determination, and refusal to allow the institution to "break him" or make him "fold" – even if it costs him additional time to serve in prison.

Jordan's attempt to preserve and document his experiences, ties to his community, and memories through the tattooing of his body – that further expose him as a vulnerable subject of the colonial-carceral state's punitive hand – serves as a testament to Jordan's refusal to relinquish his claims to preserving his humanity or human dignity. As needle touches flesh and bleeds, the skin becomes an open wound that is healed and sealed in a therapeutic green-inked ceremony. Mexican/Chicano prisoners' creative ways to resist and survive, by tapping into their culture, demonstrate the significance tattooing in prison has for the spirit of these young men – a testament to their will to live – not merely survive – in prison. Looking at tattooing practices among Mexican/Chicano prisoners within the binary logic of "self-damning" resistance or reflective of criminality and/or a criminal lifestyle, misses the larger significance that tattoos represent. In fact, it misses that "*tatuajes* (tattoos) represent a victory – a testament to the survival of the human spirit" and an expression of their human dignity (Olguin, 1997, p. 169). That is not to say that these acts and/or expressions are free from contradiction. However, looking at the intersectional relationship between the body, tattoos, the state, and captivity also demonstrates how prisoner's act of "getting blasted up" (tattooed) negates state-narrative constructions about them as a form of self-preserving resistance against the colonial gaze that allows for the production of self-dignifying counter-narrative constructions of their bodies and personhood.

Notes

1 Some names are pseudonyms based on my choice to protect individual's anonymity or upon the request of the individual(s) involved. The cases and incidents discussed here can be easily verified through an internet search due to their high profile or legal documentation through the courts; thus, it is difficult to ensure absolute anonymity. See Lubet (2017) and Jerolmack and Murphy (2017) for a discussion of the values, limitations, and obligations of anonymity in ethnographic research.
2 Gauges are a deliberate stretching of the earlobes for the purpose of wearing certain types of jewelry (i.e. gauges).
3 This is a question typically asked by gang affiliates to people they may not recognize as being part of their neighborhood and/or the gang; it can also serve as a way to verify whether the individual being

questioned claims a different gang. To break the ice a bit, I asked Jordan where he was from to signify to him that I knew he was gang affiliated and that it was okay.

4 See Brotherton (2015) for a critical discussion on how and why there has been a privileging of a pathological lens to study gangs within the past couple of decades. Also see Young (2011) and Wacquant (2009) for their discussion on how this lens reflects the power of neo-liberalism in governing US ideologies in the social sciences that also privilege positivism as the governing methodology to study marginalized communities and the urban poor.

5 See Silvia Wynter "On Disenchanting Discourse," p. 216. See also, Robinson, *Black Marxism;* Frantz Fanon, *Wretched of the Earth.*

6 I use "Mexican/Chicano" and "Brown" interchangeably throughout this chapter. I capitalize "Brown" because, like other marginalized communities (e.g. Blacks, Asians, Indigenous, Native Americans), it constitutes a culturally specific group, requiring a denotation as a proper noun. See, Crenshaw, 1988, p. 1332 n. 2, citing Mackinnon 1982, p. 516. On the other hand, I do not capitalize "white," as it is not a proper noun because whites do not make up a culturally specific group. There are times I do not capitalize "brown" because I am using it as an adjective to describe skin color

7 There are reasons I identify the true identity of places and prisons in this piece. For example, it is important to understand how the rich colonial history in the formation of Santa Barbara has shaped the geopolitical landscape of the settler city that the boys and young men in this study have to navigate. Not identifying Santa Barbara takes away from the "historical specificity" in this ethnographic project. See Kasinitz (1992, pp. 362–633) for a comment on the value of disclosing the true identity of places (e.g. neighborhoods). See Contreras (2019) for a nuanced discussion on the dangers of full disclosure of field sites and participant identities in order to replicate studies, verify accounts, and monitor social phenomenon over time for ethnographers studying violence and crime, particularly his advocacy on broadening the unmasking/masking discussion by arguing for "partial disclosure," where an ethnographer can strategically omit some data in otherwise rich biographical portraits.

8 I use Santa Barbara and Santa Bruta interchangeably.

9 While the Mexican/Chicano "gang aesthetic" has roots dating back to the 1930s and 1940s, when Mexican/Chicano gang members were identified as "pachuchos" and were typically associated with the zoot suit style, in the 21st century, Mexican/Chicano boys and men who are self- and/or state identified as gang members are stereotypically depicted wearing loose fitting khaki pants/shorts or Dickies/Ben Davis creased jeans, with white knee-high socks, a white tank top undershirt, an oversized colored (usually white) t-shirt, with athletic shoes like Nike Cortez or Airforce 1, a shaved head, and heavily tattooed.

10 Barganier, G., & Rodriguez, C. (2019, November). *From Lovelle Mixon to Oscar Grant: Rebellions against state violence.* Thematic Panel session presented at the meeting of the American Society of Criminology, San Francisco, CA.

11 See Aldama "Borders, Violence, and the Struggle for Chicana and Chicano Subjectivity" in Violence and the Body (2003). Also, Jones, N. (2016). The gender of police violence. *Tikkun, 31*(1), 25–28.

12 "Los Prietos" literally translates to "the dark ones" and can be used as an anti-Black statement or used to express disdain towards darker-skinned people within the Mexican or Black community.

13 Although I cannot verify Jordan's claim, it is not too far off from the various uncovered cases of abuse during the rise of California's juvenile justice system from the 19th to 20th centuries, when science and racism were used to justify the ideologies and practices used by state institutions in the treatment of incarcerated young people of color, including their medication and sterilization (for more, see Chávez-García, 2012). Thus, Jordan's claims merit a consideration for validity.

14 RICO is a common reference used for the Racketeer Influenced and Corrupt Organization Act, which is a United States federal law signed in 1970 by then-President Nixon that provided extended criminal penalties and a civil clause of action for acts performed as part of an ongoing criminal organization. This act was created originally to target the Mafia, but in recent times, it has been used to target gangs.

15 I am not downplaying the severity of the charges or the fact that the victim was stabbed multiple times. However, I do want to point to the punitiveness of the Santa Barbara court system when putting Mexican/Chicano boys and young men on trial.

16 In 2000, California voters (with an overwhelming 62.1 percent) voted yes to "Prop 21" to make "serious" changes to juvenile and adult criminal law. Among the more significant changes, it would lower the age of offenders to be tried as adults from 16 to 14 years old. Many psychological studies show that juvenile brains do not fully develop until the age of 23. See Elizabeth Cauffman and Laurence Steinberg, "(Im)maturity of Judgment in Adolescence: Why Adolescents May Be Less Culpable Than

Adults," *Behavioral Sciences & the Law* 18, (2000): 741–760. I will further expand on how youth of color tend to be constructed as "adult" and rarely as youth. requiring that certain juvenile offenders be held in local or state correctional facilities and increasing penalties for gang-related crimes (California State Legislature, "California Penal Code," Section 186.22.).

17 See Anderson (1999).

18 Terms and labels like "felon," "criminal," "inmate," "convict," and "prisoner" have more recently been contested in terms of being used to refer to people/individuals with convictions, those who have been formerly incarcerated, and/or those who are currently serving time. While I advocate for the use of humanizing language when referring to people with convictions or those who have been formerly incarcerated, I have elected to refer to them as prisoners because I acknowledge that some folks in prison embrace particular terms like convict and prisoner with pride as a sign of their resistance against the state's attempts to own and/or control their lives/bodies/behavior. Like McNaughton (2007), I also agree that referring to individuals as prisoners mindfully calls into question this degrading position to refer to individuals whether they are innocent or guilty of their convictions. See Leyva and Bickel (2010), Terry (2003), Cummins (1994), Bowker (1977), and Irwin (1980, 1987) for a discussion on the importance of using humanizing language to refer to individuals who are formerly and currently incarcerated.

19 For the purposes of this chapter, I am focusing on understanding the tattooing politics among Surreños (i.e. southern Mexican/Chicano gang affiliates).

20 Clemmer (1940, 1958) broadly defined 'prisonization' as the general process of assimilation to being incarcerated with the individual's acceptance/recognition of their relinquished power over their agency and control over their lives and personal choices to the state.

21 For study reception centers, see Goodman, P. (2008). "It's just Black, White, or Hispanic": an observational study of racializing moves in California's segregated prison reception centers. *Law & Society Review, 42*(4), 735–770.

22 See, Patterson, O. (2018). *Slavery and social death: A comparative study, with a new preface.* Cambridge, MA: Harvard University Press.

References

Anderson, E. (1999). *Code of the street: Decency, violence, and the moral life of the inner city.* New York, NY: WW Norton & Company.

Barganier, G. (2011). *Fanon's children: The Black Panther party and the rise of the Crips and Bloods in Los Angeles* (Doctoral dissertation). University of California, Berkeley.

Bonnycastle, K. D. (2011). The social organisation of penal tattooing in two Canadian federal male prisons: Locating sites of risk for empirically-based health care interventions. *The Howard Journal of Criminal Justice, 50*(1), 17–33.

Bowker, L. H. (1977). *Prisoner subcultures.* Lexington, MA: Lexington Books.

Brotherton, D. C. (2015). *Youth street gangs: A critical appraisal.* London; New York: Routledge.

Camarillo, A. (1979). Chicanos in a changing society; from Mexican pueblos to American barrios in Santa Barbara and Southern California 1848–1930 (No. 04; F869. S45, C3.).

Carrigan, W. D., & Webb, C. (2003). The lynching of persons of Mexican origin or descent in the United States, 1848 to 1928. *Journal of Social History,* 411–438.

Chávez-García, M. (2012). *States of delinquency: Race and science in the making of California's juvenile justice system* (Vol. 35). Berkeley and Los Angeles: University of California Press.

Clawson, A. (1995). La virgencita and los vatos locos: Tattoos and Chicano cultural identity. *The Journal of Latin American Affairs,* 37–45.

Clemmer, D. (1940). *The prison community.* New York, NY: The Christopher Publishing House.

Clemmer, D. (1958). *The prison community.* New York: Holt, Rinehart & Winston.

Collins, P. H. (2004). Assume the position: The changing contours of sexual violence. In P. H. Collins (Ed.), *Black sexual politics: African Americans, gender and the new racism* (pp. 215–246). New York, NY: Routledge.

Contreras, R. (2019, June). Transparency and unmasking issues in ethnographic crime research: methodological considerations. *Sociological Forum, 34*(2), 293–312.

Conquergood, D. (1998). Beyond the text: Toward a performative cultural politics. *The future of performance studies: Visions and revisions*, 25–36.

Crenshaw, K. W. (1988). Race, reform, and retrenchment: Transformation and legitimation in antidiscrimination law. *Harvard Law Review*, 1331–1387.

Cummins, E. (1994). *The rise and fall of California's radical prison movement*. Stanford, CA: Stanford University Press.

Decker, S. H., & Van Winkle, B. (1996). *Life in the gang: Family, friends, and violence*. New York: Cambridge University Press.

Edwards, L. F. (2004). *Beyond Black and White: Race, ethnicity, and gender in the US South and Southwest* (Vol. 35). College Station: Texas A&M University Press.

Fanon, F. (1967). *Black skin, white masks*. New York: Grove.

Garot, R. (2010). *Who you claim: Performing gang identity in school and on the streets*. New York, NY: NYU Press.

Giroux, H. A. (2003). *The abandoned generation: Democracy beyond the culture of fear*. London: Palgrave Macmillan.

Hellard, M. E., Aitken, C. K., & Hocking, J. S. (2007). Tattooing in prisons – Not such a pretty picture. *American Journal of Infection Control*, 35(7), 477–480.

Holland, S. C. (2017). *Male imprisonment tattoos: The experience of tattooing while serving time and post-incarceration* (Doctoral dissertation). Santa Barbara, CA: Fielding Graduate University.

Irwin, J. (1980). *Prisons in turmoil*. Boston, MA: Little, Brown.

Irwin, J. (1987). *The felon*. Berkeley, CA: University of California Press.

Jennings, W. G., Fox, B. H., & Farrington, D. P. (2014). Inked into crime? An examination of the causal relationship between tattoos and life-course offending among males from the Cambridge Study in Delinquent Development. *Journal of Criminal Justice*, 42(1), 77–84.

Jerolmack, C., & Murphy, A. K. (2017). The ethical dilemmas and social scientific trade-offs of masking in ethnography. *Sociological Methods & Research*. doi:10.1177/0049124117701483

Jones, N. (2014). "The regular routine": Proactive policing and adolescent development among young, poor black men. *New Directions for Child and Adolescent Development*, 2014(143), 33–54.

Kasinitz, P. (1992, June). Bringing the neighborhood back in: The new urban ethnography. *Sociological forum* 7(2), 355–363).

Leyva, M., & Bickel, C. (2010). From corrections to college: The value of a convict's voice. *Western Criminology Review*, 11, 50.

Lubet, S. (2017). *Interrogating ethnography: Why evidence matters*. Oxford: Oxford University Press.

MacKinnon, C. A. (1982). Feminism, Marxism, method, and the state: An agenda for theory. *Signs: Journal of Women in Culture and Society*, 7(3), 515–544.

Maxson, C. L., Matsuda, K. N., & Hennigan, K. (2011). "Deterrability" among gang and nongang juvenile offenders: Are gang members more (or less) deterrable than other juvenile offenders? *Crime & Delinquency*, 57(4), 516–543.

McNaughton, M. J. (2007). Hard cases: Prison tattooing as visual argument. *Argumentation and Advocacy*, 43(3–4), 133–143.

Meagher, C. (2010, August 26). Santa Bruta: How the Eastside gang was gator rolled. *Santa Barbara Independent Press*. Retrieved April 5, 2019, from www.independent.com/2010/08/26/santa-bruta/

Patterson, O. (2018). *Slavery and social death: A comparative study, with a new preface*. Cambridge, MA: Harvard University Press.

Perez, L. E. (2002). Writing on the social body: Dresses and body ornamentation in contemporary Chicana art. *Decolonial Voices: Chicana and Chicano Cultural Studies in the 21st Century*, 30–63.

Phillips, S. A. (2001). Gallo's body: Decoration and damnation in the life of a Chicano gang member. *Ethnography*, 2(3), 357–388.

Olguín, B. V. (1997). Tattoos, abjection, and the political unconscious: Toward a semiotics of the pinto visual vernacular. *Cultural Critique*, 37, 159–213.

Olguín, B. V. (2010). *La pinta: Chicana/o prisoner literature, culture, and politics*. Austin: University of Texas Press.

Rios, V., & Lopez-Aguado, P. (2012). Pelones y matones: Chicano cholos perform for a punitive audience. *Performing the US Latina and Latino Borderlands*, 382–401.

Rozycki Lozano, A. T., Morgan, R. D., Murray, D. D., & Varghese, F. (2011). Prison tattoos as a reflection of the criminal lifestyle. *International Journal of Offender Therapy and Comparative Criminology*, *55*(4), 509–529.

Santos, X. (2009). The Chicana canvas: Doing class, gender, race, and sexuality through tattooing in East Los Angeles. *NWSA Journal*, 91–120.

Schildkrout, E. (2004). Inscribing the body. *Annual Review of Anthropology*, *33*, 319–344.

Solorzano, D. G., & Bernal, D. D. (2001). Examining transformational resistance through a critical race and LatCrit theory framework: Chicana and Chicano students in an urban context. *Urban Education*, *36*(3), 308–342.

Terry, C. M. (2003). *The fellas: Overcoming prison and addiction*. Belmont, CA: Wadsworth and Thomson Learning.

Vigil, J. D. (2007). *The projects: Gang and non-gang families in East Los Angeles*. Austin, TX: University of Texas Press.

Vitale, A. S. (2017). *The end of policing*. New York: Verso Books.

Venkatesh, S. A. (2008). *Gang leader for a day: A rogue sociologist takes to the streets*. New York: Penguin Press.

Wacquant, L. (2009). *Punishing the poor: The neoliberal government of social insecurity*. Durham/London: Duke University Press.

Webb, W. P. (1965). *The Texas rangers: A century of frontier defense*. Austin, TX: University of Texas Press.

Wirth, L. (1938). Urbanism as a way of life. *American Journal of Sociology*, *44*(1), 1–24.

Yablonsky, L. (1998). *Gangsters: Fifty years of madness, drugs, and death on the streets of America*. New York: NYU Press.

Young, J. (2011). *The criminological imagination*. Cambridge: Polity Press.

40

Performance narratives of gang identity and membership

Vanessa R. Panfil

Introduction

Stereotypical thinking abounds when gangs are involved: that all gangs and gang members are the same, that gang membership is a static characteristic of an individual, that all gang members signify their group membership with publicized symbols like colored bandannas or teardrop tattoos. However, gang members' lives are much more nuanced and complex than this. More importantly, gang members actively construct gang membership and identity through their performance and narratives.

Performances of identity include personal style, speech, mannerisms, behavior, and narratives, or people's self-stories. Also known as "personal myths," narratives are acts of imagination that integrate the "remembered past, perceived present, and anticipated future" in order to make a "compelling aesthetic statement" about oneself (McAdams, 1993: 12). Talk is a critical way to craft a narrative. Talk allows us to "create, present, and sustain personal identities that are congruent with and supportive of the self-concept" (Snow and Anderson, 1987: 1348). The acknowledgement that others are hearing, viewing, and interpreting our style, speech, and behavior is one reason that these actions are referred to as performances. They are conducted for real or presumed audiences, we hope to accomplish a convincing portrayal of our identities, and we can be held accountable if our performances do not measure up to what others expect of us in a given context (Goffman, 1959). So, while gang membership can be signified through personal style like clothing, it is more likely to actually be accomplished through narratives and storytelling. This process may include individual or collective mythmaking. In the modern era, performances can happen in local neighborhoods but also for global reach on the internet. When gang members are successful in their performances of gang identity and membership, this can provide personal status and an increased sense of belonging or loyalty not just to the gang but to the gangster persona and future performances.

This chapter discusses the ways gang members perform their gang identity and membership, particularly through narratives. I engage in discussions of how personal style factors into gang identity and performance but rely primarily on gang members' own words and their descriptions of their gang identity, mostly in person but to a lesser extent online. Their narratives provide insight into the importance and meaning of the gang to its members' lives. I focus on several key points in the potential continuum of gang membership, such as their decisions to join or form gangs, the activities they engage in with their gangs, and the ways former gang members perform gang leaving via narratives. In so doing, I also cover related and relevant issues such as gang members' activities and the global cultural diffusion of gang symbolism and mythology. Throughout, I explore ways gang members negotiate performing gang identity and membership while performing other identities, which they may feel to be at odds with their gang identities.

Performance narratives of gang joining

Young people want to join gangs for a variety of reasons, many of which center around issues of protection, status, and belonging, but could include other concerns like seeking fun, excitement, money, partying, or sex (e.g., Peterson, 2012; Ward, 2013). For many young people, gangs take the place of their families of origin that were failing them, perhaps set against a backdrop of experiencing abuse, witnessing violence, and being exposed to drug/alcohol use in the home (Miller, 2001) or being emotionally neglected. Gangs can also provide support and belonging in the face of sociocultural challenges, such as facing racism, xenophobia, and poverty (Brotherton and Barrios, 2004; Durán, 2013). Socioeconomic and cultural marginalization set the stage for street socialization and gang involvement, which can provide self-esteem, identity, and belonging for marginalized youth (Vigil, 2002). This does not mean that the gangs youth join are free of infighting, abuse, neglect, and/or dysfunction, but the drive to feel included absent a loving and nurturing family and an accepting society is strong; the gang provides that belonging. One gang member noted that this was "the most important thing people need to understand about the gang" (Ward, 2013: 183). One young man in Panfil's (2017: 113) study said,

> I was excited with the more violence, the more people, the better off, I just wanted to make trouble. I feel like I wasn't getting love [from my family], so I didn't want nobody to be happy in my life, nobody. . . . I mean, my friends, my brothers, the gangs, they showed love. Whether it's the wrong kind of love, it's the love you need at that time.

While many youth seek belonging and love from their friendship groups, especially in the face of exclusion or marginalization, gang members' drive to do so is often seen as antisocial and pathological, leading to moral panics about "dangerous" youth and their alleged involvement in violent crimes that are perceived to be increasingly severe and commonplace (see, e.g., Hall et al., 1978). Young people can become scapegoats for society's ills that they personally are also responding to and negotiating.

Gangs themselves may have goals of addressing pressing social problems, such as the Almighty Latin King and Queen Nation specifying in their manifesto that their main purpose is "to show the world that we are equals and that together as one can claim the respect we deserve as human beings," and specifically as Latinos (Brotherton and Barrios, 2004: 98). Or, take the all-gay gangs in Panfil's (2017) study who formed in response to the heterosexism they experienced in their biological families and society and sought to empower their members. Thus, gang joining can be affected by the ways individuals see themselves as fitting in with the world, through lenses of race and ethnicity, class, culture, and/or sexual identity. Joining a gang makes young people "feel important, like someone who counts" (Ward, 2013: 64). Gang membership is a source of identity and reputation for many members, and gang joining also represents a shift in identity.

Although not all gangs have initiation rituals and the thought of having formal "membership" seems unusual to some (e.g., Fleisher, 2000), many do have initiation rituals. One such initiation ritual, being "beaten in" or "jumped in" by existing members of the gang, serves several functions. It increases the solidarity of the group by participating in a shared ritual, proves the recruit's toughness and fighting ability, ensures the recruit's commitment and loyalty to the gang, prepares them for what else they will encounter as a member, and can help ward off challenges from other groups (Decker, 1996; Durán, 2013). The ritual could also reflect the gang's structure, mythology, or symbolism, such as being beaten by a certain number of people or a length of time that somehow maps onto 5, 6, or 13, in the case of Bloods, Crips, or Mara Salvatrucha (MS-13), respectively (Miller, 2001; Panfil, 2017; Ward, 2013). When a gang recruit already holds significant relational ties to current members of the gang, they may forgo an initiation ritual and instead allow someone to be "blessed in," "walked in," or "crowned in" (Bolden, 2013).

Performing gang identity

Performing gangster identity through gang activities

Key components of a gang member's performance narrative include who they are and what they do. Depending on who their audience is when they recount their gang activities, gang members may focus on illegal activities or legal activities in their performance narratives. First, it is important to understand which activities typically garner reputation and respect.

Illegal activities, especially violent crimes against rival gang members and/or income-generating crimes (like drive-bys, robberies, and drug sales), are status conferring for gang members. They happen far less often than everyday activities like hanging out, eating, and sleeping, but because they represent the exciting and tough behaviors associated with gang life, they often reflect what gang members would prefer to be known for (Ward, 2013). Gang ethnographers have noted the hours of boredom in gang members' lives; entire days with virtually no "action" (e.g., Lauger, 2012; Ward, 2013). One of Fleisher's (2000) realizations after spending years in the field with a youth street gang was that although the youth did engage in and experience very serious violence, they talked about violence far more than they actually engaged in it. Katz (1988: 142) suggests that "gang members are centrally concerned with cooperative mobilization against emasculating threats to their status; in the absence of such external threats, gang members employ various collective routines, such as 'parading' – projecting collective unison through public displays of affiliation – to cope with boredom." In the gang context, violence can be used to respond to threats, either to members' safety or to turf and economic interests: trouble comes to the gang, and the gang must respond (Decker, 1996). In fact, Durán (2013: 149) identified "displaying loyalty," "responding courageously to external threats," and "promoting and defending gang status" as three important core ideals of gang culture. Engaging in gang violence, threatening it, being willing to use it, talking about it, and imagining it help create a mythology about that gang and its ability to produce a sense of threat or dread on the streets (Decker, 1996). Interpersonally, one's street image and reputation could be bolstered by a willingness to be aggressive or violent when their enactment of violence is consistent with gang violence folklore – being about retaliation, for instance (Fleisher, 2000).

Lauger (2012) delves deep into how gang members create reputations as "real" gang members, which he observed was typically tied to violence. Acts of violence helped solidify one's reputation, but in terms of frequency, a *reputation* for violence was more important than actually engaging in it. Violent incidents themselves happened sporadically. However, once that reputation was formed, there was pressure to live up to it: there was "an enduring need to prove one's rightful place within the intergang environment" (109). These performances were for their gang peers and gang rivals and included recounting violent incidents that were "relatively accurate, though skewed in their favor" (156). Gang members could usually solidify their reputation within smaller groups, but increasing their reputation within larger circles meant that they were not immune to their legitimacy being questioned, sometimes through street gossip. There was also a broader street narrative that gang members had to contend with: that gangs have lost their standards for membership and some members are just not "real," which Lauger refers to as the "dilution narrative" (78). This similarly encouraged performances as "real gangstas." Gang activities can also be recounted online, where gang members may post gang-related videos such as gang fights to build the gang's reputation (Pyrooz et al., 2015); I discuss this in depth in a later section, "Storying Gang Mythology through Media and Internet."

While Ward (2013) acknowledges that gang members typically earn respect by "putting in work" like fighting the enemy skillfully and making money, other relational factors can influence their standing in the gang, like how long they have been active, and their ability to form relationships with other gang members. Kids in the Fremont Hustlers (Fleisher, 2000) defined the group's 'members' by tightness, or the intensity of the social relationship (such as kids who hang out together and commit crimes together, who have some amount of shared social history), and the amount of time a kid spends in the neighborhood (with "everyday" or "here all the time" kids most approximating core members).

Not all gangs focus exclusively on their illegal activities, especially if the goal of that gang is to provide empowerment to its members, along with status. For example, although the gay gangs in my study wanted to become "known" in the Columbus gay scene and fighting was a way to make a name for oneself, looking good, making money, being a skilled dancer, and belonging to a well-established "family" (gay gang) were other ways to do so. When I spoke to members of the gay gangs, they often first wanted to recount the legal and positive activities their groups engaged in, followed later by descriptions of interpersonal violence, theft, and sex work. They also preferred to call their groups "cliques" or "families" instead of "gangs" but acknowledged that their groups were and could be seen as gangs. JD said this about his group:

> It's actually very supportive, we try to keep each other out of trouble, and for the most part, encourage each other to do better. Like, if somebody's not workin', then hey, get your ass up and get a job! . . . If you ain't got yo education, go to school and get it now. . . . [We] go out to eat, to the movies, out of town, things like that. Travel. . . . Things families should do. You know, be supportive of each other, and also have fun, and live life! We go to the bars, stuff like that! Parks, cookouts. . . . Even family reunions.
>
> *(Panfil, 2017: 83)*

Another member summarized their activities as "Basically what you do when you're young: Everything!" This, of course, sounds very different than many reports of gang members publicized in media and prior studies, and my book takes up a question I have gotten many times over the years, which is whether these gangs are "real." Ward (2013: 179) addressed a similar anticipated critique of focusing on relational attachments among gangs: "On the surface, it seems absurd to look at street gangs as compassionate organizations – but not for the gang members who have experienced this heart connection within their gang." Gangs may refer to themselves as "organizations" or other terms to reframe public perceptions (Miller, 2001). Some gangs, such as the Almighty Latin King and Queen Nation, have gone through reforms over time and even participated in political activity to show solidarity with other community organizations and to empower their members individually and collectively (Brotherton and Barrios, 2004). Thus, although it is clear gang members engage in a range of legal and illegal activities, certain activities help cement their reputations as "gangsters," even though those may not be the most important activities as experienced subjectively by the group's members.

Negotiating concurrent identities

Although a full discussion of concurrent identities that gang members must perform is outside the scope of this chapter, an extremely brief discussion of relevant issues is warranted. Perhaps the most obvious identity performance expected of gang members is masculine toughness, which often places young women at a disadvantage for being taken seriously as gang members. Gang girls face double standards for women and competing demands, such as that they are expected to be tough in the gang context but also to take care of and show nurturance towards male gang members (Ward, 2013). Females make up a substantial proportion of gang members but frequently are not seen as "true" gang members (Peterson, 2012). Try as some might through violence, most adolescent girls in gangs never really become "one of the guys" (Miller, 2001; but see Brotherton, 2015 for descriptions of adult women who lead gangs). And yet other young women are focused on earning respect by pursuing respectability – performing femininity in such a way that paradoxically upholds sexual double standards for women, such as shaming other girls who are sexually "promiscuous" because they believe it will negatively impact them and bring about their own sexual or gender harassment (Laidler and Hunt, 2001; see also Miller, 2001).

Expectations of normative gender expression, and specifically hypermasculinity, intersect with homophobia and transphobia to affect whether LGBTQ gang members feel they can be openly LGBTQ within their gangs. For example, Brotherton and Barrios (2004: 354) note that they encountered several gay male gang members within the Latin Kings, but these men "were afraid to 'come out' among the rest of the members due to the history of homophobia in the organization." The authors also noted that the homophobia in the Latin Kings set they studied was directed more at gay males than at lesbians. Some young gay and bisexual men feel such pressure to remain closeted and enact a masculine persona in their gang that they actually gay bash (Totten, 2000). Other men in traditional, heteronormative gangs considered coming out as gay to fellow members but feared for their physical safety and their reputation were their gangs to reject them. By contrast, men in all-gay gangs helped form their gangs and derived status as a gang partially from being openly gay and competing with rival gay crews, suggesting that gang structure and composition can also impact gang members' performances of identity (Panfil, 2017).

Something as basic as individual personalities can influence relational attachments in gangs. Although group solidarity is necessary to respond to rivals, gang members do not always get along with each other. Spending time in smaller groups within the gang allows deeper relationships and loyalties to form and provides a core group of friends a gang member can count on to provide protection (Durán, 2013; see also Conquergood, 1994 for a discussion of the small groups or "cliques" that become important). Physical fights, and even verbal duels, allow gang members to adjust social alliances within the group (Fleisher, 2000). For gangs that have formalized rules, breaking them can result in a "violation" that may include sanctions such as beatings, but not all members agree on what is a punishable offense or an acceptable sanction (Brotherton and Barrios, 2004; Ward, 2013).

Signifying gang style

In the American context, some symbolism like Bloods wear red while Crips wear blue has been widely spread through cultural diffusion. Colored bandanas or "flags" may also be used to signal gang affiliation. Sports teams' logos, designer labels, and even cartoon characters have been appropriated by gangs for their own symbolic use (e.g., Burrell, 1990). Body modifications like tattoos can also be utilized to mark gang membership, incarceration, or crimes committed. Gang symbolism may be elaborate and specific, such as using a five-point star versus a six-point star (or other symbols such as a crown or a pitchfork) or favoring the left or right side of the body for wearing one's bandana, earrings, pant leg rolled up, and so on (Conquergood, 1994; Miller, 2001). Gang graffiti also uses complex meaning systems of words, numbers, and symbols not just to mark the gang's turf or present a threat to enemy turf but to tell a story about the writer and about their gang; hand signals and gang call-outs also draw from a shared meaning system (Conquergood, 1994). Globalization has allowed for youth gangs in other countries to adopt symbols of American gangs, such as Dutch gangs wearing blue bandanas and calling themselves Crips (van Gemert, 2001), though other European gangs may not adhere to US gang fashion like colors (e.g., Van Hellemont, 2018). Gang style can intersect with other cultural or political goals. The female gang members in Mendoza-Denton's (1996) study strategically used hairstyling, makeup, and fashion to communicate not only their gang affiliation but to mark themselves as outside of both traditional Latina and Euro American hegemonic gender roles. Heavy foundation and skilled application had the added benefit of concealing bruises from gang fights. Gang girls may be less likely to wear gang colors or have visible tattoos than young men (Durán, 2013) but display their membership in ways consistent with their gender presentation.

However, not all gangs and gang members display their gang membership with colors or have tattoos; using personal style as a performance narrative provides insight into gang members' goals for doing so. For example, James, a man I interviewed for my study of gay-identified gang members, had been involved with his gang for over a decade and had obtained considerable status there. He was heavily involved in their illegal activities like drug selling and had been incarcerated for gang crimes. A member of the Bloods, he wore almost all red, had visible and prominent tattoos that included symbols from his gang's mythology and a version of its name, and even drank red-labeled Budweiser beer (Panfil, 2017). James's self-presentation as a walking advertisement for his gang illustrates his long-standing involvement and commitment to them. Contrast this to Lauger's (2012) research with gangs that suggested more established gang members might be skeptical of younger members who are ostentatious with their colors, tattoos, behavior, and insider gang knowledge since they could have come upon that knowledge via the internet and claim gang membership falsely. Names for these posers included wannabes, false flaggers, and internet gangsters. Indeed, non-gang members may adopt gang style not just to gain status but to protect themselves against becoming victims of gang violence in their communities (Burrell, 1990). This ambiguity about gang fashion and its connection to true "gangness" has led some gang members to take additional steps "to prove the truthfulness of the delinquent meaning of their fashion style and thus their overall subcultural performance" (Van Hellemont, 2018: 46). In that case, it was wearing expensive designer brands, body sculpting, and performing gangsta rap in online video clips, especially performances as a drug seller who is successful in making money.

The proliferation of knowledge about gang style, combined with the belief that gang style definitively indicates gang membership, has led to the criminalization of personal style via anti-gang statutes. Suspected "gang attire" like sagging pants or backwards hats, colors, and tattoos have been used in various locales' gang definitions, despite the fact that these have become fashionable among urban youth; these elements cannot definitively be used to distinguish gang youth from non-gang youth (Bjerregaard, 2003). Thus, even youth who are not gang affiliated are seen *by the state* to be performing gang style and thus may be criminalized for allegedly performing gang identity. School dress codes in urban areas may also prohibit wearing known gang fashion, purportedly as a way to maintain order within the school setting but which similarly results in repressive action to individuals' autonomy (Garot, 2010).

Personal style can also lead to young people being "qualified" or "certified" as an "Identified Gang Member" and entered into a gang database. Such databases allow law enforcement agencies to maintain identifying data on individuals, even if they have committed no crimes. The NYPD's criteria for certification in a gang database include several appearance-based characteristics such as tattoos/scars, colors, or hand signs. Because of the way the certification process is designed, any two of these can qualify a youth as gang involved, even absent any other evidence of membership like self-identification (see Howell, 2015). Gang databases overrepresent people of color and have been used to essentially target entire neighborhoods, with information from the databases sometimes being shared with employers or landlords, even though their information is not supposed to be publicly accessible and may be inaccurate (Vitale, 2017). Community pushback on gang databases questions their overly broad criteria; for example, in hearings on Minnesota's gang databases, community groups "asked whether the criteria used to designate gang members were 'synonymous with the urban youth culture'" (Howell, 2015: 17). Thus, people who perform urban style – but who are seen to be performing gang style – are targeted for additional surveillance by the criminal justice system.

Storying gang mythology through media and internet

Gang members' performances of gang identity are affected by cultural diffusion of gang ideology and symbolism through media. Gang-involved young people might take inspiration from movies and television shows like *Colors*, *Menace II Society* (Miller, 2001), *New Jack City*, and *The Wire* (Van Hellemont and Densley, 2019), as well as the global music industry of gangsta rap. The book *Monster: The Autobiography of an L.A. Gang Member*, was translated into several languages and made its way into the lives and homes of gang members in The Netherlands. These young men, mostly from Surinam and the Dutch Antilles, modeled their group's name (the Eight Tray Crips) after the gang described in the book, even though the name referred to a particular street in Los Angeles and had no connection to their local context (van Gemert, 2001). Congolese gangsters in Brussels sometimes use US gang signs in their online videos (Van Hellemont, 2012). Other gangs around the globe may model the language or style of American gangs while integrating references to their own neighborhoods or addresses, such as the Rollin 200 Crips in The Hague, whose graffiti exalts their "h200d" in the 200-block; their name and graffiti directly parallels Los Angeles' Rollin 40 Crips and their "h40d" (Roks, 2019). The internet also allows for gangs in different countries, such as those in the United States and Israel, to talk directly to each other and learn from each other (Sela-Shayovitz, 2012). Gang members draw on publicly available cultural references to engage in their own mythmaking about their lives as gang members, or what they believe their lives *should* be like – "the script of an imagined life" (Van Hellemont and Densley, 2019: 185).

Creating and uploading videos on the internet is also a way for gang members to perform gang membership by engaging in storytelling and mythmaking. In her ethnographic study of gang members in both their neighborhoods and in online settings, Van Hellemont (2012) found an "online gangland" driven by pursuits of status and reputation. In the videos and blogs she analyzed, gang members performed gang and criminal identities by exploiting known symbolism and mythology of gang culture but also enacted gang conflicts online. For example, in their blogs, gang members may post images of themselves displaying weapons, reference gang rivalries, describe inter-gang fights, threaten rival gang members, post images of themselves on rival gang turf in the city, and link to R.I.P. pages for murdered comrades. They may also go onto other gang members' blogs and make comments in an attempt to ruin another's reputation online;

these comments often are not deleted and thus have some permanence in the way an on-the-street scuffle might not. Comments challenging the credibility of a gang member on their blog, YouTube videos, or Facebook page may actually derail their convincing performance as a gang member (Van Hellemont, 2018). Pyrooz and colleagues (2015: 491) conclude, "In this way, gangs use the Internet much like an electronic graffiti wall." Similarly, research on online performances by American gang members finds that such environments provide a "virtual street corner" where gang members use violent imagery and rap about gang conflicts to engage in gang mythmaking and identity development, whether for the individual or the gang as a whole (Lauger and Densley, 2018: 816). Although gangs may 'advertise' online by posting videos, there is little evidence that online environments support actual illicit gang activities like drug sales or gang formation and recruitment (Pyrooz, et al., 2015; Sela-Shayovitz, 2012). However, gang members can actually experience real-world violence for going "too far" in calling out rivals or enemies on social media, and the speed with which transmissions can be composed, sent, and received can also accelerate the escalation of conflicts which may spill over into physical space (Urbanik and Haggerty, 2018).

Performing gang leaving through narratives

Gang members story their gang involvement at every stage, including their gang leaving. Exiting or former gang members focus on a number of themes in their narratives about their gang leaving, some of them very immediate. One common reason to leave a gang is experiencing victimization, whether the narrator's own harm or their fellow gang members' injury or death. Gang members report wanting to leave because of serious injuries such as beatings, stabbings, or gunshot wounds resulting in hospitalization, as well as the threat of being harmed. For example, on this subject, former gang members in Decker and Lauritsen's (2002: 57–58) study said they quit because "we might get shot," "I didn't want to die," "all my friends were getting killed that I used to hang with," and "when one of my friends got killed and you look at his face, it was hard. It could have been me."

Leaving the gang is often also conceptualized as a feature of moving into adulthood, essentially growing out of gangs as a youthful phase. Accordingly, growing out of gangs may be the result of putting additional value on and performative effort into other identities that often intersect with adulthood. These could include being a responsible parent or dependable partner. Upon the birth of their children, gang fathers re-evaluated their priorities, including their orientation toward the future, and reconsidered their gang membership were they to be a role model to their children. One young man said his kids "keep me motivated" to stay on the right track: "Before I do anything negative I always think twice." Another said, "I had never thought about a future before. My future was never important to me just besides day-to-day. It didn't matter. Now . . . I got a kid. I gotta start thinkin' about a future" (Moloney et al., 2009: 314). Fatherhood also allowed them to access and cultivate a more traditional script of masculinity instead of the violent masculinity valued in the gang context. Parenthood itself is often not enough for gang fathers or mothers to leave their gangs, especially if they have no legitimate source of income (Moloney et al., 2009), but it is an avenue by which gang parents may opt to perform gang leaving. In my own study with current and former gang members who also identify as gay, leaving the gang behind because they "grew up" or wanted a better life mapped onto other maturational processes like coming out publicly as gay (for those who had belonged to heteronormative, traditional gangs), wanting to be a respectable gay man, wanting to be a better father, or having good potential to find a future husband and/or successfully raise kids (Panfil, 2020).

As alluded to, leaving the gang and shedding membership is often a gradual process of fading away, of changing one's activities over time, or of resolving to leave but not being able to sever all ties at once. Garot (2010) identified a continuum of gang membership with several ambiguous stages, including belonging to a gang but no longer gangbanging, leading him to conclude that "conceptualizing gang identity as fluid and contingent is the rule in the inner city, not the exception" (118). A young man in Flores's (2014: 135) study who recently became involved in a gang recovery program reflected, "That gangbangin' thing is still . . . livin' in me." Gang members may find it difficult to move on from the gang identity they spent so much time cultivating; one former member in Bolden's (2013: 484) study suggested that gang involvement "becomes your whole identity." It often entails strong ties to fellow members. For example, another former member said, "I had no problem leaving it [the gang]. The only problem I had leaving it, it wasn't the fact of being in a gang, it was the friends I was leaving behind" (485). Yet another said the people in his former gang "are always going to be my buddies, and I think a lot of things through now, but I still have their back" (485). Durán (2013: 164) observes, "Older gang members often say, 'I don't bang anymore [or 'put in work'], but I'll always represent' [or 'be down for the gang']." Bolden (2013: 488) discusses this directly in relation to claims that one "cannot leave the gang," explaining,

> They may have grown up their entire lives with the same people who not only protected them on the schoolyard from bullies, but fed them when they were starving or gave them money for bills and perhaps even saved their life. Gang member relationships can be similar to what other people call family, and actually leaving one's family is much easier said than done. . . . Ultimately, the gang member's difficulty of letting go of relational attachments only illustrates their humanity and understanding of emotion.

Even those individuals who pursue conventional lives post-gang may feel existentially connected to the gang neighborhood or its people; one stated, "You can take the homeboy out of the barrio, but you can't take the barrio out of the homeboy" (Moore, 1991: 127). They may have left the gang, but in a way, the gang has not left them, especially because the gang is a representation of deeper cultural or neighborhood connections. And, those who have completely left their gangs behind may not be willing to discuss their former gang involvement (e.g., Moore, 1991) because they did not want to relive their past gang experiences and instead wanted to focus on their successful present and future. In other words, they had moved on from performing gang desistance and were instead focused on performing identities more salient to their lives in the current moment.

Just as gang members can perform gang identity through their personal style, former gang members may want to move away from gang symbolism post-gang. For example, gang members participating in recovery programs encourage each other to "grow your hair out" instead of maintaining a shaved head, wear more work-related or business casual clothing instead of sagging or baggy clothes, and to cover up gang tattoos (Flores, 2016). Tattoos especially can continue to make former gang members appear active long after their involvement, resulting in unwanted attention from law enforcement (Bjerregaard, 2003) or rival gangs. Thus, it is not surprising that Homeboy Industries, a community-based gang recovery program, offers tattoo removal as one of its comprehensive services to facilitate gang leaving (Flores, 2016).

Conclusion

Gang membership and identity are not static states of being that can be inscribed on individuals. Instead, they are dynamic characteristics that change over time, vary by person, and are resistant to rigid categorization. While gang identity and group membership can be signified through personal style, these are also storied via narratives and mythmaking, performed for real or presumed audiences in person or online, and accomplished successfully in ways that provide status and belonging (or are not accomplished at all). Gang membership and gang identity are thus performances that individuals enact through their dress, demeanor, and talk. To understand these performances, we have to understand how gang members think of their own identity and membership. Such meanings are often fluid and context dependent. Performances may also be relevant to particular times or events, such as a gang member's reasons for joining, activities engaged in with the gang, or in leaving the gang.

To assume who gang members are and what they do based on a single attribute is fueled by and perpetuates reductive, pathologizing, and dehumanizing discourses about gang members (Brotherton, 2015). Garot (2010) similarly argues we should instead shift to regarding gang membership as a "soft" version of identity, in that it is accomplished through interaction, not a fixed state of being, nor should it be pathologized. "Performance" does not mean that these groups are not 'real,' because the young people in them certainly see them as real, and performing gang identity can be quite real in its consequences (to draw from a well-known social science adage). Gang scholars, and citizens who seek a well-rounded understanding of gang identity and membership, should heed these suggestions.

References

Bjerregaard, Beth. 2003. Antigang legislation and its potential impact: The promises and the pitfalls. *Criminal Justice Policy Review* 14: 171–192.

Bolden, Christian. 2013. Tales from the hood: An emic perspective on gang joining and gang desistance. *Criminal Justice Review* 38: 473–490.

Brotherton, David C. 2015. *Youth Street Gangs: A Critical Appraisal.* New York: Routledge.

Brotherton, David C., and Luis Barrios. 2004. *The Almighty Latin King and Queen Nation: Street Politics and the Transformation of a New York City Gang.* New York: Columbia University Press.

Burrell, Susan L. 1990. Gang evidence: Issues for criminal defense. *Santa Clara Law Review* 30: 739–790.

Conquergood, Dwight. 1994. Homeboys and hoods: Gang communication and cultural space. In Lawrence R. Frey (Ed.), *Group Communication in Context: Studies of Natural Groups* (pp. 23–55). Hillsdale, NJ: Lawrence Erlbaum Associates.

Decker, Scott H. 1996. Collective and normative features of gang violence. *Justice Quarterly* 13: 243–264.

Decker, Scott H., and Janet L. Lauritsen. 2002. Leaving the gang. In C. Ronald Huff (Ed.), *Gangs in America* (3rd ed., pp. 51–70). Thousand Oaks, CA: Sage.

Durán, Robert J. 2013. *Gang Life in Two Cities: An Insider's Journey.* New York: Columbia University Press.

Fleisher, Mark. 2000. *Dead End Kids: Gang Girls and the Boys They Know.* Madison, WI: University of Wisconsin Press.

Flores, Edward Orozco. 2014. *God's Gangs: Barrio Ministry, Masculinity, and Gang Recovery.* New York: New York University Press.

Flores, Edward Orozco. 2016. "Grow your hair out": Chicano gang masculinity and embodiment in recovery. *Social Problems* 63: 590–604.

Garot, Robert. 2010. *Who You Claim: Performing Gang Identity in School and on the Streets.* New York: NYU Press.

Goffman, Erving. 1959. *The Presentation of Self in Everyday Life.* Garden City, NY: Doubleday.

Hall, Stuart, Chas Critcher, Tony Jefferson, John Clarke, and Brian Roberts. 1978. *Policing the Crisis: Mugging, the State and Law and Order.* London: The Macmillan Press.

Howell, K. Babe. 2015. Gang policing: The post stop-and-frisk justification for profile-based policing. *University of Denver Criminal Law Review* 5: 1–31.

Katz, Jack. 1988. *Seductions of Crime: Moral and Sensual Attractions in Doing Evil.* New York: BasicBooks.

Laidler, Karen Joe, and Geoffrey Hunt. 2001. Accomplishing femininity among the girls in the gang. *British Journal of Criminology* 41: 656–678.

Lauger, Timothy R. 2012. *Real Gangstas: Legitimacy, Reputation, and Violence in the Intergang Environment*. New Brunswick, NJ: Rutgers University Press.

Lauger, Timothy R., and James A. Densley. 2018. Broadcasting badness: Violence, identity, and performance in the online gang rap scene. *Justice Quarterly* 35: 816–841.

McAdams, Dan P. 1993. *The Stories We Live By: Personal Myths and the Making of the Self*. New York: Morrow.

Mendoza-Denton, Norma. 1996. "Muy macha": Gender and ideology in gang-girls' discourse about makeup. *Ethnos* 61(1/2): 47–63.

Miller, Jody. 2001. *One of the Guys: Girls, Gangs, and Gender*. New York: Oxford University Press.

Moloney, Molly, Kathleen MacKenzie, Geoffrey Hunt, and Karen Joe-Laidler. 2009. The path and promise of fatherhood for gang members. *British Journal of Criminology* 49: 305–325.

Moore, Joan W. 1991. *Going Down to the Barrio: Homeboys and Homegirls in Change*. Philadelphia, PA: Temple University Press.

Panfil, Vanessa R. 2017. *The Gang's All Queer: The Lives of Gay Gang Members*. New York: NYU Press.

Panfil, Vanessa R. 2020. "I was a homo thug, now I'm just homo": Gay gang members' desistance and persistence. *Criminology* 58: 255–279.

Peterson, Dana. 2012. Girlfriends, gun-holders, and ghetto-rats? Moving beyond narrow views of girls in gangs. In Shari Miller, Leslie D. Leve, and Patricia K. Kerig (Eds.), *Delinquent Girls: Contexts, Relationships, and Adaptation* (pp. 71–84). New York: Springer.

Pyrooz, David C., Scott H. Decker, and Richard K. Moule Jr. 2015. Criminal and routine activities in online settings: Gangs, offenders, and the internet. *Justice Quarterly* 32: 471–499.

Roks, Robert A. 2019. In the "h200d": Crips and the intersection between space and identity in the Netherlands. *Crime, Media, Culture* 15: 3–23.

Sela-Shayovitz, Revital. 2012. Gangs and the Web: Gang members' online behavior. *Journal of Contemporary Criminal Justice* 28: 389–405.

Snow, David A., and Leon Anderson. 1987. Identity work among the homeless: The verbal construction and avowal of personal identities. *American Journal of Sociology* 92: 1336–1371.

Totten, Mark D. 2000. *Guys, Gangs, and Girlfriend Abuse*. Peterborough, ON: Broadview.

Urbanik, Marta-Marika, and Kevin D. Haggerty. 2018. "#It's dangerous": The online world of drug dealers, rappers and the street code. *British Journal of Criminology* 58: 1343–1360.

van Gemert, Frank. 2001. Crips in orange: Gangs and groups in the Netherlands. In Malcolm W. Klein, Hans-Jürgen Kerner, Cheryl L. Maxson, and Elmar G. M. Weitekamp (Eds.), *The Eurogang Paradox: Street Gangs and Youth Groups in the U.S. and Europe* (pp. 145–152). Dordrecht, Germany: Kluwer Academic Publishers.

Van Hellemont, Elke. 2012. Gangland online: Performing the real imaginary world of gangstas and ghettos in Brussels. *European Journal of Crime, Criminal Law and Criminal Justice* 20: 159–173.

Van Hellemont, Elke. 2018. Legalization by commodification: The (ir)relevance of fashion styles and brands in street gangster performance. In Tereza Kuldova and Martín Sánchez-Jankowski (Eds.), *Outlaw Motorcycle Clubs and Street Gangs: Scheming Legality, Resisting Criminalization* (pp. 45–68). Cham, Switzerland: Palgrave Macmillan.

Van Hellemont, Elke, and James A. Densley. 2019. Gang glocalization: How the global mediascape creates and shapes local gang realities. *Crime, Media, Culture* 15: 169–189.

Vigil, James Diego. 2002. *A Rainbow of Gangs: Street Cultures in the Mega-City*. Austin, TX: University of Texas Press.

Vitale, Alex S. 2017. *The End of Policing*. Brooklyn, NY: Verso.

Ward, T. W. 2013. *Gangsters Without Borders: An Ethnography of a Salvadoran Street Gang*. New York: Oxford University Press.

41

California placaso[1]

The social construction of Chicanx[2] gang graffiti

Xuan Santos and Martin Leyva

A group of fuming teen muralists confront a Chicano homie by the nickname "*flako*" (skinny)[3] for defacing the mural with his neighborhood placaso (graffiti), including his moniker and affiliation with the Mountain View 13 gang. He wore his "culture," a neatly ironed white t-shirt and khaki-colored shorts with black knee-high tube socks with black ankle high Chuck Taylor sneakers. His black hair was neatly combed and gave off the unmistakable flowery scent of Three Flowers pomade. As the artists confronted and shouted obscenities at Flako for disrespecting their artwork, Flako is observed clutching a black-colored rosary that hung from his neck. He is asked why he chose to deface the mural, as it represents the Chicanx struggle. His response may explain why he seemingly turned his back on his community by defacing its representation. Flako replied in a soft-spoken voice, avoiding the earshot of other young muralists, "For weeks I came to see the piece (mural) go up, and I hoped somebody would invite me to paint. I know what I did was fucked up, but nobody bothered to include me. I just wanted to be part of the mural."

Flako's response speaks to one of the ways gang-involved Chicanx youth experience marginality in Californian communities and how their exclusion from social activities such as mural painting works to keep them from being visible. Chicanx gang members often experience discriminatory practices, police repression, exclusion, and the loss of employment opportunities. Through such treatment, Chicanx gang members become stigmatized and perceived as menaces to the community with the corporate media often contributing to those moral panics via the social construction of folk devils who threaten their barrio's moral fabric (Durán, 2018; Flores, 2016; Chastanet, 2015; Flores, 2013; Durán, 2012; St. Cyr, 2003; Zatz, 1987). Such panics are part of the process of deviance amplification through which youth become viewed as the "gang problem" (Brotherton and Gude, 2018; Young, 1971).

Flako's story is not unique in the way young men experience marginality in public spaces with the intent to paradoxically build community cohesion using the art and culture of muralism. Yet, as a young gang-involved person, he felt invisible and rejected from and by his community, prompting him to put his placaso and moniker on the mural.

In any social context, we have both dominant and subordinate groups that vary across racial, gender, sexual, class, and cultural lines. Gramsci (1971) used "subaltern" as a concept to describe those groups in the margins, excluded from social institutions through the ruling class's hegemony, a form of social domination held in place by a class ideology that promotes and maintains the dominion of one group and the subordination of another through conscious and unconscious means. The subaltern group is structurally subjugated and reproduced by the ruling class's social and economic policies and initiatives (Green, 2002).

In Spivak's (1988) article titled "Can the Subaltern Speak?" the author argues that the subaltern are voiceless due to the dominant use of the language and discourse of European intellectuals that replicates the ruling class's interests. The subaltern cannot speak for themselves because they tend to reproduce the language of the elite. However, self-expression through art acts an exception, as ordinary people use and create artistic means such as placasos to give meaning and context to their lives. The subaltern, in this case Cholxs, create their own counter-discourse through graffiti art, disrupting their silences and producing a counter-hegemonic resistance through various forms of cultural production.

Composed of shared values, norms, behavioral patterns, mindsets, and beliefs, the culture of Chicanx gang placasos represent a liberatory strategy of subaltern people not recognized or respected by those who covet the cultivated taste of the high cultured art world (Williams, 1983). Such art represents elite traditional aesthetics usually found in galleries and museums frequented, owned, and supported by the middle and upper classes. In contrast, popular culture comes to represent the working class's art that is manufactured for mass cultural appeal. Art, therefore, is emancipatory for subaltern groups and a medium that promotes social agency.

The experiences of Chicanx gang members and their production of placasos remain under-represented in academic research. In this chapter, we explore how male and female participants understand their self-concepts; their relative understanding of placasos, resistance to deviance labeling, and how the community perceives the production of graffiti.

The literature

Chicanx gang members are frequently constructed as a threat to the community. Regardless of gang members' geopolitical affiliation, for example, whether they are affiliated with the Border Brothers (Bay Area), the Bulldogs (Fresno region), or Norteños and Sureños in the various barrios of California [Boyle, 2018; Lopez-Aguado, 2018; Reynolds, 2017; Leep, 2014; Rossmann, 2012; Vigil, 2012; Boyle, 2011; Rios, 2011; Fremon, 2008; Miranda, 2003], in the literature they are widely presented as a public nuisance and an impediment to safety. This is particularly problematic, since scholars, law enforcement agencies, and policymakers do not share a common definition of the gang. Nearly all anti-gang enforcement agencies argue that these criminal gang organizations disrupt the moral fabric of society at large by wreaking havoc and threatening the citizenry's liberties through deviance amplification. Meanwhile, scholars argue that society stigmatizes and hyper-criminalizes Chicanx youth by differentially scrutinizing them for congregating with their peers, dressing different, their lexicon within the culture, and for seeking visibility and survival.

Moore's (1999) work illustrates how these "underclass" subcultures are quasi-institutionalized, emerging from barrios afflicted by discriminatory institutional practices, poverty, and economic restructuring. As the dominant society limits opportunities for Chicanx gang members, it also becomes afraid and suspicious of them. Similarly, societal reactions to Chicanx gang graffiti is often conflated with vandalism and crimes.

The Chicanx entanglement within the US legal system, institutional discrimination, and anti-Mexican sentiment have influenced the enactment of decrees seeking to expel and criminalize the entire Chicanx population in California and throughout the US Southwest (Acuña, 2014; Barrera, 1979). This discrimination has a long history. Two well-known anti-Mexican laws promoted ethnic cleansing: Greaser Laws and Operation Wetback. Both were instrumental in the ethnic cleansing project that sought to make the US Southwest exclusive for white citizens.

At the end of the two-year US/Mexico war, the 1848 Treaty of Guadalupe Hidalgo, also known as The Treaty of Peace, Friendship, Limits, and Settlement Between the United States of America and the Mexican Republic, gave rise to the annexation of present-day Southwestern US territories (California, Colorado, Nevada, New Mexico, Texas, Utah, and Wyoming) from Mexico. The majority of Mexicans living in this region became US citizens whether they wanted it or not. Mexicans were dispossessed of their lands and as a result became subjugated and relegated to low-wage work by the new European-American employing class (Acuña, 2014; Almaguer, 1994).

California's Greaser Act of 1855, for example, legally sanctioned the arrest of persons of both Spanish and Indian blood for vagrancy law violations. These laws denied working-class Mexicans privileges that white people enjoyed (Brodkin, 1998). Such laws promoted and reflected the expansion of white-nativism, increased vigilantism, and were buttressed by discriminatory legal practices against people of Mexican descent that effectively barred them from participating in California's gold rush (Gendzel, 2013). This punitive social control[4] became the norm, as police were encouraged to take the law into their own hands by turning vigilantism (including excessive force), and arresting, or deporting anyone that fit the profile of "Mexican."[5] Such legislation paved the way later by Operation Wetback in the 1950s that relied on racial profiling used to expel Mexicans from the United States.

In the 1950s Mexican laborers became the target of President Truman's mass scapegoating campaign that became the largest deportation movement in US history. The Operation Wetback decree promoted a punitive social control strategy that targeted Mexicans residing in the United States who were earlier recruited en masse to work due to labor shortages caused by World War II. In this way, Mexican laborer became the archetype of the disposable worker who participated in low-wage jobs and long shifts. Many of these workers also experienced structural discrimination and the xenophobia of whites. However, as US white military service personnel returned home, Mexican manual labor became unwanted. During this time, the US Border Patrol used military-style procedures to racially profile, arrest, and repatriate over 1.3 million undocumented immigrants and Mexicans with US citizenship of Mexican descent to Southern Mexico (away from the US borderlands region).

The systemic and historical inequalities promoted structural discrimination, repatriation, and vigilantism and continue against the descendants of Mexicans. Today Chicanx youth and young adults are subjected to the same draconian assaults that surveil and criminalize their communities, especially if they are assumed to be gang affiliated or their residences are in what are considered "gang barrios." Branded as gang infested and dilapidated, their barrios have become saturated with ordinances that criminalize the entire Chicanx community.

Mendoza-Denton (2008) uses the concept of hemispheric localism to show how Chicana homegirls conceptualize the difference between Northern and Southern gangs, paralleling the social structure that reproduces and maintains their marginality. She argues that gang members possess an understanding of how this limitation of space and territorialism relates to how society socially constructs deviants and divides them from the so-called mainstream. In their north and south identities, Chicanx gang members recognize and claim their marginality, producing cultural artifacts that carve out their uniqueness via their dress styles, graffiti, lowrider cars, and tattoos (Mendoza-Denton 2008; Moore, 1999). These contentious expressions became framed as a counter-cultural fad, similar to the way youth and adults were stigmatized and punished during the 1943 Zoot Suit Riots, stemming from a white supremacist ideology and culture that condemned zoot suit-wearing Chicanx civilians. The style of dress of that period was viewed as a threatening and rebellious leading to "witch hunts," arrests, and mass beatings of Chicanx youth and their subcultures. The same criminalization continues today through anti-graffiti laws that seek to suppress gang members (Kim, 1995).

Comparable to the preemptive strikes against immigrants, moral entrepreneurs sought to influence society by making this artistic expression deviant and a byproduct of social decay (Vanderveen and Eijk, 2016; O'Sullivan, 1994). Law enforcement and other agents of social control promoted a moral panic, a widespread fear and concern among the citizenry that gang members and graffiti artists were an imminent threat (Katz, 2011; Lane, 2002; Phillips, 1999). More recently the authors of "broken windows theory" suggest if the placaso is not addressed, it will encourage more social disorder and further serious crime (Bloch, 2019; Kelling and Coles, 2019; Muñiz, 2015). As a result, Chicanx gang members constantly experience apprehension and prosecution for their graffiti "vandalism" with punishments ranging from community service to huge fines and/or incarceration (Davis, 2014; Kramer, 2010).

Methodology

In this inquiry, we used a three-fold methodology: field research and semi-structured open-ended in-person and telephone interviews with former-Chicanx gang members, former Chicanx graffiti artists, and gang-involved Chicanx individuals in California. The participants resided in the Bay Area, the Central Valley (inland and coast), and Southern California (Los Angeles and San Diego). All participants were conveniently sampled, and most were the authors' personal acquaintances.

English was the primary language spoken during the interviews. However, we code-switched by speaking in Calo as the situation demanded. The use of Calo involves the street competency of Chicanx gang barrio slang that incorporates "Spanglish" in everyday communication (Rodriguez, 1993).

We snowball-sampled all participants by asking acquaintances for referrals. A total of 20 persons participated in this research (16 men and 4 women). Eleven in-person interviews took place at locations of our participants' choice, which included their residences, fast-food restaurants, barbershops, gasoline stations, and public parks. Participants ranged in age from 18 to 48 years, and they selected a pseudonym to protect their identities. The interviews took place from October 2018 to September 2019. The interviews ran between 45 minutes and two hours in length. Our interviews focused on (i) the socio-cultural meanings and ideologies of former and active Chicanx gang members and graffiti artists vis-à-vis the production of placasos in their barrios and (ii) how these subjects understood the social construction of their art by the wider society.

California's criminalization of gang graffiti

Daniel Ramos, a Chicano from Boyle Heights, a community east of the Los Angeles River, was one of the most reputable graffiti artists in the state of California. Ramos went by the tag name "Chaka," with his moniker appearing over 10,000 times on private and public properties all over the state, allegedly costing the taxpayer half a million dollars to cover up and restore. The 90s in Los Angeles were an era of graffiti renaissance. During this time, both tagger crews and gang members alike became active in marking their territories. While such street art experienced popularity, the police, prosecutors, and other makers of policy functioned as moral entrepreneurs,[6] lobbying publics to demonize graffiti artists and their artistic expressions, in the same way marijuana smokers were criminalized several decades before (Becker, 1963).

California's Vandalism and Graffiti Law, known as Penal Code 594 PC, was repeatedly amended during the 2000s, adding to an original law on criminal mischief passed in 1872. This statute makes it unlawful for a person to intentionally, maliciously deface and vandalize public and private property with graffiti or other inscribed material. The person who violates this law may be charged with PC 594 (a)-misdemeanor if the property damage is less than $400 and PC 594 (b)-felony if the amount exceeds $400.

Mario Lugo, a Chicano from North San Diego County who goes by the moniker "Skino," was arrested and charged under PC 594 (b) (1) a felony, vandalism, and PC 594 PC (B) (2), a misdemeanor. Although law enforcement agencies vary in the ways they investigate a graffiti incident, "Skino's" case began when someone reported the alleged vandalism on their private property. The investigator identified the exact location where the graffiti incident occurred. Once they found the graffiti, they examined the "Skino" piece to discover the identity of the perpetuator and/or his affiliation. In such cases, when the art is illegible the investigator may resort to street-level intelligence by seeking informants or witnesses. Often, the investigating officer will use the Graffiti Tracker database. This database allows persons to "identify, track, prosecute, and seek restitution from graffiti vandals" (Graffiti Tracker, 2019).

Skino's arrest report revealed that the investigator explored this database to find a record of all his alleged graffiti-related crimes through the use of his moniker. In addition, the investigator sought to determine the cost of the vandalism, including how much each incident cost to repair. It also revealed that the investigator searched the Internet, social media pages, and social media accounts to help identify the person, gang, or graffiti crew. In this case, a search warrant of "Skino's" residence was issued, where investigators looked for "piece books," graffiti paraphernalia, paint-splattered clothing, painting face masks, collapsible ladders, and paint-splattered backpacks. Skino's prosecution shines a light on the level of criminalization and surveillance of gang members and, in particular, the Othering of graffiti artists. In the following, we discuss the findings of our research as respondents describe their relationship to the culture of graffiti production and the meanings this form of art has for their lives.

Findings

Based on an analysis of the interviews with our participants three primary themes emerged that are discussed in this section: (i) From Taggers to Cholxs,[7] (ii) The Art and Culture of Cholx Placasos, and (iii) We are Here: From Resistance to Punitive Social Control. These findings inform our understanding of the social construction of neighborhoods and Cholx placasos.

i From taggers to cholxs

Several Chicanx youngsters between the ages of 12 and 24 who lived in California Barrios belonged to tagger crews[8] such as BADK (Bomb All Day Krew), GTA (Getting Too Aggressive), Metro Transit Assassins (MTA), and United Spray Painters (UPS), among other tagging crews. Across the state from the Bay Area to San Diego's Borderlands region, members sought street credibility by placing their graffiti moniker or tagger crew placaso on visible and hard-to-reach spaces, what they refer to as "getting up." Mugs, a San Diego borderlands graffiti artist expresses it like this,

> I started getting up by tagging on school desks, restroom stalls, the trolley, and buildings. I spend most of my teens traveling from downtown to South [San Diego] County. Once I got to Sidro (San Ysidro) I would cross the border to Tijuas (Tijuana, Mexico) and

spray on paredes (walls), bridges, sidewalks. I never crossed the border with spray cans, but I jacked (stole) them as I needed them. I sprayed so much shit that I stained my clothes with paint splatter. You know, I never saw what I was doing as a crime, but I saw it as my duty to be noticed, like most taggers. I think I was the real O.G. because my homies (peers) knew I was getting up in the US and Mexico; It made sense to me since I am from here and there . . . my friends would visit Tijuas and parts of San Deezy (San Diego), and they would tell me that they saw my name all over the place. I felt like I was somebody important, pinche (fuckin) ghetto superstar, because Graffiti has no borders and I felt like my world was big.

In this, Mugs tells the story of how getting up involved for him a bi-national adventure by representing his name on both sides of the border. His reputation as a transnational graffiti artist inspired other homies to form an organic tagging crew that expanded from North San Diego County to Ensenada, Baja California, Mexico.

Similarly, an LA-based tagger group became known for establishing an actual grand theft auto track record. The youth group stockpiled a plethora of G-rides[9] (Hondas and Toyotas) in their communities. Soon, their streets became saturated with stolen vehicles. Youngsters would write on their dust-filled windshields the letters GTA to let their homies know that this vehicle was available for joy riding. Once the youngsters established that they shared tagging in common, they unified under the collective identity marker by transforming the meaning of GTA acronym to Getting Too Aggressive.

GTA, like other gangs in California, increased its recruitment strategies by going to different junior high schools and high schools. As a collective group, they would identify persons ditching school and then host a series of daily ditching parties to bring into the group both female and male teenagers. Maga, now a 44-year-old father of three kids, giggled as he recollected his youthful indiscretions,

> It never failed, more or less, two or three vatos (guys) would meet at my pad (home) and then we would get a G-ride from the ally. We cruised all over the streets to hit up people and let them know we were throwing a ditch party. Even though we had alcohol, bud (marijuana), and other things, people had no idea that we were recruiting youngsters to join GTA. Some of the youngsters tagged with other homies, but here we were getting organized. We had a lot of guys join GTA, but then, to our surprise, we had chicks (women) who were down and representing our crew. The women became GTAQ (Getting Too Aggressive Queens). Our parties went from keeping it indoors to taking it out to the streets. We had a lot of spray cans and G-rides that we would travel far to get our names up. The more we spread out GTA and our names, we recruited widely. We also made enemies. We went from reppin (representing) GTA/GTAQ to crossing enemies out. The women helped bring enemies, and we straight up jumped them and made us known. People started to see us as the problem and not the barrio.
>
> *(gang)*

In the previous, Maga proudly articulates GTA's historical trajectory and how the crew grew in numbers. Everyone who joined GTA now tagged not only to express individual identity but group solidarity. It should be mentioned that GTA also included women in its organizational structure. As GTA grew in size, so did their street-level reputation. As the group's activity increased on the streets, its members took GTA as their *master status*[10] to identify themselves as tag-bangers, enabling a common pathway into delinquency. Maga expressed that he never anticipated becoming a tagger, but because of a toxic home environment, he was pushed into the streets. Once in, however, Maga found his participation in the tagger culture therapeutic and cathartic; this practice allowed him to purge his social frustrations. As he explains:

> I never wanted to do this (become a graffiti artist). I did not think it was going to happen. Frustrated, I found street art as a way of letting go of my anger issues and dealing with problems at home.

Chicanx tag-banging gained much-unwanted attention on the streets and in the larger community when a larger organizational gang created a mandate that altered the makeup of tag-banging on the streets. In the summer of 1993, a series of gang peace treaties between Chicanx gang members in Southern California were made, resulting in territorial changes among the different groups. Several small gangs became reconfigured by joining more extensive street gangs, while other gangs included tag-bangers, graffiti practitioners, and party crews where men and women joined pre-existing gang structures to avoid social ramifications or street-level sanctions. Thus, gang members became manipulated by a larger corporate gang.

The larger group mirrors Carl Taylor's (1989) typology of a corporate gang. Taylor characterizes these groups as highly organized and profit oriented. Such gangs display a corporate-like structure in the differentiated assignment of roles and responsibilities to members, who may be involved in marketing, sales, or distribution, or in more specifically criminal activities such as enforcement. Jim Boy described how the gang peace treaty changed his barrio's geopolitical make-up,

> We knew the rules of the street changed big time. Anyone who loved getting up knew that graffiti could cost them their life. The tagger glory days were over and all the chavalas (punks) were put on check. Some of the [gang] cliques grew stronger with more members. The peace treaty was no joke and the big dogs (shot callers) meant business. Graffiti or Tagging in the barrio was forbidden so if you wrote your tagger mierda (shit) you just let everyone know about your funeral. The peace treaty opened doors for heavy recruitment to organize Raza (Chicanx people) to join street gangs.

Jim Boy described how the Chicanx corporate gang structure hindered the existence of the tag-banger subculture that at one time thrived throughout California. The expansion of Chicanx gangs in California also resulted in intergenerationally creative ways to promote and shape street-level barrio politics. The art and culture of cholx placasos represents how solidarity bonds get socially constructed in the neighborhood.

ii The art and culture of cholx placasos

The art and culture of graffiti represents a street-level and subaltern aesthetic that often gets stigmatized by the public and the agents of punitive social control. In his analysis of graffiti among Chicago street gangs, Conquergood (2005) describes a community's impressions of this cultural production, "Gang graffiti is vilified by outsiders as spectacle of filth, scene of vandalism, both symptoms and source of social disorder and decay" (Pp. 354).

Similarly, Chicanx Community members usually describe cholx graffiti with disdain, especially when gang members produce it. It is common to hear community members describe graffiti as *porquerias* (filth), *chingaderas* (a piece of shit), *vandalismo* (vandalism), and *la marca del diablo* (mark of the devil), for example. They also describe gang members unfavorably as *delincuentes* (delinquents), *desgraciados* (spoiled), *hijas/os de la chingada* (daughters or sons of a bitch). Both graffiti and gang members are described in pejorative terms and seen by some as an impediment to barrio improvement and pride. Downer, a member of White Fence gang in Boyle Heights, expressed,

> Around here some people hate us (gang members), but they won't tell us shit to our face. They just try to keep their kids away from us like they are saints and we are the disease. It's like Lorenzo is going to grow horns like the devil for talking with us or Lourdes is going to go home with a devil's [pitchfork]. I hear all the alleluias (religious people) tell their kids that we are going to ruin them. When the families walk by our placasos, especially after church on Sundays, I always hear them talk shit about "el grafiti" (the graffiti) and that all we do is bring shame, property values down, and make the neighborhood look gacho.
>
> *(bad)*

Seen as harmful to the community, both Chicanx cholxs and their graffiti become categorized as a deviant group and a nuisance since outsiders lack the competency to understand street culture. Conquergood (2005) introduced the concept of "street literacy" as a way to describe a street-level school of thought that values subcultural aesthetics and modes of communication often misconstrued by people with authority and cultural outsiders. "Street literacy develops an impressive, albeit, underground, body of knowledge and skills that are based on cooperative and interdependent leaning that is embodied, coexperienced, refreshed and kept exciting through improvisation and play" (Pp 373). To gang members, placasos produced by their homies promote a cultural aesthetic that depicts in-group solidarity that promotes the social construction of community and identity. However, when outsiders mark up their neighborhood, this action gets defined as a disrespectful territorial crossing, a confrontational statement, or a feud invitation. Spanky, a veterano[11] from Big Hazard in Boyle Heights explained,

> Ramona Gardens (housing projects) means everything to the homeboys. Hazard tells everyone who are the homies in the gang, it lets the community know that we control the entire territory and who is on the outs (free and not incarcerated). We honor the homies who passed away with a Rest in Peace [memorial]. Graffiti can let the public know who our beef (troubles) is with or the enemies are on our radar. Don't get this twisted (confused), but we also have enemies disrespect us with their barrio (gang) name in our territory. When enemies put their placaso we will cross them out on sight, we want these levas (people with no respect) to know they found trouble. So, if you understand the graffiti, you can also tell who reigns supreme in the turf, it also lets you know who wants pedo (conflict), and who is trying to make a move in Hazard territory. Graffiti is the barrio periodico (newspaper) that lets you know about the politics here and there.

Spanky's testimony illustrates how graffiti produces *barrio mitote* (neighborhood gossip), street-level social media on walls for disenfranchised persons. These aerosol-sprayed discourses allow gang members to decipher meaning pertinent to the subculture. Both gang insiders and outsiders must recognize graffiti messages, and gangs must establish a consensus in maintaining a shared meaning for these messages to promote its intended power and moral belief order. Shadow, a former West Side Poros 14 member from Porterville, explains as follows:

> Most graffiti includes the hood name and their membership to let others know we have the numbers (members). The homies want people to know that the westside is our territory

and that everyone listed is down to put in work. Graffiti tells happy stories about unity, but these walls also talk about sadness and hate. The hardest thing we do is honor our fallen friends. We dogg (disrespect) some lame neighborhoods and punks by crossing them out, no disrespect to you, but we hate scraps.[12] We cross out scraps left to right, and we remind them that their lives aren't worth a nickel by writing a 187[13] by their fake placaso.

Shadow provides a storyline that demonstrates how gang graffiti promotes an "us versus them" moral code. The placasos allow them to promote solidarity and to affirm boundary maintenance in the barrio. This code represents variations that may stem from a color versus a number embedded in the graffiti. Although tag-banging has influenced cholx graffiti today, several gangs use very stylized Old English or blocked letters to mark off their geopolitical territory. In California, gang graffiti is more than markings on a wall, it can become a precursor to individual deviance. However, cholx graffiti takes on a different meaning when we explore the punitive context of gangs and their graffiti. Cholx resistance becomes a means by which social control is challenged while promoting cholx unity.

iii We are here: resistance to punitive social control

Gang-involved Chicanx men and women experience hyper-surveillance and hyper-criminalization by various community stakeholders. The targeted men and women experience policies that advance ultra-policing and repression through the use of gang injunction laws[14] and gang enhancements,[15] among other suppressive measures in communities to combat the gang situation in California. For gang members who do graffiti, they confront an unchecked punitive social control that involves an overarching system of regulating the lives of marginal groups (Swan and Bates, 2017; Rios, 2015; Stuart, Armenta, and Osborne, 2015). Gang placasos are frequently identified as vandalism and a pre-cursor to deviance. However, gang members and their ideology challenge mainstream views. Placasos as a form of social resistance allow participants to promote their existence while challenging social agents who seek to sanitize their communities through criminalizing gang members, ethnic cleansing and gentrification. Cholx social agency preemptively seeks to remind constituents and people with power that they will not be erased or placed in the margins.

Chicanx gangs as a resistance group parallel Brotherton's (2008) sociological framework showing how gangs manifest themselves as resistance groups in contexts of marginality by promoting in-group solidarity among the oppressed. This resistance becomes counter-hegemonic[16] (Carroll, 2006) by allowing Cholxs to address "conscious and/or unconscious opposition of individuals and groups to structural constraints (gang suppression strategies), be it in the form of institutional values and treatments or the micro-macro processes of cultural, physical, economic and social subjugation" (Pp. 59). As an indigenous and working-class citizenry, Cholxs engage in contentious politics via placasos to address the pushing out of subaltern people from those barrios experiencing urban renewal. Joker, from the metro area in West Los Angeles, explained,

> People think that "getting up" is criminal and that we don't have love for the streets because people say that we make our communities unsafe and ugly. Has anyone bothered to think why our communities suck? Let us talk about those fuckers wearing suits in City Hall who don't give a fuck about minorities. They don't think about putting our tax dollars to help fix our communities or to make them beautiful? It's simple. If you have browns (Chicanx) and blacks living in these communities the people in charge do not care about these neighborhoods, they just let our streets rot on purpose. But let's keep it G (real), when white

fuckers show up it all gets manicured like my hyna's (girlfriend's) fingernails. They will add a pinche (fuck'in) dog park, a few coffee shops with private security, they will let white America know that it's a great place to live. At least graffiti gives us life; it gives us a reason to do art, it gives us a reason to breathe when we don't feel alive, especially when the pigs (the police) and punksecutors (prosecutors) are on a mission to bust us. They are not here to promote their bullshit 'To Protect and To Serve,' but they are pushing us to land in a prison cell and hide us like we are a disgrace to the world.

Joker emphasizes that it is government's irresponsibility that dilapidated communities and not gang-involved persons. He believes that the city government's neglect promoted the barrio's social decay. As a result, Joker describes how People of Color experience invisibility and receive poorly distributed resources. Thus, Joker believes that placaso production allows marginal persons to feel dignity and cohesion in the face of mass evictions. He acknowledges that once the community demographics change through gentrification, then the neighborhood ceases to be invisible, but instead thrives. Nonetheless, Joker cautions that as long as the Chicanx residents remain, the community as a whole will remain super-policed and repressed. Similarly, Tweety, a homegirl from Varrio Gardens X4 in Sacramento and now a university student, stated:

We will never be silenced or forgotten. We have a hecka (a lot of) talent on the streets and several peeps (people) think we need to be underground so that we are never seen or heard. We write our names on the walls like advertisements, even if people don't know what our messages or names are about. Graffiti allows us to tell the public and those who run the show (political elites) them we aren't going anywhere. To some people graffiti is like having Christmas lights at your home way after the holiday season. They think our expression is ghetto, but we see it differently. We honor our stories, our existence, our claim to our neighborhoods. The biggest gangsters are politicians. The city always covers our pieces with a dull gray paint like Tetris game pieces. but you know that even if they cover it with nasty shades of grays, we all know they just want to bury us. These blocks of paint let everyone know that we are here. They really symbolize cemetery plots on walls that hide the social dead, but we simply keep writing over them to keep our memories, homies, and neighborhood alive. They can't stop us, we give to the world what has been handed to us. If they don't give a fuck about us why should we give a shit about them.

Thus, Chicanx Gang members do not see themselves as social misfits but as street-level, organic artists who do not fit within the conventions of the art worlds (Gans, 1999). Instead they view themselves as self-taught artists who follow a political urging to do graffiti (Becker, 1982; Campos, 2015; Lachmann, 1988; Fine, 2004). Given the simple fact that policies target black and brown bodies, graffiti becomes an instrument of resistance promoting street-level praxis and consciousness and hidden barrio aesthetics. LA Shy girl, a former member of Getting Too Aggressive, communicated to us how she emerged as a reputable street artist,

I wasn't born to be a firme (fine) artista (artist), but I love how arte (art) lets you pour your corzon (heart) and alma (soul) to the barrio like a poem (neighborhood). Ay, this shit runs deep, and it is personal, its sacred like in a confession booth at church (Catholic), where you share with a priest your sins, and like victories. But, you know, a lot of gente (people) don't give a fuck to hear us out or talk to us, so we force society to listen to us with our placasos (graffiti). A spray can, a scribe, MeanStreak, or a marker is the easiest shit to use, and on the serio (serious) tip, even if people think we use vandalism tools, the placasos speak louder than ambulance sirens screaming from Whittier Boulevard and spreading all over Boyle Heights. We proudly display our neighborhood on our terms.

LA Shy Girl laughs and pulls out a turquoise-colored Bic lighter. She proceeds to light what she refers to as her frajo (cigarette) and adds,

> We don't take art classes or have mentors who want to show us how-to pick-up skills. Ay, you know, everything we do to express who we are, how we feel, where we're from makes it the gente's (people's) art. Being an artist is not just something we are born with, we just risk it all, including going to jail to be noticed by everyone. I hate the feeling of being the invisible woman, gang members are people, just like Banksy, Mear One, Pablo Picasso, Frida, and Michelangelo. In this country, only certain people have a place to paint like at those rich people's galleries. We don't have it that good. We are like Aztecs who beautify the streets like they did in the Aztec empire. No one told Aztecs that what they painted was demonic or ugly until the Spaniards came and ruled Mexico. The same shit is happening in our streets, we are modern Aztecs putting up graffiti and the cops are like Spaniards telling us that we are doing is a crime. We all started off with no skills and being nobody in this world. We (cholx) are Americans, like everyone living in this nation.

Socially constructed as a criminal, LA Shy Girl's standpoint on gang placasos illuminates how this barrio aesthetic allows gang-involved persons to express themselves and thereby gain visibility in a world that deems them a threat to the social order. She expresses how gang placasos help maintain and produce structural resistance for marginal gang members. She posits that prominent people with resources escape stigmatization and have the cultural capital to prevent the criminalization of their art production, whereas society will always typecast persons who do not find conventional ways of producing art. Chicanx barrio artists get delegated to the cultural outsider sphere and are often demonized for producing cholx graffiti, which becomes a form of Avant-Garde or guerilla artistic expression. The latter expressions allow cholx placasos to transform their public outlook and cultural appeal.

Conclusion

Known as a leading historian of hip-hop, Henry Chalfant documented the criminalization and the rise of graffiti in the late 70s and 80s. He became fascinated by the ways the once redlined and dilapidated communities and subway cars in the Bronx and other New York City locations became canvases decorated by youngsters with street art. Chalfant remarked how graffiti crew kids, who were similar to street gangs, decorated these cityscapes as a badge of honor (Thayer, 2019). He also describes how public opinion on graffiti produces mixed standpoints where people socially construct the meaning of graffiti as art or vandalism. In this chapter, we show that while agents of social control seek to define gang members as deviant others, gang members themselves resist this systemic labeling and their oppression through the art and culture of graffiti art.

Chicanx placaso practitioners challenge negative public perceptions of their subcultural placasos. We found that Chicanx gang members engage in constructing their social identities through their placasos and in doing so become the objects of criminalization and stigmatization by dominant others. As the creation of an oppressed and disenfranchised group, placasos are not produced to promote fear and the decay of their barrios but instead are cultural artifacts utilized to make themselves visible through challenging draconian, suppressive, and repressive law enforcement. Gang members reveal subaltern agency by challenging the status quo through the construction of their placasos and social space. Hayden (1997) argues that urban neighborhoods host many vernacular arts traditions enabling different ethnic groups to claim public space.

Chicanx gang placasos speak volumes about the lives of persons who experience super-criminalization and super-surveillance in their everyday lives. The men and women who are studied in this research are subject to the ways powerful decision-makers manufacture moral panics intended to keep subaltern communities silent, demonized, and invisible. This work proves that Chicanx gang members will not stay muted; instead, they consistently find ways to speak out against the assaults visited on them.

As our communities are increasingly gentrified, we will find more attempts to erase "disposable" populations through the gross application of policies and laws seeking to make Chicanx gang members captives within the tentacles of the United States Prison Industrial Complex, a system of social control relying extensively on mass incarceration and a wide range of punitive practices. This system, which includes private corporations and the state, generates capital from the misery of marginalized persons, in this case Chicanx gang members in California.

As Chicanx gang placasos become defined as vandalism, members resist these labels by using their agency to develop social resiliency against the real and symbolic ethnic cleansing that the gentrification of their communities constitutes as they "represent" in a site where they no longer feel they belong.

Notes

1 Placasos is a Chicanx lexicon term within the culture that refers to either graffiti or tattoo.
2 The use of "X" in "Chicanx" allows for the community to be inclusive of gender and incorporates those who identify and don't identify within the gender spectrum.
3 Names and places will be replaced with pseudonyms throughout this document.
4 The structural arrangements that influence the super-criminalization of people through the social, cultural, economic, institutional, legal, political, and psychological forces.
5 Phenotypes, last names, and Spanish accents determined a person's Mexican identity.
6 Powerful persons whose interest in a cause encourage others to follow their moral stances on a concern. Moral entrepreneurs are the "rule creators" who typically argue and lobby others to believe that their concern (in this case anti-graffiti) benefits individuals and society.
7 The use of "x" in "Cholxs" allows for the community to be inclusive of gender and incorporates those who identify and do not identify within the gender spectrum.
8 Taggers are persons who write their moniker or group name on street corners, buildings, and buses, for example. Tagger crews allow graffiti artists to have an organization that seeks to obtain social recognition.
9 A stolen car.
10 This status is a social position that is the chief identifying feature of a person. In this case, belonging to a tagger crew is central to the member's character. In this case, a tag-banger is a hybrid identity that amalgamates both a tagger and gang member identity.
11 An older Chicanx youth or adult who is not actively involved in gang activity; many have respect and admiration from young gang members.
12 Disrespectful lexicon term within the Northern Chicanx gang culture to insult Southern Californian Chicanx gang members.
13 California penal code section for murder.
14 These civil court mandates attempt to suppress gang crime by using a lower legal standard, which grants the police the ability to limit gang mobility and activity in neighborhood areas called "safe zones." Gang injunction laws expand carceral captivity to the streets by making wearing team jerseys, and carrying aerosol spray cans, for example, unlawful for gang members named in the injunction.
15 California street gang enhancement laws contain two clauses: Penal Code 186.22 (a) the participation in a gang crime, which may result up to three years added to a gang members sentence; Penal Code 186.22 (b) a gang sentencing enhancement for a person who commits a felony for the gang benefit may receive 2–15 years or a life sentence in prison.
16 The challenge to a prevailing status quo and its political authority.

References

Acuña, Rodolfo F. 2014. *Occupied America: A History of Chicanos*, 8th Edition. New York: Pearson Education Inc.

Almaguer, Tomás. 1994. *Racial Fault Lines: The Historical Origins of White Supremacy in California*. Berkeley, CA: University of California Press.

Barrera, Mario. 1979. *Race and Class in the Southwest: A Theory of Racial Inequality*. Notre Dame, IN University of Notre Dame.

Becker, Howard. 1982. *Art Worlds*. Berkeley, CA: University of California Press.

Becker, Howard. 1963. *Outsider: Studies in the Sociology of Deviance*. New York: Free Press.

Bloch, Stefano. 2019. "Broken Windows Ideology and the (Mis)Reading of Graffiti." *Critical Criminology*: 1–18. Doi: 10.1007/s10612-019-09444-w.

Boyle, Gregory. 2018. *Barking to the Choir: The Power of Radical Kinship*. New York: Simon & Schuster.

Boyle, Gregory. 2011. *Tattoos on the Heart: The Power of Boundless Compassion*. New York: Free Press.

Brodkin, Karen. 1998. "Race, Class, and Gender: The Metaorganization of American Capitalism." *Transforming Anthropology* 7(2): 46–57.

Brotherton, David C. 2008. "Beyond Social Reproduction – Bringing Resistance Back in Gang Theory." *Theoretical Criminology* 12(1): 55–77.

Brotherton, David C. and Rafael Gude. 2018. *Social Inclusion from below: The Perspectives of Street Gangs and Their Possible Effects on Declining Homicide Rates in Ecuador*. Washington, DC: IABD.

Campos, Ricardo. 2015. "Youth, Graffiti, and the Aestheticization of Transgression." *Social Analysis* 59(3): 17–40.

Carroll, William K. 2006. "Hegemony, Counter-Hegemony, Anti-Hegemony." *Socialist Studies: The Journal of the Society for Socialist* Studies 2(2): 9–43.

Chastanet, François. 2015. *Cholo Writing: Latino Gang Graffiti in Los Angeles*. Sweden: Dokument Press.

Conquergood, Dwight. 2005. "Street Literacy." Pp. 354–375 in *Handbook of Research on Teaching Literacy Through the Communicative and Visual Arts*, edited by James Flood, Shirley Brice Health, and Diane Lapp. Mahwah, NJ: Lawrence Erlbaum Associates Publishers.

Davis, Kenneth A. 2014. "Views from the Field: Are We Color Blind to the Violence Behind Graffiti?" *National Gang Crime Research Center* 22(1): 43–50.

Durán, Robert J. 2018. *The Gang Paradox: Inequalities and Miracles on the U.S.-Mexico Border*. New York: Columbia University Press.

Durán, Robert J. 2012. *Gang Life in Two Cities: An Insiders' Journey*. New York: Columbia University Press.

Fine, Gary Alan. 2004. *Everyday Genius: Self-Taught Art and the Culture of Authenticity*. Chicago, IL: University of Chicago Press.

Fremon, Celeste. 2008. *G-Dog and the Homeboys: Father Greg Boyle and the Gangs of East Los Angeles*. Albuquerque, NM: University of New Mexico Press.

Flores, Edward. 2013. *God's Gangs: Barrio Ministry, Masculinity, and Gang Recovery*. New York: New York University Press.

Flores, Jerry. 2016. *Caught Up: Girls, Surveillance, and Wraparound Incarceration*. Berkeley, CA: University of California Press.

Gans, Herbert J. 1999. *Popular Culture ad High Culture: An Analysis and Evaluation of Taste*. New York: Basic Books.

Gendzel, G. 2013. "The Tortilla Curtain and California's Nativist Heritage." *Text and Performance Quarterly* 33 (April): 175–183.

Graffiti Tracker. 2019. "Graffiti Tracker." www. http://graffititracker.net.

Gramsci, Antonio. 1971. *Selections from the Prison Notebooks*. Translated and edited by Quintin Hoare and Geoffrey Nowell Smith. New York: International Publishers.

Green, Marcus. 2002. "Gramsci Cannot Speak: Presentation and Interpretations of Gramsci's Concept of the Subaltern." *Rethinking Marxism*, 14(3): 1–24.

Hayden, Dolores. 1997. *The Power of Place: Urban Landscapes as Public History*. Cambridge, MA: The MIT Press.

Katz, Karen. 2011. "The Enemy Within: The Outlaw Motorcycle Gang Moral Panic." *American Journal of Crime Justice* 36(3): 231–249.

Kelling, George L. and Catherine M. Coles. 2019. *Fixing Broken Windows: Restoring Order and Reducing Crime in Our Communities.* New York: Touchstone.

Kim, Sojin. 1995. *Chicano Graffiti and Murals: The Neighborhood Art of Peter Quesada.* Jackson, MS: University Press of Mississippi.

Kramer, Ronald. 2010. "Moral Panics and Urban Growth Machines: Official Reactions to Graffiti in New York City, 1990–2005." *Qualitative Sociology* 33: 297–311.

Lachmann, Richard. 1988. "Graffiti as Career and Ideology." *American Journal of Sociology.* 94(2): 229–250.

Lane, Jodi. 2002. "Fear of Gang Crime: A Qualitative Examination of the Four Perspectives." *Journal of Research in Crime and Delinquency* 39(4): 437–471.

Leep, Jorja. 2014. *Jumped in: What Gangs Taught Me About Violence, Drugs, Love, and Redemption.* Boston, MA: Beacon Press.

Lopez-Aguado, Patrick. 2018. *Stick Together and Come Back Home.* Berkeley, CA: University of California Press.

Mendoza-Denton, Norma. 2008. *Homegirls: Language and Cultural Practice among Latina Youth Gangs.* Malden, MA: Blackwell Publishing.

Miranda, Marie "Keta." 2003. *Homegirls in the Public Sphere.* Austin, TX: University of Texas Press.

Moore, Joan. 1999. *Going Down to the Barrio: Homeboys and Homegirls in Change.* Philadelphia, PA: Temple University Press.

Muñiz, Ana. 2015. *Police, Power, and the Production of Racial Boundaries.* New Brunswick, NJ: Rutgers University Press.

O'Sullivan, Ralph G. 1994. "Moral Entrepreneurs, Local Morality, and Labeling Processes." *Free Inquiry in Creative Sociology* 22(1): 73–77.

Phillips, Susan A. 1999. *Wallbangin': Graffiti and Gangs in L.A.* Chicago, IL: University of Chicago Press.

Reynolds, Julia. 2017. *Blood in the Fields: Ten Years Inside California's Nuestra Familia Gang.* Chicago, IL: Chicago Review Press.

Rios, Victor M. 2015. "Policed, Punished, Dehumanized: The Reality for Young Men of Color Living in America." Pp. 59–80 in *Deadly Justice: Trayvon Martin, Race, and the Criminal Justice System,* edited by Devon Johnson, Patricia Y. Warren, and Amy Farrell. New York: New York University Press.

Rios, Victor M. 2011. *Punished: Policing the Lives of Black and Latino Boys.* New York, NY: New York University Press.

Rodriguez, Luis J. 1993. *Always Running, La Vida Loca: Gang Days in L.A.* New York: Touchstone.

Rossman, Liliana Castañeda. 2012. *Transcending Gangs: Latinas Story Their Experiences.* New York: Hampton Press.

Spivak, Gayatri Chakravorty. 1988. "Can the Subaltern Speak?" In *Marxism and the Interpretation of Culture,* edited by Cary Nelson and Lawrence Grossberg. Champaigne, IL: University of Illinois Press.

St. Cyr, Jenna L. 2003. "The Folk Devil Reacts: Gangs and Moral Panic." *Criminal Justice Review* 28(1): 26–46.

Stuart, Forrest, Amada Armenta, and Melissa Osborne. 2015. "Legal Control of Marginal Groups." *Annual Review of Law and Social Science* 11: 235–254.

Swan, Richelle S. and Kristin A. Bates. 2017. "Loosening the Ties That Bind: The Hidden Harms of Civil Gang Injunctions in San Diego County." *Contemporary Justice Review* 20(1): 132–153.

Taylor, Carl. 1989. *Dangerous Society.* East Lansing: Michigan State University Press.

Thayer, Katherine. 2019. "The Artist Who Chronicled the Bronx Graffiti Boom in the 1980s." *Visual Culture.* www.artsy.net/article/artsy-editorial-artist-chronicled-bronx-graffiti-boom-1980s.

Vanderveen, Gabry and Gwen van Eijk. 2016. "Criminal but Beautiful: A Study on Graffiti and the Role of Value Judgements and Context in Perceiving Disorder." *European Journal on Criminal Policy and Research* 22(1): 107–125.

Vigil, James D. 2012. *A Rainbow of Gangs: Street Cultures in the Mega-City.* Austin, TX: University of Texas Press.

Williams, Raymond. 1983. *Keywords: A Vocabulary of Culture and Society*. Rev. ed. New York: Oxford University Press.

Young, Jock. 1971. *The Drugtakers: The Social Meaning of Drug Use*. London, UK: Paladin.

Zatz, Marjorie S. 1987. "Chicano Youth Gangs and Crime: The Creation of a Moral Panic." *Contemporary Crisis* 11: 129–158.

42

"Gangbangers are gangbangers, hustlers are hustlers"

The rap game, social media, and gang violence in Toronto

Marta-Marika Urbanik

Introduction

The increasing prevalence of social media has significantly transformed how many of us interact with the world around us. This revolution has been quite comprehensive, altering how we approach dating, job hunting, politics, networking, marketing, grieving, policing, education, and almost everything else in between. The proliferation of social media has effectively made having an online presence seem *almost mandatory* for countless aspects of our social and professional lives, so much so that many individuals have expressed it would be difficult to terminate their social media usage, or even that they are "addicted" to social media (Griffiths et al. 2014; Ryan et al. 2014). Hence, many desire or feel compelled to partake in this new stage of social relations.

One area of particular interest for criminologists is the intersection of social media, the criminal economy, and gang violence. Criminologists are only just beginning to investigate how social media has affected the gang milieu, specifically in relation to gang promotion, inter-gang dynamics, and violent victimization (see Urbanik et al. 2020 for an overview). What is notably missing from existing literature, however, is an empirical interrogation of social media's effect on *intra*-gang relations. Drawing on ethnographic data from Toronto's Regent Park neighborhood, this chapter aims to contribute to this knowledge base.

Gangs in Canada

Much criminological attention has been dedicated to unmasking and addressing the gang problem in the United States. Several prominent studies have highlighted the intimate relationship between disadvantaged and racialized American inner-city neighborhoods and the prevalence of street crime, drug trafficking, gangs, and gang violence (Anderson 1999; Bourgois 1996; Brotherton and Barrios 2004; Contreras 2013; Venkatesh 2002; Wilson 1987). Conversely, the paucity of gang research in the Canadian context has resulted in a knowledge deficit about the extent and realities of gang life and violence in Canada. Though street gangs have been a documented fixture in the country since at least the mid-twentieth century (Rogers 1945), almost

75 years later, we continue to lack data about the preponderance, activities, and experiences of Canadian street gangs.

One notable hindrance to developing a robust body of scientific knowledge on Canadian gangs is the fact that Canadian law enforcement agencies rarely release 'gang', race,[1] or even neighborhood-crime statistics to researchers or the broader public. Hence, we do not know the extent or social, racial, or spatial distribution of Canada's contemporary 'gang problem.'[2] Nevertheless, the Correctional Service of Canada claims that Canada's street and prison gang problem is growing at precipitous rates (Chettleburgh 2007; Grekul and LaBoucane-Benson 2008), and currently, 1 in 4 homicides across the country are classified as 'gang related'[3] (Beattie et al. 2018). Further, it is alleged that the number of 'gang related' homicides across Canada's largest cities have almost doubled since 2013 (Public Safety Canada 2019). Unsurprisingly, this has given rise to several government and law enforcement initiatives to contain and suppress the alleged proliferation of gang violence in Canada. Though official data on crime and 'gangs' is riddled with methodological issues and must be approached with immense caution (Best 2001; Skogan 1974), the frustrating absence of more comprehensive data makes it difficult to critically examine the legal and political priorities driving such claims and initiatives. A second contributor to the nescience on gangs in Canada is that only a handful of Canadian scholars have examined 'gangs' and criminally involved groups, resulting in a persistent near-absence of sustained, rigorous, and comparative empirical and critical investigation into our gang phenomena.

Though Canada's gang milieu varies significantly across the country, the closest resemblance to American-style, neighborhood/territory-based gangs can be found in Toronto. In recent years, Toronto's gang activity has garnered significant public concern and media attention, sparked in part by a number of high-profile shootings and a significant increase in gun violence and 'gang-related' homicides. Similar to many American cities, Toronto's gang 'hotbeds' are located within our most disadvantaged and often racialized neighborhoods – specifically, public housing projects. Toronto Community Housing (TCHC) projects such as Regent Park, Moss Park, Lawrence Heights, Jane-Finch, Galloway, and Malvern are consistently featured in the media as the epicenters of gang activity and gun violence (see also Lindgren 2009; O'Grady et al. 2010). Often missing from public rhetoric is how social-spatial closure and control (Wacquant 2001/2012) has both historically and in the present afflicted these neighborhoods and their residents, with the broader macro structures that have created spaces of concentrated poverty and exclusion remaining veiled (Berardi 2018; Urbanik 2017). A series of media exposes have, however, uncovered that Toronto's TCHC projects are also sites of concentrated victimization; residents living within TCHC projects are 4–5 times more likely to be killed than other Torontonians, and there is a disproportionate amount of homicides on TCHC properties (specifically: gun homicides) as compared to the rest of the city (Davis and Appleby 2011; Freeze 2014). Two recent ethnographic studies based within Toronto's 'projects' have revealed that some of this gun violence is related to historical neighbourhood "beefs" between gangs and criminally involved groups from rival projects (Berardi 2018; Urbanik and Haggerty 2018).

Regent Park, Toronto

One neighborhood that often dominates the conversation on gang violence in the city is Regent Park. Located just east of Toronto's downtown core, Regent Park is Canada's oldest, and until recently, was the country's largest social housing project. Prior to its ongoing revitalization, which began in 2005, the neighborhood was home to approximately 10,000 residents, with all 69 acres devoted to social housing. At the time, census data showed that Regent Park comprised the lowest and second-lowest income census tracts in the province. By 2006, almost 68% of residents lived below the low-income cut-off line, and unemployment rates doubled the rest of Toronto (TCHC 2007). Almost 80% of residents identified as "visible minorities," and 78% were foreign born, arriving predominantly from the Caribbean, Africa, and Eastern and Southern Asia (Horak and London 2010, 6). News media coverage has consistently painted Regent Park as "thoroughly ghettoized" and "a poster child for poverty" (cited in Purdy 2003, 46).

Apart from its economic and social marginalization, Regent Park has long been considered one of Toronto's – and even Canada's – most dangerous urban areas. While neighborhood-level crime statistics are usually inaccessible to researchers in Canada, Thompson (2009) found that between 1988–2003, Regent Park had the city's highest homicide rate. Although the revitalization, which is slated for completion by 2021, was expected to decrease the neighborhood's crime and violence via the social-mix model (Wilson 1987), the media maintains "gangs, drugs, and guns still rule in Regent Park" (Warmington 2013). My ethnographic research, combined with several high-profile shootings of young black neighborhood men, further highlights that at least during the interstitial stages of the revitalization, gang activity and gun violence continue to trouble the neighborhood and specifically the young men in my study (see also Urbanik et al. 2017).

Methodology

I first entered Regent Park during the summer of 2013, when I worked as a research assistant for a project examining resident experiences of the neighborhood redevelopment. Though the majority of the residents I came to know were "prosocial," I increasingly came into contact with a subset of criminally and gang-involved young men, some of whom were considered neighborhood "Old Heads" – those who controlled the underground economy. Over time, I became interested in how these men navigated changes to violence and crime in the neighborhood as a consequence of mass neighborhood change. Eventually, the men allowed me to spend time "deep hanging out" (Geertz 1998) with them, which prompted me to make Regent Park the site of my own doctoral fieldwork the following summer. Since I first arrived in the neighborhood, I have spent 2–3 months conducting ethnographic observation in Regent Park every year between 2013–2018 and have also conducted over 160 interviews to further supplement my findings.

I spent the majority of my time in the field with a group of about 25 men between 18 and 46 years old,[4] some of whom were 'Old Heads,' in and around their favorite neighborhood hangout spots. These spots changed annually but included a school yard, a basketball court, an old ice rink, a makeshift rap studio, backyards, and the entryways of their buildings. The men spent many hours each day smoking weed, drinking, selling drugs, playing dice/cards for money, freestyle rapping, and shooting hoops. The disadvantaged neighborhood setting in which most of my participants spent their entire lives largely shaped and influenced my participants' individual and collective behaviors, meaning making, and the formation of their social and delinquent groupings (Anderson 1999; Hannerz 1969), while they rarely ventured out of the neighborhood given the risks of violent victimization. Most of my participants were extensively involved in criminal activity, and some had criminal charges for drug trafficking, weapons, gun violence, robbery, and even homicide. Since the onset of my research, several of my participants have been shot or killed, and many other young black neighborhood men have also been murdered.

Most of my primary participants belonged to two neighborhood gangs: the Young Soldiers and the Rich Riderz.[5] The Young Soldiers were composed of young men from 16–28 years old, most of who were of Somali background. The Rich Riderz formed along the lines of a dwindling Caribbean group in the neighborhood, which dominated Regent Park's illicit economy prior to the Young Soldiers' emergence. While members of the Caribbean group were older and had more established reputations than the Young Soldiers, as this group dwindled because of member relocations, arrests, and aging out, the remaining group members played an active role in supporting the emergence of the Rich Riderz – often composed of their younger siblings and cousins – and eventually fused into the newer group. Though the crux of the Rich Riderz were young boys, several Old Heads coached them about the survival and hustle on the streets. Sometimes disputes erupted between members of the Young Soldiers and the Rich Riderz about drug-trafficking turf, yet they generally co-existed relatively peacefully and sometimes hung out together. In fact, their shared master status of "Regent Parker" helped to reduce much inter-group violence (Urbanik 2018).

In Toronto's broader street-involved landscape, Regent Park's reputation depended largely on the success and street cred of its local rappers, ensuring that the neighborhood maintained its violent reputation and "respect" in the city, despite its revitalization. These artists were active in producing rap music, performing, filming music videos, and/or appearing in music videos filmed in the neighborhood (Urbanik and Haggerty 2018). Some had achieved local and even international fame, with a handful garnering notable public attention for their artistry, including over a million views and tens of thousands of followers on various social media platforms. They were also intimately connected to both gangs; since their rap careers were largely influenced by the street credibility of the 'soldiers' they aligned themselves with, they widely broadcasted their gang affiliations and, in turn, other gang members prominently endorsed them. Hence, in Regent Park, the distinction between "gang member" and "rapper" was fluid at best.

Consequently, many of their online behaviors were underpinned by what is essentially the 'commodification of crime' or the 'marketing of transgression' (Van Hellemont 2018). Undeniably, social media has increased the ability of many marginalized individuals to commodify their 'identities', and specifically, sell and profit on the 'gangster' imagery they adopt (Kontos and Brotherton 2008; Ilan 2015). In addition to propelling consumerist expectations characteristic of the "crime consumerism nexus" (Hayward 2004), this also propelled a display of emotions related to consumerism; the robbery of a prized possession (like a signature gold chain) could be perceived as an attack on their individual and collective identities (Young and Brotherton 2014), sometimes leading to violence.

Early on in my fieldwork, my participants attuned me to the myriad ways social media was affecting street dynamics and violence. Consequently, I connected and communicated with many of them via various social media platforms, which allowed me to witness their online presentations and interactions and also keep abreast of happenings in their lives while away from the field, including details of their legal predicaments, rap careers, social dynamics, and street beefs. My gang-involved participants used social media for expressive and instrumental goals (Storrod and Densley 2017), and their rap connections also significantly influenced their online posts (Urbanik and Haggerty 2018), which I was therefore able to observe in real time.

This chapter draws upon data I collected during two research trips during 2018; one in the summer and one in the fall, which I spent predominantly hanging out with members of the Rich Riderz, though several Young Soldiers frequently joined us as well. Nevertheless, the analysis for this chapter is also informed by my earlier 5 years of fieldwork and social media observations, which provided additional contextualization. This chapter first describes the important ways that social media affects gang presentations and dynamics, particularly as it relates to antagonizing rap videos shared online. It then distinguishes between two roles that my gang-involved participants traditionally ascribed to – gangbangers and hustlers – and outlines how growing pressures for gang members to participate in "internet banging" (Patton et al. 2013) have diluted these distinctive roles, making many "hustlers" feel inclined to engage in behaviors that were previously reserved for "gang bangers." Specifically, this chapter outlines how social media has affected *internal* gang dynamics and expectations as they relate to featuring in antagonistic rap music videos and retaliation for insults shared online by their rivals. It concludes with cautions about the nexus between digital behaviors and offline violence and encourages gang scholars to more thoroughly examine the behind-the-scenes complexities involved in the creation and sharing of gang-related digital content, with a particular focus on how social media may affect *intra*-gang dynamics.

Gangs, rap, and social media

In recent years, gang scholars have become particularly interested in examining the role social media plays in performing gang identity, promoting gang culture and reputation, and glorifying and inciting gang violence. Social media provides gang members an additional milieu for harassing, challenging, and threatening rival gang members and law enforcement (Densley 2012; Deuchar and Holligan 2010; Patton et al. 2016, 2019; Pyrooz et al. 2015; Urbanik and Haggerty 2018). Some of this violent posturing is related to gangs' increased participation in local rap music scenes, with gang members widely disseminating antagonistic rap music videos through social media platforms such as Instagram, YouTube, Facebook, and Snap Chat. Such videos enhance their street credibility, boost the gang's reputation, and even initiate or further fuel disputes with rival groups. Researchers and law enforcement agencies have become particularly concerned with the extent to which these provocative rap videos incite retaliatory gang violence, including homicide (Johnson and Schell-Busey 2016; Patton et al. 2013; Urbanik and Haggerty 2018). Given the extent of gang bravado online – colloquially referred to as "Internet banging" (Patton et al. 2013) – and the serious consequences of such violent posturing, social media platforms can serve as an "extension of the street" for gang members (Decker and Pyrooz 2011). In fact, some scholars view antagonistic gang exchanges online as so predictive of gang violence that there are growing efforts to develop computer technologies that can mine social media posts to anticipate, and hopefully avert, future gang violence (Blandfort et al. 2018; Blevins et al. 2016; Patton et al. 2013, 2016).

Concurrently, however, several scholars have documented that many posts and interactions online are merely performative (Goffman 1959) and sometimes signal a notable departure from 'real' life (Roks 2017; Stuart 2020; Van Hellemont 2012), with social media providing a novel 'performative space' for gang members (see Conquergood 1992). Moreover, despite recent increases in studies examining the online behaviours of gang-involved individuals, we still know little about the 'real world' consequences of social media interactions – and specifically, the extent to which they affect violence in the streets (Stuart 2020; see also Lauger et al. 2019). According to Stuart (2020), much existing work on the digital presence of gangs: 1) notably overestimates the causal relationship between social media and offline gang violence, 2) neglects social media's potential to transform (and de-escalate) conflicts in the 'real world', and 3) does not include real-time observations with producers of gang-related digital content (Stuart 2020, 193). In his ethnographic work with gang-associated youth, for example, Stuart (2020) found that while social media afford youth with a means to publicly challenge rivals' street authenticity, the majority of social media challenges did not generate offline violence. My own work has also documented that while gang-involved men use social media to provoke or intimidate rivals, they simultaneously take steps to mitigate the risks of consequential violence (Urbanik and Haggerty 2018). Hence, while social media has undoubtedly transformed how gangs interact with one another and the broader public, gang scholars have yet to establish how, and which, digital presentations and interactions affect offline violence (Stuart 2020).

Further, despite the increase in scholarly attention to social media as a new platform for performing "gang-ness" (Van Hellemont 2012), little has been written about how social media has affected intra-gang relations. Specifically, it remains unclear whether and how the growing expectation that gang members "internet bang" has altered intra-group dynamics, expected roles within gangs, and gang members' relationships to violence. My ethnographic research with gang-involved men in Toronto's Regent Park demonstrates that for the Rich Riderz, gang members could be delineated as hustlers" and "gangbangers," where hustlers could traditionally limit their involvement in gang beefs – gang-related disputes with rivals sometimes pertaining to territory, money, insults, and retaliation – whereas gangbangers were expected to enthusiastically partake in them. However, the growing expectation that gang members perform and advertise their "gang-ness" online via rap music and videos has blurred these distinctions, putting increasing pressure on hustlers to participate in gang beefs, thereby altering intergang relations and potentially street-interactions in notable ways.

Gangbangers vs. hustlers

The Rich Riderz gang in Regent Park was a unique collective in the sense that group members performed distinctive roles. Contrary to the common belief that all gang members are expected to engage in inter-group conflict, these gang members apportioned themselves to positions that either adhered to this expectation or deviated from it. In an interview with Andre (26 yrs.), he illuminated these role distinctions:

> A lot of the niggas that are fucking out here, watch a lot of fucking YouTube. So, they think, 'okay, you go out there, you gang bang, make money.' No! If you know the streets, you know gangbangers are gangbangers. Hustlers are hustlers. They don't mix the two. When you mix business and pleasure, that's when you get fucked over. Right?

I asked him to further explain the differences between these roles. He replied:

> Okay so let's say I had a problem with that hood. Gangbangers supposed to be protecting me. Its more chill with the homies, make sure everything is good. Do whatever he's gotta do to make him feel like the hood is doing good. Hustlers are more the ones that make money. They're not like "raw, raw, raw" like the gangbangers, you know? They move quietly. Shit like that.

Here, Andre describes the distinctive roles that group members generally adhered to. Gangbangers are expected to handle problems with other neighborhoods, often known as gang or neighborhood "beefs". This can include "protecting" their peers when rivals come through and making sure that the "hood is doing good" in terms of its street reputation across the city. Online, this could take the form of my participants who engaged in "gang banging" posting provocative pictures and quotes inviting their rivals to "come through" the neighborhood to "find them" because their "9s [9 mm guns] are ready," suggesting the willingness to exchange gunfire. Gangbangers were also expected to deal with any loss of status to the gang due to insults posted online or strikes against them which happened on the street but were then shared online. For example, when one Regent Parker was robbed of his identifiable gold chain by a rival gang, and the rival gang posted a video of the robbery online which was shared with thousands of viewers, the 'gangbangers' spent the next few weeks increasing the severity and frequency of online threats and insults aimed at the men who stole the chain. Sometimes this retaliation increased in severity. For example, one of my participants involved in gang banging posted several videos promising to avenge the violent victimization (including homicide) of his close affiliate in the weeks following his murder: "RIP [associate's street name]. The niggas at [rival housing project] gonna taste this smoke [gunfire]. We comin for you" – essentially, a warning that the gang would soon retaliate with serious violence. On the other hand, hustlers do not typically provoke gang beefs through the back and forth "raw, raw, raw" [aggressive posturing], but instead, they "move quietly," focusing on drug dealing. They tend not to instigate problems with other gangs or neighborhoods so as to attract as little attention to themselves as possible, given "heat" [police attention] is bad for business. Since gang members' violent dispositions and behaviors can dramatically vary even within the same group (Sharp et al. 2006; Short and Strodtbeck 1963), some members may be more economically or violently inclined than others – as was the case in Regent Park.

Despite highlighting the importance of knowing one's role, that summer, I saw Andre struggle with the position that suited him best. A new father to a baby girl, he seemed caught between gangbanging and his growing desire to move away from that violent lifestyle to one focused solely on generating a profit through drug trafficking. In private conversations, he often idolized my other participants who focused on the money-making aspect of "the life" in Regent Park, admiring their ability to "stay outta the bullshit" [violence] while still being respected group members. Nevertheless, Andre's decisions at the time did not draw him further from his gangbanger identity but instead solidified it further. For example, he increasingly approached unknown men who were passing through the neighborhood and reminded them that they had to "walk softly" since they were encroaching on Rich Riderz territory. His apartment also quickly became the home base for other Rich Riderz gangbangers, which they plastered with gang memorabilia, and where many of the more violently inclined young men congregated and stored their weapons. When the police raided his apartment, my hustler participants laughed at Andre's alleged confusion about why this occurred, and told him to "stop frontin' [lying] about not being into that gang banging shit." Hence, in some cases, the neat distinctions between hustlers and gangbangers can blur, even temporarily, especially as group members 'try on' these identities.

I asked Andre to estimate what proportion of Rich Riderz fell into each group. He answered "40/60" – 40% gangbangers, and 60% hustlers, which was consistent with my own observations. Andre went on to tell me that gangbangers are:

> Mostly the young guys. The old guys got shit to live for. If you've got a kid, you're not gonna wanna be out here bangin'. My brother hustles, he has to live, right? The Banger doesn't have nothing to worry about. The young guy dies tomorrow – doesn't have any kids to worry about. Goes to jail tomorrow, doesn't have anybody to worry about.

Over my years in the neighborhood, I too recognized that age influenced, but did not determine, the roles the men adopted. Andre's older brother – Chops (39 yrs.) – is a neighborhood Old Head, a father of three, and spends much of his days selling drugs in Regent Park. Though he had a strong hold over the gang's behaviors, he himself largely refrained from getting involved in violence. Instead, his primary focus was making money that he would bring back to his kids, and I often witnessed him intervene in and try to cool neighborhood beefs and intragroup conflicts. That being said, Chops did use violence on a handful of occasions, though this violence was individualistically motivated; he reserved violence for clients who failed to pay their drug debts or who he felt had disrespected him. This use of violence was largely related to protecting his financial interests.

Conversely, neighborhood gangbangers – like Andre – were expected to adhere to more stereotypical gang behaviors, specifically those related to intergroup conflict. These were generally motivated by violent retaliation, street justice, and efforts to augment street credibility and address a perceived wrong or respond to a threat (Anderson 1999; Jacobs and Wright 2006).

Whenever I heard accounts of violence or discussions about "handling beef" which typically alluded to violent retaliation, it was my "gangbanging" participants who were usually involved, whereas my hustler participants monopolized and maintained the area's vibrant drug trade.

Though gangbangers certainly sold drugs as well, their drug trafficking was considered secondary to their "gangbanging"; their group roles were first and foremost dedicated to advancing the group's, and by extension, the neighborhood's standing in the streets. As Andre mentioned, their primary focus was the protection of the neighborhood and/or group's reputation. Gangbangers were the ones implicitly and explicitly expected to "handle" troubling situations with rivals. Despite these different behaviors, my participants still functioned as one cohesive unit. This is also how Andre made sense of how the men in my study perceived their roles against the backdrop of the other men: "At the end of the day, this takes a team. Like jail. You can't run in jail by yourself, you have to have a team." Like Andre, many of my participants understood that teamwork would not only enable their survival – in the way it might in a correctional setting – but would also enhance profits.

Nevertheless, my time in the field attuned me to the fact that social media was altering gang dynamics in such notable ways that these previously distinct roles were increasingly coalescing. Specifically, I found that the growing expectation that gang-involved men "internet bang" has compromised the relatively non-violent role of the hustler in two ways: 1) hustlers were increasingly pressured into being featured in antagonistic rap music videos widely broadcast on social media, and 2) hustlers were also increasingly expected to engage in consequent violent beefs stemming from antagonistic social media interactions and provocations.

Rollin' for the group: rap music videos

Over the years, I observed many of my "hustler" participants become frustrated with not only the serious risks posed by internet banging but also with growing expectations that they assume consequent risks. Whereas before, hustlers could focus on generating profits and could largely limit their participation in and exposure to violence, the men in my study expressed that they increasingly felt pressured to support the neighborhood's gangbangers in their online posturing and therefore became increasingly susceptible to its resulting violence (Urbanik and Haggerty 2018). For the Rich Riderz, this online posturing was intimately related to featuring in rap music videos produced by group members who were part of Toronto's vibrant rap scene and who many of my participants saw as neighborhood "reps" in the broader urban milieu.

One hot summer evening, I saw this play out first hand. Chops, Jamal (24 yrs.), Hakim (22 yrs.), and I were hanging outside one of the neighborhood buildings. This location is where my participants spent most of their time that summer, drinking beer, smoking marijuana, playing rap music off speakers, and waiting to make a "chop" [drug sale]. We saw a larger group of young neighborhood men approach us from the parking lot, followed by a camera crew:

> While I'm playing with Dawn [Jamal's baby] whose laying in my arms Chops and Hakim are arguing over which rap song they should play next. Jamal goes in through the door to make a [drug] sale to one of his regulars, then returns. I spot a group of about 8 of the younger guys approaching us from the parking lot by 18th Street. Chops looks up and says "Who is that? Where they going?" Jamal squints his eyes and says its Randy [a prominent

neighborhood rapper]. "Oh, shit eh – the man's got the whole film crew and everything! They comin' down here" says Chops. Two middle-aged white men are following behind the group with large cameras and some other equipment. Hakim comments, "Say word, he's filming right now!" Randy and his crew approach us, and he's smiling from ear to ear. "Yo! Get your Rich Riderz gear! Go get your hoodies. We filming for my new track [rap song] right now. Come by 19th Block!" He heads to us with the other young men in tow and bumps chests with the men, touches Dawn's cheek, and gives me props. "Say word! You're filming right now?" asks Jamal. He says, "Yea, nigga! Right now! Yo, get your shit, we're filming over there in 5 [minutes]!" He points to 19th Block and heads through the building door as we shuffle to make room for him to get by. Jackson – one of his closer friends waits outside with us and the others and says "Yo, come thru. You gotta support your boy. You gotta support the block!" Jamal says "Alright, give us a sec[ond], we'll come down." Randy comes out of the building and yells "come through, come through! This one's gonna be a banger" and heads in the direction of 19th Block.

Here, we see how requests for individuals to feature in rap music videos can occur rather casually, and are often framed as ways to "support" one's friends and one's neighborhood. This can put additional pressure on those asked to appear in the video to participate in its production:

When Randy's group is out of earshot, Chops, Jamal and Hakim are discussing what just happened. Chops says "Yo, I aint really tryna be in that [video] right now" as he sparks another marijuana joint. Jamal responds as he's looking through his backpack for his [Rich Riderz] hoodie, "What nigga? What the fuck you mean? We all gotta support Randy." Chops replies, "Yo, Im down to support Randy, no doubt. But I aint tryna be all up in that video man, it always brings problems. I aint about the problems and you know that. I'm too old for this shit." Hakim nods his head, "Yo, I can't be going in [being featured in the music video] either – I'm on charges still. And the last fucking time, Hillside [rival neighborhood] niggas were poppin off and tryna come through [starting beef and coming through the neighborhood]. I ain't tryna die man, I ain't tryna go back to jail. I just wanna make money and chill. I already told you that. Don't wanna be brought into this shit again. I aint about that [gangbanging] life." Jamal sucks his teeth and is visibly agitated, "Yo, one of our boys is tryna do good, you know? He's reppin for us and the team, and yet you motherfuckers don't even wanna come support? Stop being fucking goofs – the man needs us to roll right now. You know the neigbourhood is down 2–0 right now, and ya'll niggas don't wanna do nothin about it. Can't just sit back here and make easy money like that. Times have changed. Ya'll gotta show up for the squad. Marta – man tell these motherfuck-ers to stop being pussies!" I shrug, "I'm not getting involved in this. You guys figure it out."
(Field note, 2018)

The men argued amongst themselves for a few minutes. Eventually, Jamal convinced Chops and Hakim to come along to the video shoot, not too far from where we were sitting. We made our way to 19th block, where about 25 other young neighborhood men that I knew – many dressed in Rich Riderz gear – were getting ready to take part in the music video. The four of us were standing off to the side, and while Jamal looked excited as he tried to tie a bandana around his face to conceal his identity, Chops and Hakim looked less at ease than they usually did. "Let's go motherfuckers! Get your shit on! It's time for us to represent the hood!" shouted an eager Jamal. Some of the other young men around us also encouraged them to take part, with one of them – Mikey – urging Hakim to "Stop being a little bitch and support your boy!" "This is some fucking bullshit. These mandem [men] are making me get involved in their bullshit. Fuck this shit, it ain't supposed to be like this," Chops whispered to me. When Chops told me "it ain't supposed to be like this", he was referring to the fact that as a hustler, he should be able to "move quietly" and focus on hustling, instead of feeling compelled to "get involved in their bullshit" – the internet banging that occurs once these music videos are shared online.

Despite Chops' and Hakim's unwillingness to feature in the music video, they ended up reluctantly taking part; augmenting the larger group of men standing behind Randy as he rapped to his newest song that was playing from large speakers. Though they tried to hide their identities by wearing their hoodies, sunglasses, and bandanas wrapped around their faces, they were still relatively identifiable. This was not the first time that Chops appeared in a music video that he claimed to want no part of (Urbanik and Haggerty 2018). Chops and Hakim predominantly identify as "hustlers," and I've witnessed them continuously try to refrain from the violent aspect of gang life. Yet, in the music video filmed that night, if a distinction between "hustlers" and "gangbangers" existed at all, it was nominal. In that moment, I witnessed how my participants who wanted no part in broader neighborhood beefs and who prided themselves on their ability to stay out of them, or even squash them, were pressured into featuring front and center in the violent posturing of Randy's music video. Hence, it is clear that when other gang members film music videos in the neighborhood, even hustlers who have children and other "shit to live for" and who might be trying to distance themselves from the violence and/or police attention, are expected to support their Rich Riderz brothers Such examinations reveal how the borders and expectations within – but also between – gangs are "continuously negotiated, clarified, reconstructed, and contested" (Conquergood 1992, 240).

Appearing in such music videos obfuscated Chops' and Hakim's roles as hustlers since they understood that such participation could implicate them in neighborhood and gang beefs, beefs that they could have otherwise largely (though not entirely) circumvented. For example, in a conversation with Andre, he mentioned how his appearance in a music video complicated his life: "People are looking for me. I don't know about these guys, but they want something to do with me. I laugh at it cause I don't even see these kids but they know who I am. So that's what's scary." Though Andre referenced laughing at this situation, that was more an attempt at showcasing his bravado, which he then contradicts when he mentions that these unknown individuals are "scary." Many of my other participants, including Chops and Hakim, were well aware of the risks associated with diverging from their roles and engaging in widely broadcast internet banging, yet felt increasing pressure to partake in such activities because of how important signaling "gang-ness" online has become in some gang-related milieus in Toronto.

"You gotta deal with it": changing retaliation?

Another critical way that social media has affected gang dynamics is through the speed and scope that affronts, threats, and posturing are shared online. Social media has significantly expedited and broadened the dissemination of antagonistic messages and interactions; insults and threats can now travel further and significantly faster than they used to, which has significantly raised the stakes for gang-involved individuals. For my participants, social media's ability to propel and broadcast such beefs has amplifies the offence and the pressure to respond. As J-Dawg said (26 yrs.), when someone disses you online,

> It burns [hurts/embarrasses] way more. Like before, if someone dissed you or your crew, maybe like 10, 20 people would hear about it. But some nigga disses you online and now boom, people from all over the city, fuck, all the world even can hear about. Instead of 10

people knowin you got dissed, or you got robbed, now thousands of people might know. And they might know within a couple hours! So like, you gotta deal with it.

J-Dawg was clearly concerned about how significantly social media increased the velocity and reach of disrespect in Toronto's street culture and how this has intensified the expectation to "deal with" the disrespect via retaliatory violence or vengeful internet banging.

In following my participants on social media, I have witnessed many such beefs proliferate across various online platforms. Oftentimes, my participants instigated antagonistic exchanges or broadcast threats and insults directed at a rival group or neighborhood. Other times, they were the ones "losing face" because of something a rival had posted – including one inflammatory instance when a rival gang robbed one of the neighborhood men of his trademark gold chain and then proudly flaunted his chain in their newest music video. However, one incident in particular was a disturbing exemplar of how social media has changed expectations placed on "hustlers" to retaliate against insults shared online.

That summer, a young neighborhood boy (16 yrs.) was shot and killed for reasons that remain unknown. He was well loved by many neighborhood residents, including by my participants with whom he associated. Following his murder, several young men from the neighborhood released a rap song and accompanying music video to commemorate his life and grieve his untimely death. Though scholars have documented that social media has changed the grieving process for many individuals (Brubaker et al. 2012; Gibbs et al. 2014), my research suggests that for gang-involved individuals, expressing grief through the production and sharing of honorary videos online is a distinctive process which can have serious and even fatal consequences for grief-stricken young men. Though the emotional experience of gangs is often either forgotten or willfully ignored (Van Hellemont and Mills 2019, 10), ethnographic studies are often uniquely placed to draw and analyze these emotional experiences, which my data highlights. For example, while this music video was intended to be way to memorialize the young boy, several of the men in the video are depicted shooting at the camera with their fingers, a common yet symbolic feature of expressing gang-ness and the willingness to retaliate violently. In this video, the young men's grief was interwoven with demonstrations of gang power, producing drugs in trap houses, and having conspicuous sums of money. References to violent shootouts were specifically designed to intimidate the boy's killer(s) and their affiliates. Hence, like many such videos, this montage served an additional function: it was intended to increase the group's "street cred" and "save face" – as Tyson (35 yrs.) tells me – after "the group took a L (loss)" when one of their own was killed.

This mentality is of course intimately related to the "street code" (Anderson 1999) that operates in Regent Park and many disadvantaged neighborhoods like it. The street code encourages and even sometimes necessitates the threat and/or use of violence for individuals and groups to gain/maintain respect and therefore deter future disrespect and victimization. For my participants, the street code operated as a normative force that shaped most of their daily self-presentations and behaviors, including the grieving process. In a late-night conversation, Hakim explained how social media has changed the mourning process for street-involved individuals: "instead of grieving, now it breeds more violence."

However, social media's effect on grieving extends beyond how deaths are memorialized online. During my fieldwork, I experienced how grief – when broadcast online – increased the pressure to retaliate against the suspected killers. Shortly after the commemorative music video circulated across multiple social media platforms and had already garnered over 40,000 views, a young man who featured in the video shared a screenshot of an insult directed at the group from a rival gang in response to the music video. The rival group was "calling out" [provoking/

insulting] the men for wasting time making rap videos instead of avenging their friend's murder and questioned their ability and willingness to retaliate. As was undoubtedly intended, this
post rattled and infuriated several of my participants, who claimed that they now had to "deal
with" the situation to save face and prevent future disrespect to the group. Though reputation
management is not unique to gang members, it is especially important for them (McGloin and
Collins 2015), and "fear of losing face or the social death of erasure equals and sometimes over-
rides the real physical dangers of the streets" (Conquergood 1992, 244). Hence, I feared the
aftermath of this exchange.

One of the most confusing and troubling aspects of this situation was that several of my participants – like me – first encountered this provocative message not via its original poster (a rival)
but via a group member, Wayne (17 yrs.), who shared it on his own social media profile. I was
perplexed by why this young man effectively distributed an insult directed at himself and his
group to a much broader audience. It seemed nonsensical. Why one would one broadcast – and
consequently amplify – scathing disrespect to one's group? Later that week, in a conversation
with Lemarcus (19 yrs.) and Hakim, they acknowledged that they were upset that Wayne had
shared the post. Lemarcus said: "Yo, the fact that he [Wayne] shared that is fucked up! We know
what he was doin' with that. He wanted to put the pressure on us to deal with it." I asked him
what he meant, and he replied

> Even from the jump [soon after the homicide], he wanted us to go after them. And yo,
> I get it. After we shot the video, he was bent [upset] that we hadn't dealt with it [the homi-
> cide]. So he saw that nigga's post and bam! He knew if he put it out there for everyone to
> see, we would have to deal with ASAP, you know?

Hakim added,

> It's not like we was just gonna let it slide [ignore it]. Naw. But like, now that he put that
> shit out in the streets like that [shared the post online], he's making it seem like we all
> gotta bang 'em out. But it shouldn't be like that. Some of us had nothin' to do with the
> original beef. Nothing! We just lay low and try to make this paper [hustle]. I aint bout
> no gangbanging shit, for real. You see what I do. You ever seen me with a burner [gun]?
> Naw! But now? Yo, now WE [hustlers] almost have to fucking deal with. You know? It
> ain't supposed to be like that.

Here, Lemarcus and Hakim describe the intra-group tensions stemming from Wayne's sharing of the offensive image on his own page. Lemarcus and Hakim interpreted Wayne's behavior
as an effort to rally his fellow gang members, even the "hustlers," to avenge the young boy's
death. Although they participated in the music video, they did not see it as their role to "settle
the score" and were frustrated that Wayne was essentially compelled them to. These backstage
tensions highlight that "gangs need to be understood as large systems of multiple embedded
and mutually implicated units, each one impinging and shaping the contours of experiences
for all others" (Conquergood 1992, 235). Wanye's broadcasting of the insult notably magnified
the audience which in turn magnified the 'need' to respond. This situation reveals that not
only can social media instigate conflict *between* groups but, as seen through Wayne's behaviors,
can also provoke *one's own group members* to turn to violence. Again, we see how social media
dynamics are collapsing established and relatively distinct roles where certain group members
can largely refrain from violence into one – the role of the gangbanger. Previous research has
documented how relations between gang members can have a notable precipitory and even

determinative influence on violence and aggression against rivals, often motivated by efforts of status re-equilibration (Short and Strodtbeck 1963). Though new media gang scholars have yet to meaningfully unpack group processes online, it is clear that the *group processes* underpinning "online and offline environs are mutually constituted and evolve in tandem" (Urbanik and Haggerty 2018, 1357).

This situation is further indicative of how "the social experience of the individual is first and foremost constrained by the external boundary maintained by the group against outsiders" (Douglas 1982, 205; as cited in Conquergood 1992). By broadcasting the offence as widely as he did, Wayne purposefully magnified the disrespect aimed at his group, knowing that circulating the insult to his several thousand social media followers would fan the flames, thereby almost necessitating the group's violence response. It also highlights that when examining the minutiae of everyday social interactions and exchanges, gang life is characterized more by dynamic contest and struggle than static and uncontested hierarchies and roles (Conquergood 1992, 240). Though Wayne may have been motivated by the desire to avenge his friend's murder, his hopes that he could mobilize the Rich Riderz to respond to the insult with violence could have also been influenced by the street code's primary tenet: disrespect and victimization should be met with violence so as to avert future victimization (Anderson 1999).

Hence, gang scholars must remain conscious that what they may 'see' online – in the front stage – is shaped by, and in turn affects, the back stage of inter- and intra-gang dynamics (Goffman 1959). Though it may be tempting to accept what we witness online as 'real,' ethnographers of the physical and digital streets should be skeptical when their data uncovers "too much consistency, too much constancy, too little contradiction, and too high definition of account" (Young 2011, 133; see also Brotherton 2015, 40), given that the social is laden with paradoxes and complexities. While these nuances may be hidden, as highlighted previously, they may be particularly consequential in intra- and even inter-gang dynamics, and overlooking these enigmas can lead us to misunderstand and therefore misrepresent what we see. These risks may be particularly prevalent for those who limit their study of the digital streets to online gang artifacts without triangulating online portrayals with spending time with and speaking to producers of gang-related digital content (Stuart 2020; Urbanik and Roks 2020; Urbanik et al. 2020).

Cautions about inferring data from digital bravado

Much of the focus examining the role social media plays in gang dynamics has placed emphasis on the alleged positivistic connection between online performance and offline gang behaviours – and specifically violence. Though this may be the case in *some* field sites, with *some* participants, in *some* situations, it remains unclear whether this 'amplification' factor is broadly generalizable, especially in light of recent ethnographic studies which cast doubt on this claim (Stuart 2020). This assumption is also dangerous in the sense that it can cause additional harm to members of our most marginalized and racialized communities. By asserting a definite and unquestionable connection between the digital bravado of 'gang-involved' individuals and offline violence, scholars may be inadvertently legitimizing or encouraging criminal justice system actors in their conflation of presentations as reflections of reality. Law enforcement agencies already uncritically mine social media to gather 'intelligence' on criminal activities, including 'evidence on gang membership, allegiances, beefs, and violent episodes (Brayne 2017; Ferguson 2017). In New York, for example, the NYPD gang task force mobilized social media postings as 'evidence' of gang affiliation, individual culpability, and violent collective enterprise in a RICO case, extending the digital content of 14 individuals as 'evidence' against 120 defendants (Howell and Bustamante 2019). The dizzying quantity of social media content can become overwhelming for defense council, as Howell and Bustamante (2019, 8) highlight in their critical analysis, "In a world of social media posting, Facebook braggadocio, Instagram likes, Snapchat stories, and YouTube videos all provide fodder that allows statements of alleged 'co-conspirators' to be used without the benefit of cross-examination."

Do *some* interactions on social media result in real-life conflict? Certainly. Do some gang-involved individuals fear the violent repercussions of social media beefs? Yes. However, it is likely that the vast majority of social media interactions do not result in real-world violence (Stuart 2020). Any new media scholar who has examined gang interactions (and even artifacts) online can attest to the exorbitant amount of content that many gangs produce. For *some* of these groups (including my own participants), the majority of their content revolves around digital bravado, reproducing the street code, and explicitly or implicitly threatening/challenging/dissing rivals. If *all* or even *most* of these behaviours manifested in real-world violence, my participants would be so preoccupied with physically responding to the dizzying pace of their rivals' antagonistic posts and simultaneously avoiding retaliatory violence stemming from their own posts that they would have little time to update their social media profiles.

Hence, claims relating to digital 'evidence' of gang and criminal involvement will likely disproportionally disadvantage our marginalized and racialized communities, with law enforcement re-appropriating social media as yet another tool for racial profiling and over-policing marginalized communities. This is especially concerning given that presenting as a 'gangster' has become increasingly commodified; gang fashions and styles of dress have become re-appropriated from a form of resistance to a mainstream signal of 'coolness' even for those who may have no substantive connections to gangs whatsoever (see Brotherton 2015; Kontos and Brotherton 2008). Not only are such presentations reproduced online, but 'gang-like' digital exchanges – however we conceptualize these – may also be appropriated. Social media platforms may be the newest site of over-policing and hyper-surveillance; in addition to police saturating the 'ghetto', the 'hood', the favela, the 'slum,' policing initiatives are increasingly saturating digital territories as well. This form of "gang talk" is not only problematic from a definitional or constructionist standpoint but also results in negative, tangible, and notable consequences for those subjected to these misrepresentations (Hallsworth and Young 2008; Young and Brotherton 2014).

Further, if scholars examine social media only through the lens of crime and violence, they risk overlooking the everyday, non-sensationalized interactions of gang members, even though studies have noted that street-involved persons also make use of the internet in similar ways to non–gang-involved peers (Lane 2018; Moule et al. 2014). This chapter predominantly focused on deviance-based exchanges given these made up the bulk of my participants' digital content. However, such interactions and presentations should not also be considered universally generalizable to the online behaviors of all gang members, nor should they be considered autonomously separate from the context and characteristics of those involved (Brotherton 2015; Young 2011).

Conclusion

Though gang scholars have devoted significant attention in recent years to how social media has altered interactions *between* gangs, we should also critically contemplate how social media has transformed interactions and social organization *within* gangs. Existing research reveals that a gang's social organization can change for several reasons, stemming from the arrest of a gang leader or core players, to neighborhood redevelopment, to corporatization (Brotherton and Barrios 2004; Urbanik et al. 2017; Vargas 2014; Venkatesh 2002). Such changes have not only affected levels and nature of intergroup violence but also the relationships, positions, and perceptions of safety within the neighborhoods that gangs occupy. My research demonstrates that social media dynamics can significantly affect a gang's social organization, specifically by pressuring generally non-violent gang members to participate in "internet banging." In this sense, social media – and its subsequent effects on the rap game and neighborhood beefs – complicate the previous organizations of many street gangs and highlight the nuances of offline and online group member relations. No longer can certain gang members generally avoid the consequences of online feuds; like my participants, they may face increasing pressure to "roll for their group" online, just as much or even more than they do on the streets.

Undoubtedly, social media has magnified the visibility of many individuals and groups, including populations that have traditionally been difficult to access. In the same way that many individuals – especially youth – might feel like they *have* to have an online presence for social or professional reasons (Beyens et al. 2016; boyd 2014; Burke and Kraut 2013), my research finds that gang-involved men experience similar pressures. What is particularly notable here, however, is that for gang-involved men, this online presence is intimately related to performances of "gang-ness," which, when broadcast to vast and unknown audiences, can sometimes have fatal consequences. These pressures may supersede the risks associated with "internet banging," even for gang members who endeavor to refrain from participating in this new gang milieu, and the volatility and dynamism of social media complicate the experience of gang members (Urbanik and Haggerty 2018). Hence, though it is important that gang scholars studying the intersection of the physical streets with the "digital street" (Lane 2016, 2018) focus their attention to those directly involved in the production of social media postings and/or music videos that promote gang culture and beefs, our analyses should not stop there. Scholars should not merely draw a hard line between those who are directly implicated in "gang banging" and those who are not; in many disadvantaged neighborhoods, such as in Regent Park, such clear separations may be difficult – or even futile – to draw.

Future research should interrogate how the rise of social media usage among gang members has changed gang structures and intra-gang dynamics. Our understandings of the lived realities of gang members can be significantly augmented by a closer analysis of how social media has altered the roles and expectations surrounding retaliatory gang violence. While 'snippets' of data such can serve as a caricature of how gang and street-involved individuals are experiencing the digital street, we should be cautious not to present these as occurring "on an empty stage upon which the actors – police and drug dealers – appear out of nowhere" (Young 2011, 14). What we are largely missing at the present is a rich and nuanced work which not only does greater justice to our participants' placement in the social structure but which also examines how our own positionality as researchers – our class, gender, race, age – affects what we absorb, reflect, and/or participate in online, where the researcher becomes 'invisible' (c.f.; Lane 2018; see also Brotherton 2015; Young 2011). As our predispositions and positions can affect and guide our research and what we share, we should consider how these interactions are affected by class and political economy instead of predominantly focusing on the "chosen pathway of the individual and the ever-troubling prevalence of criminal transgressions by the most naturally criminogenic lower orders predictably found in the same criminogenic environments" (Brotherton 2015, 43).

Notes

1 With the notable exception of incarceration rates of Indigenous peoples.
2 One dated study of police agencies in 2002, found that at the time, Canadian police identified 484 different youth gangs within the country (Chettleburgh 2003). This number paled in comparison to the estimated 21,800 gangs in the United States that same year (National Gang Center 2017).

3 Characterized as such when law enforcement "confirm or suspect that the accused person and/or victim involved in the homicide was either a member, or a prospective member, of an organized crime group or street gang or was somehow associated with an organized crime group or street gang, and the homicide was carried out as a result of this association" (Beattie et al. 2018).
4 Over the years, I have spent my time with a group of about 25 men between 18 and 46 years old, though about half of the make-up of this group has varied from year to year, given that some of my original participants have been killed, others were in and out of jail, some were legally banned from the neighborhood, and others were forced to relocate as a result of the revitalization.
5 Names of neighborhood gangs and participants are pseudonyms. Biographical details such as ages have been changed to further protect my participants' identities.

References

Anderson, Elijah. *Code of the Street: Decency, Violence, and the Moral Life of the Inner City*. (1999). New York: W.W. Norton and Co.

Beattie, Sara, Jean-Denis David, and Joel Roy. "Homicide in Canada, 2017." *Statistics Canada*. (November 21, 2018). https://www150.statcan.gc.ca/n1/pub/85-002-x/2018001/article/54980-eng.htm.

Berardi, Luca. "*Shots Fired: Experiences of Gun Violence and Victimization in Toronto Social Housing*." PhD dissertation, University of Alberta (2018).

Best, J. *Damned Lies and Statistics: Untangling Numbers from the Media, Politicians, and Activists*. (2001). Berkeley, CA: University of California Press.

Beyens Ine, Eline Frison, and Steven Eggermont. "'I Don't Want to Miss a Thing': Adolescents' Fear of Missing Out and Its Relationship to Adolescents' Social Needs, Facebook Use, and Facebook Related Stress." *Comput Human Behav*, 64 (November 2016): 1–8. Elsevier.

Blandfort, Philipp, Desmond U. Patton, William R. Frey, Svebor Karaman, Surabhi Bhargava, Fei-Tzin Lee, Siddharth Varia, et al. "Multimodal Social Media Analysis for Gang Violence Prevention." *arXiv preprint arXiv:1807.08465* (July 23, 2018). Cornell University.

Blevins, Terra, Robert Kwiatkowski, Jamie MacBeth, Kathleen McKeown, Desmond U. Patton, and Owen Rambow. "Automatically Processing Tweets from Gang-Involved Youth." *Proceedings of the 26th International Conference on Computational Linguistics* (December 2016): 2196–2206. Osaka, Japan: The COLING 2016 Organizing Committee.

Bourgois, Phillipe. 1996. *In Search of Respect: Selling Crack in El Barrio*. Vol. 10. (2003). Cambridge, UK: Cambridge University Press.

boyd, danah. *It's Complicated: The Social Lives of Networked Teens*. (2014). New Haven, CT: Yale University Press.

Brayne, Sarah. "Big Data Surveillance: The Case of Policing." *American Sociological Review*, 82, 5. (2017): 977–1008.

Brotherton, David. *Youth Street Gangs: A Critical Appraisal*. (2015). New York: Routledge.

Brotherton, David, and Luis Barrios. *The Almighty Latin King and Queen Nation: Street Politics and the Transformation of a New York City Gang*. (2004). New York: Columbia University Press.

Brubaker, Jed R., Funda Kivran-Swaine, Lee Taber, and Gillian R. Hayes. "Grief-Stricken in a Crowd: The Language of Bereavement and Distress in Social Media." *Proceedings of the Sixth International AAAI Conference on Weblogs and Social Media*. (2012): 42–49. Association for the Advancement of Artificial Intelligence.

Burke, Moira, and Robert Kraut. "Using Facebook After Losing a Job: Differential Benefits of Strong and Weak Ties. *Proceedings of the 2013 Conference on Computer Supported Cooperative Work (CSCW '13)*. (2013): 1419–1430. New York, NY: ACM Press.

Chettleburgh, Michael, C. "The 2002 Canadian Police Survey on Youth Gangs (Cat no. PS4/4–2002)." *Public Safety and Emergency Preparedness Canada*. (2003). Ottawa, ON: Astwood Strategy Corporation.

Chettleburgh, Michael, C. *Young Thugs: Inside the Dangerous World of Canadian Street Gangs*. (2007). Ontario, ON: HarperCollins Canada.

Contreras, Randol. *The Stickup Kids: Race, Drugs, Violence, and the American Dream*. Berkeley: University of California Press. (2013).

Conquergood, Dwight. "Homeboys and Hoods: Gang Communication and Cultural Space." In *Group Communication in Context: Studies of Natural Groups*, L. R. Frey (Ed.) (1992): 224–260. Hillsdale, NJ: Lawrence Erlbaum Associates.

Davis, Stephen Spencer, and Timothy Appleby. "Residents of Toronto Public Housing Four Times More Likely to be Murder Victims." *The Globe and Mail* (June 3, 2011).

Decker, Scott H., and C. David. Pyrooz. *Leaving the Gang, Logging off and Moving on.* (2011). New York: Council on Foreign Relations.

Densley, James A. "The Organization of London's Street Gangs." *Global Crime*, 13. (2012): 42–64.

Deuchar, Ross, and Chris Holligan. "Gangs, Sectarianism, and Social Capital." *Sociology*, 44 (2010): 13–30.

Ferguson, Andrew Gurthrie. *The Rise of Big Data Policing: Surveillance, Race, and the Future of Law Enforcement.* (2017). New York: New York University Press.

Freeze Colin. "At Toronto Community Housing, a History of Violence." *The Globe and Mail.* (2014). www.theglobeandmail.com/news/toronto/toronto-community-housings-history-of-violence/article16908806/. Accessed 10 January 2018.

Geertz, Clifford. "Deep Hanging Out." *The New York Review of Books,* 45, 16. (1998): 69–72.

Gibbs, Martin, James Meese, Michael Arnold, Bjorn Nansen, Marcus Carter. "#Funeral and Instagram: Death, Social Media, and Platform Vernacular." *Information, Communication & Society,* 18, 3. (2014): 255–268.

Goffman, Erving. *The Presentation of Self in Everyday Life.* (1959). London: Penguin.

The Globe and Mail. "Residents of Toronto Public Housing Four Times More Likely to Be Murder Victims." (2011). www.theglobeandmail.com/news/toronto/residents-of-toronto-public-housing-four-times-more-likely-to-be-murder-victims/article586043/. Accessed 10 January 2018.

Grekul, Jana and Patti LaBoucane-Benson. "Aboriginal Gangs and their (Dis)placement: Contextualizing Recruitment, Membership, and Status." *Canadian Journal of Criminology and Criminal Justice*, 50, 1. (2008): 59–82.

Griffiths, Mark, Daria J. Kuss, and Zsolt Demetrovics. "Social Networking Addiction: An Overview of Preliminary Findings." *Behavioral addictions: Criteria, Evidence, and Treatment.* (2014): 119–141. London: Academic Press.

Hallsworth, S. and T. Young. "Gang Talk and Gang Talkers: A Critique." *Crime, Media, Culture.* (2008): 4(2): 175–195.

Hannerz, Ulf. *Soulside: Inquiries into Ghetto Culture and Community.* (1969). Chicago: University of Chicago Press.

Hayward, K. *City Limits: Crime, Consumer Culture and the Urban Experience.* (2004). London: Glasshouse Press.

Horak, Martin, and O. N. London. "Understanding Neighbourhood Revitalization in Toronto. Neighbourhoods." *Panel at Canadian Political Science Association 2010 Annual Meeting, Montreal.* (2010): 1–22.

Howell, Babe and Priscilla, Bustamante. "Report on the Bronx 120 Mass 'Gang' Prosecution." (2019). https://static1.squarespace.com/static/5caf6f4fb7c92ca13c9903e3/t/5cf914a3db738b00010598b8/1559827620344/Bronx%2B120%2BReport.pdf.

Ilan, J. *Understanding Street Culture: Poverty, Crime, Youth and Cool.* (2015). London: Palgrave Macmillan.

Jacobs, Bruce A., and Richard Wright. *Street Justice: Retaliation in the Criminal Underworld.* (2006). New York: Cambridge University Press.

Johnson, J.D., and N. Schell-Busey. "Old Message in a New Bottle: Taking Gang Rivalries Online Through Rap Battle Music Videos on YouTube." *Journal of Qualitative Criminal Justice & Criminology,* 4, 1. (2016): 42–81.

Kontos, L., and D. Brotherton. *Encyclopedia of Gangs.* (2008). New Haven, CT.: Greenwood Press.

Lane, Jeffrey. "The Digital Street: An Ethnographic Study of Networked Street Life in Harlem." *American Behavioral Scientist*, 60, 1. (2016): 43–58.

Lane, Jeffrey. *The Digital Street.* (2018). New York: Oxford University Press.

Lauger, T., J. Densley, and R. Moule. Social Media, Strain, and Technologically-Facilitated Gang Violence. In *The Palgrave Handbook of International Cybercrime and Cyberdeviance*, A. Bossler and T. Holt (Eds.) (2019): 1376–1395. Cham, Switzerland: Palgrave Macmillan.

Lindgren, April. "News, Geography and Disadvantage: Mapping Newspaper Coverage of High-Needs Neighborhoods in Toronto, Canada." *Canadian Journal of Urban Research*, 18, 1. (2009): 74–97.

McGloin, Jean M., and Megan E. Collins. "Micro-Level Processes of the Gang." In *The Handbook of Gangs*, S.H. Decker and D.C. Pyrooz (Eds.) (2015): 276–293. New York: Wiley.

Moule Jr, Richard K., David C. Pyrooz, and Scott H. Decker. "Internet Adoption and Online Behaviour Among American Street Gangs: Integrating Gangs and Organizational Theory." *British Journal of Criminology* 54, 6. (2014): 1186–1206.

National Gang Center. National Youth Gang Survey Analysis. (2017). www.nationalgangcenter.gov/Survey-Analysis. Accessed 17 June 2017.

O'Grady, William, Patrick F. Parnaby, and Justin Schikschneit. "Guns, Gangs, and the Underclass: A Constructionist Analysis of Gun Violence in a Toronto High School." *Canadian Journal of Criminology and Criminal Justice*, 52, 21. (2010): 55–77.

Patton, Desmond U., Robert D. Eschmann, and Dirk A. Butler. "Internet Banging: New Trends in Social Media, Gang Violence, Masculinity and Hip Hop." *Computers in Human Behavior*, 29, 5. (2013): A54–A59.

Patton, Desmond U., Jeffery Lane, Patrick Leonard, and Jocelyn R. Smith Lee. "Gang Violence on the Digital Street: Case Study of a South Side Chicago Gang Member's Twitter Communication." *New Media & Society*, 19, 7. (2017): 1000–1018.

Patton, Desmond U., David Pyrooz, Scott Decker, William R. Frey, and Patrick Leonard. "When Twitter Fingers Turn to Trigger Fingers: A Qualitative Study of Social Media-Related Gang Violence." *International Journal of Bullying Prevention*. (2019): 1–13.

Public Safety Canada, Gun and Gang Violence. (2019). www.publicsafety.gc.ca/cnt/cntrng-crm/gn-crm-frrms/index-en.aspx.

Purdy, Sean. ""Ripped off" by the System: Housing Policy, Poverty, and Territorial Stigmatization in Regent Park Housing Project, 1951–1991." *Labour/Le Travail*, 52. (2003): 45–108.

Pyrooz, David C., Scott H. Decker, and Richard K. Moule Jr. "Criminal and Routine Activities in Online Settings." *Justice Quarterly*, 32, 3. (2015): 471–499.

Roks, Robert A. "In the 'H200d': Crips and the Intersection between Space and Identity in the Netherlands." *Crime, Media, Culture*, 15, 1. (2017): 3-23.

Rogers, Kenneth H. *Street Gangs in Toronto: A Study of the Forgotten Boy.* (1945). Toronto: Ryerson Press.

Ryan, Tracii, Andrea Chester, John Reece, and Sophia Xenos. "The Uses and Abuses of Facebook: A Review of Facebook Addiction." *Journal of Behavioral Addictions*, 3. (2014): 133–148.

Sharp, P., J. Aldridge, and J. Medina. "Delinquent Youth Groups and Offending Behaviour: Findings from the 2004 Offending, Crime and Justice Survey." (2006). Home Office Online Report.

Short, James F., Jr., and Fred L. Strodtbeck. "The Response of Gang Leaders to Status Threats: An Observation on Group Process and Delinquent Behavior." *American Journal of Sociology.* 68. (1963): 571–579.

Skogan, Wesley. "The Validity of Official Crime Statistics: An Empirical Investigation." *Social Science Quarterly*, 55. (1974): 25–38.

Storrod, Michelle L. and James A. Densley. "'Going Viral' and 'Going Country': The Expressive and Instrumental Activities of Street Gangs on Social Media." *Journal of Youth Studies*, 20, 6. (2017): 677–669.

Stuart, Forrest. "Code of the Tweet: Urban Gang Violence in the Social Media Age." *Social Problems*, 67, 2. (2020): 191–207.

Thompson, Sara Kerr. "The Social Ecology and Spatial Distribution of Lethal Violence in Toronto, 1988–2003." Doctoral dissertation, Toronto: University of Toronto. (2009).

Toronto Community Housing Corporation [TCHC]. "Regent Park Social Development Plan." (2007). www.torontohousing.ca/webfm_send/4213/1.

Urbanik, Marta-Marika. "Drawing Boundaries or Drawing Weapons? Neighborhood Master Status as Suppressor of Gang Violence." *Qualitative Sociology*, 41, 4. (2018): 497–519.

Urbanik, Marta-Marika, and Kevin D. Haggerty. "#It's Dangerous: The Online World of Drug Dealers, Rappers, and the Street Code." *British Journal of Criminology*, 58, 6. (2018): 1343–1360.

Urbanik, Marta-Marika, Sara K. Thompson, and Sandra M. Bucerius. "'Before There Was Danger But There Was Rules. And Safety in Those Rules.' Effects of Neighbourhood Redevelopment on Criminal Structures." *British Journal of Criminology*, 57, 2. (2017): 422–440.

Urbanik, Marta-Marika and Robert A. Roks. "GangstaLife: Fusing Urban Ethnography with Netnography in Gang Studies." *Qualitative Sociology*, 43 (2020): 213–233.

Urbanik, Marta-Marika, Robert A. Roks, Michelle Lyttle Storrod, and James Densley. "Ethical and Methodological Issues in Gang Ethnography in the Digital Age: Lessons from Four Studies in an Emerging Field." In *Gangs in the Era of Internet and Social Media*, C. Melde and F. Weerman (Eds.) (2020). Cham: Switzerland: Springer.

Van Hellemont, E. "Gangland Online: Performing the Real Imaginary World of Gangstas and Ghettos in Brussels." *European Journal of Crime, Criminal Law and Criminal Justice*, 20. (2012): 159–173.

Van Hellemont, E. "Legalization by Commodification: The (Ir) relevance of Fashion Styles and Brands in Street Gangster Performance." *Outlaw Motorcycle Clubs and Street Gangs: Scheming Legality, Resisting Criminalization* (2018): 45–68.

Van Hellemont, E. and M. Mills. "Cultural Criminology and Gangs: Street Elitism and Politics in Late Modernity." In *International Handbook of Critical Gang Studies*, David Brotherton and Rafael Gude (Eds.) (2019). New York: Routledge.

Vargas, Robert. "Criminal Group Embeddedness and the Adverse Effects of Arresting a Gang's Leader: A Comparative Case Study." *Criminology*, 52, 2. (2014): 143–168.

Venkatesh, Sudhir Alladi. *American Project: The Rise and Fall of a Modern Ghetto*. (2002). Cambridge: Harvard University Press.

Wacquant, Loïc. "Deadly Symbiosis: When Ghetto and Prison Meet and Mesh." *Punishment and Society*, 3, 1. (2001): 95–133.

Warmington, Joe. "Regent Park Revitalization Hasn't Changed Everything." *Toronto Sun*. (February 6, 2013). https://torontosun.com/2013/02/06/regent-park-revitalization-hasnt-changed-everything.

Wilson, William J. *The Truly Disadvantaged: The Inner City, the Underclass, and Public Policy*. (1987). Chicago: University of Chicago Press.

Young, J. *The Criminological Imagination*. (2011). Cambridge: Polity Press.

Young, J. and D. C. Brotherton. "Cultural Criminology and Its Practices: A Dialog Between the Theorist and the Street Researcher." *Dialectical Anthropology*, 38, 2. (2014): 117–132.

Part VI
Contexts and spaces

43

Prison gangs in the Northern Triangle

The critical contribution of prison studies to the theory of gangs

Michele Miravalle

Summary

1   *Triangulo Norte and mass incarceration. The contribution of prison studies*
2   *Prisons, maras and pandillas: a brief history of a strong relationship*
3   *The osmosis between street culture and prison culture. the untouched gangsters' habitus*
4   *The aim of prisons. the aim of gangs*
5   *Conclusion. the resistance within the wall*

The role of incarceration in a gangster's "biography" is well epitomised by a recurrent tattoo. It is the first symbol shown by Johnathan, a 16-year-old leader of *Calle 18*, detained in the big urban prison of *Gaviota* in Guatemala City.

Three black dots on his left hand, forming a triangle: they represent the only possible final destinations for gang members: hospital, cemetery or prison. No alternatives allowed. The three dots are there to remind one that gang affiliation is an ultimate choice.

The interview with Jonathan was my first individual with a gang leader, and I would soon understand how to deepen the topic of *Maras y Pandillas* (the common name of the gangs in Central-America) within the so-called *Triangolo Norte* (the area of Central America formed by El Salvador, Guatemala and Honduras). I chose the deprivation of liberty in prison as a privileged point of view.[1]

This research moves from the assumption that street and prison are becoming synonymous environments within the contemporary societies. As suggested by Wacquant (2001), prison and urban ghetto have meshed into a "carceral continuum" whereby the two institutions resemble each other, forming the so-called *hyper-ghetto* (Wacquant, 2010). But Wacquant's theory mainly applies to the Global North (North America, Europe and English-speaking countries), and it has rarely been applied in different contexts like Central America.

Therefore, the subject of this chapter is the incarceration of gangs in El Salvador, Guatemala and Honduras. Not prison gangs (Fleisher and Decker, 2001; Ortiz, 2015) but gangs in prison, which is slightly different, because it entails a forced relationship between two complex

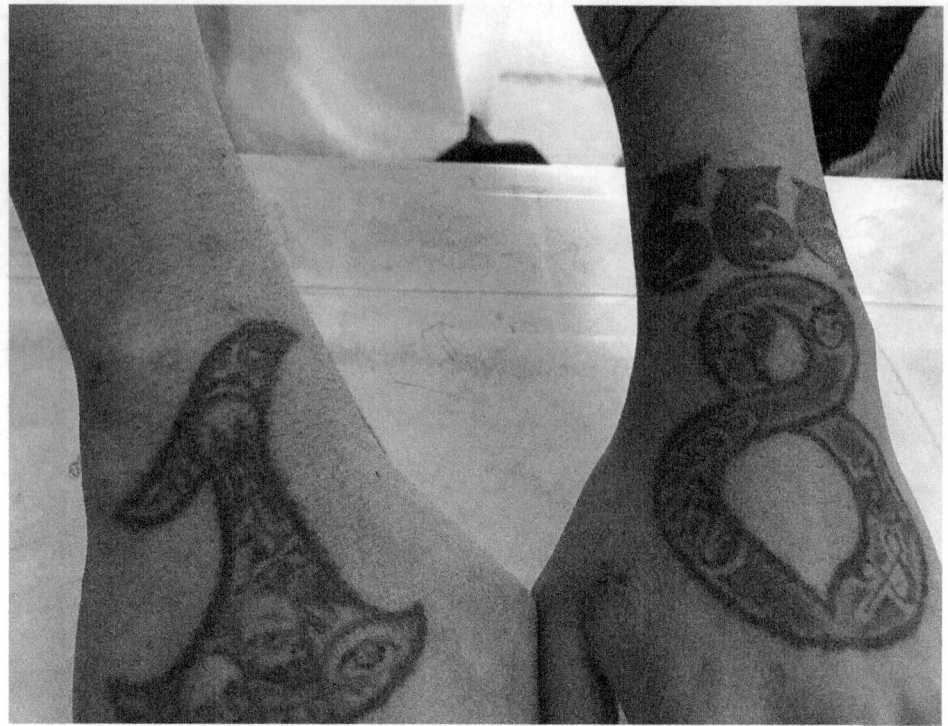

Image 43.1　Prison of *Gaviota*, Guatemala City. Black dots on the gangster's left hand

organisations, the State and its punitive apparatus on one side and the gangs, probably the most powerful non-state actor of Central America, on the other. I focused only on younger members who committed their crimes when they were minors, and for this reason, they are detained in juvenile prisons.

As noted by Fleisher and Decker, researchers "have only a rudimentary knowledge of prison gangs as social groups operating inside prisons and of the interplay between street gangs and prison gangs" (Fleisher and Decker, 2001, p. 2). The gang literature has mainly focused on street gangs while largely ignoring prison as a place where gangs "live", probably due to the traditional difficulty of empirically exploring fields of research like correctional facilities.

From a theoretical point of view, prisons for gang members are at the same time the main "technology of power" to discipline the phenomenon used by institutional actors – policy-makers and law enforcement agencies – (Foucault, 1977) and on the other side a strategic place to develop the gangs members' "careers deviance" (Becker, 1973). These are the hypotheses to be supported with empirical insights coming from the fieldwork. Following those two patterns, I will also suggest that critical criminology should strictly connect gang studies to prisons studies to improve new streams of research.

1　*Triangulo Norte* and mass incarceration. the contribution of prison studies

Within a society strongly influenced by the challenges arising from persistent security threats, crime is depicted as a generalised phenomenon, menacing citizens' daily life. In this culture of "liquid fear",[2] the criminal policy reflects the primacy (Cullen and Jonson, 2014) of a punitive and widespread use of punishment as the preferred way to organise the correctional system. Therefore, we cannot approach the study of prison and punishment without analysing the policy adopted by State.

Starting from the classical study carried out by Alexis de Tocqueville and Gustave du Beaumont (On the Penitentiary System in America and Its Applications in France, 1833) and with Emile Durkheim's first theory of punishment and social theory, it soon became clear that forms, functions and transformations of punishment were not only an instrument to react to criminality and individual deviance but an institution of power and social control, to be understood primarily in terms of its effects on the broader population and on governance. "The messages punishment communicates are aimed – not only – at criminals and potential criminals but at law-abiding citizens" (Garland, 2012).

In the 20th century, Rusche and Kirchheimer (1939) provided a first structured, critical social theory of punishment followed by a number of empirical studies that began exploring prisons as an enclosed society and as "technologies to exert power": starting from Clemmer (The Prison Community, 1940), who inspired a new sociological field of research that spread across the United States in the 1950s and 1960s (Sykes, Irwin, Goffman) and Europe in the 1960s and 1970s (Mathiesen, Christie, Cohen). The theory by Rusch and Kirchhemeir in the 1980s was further developed by Melossi and Pavarini in "Prison and The Factory" (1981), a milestone of the critical criminological approach to imprisonment. Also, Foucault criticised the traditional approach to punishment but from the institutional point of view. While Rusch and Kirchhemeir and Melossi and Pavarini focused on the economy of punishment and its relation with the labour market, Foucault was more concerned by the 'modern' relation between the institutional power and society, managed through prisons.

So, whatever the theoretical background (Foucaldians, Marxists, Eliasians, Weberians, Bourdieunians or neo-Durkheimians), scholars agree that punishment is a constituent aspect of a broader social process. Nevertheless, in the 1970s, something happened: the *mass incarceration era* began.

In 1972 in the United States, the number of inmates was 326,000: by 1975, this figure had soared to 380,000, doubling in the following decade, and it continued to increase at a 10% annual rate until the beginning of the new century, when the number of people incarcerated was in excess of 2 million (if we add people on parole and on probation, the figure reaches 7 million, 1 person of every 31 US citizens).[3]

This huge amount of people incarcerated or under penal control is the most concrete consequence of mass incarceration. But from United States, it soon became a transnational phenomenon, which can be explained by the following three streams of theories:

1   *Economical reasons* underlying the rise of neo-liberalism with imprisonment as a new way to manage poverty and unemployment. In this sense, see the famous "Punishing the Poor" by Loic Wacquant (2009);
2   *Political reasons*, mainly the failure of welfarism. In this sense, western societies are moving from *welfare* to *prisonfare* (De Giorgi, 2010);
3   *Penal populism* (Pratt, 2007; Simon, 2007), which is a phenomenon whereby the fear of crime has progressively become a tool to build political consensus. For many years, policymakers – independently of the ideologies and parties they represented – have started introducing "zero tolerance" policies, where a tough stance on crime – or other forms of social disorder and anti-social behaviours – is considered the best way to increase political approval ratings.

This trend contributed to separating to a certain extent the use of incarceration and criminality rates. A tendency that is typical of post-Fordism societies (De Giorgi, 2010), it basically consists of a massive use of penal control measures, especially imprisonment (Garland, 2001) that 'disciplines' increasingly large multi-ethnic communities and harsh economic recessions. As a consequence, welfare instruments based on social inclusion are being substituted by repressive policies, even if official statistics show that numbers of crimes committed are decreasing (McCrary and Sanga, 2012; Simon and Sparks, 2012; Matthews, 2009).

Whichever theory is the most convincing, *mass imprisonment* diverted the penal system from its official goals, proclaimed worldwide in many constitutions and bills of rights,[4] which are: to reduce recidivism rates (*deterrence*), to pursue the rehabilitation of offenders, to protect victims and to develop inclusive and sustainable instruments of social control. Mass imprisonment instead encourages the neutralisation of entire groups of the population deemed 'dangerous' or seen as 'public enemies'.

This interpretation of imprisonment is adaptable even to juvenile justice, even if numbers are lower. Beyond a paternalistic approach that blends education and punishment, when dealing with juvenile offenders, researchers (see Cramer Brooks & Roush, 2014; Weiss, 2013) have identified different waves of juvenile justice reform that show a connection with the evolving attitude towards young people in general and with fear of juvenile offenders in particular.

Juvenile offenders have often been treated without considering their age or needs, maintaining an unjustified "tough on crime" stance which worsens youth issues rather than helping to solve them or tackle structural problems. The main manifestation of this approach can be found between the 1980s and the 1990s, in correlation with the spreading of moral panic fomented by an "animalistic" vision of gang-related young people (Welch, 2002) and anxiety over ethnicity and class.

This "criminalization of youth" (Cox, 2018) has produced long-term damage in the current attitude towards juvenile delinquency and ways of aggregation, creating a mix between persistent strictness and a recent opening to mildness.

Within this theoretical framework, gangs' presence in prisons appears to be one of the most challenging issues. In the United States (Miller, 2001; Pyrooz et al., 2017), "gang members are overrepresented among incarcerated populations. About 200,000 of the 1.5 million U.S. inmates are affiliated with gangs" (Pyrooz, 2018, p. 10). Whether gang membership in prison represents only a "manifestation" of membership in the street (Oddone and Palmas, 2014) or juvenile institutionalisation actually favours the "origination" or at least the "intensification" of the affiliation is something that is going to be analysed further in this chapter.

But how does this insight apply to the peculiar area of research of the *Triangulo Norte*, just outside the so-called Global North (North America, Europe and English-speaking countries)?

What kind of effects have the policies applied to contrast the phenomenon of *maras* and *pandillas* had on quantitative and qualitative dimensions of the juvenile penitentiary system?

We have to consider if the "zero tolerance" doctrine also affected the *Triangulo Norte*. We can easily find a connection with the so-called *mano dura* and *súper mano dura* strategies, developed in Central and Latin American in the early 2000s (Cruz, 2011, 2016, Davis, 2006). Driven by moral panic campaigns (Cohen, 1972), gangs were soon identified as the main reason of the high level of violence in those countries.

The state of exception (Agamben, 2005) was institutionalised (Salazar Ugarte, 2012): *war, emergency, control, order* soon became the new buzzwords used by policy-makers to justify the introduction of new measures to contrast (exceptional?) phenomena like gangs.

This process of criminalisation is based on significant legal provisions adopted in the area.

Guatemala in 2015 reduced the minimum age for criminal responsibility (at the time, president Otto Pérez Molina campaigned under the slogan "*Mano dura, cabeza y corazón*" – "Firm hand, head and heart" – advocating an hard-line approach to rising crime in the country.

In El Salvador, the decision of the *Tribunal Constitucional* was enacted on 24 August 2015, which assimilated the *maras* and *pandillas* to terroristic organisation, applying from then onwards the *Ley Especial Contra Actos de terrorismo* (LECAT). Under the supervision of a special task force based in San Salvador, even the FBI helped Central American police forces in the coordination of law enforcement operations against gang members. This was probably a step forward towards criminalisation: this judicial decision constitutes a sort of "official" recognition of the power and dangerousness of gangs. From then on, *maras* y *pandillas* become by law a form of power capable of destroying the authority of the State.

> *La sociedad salvadoreña está pagando un precio muy alto, hemos llegado a tener 23 asesinatos al día . . . Esto ha amargado la sociedad y por lo tanto los responsables políticos tenían que dar algunas respuestas tranquilizadoras, para mostrar que el Estado estaba presente, y la gente no se dejaba sola.*
>
> [The people from El Salvador are paying a high price, we have reached 23 homicides per day . . . People are afraid and policy-makers must try to calm down the situation. They had to communicate that the State was alive, that they were not alone.]
>
> *(Interview with Antonio Rodriguez, Programa Seguridad Ciudadana y Justicia Penal,*
> *Fundacion de Estudio para la Aplicación del Derecho, FESPAD)*

Honduras was the first country of the area where the *mano dura* was pioneered. In 2002, president Ricardo Maduro promoted the idea that gangs are primarily responsible for Honduras's frequent deadly violence, and he started the "war on gangs", promising to make the country safe through sheer force. Then President Juan Orlando Hernandez approved security-oriented initiatives to battle his country's rising murder rate: he created the Military Police of Public Order (PMOP); he also has successfully managed to pressure cell phone companies into creating a perimeter around prisons that cuts off satellite reception.

The impact on the prison system (both adult and juvenile) of those 'exceptional' policies has been huge: from 2000 to 2018 in El Salvador, the general prison population increased from 7,754 to 38,237 (as a percentage, it translates into a 393% increase), in Honduras from 11,500 to 17,017 (+49%), in Guatemala from 6,979 to 21,031 (+201%).[5]

2 Prisons, *maras* and *pandillas*: a brief history of a strong relationship

From a quantitative point of view, juvenile criminal justice systems well reflect the effect of those policies; indeed, it is correct to affirm that gang members are the most representative group inside the *Triangulo Norte* juvenile prison system.

Official statistics collected during research recorded in 2018 show the over-representation of gangs inside juvenile prisons: 1,067 gang members out of 1,519 juvenile inmates in El Salvador (70%), 419 out of 935 in Guatemala (44%), 300 out of 514 in Honduras (55%). The majority of the prison population is considered affiliated with gangs. Outside prisons, statistics estimate total membership between 100,000 and 140,000 individuals, mostly affiliated with *Mara Salvatrucha* (*MS* or *MS-13*) and *Calle 18* (*Dieciocho*), the largest street gangs in northern Central America and in the Central American immigrant community in the United States. They are also the two most represented gangs inside *Triangulo Norte* juvenile prison facilities.

Table 43.1 Triangulo Norte juvenile prison facilities

	El Salvador	Guatemala	Honduras
"Zero tolerance" policies. War on gangs. Effect on incarceration from 2000 to 2018	From 7,754 to 38,237 (+393%)	From 6,979 to 21,031 (+201%)	From 11,500 to 17,017 (+49%)
Prevalence of gangs Number of gang members in juvenile prison	1,067 gang members out of 1,519 inmates (70%)	419 gang members out of 935 (44%)	300 gang members out of 514 in Honduras (55%)
Organisation of prisons For juvenile gang members	Strict separation between rival groups.	Disciplinary-model. Uniform, with a white t-shirt and jumpsuits of colours that vary depending on the sections.	Self-management of prison wards by gangs.
Allocation: 'labelling process'	Formalised, written survey, fill in by prison staff, recording even the rank (called *fase*) and the place where his group *(clica)* operates.	Not formalised, oral interview by prison staff. The *barrio* of origin is the crucial information to decide allocation inside prison.	Cooperative process between prison staff, judicial authority and gang leaders, who "approved" the final allocation of "new" inmates.

Besides the quantitative aspect, it is interesting to observe how such large numbers influence the dynamics of juvenile prisons as 'total institutions', especially from the point of view of the organisation of *time*, *space* and *interactions* between the controllers and the controlled, which are the three main characteristics that make an institution "total", according to the well-known analysis by Goffman (1961).

What are the formal and informal strategies and techniques set by the institution to "control" organisations that exist both at the prison and street level?

The first strategy in common in the three countries to peacefully manage prison facilities is the strict partition between different gangs. The two most powerful gangs active within *Triangulo Norte*, MS 13 and *Calle 18*, are everywhere strictly divided, so the main informal method to allocate the young inmates appears to be their membership, even if national laws and international standards require considering mainly the judicial position – dividing people in pre-trial detention and convicted – or the family status, trying to send the person to a prison close to his or her family.

"Firstly we need to know as soon as possible who they belong to" (interview with a prison director from Honduras).

Consequently, the individual identity loses importance; the *pandillero* 'belongs' to someone: they belong to their group. For their own safety and for the safety of the staff, the institutional actors have to urgently label him.

This 'urgency' seems justify by historical reasons: in Guatemala since August 2005, when the *Pacto del Sur* between MS-13 and *Calle 18* was broken, a series of deadly attacks against staff and members of rival groups began, first at the adult prison in Escuintla and then at other prisons (including the *Gaviota* juvenile prison).

Immediately after the end of the pact, cohabitation among members from different gangs became impossible and even forbidden by their leaders. In El Salvador, strict partitions between different gangs started by the end of year 2000, when the Tonacatepeque Juvenile Detention Center was dedicated to *Mara Salvatrucha* members and El Espino (Ahuachapán) to *Pandilla 18*.

The measure, previously rejected in principle by the actors involved in juvenile criminal justice, was deemed inevitable after riots between the two gangs in the juvenile centres of San Francisco Gotera (July 1999) and Ciudad Barrios (September 1999). Segregation began to gain followers under the belief that gangs hated one another to death, and life was the ultimate good to be safeguarded, to the detriment of any ambition towards rehabilitation.

Then, in August 2004, in the worst massacre recorded in a Salvadoran prison, 32 teenagers were killed and several were beaten up or went missing. Two weeks after that massacre, the government formalised the unprecedented decision of assigning entire facilities either to *MS-13* or *Calle 18* members.

Since then, the segregation of gang members has become a milestone in the evolution of the gang phenomenon. As a consequence, while observing juvenile prisons in *Triangulo Norte*, it is common to find even in official documents next to the name of a prison the name of the gang most represented inside. Therefore, in El Salvador, there are three prisons under the responsibility of ISNA, *Instituto Salvadoreño para el Desarrollo Integral de la Niñez y Adolescencia*; in Tonacatepeque, 92% of the young people belong to MS-13; in El Espino, the totality of the detainees belongs to Calle 18 (but divided in two groups, *Revolucionarios* and *Sureños*); in the female prison, 97% of inmates have a link with a gang, and they are divided into different units by affiliation.

In Guatemala, the partition is even stricter: two facilities are dedicated to *Calle 18* (*Etapa II* and *Gaviota*, which is the biggest juvenile prison of the country) and one to MS-13 (*Anexo*). The female prison (*Gorriones*) hosts mainly girls affiliated with *Pandilla 18* and, in a different building, a small group of MS-13 girls. In all four prisons, there are special wards dedicated to non-affiliated juvenile offenders, known as *paisas*.

Even in Honduras, the strict separation is presented as the only possible way to manage juvenile prisons. But there we find a substantial difference, because affiliation is verified directly by the judicial authority and not by prison staff. So young members are sent to a specific prison directly by the judge according to affiliation.

As a consequence, at *El Carmen* Prison in San Pedro Sula, only members of *Mara Salvatrucha* are represented; at the *Renaciendo*, mainly members of *Calle 18* (and other smaller gangs like *Chirizos* and *El Combo Que No Se Deja*). Coexistence and shared use of common areas are considered impossible, and there are no ongoing experiments in this regard.

Only in the women's centre *El Sagrado Corazón de María* are people belonging to rival groups kept together, since the staff consider those inmates "committed to the State and not belonging to any group" (interview with P., psychologist of the female prison), which allows building human relationships and peaceful coexistence, but is barely tolerated by the leaders outside. The same inmates, during a focus group, comment positively on such coexistence: "For those who live outside, it is impossible to imagine how we can share the same room with a girl from a rival group, we should hate each other" (A., 18 years old). "Cohabitation forces us to live in peace, otherwise we would all be in danger" (L., 16 years old).

In Honduras, this division by groups reaches a stage of self-management of entire sections of the facilities by gang members (in particular inside *Renaciendo* and *El Carmen*). Therefore, the level of control by the staff is reduced to a minimum. There, the young inmates are in charge of surveillance and maintenance of the section, with formal shifts also at night. Even our access inside the prison units as researchers was approved by the inmates, and our movements were constantly monitored.

Nowadays strict separation seems irreversible. Recalling the labelling theory developed by the School of Chicago and by Howard Becker (1973), it is interesting to describe the 'labelling strategies' used by institutional actors, especially prison staff.

This 'labelling process' has two important meanings: on one side, it is a way to recognise the powerful hierarchy, the very existence of gangs (their "gothic sovereignty", using the definition by John Carter, 2014); on the other side, it promotes the osmosis between street culture and prison culture.

It could be understood not only as a safety measure but also as a mutual recognition between gangs and authority, the first step to achieve a permanent negotiation between institutional actors and gangs inside prisons.

Traditionally, imprisonment is shocking; upon entering a prison, the individual loses his status (student, worker, father, son, citizen) and he is forced to maintain only the 'label' of inmate.

Inmates undergo a process of 'mortification of the self' first described by Goffman. But for gang members in the *Triangulo Norte*, the shock of imprisonment (Goffman, 1961) appears less upsetting, because they basically maintain the same status and the same position in the hierarchy of the group. They are gang members both in free and captive society; their individual and collective agency is preserved (Brotherton, 2010, p. 44).

Observing the *Triangulo Norte* juvenile prison daily life, it is harder to adapt Sykes' (1958) theory about the separation between prison and free society. Sykes identified typologies of prisoners that together form a "convict social system" (Irwin, 1970). Within this social system, prisoners develop a system of 'informal' social control known as the convict code. But in *Triangulo Norte*, the convict code seems to correspond with the gang code.

On how to label inmates, each prison acts independently; therefore, the experience of the staff in charge of the so-called first-entry interview assumes a central role. This first point of contact between prisoner and staff is a crucial aspect of the punishment. According to Matza (1969) and his theory of delinquency it could be considered a ritual, the first of a series of *degradation ceremonies* the inmates must undergo after incarceration.

During the interview, the staff first considers "aesthetic" aspects (the presence of tattoos – now in sharp decline, as they are too likely to expose inmates to stigmatisation and criminalisation risks – the way of dressing, the haircut), but also the way of speaking, the use of idiomatic expressions that could reveal affiliation with a group or another.

Second, the "geographical origin" (depending on the neighbourhood or street where the juvenile offender says he lives, the interviewer deduces that he may belong to one specific gang). Therefore, many operators admit that the margin of error is large. The risk is to take for gang members even unaffiliated teenagers, maybe only because they live in a particular *barrio*. Sometimes even the other inmates are involved in the labelling process: in Honduras, inside *Renaciendo*, it happens that in case of doubt about affiliation to a group, before deciding the allocation, the young inmate is accompanied before a leader who will either recognise him or not as a *pandillero*, considering above all the use of typical idioms or tattoos on the body. In those cases, the leader grants his informal authorisation to put the juvenile offender in that sector.

Those first-entry interviews are often unrecorded; only in El Salvador has the ISNA authority introduced a sort of formalisation of the labelling process. The prison staff must fill in a survey where all information about membership is carefully noted, even the rank (called *fase*) and the place where his group *(clica)* operates.

INSTITUTO SALVADOREÑO PARA EL DESARROLLO INTEGRAL DE LA NIÑEZ Y LA ADOLESCENCIA
CENTRO DE INSERCION SOCIAL DE TONACATEPEQUE.
TEL: 2322-0231 – FAX: 2322-0734.

ENTREVISTA PREVIA PARA ADOLESCENTES.

NUEVO INGRESO: ○   REINGRESO: ○   FECHA:_____

NOMBRE: _____ALIAS:_____

F.N.:_____EDAD:_____ NIVEL ACADÉMICO: _____

JUZGADO:_____

DELITO(S):_____
_____

DIRECCION:_____
_____

NO ES MIEMBRO DE PANDILLA .   .   ☐

TIENE PROBLEMAS CON LA PANDILLA: SI ☐   NO ☐

FASE EN LA QUE SE ENCUENTRA:

    1. FAVORES (PARO)   ☐   TIEMPO DE FASE: _____
    2. OBSERVACIÓN: ☐   (Numeral 1,2,3,4)
    3. CHEQUEO: ☐
    4. PASE PARA SER MIEMBRO ACTIVO: ☐
    5. MIEMBRO ACTIVO DE LA PANDILLA: ☐ TIEMPO: _____

NOMBRE DE LA CLICA: _____

POSEE TATUAJES ALUSIVOS A LA PANDILLA: SI ☐   NO ☐

LUGAR DONDE OPERA LA CLICA: _____

_____   _____

NOMBRE DEL ADOLESCENTE.   FIRMA Y HUELLAS.

OBSERVACIÓN: _____
_____
_____
_____

_____
NOMBRE Y FIRMA DEL TÉCNICO/ORIENTADOR.

Figure 43.2 Labelling process in El Salvador. Form used by prison staff to "label" gang-member entering in prison

3 The osmosis between street culture and prison culture. the untouched gangsters' habitus

The strict spatial separation between members of different groups in prisons allows the reproduction of the same street dynamics: hierarchy, roles, symbols are faithfully reproduced inside. This osmosis between "street culture" and "penitentiary culture" helps the construction of the gangsters' *habitus* (Bourdieu, 1972): a gangster considers himself not an individual but part of a group ("*mi familia*", my family, is the recurrent definition of their gangs given by the members met during the research); is subject to the same hierarchy as in the outside world; has a well-defined space/territory to be personalised with murals, flags and symbols (Brotherton, 2015).

Prison bureaucracy transforms the facility into temporary "territory" of the gang, a place that must be conquered, controlled and defended, exactly like the *barrio* (neighbourhood) or the *calle* (street) outside. As Conquergood underlines in his studies on the relation between spaces and gangs, the spaces of prison become "socio-political domains" (Conquergood, 1997); consequently, it seems the condition of deprivation of liberty does not change the essence of "street organization" (Brotherton, 2007).

Consequently, regardless of the kind of gangs, there is constant fear – in some cases, a true obsession of *contamination*. Anything and anyone coming from the outside world (prison staff, school teachers, an unaffiliated inmate) are the enemy, a potential danger – even in terms of contact or relationship – to be avoided at any cost. This explains and justifies the self-management of the prison units tested in Honduras, where gangs are in charge of security and decide who is allowed to enter and what activities may be carried out in their prison unit.

As Carter notes "They have transformed prisons into antimonuments, sites of negation that disrupt the temporality of politics and become sites of potential futures, in which gang members reclaim sovereign violence through expressions as invigorating as they have been esoteric" (2014, p. 477). Exactly like in the *calle* outside, prison units, cells, grey courtyards are removed from state sovereignty and embezzled by gangs.

In this sense, we find a relation between how a gang member uses his body and skin (individual dimension of the affiliation) and how he uses prison spaces (collective dimension of affiliation). The connection between prison and tattoos might appear bizarre but is linked to the urge to create a "new" identity as *pandillero*. Like the body tattooed is the acme of a "process of identification" (Beneduce and Borile, 2014, p. 80), to cover prison walls with gang symbols means that from then onwards, that building is no longer a "normal" place of deprivation of liberty but the gang's home.

Those graffiti are a clear message to the world outside and to the prison staff representing that world: we will not be yours. So prisons are transformed in a sacred space rather than a place of annihilation carried out by the state, and they get inoculated "not only from the violence of the law but from any means of reform" (Carter, p. 491).

As a matter of fact, on gang members' bodies and on prison walls, we find the same symbols: clowns, screaming skulls, open wounds, grim reapers, naked girls and dragons. Satanic figures and numbers (666) next to Christian citations and holy crosses. Other "sacred" numbers (13 for MS and 18 for Pandilla 18) and also cemeteries with the names of *homies* killed, which are "not just mementos of loved ones but veneration of the pariah exterminated by those within the community of the law" (Carter, 2014, p. 491).

The visual embezzlement of the prison has become even more symbolic after gang tattooing started to be used in criminal trials as evidence of affiliation, aggravating the sanction. Therefore, within the juvenile prison population, the number of those deciding to keep their skin clear as a means of camouflage is increasing. Furthermore all across the *Triangulo Norte*,

Figure 43.3 Honduras, The Bible and the symbol of the gang inside a cell reserved to *El combo que no se deja* gang members

international cooperation (especially from the United States) is funding programmes to delete tattoos by laser.

But what is the reaction of the state (through its prison authorities) to this spatial occupation? The exhibition of gang symbols is everywhere officially prohibited by disciplinary provisions, but prison staff usually avoid enforcing infringements.

Within *Triangulo Norte* only, Guatemala deserves a separates analysis. There, the prison organisation recalls the characteristics of the 'disciplinary prison' (as explained by Michel Foucault in his studies on the history of punishment between the 18th and the 19th century, especially when he described the case study of the prison of Mettray). In fact, Guatemala is the only country of the *Triangulo Norte* where young inmates are required to wear a uniform with a white t-shirt and jumpsuits of colours that vary depending on the sections – and therefore on gang affiliation. For security reasons, inmates may not even wear proper shoes but only slippers, even when they play soccer or basketball in the courtyard (slippers are soft and less dangerous if thrown, and they do not allow one to run fast in case of escape).

Inmates are also forced to have a standard army-style haircut. They spend most of their time inside overcrowded dormitories hosting up to 40 people in the same room and one mattress every 2 or 3 people. The bathrooms have rationed water – a few minutes per day per person. In the dormitory, young people can only keep the Bible and board games. For some of them, the only activities outside the dormitory are prayers and sports activities to be carried out in a common outdoor space (usually 2 hours per day).

They also have to salute and stand at attention in the presence of the prison director every time he visits the dormitory.

Another strategy applied in Guatemala to deter gang organisation inside the prison is the separation of leaders from the rest of the inmates. Leaders are not assigned to dormitories but to a separate building, a sort of special unit, one or two per cell. The living conditions are the same, but it becomes more difficult for them to communicate with the other members of their gang.

Lunch and dinner are the only moments when gang and non-gang inmates meet, and one of the leaders may get out of the special unit: one or two representatives per dormitory are in charge of meal distribution. They are not allowed to talk, and there is strict surveillance by the *monitores* (civilians with security duties; in fact, army and police forces usually enter the prison only in case of emergency; otherwise, they patrol only the perimeter of the facility).

Considering the higher rate of "critical events" (riots, aggressions, homicides) occurring inside juvenile prisons of the country, the strategies adopted by Guatemala seem not to work, but they appear to be justified only by the desire to humiliate the inmates.

Figure 43.4 The dormitory inside the "disciplinary" prison of Guatemala

Figure 43.5 Guatemala, Gang and non-gang members (with different colours of trousers) meet only during the meal distribution

4 The aim of prison. the aim of gangs

There is one more crucial aspect influencing the relation between gangs and the prison system in the *Triangolo Norte:* the purposes pursued by prison staff (and by the institutional authority) on gang member incarceration.

I wanted to find through empirical research confirmation of the biopolitical role of punishment towards 'special' groups of inmates such as gang members. These empirical findings recall the "institutional function" of prison explored by Michel Foucault (Garland, 1990) demonstrating the rehabilitation paradigm of prison, enshrined in law, is only an insignificant veil covering the more creeping aim of prison.

I first tried to approach the topic from the side of the gang members. Poor prison conditions and the systematic violation of basic detention standards are clearly evident. In many cases, they can be easily considered a kind of inhumane and degrading treatment according to international human rights law. So I wanted to understand whether and how gang members would like to change their life in prison – in other words, how they perceived that institutionalised context. The question was direct: "What would you do if you were the director of the prison?" With few exceptions, all the answers considered material aspects of daily life behind bars (more hours of access to the soccer field, television in the cells, the possibility of listening to music).

Only in one case (in the focus group in El Salvador) did they go beyond strictly material aspects, proposing activities that would help them improve relations with the external society (specifically, a series of video testimonies about life inside prisons and about their dreams).

For young gang members detained, it seems difficult to consider long-term objectives that go beyond the mere maintenance of their power over a certain territory (the prison unit) and the desire for annihilation of rival groups. However, existing ethnographic research (Brotherton and Barrios, 2004) on the Almighty Latin King and Queen Nation, an organisation that exists both in the free world and within the correctional system, reaches the same conclusion, revealing different goals between the street organisation and the prison gang: while the street-level organisation was concerned with community service, the prison organisation focused mainly survival within the institution.

But what might appear as a nihilistic approach to detention, a non-future oriented way of living imprisonment, actually must be acknowledged as a resistance practice: the proof that you are strong enough or, at least, stronger than "them" (the prison authorities). It is "the conscious or unconscious opposition of individuals and groups to structural constraints" (Brotherton 2007, p. 59).

Detention, as we know it from the Foucauldian tradition, is the evidence clearly showing, once again, who are the enemies and what borders you have to respect, here and now.

Every gang has its own strategy of resistance inside prisons, and generalisation is never good. Briefly, the first perception, which should be further investigated, is that MS members are more sophisticated and "projective", while *Calle 18* members appear to have a more "muscular" approach. This might explain why there are fewer MS members than *Calle 18* members in prison. At the end of the interview, one of the MS leaders in Tonacatepeque (El Salvador), just before returning to his small cell, turned back and – referring to the different purposes of gangs and of prison authorities – said: "*Ambos queremos mejorar el joven, que se sienta mejor. Tenemos los mismos objetivos, también nosotros cuidamos de nuestros jóvenes. Queremos lo mejor para ellos*" ("We both want to improve the young person, so that he feels a better person. We have the same objectives, we also take care of our young people, we want the best for them"; interview with F., El Salvador, Leader MS).

This resilient attitude is even more evident when finishing serving the sentence.

> *Salgo martes. Nadie me ha dicho cómo funciona. Tengo una tía, que tiene una tienda, le preguntaré si puedo ayudarla allí mismo. Pero alguien como yo, que pasó muchos años interno no agrada a nadie, ni siquiera a la familia. Si la pandilla me llega a buscar . . . voy a tener que decidir si volver con ellos o . . . o . . . aceptar las consecuencias . . . Dios decidirá.*
>
> I'm leaving on Tuesday [the interview was held on the previous Thursday]. Nobody has told me how it works, I have an aunt, who has a store, I'll ask her if I can help her right there. But nobody likes people like me, who spent years in prison, not even the family. If the gang comes looking for me . . . I will have to decide whether to go back with them or . . . or . . . to accept the consequences . . . God will decide
>
> *(Interview with R., Calle 18, Guatemala)*

The chronic lack of actions aimed at readmitting to society after imprisonment, despite the rhetoric of rehabilitation, is actually a great indirect help to the gangs, which remain the only point of reference for the young ones bewildered by sudden freedom.

Going back to the question about the purposes of prison, the focus now shifts to prison staff, who should realise on a daily basis the concept of rehabilitation, reintegration or re-education (depending on the wording chosen by the national legislator). Choosing within the broad apparatus of treatment activities (school, sport, work, culture and spirituality), prison staff should enact the will of the law.

This is the general goal of prison, to be guaranteed without exception, regardless of whether an inmate is a member of a gang. But what is the real perception staff have? Do they consider it achievable? Do they – consciously or unconsciously – help the strategy of resistance? In our research, we found two different approaches. All prison staff in the *Triangolo Norte* could be placed somewhere in between the two antipodes.

The first could be summarised as "*La pandilla no es nuestro problema*" ("The gang is not our problem"). For the ones (apparently the majority) who adopt this stance, membership in a gang is in itself a barrier to rehabilitation. They will apply their apparatus of educational activities (school classes, work-activities, recreation and sport), but they will never mention or address in any way the topic of gangs, as if that stopped at the door of the 'institution' ("*Se detuviera en la puerta de la 'institución'*").

The recurrent justification is based on 'personal safety' concerns: despite the security measures they adopt (choose a nickname while working, cover the numberplate of their cars between their house and the prison), they are still afraid. This fear is akin to the obsession gang members have with their rivals. It is true that quite frequently prison staff are threatened or even murdered. The ones not too afraid also mention the frustration:

> *¿Qué podemos hacer? Afuera, la sociedad no ofrece esperanza a los jóvenes pandilleros . . . terminada la sanción regresan a sus contextos y empiezan de nuevo como antes. Todos nuestros esfuerzos no sirven para nada.*
>
> [What can we do? Outside, society offers no hope to young gang members . . . Once they serve their sentence, they go back to their world and they start again like before, all our efforts are useless.]

(M., social worker, Honduras)

"*El profesional no puede hacer nada, son ellos los que deben querer cambiar. Nosotros no les podemos ayudar*" ("The staff cannot do anything, they are the ones who must change, we cannot help them"; F., social worker, El Salvador). The latter position could be summarised as "*Queremos que el joven se disocie del grupo*" ("We want them to leave the gangs"). Rarely, but spread across the *Triangulo Norte*, prison staff specifically address the gang issue and strive to start a path that leads away from the gang while respecting the original personal decisions of young people to join gangs.

This approach is extremely interesting, because it opens a specific field of research over whether young gang members actually have the opportunity – and the freedom – to choose to leave the group and whether it is legitimate – and appropriate – for state authorities to facilitate the abandonment, using different methods, included any sort of 'special' prison treatment.

This is a core issue that affects all areas of the world where criminality appears to be organised in groups or collective structures. The topic is deeply debated everywhere we find a violent conflict between an institution, labelled by law as criminal, and the state authorities. It is the case of *mafia* in Italy, political-terrorist organisations in the United Kingdom or Spain or religious-oriented groups after September 11 (Varese, 2010).

Sometimes the national legislative framework provides a possible solution, declaring what the limits (or the non-limits) are for police enforcement agencies and judiciary and penitentiary authorities. In some cases, the law facilitates and in others discourages the option of breaking the pact between the member and his group. Within the *Triangulo Norte*, there are no specific laws that deal with the consequences of dissociation (with the only exception of special programmes for witness protection but strictly only for the duration of the criminal trial).

In this sense, we must distinguish the dissociation from gangs as a voluntary or forced decision according to whether it is influenced by a third actor. In the first case, some recent research shows that "The exit of the gang is not only possible, it is more common than people think, and despite the difficulties involved . . . If it is true that it is mainly a personal choice, but it is a decision in relation to which the gang must agree" (Cruz, 2017, p. 7). Indeed, for the researcher, the continuous inflow and outflow is not surprising.

Going deeper inside the rules of gangs, detecting this sort of agreement leads to another important distinction observed during the research regarding 'voluntary' quitting: on one side we found the *desistimiento* (the desertion) and the *calmarse* (literally to "calm down"); on the other side, there is the decision not to participate in the active life of the gang and its activities anymore (i.e. meetings, criminal acts, illicit traffic) while remaining a member, part of that eternal loyalty pact with the group.

From the prison perspective, desertion is more troublesome, because it is considered a true betrayal, heavily punished by gang rules, in the *Triangulo Norte* usually translating into death.

> *Cuando sucede al interior del Centro, es un problema . . . tenemos poco tiempo para salvar al joven. Por lo general, ordeno el traslado inmediato de dormitorio, a continuación, ofrezco la oportunidad al joven de informar inmediatamente a la familia . . . ellos también, en ese momento están en peligro, y es importante que la noticia del abandono no los agarre de sorpresa. En los casos más graves, esto significa deben transferirse de inmediato e ir a un lugar seguro, de lo contrario la venganza de la pandilla sería inmediata. Estamos hablando no de días, de minutos.*
>
> [When it happens in prison it is a problem . . . we have little time to save the young person. In general, I order the immediate transfer from the dormitory I then offer the young person the opportunity to immediately inform the family . . . they too, in that moment, are in danger, and it is important that they find out about the choice of desertion as soon as possible. In the most serious cases, this means they should leave immediately and move to a safe place, otherwise the revenge of the gang would be immediate, we are talking not of days but of minutes.]
>
> *(Interview with prison director, Guatemala)*

None of the countries observed have formal protocols or procedures that establish what to do if a young person expresses the will to leave gang. The simple manifestation of the wish is difficult to understand by the staff. Often, young people ask to "*hablar*" (to talk), asking for a meeting with a social worker or, more frequently, with the director, but they cannot do it openly, because they would be immediately seen by the other inmates and their behaviour considered suspicious. So it is common for them to rely on highly symbolic gestures that demonstrate the choice of desertion (running out of the bedroom or refusing to return after an activity or feigning discomfort in order to be taken to infirmary).

In case of desertion, the inmate becomes a "*retirado*" or "*ex*". This is a third group, different from to the "*activos*" (gang members) and the "*población común*" or "*paisas*" (not gang members). They live in a specific prison unit with increased safety measures to protect them from gang vengeance.

The case of *calmarse* (to calm down) is instead an accepted possibility (especially for gang leaders), and it does not usually entail negative consequences. Like an electronic device in standby, the one who chooses to "calm down" remains a gang member. What this means is perfectly explained by a "calm" gang member from El Salvador

> *Esta noche podrían venir a tocar a mi puerta y decirme, te necesitamos . . . tienes que hacernos un trabajo . . . no podría decir que no. Podría enojarme, quejarme, pero finalmente aceptaría . . . es por eso que trato de evitar los mismos lugares de cuando estaba activo. Espero que al no verme, se olviden de mi.*

[Tonight they might come to knock on my door and tell me, we need you . . . you have to do 'a job' . . . I could not say no. I could get angry, complain, but I would finally accept . . . that's why I try to avoid the same places where I used to hang around when I was active. I hope that by not seeing me, they will forget about me.]

(Interview outside prison, E., "ex" Calle 18, El Salvador)

The process to obtain the 'permission' to calm down from the leader of the gang can be long and complicated, and, in that situation, the gang member is quite submissive. Usually the gang requests one last "act", after which permission is granted. "*Hay que hablar, hablar, hablar, hablar . . . y esperar . . . pero al final tienes éxito*" (Interview with P., "ex" Calle 18, Guatemala).

Beyond the cases of voluntary choice, there are the more problematic forced decisions, in which someone outside the bilateral relationship gang/member has a crucial role. Who are the 'third actors' influencing a young gang member? During our fieldwork, I assessed the role of prison staff in the decision to quit the gang. Actually I found family as the most important driver in this process. As much as lack of a family is a decisive factor for joining the gang, the desire to create your own family, to get married and have children is a decisive factor for quitting.

This solution is actually linked to the ageing of the gang member. Although there are many adults (and elderly) involved, the gang phenomenon concerns mainly young people. Gang maturity – roughly considered to be around the age of 28 – leads to poorly withstanding risks and the "*vida loca*" (crazy life) required by gangs. Family stability is usually also associated with economic and labour stability and, therefore, entering the world of regular work compensates for the economic benefits provided by the gang. "*Cuando salgo quiero ser mecánico, me faltan siete años, voy a tener más de 25. . . . La vida en la calle no será más para mí*" ("When I go out I want to be a mechanic, I have to serve another seven years, I'm going to be more than 25 . . . Life on the street will no longer be for me"; interview with R., MS, Honduras)

In the last few years, a new way out is becoming increasingly popular; the so-called "*volverse cristianos*" (becoming Christians) is currently the most interesting (and, in a way, problematic) way to leave a gang (Brenneman, 2011). In the *Triangulo Norte*, as in many Latin American countries (Míguez, 2012; Algranti and Brardinelli, 2013; Navarro and Sozzo, 2020), the attractiveness and power of Christian churches (especially Evangelical and Pentecostal churches) is growing fast in society and subsequently in prisons (Manchado, 2019). In most prisons observed, Christian pastors and ministers are often the only "external" people allowed to enter and to carry out not only spiritual activities but also school classes, sports and training courses. All those activities that the public institution is unable to provide, mainly due to lack of funds, are provided for free by the churches.

They usually enter in small groups, and they clearly show their church membership (they often hold a bible and wear t-shirts with Christian mottos or citations from the bible on the back, with references to 'salvation' and 'absolution'). They are usually the only ones allowed to enter the dormitories and any prison unit, a possibility that is even denied to security wardens and prison staff because of the fear they could convey messages across prison sectors.

Therefore, their power is visible and acknowledged not only because they have the money to pay for important activities or building improvements but also because the directors and most staff belong to the same church or religious group.

Relying on the promise of self-esteem, these ministers have placed the problem of gang in the soul rather than on the streets, training an increasing number of eyes on atrophied wills that only the saving grace of Jesus Christ can strengthen.

(O'Neil, 2010, p. 67)

They meet the gang member beginning with a soccer match; then they move to prayers, a bible reading session or a movie: after a while, the conversion is complete. However, it is not a simple conversion and a normal participation in the rites and life of the church; it is rather a rigorous adoption of the rules of the life of the irreproachable Christian pastor, who lives as a father of the church, giving up drinking alcohol and taking drugs, leading a quiet life of prayer, without attending parties and public places. If the gang became aware of a transgression to that way of life, it would consider it a "betrayal" to be punished.

The increasing numbers of converted gang members suggested some changes in the organisation of prisons; in fact, Honduras and El Salvador started to host *Cristianos* (Christians) in specific sections, following the model adopted by other Latin American countries such as Argentina (Algranti and Brardinelli, 2013; Brardinelli, 2012). They have their dedicated spaces, their strict rules; the most charismatic soon become the leaders of their sections and are granted the privilege to conduct daily masses and to talk to the director (Algranti, 2018). During my last week of direct observation, they were starting to paint the big walls of the prison unit with big rosaries surrounding an angel holding a Bible, on one side, their (new) name: *Cristianos*. *"Es mi nueva familia"* ("It's my new family"; interview with D., "ex", Honduras).

5 Conclusion. the resistance within the wall

This research has partially started to cover the gap of ethnographic studies of gangs in prisons, underlining the need to mix prison and gang studies within a common critical theoretical framework in future research. Therefore, prisons are nowadays a total institution facing deep changes: *mass incarceration* affected the structure of prison itself not only in the Global North area, enforcing its role of "neutralisation" (Wacquant, 2009) of public enemies and dangerous classes of individuals (gangs, among others).

In particular, in the *Triangulo Norte*, the effect of mass incarceration must be strictly linked with the *mano dura* repressing policy adopted all over Central and Latin America. Because of this war on gangs, gang members quickly became the most representative group inside the correctional system. This quantitative relevance has consequentially transformed prisons in places where gangs apply their strategy of resistance. Gang members bring inside the wall their *habitus*, organisation, leadership, hierarchy and symbols, typical of that continuum between prison and *barrio* (Wacquant, 2001). But they also transform imprisonment into a 'political' collective experience, where gangs (through their leaders) experiment with relations with the public authority, sometimes negotiating with the institutions, more frequently in total contrast.

In this sense, researchers should rekindle their interest in the seminal works on resistance of the School of Birmingham (Hall and Jefferson, 1975; Hebdige, 1979; Brake, 1985), but they should consider the peculiarity of the prison environments, where the subcultures of gangs face the dominant culture of the state, represented by prison staff. Moreover, these resistance strategies seem not to change in different kinds of correctional facilities, from the disciplinary prisons of Guatemala to the self-managed jails of Honduras, but future research should delve deeper into those differences.

From this perspective, gangs should be recognised as political actors, even able to resist the inhuman and traumatic conditions of overcrowded and violent jails. This assumption could appear shocking for mainstream criminology, which considers gangs only as criminal organisations, formed by hyper-violent individuals. To "survive" in prison is probably even harder than to live in the *barrio*: the empirical materials collected in the research demonstrate the ability of gangs to adapt to some emerging (unofficial) strategies put in place by the public authority in order to "destroy" the gangs. In this sense, prisons could become an avant-garde of a "new" relationship between gangs and dominant political power. This is what happens when we observe the role of Christian churches (especially Evangelical churches) and religious groups gangs convincing young members to abandon violence. More empirical research on gangs in prisons, considering the contribution of prison studies, may assist future researchers in explaining the role of gangs in society outside the walls of prisons.

Notes

1 The empirical insights presented in the chapter are part of wider research, coordinated by the Italian Agency for International Cooperation, which involved the Italian Prison Observatory of Juvenile Prisons led by the Antigone Association in order to set a map of the juvenile prison system of Central America and the Caribbean. In 2018, during over 60 days of fieldwork in 7 countries (Belize, Costa Rica, Dominican Republic, El Salvador, Guatemala, Honduras, Panama), the author conducted a direct observation in 31 juvenile detention facilities. The observation focused on the organisation of inmates' daily life and on the respect of their human rights. Besides the observation, the researcher conducted many hours of semi-structured interviews, focus groups and informal meetings with institutional authorities and inmates, especially gang leaders or former gang members. In this chapter, the author presents a comparative analysis, concerning three of the countries observed (Guatemala, El Salvador, Honduras). All photos published in the chapter were taken by the author during the fieldwork.
2 "Whether it is the fear of natural disasters, the fear of environmental catastrophes or the fear of indiscriminate terrorist attacks, we live today in a state of constant anxiety about the dangers that could strike unannounced and at any moment" (Bauman, 2006).
3 In absolute numbers, after the United States, the other "prison state" countries currently are China (1.65 million inmates), Russia (640,000), Brazil (607,000), India (418,000), Thailand (311,000), Mexico (255,000) and Iran (225,000). For a complete overview on the statistics of incarceration, see the Word Prison Brief coordinated by the International Center for Prison Studies. For an European quantitative overview see the SPACE I-Council of Europe Annual Penal Statistics (Aebi and Tiago, 2020).
4 The most important legislative and judicial sources addressing the issue of the rehabilitation paradigm of prison in Europe are the European Convention of Human Rights, the European Prison Rules, jurisprudence and warning made by the European Court of Human Rights, The Committee for the Prevention of Torture, the Committee of Minsters of the Council of Europe; in America, the American Convention of Human Rights, the Inter-America Court of Human Rights. Worldwide the so-called "Mandela Rules" introduce UN Standard Minimum Rules for the Treatment of Prisoners (SMRs).
5 Source: World Prison Brief coordinate by the ICPS-International Center of Prison Studies.

References

Aebi M.F. & Tiago, M., 2020, *Prisons and Prisoners in Europe 2019: Key Findings of the SPACE I Report*, Strasbourg: Council of Europe.

Agamben G., 2005, *The State of Exception*, Chicago: University of Chicago Press.

Algranti J., 2018, The Making of an Evangelical Prison: Study on NeoPentecostalism and Its Leadership Processes in the Argentine Penitentiary System, *Social Compass*, vol. 65, no. 5: 549–565.

Algranti J. and Brardinelli R., 2013, *La re-invención religiosa del encierro. Hermanitos, refugiados y cachivaches en los penales bonaerenses*, Buenos Aires: Centro Cultural de la Cooperación

Bauman Z., 2006, *Liquid Fear*, Cambridge: Polity.

Becker H.S., 1973, *Outsiders: Studies in the Sociology of Deviance*, New York: Free Press.

Beneduce R. and Borile M., 2014, Lo schiaffo del vento. Minori stranieri tra dentro e fuori, in Beneduce R., Palmas L.Q. and Oddone C. (edit by), *Loro dentro. Giovani, migranti, detenuti*, Genova: Professional Dreamers, 59–83.

Bourdieu P., 1972, *Esquisse d'une théorie de la pratique: Précédé de «Trois études d'ethnologie kabyle»*, Genève: Librairie Droz.

Brake M., 1985, *Comparative Youth Cultures: The Sociology of Youth Culture and Youth Subcultures in America, Britain and Canada*, London: Routledge-Kegan Paul.

Brardinelli R., 2012, De iglesias y pabellones inventados. Paradigmas carcelarios y 'conversiones religiosas', *Revista de Ciencias Sociales, segunda época*, vol. 4, no. 22: 7–26.

Brenneman R., 2011. *Homies and Hermanos: God and Gangs in Central America*, New York: Oxford University Press.

Brotherton D.C., 2007, Beyond Social Reproduction. Bringing Resistance Back into the Theory of Gangs, *Theoretical Criminology*, vol. 12, no. 1: 55–77.

Brotherton D.C., 2010, Oltre la riproduzione sociale. Reintrodurre la resistenza nella teoria sulle bande, in Palmas L. (edit by), *Atlantico Latino*, Rome: Carrocci, 29–46.

Brotherton D.C., 2015, *Youth Street Gangs. A Critical Appraisal*, London & New York: Routledge.

Brotherton D.C. and Barrios L., 2004, *The Almighty Latin King and Queen Nation: Street Politics and the Transformation of a New York City Gang*, New York: Columbia University Press.

Carter J.H., 2014, Gothic Sovereignty: Gangs and Criminal Community in a Honduran Prison, *The South Atlantic Quarterly*, vol. 113, no. 3, Summer.

Clemmer D., 1940, *The Prison Community*, New York: Rinehart and Winston.

Cohen S., 1972, *Folk Devils and Moral Panics. The Creation of the Mods and Rockers*, London: MacGibbon and Kee.

Conquergood D., 1997, Street Literacy, in Floord J., Heat S.B. and Lapp D. (edit by), *Handbook of Research on Teaching Literacy Through the Communicative and Visual Arts*, New York: Simon & Schuster and Macmillan, 354–375.

Cox A.L., 2018, *Trapped in a Vice: The Consequences of Confinement for Young People*, New Brunswick: Rutgers University Press.

Cramer Brooks C. and Roush D., 2014, Transformation in the Justice System, *Reclaiming Children and Youth*, vol. 23, no. 1: 42–46.

Cruz J.M., 2011, Criminal Violence and Democratization in Central America: The Survival of the Violent State, *Latin American Politics and Society*, vol. 53, no. 4: 1–33.

Cruz J.M., 2016, State and Criminal Violence in Latin America, *Crime, Law and Social Change*, vol. 66, no. 4.

Cruz J.M., et al., 2017. *La nueva cara de la pandillas callejera: el fenómeno de las pandillas en El Salvador*, Florida: Florida International University.

Cullen F.T. and Jonson C.L., 2014. *Correctional Theory. Context and Consequences*, Los Angeles: Sage Publication.

Davis D.E., 2006, The Age of Insecurity. Violence and Social Disorder in the New Latin America, *Latin America Research Review*, vol. 41, no. 1: 178–197, Texas: University of Texas Press.

De Giorgi A., 2010, *Il governo dell'eccedenza. Postfordismo e il controllo della moltitudine*, Verona: Ombre Corte.

Fleisher M.S. and Decker S.H., 2001, An Overview of the Challenge of Prison Gangs, *Corrections Management Quarterly*, vol. 5, no. 1: 1–9.

Foucault M., 1977, *Discipline and Punish*, London: Allen Lane.

Garland D., 1990, *Punishment and Modern Society: A Study in Social Theory*, Oxford: Clarendon Press.

Garland D., 2001, *Culture of Control: Crime and Social Order in Contemporary Society*, Oxford: Oxford University Press.

Garland D., 2012, Punishment and Social Solidarity, in Simon J. and Sparks R. (edit by), *The SAGE Handbook of Punishment and Society*, Los Angeles: Sage Publication.

Goffman E., 1961, *Asylums*, Garden City: Doubleday.

Hall S. and Jefferson T. (edit by), 1975, *Resistance Through Rituals: Youth Subcultures in Post-War Britain*, London: Routledge.

Hebdige D., 1979, *Subculture. The Meaning of Style*, London: Methun.

Irwin, J., 1970, *The Felon*, Englewood Cliffs: Prentice-Hall Inc.

Manchado M., 2019, No nos gusta que vengan a manejarnos ellos el pabellón. Religiosidad, autonomías y desconfianza en la gestión del orden carcelario en Argentina, *Etnografías, revista del Centro de Estudios en Antropología,* vol. 5, no. 8: 13–34.

McCrary J. and Sanga S., 2012, General Equilibrium Effects of Prison on Crime: Evidence from International Comparisons, *Cato Papers on Public Policy*, vol. 2: 165–193.

Matthews R., 2009, *Doing Time. An Introduction to the Sociology of Imprisonment*, London: Palgrave Macmillan.

Matza D., 1969, *Becoming Deviant*, Englewood Cliffs: Prentice-Hall Inc.

Melossi D. e Pavarini M., 1981, *Prison and the Factory. Origins of the Penitentiary System*, New York: Rowman and Littlefield.

Míguez D., 2012, Los universos morales en el mundo del delito. Las lógicas de reconversión en contextos de institucionalización, *Revista de Ciencias Sociales, segunda época,* vol. 4, no. 22: 45–63.

Miller W.B., 2001, *The Growth of Youth Gang Problems in the United States: 1970–98*, Washington, DC: U.S. Department of Justice.

Navarro L. and Sozzo M., 2020, Pabellones evangélicos y gobierno de la prisión. Legados de Sykes para pensar la construcción del orden en las prisiones de varones en Argentina, *Cuestiones Criminales. Cuadernos de investigación: Apuntes y Claves de lectura,* vol.3, no. 3: 177–226.

Oddone C. and Palmas L.Q., 2014, Dalle gang al carcere: esperienze giovanili della detenzione, in Beneduce R., Palmas L.Q. and Oddone C. (edit by), *Loro Dentro. Giovani, migranti, detenuti*, Genoa: Professional Dreamers.

O'Neil K.L., 2010, *The Reckless Will: Prison Chaplaincy and the Problem of Mara Salvatrucha. Public Culture*, vol. 22, no. 1, 1 January: 67–88.

Ortiz, J.M., 2015, *The Power of Place: A Comparative Analysis of Prison and Street Gangs*, New York: CUNY Academic Works. Available online at https://academicworks.cuny.edu/gc_etds/1081.

Pratt J., 2007, *Penal Populism*, New York: Routledge.

Pyrooz D., et al., 2017, Consequences of Incarceration for Gang Membership: A Longitudinal Study of Serious Offenders in Philadelphia and Phoenix, *Criminology*, vol. 55, no. 2: 273–306.

Pyrooz D., 2018, Using Restrictive Housing to Manage Gangs in US Prisons, *Corrections Today*, July/August: 10–13.

Rusche G. and Kirchheimer O., 1939 (1968). *Punishment and Social Structure,* New York: Columbia University Press.

Salazar Ugarte P., 2012, *Crítica de la mano dura: cómo enfrentar la violencia y preservar nuestras libertades*, Mexico City: Oceano.

Simon J., 2007, *Governing Through Crime: How the War on Crime Transformed American Democracy and Created a Culture of Fear*, Oxford: Oxford University Press.

Simon J. and Sparks R. (edit by), 2012, *The SAGE Handbook of Punishment and Society*, Los Angeles: Sage Publication.

Sykes G.M., 1958, *The Society of Captives: A Study of a Maximum Security Prison*, Princeton: Princeton University Press.

Varese F., 2010, *Organized Crime. Critical Concepts in Criminology*, 1st edition, New York: Routledge.

Wacquant L., 2001, Deadly Symbiosis: When Ghetto and Prison Meet and Mesh, *Punishment & Society*, vol. 3, no. 1: 95–134

Wacquant L., 2009, *Punishing the Poor: The Neoliberal Government of Social Insecurity*, Durham: Duke University Press Books.

Wacquant L., 2010, Class, Race & Hyperincarceration in Revanchist America, *Daedalus*, vol. 139, no. 3: 74–90.

Weiss G., 2013, *The Fourth Wave: Juvenile Justice Reforms for the 21st Century*, New York, The National Campaign to Reform State Juvenile Justice Systems for the Juvenile Justice Funders' Collaborative (commissioned by).

Welch M. et al., 2002, Moral Panic Over Youth Violence: Wilding and the Manufacture of Menace in the Media, *Youth and Society*, vol. 34, no. 1: 3–30.

44

Doxa is dangerous

How academic doxa inhibits prison gang research

Jennifer M. Ortiz

Introduction

Over a half century ago, C. Wright Mills cautioned researchers about the dangers of abstract empiricism. Mills (1959) warned that our shifting focus towards statistical analyses and our search for objective 'facts' would cause sociologists to lose contact with social reality. Mills called on researchers to reengage the sociological imagination by incorporating historical, biographical, and cultural analyses into our study of social phenomena. In 2011, critical criminologist Jock Young offered an update to Mills' argument in his seminal book *The Criminological Imagination*. Young (2011) posited that abstract empiricism in academic research had reached a level even Mills could not foresee. Criminologists have become determined to develop quasi-scientific research that can 'predict' or address criminality without ever stepping foot into the communities directly affected by crime. Abstract empiricism leads researchers to believe they can remove the impact of social factors by using statistical controls while simultaneously ignoring the complexities of human realities. Abstract empiricism has created the false belief amongst academics that objectivity determines the validity of one's study. "Thus, paradoxically, the less their contact with the subject matter the more knowledgeable [researchers] feel" (Young, 2011, p. 12). The desire to develop objective solutions to address subjective problems (e.g., risk assessment tools to predict violence) has permeated gang research.

Katz and Jackson-Jacobs (2004) warned criminologists that the modern approach to studying street gangs results in the development of problematic views of gangs and gang members. The authors asserted that gang researchers attempt to wave an 'explanatory wand' to explain gang membership without conducting meaningful research into the lived experiences of gang members. They further posit that researchers view gangs as windows through which we can understand social problems without directly addressing gang members. Gang members are never the providers of our theories but rather have theories imposed on their lives by researchers who are far removed from the lived realities of gang life (Katz & Jackson-Jacobs, 2004). "Given the failure to describe the individually lived realities of gang social life, gang research . . . is essentially an argument over the correct description of a ghost" (Katz & Jackson-Jacobs, 2004, p. 106). A major concern is the modern researchers' abandonment of the sociological imagination (Mills, 1959) that characterized early gang research. Researchers no longer employ the sociological imagination in a quest for thick, rich ethnographic data (Geertz, 1973) to understand the complex nature of human social groups. Instead, researchers focus on developing summary descriptions of gangs that ignore historical, cultural, and social contexts. Fifteen years after Katz and Jackson-Jacobs (2004), the issues identified in the article are even more prominent in gang research and are equally applicable to prison gang research.

Gang researchers possess a rudimentary understanding of prison-based gangs (Fleisher & Decker, 2001) that is rooted in positivist frameworks. Orthodox gang researchers abandoned critical, narrative analyses in the mid-20th century in favor of quantitative studies. Gang researchers' shift towards abstract empiricism (Mills, 1959) resulted in the development of theoretically shallow analyses of gangs. Prison gang research today is largely devoid of ethnographic methodologies, which results in quantitative studies that replicate orthodox criminological ideas (Brotherton, 2015). This problematic form of inquiry leads to superficial prison gang research. The shift towards positivism caused researchers to focus on developing one-size fits all theories of gangs that fail to explore differences between gangs (Fraser & Hagedorn, 2018). Thus, gang research results in a metonymic view of gangs whereby one gang represents all gangs (Katz & Jackson-Jacobs, 2004). On the other hand, ethnographic studies suggest that gangs differ across jurisdictions and cultures (Rodgers & Jensen, 2008; Diego Vigil, 2002). Academics ignore this information in favor of positivist studies that reinforce the academic status quo. Thus, prison gang research is devoid of studies that assess cultural, historical, and geographic differences.

Although academics are complicit in our narrow understanding of prison gangs, we must also assess how the current state of academia affects critical studies. Academia hinders the emergence of contextualized, critical gang studies by operating under ideologies that favor positivist research. The academy operates under the publish-or-perish model, which measures a researcher's value based on the number of journal articles she published in top-tier journals. This model emphasizes quantifying success without concern for whether these measures of success produce substantive change in study participants' lives. The overreliance on grant funding for research further exacerbates the publish-or-perish issue. Academic institutions pressure researchers to apply for grants to conduct large-scale positivist studies that result in more publications. The government agencies that award most research grants are not interested in studies that humanize criminal offenders. Thus, dependence on grant funding makes academia complicit in stifling critical gang studies. The primary focus of academia is not alleviating the plight of marginalized individuals or developing policy that can help eradicate social issues. Publications take precedent over addressing real-world problems. Because publications are the key factor for determining individual success in academia, academic pressures force researchers to develop studies that will result in grant funding and publications. Thus, the value of critical studies is diminished in favor of replicating commonly held criminal justice narratives that will result in funding precisely *because* these narratives ignore structural variables, state-sanctioned violence, and the lived experiences of marginalized individuals.

The present chapter highlights issues within existing prison gang research and argues for a return to critical, ethnographic prison studies that center structural variables and individual voices. I begin by exploring Bourdieu's (1980) concept of doxa in the context of academic gang research. The central argument of this chapter is that doxa in the academy leads to the development of problematic prison gang research that ignores the complexity of gangs. Researchers can only fully comprehend gangs through contextualized analyses that situate the lived experiences of prison gang members. The chapter concludes with suggestions for future research.

Jennifer M. Ortiz

Academic doxa in prison gang research

Bourdieu (1980) defined doxa as a phenomenon whereby people view the natural and social world as self-evident. In other words, people tend to accept common beliefs without questioning the authenticity or origin of these beliefs. Many gang researchers engage in academic doxa by reproducing existing criminological or sociological ideas without assessing whether these ideas are factually accurate or relevant in current times. For example, one of the most often-cited sources on prison gangs is Camp and Camp's (1985) report on the impact of prison gangs within correctional facilities. In this report, Camp and Camp (1985) assert that the first prison gang in the United States was the Gypsy Jokers, who reportedly emerged in the Washington State correctional system in 1950. Dozens of prison gang studies repeat this claim and cite Camp and Camp as their source. Academic doxa caused researchers to avoid questioning the validity of Camp and Camp's findings until fairly recently. Smith (2016) conducted a historical analysis that questioned Camp and Camp's claim about the Gypsy Jokers. The analysis found no evidence that the Gypsy Jokers emerged in prison. In fact, Gypsy Joker members assert that the organization first formed in 1965 as an outlaw motorcycle gang, not as a prison gang. In spite of living Gypsy Joker members who could clarify this obvious misconception, prison gang researchers merely repeated Camp and Camp's findings. In fact, prison gang researchers often cite Camp and Camp (1985), which lends academic legitimacy to this factually inaccurate claim. If gang researchers questioned existing findings instead of merely perpetuating academic doxa, we might have discovered this error decades ago.

Prison gang researchers also engage in academic doxa when discussing prison gangs and violence. Similar to street gang research, prison gang research does not view the link between prison gang membership and violence as a discoverable phenomenon. Instead, researchers developed a tautological argument that fails to question if members of various prison gangs engage in violence. The most commonly cited definition of prison gangs reads as follows:

> An organization which operates within the prison system as a self-perpetuating *criminally oriented* entity, consisting of a select group of inmates who have established an organized chain of command and are governed by an established code of conduct. The prison gang will usually operate in secrecy and has as its goal to conduct gang activities by controlling their prison environment through *intimidation and violence* directed toward non-members.
>
> *(Lyman, 1989, p. 48, emphasis added)*

If by definition prison gangs are criminal and use violence, then researchers need not explore whether they engage in criminal behavior. Researchers can simply repeat the claim until it becomes part of gang researcher doxa that will go unquestioned for decades.

Existing prison gang research pathologizes gang membership because gang researchers operate through a criminal justice lens that focuses on violations of institutional rules while ignoring the institution's role in the creation of misconduct. Most researchers do not attempt to understand the effect of macro-structural issues within correctional institutions. Researchers largely assume that prison gangs promote violence; however, it is equally plausible that prison gangs emerge in response to the institution's inability to regulate and control existing violence. Which comes first, the prison gang or the violence? Prison gang researchers do not address this question because academic doxa tells us prison gangs are inherently violent. Orthodox gang researchers operate under the premise that prison gangs are "vicious, ruthless, violent, dangerous, anti-authority, [and] terroristic" (Fong & Buentello, 1991, p. 66). Thus, researchers need not explore whether individual prison gangs engage in violence or how macro-structural factors contribute to that violence. The primary focus of prison gang research is analyzing how institutions can "predict" gang violence and which punitive institutional policies can "eradicate" the problem. As long as researchers analyze violence as a gang issue and not a structural issue, we can feel justified in ignoring the political, social, economic, cultural, and structural variables that necessitate that violence.

Doxa relieves researchers from the burden of conducting critical analyses of macro-structural issues. Many researchers ignore the historical context in which gangs emerge and transform over time (Brotherton, 2015). Prison gang research would lead one to believe that prison gangs exist in a vacuum unaffected by the rapidly changing criminal justice landscape. There is minimal prison gang research that explores the impact of policy shifts within the criminal justice system. For example, researchers fail to account for the impact of neoliberal economic policies that reduce available resources within institutions (Black, 2009). Prison gang research also ignores the impact of sentencing laws and mass incarceration on prison gang development (see Skarbek, 2014 for an exception). The mere fact that the United States' prison population has increased 500% over the past forty years (The Sentencing Project, 2018) should cause researchers to question all preconceptions about prisons and prison gangs. Furthermore, the increase in parole revocations, which in some jurisdictions account for 50% of all prison admissions (Pew Charitable Trusts, 2018), likely affect the prison environment, as these changes have created an unending pool of individuals who cycle in and out of correctional facilities. In spite of these glaring changes to the incarcerated population, most research does not examine the impact of these polices on prison gangs. Research that does explore changes within the correctional system often focuses on whether policies achieve their desired outcome of deterrence or incapacitation. Researchers fail to consider how criminal justice policies often function as structural violence against marginalized groups within society (Wacquant, 2009; Davis, 1998). By ignoring the impact of structural issues, researchers attribute violence to individual shortcomings (Young, 2011) while failing to question the oppressive systems that lead to the establishment of prison gangs.

Although existing prison gang research focuses heavily on institutional rule violations, researchers fail to explore how institutional actors and policies promote these violations. Researchers give minimal attention to the role of correctional officers in prison gang activity (Weide, forthcoming) in spite of media coverage identifying corrupt correctional officers. For example, the federal government indicted thirteen correctional officers in Baltimore for helping the Black Guerrilla Family operate a drug ring in the local jail (Ferranti, 2014). Researchers also ignore how correctional officers create gladiator-like contests between gang members to satisfy the officers' sadistic desires. The Federal Bureau of Investigations recently investigated gladiator contests at an Idaho correctional institution (Holloway, 2014). Additionally, researchers have documented instances of correctional officers allowing vicious attacks against gang members as punishment for violating institutional rules (See Ortiz, 2015 for an example). While ignoring these examples of structural violence, researchers simultaneously ignore how prison gangs can serve as mechanisms for addressing deprivation caused by neoliberal policies.

As long as researchers continue to dehumanize gang members using stereotypical tropes (Brotherton, 2015), we can continue ignoring how the lack of basic human needs negatively affects prison gang members and other inmates. Sykes (1958) developed the concept "pains of imprisonment" to describe how deprivation of basic human experiences – liberty, goods and services, heterosexual relationships, autonomy, and security – negatively affects the incarcerated population. Mass incarceration has exacerbated the pains of imprisonment by limiting the available resources within correctional facilities, including space, medical care, food, and safety (Skarbek, 2014). Although the pains of imprisonment are documented in the literature, most research ignores the impact of these pains on prison gangs and prison gang members.

Prison gang research also ignores the beneficial role of prison gangs in institutional management. Street gang research indicates that gangs play a role in politics (Hagedorn, 2015; Venkatesh, 2008); however, prison gang researchers often ignore this crucial function of prison gangs. Ethnographic research in the Philippines indicates prison gangs are central to managing correctional institutions (Narag & Lee, 2018). In the United States, Skarbek (2014) posits that prison gangs emerge out of a need for governance brought about by the failure of formal institutional governance. Increased populations in California prisons led to a scarcity of resources and space, which increased the value of these commodities. The era of mass incarceration weakened institutional governance and the convict code – an informal set of rules meant to regulate inmate behavior – resulting in a need for prison gangs. Weakened norms and increased scarcity of resources in prisons led inmates to seek out non-traditional forms of governance that could provide membership guidelines, norms, and punishment mechanisms (Skarbek, 2014). Skarbek's (2014) findings suggest that prison gangs formed to address the structural issues caused by mass incarceration. As prison gang membership increased between 1980 and 2005 (Skarbek & Freire, 2016), the number of riots, assaults, and suicides decreased (Useem & Piehl, 2006). Although Skarbek (2014) offers an alternative explanation of prison gang formation, his analysis stills operates under the orthodox notion that prison gangs are inherently violent. Missing from Skarbek's (2014) analysis is a discussion of how subcultural aspects of gangs contribute to the reduction of violence within penal institutions.

Early prison gang research attributed to reductions in prison violence to prison gang formation. In the seminal book *Stateville*, Jacobs (1977) found that gangs reduced violence because gang leaders recognized that violence among inmates would lead to increased suppression and state-sanctioned violence. Gang leaders developed rules to regulate gang behavior to minimize and control violence within institutions. Here we see how subcultural rules benefit the institution. A recent comprehensive analysis of data from the California Department of Correction and Rehabilitation similarly found that prison gangs helped reduce the number of assaults involving weapons (Weide, forthcoming). Thus, it would appear that prison gangs and their subcultural practices are essential to developing governable institutions (Parenti, 1999), because they regulate the use of violence (Ortiz, 2018) and promote unity amongst inmates (Fleisher & Decker, 2001).

Nevertheless, existing doxa about prison gangs operates under stereotypical tropes that portray prison gangs as groupings of violent thugs who disrupt correctional management. Research does indicate, however, that prison gangs promote cooperation between inmates (Fleisher & Decker, 2001) by regulating commissary and the contraband market (Skarbek & Freire, 2016), components of prison life that serve as the basis for power within the inmate social structure (Kalinich & Stojkovic, 1985). The studies referenced previously challenge the doxic notion that prison gangs are merely groups of violent thugs who seek to disrupt correctional systems. In fact, prison gangs control the chaos caused by mass incarceration. Similar to street gang research that indicates these organization emerge in response to forms of oppression (Brotherton & Barrios, 2004), there is existing prison gang research that illustrates how prison gangs respond to state-sanctioned structural violence within institutions (Skarbek, 2014; Weide, forthcoming). Although the research exists to support this argument, orthodox gang researchers engage in confirmation bias by ignoring these studies in favor of citing positivist research that better aligns with existing doxa. Doxa allows gang researchers to exist within academic echo chambers.

Doxa also results in researchers ignoring the impact of environment on gangs. Anthropological research suggests that space and environment are essential to the understanding of cultural formation (Low & Lawrence-Zuniga, 2003). Bourdieu's (2005) notion of habitus is important to understanding how environment can influence subcultures like gangs. As individuals enter different environments, they are socialized into the appropriate habits, beliefs, and dispositions necessary in that environment. This knowledge, or habitus, affects one's behavior within that environment. Although there is extensive research assessing environmental differences between captive and free societies (Rhodes, 2001; Sykes, 1958), gang researchers do not assess the impact of environment on gangs (see Ortiz, 2018 for an exception). A qualitative, comparative analysis of prison and street gangs found that environmental factors – heightened need for security, living in confined spaces, and the desire to avoid lockdowns – affect gang membership, gang leadership, gang hierarchies, management strategies, and relationships with authority figures (Ortiz, 2018). In spite of these documented differences, gang researchers tend to impose theories developed at the theoretical center onto gangs without exploring their applicability (Katz & Jackson-Jacobs, 2004).

The combination of abstract empiricism and prison gang doxa leads researchers to ignore differences across prison gangs. Doxa tells us that prison gangs are most prominent in California but fails to question whether California-based research is applicable in other jurisdictions. California prison gangs do not represent all prison gangs, because there are unique circumstances in California – including three strikes laws and the overuse of solitary confinement for prison gang leaders – that directly affect prison gangs. California also has the distinction of housing the oldest prison gangs, which means that these gangs have had decades to establish themselves. Given these differences, it seems obvious that researchers should question if California prison gangs are inherently different from prison gangs in other states. One exploratory study found that prison gangs exert more control over correctional management at the state level than gangs do in the federal correctional system (Ortiz, 2015). Abstract empiricism, however, causes gang researchers to ignore these differences (Fraser & Hagedorn, 2018). Failure to engage in more nuanced analyses that explore differences across gangs contributes to the creation and reinforcement of doxa.

Ignoring structural issues, failing to question whether differences exist across gangs, and focusing solely on institutional rule violations while ignoring state-sanctioned violence ensure that gang researchers continue to engage in academic doxa that does not produce critical analyses. This problematic approach to studying prison gangs reinforces the use of oppressive correctional strategies, including long-term placement in solitary confinement. As long as prison gang research is devoid of cultural and historical analyses, we will continue to produce research that reinforces the status quo within correctional institutions. Problematic research leads to problematic policy. For example, one study found that non-violent street gang members were placed in maximum-security facilities due to their gang affiliation (Ortiz, 2015). This classification policy is problematic because "studies provide no clear empirical link between gang membership and prison violence" (Skarbek, 2014, p. 98). The assumption that a gang member will commit violent acts while incarcerated and therefore warrants classification into a maximum-security facility is rooted in stereotypical ideals derived from academic doxa, not substantiated facts. A government report found that the individuals most likely to commit violent acts in prison are non-violent offenders who are housed with violent offenders (California Department of Corrections, 1975). This finding suggests that housing a non-violent gang member in a maximum-security facility may actually force the individual to commit a violent act. Orthodox gang researchers do not account for this potential problem, because if by definition gangs are violent, then non-violent gang members do not even exist. As long as scholars continue to produce gang research rooted in dated studies that reinforce stereotypical, racist tropes, we are complicit in the structural violence enacted upon prison gang members. Researchers are as responsible for punitive, oppressive, dehumanizing correctional policies as the criminal justice agencies who implement the policies.

Directions for future research

Challenging current paradigms is part of the scientific process and the search for truth. Researchers must critique the academic doxa that dominates prison gang research. Doxa is dangerous precisely because it dissuades us from challenging the status quo and developing knowledge. Gang researchers must collectively reject the academic status quo that emphasizes publications and grant funding over the development of meaningful knowledge. There is a dire need to reclaim gang research from the grips of abstract empiricism and situate it within the critical lens that dominated early gang research. To achieve this goal, researchers must reengage the sociological imagination (Mills, 1959) and the criminological imagination (Young, 2011). These imaginations reject the abstract empiricism that dominates academic inquiry of social phenomena in favor of rich, ethnographic research. Researchers need to reengage with correctional institutions and the incarcerated population. We must reject the overreliance on narratives derived solely from correctional officers and prison administrators. We cannot accurately convey stories of the oppressed by highlighting the voice of the oppressors (Lorde, 2007). Equally important is the need to understand all social phenomenon within the social, cultural, and historical contexts in which they emerge (Mills, 1959). We must abandon our obsession with being "datasaurs" (Young, 2011) that develop objective truths and acknowledge that the study of all human collectives requires subjective analyses that center the complex lived realities of human life.

In returning to ethnographic study, researchers reintroduce context into the study of gangs. Prison gangs do not exist within a vacuum but rather are affected by institutional, legal, and social changes. Ethnographic examinations of prison gangs would help us understand the impact of these changes by centering the lived experiences of incarcerated persons. This approach would require us to conduct in-depth narrative analyses and field observations that accurately capture the daily lives of prison gang members and are not merely snapshots (Katz & Jackson-Jacobs, 2004) that support the criminal justice narrative. Incarceration can be mundane and ritualistic; however, if a layperson were to read orthodox criminological studies, she may be inclined to believe that prison is an institution where inmates randomly maim each other on a daily basis. This stereotypical perception of prison life is problematic and devoid of depth and understanding. We must begin to understand how prison gang membership affects the daily lives of the incarcerated population in order to develop a deeper understanding that moves beyond an examination of inmate-on-inmate violence. Abandoning stereotypical depictions of prison gangs and centering the role of structural violence will allow for an accurate exploration of gangs.

Divorcing ourselves from stereotypes of prison gangs requires that we abandon abstract empiricism. The existing literature reveals that ethnographic studies of prisons are rare because obtaining access to correctional facilities to conduct longitudinal, ethnographic studies is an arduous task. It is telling that the most-cited studies of prisons (e.g. Sykes, 1958; Irwin, 1970) predate tough on crime policies, mass incarceration, and the war on drugs, policies that directly affected the prison population and institutional structure. Researchers should challenge institutional barriers and return to the ethnographic study of prisons to develop a deeper understanding of how policy changes altered prison life and prison gangs. The effect of policy on gangs is evident in Ortiz's (2018) comparative analysis of prison and street gangs and Skarbek's (2014) assessment of governance within prisons. We cannot ignore the impact of policies on the incarcerated experience. Analyses of prison gang governance must also humanize gangs by assessing how subcultural components affect gang structure and processes. We must acknowledge that prison gangs are subcultural groups directly affected by structural changes.

Researchers can further minimize the influence of criminal justice narratives by exploring interdisciplinary analyses (Katz & Jackson-Jacobs, 2004) that introduce studies of other cultural and social groupings. We must abandon the doxic notion that gangs are inherently different from other institution-based organizations. An interdisciplinary approach that incorporates research from sociology, anthropology, psychology, and even economics would allow for the development of a multifaceted view of gangs that accounts for the complex nature of these organizations. Prison gang research could benefit from the incorporation of subcultural studies that explore legitimized human collectives such as Greek organizations. Studies comparing gangs to other social groupings would allow researchers to reengage with the subcultural components of gangs.

Assessing prison gangs as subcultural organizations affected by macro-structural changes will lead to the development of contextualized theories. There is a need to abandon studies that view prison gangs as one monolithic human collective unaffected by contextual differences. Prison gang theories should abandon abstract empiricism and doxa by highlighting differences. New research should focus on developing gang-specific studies that allow for comparison across organizations. An entire body of literature could focus on comparing gangs across jurisdictions instead of attempting to develop universal representations of prison gangs (Fraser & Hagedorn, 2018). Yet another subarea of prison gang research could focus solely on the implications of new criminal justice policies on prison gangs. These new subareas are only possible if researchers abandon the academic doxa that creates problems within gang research.

If prison gang researchers continue to perpetuate and replicate doxa without critically assessing the applicability of doxic ideas, they will continue to develop research that fails to account for social and structural changes. Without divorcing ourselves from the abstract empiricism that permeates gang research, academics will continue producing research that ignores macro-structural issues and supports the continued oppression of marginalized groups. We must break free of the academic chains that bind us to a publish-or-perish mindset and return to ethnographic research that explores the true reality of gang life.

References

Black, T. (2009). *When a heart turns rock solid*. New York: Vintage Books.

Bourdieu, P. (1980). *The logic of practice*. Cambridge: Polity Press.

Bourdieu, P. (2005). Habitus. In J. Hillier & E. Rooksby (eds.) *Habitus: A sense of place*. Aldershot: Ashgate, pp. 43–52.

Brotherton, D. (2015). *Youth street gangs: A critical appraisal*. New York: Routledge.

Brotherton, D. & Barrios, L. (2004). *The almighty Latin King and Queen Nation: Street politics and the transformation of a New York City gang*. New York: Columbia University Press.

California Department of Corrections. (1975). *Prison violence in California: Issues and alternatives*. Sacramento, CA: State of California, Department of Finance, Program Evaluation Unit.

Camp, G. M. & Camp, C. G. (1985). *Prison gangs: Their extent, nature, and impact on prisons*. Washington, DC: U.S. Government Printing Office.

Davis, A. (1998). Masked racism: Reflections on the prison industrial complex. *ColorLines*.

Diego Vigil, J. (2002). *A rainbow of gangs: Street cultures in the mega city*. Austin, TX: University of Texas Press.

Ferranti, S. (2014). How the Black Guerrilla family turned Maryland's prison system into their personal playground. *Vice*. Retrieved from www.vice.com/en_us/article/exm9q7/the-illicit-ventures-of-the-black-guerrilla-family-in-the-maryland-prison-system-1208.

Fleisher, M. S., & Decker, S. H. (2001). An overview of the challenge of prison gangs. *Corrections Management Quarterly, 5* (1): 1–9.

Fong, R. S., & Buentello, S. (1991). The detection of prison gang development: An empirical assessment. *Federal Probation, 55*: 66–69.

Fraser, A. & Hagedorn, J. M. (2018). Gangs and a global sociological imagination. *Theoretical Criminology, 22* (1): 42–62.

Geertz, C. (1973). *The interpretation of culture*. New York: Basic Books.

Hagedorn, J. M. (2015). *The in$ane Chicago way: The daring plan by Chicago gangs to create a Spanish Mafia*. Chicago, IL: University of Chicago Press.

Holloway, L. (2014). Gladiator school: FBI investigates Idaho private prison for abuse. *The Root*. Retrieved from www.theroot.com/gladiator-school-fbi-investigates-idaho-private-pris-1790874888.

Irwin, F. (1970). *The felon*. Los Angeles, CA: University of California Press.

Jacobs, J. (1977). *Stateville*. Chicago: The University of Chicago Press.

Kalinich, D. B. & Stojkovic, S. (1985). Contraband: The basis for legitimate power in a prison social system. *Criminal Justice and Behavior, 12* (4): 435–451.

Katz, J. & Jackson-Jacobs, C. (2004). The criminologists' gang. In C. Sumner (ed.) *The Blackwell companion to criminology*. Oxford, UK: Blackwell Publishing, pp. 91–124.

Lorde, A. (2007). The master's tools will never dismantle the master's house. In A. Lorde's (ed.) *Sister outsider: Essays and speeches*. Berkeley, CA: Crossing Press, pp. 110–114.

Low, S. M. & Lawrence-Zuniga, D. (2003). *The anthropology of space and place: Locating culture*. Malden, MA: Blackwell Publishing.

Lyman, M. D. (1989). *Gangland*. Springfield, IL: Charles C Thomas.

Mills, C. W. (1959). *The sociological imagination*. New York: Oxford University Press.

Narag, R. E. & Lee, S. (2018). Putting our fires: Understanding the developmental nature and roles of inmate gangs in the Philippine overcrowded jails. *International Journal of Offender Therapy and Comparative Criminology, 62* (11): 3509–3535.

Ortiz, J. (2015). The power of place: A comparative analysis of prison and street gangs. (Doctoral dissertation). Retrieved from ProQuest Dissertations and Theses database. (UMI No. 3720963).

Ortiz, J. (2018). Gangs and environment: A comparative analysis of prison and street gangs. *American Journal of Qualitative Research, 2* (1): 97–117.

Parenti, C. (1999). *Lockdown America: Police and prisons in the age of crisis*. New York: Verso.

Pew Charitable Trusts. (2018). Probation and parole systems marked by high stakes, missed opportunities. Retrieved from www.pewtrusts.org/research-and-analysis/issue-briefs/2018/09/probation-and-parole-systems-marked-by-high-stakes-missed-opportunities.

Rhodes, L. A. (2001). Toward an anthropology of prisons. *Annual Review of Anthropology, 30*: 65–83.

Rodgers, D. & Jensen, S. (2008). Revolutionaries, barbarians or war machines? Gangs in Nicaragua and South Africa. *Socialist Register, 45*: 220–238.

The Sentencing Project. (2018). Factsheet: Trends in U.S. corrections. Retrieved from www.sentencing project.org/publications/trends-in-u-s-corrections/.

Skarbek, D. (2014). *The social order of the underworld: How prison gangs govern the American penal system*. Oxford: Oxford University Press.

Skarbek, D. & Freire, D. (2016). Prison gangs. In H. Griffin & V. Woodward (eds.) *Handbook of corrections in the United States*. London: Routledge.

Smith, C. F. (2016). When is a prison gang not a prison gang: A focused review of prison gangs literature. *Journal of Gang Research, 23* (2): 41–52.

Sykes, G. M. (1958). *Society of captives*. Princeton, NJ: Princeton University Press.

Useem, B. & Piehl, A. M. (2006). Prison buildup and disorder. *Punishment & Society, 8* (1): 87–115.

Venkatesh, S. (2008). *Gang leader for a day: A rogue sociologist crosses the line*. London: Allen Lane.

Wacquant, L. (2009). *Punishing the poor: The neoliberal government of social insecurity*. Durham and London: Duke University Press.

Weide, R. D. (forthcoming). The invisible hand: A critical historical analysis of prison gangs in California. *The Prison Journal*.

Weide, R. D. (forthcoming). Structural disorganization: How prison gangs mitigate serious violence in California. *American Journal of Sociology*.

Young, J. (2011). *The criminological imagination*. Cambridge: Polity Books.

45

Prison gangs

Rise, resistance, and reentry

Calvin John Smiley

Introduction

Prison gangs are loosely defined as organizations that operate within carceral settings. Typically, these collectives are structured around race, ethnicity, or other determining factors such as neighborhood or regional location (Fleisher & Decker, 2001; Gaes, Wallace, Gilman, Klein-Saffran, & Suppa, 2002; Joyce, 2016). Prison gangs are known to engage in forms of illicit and criminal activities and live by a convict code (Lessing, 2017; Phillips, 2012; Skarbek, 2010). These groups operate narcotic distribution, forms of racketeering and extortion, and violent acts. Prison gang members are frequently identified by prison officials through both ascribed status such as racial group or achieved status such as tattoos, clothing, expressions, and gestures (Gaes, Wallace, Gilman, Klein-Saffran, & Suppa, 2002; Mackey, 2018). Politicians and other correctional officials have cited prison gangs as catalysts to violence, creating disorder; therefore, efforts to eradicate prison gangs have been a driving force within corrections (Lessing, 2016; Maxson, 2012). However, research suggests prison gangs are highly structured systems that are motivated by profit in an underground economy and in fact create order in these spaces (Skarbek, 2012, 2014). In addition, further research concludes that the preoccupation with eliminating prison gangs has had the reverse effect and metastasized these organizations into larger and more powerful units (Lessing, 2016, 2017). Therefore, this chapter takes a critical approach at understanding the rise, resistance, and reentry of prison gang members.

The aim of this chapter is to examine prison gangs in the following manner. First, it describes a brief history of the rise of prison gangs in the United States and how mass incarceration proliferated membership because of the influx of inhabitants into prisons. Second, it examines the numerous ways these gangs have participated in prison resistance. Oftentimes, gangs are portrayed as apolitical; however, various historical events indicate that these organizations are highly motivated to be recognized as having legitimate concerns. Third, it offers insight into how individuals who are affiliated or have been identified as gang members experience prisoner reentry. Through qualitative research, individuals returning to society discuss gang involvement and what that means for their reentry process. Finally, this chapter discusses prison abolition as a serious exploratory consideration as an alternative to current prison models. Abolition frameworks introduce new dialogues between prison gangs and state officials to recognize individual and group humanity, comprehend concerns, and ultimately find common ground for a more democratic and viable system.

Rise of prison gangs and mass incarceration

According to scholars and others, prison gangs in the United States began in the 1950s (Fleisher & Decker, 2001; Stastny & Tyrnauer, 1983). Some of the first and most infamous prison gangs include the Mexican Mafia, The Aryan Brotherhood, The Black Guerilla Family, and La Nuestra Familia. All of these gangs have similar histories of having shared racial and ethnic backgrounds, being formed out of a need for protection, and being founded during a time of changing cultural dynamics in the United States, particularly the Civil Rights and Black Power Movements, amongst others.

Prior to formal gang identification, an "inmate code" existed throughout penitentiaries. This code included acting tough, not interfering with other inmates, and not befriending correctional officers (Clemmer, 1958; Hayner & Ash, 1940; Irwin & Cressey, 1962; Trammel, 2012). From their inception, prisons have been violent spaces. The architects behind the construction of prisons in the late 18th and early 19th century were reformists and sought out more progressive punishments, supposedly to combat violence; however, disease and other horrendous actions persisted (James, 2014). Even in early penal institutions, ethnic identity became a significant component of self-preservation. In the earliest known memoir written by a Black prisoner in the mid-19th century, Austin Reed expresses how being a companion with Irishmen was important. He writes,

> Reader, if you are on the right side of an Irishman, you have the best friend in the world. . . . On the right side of him, and he will spill the last drop of blood for you that runs in his veins. I would rather suffer wrong from the hands of an Irishman ten thousand times, than to suffer once from the hands of a full-blooded Yankee.
>
> *(p. 43, 2016)*

In the mid-19th century, Irish immigrants were not viewed as "White." Here, two "racially inferior" groups (i.e. Black and Irish) share an alliance against their common enemy (i.e. Yankees). This is similar to modern prison gangs. For example, the Mexican Mafia has had a long-standing alliance with the Aryan Brotherhood, a violent White supremacist prison gang (Abadinsky, 2010).

Prison gangs did not form in a vacuum but rather influenced by cultural shifts and policy changes. For instance, the Black Guerilla Family's (BGF) founder, George Jackson, had close ties to Black Power groups such as the Black Panther Party, where he developed a high political consciousness. Beyond, BGF, there had been an established tradition of prisons being spaces of political awakening, such as for Malcolm X, who joined the Nation of Islam while incarcerated (Haley & X, 1965). Additionally, the Mexican Mafia formed in a youth detention center in California in the late 1950s, and the Aryan Brotherhood (AB) began in the mid-1960s when White prisoners felt a threat of losing control to minorities inside prisons (Fleisher & Decker, 2001).

As the 1960s moved into the 1970s, several occurrences happened in the United States. First, the urban landscape drastically began to change as White Americans began leaving urban centers for more spacious and newly resurrected suburban areas, known as "White flight" (Frey, 1979). Next, workers experienced de-industrialization as factory jobs left for cheaper production overseas. Finally, as Whites and jobs left inner-city areas, urban decay festered. Social disorganization theorists suggest that the lack of intervention into communities to ensure employment and guarantee affordable and safe housing creates criminogenic environments where institutions erode and poverty can worsen, exacerbating deviant and criminal cultures (Bell, 2009; Hagedorn, 2008; Kornhauser, 1978).

The Civil Rights era was a turbulent time in the United States. In the mid-1960s, several Northern cities such as Newark, New Jersey, and Detroit, Michigan, erupted in violence. President Lyndon Johnson ordered a special counsel known as the Kerner Commission to investigate these uprisings. The most glaring concern the committee put forth was racism and de facto segregation. The report recommended massive investment in housing and social programs (U.S. Riot Commission, 1968).

In November 1968, Richard M. Nixon was elected president of the United States. Using the recent events of unrests, the rising crime rates in the United States, and decade-long struggle for Civil Rights, Nixon used coded language that had a subliminal meaning to target minority groups but situated it under the guidelines of "law and order." Since then, criminal justice became the new focus, shifting emphasis from structural inequalities to individual behavior.

In 1973, New York State Governor Nelson Rockefeller passed the country's first mandatory minimum sentence guidelines, which drastically changed penalties for drug possession (Gonnerman, 2004). In 1978, New York Governor Hugh Carey passed the Juvenile Offender Act, which allowed for children as young as thirteen years of age to be tried as adults after reading a newspaper article about fifteen-year-old Willie Bosket, who had pled guilty to killing two men and shooting a third on the New York City subway (Butterfield, 2008).

During the 1988 presidential election, George H.W. Bush famously released what became known as the "Willie Horton" ad, which highlighted his support for capital punishment. The image of a Black prisoner, Willie Horton, was used as a backdrop describing the brutally violent crimes that Horton committed while on a prison furlough, a program that operated under his opponent's time as governor. The image of a dark-skinned Black male with unkempt hair became the focal point of the ad and had a two-prong impact. First, it made Bush look strong and his opponent weak. Second, it played on racial fears and stereotypes of the desensitized inherently criminal Black male. Finally, Democratic President Bill Clinton passed the Violent Crime Control and Law Enforcement Act of 1994, which was the largest bill in the history of the United States, funding the hire of over 100,000 police officers, $9.7 billion to fund the construction of prisons, and $6.1 billion in preventative programming. These and other policies passed in the latter half of the 20th century contributed to the exponential growth of the American prison system.

In 1974, the country's imprisonment rate was 102 per 100,000, and by 2007, it was 506 per 100,000 (Austin, Eisen, Cullen, Frank, & Fellow, 2016). This meant that in the early 21st century, roughly one out of every thirty-one Americans was under some form of criminal justice supervision (Pew Center on the States, 2009). Michelle Alexander (2012) argues that this drastic growth within the prison system has had lasting effects by creating a caste-like system for formerly incarcerated individuals. Western, Kleykamp, and Rosenfeld (2006) found that Black men who do not finish high school have drastically higher rates of incarceration. In New Jersey, Black residents make up over 60% of those incarcerated yet only make up about 13% of the state population (Nellis, 2016; New Jersey Department of Corrections, 2019).

America's expansion of criminal justice efforts in the mid-20th century offers insight into the growth of American prison gangs. Lessing (2016, 2017) highlights that as prisons expanded, so did gangs, and early efforts to suppress these organizations included transferring prisoners to other facilities with the hopes of neutralizing the gangs. Furthermore, prison gangs quickly began to engage in criminal enterprise, formulating symbiotic relationships with street gangs (Pyrooz, Decker, & Fleisher, 2011; Rivera, Cowles, & Dorman, 2003; Wood, Alleyne,

Mozova, & James, 2014). Lessing (2016) points out that street gang members adhere to prison gangs' commands, as they know, at some point, they might end up in prison. Despite the close relationships between street and prison gangs, there is still much less known about prison gangs. Weide (2015) offers analysis and insight into the rise of prison gangs by examining the history of carceral policies in California. Pyrooz, Decker, and Fleisher (2011) point out there are basic administrative challenges of entering prisons and that the study of prison gangs has methodological limitations.

Meanwhile, street gangs have long been studied. Herbert Asbury (1928) published *The Gangs of New York*, a comprehensive account of New York street gangs of the 19th century. Since then, a myriad of scholarship on gangs and street life has been written. Martín Sánchez-Jankowski's book (1991), *Islands in the Street: Gangs and American Urban Society*, demystifies many of the preconceived notions about gangs. David C. Brotherton and Luis Barrio's book (2004), *The Almighty Latin King and Queen Nation*, explores how gangs can transform into social movements. John M. Hagedorn's (2015) *The Insane Chicago Way: The Daring Plan by Chicago Gangs to Create a Spanish Mafia* examines how gangs attempt to become organized like other criminal enterprises. This is just a small sample, along with a plethora of other scholarship, which highlights the complexities of gang culture.

Beyond the traditional heteronormative male-centered gangs, books about women and gender non-conforming groups in gangs have been published. Anne Campbell's book (1984), *The Girls in the Gang*, explores the role of women in gangs. Jody Miller's (2001) *One of the Guys: Girls, Gangs, and Gender* looks into gender-specific issues and gendered resistance in gangs. Vanessa R. Panfil's (2017), *The Gang's All Queer* complicates traditional modalities of the heteronormative portrayals of gang members and introduces gang members who identify as gay or queer.

Finally, there is scholarship that examines urban street life, which often has ties to gangs. Victor Rios (2011), studies how young Black and Latino boys navigate punitive policies in school and community in *Punished: Policing the Lives of Black and Latino Boys*. Randol Contreras (2013) follows a group of young men who actively engage in criminal behaviors in his book, *The Stick Up Kids*, highlighting how violence is often a means to an end in street life. Finally, Jan Haldipur (2018), in *No Place on the Corner: The Costs of Aggressive Policing*, examines the impacts of New York City's protocol known as "stop, question, and frisk" and how aggressive patrolling tactics change the social ecology of street life.

While these important works examine street gangs and urban life, there is much less written about prison gangs. David Skarbek's work (2014), *The Social Order of the Underworld: How Prison Gangs Govern the American Penal System*, takes a comprehensive look into California state prison gangs. Here, he argues that prison gang members utilize rational choice in carrying out day-to-day operations and prison politics and regulate a sense of order within these facilities. While this framework is helpful, it is important to recognize the structural environment and conditions that create a social ecology for such choices. In other words, the consideration of choice might be an option for some but not all, depending on rank or status within the prison or gang. Therefore, in order to comprehend the role that prison gangs play in penal settings, the next section focuses on resistance.

Resistance, protest, and uprisings

Prison gangs are multi-faceted organizations. Skarbek (2014) argues that prison gangs create stability rather than disarray as an unofficial form of governance. At times, the definition of what qualifies as a prison gang is also blurred. For example, the Nation of Islam and the Five

Percent Nation, both self-identifying religious organizations, have been described as prison gangs (Knight, 2013). In addition, other groups that began as gangs have engaged in political organizing, such as the Latin Kings (Brotherton and Barrios, 2004), or shifted their group from a gang to a community outreach organization, such as Conservative Vice Lords (Dawley, 1992). Therefore, it is important to recognize that prison gangs are not static but rather fluid in their identities and roles.

The seminal example of resistance is the Attica prison rebellion in upstate New York in 1971. Heather Ann Thompson's (2016) book, *Blood in the Water*, chronicles and details the horrendous conditions in Attica leading up to the rebellion. Living conditions were horrible, and correctional officers policed in a sadistic manner. Thompson writes,

> the men [prisoners] there [Attica] were so desperate for time outside their cells that they would literally stand outside in the sleet and rain just to catch some fresh air. . . . Attica's correction officers barely spoke to the prisoners – preferring instead to convey their wish with the butt of their batons.
>
> *(p. 390–391, 2016)*

According to the documentary *Eyes on the Prize*, during the rebellion, a contingent of Black Muslims became the security force protecting media, correctional officials, and other outside observers who entered the facility during the takeover (Eyes on the Prize, 1987). In the end, on September 13, 1971, the state of New York retook the prison, leaving forty-three individuals dead. Nevertheless, it is paramount in recognizing what Attica did for American prisons. News reporter John Johnson, reporting live as the re-taking of the prison occurred, prophetically stated, "Whatever happens after the situation here at Attica, the penal system here in the United States and the people who are kept inside of them will never be the same" (Eyes on the Prize, 1987). The Attica Brothers, as they became known, were able to provoke institutional change. Many of the demands were met, such as better food and health services, the recruiting of minority correctional officers, and expansion of vocational and academic training (Thompson, 2016).

Inspired by the Attica uprising, prisoners at Walpole (Massachusetts) prison in 1973 staged a rebellion. At the time, Black prisoners were denied a Kwanza celebration, galvanizing a prison-wide strike. In response, correctional officers went on strike with the hopes that the prison would fall into chaos. Jamie Bissonette's (2008) *When the Prisoners Ran Walpole* highlights how the prisoners created a truce and took on roles such as medics, cooks, and other services, which curbed racial violence. One of the most significant achievements at Walpole was the creation of a prisoners' union known as the National Prisoners Reform Association (NPRA). This representative body became a voice for prisoners' rights, introducing collective bargaining for better wages, healthcare, food, and other services (Bissonette, 2008). Walpole became a model of prison abolition, revealing how prisoners could come together for a collective purpose, de-escalate violence, and thrive independently.

Prison resistance is a way to subvert the traditional modes of power and exploitation. While prisons are designed to segregate, isolate, and diminish contact between peers, prison gangs push back against this notion. In recent years, "supermax" prisons have been built to ensure solitary confinement and limited social interaction. In July 2013, a coordinated hunger strike, led by prison gangs, began in the California state prison system, and over 29,000 prisoners participated in protest of the use of solitary confinement (John, 2013). Research on solitary confinement has found that this type of punishment has both physical and psychological ramifications (Guenther, 2013).

Weide (2015) posits that prison gangs hold a unique position within carceral settings. He writes:

> In fact, with their rigid discipline, systemic organizational structure and pervasive influence both on the streets and in carceral facilities, prison gangs like the Mexican Mafia represent the greatest possible threat to carceral facilities and the capitalist State, not because of their criminal activity, but because of their political potential for radical resistance, coordinated both on the streets and in carceral facilities throughout the state. Inmates are far more organized, ten times as numerous, much more experienced in violence and have far closer connections to and control over the streets than did those inmates who rose up against the system in the social movement era of the late 1960s and early 1970s.
>
> *(p. 354)*

The concept that slave labor exists in US prisons is justified by the 13th Amendment, which states, "Neither slavery nor involuntary servitude, *except* as a punishment for crime whereof the party shall have been duly convicted, shall exist with the United States, or any place subject to their jurisdiction" (Browne-Marshall, 2010, emphasis added). Following the American Civil War, convict leasing exponentially grew under the Jim Crow system of segregation. According to Douglas Blackmon (2009), convict labor became a re-envisioned form of bondage where states would lease convicts' labor to private companies in exchange for a financial fee.

Recently, in 2016 and 2018, prisoner strikes have occurred, and the Incarcerated Workers Organizing Committee (IWOC), which is within the Industrial Workers of the World (IWW) union, has focused on organizing prison labor (IWOC, 2018). In 2018, California prisoners were paid $1 per hour and $2 per day to fight wildfires (Lopez, 2018). In search of humanity, prisoners are recognizing their collective agency and uniting behind the causes of better conditions and human rights. The next section discusses the difficulties of reentry, particularly for someone affiliated or identified as a gang member. While all persons coming out of prison have certain barriers, those with "gang" ties have their own unique set of challenges.

Prison gangs and reentry

Prisoner reentry, commonly referred to as reentry, is the transition from incarcerated settings to the community. Research suggests that roughly 95% of all persons incarcerated are released (Travis, Solomon, & Waul, 2001). Therefore, it is imperative to have a protocol for returning individuals who are leaving these settings. Prior to the 21st century, very little academic work or policy focused on reentry or reentry services. Yet, by the 2010s, over 650,000 individuals were being released annually (Department of Justice, 2018). Hence, this subfield of criminological inquiry has taken on a growing importance. Unfortunately, research (Langan & Levin, 2002) indicates that roughly just less than 70% of those who are released from prison are re-arrested or reincarcerated within three years. Dooley, Seals and Skarbek (2014) suggest that individuals with gang affiliation are likely to have higher rates of recidivism than non-affiliated individuals, offering a six percentage point increase in recidivism.

This section examines qualitative research[1] from a community-based reentry organization in Newark, New Jersey that was collected from 2010–2013. Utilizing interviews ($n = 31$), focus groups ($n = 52$), and ethnographic data, this research investigates how being gang identified impacts one's reentry process. Moving forward, all the names are pseudonyms.

This research found that gang affiliation and identification are not the same. The former refers to those who are part of either a street or prison gang. Their affiliation is pronounced in language, gesture, street wear, or other symbols such as tattoos, whereas the latter refers to those identified as being part of a gang either by other participants or by law enforcement because of mistaken tattoos, neighborhood origin, or simply stereotypes. For example, during a focus group, a young Black male, Jones, looked across the table and said to another young Black male named Rameek, "What's poppin' slime?" The response by Rameek was half-hearted. Both men in their early twenties proceeded to participate in the group. Afterwards, Rameek discussed the interaction stating, "That shit always happens to me." When asked, "What happens?" He said, "Somebody think I'm affiliated [in a gang]." Rameek explained that the phrase, "What's poppin'" is a term used by Blood gang members, which is heard in popular hip-hop lyrics such as Lil Wayne. Rameek didn't know if the guy was greeting him in a friendly way or challenging him and indicated that is why he responded cautiously. Rameek explained, "Someone always think I'm in a gang, I'm not for real. But it don't matter, I'm from Newark, been locked up, and from a neighborhood that's heavy Crip, so people just assume I'm in a gang." When asked who the people are who assume, he responded, "Everyone, like the police, COs, you know. It even says in my jacket [case file] I'm in a gang. It's bad cause then they put [me] in places I shouldn't be." Rameek's being identified as a gang member puts his livelihood at risk because its marks him by law enforcement and gang members. Recently, the New York Police Department has amassed a "gang" data bank that collects individuals' names police presume are gang affiliated, which could elevate the type of criminal charge (Speri, 2018).

For others, gang affiliation played a role in their lives. Bobby, one of the few White males, was over six feet tall, weighed nearly 250 pounds, and with the exception of his face was covered in tattoos. He explained, "All these tattoos mean something, and I had to earn them like patches. The average person might see them and probably wouldn't understand but someone who is a 1%er would know the difference." Bobby explained that he was a "1%er," which refers to being in an outlaw motorcycle club. Bobby said, "Growing up when I did it [joined the gang], if you rode a bike [motorcycle] you join a club, I just happened to join an outlaw club." According to Bobby, it was not his outlaw motorcycle club that landed him in prison but a combination of drugs, alcohol, and short temper,

> I would go out and party and get high and drunk and then fight and hurt people. All my charges are for assault, but I know it was the boozing that did it. In fact, it was a lot of my brothers [other outlaw members] that helped me get clean.

He expressed that he was no longer actively involved in the club and club affairs but still associated with friends. He stated,

> There are bars that only bikers go to and I can go in there and I know that they won't serve me and probably kick my ass if I try to drink. That's the kind of support I need, someone who will check me if I'm stupid. I know my kind [outlaw motorcycle clubs] get a bad rap but most of these guys are good guys at the end of the day.

Bobby was honest about outlaw motorcycle clubs, saying,

> I mean I know some of those guys distribute [sell drugs] but that's not my business and yeah, there aren't any Black guys in the club, I know some pretty racist guys but we aren't all like that, I got Black friends, Spanish friends, I got no problem with people.

Bobby sought out his biker club for affirmation and sobriety, yet this did not last. After several months of not attending the group, Bobby came back to the reentry center almost unrecognizable. He cut his hair short, wore a long-sleeved t-shirt, and lost almost fifty pounds. He explained,

> The biker stuff was getting old. Don't get me wrong, I still love those guys but being in bars is hard when you're trying to stay sober that atmosphere can catch up with you. Also, I had to change my style, nobody wants to hire a two-time jail bird with all these tattoos.

Smiley and Middlemass (2016) discuss Bobby[2] and how a changing of style is important to reentry. A new beginning doesn't just happen in the abstract but in tangible manners, such as changing fashion and outward presentation of self. Bobby could now present in a new way that could aide in securing employment and a relationship. He said, "I got rid of my bike [motorcycle] and got a car, better for dates."

While some like Bobby felt they could change their outer appearance, for others it was more of a challenge. Alonzo, a Black man in his mid-twenties, was affiliated with the Bloods gang. While a young man by conventional societal standards, he was an "O.G.,"[3] in his gang, having been to prison and still alive. He explained how this "O.G." status limited him in several ways. First, because he was a known gang affiliate, his parole stipulations were very restrictive. He explained,

> My P.O. [parole officer] says I can't wear anything red or carry a red bandana or hat, anything that would signify my affiliation. I also can't be around other gang members, which is like everybody on my block. And last thing, I can't have no markers or other things like spray cans in my possession.

When asked about the spray cans, he explained that this was an issue with "tagging." In the subculture of graffiti, "tagging" refers to writing one's mark on public or private property (Ferrell, 1993; Ilan, 2015). Many gang members "tag" buildings to show territorial boundaries and turf (Conquergood, 2013). Second, Alonzo had facial tattoos, which consisted of teardrops on both sides of his face. These small but distinct pieces of art were outlined in black ink and filled in red. Alonzo said, "I know people see these [tattoos] and judge me, but that doesn't mean I can't work or do a job right. They always preaching don't judge a book by its cover, but that's exactly what happening to me." Months later, Alonzo was still searching for a full-time job but had been getting some part-time work. It was becoming clear his gang affiliation was disrupting employment opportunities and reentry.

It was not just male clients who described being gang affiliated. Tina, a light-skinned Black woman in her early twenties, openly discussed being a Gangster Disciple (G.D.). Upon her release, Tina's primary concern was to find stable housing and retain custody of her young son. She voluntarily offered her gang affiliation, stating, "I'm G.D. been in since I was like thirteen and them niggas is my family. My baby's father is G.D. too." Tina explained that her ex-boyfriend was serving a long sentence, saying, "He got some serious time, twenty-five years or something like that. The feds don't play when you heavy in this gang shit." Her remarks alluded to the fact that being gang affiliated increased the risk of prison time. Tina described still being "cool" with many of her G.D. family but also felt some distancing needed to take place to get her life on track. She said,

> I love them, they always look out and make sure I'm good, but when I'm around them niggas all I wanna do is party and bullshit. I pop hella pills when I'm with them niggas, it's just what we do and right now, I got to stay clean 'cause I'm on parole, trying to get my son, and just get my life together.

Tina discussed using makeup to cover her gang tattoo that was on the inside of her forearm, saying,

> I got this right before I got locked up, it was good and bad. It was good 'cause nobody messed with me when I was locked up 'cause they knew what it meant, but it's bad now 'cause I got to cover it up since that's not who I'm trying to be anymore. I want to change my people, places, and things and this tattoo doesn't help that.

Utilizing vernacular learned in recovery meeting groups, Tina's focus on sobriety and recognizing her gang affiliation as a trigger was an important step for her desistance.

While many clients described their street gang connections, others talked more in detail about being in a prison gang. Yusef, a Black male in his mid-40s, proudly spoke of being affiliated with a Crips set. Yusef was "jumped-in"[4] while in prison. He recounted,

> I went to prison the first time when I was nine years old, I was a baby. From that time until my early twenties I was in and out of [New] Jersey prisons, I probably been to every jail in the state 'cause I was wild. Then in the early 90s I caught a federal case.

Yusef was arrested and convicted of carjacking, which is forced removal from an automobile. In 1992, US Congress passed the Federal Anti-Car Theft Act (FACTA), which made this an offense punishable up to life in prison (Cherbonneau, 2008). Yusef said,

> I was one of the first to get hit with this fed [federal] charge so I got twenty years and they sent me to California, because when you in the feds they can put you anywhere, so I did most these last twenty years in California.

Yusef went on to describe his gang entrance, saying:

> When I got out to California I didn't know what to expect, but I knew it was gang heavy out there. Over here in Jersey when I was doing time, we didn't really have no gangs like that. There was the Muslims and Five Percenters and some Spanish gangs but the Bloods and Crips wasn't big like they are now. Anyway, I knew I could hold my own but some niggas was looking out, made sure I had shower shoes, tooth brush, toilet tissue, shit like that, so I cliqued up and I'm Crip and been Crip last twenty years.

Yusef discussed how being in a gang had its benefits and shortcomings while incarcerated, stating,

> I ride for mines, even now, I still get down that will never change but the one thing that always messed with me the most was that we had to bang against everybody: Whites, Mexicans, and other Blacks. All these other races are unified but us [Black people].

Yusef's experience was similar to Larry, who was thirty-three and just completed eleven years in the federal prison system. Like Yusef, Larry said the majority of his time in prison was spent between prisons in Texas and California. In relation to his gang affiliation, Larry described, "I was already Crip before I went to prison so I figured I would be good with the big homies [friends] wherever I was at. If they was Crip and I showed heart it would be cool." Larry was only nineteen when he went to federal prison and discussed how age played a role in how he did his time. He said:

> You know I was young when I got there and that meant I was a soldier and the prison shit set up differently, you don't ask no questions from the O.G.s, you just follow orders, which I did and I mean I caught some jail charges and shit but that's the environment you are in. You gotta remember, dudes think they tough 'cause they from Newark and go to state prison, when you in the feds you doing time with niggas from all over the country and when you all the way out in California, nobody care about no Newark. It was like Newark, Philly and New York niggas had to stick together out there.

Larry explained how he felt that the federal system is a horrible place because prison gangs control them and he hoped never to go back. He stated:

> I'm really happy to be out of the chaos, I can't wear no gang colors and that's fine, I can wear other stuff because you know being in those places you see the worst in people. Like forreal, I want to work with the dudes out here now because if you get sent to the feds you see that Mexicans and Krackas [Whites] in prison really don't see Black people as human. I seen guys kill Black men in prison like they were taking out the garbage. After seeing all that violence, I could never hurt another Black man again in my life.

Larry's vulnerability and openness about being in a prison gang, actively participating in prison gang culture, and the impact on his life are profound. DeVeaux (2013) recounts how past traumas from his prison experience impact his livelihood. It is important to remember and recognize that prison experiences do not remain inside prison walls but carry on with individuals as they reenter society. Therefore, it is important to institute therapy, counseling, and other forms of mental healing, along with physical healing into the reentry process.

Conclusion

Law enforcement is constantly seeking new and innovative ways to reduce the presence of prison gangs. The most obvious way of eliminating prison gangs is to eliminate prisons. Prison abolition could prove useful in furthering the discourse surrounding prisons, gangs, and the types of toxic environments they promote. At this point, it is hard to distinguish where the street gang ends and the prison gang starts and where the prison gang starts and the street gang ends (Pyrooz, Decker, and Fleisher, 2011). In fact, Loic Wacquant (2001) argues that hyper-incarceration has made for what he calls a "deadly symbiosis" where American "ghettos" and prisons have meshed, making carceral spaces look like our communities and our communities look like our carceral spaces.

The criminal justice system is ripe to shift to alternative forms of justice. While it is beyond the scope of this chapter, there are international perspectives that could guide intervention (Brotherton, 2007; Brotherton & Gude, 2018; Farah, 2012; Lessing, 2016, 2019; Rostami, Leinfelt, & Brotherton, 2012). In some cases, dialogues between gangs and the state have created better living environments for the prisoners and diminished violence both inside and out of the prison setting. The reality is that prison gangs are not going to just disappear, and hoping for that to happen would be both naïve and short-sighted. Prison gangs, like many subcultures, play an important role in individuals' lives, offering identity, culture, and protection. Therefore, steps need to be taken to create a space of dialogue, understanding, and change that promote positive outcomes for various stakeholders in society.

First, a truce amongst prison gangs is needed. While it seems like a futile effort on the surface, precedence would indicate that this could happen. Gangs have been open to ending violence, and a treaty should not be doubted or seen as a charade but taken seriously by the state. For example, in El Salvador, rival gangs MS-13 and Barrio 18 were able to broker a truce and implemented peace zones, which dramatically curtailed violence, cutting homicide rates nearly in half in 2012 (Brodzinsky, 2013). Unfortunately, the state pushed back against this truce and declared war on the street gangs, which are heavily controlled by leaders who are incarcerated (Hernández & Hamilton, 2016; Moss, 2015). Yet this instance sets a precedent that truce is possible and could be implemented.

Second, dialogues between the state and gangs should be pursued. Similar to the Walpole rebellion, prison gangs could very well be considered prison unions that represent the interests of those incarcerated. Here, aspects of restorative justice might be incorporated and mechanisms for healing introduced into prison environments (Nowotny & Carrara, 2018). By having a voice, prisoners are given some agency over their lives, which could have profound impacts on feeling included and accepted in society.

Next, concerns of prisoners need to be taken seriously, such as calls for education, vocational training, quality health services, visits from family and friends, and upgraded and sanitary living conditions. There are models of reform that could be used, particularly looking at Scandinavian prisons (Larson, 2013). No longer are we in the days that prisons must be dreary and dreadful sites, but rather, they could have a location that is incentivizing and inspiring. Angela Y. Davis, a preeminent prison scholar, activist, and abolitionist, argues that in the pursuit of abolition, an abolitionist can accept reform efforts if it makes the overall quality of life better for all within the prison environment (2011).

Finally, prison abolition must be the end goal. While working on the previous efforts, the constant amongst all these entities is to one day move away from conventional prison models and replace them with facilities, programs, and other actions that do not seek revenge but rather understanding and restoration. Under this innovation system, inspiration and incorporation of gangs into society could be viable and channel energies into various skill sets and societal needs that would reframe the notion of "gang."

Notes

1 The research data for this chapter is drawn from a larger study that examines how individual navigate and negotiate their reentry experiences with diminished legal rights and amplified social stigmas.
2 Different pseudonym used.
3 Traditionally refers to "original gangster" or someone who is respected in their gang. Others have acknowledged that the term comes from Five Percenter vernacular meaning "O.G." or rather "original god."
4 Joined the gang

References

Abadinsky, H. (2010). *Organized crime* (9th ed.). Belmont, CA: Wadesworth Publishing.

Alexander, M. (2012). *The new Jim Crow: Mass incarceration in the age of colorblindness.* New York: The New Press.

Asbury, H. ([1928] 1989). *The gangs of New York: An informal history of the New York underworld.* New York, NY: Dorset Press.

Austin, J. B., Eisen, L. B., Cullen, J., Frank, J., & Fellow, L. (2016). *How many Americans are unnecessarily incarcerated?* New York: Brennan Center for Justice.

Bell, K. E. (2009). Gender and gangs: A quantitative comparison. *Crime & Delinquency, 55*(3), 363–387.

Bissonette, J. (2008). *When the prisoners ran Walpole: A true story in the movement for prison abolition.* Cambridge, MA: South End Press.

Blackmon, D. A. (2009). *Slavery by another name: The re-enslavement of black Americans from the Civil War to World War II.* New York: Anchor.

Brodzinsky, S. (2013, May 15). El Salvador gang truce leads to plummeting murder rates. *The Guardian.* Retrieved September 27, 2019, from www.theguardian.com/world/2013/may/15/el-salvador-gang-truce.

Brotherton, D. C. (2007). Proceedings from the transnational street gang/organization seminar. *Crime, Media, Culture, 3*(3), 372–381.

Brotherton, D. C., & Barrios, L. (2004). *The almighty Latin King and Queen Nation: Street politics and the transformation of a New York City gang.* New York: Columbia University Press.

Brotherton, D. C., & Gude, R. (2018). *Social inclusion from below: The perspectives of street gangs and their possible effects on declining homicide rates in Ecuador* (No. IDB-DP-00578). Inter-American Development Bank.

Browne-Marshall, Gloria J. (2010). The U.S. constitution: An African American context (2nd ed.). New York: Law and Policy Group Press.

Butterfield, F. (2008). *All God's children: The Bosket family and the American tradition of violence.* New York: Vintage.

Campbell, A. (1984). *The girls in the gang.* New York: Blackwell.

Cherbonneau, M. (2008). Carjacking. In *Encyclopedia of social problems,* edited by Vincent N. Parrillo (pp. 110–111). Thousand Oaks, CA: Sage Publications.

Clemmer, D. (1958). *The prison community.* New York: Holt, Rinehart, and Winston.

Conquergood, D. (2013). *Cultural struggles: Performance, ethnography, praxis.* Ann Arbor: University of Michigan Press.

Contreras, R. (2013). *The stickup kids: Race, drugs, violence, and the American dream.* Berkeley: University of California Press.

Davis, A. Y. (2011). *Are prisons obsolete?* New York: Seven Stories Press.

Dawley, D. (1992). *A nation of lords: The autobiography of the vice lords* (2nd ed.). Prospect Heights, IL: Waveland Press.

Department of Justice. (2018). Prisoners and prisoner re-entry. Retrieved from www.justice.gov/archive/fbci/progmenu_reentry.html.

DeVeaux, Mika'il. (2013). The trauma of the incarceration experience. *Harvard Civil Rights-Civil Liberties Law Review, 48,* 257–277.

Dooley, B. D., Seals, A., & Skarbek, D. (2014). The effect of prison gang membership on recidivism. *Journal of Criminal Justice, 42*(3), 267–275.

Eyes on the Prize. (1987). A nation of law? (1968–1971). Transcript, *Eyes on the Prize.*

Farah, D. (2012, June 22). The transformation of El Salvador's gangs into political actors. *Transformation.*

Ferrell, J. (1993). *Crimes of style: Urban graffiti and the politics of criminality.* New York: Garland.

Fleisher, M. S., & Decker, S. H. (2001). An overview of the challenge of prison gangs. *Corrections Management Quarterly, 5,* 1–9.

Frey, W. H. (1979). Central city white flight: Racial and nonracial causes. *American Sociological Review,* 425–448.

Gaes, G. G., Wallace, S., Gilman, E., Klein-Saffran, J., & Suppa, S. (2002). The influence of prison gang affiliation on violence and other prison misconduct. *The Prison Journal, 82*(3), 359–385.

Gonnerman, J. (2004). *Life on the outside: The prison odyssey of Elaine Bartlett.* New York: Picador.

Guenther, L. (2013). *Solitary confinement: Social death and its afterlives.* Minneapolis: University of Minnesota Press.

Hagedorn, J. M. (2008). *A world of gangs: Armed young men and gangsta culture.* Minneapolis: University of Minnesota Press.

Hagedorn, J. M. (2015). *The insane Chicago way: The daring plan by Chicago gangs to create a Spanish mafia.* Chicago: University of Chicago Press.

Haldipur, J. (2018). *No place on the corner: The costs of aggressive policing.* New York: NYU Press.

Haley, A., & X, M. (1965). *The autobiography of Malcolm X.* New York: Ballantine Books.

Hayner, N. S., & Ash, E. (1940). The prison as a community. *American Sociological Review, 5*(4), 577–583.

Hernández, A., & Hamilton, K. (2016, March 31). El Salvador's gangs offered a truce – And the government declared war. *Vice.* Retrieved September 27, 2019, from www.vice.com/en_us/article/j59an4/el-salvador-gangs-offered-a-truce-the-government-declared-war.

Ilan, J. (2015). *Understanding street culture: Poverty, crime, youth and cool.* New York: Macmillan International Higher Education.

Irwin, J., & Cressey, D. R. (1962). Thieves, convicts and the inmate culture. *Social Problems, 10*, 142.

IWOC. (2018, August 24). Incarcerated workers organizing committee. About. Retrieved March 1, 2019, from https://incarceratedworkers.org/about.

James, Kirk A. (2014). The history of prisons in America. *Medium*, November 18. https://medium.com/@kirkajames/the-history-of-prisons-in-america-618a8247348.

Jankowski, M. S. (1991). *Islands in the street: Gangs and American urban society* (Vol. 159). Berkeley: University of California Press.

John, P. S. (2013, September 05). Inmates end California prison hunger strike. *Los Angeles Times.* Retrieved February 23, 2019, from http://articles.latimes.com/2013/sep/05/local/la-me-ff-prison-strike-20130906.

Joyce, K. L. (2016). Stars, dragons, and the letter M: Consequential symbols in California prison gang policy. *California Law Review, 104*, 733.

Knight, M. M. (2013). *The five percenters: Islam, hip-hop and the Gods of New York.* London: Oneworld Publications.

Kornhauser, Ruth. (1978). *Social sources of delinquency.* Chicago: University of Chicago Press.

Langan, P. A., & Levin, D. J. (2002). *Recidivism of prisoners released in 1994. NCJ 193427.* Washington, DC: U.S. Department of Justice, Bureau of Justice Statistics.

Larson, D. (2013, September 24). Why Scandinavian Prisons Are Superior. *The Atlantic.* Retrieved March 5, 2019, from www.theatlantic.com/international/archive/2013/09/why-scandinavian-prisons-are-superior/279949/.

Lessing, B. (2016). *Inside out: The challenge of prison-based criminal organizations.* Washington, DC: The Brookings Institution.

Lessing, B. (2017). Counterproductive punishment: How prison gangs undermine state authority. *Rationality and Society, 29*(3), 257–297.

Lessing, B. (2019, January 28). Brazil's prison massacres are a frightening window into gang warfare. *The Washington Post.* Retrieved January 30, 2019, from www.washingtonpost.com/news/monkey-cage/wp/2017/01/17/brazils-prison-massacres-are-a-frightening-window-into-gang-warfare/?utm_term=.480d185c992c.

Lopez, G. (2018, August 09). California is using prison labor to fight its record wildfires. *Vox.* Retrieved February 20, 2019, from www.vox.com/2018/8/9/17670494/california-prison-labor-mendocino-carr-ferguson-wildfires.

Mackey, D. (2018, November 17). What happens when a Barrio 18 soldier tries to leave the gang. *The Intercept.* Retrieved November 21, 2018, from https://theintercept.com/2018/11/17/el-salvador-barrio-18-ms-13-leave-gang/.

Maxson, C. L. (2012). Betwixt and between street and prison gangs: Defining gangs and structures in youth correctional facilities. In *Youth gangs in international perspective*, edited by Finn-Aage Esbensen and Cheryl L. Maxson (pp. 107–124). New York: Springer.

Miller, J. (2001). *One of the guys: Girls, gangs, and gender.* New York: Oxford University Press.

Moss, S. (2015, September 4). The gangs of El Salvador: Inside the prison the guards are too afraid to enter. *The Guardian.* Retrieved September 27, 2019, from www.theguardian.com/artanddesign/2015/sep/04/adam-hinton-el-salvador-ms-13-gangs-prison-portraits.

Nellis, A. (2016). *The color of justice: Racial and ethnic disparity in state prisons.* Washington, DC: Sentencing Project.

New Jersey Department of Corrections. (2019). Offenders in correctional institutions by race/ethnic identification. Retrieved March 5, 2019, from www.state.nj.us/corrections/pdf/offender_statistics/2019/Race%20Ethnic%20Identification%20-%20Offender%20Characteristics%20Report.pdf.

Nowotny, J. J., & Carrara, M. (2018). The use of restorative practices to reduce prison gang violence: Lessons on transforming cultures of violence. *Conflict Resolution Quarterly, 36*(2), 131–144.

Panfil, V. R. (2017). *The gang's all queer: The lives of gay gang members.* New York: NYU Press.

Pew Center on the States. (2009). *One in 31: The long reach of American corrections.* Washington, DC: Pew Charitable Trusts.

Phillips, C. (2012). 'It ain't nothing like America with the Bloods and the Crips': Gang narratives inside two English prisons. *Punishment & Society, 14*(1), 51–68.

Pyrooz, D., Decker, S., & Fleisher, M. (2011). From the street to the prison, from the prison to the street: Understanding and responding to prison gangs. *Journal of Aggression, Conflict and Peace Research, 3*(1), 12–24.

Reed, Austin. (2016). *The life and adventures of a haunted convict,* edited by Caleb Smith. New York: Random House.

Rios, V. M. (2011). *Punished: Policing the lives of Black and Latino boys.* New York: NYU Press.

Rivera, B. D., Cowles, E. L., & Dorman, L. G. (2003). An exploratory study of institutional change: Personal control and environmental satisfaction in a gang-free prison. *The Prison Journal, 83*(2), 149–170.

Rostami, A., Leinfelt, F., & Brotherton, D. C. (2012). Understanding gang leaders: Characteristics and driving forces of street gang leaders in Sweden. *Free Inquiry in Creative Sociology, 40*(2), 1–20.

Skarbek, D. (2010). Putting the "con" into constitutions: The economics of prison gangs. *The Journal of Law, Economics, & Organization, 26*(2), 183–211.

Skarbek, D. (2012). Prison gangs, norms, and organizations. *Journal of Economic Behavior & Organization, 82*(1), 96–109.

Skarbek, D. (2014). *The social order of the underworld: How prison gangs govern the American penal system.* New York: Oxford University Press.

Smiley, C. J., & Middlemass, K. M. (2016). Clothing makes the man: Impression management and prisoner reentry. *Punishment & Society, 18*(2), 220–243.

Speri, A. (2018, December 05). NYPD gang database can turn unsuspecting New Yorkers into instant felons. *The Intercept.* Retrieved January 29, 2019, from https://theintercept.com/2018/12/05/nypd-gang-database/.

Stastny, C., & Tyrnauer, G. (1983). *Who rules the joint? The changing political culture of maximum-security prisons in America.* New York: Lexington Books.

Thompson, H. A. (2016). *Blood in the water: The Attica prison uprising of 1971 and its legacy.* New York: Vintage.

Trammell, R. (2012). *Enforcing the convict code: Violence and prison culture.* Boulder, CO: Lynne Rienner Publishers.

Travis, J., Solomon, A. L., & Waul, M. (2001). *From prison to home: The dimensions and consequences of prisoner reentry.* Washington, DC: The Urban Institute.

U.S. Riot Commission. (1968). *Report of the National Advisory Commission on Civil Disorders.* New York: Bantam Books.

Wacquant, L. (2001). Deadly symbiosis: When ghetto and prison meet and mesh. *Punishment & Society, 3*(1), 95–133.

Weide, R. D. (2015). *Race war? Inter-racial conflict between black and Latino gang members in Los Angeles county* (Order No. 3685926). Available from ProQuest Dissertations & Theses A&I. (1666394735). Retrieved from https://search.proquest.com/docview/1666394735?accountid=27495.

Western, B., Kleykamp, M., & Rosenfeld, J. (2006). Did falling wages and employment increase US imprisonment? *Social Forces, 84*(4), 2291–2311.

Wood, J. L., Alleyne, E., Mozova, K., & James, M. (2014). Predicting involvement in prison gang activity: Street gang membership, social and psychological factors. *Law and Human Behavior, 38*(3), 203.

46

A legacy of mapping gang neighborhoods in LA

Susan Phillips and Stefano Bloch

Introduction

Los Angeles gangs have claimed neighborhoods scattershot throughout the city since the early 20th century, creating a quasi-autonomous geography of enmity and alliance that authorities and the public all-too-simplistically see as produced unidirectionally from the bottom up. In scaling out, we see that periodic state intrusion and withdrawal has punctuated 20th- and 21st-century urban neighborhoods in Los Angeles, cementing an alternative landscape of marginality in which gangs have flourished intergenerationally. Housing policies, interstate highway construction, shifting employment patterns, changes in education and school funding, urban restructuring, both over-policing and under-policing, and mass incarceration have constituted broad-scale social legacies and ongoing patterns of top-down violence in the form of both aggression and neglect.

Put simply, the place-based, neighborhood-rooted aspects of gang formation have their origins in local, state-level, and federal policy. Colloquial and scholarly accounts suggest that streets gangs in the United States are an epiphenomenon of economic and social restructuring and deindustrializaiton in the 1970s, which includes the decline of the nuclear family and gang members' direct involvement in the burgeoning drug trade (Coughlin and Venkatesh 2003; Hagedorn 1988). However, gangs in Los Angeles and many other North American cities predate this era of crisis by decades (see, for example, Thrasher 1927; Bogardus 1926; Vigil 1988; McWilliams 2016). As geographer Alex Alonso states, "What is most striking about the corpus of gang formation research is the limited discussion of how race and structure have worked together to create communities that have produced gangs" (2004: 662). Furthering this scholarly discourse through case studies in South Central Los Angeles and LA's San Fernando Valley, we examine how the categorization of neighborhoods by state-supported real estate assessors amplified policy-driven social inequality connected to housing policy specifically, giving rise to the formation of disenfranchised urban spaces that would become ripe for gang formation (see also Alonso 2010). Because segregation and entrenched poverty are key legacies of public-private decisions informed through bank lending and real estate policy, the development of gang neighborhoods must be reexamined as a key outcome of the Home Owners' Loan Corporation's (HOLC) cartographic practices beginning in New Deal America.

Gangs, like other community social formations, function in tandem with the delineation of urban space conceived at federal, state, and local levels. We combine our knowledge of street gangs gleaned through decades-long qualitative fieldwork with an analysis of HOLC mapping data, Housing Authority of the City of Los Angeles (HACLA) documentation, and, finally, Los Angeles District Attorney gang maps – in particular designated gang injunction "safety zones" – in order to reveal some of the historically hidden building blocks and enduring structures at play in the top-down formation of gang neighborhoods. While acknowledging the importance of a bottom-up production of gang identity, we provide a needed analysis of top-down urban development for better understanding some of the structural contributors to gang territoriality.

For us, the urgency of understanding structural contributors to gang violence is informed by personal as well as academic impulses. We have both been witness to and directly affected by gang violence in different ways. For Bloch, members of a Pacoima gang that we write about subsequently killed his best friend growing up, and he was witness throughout his childhood to many other direct acts of gang violence that devastated his own family and the families around him. During her almost thirty years of field work with gangs, Phillips lost several close friends to gang violence, and she similarly witnessed its devastating toll on families. Both authors are intimately acquainted with the kinds of toxic masculinities that gangs foment in communities. Likewise, both authors have found in self-identified gang members close friends, family members, and confidants whom we love and respect. In part due to our backgrounds as participant observers, we easily see how gang spatial formations seem to justify urban social inequality and how gang violence in particular makes it seem as though suffering is solely the fault of the people who enact that violence (see also Bourgois 2003). As academics who draw from first-hand experiences with gang members and gang violence, we understand individualistic explanations to be surface level – inadequate because they contribute to "a view of gang behavior that could be called social reproductionist and unwittingly pathologizing" (Brotherton 2008: 56). Critiquing top-down structures is urgently needed in gang studies, because official strategies play an equally significant role in engendering the violent interactions that we have seen destroy communities and individual lives.

Housing is but one window into the greater project of creating a critical gang studies that establishes theoretical and empirical counternarratives to contemporary gang research, including the lack of historical perspectives (Brotherton 2015: 4). Because gang neighborhoods are neighborhoods first and foremost, housing is a crucial place to begin understanding historic oppression that leads to inward-facing social groups like gangs. We thus treat HOLC ratings and accompanying maps as an example of how inequality is embedded in cartographic practice. By illuminating the formative role played by mapping and housing practices in the physical manifestation of class and race-based social division, we are offering a critical lens through which to understand gang formation.

A truism in the academic literature is the stratifying feature of metropolitan places (Chetty et al. 2018; Nicolaides and Wiese 2013, 2017; Logan 1978). This means that built environments tend to hold onto social advantages and disadvantages through time. Once historical patterns are established, successive waves of socio-economic pressure reify advantage or disadvantage in ways that "tend to keep things moving in the same direction" (Nicolaides and Wiese 2013). This is how inequality becomes spatialized, rooted in landscape. In this equation, high property values are linked to high-achieving schools and the further boosting of local property values. Conversely, systematic segregation ensured through redlining, racially restrictive covenants, slum clearance, and white flight have held property values down, which, along with other legal place-making policies, limited investment in communities, enervated school funding, and prevented families from building intergenerational wealth. In a place like Los Angeles, modern urban development was relatively late to start given its geopolitical proximity to a fluctuating border and its location on the south-west coast of a still-growing nation state into the 19th century. As a prime destination for internal and international migrants well into the 20th century, post-WWII racialized restructuring and ghettoization contributed directly to the city's uneven growth and patchwork urban landscape that is still strikingly evident in the 21st century (see, for example, Flamming 2005; Hise 2004; Hunt and Ramón 2010; Kurashige 2010).

The correlation of stratification and place is far from absolute, but, more often than not, advantages and disadvantages are passed onto the next generation. Security maps and accompanying home loan decisions that worked through the determination of risk created broad-scale eliminations, in which references to "negros," "low-class Italians," and "subversive racial elements" became the de jure and de facto practices that led to cemented segregation and growing inequality (Nicolaides 2002). Such practices of withholding investment and ensuring downstream divestment were put upon neighborhoods by an out-of-control private sector fixated on profit maximization. As Richard Rothstein (2017) shows, this racialized quest for profit was accomplished with the full force and support of the federal government.

Redlining, public housing, and gang formation

In 1933, under the auspices of New Deal restructuring, the Home Owners Loan Corporation embarked on a nationwide survey of nearly 250 cities to determine creditworthiness at the scale of the neighborhood. The government-sponsored corporation hired mortgage lenders, real-estate appraisers, and land developers to create color-coded maps indicating the current and forecasted quality of housing and community stock. These maps and their accompanying documentation helped to determine neighborhood credit worth and to guide race- and class-based real-estate practices across the United States for the next eight decades, often with dire and continuing consequences for whole communities.

Risk was determined based on an area's building quality, the suitability of its topography for new construction, the existing residents' incomes, and the value of prior land and structure sales. However, each "Area Description" form begins by assessing local demographics, including population growth or decline, hetero- or homogeneity, the "class and occupation" of residents, the percentage of foreign-born families, their corresponding nationalities, the percentage of "Negro" residents, and information determining "infiltration" of unwanted population groups. Based on those criteria, an area was issued a rating and corresponding color: Best (green), Still Desirable (blue), Definitely Declining (yellow), and Hazardous (red). A red color-coding became what urbanists to this day refer to as a "redlined" neighborhood.

Urban historian Kenneth Jackson described the federal imprint on urban and suburban housing patterns through this mechanism to be "enormous" (1980: 420; see also Jackson 1987). Scholarship in the decades since Jackson's pivotal work has built a nuanced portrait of links between inequality, lending patterns, race-based opportunity, and racialized concepts of risk in particular cities (see, for example, Aaronson et al. 2017; Crossney and Bartelt 2005; Hillier 2003; Lipsitz 2006; Michney and Winling 2019; Nicolaides 2002; Rothstein 2017).

Through the HOLC, redlining charted formalized economic disinvestment that ghettoized communities through the refusal of investment. Part of the motivation for this work was the federal Housing Act of 1937, which was created to support cities that sought better housing for low-income people. Progressive housing initiatives aimed to alleviate the plight of the poor had unintended negative consequences due to their deficit-based approaches to communities as slums with decrepit housing that were breeding grounds for degeneracy. Sociological evidence of the time sometimes countered these dominant narratives, depicting "poor yet functional

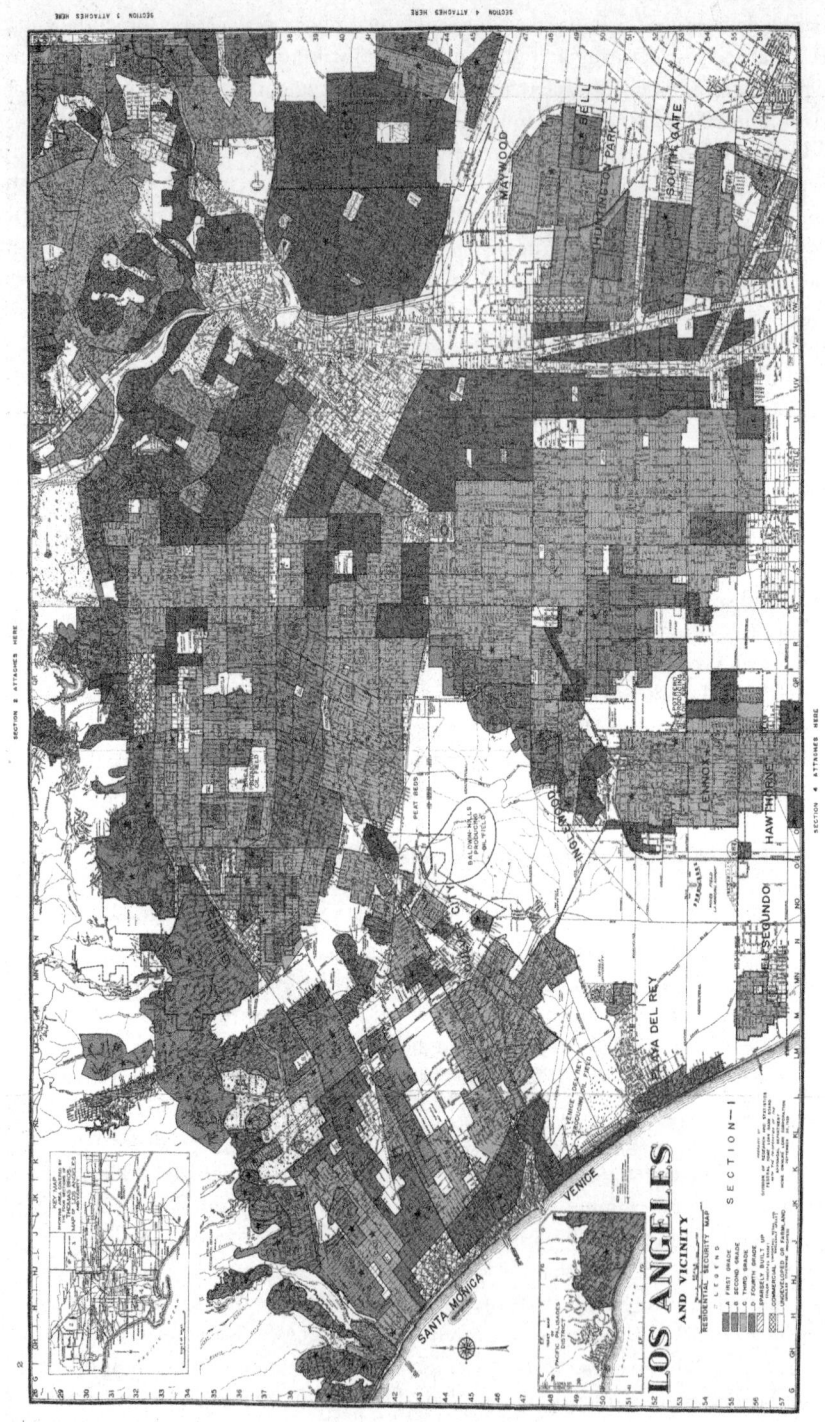

Figure 46.1 Owners' Loan Corporation Map of Los Angeles, 1939

Source: Published and sold by Thomas Bros. map company

communities" and picking apart the rhetorical strategies of progressive housing proponents (Spalding 1992: 107; see also Gans 1982).

While not every neighborhood with a red grading became host to gangs, whereas some blue and green areas did transform into neighborhoods with gang presence, key redlined areas of Los Angeles, including those throughout South Los Angeles, East Los Angeles, and parts of the San Fernando Valley, demonstrate the pattern in which gangs became entrenched through persistent housing segregation, slum designation and subsequent clearance, the construction of public housing developments, and ongoing patterns of racialized policing – which together constitute a virulent form of urban structural violence. While the first two regions, South Central LA and East LA, are well known due to their heightened levels of violence and widespread televisual representation, the San Fernando Valley is a lesser-known LA gang landscape. And while both South Central LA and East LA were redlined due to the presence of racial mixing and African American residences, the few red-rated neighborhoods of the then less-developed Valley provide a smaller-scale picture of the ways in which inequality and real estate appraisal contributed to the underpinnings of gang neighborhood formation.

The most extreme pattern is that specific areas within redlined zones underwent further photographic documentation by the Housing Authority of the City of Los Angeles in the late 1930s and early 40s. HACLA independently documented so-called slum conditions so that public housing could be built. Public housing was part of a progressive agenda in its time, but the designation and demolition of neighborhoods also destroyed the existing fabric of neighborhoods and the networks that supported residents. HACLA representatives attempted to look for areas that were overcrowded shantytowns lacking supportive infrastructure or underdeveloped areas with vacant open space that could be appropriated for housing without displacing as many residents. But often they razed entire neighborhoods wholesale – a process that was mirrored in other cities (Schill and Wachter 1995; Goetz 2000). The disruption of the existing social fabric combined with the clustering of people in extreme poverty had far-reaching consequences. All major public housing developments in Los Angeles have embedded gangs associated with them, and project-based gangs have been mainstays of the gang landscape since the 1960s and 70s (Smith 2005; Vigil 2007).

Red-lining and public housing construction both cemented immobility and intensified segregation, and the development of gangs rooted in neighborhoods mirrored these racialized, residential patterns. Today, gang neighborhoods in and out of the projects interweave gang ideological identity with in-situ opportunities for economic and social gain. Gang members fuse the neighborhood landscape of drug addiction with drug sales; endemic violence with the gun trade; and the practice of taxing people, such as street vendors or business owners, within the broader formal or informal economy. Many factors contribute to gang violence, including relationship problems, thefts, drugs, insults, the drug trade, or prison gang politics (see Brotherton 2015). Ultimately, the causes of gang violence include state policies, changing economic contexts, segregation, and inequality. All of these are enacted simultaneously at the neighborhood level. The specifics of these ultimate causes and the way they intersect with neighborhood culture are often overlooked other than to be rendered in broad strokes. We thus take a spatial view of gang neighborhoods to situate them within housing policy in particular and note the way in which mapping of so-called degenerate neighborhoods carries forward into the present. As we show in the following, these maps overlay in a way that reveals the geographic durability of neighborhood stigma.

In 1992, then-District Attorney Ira Reiner reported internal findings that half of the young black men in Los Angeles were in gangs (Stolberg 1992). Strikingly similar to the HOLC's map from the 1930s, their color scheme ranged from beige and green to light and characteristic dark

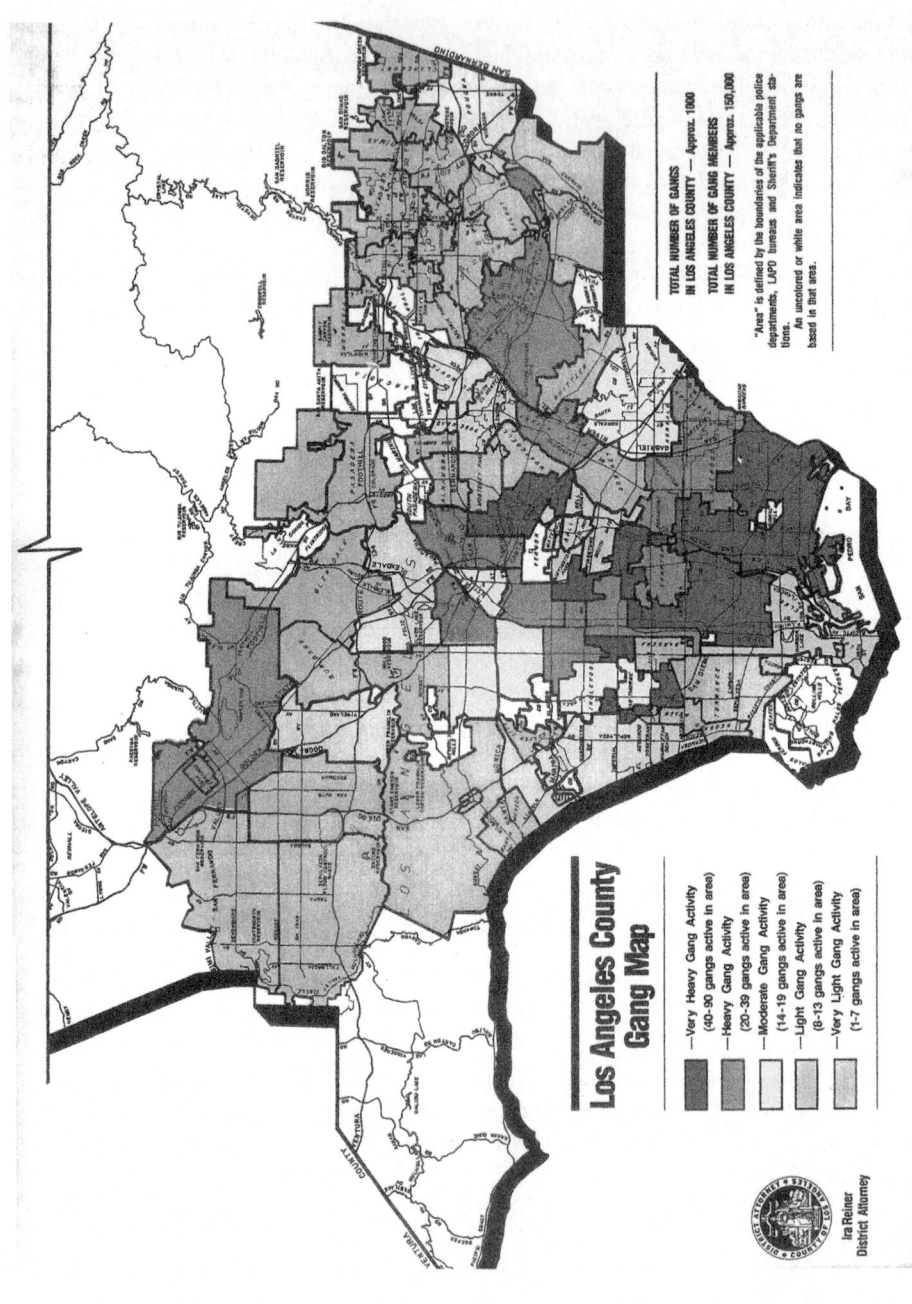

Figure 46.2 Los Angeles County Gang Map, 1992, showing relative gang density. From the report "Gangs, Crime and Violence in Los Angeles"

Source: Office of the District Attorney, County of Los Angeles

red to chart gang density. Juxtaposing the DA's map with the original HOLC map makes our point in terms of cartographic practice. Many red-lined areas, including South Central LA, East Los Angeles, and parts of the San Fernando Valley, became key gang areas with high gang density. Both types of maps represent perception as much as reality when it comes to poverty, degeneracy, and the gang life. Like East Los Angeles, South Central Los Angeles is incredibly gang dense, with hundreds of groups in the equivalent range – all of which was red-lined in the 1930s. In the San Fernando Valley, fewer gangs are spread over wider geographical reaches, but their lives are no less caught up in and contributive to neighborhood violence. We take each example in turn in the following sections.

South Central

Because of its historic association with the black population, we focus our examination of South Central LA on the development of African American Bloods and Crips. Not much is known about 1920s black gang activities in Los Angeles, other than that gangs were fairly independent and seemed to lack strong territorial aspects. LA's black population was still fairly small. By the 40s, industrialization had attracted considerable black migration to Los Angeles. For black Americans fleeing from the South, LA was perceived to be more open and amenable to black upward mobility than the southern United States (Alonso 2004; Flamming 2005). But black Angelenos soon realized that the lines of race were just as violently enforced, even if they were less visible at first (Hernández 2017). Black communities enjoyed few opportunities for the investment, integration, and belonging to which whites felt entitled upon settling in the area.

Area D-52, the Central Avenue District, bears the following description:

> This is the "melting pot" area of Los Angeles, and has long been thoroughly blighted. The Negro concentration is largely in the eastern two thirds of the area. Original construction was evidently of fair quality but lack of proper maintenance is notable. Population is uniformly of poor quality and many improvements are in a state of dilapidation. This is a fit location for a slum clearance project. The area is accorded a "low red" grade.
>
> *(Marciano et al. 1939)*

The area is said to be populated by WPA workers, laborers, low-scale clerical workers, and factory workers, with a 50% Negro population. The area is only 20% owner occupied. Notations indicate that "the encroachment of industry is a threat." Contained in this language is the confusion of a "poor quality" population with poor quality housing. This association became a self-fulfilling prophecy. The area's low red D rating would disallow home loans that might have otherwise allowed homeowners to improve housing stock or with which resident renters could become homeowners. With burgeoning environmental justice issues in the form of exposure to industrial hazards (Pulido 2000), the low-red grade insured that the area continued to face residential challenges. Simultaneously, racially restrictive housing covenants – many written directly onto homeowner's deeds – protected in perpetuity against the spread of "subversive racial elements" – which prevented black residents or other residents of color from relocating to other areas even if they could afford it.

Outside of pockets like Pasadena or Altadena and further south in Watts, black residences were historically concentrated in the area around Central Avenue, where African Americans of all classes lived together and where a vibrant social scene had developed (Bryant et al. 1999; Robinson 2010). Slauson Avenue was said to be the "Mason Dixon Line" of Los Angeles. While 50% of the population of the Central Avenue District was African American, the district

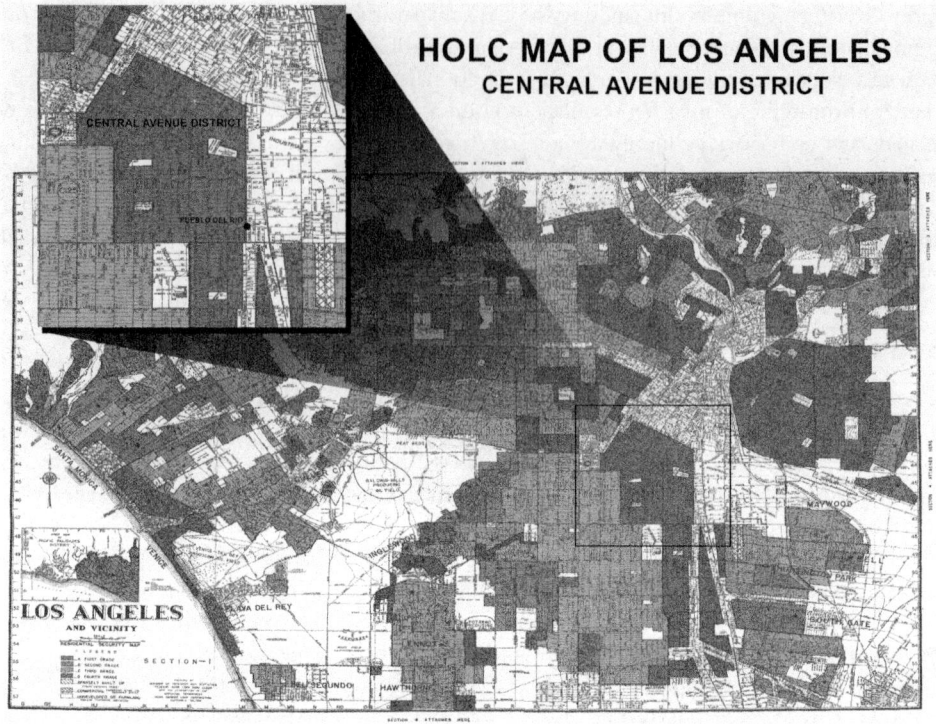

Figure 46.3 HOLC Map of Los Angeles with Central Avenue District highlighted

below Slauson Avenue had a population of mostly Mexicans and Italians, with a 3% black population. This number accompanied a paranoid description regarding the "*shifting or infiltration of more Negroes or other subversive racial elements*" (emphasis in original). This area merited a "medial red" grade, a slightly higher grade than the densely African American neighborhoods previously, but the area was still considered a poor bet for loans.

By the mid-1950s, the black population had doubled, but the infrastructure supporting this community began to decline. The lifting of racially restrictive housing covenants by the US Supreme Court in 1948 impacted the area greatly. Most people with means moved west, and those who remained were left with crumbling housing infrastructure in more uniformly impoverished areas. Simultaneously, white flight from the neighborhoods surrounding South Los Angeles had begun in part because of post-war suburbanization and through real estate speculative practices such as blockbusting (Brown and Chung 2006). Residential patterns in the first half of the 20th century that took shape courtesy of the HOLC and Housing Authority helped to create the ghettoization in which gangs became entrenched.

While the earliest black gangs took advantage of informal economic and social opportunities prior to 1950, a second generation of gangs after 1950 developed into more neighborhood-based entities at least partially in relation to racial concerns, in particular in response to white youth hate groups. Black gangs in the 1950s also cemented a pattern of inwardly facing competition in circumstances of intense sequestration, substandard schooling, and federal policies that favored suburban over urban development. Black youth were hounded by each other, sometimes by white youth, and by the LAPD, who policed residential segregation with fierce dedication (Alonso 2010; Barganier 2011).

By the 1960s, gang groups in broader South Los Angeles had been influenced by or had become members of the Black Panther Party, which subsequently was subject to the disruptions of the Federal Bureau of Investigation's COINTELPRO. The 1965 Watts Riots destroyed the system of older gangs like the Slausons, Businessmen, and D'Italians, which morphed easily into Panther politics, only then to be destroyed by massive federal and local law enforcement intrusions designed to disrupt black unity (Davis 1990; Sloan 2005; Alonso 2010; Barganier 2011). The Black Panther Party headquarters was on 41st Street and Central Avenue, and the Alprentice Bunchy Carter Free Clinic and Black Panther Party Community Information Center were located at 3223 South Central Ave, on 32nd Street – both locales were squarely within the HOLC's red-rated Central Avenue District. The headquarters on 41st and Central was the location of the infamous shootout between Panthers and the Los Angeles Police Department's newly formed Special Weapons and Tactics Unit, or SWAT – the quasi-military policing unit that would chart the course of anti-gang policing for decades to come.

A third generation of black gangs formed in 1969 with the birth of the Crips. Bloods soon followed, and with them the rising violence of the 1970s–1990s. The Central Avenue District as well as other areas became home to Blood and Crip gangs that have become intergenerational features of the landscape in the time since. In the absence of Panther ideology, militancy morphed into rapaciousness, and revolutionary warfare gave way to internecine violence. Most analyses of Crips and Bloods recount this shift from organizations that had the potential for social movement and political participation to groups vilified through moral panics and subsequent over-policing (for a discussion of gang political and economic organization in Chicago, see Hagedorn 2015; Venkatesh 1997). It can be tempting to view these progressions as binary or linear, an unfortunate either/or where politicization lost out to disorganization. We view this gang lineage of Los Angeles as the tip of an iceberg. The year 1969 is the moment where black gangs begin their visibility in the current period but where the previous legacy of housing and segregation in creating that moment has been rendered invisible in most of the literature.

In the early 1940s, the Housing Authority of the City of Los Angeles began to enact the HOLC's suggestion that the Central Avenue District was ripe for slum clearance. The Housing Authority identified locations, hired photographers to document further proposed areas for slum clearance, made arguments, and used eminent domain to obtain properties and land. The homes they identified were in the 50s blocks just east of Central Avenue between Long Beach Avenue and Alameda – just crossing the border from the Central Avenue District into a neighboring industrial area. The Housing Authority employed a team of renowned modern architects including Paul Revere Williams and Richard Neutra to design and build the Pueblo del Rio housing projects. Photographs of the area around Pueblo del Rio during and prior to project construction paint a fairly diverse portrait. Several available photographs were taken after the existing bungalows had already been razed. Other photographs include the railroad tracks that would later bisect the Pueblos original 1942 projects and a later 1950 extension. One picture depicts several residences designated as slums, which are clearly good-quality houses, rather than the slapdash structures often evident in HACLA documentation in other parts of the city. Several later photographs from 1950 used to justify the project extension show "slum dwelling exteriors" but are shots of unpaved alleys and backyards rather than front yard areas. Like HOLC documentation, HACLA photographs served a clearly rhetorical purpose (Bloch 2012; Spalding 1992). In May 1942, the original 400 units of Pueblo del Rio were completed for the explicit purpose of housing black servicemen and their families. While other public housing projects housed white military in white or mixed areas such as San Pedro, the problem of housing black servicemen necessitated the construction of wartime housing in an already segregated residential zone.

Figure 46.4   Photograph of housing deemed "slum dwellings" demolished for the construction of Pueblo Del Rio. 1941

Source: Courtesy of the Los Angeles Public Library Photo Collection

The project's history in the post-war years is telling. The first gang, the Pueblo Players, is said to have formed in the mythical birth year that mirrors the Pueblo's primary street name: 1952 for 52nd Street. In the 1960s, the "Pueblos," as they became known, split briefly into two factions. The Block Boys occupied the original 1942 side of the projects, and Slauson Park claimed the 1950 housing extension across the railroad tracks adjacent Slauson Park. Later reunified as a single gang, the "Pueblos" pre-dated Bloods and Crips and was one of the few South Central gangs to carry its name into the 1970s. Identifying today as Bloods, the gang primarily claims 52 Pueblo Bishops Bloods, named in part for their historic alliance with the 92 Bishops further south. Since the 1990s, the projects have begun a demographic shift with the rest of South Central LA from black to Latino. Clinging tenaciously to "the bricks," or the "low bottoms," as the projects are called, the Pueblo Bishops have been the subject of two federal gang indictments: one anti-drug operation in 2003 and a Racketeer Influenced and Corrupt Organization (RICO) operation in 2010 (Phillips 2012). It was the first time RICO, designed to fight entities like the Italian Mafia, was used against an African American gang. Even earlier, in 2008, the Pueblo del Rio neighborhood became part of the Florence-Pueblo Del Rio Safety Zone gang injunction, along with five additional gangs: All For Crime, Barrio Mojados, Blood Stone Villains, Florencia 13, and Oriental Boyz. The geographic parameters of this injunction encompass the eastern portion of the Central Avenue District – that area noted in the HOLC Area Description to be occupied by majority African American residents.

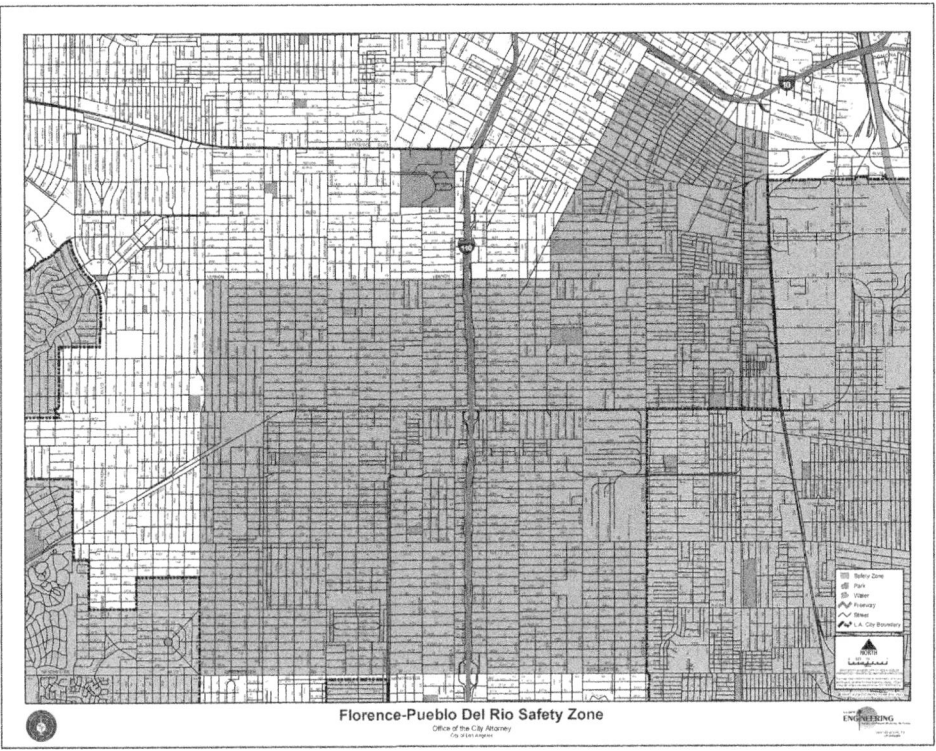

Florence-Pueblo Del Rio Safety Zone
Office of the City Attorney
City of Los Angeles

Figure 46.5   Map of Florence-Pueblo Del Rio Safety Zone
Source: Los Angeles City Attorney's Office

In Los Angeles' black community, 70,000 blue-color jobs were lost between 1978 and 1982, most of which were located along South LA's Alameda corridor (Sides 2004). Working-class labor was replaced by a punitive war on drugs that housed the newly surplus population in prisons (Gilmore 2007). Welfare reform, the decline in low-income housing, and the withdrawal of state supportive services cemented cycles of poverty and family breakdown, weakening the social fabric of already vulnerable communities. In another twist, black residents who would have once been redlined out of home loans beginning in the 1940s became the targets of predatory lending practices in the 2000s – creating a wave of foreclosures in places like the Inland Empire of California, where residents had attempted to escape the violence of inner-city life. After the real estate bubble burst, so-called "re-redlining" has occurred – once again barring black residents and other communities of color from accessing home loans. Despite decades of civil rights work, housing situations remain challenging for African Americans, particularly given the impact of carceral institutions.

San Fernando Valley

Like the region known more broadly as "South LA," the San Fernando Valley is a patchwork of incorporated and unincorporated municipalities and dozens of officially designated as well as locally construed neighborhoods on the north end of Los Angeles. At 260 square miles, the San

Fernando Valley makes up over half of the City of Los Angeles's 503 square mile area, and its 1.78 million residents account for just under 45 percent of LA City's 3.99 million inhabitants.

Aside from the role it plays in LA historical and cultural imaginaries as a white-washed, water-deprived, and sub-divided suburban enclave that was still covered by orange groves and horse stables well into the 20th century (Barraclough 2011; Jackson 1987), "the Valley" is also home to some of LA's oldest and geographically well-defined gangs. In addition to being the original home to gangs such as Barrio Van Nuys, Varrio San Fer, Pacoima 13, and Blythe Street, some of which date back to at least the 1940s, neighborhoods in the Valley were also the first places outside of their original locales to develop cliques of Mara Salvatrucha (MS-13) and Dieciocho (18th Street), both of which have become transnational entities.

While the Valley has been statistically whiter and wealthier and withdrawn from many of the socio-economic realities that faced Greater LA for much of the past century, the San Fernando Valley, as urban historian Eric Avila puts it,

> shelters a heterogeneous mix of Mexicans, Salvadorans, Guatemalans, Armenians, and African Americans. The "New Valley" harbors scant traces of the suburban good life that dominated the cultural imagery of postwar Los Angeles, and its public settings now echo the cultural dissonance of the polyglot noir city
>
> *(2004)*

However, even the "New Valley" is hardly new. Like many neighborhoods around the metropolitan region, much of the San Fernando Valley's place-based identity solidified a decade before planned communities and public housing would enter the area.

When HOLC appraisers entered the Valley in 1939, it determined four of the two-dozen neighborhoods surveyed to be "hazardous," including those in San Fernando, Pacoima, Van Nuys, and North Hollywood. In each of these neighborhoods, HOLC assessors found evidence of "subversive racial elements" among "large populations of Mexican, Japanese, and WPA laborers" who possessed "no pride of occupancy" and were therefore deemed "Hazardous" as sites of investment. Not all redlined areas on HOLC maps signified "foreign born," "Negro," or "subversive" residency. Hazardous ratings were also based on building quality, topography unsuitable for construction, and areas susceptibility to flooding. But regardless of infrastructural or topographical ratings, no majority non-Anglo American community in the United States received anything other than a low-grade rating, even when all other criteria were deemed favorable for investment. Put simply, no matter the physical condition of a neighborhood or economic circumstance of a community, if an area had majority non-white or foreign-born people who lived in multi-generational households or mixed-race neighborhoods, it was colored red.

Overlaying the 80-year-old HOLC maps on a contemporary cartographic plan of the San Fernando Valley provides a visual glimpse of the origins of restructuring and a longer timeline by which to view its reverberations. In North Hollywood, a particular tract was redlined based on population despite the assessors' acknowledgement that there were "no construction hazards or flood risks" and that the "level terrain" possessed "conveniences" that were "readily available." This area, which today supports light industrial facilities, warehouse and storage spaces, and several dance studios and motion picture service providers, is also the confluence of the mutually antagonistic and long-warring Vineland Boys and North Hollywood Boys gangs. At the time of assessment in 1939, it was deemed "utterly blighted" due to its residential population consisting "100% of subversive racial elements" and WPA workers, 70% of whom were identified as Mexican and 15% of whom were identified as Japanese – who just three years later would be imprisoned in so-called "internment" camps.

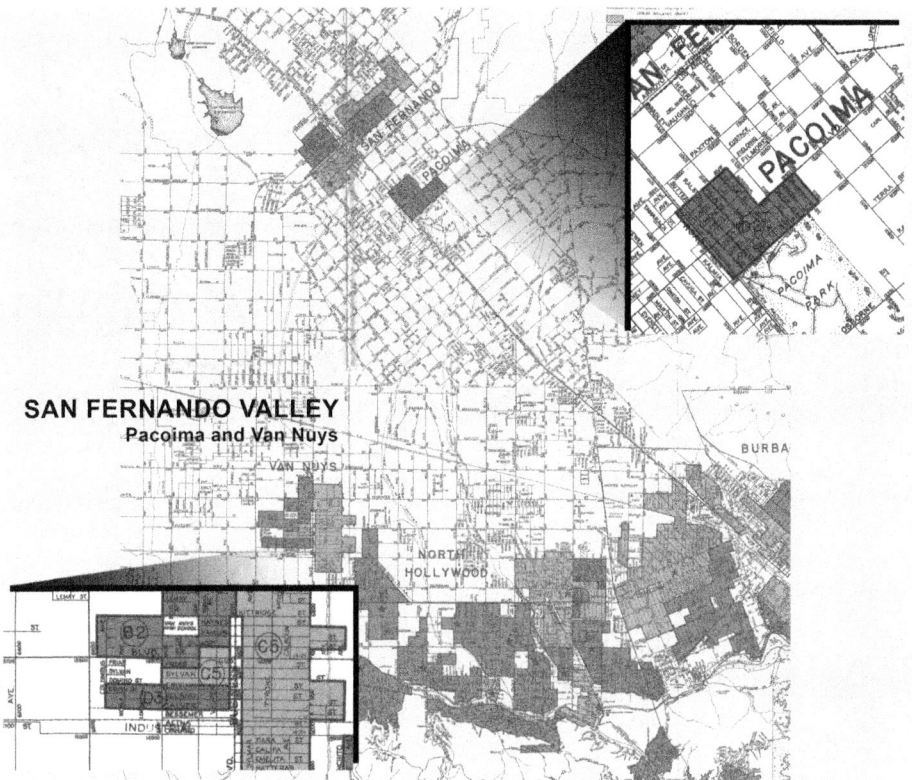

Figure 46.6 HOLC Map (Section 2) of Los Angeles's San Fernando Valley, profiling Pacoima and Van Nuys

Just eight miles to the north in Pacoima, much of the then-rural subdivision was deemed hazardous due to it being occupied by a majority "foreign born" population of orchard workers. The HOLC Area Description notes areas where "goats graze in the streets and cactus plants are greatly in evidence." The assessors state that the area was previously promoted as a "high class suburban resort," but after being abandoned by investors, it had become occupied by Mexican farm laborers who lived on and worked the land. Although Pacoima was also deemed a community with "no construction hazards" or other evidence of structural blight, the area would be cleared for the construction of public housing in the 1950s.

In the 1940s, HACLA had built the first racially integrated public housing projects – Basilone Homes – on the site of a former army barracks as a temporary solution to the lack of affordable post-war housing but demolished the homes in the late 1950s (Delgadillo 2015). When HACLA began looking for an area in which to develop permanent public housing in the 1950s, residents of the existing barrio of Pacoima pushed back against this plan, arguing that they wanted to beautify their neighborhood instead of destroying it to build another. But HACLA managed to appropriate the necessary acreage on which to build San Fernando Gardens, completed in 1955. The Valley had continued to grow. A new population of workers had been lured to the area by a combination of employment and military opportunities, the fusion of which was represented by entities such as nearby Lockheed-Martin. By the 1950s, Pacoima would house its traditional

Figure 46.7　HACLA photograph of Pacoima, Los Angeles, California at the intersection of Jouett Street and Morris Avenue. This area was developed into the public housing
project San Fernando Gardens

Source: Photograph by Leonard Nadel, July 13, 1950. Courtesy of Southern California Library for Social
Studies and Research

Mexican residents as well as a newer population of African American residents, becoming the
only sizable African American enclave in the Valley.

By this point, several different gangs existed in Pacoima, and some gang presence is evident
dating back to 1940s (see Ponce 2006). San Fernando Gardens and the residential blocks immediately surrounding it would eventually become the namesake neighborhood of four gangs, the
Pacoima Project Boys, the Pacoima Project Flats, Latin Times Pacoima, and Pacas 13. By 2001,
after a decade of boasting some of the highest violent crime rates in the city, that same parcel of
land that was red-lined, razed, redeveloped, and cleared of Mexican workers would be declared
a gang injunction safety zone by the LA City Attorney. On that single parcel of residential land,
a dozen men and boys with Spanish surnames and 100 unnamed and enjoined "affiliates," would
be legally barred from occupying public space as declared nuisances given their gang status.

Conclusion

Subsequent to decades of economic disinvestment as a result of New Deal–era stigmatization
based largely on race, many of those same Valley and South LA neighborhoods redlined in 1939
would be geographically bounded and policed as gang-injunction "safety zones" fifty years

Figure 46.8 Pacoima Projects Boys gang injunction safety zone, showing Jouett Street at center-bottom, as in Figure 46.7, 2001

Source: Available at www.lacityattorney.org/gang-injunction

later. The city's "gang problem," it appears, did not start in the hearts and minds of would-be gang members during 20th-century rampant economic downturn, mass migration from the US South and Latin America, or even job loss and the "decline of the family," as are all commonly held. Rather, the location of South LA and the San Fernando Valley's gang neighborhoods, like those located on the west and east sides of the city, had been predetermined, charted out on cartographic paper, ensured by lenders, and accepted as fact by government leaders for more than two generations.

Adding to the legacy of over 50 years of marking and perhaps unwittingly mapping gang neighborhoods was, by 1987, the implementation of a form of direct gang neighborhood mapping. In that year, the city began a decades-long project of gang abatement measures that, instead of focusing on housing in neighborhoods, focused on people in neighborhoods, creating legal stigmatization that would contribute to mass incarceration and eviction through police repression. This contemporary form of mapping accompanies the legal tactic known as the civil gang injunction.

Los Angeles's first formal gang injunction was filed by LA City Attorney James Hahn and was a direct precursor to the California-wide Street Terrorism and Enforcement Protection (STEP) act of 1988. STEP legislation sought to define a gang, increase the systematic categorization of gang members by relying on new tracking technology to make it easier to arrest purported gang members, and "enhance" prison sentences for those convicted of gang-related felonies (Muñiz 2014). For the next decade after their implementation, gang injunctions, which operate like civil restraining orders, survived constitutional challenges regarding due process and civil rights (Caldwell 2009; Werdegar 1999; Yoo 1994). One of the ways to make the policing tactic constitutionally sound was to map a specific geography in which individually named gang members would be legally forbidden from engaging in otherwise legal acts of occupying public space. The spatially defined "safety zones" accompanying many of the forty-six "permanent injunctions" that enjoin the activities of seventy-nine street gangs in much of LA overlay or are in the immediate vicinity of areas that had been stigmatized and economically disenfranchised by HOLC assessors over a generation earlier.

Looking back at the HOLC maps of the Valley, each of the Barrio Van Nuys, Pacoima Project Boys, and San Fer gang injunction safety zones are located within the precise areas that were redlined in 1939. Likewise, many of South LA's injunction safety zone neighborhoods were color-coded red long before gang members began to make their bottom-up claims to space.

Drawing links between 1930s materials and current forms of neighborhood restructuring motivated by private sector sensibilities in local government provides the connective tissue of gang neighborhood creation through time. The notion of a gang neighborhood has now been morphed by injunctions, which often work in tandem with gentrification, place-based predictive policing, which create maps of different kinds in order to enforce social order. We see these as cut of the same cloth – as forms of mapping with agendas that seem positive for public safety and that wind up re-creating racialized agendas, ramping up the problems and abuses associated with residential segregation and displacement. The intensification of race-based, residential segregation via the HOLC and public housing initiatives should be considered foundational elements of gang formation, not just in Los Angeles but in the United States as a whole.

For us personally, intimate exposure to living and working with families in formerly redlined areas exposes us daily to the challenges of segregated circumstances both by entrenched poverty and by disrespect at the hands of the police relying on their own maps of where to focus their efforts. Our case studies of South Los Angeles and the San Fernando Valley demonstrate the critical importance of research on the top-down mechanisms that contribute to gangs as neighborhood-based socio-spatial formations in order to present a counter-narrative to dominant narratives in gang scholarship, punitive discourses in government documents, and sensationalist news media depictions.

References

Aaronson, D., Hartley, D. A., & Mazumder, B. (2017). The Effects of the 1930s HOLC "Redlining" Maps. Working Paper. https://economie.esg.uqam.ca/wp-content/uploads/sites/54/2017/09/Hartley_Daniel_Oct2017.pdf.

Alonso, A. A. (2004). Racialized Identitites (sic) and the Formation of Black Gangs in Los Angeles. *Urban Geography, 25*(7), 658–674.

Alonso, A. A. (2010). Out of the Void: Street Gangs in Black Los Angeles. In Hunt, D., & Ramón, A. C. (Eds.). *Black Los Angeles: American Dreams and Racial Realities.* New York: New York University Press.

Avila, E. (2004). *Popular Culture in the Age of White Flight: Fear and Fantasy in Suburban Los Angeles.* Los Angeles: University of California Press.

Barganier, G. (2011). *Fanon's Children: The Black Panther Party and the Rise of the Crips and Bloods in Los Angeles* (Doctoral dissertation, UC Berkeley). https://escholarship.org/uc/item/3x85t70g.

Barraclough, L. R. (2011). *Making the San Fernando Valley: Rural Landscapes, Urban Development, and White Privilege.* Athens: University of Georgia Press.

Bloch, S. (2012). Considering the Photography of Leonard Nadel. *Yearbook of the Association of Pacific Coast Geographers, 74*(1), 76–95.

Bogardus, E. S. (1926). *The City Boy and His Problems*. Los Angeles, CA: House of Ralston Printers.

Bogardus, E. S. (1943). Gangs of Mexican-American Youth. *Sociology and Social Research, 28*(1), 55–66.

Bourgois, P. (2003). *In Search of Respect: Selling Crack in El Barrio*. Cambridge: Cambridge University Press.

Brotherton, D. C. (2008). Beyond Social Reproduction: Bringing Resistance Back in Gang Theory. *Theoretical Criminology, 12*(1).

Brotherton, D. C. (2015). *Youth Street Gangs: A Critical Appraisal*. London: Routledge.

Brown, L. A., & Chung, S. Y. (2006). Spatial Segregation, Segregation Indices and the Geographical Perspective. *Population, Space and Place, 12*(2), 125–143.

Bryant, C., Collette, B., Green, W., Isoardi, S., & Young, M. (Eds.). (1999). *Central Avenue Sounds: Jazz in Los Angeles*. Los Angeles: University of California Press.

Caldwell, B. (2009). Criminalizing Day-to-Day Life: A Socio-Legal Critique of Gang Injunctions. *American Journal of Criminal Law, 37*, 241.

Chetty, R., Friedman, J. N., Hendren, N., Jones, M. R., & Porter, S. R. (2018). *The Opportunity Atlas: Mapping the Childhood Roots of Social Mobility* (No. w25147). Cambridge: National Bureau of Economic Research.

Coughlin, B. C., & Venkatesh, S. A. (2003). The Urban Street Gang after 1970. *Annual Review of Sociology, 29*(1), 41–64.

Crossney, K. B., & Bartelt, D. W. (2005). The Legacy of the Home Owners' Loan Corporation. *Housing Policy Debate, 16*(3–4), 547–574.

Davis, M. (1990). *City of Quartz: Excavating the Future*. Los Angeles. London: Verso.

Delgadillo, S. (2015). *Identifying and Conserving Pacoima: A Heritage Conservation Study of a Minority Enclave in the San Fernando Valley* (Doctoral dissertation, University of Southern California).

Flamming, D. (2005). *Bound for Freedom: Black Los Angeles in Jim Crow America*. Los Angeles: University of California Press.

Gans, H. J. (1982). *Urban Villagers*. New York: Simon and Schuster.

Gilmore, R. W. (2007). *Golden Gulag: Prisons, Surplus, Crisis, and Opposition in Globalizing California*. Los Angeles: University of California Press.

Goetz, E. G. (2000). The Politics of Poverty Deconcentration and Housing Demolition. *Journal of Urban Affairs, 22*(2), 157–173.

Hagedorn, J. M. (1988). *People and Folks: Gangs, Crime and the Underclass in a Rustbelt City*. Chicago: Lake View Press.

Hagedorn, J. M. (2015). *The Insane Chicago Way: The Daring Plan by Chicago Gangs to Create a Spanish Mafia*. Chicago: University of Chicago Press.

Hernández, K. L. (2017). *City of Inmates: Conquest, Rebellion, and the Rise of Human Caging in Los Angeles, 1771–1965*. Chapel Hill: UNC Press.

Hillier, A. E. (2003). Redlining and the Home Owners' Loan Corporation. *Journal of Urban History, 29*(4), 394–420.

Hise, G. (2004). Border City: Race and Social Distance in Los Angeles. *American Quarterly, 56*(3), 545–558.

Hunt, D., & Ramón, A. C. (Eds.). (2010). *Black Los Angeles: American Dreams and Racial Realities*. New York: NYU Press.

Jackson, K. T. (1980). Race, Ethnicity, and Real Estate Appraisal: The Home Owners Loan Corporation and the Federal Housing Administration. *Journal of Urban History, 6*(4), 419–452.

Jackson, K. T. (1987). *Crabgrass Frontier: The Suburbanization of the United States*. Oxford: Oxford University Press.

Kurashige, S. (2010). *The Shifting Grounds of Race: Black and Japanese Americans in the Making of Multiethnic Los Angeles*. Princeton, NJ: Princeton University Press.

Lipsitz, G. (2006). *The Possessive Investment in Whiteness: How White People Profit from Identity Politics*. Philadelphia, PA: Temple University Press.

Logan, J. R. (1978). Growth, Politics, and the Stratification of Places. *American Journal of Sociology, 84*(2), 404–416.

Marciano, R., Connolly, N., et al. (1939). Mapping Inequality. In R. K. Nelson & E. L. Ayers (Eds.). *American Panorama*. https://dsl.richmond.edu/panorama/redlining/

McWilliams, C., Meier, M. S., & García, A. M. (2016). *North from Mexico: The Spanish-Speaking People of the United States: The Spanish-Speaking People of the United States*. Santa Barabra, CA: ABC-CLIO.

Michney, T. M., & Winling, L. (2019). New Perspectives on New Deal Housing Policy: Explicating and Mapping HOLC Loans to African Americans. *Journal of Urban History*, *25*(2), 1–31.

Muñiz, A. (2014). Maintaining Racial Boundaries: Criminalization, Neighborhood Context, and the Origins of Gang Injunctions. *Social Problems*, *61*(2), 216–236.

Nicolaides, B. (2002). *My Blue Heaven: Life and Politics in the Working-Class Suburbs of Los Angeles, 1920–1965*. Chicago: University of Chicago Press.

Nicolaides, B., & Wiese, A. (2013). Suburban Disequilibrium. *New York Times*, April 6.

Nicolaides, B., & Wiese, A. (2017). Suburbanization in the United States after 1945. In *Oxford Research Encyclopedia of American History*. Oxford: Oxford University Press.

People vs. Blythe Street Gang, Superior Court of the State of California, LC020525, 2000.

Phillips, S. A. (2012). *Operation Fly Trap: LA Gangs, Drugs, and the Law*. Chicago: University of Chicago Press.

Ponce, M. H. (2006). *Hoyt Street: An Autobiography*. Albuquerque: University of New Mexico Press.

Pulido, L. (2000). Rethinking Environmental Racism: White Privilege and Urban Development in Southern California. *Annals of the Association of American Geographers*, *90*(1), 12–40.

Robinson, P. (2010). Race, Space, and the Evolution of Black Los Angeles. In Hunt, D., & Ramón, A. C. (Eds.). *Black Los Angeles: American Dreams and Racial Realities*. New York: NYU Press, pp. 21–59.

Rothstein, R. (2017). *The Color of Law: A Forgotten History of How Our Government Segregated America*. New York: Liveright Publishing.

Schill, M. H., & Wachter, S. M. (1995). The Spatial Bias of Federal Housing Law and Policy: Concentrated Poverty in Urban America. *University of Pennsylvania Law Review*, *143*(5), 1285–1342.

Sides, J. (2004). Straight into Compton: American Dreams, Urban Nightmares, and the Metamorphosis of a Black Suburb. *American Quarterly*, *56*(3), 583–605.

Sloan, C. S. (2005). *Bastards of the Party* (Documentary film) HBO. 95 mins.

Smith, N. (2005). *The New Urban Frontier: Gentrification and the Revanchist City*. London: Routledge.

Spalding, S. (1992). The Myth of the Classic Slum: Contradictory Perceptions of Boyle Heights Flats, 1900–1991. *Journal of Architectural Education*, *45*(2), 107–119. DOI: 10.1080/10464883.1992.10734496.

Stolberg, S. (1992). 150,000 Are in Gangs, Report by D.A. Claims: Reiner's Study Says Half of Young Blacks Are Members. *Los Angeles Times*, May 22.

Thrasher, F. (1927). *The Gang: A Study of 1,313 Gangs in Chicago*. Chicago: The University of Chicago Press.

Venkatesh, S. A. (1997). The Social Organization of Street Gang Activity in an Urban Ghetto. *American Journal of Sociology*, *103*(1), 82–111.

Vigil, J. D. (1988). *Barrio Gangs: Street Life and Identity in Southern California*. Austin: University of Texas Press.

Vigil, J. D. (2007). *The Projects: Gang and Non-Gang Families in East Los Angeles*. Austin: University of Texas Press.

Vigil, J. D. (2010). *Barrio Gangs: Street Life and Identity in Southern California*. Austin: University of Texas Press.

Werdegar, M. M. (1999). Enjoining the Constitution: The Use of Public Nuisance Abatement Injunctions Against Urban Street Gangs. *Stanford Law Review*, 409–445.

Yoo, C. S. (1994). Constitutionality of Enjoining Criminal Street Gangs as Public Nuisances. *Northwestern University Law Review*, *89*, 212.

Part VII
Critical appraisals of major figures in gang research

47

Dwight Conquergood

An appreciation of his intellectual life and contribution to critical gang studies

Kamran Afary and David C. Brotherton

Lorne Dwight Conquergood (1949–2004) was a pioneer and a foundational theorist in the field of performance studies. An associate professor at Northwestern University, Conquergood's performance ethnographies brought together ideas from several fields, including critical theory, cultural anthropology, critical race studies, and theater. This confluence of theory and practical performance widely influenced the scholarship of several contemporary performance scholars both during the course of Conquergood's life and in the decade and a half after his death. Conquergood articulated some of the key principles of performance studies, in particular the ethical dimensions of using performance as a lens through which one conducts research in the humanities.

Conquergood's many groundbreaking essays and ethnographic publications were collected into an edited volume by E. Patrick Johnson and published posthumously (see Johnson 2013; Conquergood 2013). The collection also contains a comprehensive Introduction and several tributes to Conquergood by a number of scholars, highlighting his unique qualities and contributions. This resource has proved invaluable for this chapter.

Conquergood was born in Ontario, Canada, and grew up on a farm in rural Indiana. He attended Indiana State University in Terre Haute for his undergraduate degree in speech communication and English, and subsequently moved to University of Utah, where he received his master's degree in 1972. He received his doctorate at Northwestern University in the former Department of Interpretation, currently Performance Studies. By the time he graduated, he was a multitalented and skilled scholar and filmmaker, having been mentored by scholars in interpretation and rhetoric. As a medievalist, he wrote his dissertation on Beowulf and the Anglo-Saxon Boast. This would foreshadow his later ethnographic work with gang youth on street literacy and his close reading of gang graffiti (Roach 2013). After graduating, Dwight began working at Northwestern in 1978, where he continued to teach for 26 years until his death in 2004, a career span that changed not only his department at Northwestern but also impacted the field of performance studies and communication studies.

His presentations at the National Communication Association conferences were often packed, and audiences were moved by his clear and articulate voice – speaking out against oppressive norms and advocating for the artistic creativity of the youth in Chicago whose affiliation with gangs was criminalized. He set out to document the many creative ways gang youth claimed public spaces in the face of severe repression and criminalization of their sense of identity and belonging (Conquergood 2020). Dwight's writings and presentations at conferences demonstrate his tremendous commitments to not only social justice but also to civic engagement in a way that did not separate theory from practice. His ethnographic essays span several continents: Laotian refugee camps in Thailand, where he wrote about Health Theater; Palestinian refugee camps, where he focused on language; and Chicago's multiethnic new immigrant and refugee neighborhoods, where he wrote about housing conditions and street gangs while he served on numerous boards and consulted with many human rights organizations (Conquergood 1988, 2004, 2013, 2020).

Conquergood developed a reputation as a profound and influential pedagogue, winning Illinois Professor of the Year Award in 1993. His courses were vigorous and challenging, and his assignments always demanded artistic creativity and reflexivity. Importantly, he refused to segregate the process of analysis in critical theory from creativity in producing artistic artifacts and always encouraged the creation of a classroom community through dialogic exercises, small group field research, and performance assignments. In the following, we recount his extraordinary contributions to the foundations and development of performance studies and segue into his equally crucial impact on the development of critical gang studies.

Conquergood as a pioneer of performance studies

Although Dwight passed away at the young age of 55 years, he left a tremendous body of writings, documentary films, and performances. The publication of a collection of his works provides insight into the disciplinary and methodological debates in which he participated and the relationship between performance studies and his interpretation of critical ethnography. In his introduction to the life and works of Conquergood, Johnson (2013) advances a three-part approach to better understand how he brought theory, method, and field research together.

First, in what Johnson (2013, p. 6) calls "performance ethnography as theory", Conquergood's role as a foundational figure in the emergence of performance studies as a field of study is firmly established. In achieving this task, Conquergood was an unrelenting critic of positivist and conservative scholarship, demonstrated through his countless presentations at academic conferences and in numerous essays; he often critiqued dominant social science and empirical methods and epistemologies for their inability to appreciate or even consider performance as a site and object of study.

The second major theme is highlighted in what Johnson (2013, p. 7) calls "performance as method" and has three interrelated dimensions – economics, cultural, and spatial. For Conquergood, who was deeply influenced by Victor Turner's (1977) cultural anthropology, the processual construction of cultures and identities through rituals, rites of passage, and social dramas was critical, particularly as it relates to the way subaltern populations construct a sense of meaning and resist oppressive social norms. He advocated for engaging subaltern agency in ethnographic research through the lens of how identities are performed – in particular, how subaltern populations create and perform identities in rituals and rites of passage through social and personal dramas. The approach is rooted in material relationships – both as institutions in the larger political economy and as interactions in interpersonal communications. For Conquergood (2006b, pp. 352–355), performances of identities are a way to understand cultural creativity and human agency, situated within fluid and evolving locations, as bodies in motion in displacement and diasporas.

Conquergood was not only appropriating ethnographic methods for performance studies, he was also adding an indispensable lens to deepen research methodology. Performance allows the researcher to reach a deeper dialogical relationship, through complicating who and what is being researched and by whom. Performance dispenses with the notion that the subject of research is there waiting to be documented and preserved and instead reveals a more embodied realm in which history, memory, and rituals are preserved. Conquergood advocated for self-reflexivity as a more dialogical form of encounter, in which both researchers and those they study are engaged in the process of representation and meaning making.

This insight has extended Conquergood's influence in such fields as social psychology. For example, Robert Lecusay (2015) focuses on the therapeutic dimension of Conquergood's contribution through the development of a research praxis that is also self-reflexive through his studies on both meaning making practices and the transformation of consciousness for all concerned. At the heart of this practice is the intersubjective relationship between the researcher, the researched, community partners, and the audience for whom the research is staged. Because this embodied interaction includes performing histories of marginalized individuals, it can also serve to scaffold the learning of real problem-solving practices. Furthermore, by moving performance into the research process itself, performance ethnography constructs and sustains an environment of creativity with participants oriented to looking for novel solutions to complicated problems where conflicts and disagreements, contradictions and dilemmas are imaginatively addressed.

Maintaining an environment for creative performances teaches all participants to pay closer attention to their interrelatedness, orchestrating people, their symbolic practices, and the available materials at all times, whereby everyone involved can enter the stage and act as an agent of self-transformation. Lecusay (2015) calls this a "dialogic form of ethnography, one grounded in an ethic of reciprocal exchange among community partners, audiences, and researchers. The aim is to collaboratively rethink everyday practices and as a consequence create, transform, and represent new practices".

In 1985, Conquergood articulated this notion of a dialogic performance in his essay titled "Performance as a Moral Act: Ethical Dimensions of the Ethnography of Performance" (Conquergood 2013, pp. 65–81). Although this particular articulation of ethics of research has received the most attention among scholars, over time, Conquergood moved away from centering the relationship on *dialogue* and toward *coperformative witnessing*. Dialogue was "too thin" a trope, Johnson (2013, p. 9) argues, for the complicated and contested dynamic between the researcher and the researched. This move can also be seen in later articulations, such as in "Rethinking Ethnography: Towards a Critical Cultural Politics", where Conquergood (2006b, pp. 351–365) calls on communication studies researchers to be more reflexive about their practices and to move from the gaze of an observer to the engagement of coperformance.

While Conquergood lived in a housing tenement in Chicago, he produced research that captured the way global and local political economies impacted the Albany Park neighborhood. Both material conditions and human practices that created metaphoric meanings were accounted for with his work deeply influenced by Zora Neale Hurston's performance ethnographies. As Judith Hamera (2013) has argued, Conquergood did not just move to study residents as objects but to understand through his own body what it is like to live under siege. Thus, his account of life conditions is riveting but not sensationalistic, while his academic credentials helped him to undermine structures of power, and advocate for those who did not have access to the same kind of power to employ in their own defense.

Micaela di Leonardo (2013, p. 303) most appreciated his "performative political economy", explaining that while Conquergood was firmly anchored in Marx's break from classical political economy and its assumptions about capital, labor, property, and power, he did not separate cultural form from economic analysis. Indeed, by adding an organic *performative lens*, he was able to focus on how human bodies make meanings as they *move* in urban spaces of domination and inequality.

To demonstrate this, di Leonardo (2013) points to the work mentioned previously when Conquergood was living in "Big Red" among the Hmong populations in Chicago and that resulted in several years of ethnographic research showing how global forces shape neighborhood human interactions. In gathering empirical data on labor, property, and the history of the neighborhood, as well as in ethnographic narratives of people "making do" in everyday life, di Leonardo writes that:

> [t]hese narratives, more often than not, gave us windows onto the contingent, bricolage performances of the urban poor-turning an alley into a bracero party site, indoor hallways into sociability havens, an outside courtyard into a safe children's playground, policed ironically by gang members.
>
> *(di Leonardo 2013, p. 304)*

Another example of Conquergood's ethnographic work that exemplified this *performative political economy* is a film Conquergood coproduced with Taggart Siegel (1990), *The Heart Broken in Half: Street Gangs in Urban America*. This documentary on Chicago's neighborhood of Albany Park addresses issues of gentrification and the ways in which young Latino King gang members carve out and claim a public space through their graffiti art work. With this and other works, he continued to develop this work on gang youth performances and critical political economy throughout the 1990s. But, as unique as his *performative political economy* is, it is Conquergood's "deep, highly-political, openhearted engagement with human beings globally", writes di Leonardo, "who are caught on the losing ends of neoliberal globalization, and who act collectively against their fates", that makes his legacy ever more relevant today (di Leonardo 2013, p. 305).

Hamera has written extensively on Conquergood's contributions. In addressing Conquergood's work, she highlights his contributions in developing an "epistemology of ethical obligations" through which performance requires answerability and vulnerability. In this way, performance opens up a deeper relationship between the performer and the audience built upon mutual vulnerability between a self and an other. For Conquergood, both the self and the other are often marginalized and traumatized by social structures, thereby creating the conflict and resonance of the performance (Hamera 2013, p. 307).

Conquergood's heightened appreciation for the voice of others and his years of training and experience in performance studies helped him in theorizing the ethical dimensions of the interaction between the researcher, advocating a rigorous accuracy and the subject being listened to and represented. His celebrated "moral map" created a new methodology and a language in order to allow the ethnographer and performer to negotiate these gaps between the researcher and the researched. As Hamera points out, rather than "avoiding the *enthusiast's infatuated* insistence that the[se gaps] don't exist and the *cynic's refusal* to even approach them, negotiating the approach means resisting *exhibitionist* and *entrepreneurial* motives" (Hamera 2013, p. 307 [emphasis in original]).

Another theme that comes across through several of Conquergood's tributes is that of vulnerability (Hamera 2013, p. 308), seeing this as a prerequisite to doing performance ethnography and a willingness to remake oneself through the necessary exposure of working with others. In an unpublished manuscript, Conquergood writes:

> Performers . . . submit themselves to the gaze of multiple onlookers, offering themselves to the variable apprehensions of audiences. . . . For performing researchers the body becomes the porous boundary of exchange, the interface.
>
> *(Conquergood quoted in Hamera 2013, p. 308)*

Conquergood navigated disciplinary boundaries in an eclectic and fruitful manner and was deeply engaged in creating an interdisciplinary approach to the many forms of performance in the humanities. He was interested in all dimensions of performance, including those of the aesthetic, communicative, oral, embodied, and narrative. Conquergood's writings, as Jackson (2013) points out, opened up meta and actual spaces for theorizing and performing with his sites of performance a testament to his search for new ways to embody performance scholarship in uncharacteristic places. Jackson also highlights Conquergood's moral mapping of the ethnographer's encounter and writes that:

> [h]e worried about the danger of cross-cultural theft as much as he argued for the importance of cross-cultural knowledge. He was as adamantly against scholarly appropriation as he was against scholarly cynicism.
>
> *(Jackson quoted in Conquergood 2013, p. 311)*

Conquergood's anti-racist scholarship and activism are most attested to by D. Soyini Madison (2013, pp. 314–319), focusing on his legacy in refusing to ignore racial differences and making sure those differences were posed in a way that would help bring about racial justice. Conquergood's (2006a) anti-racism is demonstrated not only internationally – in his fieldwork with Laotian refugees in Thailand, Palestinian refugees in Gaza camps, and Latino youth in Chicago – but also in his recuperating voices of Black freedom fighters in earlier periods of history. In reflecting on Conquergood's principled anti-racist activism and allyship, Madison (2013, p. 313) writes that, "Dwight was always aware of his own white privilege and his status as a white male, it ironically made his racial phenotype rescind under the mighty weight of his racial principles".

Commenting on Conquergood's (2013, pp. 104–127) essay "Rethinking Elocution . . .", Madison (2013, p 316) argues that he highlighted the oral traditions introduced by Black Abolitionists who, even when they "seized a written text, learned and deciphered its words", nevertheless broke the rules of White elocutionists by using it in the service of uprooting slavery. According to Madison (2013), Conquergood makes a compelling case of simultaneously racing theory and advocating for racial justice while criticizing text-centered ways of knowing. Conquergood's "Rethinking Elocution . . ." contrasts the stratification and intensified hierarchies between forms of black literacy in performances by formerly enslaved abolitionists and the so-called refinements and civilizing effects of the elocutionary movement and situates this tension in the political economy of the time, a new stage of industrial capitalism and the rise of new forms of chattel slavery. However, Conquergood complicates the history and practices of the elocutionary movement as it sought to regulate and refine the illiterate poor and to teach the enslaved how to enact proper decorum, rejoining:

> class and race back to its more true, troubled, and complicated political history . . . where rules of conduct, the aesthetics of public speech, and the materiality of voice become inseparable from the social-political milieu of industrial capitalism's affective grip in the distribution and disciplining of labor and race in America-slave wages and enslaved persons.
>
> *(Madison 2013, p. 316)*

Conquergood and his impact on gang studies

Thus far, we have discussed Conquergood's extraordinary contribution to a range of scholarship but primarily emphasizing his role in the evolution of the interdisciplinary performance studies. Within his overall oeuvre of research and pedagogy, however, a substantial amount of his time and energy was given over to the study of gang subcultures in Chicago, with a particular focus on that city's Latin Kings. This work emerged from his long-term ethnographic study within the tenement "Big Red", as mentioned previously, from which he produced a series of highly influential publications that cemented his reputation as a theoretically astute ethnographer, combining the literatures of sociology, anthropology, social geography, and theater, who was able to document, interpret, and critically analyze the lived culture of this group set in its community context. In the following, we consider Conquergood's impact through three domains: space, culture, and theory.

Gang spaces

The creation of urban space occupied by street gangs was a major focus of Conquergood's (2004) work as he approached what he called these highly charged, sociopolitical domains. For Conquergood, these are largely public spaces where the state and its agents have created a plethora of interlocking legal and para-legal devices and strategies to control the autonomous behavior of gangs recruited from the working-class and the poor. He saw these subcultures as street organizations (Brotherton and Barrios 2004), what he termed "bonded communitarians" (Conquergood 2004), eking out physical and symbolic areas for themselves, sometimes in competition with other groups but always in competition with agents of the state, most notably the Chicago police. As Conquergood (2004) saw it, the gangs consisted of members drawn from the entire mosaic of race and ethnicities within the local population, in effect transgressing the racially and ethnically segregated domains designated by the city's dominant class, and in their own way contesting the contradictions from below of an imposed urban grid that racially divided the poor.

For Conquergood, it was imperative to understand the construction of spaces over time to grasp the evolving meanings, rituals, and practices of gangs and gang life. Any theorizing of the gang that does not contemplate the role and the politics of the built spaces within which gangs coexist will be necessarily flawed and will only describe and imagine these subcultures outside of the historically constituted political economy of space within which these groups emerge and proliferate. For Conquergood, such contested space is neither well documented nor critically engaged, and as a result, his work still remains a major exception to the rule, continuing to demonstrate how we might reconceptualize gangs across different sociogeographic domains. For example, once we think outside of the usual landscapes within which gangs are framed and frozen, we might entertain other kinds of space such as: (1) institutionalized versus non-institutionalized spaces, (2) incarcerated vs free spaces, (3) exiled versus citizenship spaces, and (4) public versus private spaces (see Brotherton 2015).

Gang cultures

Most gang criminological studies treat culture as something that is tied to structure and usually amounts to little more than a discourse on values, that is, class, race/ethnic, and/ or gendered values. For Conquergood, a critical culturalist approach is key to the research project for he was interested in the meanings attached to a panoply of behaviors viewed as individual and collective interpretations of material circumstances and traditions, as in di Leonardo's (2013) reading of his performance political economy. The rehearsed and self-created symbols of everyday life and the rites and rituals that characterize, organize, and lend meaning to gang life were his paramount concerns, as he immersed himself in and surveilled the surrounding community and its environs during his field work. Culture, for Conquergood (2013), was made, lived, and mediated and was considered a verb, not a noun, a tenet of his critical methodological approach of which he consistently reminded us. Consequently, gang culture should be viewed as a rich assemblage of properties and of processes in production, in flux and in context. Its forms should be represented and interpreted in a way that highlights its various influences and linkages, not as an example of exotica or self-contained deviance but as an outgrowth of struggle for social autonomy and human dignity, as well as social reproduction.

Consistently in his work, gang culture was understood as the expressivity of a subaltern population that has multiple dimensions – physical, textual, and virtual. He saw that the cultural and symbolic repertoire of such groups were located and embedded within a colonized and postcolonized set of relations that circumscribed their liminality; that is, groups are positioned between internal and external borders, low and high cultures, and linguistic structures. Conquergood was particularly influenced by the literature coming out of the Birmingham School which emphasized how youth subcultures intersected strongly with and are infused by a range of values, ideologies, and norms from below and from above. For example, they are simultaneously influenced by the commodified seductions of the leisure industry and youth marketing as well as by the social obligations of their parents and peers. He thought that such subcultures took from these cultural vistas and practices a range of meanings and symbolic attachments that had to be appropriated, interpreted, and reincorporated through a process of bricolage, resulting in highly innovative individual and collective meanings, not just routinized action.

It was Conquergood (2004) who was one of the first to shine a light on the complex communicative systems used by gangs to convey their innermost meanings to each other and to the outside society. What was often misread simply as primitive graffiti by outsiders (particularly the police) was interpreted by Conquergood as a deep expression of the subculture's place in society and its internal economy of signs used to convey threat, sorrow, hope, peace, disapproval, and other displays of collective emotion and identity. He called this a form of "street literacy" and contrasted it to the texts and codes produced by the dominant culture which were frequently used to marginalize, control, and criminalize gang members in communities that felt like occupied zones (Conquergood 2004). Drawing on his wide reading from multiple disciplinary sources, his research became foundational in the growing field of urban communications as he discursively introduced the gang not through their usual stereotypes of violent bodies and actions but through their texts, speeches, gestures, graffiti, clothing styles, and corporal adornments that combine to form a coherent system created over time within a field of complexly contested urban power relations.

Both his written and visual analyses of communications vis-à-vis gangs (2004, 2013, 2020) are critical texts in a world saturated by images and simulacra of the Other and the various struggles for authenticity. As we have seen in his praxis of performance studies more generally, a critical study must draw on the everyday activities, practices, and elements of the coperforming research subjects, and so it was in his ethnographic forays into gang culture. What sets his work apart is his radical listening and acute observations of these urban cultural creators as he archived their practices while documenting the impacts they have on both the micro and the macro levels of society (for example, the torrent of images that are created as societies go to war against the gang Other and the reaction of the gang to such images, or the rise of global hip-hop and the powerful influence of gangs as subjects, progenitors, and settings).

Conquergood insisted that it was difficult to capture adequately the "moral outrage and repression"[1] that street gang literacy spoke to, considering such cultural products part of a gang's subjugated knowledge base that consisted of: "street sense, survival wisdom, underground history, cultural codes, and protocols of communication" (Conquergood, personal communication with Brotherton 1999). In an articulation of the felt exclusion/inclusion dialectic of gang members living under the constant gaze of the state, he wrote in his inimitable style:

> The insult of effacement is compounded by surveillance. In the ocular politics of the ruling classes, subordinate groups are expunged from spaces of respectability, and then rendered hypervisible in the surreal zone of the panoptic power.
>
> *(Conquergood 2004, p. 355)*

In responding to such pressures and infiltrations, gangs produce communications that are contradictory, that is, both overt and secret, opaque and transparently clear, camouflaged and pointedly direct. He felt that these subjugated knowledges could be seen as constituting an alternative street curriculum including "all the manifold genres of cultural performance" (Conquergood, personal communication with Brotherton 1999). Thus, there is no better place to start a critical study of gang communications than with Conquergood's rich theoretical and empirical legacy.

Gang theory

Conquergood's long-term in situ documentation of neighborhood Latin Kings in Chicago has produced a number of highly innovative cultural interpretations of the customs, rituals, and symbolic universes of gang members (Conquergood and Siegel 1990, Conquergood 2004, 2013, pp. 170–223, 2020, pp. 224–263). Borrowing equally from the British school of cultural resistance studies (for example, Hall et al. 1978; Hall and Jefferson 1975; Willis 1977), from the labeling theories of Howard S. Becker (1963), and from the interdisciplinary discourses of performance studies (for example, Turner 1977; Rosaldo 1989; Clifford 1988; Bakhtin 1981; Geertz 1983), Conquergood alerts us to the actively produced and reproduced worlds of gangs. For him, gang members are not viewed as adapting either fatalistically or pathologically – or simply innovatively – to their environment but rather as social actors consciously making their culture in between the structures and crevices of an imposed bourgeois social order. As Conquergood phrases it:

> The homeboys are keenly aware of class difference in communication style, and are critical of what they take to be the tepid, distant, interpersonal mode of the middle class. . . . Against a dominant world that displaces, stifles, and erases identity, the homeboys create, through their communications practices, a hood: a subterranean space of life-sustaining warmth, intimacy, and protection.
>
> *(Conquergood 2013, p. 247)*

Today Conquergood's work stands in stark contrast to the bulk of orthodox gang studies, not least because he requires us (the actor, the student, the observer, the listener, etc.) to unearth the hidden and the opaque while questioning our own expert positionality (Rosaldo 1989). In a series of probing questions, Conquergood asks:

What are the differences between reading an analysis of fieldwork data, and hearing the voices from the field interpretively filtered through the voice of the researcher? For the listening audience of peers? For the performing ethnographer? For the people whose lived experience is the subject matter of the ethnography? What about enabling the people themselves to perform their own experience?

(Conquergood 2013, p. 96)

Thus, Conquergood calls upon the research community to see gangs as social and cultural agents who function both as subjects and as objects in their own theater of operations as well as in the gaze of the researcher. For a variety of reasons, however, Conquergood's perspective of gangs is still considered heretical, evidenced by the fact that, with the exception of a few gang researchers within the critical realm (for example, Fraser 2015; Venkatesh 1997; Brotherton 2015; Garot 2010), there are few if any references to his considerable theoretical and empirical contributions in the countless gang articles produced by orthodox pens. Following is a summary of some of the major conceptual differences between Conquergood's approach and those of mainstream criminology compared across the analytical categories of (1) social agency, (2) processes of cultural construction, (3) presumed character of society, and (4) perceived relations between the gang and the community.

Table 47.1 Comparison between Conquergood's approach to gangs and that of orthodox criminology across four analytical categories

	(I) Social agency	(II) Cultural processes	(III) Character of society	(IV) Gang-community relations
Conquergood	Active, purposive, resistant, empowering, and spatially transformative	Symbolically appropriating from dominant, hostile culture; rational self-articulating; performed	Capitalist mode of production; class- and racial-based hierarchies; coercive apparatuses of bourgeois state control used to exclude, demonize, and contain lower-class "other"	Organically emergent; contradictory
Orthodox criminology	Adaptive Reproducing itself pathologically	Learned in interactions with juveniles and adults Regenerative Learned criminal deviance Cultures and subcultures of poverty Apart lower-class cultural milieu, mainly juvenile peer-influenced	Non-defined, modern, industrial, disorganized, rapidly changing, naturally poverty producing, transhistorical	Strained with mainstream, reflective of community pathologies, fundamentally anomic

Conclusion

As the previous has made manifest, it is our opinion that Conquergood was a giant among gang researchers who has still to be fully appreciated by the many researchers active in the field or by the young students beginning their journey in this endeavor. His insights into gang life-worlds are unparalleled within the ethnographic literature, as he drew on a vast interdisciplinary literature to help us see the all-sidedness of the shared practices and meanings of gang members situated in specifically structured social, economic, and political contexts. His academic training and influence in the burgeoning discipline of performance studies gave him a different vantage point from which to observe his research subjects as well as the webs of urban subcultural networks within which they were immersed that were distinct from most gang studies coming from sociology and criminology and completely in tension with anything related to a criminal justice perspective.

Both methodologically and theoretically, he has left for us a firm foundation on which to build the new traditions of critical gang discourse. Meanwhile, his principled commitment to those who are marginalized and disenfranchised will continue to be a model of activist research praxis that brooks no compromise with the goals of social scientific excellence and integrity. For those inquiring minds seeking alternatives to the staid conventions of so much published gang research that dutifully repeat the same old criminogenic tropes within which the gang phenomenon has been contained, then with the texts and documentaries of Conquergood, there is no better place to start.

Note

1 Who other than Conquergood would talk about the "moral outrage" of gang members? Most outsiders would see such subjects as either immoral or amoral, but Conquergood again and again pointed out the deeply human personal and social properties of these groups and, if anything, saw the dominant society as largely immoral and amoral, which is one reason he was so committed to exposing the barbaric practice of the death penalty See Conquergood (2002a, pp. 339–367), "Lethal Theatre: Performance, Punishment, and the Death Penalty", repr. (2013, pp. 264–301).

Bibliography

Bakhtin, M (1981). *The dialogic imagination: four essays*. Holquist, M (ed.) Austin: University of Texas Press.

Becker, HS (1963). *Outsiders: studies in the sociology of deviance*. New York: Free Press.

Brotherton, DC (2015). *Youth street gangs: a critical appraisal*. London: Routledge.

Brotherton, DC & Barrios, L (2004). *The Almighty Latin King and Queen Nation: street politics and the transformation of a New York City gang*. New York: Columbia University Press.

Clifford, J (1988). *The predicament of culture: twentieth-century ethnography, literature, and art*. Cambridge, MA: Harvard University Press.

Conquergood, D (1988). "Health theatre in a Hmong refugee camp: performance, communication, and culture". *TDR: The Drama Review*, vol. 32, no. 3, pp. 174–208. www.jstor.org/stable/1145914.

Conquergood, D (1999). Personal emails to David C. Brotherton. <may not be needed in bibliography>.

Conquergood, D (2002a). "Lethal theatre: performance, punishment, and the death penalty". *Theatre Journal*, vol. 54, no. 3, pp. 339–367. Reprint (2013), pp. 264–301. www.jstor.org/stable/info/25069091.

Conquergood, D (2004). "Street literacy". In Flood, JH, Heath, SB & Lapp, D (eds.) *Handbook of research on teaching literacy through the communicative and visual arts*. New York: Routledge, pp. 354–375.

Conquergood, D (2006a). "Rethinking elocution: The trope of the talking book and other figures of speech". In Hamera, J (ed.) *Opening acts: performance in/as communication and cultural studies*. Thousand Oaks, CA: Sage, pp. 141–161.

Conquergood, D (2006b). "Rethinking ethnography: towards a critical cultural politics". in Madison, DS & Hamera, J (eds.) *The SAGE handbook of performance studies*. Thousand Oaks, CA: Sage, pp. 351–365 (Original work published 1991).

Conquergood, D (2013). *Cultural struggles: performance, ethnography, praxis*. Johnson, EP (ed. and intro.) Ann Arbor: University of Michigan Press.

Conquergood, D (2020). "Drama therapy". Presentation at Globalizing the Streets Conference in New York, May 2001. Conference organized by David C Brotherton and Luis Barrios at the John Jay College of Criminal Justice. Afary, K (recorded); Galan, I (ed.). www.youtube.com/watch?v=xBcRmNb M6Po&feature=youtu.be (accessed January 6, 2020).

Conquergood, D & Siegel, T (1990). *The heart broken in half: street gangs in urban America*. San Francisco: Collective Eye Films. www.kanopy.com/product/heart-broken-half (accessed January 19, 2020).

di Leonardo, M (2013). "Dwight Conquergood and performative political economy". In Johnson, EP (ed.) *Cultural struggles: performance, ethnography, praxis*, by Conquergood, D. Ann Arbor: University of Michigan Press, pp. 303–305.

Fraser, A (2015). *Urban legends: gang identity in the post-industrial city*. Oxford: Oxford University Press.

Garot, R (2010). *Who you claim: performing gang identity in school and on the streets*. New York: New York University Press.

Geertz, C. (1983) "Notions of Primitive Thought: Dialogue with Clifford Geertz." In *States of Mind*. ed. & comp. Jonathan Miller. New York: Pantheon, pp. 192–210.

Hall, S, Critcher, C, Jefferson, T, Clarke, J & Roberts, B (1978). *Policing the crisis: mugging, the state and law and order*. New York: Holmes and Meier.

Hall, S & Jefferson, T (eds.). (1975). *Resistance through rituals: youth subcultures in post-war Britain*. London: Routledge.

Hamera, J (2013). "Response-ability, vulnerability, and other(s') bodies". In Johnson, JP (ed.) *Cultural struggles: performance, ethnography, praxis*, by Conquergood, D. Ann Arbor: University of Michigan Press, pp. 306–309.

Jackson, S (2013). "Caravans continued: in memory of Dwight Conquergood". In Johnson, JP (ed.) *Cultural struggles: performance, ethnography, praxis*, by Conquergood, D. Ann Arbor: University Michigan Press, pp. 310–313.

Johnson, EP (ed.). (2013). "Introduction: opening and interpreting lives". In *Cultural struggles: performance, ethnography, praxis*, by Conquergood, D. Ann Arbor: University of Michigan Press, pp. 1–14.

Lecusay, R (2015). "The contributions of Dwight Conquergood's performance theory to the practice of socio-cultural historical psychology". Research draft. www.researchgate.net/publication/280732703_ The_Contributions_of_Dwight_Conquergood's_Performance_Theory_to_the_Practice_of_Socio-Cultural_Historical_Psychology (accessed January 19, 2020). <replaced website; previous link not active; this is a draft version>.

Madison, DS (2013). "'Is Dwight White?!'or black transgressions and the preeminent performance of whiteness". In Johnson, EP (ed.) *Cultural struggles: performance, ethnography, praxis*, by Conquergood, D. Ann Arbor: University of Michigan Press, pp. 314–319.

Roach, R (2013). "Eloquence and vocation: Dwight's calling". In Johnson, EP (ed.) *Cultural struggles: performance, ethnography, praxis*, by Conquergood, D. Ann Arbor: University of Michigan Press, pp. 328–331.

Rosaldo, R (1989). *Culture & truth: the remaking of social analysis*. Boston: Beacon.

Turner, V (1977). *The ritual process: structure and anti-structure*. Ithaca, NY: Cornell University Press.

Venkatesh, SA (1997). "The social organization of street gang activity in an urban ghetto". *American Journal of Sociology*, vol. 103, no. 1, pp. 82–111. https://doi.org/10.1086/231172.

Willis, PE (1977). *Learning to labor: how working-class kids get working class jobs*. Farnborough, UK: Saxon House.

48

The legacy of Joan Moore

A revolution in gang research

Jorge David Mancillas and Robert Donald Weide

The scholarly career of Dr. Joan Moore, Distinguished Professor Emerita at the University of Wisconsin, Milwaukee, represents an unmistakable revolution in the field of gang research, and both her personal and scholarly legacy evince a gentle empathy and humility that characterized her career. The implications of the revolutionary methodological approach to her research on barrio gangs in Los Angeles particularly also engendered corresponding theoretical innovations that framed the perspective and praxis of her fieldwork. Her work humanized gang members in a way all previous scholarly research had failed to do, conceptualizing gang members as full partners and active accomplices in the process of data collection and critical analysis rather than as passive subjects. Instead of conceiving of gang members as inherently criminogenic and essentially incorrigible, Joan saw us as human beings who are just as capable of engaging in research and analysis as scholars like herself from more privileged backgrounds who come into our communities from the outside to study us. It might be fair to say that Joan was the first truly modern critical gang scholar, and her legacy extends into the future across generations of critical gang scholars who have followed in her footsteps.

Joan's legacy has been carried and further progressed faithfully by a line of critical gang scholars who have likewise published seminal works in the critical gang studies tradition established by Joan, including James Diego Vigil,[1] John Hagedorn,[2] Avelardo Valdez,[3] David C. Brotherton,[4] Susan Phillips,[5] Alex Alonso,[6] Robert Durán,[7] Randol Contreras,[8] Roberto R. Aspholm[9] and hopefully, someday, ourselves and many others as well. The progeny of Joan's legacy live on through these critical gang scholars who were directly influenced and mentored by Joan, and through their students like us, whose research and publications embody the humanistic critical perspective on gangs that Joan's trailblazing career established. We are now in our third and fourth generations removed from Joan, but her example continues to influence the way we conduct qualitative research, the way we conceptualize the populations we work with and the way we communicate that to our own students, the public and our colleagues. The example set by Joan and passed down to our students by each generation of critical gang scholars will no doubt be a beacon for generations to come. She is unmistakably our *Madrena*.

In this chapter, we present the inspiring story of an amazing woman whose steadfast perseverance, impenetrable dignity and indomitable resilience enabled her to surmount innumerable barriers and, in the process, carve out a place for herself and for us all in the ivory tower of the academy. We were fortunate enough to have the opportunity to interview Joan in the spring of 2019 and include a number of direct quotes from that interview in this chapter. We also interviewed two of her most important students who were directly mentored by her and who have been unfailing mentors to us as well, Dr. James Diego Vigil and Dr. John Hagedorn. We present her story as told to us by her and by them, offering our own consideration of the positionality and importance of her career for the development of critical gang studies within the wider fields of criminology and sociology.

An unlikely revolutionary

It was no foregone conclusion that Joan would play such a pivotal role in critical gang studies. Born in Manhattan in 1929, her father had been an émigré from Wisconsin and was trained and employed by the New York City Department of Education as an architect. Unfortunately, the Great Depression started shortly after she was born, and her father lost his employment as a result. In order to make ends meet, the young family moved across the Hudson River with Joan's maternal grandparents, who had a small butcher shop and bodega in Jersey City. As the nation was pulled out of the Great Depression by World War II, her father again found employment as an architect with the New Deal agency, the Works Progress Administration. As a result, when Joan was about to start high school, her parents managed to move back to Manhattan in the Morningside Heights neighborhood on the Upper West Side, then a predominantly white working-class community. After two years at George Washington High School, Joan enrolled in a local experimental high school run by Columbia University where high school students finished their last two years taking courses at Columbia University. As a result of this unique opportunity and Joan's exemplary performance, she was offered a scholarship to attend the University of Chicago for her bachelor's degree in 1945. At Chicago, she found herself surrounded by GIs much older than herself returning home from the war, using their GI scholarships to pursue higher education. As she recounted, "I was married in three years."

She quickly found a home in the Department of Sociology at the University of Chicago. Her first research assistantship was with Lloyd Warner, a renowned scholar of social class, who later became the chair for her dissertation committee. She took classes with Everett Hughes, who became her master's thesis advisor, and even took a methods course with Ernest Burgess, who was brought back as emerita at the time to teach. Her most pertinent memory of the course was another student's service dog yawning repeatedly throughout each lecture. The methodological training she received emphasized a comprehensive empiricism that provided a blueprint for urban research: select a community, conduct an in-depth participant observation ethnography, interview as many residents as possible, sit in on local agencies in the community, collect every bit of census and statistical data that can be found and essentially treat the community as a laboratory, employing the full panoply of methods to examine every aspect of the community being studied. Joan credits her training in this regard to Hughes and anthropologist Robert Redfield, as well as to Warner, who was himself an accomplished anthropologist when he found an interest in social class mid-career.

Joan earned her master's degree in 1953 and her doctorate in 1959. She recalls having "no particular interest in anything" after having her first child while she was in her master's program and settled on the topic for her dissertation, voluntary associations of upper-class women in Chicago, primarily at her advisors' suggestion. Joan's husband was originally from California and yearned to return, and she hadn't found a passion for studying anything in Chicago, so in 1961, she secured a one-year lecturer position in sociology at the University of California, Los Angeles. However, as a result of her second pregnancy, she had to write the chair of the department and request that her appointment be postponed to 1962, which is when they made the move to sunny Southern California. She later ran into him at an American Sociological Association (ASA hereafter) annual meeting and, perhaps as a result of inebriation, he remarked to her that as a result of his experience with her asking to defer her appointment for a year, he would "never hire a woman again." Needless to say, her appointment was not renewed the following year, but she was fortunate to be offered a joint appointment at University of California, Riverside, in 1963 that matured into a tenure-track appointment in the Department of Sociology.

It was while at UC Riverside that Joan embarked on the first step of what would evolve into her primary research agenda that distinguished her career as a critical gang scholar. In 1964, Joan was hired as Associate Director of the Mexican American Study Project (MASP hereafter), which was funded by the Ford Foundation and included Director Leo Grebler (UCLA) and Ralph Guzman, then a doctoral candidate in political science at UCLA. They needed someone who was actually a real Mexican American on the project, and with a dearth of Chicano academics holding a PhD at the time, even though Guzman was still in graduate school, he was the most qualified candidate to assume the position. All of the others who worked on the project were Anglos, most of whom were men. It was with MASP that Joan first became aware of the marginalization suffered by the Chicano population of the American Southwest, as she implemented a massive multi-year research project that included community interviews in Los Angeles and San Antonio, Texas. MASP culminated in two book length publications, among others, *The Mexican-American People: The Nation's Second Largest Minority* and *Mexican Americans*, of which she was coauthor and sole author, respectively.[10]

In the spring of 1968, the Chicano movement exploded in Los Angeles with the East LA Walkouts and subsequent criminal prosecutions of the student leaders of the walkouts, collectively known as the East LA Thirteen (one of whom was James Diego Vigil's brother Richard Vigil). The story of the walkouts and their aftermath is told by Ian Haney-Lopez in his book *Racism on Trial: The Fight for Chicano Justice* (2003). The students were tried on serious felony conspiracy charges and chose as their lawyer an eccentric Chicano activist attorney, Oscar Acosta. Acosta was known for his colorful suits and a penchant for psychedelic experiences, as recounted in his fellow adventurer Hunter Thompson's counter-culture classic, *Fear and Loathing in Las Vegas*. However, he had never tried a felony case in open court. His was a most unorthodox defense strategy in that rather than disputing the facts of the case, Acosta endeavored to put the entire racist system on trial, arguing that the court system, and American society for that matter, were irredeemably racist and as such had no legitimacy to prosecute the defendants for the crimes they were accused of. It was a daring and dangerous strategy for both Acosta and the defendants that required the testimony of academic experts as to the marginalization and oppression experienced by the Chicano community. Having recently secured a precarious academic appointment at California State University, Los Angeles and having started the Mexican American Study Program there, which later evolved into the Department of Chicano Studies in 1971 (now Chicano and Latino Studies), Guzman deferred out of fear that he might endanger his position and referred Acosta to Joan in lieu of himself testifying. Certainly, the testimony of a middle-class white woman would go over better in court than that of a Chicano at the time as well.

Her testimony in the case, which ultimately ended in acquittals for the defendants, made Joan realize the imperative of sociology as a public discipline. For the first time in her career, she realized that her work as a sociologist could have a direct impact on people's lives other than by publishing academic articles, and she took that as her torch to carry. This epiphany motivated her to get involved in the Chicano community as both an academic, and although she is too modest to acknowledge it, an activist for the rights of the Chicano community in Los Angeles. In our interview with Vigil, he fondly recalled the moxie of her plucky comments at City Council meetings and other public venues, where he described her as being rather outspoken, in her own graceful manner. "She was no wall flower", he recalled with a laugh. In addition to her academic contributions to our field, Joan also deserves recognition as a steadfast accomplice in the Chicano movement, ever the bugaboo to those who would have rather preferred to ignore or dismiss Chicanismo as the machinations of incorrigible Mexican miscreants. It was this relationship that compelled Joan to get involved in the Chicano community and that ultimately led her to her work on barrio gangs in Los Angeles.

In 1966, President Lyndon Johnson's administration implemented the Model Cities Program as part of his Great Society and War on Poverty initiatives that were the hallmarks of his domestic policy during his tenure in office. The Model Cities Program funded over 100 different programs in American cities throughout the country. One of the programs that was funded in Los Angeles was called Community Concern, and even more so than the Homeboy Industries program we are familiar with in Los Angeles today, Community Concern was run entirely by gang members at every level of the organization.[11] Joan also ingratiated herself with another associated *pinto*-run organization that had been started in San Quentin State Prison called LUCHA, League of United Citizens to Help Addicts, which was led by *Señor* Eduardo "Moe" Aguirre, a respected *pinto* leader both in the California prison system and on the streets. While she was rebuffed as an outsider by many of the other "respectable" organizations she had tried to establish contact with in the Chicano community, the *pintos* found in her a sincere and willing accomplice to aid in their resistance to the criminalization they had experienced.

The marginality and exclusion Community Concern and LUCHA experienced from the "respectable" community in East Los Angeles also must have played a role in their inclination to embrace her as an accomplice. Joan recalled a particular City Council meeting in Los Angeles that she had attended to support Community Concern, and their opponents were livid, screaming and yelling their objections to the program being funded, while their supporters voiced their support in the most genteel manner. Community Concern and LUCHA shared a familiar station with Joan, as outsiders excluded from "respectable" political engagement. Joan was all too happy to be welcomed into these organizations and to collaborate with them both in their activism and as full-fledged research partners, and the *pintos* were all too happy to have a willing and capable vehicle for the humanist redemption narrative they were trying to build. As Joan recounted, *pintos* both in the prisons and the streets "really wanted the story of possible rehabilitation told, and I was in effect their vehicle".

Shattering paradigms

With the support of the *pintos* she was working with in Community Concern and LUCHA, Joan submitted a research proposal to the National Institute of Drug Abuse (NIDA) proposing to use gang members as field researchers to do interviews with gang members in gang neighborhoods, a rather unconventional approach compared to methodologies employed in gang research at the time. No one had ever endeavored to use "subjects" as researchers. No one had ever considered the possibility that the populations who are the subjects of research could be equal partners in the research process as field researchers and analysts themselves. By even conceptualizing such a research design, Joan and her accomplices in Community Concern and LUCHA shattered the colonial gaze that perceives researchers as a separate class distinct from subjects. To their credit, NIDA was ahead of its time, even by today's standards, in awarding Joan the grant to execute the research project she and her accomplices had proposed, which culminated in the book that defined her career, *Homeboys: Gangs, Drugs, and Prison in the Barrios of Los Angeles*, published in 1978 by Temple University Press. Even today, most major research grant funders might be reticent to provide funds to a research team consisting of over a dozen convicted felons.

The research project was as much conceived by the homeboys Joan worked with as by her. She merely functioned as the instrument to realize their desire to publish research that served to humanize themselves and their communities rather than criminalizing them. Joan had the academic title, training and writing capability that they lacked, and they had the access she needed. It was a collaborative project by design from its conception, and she gave her accomplices all the credit they deserved, including listing four of them as coauthors: Robert Garcia (White Fence), Carlos Garcia (Hoyo Maravilla), Luis Cerda (San Fer) and Frank Valencia (Happy Valley), a rather unorthodox and unheard-of practice at the time. Also significant, and another clear break from mainstream methodological practices in gang research, Joan's research team was made up of some of the most respected *pintos* from each of their respective neighborhoods that were the field sites for the field work, White Fence, El Hoyo Maravilla and San Fer(nando). These people weren't mere corner boys on the block, or junior gang members with only an incipient knowledge and perspective of their own communities. These were *pintos* who were widely recognized as leaders in their criminalized communities, both in the prisons and on the streets. The research team later incorporated as The Chicano Pinto Research Project while Joan was at USC.

Pintos were instrumental in establishing the fieldwork protocol, composing the questionnaires used for formal interviews and selecting field sites, and the *pintos* conducted all of the interviews themselves. As Joan argued in an essay written with *Homeboys* coauthor Robert Garcia, having members of the community actually do the interviews themselves neutralized the tendency of respondents to perform to the perceived expectations of researchers who are outsiders.[12] However, most importantly, the *pintos* participated as full research partners in the analysis of the data that they themselves had gathered. This collaborative research reflexivity is perhaps Joan's most significant contribution to the critical gang research tradition in our view. The revolutionary collaborative reflexive methodological approach she employed exposed the flaws of the colonial gaze in qualitative fieldwork that had always granted the final word to researchers who were outsiders in the contexts and communities they studied. Furthermore, it demonstrated that gang members are just as capable as scholars, if not more so, of collecting meaningful data and of analyzing that data because of their positionality and the indigenous perspective they alone possess of their respective criminalized communities. The data they produced was an impressive catalogue of the experiences of criminalized barrio youth expressed in their own words and writing analyzed by *pintos* who had themselves endured the same experiences. The project was far ahead of its time in the field. For example, although he neglected to cite *Homeboys*, Joan's discussion of the multiple axes of state marginalization that worked in conjunction to produce the criminalization of barrio youth, from the police and courts, to schools and counselors, to health and welfare agencies, preempted Victor Rios's *youth control complex* framework by over three decades.[13]

The collaborative reflexive research model Joan employed had equally significant theoretical implications, which were reflected in her gentle humanist analysis. Joan conceptualized gang members not as incorrigibly criminogenic by nature but as products of the historically situated disadvantaged circumstances they faced, which were beyond their control. Using gang members as field researchers and analysts wasn't just a methodological stratagem to gain access for data collection and perspective for analysis. It was a substantive demonstration of the analysis she presented, that gang members were redeemable members of society. They were products of their environments, environments that could be improved by benevolent public policy. While her reformist approach to ameliorating the circumstances faced by gang members was short of revolutionary, her groundbreaking methodological approach and analysis represented a revolution in gang research that laid the foundation for the humanistic perspective that exemplifies the critical gang studies tradition today.

In reaction to the Civil Rights Movement in the 1960s, a debate emerged in the field of sociology around the issue of "going native" and "politicizing" research, that is, of losing the façade of objectivity that enables the field of sociology to maintain a plausible claim to scientifiosity. Joan came down clearly on the side of disregarding these apprehensions. In contrast, she conceived of gang members as active partners rather than passive subjects, accomplices rather than allies. While Joan herself conceptualizes her perspective as merely an extension of the pre-war Chicago empirical tradition she was trained in, her work represents a significant break from the kind of colonial gaze that characterized urban research, particularly research on gangs, up until that time. She wasn't casting a colonial gaze conceptualizing herself as researcher, the objects of her research as subjects and her field site as a laboratory. Instead she transformed subjects into researchers, thereby relocating the agency in research from the academy to the community.

Her refusal to abide by hegemonic methodological and conceptual expectations in the field at the time, especially as a woman daring to deviate from the work done by men in the field who were her seniors, should rightly be recognized as revolutionary in the field of gang research and the wider fields of sociology and criminology, for that matter. The methodologies she employed, her humanistic conceptualization of gang members and her unrepentant gumption shattered dominant methodological and theoretical paradigms, as well as social expectations about the place of women in the academy at the time. Unfortunately, despite her many academic accomplishments and the very public sociology she practiced, her willingness to violate academic and social expectations with the work she did caused her to suffer repercussions in the course of her career more significant than being insulted by some chauvinist inebriate at a cocktail party.

No good deed goes unpunished

In 1972, while what became the Chicano Pinto Research Project was being conceived, Joan was offered a three-year appointment at the University of Southern California in the new Urban Studies Program. She gave up her tenured position at UC Riverside in order to make the move back to Los Angeles and accept the position at USC. The interdisciplinary program combined faculty from different fields, however not all in the same location. Existing affiliated faculty remained in their department offices on campus, while new faculty who had been hired for the program were housed in offices outside the main USC campus, just east of the 110 Freeway. As such, Joan had virtually no contact with anyone in the Department of Sociology to which she was nominally affiliated and only interacted with colleagues who were demographers housed in the same off site offices. Joan recalled that she had no compunctions about leaving her tenured position at UC Riverside to come to USC because it had not occurred to her that she could possibly be denied tenure at USC after her three-year contract expired. She had successfully seen the MASP to completion, received major grants from NIDA and the National Science Foundation in her second year at USC to support the Pinto Project, published numerous articles in peer-reviewed journals and served on ASA committees, all of which should have easily been adequate for tenure. However, a vindictive campaign perpetrated by a senior member of the Department of Sociology, Malcolm Klein, led to her appointment being surreptitiously terminated.

Hagedorn recalled,

> He hated her guts. And he is the reason she doesn't get tenure, he sabotaged her tenure. . . .
> And the reason was this collaborative research model that she had and that she worked on
> the project and she was very deeply involved with the *Pintos*. . . . Klein saw it as a threat
> to his research and indeed it was. I mean, theoretically it was absolutely critical of Latino
> ills and the stuff Klein was doing and certainly diametrically opposed to his notion of the
> way he conceptualized gang members and that they could be active contributors to the
> research project and the development of knowledge, that they were a force that needed to
> be empowered, not imprisoned. So, he was extremely upset with her, and when her tenure
> came up, when she went there (USC), she had tenure at Riverside, she went to USC with-
> out tenure but with an offer that they would tenure her. And so, she gave up her tenure at
> Riverside, she went to USC and then in 1975 they withdrew their offer of tenure under
> pressure from Klein.

While Joan's approach to gang research humanized gang members and collaborated with
them as research partners, Klein had made his career by demonizing and criminalizing gang
members and gang workers.[14] Joan never spoke to Klein, either before or after her termination. The idea that gang members could actually design and implement a research project;
conduct the fieldwork, interviews and data collection for the research; and have agency
in the analysis of the data they themselves had collected must have seemed horrifyingly
corrupt from Klein's perspective that gang members were inherently criminal and could
not be trusted. From Klein's perspective, the idea that gang members could guide research
themselves and have a say in the analysis must have seemed a ghastly abomination enabling
gang members to feign humanity when they were, in his view, incorrigible criminals. He
was even more perturbed by Joan's habit of being accompanied by a crew of *pintos* when in
public, colloquially known as "Joan's *Pistoleros*". Klein must have been rather intimidated by
the presence of actual gang members on the campus of USC, an elite private school located
in the middle of one of the largest ghettos in the United States. Unbeknownst to her at the
time, two of the *pintos* she had been working with on the Chicano Pinto Research Project
at USC made a desperate effort to meet with Klein personally to appeal for Joan to remain
at USC. The idea that two *pintos*, one with only one eye, could possibly convince Klein of
anything is rather comical in retrospect. We imagine the experience must have been terrifying to him.

While it was certainly unanticipated by Joan at the time of her termination, it ought to be
no surprise to anyone who is familiar with Klein's career that he saw Joan as a threat, and rightly
so. As a public sociologist who was both outspoken and independent, Joan was a threat to his
chauvinist sensibilities that demanded subordination of junior (especially female) faculty. As a
researcher sympathizing and collaborating with convicted felons, she was, from Klein's perspective, an active accomplice in their criminality. As a sympathetic expert on gangs with a level of
access a hostile outsider like Klein could never hope to attain, her expertise presented a challenge to his reactionary perspective on gangs. Finally, he must have been concerned that her
progeny could eventually grow to be a threat to his own, an apprehension that the volume this
chapter is published in represents.

While Joan, in her unwavering humility, prefers to avoid the subject, the shameful and
abominable experience Joan suffered at USC is important to consider not only because contemporary gang researchers should know what kind of a person Klein was but moreover
because her experience and her resilience in the wake of such a terrifying attempt at career

assassination is instructive to those of us in the critical gang studies field who follow in her footsteps and, as such, represent a threat to the status quo. Rather than perceive the way Joan was treated as an anomaly, her experiences should instead interpret it as a symbol of the suppression critical scholars should expect to face over the course of their careers. Critical gang scholars should not be surprised as Joan was when they become the targets of vindictive reprisals by those who are threatened by critical ideas and praxis. They should expect it. Career assassination attempts should be worn with a badge of honor, as proof that the scholarship produced by critical gang scholars is rightly recognized as a threat to the status quo. Moreover, for every critical scholar who ever has or ever will suffer threats to their scholarly careers, Joan is a role model in how to endure such turmoil and humiliation with the kind of steadfast perseverance, impenetrable dignity and indomitable resilience that she always demonstrated.

Steadfast perseverance

While her termination at USC was a daunting experience for Joan professionally, it also represented a substantive threat to the financial viability of her humble family, for which she was the primary breadwinner. Joan immediately went on the job market and was fortunate to be offered a tenure track position at the University of Wisconsin-Milwaukee in the Department of Sociology, where she taught in another new urban studies doctoral program. Despite the family's move to distant Milwaukee, Joan continued her work in Los Angeles for another ten years, renting a house (with a pool if possible) each summer to provide hands-on guidance for the continuing Pinto Project research that was ongoing over those years.

Her flagship work *Homeboys* was followed by numerous articles and eventually a second book, *Going Down to the Barrio: Homeboys and Homegirls in Change* (Moore 1991). The intention of this second volume was to follow up with two of the gangs that had been examined in *Homeboys*, White Fence and Hoyo Maravilla, in order to provide some longitudinal perspective on the trajectory of the gangs and important issues pertaining to them, like drug use and violence. The second book and a number of companion articles addressed what had not been considered in *Homeboys*, the experiences of young women who were involved in gangs and drugs.[15] Joan's second book examined a number of issues that concerned young women and gangs, including the proportion of women to men in gangs, the role of women in gangs, the relationships between men and women in gangs, the extent of involvement of women in criminal activity, the relationships between women in gangs and their often patriarchal families and more generally the role of patriarchy in determining women's position in the gang subculture. The discussions concerning the effects of machismo and patriarchy on young women in gangs were particularly prescient.

Joan's treatment of young women in gangs in *Going Down to the Barrio* also reflected another significant theoretical contribution that has been largely overlooked, her conceptualization of women in gangs as "doubly deviant".[16] We see this conceptualization of the duality of deviance that female gang members were subjected to, as gang members suffering from racialized criminalization and as women suffering from patriarchal domination, in the same theoretical vein as Vigil's concept of multiple marginality and Kimberlé Crenshaw's legal concept of intersectionality.[17] As Vigil and Crenshaw had previously, Joan analyzed women in gangs she looked along each of the multiple facets of marginality that intersected in their lives: patriarchy, poverty, criminalization, racism, gang violence, cultural praxis and drug addiction. Joan deserves to be recognized as an early voice who recognized the theoretical framework that is now popularly known as intersectionality.

A living legacy

As the first truly critical gang scholar of the modern era, Joan's legacy lives on through her direct students, those she influenced indirectly, and their students – ourselves included. Her work on gangs has been widely cited in both academic and popular literature on gangs that can be included in the critical gang studies tradition.[18] Joan was characteristically modest in her evaluation of her role in the careers of students she mentored directly, "My influence on students was virtually nil, right? Zero!" Despite her modesty, there are a handful of significant scholars in the field of critical gang research who were directly mentored by her to one extent or another. Perhaps the two who were most directly mentored by her were James Diego Vigil and John Hagedorn. Joan coauthored multiple publications with both of them, as well as *Homeboys* coauthor Robert Garcia, in an effort to support their scholarship and advance their academic careers.[19]

Vigil found his way to Joan while she was in Los Angeles one summer doing follow-up research for the Pinto Project after she had been fired from USC. He sought her guidance for his interest in gangs, which developed into an impressive publication record of three books and numerous articles on gangs in Los Angeles. Vigil's work followed in Joan's footsteps, incorporating her research strategy in the sense that, although he wasn't a *pinto*, he grew up in the barrios of what is now popularly known as South Central Los Angeles, just south of the 10 Freeway. As Joan had demonstrated that *pintos* were capable of doing scholarly research, Vigil represented the first generation of Chicano scholars who grew up around gangs to do research on the gangs he was already familiar with as a barrio resident. While he was trained as an anthropologist, and she a sociologist, Joan served an informal but important mentor for Vigil throughout his career. Each of his three books on gangs, and his book on Chicano history, reflect the influence Joan had on Vigil.[20] Each were composed of the kind of thick descriptions that characterize Joan's work and considered the historical socio-economic circumstances faced by barrio gang members. However, in his first two books, *Barrio Gangs* and *A Rainbow of Gangs*, Vigil uses micro analyses of life histories rather than micro analyses of individual gangs.[21] In his third book, *The Projects*, Vigil employed the same kind of historical analysis of the gang and its community as Joan had in her work.[22] Joan's work was not merely a citation but a model for the work that Vigil did throughout his career, but perhaps more importantly for a trailblazer like him, Joan's support and encouragement gave him the confidence to carve a place for himself and successive generations in the ivory towers of the academy.

John Hagedorn was perhaps the only one of Joan's direct mentees who was actually her student in a formal sense. Joan invited Hagedorn to take a few courses in the Department of Sociology and served as chair for his thesis in order for him to finish his degree after it was rejected by his original Department of Criminal Justice. The book that he eventually published as *People and Folks* in 1988 best exemplifies the influence of Joan's research model in numerous regards. Hagedorn provided a detailed historical analysis of the socio-economic conditions that contextualized the communities his respondents existed in. Hagedorn stresses the effects of socio-economic disenfranchisement and the market for narcotics that Joan's work had emphasized. He also preempted her focus on women in gangs in *Going Down to the Barrio*. Although Joan adamantly denies any credit for the work, Hagedorn credits her as his most significant academic influence. He even reminisced that the interview questionnaires he used were copied from the ones her team used for *Homeboys*. While Hagedorn's second book, *A World of Gangs*, published in 2008, wasn't a field study, Joan's emphasis on historical analysis of socio-economic conditions and her humanization of gang members were clearly strong influences on Hagedorn's analysis of the spread of gang culture around the world. In his third book, *The Insane Chicago Way*, published in 2015, Hagedorn returned to the type of detailed case study model Joan bequeathed to him from her old Chicago School training. With a focus on a particular constellation of gangs and the use of a key collaborative informant who had been deeply involved in every aspect of the book, *Insane* is reminiscent of Sutherland's (1937) classic *The Thief*.

While never a direct student of hers, Joan had a significant influence on USC gang researcher Avelardo (Lalo) Valdez, himself a Milwaukee native. Joan recalled that he had reached out to her after she had been working in Milwaukee for some time, and she had supported, mentored and encouraged him the same way she had for Vigil and Hagedorn. Her influence is perhaps most apparent in his 2007 book, *Mexican American Girls and Gang Violence*, for which Joan wrote the foreword. The book mirrors *Homeboys* in its focus on the intersections of gang identity, poverty and drug use in the barrios of San Antonio, Texas. Valdez faithfully recreated Joan's research model by assembling a team of community members who had the access to make contact and build rapport with the young women in his study, as Joan's fieldworkers had two decades before. The book also faithfully reexamines many of the issues concerning patriarchy that Joan had raised in *Going Down to the Barrio*, including the role of women in gangs, the relationships between men and women in gangs, the extent of involvement of women in criminal activity and the relationships between women in gangs and their often patriarchal families, as well as the sexual and physical victimization of women involved in gangs.

Joan also had an obvious influence on the work of numerous scholars for whom she did not have any substantive interaction with as mentees or students. The influence of Joan's work concerning female gang members on audiences outside her own field and outside the United States is apparent in two of Valdez's contemporary publications on female gang members, Norma Mendoza-Denton's *Homegirls* and Michel Dorais and Patrice Corriveau's *Gangs and Girls*.[23] Joan's collaborative research strategy and humanistic approach are also clearly apparent and credited in the work of David Charles Brotherton and Luis Barrios as well.[24] In his recent critical history of gang research, Brotherton situates Joan as a central figure in the emergence of critical gangs studies.[25]

However, perhaps the most significant progeny of Joan's work is Robert Durán, whose dissertation committee Joan served on and who is the first barrio gang member to research and write now two books on barrio gangs using his own experiences as a gang member to both inform his fieldwork and his analysis.[26] Duran's work is the logical conclusion of the gang member as researcher model established by the legacy of Joan's foundational work. Durán also reflects Joan's example in his humanization of gang members and in his treatment of the colonial history that underpins barrio gangs, especially in his second book, *The Gang Paradox*. Durán also explicitly models his research design for both books after Joan's reflexive collaborative research model, involving community and gang members directly in the data collection process. In fact, Durán dedicates a whole chapter to explicating his employment of the collaborative method in his second book, *The Gang Paradox*.

While he denies direct involvement in the crimes he writes about, Randol Contreras's work on robbery crews in the South Bronx and forthcoming work on one of the communities Joan examined, Maravilla in unincorporated East Los Angeles, represents yet another example of research on gangs done by someone who was intimately involved in them.[27] Like these notable emergent scholars, the work of a burgeoning cohort of gang-involved and formerly incarcerated junior scholars attests to the lasting influence Joan's career has had on the field of critical gang studies and the flourishing cohort of scholars who were directly involved with gangs and have gone on to pursue academic careers.

Joan's refusal to abide by hegemonic methodological and conceptual expectations in the field at the time, especially as a woman, should rightly be recognized as revolutionary in the field of gang research and the wider fields of sociology and criminology. The methodologies she employed, her humanistic conceptualization of gang members and her unrepentant gumption shattered dominant methodological and theoretical paradigms, as well as social expectations about the place of women in the academy at the time. After having pursued a doctoral dissertation on what was thought to be a more "appropriate" topic of inquiry for a woman by her advisors, Joan broke down barriers by entering what was at the time an exclusively male-dominated gang research field. As one of the first generation of women to penetrate the field of gang research, and a woman who did not think twice to challenge senior male scholars and assume objectionable perspectives, Joan endured innumerable indignations throughout her early career with steadfast persistence, impenetrable dignity and an indomitable resilience. Joan's work, her career and the way she conducted herself through it all will forever be an example for those whose careers were made possible by the woman whose footsteps we follow in.

Notes

1 Vigil 1988, 2002, 2007
2 Hagedorn 1988, 2008, 2015
3 Valdez 2007
4 Brotherton and Barrios 2004; Brotherton 2015
5 Phillips 1999, 2019
6 Alonso 1999, 2004, 2010
7 Durán 2013, 2018
8 Contreras 2012
9 Aspholm 2019
10 Grebler, Moore and Guzman 1970; Moore 1976
11 The word *pinto* implies both gang membership and prior incarceration, with some likelihood of drug addiction.
12 Moore and Garcia 1979
13 Moore 1978, pp. 103–106; Rios 2011
14 Klein 1971
15 Moore 1994; Moore and Hagedorn 1996, 2001
16 Hagedorn 2010
17 Vigil 1988; Crenshaw 1989
18 Hagedorn 1988, 2008, 2015; Padilla 1992; Brotherton and Barrios 2004; Hayden 2004; Umemoto 2006; Lauger 2012; Flores 2014; Brotherton 2015; Tapia 2017; Lopez-Aguado 2018
19 Moore and Garcia 1979; Moore, Vigil and Garcia 1983; Moore and Vigil 1993; Moore and Hagedorn 1996
20 Vigil 1980, 1988, 2002, 2007
21 Vigil 1988, 2002
22 Vigil 2007
23 Mendoza-Denton 2008; Dorais and Coriveau 2009
24 Brotherton and Barrios 2004; Brotherton 2015
25 Brotherton and Barrios 2004; Brotherton 2015
26 Durán 2013, 2018
27 Contreras 2012

References

Alonso, Alejandro A. 1999. "Territoriality Among African American Gangs in Los Angeles." Master's Thesis, University of Southern California.
Alonso, Alex. 2004. "Racialized Identities and the Formation of Black Gangs in Los Angeles." *Urban Geography*. 25(7): 658–674.
Alonso, Alex. 2010. "Out of the Void: Street Gangs in Black Los Angeles." In Darnell Hunt and Ana-Christina Ramon (Eds.) *Black Los Angeles: American Dreams and Racial Realities*. New York, NY: NYU Press.

Aspholm, Roberto. 2019. *Views from the Street: The Transformation of Gangs and Violence on Chicago's South Side*. New York, NY: Columbia University Press.

Brotherton, David Charles and Luis Barrios. 2004. *The Almighty Latin King and Queen Nation: Street Politics and the Transformation of a New York City Street Gang*. New York, NY: Columbia University Press.

Brotherton, David Charles. 2015. *Youth Street Gangs: A Critical Appraisal*. New York, NY: Routledge.

Contreras, Randol. 2012. *The Stickup Kids: Race, Drugs, Violence and the American Dream*. Berkeley, CA: UC Press.

Crenshaw, Kimberlé. 1989. "Demarginalizing the Intersection of Race and Sex: A Black Feminist Critique of Antidiscrimination Doctrine, Feminist Theory and Antiracist Politics." *University of Chicago Legal Forum*. 1989(1) Article 8.

Dorais, Michel, and Patrice Coriveau. 2009. *Girls and Gangs*. Quebec, CAN: McGill-Queen's University Press.

Durán, Robert J. 2013. *Gang Life in Two Cities: An Insider's Journey*. New York, NY: Columbia University Press.

Flores, Edward, Orozco. 2013. *God's Gangs: Barrio Ministry, Masculinity, and Gang Recovery*. New York: NYU Press.

Durán, Robert J. 2018. *The Gang Paradox: Inequalities and Miracles on the US-Mexico Border*. New York, NY: Columbia University Press.

Grebler, Leo, Joan W. Moore, and Ralph C Guzman. 1970. *The Mexican-American People: The Nation's Second Largest Minority*. New York, NY: The Free Press.

Hagedorn, John M. 1988. *People and Folks: Gangs, Crime and the Underclass in a Rustbelt City*. Chicago, IL: Lake View Press.

Hagedorn, John M. 2008. *A World of Gangs: Armed Young Men and Gangsta Culture*. Minneapolis, MN: University of Minnesota Press.

Hagedorn, John M. 2015. *The Insane Chicago Way: The Daring Plan by Chicago Gangs to Create a Spanish Mafia*. Chicago, IL: University of Chicago Press.

Hagedorn, John. 2010. "Moore, Joan W.: Homeboys and Homegirls in the Barrio." In Francis Cullen and Pamela Wilcox (Eds.) *Encyclopedia of Criminological Theory*. Thousand Oaks, CA: Sage, pp. 650–653.

Haney-Lopez, Ian. 2003. *Racism on Trial: The Chicano Fight for Justice*. Cambridge, MA: Belknap-Harvard University Press.

Hayden, Tom. *Street Wars: Gangs and the Future of Violence*. New York: New Press.

Klein, Malcolm. 1971. *Street Gangs and Street Workers*. Englewood Cliffs, NJ: Prentice Hall.

Lauger, Timothy, R. 2012. *Real Gangstas: Legitimacy, Reputation, and Violence in the Intergang Environment*. New Brunswick, N.J.: Rutgers University Press.

Lopez-Aguado, Patrick. 2018. *Stick Together and Come Back Home: Racial Sorting and the Spillover of Carceral Identity*. Berkeley, CA: UC Press.

Mendoza-Denton, Norma. 2008. *Homegirls: Language and Cultural Practice among Latina Youth Gangs*. Malden, MA: Blackwell Publishing.

Moore, Joan W. 1991. *Going Down to the Barrio: Homeboys and Homegirls in Change*. Philadelphia, PA: Temple University Press.

Moore, Joan W. 1994. "The Chola Life Course: Chicana Heroin Users and the Barrio Gang. *International Journal of Addictions*. 29: 1115–1126.

Moore, Joan W., and Robert Garcia. 1979. *Research in Minority Communities: Collaborative and Street Ethnography Models Compared*. Milwaukee, WI: University of Wisconsin-Milwaukee Urban Research Center.

Moore, Joan W., Robert Garcia, Carlos Garcia, Luis Cerda, and Frank Valencia. 1978. *Homeboys: Gangs, Drugs, and Prisons in the Barrios of Los Angeles*. Philadelphia, PA: Temple University Press.

Moore, Joan W., and John Hagedorn. 1996. "What Happens to Girls in Gangs?" In C. Ron Huff (Ed.) *Gangs in America* (2nd Edition). Thousand Oaks, CA: Sage.

Moore, Joan W., and John Hagedorn. 2001. *Female Gangs a Focus on Research*. Office of juvenile Justice and Delinquency Prevention. Washington, DC: US Department of Justice, Office of Justice Programs.

Moore, Joan W., and Harry Pachon. 1976. *Mexican Americans* (2nd Edition). Ethnic Groups in American Life Series. Englewood Cliffs, NJ: Prentice Hall.

Moore, Joan W., and James Diego Vigil. 1993. "Barrios in Transition." In Joan Moore and Raquel Pinder-hughes (Eds.) *In the Barrios: Latinos and the Underclass Debate*. New York, NY: Russel Sage Publications.

Moore, Joan W., James Diego Vigil, and Robert Garcia. 1983. "Residence and Territoriality in Chicano Gangs." *Social Problems*. 31(2): 182–194.

Padilla, F. M. 1992. *The Gang as an American Enterprise. New* Brunswick, N.J.: Rutgers University Press.

Phillips, Susan A. 1999. *Wallbangin": Graffiti and Gangs in L.A.* Chicago, IL: University of Chicago Press.

Phillips, Susan A. 2019. *The City Beneath: A Century of Los Angeles Graffiti*. New Haven, CT: Yale University Press.

Rios, Victor. 2011. *Punished: Policing the Lives of Black and Latino Boys*. New York, NY: NYU Press.

Sutherland, Edwin. 1937. *The Professional Thief*. Chicago, IL: University of Chicago Press.

Tapia, Mike. 2017. *The Barrio Gangs of San Antonio, 1915-2015*. Fort Worth: Texas Christian University Press.

Umemoto, Karen. 2006. *The Truce: Lessons from an L.A. War*. Ithaca: Cornel University Press.

Valdez, Avelardo. 2007. *Mexican American Girls and Gang Violence: Beyond Risk*. New York, NY: Palgrave MacMillan.

Vigil, James Diego. 1980. *From Indians to Chicanos: The Dynamics of Mexican-American Culture*. Long Grove, IL: Waveland Press.

Vigil, James Diego. 1988. *Barrio Gangs: Street Life and Identity in Southern California*. Austin, TX: University of Austin Press.

Vigil, James Diego. 2002. *A Rainbow of Gangs: Street Cultures in the Mega-City*. Austin, TX: University of Austin Press.

Vigil, James Diego. 2007. *The Projects: Gang and Non-Gang Families in East Los Angeles*. Austin, TX: University of Austin Press.

49

The legacy of James Diego Vigil

Rebelde con causa

Robert Donald Weide

The scholarly career of Dr. James Diego Vigil, Professor Emerita at the University of California, Irvine, represents the first generation of barrio scholars to penetrate the academy and write about barrio communities from an *indigenas* perspective. His work and his career represent a significant break from all prior research on gangs in that Diego was intimately involved and experienced with gangs himself, having been raised in the heart of post-WWII Los Angeles. His positionality as a homeboy doing research in the barrios of Los Angeles where he grew up was revolutionary in the field, both for the access he was able to achieve with one of the most marginalized populations in our society but moreover for the *multiple marginality* theoretical framework he established that remains as germane today as it was when it was first published over 30 years ago. His work was sharply critical when compared to the criminalizing perspectives of his mainstream predecessors and contemporaries in the gang studies field, and he should rightly be recognized as one of the early progenitors of critical gang studies. Diego's career was the next step along the logical progression emanating from the work of his primary mentor, Joan Moore, whose groundbreaking work on gangs in the barrios of Los Angeles employed actual gang members and residents of their communities to participate in the research process.[1] Diego was the first such homeboy from the barrio to earn a PhD and embark on a career researching barrio gangs as a bona fide principal investigator. He has published a total of twelve books and numerous academic journal articles and book chapters for edited volumes on Chicano history, gangs and urban communities throughout his prodigious scholarly career spanning 1970 to the present.[2] Diego demonstrated by his own example that street kids from the most marginalized communities in our society could grow up to earn doctorates, conduct important research, conceive new theoretical analyses and have a say in issues affecting their own communities. He was the first of a now-growing cohort of organic intellectuals who came from the hood and stayed from the hood. Diego never lost his sense of his own humble origins, dedicating his life in service to barrio communities like the one in which he grew up. While Joan was the first to open the door to the ivory tower, Diego was the first to walk through, and in the process, he laid the footsteps for multiple cohorts of gang members now turned researchers to proudly walk in.

Diego's work had a profound influence on his contemporaries in critical gang research, including notable scholars like John Hagedorn,[3] Avelardo Valdez[4] and David C. Brotherton.[5] Diego's legacy has been continued by a new generation of young scholars from barrio communities around the United States who have been involved in street gangs and other comparable street-oriented groups and now find themselves following his example in the academy, including but not limited to Alex Alonso,[6] Victor Rios,[7] Randol Contreras,[8] Robert Durán[9] and myself.[10] Diego has likewise served as a direct mentor or indirect role model to other contemporary scholars of gangs and urban life who were not themselves directly involved in gangs, such as Susan Phillips,[11] Cid Martinez,[12] Mike Tapia[13] and Roberto R. Aspholm.[14] Our generation will soon be succeeded by a generation of upcoming organic barrio intellectuals who have likewise been personally involved in gangs, a number of whom have served significant time in prison as a result. As each successive generation of critical gang scholars emerges, we recognize and pay homage to those who opened the doors of the ivory tower and led us to the other side. We can never forget the travails they endured and the dignity and perseverance with which they faced the challenges that awaited them. From his days in the Brown Berets to his ascent up the ivory tower, Diego has not only served as an academic role model and mentor, but moreover, his life and career have been a model of resistance and dignity for generations to come.

In this chapter, I offer a narrative of an unassuming man who dedicated his life and career to serving and speaking for barrio communities during an era when mainstream America wanted to hear those voices even less than it does now. I had the honor of interviewing him in his home in the summer of 2019, where I have spent numerous evenings and holidays with him and his family, who have always been gracious and generous hosts to me and my partner. The content for this chapter is based on that interview, as well as the more than 15-year relationship I have had with Diego as a direct academic mentor, as well as my proliferous knowledge of his contributions to the academic literature and his personal life story. His is a riveting personal and professional narrative of steadfast resistance and perseverance. Diego was on the front lines of *El Movemiento* during the Civil Rights Era and went on to use his academic career as a vehicle to retrieve and revive our knowledge of our history, establishing a framework for understanding our experiences in the barrios of *Alta Mexico*. His legacy is not an inheritance bequeathed to the privileged and the powerful but rather a gift to the most excluded and the most marginalized populations in our postcolonial society. It was Diego who was the first to recognize the multiple marginality of our collective experience, and it is incumbent upon us to give him the recognition he deserves.

Humble origins

Diego was born in 1938, the sixth child of Mr. Patrick Vigil and Mrs. Magdalena Vigil. His father was from El Paso, Texas, where the Vigil clan had long established roots dating to before the annexation of half of Mexico to the United States in the wake of the Mexican American War. Diego's grandfather had been a merchant who ran the wagon train between Chihuahua and El Paso, resupplying the community back when Texas was the northern frontier of an independent Mexican State that stretched from *Alta California* to the Yucatan. Diego's mother was born in San Angelo, Texas, just north of San Antonio. She moved to El Paso with her family by covered wagon train when she was only five years at the turn of the century, a perilous trip at that time that family lore recalls took three weeks of hard travel. She was subsequently orphaned as a child and lost most of her family along with her parents after arriving in El Paso in the swine flu epidemic that swept across Texas in the pre-WWI years. She and her sister, along with two uncles, were the only survivors out of the extended family that had made the trip from San Angelo by covered wagon train only a few years prior.

The Vigils met and married in El Paso and honeymooned on the white sand beaches of sunny Los Angeles. While the Vigil family are many and well regarded in El Paso and surrounding communities, Diego's parents decided to move their small family to Los Angeles around 1930. Mr. Vigil had suffered the indignity of the kind of transparent racial bigotry that was all too common in the American workplace prior to the Civil Rights Acts of the 1960s. Working at the local railroad terminal, he had been passed over for advancement by an Anglo who was lacking both in expertise and experience for the job. To add insult to injury, Mr. Vigil had been given the ignominious task of training his new superior. The humiliation of that unfortunate experience compelled the family patriarch to seek a better life for himself and his family in Los Angeles, where he and his wife had enjoyed the temperate weather and beautiful beaches during their honeymoon a few years prior.

They arrived from El Paso with their two elder children. Diego was born in Los Angeles at White Memorial Hospital in the heart of Boyle Heights. The family settled in a humble working-class community on what was then the southern edge of downtown at 2221 Maple Avenue, a site that is now occupied by the track and field for Santee High School, which was built decades later. Contemporary Angelenos might consider that neighborhood the northern part of South-Central Los Angeles, because it sits south of the I-10 Freeway, but of course the I-10 Freeway had not yet been built when Diego grew up there in the 1940s and early 1950s. In 1957, the I-10 was erected, cutting a swath through black and Chicano communities from the East Side to the Pacific Ocean, and permanently excising the working-class community Diego was raised in from downtown proper.[15]

Mr. Vigil was able to transfer his employment with the railroad to Union Station, where he worked as currency clerk over the course of his career. The Vigil family also opened a restaurant and nightclub downtown called Club Fandango on Commercial and Los Angeles Streets, a block east of City Hall where the Children's Museum was located when I was a child growing up in Los Angeles in the 1980s. Diego's mother was always a housewife, back in an era when one working-class income was enough to raise a family of seven children.

The neighborhood Diego grew up in was an eclectic cosmopolitan community, where poor and working-class blacks, whites, Asians and Chicanos lived together in close physical and cultural proximity. He went to San Pedro Elementary and John Adams Middle Schools, both of which still exist. Along with the other street-oriented youth in his community, Diego grew up taking the streetcar or simply walking the short distance to downtown and neighboring communities to play the penny arcade, watch a movie or just play hooky. Diego recalls a lack of class or race consciousness in his own neighborhood, but he first began to witness class bias and racial bigotry as a child when traveling outside of his neighborhood. He recalls he and his friends had to sneak in the back entrance to the circus when it came to town with the police constantly shooing them away, while middle- and upper-class white families were able to buy tickets for their children who entered through the front entrance and were catered to exclusively by circus staff. Being of relatively moderate complexion, Diego enjoyed the privilege of passing during an era when Chicanos were nominally white but functionally non-white in many contexts. The grey area in the racial hierarchy of mid-20th-century America allowed him to pass unmolested in public, but he vividly recalls his Chicano childhood friends of darker hue were not so fortunate. The most disturbing memory he had of explicit racial exclusion was when he and a cohort of boys from his neighborhood took the streetcar over to Vermont Avenue to the public pools at Bimini Baths. He and the other light- to medium-hued boys were allowed in, but one of the boys who had a dark complexion, whom we would now recognize as *Afro-Mestizo* (although no one was conscious of that category at the time), was refused entry and had to wait on the sidewalk while the other boys enjoyed themselves. The sense of injustice he felt for his friend ruined the day for young Diego, and the experience stuck with him as he grew into a young man with an acute social conscience.

While Diego had numerous neighborhood friends from the 32nd Street gang in his own neighborhood on Maple Street, he also made friends with *vatos* from the 39th Street gang, whose barrio was about two miles southwest of his own, near the Coliseum along what was called Santa Barbara Boulevard, later christened Martin Luther King Boulevard. In the 1940s and 1950s, gangs were often multi-ethnic, with white, Chicano and Asian boys in the same gangs. There were no African American gangs in the 1940s in Los Angeles that he was aware of, but Diego recalls that black clubs like the Slausons and Roman Twenties started in the 1950s. The worst trouble the boys got into was being pulled over by the LAPD, lined up on a wall and berated with bigotry, "Mexicans this, and Mexicans that". Gangs during that era were not the hyper-criminalized progenitors of nihilistic violence that they became during my own child-hood in the 1980s and 1990s. It was unheard of for someone to use a firearm in a gang fight, and the use of even handheld weapons during that era was extremely rare. In the wake of the infamous Sleepy Lagoon murder and so-called "Zoot Suit Riots", gang members and the wider Chicano community had little inclination for serious violence. Diego recalls that fights were not altogether uncommon but never life threatening.

Fortunately, Diego's choice of athletic endeavors spared him from being picked on, and he never got into any serious street fights because of it. As a boy he would go over to an older neighbor's house in the neighborhood who had a punching bag hung up in his backyard – Benny Contreras, known colloquially as *Moco Verde* (green snot). After getting his form right through practicing on the bag under Benny's tutelage, Benny took him over to *Santo Nino*, where there was a boxing program sponsored by the Catholic Youth Organization. The CYO was the Catholic Archdiocese's response to the so-called "Zoot Suit Riots" a few years prior. Without any experience actually hitting a real person and being hit, the CYO coach threw him in the ring with another boy, and Diego quickly had to learn to sink or spar. He competed in three competitive boxing matches in the youth league organized by the CYO, unfortunately losing all three. However, undeterred, later he continued on to fight all over the city in his early teens. He even fought a match with Johnny Gallardo to a draw, father to *Senór* David "Smilon" Gallardo of the Ramona Gardens barrio. After catching a mean hook that left him with a chronic earache in a match with a fighter from Bell Gardens, known colloquially as *Palos Verde*, Diego finally decided to hang up his gloves and put on his cleats instead to play American football.

When Diego was in his early teens, in 1954, his father decided to move the family to Nor-walk, then a primarily white middle-class suburb, save for a couple pockets of barrio *colonia* communities leftover from migrant agricultural worker families when the area was primarily occupied by orange orchards – Carmelas and Varrio Norwalk. Diego excelled in high school athletics and due to his interest in sports decided to continue his education majoring in physical education at the local Cerritos College in 1957, playing on the football team. Being the only sibling who had any interest in a college education, his father made every effort to provide for his education, paying for his books, gas and registration fees so Diego could focus on his education.

From Mexican American to Chicano

After finishing his associate degree at Cerritos College, Diego went on to Long Beach State, where he played on the football team for one season. He finished his BA in history in 1962. After college, Diego had been working as a public school teacher for a few years when he got turned on to the burgeoning Chicano movement in 1966. His first serious interest in politics was spurred by a Jewish classmate named Arnie Abrams, his brother Richard's best friend and valedictorian at their high school in Norwalk. Arnie went on to college at UC Berkeley in the early 1960s, returning to Norwalk obsessed with the progressive politics of the era that he passed on to Diego and Richard. Diego's father and eldest brother had supported progressive Democratic candidate Henry Wallace in the late 1940s, so it was a natural extension of the family's political persuasion.

In 1965, Diego joined AMAE, the Association of Mexican American Educators, a grassroots teacher run education advocacy organization that had its meetings where Diego now resides in the city of Whittier, just east of East LA. In the summer of 1966, he started working for Lyndon B. Johnson's War on Poverty program, which introduced him to another young professional proto-Chicano organization called MAAC, the Mexican American Action Committee. While he was involved in MAAC, they provided money to David Sanchez's Young Chicanos for Community Action, a predecessor to the Brown Berets. Like many other incipient Chicano radicals, Diego hung around at the Brown Berets' de facto headquarters, La Piranha Coffee House, talking politics and getting acquainted with other young Chicano activists. Eventually they both joined the Brown Berets, with Diego's brother Richard becoming minister of defense due to his military background. However, it was Diego who had introduced Richard to the Berets by bringing him to La Piranha after Richard returned from active duty as a paratrooper in the US Army. They were both radical *Chicanismos* who favored a militant approach to *El Movimiento*. Diego recalls fondly that his primary role model was Malcolm X and felt strongly connected to the Black Civil Rights Movement as well.

Diego could not recall where he first heard the term Chicano used as a self-identifier, but when it hit the streets, it took off like wildfire. An entire population that had up to that point uncritically assumed its inevitable assimilation was suddenly confronted with an identity crisis. Almost overnight, an entire population was presented with a choice they had to consciously make, whether they were Mexican American as they had uncritically assumed for decades, or whether they were Chicanos. Some, like Diego's eldest brother, who was a WWII veteran and distanced himself from Diego and Richard, felt the Chicano identifier was too radical and provocative. In contrast, Diego and Richard adopted *Chicanismo* with vigor, embracing the new identifier as an expression of resistance to the class oppression and racial exclusion they had witnessed and experienced throughout their young lives.

Both Diego and his brother were charged in the notorious conspiracy cases pursued against Chicano activists in the wake of the infamous East LA School Walkouts on March 6, 1968, and the (attempted) disruption of Governor Ronald Reagan's speech at the posh Biltmore Hotel downtown on April 24, 1969.[16] Richard was one of the East LA 13 who had been criminally charged for organizing the walkouts, while Diego was charged for disrupting Reagan's speech at the Biltmore, where Carlos Montes and undercover LAPD officer Fernando Sumaya allegedly had set a small towel on fire on an upper floor, which was used as a pretext to bring conspiracy charges against the activists that could have potentially have resulted in life imprisonment. Most of the defendants, including those who were tried in the cases, chose the colorful Chicano activist attorney Oscar Acosta to represent them. While Acosta was better known for his psychedelic wardrobe and adventures with counterculture writer Hunter Thompson, as depicted in the book and cult classic film, *Fear and Loathing in Las Vegas*, he had never actually tried a case in open court. He ultimately prevailed with a daring legal strategy of using the cases to put the entire racist American legal system on trial.

However, Diego decided to go the more conventional route and chose as his attorney an elder and experienced Chicano attorney named Manuel Ruiz, who had represented defendants a generation before in the so-called Zoot Suit Riots. None of the defendants in the cases, including Diego, were convicted of any serious charges, but the circumstances of his prosecution eventually forced him out of his teaching position surreptitiously, by which time he had already decided to pursue a PhD.

From the streets to the ivory tower

During the peak of *El Movimiento* when Diego, his brother Richard and their Brown Berets *camaradas* were being prosecuted, Diego was pursing his MA in social studies at California State University, Sacramento. One of the perks of the program was that it included a six-week trip throughout Mexico, which was Diego's first pilgrimage to Mexico proper. He had the opportunity to visit Mexico City, Guadalajara, Oaxaca and Chiapas during the trip, which had a profound effect on his conceptualization of his identity as a Chicano, born and raised under Anglo occupation. The trip served as the foundation for his research on Chicano anthropological history that culminated in the publication of *From Indians to Chicanos* in 1980.[17]

In 1969, after completing his MA, Diego got a job teaching in the High Potential Program at UCLA, which was the predecessor to ethnic studies, intended to help students from marginalized communities acclimate to a university environment. Being at UCLA teaching, in 1970, Diego applied to and was accepted for the doctoral program in the Department of History, where he began taking classes towards his PhD. When the High Potential Program ended, Diego found himself out of a job in a doctoral program with a young family to support. After a frantic search for employment, he finally found a half-time position as a lecturer in Mexican American Studies at Chaffey College in 1971, out in Rancho Cucamonga in the Inland Empire, an hour east of downtown where he grew up. After starting in the doctoral program in history at UCLA, a friend of his who was in the doctoral program in anthropology suggested Diego apply for a Rockefeller-sponsored fellowship in anthropology that he was vacating. Diego was awarded the prestigious fellowship, which came with a much-needed full tuition waiver and generous stipend for books and expenses, and he transferred into the Department of Anthropology at UCLA in fall of 1971.

Financial security dictated Diego's career choice to an extent. He had four children from a prior marriage at that point and was dedicated to providing for them, and he had met the love of his life, his lovely wife Polly, shortly after starting graduate school. As the primary provider for a growing family, he was able to piece together a stable income between the half-time position at Chaffey and the Rockefeller fellowship at UCLA. Despite his career choice being the progeny of necessity, Diego found a stimulating intellectual environment in anthropology. He was naturally inclined towards historical and especially cultural anthropology, and his academic training in the field informed the impressive body of literature Diego produced over the course of his scholarly career. His dissertation in anthropology at UCLA, defended in 1976, was written on acculturation and school performance – a fitting topic given his prior career as a high school teacher and his history of militant anti-assimilationist *Chicanismo* politics.

Diego's dissertation was the foundation of a later book published in 1997, *Personas Mexicanas: Chicano High Schoolers in a Changing Los Angeles*, which, characteristically of his work on gangs, compared different working class Chicano communities, urban and suburban, using high schools in East LA and Southeast Los Angeles County as case studies. The book uses samples collected in 1974 during his dissertation and a follow-up sample taken in 1988 after *Barrio Gangs* was published.

Throughout his involvement in *El Movemiento* and graduate school, especially after his pilgrimage to Mexico in 1969, Diego had been avidly researching the history of colonialism and the historical roots of contemporary Chicano populations. His research on his own historical roots culminated in the publication of *From Indians to Chicanos* in 1980. This first book was the culmination of everything he had read and learned up to that point when it was first published in 1980. The book is now in its third edition, with revisions made for each progressive edition, the most recent in 2012. It was one of the first books on Chicano history and identity published by a Chicano sole author, and it remains a foundational work in the fields of Chicano/Latino studies and historical anthropology. The book was unmistakably influenced by his mentor Joan Moore's prior work on the Mexican American community and her activism throughout the 1960s and 1970s.[18]

After finishing graduate school, Diego was fortunate to be offered a lecturer position at the University of Southern California, which matured into a tenure-track position two years later in 1978. He received tenure at USC in 1984, a feat all the more impressive after Diego's mentor Joan Moore had been blackballed out of USC a decade prior.[19] He kept his tenure at Chaffey College throughout in order to maximize his income to provide for his six children at the time but resigned from Chaffey when he was granted tenure at USC and moved back to Los Angeles from the closet community of Upland, where he and Polly had been raising their family.

Back to the barrio

Diego's work on gangs grew naturally out of his lifelong experiences with gang members as a child, during his teaching years and as a college-level instructor. He had fraternized with gang members as a child and young man growing up in South Los Angeles, he had worked with gang members while he was employed in the War on Poverty and while he was teaching at Chaffey College, he found that many of his students had friends and family who were involved in local gangs. He had even included a section on gangs for his comprehensive exams in his doctoral program at UCLA in order to demonstrate his mastery of the literature. When students at Chaffey expressed in his classes the importance of gangs to their lived experience growing up in the *colonia* barrios of Rancho Cucamonga, Pomona, Ontario, Chino, Fontana and Corona, among others, Diego decided to assign them to write about their experiences. This led to contacts with friends and family members of his students who were involved in gangs throughout the 1970s and compelled Diego to seek out Joan Moore for her guidance and mentorship in 1977.

In addition to the mentorship of a senior scholar who had published the only academic account of gang life in the barrios of Los Angeles up to that point, Joan was able to introduce Diego to a network of gang members – "Joan's *Pistoleros*" – who provided him with access to respondents who were members of gangs in Los Angeles, particularly East Los Angeles. Diego always felt at home in the barrio and felt the kind of longing for the barrio. With his impressive network of contacts and respondents in the Inland Empire and Los Angeles proper, his initial research on gangs in the 1970s and 1980s replicated the kind of urban versus suburban comparative analysis he had employed in his dissertation, with case histories and ethnographic analysis of barrio life in Southern California both in the urban core of Los Angeles, as well as its satellite post-rural suburbs.

The book that came out of this initial fieldwork on gangs during the 1970s and 1980s, *Barrio Gangs: Street Life and Identity in Southern California*, was published in 1988 and is widely and rightly perceived as Diego's *magnum opus*.[20] *Barrio Gangs* represents the first book-length academic publication written by someone who grew up in the barrios of Los Angeles and for that reason is a historic precedent in the field of critical gang studies and the larger field of criminology. The influence of Joan Moore on the book is unmistakable, and Diego recognizes her as his primary academic mentor. He even went up to Milwaukee for a couple of months during his postdoc and nearly froze to death living in an attic so that he could benefit from her direct guidance while he was working on *Barrio Gangs*. However, Diego employed a slightly different research design that he had acquired from his anthropology training, including detailed life histories of individual gang members across the urban/suburban divide, which were representative of their wider communities and provided a deeper layer of insight into the lives of gang members than even Joan's *Homeboys* had. While Joan had humanized gang members by including them in the research and analysis process, Diego was humanizing them on the page with poignant and detailed narratives of the challenges and indignities they endured growing up in the barrios of Southern California.

Multiple marginality and intersectionality

Diego's positionality had significant ramifications for both his fieldwork and analysis. As someone who had grown up around gang members in a barrio community, Diego genuinely shared their habitus. He understood his respondents and could relate to them on their own terms and represent their experiences in writing in a way that humanized them to the reader. His authenticity and sincerity were perceived by his respondents, which allowed his respondents the ability to let their guard down and open up their lives to him the way they never would for someone perceived as an outsider. For the first time, barrio youth were writing their own story with their own hand, *sin Anglo*.

Beyond mere access, however, Diego's positionality as a genuine organic intellectual had important implications for his analysis and the multiple marginality theoretical framework he established in *Barrio Gangs*. Having been raised in a working-class barrio community, Diego had himself faced and had witnessed others facing the twin challenges of class exploitation and racial oppression. He had the perspective to recognize the panoply of dilemmas created by poverty that working-class populations like the barrio gang members he studied experienced every day of their lives. He had witnessed and experienced the indignity of racial exclusion and repression, not to mention the jingoistic xenophobia experienced by immigrants on stolen land. The idea of studying societies from the perspective of only a single causal factor never sat well with Diego in graduate school, and he was determined to take a more holistic multidimensional multidisciplinary perspective on causation in his work on gangs – a hallmark of the critical gang studies tradition. Diego could not only recognize the importance of each and every one of the facets of marginality barrio gang members faced in Southern California, even more importantly, he recognized how different aspects of marginalization interact to reinforce and amplify the impact and effect of each individually – an analysis that has since been co-opted under the banner of intersectionality, appropriated from the work of critical race studies legal scholar Kimberlé Crenshaw.

While Crenshaw's legal concept of intersectionality as it applies to court decisions affecting marginalized groups has been widely appropriated in the social sciences, the theoretical framework provided by the multiple marginality perspective was proposed by Diego *within* the social sciences of anthropology and criminology prior to Crenshaw yet has been largely ignored outside of the critical gang studies subfield. A prominent criminologist even published a book on intersectionality in criminology extolling the field to integrate intersectionality into criminological research and theory but failed to cite Diego's multiple marginality framework as an obvious predecessor.[21] Of course, to do so would require giving Diego the credit as the progenitor of the idea that multiple facets of marginality intersect to reinforce and amplify oppression experienced by members of marginalized communities. In fact, Diego's multiple marginality framework was published the year before Crenshaw's infamous article. Crenshaw's original article, entitled "Demarginalizing the Intersection of Race and Sex: A Black Feminist Critique of Antidiscrimination Doctrine, Feminist Theory and Antiracist Politics", even used the same terminology of marginality to analyze the multiple facets of oppression as Vigil had the year prior.[22] It is incumbent upon the field to recognize the indisputable fact that these two theoretical frameworks are essentially one and the same, each recognizing that marginalization and exclusion occurs along multiple axes of oppression and that each axis has a multiplier effect in combination on the experiences of marginalized populations. Most importantly, both centralize racial/ethnic identities as a primary axis of marginalization.

However, each in their original presentation is lacking in their own regard. Being a cis-male doing ethnographic research on the hyper-masculine *machismo cholo* culture, Diego's respondents were uniformly male, and so he failed to include the marginality of gender oppression in his presentation of multiple marginality as a theoretical framework. This is a cardinal sin in the intersectionality framework as it is popularly conceived in the social sciences and an embarrassing gaffe from a contemporary perspective. Diego was focused on hardcore gang members who, during the hyper *machismo* era he conducted his research, were exclusively male.

Likewise, Crenshaw's iteration of intersectionality is equally devoid of any class analysis, which is consequently a central component of the multiple marginality framework. This could be the result of her taking for granted her own privileged class position, much as Diego took for granted his cis-male gender identity in neglecting to include gender as an axis of marginality in his conceptualization of the multiple marginality framework. Of course, Crenshaw could also have neglected to include class analysis in her presentation of the intersectionality framework because western legal systems do not acknowledge class as a protected identity. It is simply not a legal issue. In fact, since the 19th century, western legal systems have been recognized as being explicitly designed to protect class privilege and therefore cannot be reformed to undermine or even acknowledge class oppression.[23] Therefore, it is entirely understandable that Crenshaw did not include class oppression in her conceptualization of the intersectionality matrix, because class is not an identity that has ever had legal standing or likely ever will under the current capitalist settler colonial legal system in which we live.

In any case, the combination of these two independently conceived and individually inadequate frameworks produces a more comprehensive framework that can account for multiple axes of oppression experienced by marginalized populations. Vigil deserves recognition and praise for being the first to conceive and publish this framework, and Crenshaw should be recognized and praised for her addition of gender identity to the matrix of axes of oppression that marginalized populations experience. Despite their disciplinary distance, Vigil an anthropologist/criminologist and Crenshaw a legal scholar, the evolution of this idea has been among the more significant theoretical developments in social science scholarship in the past generation. It is long since time for Diego's multiple marginality framework to receive the recognition it is due.

The evolution of multiple marginality

In 1995, Diego left USC in order to take a tenured position in anthropology at his alma mater, as well as to serve as Associate Director of the Center for the Study of Urban Poverty at UCLA. In 2000, while he was working on his second book on gangs, Diego decided to leave UCLA and took a position at the newly emerging Department of Criminology, Law and Society at the University of California, Irvine. It had always occurred to Diego that no one was doing work on gangs in black, Central American or Asian diaspora communities in Los Angeles. He had received a small grant to do some interviews with Vietnamese gang members in the 1980s and decided to write the first inter-racial comparative analysis of gangs, which was published as *A Rainbow of Gangs: Street Cultures in the Mega-City*.

The book follows the model set by *Barrio Gangs* in many ways. *Rainbow of Gangs* employs Diego's characteristic comparative analysis and uses his multiple marginality framework to explore the intersection of multiple marginalities that gang members from different racial/ethnic backgrounds endure, suggesting the commonality of their experiences at the bottom of the American social stratification hierarchy. Whereas *Barrio Gangs* had employed life histories in a single chapter, *Rainbow of Gangs* employed detailed individual life histories as whole chapters providing context for his analysis of the marginality endured by Chicano, black, Vietnamese and Salvadoran gang members in each of their distinctive communities. Unfortunately, like much of Diego's work aside from *Barrio Gangs*, *Rainbow of Gangs* has often been ignored by contemporary scholars of inter-racial gang conflict.[24]

Diego's third book on gangs, *The Projects: Gang and Non-Gang Families in East Los Angeles*, published in 2007, was the result of a grant opportunity he was offered by the US Department of Health and Human Services. DHHS was interested in funding research on families, which was opportune given Diego's recent work in the Pico Gardens/Aliso Village housing projects. In 1991, after having conducted an on-site evaluation of a Los Angeles Housing Authority drug intervention program for the Housing Authority, Diego reached out to Father Gregory Boyle for help initiating a long-term study at Pico Aliso. Father Boyle, or Father G, as he is known colloquially, was the Jesuit parish priest at Dolores Mission Catholic Church in Boyle Heights on the edge of downtown and is the founder of Homeboy Industries, the largest gang intervention organization in the world, which rehabilitates gang members by addressing their trauma and feeding them into vocational and academic careers. We have dozens of friends, family and students who work for Homeboy Industries, so it was a natural connection for Diego to have made when Homeboy Industries was in its infancy. The Pico Aliso community is also distinct in that, unlike the other major housing projects in East Los Angeles, Ramona Gardens and Estrada Courts, numerous rival gangs share Pico Aliso and the surrounding warren of backstreets as their territory. Diego chose to focus his analysis primarily, though not exclusively, on Cuatro Flats, the oldest gang in Pico Aliso that predates the construction of the housing project.

While it hasn't received the attention in the field that it deserves, *The Projects* represents an evolution in both Diego's work and the larger critical gang studies tradition. First of all, he includes a lengthy detailed historical analysis in the first part of the book of the primary gang he focuses on stretching back to the 1930s, a primary element of the critical gang studies tradition as suggested by Brotherton in his recent guide to critical gang research.[25] Second, Diego includes the multiple marginalities endured by female gang members, with a chapter dedicated exclusively to the experiences of *Cholas* in Pico Aliso. Moreover, with a wider focus on the families and the whole community, *The Projects* provides a window into the perspective of residents who are not gang members. Taking a novel approach to gang research, Diego counterposed these non-gang affiliated residents and their families with gang members and their families in his comparative analysis for the book. While his conclusion, complete with policy recommendations, is decidedly reformist, not unlike his conclusion in *Rainbow of Gangs*, *The Projects* represents another important evolution in the application of the multiple marginality framework and the wider critical gang studies tradition by extension.

A living legacy

The legacy of Diego's life, activism and academic career lives on through his students and through their students. Diego was the first scholar in the gang research field who grew up in barrio communities to enter through the door that Joan Moore opened into the ivory tower. It is in his footsteps that we walk today, and there are a number of us who have been directly and indirectly influenced by Diego and his work, some of us having personal experience with gangs and others not. Following behind is a much larger cohort of young scholars who have personal involvement with gangs, many of whom have been incarcerated for extensive periods. All of us walk on a path laid for us by Diego's groundbreaking work.

Diego's work on gangs has been widely cited in both academic and popular literature on gangs that can be included in the critical gang studies tradition.[26] However, surely the most accomplished of Diego's direct progeny is Victor Rios, who has risen to become one of the brightest stars in the wider field of sociology. As the first bona fide gang member to do research on his own community and write now two academic books dealing with issues that he himself experienced growing up, it should be apparent that Rios is not only the most prominent but also the first of Diego's direct progeny. Rios's first book, *Punished*, has become one of the best-selling books in the history of the field and will no doubt be considered a classic of the current era. In it, Rios explicitly acknowledges Diego as predecessor to his own insider positionality. Rios likewise cites Diego in the methodological appendix to his follow-up book, *Human Targets*, that more explicitly addresses gangs and for which Diego wrote the foreword. While Rios doesn't cite Diego in the chapter on "Multiple Manhoods", the obvious influence of Diego's multiple marginality framework is indisputable. Rios has maintained a close personal relationship with Diego, who has served as a mentor to him since his days as a doctoral candidate at UC Berkeley, and they maintain close contact to the present day. Another contemporary scholar of note who has been directly mentored by Diego is Rios's cohort colleague from graduate school at Berkeley, Cid Martinez. Martinez not only cites Diego in his recent book but has also maintained close personal contact with Diego and considers him a significant mentor as well.

Probably the most significant progeny of Diego's in the critical gang study tradition thus far is Robert Durán, who is the first bona fide gang member to write a book about gang life that he himself was involved in, *Gang Life in Two Cities*, published in 2013. Durán was the direct student of both the distinguished ethnographer Patricia Adler at the University of Colorado and Joan Moore, who served on his dissertation committee. Durán routinely cites Diego as predecessor to his own work on gangs, firmly situating himself in the footsteps laid by Joan and Diego. Durán faithfully cites all three of Diego's books on gangs in both of his recent books on gangs in the Midwest and Southwest. Durán's critical analysis in *Gang Life in Two Cities* also bears the hallmarks of the critical gang tradition pioneered by Diego and Joan Moore. Durán contextualizes the historical circumstances of his field sites in Denver and Ogden going back to the pre-WWII period, just as Diego had in *The Projects*. Furthermore, his critical analysis of the racial oppression endured by gang members also represents a further evolution of Diego's multiple marginality framework applied to different context from the Los Angeles area gangs Diego focused on exclusively, showing that the multiple marginality framework carries validity in other contexts as well. Durán's second book on gangs in cities along the Mexican border, *The Gang Paradox*, published in 2018, represents an even further evolution of the critical gang studies tradition, boasting an even more sophisticated historical analysis of the contextual circumstances gang members living along the Mexican border face as a result of the double colonization they have experienced historically. Durán also explicitly credits the multiple marginality framework as "one of the central frameworks for explaining the development of gangs."[27]

Diego also had a significant impact on the work and career of the prominent scholar of Los Angeles gang graffiti, Susan Phillips. Phillips was a doctoral student in anthropology at UCLA when Diego left USC and accepted a tenure track position at his alma mater in 1995. Like him, Phillips is a cultural anthropologist whose work focuses on gang culture in Los Angeles. As such, Diego was an important mentor and dissertation committee member for Phillips and was a valuable advisor for her popular 1999 book on Los Angeles gang graffiti, *Wallbangin'*.

Her forthcoming magnum opus supported by over 30 years of ethnographic research, *The City Beneath: A Century of Los Angeles Graffiti*, likewise reflects Diego's mentorship and influence.

Another significant direct mentee of Diego's who has known him longer than any of us, since his tenure at USC, is the scholarly authority on Crip- and Blood-affiliated African American gangs in Los Angeles, Alex Alonso. Alonso is also the owner/operator of the world's most trafficked website on gangs, StreetGangs.com, which he uses as a repository for his unparalleled collection of interviews with gang members the world over. Alonso has maintained a decades-long relationship with Diego and has faithfully cited him in each of his flagship article and book chapter publications on the origins and trajectory of African American gangs in Los Angeles.[28] Alonso considers Diego the world's foremost authority on Chicano gangs in Los Angeles and has worked alongside him as an expert witness on behalf of the accused in countless criminal proceedings related to gangs.

Finally, probably the least significant progeny of Diego's at the time of this writing is me. I first met Diego when he recruited me as a doctoral candidate at UC Irvine. While I chose to accept an offer from NYU instead, I remained in close contact with Diego throughout my doctoral program at NYU, and he served on my dissertation committee. Diego's influence on my dissertation is apparent in both my positionality and historical foundation, but perhaps more important is the influence of his multiple marginality perspective on my analysis. Recognizing the intersections of multiple marginalities that both black and Latino gang members endure growing up in Los Angeles, my analysis argues for solidarity between black and Latino gang members on the grounds of those shared experiences. My first book, largely drawn from my dissertation, entitled *Divide and Conquer: Inter-Racial Gang Conflict in Los Angeles*, is under contract with Temple University Press. In it, I offer a slightly more sophisticated historical background and theoretical analysis than I had conceived in my dissertation but which is solidly grounded in the multiple marginality framework bequeathed to me by Diego.

Diego has served and continues to serve as a humble role model and mentor for progressive generations of critical scholars, many of whom now and surely into the future will come to the academy with personal experience with gangs. Diego should be rightly recognized as a progenitor of the critical gang studies tradition that this volume celebrates, moving the field forward from the foundational work of his mentor Joan Moore and making numerous contributions to the core traditions in critical gang studies. Diego was the first generation of researchers from the barrio who went back to the barrio to study and write about communities like the one he had grown up in. His humble upbringing in the core of Los Angeles and history of militant activism during the civil rights era conferred an authenticity that had been severely lacking in the academy. The multiple marginality framework he developed as a result of this positionality remains the core theoretical foundation in the field of critical gang studies and will likely remain so for the foreseeable future. Diego reintroduced anthropological perspectives and methodologies into the field, including extended individual case studies and detailed historical analysis in order to establish context. Perhaps most important, though, are the dignity and humanity that Diego's work bestows upon perhaps the most marginalized members of our society, who continue to suffer indefinitely at the intersections of poverty, racism, xenophobia, patriarchy and hyper-criminalization.

Notes

1 Moore 1978, 1991
2 Vigil 1980, 1982,1988, 1993, 1997, 2002, 2003 2007, 2011; Moore, Vigil and Garcia 1983; Moore and Vigil 1987, 1993; Vigil and Long 1990; Vigil and Yun 1990

3 Hagedorn 1988, 2008, 2015
4 Valdez 2007
5 Brotherton and Barrios 2004; Brotherton 2015
6 Alonso 1999, 2004, 2010
7 Rios 2011, 2017
8 Contreras 2012
9 Durán 2013, 2018
10 Weide 2021 (forthcoming)
11 Phillips 1999, 2019
12 Martinez 2016
13 Tapia 2017
14 Aspholm 2019
15 Chapple 2010
16 Haney-Lopez 2003
17 Vigil 1980
18 Greber, Moore, and Guzman 1970; Moore and Pachon 1976
19 See prior chapter on the career and legacy of Joan Moore
20 Vigil 1988
21 Potter 2015
22 Crenshaw 1989
23 Kropotkin 1886
24 Umemoto 2006; Martinez 2016; Sanchez-Jankowski 2016
25 Brotherton 2015
26 Hagedorn 1988, 2008, 2015; Padilla 1992; Brotherton and Barrios 2004; Hayden 2004; Umemoto 2006; Garot 2010; Lauger 2012; Hallsworth 2013; Flores 2014; Brotherton 2015; Tapia 2017
27 Durán 2018, p. 41
28 Alonso 1999, 2004, 2010

References

Alonso, Alejandro A. 1999. "Territoriality Among African American Gangs in Los Angeles." Master's Thesis, University of Southern California.

Alonso, Alex. 2004. "Racialized Identities and the Formation of Black Gangs in Los Angeles." *Urban Geography*. 25(7): 658–674.

Alonso, Alex. 2010. "Out of the Void: Street Gangs in Black Los Angeles." In Darnell Hunt and Ana-Christina Ramon (Eds.) *Black Los Angeles: American Dreams and Racial Realities*. New York, NY: NYU Press.

Aspholm, Roberto. 2019. *Views from the Street: The Transformation of Gangs and Violence on Chicago's South Side*. New York, NY: Columbia University Press.

Brotherton, David Charles and Luis Barrios. 2004. *The Almighty Latin King and Queen Nation: Street Politics and the Transformation of a New York City Street Gang*. New York, NY: Columbia University Press.

Brotherton, David Charles. 2015. *Youth Street Gangs: A Critical Appraisal*. New York, NY: Routledge.

Chapple, Reginald. 2010. "From Central Avenue to Leimert Park: The Shifting Center of Black Los Angeles." In Darnell Hunt and Ana-Christina Ramon (Eds.) *Black Los Angeles: American Dreams and Racial Realities*. New York, NY: NYU Press.

Crenshaw, Kimberlé. 1989. "Demarginalizing the Intersection of Race and Sex: A Black Feminist Critique of Antidiscrimination Doctrine, Feminist Theory and Antiracist Politics." *University of Chicago Legal Forum*. 1989(1) Article 8.

Durán, Robert J. 2013. *Gang Life in Two Cities: An Insider's Journey*. New York, NY: Columbia University Press.

Durán, Robert J. 2018. *The Gang Paradox: Inequalities and Miracles on the US-Mexico Border*. New York, NY: Columbia University Press.

Flores, Edward Orozco. 2014. *God's Gangs: Barrio Ministry, Masculinity and gang Recovery*. New York, NY: NYU Press.

Garot, Robert. 2010. *Who You Claim: Performing Gang Identity in School and on the Streets*. New York, NY: NYU Press.

Grebler, Leo, Joan W. Moore, and Ralph C Guzman. 1970. *The Mexican-American People: The Nation's Second Largest Minority*. New York, NY: The Free Press.

Hagedorn, John M. 1988. *People and Folks: Gangs, Crime and the Underclass in a Rustbelt City*. Chicago, IL: Lake View Press.

Hagedorn, John M. 2008. *A World of Gangs: Armed Young Men and Gangsta Culture*. Minneapolis, MN: University of Minnesota Press.

Hagedorn, John M. 2015. *The Insane Chicago Way: The Daring Plan by Chicago Gangs to Create a Spanish Mafia*. Chicago, IL: University of Chicago Press.

Hallsworth, Simon. 2013. *The Gang & Beyond: Interpreting Violent Street Worlds*. New York, NY: Palgrave Macmillan.

Haney-Lopez, Ian. 2003. *Racism on Trial: The Chicano Fight for Justice*. Cambridge, MA: Belknap-Harvard University Press.

Hayden, Tom. 2004. *Street Wars: Gangs and the Future of Violence*. New York, NY: The Free Press.

Kropotkin, Pyotr. 1886. "Law and Authority." In Roger N. Baldwin (Ed.) *Kropotkin's Revolutionary Pamphlets*. Vanguard Press, 1927.

Lauger, Timothy R. 2012. *Real Gangstas: Legitimacy, Reputation and Violence in the Intergang Environment*. New Brunswick, NJ: Rutgers University Press.

Martinez, Cid Gregory. 2016. *The Neighborhood Has Its Own Rules: Latinos and African Americans in South Los Angeles*. New York, NY: NYU Press.

Moore, Joan W. 1991. *Going Down to the Barrio: Homeboys and Homegirls in Change*. Philadelphia, PA: Temple University Press.

Moore, Joan W., Robert Garcia, Carlos Garcia, Luis Cerda, and Frank Valencia. 1978. *Homeboys: Gangs, Drugs, and Prisons in the Barrios of Los Angeles*. Philadelphia, PA: Temple University Press.

Moore, Joan W., and Harry Pachon. 1976. *Mexican Americans* (2nd Edition). Ethnic Groups in American Life Series. Englewood Cliffs, NJ: Prentice Hall.

Moore, Joan W., and James Diego Vigil. 1987. "Chicano Gangs: Group Norms and Individual Factors Related to Adult Criminality." *Aztlan*. 18(2): 27–44.

Moore, Joan W., and James Diego Vigil. 1993. "Barrios in Transition." In Joan Moore and Raquel Pinderhughes (Eds.) *In the Barrios: Latinos and the Underclass Debate*. New York, NY: Russel Sage Publications.

Moore, Joan W., James Diego Vigil, and Robert Garcia. 1983. "Residence and Territoriality in Chicano Gangs." *Social Problems*. 31(2): 182–194.

Padilla, Felix M. 1992. *The Gang as an American Enterprise*. New Brunswick, NJ: Rutgers University Press.

Phillips, Susan A. 1999. *Wallbangin'": Graffiti and Gangs in L.A.* Chicago, IL: University of Chicago Press.

Phillips, Susan A. 2019. *The City Beneath: A Century of Los Angeles Graffiti*. New Haven, CT: Yale University Press.

Potter, Hillary. 2015. *Intersectionality and Criminology*. New York, NY: Routledge.

Rios, Victor. 2011. *Punished: Policing the Lives of Black and Latino Boys*. New York, NY: NYU Press.

Rios, Victor. 2017. *Human Targets: Schools, Police, and the Criminalization of Latino Youth*. Chicago, IL: University of Chicago Press.

Sanchez-Jankowski, Martin. 2016. *Burning Dislike: Ethnic Violence in High Schools*. Berkeley, CA: UC Press.

Tapia, Mike. 2017. *The Barrio Gangs of San Antonio 1915–2015*. Fort Worth, TX: TCU Press.

Umemoto, Karen. 2006. *The Truce: Lessons from an LA Gang War*. Ithaca, NY: Cornell University Press.

Valdez, Avelardo. 2007. *Mexican American Girls and Gang Violence: Beyond Risk*. New York, NY: Palgrave Macmillan.

Vigil, James Diego. 1980. *From Indians to Chicanos: The Dynamics of Mexican-American Culture*. Long Grove, IL: Waveland Press.

Vigil, James Diego. 1982. "Human Revitalization: The Six Tasks of Victory Outreach." *The Drew Gateway*. 52(3): 49–59.

Vigil, James Diego. 1988. *Barrio Gangs: Street Life and Identity in Southern California*. Austin, TX: University of Austin Press.

Vigil, James Diego. 1993. "The Established Gangs." In Scott Jennings and David J. Monti (Eds.) *Gangs: The Origins and Impact of Contemporary Youth Gangs in the United States*. Albany, NY: SUNY Press.

Vigil, James Diego. 1997. *Personas Mexicanas: Chicano High Schoolers in a Changing Los Angeles*. Fort Worth, TX: Harcourt College Publishers.

Vigil, James Diego. 2002. *A Rainbow of Gangs: Street Cultures in the Mega-City*. Austin, TX: University of Austin Press.

Vigil, James Diego. 2003. "Urban Violence and Street Gangs." *Annual Review of Anthropology*. 32: 225–242.

Vigil, James Diego. 2007. *The Projects: Gang and Non-Gang Families in East Los Angeles*. Austin, TX: University of Austin Press.

Vigil, James Diego. 2011. "Ethnic Succession and Ethnic Conflict." In Edward Telles, Mark Sawyer and Gaspar Rivera-Salgado (Eds.) *Just Neighbors? Research on African American and Latino Relations*. New York, NY: Russell Sage Foundation.

Vigil, James Diego, and John M. Long. 1990. "Emic and Etic Perspectives on Gang Culture: The Chicano Case." In C. Ronald Huff (Ed.) *Gangs in America*. Newbury Park, CA: Sage.

Vigil, James Diego, and Steve Chong Yun. 1990. "Vietnam Youth Gangs in Southern California." In Scott Cummings and Daniel J. Monti (Eds.) *Gangs in America*. Albany, NY: SUNY Press.

Weide, Robert. Forthcoming. *Divide and Conquer: Inter-Racial Gang Conflict in Los Angeles*. Philadelphia: Temple University Press.

Index

Page numbers in *italic* indicate a figure, and page numbers in **bold** indicate a table on the corresponding page.

9/11 20, 23
1845 ordinance 353–355
1932 Ordinance 356–358

Aboriginal-based organized crime (ABOC): *see* Indigenous gangs
abstract empiricism 624, 629
abstract space 99–103
academic doxa: directions for future research 630–631; introduction 624–625; in prison gang research 626–629; violence and 626–627
access to the gang scene 155–156, 162n5
Acosta, O. 680
Adler, P. 701
Afary, K. 667
affected/affection 59, 61, 69–71, 71n4
African Americans: controlled integration 260; drug economy 250–251, 252, 253–254; dual marginalization 249, 252, 253–254; economic marginalization 36; ghetto collapse 9; in Hartford 259; political consciousness 37; segregation 102; unemployment 244, 253; war on drugs 37–38
African Caribbean communities 9
Afrika Bambaataa 302, 322
Afro-Caribbean santeria 313n13
Agamben, G. 23, 64, 221
Agozino, B. 352
Aguirre, E. 311
Aguirre, E. "Moe" 681
Ain't No Making It (MacLeod) 133
Alas, J. L. E. 82
Aldridge, J. 7
Alexander, M. 37, 38, 532, 635
Alfredo, M. 274
ALK(Q) N 51
Allport, G. W. 166
Almeida, J. G. 313n13
Almighty Latin and Queen Nation: *see* Latin Kings
Almighty Latin King and Queen Nation, The (Brotherton and Barrios) 122, 636

Alonso, A. A. 647, 692, 702
Althusser, L. 11
Amarildo scandal 215–216
American interactionist tradition 111
Andell, P. 3, 9
Anderson, B. 70
Anderson E. 162n2
Andrade, C.: *see* King Manaba
Andrade, X. 455
Angel (Crips leader) 388
anonymity 144–145
Antillano, A. 473
Antiterrorism and Effective Death Penalty Act 199
Antle, B. J. 138
Appadurai, A. 462
Apprenticeship in Critical Ethnographic Practice (Lave) 145
arboreal framework 6
Arcades Project, The (Benjamin) 18
Arias, E. D. 400, 414, 486n18
Asanza, G. 460
Asbury, H. 636
Asbury, J. 16
Ashcroft, B. 9, 11
Asian criminology 352, 373
Aspholm, R. R. 243, 692
Atkinson-Sheppard, S. 364, 367
Attica prison rebellion 637
autonomous human individual 11
Ávalos, J. V. R. 478
Avila, E. 658
Awami League (AL) 370
Azcona, J. 19

Baird, A. 371, 386, 387
Baker, M. K. 276
Baker, P. 40
Baktin, M. M. 308
Banaji, M. R. 167
Bangladesh: context 367–368; gangs in 369–370, 371–372; Gulshan boys 369; introduction 364–365; literature on gangs 367; *mastaans* 367,

369–370; new landscape of gangs 371–372; organized crime in 367, 369, 370, 371; research methods 368–369

Bangladesh National Party (BNP) 370

Banks, S. 47

Barajas, F. P. 276

Barcelona 153–163, 463–464

Barganier, G. 538, 541

Barnes, N. 474, 485n7

Barrio 18 21, 24, 76, 341, 345–347, 415; *see also* Eighteenth Street gang

Barrio Gangs (Vigil) 686, 697, 700

Barrios, L. 34–35, 62, 122, 133, 278, 299, 300, 364, 395, 505, 560, 636, 687

Becker, H. S. 674

Belize: active gangs *394*; Bloods and Crips 388–389, 395, 396; *Crimes Commission* 390; cultural transfer 389–390; drugs 391; gang evolution 393–396; gang fragmentation 390–393; gang institutionalization 392; introduction 386–387; literature on 387; methodology 387–388; murder in 391; organized crime in 391; transnationalism 388–390, 395; violence in 386, 389, 390–393, 391, *393*, 396

Bell, D. 167

Bellevue Square 260–261

Benjamin, W. 16; background 17–18; "Critique of Violence" 20, 21; *One-Way Street* 18; political theology 23–24; reflections on violence 20–23; sovereignty 21–23; "Theses on the Philosophy of History" 25

Berg, L. A. 419, 423n26

Bernal, D. D. 539

Bernstein B. 155

Berrios, R. 66

Beske, M. 395

Bharara, P. 185

Big Bird (Solids leader) 264, 265, 267

"From Biker to Academic" (Mørck and Hansen) 145

Biondi, K. 444

Birmingham School: consumption and 115; cultural criminology and 111, 673; gang bangers and muggers 39–41; introduction 29; origins of 29–30; pessimism of 33–34; *Policing the Crisis* (Hall et al.) 36–39; resistance 31–33, 365, 620; subcultures and 30–36

Bishops, The 259

Bissonette, J. 637

Black and Gold (documentary) 300

Black Hand 51–52

Black Jackets 318

Black Panther Party 226, 258, 259

Black Skin, White Masks (Fanon) 539

Blackstone Rangers 259

Bloch, S. 647, 648

"blood in blood out" stereotype 168, 170

Blood in the Water (Thompson) 637

Bloods: in Belize 386, 388–389, 395, 396; in Europe 330; gang mapping and 653, 654, 656; literature on 387

Blumer, H. 128

Bohannan, P. 64

Bolden, C. 564

Bolivarian Revolution 475

Bolland, N. 389

Bolton, K. 358

Bonil 213

Bonilla, M. L. 213

Bordenkircher v. Hayes 186

Bourdieu, P. 10–12, 11, 91, 122, 132, 154, 155, 625, 626, 628

Bourgois, P. 34, 62, 69

Boyle, G. 174, 278, 700

Branch, C. 505

Bras, J. M. 66

Brazil: Bahia and the Bonde do Maluco 447–448; citizenship role of gangs 400; *Comando Vermelho* 439, 442–443, 448; COMPAJ massacre 439, 440; current landscape 446–448; *facções* 446–448; *Família do Norte* 439, 444–445; *Família Esparta 300* 445; femicide 442; *Guardiões do Estado* 447; homicides 446; introduction 439–441; *milícias* 445–446; military involvement 214–216, 217; *Okaida* 447; organized crime 443, 448; Police Pacification Units (Unidades de Polícia Pacificadora) 214–216; *Primeiro Comando da Capital* 439, 444, 445; primer on gangs 442–445; prisons 439, 443, 444, 445, 446; Rio de Janeiro 214–216, 217, 219, 221; secret society 444; *Sindicato do Crime* 447; the South 448; spatial reconfigurations 446–448; translations and cultural context 441–442; transnationality 461–463; violence in 446–448

Brenneman, R. 82

Brenner, N. 89

bricolage 32–33

Bright, F. 172

Bronx 120 185, 187, 189, 190, 228

Brotherton, D. 278, 299, 330, 352, 364, 395, 505, 560, 575, 636, 687, 691

Brotherton, D. C. 34–35, 40, 62, 90, 122, 123, 128, 133, 146, 667

Brown, S. 357

Bucerius, S. M. 284

Buddle, K. 288

Bugli, V. 343

Burgess, E. 679

Burgos, M. 439

Buscando Respeto (documentary) 153, 154, 159–161

Bush, G. H. 635

Bustamante, J. 486n19

Bustamante, P. 228, 595

Butts, R. 172

Cabral, S. 214

Cain, M. 356

Caldeira, T. 455

Calderón, F. 505

California: prison studies 444, 629; prison
    wages 638; *Social Order of the Underworld, The*
    (Skarbek) 636; *see also* Los Angeles

Calogirou, C. 320

Camorra 444

Campbell, A. 636

Camp, C. G. 626

Camp, G. M. 626

Campos, J. A. 271, 273

Canada 582–583, 596n2; *see also* Toronto

"Can the Subaltern Speak?" (Spivak) 568

capitalism 31, 32, 33

Capone, A. 54

Carey, H. 635

Caritas 84–85

Carl (community activist) 263–264, 265

Carlen, P. 5

Carranza, M. 419, 423n26

Carrington, K. 5, 6, 10

Carter, J. H. 16, 612

Cassius (Outlaw Gangster Disciple) 246

Castells, M. 516

Castel, R. 323

categorization 146–149, 165, 166–168; *see also*
    labeling

Catholic Church: Christian reconciliation 80–82;
    introduction 74–75; liberation theology 77–80,
    82–83; stances and strategies 82–85; theological
    keys 77–82

Center for Contemporary Cultural Studies
    (CCCS) 29

Central America: Barrio 18 341; context
    198–200, 426–427, 428–429; data gaps
    198–199; de-securitizing gangs 206; gangs,
    insurgents and terrorists 203–206; history of
    gangs 428–429; homicides 412; introduction
    197–198, 426; local power brokers 433–434;
    Mano Dura (Iron Fist) 429–430; Mara
    Salvatrucha (MS-13) 341; New Right 201;
    Northern Triangle 199–200; political theology
    23–24; roots of transnational gangs 426–429;
    securitization 200–203; state of emergency
    18–20; threat perception 197–198, 202–203;
    violence in 426; war on gangs 203; Weimar
    Republic and 16; *see also specific countries*

Cerbino, M. 453

Cerda, L. 682

Césaire, A. 4

Chalas, D. M. 290

Chalfant, H. 577

Chambliss, W. 5

Chambliss, W. J. 365

Chamboredon J.-C. 320

Chan, P. Y. 356

Chan, W. S. 358, 359

Chavez, L. R 271

Chesney-Lind, M. 520

Chicago: Black Panther Party 226;
    deindustrialization 244–245; dual
    marginalization 249–253; FBI prosecutions
    248–249; gang governance 399, 408;
    institutionalized gangs 244; *Plan for
    Transformation* 247; playground sign 96–97;
    police activities 226; police database 230; public
    housing redevelopment 101–103, 247, 248;
    Robert Taylor Homes 96, 123; transforming
    drug markets 245–249; underground mobility
    245–249; unemployment 252–253

Chicago School 104, 365, 427

Chicanas: conceptual model of gang affiliation
    526; definition of 521–522; Estefania 527–528;
    introduction 518–519; Leticia 530; life course
    theoretical application *522*; Lorena 528–529;
    Mayra 518–519, 530; Patricia 529; reflexivity
    525; research methodology 523–525, *523*;
    violence and 521–523; a welfare case 527–529;
    women in gangs 519–521

Chicanx gang graffiti: Chaka (graffiti artist) 570; Cholx
    placasos 573–575; criminalization of 570–571,
    578n15; Downer (White Fence member) 574;
    findings 571–577; Flako (graffiti artist) 567; GTA
    572–573; introduction 567–568; Jim Boy (gang
    member) 573; Joker (gang member) 575–576; LA
    Shy girl (ex-gang member) 576–577; literature
    on 568–570; Lugo, M. (graffiti artist) 571; Maga
    (GTA member) 572–573; Mugs (graffiti artist)
    571–572; Ramos, D. (graffiti artist) 570; research
    methodology 570–571; as resistance 575–577;
    Shadow (gang member) 574–575; Skino (graffiti
    artist) 571; Spanky (gang member) 574; from
    taggers to cholxs 571–573; Tweety (homegirl) 576

Chico gang 231–232

child welfare system 527–529

China: context 367–368; gangs in 370–372;
    introduction 364–365; literature on gangs 367;
    new landscape of gangs 371–372; organized
    crime in 371; research methodology 368–369

Cholo gangs 48, 50–51

Cholx placasos 573–575

Chombart de Lauwe, P.-H. 318

Christensen, T. W. 146

Christian reconciliation 80–82

churches 74–75, 82, 84, 85, 619–620, 621; *see also*
    Catholic Church

Cintron, R. 337

City Beneath, The (Phillips) 702

City of Inmates (Hernández) 273

civilized socialism 20

Clarke, J. 32, 33

class socialization 132

Clemmer D. 605

Clifford, J. 462

Clinton, B. 635
Clinton, W. 54
Cloward, R. A. 131
codes 155, 378
Codici 342, 344–345
Cohen, A.K. 48, 133
Cohen, P. 31
Cohen, S. 5, 6, 271
COINTEL Program 226
Collins, P. H. 272, 542
Colonia el Romero 212–214, 217, 218, 219, 221
colonialism 538, 540, 541, 546, 552n7, 569
colours 313n13, 560–561
Comack, E. 288
Comando Vermelho 439, 442–443, 448
Comaroff, J. 221
Comaroff, J. L. 221
commodification of gangs 114–116
community 30, 31, 32, 35, 96, 377
Community Concern 681
Community-Oriented Policing (COP) reforms 211
Comunale, T. 346
conceptual model of gang affiliation 526
Connell, R. 5
Conquergood, D. 35, 113, 116, 122, 129, 130–131, 132, 160, 410n2, 573, 574, 612, 667–675; anti-racist scholarship and activism 671; gang cultures 672–674; gang spaces 672; gang theory 674–675, 675; impact on gang studies 672–675; introduction 667–668; as pioneer 668–671
conspiracy indictments 183–184
conspiracy trials: evidence 188–190; procedural and evidentiary advantages 187–188
consumerism 115
Conte, M. 342–343, 346
contradictory consciousness 545–547
Contreras, R. 552n7, 636, 687, 692
controlled integration 260
convict social system 610
convivencia 61, 65–67, 68
cooperator testimony 188
coperformative witnessing 669
Cornwall, P. 168
corporate gangs 573
Correa, R. 464, 471, 472
Corriveau, P. 687
Corten, A. 78
courts, dehumanization in: see dehumanization in courts
crack cocaine 245–246
CRASH Unit 226
Crenshaw, K. 685, 698, 699
crime-consumerism nexus 115
crime, functions of 37
criminal insurgencies 204
"criminal label" 37
criminal politics 474
Criminological Imagination, The (Young) 624

Criminologists' Gang, The (Katz and Jackson-Jacobs) 328
criminology: abstract empiricism in 624–625; Asian 352, 373; categories of 675; cultural 113–118; decentring of 352; of gangs and organized crime in Brazil 439–448; as imperialist science 352; orthodox 365; Southern criminology 352, 365–367; Soviet 379
Crips: in Belize 386, 388–389, 395, 396; Dutch Crips see Dutch Crips; in Europe 328, 330; gang mapping and 653, 654; literature on 387
critical realism 9
"Critique of Violence" (Benjamin) 20, 21
Cruz, J. M. 75, 482, 484
cultural capital 154
cultural criminology: cultural space 113–114; digitalisation and commodification of gangs 114–116; gang ontology 112–113; introduction 111–112; lost gang 116–118; politics of meaning 116–118
cultural space 113–114
cultural transfer 389–390
culture 672–674
culture wars 52–54
Cummings, L. L. 50
Cunneen, C. 352
Curtis, R. 63

Daley, R. J. 244
Damasio, A. 128
Danish biker gangs 138–151
da Silva, L 216
databases: California 230; gang style and 562; New York City 179–181, 226, 228–230, 230, 562; United Kingdom 230
data on alleged gang members 191n2
Davis, A. 169, 174n1
Davis, A. Y. 643
Davis, J. 354
D'Cruz, H. 139, 150n2
de Aquino, J. P. D. 447
de Beauvoir, S. 60
De Certeau, M. 155, 462
Decker, H. S. 49
Decker, S. 636
Decker, S. H. 12, 122, 330, 563, 604
decolonial framework 538, 540
De Corazón 67–68
dehumanization in courts: categorization 166–168; critical gang studies 173–174; demonization as strategy 171–172; effectiveness of 172–173; examples of 168–171; frames and 167, 170; fundamental attributional error 166; prejudice 166–168; stereotypes 164–165, 166–168; terminology 164
Deleuze, G. 79
"Demarginalizing the Intersection of Race and Sex" (Crenshaw) 698

de Martino, E. 309
Dempsey, V. 233
Den, D. P. 71n13
Densley, J. 330
Densley, J.A. 366, 387
deportations 199–200, 415, 426, 428
Derrida, J. 26
de Sá, L. D. 447
Descartes' Error (Damasio) 128
de-securitizing gangs 206
d'Estaing, V. G. 319
de Tocqueville, A. 605
Deuchar, R. 139, 143, 144
Devitt, M. 170
dialectics of space 93–99
Dialogic Imagination, The (Bakhtin) 308
dialogue 669
diaspora 462
DiChiara, A. 257
Dickens, C. 16
Dictatorship (Schmitt) 22
digitalisation and commodification of gangs 114–116
di Leonardo, M. 670, 671, 673
dilution narrative 332
Dips: *convivencia* 65; joining Ñetas 61–62; La Sombra and 66; leaving Ñetas 69; *mesa disciplinaria* 58–59; progress in Ñetas 63
discriminatory society 75–77
disengagement from gangs 334–335, 518–533, 563–564, 618–620
dispossessed inheritors 31
Distinction (Bourdieu) 122
Divide and Conquer (Weide) 702
divine violence 22–23, 25, 26
domination 59–61, 71n3
Dominicans in New York City 507
Donovan, K. 302
Dooley, B. D. 638
Dorais, M. 687
Doueiri, Z. 400
doxa: *see* academic doxa
Druckman, J. A. 167
drug economy 245–249, 250–251, 253–254
dualistic discursive misrepresentation 146–147
du Beaumont, G. 605
Dubet, F. 320, 321
Du Bois, W. E. B. 4, 38, 365
Durán-Martínez, A. 484
Durán, R. J. 132–133, 271, 273, 558, 687, 692, 701
Durkheim, E. 605
Dutch Crips: analysis of 330; compared to U.S. Crips 330; gang disengagement 334–335; "h200d" 333; "h200d" 333–334, 562; media coverage 336; murder of Sin 331–332; mythmaking of 331, 336–337; research design 330; transcendental "realness" 335–336, 337; violence in 334–335, 336

Eagleton, T. 382
economic capital 154
economic marginalization: deindustrialization 244–245; dual marginalization 249–253; introduction 243; transforming drug markets 245–249; underground mobility 245–249
Ecuador: 2007–2017 464–466; context 454–456; current situation 466–467; homicides 470; introduction 453–454; Latin Kings 302, 303, 304; Latin Kings, beginnings of 456–458; Latin Kings, phases of 458–461; marginality and exclusion 456; Masters of the Street 469–470; peace processes in 469–472; political change in 463–464; recognition of Latin Kings 463; Secretaría del Pueblo 472; Ser Paz 470–471, 472n3; urban setting 455–456; violence in 470
Eighteenth Street gang 426, 427, 428; *see also* Barrio 18
Eisner, M. 423n5
Elden, S. 94
El Grito 508, *508*
Ellacuría, I. 77, 78, 79, 82, 86
El Romero 212–214, 217, 218, 219, 221
El Rukns 50
El Salvador: 22 de Abril 21; armed forces gang ties 433; Catholic Church in 82–85; Christian reconciliation 80–82; context 413–414, 421–422; counterinsurgency policing 205; deportation 200; de-securitizing gangs 206; discriminatory society 75–77; extortion practices 416–417; functions of gang violence 419–421, **420**, 422; gang development in 76–77; gang truce 83, 418, 430–433, 478, 484; homicides in 417–418, 431–432; Homies Unidos-El Salvador 430; institutionalization of gangs 416–418; introduction 74–75, 412–413; liberation theology 77–80; local government gang relationships 434; Mano Dura (Iron Fist) 432; *mareros* in 341–342; Milan and 345; military hold on 220; Nueva Concepción 412, 415, 417, 418; post-war growth of gangs 414–416; prisons in 201, 416, 417–418, 423n10, 607, 607–611, **608**; Special Reaction Forces 211; terrorism 78, 205, 607; transformations of gang violence 414–418; *Tribunal Constitucional* 607; U.S. policy and 427; violence in 76, 412–422, 430–431
emergentism 10–12
empirical approaches 8–9
England 5, 7
enhanced bail 234–235
Enlightenment thinking 11
Erikson, K. T. 46
Espadaler, R. 301
Espagne, M. 389, 390
Esparza, M. 299
Esteban, A. 310

Esterle-Hédibel, M. 320
Estrela, R. 446
ethics: *see* social practice ethics
ethnic identity: *see* race
ethnography 122–124, 630, 669
"Eurogang paradox" 239
Evangelical churches 74–75, 82, 85, 86
Evangelii Gaudium 79
evidence: in conspiracy defense 188–190;
    cooperator testimony 188; experts 190; forensic
    189; NYPD testimony 189; prior convictions
    and arrests 189–190; social media posts 188–189
Eyes on the Prize (documentary) 637

Fahlberg, A.N. 217
Família do Norte 439, 444–445
Família Esparta 300 445
Fanon, F. 4, 9, 10, 539
Fear and Loathing in Las Vegas (Thompson) 680, 695
Feixa, C. 298
Feltran, G. 444
female gang members: *see* women in gangs
Ferrarotti, F. 307
Ferrell, J. 116, 117
field theory 11–12
filming: *see* visual sociology
Fiske, S. T. 166, 171
Fize, M. 319, 321
Flako (graffiti artist) 567
Fleisher, M. 366, 558, 636
Fleisher, M. S 604
Flores, E. O. 278, 564
Flores, J. 529
Floyd (Black Disciple) 252
Fontes, A. 348
Fontes, A. W. 202
forgiveness 81–82
formers 139
Fort, J. 50
foster care 527–529
Foucault, M. 605, 613, 615
frames 167, 170
France: 1980s 319–321; 2000s 323–325; Black
    Jackets 318; emergence of ethnic gangs
    321–323; gangs caught up by immigration
    318–319; housing projects 318, 320, 322;
    introduction 316–317; Loubards 318; race
    in 316–324; segregation 318; sociological
    studies 316, 318; threat perception 320; white
    supremacists groups 322; "Zulus" generation 322
Franco, M. 216
Frankfurt School 32
Fraser, A. 351, 372
Freikorps 22
Freire, P. 513, 514
Fremont Hustlers 559
Freud, S. 11, 60

friendship groups 128–129
frustration 48–49
Fuerza de Tarea Maya (Task Force Maya) 212–214
functions of crime 37
fundamental attributional error 166
Funes, M. 431, 432

Gallisá, C. 66
Galtung, J. 521
Gang as an American Enterprise, The (Padilla) 129
gang bangers and muggers 39–41
gangbangers vs. hustlers 587–589
"gang call-ins" 8
gang cultures 672–674
gang definitions 71n5, 178–179, 366, 369, 370,
    428, 626
Gang Life in Two Cities (Durán) 132, 701
gang member makeup 271
gang narratives 177–193
"gang-ness" 328–337
gang ontology 112–113
Gang Paradox, The (Durán) 687, 701
gang policing 53–54
Gang's All Queer, The (Panfil) 636
Gangs and Girls (Corriveau) 687
Gangs of New York, The (Asbury) 636
Gangs on Trial (Hagedorn) 165
gang spaces 672
"gangsta culture" 36
Gangster Disciples 169, 172, 244
gang talk 116–117
gang theory 674–675, **675**
Gang, The (Thrasher) 302
Ganpat, S.M. 335
Garcia, C. 682
García Díaz, F. J. 469
Garcia, M. 59–60
Garcia, R. 682, 686
Garcia, S. 168
Garot, R. 122, 330, 564
garrison state: defined 220; gang policing and
    security politics 220–221; introduction 210–211
Gatti, U. 366
Gayle, H. 386, 387
gays in gangs 557, 559, 560, 636
Geanie (Solids leader) 264, 265, 267
Geffray, C. 401
generic insurgency concept 204
Geneva Declaration 419
Germany 17, 22 23
Ghetto Brothers 258
ghettos 36, 37
Giammettei, A. 214
Giddens, A. 127
Gilligan, J. 76–77
Gillingham, P. 139, 150n2
Gilovich, T. 167

Gilroy, P. 4
girls: *see* women in gangs
Girls in the Gang, The (Campbell) 636
Giuliani, R. 58, 62, 302, 311
globalilzation of indifference 79
Global War on Terror (GWOT) 198, 203–206, 205
Gluckman, M. 64
Godnick, W. 486n19
Goeury, Hugo 29
Goffman, E. 134, 610
Going Down to the Barrio (Moore) 685, 686
Go, J. 4, 9, 10, 11
Gómez, L. 478
gopniks 380
governance of gangs: introduction 399–400; literature on 399–400; nature of 409; political economy of 408–409
graffiti: Chicanx gang graffiti *see* Chicanx gang graffiti; criminalization of 570–571, 578n15; identity and 35, 561, 612, 673; in prisons 612; as street literacy 547, 673
Gramsci, A. 31, 33, 38, 309, 382, 464, 567
Grassi, P. 340
Gray, P. 357
Greaser Act 569
Greenblatt, S. 389
Greenwald, A. G. 167
Grekul, J. 290, 291
Gringo Justice (Mirandé) 278
Grito 59, 66, 71n1
GTA 572–573
Guardiões do Estado 447
Guatemala: age of criminal responsibility 607; *Calle 18* 603; Colonia el Romero 212–214, 217, 218, 219, 221; law enforcement collusion 433; military involvement 205; *Pacto del Sur* 608–609; prisons in 201, 202, 607, 607–611, **608**, 613–614, *614*, *615*; securitization 201; terrorism 206; U.S. policy and 427
Guattari, F. 79
Guevara, E. C. 58
Gulshan boys 369
Gupta, A. 485n6
Gutierrez, G. 77
Gypsy Jokers 626

habitus 628–629
Hagedorn, J. 364, 372, 684, 686
Hagedorn, J. M. 91, 101, 164, 244, 401, 441, 445, 448, 636, 691
Haggerty, K. D. 284
Hague, The 328–329, 333–334
Haldipur, J. 636
hall of mirrors 113–114
Hall, S. 29, 36, 37
Hallsworth, S. 6, 7, 9, 50, 95, 366
Hamera, J. 669, 671

Hamm, M. S. 49–50
Hampton, F. 226
Hanson, R. 473, 478
harassment 232–234
Harper, S. 286
Harrington, M. 182
Hartford: Black radicalism 259–262; gang formation in 258–259; Greater Hartford Process 259; housing projects 258, 259–262; insights from 267; introduction 257–258; pastoral state and social welfare system 265–266; segregation 102, 266; Solids 262–265
Hartford Public Library 260, 261
Hayward, K. 115, 239, 367
H.D, Lasswell, 211
Heart Broken in Half (documentary) 670
From the Heart (Solids video) 265
Hebdige, D. 32, 33, 34, 131, 365
hegemony 31–32, 38
Hernandez, J. O. 26, 607
Hernández, K. L. 273
Herron, R. 230–231
Herrou, A. 66
Hill, B. 544
history of gangs: Hong Kong 353; Luis Fanor Hernández gang 401; New York City 285–287; in the U.S. 427–428
Hobsbawm, E. 16, 462
Hoggart, R. 29–30, 32
Hogg, R. 5
Homeboy Industries 564
Homeboys (Moore) 682
Home Owners' Loan Corporation's (HOLC) 647, 649, *650*
Honduras: Bible and gang symbol *613*; changes in gang life 26; Contras in 19; law enforcement collusion 433; Mano Dura (Iron Fist) 607; militarization 205–206; political theology 23; prisons in 24–25, 201–202, 607, 607–611, **608**; states of emergency 18; tattooing practices 24; U.S. policy and 427; war on gangs 21
Hong Kong: 1845 ordinance 353–355; 1888 European District Ordinance 355; 1932 Ordinance 356–358; 1974 foundation 358–360; corruption in 358; genealogy of gangs 353–360; history 353; introduction 351; recentring the world of gangs 351–353; reform 358; research in 353; triads 353–355, 357–359, 360
hope 513–515
Horn, R. 172
housing 648, 649; *see also* public housing
Howell, B. 177, 595
Howell, B. K. 53, 228
How Emotions Work (Katz) 130
Hughes, E. 679
Human Targets (Rios) 701
Hurston, Z. N. 669

hybrid gangs 48
hyper-ghetto 603
hyper-policing 232–234
hyper-strain 115

idealism 7–8
idealist literature 7
identity: concurrent identities 560; gang activities
    and 558–560; gang style and 560–562; gender
    expression 560; hope and 513–515; importance
    of 505–506; Latinization of 506–512; spirituality
    and 515–516; *see also* performance narratives
Illegal Immigration Reform and Immigration
    Responsibility Act 199
image 112
Immigration Reform and Immigrant
    Responsibility Act (IIRIRA) 428
Incarcerated Workers Organizing Committee
    (IWOC) 638
From Indians to Chicanos (Vigil) 696
Indigenous gangs: Alberta Warriors 290, 294; ASAP
    294; expansion 289–290, 292; Indian Posse 289,
    290, 291, 293, 294; introduction 284; Manitoba
    Warriors 289, 290, 291; origins of 288–289;
    overview 287–288; in prisons 290–292; Redd
    Alert 293; research lack 294–295; research
    methodology 288; on the streets 292–294
Indigenous people: assimilationist policies 286;
    history 285–287; overrepresentation in criminal
    justice system 284–285, 286–287; peace and
    justice 285
informed consent 143–144
initiation rituals 557–558
Insane Chicago Way, The (Hagedorn) 636, 686
Institute for Violence Reduction 265
institutionalized gangs 244, 416–418, 441
institutional violence 518–533
insurgents 203–206
"integral state" 38
internationalization 199, 202
Internet 562–563
Internet banging 586
intersectionality 522, 685, 698–700
interviewing: discursive 133–135; emotions, centrality
    of 128–131; empowerment 125; focused interview
    127; introduction 122–124; methodological 124,
    126, 127; methods textbooks 124–126; phatic
    communication 131; phenomenological 127;
    pre-theorization 127, 135; qualitative 124, 126;
    re-conceptualization of 126–128; repeat questioning
    124, 127, 129, 130, 135; sequential narrative 130;
    "studying down" 134; symbolic interactionist fallacy
    130; wider social context 131–133
Islam 49–50
Islands in the Street (Sánchez-Jankowski) 122, 636
Italy: *see* Milan
ITSTIME 346

Jabaar 390
Jackman, D. 367
Jackson, A. 171
Jackson, J. 187
Jackson, K. T. 649
Jackson, P. I. 271
Jackson, S. 671
Jackson-Jacobs. C. 131, 328, 330, 624
Jacobs, J. 628
Jaffe, R. 400
Jamaica 34, 211, 400
James (Black P Stone) 251
James, K. 49
Jankowski 122
JD (research participant) 559
Jensen, S. 34, 79, 400
Jephcott, P. 356
Jessop, B. 91
JK (rapper) 390–391, 393–394, 395
Johannesburg 400
Johns, A. 387, 395
Johnson, E. P. 668
Johnson, J. 637
Johnson, L. 635, 681
joint ventures 140–141
Jones, D. J. 284
Jordan (ex-gang member) 537–538, 540–545,
    547–551, *550*
Juarez, R. 544–545
*Judicial Process among the Barotse of Northern
    Rhodesia, The* (Gluckman) 64
justice 81
Justice and Judgement among the Tiv (Bohannan) 64
juvenile delinquency 606
Juvenile Offender Act 635

Kahneman, D. 171
Katone, M. 203
Katz, J. 7, 112, 125, 128, 130, 328, 330, 558, 624
Kefauver Committee 52
Kelly, R. 226
Kelsen, H. 22
Kemp, R. 386
Kenya: Al Shabaab 497–498; ethnic politics
    496–497; gang definitions 490; gang identity
    and function 490–492; gangs and manhood
    494–497; gangs and politics 495–496; illegal
    alcohol 492–494; introduction 489–490; Kenya
    African National Union (KANU) 491–492;
    Mathare 493–494; Mungiki movement 489,
    491; police killings 490–491; political gangs
    489, 491; security 497–498, 499; Sungu Sungu
    498; vigilantism 492; violence in 490–491;
    working gangs 489–490, 492–497
Kerner Commission 635
King Boy Gean 302
King Charly 456

Kingism 51

King Manaba: chronotype 308; horizontal synthesis 307; introduction 298–300; postscripts 310–312; reading keys 307–309; research assistant 301, 304; subaltern story 309; three lives of 304–307; trial of 312; vertical synthesis 307

King, R. 173, 199

King's Constitution Manifesto 298

King Wolverine 302, 303

Kipling, R. 166

Kirchheimer O. 605

Klein, M. W. 276, 329, 335, 366, 683–684

Kleykamp, M. 635

Kokoreff, M. 321

Kontos, L. 45

Kraska, P.B. 211

Krulewitch v. United States 187

Kushner, K. 541, 542

Kwok, N. Y. 359, 360

La Asociación Pro-Derechos del Confinado: see Ñetas

labeling 37, 232–237, 274, 553n18, **608**, 610, *611; see also* categorization

La Boétie 60

Laboucane-Benson, P. 291

Lacalle, F. S. 82

Lagrée, J.-C. 320

Lahosa, J. M. 299

Laidler, K. 351

Lakoff, G. 170, 171

Lamotte, Martin 58

Lane, J. 275

language: *see* terminology

Lapeyronnie, D. 324

La Piedad 475–476, 479–480

La Sombra, C. 58, 63, 66–67, 71n1

Lasswell, H. D. 220

Latin America 211–216; Brazil 214–216; Colonia el Romero 212–214; *Fuerza de Tarea Maya* (Task Force Maya) 212–214; gang policing and security politics 220–221; Guatemala 212–214; introduction 210–211; Milan and 343, 344, 345; Police Pacification Units (Unidades de Policía Pacificadora) 214–216; religious governance 400; urban margins 216–219; *see also* Central America; Latinos; *specific countries*

Latinization of identity: appropriation of Latino heritage 506–509; against invisibility 509–512

Latin Kings: ALK(Q) N 51; Barcelona 299–300, 463–464; from criminal gang to cultural organization 300–302; in Ecuador *see* Latin Kings in Ecuador; filming 158, 161; history of 302–304, 461; King Manaba *see* King Manaba; King Tone 162n5; *Manifesto* 511, 516, 557; origin and spread of 278; political activity 559; *Sagrada Tribe Atahualpa Ecuador* (STAE) 302; *Sagrada Tribu América Spain* (STAS) 302; in Spain 463–464

Latin Kings in Ecuador: 2007–2017 464–466; beginnings of 456–457; conservative period 458–461; context 454–456; current views 466–467; introduction 453–454; King Boy Gean 457, 459, 460–461; King Charly 456; King Chino Ice 458, 460; King Eric 461; King Lucky 459, 460–461; King M. 457, 458; King Moonface 461; planting the flag 457–458, 458; primitive period 458–461; recognition and status 463–464; as transnational nations 461–463

Latin Kings in New York: *El Grito* 508, *508*; identity and hope 513–515; identity and spirituality 515–516; introduction 505–506; King B. 509; King C. 507; King D. 514; King F. 511; King H. 512, 514; King M. 512; King R. 505; King S. 514; King Tone 510, 515–516; Latinization of identity 506–512; *Manifesto* 511, 516; prayer 515; Queen A. 509, 514; Queen C. 515; Queen D. 509; Queen H. 506; Queen J. 507; Queen M. 510; Queen Z. 510; visibility 509–512

Latinos: identity 506–512; *Punished* (Rios) 636; as resistance institutions 276–280, *277*; state use of gangs to enhance criminalization 275–276; threat perception 271–272, 274–275, 280; *see also* Central America; Latin America; *specific countries*

Laub, J. H. 522

Lauger, T. 558–559

Lauger, T. R. 329, 330, 332, 561

Lauritson, J. L. 563

Lave, J. 144, 145

La Vida Loca (film) 300

law-making violence 21

law-preserving violence 21

League of United Citizens to Help Addicts 681

Learning to Labour (Willis) 33

leaving a gang: *see* disengagement from gangs

Lecusay, R. 669

Lefebvre, H.: abstract space 99–103; dialectics of space 93–99; *Production of Space, The* (Lefebvre) 89, 90, 92, 104; spatial theory 89–90, 92

Left Realists 10

Lemaire M. 318

Lessing, B. 446, 482, 635–636

Leung, H. 351

Levenson, D. 79

Lévi-Strauss 32

Lew-Fai, P. 320

Lewis, D. 367

Leyva, M. 567

liberation theology 77–80, 82–83, 516

Liderato: book 62–63; code 63–64; *convivencia* 65–67

Li, E. 360

Liem, M. C. 335

Life Conduct List 145

life course criminalization 532

life course theory 522, *522*

liminal redemption 348n1

Linare, L. A. 544

Link, B. G. 520

Lippmann, W. 170

"Lived Ethics" (video) 144

Lok, L. 358

London 9

Lopez-Aguado, P. 549

Los Angeles 278; Chicana mothers *see* Chicanas; CRASH Unit 226; deportations 415; gang numbers 523; gang origins 427; housing projects 654, *656*; Mara Salvatrucha (MS–13) 76, 272; Pacoima 659–660, *661*; public housing 654; research methodology 523–525, **523**; Rollin 40 Crips 333; San Fernando Valley 657–660, *659*; South Central 519, 521–524, 651, 653–657; violence in 521–523; women in gangs 519–521

Los Angeles gang mapping: 1939 *650*; 1992 *652*; Central Avenue District *654*; introduction 647–649; Pacoima 659–660, *660*, *661*; public housing 651, 659–660, *660*; Pueblo del Rio 655–657, *656*, *657*; race and 649, 651, 653–654; red lining 649–651; San Fernando Valley 657–660, *659*; South Central 653–657

Los Solidos Handbook 262

lost gang 116–118

Lo, T. W. 359

Loubards 318

love 60, 67–68, 69, 71n12

Luis Fanor Hernández gang: combo phase 406–407; drug-dealing phase 403–404; emergent phase 402; evolution of 408; gang history 401; 'Golden Era' phase 402–403; pacification phase 404–405; political economy of gang governance 408–409; post-April 2018 407–408; revival phase 405–406

Luke, D. 444

Lyman, M. D. 626

MacClean, B. 172

MacLeod, J. 133

Macmillan, H. 31

Madison, D. S. 671

Maduro, N. 473, 482

Maduro, R. 20, 607

Mafia 51–52, 366, 444

Magaloni, B. 215

Magnificent 20s 258

Making of the English Working Class, The (Thompson) 30

Maldonado-Fabela, K. L. 518

Mancillas, J. D. 678

Mano Dura (Iron Fist) 19, 23–24, 429–430, 432, 473, 483, 484

Manso, B. P. 444

Manwaring, M. G. 203

mapping gang neighborhoods: 1939 *650*; 1992 *652*; Central Avenue District *654*; introduction 647–649; Pacoima 659–660, *660*, *661*; public housing 659–660, *660*; Pueblo del Rio 655–657, *656*, *657*; race and 649, 651, 653–654; red lining 649–651; San Fernando Valley 657–660, *659*; South Central 653–657

Mara Salvatrucha (MS–13): in El Salvador 341, 415; in Italy 345–347; Los Angeles 76; origins of 19, 76, 426, 427; self-mythology 51; tattooing practices 24; as terrorists 198; threat perception 53; Trump, D. and 39–40, 165, 197, 272; in the U.S. 428, 431

Marchena, M. 312

Marciano, R. 653

Marco (Black Disciple) 250

Martín-Baró, J. I. 75

Martin, C. 203

Martinez, A. A. 537

Martinez, C. G. 692, 701

Martínez, E. 278

Martínez, L. 432

Marx, K. 11

Massey, D. 91, 92

mass incarceration 604–607, 620, 627, 628, 634–636

mastaans 367, 369–370

Masters of the Street 469–470

Matthews, R. 111

Matza, D. 48, 52, 133, 610

Mauger, G. 321

Maxson, C. L. 366

Maze, D. 292

McCarthy Committee 52

McKay, H. D. 46, 100

McLehose, M. 358

McNaughton, M. J. 553n18

Meagher, C. 543

Medellín conference 77

media 114–116, 158, 430, 455, 562–563

Melgar, M. 431

Melossi D. 605

Mendoza-Denton, N. 395, 561, 569, 687

Menesses, R. 433

Menjivar, C. 521

Merton, R. 36, 54, 115, 127

mesa disciplinaria 59, 64

Messiah (dancehall singer) 390–391, 393–394, 395

methodological politics 117

Mexican American Girls and Gang Violence (Valdez) 687

Michelutti, L. 70

Middlemass, K. M. 640

Milan: economic statistics 349n7; gang expansion in 342; immigrants in 344, 349n6, 349n13; Latin American gangs in 343, 344, 345; *mareros* in 340, 346–347; research in 342, 343–344, 346

milícias 445–446

Miller, J. 636
Miller, J.-A. 382
Miller, M. 46
Miller Matthei, L. 387
Miller v Alabama 168
Mills, C. 5
Mills, C. W. 624
Mills, Michael 111
Mirandé, A. 278
Miravalle, M. 603
misrepresentation 146, 147–148
Model Cities Program 681
Mohammed, M. 316, 324
Moignard, B. 324
Moland, J. Jr. 50
Molina, O. P. 201, 213, 607
Mombasa Republican Council (MRC) 496–497
Monod, J. 318, 319
Monster (book) 562
Montañez, J. 164, 168–169, 171
Montejano, D. 278
Moore, J. 122, 568, 691, 697, 701, 702; Chicano
    Pinto Research Project 683, 684; gang research
    678–688; introduction 678–679; legacy of
    686–688; Malcolm Klein and 683–684;
    perseverance of 685; research methods
    681–683; as revolutionary 679–681; shattering
    paradigms 681–683
Moore, J.W. 365
Moosavi, L. 352
Moral entrepreneurs 578n6
Morales, J. 214
moral outrage 675n1
moral panics 6, 36, 38, 41, 271, 275, 379
Moran, K. 117, 122
Mørck, L. L. 138
Moreno, L. 310
Morgan, M. J. 220
Moro, S. 446
Morris, A. 365
MS–13: *see* Mara Salvatrucha (MS–13)
"mugging crisis" 36–37, 38, 39
Muhammad, N. 390, 395
Müller, Markus-Michael 197
Müller, M.-M. 201
multiple marginality 691, 698–700
Munguía Payés, D. 431, 432
Murphy, T. "Bam," Jr. 227
Murphy, T. "Chicken" 227
Murphy, T., Sr. 227
music 158–159
mythical violence 21–22, 25
mythmaking 330, 331, 336–337

Nabil (co-researcher) 140, 141, 142, 147, 148–149
Naepels, M. 60
naive realism 8–9

Nakano, G. E. 273
National Crime Agency 6
National Gang Intelligence Centre 428
National Gang Report 428
National Inter-institutional Security Force 204
National Prisoners Reform Association (NPRA) 637
National Youth Gang Survey 271
nativism 52, 53, 54–55
natural law 21
Nature of Prejudice, The (Allport) 166
Navalny, A. 381
Navarro, A. 278
Nayak, A. 395
Neither War Nor Peace (Dowdney) 444
Ñetas: affection 61; *convivencia* 65–67; De Corazón
    67–68; filming 158; *Grito* 59; hierarchy 68–69;
    law 64–65; laws *see Liderato*; love 67–68;
    paternal figure 68–69; power relationships
    68–69; rap text 158; rules 67; rules of 59
Netherlands: Dutch Crips *see* Dutch Crips; gang
    disengagement 334–335; "h200d" 333–334,
    562; homicides 335; introduction 328–329;
    "real" gangs in Europe 329–330; Rollin
    200 Crips 328; Soetosenojo, Q. "Sin" 239,
    331–332, 335–336; transformative "realness"
    332, 334; violence, role of 334–335
Neuberger, J. 378
New Deal America 647, 649
new landscape of gangs 371–372
new military urbanism 211
New York City: changes in policing 226; Chico
    gang 231–232; Criminal Group Database 226;
    enhanced bail 234–235; gang database 179–181,
    226, 228–230; gang definition 178–179,
    228–229; gang raids 227–228; harassment
    232–234; history with gangs 225; hyper-
    policing 232–234; indictments, trials, and plea
    deals 235–237; introduction 177–178; inventing
    gangs 230–231; labeling, consequences of
    232–237; Mobile Trauma Units 238; *No Place
    on the Corner* (Haldipur) 636; Operation Crew
    Cut 177, 191n1, 226; police misconduct
    230; prosecution 183–190; reasons for youth
    violence 237–238; school safety agents 181;
    SMART program 181; social media surveillance
    181; street interactions, arrests, debriefings
    181–183; "targeted" policing 181
Nicaragua: *cartelito* 404–405, 408, 409; *Combos*
    406–407, 409; el Indio Viejo 403, 404, 405;
    gang governance 399–409; introduction 399;
    Los Dantos 406, 408, 409; *Los Dragones* 404; *Los
    Sobrevivientes* 403; Luis Fanor Hernández *see* Luis
    Fanor Hernández gang; *Sandinistas* 401, 402, 407;
    uprising 407; U.S. policy and 427; violence in
    402, 403, 404, 405, 406; *see also* Central America
Niederhofer, A. 46
Nissen, M. 140

Nixon, R. M. 635
Nobles 50
No Place on the Corner (Haldipur) 636
Northern Triangle 199–200, 429, 603–621;
    see also El Salvador; Guatemala; Honduras
Nunes, C. 444

Obama, B. 40, 54, 55
Occidentalism 356
Ochoa, F. 544
Off the Books (Vehkatesh) 243
Ohlin, L. E. 131
Okaida 447
O'Neill, K. L. 619
One of the Guys (Miller) 636
One-Way Street (Benjamin) 18
online culture 116, 118; *see also* social media
ontological individualism 132
Operación de Liberación y Protección del Pueblo (OLP)
    475–476
Operation Crew Cut 177, 191n1, 226
Operation Gator Roll 543–544
Operation Wetback 569
organized crime: in Bangladesh 367, 369, 370, 371;
    in Belize 391; in Brazil 443, 448; in China 371;
    defined 366; versus gangs 365; in Russia 380
Orientalism (Said) 165, 356
orthodox criminology 365
Ortiz, J. 630
Ortiz, J. M. 624
Oscar (*marero*): change effort 347–348; in El Salvador
    341–342; introduction 340; in Milan 343–345;
    post-prison life 345–347; in prison 345
Osvaldo (gang leader) 159
Oualhaci, A. 316
Oww Oww Gang 230–231, 233

Padilla, F. M. 129, 130, 134
pains of imprisonment 627
Paiva, L. F. S. 441, 446
Palmas, L. Q. 153, 342, 344, 465
Palmer, S. 9
Panfil, V. R. 556, 557, 559, 636
Parker, K. K. 204
Park, R. E. 365
parliamentary socialism 20
Pasolini, P. P. 309, 342
pastoral state 265–266
Pavarini M. 605
peace accords 74, 221, 429
peace-making efforts 434–435
Pekin (Solids president) 264
penitentiary culture 612–615
*On the Penitentiary System in America and Its
    Applications in France* (de Tocqueville and du
    Beaumont) 605
Pentecostal churches 74, 84, 85

People and Folks (Hagedorn) 165, 686
People of New York vs. Robert Cartagena 228
Perez, E. 258
Perez, L. E. 546
performance narratives: concurrent identities
    560; gang activities 558–560; of gang joining
    557–558; gang leaving 563–564; gangster
    identity 558–560; gang style 560–562; gender
    expression 560; initiation rituals 557–558;
    introduction 556–557; JD (research participant)
    559; *Manifesto* 557; media and internet
    562–563; talk 556
performance studies 668–671
performing "gang-ness" 328–337
personal myths: *see* performance narratives
Personas Mexicanas (Vigil) 696
pessimism 33–34
Peter (co-researcher) 141, 142–143, 144, 145, 147
Pétonnet, C. 319
Petrovskaya, I. 381
phatic communication 131
Phelan, J. C. 520
phenomenological analysis 127
Philippines 628
Phillips, L. 520
Phillips, S. 647, 648, 701
Phillips, S. A. 545, 692
Phoenix 274
Pirie, F. 62, 65
Piscitelli, A. 505
Pitts, J. 9
placasos: *see* graffiti
plea bargaining 186–187
Police Pacification Units (Unidades de Policía
    Pacificadora) 214–216, 217, 218, 219
Policing the Crisis (Hall et al.) 29, 36–39
political praxis 12–13
political theology 23–24
Political Theology (Schmitt) 22
politics of meaning 116–118
Pope Benedict XVI 82
Pope Francis 79, 82
Pope John Paul II 82, 83
Pope John XXIII 82
Pope Paul VI 82
Portland, Oregon 226, 230
positive law 21
post-colonial criminology 4
postcolonial rationalism 9
postcolonial realism 9
postcolonial theory 4, 5
postnational identities 298–313
post-positivist realism 10
post-war context 30–31
Poveda, C. 300
poverty 78
power relationships 419, **420**

practice research 140–142
pre-dawn raids 184–186
prejudice 166–168
pre-trial detention 185–186, 191n6, 191n7
Prigge, W. 94, 96
Primeiro Comando da Capital 439, 444, 445
Prison and The Factory (Melossi and Pavarini) 605
prison arrests 185
Prison Community, The (Clemmer) 605
prison gangs: affiliation vs identification 638–642;
    Alonzo (research participant) 640; beneficial
    role of 628, 636; Bobby (research participant)
    639–640; definition of 626, 633, 636–637;
    gang strengthening and 416; Indigenous
    gangs 290–292; introduction 633–634;
    Larry (research participant) 641–642; mass
    incarceration and 634–636; prison reform and
    643; Rameek (research participant) 639; reentry
    and 638–642; resistance, protest, and uprisings
    636–638; Tina (research participant) 640–641;
    violence and 626–627, 628; Yusef (research
    participant) 641
Prison Notebooks (Gramsci) 309
prisons: abolition of 643; Attica prison rebellion
    637; in Brazil 439, 443, 444, 445, 446;
    churches and 621; in El Salvador 416, 417–418,
    423n10, 607–611, **608**; ethnic identity and
    self-preservation in 634–635; graffiti 612; in
    Guatemala 607–611, **608**, 613–614, *614*,
    615; in Honduras 607–611, **608**; incarceration
    data 605, 621n3, 627, 635, 638; labeling in
    610, *611*; mass incarceration 604–607, 620,
    627, 628; in Northern Triangle 603–621;
    overcrowding 201–202; overrepresentation
    of gang members 606, 607–608;
    overrepresentation of Indigenous people 284;
    radicalization in 49; reform 643; resistance as
    self-preservation 547–549; restorative justice
    643; segregation in 609; slave labor in 638;
    strikes 66, 638; tattooing practices 538–539,
    540, 547–549, 612; truces 643; in Venezuela
    477; violence in 634; Walpole rebellion 637,
    643; *see also* prison studies
prison studies: abstract empiricism in 624–625,
    629; academic doxa in 626–629; aim of prison/
    aim of gangs 615–620; churches and 619–620;
    convict social system 610; directions for future
    research 630–631; disengagement from gangs
    618–620; habitus 628–629; introduction
    624–625; Jonathan (research participant) 603;
    osmosis between street and prison culture
    612–615; prisons, maras, and pandillas
    607–611; resistance 620–621; summary
    603–604; *Triangulo Norte* and mass incarceration
    604–607
Production of Space, The (Lefebvre) 89, 92, 104
Professional Thief, The (Sutherland) 687

Projects, The (Vigil) 686, 700, 701
Prop 21 45, 552n16
prosecutions: conspiracy indictments 183–184;
    conspiracy trials 187–190; plea bargaining
    186–187; pre-dawn raids 184–186
proximity policing 215
Pryce, K. 9
public housing 101–103, 247, 248, 583–584, 651,
    654, *656*, 659–660, *660*; *see also* housing
Pueblo del Rio 655–657, *656*, *657*
Puerto Ricans: in Hartford 259, 262–263, 263,
    264, 265–266; Latin Kings and Queens 278; in
    New York City 62, 506–507; Solids 267
Puerto Rico 34, 58, 58–59, 61, 66, 272
Punished (Rios) 636, 701
punishment 605, 615
Putin, V. 381
Pyrooz, D. 636
Pyrooz, D. C. 49, 122

Quagliaro, C. 486n19
Quebec Biker War 284
Queen J. 513
Queirolo Palmas, L. 462

race: culture wars 52–53; data on alleged gang
    members 179–181; in France 316–324; gang
    member makeup 271; homogeneous concept
    and 39–40; Latinos, racialization of 272; moral
    panics and 38; prisons and 634–635; racialized
    other 40, 171; racial schema 166–167; real-
    estate practices and 649, 651, 653–654, 658;
    segregation 102
racialized dehumanization 538–539, 541–542, 547
Racketeer Influenced and Corrupt Organisations
    (RICO) Act 428, 656
radicalization 49, 50
Ragazzi di vita (Pasolini) 342
Rahman, M.H. 367
raids 184–186
Rainbow of Gangs, A (Vigil) 686, 699, 700
rap music 585, 586, 589–591
Rastafrian/Rude Boy subcultures 34
Ratzinger, J. 82
"real" gangs in Europe 329–330
"Real Gangstas" (Lauger) 332
"realness" 332, 334
Redfield, R. 679
red lining 649–651
reductionism, opposing 3–5
Reed, A. 634
reentry 638–642
Reflections on Violence (Sorel) 20, 24
reflexivity 139, 150–151n2, 525
Regehr, C. 138
Reiner, I. 651
relationalism 10–12

religious governance 400

representations of space 93, 94–95, 95–96

research design: discursive 133–135; emotions, centrality of 128–131; gang thematic considerations 128–135; interview methods textbooks 124–126; introduction 122–124; re-conceptualizing the interview 126–128; "studying down" 134; wider social context 131–133

researcher codexes 143–144

research ethics: *see* social practice ethics

resistance: Attica prison rebellion 637; gangs as institutions cultivating resistance 276–280, *277*; graffiti 575–577; introduction 537–540; Jordan (ex-gang member) 537–538, 540–545; in prisons 620–621, 636–638; self-damning 538, 540, 551; self-defeating 538, 539, 540, 542; as self-preservation 547–549; tattooing practices 538–539, 540, 545–547, *546*, *548*; through rituals 31–33

Resistance through Rituals (Hall and Jefferson) 36, 365

restorative justice 643

"Rethinking Elocution. . . " (Conquergood) 671

"Rethinking Ethnography" (Conquergood) 669

revolutionary violence 79

Reyna, J. L. 505

rhizomic knowledge 6

Richie, B. E. 519

Rio de Janeiro 214–216, 217, 219, 221; *see also* Brazil

Rios, V. 549, 636, 692, 701

risk 146–150

Rivera, A. 310

Rivera y Damas, A. 82

Roberto (mentor) 263, 265

Roberts, D. K. 258

Robert Taylor Homes 96, 123

Robinson, W. I. 200

Rocha, J.-L. 405

Rockefeller, N. 635

Rodgers, D. 79, 371, 399, 400, 405

Rodney King riots 199

Rodrigues, R. 216

Rodríguez, A. 453

Rodriguez, C. 541

Roediger, D. 38

Roks, R. A. 328, 387

Rollin 40 Crips 333

Rollin 200 Crips 562; *see also* Dutch Crips

Romero, M. 274

Romero, O. A. 77, 78, 79, 82

Rosenbaum, R. J. 276

Rosenfeld, J. 635

Rothstein, R. 102

Rouch, J. 161

Roulston, K. 125

Roy, O. 321

Ruiz, M. 695

Rusche G. 605

Russia: AUE 380; criminology 379; gopniks 380; introduction 376; moral panics 379; organized crime 380; political uses of street gangs 381–382; social construction of street gang 378–380; street codes 378; street gangs as male socialization 376–378, 382; territoriality 377

Saca, A. 201

Sagrada Tribe Atahualpa Ecuador (STAE) 302

Sagrada Tribu América Spain (STAS) 302

Said, E. 165, 174, 356

Saints and Roughnecks (Chambliss) 365

Salinas, California 204

Sampson, R. 522

Sánchez, A. 84–85

Sánchez Cerén, S. 432

Sánchez-Jankowski, M. 122, 636

Sánchez, P. 310

sanctuary cities 53

San Fernando Valley 657–660, *659*

Santa Barbara 540, 543, 552n7

Santos, X. 567

Saunders-Hastings, K. 210

Sauvadet, T. 162n3, 324

Savenije, W. 413

scene, concept of 162n2

Scheper-Hughes, N. 69

Schmid, C. 93

Schmitt, C. 17, 22, 24, 25

school safety agents 181

Schwab, Benjamin Jonathan 74

Schwarze, Tilman 89

Scott J. 155

Scrappy, L. 546

Seals, A. 638

Second Vatican Council 77, 82, 85

Secretaría del Pueblo 472

secretive organizations. 45–47

secret society: in Brazil 444; culture wars 52–54; gang as 47–49; introduction 45–47; nativism 52; terrorism and 49–50; transparency, illusion of 50–52

securitization: context 198–200; defined 198; de-securitizing gangs 206; discussion of 200–203; gangs, insurgents and terrorists 203–206

Seelke, R. 205

segregation 102, 266, 318, 609–610

Sessions, J. 54, 198

Sex Pistols 33

Shafi, S.A. 367

shared writing 156–157

Shaw, C. R. 46, 100

Shea, D. 182, 229

Shermer, M. 168

Shoman, A. 389

Short, J. 50
Sibley, D. 455
Siegel, T. 670
Simmel, G. 45, 46, 47, 54
Simone, A. 400
"Sin": *see* Soetosenojo, Q. "Sin"
Sindicato do Crime 447
situated dialogue 143–144
situated ethics 150n2
situated knowledge 10
Skarbek, D. 444, 628, 630, 636, 638
Sleepy Lagoon murder trial 427
SMART program 181
Smiley, C. J. 633, 640
Smith, C. F. 626
Smith, D. 387
Smith, D. L. 172
Smurf (Solids speaker) 264, 265, 267
Snodgrass, J. 100
Sobrino, J. 77, 78, 79, 80
social bases 417
social capital 154
social disorganization 31
social ecology approach 100
socialism, civilized 20
socialism, parliamentary 20
social media: as evidence in trials 188–189;
    grieving and 592; influence of 585; intelligence
    gathering and 594–595; introduction 582;
    NYPD task force 594; performance narratives
    596; retaliation and 591–594; role of 586–587;
    surveillance 181
Social Order of the Underworld, The (Skarbek) 444, 636
social practice ethics: anonymity 144–145;
    beyond dualistic discursive representations
    146–147; case analysis 142–149; categorizations
    and risk 146–149; co-researchers 140,
    141–142; co-researching with publicly
    known formers 142–146; ethical dilemmas
    and possibilities for action 142–149; gang
    policies 149–150; informed consent 143–144;
    introduction 138–140; joint ventures 140–141;
    misrepresentation 146, 147–148; participants
    backgrounds 141–142; practice research
    140–142; public dialogue 147–149; reflexivity
    139; research apprentices 145–146; researcher
    codexes 143–144; risk assessment 149; situated
    dialogue 143–144
social space 89
social theory 4
social welfare system 265–266
socio-political domains 612
Soei, A. 149
Soetosenojo, Q. "Sin" 329, 331–332, 335–336, 337
Solids 257, 258, 262–266, 267
Solorzano, D. G. 539
Sorel, G. 17, 20–21, 24

South Africa 211, 400
South Arsenal Neighborhood Development
    (SAND) 258
South Central LA 519, 521–524, 651, 653–657
Southern criminology: approach of 5–6;
    Bangladesh 364–373; China 364–373; critical
    realism 9; emergentism 10–12; idealism
    and gangs 7–8; naive realism 8–9; need
    for 365–367; opposing reductionism 3–5;
    political praxis 12–13; postcolonial realism 9;
    relationalism 10–12; strategic essentialism 10;
    UK Gang Thesis Debate and 6–7
South LA 657–660, *659*
sovereignty 21–23
space 46, 113–114; *see also* spatial theory
spaces of representation 93, 95, 672
Spade 69, 70
Spain 302–303, 463–464
Spartaco (Latin King member) 161
spatial practices 93, 94, 96–98
spatial theory: abstract space 99–103; application
    to gangs 95–99; dialectics of space 93–99;
    gang research and 90–93; introduction 89–90;
    meaning of space 91–92; production of space
    93–94; representations of space 93, 94–95;
    spaces of representation 93, 95, 98–99; spatial
    practices 93, 94, 96–98
spatial violence 98
Special Response Team and Intelligence Troop 204
Spence, J. 289
spirituality 515–516
Spivak G.C. 9, 10–11, 153, 568
Springfield, Massachusetts 204
Stanek, L. 94
Stanley, C. 544
Stanley, W. 220
states of emergency: background 17–18;
    Benjamin, W. 17–18; exception to the
    exception 24–25; Honduras 18–19;
    introduction 16–17; political theology 23–24;
    reflections on violence 19; sovereignty 21–23
Stateville (Jacobs) 628
status frustration 48–49
Steele, C. 171
Stephens, D. P. 520
Stephenson, S. 376
stereotypes 164–165, 166–171
Stewart, K. 25
Stick Up Kids, The (Contreras) 636
stigmatization 520
Stoler, A. 61, 70
Stone, R. 169
stop-and-frisk 53
Stoutmire, K. 169, 170–171
Stout, P. 172
Strapped 'N Strong (documentary) 336
strategic essentialism 9, 10

stratification 648–649

street codes 378, 592

street culture 612–615

street literacy 574, 673; *see also* graffiti

street organization 34

streets, the 113–114, 115

Street Terrorism and Enforcement Protection (STEP) 661–662

structural sin 77–78

structural violence 77, 103, 525–531, 627

Stuart, F. 586

"studying down" 134

subaltern studies 9, 10–11, 309, 567–568

Subculture (Hebdige) 365

subcultures: gang studies and 34–36; post-war context 30–31; symbolic resistance and 31–34

submission 59–60, 71

Super Dave (Solids leader) 266

Sutherland, E. 46, 687

Suttles, G. D. 399

Sweet, P. 9

Sykes, G. M. 48, 52, 610, 627

symbolic interactionist fallacy 130

symbolic violence 103

symbolism 50, 560–561

Sysuev, O. 381

Tanter A. 323

Tapia, M. 275, 692

Tapias, R. 299

"targeted" policing 181

tattooing practices *546, 548*; *Calle 18*, Guatemala *604*; labeling and 545–547; prison and 612; as resistance 538–539, 540; self-damning 538, 547; self-defeating 538, 547; symbolism of 603

taxonomic categories 6

Taylor, C. 573

Taylor Homes 96, 123

Taylor, I. 5

Taylor, R. 139

terminology 6, 34, 71n5, 156, 162n2, 164, 182, 191n5, 553n18

Terrence (Mickey Cobra) 247–248

territoriality 35

terrorism 49–50, 78, 203–206, 205–206

theological keys 77–82

"Theses on the Philosophy of History" (Benjamin) 25

Thompson, E.P. 29, 30, 31

Thompson, H. 680, 695

Thompson, H. A. 637

Thompson, S. K. 584

Thrasher, F. M. 45, 48, 128, 302, 334, 364, 365, 408

threat perception 197–198, 202–203, 271, 274–275, 280, 320

threshold 16

Tiger 395–396

Tomlinson, J. 389

Toronto: Andre (Rich Riderz member) 588, 589; Chops (Old Head) 588, 589–591; gangbangers vs. hustlers 587–589; gangs in Canada 582–583; Hakim (research participant) 589–591, 593; homicides 584; introduction 582; J-Dawg (research participant) 591–592; Lemarcus (research participant) 593; rap music 585, 586, 589–591; Regent Park 583–584; research methodology 584–586; retaliation 591–594; Rich Riderz 584–585, 587, 588, 589; social media 585, 586–587; violence in 588–589; Wayne (research participant) 593–594; Young Soldiers 584–585

Torre, A. 342

Torres, A. 442

Toubon J.-C. 323

trails of violence: conceptual model of gang affiliation *526*; Estefania 527–528; introduction 518–519; Leticia 530; Lorena 528–529; Mayra 518–519, 530; Patricia 529; reconceptualization of 521; reflexivity 525; research methodology 523–525, **523**; structural violence 525–531; violence in barrio South Central 521–523; a welfare case 527–529; women in gangs 519–521

Transformadors Youth Centre 301

transformations of the post-war context 30–31

transformative "realness" 332

TRANSGANG project 302, 304, 312

translocality 462

transnationality/transnationalism: in Belize 386, 389–390, 395, 396; in Brazil 461–463; in Central America 199, 426–429; as cultural transfer 389–390; Latin Kings 298–313; literature on 387; MS–13 and 18th Street 202; in the U.S. 428

transparency, illusion of 50–52

Travers, M. 3, 4, 9

triad gangs 353–355, 357–359, 360

Triangolo Norte: *see* Northern Triangle

Trujillo, Josmar 225

Trujillo, L. 82

Truly Disadvantaged (Wilson) 244

Truman, H. S. 569

Trump, D. 39–40, 52–53, 54–55, 165, 197, 271, 272

truth 80–81

Turner, V. 668

typologies 485n7

UK Gang Thesis Debate 3, 6–7

United Kingdom: context 31; drug distribution networks 12; Gangs Matrix system 230; juvenile delinquency 357; moral panics 36–37; "mugging crisis" 36–37, 38, 39; rehabilitation model 356

United Nations International Children's Emergency Fund (UNICEF) 198

United States: history of gangs 427–428; incarceration data 605
University of Alberta Prison Project (UAPP) 288
UPP social 215
urban gang suppression strategies 211–216
Urbanik, M. 582

Vagg, J. 357
Valdez, A. 687, 691
Valencia, F. 682
Valencia, R. 346
Vance, C. 227, 231
Vandenberghe, F. 4
van der Borgh, C. 412
Van Gemert, F. 330
van Gemert, F. 366
Van Hellemont, E. 111, 330, 337, 562
van Stapele, V. 489
Varela, L. 311
Venezuela: Bolivarian Revolution 475; confrontation and instrumental negotiation 480–483; Doni (gang leader) 477, 479, 481; failed integration 477–480; homicides 475, 477; impact of militarized policing 483–485; introduction 473–475; La Piedad 475–476, 479–480, 481–482, 483, 484; *mano dura* 473, 483, 484; militarization, violent enforcement, persecution and imprisonment 476–477; Misión a Toda Vida Venezuela 478, 486n16; before the OLP 475–476; *Operación de Liberación y Protección del Pueblo* (OLP) 473, 480–483, 484–485; Peace Territories 478–480; People's Liberation and Protection Operation 473, 480–483, 484–485; prisons 477; research methodology 474–475; violence in 473, 475–476
Venkatesh, S. A. 95, 123, 243
Vice Lords 50
Video Interactive Patrol Enhanced Response (VIPER) 227
Vigil, D. J. 48, 122, 685, 686; academic career 696–697; back to the barrio 697–698; humble origins 692–694; intersectionality 698–700; introduction 691–692; legacy of 691–702, 700–702; multiple marginality 698–700; self-identification as Chicano 694–696
violence: academic doxa and 626–627; in Belize 386, 389, 390–393, 391, *393*, 396; in Brazil 439–440, 446–448; categorization of 419, **420**; causes of 651; in Central America 412, 426; context and 412, 413, 421–422; diversification of 416–418; in Dutch gangs 334–335, 336; in Ecuador 470; in El Salvador 412–422, 430–431; female gang members and 521; forms of 21; functions of 76–77, 413–414, 419–421, **420**, 422; identity and 558–559; in

Kenya 490–491; liberation theology and 77–80; in Los Angeles 521–523; in Nicaragua 402, 403, 404, 405, 406; in prisons 626–627, 628, 634; reconceptualization of 521; revolutionary violence 79; spatial violence 98; structural violence 77, 103, 525–531, 627 *see also* trails of violence; symbolic violence 103; talking about 558; in Toronto 588–589; transformations of 414–418; understanding of 21; in Venezuela 473, 475–476
Violent Crime Control and Law Enforcement Act 635
visual sociology: access to the field 155–156, 162n5; ambiguity and 157–161; fiction and 157; objectification and 157–161; shared writing 156–157; subalterns and 153–154; usefulness of 162
Vitale, Alex S. 225
vulnerability 670–671

Wachtler, S. 183
Wacquant, L. 9, 11, 603, 642
Wales 5, 7
Wallbangin' (Phillips) 701
Walpole rebellion 637, 643
Walton, P. 5
Wang, P. 367
Ward, T. W. 559
Warner, L. 679
war on drugs 37–38
war on gangs: in Central America 203; gangs as institutions cultivating resistance 276–280, 277; introduction 271–273; state use of gangs to enhance criminalization 275–276; threat perception 274–275, 280
warrior capital 154, 162n3
Warrior Capital (Sauvadet) 324
Weber, M. 22
Weerman, F. 366
Weide, R. D. 636, 638, 678, 691, 702
Weimar Republic 16, 18–20, 22
Wennmann, A 485n7
West Beyrouth (film) 400
Western, B. 635
West Harlem sweep 227–228
When the Prisoners Ran Walpole (Bissonette) 637
When Work Disappears (Wilson) 244
Whyte, W. F. 46
Williams, A. 232–233
Williams, R. 29, 30, 230–231, 233–234
"Willie Horton" as 635
Willis, P. 33
Wilson, M. 172
Wilson, W. J. 244
Wing, Lo, T. 367, 371
Winter, N. J. G. 166

Winton, A. 91, 352, 366
Witter, T. V. 377
Wolf, S. 199, 206, 426
women in gangs: Chicanas 518–533;
    double standards 560; gang style and 561, 569;
    identity and 560; literature on 636; violence
    and 521
working-class culture 29–30, 31, 32
World Economic Forum 200
worlding 25
World of Gangs, A (Hagedorn) 686
World Prison Brief 201
Woytila, K. 82
wraparound incarceration 529
written informed consent 143–144
Wyneken, G. 18

X (co-researcher) 141–142, 147–148

Young, J. 5, 8–9, 33–34, 624
Young, T. 7, 95, 366
Youth Justice Board 7
Youth Street Gangs (Brotherton) 123, 128

Zafarullah, H. 367
Zatz, M. 40
Zatz, M. S. 274
Zero Tolerance 58, 62
Zilberg, E. 34, 40, 364
Zolotov, V. 381
Zoot Suit Riots 427, 569
Zubillaga, V. 473
"Zulus" generation 322

Printed in Great Britain
by Amazon

37865387R00416